W9-AVD-202

American Government

The Essentials

American Government

The Essentials

TENTH EDITION

James Q. Wilson

University of California, Los Angeles
Pepperdine University

John J. DiIulio, Jr.

University of Pennsylvania

Houghton Mifflin Company
Boston   New York

For Roberta, Matthew, Rebecca, Annie, and Bob
and Clementine and Sara
J. Q. W.

Dedicated to the memory of Aaron H. Crasner
J. J. D.

Publisher: Charles Hartford
Sponsoring Editor: Katherine Meisenheimer
Development Editor: Lisa Kalner Williams
Senior Project Editor: Carol Newman
Editorial Assistant: Kristin Craib
Editorial Assistant: Robert Woo
Composition Buyer: Chuck Dutton
Senior Art Editor: Jill Haber
Senior Photo Editor: Jennifer Meyer Dare
Executive Marketing Coordinator: Nicola Poser
Marketing Associate: Kathleen Mellon

Cover image: Jim Wehtje/Getty Images

Copyright © 2006 by Houghton Mifflin Company

No part of this work may be reproduced or transmitted in any form or by any
means, electronic or mechanical, including photocopying and recording, or by
any information storage retrieval system without the prior written permission
of Houghton Mifflin Company unless such copying is expressly permitted by
federal copyright law. Address inquiries to College Permissions, Houghton
Mifflin Company, 222 Berkeley Street, Boston, MA 02116-3764.

Printed in U.S.A.

Library of Congress Catalog Number: 2005929292

ISBN: 0-618-56245-1

2 3 4 5 6 7 8 9 0–VH–09 08 07 06

★ BRIEF CONTENTS

PART I

THE AMERICAN SYSTEM 1

1 The Study of American Government 2
2 The Constitution 16
3 Federalism 48
4 American Political Culture 75
5 Civil Liberties 97
6 Civil Rights 124

PART II

OPINIONS, INTERESTS, AND ORGANIZATIONS 153

7 Public Opinion 154
8 Political Participation 177
9 Political Parties 197
10 Elections and Campaigns 230
11 Interest Groups 264
12 The Media 291

PART III

INSTITUTIONS OF GOVERNMENT 315

13 Congress 316
14 The Presidency 367
15 The Bureaucracy 409
16 The Judiciary 437

PART IV

THE POLITICS OF PUBLIC POLICY 467

17 Politics and Public Policy 468

☆ CONTENTS

PREFACE   xiii
ABOUT THE AUTHORS   xv

PART I
THE AMERICAN SYSTEM   1

1   The Study of American Government   2

What Is Political Power?   4
What Is Democracy?   6
Is Representative Democracy Best?   7
How Is Political Power Distributed?   8
Is Democracy Driven by Self-Interest?   10
What Explains Political Change?   11
The Nature of Politics   12

2   The Constitution   16

The Problem of Liberty   17
  The Colonial Mind   18
  The Real Revolution   20
  Weaknesses of the Confederation   21
The Constitutional Convention   22
  The Lessons of Experience   22
  The Framers   24
The Challenge   25
  The Virginia Plan   25
  The New Jersey Plan   25
  The Compromise   26
The Constitution and Democracy   27
  Key Principles   28
  Government and Human Nature   29
The Constitution and Liberty   30
  The Antifederalist View   31
  Need for a Bill of Rights   35
  The Constitution and Slavery   36

The Motives of the Framers   37
  Economic Interests at the Convention   37
  Economic Interests and Ratification   38
  The Constitution and Equality   39
Constitutional Reform: Modern Views   40
  Reducing the Separation of Powers   40
  Making the System Less Democratic   43
  Who Is Right?   45

3   Federalism   48

Governmental Structure   50
  Federalism: Good or Bad?   50
  Increased Political Activity   52
The Founding   52
  A Bold, New Plan   52
  Elastic Language   53
The Debate on the Meaning of Federalism   54
  The Supreme Court Speaks   54
  Nullification   56
  Dual Federalism   57
  State Sovereignty   58
Federal-State Relations   60
  Grants-in-Aid   60
  Meeting National Needs   61
  The Intergovernmental Lobby   62
  Categorical Grants Versus Revenue Sharing   63
  Rivalry Among the States   65
Federal Aid and Federal Control   66
  Mandates   66
  Conditions of Aid   67
A Devolution Revolution?   68
  Block Grants for Entitlements   69
  What's Driving Devolution?   70
Congress and Federalism   70

4 **American Political Culture** 75

Political Culture 76
 The Political System 77
 The Economic System 79
Comparing America with Other Nations 80
 The Political System 80
 The Economic System 81
 The Civic Role of Religion 82
 Religion and Politics 83
The Sources of Political Culture 84
 The Culture War 86
Mistrust of Government 87
Political Efficacy 89
Political Tolerance 91

5 **Civil Liberties** 97

Culture and Civil Liberties 99
 Rights in Conflict 99
 Cultural Conflicts 100
 Applying the Bill of Rights to the States 102
Interpreting and Applying the First Amendment
 102
 Speech and National Security 102
What Is Speech? 105
 Libel 105
 Obscenity 105
 Symbolic Speech 108
Who Is a Person? 108
Church and State 110
 The Free-Exercise Clause 110
 The Establishment Clause 111
Crime and Due Process 113
 The Exclusionary Rule 114
 Search and Seizure 116
 Confessions and Self-Incrimination 117
 Relaxing the Exclusionary Rule 118
 Terrorism and Civil Liberties 119

6 **Civil Rights** 124

The Black Predicament 126
The Campaign in the Courts 127
 "Separate but Equal" 128
 Can Separate Schools Be Equal? 129
 Brown v. Board of Education 129
The Campaign in Congress 134
 Racial Profiling 139
Women and Equal Rights 139
 Sexual Harassment 142
 Privacy and Sex 142
Affirmative Action 144
 Equality of Results 144
 Equality of Opportunity 145
Gays and the Constitution 149

P A R T   I I
OPINIONS, INTERESTS, AND
ORGANIZATIONS 153

7 **Public Opinion** 154

What Is Public Opinion? 156
 How Polling Works 157
 How Opinions Differ 157
Political Socialization: The Family 158
 Religion 159
 The Gender Gap 160
 Schooling and Information 161
Cleavages in Public Opinion 162
 Social Class 163
 Race and Ethnicity 164
 Region 167
Political Ideology 167
 Consistent Attitudes 168
 What Do Liberalism and Conservatism Mean? 168
 Various Categories 169
 Analyzing Consistency 169
 Political Elites 171
Political Elites, Public Opinion, and Public Policy
 172

8 Political Participation   177

A Closer Look at Nonvoting   178
The Rise of the American Electorate   180
   From State to Federal Control   181
   Voter Turnout   184
Who Participates in Politics?   187
   Forms of Participation   187
   The Causes of Participation   188
   The Meaning of Participation Rates   191

9 Political Parties   197

Parties—Here and Abroad   198
   Political Culture   200
The Rise and Decline of the Political Party   201
   The Founding   201
   The Jacksonians   202
   The Civil War and Sectionalism   203
   The Era of Reform   204
   Party Realignments   205
   Party Decline   207
The National Party Structure Today   207
   National Conventions   209
State and Local Parties   213
   The Machine   213
   Ideological Parties   215
   Solidary Groups   215
   Sponsored Parties   216
   Personal Following   216
The Two-Party System   217
Minor Parties   220
Nominating a President   223
   Are the Delegates Representative of the Voters?
      224
   Who Votes in Primaries?   224
   Who Are the New Delegates?   225
Parties Versus Voters   225

10 Elections and Campaigns   230

Presidential Versus Congressional Campaigns   232
   Running for President   232
   Getting Elected to Congress   234
Primary Versus General Campaigns   237
   Two Kinds of Campaign Issues   239
   Television, Debates, and Direct Mail   240
Money   244
   The Sources of Campaign Money   244
   Campaign Finance Rules   246
   A Second Campaign Finance Reform   250
   New Sources of Money   251
   Money and Winning   252
What Decides the Election?   253
   Party   254
   Issues, Especially the Economy   255
   The Campaign   256
   Finding a Winning Coalition   257
The Effects of Elections on Policy   259

11 Interest Groups   264

Explaining Proliferation   265
The Birth of Interest Groups   266
Kinds of Organizations   268
   Institutional Interests   268
   Membership Interests   269
   Incentives to Join   270
   The Influence of the Staff   272
Interest Groups and Social Movements   273
   The Environmental Movement   274
   The Feminist Movement   274
   The Union Movement   275
Funds for Interest Groups   276
   Foundation Grants   276
   Federal Grants and Contracts   276
   Direct Mail   277
The Problem of Bias   278

The Activities of Interest Groups   279
   Information   279
   Public Support: The Rise of the New Politics   280
   Money and PACs   282
   The "Revolving Door"   284
   Trouble   285
Regulating Interest Groups   286

12 **The Media**   291

Journalism in American Political History   293
   The Party Press   294
   The Popular Press   295
   Magazines of Opinion   295
   Electronic Journalism   296
   The Internet   297
The Structure of the Media   298
   Degree of Competition   298
   The National Media   299
Rules Governing the Media   300
   Confidentiality of Sources   301
   Regulating Broadcasting   301
   Campaigning   302
Are the National Media Biased?   303
Government and the News   307
   Prominence of the President   307
   Coverage of Congress   308
   Why Do We Have So Many News Leaks?   308
   Sensationalism in the Media   310
   Government Constraints on Journalists   311

PART III
INSTITUTIONS OF GOVERNMENT
315

13 **Congress**   316

Congress Versus Parliament   318
The Evolution of Congress   321
Who Is in Congress?   325
   Sex and Race   325
   Incumbency   326
   Party   328

Do Members Represent Their Voters?   330
   Representational View   331
   Organizational View   332
   Attitudinal View   332
Ideology and Civility in Congress   333
The Organization of Congress: Parties and Caucuses   334
   Party Organization of the Senate   334
   Party Structure in the House   335
   The Strength of Party Structures   337
   Party Unity   338
   Caucuses   340
The Organization of Congress: Committees   341
The Organization of Congress: Staffs and Specialized Offices   345
   Tasks of Staff Members   346
   Staff Agencies   347
How a Bill Becomes Law   347
   Introducing a Bill   350
   Study by Committees   350
   Floor Debate—The House   353
   Floor Debate—The Senate   353
   Methods of Voting   355
Reducing Power and Perks   358
The Post-9/11 Congress   359

14 **The Presidency**   367

Presidents and Prime Ministers   368
Divided Government   370
   Does Gridlock Matter?   371
   Is Policy Gridlock Bad?   371
The Evolution of the Presidency   372
   Concerns of the Founders   372
   The Electoral College   373
   The President's Term of Office   373
   The First Presidents   374
   The Jacksonians   375
   The Reemergence of Congress   377
The Powers of the President   379
The Office of the President   380
   The White House Office   381
   The Executive Office of the President   383

The Cabinet   384

Independent Agencies, Commissions, and Judgeships
385

Who Gets Appointed   385

Presidential Character   388

The Power to Persuade   390

The Three Audiences   390

Popularity and Influence   390

The Decline in Popularity   392

The Power to Say No   394

Veto   394

Executive Privilege   396

Impoundment of Funds   396

The President's Program   397

Putting Together a Program   397

Attempts to Reorganize   399

Presidential Transition   401

The Vice President   401

Problems of Succession   402

Impeachment   403

How Powerful Is the President?   406

15 **The Bureaucracy   409**

Distinctiveness of the American Bureaucracy   410

The Growth of the Bureaucracy   411

The Appointment of Officials   412

A Service Role   412

A Change in Role   414

The Federal Bureaucracy Today   414

Recruitment and Retention   415

Personal Attributes   421

Do Bureaucrats Sabotage Their Political Bosses?   422

Culture and Careers   423

Constraints   424

Agency Allies   426

Congressional Oversight   427

The Appropriations Committee and Legislative
Committees   428

The Legislative Veto   429

Congressional Investigations   429

Bureaucratic "Pathologies"   430

Reforming the Bureaucracy   432

16 **The Judiciary   437**

The Development of the Federal Courts   439

National Supremacy and Slavery   441

Government and the Economy   442

Government and Political Liberty   443

The Revival of State Sovereignty   445

The Structure of the Federal Courts   446

Selecting Judges   446

The Jurisdiction of the Federal Courts   448

Getting to Court   451

Fee Shifting   452

Standing   452

Class-Action Suits   453

The Supreme Court in Action   454

The Power of the Federal Courts   456

The Power to Make Policy   456

Views of Judicial Activism   459

Legislation and the Courts   460

Checks on Judicial Power   460

Congress and the Courts   461

Public Opinion and the Courts   463

PART IV

THE POLITICS OF PUBLIC POLICY
467

17 **Politics and Public Policy   468**

How the American System Affects Policy-Making
467 470

How the American System Has Changed   472

Restraints on Growth   474

Relaxing the Restraints   474

The Old System   475

The New System   476

Polarized Politics   479

Should the System Be Changed?   480

Reducing the Barriers to Action   480

Increasing the Barriers to Action   482

Term Limits   483

Who is Right?   483

Appendix   A1

The Declaration of Independence   A1
The Constitution of the United States   A4
The *Federalist* No. 10   A21
The *Federalist* No. 51   A26
Presidents and Congresses, 1789–2006   A30

GLOSSARY   G1
NOTES   N1
INDEX   I1
CREDITS   C1

☆ PREFACE

This Tenth Edition of *American Government* offers students its classic hallmark features and the latest in politics in America. As before, we show not only who governs but also what difference—in policies adopted or rejected—it makes in who governs. We again stress the historical evolution of our practices and institutions, focusing on the importance of the Constitution and American political culture in shaping governmental activities. Whenever appropriate, we compare our institutions with other democratic institutions around the globe.

This edition, while retaining the above themes, has been revised to fit even more closely to how this course is often taught. For example, we have moved the chapters on civil liberties and civil rights earlier in the text; they have now become Chapters 5 and 6. In order to provide a clearer set of arguments that link all of the chapters to the central arguments of Chapter 1, "The Study of American Government," we begin each chapter with the questions "Who Governs?" and "To What Ends?"; we end each chapter with corresponding summaries ("Reconsidering Who Governs" and "Reconsidering To What Ends") of what the reader will have learned about the chapter opening questions. Naturally, the text has been revised to reflect American government since the publication of the Ninth Edition. Timely updates include, among others, the Post-9/11 Congress (including the 9/11 Commission); the effect of campaign finance reform on civil liberties; a thorough examination of the 2004 presidential election, including voter opinions and turnout; the role of 527s on political contributions; and the impact of the Internet on raising election funds and disseminating news.

This edition keeps the number of boxed items few in number and clear in focus. For example, each substantive chapter features a "What Would You Do?" box; this popular feature encourages classroom discussion by highlighting an important policy question and briefly stating the arguments for and against each major option. We still offer select "How Things Work" boxes to give students an understanding of such procedures in American politics as amending the Constitution, becoming a U.S. citizen, and qualifying to become a Congressperson. A number of our "Politically Speaking," "Trivia," and "The 'Rules' of Politics" boxes are now incorporated in the narrative of the text or are available online.

Each chapter ends with a Summary, World Wide Web Resources, and Suggested Readings that provide students with reference material and preparation for classroom lectures and examinations.

Learning and Teaching Ancillaries

The program for *American Government*, Tenth Edition includes a number of useful learning and teaching aids. These ancillaries are designed to provide instructors with useful course management and presentation tools and to help students get the most from their American Government course.

For the Instructor

The **Instructor's Resource Manual** helps instructors plan their course, lectures, and discussion sections. Mary Beth Melchior (Florida International University) has integrated the IRM with the textbook. Elements new to this edition have been summarized, and the resources and references sections have been thoroughly updated.

The **Test Item File,** revised by P.S. Ruckman, Jr. (Rock Valley College) contains over 4,000 multiple choice, true/false, and essay questions for classroom use. **HM Testing™,** a computerized version of the Test Item File with flexible test-editing capabilities, is available on the **HM ClassPrep CD-ROM.**

In addition to HM Testing, the HM ClassPrep CD-ROM features other classroom presentation tools, including an online version of the Instructor's Resource Manual, video and audio clips, and a set of PowerPoint® slides of key charts and graphs. PowerPoint® slides can also be downloaded from the **Instructor's Resource Page** (http://politicalscience.college.hmco.com/instructors).

A newly revised **State and Local Government Supplement,** packaged at no cost with *American Government,* Tenth Edition, offers material for those courses that include a unit on state and local politics.

The ***American Government,*** **Tenth Edition Web Site,** online at http://politicalscience.college.hmco.com/students, contains other aids for students, including chapter outlines, ACE self-quizzes, *What Would You Do?* interactive simulations, additional "Trivia," "Rules of Politics," and "Politically Speaking" features, and chapter-specific web links. The site also links to **Crosstabs 4.0.** Crosstabs allows students to cross-tabulate survey data on the recent Presidential election and the Congressional voting records in order to analyze voter attitudes and behaviors.

For the Student

The **Student Handbook** has been thoroughly updated by P.S. Ruckman, Jr. (Rock Valley College) to help students master the facts and principles in *American Government* and prepare for examinations. For each chapter, the handbook includes focus points, a study outline, key terms, notes about possible misconceptions, a data check, practice exam questions, and special application projects, as well as answers to all the chapter exercises (excluding the essay questions).

Acknowledgements

A number of scholars reviewed the Ninth Edition and made useful suggestions for the Tenth. They include William Bianco, Pennsylvania State University; Melvin A. Kulbicki, York College of Pennsylvania; Jeff Gulati, Wellesley College; Edward B. Hasecke, Cleveland State University; Richard Himelfarb, Hofstra University; Thomas Masterson, Butte College; L. Marvin Overby, University of Missouri; Donald P. Racheter, Central College. Additional thanks go to Marc Siegal for his research assistance.

James Q. Wilson

James Q. Wilson now teaches at Pepperdine University. He is an emeritus professor of management and public policy at the University of California, Los Angeles, and from 1961 to 1987 was a professor of government at Harvard University. Raised in California, he received a B.A. degree from the University of Redlands and Ph.D. from the University of Chicago. Wilson is the author or coauthor of fourteen books, including *The Marriage Problem* (2002), *Moral Judgment* (1997), *The Moral Sense* (1993), *Bureaucracy* (1989), *Crime and Human Nature* (1985, with Richard J. Herrnstein), *Thinking about Crime* (1983), and *Political Organizations* (1974).

Wilson has served in a number of advisory posts in the federal government. He was chairman of the White House Task Force on Crime in 1967, chairman of the National Advisory Council on Drug Abuse Prevention in 1972–1973, a member of the Attorney General's Task Force on Violent Crime in 1981, and a member of the President's Foreign Intelligence Advisory Board in 1986–1990.

In 1977 the American Political Science Association conferred on him the Charles E. Merriam Award for advancing the art of government through the application of social science knowledge and in 1990 the James Madison Award for distinguished scholarship. In 1991–1992 he was President of the Association.

He is a Fellow of the American Academy of Arts and Sciences and a member of the American Philosophical Society. When not writing, teaching, or advising, he goes scuba diving. In 2003 Wilson received the Presidential Medal of Freedom, this nation's highest civilian award.

John J. DiIulio, Jr.

John J. DiIulio, Jr. is a professor of political science at the University of Pennsylvania and a senior fellow at the Brookings Institution. From 1986 to 1999, he was a professor of politics and public affairs at Princeton University's Woodrow Wilson School of Public and International Affairs. He received B.A. and M.A. degrees from the University of Pennsylvania and M.A. and Ph.D. degrees from Harvard University. He is the author, coauthor, or editor of a dozen books, including *What's God Got to Do with the American Experiment?* (2000, with E.J. Dionne); *Medicaid and Devolution* (1998, with Frank Thompson); and *Deregulating the Public Service* (1994).

DiIulio advised both Vice President Al Gore and Governor George W. Bush during the 2000 Presidential campaign. While on leave in academic year 2000–2001, he served as Assistant to the President of the United States. Over the last decade, he has advised officials at the National Performance Review, the Office of Management and Budget, the General Accounting Office, the U.S. Department of Justice, and other federal agencies. He has served on the boards of Big Brothers Big Sisters of America and other national nonprofit organizations.

In 1995 the Association of Public Policy Analysis and Management conferred on him the David N. Kershaw Award for outstanding research achievements and in 1987 he received the American Political Science Association's Leonard D. White Award in public administration. In 1991–1994 he chaired the latter association's standing committee on professional ethics.

American Government

The Essentials

PART I

The American System

*In framing a government which is to
be administered by men over men,
the great difficulty lies in this:
You must first enable the government
to control the governed; and in the
next place oblige it to control itself.*

FEDERALIST No. 51

CHAPTER 1

The Study of American Government

What Is Political Power?

What Is Democracy?

Is Representative Democracy Best?

How Is Power Distributed in a Democracy?

How Is Political Power Distributed?

Is Democracy Driven by Self-Interest?

What Explains Political Change?

The Nature of Politics

WHO GOVERNS?

1. How is political power actually distributed in America?
2. What explains major political change?

TO WHAT ENDS?

1. What value or values matter most in American democracy?
2. Are trade-offs among political purposes inevitable?

When you read the report of the National Commission on Terrorist Attacks Upon the United States, better known as the 9/11 Commission, you may wonder why many government agencies failed to alert us.[1] You may be depressed by the many stories of divided authority, weak congressional oversight, federal bureaucracies not talking to one another, and countless state and local agencies with no central leadership. You may well decide, as the Commission did, that the nation has to unify all of these groups.[2]

But unity is rare in American politics. You may think this is the result of idiots failing to do their jobs. But if you think that, you have not read this book.

Politics exists in part because people differ about two things: who should govern, and the ends toward which they should work.

We want to know the answer to the first question because we believe that those who rule—their personalities and beliefs, their virtues and vices— will affect what they do to and for us. Many people think they already know the answer to the question, and they are prepared to talk and vote on that basis. That is their right, and the opinions they express may be correct. But they may also be wrong. Indeed, many of these opinions *must* be wrong because they are in conflict. When asked, "Who governs?" some people will say "the unions" and some will say "big business"; others will say "the politicians," "the people," or "the special interests." Still others will say "Wall Street," "the military," "crackpot liberals," "the media," "the bureaucrats," or "white males." Not all these answers can be correct—at least not all of the time.

The answer to the second question is important because it tells us how government affects our lives. We want to know not only who governs, but what difference it makes who governs. In our day-to-day lives we may not think government makes much difference at all. In one sense that is right, because our most pressing personal concerns—work, play, love, family, health—are essentially private matters on which government touches but slightly. But in a larger and longer perspective government makes a substantial difference. Consider: in 1935, 96 percent of all American families paid no federal income tax, and for the 4 percent or so who did pay, the average rate was only about 4 percent of their incomes. Today almost all families pay federal payroll taxes, and the average rate is 21 percent of their incomes. Or consider: in 1960, in many parts of the country, African Americans could ride only in the backs of buses, had to use washrooms and

Why Government Matters: A Top Ten List

Based on a survey of 450 history and political science professors and an analysis of over 500 public statutes, here is one list of the government's top ten post-1950 achievements.

10. Promoted financial security in retirement
9. Reduced the federal budget deficit
8. Increased access to health care for older Americans
7. Strengthened the nation's highway system
6. Ensured safe food and drinking water
5. Reduced workplace discrimination
4. Reduced disease
3. Promoted equal access to public accommodations
2. Expanded the right to vote
1. Rebuilt Europe after World War II

As you read this book (especially Chapters 17 through 21 on public policy issues) and study American government, ponder what might be on the top ten list for the first quarter of the twenty-first century.

Source: Adapted from Paul C. Light, "Government's Greatest Achievements of the Past Half Century," Reform Watch Brief #2, Brookings Institution, Washington, D.C., November 2000. Reprinted by permission of the Brookings Institution.

---

drinking fountains that were labeled "colored," and could not be served in most public restaurants. Such restrictions have been almost eliminated, in large part because of decisions by the federal government.

It is important to bear in mind that we wish to answer two different questions, and not two versions of the same question. You cannot always predict what goals government will establish knowing only who governs, nor can you always tell who governs by knowing what activities government undertakes. Most people holding national political office are middle-class, middle-aged, white Protestant males, but we cannot then conclude that the government will adopt only policies that are to the narrow advantage of the middle class, the middle-aged, whites, Protestants, or men. If we thought that, we would be at a loss to explain why the rich are taxed more heavily than the poor, why the War on Poverty was declared, why constitutional amendments giving rights to African Americans and women passed Congress by large majorities, or why Catholics and Jews have been appointed to so many important governmental posts.

This book is chiefly devoted to answering the question, Who governs? It is written in the belief that this question cannot be answered without looking at how government makes—or fails to make—decisions about a large variety of concrete issues. Thus in this book we shall inspect government policies to see what individuals, groups, and institutions seem to exert the greatest power in the continuous struggle to define the purposes of government. We shall see that power and purpose are inextricably intertwined.

What Is Political Power?

By **power** we mean the ability of one person to get another person to act in accordance with the first person's intentions. Sometimes an exercise of power is obvious, as when the president tells the air force that it cannot build a new bomber or orders soldiers into combat in a foreign land. Some claim it is exercised in subtle ways that may not be evident even to the participants, as when the president's junior speechwriters, reflecting their own evolving views, adopt a new tone when writing for their boss about controversial social issues like abortion. The speechwriters may not think they are using power—after all, they are the president's subordinates and may rarely see him face-to-face. But if the president lets their words exit his mouth in public, they have used power.

Power is found in all human relationships, but we shall be concerned here only with power as it is used to affect who will hold government office and how

---

power   The ability of one person to get another person to act in accordance with the first person's intentions.

government will behave. This fails to take into account many important things. If a corporation closes a factory in a small town where it was the major employer, it is using power in ways that affect deeply the lives of people. When a university refuses to admit a student or a medical society refuses to license a would-be physician, it is also using power. But to explain how all these things happen would be tantamount to explaining how society as a whole, and in all its particulars, operates. We limit our view here to government, and chiefly to the American federal government. However, we shall repeatedly pay special attention to how things once thought to be "private" matters become "public"—that is, how they manage to become objects of governmental action. Indeed, one of the most striking transformations of American politics has been the extent to which, in recent decades, almost every aspect of human life has found its way onto the governmental agenda. In the 1950s the federal government would have displayed no interest in a factory closing its doors, a university refusing an applicant, or a profession not accrediting a member. Now government actions can and do affect all these things.

People who exercise political power may or may not have the authority to do so. By **authority** we mean the right to use power. The exercise of rightful power—that is, of authority—is ordinarily easier than the exercise of power that is not supported by any persuasive claim of right. We accept decisions, often without question, if they are made by people who we believe have the right to make them; we may bow to naked power because we cannot resist it, but by our recalcitrance or our resentment we put the users of naked power to greater trouble than the wielders of authority. In this book we will on occasion speak of "formal authority." By this we mean that the right to exercise power is vested in a governmental office. A president, a senator, and a federal judge have formal authority to take certain actions.

What makes power rightful varies from time to time and from country to country. In the United States we usually say that a person has political authority if his or her right to act in a certain way is conferred by a law or by a state or national constitution. But what makes a law or constitution a source of right? That is the question of **legitimacy.** In the United States the Constitution today is widely, if not unanimously, accepted as a source of legitimate authority, but that was not always the case.

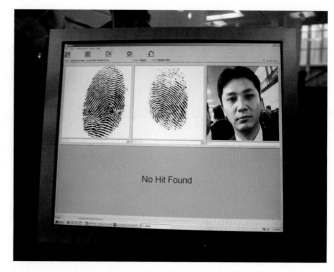

To enter the United States, foreigners must now produce a photograph and fingerprints.

Much of American political history has been a struggle over what constitutes legitimate authority. The Constitutional Convention in 1787 was an effort to see whether a new, more powerful federal government could be made legitimate; the succeeding administrations of George Washington, John Adams, and Thomas Jefferson were in large measure preoccupied with disputes over the kinds of decisions that were legitimate for the federal government to make. The Civil War was a bloody struggle over the legitimacy of the federal union; the New Deal of Franklin Roosevelt was hotly debated by those who disagreed over whether it was legitimate for the federal government to intervene deeply in the economy.

During the 2004 presidential contest, even many citizens who took the same view on a hot-button question like gay marriage disagreed over whether it was legitimate to address the issue through an amendment to the Constitution that banned it nationally or whether the matter ought to be left for each state to decide.

On one thing, however, virtually all Americans seem to agree: no exercise of political power by government at any level is legitimate if it is not in some

---

authority   The right to use power.
legitimacy   Political authority conferred by law or by a state or national constitution.

Iraqis cheer American soldiers who were helping distribute humanitarian aid.

sense democratic. That was hardly always the prevailing view. In 1787, as the Constitution was being debated, Alexander Hamilton worried that the new government he helped create might be too democratic, while George Mason, who refused to sign the Constitution, worried that it was not democratic enough. Today, however, almost everyone believes that democratic government is the only proper kind. Most people believe that American government is democratic; some believe that other institutions of public life—schools, universities, corporations, trade unions, churches—should also be run on democratic principles if they are to be legitimate; and some insist that promoting democracy abroad ought to be a primary purpose of U.S. foreign policy.

Whether democracy is the best way of governing all institutions and whether promoting democracy either has been or ought to be a major objective of U.S. foreign policy are both worthwhile questions. The former question goes beyond the scope of this book, but we will touch upon the latter question in Chapter 20.

---

democracy   The rule of the many.

direct or participatory democracy   A government in which all or most citizens participate directly.

representative democracy   A government in which leaders make decisions by winning a competitive struggle for the popular vote.

☆ What Is Democracy?

Democracy is a word with at least two different meanings. First, the term *democracy* is used to describe those regimes that come as close as possible to Aristotle's definition—the "rule of the many."[3] A government is democratic if all, or most, of its citizens participate directly in either holding office or making policy. This is often called **direct or participatory democracy.** In Aristotle's time—Greece in the fourth century B.C.—such a government was possible. The Greek city-state, or *polis,* was quite small, and within it citizenship was extended to all free adult male property holders. (Slaves, women, minors, and those without property were excluded from participation in government.) In more recent times the New England town meeting approximates the Aristotelian ideal. In such a meeting the adult citizens of a community gather once or twice a year to vote directly on all major issues and expenditures of the town. As towns have become larger and issues more complicated, many town governments have abandoned the pure town meeting in favor of either the representative town meeting (in which a large number of elected representatives, perhaps two or three hundred, meet to vote on town affairs) or representative government (in which a small number of elected city councilors make decisions).

The second definition of democracy is the principle of governance of most nations that are called democratic. It was most concisely stated by the economist Joseph Schumpeter: "The democratic method is that institutional arrangement for arriving at political decisions in which individuals [that is, leaders] acquire the power to decide by means of a competitive struggle for the people's vote."[4] Sometimes this method is called, approvingly, **representative democracy;** at other times it is referred to, disapprovingly, as the elitist theory of democracy. It is justified by one or both of two arguments: First, it is impractical, owing to limits of time, information, energy, interest, and expertise, for the people to decide on public policy, but it is not impractical to expect them to make reasonable choices among competing leadership groups. Second, some people (including, as we shall see in the next chapter, many of the Framers of the Constitution) believe that direct democracy is likely to lead to bad decisions, because people often decide large issues on the basis of fleet-

Can a Democracy Fight a War Against Terrorists?

Americans felt powerfully connected to their fellow citizens in the immediate aftermath of 9/11.

On September 11, 2001, a date that will forever more be referred to as 9/11, war came to the United States when terrorists crashed four hijacked airliners, filled with passengers, into the two towers of the World Trade Center in New York City, into the Pentagon in Washington, D.C., and into some empty land in Pennsylvania. About three thousand people were killed.

How can a democratic nation respond to a war waged, not by an enemy nation, but by a loose collection of terrorists with cells in many parts of the world? America's new war against terrorism is much more difficult to fight than the one against Nazi Germany and the Japanese warlords in 1941.

- How can we reorganize the military so that it can respond swiftly and effectively against small targets?
- Is it constitutional to try captured terrorists in military tribunals?
- How much new law enforcement authority should be given to police and investigative agencies?
- Should America invade nations that support terrorists?

In the years ahead, these questions will raise profound challenges for American democracy.

ing passions and in response to popular demagogues. This concern about direct democracy persists today, as can be seen from the statements of leaders who do not like what voters have decided. For example, in 2000 voters in Michigan overwhelmingly rejected a referendum that would have increased public funding for private schools. Politicians who opposed the defeated referendum spoke approvingly of the "will of the people," but politicians who favored it spoke disdainfully of "mass misunderstanding."

☆ Is Representative Democracy Best?

Whenever the word *democracy* is used alone in this book, it will have the meaning Schumpeter gave it.

As we discuss in the next chapter, the men who wrote the Constitution did not use the word *democracy* in that document. They wrote instead of a "republican form of government," but by that they meant what we call "representative democracy." Whenever we refer to that form of democracy involving the direct participation of all or most citizens, we shall use the term *direct* or *participatory* democracy.

For representative government to work, there must, of course, be an opportunity for genuine leadership competition. This requires in turn that individuals and parties be able to run for office, that communication (through speeches or the press, and in meetings) be free, and that the voters perceive that a meaningful choice exists. Many questions still remain to be answered. For instance: How many offices should be elective and how many appointive? How many candidates or parties can exist before the choices become hopelessly confused? Where will the money come from to finance electoral campaigns? There is more than one answer to such questions. In some European democracies, for example, very few offices—often just those in the national or local legislature—are elective, and much of the money for campaigning for these offices comes from the government. In the United States many offices—executive and judicial as well as legislative—are elective, and most of the money the candidates use for campaigning comes from industry, labor unions, and private individuals.

Some people have argued that the virtues of direct or participatory democracy can and should be reclaimed even in a modern, complex society. This can be done either by allowing individual neighborhoods in big cities to govern themselves (community control) or by requiring those affected by some government program to participate in its formulation (citizen participation). In many states a measure of direct democracy exists when voters can decide on referendum issues—that is, policy choices that appear on the ballot. The proponents of direct democracy defend it as the only way to ensure that the "will of the people" prevails.

The Framers of the Constitution did not think that the "will of the people" was synonymous with the "common interest" or the "public good." They strongly favored representative democracy over direct democracy. They believed that government should mediate, not mirror, popular views, and that elected officials should represent, not register, majority sentiments. They supposed that most citizens did not have the time, information, interest, and expertise to make reasonable choices among competing policy positions. They suspected that even highly educated people could be manipulated by demagogic leaders who played on their fears and prejudices. They granted that representative democracy often proceeds slowly and prevents sweeping changes in policy, but they cautioned that a government capable of doing great good quickly also can do great harm quickly. They agreed that majority opinion should figure in the enactment of many or most government policies, but they insisted that the protection of civil rights and civil liberties—the right to a fair trial; the freedom of speech, press, and religion; or the right to vote itself—ought never to hinge on a popular vote. Above all, they embraced representative democracy because they saw it as a way of minimizing the chances that power would be abused either by a tyrannical popular majority or by self-serving officeholders.

Clearly, the Framers of the Constitution thought that representative democracy was best, but were they right? Any answer must address two related questions: first, even if the Framers' assumptions about direct democracy being impractical and likely to lead to bad decisions were correct for their time, are they equally correct in ours?; and, second, should American political history be read more nearly to justify or to jettison the Framers' faith that representative democracy would help to protect minority rights and prevent politicians from using public offices for private gains?

The first question asks whether people today have more time, information, energy, interest, and expertise, or more ability to gather together for collective decision-making, than they did when the Constitution was adopted. To decide, one should know how the Internet has vastly expanded access to political information as well as how little most people consume political news.

☆ How Is Political Power Distributed?

The second question asks how political power has actually been distributed in America's representative democracy. Scholars differ in their interpretations of the American political experience. Where some see a steady march of democracy, others see no such thing; where some emphasize how voting and other rights have been steadily expanded, others stress how they were denied to so many for so long, and so forth. Short of attempting to reconcile these competing historical interpretations, let us step back now for a moment to our definition of representative democracy and four competing views about how political power has been distributed in America.

Representative democracy is defined as any system of government in which leaders are authorized to make decisions—and thereby to wield political power—by winning a competitive struggle for the popular vote. It is obvious then that very different sets of hands can control political power, depending on what kinds of people can become leaders, how the struggle for votes is carried on, how much freedom to act is given to those who win the struggle, and what other sorts of influence (besides the desire for popular approval) affect the leaders' actions.

In some cases the leaders will be so sharply constrained by what most people want that the actions of officeholders will follow the preferences of citizens very closely. We shall call such cases examples of *majoritarian politics*. In this case elected officials are the delegates of the people, acting as the people (or a majority of them) would act were the matter put to a popular vote. The issues handled in a majoritarian fashion can be only those that are sufficiently important to command the attention of most citizens, sufficiently clear to elicit an informed opinion from citizens, and sufficiently feasible to address so that what citizens want done can in fact be done.

When circumstances do not permit majoritarian decision-making, then some group of officials will have to act without knowing (and perhaps without caring) exactly what people want. Indeed, even on issues that do evoke a clear opinion from a majority of citizens, the shaping of the details of a policy will reflect the views of those people who are sufficiently motivated to go to the trouble of becoming active participants in policy-making. These active participants usually will be a small, and probably an unrepresentative, minority. Thus the actual distribution of political power, even in a democracy, will depend importantly on the composition of the political elites who are actually involved in the struggles over policy. By **elite** we mean an identifiable group of persons who possess a disproportionate share of some valued resource—in this case, political power.

There are at least four different schools of thought about political elites and how power has actually been distributed in America's representative democracy: *Marxist, power elite, bureaucratic,* and *pluralist.* The German philosopher Karl Marx (1818–1883) was the founder of modern socialist thought. There are many variants of Marxist ideology. Essentially, however, the **Marxist view** is that government, even if democratic in form, is merely a reflection of underlying economic forces.[5] Marxists hold that in modern societies, two economic classes contend for power—capitalists (business owners or the "bourgeoise") and workers (laborers or the "proletariat"). Whichever class dominates the economy also controls the government, which is, they reckon, nothing more than a piece of machinery designed to express and give legal effect to underlying class interests. In the United States, Marxists maintain, capitalists (especially "big business" and today's "multinational corporations" headquartered in America) have generally dominated the economy and hence the government.

A second theory, closely related to the first, was started by C. Wright Mills, a famous mid-twentieth-century American sociologist. To him, a coalition of three groups—corporate leaders, top military officers, and a handful of elected officials—dominate politics and government.[6] Today, some add to Mills's triumvirate major communications media chiefs, top labor union officials, the heads of various special-interest groups, and others. But the essential **power elite view** is the same: American democracy is actually dominated by a few top leaders, most of whom are outside of government and enjoy great advantages in wealth, status, or organizational position.

The third theory was shaped by the German scholar, Max Weber (1864–1920), a founder of sociology. To Weber, the dominant social and political reality of modern times was that all institutions, governmental and nongovernmental, have fallen under the control of large bureaucracies whose expertise and competence are essential to the management of contemporary affairs.[7] Capitalists or workers may come to power (as in the Marxist view), or coalitions of well-positioned elites may dominate government and the legislative process (as in the power elite view), but the government they create and the laws they enact will be dominated in either case by bureaucrats who staff and operate the government on a daily basis. This **bureaucratic view** suggests that power is mainly in the hands, not of American democracy's elected representatives, but in those of its appointed officials, career government workers who, though they may be virtually invisible to most average citizens and unknown to most elites, nonetheless exercise vast power by deciding how to translate public laws into administrative actions. In this view, government bureaucrats do not merely implement public policies, they effectively "make" them as suits their own ideas and interests.

Fourth is the **pluralist view.** It has no single intellectual parent, but it has many followers in

---

elite   Persons who possess a disproportionate share of some valued resource, like money or power.

Marxist view   View that the government is dominated by capitalists.

power elite view   View that the government is dominated by a few top leaders, most of whom are outside of government.

bureaucratic view   View that the government is dominated by appointed officials.

pluralist view   The belief that competition among all affected interests shapes public policy.

contemporary political science and in journalism. Pluralists acknowledge that big businesses, cozy elites, or career bureaucrats may dominate on some issues, but stress that political resources, such as money, prestige, expertise, organizational position, and access to the mass media, are so widely scattered in American society that no single elite has anything like a monopoly on them.[8] Furthermore, pluralists point out, in America, there are so many governmental institutions in which power may be exercised—city, state, and federal governments and, within these, the offices of mayors, managers, legislators, governors, presidents, judges, bureaucrats—that no single group, even if it had many political resources, could dominate most, or even much, of the political process. Instead, many policies are the outcome of a complex pattern of political haggling, innumerable compromises, and shifting alliances. What government does is affected to varying degrees not only by competing groups of elites inside or outside government but by mass public opinion as well.

Pluralists do not go so far as to argue that political resources are distributed equally—that would be tantamount to saying that all decisions are made on a majoritarian basis. After reviewing recent evidence, in 2004 the American Political Science Association's Task Force on Inequality and American Democracy concluded that "political input" and the "exercise of political voice" in American democracy are "extremely unequal" and "stratified most fundamentally by social class."[9] But the APSA task force also noted that, though such inequalities seem "especially pronounced in the United States," they exist "in all democracies."[10] It also expressed uncertainty about whether recent increases in economic inequality had much, if any, impact either on long-observed socioeconomic differences in patterns of political participation, or on particular government policies and programs.

Thus, acknowledging strong evidence about inequalities in American democracy, pluralists maintain that political resources nonetheless remain sufficiently divided among such different kinds of elites (business people, politicians, union leaders, journalists, bureaucrats, professors, environmentalists, lawyers, and whomever else) that all, or almost all, relevant interests have a chance to affect the outcome of decisions. Not only are the elites divided, they are responsive to their followers' interests, and thus they provide representation to almost all citizens affected by a policy.

☆ Is Democracy Driven by Self-Interest?

Of the four views of how political power has been distributed in the United States, the pluralist view does the most to reassure one that America has been, and continues to be, a democracy in more than name only. But the pluralist view, not less than the other three, may lead some people to the cynical conclusion that, whichever view is correct, politics is a self-seeking enterprise in which everybody is out for personal gain. Though there is surely plenty of self-interest among political elites (at least as much as there is among college or high school students!), it does not necessarily follow that the resulting policies will be wholly self-serving. Nor does it follow that democracy itself is driven mainly or solely by people's baser motives or selfish desires.

For one thing, a policy may be good or bad independent of the motives of the person who decided it, just as a product sold on the market may be useful or useless regardless of the profit-seeking or wage-seeking motives of those who produced it. For another thing, the self-interest of individuals is often an incomplete guide to their actions. People must frequently choose between two courses of action, neither of which has an obvious "payoff" to them. We caution against the cynical explanation of politics that Americans seem especially prone to adopt. Alexis de Tocqueville, the French author of a perceptive account of American life and politics in the early nineteenth century, noticed this trait among us.

> Americans . . . are fond of explaining almost all the actions of their lives by the principle of self-interest rightly understood. . . . In this respect I think they frequently fail to do themselves justice; for in the United States as well as elsewhere people are sometimes seen to give way to those disinterested and spontaneous impulses that are natural to man; but the Americans seldom admit that they yield to emotions of this kind; they are more anxious to do honor to their philosophy than to themselves.[11]

The belief that people will usually act on the basis of their self-interest, narrowly defined, is a theory to be tested, not an assumption to be made. Sometimes, as happened in New York City on September 11, 2001, elected officials, government workers, and average citizens behave in ways that plainly transcend personal or professional self-interest. There are countless other far less dramatic but still telling examples of people acting publicly in ways that seem anything but self-interested. For example, in the 1960s leaders of the AFL-CIO in Washington were among the most influential forces lobbying Congress for the passage of certain civil rights bills. Yet at the time they did this, the leaders did not stand to benefit either personally (they were almost all white) or organizationally (rank-and-file labor union members were not enthusiastic about such measures).[12] To understand why they took these positions, it is not enough to know their incomes or their jobs; one must also know something about their attitudes, their allies, and the temper of the times. In short, political preferences cannot invariably be predicted simply by knowing economic or organizational position.

Yet another reason to resist interpreting American democracy as if it were always and everywhere driven by narrowly self-interested individuals and groups is that many of the most important political happenings in U.S. history—the revolutionary movement of the 1770s and 1780s, the battle for civil rights in the 1950s and 1960s, to name just two—were led against long odds by people who risked much knowing that they might not succeed and suspecting that, even if they did succeed, generations might pass before their efforts truly benefited anyone. As we shall see, self-interest figures mightily in politics, but so do ideas about the common good and public-spirited behavior.

☆ What Explains Political Change?

When we see American democracy from the perspective of the past, we will find it hard to accept as generally true any simple interpretation of politics. Economic interests, powerful elites, entrenched bureaucrats, competing pressure groups, and morally impassioned individuals have all played a part in shaping our government and its policies. But the great shifts in the character of our government—its size, scope, institutional arrangements, and the direction of its policies—have reflected complex and sometimes sudden changes in elite or mass *beliefs* about what government is supposed to do.

In the 1920s it was widely assumed that the federal government would play a small role in our lives. From the 1930s through the 1970s it was generally

New York City Mayor Rudy Giuliani discusses the fallen World Trade Center towers with President George Bush, Senator Charles Schumer, and New York Fire Commissioner Thomas Van Essen.

believed that the federal government would try to solve whatever social or economic problem existed. From 1981 through 1988 the administration of Ronald Reagan sought to reverse that assumption and to cut back on the taxes Washington levied, the money it spent, and the regulations it imposed. It is clear that no simple theory of politics is likely to explain both the growth of federal power after 1932 and the effort to cut back on that power starting in 1981. Every student of politics sooner or later learns that the hardest things to explain are usually the most important ones.

Take the case of foreign affairs. During certain periods in our history we have taken an active interest in the outside world—at the time the nation was founded, when France and England seemed to have it in their power to determine whether or not America would survive as a nation; in the 1840s, when we sought to expand the nation into areas where Mexico and Canada had claims; in the late 1890s, when many leaders believed we had an obligation to acquire an overseas empire in the Caribbean and the Pacific; and in the period from the 1940s to the 1960s, when we openly accepted the role of the world's police officer. At other times America has looked inward, spurning opportunities for expansion and virtually ignoring events that in other periods would have been a cause for war, or at least mobilization. Today, America seems to be looking outward once again, spurred, on the one side, by unprecedented terrorist attacks against the country and, on the other side, by historic opportunities to make new friends with old foreign foes.

Deep-seated beliefs, major economic developments, and widely shared (or competing) opinions about what constitutes the dominant political problem of the time shape the nature of day-to-day political conflict. What this means is that, in any broad historical or comparative perspective, politics is not just about "who gets what," though that is part of the story. It is about how people, or elites claiming to speak for people, define the public interest. Lest one think that such definitions are mere window dressing, signifying nothing of importance, bear in mind that on occasion men and women have been prepared to fight and die for one definition or another. Suppose you had been alive in 1861. Do you think you would have viewed slavery as a matter of gains and losses, costs and benefits, winners and losers? Some people did. Or do you think you would have been willing to fight to abolish or preserve it? Many others did just that. The differences in these ways of thinking about such an issue are at least as important as how institutions are organized or elections conducted.

☆ The Nature of Politics

Ideally, political scientists ought to be able to give clear answers, amply supported by evidence, to the questions we have posed about American democracy, starting with "who governs?" In reality they can (at best) give partial, contingent, and controversial answers. The reason is to be found in the nature of our subject. Unlike economists, who assume that people have more or less stable preferences and can compare ways of satisfying those preferences by looking at the relative prices of various goods and services, political scientists are interested in how preferences are formed, especially for those kinds of services, such as national defense or pollution control, that cannot be evaluated chiefly in terms of monetary costs.

Understanding preferences is vital to understanding power. Who did what in government is not hard to find out, but who wielded power—that is, who made a difference in the outcome and for what reason—is much harder to discover. *Power* is a word that conjures up images of deals, bribes, power plays, and arm-twisting. In fact, most power exists because of shared understanding, common friendships, communal or organiza-

tional loyalties, and different degrees of prestige. These are hard to identify and almost impossible to quantify.

Nor can the distribution of political power be inferred simply by knowing what laws are on the books or what administrative actions have been taken. The enactment of a consumer protection law does not mean that consumers are powerful, any more than the absence of such a law means that corporations are powerful. The passage of such a law could reflect an aroused public opinion, the lobbying of a small group claiming to speak for consumers, the ambitions of a senator, or the intrigues of one business firm seeking to gain a competitive advantage over another. A close analysis of what the law entails and how it was passed and administered is necessary before much of anything can be said.

This book will avoid sweeping claims that we have an "imperial" presidency (or an impotent one), an "obstructionist" Congress (or an innovative one), or "captured" regulatory agencies. Such labels do an injustice to the different roles that presidents, members of Congress, and administrators play in different kinds of issues and in different historical periods.

The view taken in this book is that judgements about institutions and interests can be made only after one has seen how they behave on a variety of important issues or potential issues, such as economic policy, the regulation of business, social welfare, civil rights and liberties, and foreign and military affairs. The policies adopted or blocked, the groups heeded or ignored, the values embraced or rejected—these constitute the raw material out of which one can fashion an answer to the central questions we have asked: Who governs? and To what ends?

The way in which our institutions of government handle social welfare, for example, differs from the way other democratic nations handle it, and it differs as well from the way our own institutions once treated it. The description of our institutions in Part III will therefore include not only an account of how they work today but also a brief historical background on their workings and a comparison with similar institutions in other countries. There is a tendency to assume that how we do things today is the only way they could possibly be done. In fact, there are other ways to operate a government based on some measure of popular rule. History, tradition, and belief weigh heavily on all that we do.

Although political change is not always accompanied by changes in public laws, the policy process is arguably one of the best barometers of changes in who

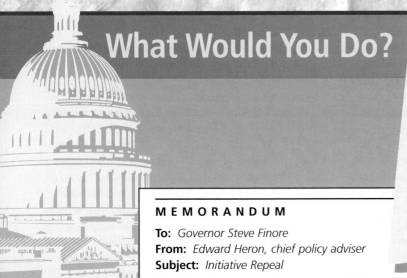

What Would You Do?

Legal and Policy Experts Call for a Ban on Ballot Initiatives

December 11
SACRAMENTO, CA

A report released yesterday and signed by more than 100 law and public policy professors statewide urges that the state's constitution be amended to ban legislation by initiative. The initiative allows state voters to place legislative measures directly on the ballot by getting enough signatures. The initiative "has led to disastrous policy decisions on taxes, crime, and other issues," the report declared . . .

MEMORANDUM

To: *Governor Steve Finore*
From: *Edward Heron, chief policy adviser*
Subject: *Initiative Repeal*

You have supported several successful initiatives (life imprisonment for thrice-convicted violent felons, property tax limits), but you have never publicly stated a view on the initiative itself, and the repeal proposal will probably surface during tomorrow's press briefing.

Arguments for a ban:

1. Ours is a representative, not a direct, democracy in which voters elect leaders and elected leaders make policy decisions subject to review by the courts.
2. Voters are often neither rational nor respectful of constitutional rights. For example, many people demand both lower taxes and more government services, and polls find that most voters would prohibit people with certain views from speaking and deprive all persons accused of a violent crime from getting out on bail while awaiting trial.
3. Over the past 100 years nearly 800 statewide ballot initiatives have been passed in 24 states, including 35 in 1998 alone. Rather than giving power to the people, special-interest groups have spent billions of dollars manipulating voters to pass initiatives that enrich or benefit them, not the public at large.

Arguments against a ban:

1. When elected officials fail to respond to persistent public majorities favoring tougher crime measures, lower property taxes, and other popular concerns, direct democracy via the initiative is legitimate, and the courts can still review the law.
2. More Americans than ever have college degrees and easy access to information about public affairs. Studies find that most average citizens are able to figure out which candidates, parties, or advocacy groups come closest to supporting their own economic interests and personal values.
3. All told, the 24 states that passed 35 laws by initiative in 1998 also passed more than 14,000 laws by the regular legislative process (out of more than 70,000 bills they considered). Studies find that special-interest groups are severely limited in their ability to pass new laws by initiative, while citizens' groups with broad-based public support are behind most initiatives that pass.

Your decision:

Favor ban _____ Oppose ban _____

governs. In Chapter 15, we offer a way of classifying and explaining the politics of different policy issues. The model we present there has been developed, refined, and tested over more than two decades (longer than most of our readers have been alive!). Our own students and others have valued it mainly because, they have found, it helps to answer such questions about who governs: How do political issues get on the public agenda in the first place? How, for example, did sexual harassment, which was hardly ever discussed or debated by Congress, burst onto the public agenda? Once on the agenda, how does the politics of issues like income security for older Americans—for example, the politics of Social Security, a program that has been on the federal books since 1935 (see Chapter 19)— change over time? And if, today, one cares about expanding civil liberties (see Chapter 5) or protecting civil rights (see Chapter 6), what political obstacles and opportunities are you likely to face, and what role are public opinion, organized interest groups, the media, the courts, political parties, and other institutions likely to play in frustrating or fostering your particular policy preferences, whatever they might be?

Peek ahead, if you wish, to the book's policy chapters, but understand that the place to begin a search for how power is distributed in national politics and what purposes that power serves is with the founding of the federal government in 1787: the Constitutional Convention and the events leading up to it. Though the decisions of that time were not made by philosophers or professors, the practical men who made them had a philosophic and professorial cast of mind, and thus they left behind a fairly explicit account of what values they sought to protect and what arrangements they thought ought to be made for the allocation of political power.

☆ SUMMARY

*T*here are two major questions about politics: Who governs? To what ends? This book focuses mainly on answering the first.

Four answers have traditionally been given to the question of who governs.

- The *Marxist*—those who control the economic system will control the political one.
- The *elitist*—a few top leaders, not all of them drawn from business, make the key decisions without reference to popular desires.
- The *bureaucratic*—appointed civil servants run things.
- The *pluralist*—competition among affected interests shapes public policy.

To choose among these theories or to devise new ones requires more than describing governmental institutions and processes. In addition one must examine the kinds of issues that do (or do not) get taken up by the political system and how that system resolves them.

The distinction between different types of democracies is important. The Framers of the Constitution intended that America be a representative democracy in which the power to make decisions is determined by means of a free and competitive struggle for the citizens' votes.

RECONSIDERING WHO GOVERNS?

1. How is political power actually distributed in America?

Some believe that political power in America is monopolized by wealthy business leaders, by other powerful elites, or by entrenched government bureaucrats. Others believe that political resources such as money, prestige, expertise, organizational position, and access to the mass media are so widely dispersed in American society, and the governmental institutions and offices in which power many be exercised so numerous and varied, that no single group truly has all or most political power. In this view, political power in America is distributed more or less widely. No one, however, argues that political resources are distributed equally in America.

2. What explains major political change?

The great shifts in the character of American government—its size, scope, institutional arrangements, and the direction of its policies—have reflected complex and sometimes sudden changes in elite or mass beliefs about what government is supposed to do. For instance, before Franklin Roosevelt's New Deal, most leaders and citizens did not automatically look to the federal government to improve the economy, and many doubted that Washington had any legitimate role to play in managing economic affairs. Today, however, leaders in both political parties assume that Washington must help reduce unemployment, create jobs, and otherwise actively manage the country's economy. The federal government now has policies on street crime, the environment, homeland security, and many other issues that were not on the federal agenda a half-century (or, in the case of homeland security, a mere half-decade) ago.

RECONSIDERING TO WHAT ENDS?

1. What value or values matter most in American democracy?

The Framers of the Constitution had their vision of American democracy and favored certain values, but neither they nor the Constitution specify what values matter most or how best to make trade-offs among or between competing political ends.

2. Are trade-offs among political purposes inevitable?

Yes. For instance, the government cannot spend more on health care without spending less on something else we may also desire—college loans, police patrols, or toxic waste cleanups. Nor can it maximize one value or purpose (say respecting the rights of persons suspected or accused of terrorist acts) without minimizing others (like liberty and associated legal rights). And, even if everyone agreed that the same one value—say liberty—was supreme, we could not all exercise it at the same time or to the fullest or just as we pleased without all losing it in the bargain: if everybody is at liberty to shout simultaneously, nobody is at liberty to be heard individually. We often cannot have more of some things we desire without having less of other things we desire, too. That is as true in politics and government, and as true for American democracy, as it is in other parts of life.

SUGGESTED READINGS

Banfield, Edward C. *Political Influence*. New York: Free Press, 1961. A method of analyzing politics—in this case, in the city of Chicago—comparable to the approach adopted in this book.

Crick, Bernard, *The American Science of Politics*. London: Routledge & Kegan Paul, 1959. A critical review of the methods of studying government and politics.

Marx, Karl, and Friedrich Engels. "The Manifesto of the Communist Party." In *The Marx-Engels Reader*, 2d ed., edited by Robert C. Tucker. New York: Norton, 1978, 469–500. The classic statement of the Marxist view of history and politics. Should be read in conjunction with Engels, "Socialism: Utopian and Scientific," in the same collection, 683–717.

Mills, C. Wright. *The Power Elite*. New York: Oxford University Press, 1956. An argument that self-serving elites dominate American politics.

Schumpeter, Joseph A. *Capitalism, Socialism, and Democracy*. 3d ed. New York: Harper Torchbooks, 1950, chs. 20–23. A lucid statement of the theory of representative democracy and how it differs from participatory democracy.

Truman, David B. *The Governmental Process*. 2d ed. New York: Knopf, 1971. A pluralist interpretation of American politics.

Weber, Max. *From Max Weber: Essays in Sociology*. Translated and edited by H. H. Gerth and C. Wright Mills. London: Routledge & Kegan Paul, 1948, ch. 8. A theory of bureaucracy and its power.

CHAPTER 2

The Constitution

The Problem of Liberty
The Colonial Mind ● The Real
Revolution ● Weaknesses of the
Confederation

The Constitutional Convention
The Lessons of Experience ●
The Framers

The Challenge
The Virginia Plan ● The New Jersey
Plan ● The Compromise

The Constitution and Democracy
Key Principles ● Government and
Human Nature

The Constitution and Liberty
The Antifederalist View ● Need for
a Bill of Rights ● The Constitution
and Slavery

The Motives of the Framers
Economic Interests at the Convention ●
Economic Interests and Ratification ●
The Constitution and Equality

Constitutional Reform: Modern Views
Reducing the Separation of Powers ●
Making the System Less Democratic ●
Who Is Right?

WHO GOVERNS?

1. What is the difference between a democracy and a republic?
2. What branch of government has the greatest power?

TO WHAT ENDS?

1. Does the Constitution tell us what goals the government should serve?
2. Whose freedom does the Constitution protect?

*I*f you had been alive in 1787, you might have wondered what was going on in Philadelphia. A small group of men (all white) were meeting to discuss how the country should be run. They were not chosen by popular election and they were meeting in secret. There was no press coverage. A few famous men, such as Patrick Henry of Virginia, had refused to be a delegate, and one state, Rhode Island, sent no delegates at all.

And just what were these men going to do? They were supposed to fix the defects in the Articles of Confederation, the arrangement under which the former American colonies had waged war against England. But when the convention was over, no defects in the Articles had been fixed; instead, a wholly new constitution had been proposed. And it was a constitution that in the eyes of some people gave too much power to a new national government.

The goal of the American Revolution was liberty. It was not the first revolution with that object; it may not have been the last; but it was perhaps the clearest case of a people altering the political order violently, simply in order to protect their liberties. Subsequent revolutions had more complicated, or utterly different, objectives. The French Revolution in 1789 sought not only liberty, but "equality and fraternity." The Russian Revolution (1917) and the Chinese Revolution (culminating in 1949) chiefly sought equality and were little concerned with liberty as we understand it.

☆ The Problem of Liberty

What the American colonists sought to protect when they signed the Declaration of Independence in 1776 were the traditional liberties to which they thought they were entitled as British subjects. These liberties included the right to bring their legal cases before truly independent judges rather than ones subordinate to the king; to be free of the burden of having British troops quartered in their homes; to engage in trade without burdensome restrictions; and, of course, to pay no taxes voted by a British Parliament in which they had no direct representation. During the ten years or more of agitation and argument leading up to the War of Independence, most colonists believed that their liberties could be protected while they remained a part of the British Empire.

Slowly but surely opinion shifted. By the time war broke out in 1775, a large number of colonists (though perhaps not a majority) had reached the conclusion that the colonies would have to become independent of Great

17

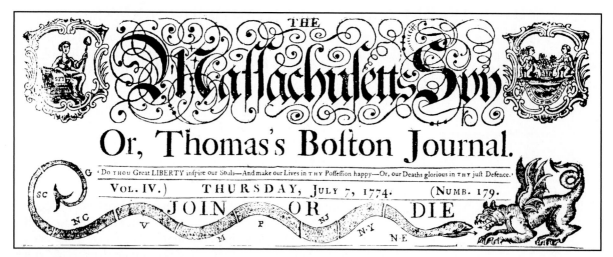

Even before the Revolutionary War, many felt that some form of union would be necessary if the rebellious colonies were to survive. In 1774, the Massachusetts Spy *portrayed the colonies as segments of a snake that must "Join or Die."*

Britain if their liberties were to be assured. The colonists had many reasons for regarding independence as the only solution, but one is especially important: they no longer had confidence in the English constitution. This constitution was not a single written document but rather a collection of laws, charters, and traditional understandings that proclaimed the liberties of British subjects. Yet these liberties, in the eyes of the colonists, were regularly violated despite their constitutional protection. Clearly, then, the English constitution was an inadequate check on the abuses of political power. The revolutionary leaders sought an explanation of the insufficiency of the constitution and found it in human nature.

The Colonial Mind

"A lust for domination is more or less natural to all parties," one colonist wrote.[1] Men will seek power, many colonists believed, because they are ambitious, greedy, and easily corrupted. John Adams denounced the "luxury, effeminacy, and venality" of English politics; Patrick Henry spoke scathingly of the "corrupt House of Commons"; and Alexander Hamilton described England as "an old, wrinkled, withered, worn-out hag."[2] This was in part flamboyant rhetoric designed to whip up enthusiasm for the conflict, but it was also deeply revealing of the colonial mind. Their belief that English politicians—and by implication, most politicians—tended to be corrupt was the colonists' explanation of why the English constitution

was not an adequate guarantee of the liberty of the citizens. This opinion was to persist and, as we shall see, profoundly affect the way the Americans went about designing their own governments.

The liberties the colonists fought to protect were, they thought, widely understood. They were based not on the generosity of the king or the language of statutes but on a "higher law" embodying "natural rights" that were ordained by God, discoverable in nature and history, and essential to human progress. These rights, John Dickinson wrote, "are born with us; exist with us; and cannot be taken away from us by any human power."[3] There was general agreement that the essential rights included life, liberty, and property long before Thomas Jefferson wrote them into the Declaration of Independence. (Jefferson changed "property" to "the pursuit of happiness," but almost everybody else went on talking about property.)

This emphasis on property did not mean that the American Revolution was thought up by the rich and wellborn to protect their interests or that there was a struggle between property owners and the propertyless. In late-eighteenth-century America most people (except the black slaves) had property of some kind. The overwhelming majority of citizens were self-employed—as farmers or artisans—and rather few people benefited financially by gaining independence from England. Taxes were higher during and after the war than before, trade was disrupted by the conflict, and debts mounted perilously as various expedients

The American colonists' desire to assert their liberties led in time to a deep hostility to British government, as when these New Yorkers toppled a statue of King George III, melted it down, and used the metal to make bullets.

were invented to pay for the struggle. There were, of course, war profiteers and those who tried to manipulate the currency to their own advantage, but most Americans at the time of the war saw the conflict clearly in terms of political rather than economic issues. It was a war of ideology.

Everyone recognizes the glowing language with which Jefferson set out the case for independence in the second paragraph of the Declaration:

> We hold these truths to be self-evident, that all men are created equal, that they are endowed by their Creator with certain unalienable Rights, that among these are Life, Liberty, and the pursuit of Happiness.—That to secure these rights, Governments are instituted among Men, deriving their just powers from the consent of the governed—that whenever any Form of Government becomes destructive of these ends, it is the Right of the People to alter or to abolish it, and to institute new Government, having its foundation on such principles, and organizing its powers in such form, as to them shall seem most likely to effect their Safety and Happiness.

What almost no one recalls, but what are an essential part of the Declaration, are the next twenty-seven paragraphs, in which Jefferson listed, item by item, the specific complaints the colonists had against George III and his ministers. None of these items spoke of social or economic conditions in the colonies; all spoke instead of specific violations of political liberties. The Declaration was in essence a lawyer's brief prefaced by a stirring philosophical claim that the rights being violated were **unalienable**—that is, based on nature and Providence, and not on the whims or preferences of people. Jefferson, in his original draft, added a twenty-eighth complaint—that the king had allowed the slave trade to continue *and* was inciting slaves to revolt against their masters. Congress, faced with so contradictory a charge, decided to include a muted reference to slave insurrections and omit all reference to the slave trade.

---

unalienable   A human right based on nature or God.

North America in 1787

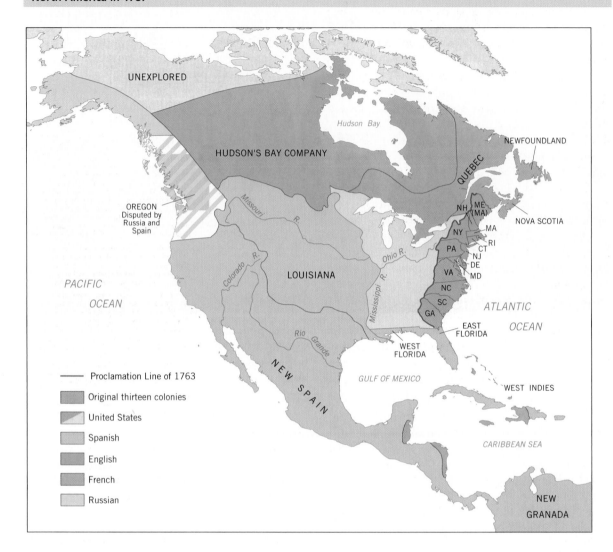

The Real Revolution

The Revolution was more than the War of Independence. It began before the war, continued after it, and involved more than driving out the British army by force of arms. The *real* Revolution, as John Adams afterward explained in a letter to a friend, was the "radical change in the principles, opinions, sentiments, and affections of the people."[4] This radical change had to do with a new vision of what could make political authority legitimate and personal liberties secure. Government by royal prerogative was rejected; instead legitimate government would require the consent of the governed. Political power could not be exercised on the basis of tradition but only as a result of a direct grant of power contained in a written constitution. Human liberty existed before government was organized, and government must respect that liberty. The legislative branch of government, in which the people were directly represented, should be superior to the executive branch.

These were indeed revolutionary ideas. No government at the time had been organized on the basis of these principles. And to the colonists such notions were not empty words but rules to be put into immediate practice. In 1776 eight states adopted written constitutions. Within a few years every former colony had adopted one except Connecticut and

Rhode Island, two states that continued to rely on their colonial charters. Most state constitutions had detailed bills of rights defining personal liberties, and most placed the highest political power in the hands of elected representatives.

Written constitutions, representatives, and bills of rights are so familiar to us now that we forget how bold and unprecedented those innovations were in 1776. Indeed, many Americans did not think they would succeed: such arrangements would be either so strong that they would threaten liberty or so weak that they would permit chaos.

The eleven years that elapsed between the Declaration of Independence and the signing of the Constitution in 1787 were years of turmoil, uncertainty, and fear. George Washington had to wage a bitter, protracted war without anything resembling a strong national government to support him. The supply and financing of his army were based on a series of hasty improvisations, most badly administered and few adequately supported by the fiercely independent states. When peace came, many parts of the nation were a shambles. At least a quarter of New York City was in ruins, and many other communities were nearly devastated. Though the British lost the war, they still were powerful on the North American continent, with an army available in Canada (where many Americans loyal to Britain had fled) and a large navy at sea. Spain claimed the Mississippi River valley and occupied what are now Florida and California. Men who had left their farms to fight came back to discover themselves in debt with no money and heavy taxes. The paper money printed to finance the war was now virtually worthless.

Weaknesses of the Confederation

The thirteen states had formed only a faint semblance of a national government with which to bring order to the nation. The **Articles of Confederation,** which went into effect in 1781, created little more than a "league of friendship" that could not levy taxes or regulate commerce. Each state retained its sovereignty and independence, each state (regardless of size) had one vote in Congress, nine (of thirteen) votes were required to pass any measure, and the delegates who cast these votes were picked and paid for by the state legislatures. Congress did have the power to make peace, and thus it was able to ratify the treaty with England in 1783. It could coin money, but there

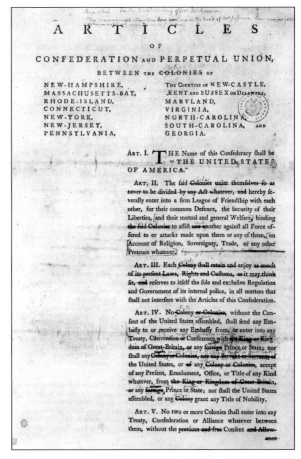

The Articles of Confederation had made it plain that the United States was not to have a true national government but was to be governed by a compact among sovereign and independent states.

was precious little to coin; it could appoint the key army officers, but the army was small and dependent for support on independent state militias; it was allowed to run the post office, then, as now, a thankless task that nobody else wanted. John Hancock, who in 1785 was elected to the meaningless office of "president" under the Articles, never showed up to take the job. Several states claimed the unsettled lands in the West, and they occasionally pressed those claims with guns. Pennsylvania and Virginia went to

Articles of Confederation A weak constitution that governed America during the Revolutionary War.

John Hancock was proud to have signed the Declaration of Independence but thought so little of the presidency under the Articles of Confederation that he never bothered to accept the job.

war near Pittsburgh, and Vermont threatened to become part of Canada. There was no national judicial system to settle these or other claims among the states. To amend the Articles of Confederation, all thirteen states had to agree.

Many of the leaders of the Revolution, such as George Washington and Alexander Hamilton, believed that a stronger national government was essential. They lamented the disruption of commerce and travel caused by the quarrelsome states and deeply feared the possibility of foreign military intervention, with England or France playing one state off against another. A small group of men, conferring at Washington's home at Mount Vernon in 1785, decided to call a meeting to discuss trade regulation. That meeting, held at Annapolis, Maryland, in September 1786, was not well attended (no delegates arrived from New England), and so another meeting, this one in Philadelphia, was called for the following spring—in May 1787—to consider ways of remedying the defects of the Confederation.

Constitutional Convention   Meeting in Philadelphia in 1787 that produced a new constitution.

☆ The Constitutional Convention

The delegates assembled at Philadelphia at the **Constitutional Convention,** for what was advertised (and authorized by Congress) as a meeting to revise the Articles; they adjourned four months later having written a wholly new constitution. When they met, they were keenly aware of the problems of the confederacy but far from agreeing as to what should be done about those problems. The protection of life, liberty, and property was their objective in 1787 as it had been in 1776, but they had no accepted political theory that would tell them what kind of national government, if any, would serve that goal.

The Lessons of Experience

They had read ancient and modern political history, only to learn that nothing seemed to work. James Madison spent a good part of 1786 studying books sent to him by Thomas Jefferson, then in Paris, in hopes of finding some model for a workable American republic. He took careful notes on various confederacies in ancient Greece and on the more modern confederacy of the United Netherlands. He reviewed the history of Switzerland and Poland and the ups and downs of the Roman republic. He concluded that there was no model; as he later put it in one of the *Federalist* papers, history consists only of beacon lights "which give warning of the course to be shunned, without pointing out that which ought to be pursued."[5] The problem seemed to be that confederacies were too weak to govern and tended to collapse from internal dissension, while all stronger forms of government were so powerful as to trample the liberties of the citizens.

■ **State Constitutions**   Madison and the others did not need to consult history, or even the defects of the Articles of Confederation, for illustrations of the problem. These could be found in the government of the American states at the time. Pennsylvania and Massachusetts exemplified two aspects of the problem. The Pennsylvania constitution, adopted in 1776, created the most radically democratic of the new state regimes. All power was given to a one-house (unicameral) legislature, the Assembly, the members of which were elected annually for one-year terms. No legislator could serve more than four years. There was no governor or president, only an Executive Council that had few powers. Thomas Paine, whose pamphlets had helped precipitate the break with England, thought the Pennsylvania constitution was the best in America, and in France philosophers hailed it as the very embodiment of the principle of rule by the people. Though popular in France, it was a good deal less popular in Philadelphia. The Assembly disfranchised the Quakers, persecuted conscientious objectors to the war, ignored the requirement of trial by juries, and manipulated the judiciary.[6] To Madison and his friends the Pennsylvania constitution demonstrated how a government, though democratic, could be tyrannical as a result of concentrating all powers into one set of hands.

The Massachusetts constitution, adopted in 1780, was a good deal less democratic. There was a clear separation of powers among the various branches of government, the directly elected governor could veto acts of the legislature, and judges served for life. Both voters and elected officials had to be property owners; the governor, in fact, had to own at least £1,000 worth of property. The principal officeholders had to swear that they were Christians.

■ **Shays's Rebellion** But if the government of Pennsylvania was thought to be too strong, that of Massachusetts seemed too weak, despite its "conservative" features. In January 1787 a group of ex-Revolutionary War soldiers and officers, plagued by debts and high taxes and fearful of losing their property to creditors and tax collectors, forcibly prevented the courts in western Massachusetts from sitting. This became known as **Shays's Rebellion,** after one of the officers, Daniel Shays. The governor of Massachusetts asked the Continental Congress to send troops to suppress the rebellion, but it could not raise the money or the manpower. Then he turned to his own state militia, but discovered he did not have one. In desperation private funds were collected to hire a volunteer army, which marched on Springfield and, with the firing of a few shots, dispersed the rebels, who fled into neighboring states.

Shays's Rebellion, occurring between the aborted Annapolis and the coming Philadelphia conventions, had a powerful effect on opinion. Delegates who might have been reluctant to attend the Philadelphia

The presiding officer at the Constitutional Convention was George Washington (1732–1799). He participated just once in the debates, but the effect of his presence was great. He was a national military hero, and it was generally expected that he would be the nation's first president.

meeting, especially those from New England, were galvanized by the fear that state governments were about to collapse from internal dissension. George Washington wrote a friend despairingly: "For God's sake, if they [the rebels] have *real* grievances, redress them; if they have not, employ the force of government against them at once."[7] Thomas Jefferson, living in Paris, took a more detached view: "A little rebellion now and then is a good thing," he wrote. "The tree of liberty must be refreshed from time to time with the blood of patriots and tyrants."[8] Though Jefferson's detachment might be explained by the fact that he was in Paris and not in Springfield, there were others, like Governor George Clinton of New York, who shared the view that no strong central government was required. (Whether Clinton would have agreed about the virtues of spilled blood, especially his, is another matter.)

> **Shays's Rebellion** A 1787 rebellion in which ex-Revolutionary War soldiers attempted to prevent foreclosures of farms as a result of high interest rates and taxes.

Shays's Rebellion in western Massachusetts in 1786–1787 stirred deep fears of anarchy in America. The ruckus was put down by a hastily assembled militia, and the rebels were eventually pardoned.

The Framers

The Philadelphia convention attracted fifty-five delegates, only about thirty of whom participated regularly in the proceedings. One state, Rhode Island, refused to send anyone. The convention met during a miserably hot Philadelphia summer, with the delegates pledged to keep their deliberations secret. The talkative and party-loving Benjamin Franklin was often accompanied by other delegates to make sure that neither wine nor his delight in telling stories would lead him to divulge delicate secrets.

Those who attended were for the most part young (Hamilton was thirty; Madison thirty-six) but experienced. Eight delegates had signed the Declaration of Independence, seven had been governors, thirty-four were lawyers and reasonably well-to-do, a few were wealthy. They were not "intellectuals," but men of practical affairs. Thirty-nine had served in the ineffectual Congress of the Confederation; a third were veterans of the Continental Army.

Some names made famous by the Revolution were conspicuously absent. Thomas Jefferson and John Adams were serving as ministers abroad; Samuel Adams was ill; Patrick Henry was chosen to attend but refused, commenting that he "smelled a rat in Philadelphia, tending toward monarchy."

The convention produced not a revision of the Articles of Confederation, as it had been authorized to do, but instead a wholly new written constitution creating a true national government unlike any that had existed before. That document is today the world's oldest written national constitution. Those who wrote it were neither saints nor schemers, and the deliberations were not always lofty or philosophical—much hard bargaining, not a little confusion, and the accidents of personality and time helped shape the final product. The delegates were split on many issues—what powers should be given to a central government, how the states should be represented, what was to be done about slavery, the role of the people—each of which was resolved by a compromise. The speeches of the delegates (known to us from the detailed notes kept by Madison) did not explicitly draw on political philosophy or quote from the writings of philosophers. Everybody present was quite familiar with the traditional arguments and, on the whole, well read in history. But though the leading political philosophers were only rarely mentioned, the debate was profoundly influenced by philosophical beliefs, some formed by the revolutionary experience and others by the eleven-year attempt at self-government.

From the debates leading up to the Revolution, the delegates had drawn a commitment to liberty, which, despite the abuses sometimes committed in its name, they continued to share. Their defense of liberty as a natural right was derived from the writings of the English philosopher John Locke and based on his view that such rights are discoverable by reason. In a "state of nature," Locke argued, all men cherish and seek to protect their life, liberty, and property. But in a state of nature—that is, a society without a government—the strong can use their liberty to deprive the weak of theirs. The instinct for self-preservation leads people to want a government that will prevent this exploitation. But if the government is not itself to deprive its subjects of their liberty, it must be limited. The chief limitation on it, he said, should derive from the fact that it is created, and governs, by the consent of the governed. People will not agree to be ruled by a government that threatens their liberty; therefore the government to which they freely choose to submit themselves will be a limited government designed to protect liberty.

The Pennsylvania experience as well as the history of British government led the Framers to doubt whether popular consent alone would be a sufficient guarantor of liberty. A popular government may prove too weak (as in Massachusetts) to prevent one faction from abusing another, or a popular majority can be tyrannical (as in Pennsylvania). In fact the tyranny of the majority can be an even graver threat than rule by the few. In the former case there may be no defenses for the individual—one lone person cannot count on the succor of public opinion or the possibility of popular revolt.

The problem, then, was a delicate one: how to devise a government strong enough to preserve order but not so strong that it would threaten liberty. The answer, the delegates believed, was not "democracy" as it was then understood. To many conservatives in the late eighteenth century, democracy meant mob rule—it meant, in short, Shays's Rebellion (or, if they had been candid about it, the Boston Tea Party). On the other hand, *aristocracy*—the rule of the few—was no solution, since the few were likely to be self-seeking. Madison, writing later in the *Federalist* papers, put the problem this way:

> If men were angels, no government would be necessary. If angels were to govern men, neither external nor internal controls on government would be necessary. In framing a government which is to be administered by men over men, the great difficulty lies in this: you must first enable the government to control the governed; and in the next place oblige it to control itself.[9]

Striking this balance could not be done, Madison believed, simply by writing a constitution that set limits on what government could do. The example of British rule over the colonies proved that laws and customs were inadequate checks on political power. As he expressed it, "A mere demarcation on parchment of the constitutional limits [of government] is not a sufficient guard against those encroachments which lead to a tyrannical concentration of all the powers of government in the same hands."[10]

☆ The Challenge

The resolution of political issues, great and small, often depends crucially on how the central question is phrased. The delegates came to Philadelphia in general agreement that there were defects in the Articles of Confederation that ought to be remedied.

Had they, after convening, decided to make their business that of listing these defects and debating alternative remedies for them, the document that emerged would in all likelihood have been very different from what in fact was adopted. But immediately after the convention had organized itself and chosen Washington to be its presiding officer, the Virginia delegation, led by Governor Edmund Randolph but relying heavily on the draftsmanship of James Madison, presented to the convention a comprehensive plan for a wholly new national government. The plan quickly became the major item of business of the meeting; it, and little else, was debated for the next two weeks.

The Virginia Plan

When the convention decided to make the **Virginia Plan** its agenda, it had fundamentally altered the nature of its task. The business at hand was not to be the Articles and their defects, but rather how one should go about designing a true national government. The Virginia Plan called for a strong national union organized into three governmental branches—the legislative, executive, and judicial. The legislature was to be composed of two houses, the first elected directly by the people and the second chosen by the first house from among the people nominated by state legislatures. The executive was to be chosen by the national legislature, as were members of a national judiciary. The executive and some members of the judiciary were to constitute a "council of revision" that could veto acts of the legislature; that veto, in turn, could be overridden by the legislature. There were other interesting details, but the key features of the Virginia Plan were two: (1) a national legislature would have supreme powers on all matters on which the separate states were not competent to act, as well as the power to veto any and all state laws, and (2) at least one house of the legislature would be elected directly by the people.

The New Jersey Plan

As the debate went on, the representatives of New Jersey and other small states became increasingly worried that the convention was going to write a

Virginia Plan   Proposal to create a strong national government.

constitution in which the states would be represented in both houses of Congress on the basis of population. If this happened, the smaller states feared they would always be outvoted by the larger ones, and so, with William Paterson of New Jersey as their spokesman, they introduced a new plan. The **New Jersey Plan** proposed to amend, not replace, the old Articles of Confederation. It enhanced the power of the national government (though not as much as the Virginia Plan), but it did so in a way that left the states' representation in Congress unchanged from the Articles—each state would have one vote. Thus not only would the interests of the small states be protected, but Congress itself would remain to a substantial degree the creature of state governments.

If the New Jersey resolutions had been presented first and taken up as the major item of business, it is quite possible that they would have become the framework for the document that finally emerged. But they were not. Offered after the convention had been discussing the Virginia Plan for two weeks, the resolutions encountered a reception very different from what they would have received if introduced earlier. The debate had the delegates already thinking in terms of a national government that was more independent of the states, and thus it had accustomed them to proposals that, under other circumstances, might have seemed quite radical. On June 19 the first decisive vote of the convention was taken: seven states preferred the Virginia Plan, three states the New Jersey Plan, and one state was split.

With the tide running in favor of a strong national government, the supporters of the small states had to shift their strategy. They now began to focus their efforts on ensuring that the small states could not be outvoted by the larger ones in Congress. One way was to have the members of the lower house elected by the state legislatures rather than the people, with each state getting the same number of seats rather than seats proportional to its population.

The debate was long and feelings ran high, so much so that Benjamin Franklin, at eighty-one the oldest delegate present, suggested that each day's

Independence Hall in Philadelphia, where the Declaration of Independence and the Constitution were signed.

meeting begin with a prayer. It turned out that the convention could not even agree on this: Hamilton is supposed to have objected that the convention did not need "foreign aid," and others pointed out that the group had no funds with which to hire a minister. And so the argument continued.

The Compromise

Finally, a committee was appointed to meet during the Fourth of July holidays to work out a compromise, and the convention adjourned to await its report. Little is known of what went on in that committee's session, though some were later to say that Franklin played a key role in hammering out the plan that finally emerged. That compromise, the most important reached at the convention, and later called the **Great Compromise** (or sometimes the Connecticut Compromise), was submitted to the full convention on July 5 and debated for another week and a half.

New Jersey Plan   Proposal to create a weak national government.

Great Compromise   Plan to have a popularly elected House based on state population and a state-selected Senate, with two members for each state.

The debate might have gone on even longer, but suddenly the hot weather moderated, and Monday, July 16, dawned cool and fresh after a month of misery. On that day the plan was adopted: five states were in favor, four were opposed, and two did not vote.* Thus, by the narrowest of margins, the structure of the national legislature was set as follows:

- A House of Representatives consisting initially of sixty-five members apportioned among the states roughly on the basis of population and elected by the people
- A Senate consisting of two senators from each state to be chosen by the state legislatures

The Great Compromise reconciled the interests of small and large states by allowing the former to predominate in the Senate and the latter in the House. This reconciliation was necessary to ensure that there would be support for a strong national government from small as well as large states. It represented major concessions on the part of several groups. Madison, for one, was deeply opposed to the idea of having the states equally represented in the Senate. He saw in that a way for the states to hamstring the national government and much preferred some measure of proportional representation in both houses. Delegates from other states worried that representation on the basis of population in the House of Representatives would enable the large states to dominate legislative affairs. Although the margin by which the compromise was accepted was razor-thin, it held firm. In time most of the delegates from the dissenting states accepted it.

After the Great Compromise many more issues had to be resolved, but by now a spirit of accommodation had developed. When one delegate proposed having Congress choose the president, another, James Wilson, proposed that he be elected directly by the people. When neither side of that argument prevailed, a committee invented a plan for an "electoral college" that would choose the president. When some delegates wanted the president chosen for a life term, others proposed a seven-year term, and still others wanted the term limited to three years without eligibility for reelection. The convention settled on a four-year term with no bar to reelection. Some states wanted the Supreme Court picked by the Senate; others wanted it chosen by the president. They finally agreed to let the justices be nominated by the president and then confirmed by the Senate.

Finally, on July 26, the proposals that were already accepted, together with a bundle of unresolved issues, were handed over to the Committee of Detail, consisting of five delegates. This committee included Madison and Gouverneur Morris, who was to be the chief draftsman of the document that finally emerged. The committee hardly contented itself with mere "details," however. It inserted some new proposals and made changes in old ones, drawing for inspiration on existing state constitutions and the members' beliefs as to what the other delegates might accept. On August 6 the report—the first complete draft of the Constitution—was submitted to the convention. There it was debated, item by item, revised, amended, and finally, on September 17, approved by all twelve states in attendance. (Not all *delegates* approved, however; three, including Edmund Randolph, who first submitted the Virginia Plan, refused to sign.)

☆ The Constitution and Democracy

A debate continues to rage over whether the Constitution created, or was even intended to create, a democratic government. The answer is complex. The Framers did not intend to create a "pure democracy"—one in which the people rule directly. For one thing the size of the country and the distances between settlements would have made that physically impossible. But more important the Framers worried that a government in which all citizens directly participate, as in the New England town meeting, would be a government excessively subject to temporary popular passions and one in which minority rights would be insecure. They intended instead to create a **republic,** by which they meant a government in which a system of representation operates. In designing that system the Framers chose, not

---

*The states in favor were Connecticut, Delaware, Maryland, New Jersey, and North Carolina. Those opposed were Georgia, Pennsylvania, South Carolina, and Virginia. Massachusetts was split down the middle; the New York delegates had left the convention. New Hampshire and Rhode Island were absent.

republic A government in which elected representatives make the decisions.

without argument, to have the members of the House of Representatives elected directly by the people. Some delegates did not want to go even that far. Elbridge Gerry of Massachusetts, who refused to sign the Constitution, argued that though "the people do not want [that is, lack] virtue," they are often the "dupes of pretended patriots." Roger Sherman of Connecticut agreed. But George Mason of Virginia and James Wilson of Pennsylvania carried the day when they argued that "no government could long subsist without the confidence of the people," and this required "drawing the most numerous branch of the legislature directly from the people." Popular elections for the House were approved: six states were in favor, two opposed.

But though popular rule was to be one element of the new government, it was not to be the only one. State legislatures, not the people, would choose the senators; electors, not the people directly, would choose the president. As we have seen, without these arrangements, there would have been no Constitution at all, for the small states adamantly opposed any proposal that would have given undue power to the large ones. And direct popular election of the president would clearly have made the populous states the dominant ones. In short the Framers wished to observe the principle of majority rule, but they felt that, on the most important questions, two kinds of majorities were essential—a majority of the voters and a majority of the states.

The power of the Supreme Court to declare an act of Congress unconstitutional—**judicial review**—is also a way of limiting the power of popular majorities. It is not clear whether the Framers intended that there be judicial review, but there is little doubt that in the Framers' minds the fundamental law, the Constitution, had to be safeguarded against popular passions. They made the process for amending the Constitution easier than it had been under the Articles but still relatively difficult.

An amendment can be proposed either by a two-thirds vote of both houses of Congress *or* by a national convention called by Congress at the request of two-thirds of the states.* Once proposed, an amendment must be ratified by three-fourths of the states, either through their legislatures or through special ratifying conventions in each state. Twenty-seven amendments have survived this process, all of them proposed by Congress and all but one (the Twenty-first Amendment) ratified by state legislatures rather than state conventions.

In short the answer to the question of whether the Constitution brought into being a democratic government is yes, if by *democracy* one means a system of representative government based on popular consent. The degree of that consent has changed since 1787, and the institutions embodying that consent can take different forms. One form, rejected in 1787, gives all political authority to one set of representatives, directly elected by the people. (That is the case, for example, in most parliamentary regimes, such as Great Britain, and in some city governments in the United States.) The other form of democracy is one in which different sets of officials, chosen directly or indirectly by different groups of people, share politcal power. (That is the case with the United States and a few other nations where the separation of powers is intended to operate.)

Key Principles

The American version of representative democracy was based on two major principles, the separation of powers and federalism. In America political power was to be shared by three separate branches of government; in parliamentary democracies that power was concentrated in a single, supreme legislature. In America political authority was divided between a national government and several state governments—**federalism**—whereas in most European systems authority was centralized in the national government. Neither of these principles was especially controversial at Philadelphia. The delegates began their work in broad agreement that separated powers and some measure of federalism were necessary, and both the

---

judicial review   The power of the courts to declare laws unconstitutional.

federalism   Government authority shared by national and state governments.

---

*There have been many attempts to get a new constitutional convention. In the 1960s thirty-three states, one short of the required number, requested a convention to consider the reapportionment of state legislatures. In the 1980s efforts were made to call a convention to consider amendments to ban abortions and to require a balanced federal budget.

★ HOW THINGS WORK ★

Checks and Balances

The Constitution creates a system of *separate* institutions that *share* powers. Because the three branches of government share powers, each can (partially) check the powers of the others. This is the system of **checks and balances**. The major checks possessed by each branch are listed below.

Congress

1. Can check the president in these ways:
   a. By refusing to pass a bill the president wants
   b. By passing a law over the president's veto
   c. By using the impeachment powers to remove the president from office
   d. By refusing to approve a presidential appointment (Senate only)
   e. By refusing to ratify a treaty the president has signed (Senate only)

2. Can check the federal courts in these ways:
   a. By changing the number and jurisdiction of the lower courts
   b. By using the impeachment powers to remove a judge from office
   c. By refusing to approve a person nominated to be a judge (Senate only)

The President

1. Can check Congress by vetoing a bill it has passed
2. Can check the federal courts by nominating judges

The Courts

1. Can check Congress by declaring a law unconstitutional
2. Can check the president by declaring actions by him or his subordinates to be unconstitutional or not authorized by law

In addition to these checks specifically provided for in the Constitution, each branch has informal ways of checking the others. For example, the president can try to withhold information from Congress (on the grounds of "executive privilege"), and Congress can try to get information by mounting an investigation.

The exact meaning of the various checks is explained in Chapter 13 on Congress, Chapter 14 on the presidency, and Chapter 16 on the courts.

Virginia and New Jersey plans contained a version of each. How much federalism should be written into the Constitution was quite controversial, however.

Under these two principles, governmental powers in this country can be divided into three categories. The powers that are given to the national government exclusively are the delegated or **enumerated powers.** They include the authority to print money, declare war, make treaties, conduct foreign affairs, and regulate commerce among the states and with foreign nations. Those that are given exclusively to the states are the **reserved powers** and include the power to issue licenses and to regulate commerce wholly within a state. Those that are shared by both the national and the state governments are called **concurrent powers** and include collecting taxes, building roads, borrowing money, and having courts.

Government and Human Nature

The desirability of separating powers and leaving the states equipped with a broad array of rights and responsibilities was not controversial at the Philadelphia convention because the Framers' experiences

checks and balances Authority shared by three branches of government.
enumerated powers Powers given to the national government alone.
reserved powers Powers given to the state government alone.
concurrent powers Powers shared by the national and state governments.

with British rule and state government under the Articles had shaped their view of human nature.

These experiences had taught most of the Framers that people would seek their own advantage in and out of politics; this pursuit of self-interest, unchecked, would lead some people to exploit others. Human nature was good enough to make it possible to have a decent government that was based on popular consent, but it was not good enough to make it inevitable. One solution to this problem would be to improve human nature. Ancient political philosophers such as Aristotle believed that the first task of any government was to cultivate virtue among the governed.

Many Americans were of the same mind. To them Americans would first have to become good people before they could have a good government. Samuel Adams, a leader of the Boston Tea Party, said that the new nation must become a "Christian Sparta." Others spoke of the need to cultivate frugality, industry, temperance, and simplicity.

But to James Madison and the other architects of the Constitution, the deliberate cultivation of virtue would require a government too strong and thus too dangerous to liberty, at least at the national level. Self-interest, freely pursued within reasonable limits, was a more practical and durable solution to the problem of government than any effort to improve the virtue of the citizenry. He wanted, he said, to make republican government possible "even in the absence of political virtue."

Madison argued that the very self-interest that leads people toward factionalism and tyranny might, if properly harnessed by appropriate constitutional arrangements, provide a source of unity and a guarantee of liberty. This harnessing was to be accomplished by dividing the offices of the new government among many people and giving to the holder of each

office the "necessary means and personal motives to resist encroachments of the others." In this way "ambition must be made to counteract ambition" so that "the private interest of every individual may be a sentinel over the public rights."[11] If men were angels, all this would be unnecessary. But Madison and the other delegates pragmatically insisted on taking human nature pretty much as it was, and therefore they adopted "this policy of supplying, by opposite and rival interests, the defect of better motives."[12] The **separation of powers** would work, not in spite of the imperfections of human nature, but because of them.

So also with federalism. By dividing power between the states and the national government, one level of government can serve as a check on the other. This should provide a "double security" to the rights of the people: "The different governments will control each other, at the same time that each will be controlled by itself."[13] This was especially likely to happen in America, Madison thought, because it was a large country filled with diverse interests—rich and poor, Protestant and Catholic, northerner and southerner, farmer and merchant, creditor and debtor. Each of these interests would constitute a **faction** that would seek its own advantage. One faction might come to dominate government, or a part of government, in one place, and a different and rival faction might dominate it in another. The pulling and hauling among these factions would prevent any single government—say, that of New York—from dominating all of government. The division of powers among several governments would give to virtually every faction an opportunity to gain some—but not full—power.

☆ The Constitution and Liberty

A more difficult question is whether the Constitution created a system of government that would respect personal liberties. And that in fact is the question that was debated in the states when the document was presented for ratification. The proponents of the Constitution called themselves the **Federalists** (though they might more accurately have been called "nationalists"). The opponents came to be known as the **Antifederalists** (though they might

separation of powers Constitutional authority is shared by three different branches of government.

faction A group with a distinct political interest.

Federalists Those who favor a stronger national government.

Antifederalists Those who favor a weaker national government.

more accurately have been called "states' righters").* To be put into effect, the Constitution had to be approved at ratifying conventions in at least nine states. This was perhaps the most democratic feature of the Constitution: it had to be accepted, not by the existing Congress (still limping along under the Articles of Confederation), nor by the state legislatures, but by special conventions elected by the people.

Though democratic, the process established by the Framers for ratifying the Constitution was technically illegal. The Articles of Confederation, which still governed, could be amended only with the approval of all thirteen state legislatures. The Framers wanted to bypass these legislatures because they feared that, for reasons of ideology or out of a desire to retain their powers, the legislators would oppose the Constitution. The Framers wanted ratification with less than the consent of all thirteen states because they knew that such unanimity could not be attained. And indeed the conventions in North Carolina and Rhode Island did initially reject the Constitution.

The Antifederalist View

The great issue before the state conventions was liberty, not democracy. The opponents of the new Constitution, the Antifederalists, had a variety of objections but were in general united by the belief that liberty could be secure only in a small republic in which the rulers were physically close to—and closely checked by—the ruled. Their central objection was stated by a group of Antifederalists at the ratifying convention in an essay published just after they had lost: "a very extensive territory cannot be governed on the principles of freedom, otherwise than by a confederation of republics."[14]

These dissenters argued that a strong national government would be distant from the people and would use its powers to annihilate or absorb the functions that properly belonged to the states. Con-

---

*To the delegates a truly "federal" system was one, like the New Jersey Plan, that allowed for very strong states and a weak national government. When the New Jersey Plan lost, the delegates who defeated it began using the word *federal* to describe their plan even though it called for a stronger national government. Thus men who began as "Federalists" at the convention ultimately became known as "Antifederalists" during the struggle over ratification.

Ratification of the Federal Constitution by State Conventions, 1787–1790

Strongly in favor, ratified early

Initially opposed, later ratified

Ratified initially after close struggle

gress would tax heavily, the Supreme Court would overrule state courts, and the president would come to head a large standing army. (Since all these things have occurred, we cannot dismiss the Antifederalists as cranky obstructionists who opposed without justification the plans of the Framers.) These critics argued that the nation needed, at best, a loose confederation of states, with most of the powers of government kept firmly in the hands of state legislatures and state courts.

But if a stronger national government was to be created, the Antifederalists argued, it should be hedged about with many more restrictions than those in the constitution then under consideration. They proposed several such limitations, including narrowing the jurisdiction of the Supreme Court,

The *Federalist* Papers

In 1787, to help win ratification of the new Constitution in the New York state convention, Alexander Hamilton decided to publish a series of articles defending and explaining the document in the New York City newspapers. He recruited John Jay and James Madison to help him, and the three of them, under the pen name "Publius," wrote eighty-five articles that appeared from late 1787 through 1788. The identity of the authors was kept secret at the time, but we now know that Hamilton wrote fifty-one of them, Madison twenty-six, and Jay five, and that Hamilton and Madison jointly authored three.

The *Federalist* papers probably played only a small role in securing ratification. Like most legislative battles, this one was not decisively influenced by philosophical writings. But these essays have had a lasting value as an authoritative and profound explanation of the Constitution. Though written for political purposes, the *Federalist* has become the single most important piece of American political philosophy ever produced. Ironically Hamilton and Madison were later to become political enemies; even at the Philadelphia convention they had different views of the kind of government that should be created. But in 1787–1788 they were united in the belief that the new constitution was the best that could have been obtained under the circumstances.

Although Hamilton wrote most of the *Federalist* papers, Madison wrote the two most famous articles—Nos. 10 and 51, reprinted here in the Appendix. After you have finished this chapter, turn to the Appendix and try to read them. On your first reading of the papers you may find Madison's language difficult to understand and his ideas overly complex. The following pointers will help you decipher his meaning.

In *Federalist* No. 10 Madison begins by stating that "a well constructed Union" can "break and control the violence of faction." He goes on to define a "faction" as any group of citizens who attempt to advance their ideas or economic interests at the expense of other citizens, or in ways that

James Madison

John Jay

Alexander Hamilton

conflict with "the permanent and aggregate interests of the community" or "public good." Thus what Madison terms "factions" are what we today call "special interests."

One way to defeat factions, according to Madison, is to remove whatever causes them to arise in the first place. This can be attempted in two ways. First, government can deprive people of the liberty they need to organize: "Liberty is to faction what air is to fire." But that is surely a cure "worse than the disease." Second, measures can be taken to make all citizens share the same ideas, feelings, and economic interests. However, as Madison observes, some people are smarter or more hard working than others, and this "diversity in the faculties" of citizens is bound to result

For the Independent Journal.

The FŒDERALIST. No. X.

To the People of the State of New-York.

AMONG the numerous advantages promised by a well constructed Union, none deserves to be more accurately developped than its tendency to break and control the violence of faction. The friend of popular governments, never finds himself so much alarmed for their character and fate, as when he contemplates their propensity to this dangerous vice. He will not fail therefore to set a due value on any plan which, without violating the principles to which he is attached, provides a proper cure for it. The instability, injustice and confusion introduced into the public councils, have in truth been the mortal diseases under which popular governments have every where perished; as they continue to be the favorite and fruitful topics from which the adversaries to liberty derive their most specious declamations. The valuable improvements made by the American Constitutions on the popular models, both ancient and modern, cannot certainly be too much admired; but it would be an unwarrantable partiality, to contend that they have as effectually obviated the danger on this side as was wished and expected. Complaints are every where heard from our most considerate and virtuous citizens, equally the friends of public and private faith, and of public and personal liberty; that our governments are too unstable; that the public good is disregarded in the conflicts of rival parties; and that measures are too often decided, not according to the rules of justice, and the rights of the minor party; but by the superior force of an interested and over-bearing majority. However anxiously we may

Madison thus proposes a second and, he thinks, more practical and desirable way of defeating faction. The way to cure "the mischiefs of faction" is not by removing its causes but by "controlling its effects." Factions will always exist, so the trick is to establish a form of government that is likely to serve the public good through the even-handed "regulation of these various and interfering interests." Wise and public-spirited leaders can "adjust these clashing interests and render them all subservient to the public good," but, he cautions, "enlightened statesmen will not always be at the helm." (Madison implies that "enlightened statesmen"—such as himself, Washington, and Jefferson—were at the "helm" of government in 1787.)

Madison's proposed cure for the evils of factions is in fact nothing other than a republican form of government. Use the following questions to guide your own analysis of Madison's ideas. Why does Madison think the problem of a "minority" faction is easy to handle? Conversely, why is he so troubled by the potential of a majority faction? How does he distinguish direct democracy from republican government? What is he getting at when he terms elected representatives "proper guardians of the public weal," and why does he think that "extensive republics" are more likely to produce such representatives than small ones?

When you are finished with *Federalist* No. 10, try your hand at *Federalist* No. 51. You will find that the ideas in the former paper anticipate many of those in the latter. And you will find many points on which you may or may not agree with Madison. For example, do you agree with his assumption that people—even your best friends or college roommates—are factious by nature? Likewise, do you agree with his view that government is "the greatest of all reflections on human nature"?

By attempting to meet the mind of James Madison, you can sharpen your own mind and deepen your understanding of American government.

in different economic interests as some people acquire more property than others. Consequently, protecting property rights, not equalizing property ownership, "is the first object of government." Even if everyone shared the same basic economic interests, they would still find reasons "to vex and oppress each other" rather than cooperate "for their common good." Religious differences, loyalties to different leaders, even "frivolous and fanciful distinctions" (not liking how other people dress or their taste in music) can be fertile soil for factions. In Madison's view people are factious by nature; the "causes of faction" are "sown" into their very being.

checking the president's power by creating a council that would review his actions, leaving military affairs in the hands of the state militias, increasing the size of the House of Representatives so that it would reflect a greater variety of popular interests, and reducing or eliminating the power of Congress to levy taxes. And some of them insisted that a *bill of rights* be added to the Constitution.

James Madison gave his answer to these criticisms in *Federalist* No. 10 and No. 51 (reprinted in the Appendix). It was a bold answer, for it flew squarely in the face of widespread popular sentiment and much philosophical writing. Following the great French political philosopher Montesquieu, many Americans believed that liberty was safe only in small societies governed either by direct democracy or by large legislatures with small districts and frequent turnover among members.

Madison argued quite the opposite—that liberty is safest in *large* (or as he put it, "extended") republics. In a small community, he said, there will be relatively few differences in opinion or interest; people will tend to see the world in much the same way. If anyone dissents or pursues an individual interest, he or she will be confronted by a massive majority and will have few, if any, allies. But in a large republic there will be many opinions and interests; as a result it will be hard for a tyrannical majority to form or organize, and anyone with an unpopular view will find it easier to acquire allies. If Madison's argument seems strange or abstract, ask yourself the following question: if I have an unpopular opinion, an exotic lifestyle, or an unconventional interest, will I find greater security living in a small town or a big city?

By favoring a large republic Madison was not trying to stifle democracy. Rather he was attempting to show how democratic government really works, and what can make it work better. To rule, different interests must come together and form a **coalition**—that is, an alliance. In *Federalist* No. 51 he argued that the coalitions that formed in a large republic would be more moderate than those that formed in a small one because the bigger the republic, the greater the variety of interests, and thus the more a coalition of the majority would have to accommodate a diversity of

---

coalition   An alliance of factions.

---

interests and opinions if it hoped to succeed. He concluded that in a nation the size of the United States, with its enormous variety of interests, "a coalition of a majority of the whole society could seldom take place on any other principles than those of justice and the general good." Whether he was right in that prediction is a matter to which we shall return repeatedly.

The implication of Madison's arguments was daring, for he was suggesting that the national government should be at some distance from the people and insulated from their momentary passions, because the people did not always want to do the right thing. Liberty was threatened as much (or even more) by public passions and popularly based factions as by strong governments. Now the Antifederalists themselves had no very lofty view of human nature, as is evidenced by the deep suspicion with which they viewed "power-seeking" officeholders. What Madison did was take this view to its logical conclusion, arguing that if people could be corrupted by office, they could also be corrupted by factional self-interest. Thus the government had to be designed to prevent both the politicians and the people from using it for ill-considered or unjust purposes.

To argue in 1787 against the virtues of small democracies was like arguing against motherhood, but the argument prevailed, probably because many citizens were convinced that a reasonably strong national government was essential if the nation were to stand united against foreign enemies, facilitate commerce among the states, guard against domestic insurrections, and keep one faction from oppressing another. The political realities of the moment and the recent bitter experiences with the Articles probably counted for more in ratifying the Constitution than did Madison's arguments. His cause was helped by the fact that, for all their legitimate concerns and their uncanny instinct for what the future might bring, the Antifederalists could offer no agreed-upon alternative to the new Constitution. In politics, then as now, you cannot beat something with nothing.

But this does not explain why the Framers failed to add a bill of rights to the Constitution. If they were so preoccupied with liberty, why didn't they take this most obvious step toward protecting liberty, especially since the Antifederalists were demanding it? Some historians have suggested that this omission was evidence that liberty was not as important to the Framers as they claimed. In fact when one delegate suggested that a bill of rights be drawn up, the state delegations at the convention unanimously voted the idea down. There were several reasons for this.

First, the Constitution, as written, *did* contain a number of specific guarantees of individual liberty, including the right of trial by jury in criminal cases and the privilege of the writ of habeas corpus. The liberties guaranteed in the Constitution (before the **Bill of Rights** was added) are listed below.

- Writ of **habeas corpus** may not be suspended (except during invasion or rebellion).
- No **bill of attainder** may be passed by Congress or the states.
- No **ex post facto law** may be passed by Congress or the states.
- Right of trial by jury in criminal cases is guaranteed.
- The citizens of each state are entitled to the privileges and immunities of the citizens of every other state.
- No religious test or qualification for holding federal office is imposed.
- No law impairing the obligation of contracts may be passed by the states.

Second, most states in 1787 had bills of rights. When Elbridge Gerry proposed to the convention that a federal bill of rights be drafted, Roger Sherman rose to observe that it was unnecessary because the state bills of rights were sufficient.[15]

But third, and perhaps most important, the Framers thought they were creating a government with specific, limited powers. It could do, they thought, only what the Constitution gave it the power to do, and nowhere in that document was there permission to infringe on freedom of speech or of the press or to impose cruel and unusual punishments. Some delegates probably feared that if any serious effort were made to list the rights that were guaranteed, later officials might assume that they had the power to do anything not explicitly forbidden.

Need for a Bill of Rights

Whatever their reasons, the Framers made at least a tactical and perhaps a fundamental mistake. It quickly became clear that without at least the promise of a bill of rights, the Constitution would not be ratified. Though the small states, pleased by their equal representation in the Senate, quickly ratified (in Delaware, New Jersey, and Georgia, the vote in

the conventions was unanimous), the battle in the large states was intense and the outcome uncertain. In Pennsylvania Federalist supporters dragged boycotting Antifederalists to the legislature in order to ensure that a quorum was present so that a convention could be called. There were rumors of other rough tactics.

In Massachusetts the Constitution was approved by a narrow majority, but only after key leaders promised to obtain a bill of rights. In Virginia James Madison fought against the fiery Patrick Henry, whose climactic speech against ratification was dramatically punctuated by a noisy thunderstorm outside. The Federalists won by ten votes. In New York Alexander Hamilton argued the case for six weeks against the determined opposition of most of the state's key political leaders; he carried the day, but only by three votes, and then only after New York City threatened to secede from the state if it did not ratify. By June 21, 1788, the ninth state—New Hampshire—had ratified, and the Constitution was law.

Despite the bitterness of the ratification struggle, the new government that took office in 1789–1790, headed by President Washington, was greeted enthusiastically. By the spring of 1790 all thirteen states had ratified. There remained, however, the task of fulfilling the promise of a bill of rights. To that end James Madison introduced into the first session of the First Congress a set of proposals, many based on the existing Virginia bill of rights. Twelve were approved by Congress; ten of these were ratified by the states and went into effect in 1791. These amendments did not limit the power of state governments over citizens, only the power of the federal government. Later the Fourteenth Amendment, as interpreted by the Supreme Court, extended many of the guarantees of the Bill of Rights to cover state governmental action.

---

habeas corpus An order to produce an arrested person before a judge.

bill of attainder A law that declares a person, without a trial, to be guilty of a crime.

ex post facto law A law that makes an act criminal although the act was legal when it was committed.

Bill of Rights First ten amendments to the Constitution.

★ HOW THINGS WORK ★

The Bill of Rights

The First Ten Amendments to the Constitution Grouped by Topic and Purpose

Protections Afforded Citizens to Participate in the Political Process

Amendment 1: Freedom of religion, speech, press, and assembly; the right to petition the government.

Protections Against Arbitrary Police and Court Action

Amendment 4: No unreasonable searches or seizures.

Amendment 5: Grand jury indictment required to prosecute a person for a serious crime.

No "double jeopardy" (being tried twice for the same offense).

Forcing a person to testify against himself or herself prohibited.

No loss of life, liberty, or property without due process.

Amendment 6: Right to speedy, public, impartial trial with defense counsel and right to cross-examine witnesses.

Amendment 7: Jury trials in civil suits where value exceeds $20.

Amendment 8: No excessive bail or fines, no cruel and unusual punishments.

Protections of States' Rights and Unnamed Rights of People

Amendment 9: Unlisted rights are not necessarily denied.

Amendment 10: Powers not delegated to the United States or denied to states are reserved to the states.

Other Amendments

Amendment 2: Right to bear arms.

Amendment 3: Troops may not be quartered in homes in peacetime.

The Constitution and Slavery

Though black slaves amounted to one-third of the population of the five southern states, nowhere in the Constitution can one find the word *slave* or *slavery.*

To some the failure of the Constitution to address the question of slavery was a great betrayal of the promise of the Declaration of Independence that "all men are created equal."[16] For the Constitution to be silent on the subject of slavery, and thereby to allow that odious practice to continue, was to convert, by implication, the wording of the Declaration to "all white men are created equal."

It is easy to accuse the signers of the Declaration and the Constitution of hypocrisy. They knew of slavery, many of them owned slaves, and yet they were silent. Indeed, British opponents of the independence movement took special delight in taunting the colonists about their complaints of being "enslaved" to the British Empire while ignoring the slavery in their very

midst. Increasingly, revolutionary leaders during this period spoke to this issue. Thomas Jefferson had tried to get a clause opposing the slave trade put into the Declaration of Independence. James Otis of Boston had attacked slavery and argued that black as well as white men should be free. As revolutionary fervor mounted, so did northern criticism of slavery. The Massachusetts legislature and then the Continental Congress voted to end the slave trade; Delaware prohibited the importation of slaves; Pennsylvania voted to tax it out of existence; and Connecticut and Rhode Island decided that all slaves brought into those states would automatically become free.

Slavery continued unabated in the South, defended by some whites because they thought it right, by others because they found it useful. But even in the South there were opponents, though rarely conspicuous ones. George Mason, a large Virginia slaveholder and a delegate to the convention, warned prophetically that "by an inevitable chain of causes

The Constitution was silent on slavery, and so buying and selling slaves continued for many years.

and effects, providence punishes national sins [slavery] by national calamities."[17]

The blunt fact, however, was that any effort to use the Constitution to end slavery would have meant the end of the Constitution. The southern states would never have signed a document that seriously interfered with slavery. Without the southern states there would have been a continuation of the Articles of Confederation, which would have left each state entirely sovereign and thus entirely free of any prospective challenge to slavery.

Thus the Framers compromised with slavery; political scientist Theodore Lowi calls this their Greatest Compromise.[18] Slavery is dealt with in three places in the Constitution, though never by name. In determining the representation each state was to have in the House, "three-fifths of all other persons" (that is, of slaves) are to be added to "the whole number of free persons."[19] The South originally wanted slaves to count fully even though, of course, none would be elected to the House; they settled for counting 60 percent of them. The convention also agreed not to allow the new government by law or even constitutional amendment to prohibit the importation of slaves until the year 1808.[20] The South thus had twenty years in which it could acquire more slaves from abroad; after that Congress was free (but not required) to end the importation.

Finally, the Constitution guaranteed that if a slave were to escape his or her master and flee to a nonslave state, the slave would be returned by that state to "the party to whom . . . service or labour may be due."[21]

The unresolved issue of slavery was to prove the most explosive question of all. Allowing slavery to continue was a fateful decision, one that led to the worst social and political catastrophe in the nation's history—the Civil War. The Framers chose to sidestep the issue in order to create a union that, they hoped, would eventually be strong enough to deal with the problem when it could no longer be postponed. The legacy of that choice continues to this day.

☆ The Motives of the Framers

The Framers were not saints or demigods. They were men with political opinions who also had economic interests and human failings. It would be a mistake to conclude that everything they did in 1787 was motivated by a disinterested commitment to the public good. But it would be an equally great mistake to think that what they did was nothing but an effort to line their pockets by producing a government that would serve their own narrow interests. As in almost all human endeavors, the Framers acted out of a mixture of

This late eighteenth century cartoon shows the enthusiasm many people had for the new Constitution.

motives. What is truly astonishing is that economic interests played only a modest role in their deliberations.

Economic Interests at the Convention

Some of the Framers were wealthy; some were not. Some owned slaves; some had none. Some were creditors (having loaned money to the Continental Congress or to private parties); some were deeply in debt. For nearly a century scholars have argued over just how important these personal interests were in shaping the provisions of the Constitution.

In 1913 Charles Beard, a historian, published a book—*An Economic Interpretation of the Constitution*—arguing that the better-off urban and commercial classes, especially those members who held the IOUs issued by the government to pay for the Revolutionary War, favored the new Constitution because they stood to benefit from it.[22] But in the 1950s that view was challenged by historians who, after looking carefully at what the Framers owned or owed, concluded that one could not explain the Constitution exclusively or even largely in terms of the economic interests of those who wrote it.[23] Some of the richest delegates, such as Elbridge Gerry of Massachusetts and George Mason of Virginia, refused to sign the document, while many of its key backers—James Madison and James Wilson, for example—were men of modest means or heavy debts.

In the 1980s a new group of scholars, primarily economists applying more advanced statistical techniques, found evidence that some economic considerations influenced how the Framers voted on some issues during the Philadelphia convention. Interestingly, however, the economic position of the *states* from which they came had a greater effect on their votes than did their *own* monetary condition.[24]

We have already seen how delegates from small states fought to reduce the power of large states and how those from slaveowning states made certain that the Constitution would contain no provision that would threaten slavery.

But contrary to what Beard asserted, the individual interests of the Framers themselves did not dominate the convention except in a few cases where a constitutional provision would have affected them directly. As you might expect, all slaveowning delegates, even those who did not live in states where slavery was commonplace (and several northern delegates owned slaves), tended to vote for provisions that would have kept the national government's power over slavery as weak as possible. However, the effects of other personal business interests were surprisingly weak. Some delegates owned a lot of public debt that they had purchased for low prices. A strong national government of the sort envisaged by the Constitution was more likely than the weak Continental Congress to pay off this debt at face value, thus making the delegates who owned it much richer. Despite this, the ownership of public debt had no significant effect on how the Framers voted in Philadelphia. For example, five men who among them owned one-third of all the public securities held by all the delegates voted against the Constitution. Nor did the big land speculators vote their interests. Some, such as George Washington and Robert Morris, favored the Constitution, while others, such as George Mason and William Blount, opposed it.[25]

In sum the Framers tended to represent their states' interests on important matters. Since they were picked by the states to do so, this is exactly what one would expect. If they had not met in secret, perhaps they would have voted even more often as their constituents wanted. But except with respect to slavery, they usually did not vote their own economic interests. They were reasonably but not wholly disinterested delegates who were probably influenced as much by personal beliefs as by economics.

Economic Interests and Ratification

At the popularly elected state ratifying conventions, economic factors played a larger role. Delegates who were merchants, who lived in cities, who owned large amounts of western land, who held government IOUs, and who did not own slaves were more likely to vote to ratify the new Constitution than were delegates who were farmers, who did not own public debt, and who did own slaves.[26] There were plenty of exceptions, however. Small farmers dominated the conventions in some states where the vote to ratify was unanimous.

Though interests made a difference, they were not simply elite interests. In most states the great majority of adult white males could vote for delegates to the ratifying conventions. This means that women and blacks were excluded from the debates, but by the standards of the time—standards that did not change for over a century—the ratification process was remarkably democratic.

The Constitution and Equality

Ideas counted for as much as interests. At stake were two views of the public good. One, espoused by the Federalists, was that a reasonable balance of liberty,

order, and progress required a strong national government. The other, defended by the Antifederalists, was that liberty would not be secure in the hands of a powerful, distant government; freedom required decentralization.

Today that debate has a new focus. The defect of the Constitution, to some contemporary critics, is not that the government it created is too strong but that it is too weak. In particular the national government is too weak to resist the pressures of special interests that reflect and perpetuate social inequality.

This criticism reveals how our understanding of the relationship between liberty and equality has changed since the Founding. To Jefferson and Madison citizens naturally differed in their talents and qualities. What had to be guarded against was the use of governmental power to create unnatural and undesirable inequalities. This might happen, for example, if political power was concentrated in the hands of a few people (who could use that power to give themselves special privileges) or if it was used in ways that allowed some private parties to acquire exclusive charters and monopolies. To prevent the inequality that might result from having too strong a government, its powers must be kept strictly limited.

Elbridge Gerry (left, 1744–1814) was a wealthy Massachusetts merchant and politician who participated in the convention but refused to sign the Constitution. James Wilson (right, 1742–1798) of Pennsylvania, a brilliant lawyer and terrible businessman, was the principal champion of the popular election of the House. Near the end of his life he was jailed repeatedly for debts incurred as a result of his business speculations.

Today some people think of inequality quite differently. To them it is the natural social order—the marketplace and the acquisitive talents of people operating in that marketplace—that leads to undesirable inequalities, especially in economic power. The government should be powerful enough to restrain these natural tendencies and produce, by law, a greater degree of equality than society allows when left alone.

To the Framers liberty and (political) equality were not in conflict; to some people today these two principles are deeply in conflict. To the Framers the task was to keep government so limited as to prevent it from creating the worst inequality—political privilege. To some modern observers the task is to make government strong enough to reduce what they believe is the worst inequality—differences in wealth.

☆ Constitutional Reform: Modern Views

Almost from the day it was ratified, the Constitution has been the object of debate over ways in which it might be improved. These debates have rarely involved the average citizen, who tends to revere the document even if he or she cannot recall all its details. Because of this deep and broad popular support, scholars and politicians have been wary of attacking the Constitution or suggesting many wholesale changes. But such attacks have occurred. During the 1980s—the decade in which we celebrated the bicentennial of its adoption—we heard a variety of suggestions for improving the Constitution, ranging from particular amendments to wholesale revisions. In general there are today, as in the eighteenth century, two kinds of critics: those who think the federal government is too weak and those who think it is too strong.

Reducing the Separation of Powers

To the first kind of critic the chief difficulty with the Constitution is the separation of powers. By making every decision the uncertain outcome of the pulling and hauling between the president and Congress, the Constitution precludes the emergence—except perhaps in times of crisis—of the kind of effective national leadership the country needs. In this view our nation today faces a number of challenges that require prompt, decisive, and comprehensive action.

Our problem is gridlock. Our position of international leadership, the dangerous and unprecedented proliferation of nuclear weapons among the nations of the globe, and the need to find ways of stimulating economic growth while reducing our deficit and conserving our environment—all these situations require that the president be able to formulate and carry out policies free of some of the pressures and delays from interest groups and members of Congress tied to local interests.

Not only would this increase in presidential authority make for better policies, these critics argue, it would also help the voters hold the president and his party accountable for their actions. As matters now stand, nobody in government can be held responsible for policies: everybody takes the credit for successes and nobody takes the blame for failures. Typically the president, who tends to be the major source of new programs, cannot get his policies adopted by Congress without long delays and much bargaining, the result of which often is some watered-down compromise that neither the president nor Congress really likes but that each must settle for if anything is to be done at all.

Finally, critics of the separation of powers complain that the government agencies responsible for implementing a program are exposed to undue interference from legislators and special interests. In this view the president is supposed to be in charge of the bureaucracy but in fact must share this authority with countless members of Congress and congressional committees.

Not all critics of the separation of powers agree with all these points, nor do they all agree on what should be done about the problems. But they all have in common a fear that the separation of powers makes the president too weak and insufficiently accountable. Their proposals for reducing the separation of powers include the following:

- Allow the president to appoint members of Congress to serve in the cabinet (the Constitution forbids members of Congress from holding any federal appointive office while in Congress).
- Allow the president to dissolve Congress and call for a special election (elections now can be held only on the schedule determined by the calendar).
- Allow Congress to require a president who has lost its confidence to face the country in a special election before his term would normally end.

Were Women Left Out of the Constitution?

In one sense, yes: Women were nowhere mentioned in the Constitution when it was written in 1787. Moreover, Article I, which set forth the provisions for electing members of the House of Representatives, granted the vote to those people who were allowed to vote for members of the lower house of the legislature in the states in which they resided. In no state at the time could women participate in those elections. In no state could they vote in any elections or hold any offices. Furthermore, wherever the Constitution uses a pronoun, it uses the masculine form—*he* or *him.*

In another sense, no: Wherever the Constitution or the Bill of Rights defines a right that people are to have, it either grants that right to "persons" or "citizens," not to "men," or it makes no mention at all of people or gender. For example:

- "The *citizens* of each State shall be entitled to all privileges and immunities of citizens of the several States."   [Art. I, sec. 9]

- "No *person* shall be convicted of treason unless on the testimony of two witnesses to the same overt act, or on confession in open court."   [Art. III, sec. 3]

- "No bill of attainder or ex post facto law shall be passed."   [Art. I, sec. 9]

- "The right of the *people* to be secure in their persons, houses, papers, and effects, against unreasonable searches and seizures, shall not be violated."   [Amend. IV]

- "No *person* shall be held to answer for a capital, or otherwise infamous crime, unless on presentment or indictment of a grand jury . . . nor shall any *person* be subject for the same offense to be twice put in jeopardy of life or limb; . . . nor be deprived of life, liberty, or property, without due process of law."   [Amend. V]

- "In all criminal prosecutions the *accused* shall enjoy the right to a speedy and public trial, by an impartial jury."   [Amend. VI]

Moreover, when the qualifications for elective office are stated, the word *person*, not *man*, is used.

- "No *person* shall be a Representative who shall not have attained to the age of twenty-five years."   [Art. I, sec. 2]

- "No *person* shall be a Senator who shall not have attained to the age of thirty years."   [Art. I, sec. 3]

- "No *person* except a natural born citizen . . . shall be eligible to the office of President; neither shall any *person* be eligible to that office who shall not have attained to the age of thirty-five years."   [Art. II, sec. 1]

In places the Constitution and the Bill of Rights used the pronoun *he,* but always in the context of referring back to a *person* or *citizen.* At the time, and until quite recently, the male pronoun was often used in legal documents to refer generically to both men and women.

Thus, though the Constitution did not give women the right to vote until the Nineteenth Amendment was ratified in 1920, it did use language that extended fundamental rights, and access to office, to women and men equally.

Of course what the Constitution permitted did not necessarily occur. State and local laws denied to women rights that in principle they ought to have enjoyed. Except for a brief period in New Jersey, no women voted in statewide elections until, in 1869, they were given the right to cast ballots in territorial elections in Wyoming.

When women were first elected to Congress, there was no need to change the Constitution; nothing in it restricted officeholding to men.

When women were given the right to vote by constitutional amendment, it was not necessary to amend any existing language in the Constitution, because nothing in the Constitution itself denied women the right to vote; the amendment simply added a new right:

- "The right of citizens of the United States to vote shall not be denied or abridged by the United States or any state on account of sex."   [Amend. XIX]

Source: Adapted from Robert Goldwin, "Why Blacks, Women and Jews Are Not Mentioned in the Constitution," *Commentary* (May 1987): 28–33.

☆ HOW THINGS WORK ☆

Ways of Amending the Constitution

Under Article V there are two ways to *propose* amendments to the Constitution and two ways to *ratify* them.

To Propose an Amendment

1. Two-thirds of both houses of Congress vote to propose an amendment, *or*
2. Two-thirds of the state legislatures ask Congress to call a national convention to propose amendments.

To Ratify an Amendment

1. Three-fourths of the state legislatures approve it, *or*
2. Ratifying conventions in three-fourths of the states approve it.

Some Key Facts

- Only the first method of proposing an amendment has been used.
- The second method of ratification has been used only once, to ratify the Twenty-first Amendment (repealing Prohibition).
- Congress may limit the time within which a proposed amendment must be ratified. The usual limitation has been seven years.
- Thousands of proposals have been made, but only thirty-three have obtained the necessary two-thirds vote in Congress.
- Twenty-seven amendments have been ratified.
- The first ten amendments, ratified on December 15, 1791, are known as the Bill of Rights.

- Require the presidential and congressional candidates to run as a team in each congressional district; thus a presidential candidate who carries a given district could be sure that the congressional candidate of his party would also win in that district.
- Have the president serve a single six-year term instead of being eligible for up to two four-year terms; this would presumably free the president to lead without having to worry about reelection.
- Lengthen the terms of members of the House of Representatives from two to four years so that the entire House would stand for reelection at the same time as the president.[27]

Some of these proposals are offered by critics out of a desire to make the American system of government work more like the British parliamentary system, in which, as we shall see in Chapters 13 and 14, the prime minister is the undisputed leader of the majority in the British Parliament. The parliamentary system is the major alternative in the world today to the American separation-of-powers system.

Both the diagnosis and the remedies proposed by these critics of the separation of powers have been challenged. Many defenders of our present constitutional system believe that nations, such as Great Britain, with a different, more unified political system have done no better than the United States in dealing with the problems of economic growth, national security, and environmental protection. Moreover, they argue, close congressional scrutiny of presidential proposals has improved these policies more often than it has weakened them. Finally, congressional "interference" in the work of government agencies is a good way of ensuring that the average citizen can fight back against the bureaucracy; without that so-called interference, citizens and interest groups might be helpless before big and powerful agencies.

Each of the specific proposals, defenders of the present constitutional system argue, would either make matters worse or have, at best, uncertain effects. Adding a few members of Congress to the president's cabinet would not provide much help in

---

amendment   A new provision in the Constitution that has been ratified by the states.

getting his program through Congress; there are 535 senators and representatives, and probably only about half a dozen would be in the cabinet. Giving either the president or Congress the power to call a special election in between the regular elections (every two or four years) would cause needless confusion and great expense; the country would live under the threat of being in a perpetual political campaign with even weaker political parties. Linking the fate of the president and congressional candidates by having them run as a team in each district would reduce the stabilizing and moderating effect of having them elected separately. A Republican presidential candidate who wins in the new system would have a Republican majority in the House; a Democratic candidate winner would have a Democratic majority. We might as a result expect dramatic changes in policy as the political pendulum swung back and forth. Giving presidents a single six-year term would indeed free them from the need to worry about reelection, but it is precisely that worry that keeps presidents reasonably concerned about what the American people want.

Making the System Less Democratic

The second kind of critic of the Constitution thinks the government does too much, not too little. Though the separation of powers at one time may have slowed the growth of government and moderated the policies it adopted, in the last few decades government has grown helter-skelter. The problem, these critics argue, is not that democracy is a bad idea but that democracy can produce bad, or at least unintended, results if the government caters to the special-interest claims of the citizens rather than to their long-term values.

To see how these unintended results might occur, imagine a situation in which every citizen thinks the government grows too big, taxes too heavily, and spends too much. Each citizen wants the government made smaller by reducing the benefits other people get—but not by reducing the benefits he or she gets. In fact such citizens may even be willing to see their own benefits cut, provided everybody else's are cut as well, and by a like amount.

But the political system attends to individual wants, not general preferences. It gives aid to farmers, contracts to industry, grants to professors, pensions to the elderly, and loans to students. As someone once said, the government is like an adding machine: during elections candidates campaign by promising to do more for whatever group is dissatisfied with what the incumbents are doing for it. As a result most elections bring to office men and women who are committed to doing more for somebody. The grand total of all these additions is more for everybody. Few politicians have an incentive to do less for anybody.

To remedy this state of affairs, these critics suggest various mechanisms, but principally a constitutional amendment that would either set a limit on the amount of money the government could collect in taxes each year or require that each year the government have a balanced budget (that is, not spend more than it takes in in taxes), or both. In some versions of these plans an extraordinary majority (say, 60 percent) of Congress could override these limits, and the limits would not apply in wartime.

The effect of such amendments, the proponents claim, would be to force Congress and the president to look at the big picture—the grand total of what they are spending—rather than just to operate the adding machine by pushing the "add" button over and over again. If they could spend only so much during a given year, they would have to allocate what they spend among all rival claimants. For example, if more money were to be spent on the poor, less could then be spent on the military, or vice versa.

Some critics of an overly powerful federal government think these amendments will not be passed or may prove unworkable; instead they favor enhancing the president's power to block spending by giving him a **line-item veto.** Most state governors can veto a particular part of a bill and approve the rest using a line-item veto. The theory is that such a veto would better equip the president to stop unwarranted spending without vetoing the other provisions of a bill. In 1996 President Clinton signed the Line Item Veto Act, passed by the 104th Congress. But despite its name, the new law did not give the president full line-item veto power (only a change in the Constitution could confer that power). Instead the law gave the president authority to selectively eliminate individual items in large appropriations bills, expansions

---

line-item veto   An executive's ability to block a particular provision in a bill passed by the legislature.

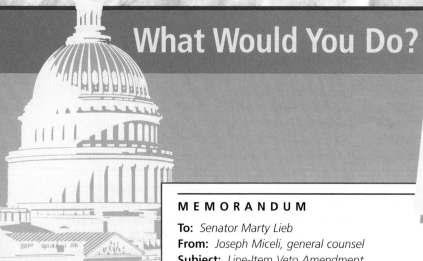

House Backs Amendment to Give President New Veto Power

June 27
WASHINGTON

Yesterday the House of Representatives, by a 315-to-120 vote, proposed an amendment to the U.S. Constitution that would give future presidents the power to veto a particular part of a bill and approve the rest. The Senate will debate the bill next week . . .

MEMORANDUM

To: *Senator Marty Lieb*
From: *Joseph Miceli, general counsel*
Subject: *Line-Item Veto Amendment*

In 1996 you voted in favor of the Line Item Veto Act, which authorized the president to selectively eliminate items in certain appropriations bills subject to such exemptions as Congress might make. Despite its narrow application, the Supreme Court has declared the law unconstitutional. The amendment being debated next week would confer full line-item veto power on the president.

Arguments for:

1. Forty-three state constitutions, most of them explicitly modeled on the U.S. Constitution, confer line-item veto power on governors.
2. The line-item veto has equipped many governors to stop unwarranted spending without stopping the sensible provisions of a bill.
3. Most people favor giving the president this authority and holding him accountable.

Arguments against:

1. The national government is different. The Founding Fathers considered many veto alternatives and limited the president's "qualified negative" power to rejecting a bill in its entirety, subject to an override by a two-thirds vote of Congress.
2. There is no clear evidence that the line-item veto restrains state spending or that the aforementioned 1996 law restrained federal spending.
3. Popular support for the line-item veto dwindles when people are reminded about our system's separation of powers and checks and balances.

Your decision:

Favor amendment _____
Oppose amendment _____

in certain income-transfer programs, and tax breaks (giving the president what budget experts call *enhanced rescission authority*). But it also left Congress free to craft bills in ways that would give the president few opportunities to veto (or *rescind*) favored items. For example, Congress could still force the president to accept or reject an entire appropriations bill simply by tagging on this sentence: "Appropriations provided under this act (or title or section) shall not be subject to the provisions of the Line Item Veto Act." In *Clinton et al. v. New York et al.* (1998), the Supreme Court struck down the 1996 law, holding 6 to 3 that the Constitution does not allow the president to cancel specific items in tax and spending legislation.

Finally, some of these critics of a powerful government feel that the real problem arises not from an excess of "adding-machine" democracy but from the growth in the power of the federal courts, as described in Chapter 16. What these critics would like to do is devise a set of laws or constitutional amendments that would narrow the authority of federal courts.

The opponents of these suggestions argue that constitutional amendments to restrict the level of taxes or to require a balanced budget are unworkable, even assuming—which they do not—that a smaller government is desirable. There is no precise, agreed-upon way to measure how much the government spends or to predict in advance how much it will receive in taxes during the year; thus defining and enforcing a "balanced budget" is no easy matter. Since the government can always borrow money, it might easily evade any spending limits. It has also shown great ingenuity in spending money in ways that never appear as part of the regular budget.

The line-item veto may or may not be a good idea. Unless the Constitution is amended to permit it, future presidents will have to do without it. The states, where some governors have long had the veto, are quite different from the federal government in power and responsibilities. Whether a line-item veto would work as well in Washington, D.C., as it does in many state capitals is something that we may simply never know.

Finally, proposals to curtail judicial power are thinly veiled attacks, the opponents argue, on the ability of the courts to protect essential citizen rights. If Congress and the people do not like the way the Supreme Court has interpreted the Constitution, they can always amend the Constitution to change a specific ruling; there is no need to adopt some across-the-board limitation on court powers.

Who Is Right?

Some of the arguments of these two sets of critics of the Constitution may strike you as plausible or even entirely convincing. Whatever you may ultimately decide, decide nothing for now. One cannot make or remake a constitution based entirely on abstract reasoning or unproven factual arguments. Even when the Constitution was first written in 1787, it was not an exercise in abstract philosophy but rather an effort to solve pressing, practical problems in the light of a theory of human nature, the lessons of past experience, and a close consideration of how governments in other countries and at other times had worked.

Just because the Constitution is over two hundred years old does not mean that it is out-of-date. The crucial questions are these: How well has it worked over the long sweep of American history? How well has it worked compared to the constitutions of other democratic nations?

The only way to answer those questions is to study American government closely—with special attention to its historical evolution and to the practices of other nations. That is what this book is about. Of course, even after close study, people will still disagree about whether our system should be changed. People want different things and evaluate human experience according to different beliefs. But if we first understand how, in fact, the government works and why it has produced the policies it has, we can then argue more intelligently about how best to achieve our wants and give expression to our beliefs.

☆ SUMMARY

The Framers of the Constitution sought to create a government capable of protecting both liberty and order. The solution they chose—one without precedent at that time—was a government that was based on a written constitution that combined the principles of popular consent, the separation of powers, and federalism.

Popular consent was embodied in the procedure for choosing the House of Representatives but limited by the indirect election of senators and the electoral college system for selecting the president. Political authority was to be shared by three branches of government in a manner deliberately intended to produce conflict among these branches. This conflict, motivated by the self-interest of the people occupying each branch, would, it was hoped, prevent tyranny, even by a popular majority.

Federalism came to mean a system in which both the national and state governments had independent authority. Allocating powers between the two levels of government and devising means to ensure that neither large nor small states would dominate the national government required the most delicate compromises at the Philadelphia convention. The decision to do nothing about slavery was another such compromise.

In the drafting of the Constitution and the struggle over its ratification in the states, the positions people took were chiefly determined not by their economic interests but by a variety of factors. Among these were profound differences of opinion over whether the state governments or the national government would be the best protector of personal liberty.

RECONSIDERING WHO GOVERNS?

1. What is the difference between a democracy and a republic?

A democracy means rule by the people; direct democracy means letting every important issue be decided by popular vote. A republic is a government in which authority has been given to elected representatives. The United States is a republic in which members of the House of Representatives are selected in democratic elections, members of the Senate

(at least initially) were selected by state legislatures, and the courts are staffed by appointed judges.

2. What branch of government has the greatest power?

Initially, Congress had the most authority. As we shall see in later chapters, the president and the federal courts grew in power, but even so Congress remains the most important institution.

RECONSIDERING TO WHAT ENDS?

1. Does the Constitution tell us what goals the government should serve?

Not really. The preface tells us what the Founders hoped the federal government would do, but that preface has no legal authority. By and large, the government has to set its own goals.

2. Whose freedom does the Constitution protect?

It was intended to protect everybody's freedom, except that of slaves. To create a national government, it was necessary that the Constitution do

nothing about slavery, but without the Constitution, there would have been no national government to challenge slavery during the Civil War. Though women are not mentioned, in fact there is nothing in the Constitution to prevent them from holding national office or from voting in federal elections. Voting was to be decided by each state until the passage of a constitutional amendment (the Nineteenth, ratified in 1920) that prohibited the states from denying the vote to women.

WORLD WIDE WEB RESOURCES

To find historical and legal documents:

FedLaw's constitutional and early government documents: **www.thecre.com/fedlaw/legal9.htm**

TeachingAmericanHistory.org

National Constitution Center: **www.constitutioncenter.org**

Congress: **thomas.loc.gov/** (choose Historical Documents)

To look at court cases about the Constitution:

Cornell University: **supct.law.cornell.edu/supct/index.html**

SUGGESTED READINGS

Bailyn, Bernard. *The Ideological Origins of the American Revolution.* Cambridge: Harvard University Press, 1967. A brilliant account of how the American colonists formed and justified the idea of independence.

Becker, Carl L. *The Declaration of Independence.* New York: Vintage, 1942. The classic account of the meaning of the Declaration.

Farrand, Max. *The Framing of the Constitution of the United States.* New Haven, Conn.: Yale University Press, 1913. A good, brief account of the Philadelphia convention by the editor of Madison's notes on the convention.

Federalist papers. By Alexander Hamilton, James Madison, and John Jay. The definitive edition, edited by Jacob E. Cooke, was published in Middletown, Conn., in 1961, by the Wesleyan University Press.

Goldwin, Robert A., and William A. Schambra, eds. *How Capitalistic Is the Constitution?* Washington, D.C.: American Enterprise Institute, 1982. Essays from different viewpoints discussing the relationship between the Constitution and the economic order.

————. *How Democratic Is the Constitution?* Washington, D.C.: American Enterprise Institute, 1980. Collection of essays offering different interpretations of the political meaning of the Constitution.

McDonald, Forrest. *Novus Ordo Seclorum.* Lawrence: University of Kansas Press, 1985. A careful study of the intellectual origins of the Constitution. The Latin title means "New World Order," which is what the Framers hoped they were creating.

Robinson, Donald L., ed. *Reforming American Government.* Boulder, Colo.: Westview Press, 1985. Collection of essays advocating constitutional reform.

Sheldon, Garrett W. *The Political Philosophy of James Madison.* Baltimore: Johns Hopkins University Press, 2001. Masterful account of Madison's political thought and its roots in classical republicanism and Christianity.

Storing, Herbert J. *What the Anti-Federalists Were For.* Chicago: University of Chicago Press, 1981. Close analysis of the political views of those opposed to the ratification of the Constitution.

Wood, Gordon S. *The Creation of the American Republic.* Chapel Hill: University of North Carolina Press, 1969. A detailed study of American political thought before the Philadelphia convention.

————. *The Radicalism of the American Revolution.* New York: Knopf, 1992. Magisterial study of the nature and effects of the American Revolution and the relationship between the socially radical Revolution and the Constitution.

CHAPTER 3

Federalism

Governmental Structure
Federalism: Good or Bad? ● Increased Political Activity

The Founding
A Bold, New Plan ● Elastic Language

The Debate on the Meaning of Federalism
The Supreme Court Speaks ● Nullification ● Dual Federalism ● State Sovereignty

Federal-State Relations
Grants-in-Aid ● Meeting National Needs ● The Intergovernmental Lobby ● Categorical Grants Versus Revenue Sharing ● Rivalry Among the States

Federal Aid and Federal Control
Mandates ● Conditions of Aid

A Devolution Revolution?
Block Grants for Entitlements ● What's Driving Devolution?

Congress and Federalism

WHO GOVERNS?

1. Where is sovereignty located in the American political system?
2. How is power divided between the national government and the states under the Constitution?

TO WHAT ENDS?

1. What competing values are at stake in federalism?
2. Who should decide what matters ought to be governed mainly or solely by national laws?

*T*he average citizen wants more protection against terrorist attacks. The major targets for such attacks are probably to be found in big cities, major sea ports, and important airports. But in our system of government, it is hard to send money to only a few key locations. Just a few months after the Department of Homeland Security (DHS) was created, some governors complained that not enough DHS money was going to suburbs, small towns, and rural areas.

This struggle is not new. Since the adoption of the Constitution in 1787, the single most persistent source of political conflict has been the relations between the national and state governments. The political conflict over slavery, for example, was intensified because some state governments condoned or supported slavery, while others took action to discourage it. The proponents and opponents of slavery were thus given territorial power centers from which to carry on the dispute. Other issues, such as the regulation of business and the provision of social welfare programs, were in large part fought out, for well over a century, in terms of "national interests" versus "states' rights." While other nations, such as Great Britain, were debating the question of whether the national government *ought* to provide old-age pensions or regulate the railroads, the United States debated a different question—whether the national government *had the right* to do these things. Even after these debates had ended—almost invariably with a decision favorable to the national government—the administration and financing of the programs that resulted have usually involved a large role for the states.

Today an effort is under way to scale back the size and activities of the national government and to shift responsibility for a wide range of domestic programs from Washington to the states. The effort to devolve onto the states the national government's functions in areas such as welfare, health care, and job training has become known as **devolution.** In the 104th Congress (1994–1996) Republican majorities in the House and Senate made proposals, several of them enacted into law, to accelerate the devolution of national power. Many of these proposals involved giving the states **block grants**—money from the national government for programs in certain general areas that the states can use at their discretion within broad guidelines set by Congress or responsible federal agencies.

In 1908 Woodrow Wilson observed that how we structure the relationship between the national government and the states "is the cardinal question of our constitutional system," a question that cannot be settled by "one generation,

49

because it is a question of growth, and every successive stage of our political and economic development gives it a new aspect, makes it a new question."[1]

Today, in the twenty-first century, is the American political system in the early stages of a "devolution revolution" that will make the states, not the national government, the dominant force in domestic affairs? Do most Americans support devolution? Have recent court decisions returned power to the states? What, if any, differences will devolution reforms make in who governs and to what ends? Before one can begin to address these questions, it is important to master the basic concepts and understand the political history of federalism.

☆ Governmental Structure

Federalism refers to a political system in which there are local (territorial, regional, provincial, state, or municipal) units of government, as well as a national government, that can make final decisions with respect to at least some governmental activities and whose existence is specially protected.[2] Almost every nation in the world has local units of government of some kind, if for no other reason than to decentralize the administrative burdens of governing. But these governments are not federal unless the local units exist independent of the preferences of the national government and can make decisions on at least some matters without regard to those preferences.

The United States, Canada, Australia, India, Germany, and Switzerland are federal systems, as are a few other nations. France, Great Britain, Italy, and Sweden are not: they are unitary systems, because such local governments as they possess can be altered or even abolished by the national government and cannot plausibly claim to have final authority over any significant governmental activities.

The special protection that subnational governments enjoy in a federal system derives in part from the constitution of the country but also from the habits, preferences, and dispositions of the citizens

devolution   The effort to transfer responsibility for many public programs and services from the federal government to the states.

block grants   Money from the national government that states can spend within broad guidelines determined by Washington.

and the actual distribution of political power in society. The constitution of the former Soviet Union in theory created a federal system, as claimed by that country's full name—the Union of Soviet Socialist Republics—but for most of their history, none of these "socialist republics" were in the slightest degree independent of the central government. Were the American Constitution the only guarantee of the independence of the American states, they would long since have become mere administrative subunits of the government in Washington. Their independence results in large measure from the commitment of Americans to the idea of local self-government and from the fact that Congress consists of people who are selected by and responsive to local constituencies.

"The basic political fact of federalism," writes David B. Truman, "is that it creates separate, self-sustaining centers of power, prestige, and profit."[3] Political power is locally acquired by people whose careers depend for the most part on satisfying local interests. As a result, though the national government has come to have vast powers, it exercises many of those powers through state governments. What many of us forget when we think about "the government in Washington" is that it spends much of its money and enforces most of its rules not on citizens directly but on other, local units of government. A large part of the welfare system, all of the interstate highway system, virtually every aspect of programs to improve cities, the largest part of the effort to supply jobs to the unemployed, the entire program to clean up our water, and even much of our military manpower (in the form of the National Guard) are enterprises in which the national government does not govern so much as it seeks, by regulation, grant, plan, argument, and cajolery, to get the states to govern in accordance with nationally defined (though often vaguely defined) goals.

In France welfare, highways, education, the police, and the use of land are all matters that are directed nationally. In the United States highways and some welfare programs are largely state functions (though they make use of federal money), while education, policing, and land-use controls are primarily local (city, county, or special-district) functions.

Federalism: Good or Bad?

A measure of the importance of federalism is the controversy that surrounds it. To some, federalism means allowing states to block action, prevent progress, upset national plans, protect powerful local interests, and cater to the self-interest of hack politicians. Harold Laski, a British observer, described American states as "parasitic and poisonous,"[4] and William H. Riker, an American political scientist, argued that "the main effect of federalism since the Civil War has been to perpetuate racism."[5] By contrast, another political scientist, Daniel J. Elazar, argued that the "virtue of the federal system lies in its ability to develop and maintain mechanisms vital to the perpetuation of the unique combination of governmental strength, political flexibility, and individual liberty, which has been the central concern of American politics."[6]

So diametrically opposed are the Riker and Elazar views that one wonders whether they are talking about the same subject. They are, of course, but they are stressing different aspects of the same phenomenon. Whenever the opportunity to exercise political power is widely available (as among the fifty states, three thousand counties, and many thousands of municipalities in the United States), it is obvious that in different places different people will make use of that power for different purposes. There is no question that allowing states and cities to make autonomous, binding political decisions will allow some people in some places to make those decisions in ways that maintain racial segregation, protect vested interests, and facilitate corruption. It is equally true, however, that this arrangement also enables other people in other places to pass laws that attack segregation, regulate harmful economic practices, and purify politics, often long before these ideas gain national support or become national policy.

For example, in a unitary political system, such as that of France, a small but intensely motivated group could not have blocked civil rights legislation for as long as some southern senators blocked it in this country. But by the same token it would have been equally difficult for another small but intensely motivated group to block plans to operate a nuclear power plant in their neighborhood, as citizens have done in this country but not in France.

The existence of independent state and local governments means that different political groups pursuing different political purposes will come to power in different places. The smaller the political unit, the more likely it is to be dominated by a single political faction. James Madison understood this fact perfectly and used it to argue (in *Federalist* No. 10) that it

☆ POLITICALLY SPEAKING ☆

Sovereignty, Federalism, and the Constitution

Sovereignty means supreme or ultimate political authority: A sovereign government is one that is legally and politically independent of any other government.

A **unitary system** is one in which sovereignty is wholly in the hands of the national government, so that the states and localities are dependent on its will.

A **confederation or confederal system** is one in which the states are sovereign and the national government is allowed to do only that which the states permit.

A **federal system** is one in which sovereignty is shared, so that in some matters the national government is supreme and in other matters the states are supreme.

The Founding Fathers often took *confederal* and *federal* to mean much the same thing. Rather than establishing a government in which there was a clear division of sovereign authority between the national and state governments, they saw themselves as creating a government that combined some characteristics of a unitary regime with some of a confederal one. Or, as James Madison expressed the idea in *Federalist* No. 39, the Constitution "is, in strictness, neither a national nor a federal Constitution, but a composition of both." Where sovereignty is located in this system is a matter that the Founders did not clearly answer.

In this text, a **federal regime** is defined in the simplest possible terms—as one in which local units of government have a specially protected existence and can make some final decisions over some governmental activities.

would be in a large (or "extended") republic, such as the United States as a whole, that one would find the greatest opportunity for all relevant interests to be heard. When William Riker condemns federalism, he is thinking of the fact that in some places the ruling factions in cities and states have opposed granting equal rights to African Americans. When Daniel Elazar praises federalism, he is recalling that, in other states and cities, the ruling factions have taken the lead (long in advance of the federal government) in developing measures to protect the environment,

Federalism has permitted experimentation. Women were able to vote in the Wyoming Territory in 1888, long before they could do so in most states.

extend civil rights, and improve social conditions. If you live in California, whether you like federalism depends in part on whether you like the fact that California has, independent of the federal government, cut property taxes, strictly controlled coastal land use, heavily regulated electric utilities, and increased (at one time) and decreased (at another time) its welfare rolls.

Increased Political Activity

Federalism has many effects, but its most obvious effect has been to facilitate the mobilization of political activity. Unlike Don Quixote, the average citizen does not tilt at windmills. He or she is more likely to become involved in organized political activity if he or she feels there is a reasonable chance of having a practical effect. The chances of having such an effect are greater where there are many elected officials and independent governmental bodies, each with a relatively small constituency, than where there are

few elected officials, most of whom have the nation as a whole for a constituency. In short a federal system, by virtue of the decentralization of authority, lowers the cost of organized political activity; a unitary system, because of the centralization of authority, raises the cost. We may disagree about the purposes of organized political activity, but the fact of widespread organized activity can scarcely be doubted—or if it can be doubted, it is only because you have not yet read Chapters 8 and 11.

It is impossible to say whether the Founders, when they wrote the Constitution, planned to produce such widespread opportunities for political participation. Unfortunately they were not very clear (at least in writing) about how the federal system was supposed to work, and thus most of the interesting questions about the jurisdiction and powers of our national and state governments had to be settled by a century and a half of protracted, often bitter, conflict.

☆ The Founding

The goal of the Founders seems clear: federalism was one device whereby personal liberty was to be protected. (The separation of powers was another.) They feared that placing final political authority in any one set of hands, even in the hands of persons popularly elected, would so concentrate power as to risk tyranny. But they had seen what happened when independent states tried to form a compact, as under the Articles of Confederation; what the states put together, they could also take apart. The alliance among the states that existed from 1776 to 1787 was a confederation: that is, a system of government in which the people create state governments, which, in turn, create and operate a national government (see Figure 3.1). Since the national government in a confederation derives its powers from the states, it is dependent on their continued cooperation for its survival. By 1786 that cooperation was barely forthcoming.

A Bold, New Plan

A federation—or a "federal republic," as the Founders called it—derives its powers directly from the people, as do the state governments. As the Founders envisioned it, both levels of government, the national and the state, would have certain powers, but neither would have supreme authority over the other. Madison, writing in *Federalist* No. 46, said that both the state and federal governments "are in fact but different agents and trustees of the people, constituted with different powers." In *Federalist* No. 28 Hamilton explained how he thought the system would work: The people could shift their support between state and federal levels of government as needed to keep the two in balance. "If their rights are invaded by either, they can make use of the other as the instrument of redress."

It was an entirely new plan, for which no historical precedent existed. Nobody came to the Philadelphia convention with a clear idea of what a federal (as opposed to a unitary or a confederal) system would look like, and there was not much discussion at Philadelphia of how the system would work in practice. Few delegates then used the word *federalism* in the sense in which we now employ it (it was originally used as a synonym for *confederation* and only later came to stand for something different).[7] The Constitution does not spell out the powers that the states are to have, and until the Tenth Amendment was added at the insistence of various states, there was not even a clause in it saying (as did the amendment) that "the powers not delegated to the United States by the Constitution, nor prohibited by it to the states, are reserved to the states respectively, or to the people." The Founders assumed from the outset that the federal government would have only those powers given to it by the Constitution; the Tenth Amendment was an afterthought, added to make that assumption explicit and allay fears that something else was intended.[8]

The Tenth Amendment has rarely had much practical significance, however. From time to time the Supreme Court has tried to interpret that amendment as putting certain state activities beyond the reach of the federal government, but invariably the Court has later changed its mind and allowed Washington to regulate such matters as the hours that employees of a city-owned mass-transit system may work. The Court did not find that running such a transportation system was one of the powers "reserved to the states."[9] But, as we explain later in this chapter, the Court has begun to give new life to the Tenth Amendment and the doctrine of state sovereignty.

Elastic Language

The need to reconcile the competing interests of large and small states and of northern and southern

Figure 3.1 Lines of Power in Three Systems of Government

UNITARY SYSTEM

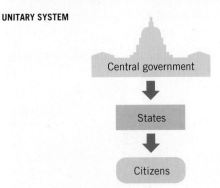

Power centralized.
State or regional governments derive authority from central government.
Examples: United Kingdom, France.

FEDERAL SYSTEM

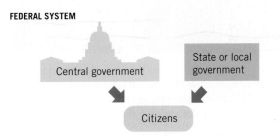

Power divided between central and state or local governments.
Both the government and constituent governments act directly upon the citizens.
Both must agree to constitutional change.
Examples: Canada, United States since adoption of Constitution.

CONFEDERAL SYSTEM (or CONFEDERATION)

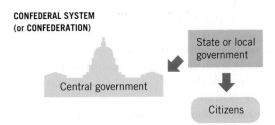

Power held by independent states.
Central government is a creature of the constituent governments.
Example: United States under the Articles of Confederation.

states, especially as they affected the organization of Congress, was sufficiently difficult without trying to spell out exactly what relationship ought to exist between the national and state systems. For example, Congress was given the power to regulate commerce

Thomas Jefferson (1743–1826) was not at the Constitutional Convention. His doubts about the new national government led him to oppose the Federalist administration of John Adams and to become an ardent champion of states' rights.

"among the several states." The Philadelphia convention would have gone on for four years rather than four months if the Founders had decided that it was necessary to describe, in clear language, how one was to tell where commerce *among* the states ended and commerce wholly *within* a single state began. The Supreme Court, as we shall see, devoted over a century to that task before giving up.

Though some clauses bearing on federal-state relations were reasonably clear (see the box on page 55), other clauses were quite vague. The Founders knew, correctly, that they could not make an exact and exhaustive list of everything the federal government was empowered to do—circumstances would change, new exigencies would arise. Thus they added the following elastic language to Article I: Congress shall have the power to "make all laws which shall be necessary and proper for carrying into execution the foregoing powers."

The Founders themselves carried away from Philadelphia different views of what federalism meant. One view was championed by Hamilton. Since the people had created the national govern-

ment, since the laws and treaties made pursuant to the Constitution were "the supreme law of the land" (Article VI), and since the most pressing needs were the development of a national economy and the conduct of foreign affairs, Hamilton thought that the national government was the superior and leading force in political affairs and that its powers ought to be broadly defined and liberally construed.

The other view, championed by Jefferson, was that the federal government, though important, was the product of an agreement among the states; and though "the people" were the ultimate sovereigns, the principal threat to their liberties was likely to come from the national government. (Madison, a strong supporter of national supremacy at the convention, later became a champion of states' rights.) Thus the powers of the federal government should be narrowly construed and strictly limited. As Madison put it in *Federalist* No. 45, in language that probably made Hamilton wince, "The powers delegated by the proposed Constitution to the federal government are few and defined. Those which are to remain in the State governments are numerous and indefinite."

Hamilton argued for national supremacy, Jefferson for states' rights. Though their differences were greater in theory than in practice (as we shall see in Chapter 14, Jefferson while president sometimes acted in a positively Hamiltonian manner), the differing interpretations they offered of the Constitution were to shape political debate in this country until well into the 1960s.

★ The Debate on the Meaning of Federalism

The Civil War was fought, in part, over the issue of national supremacy versus states' rights, but it settled only one part of that argument—namely, that the national government was supreme, its sovereignty derived directly from the people, and thus the states could not lawfully secede from the Union. Virtually every other aspect of the national-supremacy issue continued to animate political and legal debate for another century.

The Supreme Court Speaks

As arbiter of what the Constitution means, the Supreme Court became the focal point of that debate. In Chapter 16 we shall see in some detail how the

---

★ **HOW THINGS WORK** ★

The States and the Constitution

The Framers made some attempt to define the relations between the states and the federal government and how the states were to relate to one another. The following points were made in the original Constitution—before the Bill of Rights was added.

Restrictions on Powers of the States
States may not make treaties with foreign nations, coin money, issue paper currency, grant titles of nobility, pass a bill of attainder or an ex post facto law, or, without the consent of Congress, levy any taxes on imports or exports, keep troops and ships in time of peace, or enter into an agreement with another state or with a foreign power.

[Art. I, sec. 10]

Guarantees by the Federal Government to the States
The national government guarantees to every state a "republican form of government" and protection against foreign invasion and (provided the states request it) protection against domestic insurrection.

[Art. IV, sec. 4]

An existing state will not be broken up into two or more states or merged with all or part of another state without that state's consent.

[Art. IV, sec. 3]

Congress may admit new states into the Union.

[Art. IV, sec. 3]

Taxes levied by Congress must be uniform throughout the United States: they may not be levied on some states but not others.

[Art. I, sec. 8]

The Constitution may not be amended to give states unequal representation in the Senate.

[Art. V]

Rules Governing How States Deal with Each Other
"Full faith and credit" shall be given by each state to the laws, records, and court decisions of other states. (For example, a civil case settled in the courts of one state cannot be retried in the courts of another.)

[Art. IV, sec. 1]

The citizens of each state shall have the "privileges and immunities" of the citizens of every other state. (No one is quite sure what this is supposed to mean.)

[Art. IV, sec. 2]

If a person charged with a crime by one state flees to another, he or she is subjected to extradition—that is, the governor of the state that finds the fugitive is supposed to return the person to the governor of the state that wants him or her.

[Art. IV, sec. 2]

Court made its decisions. For now it is enough to know that during the formative years of the new Republic, the Supreme Court was led by a staunch and brilliant advocate of Hamilton's position, Chief Justice John Marshall. In a series of decisions he and the Court powerfully defended the national-supremacy view of the newly formed federal government.

The most important decision was in a case, seemingly trivial in its origins, that arose when James McCulloch, the cashier of the Baltimore branch of the Bank of the United States, which had been created by Congress, refused to pay a tax levied on that bank by the state of Maryland. He was hauled into state court and convicted of failing to pay a tax. In 1819 McCulloch appealed all the way to the Supreme Court in a case known as *McCulloch v. Maryland.* The Court, in a unanimous opinion, answered two questions in ways that expanded the powers of Congress and confirmed the supremacy of the federal government in the exercise of those powers.

The first question was whether Congress had the right to set up a bank, or any other corporation, since such a right is nowhere explicitly mentioned in the Constitution. Marshall said that, though the federal government possessed only those powers enumerated in the Constitution, the "extent"—that is, the meaning—of those powers required interpretation. Though the word *bank* is not in that document, one finds there the power to manage money: to lay and collect taxes, issue a currency, and borrow funds. To

At one time the states could issue their own paper money, such as this New York currency worth twenty-five cents in 1776. Under the Constitution this power was reserved to Congress.

carry out these powers Congress may reasonably decide that chartering a national bank is "necessary and proper." Marshall's words were carefully chosen to endow the **"necessary and proper" clause** with the widest possible sweep:

> Let the end be legitimate, let it be within the scope of the Constitution, and all means which are appropriate, which are plainly adapted to that end, which are not prohibited, but consistent with the letter and spirit of the Constitution, are constitutional.[10]

The second question was whether a federal bank could lawfully be taxed by a state. To answer it, Marshall went back to first principles. The government of the United States was not established by the states, but by the people, and thus the federal government was supreme in the exercise of those powers conferred upon it. Having already concluded that chartering a bank was within the powers of Congress, Marshall then argued that the only way for such pow-

---

"necessary and proper" clause   Section of the Constitution allowing Congress to pass all laws "necessary and proper" to its duties, and which has permitted Congress to exercise powers not specifically given to it (enumerated) by the Constitution.

nullification   The doctrine that a state can declare null and void a federal law that, in the state's opinion, violates the Constitution.

---

ers to be supreme was for their use to be immune from state challenge and for the products of their use to be protected against state destruction. Since "the power to tax involves the power to destroy," and since the power to destroy a federal agency would confer upon the states using its supremacy over the federal government, the states may not tax any federal instrument. Hence the Maryland law was unconstitutional.

McCulloch won, and so did the federal government. Half a century later the Court decided that what was sauce for the goose was sauce for the gander. It held that just as state governments could not tax federal bonds, the federal government could not tax the interest people earn on state and municipal bonds. In 1988 the Supreme Court changed its mind and decided that Congress was now free, if it wished, to tax the interest on such state and local bonds.[11] Municipal bonds, which for nearly a century were a tax-exempt investment protected, so their holders thought, by the Constitution, were now protected only by politics. So far Congress hasn't wanted to tax them.

Nullification

The Supreme Court can decide a case without settling the issue. The struggle over states' rights versus national supremacy continued to rage in Congress, during presidential elections, and ultimately on the battlefield. The issue came to center on the doctrine of **nullification.** When Congress passed laws (in 1798) to punish newspaper editors who published stories critical of the federal government, James Madison and Thomas Jefferson opposed the laws, suggesting (in statements known as the Virginia and Kentucky Resolutions) that the states had the right to "nullify" (that is, declare null and void) a federal law that, in the states' opinion, violated the Constitution. The laws expired before the claim of nullification could be settled in the courts.

Later the doctrine of nullification was revived by John C. Calhoun of South Carolina, first in opposition to a tariff enacted by the federal government and later in opposition to federal efforts to restrict slavery. Calhoun argued that if Washington attempted to ban slavery, the states had the right to declare such acts unconstitutional and thus null and void. This time the issue was settled—by war. The northern victory in the Civil War determined once and for all that the federal union is indissoluble and that states cannot declare acts of Congress unconstitutional, a view later confirmed by the Supreme Court.[12]

Dual Federalism

After the Civil War the debate about the meaning of federalism focused on the interpretation of the commerce clause of the Constitution. Out of this debate there emerged the doctrine of **dual federalism,** which held that though the national government was supreme in its sphere, the states were equally supreme in theirs, and that these two spheres of action should and could be kept separate. Applied to commerce the concept of dual federalism implied that there were such things as *inter*state commerce, which Congress could regulate, and *intra*state commerce, which only the states could regulate, and that the Court could tell which was which.

For a long period the Court tried to decide what was interstate commerce based on the kind of business that was being conducted. Transporting things between states was obviously interstate commerce, and so subject to federal regulation. Thus federal laws affecting the interstate shipment of lottery tickets,[13] prostitutes,[14] liquor,[15] and harmful foods and drugs[16] were upheld. On the other hand, manufacturing,[17] insurance,[18] and farming[19] were in the past considered *intra*state commerce, and so only the state governments were allowed to regulate them.

Such product-based distinctions turned out to be hard to sustain. For example, if you ship a case of whiskey from Kentucky to Kansas, how long is it in interstate commerce (and thus subject to federal law), and when does it enter intrastate commerce and become subject only to state law? For a while the Court's answer was that the whiskey was in interstate commerce so long as it was in its "original package,"[20] but that only precipitated long quarrels as to what was the original package and how one is to treat things, like gas and grain, that may not be shipped in packages at all. And how could one distinguish between manufacturing and transportation when one company did both or when a single manufacturing corporation owned factories in different states? And if an insurance company sold policies to customers both inside and outside a given state, were there to be different laws regulating identical policies that happened to be purchased from the same company by persons in different states?

> **dual federalism**   Doctrine holding that the national government is supreme in its sphere, the states are supreme in theirs, and the two spheres should be kept separate.

☆ **POLITICALLY SPEAKING** ☆

The Terms of Local Governance

Legally a **city** is a **municipal corporation or municipality** that has been chartered by a state to exercise certain defined powers and provide certain specific services. There are two kinds of charters: special-act charters and general-act charters.

A **special-act charter** applies to a certain city (for example, New York City) and lists what that city can and cannot do. A **general-act charter** applies to a number of cities that fall within a certain classification, usually based on city population. Thus in some states all cities over 100,000 population will be governed on the basis of one charter, while all cities between 50,000 and 99,999 population will be governed on the basis of a different one.

Under **Dillon's rule** the terms of these charters are to be interpreted very narrowly. This rule (named after a lawyer who wrote a book on the subject in 1911) authorizes a municipality to exercise only those powers expressly given, implied by, or essential to the accomplishment of its enumerated powers. This means, for example, that a city cannot so much as operate a peanut stand at the city zoo unless the state has specifically given the city that power by law or charter.

A **home-rule charter,** now in effect in many cities, reverses Dillon's rule and allows a city government to do anything that is not prohibited by the charter or state law. Even under a home-rule charter, however, city laws (called **ordinances**) cannot be in conflict with state laws, and the states can pass laws that preempt or interfere with what home-rule cities want to do.

There are in this country more than 87,500 local governments, less than one-fourth (19,000) of which are cities or municipalities. **Counties** (3,000) are the largest territorial units between a state and a city or town. Every state but Connecticut and Rhode Island has county governments. (In Louisiana counties are called parishes, in Alaska boroughs.)

There are more than 35,000 **special-district governments or authorities,** which have responsibility for some single governmental function—handling sewage treatment, managing airports, or getting rid of mosquitoes, for example. **School districts** (more than 13,500) are the most familiar special-district governments. Often the voters elect school board members, who then choose a school superintendent.

In time the effort to find some clear principles that distinguished interstate from intrastate commerce was pretty much abandoned. Commerce was like a stream flowing through the country, drawing to itself contributions from thousands of scattered enterprises and depositing its products in millions of individual homes. The Court began to permit the federal government to regulate almost anything that affected this stream, so that by the 1940s not only had farming and manufacturing been redefined as part of interstate commerce,[21] but even the janitors and window washers in buildings that housed companies engaged in interstate commerce were now said to be part of that stream.[22]

Today lawyers are engaged in interstate commerce but professional baseball players are not. If your state has approved marijuana use for medical purposes, you can still be penalized under federal law even when the marijuana you consume was grown in a small pot in your backyard.[23]

State Sovereignty

It would be a mistake to think that the doctrine of dual federalism is entirely dead. Until recently Congress, provided that it had a good reason, could pass a law regulating almost any kind of economic activity anywhere in the country, and the Supreme Court would call it constitutional. But in *United States v. Lopez* (1995) the Court held that Congress had exceeded its commerce clause power by prohibiting guns in a school zone.

The Court reaffirmed the view that the commerce clause does not justify any federal action when, in May 2000, it overturned the Violence Against Women Act of 1994. This law allowed women who were the victims of a crime of violence motivated by gender to sue the guilty party in federal court. In *United States v. Morrison* the Court, in a five-to-four decision, said that attacks against women are not, and do not substantially affect, interstate commerce, and hence Congress cannot constitutionally pass such a law. Chief Justice William Rehnquist said that "the Constitution requires a distinction between what is truly national and what is truly local." The states, of course, can pass such laws, and many have.

The Court has moved to strengthen states' rights on other grounds as well. In *Printz v. United States* (1997) the Court invalidated a federal law that required local police to conduct background checks on all gun pur-

chasers. The Court ruled that the law violated the Tenth Amendment by commanding state governments to carry out a federal regulatory program. Writing for the five-to-four majority, Justice Antonin Scalia declared, "The Federal government may neither issue directives requiring the states to address particular problems, nor command the states' officers, or those of their political subdivisions, to administer or enforce a Federal regulatory program. . . . Such commands are fundamentally incompatible with our constitutional system of dual sovereignty."

The Court has also given new life to the Eleventh Amendment, which protects states from lawsuits by citizens of other states or foreign nations. In 1999 the Court shielded states from suits by copyright owners who claimed infringement from state agencies and immunized states from lawsuits by people who argued that state regulations create unfair economic competition. In *Alden v. Maine* (1999) the Court held that state employees could not sue to force state compliance with federal fair-labor laws. In the Court's five-to-four majority opinion, Justice Anthony M. Kennedy stated, "Although the Constitution grants broad powers to Congress, our federalism requires that Congress treat the states in a manner consistent with their status as residuary sovereigns and joint participants in the governance of the nation." A few years later, in *Federal Maritime Commission v. South Carolina Ports Authority* (2002), the Court further expanded states' sovereign immunity from private lawsuits. Writing for the five-to-four majority, Justice Clarence Thomas declared that dual sovereignty "is a defining feature of our nation's constitutional blueprint," adding that the states "did not consent to become mere appendages of the federal government" when they ratified the Constitution.

Not all recent Court decisions, however, support greater state sovereignty. In 1999, for example, the Court ruled seven to two that state welfare programs may not restrict new residents to the welfare benefits they would have received in the states from which they moved. In addition, each of the Court's major prostate sovereignty decisions has been decided by a tenuous five-to-four margin. More generally, to empower states is not to disempower Congress, which, as it has done since the late 1930s, can still make federal laws on almost anything as long as it does not go too far in "commandeering" state resources or gutting states' rights.

New debates over state sovereignty call forth old truths about the constitutional basis of state and local government. In general a state can do anything that is not prohibited by the Constitution or preempted by federal policy and that is consistent with its own constitution. One generally recognized state power is the **police power,** which refers to those laws and regulations, not otherwise unconstitutional, that promote health, safety, and morals. Thus the states can enact and enforce criminal codes, require children to attend school and citizens to be vaccinated, and restrict (subject to many limitations) the availability of pornographic materials or the activities of prostitutes and drug dealers.

As a practical matter the most important activities of state and local governments involve public education, law enforcement and criminal justice, health and hospitals, roads and highways, public welfare, and control over the use of public land and water supplies. On these and many other matters, state constitutions tend to be far more detailed than the federal Constitution, and to embody a more expansive view of both governmental responsibilities and individual rights than it does. For instance, California's lengthy state constitution includes an explicit right to "privacy," specifies that "non-citizens have the same property rights as citizens," directs the state's legislature to use "all suitable means" to support public education, and contains language governing public housing for low-income citizens. Many state constitutions contain kindred provisions. In part for this reason, state courts are now believed by some to be on the whole more progressive in their holdings on abortion rights (authorizing fewer restrictions on minors), welfare payments (permitting fewer limits on eligibility), employment discrimination (prohibiting discrimination based on sexual preference), and many other matters than federal courts generally are.

As we saw in Chapter 2, the federal Constitution is based on a republican, not a democratic, principle: laws are to be made by the representatives of citizens, not by the citizens directly. But many state constitutions open one or more of three doors to direct democracy. About half of the states provide for some form of legislation by initiative. The **initiative** allows voters to place legislative measures (and sometimes constitutional amendments) directly on the ballot by getting enough signatures (usually between 5 and 15 percent of those who voted in the last election) on a petition. About half of the states permit the **referendum,** a procedure that enables voters to reject a measure adopted by the legislature. Sometimes the state constitution specifies that certain kinds of legislation (for example, tax increases) must be subject to a referendum whether the legislature wishes it or not. The **recall** is a procedure, in effect in over twenty states, whereby voters can remove an elected official from office. If enough signatures are gathered on a petition, the official must go before voters, who can vote to leave the person in office, remove the person from office, or remove the person and replace him or her with someone else.

The existence of the states is guaranteed by the federal Constitution: no state can be divided without its consent, each state must have two representatives in the Senate (the only provision of the Constitution that may not be amended), every state is assured of a republican form of government, and the powers not granted to Congress are reserved for the states. By contrast, cities, towns, and counties enjoy no such protection; they exist at the pleasure of the states. Indeed, states have frequently abolished certain kinds of local governments, such as independent school districts. Without exception the legal terms of local governance (see the box on page 57) are determined by the states.

This explains why there is no debate about city sovereignty comparable to the debate about state sovereignty. The constitutional division of power between them is settled: the state is supreme. But federal-state relations can be complicated, because the Constitution invites elected leaders to struggle over sovereignty. Which level of government has the ultimate power to decide where nuclear waste gets stored, how much welfare beneficiaries are paid, what rights prisoners enjoy, or whether supersonic jets can land at local airports? American federalism answers such questions, but on a case-by-case basis through intergovernmental politics and court decisions.

---

police power   State power to enact laws promoting health, safety, and morals.

initiative   Process that permits voters to put legislative measures directly on the ballot.

referendum   Procedure enabling voters to reject a measure passed by the legislature.

recall   Procedure whereby voters can remove an elected official from office.

☆ Federal-State Relations

Though constitutionally the federal government may be supreme, politically it must take into account the fact that the laws it passes have to be approved by members of Congress selected from, and responsive to, state and local constituencies. Thus what Washington lawfully may do is not the same thing as what it politically may wish to do. For example, in 1947 the Supreme Court decided that the federal government and not the states had supreme authority over oil beneath the ocean off the nation's coasts.[24] Six years later, after an intense debate, Congress passed and the president signed a law transferring title to these tideland oil reserves back to the states.

Grants-in-Aid

The best illustration of how political realities modify legal authority can be found in federal **grants-in-aid.** The first of these programs began even before the Constitution was adopted, in the form of land grants made by the national government to the states in order to finance education. (State universities all over the country were built with the proceeds from the sale of these land grants; hence the name *land-grant colleges.*) Land grants were also made to support the building of wagon roads, canals, railroads, and flood-control projects. These measures were hotly debated in Congress (President Madison thought some were unconstitutional), even though the use to which the grants were put was left almost entirely to the states.

Cash grants-in-aid began almost as early. In 1808 Congress gave $200,000 to the states to pay for their militias, with the states in charge of the size, deployment, and command of these troops. However, grant-in-aid programs remained few in number and small in price until the twentieth century, when scores of new ones came into being. In 1915 less than $6 million was spent per year in grants-in-aid; by 1925 over $114 million was spent; by 1937 the figure was nearly $300 million.[25] But the greatest growth began in the 1960s and has continued almost unabated ever since. Between 1960 and

Some of the nation's greatest universities, such as the University of California at Los Angeles, began as land-grant colleges.

1975, total federal grants to the states and localities increased eightfold. By 1985 they amounted to over $100 billion a year, and by 2003 they had risen to about $400 billion a year and provided state and local governments with roughly a fifth of their annual budgets. Today, federal grants go to hundreds of programs, including such giant federal-state programs as Medicaid.[26]

The grants-in-aid system, once under way, grew rapidly because it helped state and local officials resolve a dilemma. On the one hand they wanted access to the superior taxing power of the federal government. On the other hand prevailing constitutional interpretation, at least until the late 1930s, held that the federal government could not spend money for purposes not authorized by the Constitution. The solution was obviously to have federal

---

grants-in-aid   Money given by the national government to the states.

money put into state hands: Washington would pay the bills; the states would run the programs.

Federal money seemed, to state officials, so attractive for four reasons. First, the money was there. Thanks to the high-tariff policies of the Republicans, in the 1880s Washington had huge budget surpluses. Second, in the 1920s, as those surpluses dwindled, Washington inaugurated the federal income tax. It automatically brought in more money as economic activity (and thus personal income) grew. Third, the federal government, unlike the states, managed the currency and could print more at will. (Technically, it borrowed this money, but it was under no obligation to pay it all back, because, as a practical matter, it had borrowed from itself.) States could not do this: if they borrowed money (and many could not), they had to pay it back, in full.

These three economic reasons for the attractiveness of federal grants were probably not as important as a fourth reason: politics. Federal money seemed to a state official to be "free" money. Governors did not have to propose, collect, or take responsibility for federal taxes. Instead, a governor could denounce the federal government for being profligate in its use of the people's money. Meanwhile he or she could claim credit for a new public works or other project funded by Washington and, until recent decades, expect little or no federal supervision in the bargain.[27]

That every state had an incentive to ask for federal money to pay for local programs meant, of course, that it would be very difficult for one state to get money for a given program without every state's getting it. The senator from Alabama who votes for the project to improve navigation on the Tombigbee will have to vote in favor of projects improving navigation on every other river in the country if the senator expects his or her Senate colleagues to support such a request. Federalism as practiced in the United States means that when Washington wants to send money to one state or congressional district, it must send money to many states and districts.

Shortly after September 11, 2001, for example, President George W. Bush and congressional leaders in both parties pledged new federal funds to increase public safety payrolls, purchase the latest equipment to detect bioterror attacks, and so on. Since then New York City and other big cities have received tens of millions of federal dollars for such purposes, but so have scores of smaller cities and towns. In 2003 and

The terrorist threat has enhanced national law enforcement, such as this truck operated by the Secret Service.

2004 the grants allocated by the Department of Homeland Security were based on so-called fair-share formulas mandated by Congress, which are basically the same formulas the federal government uses to allocate certain highway and other funds among the states. These funding formulas not only spread money around but generally skew funding toward states and cities with low populations. Thus in 2003 Wyoming received seven times as much federal homeland security funding per capita as New York State did, and Grand Forks County, North Dakota (population 70,000), received $1.5 million to purchase biochemical suits, a semiarmored van, decontamination tents, and other equipment to deal with weapons of mass destruction.[28]

Meeting National Needs

Until the 1960s most federal grants-in-aid were conceived by or in cooperation with the states and were designed to serve essentially state purposes. Large blocs of voters and a variety of organized interests would press for grants to help farmers, build highways, or support vocational education. During the 1960s, however, an important change occurred: the federal government began devising grant programs based less on what states were demanding and more on what federal officials perceived to be important *national* needs (see Figure 3.2). Federal officials, not state and local ones, were the principal proponents of grant programs to aid the urban poor, combat crime, reduce pollution, and deal with drug abuse. Some of

ments increased in the 1990s and reached new highs after 2000 (see Figure 3.3).

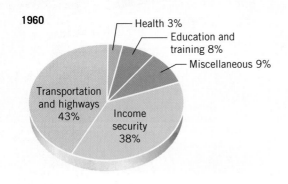

Figure 3.2 The Changing Purpose of Federal Grants to State and Local Governments

1960

- Health 3%
- Education and training 8%
- Miscellaneous 9%
- Transportation and highways 43%
- Income security 38%

2003

- Transportation and highways 11%
- Income security 22%
- Health 45%
- Education and training 13%
- Miscellaneous 9%

Note: Totals may not add up to 100 percent because of rounding.
Source: Budget of the U.S. Government, Fiscal Year 2005, table 12.2.

The Intergovernmental Lobby

State and local officials, both elected and appointed, began to form an important new lobby—the "intergovernmental lobby," made up of mayors, governors, superintendents of schools, state directors of public health, county highway commissioners, local police chiefs, and others who had come to count on federal funds.[29] Today, federal agencies responsible for health care, criminal justice, environmental protection, and other programs have people on staff who specialize in providing information, technical assistance, and financial support to state and local organizations, including the "Big 7": the U.S. Conference of Mayors; the National Governors Association; the National Association of Counties; the National League of Cities; the Council of State Governments; the International City/County Management Association; and the National Conference of State Legislatures. Reports by these groups and publications like *Governing* magazine are read routinely by many federal officials to keep a handle on issues and trends in state and local government.

National organizations of governors or mayors press for more federal money, but not for increased funding for any particular city or state. Thus most states, dozens of counties, and over one hundred cities have their own offices in Washington, D.C. Some are small, some share staff with other jurisdictions, but a few are quite large and boast several dozen full-time employees. Back home, state and local governments have created new positions, or redefined old ones, in response to new or changed federal funding opportunities. For example, in 2001, after the U.S. Conference of Mayors endorsed President George W. Bush's plan to increase federal funding for local community-serving organizations, over a hundred mayors hired or designated someone on their staff (such as a deputy mayor) to work with the new White House Office of Faith-Based and Community Initiatives and its centers in several federal departments.

The purpose of the intergovernmental lobby has been the same as that of any private lobby—to obtain more federal money with fewer strings attached. For a while the cities and states did in fact get more money, but since the early 1980s their success in getting federal grants has been more checkered.

these programs even attempted to bypass the states, providing money directly to cities or even to local citizen groups. These were worrisome developments for governors, who were accustomed to being the conduit for money on its way from Washington to local communities.

The rise in federal activism in setting goals and the efforts, on occasion, to bypass state officials occurred at a time when the total amount of federal aid to states and localities had become so vast that many jurisdictions were completely dependent on it for the support of vital services. Whereas federal aid amounted to less than 2 percent of state and local spending in 1927, by 1980 it amounted to 26 percent, and total aid to state and local governments was 15.4 percent of the federal budget. After stabilizing and dipping slightly in the 1980s, Washington's grants to state and local govern-

Figure 3.3   Federal Grants to State and Local Governments, 1984–2004

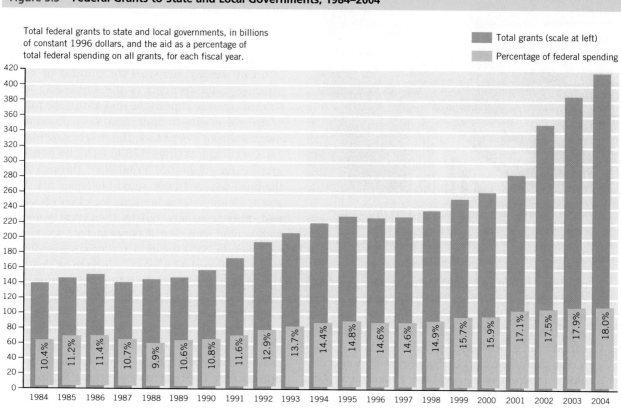

Total federal grants to state and local governments, in billions of constant 1996 dollars, and the aid as a percentage of total federal spending on all grants, for each fiscal year.

■ Total grants (scale at left)
■ Percentage of federal spending

Note: Data for the year 2004 is estimated.
Source: Budget of the U.S. Government, Fiscal Year 2002, Historical Tables, table 6.1, and Budget of the U.S. Government, Fiscal Year 2005, table 12.1.

Categorical Grants Versus Revenue Sharing

The effort to loosen the strings took the form of shifting, as much as possible, the federal aid from **categorical grants** to block grants or to **revenue sharing.** A categorical grant is one for a specific purpose defined by federal law: to build an airport or a college dormitory, for example, or to make welfare payments to low-income mothers. Such grants usually require that the state or locality put up money to "match" some part of the federal grant, though the amount of matching funds can be quite small. (In the federal highway program Washington pays about 90 percent of the construction costs and the states only about 10 percent.) Governors and mayors complained about these categorical grants because their purposes were often so narrow that it was

impossible for a state to adapt federal grants to local needs. A mayor seeking federal money to build parks might have discovered that the city could get money only if it launched an urban-renewal program that entailed bulldozing several blocks of housing or small businesses.

One response to this problem was to consolidate several categorical or project grant programs into a single block grant devoted to some general purpose and with fewer restrictions on its use. Block grants (sometimes called *special revenue sharing* or *broad-based*

categorical grants   Federal grants for specific purposes, such as building an airport.
revenue sharing   Federal sharing of a fixed percentage of its revenue with the states.

The Federal Department of Housing and Urban Development works with state housing authorities to create affordable places to live, such as this new mixed-income community in Atlanta.

aid) began in the mid-1960s, when such a grant was created in the health field. Though many block grants were proposed between 1966 and 1980, only five were enacted. Of the three largest, one consolidated various categorical grant programs aimed at cities (Community Development Block Grants), another created a program to aid local law enforcement (Law Enforcement Assistance Act), and a third authorized new kinds of locally managed programs for the unemployed (CETA, or the Comprehensive Employment and Training Act). Between 1980 and 1995 the number of block grants in effect rose from five to sixteen.

Revenue sharing (sometimes called *general revenue sharing*, or GRS) was even more permissive. Adopted in 1972 with the passage of the State and Local Fiscal Assistance Act, GRS provided for the distribution of about $6 billion a year in federal funds to states and localities, with no requirement as to matching funds and freedom to spend the money on almost any governmental purpose. Distribution of the money was determined by a statistical formula that took into account population, local tax effort, and the wealth of the state in a way intended to send more money to poorer, heavily taxed states and less to richer, lightly taxed ones. In 1986 the program was ended after having distributed about $85 billion over a fourteen-year period.

In theory block grants and revenue sharing were supposed to give the states and cities considerable freedom in deciding how to spend the money while helping to relieve their tax burdens. To some extent they did. However, neither the goal of "no strings" nor the one of fiscal relief was really attained. First, the amount of money available from block grants and revenue sharing did not grow as fast as the states had hoped nor as quickly as did the money available through categorical grants. Second, the federal government steadily increased the number of strings attached to the spending of this supposedly "unrestricted" money. Thus in the mid-1990s the number of federal grants to state and local governments increased from 599 to 633. The entire growth was in categorical grants (from 578 to 618); no new block grants were established. From 2001 through 2003, the Bush administration sought to create new block grants for low-income housing, preschool education, and other programs, but by then most governors were coping with steep declines in state government revenues. In 2004 the drop in state government revenues, combined with federal efforts to ratchet down state and local domestic spending, led many states to cut or freeze even widely popular children's health and other state programs.

Block grants grew more slowly than categorical grants because of the different kinds of political coalitions supporting each. Congress and the federal bureaucracy liked categorical grants for the same reason the states disliked them—the specificity of these programs enhanced federal control over how the money was to be used. Federal officials, joined by liberal interest groups and organized labor, tended to distrust state governments. Whenever Congress wanted to address some national problem, its natural inclination was to create a categorical grant program so that it, and not the states, would decide how the money would be spent.

Moreover, even though governors and mayors like block grants and revenue sharing, these programs cover such a broad range of activities that no single interest group has a vital stake in pressing for their enlargement. Revenue sharing, for example, provided a little money to many city agencies but rarely provided all or even most of the money for any single agency. Thus no single agency acted as if the expansion of revenue sharing were a life-and-death matter. Categorical grants, on the other hand, are often a matter of life and death for many agencies—state departments of welfare, of highways, and of health, for example, are utterly dependent on federal aid. Accordingly, the administrators in charge of these programs will press strenuously for their expansion. Moreover, categorical programs are supervised by special committees of Congress, and as we shall see in Chapter 13, many of these committees have an interest in seeing their programs grow.

Rivalry Among the States

The more important that federal money becomes to the states, the more likely they are to compete among themselves for the largest share of it. For a century or better the growth of the United States—in population, business, and income—was concentrated in the industrial Northeast. In recent decades, however, that growth—at least in population and employment, if not in income—has shifted to the South, Southwest, and Far West. This change has precipitated an intense debate over whether the federal government, by the way it distributes its funds and awards its contracts, is unfairly helping some regions and states at the expense of others. Journalists and politicians have dubbed the struggle as one between Snowbelt (or Frostbelt) and Sunbelt states.

Whether in fact there is anything worth arguing about is far from clear: the federal government has had great difficulty in figuring out where it ultimately spends what funds for what purposes. For example, a $1 billion defense contract may go to a company with headquarters in California, but much of the money may actually be spent in Connecticut or New York, as the prime contractor in California buys from subcontractors in the other states. It is even less clear whether federal funds actually affect the growth rate of the regions. The uncertainty about the facts has not prevented a debate about the issue, however. That debate focuses on the formulas written into federal laws by which block grants are allocated. These formulas take into account such factors as a county's or city's population, personal income in the area, and housing quality. A slight change in a formula can shift millions of dollars in grants in ways that favor either the older, declining cities of the Northeast or the newer, still-growing cities of the Southwest.

With the advent of grants based on distributional formulas (as opposed to grants for a particular project), the results of the census, taken every ten years, assume monumental importance. A city or state shown to be losing population may, as a result, forfeit millions of dollars in federal aid. There are over one hundred programs (out of over five hundred federal grant programs in all) that distribute money on the basis of population. When the director of the census in 1960 announced figures showing that many big

The federal government helps shape the character of cities by giving money to build parts of the federal highway system.

cities had lost population, he was generally ignored. When he made the same announcement in 1980, after the explosion in federal grants, he was roundly denounced by the mayors of those cities.

Senators and representatives now have access to computers that can tell them instantly the effect on their states and districts of even minor changes in a formula by which federal aid is distributed. These formulas rely on objective measures, but the exact measure is selected with an eye to its political consequences. There is nothing wrong with this in principle, since any political system must provide some benefits for everybody if it is to stay together. Given the competition among states in a federal system, however, the struggle over allocation formulas becomes especially acute. The results are sometimes plausible, as when Congress decides to distribute money intended to help disadvantaged local school systems in large part on the basis of the proportion of poor children in each school district. But sometimes the results are a bit strange, as when the formula by which federal aid for mass transit is determined gives New York, a city utterly dependent on mass transit, a federal subsidy of two cents per transit passenger but gives Grand Rapids, a city that relies chiefly on the automobile, a subsidy of forty-five cents per passenger.[30]

☆ Federal Aid and Federal Control

So important has federal aid become for state and local governments that mayors and governors, along with others, began to fear that Washington was well on its way to controlling other levels of government. "He who pays the piper calls the tune," they muttered. In this view the constitutional protection of state government to be found in the Tenth Amendment was in jeopardy as a result of the strings being attached to the grants-in-aid on which the states were increasingly dependent.

Block grants and revenue sharing were efforts to reverse this trend by allowing the states and localities freedom (considerable in the case of block grants; almost unlimited in the case of revenue sharing) to spend money as they wished. But as we have seen, these new devices did not in fact reverse the trend. Categorical grants—those with strings attached—continued to grow even faster.

There are two kinds of federal controls on state governmental activities. The traditional control tells the state government what it must do if it wants to get some grant money. These strings are often called **conditions of aid.** The newer form of control tells the state government what it must do, period. These rules are called **mandates.** Most mandates have little or nothing to do with federal aid—they apply to all state governments whether or not they accept grants.

> **conditions of aid**   Terms set by the national government that states must meet if they are to receive certain federal funds.
>
> **mandates**   Terms set by the national government that states must meet whether or not they accept federal grants.

Mandates

Most mandates concern civil rights and environmental protection. States may not discriminate in the operation of their programs, no matter who pays for them. Initially the antidiscrimination rules applied chiefly to distinctions based on race, sex, age, and ethnicity, but of late they have been broadened to include physical and mental disabilities as well. Various pollution control laws require the states to comply with federal standards for clean air, pure drinking water, and sewage treatment.[31]

Stated in general terms, these mandates seem reasonable enough. It is hard to imagine anyone arguing that state governments should be free to discriminate against people because of their race or national origin. In practice, however, some mandates create administrative and financial problems, especially when the mandates are written in vague language, thereby giving federal administrative agencies the power to decide for themselves what state and local governments are supposed to do.

In 1980 there were thirty-six mandates affecting state and local governments, twenty-two of them enacted in the 1970s. Both the Reagan administration and the administration of Bush the elder opposed the growth of mandates. Nevertheless, between 1981 and 1986 some 140 regulations, representing nearly six thousand new requirements on state and local government, were added to eighteen existing mandates. Over the last two decades, Congress has passed several dozen additional mandates.

All mandates are not created equal. Some mandates take the form of regulatory statutes and amendments that expand on previous legislation; the 1982 Voting Rights Act Amendments were based on federal civil rights laws dating back to the 1960s. Other mandates represent new areas of federal involvement. For example, the 1986 Handicapped Children's Protection Act introduced federal regulations intended to improve the life prospects of disabled youngsters. Some mandates are easy to understand, simple to administer, and relatively inexpensive—for example, the 1988 Ocean Dumping Ban Act, which prohibits any additional dumping of municipal sewage sludge in ocean waters. However, many mandates are hard to interpret, difficult to administer, and have high or uncertain costs. The 1990 Americans with Disabilities Act (ADA), which required businesses and state and local governments to provide the disabled with equal access to services, employment, buildings, and transportation systems, was one of twenty mandates signed into law by President Bush the elder in 1990. Unfortunately, the ADA was enacted with no clear-cut definition of "equal access," no unambiguous blueprint of how it was to be administered, and no reliable estimates of how much it would cost to implement.

Mandates are not the only way in which the federal government imposes costs on state and local governments. Certain federal tax and regulatory policies make it difficult or expensive for state and local governments to raise revenues, borrow funds, or privatize public functions. Other federal laws expose state and local governments to financial liability, and numerous federal court decisions and administrative regulations require state and local governments to do or not do various things, either by statute or through an implied constitutional obligation.[32]

It is clear that the federal courts have helped fuel the growth of mandates. As interpreted in this century by the U.S. Supreme Court, the Tenth Amendment provides state and local officials no protection against the march of mandates. Indeed, many of the more controversial mandates result not from congressional action but from court decisions. For example, many state prison systems have been, at one time or another, under the control of federal judges who required major changes in prison construction and management in order to meet standards the judges derived from their reading of the Constitution.

School-desegregation plans are of course the best-known example of federal mandates. Those involving busing—an unpopular policy—have typically been the result of court orders rather than of federal law or regulation.

Judges—usually, but not always, in federal courts—ordered Massachusetts to change the way it hires fire fighters, required Philadelphia to institute new procedures to handle complaints of police brutality, and altered the location in which Chicago was planning to build housing projects. Note that in most of these cases nobody in Washington was placing a mandate on a local government; rather a local citizen was using the federal courts to change a local practice.

The Supreme Court has made it much easier of late for citizens to control the behavior of local officials. A federal law, passed in the 1870s to protect newly freed slaves, makes it possible for a citizen to sue any state or local official who deprives that citizen of any "rights, privileges, or immunities secured by the Constitution and laws" of the United States. In 1980 the Court decided that this law permitted a citizen to sue a local official if the official deprived the citizen of *anything* to which the citizen was entitled under federal law (and not just those federal laws protecting civil rights). For example, a citizen can now use the federal courts to obtain from a state welfare office a payment to which he or she may be entitled under federal law. No one yet knows how this development will affect the way local government operates.

Conditions of Aid

By far the most important federal restrictions on state action are the conditions attached to the grants the states receive. In theory accepting these conditions is voluntary—if you don't want the strings, don't take the money. But when the typical state depends for a quarter or more of its budget on federal grants, many of which it has received for years and on which many of its citizens depend for their livelihoods, it is not clear exactly how "voluntary" such acceptance is. During the 1960s some strings were added, the most important of which had to do with civil rights. But beginning in the 1970s the number of conditions began to proliferate and have expanded in each subsequent decade down to the present.

Some conditions are specific to particular programs, but most are not. For instance, if a state builds something with federal money, it must first conduct an environmental impact study, it must pay construction workers the "prevailing wage" in the area, it often must provide an opportunity for citizen participation in some aspects of the design or location of the project, and it must ensure that the contractors who build the project have nondiscriminatory hiring policies.

The states and the federal government, not surprisingly, disagree about the costs and benefits of such rules. Members of Congress and federal officials feel they have an obligation to develop uniform national policies with respect to important matters and to prevent states and cities from misspending federal tax dollars. State officials, on the other hand, feel these national rules fail to take into account diverse local conditions, require the states to do things that the states must then pay for, and create serious inefficiencies.

The National Guard, a state-run activity, not only sends troops to combat but hands out emergency supplies, as here in Florida after a hurricane in 2004.

What state and local officials discovered, in short, was that "free" federal money was not quite free after all. In the 1960s federal aid seemed to be entirely beneficial; what mayor or governor would not want such money? But just as local officials found it attractive to do things that another level of government then paid for, in time federal officials learned the same thing. Passing laws to meet the concerns of national constituencies—leaving the cities and states to pay the bills and manage the problems—began to seem attractive to Congress.

Because they face different demands, federal and local officials find themselves in a bargaining situation in which each side is trying to get some benefit (solving a problem, satisfying a pressure group) while passing on to the other side most of the costs (taxes, administrative problems).

The bargains struck in this process used to favor the local officials, because members of Congress were essentially servants of local interests: they were elected by local political parties, they were part of local political organizations, and they supported local autonomy. Beginning in the 1960s, however, changes in American politics that will be described in later chapters—especially the weakening of political parties, the growth of public-interest lobbies in

Washington, and the increased activism of the courts—shifted the orientation of many in Congress toward favoring Washington's needs over local needs.

In 1981 President Reagan tried to reverse this trend. He asked Congress to consolidate eighty-three categorical grants into six large block grants. The Reagan-era cutbacks in the amount of federal money, and the threat of more to come, led many governors and mayors to find new ways of delivering old services. Many cities turned over trash collection and other tasks to private firms, often realizing financial savings. Many states experimented with ways of inducing welfare recipients to take jobs, thereby saving on welfare payments. During the prosperous 1980s the cutback in federal aid was made easier to bear because the economy brought in more tax money to the states without their having to raise new taxes. In tough times, such as the early 1990s, the states struggled to make ends meet. By the mid-1990s, however, the economy was back on track, and the effort begun by the Reagan administration to devolve federal power to the states got a powerful new push by the 104th Congress.

☆ A Devolution Revolution?

With the election of Republican majorities in the House and Senate in 1994, a renewed effort was led by Congress to shift important functions back to the states. The key first issue was welfare—that is, Aid to Families with Dependent Children (AFDC). Since 1935 there had been a federal guarantee of cash assistance to states that offered support to low-income, unmarried mothers and their children. AFDC had become bitterly controversial as the number of women using it and the proportion of births out of wedlock rose dramatically. President Clinton vetoed the first two bills to cut it back but signed the third. It ended any federal guarantee of support and, subject to certain rules, turned the management of the program entirely over to the states, aided by federal block grants. The rules said that every aided woman should begin working within two years and no woman could receive benefits for more than five years.

These and other Republican initiatives were part of a new effort called devolution, which aimed to pass on to the states many federal functions. It is an old idea but one that acquired new vitality because

Congress, rather than the president, was leading the effort. Traditionally members of Congress liked voting for federal programs and categorical grants; that way members could take credit for what they were doing for particular constituencies. Under its new conservative leadership, Congress, and especially the House, was looking for ways to scale back the size and activities of the national government. Even Clinton seemed to agree when, in his 1996 State of the Union address, he said that the era of big national government was over. But whatever politicians say, no one really knows how best to divide the responsibility between Washington and the states.

Block Grants for Entitlements

Consider what happened with block grants. Basically, there are three types of block grants: *operational grants,* for purposes such as running state child-care programs; *capital grants,* for purposes such as building local wastewater treatment plants; and *entitlement grants,* for transferring income to families and individuals. From 1966 to 1994 a total of twenty-three block grants were enacted, and fifteen were still in place when the 104th Congress came to power. But all of these block grants, including all nine of the Reagan-era block grants, were for operating and capital purposes; none were for major entitlement programs.

The federal government's two biggest grant-in-aid programs—the now defunct AFDC, often referred to simply as "welfare," which provided cash assistance to the poor, and Medicaid, which finances the majority of medical and long-term care services for low-income and disabled adults and children—were not created as block grant programs. Together AFDC and Medicaid accounted for half of all federal grant-in-aid spending. Both AFDC and Medicaid were operated as entitlement programs. Each state was entitled to federal dollars for AFDC and Medicaid based on the amount of money it paid to poor families and individuals. In turn each state determined the level and range of benefits eligible individuals received, within a framework defined by federal laws and regulations.

Republicans in the 104th Congress made a flurry of proposals for making *both* AFDC and Medicaid into block grant programs, as well as federal job training, vocational education, employment, childcare, foster care, school nutrition, and food programs. All told these proposals, had they been enacted, would have increased federal block grants to about $183 billion

and catapulted the amount of block grant funds in income-transfer programs from only 4 percent to nearly 79 percent.

In the end the devolution revolutionaries of the 104th Congress did not succeed in turning Medicaid into a block grant program. But they did succeed with AFDC and a number of related programs. And they did put the devolution of Medicaid and other important federal programs squarely on the national political agenda, possibly to stay.

There is also some early evidence that the devolution of federal welfare programs has triggered second-order devolution, a flow of power and responsibility from the states to local governments, and third-order devolution, the increased role of nonprofit organizations and private groups in policy implementation. For example, until the 1996 federal welfare reform law took effect, few states administered their welfare systems in close working partnerships with city or county governments. By 2000, however, fifteen states, including two of the biggest (California and New York), were using so-called county-administered systems. Subject to state direction, scores of local governments are now designing and administering welfare programs (job placement, job training, childcare, and others) through for-profit firms and a wide variety of nonprofit organizations, including local religious congregations. For example, a 2004 study found that in some big cities over a quarter of welfare-to-work programs were being administered through public-private partnerships that included various local community-based organizations as grantees.[33]

From 1996, when federal welfare reform law took effect, to 2002, when the law received its required five-year renewal, the nation's welfare caseload declined by 57 percent to just over 2 million families.[34] Observers disagree about how much the devolution of welfare policy (independent of good economic times and other factors) had to do with these drops. But one thing is clear: with fewer people on welfare rolls receiving cash assistance, states amassed billions of dollars in unspent federal welfare funds. In the late 1990s, these so-called welfare surpluses, together with booming economic conditions in many places, permitted most states to increase spending. But the good times were short-lived. By 2002, growth in state Medicaid costs fueled in part by new federal laws making the program more generous and covering more people, a shortfall

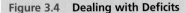

Figure 3.4   Dealing with Deficits

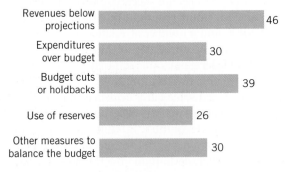

Key fiscal developments by number
of states, as of January 2002:

- Revenues below projections — 46
- Expenditures over budget — 30
- Budget cuts or holdbacks — 39
- Use of reserves — 26
- Other measures to balance the budget — 30

Source: From "Dealing With Deficit," Council of State Governments, National Conference of State Legislatures, as reported in Governing, May 2002, p. 22. Reprinted with permission.

in revenues states were projected to receive in tobacco-settlement payments from big cigarette companies (the payments were keyed to the companies' sales, which have been falling), and a sudden surge in funding for state police and other post–September 11 homeland security measures, among other factors, found most states dealing with budget deficits and raiding fiscal reserves (see Figure 3.4).

What's Driving Devolution?

The drive for devolution has complex roots, but three forces stand out: the beliefs of devolution's proponents, the realities of deficit politics, and the views of most citizens. According to R. Kent Weaver, the House Republicans who spearheaded the devolution effort harbored a "deep-seated ideological mistrust of the federal government reinforced by the belief that governments closer to the people were more responsive to popular sentiment, and more likely to constrain the growth of programs that were wasteful and redistributive."[35] At the same time, by 1994 many governors of both parties were convinced that the time had come to let state capitals take the lead in figuring out how best to address social problems and administer public health and welfare programs.

But deficit politics also played a role. Congressional Republicans sought not only to fund entitlement pro-grams with block grants instead of categorical grants but also to make major cuts in entitlement spending. For example, one of their bills would have reduced Medicaid spending by $163 billion and various welfare entitlements by $175 billion over seven years.

Many Americans favor devolution, at least in theory. But it remains unclear how deep public sentiment in favor of devolution runs when "shifting responsibility to the states" also means cutting specific program benefits. For example, when asked in 1995 which federal programs "should be cut back in order to reduce the federal budget deficit," most Americans opposed cuts in Medicaid (73 percent), environmental spending (67 percent), unemployment insurance (64 percent), and many other programs. The one main exception was AFDC (only 35 percent opposed cutting it).[36] In 2004, amid projections by the Congressional Budget Office that the year's federal deficit would reach over $440 billion, an all-time high, and total some $2.3 trillion over the next decade, polls still found little mass support for cutting Social Security benefits or specific social programs to aid the old or disabled, and both major presidential candidates endorsed policies that betokened greater future domestic and defense spending.

☆ Congress and Federalism

Just as it remains to be seen whether the Supreme Court will continue to revive the doctrine of state sovereignty, so it is not yet clear whether the devolution movement will gain momentum, stall, or be reversed. But whatever the movement's fate, the United States will not become a wholly centralized nation. There remains more political and policy diversity in America than one is likely to find in any other large industrialized nation. The reason is not only that state and local governments have retained certain constitutional protections but also that members of Congress continue to think of themselves as the representatives of localities *to* Washington and not as the representatives *of* Washington to the localities. As we shall see in Chapter 13, American politics, even at the national level, remains local in its orientation.

But if this is true, why do these same members of Congress pass laws that create so many problems for, and stimulate so many complaints from, mayors and

What Would You Do?

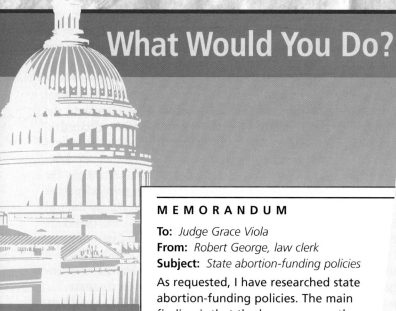

Out-of-Towner with Twins to Sue State for Failing to Fund Abortion

January 4
PIERRE, SD

An abortion rights group has filed a multimillion-dollar federal lawsuit against the South Dakota Department of Human Services. The suit is brought on behalf of a welfare-dependent Minnesota woman who was denied public funding for an abortion. In Minnesota, public funding for abortions is available to adult welfare recipients in all or most circumstances, but in South Dakota it is available only in cases of life endangerment. The woman claimed that while her life was not endangered, the abortion that she sought was "medically necessary" because she had previously been diagnosed as suffering from chronic fatigue syndrome. Agency doctors disagreed and denied her the procedure. While in the state seeking work, she went into premature labor and gave birth to twins . . .

MEMORANDUM

To: *Judge Grace Viola*
From: *Robert George, law clerk*
Subject: *State abortion-funding policies*

As requested, I have researched state abortion-funding policies. The main finding is that the laws vary greatly. The first question before you is whether to accept the case for review.

Arguments for:

1. Three states provide public financing for abortion only in cases of life endangerment. Sixteen states provide it in all or most circumstances.
2. About two hundred thousand women nationwide receive government-funded abortions each year.
3. Advocates argue that just as the federal courts have narrowed state discretion in domains such as state prisoners' appeal rights, the courts should set and enforce national standards for women's abortion rights. Who gets what should not depend on who lives where.

Arguments against:

1. Twenty-six states provide public financing for abortions only in cases of rape, incest, or life endangerment. Only five provide it under those and other health circumstances.
2. About 85 percent of all abortions are privately funded, and federal courts have consistently upheld the right of states to restrict abortions and withhold public funding.
3. Opponents argue that just as the Supreme Court has begun to restore state sovereignty and revive the Eleventh Amendment, it would be a mistake, especially on such a morally controversial issue as abortion, to prevent the citizens of each state from setting and enforcing policies that are in accord with their preferences. Who gets what should sometimes depend on who lives where.

Your decision:

Accept case _____

Reject case _____

governors? One reason is that members of Congress represent different constituencies from the same localities. For example, one member of Congress from Los Angeles may think of the city as a collection of business people, homeowners, and taxpayers, while another may think of it as a group of African Americans, Hispanics, and nature lovers. If Washington wants to simply send money to Los Angeles, these two representatives could be expected to vote together. But if Washington wants to impose mandates or restrictions on the city, they might very well vote on opposite sides, each voting as his or her constituents would most likely prefer.

Another reason is that the organizations that once linked members of Congress to local groups have eroded. As we shall see in Chapter 9, the political parties, which once allowed many localities to speak with a single voice in Washington, have decayed to the point where most members of Congress now operate as free agents, judging local needs and national moods independently. In the 1960s these needs and moods seemed to require creating new grant programs; in the 1970s they seemed to require voting for new mandates; in the 1980s and 1990s they seemed to require letting the cities and states alone to experiment with new ways of meeting their needs; and today some say they require rethinking devolution before it goes "too far."

There are exceptions. In some states the parties continue to be strong, to dominate decision-making in the state legislatures, and to significantly affect the way their congressional delegations behave. Democratic members of Congress from Chicago, for example, typically have a common background in party politics and share at least some allegiance to important party leaders.

But these exceptions are becoming fewer and fewer. As a result, when somebody tries to speak "for" a city or state in Washington, that person has little claim to any real authority. The mayor of Philadelphia may favor one program, the governor of Pennsylvania may favor another, and individual local and state officials—school superintendents, the insurance commissioner, public health administrators—may favor still others. In bidding for federal aid, those parts of the state or city that are best-organized often do the best, and increasingly the best-organized groups are not the political parties but rather specialized occupational groups such as doctors or schoolteachers. If one is to ask, therefore, why a member of Congress does not listen to his or her state anymore, the answer is, "What do you mean by *the state*? Which official, which occupational group, which party leader speaks for the state?"

Finally, Americans differ in the extent to which we like federal as opposed to local decisions. When people are asked which level of government gives them the most for their money, relatively poor citizens are likely to mention the federal government first, whereas relatively well-to-do citizens are more likely to mention local government. If we add to income other measures of social diversity—race, religion, and region—there emerge even sharper differences of opinion about which level of government works best. It is this social diversity, and the fact that it is represented not only by state and local leaders but also by members of Congress, that keeps federalism alive and makes it so important. Americans simply do not agree on enough things, or even on which level of government ought to decide on those things, to make possible a unitary system.

☆ SUMMARY

States participate actively both in determining national policy and in administering national programs. Moreover, they reserve to themselves or the localities within them important powers over public services, such as schooling and law enforcement, and public decisions, such as land-use control, that in unitary systems are dominated by the national government.

Debates about federalism are as old as the republic itself. After the Civil War, the doctrine of dual feder-

alism emerged, which held that though the national government was supreme in its sphere, the states were equally supreme in theirs. For most of the twentieth century, however, changes in public law and court decisions favored national over state power.

After the 1960s states became increasingly dependent on Washington to fund many activities and programs. Today, however, there is once again a lively debate about the limits of national power, how closely the federal government ought to regulate its grants to states, and the wisdom of devolving ever more federal responsibilities onto state and local governments.

Evaluating federalism is difficult. On the one hand, there is the sordid history of states' rights and legalized racism. On the other hand, there is the open opportunity for political participation afforded by today's fifty states and thousands of local govern-ments. Naturally, federalism permits laws and poli-cies on important public matters to vary from state to state and town to town. But how much, if at all, they should vary on given matters, and who should decide, are questions that every generation of Amer-icans must answer anew.

RECONSIDERING WHO GOVERNS?

1. *Where is sovereignty located in the American political system?*

Strictly speaking, the answer is "nowhere." Sover-eignty means supreme or ultimate political authori-ty. A sovereign government is one that is legally and politically independent of any other government. No government in America, including the national gov-ernment headquartered in Washington, D.C., meets that definition. In the American political system, fed-eral and state governments share sovereignty in complicated and ever-changing ways. Both constitu-tional tradition (the doctrine of dual sovereignty) and everyday politicking (fights over federal grants, mandates, and conditions of aid) render the national government supreme in some matters (national defense, for example) and the states supreme in oth-ers (education, for instance).

2. *How is power divided between the national gov-ernment and the states under the Constitution?*

Early in American history, local governments and the states had most of it. In the twentieth century, the national government gained power. In the last two decades the states have won back some of their power because of Supreme Court decisions and leg-islative efforts to devolve certain federal programs to the states. But the distribution of power between the national government and the states is never as sim-ple or as settled as it may appear to be.

RECONSIDERING TO WHAT ENDS?

1. *What competing values are at stake in federalism?*

Basically two: equality versus participation. Federal-ism means that citizens living in different parts of the country will be treated differently, not only in spending programs, such as welfare, but in legal sys-tems that assign in different places different penal-ties to similar offenses or that differentially enforce civil rights laws. But federalism also means that there are more opportunities for participation in making decisions—in influencing what is taught in the schools and in deciding where highways and government projects are to be built. Indeed, differ-ences in public policy—that is, unequal treatment—are in large part the result of participation in decision-making. It is difficult, perhaps impossible, to have more of one of these values without having less of the other.

2. *Who should decide what matters ought to be gov-erned mainly or solely by national laws?*

In practice, the federal courts have often been the main or final arbiters of federalism. As we shall see in Chap-ter 6, it was the U.S. Supreme Court that decided to out-law state and local laws that kept children in racially segregated public schools. Constitutional amendments initiated by members of Congress have also been used to apply legally enforceable national standards to mat-ters once left to state or local governments. Examples would include the Twenty-sixth Amendment, which gave eighteen-year-old citizens the right to vote. Not surprisingly, when state and local officials have been permitted to decide, they have usually favored national laws or standards when it served their political interests or desire for "free" money, but decried them as "intru-sive" or worse when they have not.

WORLD WIDE WEB RESOURCES

State news: **www.stateline.org**

Council of State Governments: **www.csg.org**

National Governors' Association: **www.nga.org**

Supreme Court decisions:
www.findlaw.com/casecode/supreme.html

SUGGESTED READINGS

Beer, Samuel H. *To Make a Nation: The Rediscovery of American Federalism*. Cambridge: Harvard University Press, 1993. The definitive study of the philosophical bases of American federalism.

Conlan, Timothy. *From New Federalism to Devolution.* Washington, D.C.: Brookings Institution, 1998. A masterful overview of the politics of federalism from Richard Nixon to Bill Clinton.

Derthick, Martha N. *Keeping the Compound Republic.* Washington, D.C.: Brookings Institution, 2001. A masterful analysis of trends in American federalism from the Founding to the present.

Diamond, Martin. "The Federalist's View of Federalism." In *Essays in Federalism,* edited by George C.S. Benson. Claremont, Calif.: Institute for Studies in Federalism of Claremont Men's College, 1961, 21–64. A profound analysis of what the Founders meant by federalism.

Grodzins, Morton. *The American System.* Chicago: Rand McNally, 1966. Argues that American federalism has always involved extensive sharing of functions between national and state governments.

Melnick, R. Shep. *Between the Lines: Interpreting Welfare Rights.* Washington, D.C.: Brookings Institution, 1994. An examination of how trends in statutory interpretation have affected broader policy developments, including the expansion of the agenda of national government, the persistence of divided government, and the resurgence and decentralization of Congress.

Riker, William H. *Federalism: Origin, Operation, Significance.* Boston: Little, Brown, 1964. A classic explanation and critical analysis of federalism here and abroad.

American Political Culture

Political Culture
The Political System ● The Economic System

Comparing America with Other Nations
The Political System ● The Economic System ●
The Civic Role of Religion ● Religion and Politics

The Sources of Political Culture
The Culture War

Mistrust of Government

Political Efficacy

Political Tolerance

WHO GOVERNS?

1. Do Americans trust their government?
2. Why do we accept great differences in wealth and income?

TO WHAT ENDS?

1. Why does our government behave differently than governments in countries with similar constitutions?

*I*f you have lived in Argentina, Brazil, Mexico, or the Philippines, you might wonder why these countries, whose constitutions are very much like the American one, have had so much trouble with corruption, military takeovers, and the rise of demagogues. All of these nations have had periods of democratic rule, but only for rather short periods of time. If these nations have an elected president, a separately elected congress, and an independent judiciary, and if all promise personal freedom to their people, why do they have so much trouble?

This is an old problem. Alexis de Tocqueville, the perceptive French observer of American politics, noticed this as early as the 1830s. One reason a democratic republic took root in the United States but not in other countries that copied its constitution was that this country offered more abundant and fertile soil in which the roots could grow.[1] The vast territory of the United States created innumerable opportunities for people to acquire land and make a living. No feudal aristocracy monopolized the land, the government imposed only minimal taxes, and few legal restraints existed. As one place after another filled up, people kept pushing west to find new opportunities. A nation of small, independent farmers, unlike the traditional European one of landless peasants and indentured servants, could make democracy work.

But other nations that were similarly favored did not achieve the same result. As Tocqueville noted, much of South America contains fertile land and rich resources, but democracy has not flourished there.[2] Had he returned to the United States fifty years later, when the frontier was no longer expanding and Americans were crowding into big cities, he would have found that democratic government was still more or less intact.

The Constitution and the physical advantages of the land cannot by themselves explain the persistence of the nation's democratic institutions. In addition we must consider the customs of the people—what Tocqueville called their "moral and intellectual characteristics"[3] and what modern social scientists call our political culture.

☆ Political Culture

If you travel abroad, you will quickly become aware that other people often behave differently from Americans. Spaniards may eat dinner at 10:00 P.M., whereas Americans eat at 6:00 or 7:00 P.M. Italians may close their shops

Alexis de Tocqueville (1805–1859) was a young French aristocrat who came to the United States to study the American prison system. He wrote the brilliant Democracy in America *(2 vols., 1835–1840), a profound analysis of our political culture.*

for three hours in the middle of the day, while American shops are open continuously from 9:00 to 5:00. Germans address people more formally than Americans, using last names when we would use first names. Japanese business executives attach a lot of importance to working together as a group, while their American counterparts often are more individualistic. In these and countless other ways we can observe cultural differences among people.

Such differences are not limited to eating, shopkeeping, or manners. They include differences in political culture as well. A **political culture** is a distinctive and patterned way of thinking about how political and economic life ought to be carried out. Beliefs about economic life are part of the political culture because politics affects economics.

Americans do not judge their political and economic systems in the same way. As we shall see, this difference makes them somewhat unique, for in many other nations people apply the same standards to both systems. For example, Americans think it very important that everybody should be equal politically, but they do not think it important that everybody should be equal economically. By contrast, people in some other nations believe that the principle of equality should be applied to both economic and political life.

The Political System

There are at least five important elements in the American view of the political system:

- *Liberty:* Americans are preoccupied with their rights. They believe they should be free to do pretty much as they please, with some exceptions, so long as they don't hurt other people.
- *Equality:* Americans believe everybody should have an equal vote and an equal chance to participate and succeed.
- *Democracy:* Americans think government officials should be accountable to the people.
- *Civic duty:* Americans generally feel people ought to take community affairs seriously and help out when they can.[4]
- *Individual responsibility:* A characteristically American view is that, barring some disability, individuals are responsible for their own actions and well-being.

By vast majorities Americans believe that every citizen should have an equal chance to influence government policy and to hold public office, and they oppose the idea of letting people have titles such as "Lord" or "Duke," as in England. By somewhat smaller majorities they believe that people should be allowed to vote even if they can't read or write or vote intelligently.[5] Though Americans recognize that people differ in their abilities, they overwhelmingly agree with the statement that "teaching children that all people are really equal recognizes that all people are equally worthy and deserve equal treatment."[6]

At least three questions can be raised about this political culture. First, how do we know that the American people share these beliefs? For most of our history there were no public opinion polls, and even after they became commonplace, they were rather crude tools for measuring the existence and meaning

political culture A coherent way of thinking about how politics and government ought to be carried out.

At the height of immigration to this country there was a striking emphasis on creating a shared political culture. Schoolchildren, whatever their national origin, were taught to salute this country's flag.

of complex, abstract ideas. There is in fact no way to prove that values such as those listed above are important to Americans. But neither is there good reason for dismissing the list out of hand. One can infer, as have many scholars, the existence of certain values by a close study of the kinds of books Americans read, the speeches they hear, the slogans to which they respond, and the political choices they make, as well as by noting the observations of insightful foreign visitors. Personality tests as well as opinion polls, particularly those asking similar questions in different countries, also supply useful evidence, some of which will be reviewed in the following paragraphs.

Second, if these values are important to Americans, how can we explain the existence in our society of behavior that is obviously inconsistent with them? For example, if white Americans believe in equality of opportunity, why did so many of them for so long deny that equality to African Americans? That people act contrary to their professed beliefs is an everyday fact of life: people believe in honesty, yet they steal from their employers and sometimes underreport their taxable income. Besides values, self-interest and social circumstances also shape behavior. Gunnar Myrdal, a Swedish observer of American society, described race relations in this country as "an American dilemma" resulting from the conflict between the "American creed" (a belief in equality of opportunity) and American behavior (denying African Americans full citizenship).[7] But the creed remains important because it is a source of change: as more and more

people become aware of the inconsistency between their values and their behavior, that behavior slowly changes.[8] Race relations in this country would take a very different course if instead of an abstract but widespread belief in equality there were an equally widespread belief that one race is inherently inferior to another. (No doubt some Americans believe that, but most do not.)

Third, if there is agreement among Americans on certain political values, why has there been so much political conflict in our history? How could a people who agree on such fundamentals fight a bloody civil war, engage in violent labor-management disputes, take to the streets in riots and demonstrations, and sue each other in countless court battles? Conflict, even violent struggles, can occur over specific policies even among those who share, at some level of abstraction, common beliefs. Many political values may be irrelevant to specific controversies: there is no abstract value, for example, that would settle the question of whether steelworkers ought to organize unions. More important, much of our conflict has occurred precisely because we have strong beliefs that happen, as each of us interprets them, to be in conflict. Equality of opportunity seems an attractive idea, but sometimes it can be pursued only by curtailing personal liberty, another attractive idea. The states went to war in 1861 over one aspect of that conflict—the rights of slaves versus the rights of slaveowners.

Indeed, the Civil War illustrates the way certain fundamental beliefs about how a democratic regime ought to be organized have persisted despite bitter conflict over the policies adopted by particular governments. When the southern states seceded from the Union, they formed not a wholly different government but one modeled, despite some important differences, on the U.S. Constitution. Even some of the language of the Constitution was duplicated, suggesting that the southern states believed not that a new form of government or a different political culture ought to be created but that the South was the true repository of the existing constitutional and cultural order.[9]

Perhaps the most frequently encountered evidence that Americans believe themselves bound by common values and common hopes has been the persistence of the word *Americanism* in our political vocabulary. Throughout the nineteenth and most of the twentieth centuries *Americanism* and *American way of life* were familiar terms not only in Fourth of July speeches but also in everyday discourse. For many years the House of Representatives had a committee called the House Un-American Activities Committee. There is hardly any example to be found abroad of such a way of thinking: There is no "Britishism" or "Frenchism," and when Britons and French people become worried about subversion, they call it a problem of internal security, not a manifestation of "un-British" or "un-French" activities.

The Economic System

Americans judge the economic system using many of the same standards by which they judge the political system, albeit with some very important differences. As it is in American politics, liberty is important in the U.S. economy. Thus Americans support the idea of a free-enterprise economic system, calling the nation's economy "generally fair and efficient" and denying that it "survives by keeping the poor down."[10] However, there are limits to how much freedom they think should exist in the marketplace. People support government regulation of business in order to keep some firms from becoming too powerful and to correct specific abuses.[11]

Americans are more willing to tolerate economic inequality than political inequality. They believe in maintaining "equality of opportunity" in the economy but not "equality of results." If everyone has an equal opportunity to get ahead, then it is all right for people with more ability to earn higher salaries and for wages to be set based on how hard people work rather than on their economic needs.[12] Hardly anyone is upset by the fact that Bill Gates, Warren Buffett, and Mel Gibson are rich men. Although Americans are quite willing to support education and training programs to help disadvantaged people get ahead, they are strongly opposed to anything that looks like preferential treatment (for example, hiring quotas) in the workplace.[13]

The leaders of very liberal political groups, such as civil rights and feminist organizations, are more willing than the average American to support preferential treatment in the hiring and promoting of minorities and women. They do so because, unlike most citizens, they believe that whatever disadvantages minorities and women face are the result of failures of the economic system rather than the fault of individuals.[14] Even so, these leaders strongly support the idea that earnings should be based on ability and oppose the idea of having any top limit on what people can earn.[15]

This popular commitment to economic individualism and personal responsibility may help explain

In the 1950s Senator Joseph McCarthy of Wisconsin was the inspiration for the word "McCarthyism" after his highly publicized attacks on alleged communists working in the federal government.

how Americans think about particular public policies, such as welfare and civil rights. Polls show that Americans are willing to help people "truly in need" (this includes the elderly and the disabled) but not those deemed "able to take care of themselves" (this includes, in the public's mind, people "on welfare"). Also, Americans dislike preferential hiring programs and the use of quotas to deal with racial inequality.

At the core of these policy attitudes is a widely (but not universally) shared commitment to economic individualism and personal responsibility. Some scholars, among them Donald Kinder and David Sears, interpret these individualistic values as "symbolic racism"—a kind of plausible camouflage for antiblack attitudes.[16] But other scholars, such as Paul M. Sniderman and Michael Gray Hagen, argue that these views are not a smoke screen for bigotry or insensitivity but a genuine commitment to the ethic of self-reliance.[17] Since there are many Americans on both sides of this issue, debates about welfare and civil rights tend to be especially intense. What is striking about the American political culture is that in this country the individualist view of social policy is by far the most popular.[18]

Views about specific economic policies change. Americans now are much more inclined than they once were to believe that the government should help the needy and regulate business. But the commitment to certain underlying principles has been remarkably enduring. In 1924 almost half of the high school students in Muncie, Indiana, said that "it is entirely the fault of the man himself if he cannot succeed" and disagreed with the view that differences in wealth showed that the system was unjust. Over half a century later, the students in this same high school were asked the same questions again, with the same results.[19]

☆ Comparing America with Other Nations

The best way to learn what is distinctive about the American political culture is to compare it with that of other nations. This comparison shows that Americans have somewhat different beliefs about the political system, the economic system, and religion.

The Political System

Sweden has a well-developed democratic government, with a constitution, free speech, an elected legislature, competing political parties, and a reasonably honest and nonpartisan bureaucracy. But the Swedish political culture is significantly different from ours; it is more deferential than participatory. Though almost all adult Swedes vote in national elections, few participate in politics in any other way. They defer to the decisions of experts and specialists who work for the government, rarely challenge governmental decisions in court, believe leaders and legislators ought to decide issues on the basis of "what is best" more than on "what the people want," and value equality as much as (or more than) liberty.[20] Whereas Americans are contentious, Swedes value harmony; while Americans tend to assert their rights, Swedes tend to observe their obligations.

The contrast in political cultures is even greater when one looks at a nation, such as Japan, with a wholly different history and set of traditions. One study compared the values expressed by a small number of upper-status Japanese with those of some similarly situated Americans. Whereas the Americans emphasized the virtues of individualism, com-

petition, and equality in their political, economic, and social relations, the Japanese attached greater value to maintaining good relations with colleagues, having decisions made by groups, preserving social harmony, and displaying respect for hierarchy. The Americans were more concerned than the Japanese with rules and with treating others fairly but impersonally, with due regard for their rights. The Japanese, on the other hand, stressed the importance of being sensitive to the personal needs of others, avoiding conflict, and reaching decisions through discussion rather than the application of rules.[21] These cultural differences affect in profound but hard-to-measure ways the workings of the political and economic systems of the two countries, making them function quite differently despite the fact that both are industrialized, capitalist nations.

It is easy to become carried away by the more obvious differences among national cultures and to overgeneralize from them. Thinking in stereotypes about the typical American, the typical Swede, or the typical Japanese is as risky as thinking of the typical white or the typical black American. This can be especially misleading in nations, such as the United States and Canada, that have been settled by a variety of ethnic and religious groups (English-speaking versus French-speaking Canadians, for example, or Jewish, Protestant, and Catholic Americans). But it is equally misleading to suppose that the operation of a political system can be understood entirely from the nation's objective features—its laws, economy, or physical terrain.

In 1959–1960 Gabriel Almond and Sidney Verba published a study of political culture in five nations. In general they found that Americans, and to a lesser degree citizens of Great Britain, had a stronger sense of **civic duty** (a belief that one has an obligation to participate in civic and political affairs) and a stronger sense of **civic competence** (a belief that one can affect government policies) than did the citizens of Germany, Italy, or Mexico. Over half of all Americans and a third of all Britons believed that the average citizen ought to "be active in one's community," compared to only a tenth in Italy and a fifth in Germany. Moreover, many more Americans and Britons than Germans, Italians, or Mexicans believed that they could "do something" about an unjust national law or local regulation.[22] Since 1960 nobody has asked people in these five countries the same questions, and hence we do not know whether these views have changed in recent years. But in a 1995 study of citizen participation in politics, Verba and others report-

---

civic duty   A belief that one has an obligation to participate in civic and political affairs.

civic competence   A belief that one can affect government policies.

ed that while America lagged behind Austria, the Netherlands, West Germany, and the United Kingdom in voter participation, when it came to campaigning, attending political meetings, becoming active in the local community, and contacting government officials, Americans were as active—or substantially more active—than citizens elsewhere.[23]

Today the American people have less trust in government than they once did. But even so, popular confidence in political institutions remains higher here than in many places abroad. In cross-national surveys conducted in the 1990s in the United States and sixteen other democracies, Americans expressed more confidence in public institutions (Congress/Parliament, the police, the armed forces, the legal system, and the civil service) than did the citizens of all but four other countries (Denmark, Ireland, Northern Ireland, and Norway), and greater confidence in private institutions (the church, major companies, the press, trade unions) than did the citizens of any other nation.[24] In other cross-national surveys conducted in the 1990s, Americans were more likely than the French or Germans to say they were "very patriotic" (see Table 4.1). Of course, Americans know that their country has a lot of faults. But even the most disaffected voters believe the United States needs to change only certain policies, not its system of government.[25]

The Economic System

The political culture of Sweden is not only more deferential than ours but also more inclined to favor equality of results over equality of opportunity. Sidney Verba and Gary Orren compared the views of Swedish and American trade union and political party leaders on a variety of economic issues. In both countries the leaders were chosen from either blue-collar unions or the major liberal political party (the Democrats in the United States, the Social Democrats in Sweden).

The British House of Commons reflects a different political culture from that found in the United States.

The results (see Table 4.2) are quite striking. By margins of four or five to one the Swedish leaders were more likely to believe in giving workers equal pay than were their American counterparts. Moreover, by margins of at least three to one, the Swedes were more likely than the Americans to favor putting a top limit on incomes.[26]

Just what these differences in beliefs mean in dollars-and-cents terms was revealed by the answers to another question. Each group was asked what should be the ratio between the income of an executive and that of a menial worker (a dishwasher in Sweden, an elevator operator in the United States). The Swedish leaders said the ratio should be a little over two to one. That is, if the dishwasher earned $200 a week, the executive should earn no more than $440 to $480 a week. But the American leaders were ready to let the executive earn between $2,260 and $3,040 per week when the elevator operator was earning $200.

Table 4.1	Patriotism in America, France, and Germany		
	Percentage Agreeing		
Statement	**U.S.**	**France**	**Germany**
I am very patriotic.	51%	27%	26%
I am proud to be (American, etc.).	74	25	23
We should be willing to fight for our country whether it is right or wrong.	22	17	5

Source: Adapted from *The Public Perspective* (April/May 1999): 23.

Table 4.2	Commitment to Income Equity in Sweden and the United States			
	Political Party Leaders		**Blue-Collar Union Leaders**	
	Sweden (Social Democrats)	**U.S. (Democrats)**	**Sweden**	**U.S.**
Favor equality of results (%)	21%	9%	14%	4%
Favor equal pay (%)	58	12	68	11
Favor top limit on income (%)	44	17	51	13
Fair income ratio of executive to menial worker*	2:1	15:1	2:1	11:1

*In Sweden menial worker was a dishwasher; in U.S. menial worker was an elevator operator.

Source: Reprinted by permission of the publisher from *Equality in America: The View from the Top* by Sidney Verba and Gary R. Orren, Cambridge: Harvard University Press, Copyright © 1985 by the Presidents and Fellows of Harvard College.

Americans, compared to people in many other countries, are more likely to think that freedom is more important than equality and less likely to think that hard work goes unrewarded or that the government should guarantee citizens a basic standard of living (see Table 4.3). These cultural differences make a difference in politics. In fact there is less income inequality in Sweden than in the United States—the government sees to that.

The Civic Role of Religion

In the 1830s Tocqueville was amazed at how religious Americans were in comparison to his fellow Europeans. From the first days of the new Republic right down to the present, America has been among the most religious countries in the world.[27] The average American is more likely than the average European to believe in God, to pray on a daily basis, and to acknowledge clear standards of right and wrong (see Table 4.4).

There is some evidence that Americans are becoming more religious. It is doubtful that this is true for American elites (see Chapter 7) but it seems clear that mass religiosity has increased somewhat over the last two decades. For example, the percentage of Americans who "completely agree" that "God really exists" rose from 68 percent in 1987 to 79 percent in 1997, and, over the same period, the percentage who "completely agree" that "prayer is an important part of my daily life" rose from 41 percent to 53 percent.[28] It is clear that America remains a highly religious nation, both in absolute terms and relative to most European countries (see Tables 4.5 and 4.6).

Many present-day Americans, however, are attracted to religion as much for its civic as for its spiritual significance. Churches, synagogues, mosques, and other religious organizations are the country's major source of volunteer and community services: Half of their members do unpaid community work each year; nine in ten give money to charity; and eight in ten give goods, clothing, or other property to charity.[29] In many urban communities all across the country, religious organizations are major or sole providers of myriad social and health care services to low-income children, youth, and families.[30]

Table 4.3	Attitudes toward Economic Equality in America and Europe				
	Percentage Agreeing				
Statement	**U.S.**	**Great Britain**	**Germany**	**Italy**	**France**
It is government's responsibility to take care of the very poor who can't take care of themselves.	23%	62%	50%	66%	62%
Hard work guarantees success.	63	46	38	51	46
Government should *not* guarantee every citizen food and basic shelter.	34	9	13	14	10

Source: Adapted from *The Public Perspective* (November/December 1991): 5, 7. © *The Public Perspective,* a publication of the Roper Center for Public Opinion Research, University of Connecticut, Storrs. Reprinted with permission.

Table 4.4   Religious Belief in America and Europe

	Percentage Agreeing				
Statement	U.S.	Great Britain	Germany	Italy	France
I never doubt the existence of God.	60%	31%	20%	56%	29%
Prayer is an important part of my daily life.	77	37	44	69	32
There are clear guidelines about what is good and evil.	79	65	54	56	64

Source: Adapted from *The Public Perspective* (November/December 1991): 5, 8. Reprinted by permission of *The Public Perspective,* a publication of the Roper Center for Public Opinion Research, University of Connecticut.

Table 4.5   Religion in America Today

	Percentage of Adult Americans
Believe in God	96%
Say they have a personal relationship with God	80
Never doubt God's existence	79
Say they are seeking to grow in religious faith	76
Pray at least daily	75
Are a member of a church, synagogue, mosque, or other organized religious group	64
Say religion can solve all or most of today's problems	61
Attend worship services more than once a month	54

Source: Adapted from George Gallup, Jr., and Timothy Jones, *The Next American Spirituality* (Colorado Springs, Colo: Cook, 2000), ch. 1, appendices 1 and 2.

Religion and Politics

Religious beliefs have always played a significant role in American politics. The religious revivalist movement of the late 1730s and early 1740s (known as the First Great Awakening) transformed the political life of the American colonies. Religious ideas fueled the break with England, which, in the words of the Declaration of Independence, had violated "the laws of nature and nature's God." Religious leaders were central to the struggle over slavery in the nineteenth century and the temperance movement of the early twentieth century.

Both liberals and conservatives have used the pulpit to promote political change. The civil rights movement of the 1950s and 1960s was led mainly by black religious leaders, most prominently Martin Luther King, Jr. In the 1980s a conservative religious group known as the Moral Majority advocated constitutional amendments that would allow prayer in public schools and ban abortion. In the 1990s another conservative religious group, the Christian Coalition, attracted an enormous amount of media attention and became a prominent force in many national, state, and local elections.

Candidates for national office in most contemporary democracies mention religion rarely if they mention it at all. Not so in America. During the 2000 presidential

America is much more religious than almost any European democracy.

Table 4.6 Religion in Industrial Nations, 1990–1993								
	Percentage Answering Yes							
Statement	**U.S.**	**Sweden**	**France**	**W. Germany**	**Britain**	**Spain**	**Canada**	**Mexico**
Would you say you are. . .								
A religious person?	82%	29%	48%	54%	55%	64%	69%	72%
Not a religious person?	15	56	36	27	37	27	26	22
A convinced atheist?	1	7	11	2	4	4	3	2
Not sure	2	9	5	17	4	5	2	4

Source: Adapted from *The Public Perspective,* reporting data from surveys conducted from 1990 to 1993 by the Inter-University Consortium for Political and Social Research. *The Public Perspective* (Storrs: Roper Center for Public Opinion Research, University of Connecticut, April/May 1995): 2. © The Public Perspective. Reprinted by permission.

campaign, for example, both Democratic candidate Al Gore and Republican candidate George W. Bush the younger gave major speeches extolling the virtues of religion and advocating the right of religious organizations that deliver social services to receive government funding on the same basis as all other nonprofit organizations. Both Bush and Gore were responding in part to public support for so-called faith-based approaches to solving social ills. In 2000, three-quarters of all Americans favored allowing churches, synagogues, mosques, and other houses of worship to apply for government funding to provide social services such as homeless shelters, job training, or drug treatment counseling to people who need them.[31] When asked, in general, who can do the best job of providing social services to those in need, 40 percent of Americans said faith-based organizations, 28 percent chose federal and state government agencies, and 25 percent opted for secular community groups.[32]

The general feeling about religion became apparent when a federal appeals court in 2002 tried to ban the Pledge of Allegiance because it contained the phrase "under God." There was an overwhelming and bipartisan condemnation of the ruling. To a degree that would be almost unthinkable in many other democracies, religious beliefs will probably continue to shape political culture in America for many generations to come.

☆ The Sources of Political Culture

That Americans bring a distinctive way of thinking to their political life is easier to demonstrate than to explain. But even a brief, and necessarily superficial, effort to understand the sources of our political culture can help make its significance clearer.

The American Revolution, as we discussed in Chapter 2, was essentially a war fought over liberty: an assertion by the colonists of what they took to be their rights. Though the Constitution, produced eleven years after the Revolution, had to deal with other issues as well, its animating spirit reflected the effort to reconcile personal liberty with the needs of social control. These founding experiences, and the political disputes that followed, have given to American political thought and culture a preoccupation with the assertion and maintenance of rights. This tradition has imbued the daily conduct of U.S. politics with a kind of adversarial spirit quite foreign to the political life of countries that did not undergo a libertarian revolution or that were formed out of an interest in other goals, such as social equality, national independence, or ethnic supremacy.

The adversarial spirit of the American political culture reflects not only our preoccupation with rights but also our long-standing distrust of authority and of people wielding power. The colonies' experiences with British rule was one source of that distrust. But another, older source was the religious belief of many Americans, which saw human nature as fundamentally depraved. To the colonists all of mankind suffered from original sin, symbolized by Adam and Eve eating the forbidden fruit in the Garden of Eden. Since no one was born innocent, no one could be trusted with power. Thus the Constitution had to be designed in such a way as to curb the darker side of human nature. Otherwise everyone's rights would be in jeopardy.

The contentiousness of a people animated by a suspicion of government and devoted to individualism could easily have made democratic politics so tumultuous as to be impossible. After all one must be willing to trust others with power if there is to be any kind of democratic government, and sometimes those others will be people not of one's own choosing. The first great test case took place around 1800 in a battle between the Federalists, led by John Adams and Alexander Hamilton, and the Democratic-Republicans, led by Thomas Jefferson and James Madison. The two factions deeply distrusted each other: The Federalists had passed laws designed to suppress Jeffersonian journalists; Jefferson suspected the Federalists were out to subvert the Constitution; and the Federalists believed Jefferson intended to sell out the country to France. But as we shall see in Chapter 9, the threat of civil war never materialized, and the Jeffersonians came to power peacefully. Within a few years the role of an opposition party became legitimate, and people abandoned the idea of making serious efforts to suppress their opponents. By happy circumstance people came to accept that liberty and orderly political change could coexist.

The Constitution, by creating a federal system and dividing political authority among competing institutions, provided ample opportunity for widespread—though hardly universal—participation in politics. The election of Jefferson in 1800 produced no political catastrophe, and those who had predicted one were, to a degree, discredited. But other, more fundamental features of American life contributed to the same end. One of the most important of these was religious diversity.

The absence of an established or official religion for the nation as a whole, reinforced by a constitutional prohibition of such an establishment and by the migration to this country of people with different religious backgrounds, meant that religious diversity was inevitable. Since there could be no orthodox or official religion, it became difficult for a corresponding political orthodoxy to emerge. Moreover, the conflict between the Puritan tradition, with its emphasis on faith and hard work, and the Catholic Church, with its devotion to the sacraments and priestly authority, provided a recurrent source of cleavage in American public life. The differences in values between these two groups showed up not only in their religious practices but also in areas involving the regulation of manners and morals, and even in people's choice of political party. For more than a century candidates for state and national office were deeply divided over whether the sale of liquor should be prohibited, a question that arose ultimately out of competing religious doctrines.

Even though there was no established church, there was certainly a dominant religious tradition—Protestantism, and especially Puritanism. The Protestant churches provided people with both a set of beliefs and an organizational experience that had profound effects on American political culture. Those beliefs encouraged, or even required, a life of personal achievement as well as religious conviction: a believer had an obligation to work, save money, obey the secular law, and do good works. Max Weber explained the rise of capitalism in part by what he called the Protestant ethic—what we now sometimes call the work ethic.[33] Such values had political consequences, as people holding them were motivated to engage in civic and communal action.

Churches offered ready opportunities for developing and practicing civic and political skills. Since most Protestant churches were organized along congregational lines—that is, the church was controlled by its members, who put up the building, hired the preacher, and supervised the finances—they were, in effect, miniature political systems, with leaders and committees, conflict and consensus. Developing a participatory political culture was undoubtedly made easier by the existence of a participatory religious culture. Even some Catholic churches in early America were under a degree of lay control. Parishioners owned the church property, negotiated with priests, and conducted church business.

All aspects of culture, including the political, are preserved and transmitted to new generations primarily by the family. Though some believe that the weakening of the family unit has eroded the extent to which it transmits anything, particularly culture, and has enlarged the power of other sources of values—the mass media and the world of friends and fashion, leisure and entertainment—there is still little doubt that the ways in which we think about the world are largely acquired within the family. In Chapter 7 we shall see that the family is the primary source of one kind of political attitude—identification with one or another political party. Even more important, the family shapes in subtle ways how we think and act on political matters. Erik Erikson, the psychologist, noted certain traits that are more characteristic of American than of European families—the greater freedom enjoyed by children, for example, and the larger measure of equality among family members. These familial characteristics promote a belief, carried through life, that every person has rights deserving protection and that a variety of interests have a legitimate claim to consideration when decisions are made. [34]

The combined effect of religious and ethnic diversity, an individualistic philosophy, fragmented political authority, and the relatively egalitarian American family can be seen in the absence of a high degree of **class consciousness** among Americans. Class consciousness means thinking of oneself as a worker whose interests are in opposition to those of management, or vice versa. In this country most people, whatever their jobs, think of themselves as "middle class."

Though the writings of Horatio Alger are no longer popular, Americans still seem to believe in the message of those stories—that the opportunity for success is available to people who work hard. This may help explain why the United States is the only large industrial democracy without a significant socialist party and why the nation has been slow to adopt certain welfare programs.

The Culture War

Almost all Americans share some elements of a common political culture. Why, then, is there so much cultural conflict in American politics? For many years, the most explosive political issues have included abortion, gay rights, drug use, school prayer, and pornography. Viewed from a Marxist perspective, politics in the United States is utterly baffling: instead of two economic classes engaged in a bitter struggle over wealth, we have two cultural classes locked in a war over values.

To say that there are two cultural classes is, of course, an oversimplification, but to say that there is a culture war is not an exaggeration. [35] Groups supporting and opposing the right to abortion have had

---

class consciousness   A belief that you are a member of an economic group whose interests are opposed to people in other such groups.
orthodox   A belief that morality and religion ought to be of decisive importance.
progressive   A belief that personal freedom and solving social problems are more important than religion.

---

many angry confrontations in recent years. The latter have been arrested while attempting to block access to abortion clinics; some clinics have been firebombed; and at least seven physicians have been killed. A controversy over what schoolchildren should be taught about homosexuals was responsible, in part, for the firing of the head of the New York City school system; in other states there have been fierce arguments in state legislatures and before the courts over whether gay and lesbian couples should be allowed to marry or adopt children. Although most Americans want to keep heroin, cocaine, and other drugs illegal, a significant number of people want to legalize (or at least decriminalize) their use. The Supreme Court has ruled that children cannot pray in public schools, but this has not stopped many parents and school authorities from trying to reinstate school prayer, or at least prayerlike moments of silence. The discovery that a federal agency, the National Endowment for the Arts, had given money to support exhibitions and performances that many people thought were obscene led to a furious congressional struggle over the future of the agency.

The culture war differs from other political disputes (over such matters as taxes, business regulations, and foreign policy) in several ways: money is not at stake, compromises are almost impossible to arrange, and the conflict is more profound. It is animated by deep differences in people's beliefs about private and public morality—that is, about the standards that ought to govern individual behavior and social arrangements. It is about what kind of country we ought to live in, not just about what kinds of policies our government ought to adopt.

To simplify, there are two opposed camps, the **orthodox** and the **progressive.** On the orthodox side are people who believe that morality is as important as, or more important than, self-expression and that moral rules derive from the commands of God or the laws of nature—commands and laws that are relatively clear, unchanging, and independent of individual preferences. On the progressive side are people who think that personal freedom is as important as, or more important than, certain traditional moral rules and that those rules must be evaluated in light of the circumstances of modern life—circumstances that are quite complex, changeable, and dependent on individual preferences.

Most conspicuous among the orthodox are fundamentalist Protestants and evangelical Christians, and so critics who dislike orthodox views often dismiss them as the fanatical expressions of "the Religious Right." But many people who hold orthodox views are not fanatical or deeply religious or right-wing on most issues; they simply have strong views about drugs, pornography, and sexual morality. Similarly, the progressive side often includes members of liberal Protestant denominations (for example, Episcopalians and Unitarians) and people with no strong religious beliefs, and so their critics often denounce them as immoral, anti-Christian radicals who have embraced the ideology of secular humanism, the belief that moral standards do not require religious justification. But in all likelihood few progressives are immoral or anti-Christian, and most do not regard secular humanism as their defining ideology.

Moreover, the culture war is occurring not just between different religious denominations but also within them. Catholic, Protestant, and Jewish leaders with an orthodox perspective tend to assign great importance to two-parent families, condemn pornography, denounce homosexuality, and think the United States is in general a force for good in the world. Leaders of the same faiths who have a progressive outlook are more likely to say that many legitimate alternatives to the traditional two-parent family exist, that pornography and homosexuality are private matters protected by individual rights, and that the United States has been at best a neutral and at worst a bad force in world affairs.[36] This conflict between the orthodox and progressive view of American culture is similar to, and has many of the same causes, as the cleavage (described in Chapter 5) between the traditional middle class and the new middle class.

American history has always had conflicts of this sort, but they have acquired special importance today as a result of two major changes in American society. The first is the great increase in the proportion of people who consider themselves progressive. Once almost everyone was religiously orthodox, even if politically liberal; today fewer are. The second factor is the rise of media (such as television, direct-mail advertising, and the Internet) that make it easy to wage a cultural war on a large scale. In the past preachers, writers, and lecturers could reach at most a few hundred people at a time; today television evangelists, radio talk-show hosts, and the authors of direct-mail messages or web sites can wage a furious war of words reaching tens of millions of people and

recruiting hundreds of thousands of followers. A cultural war that once enlisted only a few activists can now mobilize mass armies.

☆ Mistrust of Government

There is one aspect of public opinion that worries many people. Since the late 1950s there has been a more or less steady decline in the proportion of Americans who say they trust the government in Washington to do the right thing. In the past, polls showed that about three-quarters of Americans said they trusted Washington most of the time or just about always, but by 1980 that proportion had declined sharply to about one-quarter. The level of trust briefly rose during the Reagan administration but sank back down about the time he left office. Another measure pollsters use shows pretty much the same thing. Between 1952 and 1992 the fraction of Americans who said public officials did not care what the public thought doubled from one-third to two-thirds (see Figure 4.1 on page 89).[37]

Before we get too upset about this, we should remember that people are talking about government officials, not the system of government. Americans are much more supportive of the country and its institutions than Europeans are of theirs. Even so, the decline in confidence in officials is striking. There are all sorts of explanations for why it has happened. In the 1960s there was our unhappy war in Vietnam, in the 1970s President Nixon had to resign because of his involvement in the Watergate scandal, and in the 1990s President Clinton went through scandals that led to his being impeached by the House of Representatives (but not convicted of that charge by the Senate).

But there is another way of looking at the matter. Maybe in the 1950s we had an abnormally *high* level of confidence in government, one that could never be expected to last no matter what any president did. After all, when President Eisenhower took office in 1952, we had won a war against fascism, overcome the Depression of the 1930s, possessed a near monopoly of the atom bomb, had a currency that was the envy of the world, and dominated international trade. Moreover, in those days not much was expected out of Washington. Hardly anybody thought that there should be important federal laws about civil rights, crime, illegal drugs, the environment, the role

*Protests and demonstrations are a common feature of American politics, as with this attack in
Seattle on American membership in the World Trade Organization in November 2001. Yet, despite
disagreements Americans are a patriotic people, as seen in this photo of baseball fans
waving flags and singing "God Bless America," taken a few days after 9/11.*

of women, highway safety, or almost anything else one now finds on the national agenda. Since nobody expected much out of Washington, nobody was upset that they didn't get much out of it.

The 1960s and 1970s changed all of that. Domestic turmoil, urban riots, a civil rights revolution, the war in Vietnam, economic inflation, and a new concern for the environment dramatically increased what we expected Washington to do. And since these problems are very difficult ones to solve, a lot of people became convinced that our politicians couldn't do much.

Those events also pushed the feelings Americans had about their country—that is, their patriotism—into the background. We liked the country, but there weren't many occasions when expressing that approval seemed to make much sense. But on September 11, 2001, when hijacked airliners were crashed by terrorists into the World Trade Center in New York City and the Pentagon in Washington, all of that changed. There was an extraordinary outburst of patriotic fervor, with flags displayed everywhere, fire and police heroes widely celebrated, and strong national support for our going to war in Afghanistan to find the key terrorist, Osama bin Laden, and destroy the tyrannical Taliban regime that he supported. By November of that year about half of all Americans of both political parties said that they trusted Washington officials to do what is right most of the time, the highest level in many years.

Those who had hoped or predicted that this new level of support would last, not ebb and flow, have been disappointed. In October 2001, 57 percent of Americans (up from just 29 percent in July 2001) said they trusted the federal government to do what is right just about always or most of the time. But by May 2002, only 40 percent expresssed such trust in the federal government, and 57 percent said they trusted Washington only some of the time or never.[38] Still, it is premature to conclude that we have seen the last of post–September 11 surges in support for the federal government. Much will depend on how citizens will evaluate overall government performance, whether Washington will be widely credited with foiling terrorist attacks in the future, and how people will understand and respond to specific proposals.

As Figure 4.2 shows, public confidence in many institutions, such as Congress, newspapers, churches, and the Supreme Court, does not change much: Congress and newspapers have rather little support; churches and the Supreme Court have a lot. But support for the military and the presidency changes quite a bit: backing for the military increased dramatically after we went to war in Afghanistan and Iraq, and backing for the presidency rose after the scandals touching the Clinton administration had passed.

There are differences in how much confidence various groups have. African Americans, for exam-

Figure 4.1   Trust in the Federal Government, 1958–2002

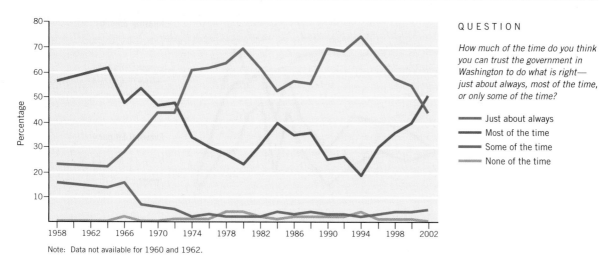

QUESTION

How much of the time do you think you can trust the government in Washington to do what is right— just about always, most of the time, or only some of the time?

— Just about always
— Most of the time
— Some of the time
— None of the time

Note: Data not available for 1960 and 1962.

Source: University of Michigan, *The National Election Studies.*

ple, have more confidence in organized religion and less confidence in the criminal justice system than do white Americans. But both blacks and whites have far more confidence in churches than they do in

criminal courts. Three-quarters of both say that they are "proud to live under our political system," and 95 percent of both say that there are no "countries better than the United States."[39] In sum, without regard to race or other factors, most Americans no longer give to political leaders and their policies the kind of support they gave in the 1950s, but they have never lost confidence in either the political system or each other.

Figure 4.2   Public Confidence in Institutions, 1981–2004

— Churches
— Military
— Supreme Court
— President
— Newspapers
— Congress

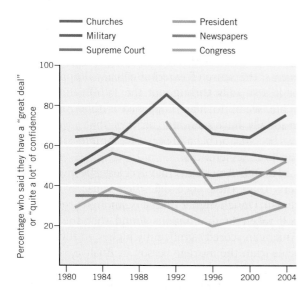

Source: Gallup Poll, poll dated May 21–23, 2004.

☆ Political Efficacy

Perhaps the most worrisome aspect of recent changes in the American political culture is the decline in the extent to which citizens feel that the political system will respond to their needs and beliefs. These changes are in what scholars call a citizen's sense of **political efficacy**, by which they mean a citizen's capacity to understand and influence political events.

political efficacy   A belief that you can take part in politics (internal efficacy) or that the government will respond to the citizenry (external efficacy).

Figure 4.3   Changes in the Sense of Political Efficacy, 1952–2002

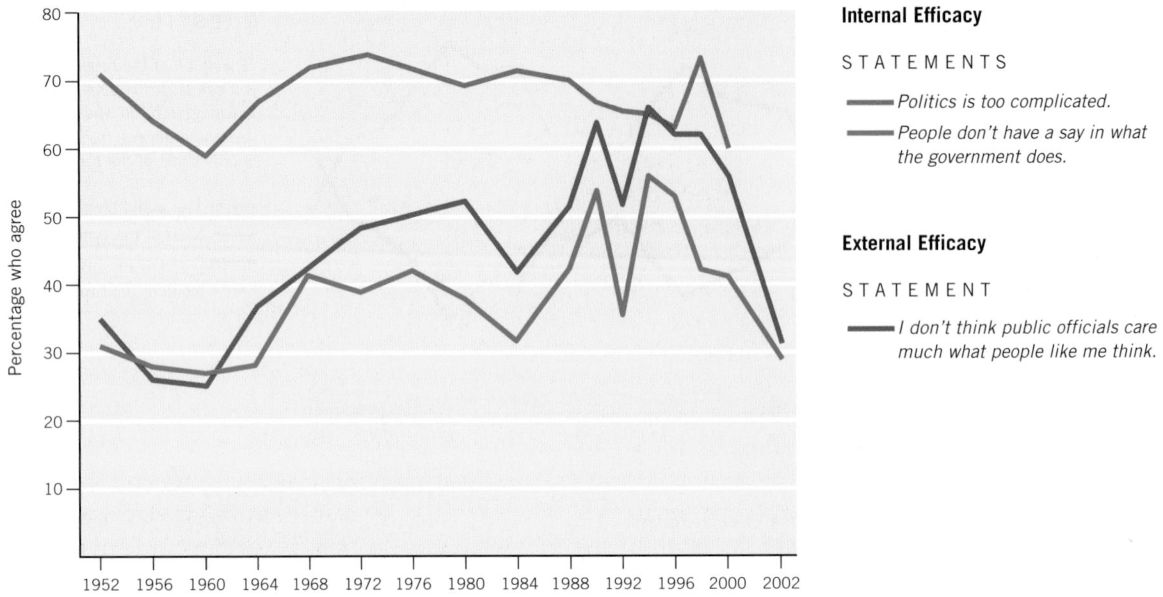

Internal Efficacy

STATEMENTS

— *Politics is too complicated.*
— *People don't have a say in what the government does.*

External Efficacy

STATEMENT

— *I don't think public officials care much what people like me think.*

Source: University of Michigan, *The National Election Studies.*

This sense of efficacy has two parts—**internal efficacy** (the ability to understand and take part in political affairs) and **external efficacy** (the ability to make the system respond to the citizenry). Since the mid-1960s there has been a fairly sharp drop in the sense of external efficacy (or system responsiveness) but not much change in the sense of internal efficacy (personal competence).

As we can see in Figure 4.3, people today are not much different from people in 1952 with respect to whether they can understand what is going on in government (most find it too complicated to fathom) and whether they have much say in what the government does. But there has been a big change in how responsive people think the government is to their interests. Between 2000 and 2002, the confi-

dence people have in American government went up, also surely because the government was struggling to cope with a national crisis—the destruction of buildings by the terrorist attacks on September 11, 2001. But after 2002, confidence in the government began to drop again.

Unlike the increase in the mistrust of government, the increase in the feeling that government is unresponsive has not been shaped by any particular events; the sense of external efficacy dropped more or less steadily throughout the 1960s and 1970s. What seems to have happened is that Americans gradually have come to the view that government has become too big and pervasive for it to be sensitive to citizen preferences.

Though Americans may feel less effective as citizens than they once did, their sense of efficacy remains much higher than it is among Europeans. A poll taken in five nations found that the average American scored significantly higher on the efficacy scale than the average person in Austria, Germany, Great Britain, or the Netherlands. Moreover, Americans were much more likely than Europeans to say

internal efficacy   The ability to understand and take part in politics.

external efficacy   The willingness of the state to respond to the citizenry.

that they regularly discussed politics, signed petitions, and worked to solve community problems.[40] Though Americans are less likely to vote than Europeans, they are more likely to do the harder chores that make up democratic politics.

Because Americans are less likely than they once were to hold their leaders in high esteem, to have confidence in government policies, and to believe the system will be responsive to popular wishes, some observers like to say that Americans today are more "alienated" from politics. Perhaps, but careful studies of the subject have not yet been able, for example, to demonstrate any relationship between overall levels of public trust in government or confidence in leaders, on the one hand, and the rates at which people come out to vote, on the other. There is, however, some evidence that the less voters trust political institutions and leaders, the more likely they are to support candidates from the nonincumbent major party (in two-candidate races) and third-party candidates.[41] If this is so, it helps to explain why the incumbent party has lost, and third parties have strongly contested, five of the last nine presidential elections (1968–2000).

☆ Political Tolerance

Democratic politics depends crucially on citizens' being reasonably tolerant of the opinions and actions of others. If unpopular speakers were always shouted down, if government efforts to censor newspapers were usually met with popular support or even public indifference, if peaceful demonstrations were regularly broken up by hostile mobs, if the losing candidates in an election refused to allow their victorious opponents to take office, then the essential elements of a democratic political culture would be missing, and democracy would fail. Democracy does not require perfect tolerance; if it did, the passions of human nature would make democracy forever impossible. But at a minimum citizens must have a political culture that allows the discussion of ideas and the selection of rulers in an atmosphere reasonably free of oppression.

Public opinion surveys show that the overwhelming majority of Americans agree with concepts such as freedom of speech, majority rule, and the right to

circulate petitions—at least in the abstract.[42] But when we get down to concrete cases, a good many Americans are not very tolerant of groups they dislike. Suppose you must decide which groups will be permitted to espouse their causes at meetings held in your community's civic auditorium. Which of these groups would *you* allow to run such a meeting?

1. Protestants holding a revival meeting
2. Right-to-life groups opposing abortion
3. People protesting a nuclear power plant
4. Feminists organizing a march for the Equal Rights Amendment
5. Gays organizing for homosexual rights
6. Atheists preaching against God
7. Students organizing a sit-in to shut down city hall

In general, Americans have become a bit more tolerant. As you can see in Figure 4.4, we say (perhaps accurately) that we are more willing to tolerate Communists, people who teach against churches and religions, advocates of government ownership of industries, and people who think that blacks are genetically inferior. In Figure 4.6 we see that people are today more likely than in the past to say they are willing to vote for an otherwise qualified person who ran for president even if the candidate was a Catholic, a Jew, a woman, a black, or a homosexual.[43]

One person's civic intolerance can be another person's heartfelt display of civic concern. As is suggested by Figure 4.5, most Americans believe that serious civic problems are rooted in a breakdown of moral values. Correctly or not, most citizens worry that the nation is becoming too tolerant of behaviors that harm society, and they favor defending common moral standards over protecting individual rights.

Nonetheless, this majority tolerance for many causes should not blind us to the fact that for most of us there is some group or cause from which we are willing to withhold political liberties—even though we endorse those liberties in the abstract.

If most people dislike one or another group strongly enough to deny it certain political rights that we usually take for granted, how is it that such groups (and such rights) survive? The answer, in part, is that most of us don't act on our beliefs. We rarely take the trouble—or have the chance—to block another person from making a speech or

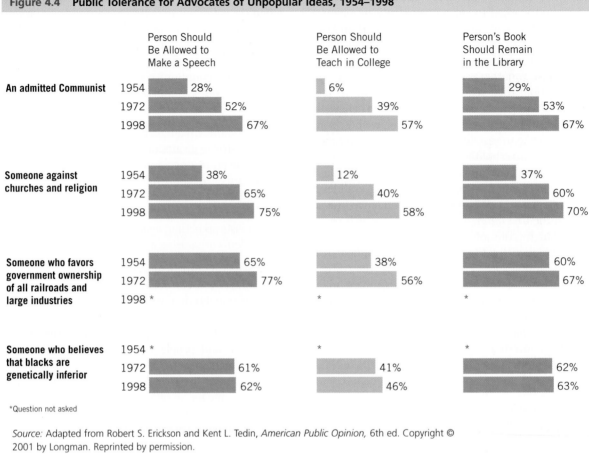

Figure 4.4   Public Tolerance for Advocates of Unpopular Ideas, 1954–1998

	Person Should Be Allowed to Make a Speech	Person Should Be Allowed to Teach in College	Person's Book Should Remain in the Library
An admitted Communist 1954	28%	6%	29%
1972	52%	39%	53%
1998	67%	57%	67%
Someone against churches and religion 1954	38%	12%	37%
1972	65%	40%	60%
1998	75%	58%	70%
Someone who favors government ownership of all railroads and large industries 1954	65%	38%	60%
1972	77%	56%	67%
1998	*	*	*
Someone who believes that blacks are genetically inferior 1954	*	*	*
1972	61%	41%	62%
1998	62%	46%	63%

*Question not asked

Source: Adapted from Robert S. Erickson and Kent L. Tedin, *American Public Opinion,* 6th ed. Copyright © 2001 by Longman. Reprinted by permission.

teaching school. Some scholars have argued that among people who are in a position to deny other people rights—officeholders and political activists, for example—the level of political tolerance is somewhat greater than among the public at large, but that claim has been strongly disputed.[44]

But another reason may be just as important. Most of us are ready to deny *some* group its rights, but we usually can't agree on which group that should be. Sometimes we can agree, and then the disliked group may be in for real trouble. There have been times (1919–1920, and again in the early 1950s) when socialists or communists were disliked by most people in the United States. The government on each occasion took strong actions against them. Today fewer people agree that these left-wing groups

are a major domestic threat, and so their rights are now more secure.

Finally, the courts are sufficiently insulated from public opinion that they can act against majority sentiments and enforce constitutional protections (see Chapter 16). Most of us are not willing to give all rights to all groups, but most of us are not judges.

These facts should be a sober reminder that political liberty cannot be taken for granted. Men and women are not, it would seem, born with an inclination to live and let live, at least politically, and many—possibly most—never acquire that inclination. Liberty must be learned and protected. Happily the United States during much of its recent history has not been consumed by a revulsion for any one

Figure 4.5 Views of Toleration and Morality

QUESTION

Which worries you more, that the country will become too tolerant of behaviors that are bad for sociey, or that the country will become too intolerant of behaviors that don't do any real harm to society?

1998

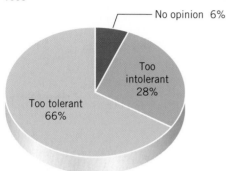

No opinion 6%

Too intolerant 28%

Too tolerant 66%

QUESTION

Is it more important to defend standards of right and wrong, to protect the rights of individuals, or are both equally important?

1998

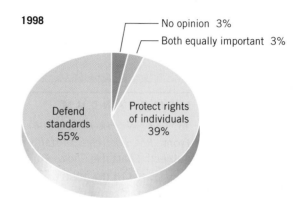

No opinion 3%

Both equally important 3%

Defend standards 55%

Protect rights of individuals 39%

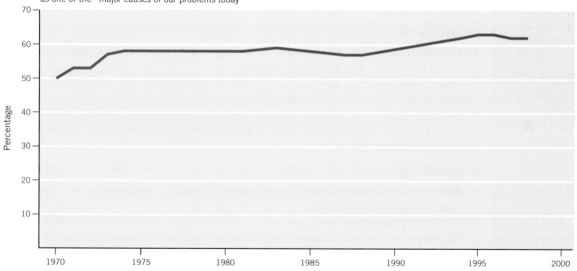

Americans who pick out "a letdown in moral values" as one of the "major causes of our problems today"

Source: The American Enterprise (January/February 1999): 37, reporting data from Roper, *Washington Post,* Harvard, and Kaiser Family Foundation polls.

group that has been strong enough to place the group's rights in jeopardy.

Nor should any part of society pretend that it is always more tolerant than another. In the 1950s, for example, ultraconservatives outside the universities were attacking the rights of professors to say and teach certain things. In the 1960s and 1970s ultraliberal students and professors inside the universities were attacking the rights of other students and professors to say certain things.

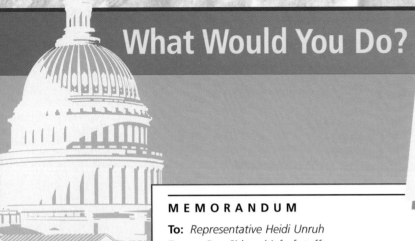

What Would You Do?

Religious Leaders Rally to Expand Federal Funding for "Charitable Choice"

August 28
WASHINGTON

Yesterday an interfaith coalition of religious leaders conducted an all-day prayer vigil on Capitol Hill and called for increased federal funding for antipoverty programs run by local religious congregations . . .

MEMORANDUM

To: *Representative Heidi Unruh*
From: *Ron Sider, chief of staff*
Subject: *Charitable Choice Expansion Act*

Section 104 of the 1996 federal welfare reform law encouraged states to utilize "faith-based organizations" as providers of federal welfare services. Known as Charitable Choice, the law prohibits participating organizations from discriminating against beneficiaries on the basis of religion but permits them to control "the definition, development, practice, and expression" of their religious convictions. The proposed act would expand Charitable Choice to crime prevention and other areas.

Arguments for:

1. Over 90 percent of Americans believe in God, and 80 percent favor government funding for faith-based social programs.
2. Local religious groups are the main nongovernmental providers of social services in poor urban neighborhoods. The primary beneficiaries of faith-based programs are needy neighborhood children who are not affiliated with any congregation.
3. So long as the religious organizations serve civic purposes and do not proselytize, the law is constitutional.

Arguments against:

1. Americans are a richly religious people precisely because we have never mixed church and state in this way.
2. Community-serving religious groups succeed because over 97 percent of their funding is private and they can flexibly respond to people's needs without government or other interference.
3. Constitutional or not, the law threatens to undermine both church and state: Children will have religion slid (if not jammed) down their throats, and religious leaders will be tempted to compromise their convictions.

Your decision:

Favor expansion _____
Oppose expansion _____

Figure 4.6   Changes in Levels of Political Tolerance, 1930–1999

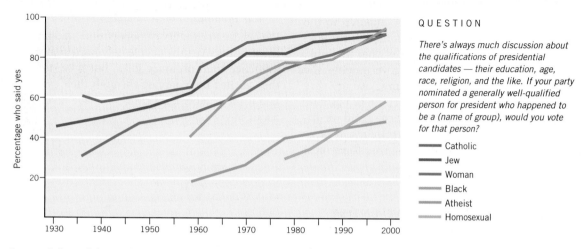

QUESTION

There's always much discussion about the qualifications of presidential candidates — their education, age, race, religion, and the like. If your party nominated a generally well-qualified person for president who happened to be a (name of group), would you vote for that person?

— Catholic
— Jew
— Woman
— Black
— Atheist
— Homosexual

Sources: Gallup poll data, various years, as compiled by Professor John Zaller, Department of Political Science, UCLA; The Gallup Organization, *Poll Releases* (March 29, 1999), 2–6.

☆ SUMMARY

The American system of government is supported by a political culture that fosters a sense of civic duty, takes pride in the nation's constitutional arrangements, and provides support for the exercise of essential civil liberties (albeit out of indifference or diversity more than principle at times). In recent decades mistrust of government officials (though not of the system itself) has increased, and confidence in their responsiveness to popular feelings has declined.

Although Americans value liberty in both the political system and the economy, they believe equality is important in the political realm. In economic affairs they wish to see equality of opportunity but accept inequality of results.

Not only is our culture generally supportive of democratic rule, it also has certain distinctive features that make our way of governing different from what one finds in other democracies. Americans are preoccupied with their rights, and this fact, com-

bined with a political system that (as we shall see) encourages the vigorous exercise of rights and claims, gives to our political life an *adversarial* style. Unlike Swedes or Japanese, we do not generally reach political decisions by consensus, and we often do not defer to the authority of administrative agencies. American politics, more than that of many other nations, is shot through at every stage with protracted conflict.

But as we shall learn in the next chapter, that conflict is not easily described as always pitting liberals against conservatives. Not only do we have a lot of conflict, it is often messy conflict, a kind of political Tower of Babel. Foreign observers sometimes ask how we stand the confusion. The answer, of course, is that we have been doing it for over two hundred years. Maybe our Constitution is two centuries old not in spite of this confusion but because of it. We shall see.

RECONSIDERING WHO GOVERNS?

1. *Do Americans trust their government?*

More than it sometimes appears. Compared to the 1950s, we are much less likely to think that the government does the right thing or cares what we think. But when we look at our system of government—the Constitution and our political culture—we are very pleased with it. Americans are much more patriotic than people in many other democracies. And we display a great deal of support for churches in large measure because we are more religious than most Europeans.

2. *Why do we accept great differences in wealth and income?*

We believe in equality of opportunity and not equality of result. Wealthy people may have more political influence than ordinary folks, but if we think that they earned their money through their own efforts and if they follow legal rules, we have no complaint about their wealth.

RECONSIDERING TO WHAT ENDS?

1. *Why does our government behave differently than governments in countries with similar constitutions?*

Our political culture has imbued it with more tolerance and a greater respect for orderly procedures and personal rights than can be found in nations with constitutions like ours. We are willing to let whoever wins an election govern without putting up a fuss, and our military does not intervene.

WORLD WIDE WEB RESOURCES

Polling organizations that frequently measure aspects of political culture:
www.roper.com
www.gallup.com
U.S. Census Bureau: **www.census.gov**

SUGGESTED READINGS

Almond, Gabriel, and Sidney Verba. *The Civic Culture.* Princeton, N.J.: Princeton University Press, 1963. A survey of the political cultures of five nations—the United States, Germany, Great Britain, Italy, and Mexico—as they were in 1959.

Fiorina, Morris. *Culture War? The Myth of a Polarized America.* New York: Pearson Longman, 2004. Argues that Americans are not deeply polarized in their political views.

Hartz, Louis. *The Liberal Tradition in America.* New York: Harcourt Brace Jovanovich, 1955. A stimulating interpretation of American political thought since the Founding, emphasizing the notion of a liberal consensus.

Lipset, Seymour Martin. *The First New Nation.* Rev. ed. New York: Norton, 1979. How the origins of American society gave rise to the partially competing values of equality and achievement and the ways in which these values shape political institutions.

McClosky, Herbert, and Alida Brill. *Dimensions of Tolerance: What Americans Believe About Civil Liberties.* New York: Russell Sage Foundation, 1983. How—and whether—different kinds of Americans learn political tolerance.

McClosky, Herbert, and John Zaller. *The American Ethos: Public Attitudes Toward Capitalism and Democracy.* Cambridge: Harvard University Press, 1984. Study of the ways in which Americans evaluate political and economic arrangements.

Nye, Joseph S., Philip D. Zelikow, and David C. King. *Why People Don't Trust Government.* Cambridge: Harvard University Press, 1997. An effort to explain distrust.

Putnam, Robert D. *Bowling Alone: The Collapse and Revival of American Community.* New York: Simon & Schuster, 2000. An important argument that American political culture has been harmed by the decline in membership in organizations that bring people together for communal activities.

Tocqueville, Alexis de. *Democracy in America.* Edited by Phillips Bradley. 2 vols. New York: Knopf, 1951. First published in 1835–1840, this was and remains the greatest single interpretation of American political culture.

Verba, Sidney, and Gary R. Orren. *Equality in America: The View from the Top.* Cambridge: Harvard University Press, 1985. Elite views on political and economic equality.

Civil Liberties

Culture and Civil Liberties

Rights in Conflict ● Cultural Conflicts
● Applying the Bill of Rights to
the States

**Interpreting and Applying the First
Amendment**

Speech and National Security

What Is Speech?

Libel ● Obscenity ● Symbolic Speech

Who Is a Person?

Church and State

The Free-Exercise Clause ●
The Establishment Clause

Crime and Due Process

The Exclusionary Rule ● Search
and Seizure ● Confessions and
Self-Incrimination ● Relaxing the
Exclusionary Rule ● Terrorism and
Civil Liberties

WHO GOVERNS?

1. Why do the courts play so large a role in deciding what our civil liberties should be?

TO WHAT ENDS?

1. Why not display religious symbols on government property?
2. If a person confesses to committing a crime, why is that confession sometimes not used in court?
3. Does the Patriot Act reduce our liberties?

Dogs trained to sniff out drugs go down your high school corridors and detect marijuana in some lockers. The school authorities open and search your locker without permission or a court order. You are expelled from school without any hearing. Have your liberties been violated?

Angry at what you consider unfair treatment, you decide to wear a cloth American flag sewn to the seat of your pants, and your fellow students decide to wear black armbands to class to protest how you were treated. The police arrest you for wearing a flag on your seat, and the school punishes your classmates for wearing armbands contrary to school regulations. Have your liberties, or theirs, been violated?

You go into federal court to find out. We cannot be certain how the court would decide the issues in this particular case, but in similar cases in the past the courts have held that school authorities can use dogs to detect drugs in schools and that these officials can conduct a "reasonable" search of you and your effects if they have a "reasonable suspicion" that you are violating a school rule. But they cannot punish your classmates for wearing black armbands, they cannot expel you without a hearing, and the state cannot make it illegal to treat the flag "contemptuously" (by sewing it to the seat of your pants, for example).[1]

Your claim that these actions violated your constitutional rights would have astonished the Framers of the Constitution. They thought that they had written a document that stated what the federal government *could* do, not one that specified what state governments (such as school systems) *could not* do. And they thought that they had created a national government of such limited powers that it was not even necessary to add a list—a bill of rights—stating what that government was forbidden from doing. It would be enough, for example, that the Constitution did not authorize the federal government to censor newspapers; an amendment prohibiting censorship would be superfluous.

The people who gathered in the state ratifying conventions weren't so optimistic. They suspected—rightly, as it turned out—that the federal government might well try to do things that it was not authorized to do, and so they insisted that the Bill of Rights be added to the Constitution. But even they never imagined that the Bill of Rights would affect what *state* governments could do. Each state would decide that for itself, in its own constitution. And if by chance the Bill of Rights did apply to the states, surely its guarantees of free speech and freedom from unreasonable searches and seizures would apply to big issues—the freedom to attack the government in a newspaper editorial, for example, or to keep the police from breaking down the door of your home without a warrant. The courts would not be deciding who could wear what kinds of armbands or under what circumstances a school could expel a student.

Civil liberties are the protections the Constitution provides against the abuse of government power by, for example, censoring your speech. Civil rights, to be discussed in the next chapter, usually refers to protecting certain groups, such as women, gays, and African Americans, against discrimination. In practice, however, there is no clear line between civil liberties and civil rights. For example, is the right to an abortion a civil liberty or a civil right? In this chapter, we take a look at free speech, free press, religious freedom, and the rights of the accused. In the next one we look at discrimination and abortion.

☆ Culture and Civil Liberties

Rights in Conflict

We often think of "civil liberties" as a set of principles that protect the freedoms of all of us all of the time. That is true—up to a point. But in fact the Constitution and the Bill of Rights contain a list of *competing* rights and duties. That competition becomes obvious when one person asserts one constitutional right or duty and another person asserts a different one. For example:

- Dr. Samuel H. Sheppard of Cleveland, Ohio, asserted his right to have a fair trial on the charge of having murdered his wife. Bob Considine and Walter Winchell, two radio commentators, as well as other reporters, asserted their right to broadcast whatever facts and rumors they heard about Dr. Sheppard and his love life. Two rights in conflict.
- The U.S. government has an obligation to "provide for the common defense" and, in pursuit of that duty, has claimed the right to keep secret certain military and diplomatic information. The *New York Times* claimed the right to publish such secrets as the "Pentagon Papers" without censorship, citing the Constitution's guarantee of freedom of the press. A duty and a right in conflict.
- Carl Jacob Kunz delivered inflammatory anti-Jewish speeches on the street corners of a Jewish neighborhood in New York City, suggesting,

among other things, that Jews be "burnt in incinerators." The Jewish people living in that area were outraged. The New York police commissioner revoked Kunz's license to hold public meetings on the streets. When he continued to air his views on the public streets, Kunz was arrested for speaking without a permit. Freedom of speech versus the preservation of public order.

Even a disruptive high school student's right not to be a victim of arbitrary or unjustifiable expulsion is in partial conflict with the school's obligation to maintain an orderly environment in which learning can take place.

Political struggles over civil liberties follow much the same pattern as interest group politics involving economic issues, even though the claims in question are made by individuals. Indeed, there are formal, organized interest groups concerned with civil liberties. The Fraternal Order of the Police complains about restrictions on police powers, whereas the American Civil Liberties Union defends and seeks to enlarge those restrictions. Catholics have pressed for public support of parochial schools; Protestants and Jews have argued against it. Sometimes the opposed groups are entirely private; sometimes one or both are government agencies. Often their clashes end up in the courts. (When the Supreme Court decided the cases given earlier, Sheppard, the *New York Times*, and Kunz all won.[2])

A 1919 cartoon expresses popular fears of "Reds" (that is, leftist radicals) threatening American institutions.

War has usually been the crisis that has restricted the liberty of some minority. For example:

- The Sedition Act was passed in 1798, making it a crime to write, utter, or publish "any false, scandalous, and malicious writing" with the intention of defaming the president, Congress, or the government or of exciting against the government "the hatred of the people." The occasion was a kind of half-war between the United States and France, stimulated by fear in this country of the violence following the French Revolution of 1789. The policy entrepreneurs were Federalist politicians who believed that Thomas Jefferson and his followers were supporters of the French Revolution and would, if they came to power, encourage here the kind of anarchy that seemed to be occurring in France.

- The Espionage and Sedition Acts were passed in 1917–1918, making it a crime to utter false statements that would interfere with the American military, to send through the mails material "advocating or urging treason, insurrection, or forcible resistance to any law of the United States," or to utter or write any disloyal, profane, scurrilous, or abusive language intended to incite resistance to the United States or to curtail war production. The occasion was World War I; the impetus was the fear that Germans in this country were spies and that radicals were seeking to overthrow the government. Under these laws more than two thousand persons were prosecuted (about half were convicted), and thousands of aliens were rounded up and deported. The policy entrepreneur leading this massive crackdown (the so-called Red Scare) was Attorney General A. Mitchell Palmer.

- The Smith Act was passed in 1940, the Internal Security Act in 1950, and the Communist Control Act in 1954. These laws made it illegal to advocate the overthrow of the U.S. government by force or violence (Smith Act), required members of the Communist Party to register with the government (Internal Security Act), and declared the Communist Party to be part of a conspiracy to overthrow the government (Communist Control Act). The occasion was World War II and the Korean War, which, like earlier wars, inspired fears that foreign agents (Nazi and Soviet) were trying to subvert the government. For the latter two laws the policy entrepreneur was Senator Joseph McCarthy, who attracted a great deal of attention with his repeated (and sometimes inaccurate) claims that Soviet agents were working inside the U.S. government.

These laws had in common an effort to protect the nation from threats, real and imagined, posed by people who claimed to be exercising their freedom to speak, publish, organize, and assemble. In each case a real threat (a war) led the government to narrow the limits of permissible speech and activity. Almost every time such restrictions were imposed, the Supreme Court was called upon to decide whether Congress (or sometimes state legislatures) had drawn those limits properly. In most instances the Court tended to uphold the legislatures. But as time passed and the war or crisis ended, popular passions abated and many of the laws proved to be unimportant.

Though it is uncommon, some use is still made of the sedition laws. In the 1980s various white supremacists and Puerto Rican nationalists were charged with sedition. In each case the government alleged that the accused had not only spoken in favor of overthrowing the government but had actually engaged in violent actions such as bombings. Later in this chapter we shall see how the Court has increasingly restricted the power of Congress and state legislatures to outlaw political speech; to be found guilty of sedition now it is usually necessary to do something more serious than just talk about it.

Cultural Conflicts

In the main the United States was originally the creation of white European Protestants. Blacks were, in most cases, slaves, and American Indians were not citizens. Catholics and Jews in the colonies composed a small minority, and often a persecuted one. The early schools tended to be religious—that is, Protestant—ones, many of them receiving state aid. It is not surprising that under these circumstances a view of America arose that equated "Americanism" with the values and habits of white Anglo-Saxon Protestants.

But immigration to this country brought a flood of new settlers, many of them coming from very different backgrounds (see Figure 5.1). In the mid-nineteenth century the potato famine led millions of Irish Catholics to migrate here. At the turn of the century religious persecution and economic disadvantage brought more millions of people, many Catholic or Jewish, from southern and eastern Europe.

In recent decades political conflict and economic want have led Hispanics (mostly from Mexico but increasingly from all parts of Latin America),

Figure 5.1 Annual Immigration, 1840–1996

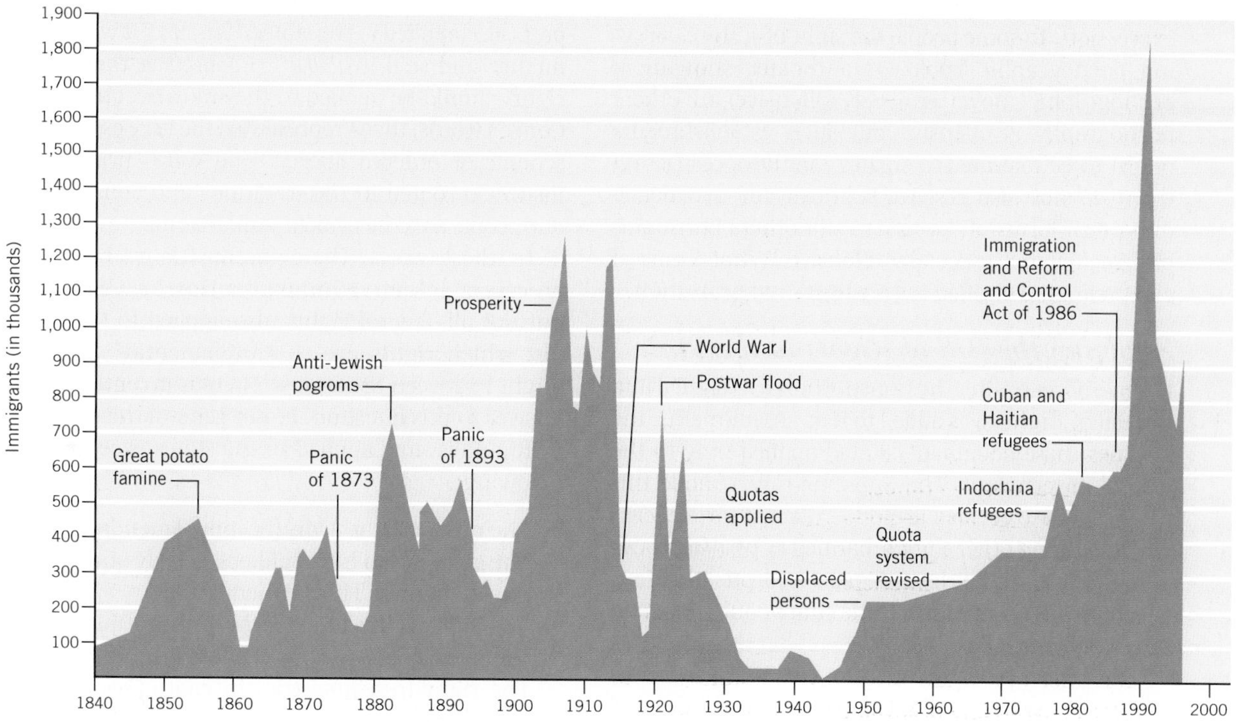

Note: Figures for 1989 and 1990 include persons who were granted permanent residence under the legalization program of the Immigration and Reform and Control Act of 1986.
Source: Statistical Abstract of the United States, 1998, 10.

Caribbeans, Africans, Middle Easterners, Southeast Asians, and Asians to cross our borders—some legally, some illegally. Among them have been Buddhists, Catholics, Muslims, and members of many other religious and cultural groups.

Ethnic, religious, and cultural differences have given rise to different views as to the meaning and scope of certain constitutionally protected freedoms. For example:

- Many Jewish groups find it offensive for a crèche (that is, a scene depicting the birth of Christ in a manger) to be displayed in front of a government building such as city hall at Christmastime, while many Catholics and Protestants regard such displays as an important part of our cultural heritage. Does a religious display on public property violate the First Amendment requirement that the government pass no law "respecting an establishment of religion"?

- Many English-speaking people believe that the public schools ought to teach all students to speak and write English, because the language is part of our nation's cultural heritage. Some Hispanic groups argue that the schools should teach pupils in both English and Spanish, since Spanish is part of the Hispanic cultural heritage. Is bilingual education constitutionally required?

- The Boy Scouts of America refuses to allow homosexual men to become scout leaders even though federal law says that homosexuals may not be the victims of discrimination. Many civil libertarians and homosexuals challenged this policy because it discriminated against gays, while the Boy Scouts defended it because their organization was a private association free to make its own rules. (The Supreme Court in 2000 upheld the Boy Scouts on the grounds of their right to associate freely.)

Even within a given cultural tradition there are important differences of opinion as to the balance between community sensitivities and personal self-expression. To some people the sight of a store carrying pornographic books or a theater showing a pornographic movie is deeply offensive; to others pornography is offensive but such establishments ought to be tolerated to ensure that laws restricting them do not also restrict politically or artistically important forms of speech; to still others pornography itself is not especially offensive. What forms of expression are entitled to constitutional protection?

Applying the Bill of Rights to the States

For many years after the Constitution was signed and the Bill of Rights was added to it as amendments, the liberties these documents stated applied only to the federal government. The Supreme Court made this clear in a case decided in 1833.[3] Except for Article I which, among other things, banned *ex post facto* laws and guaranteed the right of habeas corpus, the Constitution was silent on what the states could not do to their residents.

This began to change after the Civil War when new amendments were ratified in order to ban slavery and protect newly freed slaves. The Fourteenth Amendment, ratified in 1868, was the most important addition. It said that no state shall "deprive any person of life, liberty, or property without **due process of law**" (a phrase now known as the "due process clause") and that no state shall "deny to any person within its jurisdiction the **equal protection of the laws**" (a phrase now known as the "equal protection clause").

Beginning in 1897, the Supreme Court started to use these two phrases as a way of applying certain rights to state governments. It first said that no state

could take private property without paying just compensation, and then in 1925 held, in the *Gitlow* case that the federal guarantees of free speech and free press also applied to the states.[4] In 1937 it went much further and said in *Palko v. Connecticut* that certain rights should be applied to the states because, in the Court's words, they "represented the very essence of a scheme of ordered liberty" and were "principles of justice so rooted in the traditions and conscience of our people as to be ranked fundamental."[5]

In these cases, the Supreme Court began the process of **selective incorporation** by which some, but not all, federal rights also applied to the states. But which rights are so "fundamental" that they ought to govern the states? There is no entirely clear answer to this question, but in general the entire Bill of Rights is now applied to the states except for the following:

- The right to bear arms (Second Amendment)
- The right not to have soldiers forcibly quartered in private homes (Third Amendment)
- The right to be indicted by a grand jury before being tried for a serious crime (Fifth Amendment)
- The right to a jury trial in civil cases (Seventh Amendment)
- The ban on excessive bail and fines (Eighth Amendment)

And as we shall see, when the Court creates a new right, such as the right to "privacy," the justices have applied it to both state and national governments.

☆ Interpreting and Applying the First Amendment

The First Amendment contains the language that has been at issue in most of the cases to which we have thus far referred. It has roughly two parts: one protecting **freedom of expression** ("Congress shall make no law . . . abridging the freedom of speech, or of the press, or the right of people peaceably to assemble, and to petition the government for a redress of grievances") and the other protecting **freedom of religion** ("Congress shall make no law respecting an establishment of religion; or abridging the free exercise thereof").

Speech and National Security

The traditional view of free speech and a free press was expressed by William Blackstone, the great Eng-

due process of law   Denies the government the right, without due process, to deprive people of life, liberty, and property.

equal protection of the law   A standard of equal treatment that must be observed by the government.

selective incorporation   Court cases that apply Bill of Rights to states.

freedom of expression   Right of people to speak, publish, and assemble.

freedom of religion   People shall be free to exercise their religion, and government may not establish a religion.

LANDMARK CASES

Incorporation

- *Gitlow v. New York* **(1925)**: Supreme Court says the First Amendment applies to states.
- *Palko v. Connecticut* **(1937)**: Supreme Court says that states must observe all "fundamental" liberties.

lish jurist, in his *Commentaries*, published in 1765. A free press is essential to a free state, he wrote, but the freedom that the press should enjoy is the freedom from **prior restraint**—that is, freedom from censorship, or rules telling a newspaper in advance what it can publish. Once a newspaper has published an article or a person has delivered a speech, that paper or speaker has to take the consequences if what was written or said proves to be "improper, mischievous, or illegal."[6]

The U.S. Sedition Act of 1798 was in keeping with traditional English law. Like it, the act imposed no prior restraint on publishers; it did, however, make them liable to punishment after the fact. The act was an improvement over the English law, however, because unlike the British model, it entrusted the decision to a jury, not a judge, and allowed the defendant to be acquitted if he or she could prove the truth of what had been published. Although several newspaper publishers were convicted under the act, none of these cases reached the Supreme Court. When Jefferson became president in 1801, he pardoned everyone who had been convicted under the Sedition Act. Though Jeffersonians objected vehemently to the law, their principal objection was not to the idea of holding newspapers accountable for what they published but to letting the *federal* government do this. Jefferson was perfectly prepared to have the *states* punish what he called the "overwhelming torrent of slander" by means of "a few prosecutions of the most prominent offenders."[7]

It would be another century before the federal government would attempt to define the limits of free speech and writing. Perhaps recalling the widespread opposition to the sweep of the 1798 act, Congress in 1917–1918 placed restrictions not on publications that were critical of the government but only on those that advocated "treason, insurrection, or forcible resistance" to federal laws or attempted to foment disloyalty or mutiny in the armed services.

In 1919 this new law was examined by the Supreme Court when it heard the case of Charles T. Schenck, who had been convicted of violating the Espionage Act because he had mailed circulars to men eligible for the draft, urging them to resist. At issue was the constitutionality of the Espionage Act and, more broadly, the scope of Congress's power to control speech. One view held that the First Amendment prevented Congress from passing *any* law restricting speech; the other held that Congress could punish dangerous speech. For a unanimous Supreme Court, Justice Oliver Wendell Holmes announced a rule by which to settle the matter. It soon became known as the **clear-and-present-danger test:**

> The question in every case is whether the words used are used in such circumstances and are of such a nature as to create a clear and present danger that they will bring about the substantive evils that Congress has a right to prevent.[8]

The Court held that Schenck's leaflets did create such a danger, and so his conviction was upheld. In explaining why, Holmes said that not even the Constitution protects a person who has been "falsely shouting fire in a theatre and causing a panic." In this case things that might safely be said in peacetime may be punished in wartime.

---

prior restraint   Censorship of a publication.
clear-and-present-danger test   Law should not punish speech unless there was a clear and present danger of producing harmful actions.

Women picketed in front of the White House, urging President Warren Harding to release political radicals arrested during his administration.

The clear-and-present-danger test may have clarified the law, but it kept no one out of jail. Schenck went, and so did the defendants in five other cases in the period 1919–1927, even though during this time Holmes, the author of the test, shifted his position and began writing dissenting opinions in which he urged that the test had not been met and so the defendant should go free.

In 1925 Benjamin Gitlow was convicted of violating New York's sedition law—a law similar to the federal Sedition Act of 1918—by passing out some leaflets. The Supreme Court upheld his conviction but added, as we have seen, a statement that changed constitutional history: freedom of speech and of the press were now among the "fundamental personal rights" protected by the due-process clause of the Fourteenth Amendment from infringements by *state* action.[9] Thereafter state laws involving speech, the press, and peaceful assembly were struck down by the Supreme Court for being in violation of the freedom-of-expression guarantees of the First Amendment, made applicable to the states by the Fourteenth Amendment.[10]

The clear-and-present-danger test was a way of balancing the competing demands of free expression

and national security. As the memory of World War I and the ensuing Red Scare evaporated, the Court began to develop other tests, ones that shifted the balance more toward free expression. Some of these tests are listed in the box on page 107.

But when a crisis reappears, as it did in World War II and the Korean conflict, the Court has tended to defer, up to a point, to legislative judgments about the need to protect national security. For example, it upheld the conviction of eleven leaders of the Communist Party for having advocated the violent overthrow of the U.S. government, a violation of the Smith Act of 1940.

This conviction once again raised the hard question of the circumstances under which words can be punished. Hardly anybody would deny that actually *trying* to overthrow the government is a crime; the question is whether *advocating* its overthrow is a crime. In the case of the eleven communist leaders, the Court said that the government did not have to wait to protect itself until "the *putsch* [rebellion] is about to be executed, the plans have been laid and the signal is awaited." Even if the communists were not likely to be successful in their effort, the Court held that specifically advocating violent overthrow could be punished. "In each case," the opinion read, the courts "must ask whether the gravity of the 'evil,' discounted by its improbability, justifies such invasion of free speech as is necessary to avoid the danger."[11]

But as the popular worries about communists began to subside and the membership of the Supreme Court changed, the Court began to tip the balance even farther toward free expression. By 1957 the Court made it clear that for advocacy to be punished, the government would have to show not just that a person believed in the overthrow of the government but also that he or she was using words "calculated to incite" that overthrow.[12]

By 1969 the pendulum had swung to the point where the speech would have to be judged likely to incite "imminent" unlawful action. In this case Clarence Brandenburg, a leader of the Ku Klux Klan in Ohio, staged a cross-burning rally during which he reviled blacks and Jews. The police told him to clear the street; as he left, he said, "We'll take the [expletive] street later." He was convicted of attempting to incite lawless mob action. The Supreme Court overturned the conviction, holding that any speech that does not call for illegal action is protected, and even speech that *does* call for illegal action is protected if the action is not "imminent" or there is reason to believe that the listeners will not take action.[13]

This means that no matter how offensive or provocative some forms of expression may be, this expression has powerful constitutional protections. In 1977 a group of American Nazis wanted to parade through the streets of Skokie, Illinois, a community with a large Jewish population. The residents, outraged, sought to ban the march. Many feared violence if it occurred. But the lower courts, under prodding from the Supreme Court, held that, noxious and provocative as the anti-Semitic slogans of the Nazis may be, the Nazi party had a constitutional right to speak and parade peacefully.[14]

Similar reasoning led the Supreme Court in 1992 to overturn a Minnesota statute that made it a crime to display symbols or objects, such as a Nazi swastika or a burning cross, that are likely to cause alarm or resentment among an ethnic or racial group, such as Jews or African Americans.[15] On the other hand, if you are convicted of actually hurting someone, you may be given a tougher sentence if it can be shown that you were motivated to assault them by racial or ethnic hatred.[16] To be punished for such a hate crime, your bigotry must result in some direct and physical harm and not just the display of an odious symbol.

☆ What Is Speech?

If most political speaking or writing is permissible, save that which actually incites someone to take illegal actions, what *kinds* of speaking and writing qualify for this broad protection? Though the Constitution says that the legislature may make "no law" abridging freedom of speech or the press, and although some justices have argued that this means literally *no* law, the Court has held that there are at least four forms of speaking and writing that are not automatically granted full constitutional protection: libel, obscenity, symbolic speech, and false advertising.

Libel

A **libel** is a written statement that defames the character of another person. (If the statement is oral, it is called a slander.) In some countries, such as England, it is easy to sue another person for libel and to collect. In this country it is much harder. For one thing, you must show that the libelous statement was false. If it

A Ku Klux Klan member uses his constitutional right to free speech to utter "white power" chants in Skokie, Illinois.

was true, you cannot collect no matter how badly it harmed you.

A beauty contest winner was awarded $14 million (later reduced on appeal) when she proved that *Penthouse* magazine had libeled her. The actress Carol Burnett collected a large sum from a libel suit brought against a gossip newspaper. But when Theodore Roosevelt sued a newspaper for falsely claiming that he was a drunk, the jury awarded him damages of only six cents.[17]

If you are a public figure, it is much harder to win a libel suit. A public figure such as an elected official, an army general, or a well-known celebrity must prove not only that the publication was false and damaging but also that the words were published with "actual malice"—that is, with reckless disregard for their truth or falsity or with knowledge that they were false.[18] General Ariel Sharon was able to prove that the statements made about him by *Time* magazine were false and damaging but not that they were the result of "actual malice."

Obscenity

Obscenity is not protected by the First Amendment. The Court has always held that obscene materials, because they have no redeeming social value and are

---

libel   Writing that falsely injures another person.

calculated chiefly to appeal to one's sexual rather than political or literary interests, can be regulated by the state. The problem, of course, arises with the meaning of *obscene*. In the eleven-year period from 1957 to 1968 the Court decided thirteen major cases involving the definition of obscenity, which resulted in fifty-five separate opinions.[19] Some justices, such as Hugo Black, believed that the First Amendment protected all publications, even wholly obscene ones. Others believed that obscenity deserved no protection and struggled heroically to define the term. Still others shared the view of former Justice Potter Stewart, who objected to "hard-core pornography" but admitted that the best definition he could offer was "I know it when I see it."[20]

It is unnecessary to review in detail the many attempts by the Court at defining obscenity. The justices have made it clear that nudity and sex are not, by definition, obscene and that they will provide First Amendment protection to anything that has political, literary, or artistic merit, allowing the government to punish only the distribution of "hard-core pornography." Their most recent definition of this is as follows: to be obscene, the work, taken as a whole, must be judged by "the average person applying contemporary community standards" to appeal to the "prurient interest" or to depict "in a patently offensive way, sexual conduct specifically defined by applicable state law" and to lack "serious literary, artistic, political, or scientific value."[21]

After Albany, Georgia, decided that the movie *Carnal Knowledge* was obscene by contemporary local standards, the Supreme Court overturned the distributor's conviction on the grounds that the authorities in Albany failed to show that the film depicted "patently offensive hard-core sexual conduct."[22]

It is easy to make sport of the problems the Court has faced in trying to decide obscenity cases (one conjures up images of black-robed justices leafing through the pages of *Hustler* magazine, taking notes), but these problems reveal, as do other civil liberties cases, the continuing problem of balancing competing claims. One part of the community wants to read or see whatever it wishes; another part wants to protect private acts from public degradation. The first part cherishes liberty above all; the second values decency above liberty. The former fears that *any* restriction on literature will lead to *pervasive* restrictions; the latter believes that reasonable people can distinguish (or reasonable laws can require them to

distinguish) between patently offensive and artistically serious work.

Anyone strolling today through an "adult" bookstore must suppose that no restrictions at all exist on the distribution of pornographic works. This condition does not arise simply from the doctrines of the Court. Other factors operate as well, including the priorities of local law enforcement officials, the political climate of the community, the procedures that must be followed to bring a viable court case, the clarity and workability of state and local laws on the subject, and the difficulty of changing the behavior of many people by prosecuting one person. The current view of the Court is that localities can decide for themselves whether to tolerate hard-core pornography; but if they choose not to, they must meet some fairly strict constitutional tests.

The protections given by the Court to expressions of sexual or erotic interest have not been limited to books, magazines, or films. Almost any form of visual or auditory communication can be considered "speech" and thus protected by the First Amendment. In one case even nude dancing was given protection as a form of "speech,"[23] although in 1991 the Court held that nude dancing was only "marginally" within the purview of First Amendment protections, and so it upheld an Indiana statute that banned *totally* nude dancing.[24]

Of late some feminist organizations have attacked pornography on the grounds that it exploits and degrades women. They persuaded Indianapolis to pass an ordinance that defined pornography as portrayals of the "graphic, sexually explicit subordination of women" and allowed people to sue the producers of such material. Sexually explicit portrayals of women in positions of equality were not defined as pornography. The Court disagreed. In 1986 it affirmed a lower-court ruling that such an ordinance was a violation of the First Amendment because it represented a legislative preference for one form of expression (women in positions of equality) over another (women in positions of subordination).[25]

One constitutionally permissible way to limit the spread of pornographic materials has been to establish rules governing where in a city they can be sold. When one city adopted a zoning ordinance prohibiting an "adult" movie theater from locating within one thousand feet of any church, school, park, or residential area, the Court upheld the ordinance, noting that the purpose of the law was not to regu-

HOW THINGS WORK

Testing Restrictions on Expression

The Supreme Court has employed various standards and tests to decide whether a restriction on freedom of expression is constitutionally permissible.

1. **Preferred position** The right of free expression, though not absolute, occupies a higher, or more preferred, position than many other constitutional rights, such as property rights. This is still a controversial rule; nonetheless, the Court always approaches a restriction on expression skeptically.
2. **Prior restraint** With scarcely any exceptions, the Court will not tolerate a prior restraint on expression, such as censorship, even when it will allow subsequent punishment of improper expressions (such as libel).
3. **Imminent danger** Punishment for uttering inflammatory sentiments will be allowed only if there is an imminent danger that the utterances will incite an unlawful act.
4. **Neutrality** Any restriction on speech, such as a requirement that parades or demonstrations not disrupt other people in the exercise of their rights, must be neutral—that is, it must not favor one group more than another.
5. **Clarity** If you must obtain a permit to hold a parade, the law must set forth clear (as well as neutral) standards to guide administrators in issuing that permit. Similarly, a law punishing obscenity must contain a clear definition of obscenity.
6. **Least-restrictive means** If it is necessary to restrict the exercise of one right to protect the exercise of another, the restriction should employ the least-restrictive means to achieve its end. For example, if press coverage threatens a person's right to a fair trial, the judge may only do what is minimally necessary to that end, such as transferring the case to another town rather than issuing a "gag order."

Cases cited, by item: (1) *United States v. Carolene Products,* 304 U.S. 144 (1938). (2) *Near v. Minnesota,* 283 U.S. 697 (1931). (3) *Brandenburg v. Ohio,* 395 U.S. 444 (1969). (4) *Kunz v. New York,* 340 U.S. 290 (1951). (5) *Hynes v. Mayor and Council of Oradell,* 425 U.S. 610 (1976). (6) *Nebraska Press Association v. Stuart,* 427 U.S. 539 (1976).

late speech but to regulate the use of land. And in any case the adult theaters still had much of the city's land area in which to find a location.[26]

With the advent of the Internet it has become more difficult for the government to regulate obscenity. The Internet spans the globe. It offers an amazing variety of materials—some educational, some entertaining, some sexually explicit. But it is difficult to apply the Supreme Court's standard for judging whether sexual material is obscene—the "average person" applying "contemporary community standards"—to the Internet, because there is no easy way to tell what "the community" is. Is it the place where the recipient lives or the place where the material originates? And since no one is in charge of the Internet, who can be held responsible for controlling offensive material? Since anybody can send anything to anybody else without knowing the age or location of the recipient, how can the Internet protect children? When Congress tried to ban obscene, indecent, or "patently offensive" materials from the Internet, the Supreme Court struck down the law as unconstitutional. The Court went even further with child pornography. Though it has long held that child pornography is illegal even if it is not obscene because of the government's interest in protecting children, it would not let Congress ban pornography involving computer-designed children. Under the 1996 law, it would be illegal to display computer simulations of children engaged in sex even if no real children were involved. The Court said "no." It held that Congress could not ban "virtual" child pornography without violating the First Amendment because, in its view, the law might bar even harmless depictions of children and sex (for example, in a book on child psychology).[27]

"Symbolic speech": when young men burned their draft cards during the 1960s to protest the Vietnam War, the Supreme Court ruled that it was an illegal act for which they could be punished.

Symbolic Speech

You cannot ordinarily claim that an illegal act should be protected because that action is meant to convey a political message. For example, if you burn your draft card in protest against the foreign policy of the United States, you can be punished for the illegal act (burning the card), even if your intent was to communicate your beliefs. The Court reasoned that giving such **symbolic speech** the same protection as real speech would open the door to permitting all manner of illegal actions—murder, arson, rape—if the perpetrator meant thereby to send a message.[28]

On the other hand, a statute that makes it illegal to burn the American flag is an unconstitutional infringement of free speech.[29] Why is there a difference between a draft card and the flag? The Court argues that the government has a right to run a military draft and so can protect draft cards, even if this incidentally restricts speech. But the only motive that the government has in banning flag-burning is to restrict this form of speech, and that would make such a restriction improper.

The American people were outraged by the flag-burning decision, and in response the House and Senate passed by huge majorities (380 to 38 and 91 to 9) a law making it a federal crime to burn the flag.

---

symbolic speech   An act that conveys a political message.

But the Court struck this law down as unconstitutional.[30] Now that it was clear that only a constitutional amendment could make flag-burning illegal, Congress was asked to propose one. But it would not. Earlier members of the House and Senate had supported a law banning flag-burning with over 90 percent of their votes, but when asked to make that law a constitutional amendment they could not muster the necessary two-thirds majorities. The reason is that Congress is much more reluctant to amend the Constitution than to pass new laws. Several members decided that flag-burning was wrong, but not so wrong or so common as to justify an amendment.

☆ Who Is a Person?

If people have a right to speak and publish, do corporations, interest groups, and children have the same right? By and large the answer is yes, though there are some exceptions.

When the attorney general of Massachusetts tried to prevent the First National Bank of Boston from spending money to influence votes in a local election, the Court stepped in and blocked him. The Court held that a corporation, like a person, has certain First Amendment rights. Similarly, when the federal government tried to limit the spending of a group called Massachusetts Citizens for Life (an antiabortion organization), the Court held that such organizations have First Amendment rights.[31] The Court has also told states that they cannot forbid liquor stores to advertise their prices and informed federal authorities that they cannot prohibit casinos from plugging gambling.[32]

When the California Public Utility Commission tried to compel one of the utilities that it regulates, the Pacific Gas and Electric Company, to enclose in its monthly bills to customers statements written by groups attacking the utility, the Supreme Court blocked the agency, saying that forcing it to disseminate political statements violated the firm's free speech rights. "The identity of the speaker is not decisive in determining whether speech is protected," the Court said. "Corporations and other associations, like individuals, contribute to the 'discussion, debate, and the dissemination of information and ideas' that the First Amendment seeks to foster." In this case the right to speak includes the choice of what *not* to say.[33]

Even though corporations have some First Amendment rights, the government can place more

LANDMARK CASES

Free Speech and Free Press

- *Chaplinksy v. New Hampshire* (1942): "Fighting words" are not protected by the First Amendment.

- *Collin v. Smith* (1978): The Nazi Party may march through a largely Jewish neighborhood.

- *McConnell v. Federal Election Commission* (2003): Upholds 2002 campaign finance reform law.

- *Miller v. California* (1973): Obscenity defined as appealing to prurient interests of an average person with materials that lack literary, artistic, political, or scientific value.

- *New York Times v. Sullivan* (1964): To libel a public figure, there must be "actual malice."

- *Reno v. ACLU* (1997): A law that bans sending "indecent" material to minors over the Internet is unconstitutional because "indecent" is too vague and broad a term.

- *Schenck v. United States* (1919): Speech may be punished if it creates a clear-and-present-danger test of illegal acts.

- *Texas v. Johnson* (1989): There may not be a law to ban flag-burning.

limits on commercial than on noncommercial speech. The legislature can place restrictions on advertisements for cigarettes, liquor, and gambling; it can even regulate advertising for some less harmful products provided that the regulations are narrowly tailored and serve a substantial public interest.[34] If the regulations are too broad or do not serve a clear interest, then ads are entitled to some constitutional protection. For example, the states cannot bar lawyers from advertising or accountants from personally soliciting clients.[35]

A big exception to the free-speech rights of corporations and labor unions groups was imposed by the McCain-Feingold campaign finance reform law passed in 2002. Many groups, ranging from the American Civil Liberties Union and the AFL-CIO to the National Rifle Association and the Chamber of Commerce, felt that the law banned legitimate speech. Under its terms, organizations could not pay for "electioneering communications" on radio or television that "refer" to candidate for federal office within sixty days before the election. But the Supreme Court struck down these arguments, upholding the law in *McConnell v. Federal Election Commission*. The Court said that ads that only mentioned but did not "expressly advocate" a candidate

were ways of influencing the election. Some dissenting opinion complained that a Court that had once given free speech protection to nude dancing ought to give it to political speech.[36] In Chapter 11 we shall look at this issue more closely.

Under certain circumstances, young people may have less freedom of expression than adults. In 1988 the Supreme Court held that the principal of Hazelwood High School could censor articles appearing in the student-edited newspaper. The newspaper was published using school funds and was part of a journalism class. The principal ordered the deletion of stories dealing with student pregnancies and the impact of parental divorce on students. The student editors sued, claiming their First Amendment rights had been violated. The Court agreed that students do not "shed their constitutional rights to freedom of speech or expression at the schoolhouse gate" and that they cannot be punished for expressing on campus their personal views. But students do not have exactly the same rights as adults if the exercise of those rights impedes the educational mission of the school. Students may lawfully say things on campus, as individuals, that they cannot say if they are part of school-sponsored activities, such as plays or school-run newspapers, that are part of the curriculum.

School-sponsored activities can be controlled so long as the controls are "reasonably related to legitimate pedagogical concerns."[37]

☆ Church and State

Everybody knows, correctly, the language of the First Amendment that protects freedom of speech and the press, though most people are not aware of how complex the legal interpretations of these provisions have become. But many people also believe, wrongly, that the language of the First Amendment clearly requires the "separation of church and state." It does not.

What that amendment actually says is quite different and maddeningly unclear. It has two parts. The first, often referred to as the **free-exercise clause,** states that Congress shall make no law prohibiting the "free exercise" of religion. The second, which is called the **establishment clause,** states that Congress shall make no law "respecting an establishment of religion."

The Free-Exercise Clause

The free-exercise clause is the clearer of the two, though by no means is it lacking in ambiguity. It obviously means that Congress cannot pass a law prohibiting Catholics from celebrating Mass, requiring Baptists to become Episcopalians, or preventing Jews from holding a bar mitzvah. Since the First Amendment has been applied to the states via the due-process clause of the Fourteenth Amendment, it means that state governments cannot pass such laws either. In general the courts have treated religion like speech: you can pretty much do or say what you want so long as it does not cause some serious harm to others.

Even some laws that do not appear on their face to apply to churches may be unconstitutional if their enforcement imposes particular burdens on churches or greater burdens on some churches than others. For example, a state cannot apply a license fee on

free-exercise clause   First Amendment requirement that law cannot prevent free exercise of religion.
establishment clause   First Amendment ban on laws "respecting an establishment of religion."

door-to-door solicitors when the solicitor is a Jehovah's Witness selling religious tracts.[38] By the same token, the courts ruled that the city of Hialeah, Florida, cannot ban animal sacrifices by members of an Afro-Caribbean religion called Santeria. Since killing animals is generally not illegal (if it were, there could be no hamburgers or chicken sandwiches served in Hialeah's restaurants, and rat traps would be unlawful), the ban in this case was clearly directed against a specific religion and hence was unconstitutional.[39]

Having the right to exercise your religion freely does not mean, however, that you are exempt from laws binding other citizens, even when the law goes against your religious beliefs. A man cannot have more than one wife, even if (as once was the case with Mormons) polygamy is thought desirable on religious grounds.[40] For religious reasons you may oppose being vaccinated or having blood transfusions, but if the state passes a compulsory vaccination law or orders that a blood transfusion be given to a sick child, the courts will not block them on grounds of religious liberty.[41] Similarly, if you belong to an Indian tribe that uses a drug, peyote, in religious ceremonies, you cannot claim that your freedom was abridged if the state decides to ban the use of peyote, provided the law applies equally to all.[42] Since airports have a legitimate need for tight security measures, begging can be outlawed in them even if some of the people doing the begging are part of a religious group (in this case, the Hare Krishnas).[43]

Unfortunately some conflicts between religious belief and public policy are even more difficult to settle. What if you believe on religious grounds that war is immoral? The draft laws have always exempted a conscientious objector from military duty, and the Court has upheld such exemptions. But the Court has gone further: it has said that people cannot be drafted even if they do not believe in a Supreme Being or belong to any religious tradition, so long as their "consciences, spurred by deeply held moral, ethical, or religious beliefs, would give them no rest or peace if they allowed themselves to become part of an instrument of war."[44] Do exemptions on such grounds create an opportunity for some people to evade the draft because of their political preferences? In trying to answer such questions, the courts often have had to try to define a religion—no easy task.

And even when there is no question about your membership in a bona fide religion, the circumstances under which you may claim exemption from laws that apply to everybody else are not really clear. What if you, a member of the Seventh-Day Adventists, are fired by your employer for refusing on religious grounds to work on Saturday, and then it turns out that you cannot collect unemployment insurance because you refuse to take an available job—one that also requires you to work on Saturday? Or what if you are a member of the Amish sect, which refuses, contrary to state law, to send its children to public schools past the eighth grade? The Court has ruled that the state must pay you unemployment compensation and cannot require you to send your children to public schools beyond the eighth grade.[45]

These last two decisions, and others like them, show that even the "simple" principle of freedom of religion gets complicated in practice and can lead to the courts' giving, in effect, preference to members of one church over members of another.

The Establishment Clause

What in the world did the members of the First Congress mean when they wrote into the First Amendment language prohibiting Congress from making a law "respecting" an "establishment" of religion? The Supreme Court has more or less consistently interpreted this vague phrase to mean that the Constitution erects a "wall of separation" between church and state.

That phrase, so often quoted, is not in the Bill of Rights nor in the debates in the First Congress that drafted the Bill of Rights; it comes from the pen of Thomas Jefferson, who was opposed to having the Church of England as the established church of his native Virginia. (At the time of the Revolutionary War there were established churches—that is, official, state-supported churches—in at least eight of the thirteen former colonies.) But it is not clear that Jefferson's view was the majority view.

During much of the debate in Congress the wording of this part of the First Amendment was quite different and much plainer than what finally emerged. Up to the last minute the clause was intended to read "no religion shall be established by law" or "no national religion shall be established." The meaning of those words seems quite clear: whatever the states may do, the federal government cannot create an official, national religion or give support to one religion in preference to another.[46]

But Congress instead adopted an ambiguous phrase, and so the Supreme Court had to decide what

Students pray in front of a high school in Virginia. The Supreme Court will not let this happen inside a public school.

it meant. It has declared that these words do not simply mean "no national religion" but mean as well no government involvement with religion at all, even on a nonpreferential basis. They mean, in short, erecting a "wall of separation" between church and state.[47] Though the interpretation of the establishment clause remains a topic of great controversy among judges and scholars, the Supreme Court has more or less consistently adopted this **wall-of-separation** principle.

Its first statement of this interpretation was in 1947. The case involved a New Jersey town that reimbursed parents for the costs of transporting their children to school, including parochial (in this case Catholic) schools. The Court decided that this reimbursement was constitutional, but it made it clear that the establishment clause of the First Amendment applied (via the Fourteenth Amendment) to the states and that it meant, among other things, that the government cannot require a person to profess a belief or disbelief in any religion; it cannot aid one religion, some religions, or all religions; and it cannot spend any tax money, however small the amount might be, in support of any religious activities or institutions.[48] The reader may wonder, in view of the Court's reasoning, why it allowed the

wall of separation Court ruling that government cannot be involved with religion.

town to pay for busing children to Catholic schools. The answer that it gave is that busing is a religiously neutral activity, akin to providing fire and police protection to Catholic schools. Busing, available to public- and private-school children alike, does not breach the wall of separation.

Since 1947 the Court has applied the wall-of-separation theory to strike down as unconstitutional every effort to have any form of prayer in public schools, even if it is nonsectarian,[49] voluntary,[50] or limited to reading a passage of the Bible.[51] Since 1992 it has even been unconstitutional for a public school to ask a rabbi or minister to offer a prayer—an invocation or a benediction—at the school's graduation ceremony, and since 2001 it has been unconstitutional for a student, elected by other students, to lead a voluntary prayer at the beginning of a high school football game.[52] Moreover, the Court has held that laws prohibiting teaching the theory of evolution or requiring giving equal time to "creationism" (the biblical doctrine that God created mankind) are religiously inspired and thus unconstitutional.[53] A public school may not allow its pupils to take time out from their regular classes for religious instruction if this occurs within the schools, though "released-time" instruction is all right if it is done outside the public school building.[54] The school prayer decisions in particular have provoked a storm of controversy, but efforts to get Congress to propose to the states a constitutional amendment authorizing such prayers have failed.

Almost as controversial have been Court-imposed restrictions on public aid to parochial schools, though here the wall-of-separation principle has not been used to forbid any and all forms of aid. For example, it is permissible for the federal government to provide aid for constructing buildings on denominational (as well as nondenominational) college campuses[55] and for state governments to loan free textbooks to parochial-school pupils,[56] grant tax-exempt status to parochial schools,[57] allow parents of parochial-school children to deduct their tuition payments on a state's income tax returns,[58] and pay for computers and a deaf child's sign language interpreter at private and religious schools.[59] But the government cannot pay a salary supplement to teachers who teach secular subjects in parochial schools,[60] reimburse parents for the cost of parochial-school tuition,[61] supply parochial schools with services such as counseling,[62] give money with which to purchase instructional materials, require that "creationism" be taught in public schools, or create a special school district for Hasidic Jews.[63]

The Court sometimes changes its mind on these matters. In 1985 it said that the states could not send teachers into parochial schools to teach remedial courses for needy children, but twelve years later it decided that they could. "We no longer presume," the Court wrote, "that public employees will inculcate religion simply because they happen to be in a sectarian environment."[64]

Perhaps the most important establishment-clause decision in recent times was the Court ruling that vouchers can be used to pay for children being educated at religious and other private schools. The case began in Cleveland, Ohio, where the state offered money to any family (especially poor ones) whose children attended a school that had done so badly that it was under a federal court order requiring it to be managed directly by the state superintendent of schools. The money, a voucher, could be used to send a child to any other public or private school, including one run by a religious group. The Court held that this plan did not violate the establishment clause because the aid went, not to the school, but to the families who were to choose a school.[65]

If you find it confusing to follow the twists and turns of Court policy in this area, you are not alone. The wall-of-separation principle has not been easy to apply, and the Court has begun to alter its position on church-state matters. (Justices O'Connor, Rehnquist, Scalia, Kennedy, and Thomas have generally supported lowering—or perhaps perforating—the wall a bit.) The Court has tried to sort out the confusion by developing a three-part test to decide under what circumstances government involvement in religious activities is improper.[66] That involvement is constitutional if it meets these tests:

1. It has a secular purpose.
2. Its primary effect neither advances nor inhibits religion.
3. It does not foster an excessive government entanglement with religion.

No sooner had the test been developed than the Court decided that it was all right for the government of Pawtucket, Rhode Island, to erect a Nativity scene as part of a Christmas display in a local park. But five years later it said that Pittsburgh could not put a Nativity scene in front of the courthouse but could

How Would You Decide?

Suppose that you are on the Supreme Court. In each of the actual cases summarized below, you are asked to decide whether the First Amendment to the Constitution permits or prohibits a particular action. What would be your decision? (How the Supreme Court actually decided is given on page 117.)

Case 1:   Jacksonville, Florida, passed a city ordinance prohibiting drive-in movies from showing films containing nudity if the screen was visible to passersby on the street. A movie theater manager protested, claiming that he had a First Amendment right to show such films, even if they could be seen from the street. Who is correct?

Case 2:   Dr. Benjamin Spock wanted to enter Fort Dix Military Reservation in New Jersey to pass out campaign literature and discuss issues with service personnel. The military denied him access on grounds that regulations prohibit partisan campaigning on military bases. Who is correct?

Case 3:   A town passed an ordinance forbidding the placing of "For Sale" or "Sold" signs in front of homes in racially changing neighborhoods. The purpose was to reduce "white flight" and panic selling. A realty firm protested, claiming that its freedom of speech was being abridged. Who is correct?

Case 4:   A girl in Georgia was raped and died. A local television station broadcast the name of the girl, having obtained it from court records. Her father sued, claiming that his family's right to privacy had been violated, and pointed to a Georgia law that made it a crime to broadcast the name of a rape victim. The television station claimed that it had a right under the First Amendment to broadcast the name. Who is correct?

Case 5:   Florida passed a law giving a political candidate the right to equal space in a newspaper that had published attacks on him. A newspaper claimed that this violated the freedom of the press to publish what it wants. Who is correct?

Case 6:   Zacchini is a "human cannonball" whose entire fifteen-second act was filmed and broadcast by an Ohio television station. Zacchini sued the station, claiming that his earning power had been reduced by the film because the station showed for free what he charges people to see at county fairs. The station replied that it had a First Amendment right to broadcast such events. Who is correct?

display a menorah (a Jewish symbol of Chanukah) next to a Christmas tree and a sign extolling liberty. The Court claimed that the crèche had to go (because, being too close to the courthouse, a government endorsement was implied) but the menorah could stay (because, being next to a Christmas tree, it would not lead people to think that Pittsburgh was endorsing Judaism).[67]

Confused? It gets worse. Though the Court has struck down prayer in public schools, it has upheld prayer in Congress (since 1789, the House and Senate open each session with a prayer).[68] A public school cannot have a chaplain, but the armed services can. The Court has said that the government cannot "advance" religion, but it has not objected to the printing of the phrase "In God We Trust" on the back of every dollar bill.

It is obvious that despite its efforts to set forth clear rules governing church-state relations, the Court's actual decisions are hard to summarize. It is deeply divided—some would say deeply confused—on these matters, and so the efforts to define the "wall of separation" will continue to prove to be as difficult as the Court's earlier efforts to decide what is interstate and what is local commerce (see Chapter 3).

☆ Crime and Due Process

Whereas the central problem in interpreting the religion clauses of the First Amendment has been to decide what they mean, the central problems in interpreting those parts of the Bill of Rights that affect people accused of a crime have been to decide not only what they mean but also how to put them into effect. It is not obvious what constitutes an "unreasonable search," but even if we settle that question, we still must decide how best to protect

LANDMARK CASES

Religious Freedom

- *Engel v. Vitale* (1962): There may not be a prayer, even a nondenominational one, in public schools.
- *Everson v. Board of Education* (1947): The wall-of-separation principle is announced.
- *Lee v. Weisman* (1992): Public schools may not have clergy lead prayers at graduation ceremonies.
- *Lemon v. Kurtzman,* 403 U.S. 602 (1971): Three tests are described for deciding whether the government is improperly involved with religion.
- *Santa Fe Independent School District v. Doe* (2000): Students may not lead prayers before the start of a football game at a public school.
- *Zelman v. Simmons-Harris,* 536 U.S. 639 (2000): Voucher plan to pay school bills is upheld.
- *Zorauch v. Clauson* (1952): States may allow students to be released from public schools to attend religious instruction.

people against such searches in ways that do not unduly hinder criminal investigations.

There are at least two ways to provide that protection. One is to let the police introduce in court evidence relevant to the guilt or innocence of a person, no matter how it was obtained and then, after the case is settled, punish the police officer (or his or her superiors) if the evidence was gathered improperly (for example, by an unreasonable search). The other way is to exclude improperly gathered evidence from the trial in the first place, even if it is relevant to determining the guilt or innocence of the accused.

Most democratic nations, including England, use the first method; the United States uses the second. Because of this, many of the landmark cases decided by the Supreme Court have been bitterly controversial. Opponents of these decisions have argued that a guilty person should not go free just because the police officer blundered, especially if the mistake was minor. Supporters rejoin that there is no way to punish errant police officers effectively other than by excluding tainted evidence; moreover, nobody

should be convicted of a crime except by evidence that is above reproach.[69]

The Exclusionary Rule

The American method relies on what is called the **exclusionary rule.** That rule holds that evidence gathered in violation of the Constitution cannot be used in a trial. The rule has been used to implement two provisions of the Bill of Rights—the right to be free from unreasonable searches and seizures (Fourth Amendment) and the right not to be compelled to give evidence against oneself (Fifth Amendment).*

Not until 1949 did the Supreme Court consider whether to apply the exclusionary rule to the states. In a case decided that year the Court made it clear that the Fourth Amendment prohibited the police from carrying out unreasonable searches and obtaining improper confessions but held that it was

---

exclusionary rule   Improperly gathered evidence may not be introduced in a criminal trial.

---

*We shall consider here only two constitutional limits—those bearing on searches and confessions. Thus we will omit many other important constitutional provisions affecting criminal cases, such as rules governing wiretapping, prisoner rights, the right to bail and to a jury trial, the bar on ex post facto laws, the right to be represented by a lawyer in court, the ban on "cruel and unusual" punishment, and the rule against double jeopardy.

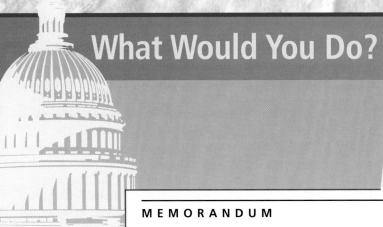

What Would You Do?

Congress Debates the Exclusionary Rule

October 15
WASHINGTON

Congress takes up tomorrow a proposed constitutional amendment that would ban the exclusionary rule from trials. The Supreme Court has required courts to exclude improperly gathered evidence from criminal cases . . .

MEMORANDUM

To: *Senator Edward Cortez*
From: *Mary Briscoe, legislative assistant*

Federal courts have been required to exclude improperly gathered evidence since 1886 and state courts since 1961. The rule is an effort to prevent unconstitutional searches and seizures. The constitutional amendment would ban the rule and create instead a procedure for punishing police officers who violate the Constitution.

Arguments for:

1. The rule makes it easy for defense attorneys to attack police evidence by having the judge declare it inadmissible. As a result a guilty person may go free because a police officer made a mistake.
2. The rule does not punish a police officer who violates the Constitution. Instead it benefits only accused persons.
3. No other democratic country uses the exclusionary rule.

Arguments against:

1. The rule protects the privacy of every individual by discouraging illegal searches.
2. There is no easy way to punish police officers who gather illegal evidence except by preventing them from using it in court.
3. There is no strong evidence that guilty people go free because of the rule.

Your decision:

Favor amendment _____
Oppose amendment _____

not necessary to use the exclusionary rule to enforce those prohibitions. It noted that other nations did not require that evidence improperly gathered had to be excluded from a criminal trial. The Court said that the local police should not improperly gather and use evidence, but if they did, the remedy was to sue the police department or punish the officer.[70]

But in 1961 the Supreme Court changed its mind about the use of the exclusionary rule. It all began when the Cleveland police broke into the home of Dollree Mapp in search of drugs and, finding none, arrested her for possessing some obscene pictures that they found there. The Court held that this was an unreasonable search and seizure because the police had not obtained a search warrant, though they had had ample time to do so. Furthermore, such illegally gathered evidence could not be used in the trial of Mapp.[71] Beginning with this case—*Mapp v. Ohio*—the Supreme Court required the use of the exclusionary rule as a way of enforcing a variety of constitutional guarantees.

Search and Seizure

After the Court decided to exclude improperly gathered evidence, the next problem was to decide what evidence was improper. What happened to Dollree Mapp was an easy case: hardly anybody argued that it was reasonable for the police to break into someone's home without a warrant, ransack their belongings, and take whatever they could find that might be incriminating. But that left a lot of hard choices still to be made.

When can the police search you without its being unreasonable? Under two circumstances—when they have a search warrant and when they have lawfully arrested you. A **search warrant** is an order from a judge authorizing the search of a place; the order must describe what is to be searched and seized, and the judge can issue it only if he or she is persuaded by the police that good reason **(probable cause)** exists to believe that a crime has been committed and that the evidence bearing on that crime will be found at a certain location. (The police can also search a building if the occupant gives them permission.)

---

search warrant   A judge's order authorizing a search.

probable cause   Reasonable cause for issuing a search warrant or making an arrest; more than mere suspicion.

In addition, you can be searched if the search occurs when you are being lawfully arrested. When can you be arrested? You can be arrested if a judge has issued an arrest warrant for you, if you commit a crime in the presence of a police officer, or if the officer has probable cause to believe that you have committed a serious crime (usually a felony). If you are arrested and no search warrant has been issued, the police, and not a judge, decide what they can search. What rules should they follow?

In trying to answer that question, the courts have elaborated a set of rules that are complex, subject to frequent change, and quite controversial. In general the police, after arresting you, can search:

- You
- Things in plain view
- Things or places under your immediate control

As a practical matter, things "in plain view" or "under your immediate control" mean the room in which you are arrested but not other rooms of the house.[72] If the police want to search the rest of your house or a car parked in your driveway, they will first have to go to a judge to obtain a search warrant. But if the police arrest a college student on campus for drinking under age and then accompany that student back to his or her dormitory room so that the student can get proof that he or she was old enough to drink, the police can seize drugs that are in plain view in that room.[73] And if marijuana is growing in plain view in an open field, the police can enter and search that field even though it is fenced off with a locked gate and a "No Trespassing" sign.[74]

But what if you are arrested while driving your car—how much of it can the police search? The answer to that question has changed almost yearly. In 1979 the Court ruled that the police could not search a suitcase taken from a car of an arrested person, and in 1981 it extended this protection to any "closed, opaque container" found in the car.[75] But the following year the Court decided that all parts of a car, closed or open, could be searched if the officers had probable cause to believe that they contained contraband (that is, goods illegally possessed). And recently the rules governing car searches have been relaxed even further. Officers who have probable cause to search a car can also search the things passengers are carrying in the car. And if the car is stopped to give the driver a traffic ticket, the car can be searched if the officer develops a "reasonable,

How the Court Decided

The United States Supreme Court answered the questions on page 113 in the following ways:

Case 1: The drive-in movie won. The Supreme Court, 6–3, decided that the First Amendment protects the right to show nudity; it is up to the unwilling viewer on the public streets to avert his or her eyes.
Erznoznik v. Jacksonville,
422 U.S. 205 (1975)

Case 2: The military won. The Supreme Court, 6–2, decided that military reservations are not like public streets or parks, and thus civilians can be excluded from them, especially if such exclusion prevents the military from appearing to be the handmaiden of various political causes.
Greer v. Spock,
424 U.S. 828 (1976)

Case 3: The realty firm won. The Supreme Court, 8–0, decided that the First Amendment prohibits the banning of signs, even of a commercial nature, without a strong, legitimate state interest. Banning the signs would not obviously reduce "white flight," and the government has no right to withhold information from citizens for fear that they will act unwisely.
Linmark Associates, Inc. v. Willingboro,
431 U.S. 85 (1977)

Case 4: The television station won. The Court, 8–1, decided that the First Amendment protects the right to broadcast the names of rape victims obtained from public (that is, court) records.
Cox Broadcasting Corp. v. Cohn,
420 U.S. 469 (1975)

Case 5: The newspaper won. The Supreme Court decided unanimously that the First Amendment prohibits the state from intruding into the function of editors.
Miami Herald Publishing Co. v. Tornillo,
418 U.S. 241 (1974)

Case 6: Zacchini, the human cannonball, won. The Supreme Court, 5–4, decided that broadcasting the entire act without the performer's consent jeopardized his means of livelihood, even though the First Amendment would guarantee the right of the station to broadcast newsworthy facts about the act.
Zacchini v. Scripps-Howard Broadcasting Co.,
433 U.S. 562 (1977)

articulable suspicion" that the car is involved in other illegal activity.[76]

In this confusing area of the law the Court is attempting to protect those places in which a person has a "reasonable expectation of privacy." Your body is one such place, and so the Court has held that the police cannot compel you to undergo surgery to remove a bullet that might be evidence of your guilt or innocence in a crime.[77] But the police can require you to take a Breathalyzer test to see whether you have been drinking while driving.[78] Your home is another place where you have an expectation of privacy, but a barn next to your home is not, nor is your backyard viewed from an airplane, nor is your home if it is a motor home that can be driven away, and so the police need not have a warrant to look into these places.[79]

If you work for the government, you have an expectation that your desk and files will be private;

nonetheless, your supervisor may search the desk and files without a warrant, provided that he or she is looking for something related to your work.[80] But bear in mind that the Constitution protects you only against *the government;* a private employer has a great deal of freedom to search your desk and files.

Confessions and Self-Incrimination

The constitutional ban on being forced to give evidence against oneself was originally intended to prevent the use of torture or "third-degree" police tactics to extract confessions. But it has since been extended to cover many kinds of statements uttered not out of fear of torture but from lack of awareness of one's rights, especially the right to remain silent, whether in the courtroom or in the police station.

For many decades the Supreme Court had held that involuntary confessions could not be used in

A police officer reads the Miranda warning to a man he has arrested.

federal criminal trials but had not ruled that they were barred from state trials. But in the early 1960s it changed its mind in two landmark cases—*Escobedo* and *Miranda*.[81] The story of the latter and of the controversy that it provoked is worth telling.

Ernesto A. Miranda was convicted in Arizona of the rape and kidnapping of a young woman. The conviction was based on a written confession that Miranda signed after two hours of police questioning. (The victim also identified him.) Two years earlier the Court had decided that the rule against self-incrimination applied to state courts.[82] Now the question arose of what constitutes an "involuntary" confession. The Court decided that a confession should be presumed involuntary unless the person in custody had been fully and clearly informed of his or her right to be silent, to have an attorney present during any questioning, and to have an attorney pro-

vided free of charge if he or she could not afford one. The accused may waive these rights and offer to talk, but the waiver must be truly voluntary. Since Miranda did not have a lawyer present when he was questioned and had not knowingly waived his right to a lawyer, the confession was excluded from evidence in the trial and his conviction was overturned.[83]

Miranda was tried and convicted again, this time on the basis of evidence supplied by his girlfriend, who testified that he had admitted to her that he was guilty. Nine years later he was released from prison; four years after that he was killed in a barroom fight. When the Phoenix police arrested the prime suspect in Ernesto Miranda's murder, they read him his rights from a "Miranda card."

Everyone who watches cops-and-robbers shows on television probably knows the "Miranda warning" by heart (see the box on page 119). The police now read it routinely to people whom they arrest. It is not clear whether it has much impact on who does or does not confess or what effect, if any, it may have on the crime rate.

In time the Miranda rule was extended to mean that you have a right to a lawyer when you appear in a police lineup[84] and when you are questioned by a psychiatrist to determine whether you are competent to stand trial.[85] The Court threw out the conviction of a man who had killed a child, because the accused, without being given the right to have a lawyer present, had led the police to the victim's body.[86] You do not have a right to a Miranda warning, however, if while in jail you confess a crime to another inmate who turns out to be an undercover police officer.[87]

Some police departments have tried to get around the need for a Miranda warning by training their officers to question suspects before giving them a Miranda warning and then, if the suspect confessed, giving the warning and asking the same questions over again. But the Supreme Court would not allow this and struck the practice down.[88]

Relaxing the Exclusionary Rule

Cases such as *Miranda* were highly controversial and led to efforts in Congress to modify or overrule the decisions by statute—without much coming of the attempts. But as the rules governing police conduct became increasingly more complex, pressure mounted to find an alternative. Some thought that any evidence should be admissible, with the question of

★ HOW THINGS WORK ★

The Miranda Rule

The Supreme Court has interpreted the due-process clause to require that local police departments issue warnings of the sort shown below to people whom they are arresting.

PHILADELPHIA POLICE DEPARTMENT

STANDARD POLICE INTERROGATION CARD

WARNINGS TO BE GIVEN ACCUSED

We are questioning you concerning the crime of (state specific crime).

    We have a duty to explain to you and to warn you that you have the following legal rights:

A. You have a right to remain silent and do not have to say anything at all.

B. Anything you say can and will be used against you in Court.

C. You have a right to talk to a lawyer of your own choice before we ask you any questions, and also to have a lawyer here with you while we ask questions.

D. If you cannot afford to hire a lawyer, and you want one, we will see that you have one provided to you free of charge before we ask you any questions.

E. If you are willing to give us a statement, you have a right to stop any time you wish.

75-Misc.-3   (Over)

(6-24-70)

Ernesto A. Miranda was convicted in Arizona of rape and kidnapping. When the Supreme Court overturned the conviction, it issued a set of rules—the "Miranda rules"—governing how police must conduct an arrest and interrogation.

police conduct left to lawsuits or other ways of punishing official misbehavior. Others felt that the exclusionary rule served a useful purpose but had simply become too technical to be an effective deterrent to police misconduct (the police cannot obey rules that they cannot understand). And still others felt that the exclusionary rule was a vital safeguard to essential liberties and should be kept intact. The Court has refused to let Congress abolish Miranda because it is a constitutional rule.[89]

The courts themselves began to adopt the second position, deciding a number of cases in ways that retained the exclusionary rule but modified it by limiting its coverage (police were given greater freedom to question juveniles)[90] and by incorporating what was called a **good-faith exception.** For example, if the police obtain a search warrant that they believe is valid, the evidence that they gather will not be excluded if it later turns out that the warrant was defective for some reason (such as the judge's having used the wrong form).[91] And the Court decided that

"overriding considerations of public safety" may justify questioning a person without first reading the person his or her rights.[92] Moreover, the Court changed its mind about the killer who led the police to the place where he had disposed of his victim's body. After the man was convicted a second time and again appealed, the Court in 1984 held that the body would have been discovered anyway; thus evidence will not be excluded if it can be shown that it would "inevitably" have been found.[93]

Terrorism and Civil Liberties

The attacks of September 11, 2001, raised important questions about how far the government can go in investigating and prosecuting individuals.

---

good-faith exception   An error in gathering evidence sufficiently minor that it may be used in a trial.

Although Osama bin Laden, pictured here in a video-taped address, remains at large, many of his al Queda network have been captured.

A little over one month after the attacks, Congress passed a new law, the USA Patriot Act, designed to increase federal powers to investigate terrorists.* Its main provisions are these:

- Telephone taps. The government may tap, if it has a court order, any telephone a suspect uses instead of having to get a separate order for each telephone.
- Internet taps. The government may tap, if it has a court order, Internet communications.
- Voice mail. The government, with a court order, may seize voice mail.
- Grand jury information. Investigators can now share with other government officials things learned in secret grand jury hearings.
- Immigration. The attorney general may hold any noncitizen who is thought to be a national security risk for up to seven days. If the alien cannot be charged with a crime or deported within that time, he or she may still be detained if he or she is certified to be a security risk.
- Money laundering. The government gets new powers to track the movement of money across U.S. borders and among banks.

*The name of the law is an acronym derived from the official title of the bill, drawn from the first letters of the following capitalized words: Uniting and Strengthening America by Providing Appropriate Tools Required to Intercept and Obstruct Terrorism (USA PATRIOT).

- Crime. This provision eliminates the statute of limitation on terrorist crimes and increases the penalties.

About a month later, President Bush, by executive order, proclaimed a national emergency under which any noncitizen who is believed to be a terrorist or has harbored a terrorist will be tried by a military, rather than a civilian, court.

A military trial is carried on before a commission of military officers and not a civilian jury. The tribunal can operate in secret if classified information is used in evidence. Two-thirds of the commission must agree before the suspect can be convicted and sentenced. If convicted, the suspect can appeal to the secretary of defense and the president, but not to a civilian court.

These commissions may eventually be used to try some of the men captured by the U.S. military during its campaign in Afghanistan against the Taliban regime and the al Qaeda terrorist network that was created by Osama bin Laden. These detainees were held in a prison at our Guantanamo naval base in Cuba and are not regarded by the Defense Department as ordinary prisoners of war.

The biggest legal issue created by this country's war on terrorism is whether the people we capture can be held by our government without giving them access to the courts. The traditional view, first announced during World War II, was that spies sent to this country by the Nazis could be tried by a military tribunal instead of by a civilian court. They were neither citizens nor soldiers, but "unlawful combatants."[94] The Bush administration relied on this view when it detained in our military base in Guantanamo Bay, Cuba, men seized by American forces in Afghanistan. These men were mostly members of the al Qaeda terrorist movement or of the Taliban movement that governed Afghanistan before American armed forces, together with Afghan rebels, defeated them, These men, none of them American citizens, argued that they were neither terrorists nor combatants. They demanded access to American courts. By a vote of six to three, the Supreme Court held that American courts can consider challenges to the legality of the detention of these men. The Court's opinion did not spell out what the courts should do when it hears these petitions.[95]

In another decision given the same day, the Supreme Court ruled on the case of an American citizen who

LANDMARK CASES

Criminal Charges

- *Dickerson v. United States* **(2000):** The *Mapp* decision is based on the Constitution and it cannot be altered by Congress passing a law.
- *Gideon v. Wainwright* **(1964):** Persons charged with a crime have a right to an attorney even if they cannot afford one.
- *Mapp v. Ohio* **(1961):** Evidence illegally gathered by the police may not be used in a criminal trial.
- *Miranda v. Arizona,* **384 U.S. 436 (1966):** Court describes ruling that police must give to arrested persons.
- *Rasul v. Bush,* **03-334 (2004):** Terrorist detainees must have access to a neutral court to decide if they are legally held.
- *United States v. Leon* **(1984):** Illegally obtained evidence may be used in a trial if it was gathered in good faith without violating the principles of the *Mapp* decision.

apparently was working with the Taliban regime but was captured by our forces and was imprisoned in South Carolina. The Court said that American citizens were entitled to a hearing before a neutral decision maker in order to challenge the basis for detention.[96]

No one knows what kind of courts will hear the petitions by the foreign detainees or what rules they will apply. In theory this decision may make capturing enemy prisoners a complex and time-consuming legal problem, but so far we can only guess as to how it will work out in practice.

In addition to the USA Patriot Act and the presidential order about military tribunals, key federal agencies have intensified their investigations. The Justice Department has detained many immigrants, authorized federal investigators to listen in on conversations between some federal prisoners and their lawyers, promised to help in obtaining citizenship for immigrants who help the nation identify terrorists, and (with the State Department) intensified scrutiny of applications for visas filed by people from certain countries.

Many of these measures have been criticized by civil liberties organizations and may be challenged in court. To meet some of these arguments, Congress provided that certain provisions of the Patriot Act, such as seizing voice mail in pursuance of a court order, would automatically expire in 2005.

☆ SUMMARY

Civil liberties questions are in some ways like and in some ways unlike ordinary policy debates. Like most issues, civil liberties problems often involve competing interests—in this case conflicting rights or conflicting rights and duties—and so we have groups mobilized on both sides of issues involving free speech and crime control. Like some other issues, civil liberties problems can also arise from the successful appeals of a policy entrepreneur, and so we have periodic reductions in liberty resulting from popular fears, usually aroused during or just after a war.

But civil liberties are unlike many other issues in at least one regard: more than struggles over welfare spending or defense or economic policy, debates about civil liberties reach down into our fundamental political beliefs and political culture, challenging us to define what we mean by religion, Americanism, and decency.

The most important of these challenges focuses on the meaning of the First Amendment: What is "speech"? How much of it should be free? How far can the state go in aiding religion? How do we strike a balance between national security and personal expression? The zigzag course followed by the courts in judging these matters has, on balance, tended to enlarge freedom of expression.

Almost as important has been the struggle to strike a balance between the right of society to protect itself from criminals and the right of people (including criminals) to be free from unreasonable searches and coerced confessions. As with free speech cases, the courts have generally broadened the rights at some expense to the power of the police. But in recent years the Supreme Court has pulled back from some of its more sweeping applications of the exclusionary rule.

The resolution of these issues by the courts is political in the sense that differing opinions about what is right or desirable compete, with one side or another prevailing (often by a small majority). In this competition of ideas federal judges, though not elected, are often sensitive to strong currents of popular opinion. When entrepreneurial politics has produced new action against apparently threatening minorities, judges are inclined, at least for a while, to give serious consideration to popular fears and legislative majorities. And when no strong national mood is discernible, the opinions of elites influence judicial thinking (as described in Chapter 16).

At the same time, courts resolve political conflicts in a manner that differs in important respects from the resolution of conflicts by legislatures or executives. First, the very existence of the courts, and the relative ease with which one may enter them to advance a claim, facilitates challenges to accepted values. An unpopular political or religious group may have little or no access to a legislature, but it will have substantial access to the courts. Second, judges often settle controversies about rights not simply by deciding the case at hand but by formulating a general rule to cover like cases elsewhere. This has an advantage (the law tends to become more consistent and better known) but a disadvantage as well: a rule suitable for one case may be unworkable in another. Judges reason by analogy and sometimes assume that two cases are similar when in fact there are important differences. A definition of "obscenity" or of "fighting words" may suit one situation but be inadequate in another. Third, judges interpret the Constitution, whereas legislatures often consult popular preferences or personal convictions. However much their own beliefs influence what judges read into the Constitution, almost all of them are constrained by its language.

Taken together, the desire to find and announce rules, the language of the Constitution, and the personal beliefs of judges have led to a general expansion of civil liberties. As a result, even allowing for temporary reversals and frequent redefinitions, any value that is thought to hinder freedom of expression and the rights of the accused has generally lost ground to the claims of the First, Fourth, Fifth, and Sixth Amendments.

RECONSIDERING WHO GOVERNS?

1. *Why do the courts play so large a role in deciding what our civil liberties should be?*

The courts are independent of the executive and legislative branches, both of which will respond to public pressures. In wartime or in other crisis periods, people want "something done." The president and members of Congress know this. The courts are usually a brake on their demands. But of course the courts can make mistakes or get things confused, as many people believe they have with the establishment clause and the rights of criminal defendants.

RECONSIDERING TO WHAT ENDS?

1. Why not display religious symbols on government property?

The courts believe that putting on government property a single religious symbol, such as a Nativity scene, will make Americans believe that the government endorses that religion. But if symbols from several different religions are displayed, no one thinks the government has endorsed any one of them. Of course, putting "In God We Trust" on a government dollar bill is all right. Do not look for consistency here.

2. If a person confesses to committing a crime, why is that confession sometimes not used in court?

Because the confession was improperly gathered by the police. Suspects may not be tortured, and they must be given the Miranda warning. There are other ways of protecting the right of people to be free of improper police procedures, such as admitting the confession in court and then punishing the officers who gathered it improperly. The American courts do not think that system would work in this country.

3. Does the Patriot Act reduce our liberties?

There have not yet been any court tests of the law. Passed after 9/11, it improves the ability of the police to obtain search warrants and eliminates the old tension between intelligence and law enforcement.

WORLD WIDE WEB RESOURCES

Court cases: **www.law.cornell.edu**

Civil Rights Division of the Department of Justice: **www.usdoj.gov**

American Civil Liberties Union: **www.aclu.org**

SUGGESTED READINGS

Abraham, Henry J., and Barbara A. Perry, *Freedom and the Court*. 7th ed. New York: Oxford University Press, 1998. Analysis of leading Supreme Court cases on civil liberties and civil rights.

Amar, Akhil Reed. *The Constitution and Criminal Procedure: First Principles*. New Haven, Conn.: Yale University Press, 1997. A brilliant critique of how the Supreme Court has interpreted those parts of the Constitution bearing on search warrants, the exclusionary rule, and self-incrimination.

Berns, Walter. *The First Amendment and the Future of American Democracy*. New York: Basic Books, 1976. A look at what the Founders intended by the First Amendment that takes issue with contemporary Supreme Court interpretations of it.

Clor, Harry M. *Obscenity and Public Morality*. Chicago: University of Chicago Press, 1969. Argues for the legitimacy of legal restrictions on obscenity.

Levy, Leonard W. *Legacy of Suppression: Freedom of Speech and Press in Early American History*. Rev. ed. New York: Oxford University Press, 1985. Careful study of what the Founders and the early leaders meant by freedom of speech and press.

Civil Rights

The Black Predicament

The Campaign in the Courts
   "Separate but Equal" ● Can Separate
   Schools Be Equal? ● *Brown v. Board*
   of Education

The Campaign in Congress
   Racial Profiling

Women and Equal Rights
   Sexual Harassment ● Privacy and Sex

Affirmative Action
   Equality of Results ● Equality of
   Opportunity

Gays and the Constitution

WHO GOVERNS?

1. Since Congress enacts our laws, why has it not made certain that all groups have the same rights?
2. After the Supreme Court ended racial segregation in the schools, what did the president and Congress do?

TO WHAT ENDS?

1. If the law supports equality of opportunity, why has affirmative action become so important?
2. Under what circumstances can men and women be treated differently?

*I*n 1830 Congress passed a law requiring all Indians east of the Mississippi River to move to the Indian Territory west of the river, and the army set about implementing it. In the 1850s a major political fight broke out in Boston over whether the police department should be obliged to hire an Irish officer. Until 1920 women could not vote in most elections. In the 1930s the Cornell University Medical School had a strict quota limiting the number of Jewish students who could enroll. In the 1940s the army, at the direction of President Franklin D. Roosevelt, removed all Japanese Americans from their homes in California and placed them in relocation centers far from the coast.

In all such cases some group, usually defined along racial or ethnic lines, was denied access to facilities, opportunities, or services that were available to other groups. Such cases raise the issue of **civil rights.** The pertinent question regarding civil rights is not whether the government has the authority to treat different people differently; it is whether such differences in treatment are reasonable. All laws and policies make distinctions among people—for example, the tax laws require higher-income people to pay taxes at a higher rate than lower-income ones—but not all such distinctions are defensible. The courts have long held that classifying people on the basis of their income and taxing them at different rates is quite permissible because such classifications are not arbitrary or unreasonable and are related to a legitimate public need (that is, raising revenue). Increasingly, however, the courts have said that classifying people on the basis of their race or ethnicity is unreasonable. These are **suspect classifications,** and while not every law making such classifications has been ruled unconstitutional, they have all become subject to especially **strict scrutiny.**[1]

To explain the victimization of certain groups and the methods by which they have begun to overcome it, we shall consider chiefly the case of African Americans. Black-white relations have in large measure defined the problem of civil rights in this country; most of the landmark laws and court decisions have involved black claims. The strategies employed by or on behalf of African Americans have typically set the pattern for the strategies employed by other groups. At the end of this chapter we shall look at the related but somewhat different issues of women's rights and gay rights.

A segregated bus station in Durham, North Carolina, in 1940.

☆ The Black Predicament

Though constituting more than 12 percent of the population, African Americans until fairly recently could not in many parts of the country vote, attend integrated schools, ride in the front seats of buses, or buy homes in white neighborhoods.

---

civil rights   The rights of people to be treated without unreasonable or unconstitutional differences.

suspect classifications   Classifications of people on the basis of their race or ethnicity.

strict scrutiny   A Supreme Court test to see if a law denies equal protection because it does not serve a compelling state interest and is not narrowly tailored to achieve that goal.

Although today white citizens generally do not feel threatened when a black family moves into Cicero, Illinois, a black child goes to school at Little Rock Central High School, or a black group organizes voters in Neshoba County, Mississippi, at one time most whites in Cicero, Little Rock, and Neshoba County felt deeply threatened by these things (and some whites still do). This was especially the case in those parts of the country, notably the Deep South, where blacks were often in the majority. There the politically dominant white minority felt keenly the potential competition for jobs, land, public services, and living space posed by large numbers of people of another race. But even in the North, black gains often appeared to be at the expense of lower-income whites who lived or worked near them, not at the expense of upper-status whites who lived in suburbs.

African Americans were not allowed to vote at all in many areas; they could vote only with great difficulty in others; and even in those places where voting was easy, they often lacked the material and institutional support for effective political organization. If your opponent feels deeply threatened by your demands and in addition can deny you access to the political system that will decide the fate of those demands, you are, to put it mildly, at a disadvantage. Yet from the end of Reconstruction to the 1960s—for nearly a century—many blacks in the South found themselves in just such a position.

To the dismay of those who prefer to explain political action in terms of economic motives, people often attach greater importance to the intangible costs and benefits of policies than to the tangible ones. Thus, even though the average black represented no threat to the average white, antiblack attitudes—racism—produced some appalling actions. Between 1882 and 1946, 4,715 people, about three-fourths of them African Americans, were lynched in the United States.[2] Some lynchings were carried out by small groups of vigilantes acting with much ceremony, but others were the actions of frenzied mobs. In the summer of 1911 a black man charged with murdering a white man in Livermore, Kentucky, was dragged by a mob to the local theater, where he was hanged. The audience, which had been charged admission, was invited to shoot the swaying body (those in the orchestra seats could empty their revolvers; those in the balcony were limited to a single shot).[3]

Though the public in other parts of the country was shocked by such events, little was done: lynching was a local, not a federal, crime. It obviously would not require many lynchings to convince African Americans in these localities that it would be foolhardy to try to vote or enroll in a white school. And even in those states where blacks did vote, popular attitudes were not conducive to blacks' buying homes or taking jobs on an equal basis with whites. Even among those professing to support equal rights, a substantial portion opposed African Americans' efforts to obtain them and federal action to secure them. In 1942 a national poll showed that only 30 percent of whites thought that black and white children should attend the same schools; in 1956 the proportion had risen, but only to 49 percent, still less than a majority. (In the South white support for school integration was even lower—14 percent favored it in 1956, about 31 percent in 1963.) As late as 1956 a majority of southern whites were opposed to integrated public transportation facilities. Even among whites who generally favored integration, there was in 1963 (*before* the ghetto riots) considerable opposition to the black civil rights movement: nearly half of the whites who were classified in a survey as moderate integrationists thought that demonstrations hurt the black cause; nearly two-thirds disapproved of actions taken by the civil rights movement; and over a third felt that civil rights should be left to the states.[4]

In short, the political position in which African Americans found themselves until the 1960s made it difficult for them to advance their interests through a feasible legislative strategy; their opponents were aroused, organized, and powerful. Thus if black interests were to be championed in Congress or state legislatures, blacks would have to have white allies. Though some such allies could be found, they were too few to make a difference in a political system that gives a substantial advantage to strongly motivated opponents of any new policy. For that to change, one or both of two things would have to happen: additional allies would have to be recruited (a delicate problem, given that many white integrationists disapproved of aspects of the civil rights movement), or the struggle would have to be shifted to a policy-making arena in which the opposition enjoyed less of an advantage.

Partly by plan, partly by accident, black leaders followed both of these strategies simultaneously. By publicizing their grievances and organizing a civil rights movement that (at least in its early stages) concentrated on dramatizing the denial to blacks of essential and widely accepted liberties, African Americans were able to broaden their base of support both among political elites and among the general public and thereby to raise civil rights matters from a low to a high position on the political agenda. By waging a patient, prolonged, but carefully planned legal struggle, black leaders shifted decision-making power on key civil rights issues from Congress, where they had been stymied for generations, to the federal courts.

After this strategy had achieved some substantial successes—after blacks had become enfranchised and legal barriers to equal participation in political and economic affairs had been lowered—the politics of civil rights became more conventional. African Americans were able to assert their demands directly in the legislative and executive branches of government with reasonable (though scarcely certain) prospects of success. Civil rights became less a matter of gaining entry into the political system and more one of waging interest group politics within that system. At the same time, the goals of civil rights politics were broadened. The struggle to gain entry into the system had focused on the denial of fundamental rights (to vote, to organize, to obtain equal access to schools and public facilities); later the dominant issues were manpower development, economic progress, and the improvement of housing and neighborhoods.

☆ The Campaign in the Courts

The Fourteenth Amendment was both an opportunity and a problem for black activists. Adopted in 1868, it seemed to guarantee equal rights for all: "No state shall make or enforce any law which shall abridge the privileges or immunities of citizens of the United States; nor shall any state deprive any person of life, liberty, or property, without due process of law; nor deny to any person within its jurisdiction the equal protection of the laws."

The key phrase was "equal protection of the laws." Read broadly, it might mean that the Constitution should be regarded as color-blind: no state law could have the effect of treating whites and blacks differently. Thus a law segregating blacks and whites into separate schools or neighborhoods would be unconstitutional. Read narrowly, "equal protection" might mean only that blacks and whites had certain fundamental legal rights in common, among them the right to sign contracts, to serve on juries, or to buy and sell property, but otherwise they could be treated differently.

Historians have long debated which view Congress held when it proposed the Fourteenth Amendment. What forms of racial segregation, if any, were still permissible? Segregated trains? Hotels? Schools? Neighborhoods?

The Supreme Court took the narrow view. Though in 1880 it declared unconstitutional a West Virginia law requiring juries to be composed only of white males,[5] it decided in 1883 that it was unconstitutional for Congress to prohibit racial discrimination in public accommodations such as hotels.[6] The difference between the two cases seemed, in the eyes of the Court, to be this: serving on a jury was an essential right of citizenship that the state could not deny to any person on racial grounds without violating the Fourteenth Amendment, but registering at a hotel was a convenience controlled by a private person (the hotel owner), who could treat blacks and whites differently if he or she wished.

The major decision that was to determine the legal status of the Fourteenth Amendment for over half a century was *Plessy v. Ferguson*. Louisiana had passed a law requiring blacks and whites to occupy separate cars on railroad trains operating in that state. When Adolph Plessy, who was seven-eighths white and one-eighth black, refused to obey the law, he was arrested. He appealed his conviction to the Supreme Court, claiming that the law violated the Fourteenth Amendment. In 1896 the Court rejected his claim, holding that the law treated both races equally even though it required them to be separate. The equal-protection clause guaranteed political and legal but not social equality. "Separate-but-equal" facilities were constitutional because if "one race be inferior to the other socially, the Constitution of the United States cannot put them on the same plane."[7]

> **separate-but-equal doctrine**   The doctrine established in *Plessy v. Ferguson* (1896) that African Americans could constitutionally be kept in separate but equal facilities.

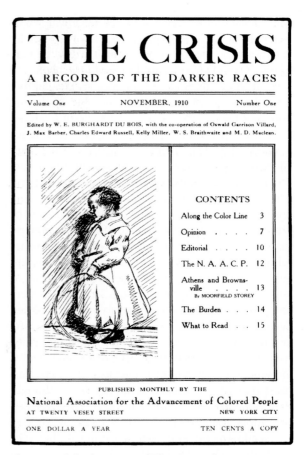

The cover of the first issue of The Crisis, *the magazine started by the NAACP in 1910 to raise African American consciousness and publicize racist acts.*

"Separate but Equal"

Thus began the **separate-but-equal doctrine.** Three years later the Court applied it to schools as well, declaring in *Cumming v. Richmond County Board of Education* that a decision in a Georgia community to close the black high school while keeping open the white high school was not a violation of the Fourteenth Amendment because blacks could always go to private schools. Here the Court seemed to be saying that not only could schools be separate, they could even be unequal.[8]

What the Court has made, the Court can unmake. But to get it to change its mind requires a long, costly, and uncertain legal battle. The National Association for the Advancement of Colored People (NAACP) was the main organization that waged that battle. Formed in 1909 by a group of whites and blacks in the aftermath of a race riot, the NAACP did many things—lobbying in Washington and publicizing black grievances, especially in the pages of *The Crisis*, a magazine edited by W.E.B. Du Bois—but its most influential role was played in the courtroom.

It was a rational strategy. Fighting legal battles does not require forming broad political alliances or changing public opinion, tasks that would have been very difficult for a small and unpopular organization. A court-based approach also enabled the organization to remain nonpartisan.

But it was a slow and difficult strategy. The Court had adopted a narrow interpretation of the Fourteenth Amendment. To get the Court to change its mind would require the NAACP to bring before it cases involving the strongest possible claims that a black had been unfairly treated—and under circumstances sufficiently different from those of earlier cases that the Court could find some grounds for changing its mind.

The steps in that strategy were these: First, persuade the Court to declare unconstitutional laws creating schools that were separate but obviously unequal. Second, persuade it to declare unconstitutional laws supporting schools that were separate but unequal in not-so-obvious ways. Third, persuade it to rule that racially separate schools were inherently unequal and hence unconstitutional.

Can Separate Schools Be Equal?

The first step was accomplished in a series of court cases stretching from 1938 to 1948. In 1938 the Court held that Lloyd Gaines had to be admitted to an all-white law school in Missouri because no black law school of equal quality existed in that state.[9] In 1948 the Court ordered the all-white University of Oklahoma Law School to admit Ada Lois Sipuel, a black, even though the state planned to build a black law school later. For education to be equal, it had to be equally available.[10] It still could be separate, however: the university admitted Ms. Sipuel but required her to attend classes in a section of the state capitol, roped off from other students, where she could meet with her law professors.

The second step was taken in two cases decided in 1950. Heman Sweatt, an African American, was treated by the University of Texas Law School much as Ada Sipuel had been treated in Oklahoma: "admitted" to the all-white school but relegated to a separate building. Another African American, George McLaurin, was allowed to study for his Ph.D. in a

"colored section" of the all-white University of Oklahoma. The Supreme Court unanimously decided that these arrangements were unconstitutional because, by imposing racially based barriers on the black students' access to professors, libraries, and other students, they created unequal educational opportunities.[11]

The third step, the climax of the entire drama, began in Topeka, Kansas, where Linda Brown wanted to enroll in her neighborhood school but could not because she was black and the school was by law reserved exclusively for whites. When the NAACP took her case to the federal district court in Kansas, the judge decided that the black school that Linda could attend was substantially equal in quality to the white school that she could not attend. Therefore denying her access to the white school was constitutional. To change that the lawyers would have to persuade the Supreme Court to overrule the district judge on the grounds that racially separate schools were unconstitutional even if they were equal. In other words, the separate-but-equal doctrine would have to be overturned by the Court.

It was a risky and controversial step to take. Many states, Kansas among them, were trying to make their all-black schools equal to those of whites by launching expensive building programs. If the NAACP succeeded in getting separate schools declared unconstitutional, the Court might well put a stop to the building of these new schools. Blacks could win a moral and legal victory but suffer a practical defeat—the loss of these new facilities. Despite these risks, the NAACP decided to go ahead with the appeal.

Brown v. Board of Education

On May 17, 1954, a unanimous Supreme Court, speaking through an opinion written and delivered by Chief Justice Earl Warren, found that "in the field of public education the doctrine of 'separate but equal' has no place" because "separate educational facilities are inherently unequal."[12] *Plessy v. Ferguson* was overruled, and "separate but equal" was dead.

The ruling was a landmark decision, but the reasons for it and the means chosen to implement it were as important and as controversial as the decision itself. There were at least three issues. First, how would the decision be implemented? Second, on what grounds were racially separate schools unconstitutional? Third, what test would a school system have to meet in order to be in conformity with the Constitution?

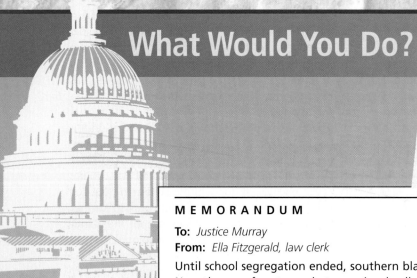

Court to Rule on Black Colleges

January 19
WASHINGTON

The Supreme Court has announced that it will decide whether all-black colleges in the South can receive state support if there are too few whites attending them. The case began in Mississippi, where . . .

MEMORANDUM

To: *Justice Murray*
From: *Ella Fitzgerald, law clerk*

Until school segregation ended, southern blacks could attend only all-black colleges. Now they are free to apply to previously all-white colleges, and these schools are integrated. But the traditional black colleges still exist, and very few whites apply to them. In 1992 the Supreme Court held that the state could not solve the problem by requiring a race-neutral admissions policy.* Now the Court must decide whether a predominantly black college can receive state support.

Arguments for all-black colleges:

1. These schools have a long tradition that ought to be preserved.
2. Many black students will learn better in an all-black environment.
3. African American organizations, in particular the United Negro College Fund, raise money for these schools.

Arguments against all-black colleges:

1. If the state once required single-race schools, it now has an obligation to dismantle them.
2. Race is a suspect classification, and no state program that chiefly serves one race can be allowed.

Your decision:

Allow all-black colleges _____
Ban all-black colleges _____

*United States v. Fordice, 505 U.S. 717 (1992).

On September 25, 1957, troops of the 101st Airborne Division escorted nine black students into Little Rock (Arkansas) Central High School to begin its integration.

■ **Implementation** The *Brown* case involved a class-action suit; that is, it applied not only to Linda Brown but to all others similarly situated. This meant that black children everywhere now had the right to attend formerly all-white schools. This change would be one of the most far-reaching and conflict-provoking events in modern American history. It could not be effected overnight or by the stroke of a pen. In 1955 the Supreme Court decided that it would let local federal district courts oversee the end of segregation by giving them the power to approve or disapprove local desegregation plans. This was to be done "with all deliberate speed."[13]

In the South "all deliberate speed" turned out to be a snail's pace. Massive resistance to desegregation broke out in many states. Some communities simply defied the Court; some sought to evade its edict by closing their public schools. In 1956 over one hundred southern members of Congress signed a "Southern Manifesto" that condemned the *Brown* decision as an "abuse of judicial power" and pledged to "use all lawful means to bring about a reversal of the decision."

In the late 1950s and early 1960s the National Guard and regular army paratroopers were used to escort black students into formerly all-white schools and universities. It was not until the 1970s that resistance collapsed and most southern schools were integrated. The use of armed force convinced people that resistance was futile; the disruption of the politics and economy of the South convinced leaders that it was imprudent; and the voting power of blacks convinced politicians that it was suicidal. In addition, federal laws began providing financial aid to integrated schools and withholding it from segregated ones. By 1970 only 14 percent of southern black schoolchildren still attended all-black schools.[14]

■ **The Rationale** As the struggle to implement the *Brown* decision continued, the importance of the rationale for that decision became apparent. The case was decided in a way that surprised many legal scholars. The Court could have said that the equal-protection clause of the Fourteenth Amendment makes the Constitution, and thus state laws, color-blind. Or it could have said that the authors of the Fourteenth Amendment meant to ban segregated schools. It did neither. Instead it said that segregated education is bad because it "has a detrimental effect upon the colored children" by generating "a feeling

In 1963 Governor George Wallace of Alabama stood in the doorway of the University of Alabama to block the entry of black students. Facing him is U.S. Deputy Attorney General Nicholas Katzenbach.

of inferiority as to their status in the community" that may "affect their hearts and minds in a way unlikely ever to be undone."[15] This conclusion was supported by a footnote reference to social science studies of the apparent impact of segregation on black children.

Why did the Court rely on social science as much as or more than the Constitution in supporting its decision? Apparently for two reasons. One was the justices' realization that the authors of the Fourteenth Amendment may *not* have intended to outlaw segregated schools. The schools in Washington, D.C., were segregated when the amendment was proposed, and when this fact was mentioned during the debate, it seems to have been made clear that the amendment was not designed to abolish this segregation. When Congress debated a civil rights act a few years later, it voted down provisions that would have ended segre-

---

de jure segregation   Racial segregation that is required by law.

de facto segregation   Racial segregation that occurs in schools, not as a result of the law, but as a result of patterns of residential settlement.

---

gation in schools.[16] The Court could not easily base its decision on a constitutional provision that had, at best, an uncertain application to schools. The other reason grew out of the first. On so important a matter the chief justice wanted to speak for a unanimous court. Some justices did not agree that the Fourteenth Amendment made the Constitution color-blind. In the interests of harmony the Court found an ambiguous rationale for its decision.

■ **Desegregation Versus Integration**   That ambiguity led to the third issue. If separate schools were inherently unequal, what would "unseparate" schools look like? Since the Court had not said that race was irrelevant, an "unseparate" school could be either one that blacks and whites were free to attend if they chose or one that blacks and whites in fact attended whether they wanted to or not. The first might be called a desegregated school, the latter an integrated school. Think of the Topeka case. Was it enough that there was now no barrier to Linda Brown's attending the white school in her neighborhood? Or was it necessary that there be black children (if not Linda, then some others) actually going to that school together with white children?

As long as the main impact of the *Brown* decision lay in the South, where laws had prevented blacks from attending white schools, this question did not seem important. Segregation by law **(de jure segregation)** was now clearly unconstitutional. But in the North laws had not kept blacks and whites apart; instead all-black and all-white schools were the result of residential segregation, preferred living patterns, informal social forces, and administrative practices (such as drawing school district lines so as to produce single-race schools). This was often called segregation in fact **(de facto segregation).**

In 1968 the Supreme Court settled the matter. In New Kent County, Virginia, the school board had created a "freedom-of-choice" plan under which every pupil would be allowed without legal restriction to attend the school of his or her choice. As it turned out, all the white children chose to remain in the all-white school, and 85 percent of the black children remained in the all-black school. The Court rejected this plan as unconstitutional because it did not produce the "ultimate end," which was a "unitary, nonracial system of education."[17] In the opinion written by Justice William Brennan, the Court seemed to be saying that the Constitution required actual racial mixing in the schools, not just the repeal of laws requiring racial separation.

This impression was confirmed three years later when the Court considered a plan in North Carolina under which pupils in Mecklenburg County (which includes Charlotte) were assigned to the nearest neighborhood school without regard to race. As a result about half the black children now attended formerly all-white schools, with the other half attending all-black schools. The federal district court held that this was inadequate and ordered some children to be bused into more distant schools in order to achieve a greater degree of integration. The Supreme Court, now led by Chief Justice Warren Burger, upheld the district judge on the grounds that the court plan was necessary to achieve a "unitary school system."[18]

This case—*Swann v. Charlotte-Mecklenburg Board of Education*—pretty much set the guidelines for all subsequent cases involving school segregation. The essential features of those guidelines are as follows:

- To violate the Constitution, a school system, by law, practice, or regulation, must have engaged in discrimination. Put another way, a plaintiff must show an intent to discriminate on the part of the public schools.
- The existence of all-white or all-black schools in a district with a history of segregation creates a presumption of intent to discriminate.
- The remedy for past discrimination will not be limited to freedom of choice, or what the Court called "the walk-in school." Remedies may include racial quotas in the assignment of teachers and pupils, redrawn district lines, and court-ordered busing.
- Not every school must reflect the social composition of the school system as a whole.

Relying on *Swann*, district courts have supervised redistricting and busing plans in localities all over the nation, often in the face of bitter opposition from the community. In Boston the control of the city schools by a federal judge, W. Arthur Garrity, lasted for more than a decade and involved him in every aspect of school administration.

One major issue not settled by *Swann* was whether busing and other remedies should cut across city and county lines. In some places the central-city schools had become virtually all black. Racial integration could be achieved only by bringing black pupils to

Antibusing protesters buried a school bus (unoccupied) to dramatize their cause.

white suburban schools or moving white pupils into central-city schools. In a series of split-vote decisions the Court ruled that court-ordered intercity busing could be authorized only if it could be demonstrated that the suburban areas as well as the central city had in fact practiced school segregation. Where that could not be shown, such intercity busing would not be required. The Court was not persuaded that intent had been proved in Atlanta, Detroit, Denver, Indianapolis, and Richmond, but it was persuaded that it had been proved in Louisville and Wilmington.[19]

The importance that the Court attaches to intent means that if a school system that was once integrated becomes all black as a result of whites' moving to the suburbs, the Court will not require that district lines constantly be redrawn or new busing plans adopted to adjust to the changing distribution

LANDMARK CASES

Civil Rights

- *Plessy v. Ferguson* (1896): Upheld separate-but-equal facilities for white and black people on railroad cars.
- *Brown v. Board of Education* (1954): Said that separate public schools are inherently unequal, thus starting racial desegregation.
- *Green v. County School Board of New Kent County* (1968): Banned a freedom-of-choice plan for integrating schools, suggesting that blacks and whites must actually attend racially mixed schools.
- *Swann v. Charlotte-Mecklenburg Board of Education* (1971): Approved busing and redrawing district lines as ways of integrating public schools.

of the population.[20] This in turn means that as long as blacks and whites live in different neighborhoods for whatever reason, there is a good chance that some schools in both areas will be heavily of one race. If mandatory busing or other integration measures cause whites to move out of a city at a faster rate than they otherwise would (a process often called "white flight"), then efforts to integrate the schools may in time create more single-race schools. Ultimately integrated schools will exist only in integrated neighborhoods or where the quality of education is so high that both blacks and whites want to enroll in the school even at some cost in terms of travel and inconvenience.

Mandatory busing to achieve racial integration has been a deeply controversial program and has generated considerable public opposition. Surveys show that a majority of people oppose it.[21] As recently as 1992 a poll showed that 48 percent of whites in the Northeast and 53 percent of southern whites felt that it was "not the business" of the federal government to ensure "that black and white children go to the same schools."[22] Presidents Nixon, Ford, and Reagan opposed busing; all three supported legislation to prevent or reduce it, and Reagan petitioned the courts to reconsider busing plans. The courts refused to reconsider, and Congress has passed only minor restrictions on busing.

The reason why Congress has not followed public opinion on this matter is complex. It has been torn between the desire to support civil rights and uphold the courts and the desire to represent the views of its constituents. Because it faces a dilemma, Congress has taken both sides of the issue simultaneously. By the late 1980s busing was a dying issue in Congress, in part because no meaningful legislation seemed possible and in part because popular passion over busing had somewhat abated.

Then, in 1992, the Supreme Court made it easier for local school systems to reclaim control over their schools from the courts. In DeKalb County, Georgia (a suburb of Atlanta), the schools had been operating under court-ordered desegregation plans for many years. Despite this effort full integration had not been achieved, largely because the county's neighborhoods had increasingly become either all black or all white. The Court held that the local schools could not be held responsible for segregation caused solely by segregated living patterns and so the courts would have to relinquish their control over the schools.[23]

☆ The Campaign in Congress

The campaign in the courts for desegregated schools, though slow and costly, was a carefully managed effort to alter the interpretation of a constitutional provision. But to get new civil rights laws out of Congress required a far more difficult and decentralized strategy, one that was aimed at mobilizing public opinion and overcoming the many congressional barriers to action.

*In 1960 black students from North Carolina Agricultural and Technical College staged the first
"sit-in" when they were refused service at a lunch counter in Greensboro (left). Twenty years
later graduates of the college returned to the same lunch counter (right). Though prices had risen,
the service had improved.*

The first problem was to get civil rights on the political agenda by convincing people that something had to be done. This could be achieved by dramatizing the problem in ways that tugged at the conscience of whites who were not racist but were ordinarily indifferent to black problems. Brutal lynchings of blacks had shocked these whites, but lynchings were becoming less frequent in the 1950s, and obviously black leaders had no desire to provoke more lynchings just to get sympathy for their cause.

Those leaders could, however, arrange for dramatic confrontations between blacks claiming some obvious right and the whites who denied it to them. Beginning in the late 1950s these confrontations began to occur in the form of sit-ins at segregated lunch counters and "freedom rides" on segregated bus lines. At about the same time, efforts were made to get blacks registered to vote in counties where whites had used intimidation and harassment to prevent it.

The best-known campaign occurred in 1955–1956 in Montgomery, Alabama, where blacks, led by a young minister named Martin Luther King, Jr., boycotted the local bus system after it had a black woman, Rosa Parks, arrested because she refused to surrender her seat on a bus to a white man.

These early demonstrations were based on the philosophy of **civil disobedience**—that is, peacefully violating a law, such as one requiring blacks to ride in a segregated section of a bus, and allowing oneself to be arrested as a result.

But the momentum of protest, once unleashed, could not be centrally directed or confined to nonviolent action. A rising tide of anger, especially among younger blacks, resulted in the formation of more militant organizations and the spontaneous eruption of violent demonstrations and riots in dozens of cities across the country. From 1964 to 1968 there were in the North as well as the South four "long, hot summers" of racial violence.

The demonstrations and rioting succeeded in getting civil rights on the national political agenda, but at a cost: many whites, opposed to the demonstrations or appalled by the riots, dug in their heels and fought against making any concessions to "law-breakers," "troublemakers," and "rioters." In 1964 and again in 1968 over two-thirds of the whites interviewed in opinion polls said that the civil rights movement was pushing too fast, had hurt the black cause, and was too violent.[24]

In short, there was a conflict between the agenda-setting and coalition-building aspects of the civil rights movement. This was especially a problem since conservative southern legislators still controlled many key congressional committees that had for

civil disobedience   Opposing a law one considers unjust by peacefully disobeying it and accepting the resultant punishment.

Figure 6.1   Changing White Attitudes Toward Differing Levels of School Integration

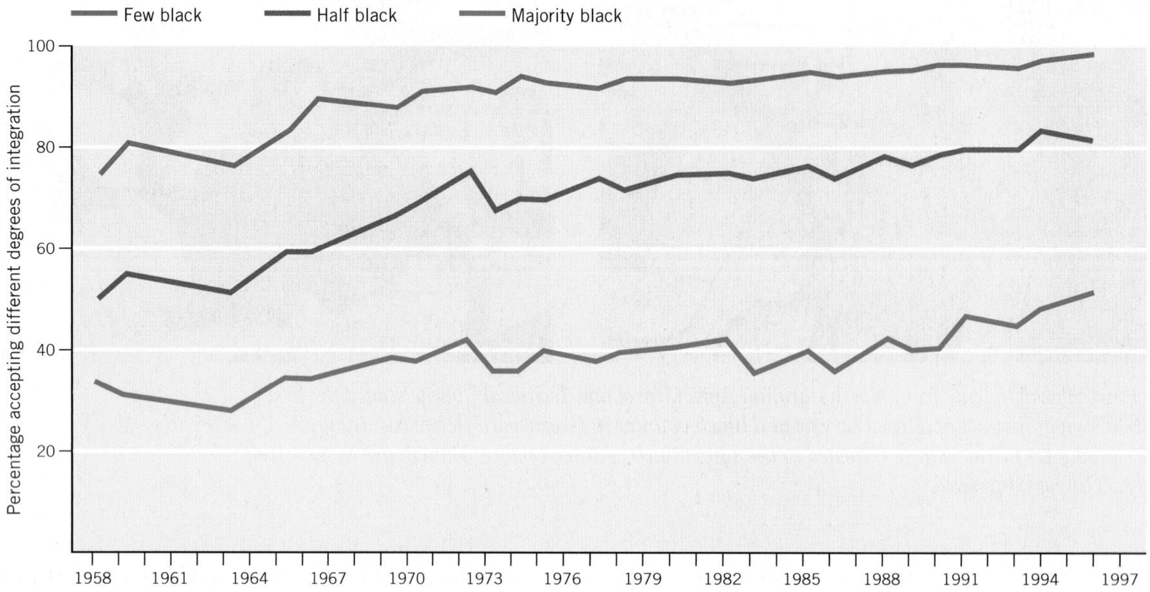

Source: Reprinted by permission of the publishing from *Racial Attitudes in America* by Howard Schuman, Charlotte Steeh, and Lawrence Bobo, p. 69, Cambridge, Mass.: Harvard University Press. Copyright © 1985, 1997, by the Presidents and Fellows of Harvard College.

years been the graveyard of civil rights legislation. The Senate Judiciary Committee was dominated by a coalition of southern Democrats and conservative Republicans, and the House Rules Committee was under the control of a chairman hostile to civil rights bills, Howard Smith of Virginia. Any bill that passed the House faced an almost certain filibuster in the Senate. Finally, President John F. Kennedy was reluctant to submit strong civil rights bills to Congress.

Four developments made it possible to break the deadlock. First, public opinion was changing. As Figure 6.1 shows, the proportion of whites who said that they were willing to have their children attend a school that was half black increased sharply (though the proportion of whites willing to have their children attend a school that was predominantly black increased by much less). About the same change could be found in attitudes toward allowing blacks equal access to hotels and buses.[25] Of course support in principle for these civil rights measures was not necessarily the same as support in practice; nonetheless, there clearly was occurring a major shift in popular approval of at least the principles of civil rights. At the leading edge of this change were young, college-educated people.[26]

Second, certain violent reactions by white segregationists to black demonstrators were vividly portrayed by the media, especially television, in ways that gave to the civil rights cause a powerful moral force. In May 1963 the head of the Birmingham police, Eugene "Bull" Connor, ordered his men to use attack dogs and high-pressure fire hoses to repulse a peaceful march by African Americans demanding desegregated public facilities and increased job opportunities. The pictures of that confrontation (such as the one on page 137) created a national sensation and contributed greatly to the massive participation, by whites and blacks alike, in the "March on Washington" that summer. About a quarter of a million people gathered in front of the Lincoln Memorial to hear Martin Luther King, Jr., deliver a stirring and widely hailed address, often called the "I Have a Dream" speech. The following summer in Neshoba County, Mississippi, three young civil rights workers (two white and one black) were brutally murdered by Klansmen aided by the local sheriff. When the FBI identified the murderers, the effect on national public opinion was galvanic; no white southern leader could any longer offer persuasive opposition to fed-

This picture of a police dog lunging at a black man during a racial demonstration in Birmingham, Alabama, in May 1963 was one of the most influential news photographs ever published. It was widely reprinted throughout the world and was frequently referred to in congressional debates on the civil rights bill of 1964.

eral laws protecting voting rights when white law enforcement officers had killed students working to protect those rights. And the next year a white woman, Viola Liuzzo, was shot and killed while driving a car used to transport civil rights workers. Her death was the subject of a presidential address.

Third, President John F. Kennedy was assassinated in Dallas, Texas, in November 1963. Many people originally (and wrongly) thought that he had been killed by a right-wing conspiracy. Even after the assassin had been caught and shown to have left-wing associations, the shock of the president's murder—in a southern city—helped build support for efforts by the new president, Lyndon B. Johnson (himself a Texan), to obtain passage of a strong civil rights bill as a memorial to the slain president.

Fourth, the 1964 elections not only returned Johnson to office with a landslide victory but also sent a huge Democratic majority to the House and

retained the large Democratic margin in the Senate. This made it possible for northern Democrats to out-vote or outmaneuver southerners in the House.

The cumulative effect of these forces led to the enactment of five civil rights laws between 1957 and 1968. Three (1957, 1960, and 1965) were chiefly directed at protecting the right to vote; one (1968) was aimed at preventing discrimination in housing; and one (1964), the most far-reaching of all, dealt with voting, employment, schooling, and public accommodations.

The passage of the 1964 act was the high point of the legislative struggle. Liberals in the House had drafted a bipartisan bill, but it was now in the House Rules Committee, where such matters had often disappeared without a trace. In the wake of Kennedy's murder a discharge petition was filed, with President Johnson's support, to take the bill out of committee and bring it to the floor of the House. But the Rules Committee, without waiting for a vote on the petition (which it probably realized it would lose), sent the bill to the floor, where it passed overwhelmingly. In the Senate an agreement between Republican minority leader Everett Dirksen and President Johnson smoothed the way for passage in several important respects. The House bill was sent directly to the Senate floor, thereby bypassing the southern-dominated Judiciary Committee. Nineteen southern senators began an eight-week filibuster against the bill. On June 10, 1964, by a vote of seventy-one to twenty-nine, cloture was invoked and the filibuster ended—the first time in history that a filibuster aimed at blocking civil rights legislation had been broken.

Since the 1960s congressional support for civil rights legislation has grown—so much so, indeed, that labeling a bill a civil rights measure, once the kiss of death, now almost guarantees its passage. For example, in 1984 the Supreme Court decided that the federal ban on discrimination in education applied only to the "program or activity" receiving federal aid and not to the entire school or university.[27] In 1988 Congress passed a bill to overturn this decision by making it clear that antidiscrimination rules applied to the entire educational institution and not just to that part (say, the physics lab) receiving federal money. When President Reagan vetoed the bill (because, in his view, it would diminish the freedom of church-affiliated schools), Congress overrode the veto. In the override vote every southern Democrat in the Senate and almost 90 percent of those

Key Provisions of Major Civil Rights Laws

1957 **Voting** Made it a federal crime to try to prevent a person from voting in a federal election. Created the Civil Rights Commission.

1960 **Voting** Authorized the attorney general to appoint federal referees to gather evidence and make findings about allegations that African Americans were being deprived of their right to vote. Made it a federal crime to use interstate commerce to threaten or carry out a bombing.

1964 **Voting** Made it more difficult to use devices such as literacy tests to bar African Americans from voting.

Public accommodations Barred discrimination on grounds of race, color, religion, or national origin in restaurants, hotels, lunch counters, gasoline stations, movie theaters, stadiums, arenas, and lodging houses with more than five rooms.

Schools Authorized the attorney general to bring suit to force the desegregation of public schools on behalf of citizens.

Employment Outlawed discrimination in hiring, firing, or paying employees on grounds of race, color, religion, national origin, or sex.

Federal funds Barred discrimination in any activity receiving federal assistance.

1965 **Voter registration** Authorized appointment by the Civil Service Commission of voting examiners who would require registration of all eligible voters in federal, state, and local elections, general or primary, in areas where discrimination was found to be practiced or where less than 50 percent of voting-age residents were registered to vote in the 1964 election. The law was to have expired in 1970, but Congress extended it; it will expire in 2007.

Literacy tests Suspended use of literacy tests or other devices to prevent African Americans from voting.

1968 **Housing** Banned, by stages, discrimination in sale or rental of most housing (excluding private owners who sell or rent their homes without the services of a real-estate broker).

Riots Made it a federal crime to use interstate commerce to organize or incite a riot.

1972 **Education** Prohibited sex discrimination in education programs receiving federal aid.

1988 **Discrimination** If any part of an organization receives federal aid, no part of that organization may discriminate on the basis of race, sex, age, or physical handicap.

1991 **Discrimination** Made it easier to sue over job discrimination and collect damages; overturned certain Supreme Court decisions. Made it illegal for the government to adjust, or "norm," test scores by race.

in the House voted for the bill. This was a dramatic change from 1964, when over 80 percent of the southern Democrats in Congress voted against the Civil Rights Act (see Figure 6.2).

This change partly reflected the growing political strength of southern blacks. In 1960 less than one-third of voting-age blacks in the South were registered to vote; by 1971 more than half were, and by 1984 two-thirds were. In 2001 over nine thousand blacks held elective office (see Table 6.1). But this was only half of the story. Attitudes among white political elites and members of Congress had also changed. This was evident as early as 1968, when Congress passed a law barring discrimination in housing even though polls showed that only 35 percent of the public supported the measure.

Civil rights is not an issue easily confined to schools, housing, and jobs. Sometimes it is extended to crime. When crack cocaine became a popular drug, it was cheap and easily sold on street corners.

President Lyndon Johnson congratulates Rev. Martin Luther King, Jr., after signing the Civil Rights Act of 1964.

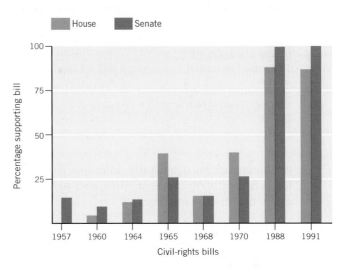

Figure 6.2 **Growing Support Among Southern Democrats in Congress for Civil Rights Bills**

Sources: Congressional Quarterly, *Congress and the Nation,* vols. 1, 2, 3, 7, 8.

When the public demanded that the police get tough on crack dealers, arrests followed. Since the great majority of arrested dealers were black, there was a sharp increase in black drug dealers going to prison. Some blacks claimed that they were being singled out by the police because of their race. The Supreme Court disagreed, holding that no evidence had been presented to show that drug dealers of other races had not been prosecuted.[28]

Racial Profiling

If law enforcement authorities are more likely to stop and question people because of their race or ethnicity, racial profiling occurs. At first glance this would seem to be a bad idea. For example, African Americans often complain that they are stopped by the police for "driving while black." This complaint became a national issue in 1998 when the governor of New Jersey fired the head of the state police for saying that blacks were stopped more frequently than whites because they broke the law more frequently. Soon President Clinton and later President Bush made statements condemning racial profiling.

But there is another side to this issue. Perhaps people of a certain race are more likely to break the speed limit or smuggle drugs in their cars; if that is the case, then stopping them more frequently, even if it means stopping more innocent people, may make sense. A study of police stops in Oakland, California,

by the RAND Corporation showed that, at least in that city, officers stopped cars without knowing the race of the occupants because the share of blacks stopped at night, when the drivers could not been seen, was the same as the share stopped during the day when they could be seen.[29]

The terrorist attacks of 9/11 added a new dimension to the issue. If young Middle Eastern men are more likely to smuggle weapons onto airplanes, searching them more carefully than one searches an elderly white Caucasian woman may make sense. But federal officials are leery of doing anything that might get them labeled as "racial profilers."

☆ Women and Equal Rights

The political and legal efforts to secure civil rights for African Americans were accompanied by efforts to expand the rights of women. There was an important difference between the two movements, however: whereas African Americans were arguing against a legal tradition that explicitly aimed to keep them in a subservient status, women had to argue against a tradition that claimed to be protecting them. For example, in 1908 the Supreme Court upheld an Oregon law that limited female laundry workers to a

Table 6.1	Increase in Number of Black Elected Officials		
Office	**1970**	**1991**	**2001**
Congress and state legislatures	182	476	633
City and county offices	715	4,493	5,456
Judges and sheriffs	213	847	1,044
Boards of education	362	1,629	1,928
Total	1,472	7,445	9,061

Sources: Statistical Abstract of the United States, 2003, Table 417.

Though many women have enlisted in the armed forces, the Supreme Court in 1981 held that Congress could exclude women from the draft.

ten-hour workday against the claim that it violated the Fourteenth Amendment. The Court justified its decision with this language:

> The two sexes differ in structure of body, in the functions to be performed by each, in the amount of physical strength, in the capacity for long-continued labor, particularly when done standing. . . . the self-reliance which enables one to assert full rights, and in the capacity to maintain the struggle for subsistence. This difference justifies a difference in legislation and upholds that which is designed to compensate for some of the burdens which rest upon her.[30]

The origin of the movement to give more rights to women was probably the Seneca Falls Convention held in 1848. Its leaders began to demand the right to vote for women. Though this was slowly granted by several states, especially in the West, it was not until 1920 that the Nineteenth Amendment made it clear that no state may deny the right to vote on the basis of sex. The great change in the status of women, however, took place during World War II when the demand for workers in our defense plants led to the employment of millions of women, such as "Rosie the Riveter," in jobs they had rarely held before. After the war, the feminist movement took flight with the publication in 1963 of *The Feminine Mystique* by Betty Friedan.

Congress responded by passing laws that required equal pay for equal work, prohibited discrimination on the basis of sex in employment and among students in any school or university receiving federal funds, and banned discrimination against pregnant women on the job.[31]

At the same time, the Supreme Court was altering the way it interpreted the Constitution. The key passage was the Fourteenth Amendment, which prohibits any state from denying to "any person" the "equal protection of the laws." For a long time the traditional standard, as we saw in the 1908 case, was a kind of protective paternalism. By the early 1970s, however, the Court had changed its mind. In deciding whether the Constitution bars all, some, or no sexual discrimination, the Court had a choice between two standards. The first is the *reasonableness* standard. This says that when the government treats some classes of people differently from others—for example, applying statutory rape laws to men but not to women—the different treatment must be reasonable and not arbitrary. The second is the strict scrutiny standard. This says that some instances of drawing distinctions between different groups of people—for example, by treating whites and blacks differently—are inherently suspect; thus the Court will subject them to strict scrutiny to ensure that they are clearly necessary to attain a legitimate state goal.

When women complained that some laws treated them unfairly, the Court adopted a standard somewhere between the reasonableness and strict scrutiny tests. Thus a law that treats men and women differently must be more than merely reasonable, but the allowable differences need not meet the strict scrutiny test.

And so in 1971 the Court held that an Idaho statute was unconstitutional because it required that males be preferred over females when choosing people to administer the estates of deceased children. To satisfy the Constitution, a law treating men and women differently "must be reasonable, not arbitrary, and must rest on some ground of difference having a fair and substantial relation to the object of legislation so that all persons similarly circumstanced shall be treated alike."[32] In later decisions some members of the Court wanted to make classifications based on sex inherently suspect and subject to the strict scrutiny test, but no majority has yet embraced this position.[33]

But sexual classifications can also be judged by a different standard. The Civil Rights Act of 1964 prohibits sex discrimination in the hiring, firing, and compensation of employees. The 1972 Civil Rights Act bans sex discrimination in local education programs receiving federal aid. These laws apply to *private* and not just government action.

Over the years the Court has decided many cases involving sexual classification. The following lists provide several examples of illegal sexual discrimination (violating either the Constitution or a civil rights act) and legal sexual distinctions (violating neither).

■ Illegal Discrimination

- A state cannot set different ages at which men and women legally become adults.[34]
- A state cannot set different ages at which men and women are allowed to buy beer.[35]
- Women cannot be barred from jobs by arbitrary height and weight requirements.[36]
- Employers cannot require women to take mandatory pregnancy leaves.[37]
- Girls cannot be barred from Little League baseball teams.[38]

- Business and service clubs, such as the Junior Chamber of Commerce and Rotary Club, cannot exclude women from membership.[39]
- Though women as a group live longer than men, an employer must pay them monthly retirement benefits equal to those received by men.[40]
- High schools must pay the coaches of girls' sports the same as they pay the coaches of boys' sports.[41]

■ Decisions Allowing Differences Based on Sex

- A law that punishes males but not females for statutory rape is permissible; men and women are not "similarly situated" with respect to sexual relations.[42]
- All-boy and all-girl public schools are permitted if enrollment is voluntary and quality is equal.[43]
- States can give widows a property-tax exemption not given to widowers.[44]
- The navy may allow women to remain officers longer than men without being promoted.[45]

The lower federal courts have been especially busy in the area of sexual distinctions. They have said that public taverns may not cater to men only and that girls may not be prevented from competing against boys in noncontact high school sports; on the other hand, hospitals may bar fathers from the delivery room. Women may continue to use their maiden names after marriage.[46]

In 1996 the Supreme Court ruled that women must be admitted to the Virginia Military Institute, until then an all-male state-supported college that had for many decades supplied what it called an "adversative method" of training to instill physical and mental discipline in cadets. In practical terms this meant being very tough on students. The Court said that for a state to justify spending tax money on a single-sex school, it must supply an "exceedingly persuasive justification" for excluding the other gender. Virginia countered by offering to support an all-female training course at another college, but this was not enough.[47] This decision came close to imposing the strict scrutiny test, and so it has raised important questions about what could happen to all-female or traditionally black colleges that accept state money.

Perhaps the most far-reaching cases defining the rights of women have involved the draft and abortion. In 1981 the Court held in *Rostker v. Goldberg* that Congress may require men but not women to

LANDMARK CASES

Women's Rights

- *Reed v. Reed* (1971): Gender discrimination violates the equal protection clause of the Constitution.
- *Craig v. Boren* (1976): Gender discrimination can only be justified if it serves "important governmental objectives" and be "substantially related to those objectives."
- *Rostker v. Goldberg* (1981): Congress can draft men without drafting women.
- *United States v. Virginia* (1996): State may not finance an all-male military school.

register for the draft without violating the due-process clause of the Fifth Amendment.[48] In the area of national defense the Court will give great deference to congressional policy (Congress had already decided to bar women from combat roles). For many years women could be pilots and sailors but not on combat aircraft or combat ships. In 1993 the secretary of defense opened air and sea combat positions to all persons regardless of gender; only ground-troop combat positions are still reserved for men. The issue played a role in preventing the ratification of the Equal Rights Amendment to the Constitution, because of fears that it would reverse *Rostker v. Goldberg*.

Sexual Harassment

When Paula Corbin Jones accused President Clinton of sexual harassment, the judge threw the case out of court because she had not submitted enough evidence such that, if the jury believed her story, she would have made a legally adequate argument that she had been sexually harassed.

What, then, is sexual harassment? Drawing on rulings by the Equal Employment Opportunities Commission, the Supreme Court has held that harassment can take one of two forms. First, it is illegal for someone to request sexual favors as a condition of employment or promotion. This is the "quid pro quo" rule. If a person does this, the employer is "strictly liable." Strict liability means that the employer can be found at fault even if he or she did not know that a subordinate was requesting sex in exchange for hiring or promotion.

Second, it is illegal for an employee to experience a work environment that has been made hostile or intimidating by a steady pattern of offensive sexual teasing, jokes, or obscenity. But employers are not strictly liable in this case; they can be found at fault only if they were "negligent"—that is, they knew about the hostile environment but did nothing about it.

In 1998 the Supreme Court decided three cases that made these rules either better or worse, depending on your point of view. In one it determined that a school system was not liable for the conduct of a teacher who seduced a female student because the student never reported the actions. In a second it held that a city was liable for a sexually hostile work environment confronting a female lifeguard even though she did not report this to her superiors. In the third it decided that a female employee who was not promoted after having rejected the sexual advances of her boss could recover financial damages from the firm. But, it added, the firm could have avoided paying this bill if it had put in place an "affirmative defense" against sexual exploitation, although the Court never said what such a policy might be.[49]

Sexual harassment is a serious matter, but because there are almost no federal laws governing it, we are left with somewhat vague and often inconsistent court and bureaucratic rules to guide us.

Privacy and Sex

Regulating sexual matters has traditionally been left up to the states, which do so by exercising their **police powers.** These powers include more than the authority to create police departments; they include all laws designed to promote public order and secure the safety and morals of the citizens. Some have argued that the Tenth Amendment to the Constitu-

---

police powers   State power to effect laws promoting health, safety, and morals.

LANDMARK CASES

Privacy and Abortion

- *Griswold v. Connecticut* **(1965):** Found a "right to privacy" in the Constitution that would ban any state law against selling contraceptives.
- *Roe v. Wade* **(1973):** State laws against abortion were unconstitutional.
- *Webster v. Reproductive Health Services* **(1989):** Allowed states to ban abortions from public hospitals and permitted doctors to test to see if fetuses were viable.
- *Planned Parenthood v. Casey* **(1992):** Reaffirmed *Roe v. Wade* but upheld certain limits on its use.
- *Stenberg v. Carhart* **(2000):** States may not ban partial birth abortions if they fail to allow an exception to protect the health of the mother.

tion, by reserving to the states all powers not delegated to the federal government, meant that states could do anything not explicitly prohibited by the Constitution. But that changed when the Supreme Court began expanding the power of Congress over business and when it started to view sexual matters under the newly discovered right to privacy.

Until that point, it had been left up to the states to decide whether and under what circumstances a woman could obtain an abortion. For example, New York allowed abortions during the first twenty-four weeks of pregnancy, while Texas banned it except when the mother's life was threatened.

That began to change in 1965 when the Supreme Court held that the states could not prevent the sale of contraceptives because by so doing it would invade a "zone of privacy." Privacy is nowhere mentioned in the Constitution, but the Court argued that it could be inferred from "penumbras" (literally, shadows) cast off by various provisions of the Bill of Rights.[50]

Eight years later the Court, in its famous *Roe v. Wade* decision, held that a "right to privacy" is "broad enough to encompass a woman's decision whether or not to terminate a pregnancy."[51] The case, which began in Texas, produced this view: during the first three months (or trimester) of pregnancy, a woman has an unfettered right to an abortion. During the second trimester, states may regulate abortions but only to protect the mother's health. In the third trimester, states might ban abortions.

In reaching this decision, the Court denied that it was trying to decide when human life began—at the moment of conception, at the moment of birth, or somewhere in between. But that is not how critics of the decision saw things. To them life begins at conception, and so the human fetus is a "person" entitled to the equal protection of the laws guaranteed by the Fourteenth Amendment. People feeling this way began to use the slogans "right to life" and "pro-life." Supporters of the Court's action saw matters differently. In their view, no one can say for certain when human life begins; what one *can* say, however, is that a woman is entitled to choose whether or not to have a baby. These people took the slogans "right to choose" and "pro-choice."

Almost immediately the congressional allies of pro-life groups introduced constitutional amendments to overturn *Roe v. Wade*, but none passed Congress. Nevertheless, abortion foes did persuade Congress, beginning in 1976, to bar the use of federal funds to pay for abortions except when the life of the mother is at stake. This provision is known as the Hyde Amendment, after its sponsor, Representative Henry Hyde. The chief effect of the amendment has been to deny the use of Medicaid funds to pay for abortions for low-income women.

Despite pro-life opposition, the Supreme Court for sixteen years steadfastly reaffirmed and even broadened its decision in *Roe v. Wade*. It struck down laws requiring, before an abortion could be performed, a woman to have the consent of her husband, an "emancipated" but underage girl to have the consent of her parents, or a woman to be advised by her doctor as to the facts about abortion.[52]

But in 1989, under the influence of justices appointed by President Reagan, it began in the *Webster* case to uphold some state restrictions on abortions. When that happened, many people predicted that in time *Roe v. Wade* would be overturned, especially if President H. W. Bush was able to appoint more justices. He appointed two (Souter and Thomas), but *Roe* survived. The key votes were cast by Justices O'Connor, Souter, and Kennedy. In 1992, in its *Casey* decision, the Court by a vote of five to four explicitly refused to overturn *Roe*, declaring that there was a right to abortion. At the same time, however, it upheld a variety of restrictions imposed by the state of Pennsylvania on women seeking abortions. These included a mandatory twenty-four-hour waiting period between the request for an abortion and the performance of it, the requirement that teenagers obtain the consent of one parent (or, in special circumstances, of a judge), and a requirement that women contemplating an abortion be given pamphlets about alternatives to it. Similar restrictions had been enacted in many other states, all of which looked to the Pennsylvania case for guidance as to whether they could be enforced. In allowing these restrictions, the Court overruled some of its own earlier decisions.[53] On the other hand, the Court did strike down a state law that would have required married women to obtain the consent of their husbands before having an abortion.

In 2000 the Court visited abortion again, and by another five-to-four vote refused to allow states to ban so-called partial birth abortions. This method is usually done to fetuses that are at least twenty weeks old.

With the right to an abortion again politically secure, the struggle over its implementation took a new turn. Antiabortion activists conducted demonstrations at many abortion clinics, and a few extremists wounded or killed some abortion doctors. This led to a demand for laws protecting the clinics. Laws were passed and court orders issued, designed to strike a balance between the activists' right to protest and the clinics' right to operate.

In 1997 the Supreme Court upheld legal orders that forbid acts of physical obstruction and that provide a "buffer zone" of fifteen feet around the entrance to a clinic within which demonstrations cannot occur.[54]

There is one irony in all of this: "Roe," the pseudonym for the woman who started the suit that became *Roe v. Wade*, never had an abortion and many years later, using her real name, Norma McCorvey, became an evangelical Christian who published a book and started a ministry to denounce abortions.

☆ Affirmative Action

A common thread running through the politics of civil rights is the argument between **equality of results** and equality of opportunity.

Equality of Results

One view, expressed by most civil rights and feminist organizations, is that the burdens of racism and sexism can be overcome only by taking race or sex into account in designing remedies. It is not enough to give rights to people; they must be given benefits. If life is a race, everybody must be brought up to the same starting line (or possibly even to the same finish line). This means that the Constitution is not and should not be color-blind or sex-neutral. In education this implies that the races must actually be mixed in the schools, by busing if necessary. In hiring it means that **affirmative action**—preferential hiring practices—must be used to find and hire women, African Americans, and other minorities. Women should not simply be free to enter the labor force; they should be given the material necessities (for example, free daycare) that will help them enter it. On payday workers' checks should reflect not just the results of people's competing in the marketplace but the results of plans designed to ensure that people earn comparable amounts for comparable jobs. Of late, affirmative action has been defended in the name of diversity or multiculturalism—the view that every institution (firm, school, or agency) and every college curriculum should reflect the cultural (that is, ethnic) diversity of the nation.

---

affirmative action   Programs designed to increase minority participation in some institution (businesses, schools, labor unions, or government agencies) by taking positive steps to appoint more minority-group members.

equality of result   Making certain that people achieve the same result.

☆ HOW THINGS WORK ☆

Becoming a Citizen

For persons born in the United States, the rights of U.S. citizenship have been ensured, in constitutional theory if not in everyday practice, since the passage of the Fourteenth Amendment in 1868 and the civil rights laws of the 1960s. The Fourteenth Amendment conferred citizenship upon "all persons born in the United States . . . and subject to the jurisdiction thereof." Subsequent laws also gave citizenship to children born outside the United States to parents who are American citizens.

But immigrants, by definition, are not born with the rights of U.S. citizenship. Instead those seeking to become U.S. citizens must, in effect, assume certain responsibilities in order to become citizens. The statutory requirements for naturalization, as they have been broadly construed by the courts, are as follows:

- Five years' residency, or three years if married to a citizen.
- Continuous residency since filing of the naturalization petition.

- Good moral character, which is loosely interpreted to mean no evidence of criminal activity.
- Attachment to constitutional principles. This means that potential citizens have to answer basic factual questions about American government (e.g., "Who was the first president of the United States?") and publicly denounce any and all allegiance to their native country and its leaders (e.g., Italy and the king of Italy), but devotion to constitutional principles is now regarded as being implicit in the act of applying for naturalization.
- Being favorably disposed to "the good order and happiness of the United States."*

Today about 97 percent of aliens who seek citizenship are successful in meeting these requirements and becoming naturalized citizens of the United States.

*8 U.S.C. 1423, 1427 (1970); *Girouard v. United States,* 328 U.S. 61 (1946).

Source: New York Times (July 25, 1993), 33. Copyright © 1993 by the *New York Times.* Reprinted by permission.

Equality of Opportunity

The second view holds that if it is wrong to discriminate *against* African Americans and women, it is equally wrong to give them preferential treatment over other groups. To do so constitutes **reverse discrimination.** The Constitution and laws should be color-blind and sex-neutral.[55] In this view allowing children to attend the school of their choice is sufficient; busing them to attain a certain racial mixture is wrong. Eliminating barriers to job opportunities is right; using numerical "targets" and "goals" to place minorities and women in specific jobs is wrong. If people wish to compete in the market, they should be satisfied with the market verdict concerning the worth of their work.

These two views are intertwined with other deep philosophical differences. Supporters of **equality of opportunity** tend to have orthodox beliefs; they favor letting private groups behave the way that they want (and so may defend the right of a men's club to

exclude women). Supporters of the opposite view are likely to be progressive in their beliefs and insist that private clubs meet the same standards as schools or business firms. Adherents to the equality-of-opportunity view often attach great importance to traditional models of the family and so are skeptical of daycare and federally funded abortions. Adherents to the equality-of-results view prefer greater freedom of choice in lifestyle questions and so take the opposite position on daycare and abortion.

Of course the debate is more complex than this simple contrast suggests. Take, for example, the question of affirmative action. Both the advocates of equality of opportunity and those of equality of

---

reverse discrimination   Using race or sex to give preferential treatment to some people.

equality of opportunity   Giving people an equal chance to succeed.

★ HOW THINGS WORK ★

The Rights of Aliens

America is a nation of immigrants. Some have arrived legally, others illegally. An illegal, or undocumented, alien is subject to being deported. With the passage in 1986 of the Immigration Reform and Control Act, illegal aliens who have resided in this country continuously since before January 1, 1982, are entitled to amnesty—that is, they can become legal residents. However, the same legislation stipulated that employers (who once could hire undocumented aliens without fear of penalty) must now verify the legal status of all newly hired employees; if they knowingly hire an illegal alien, they face civil and criminal penalties.

Aliens—people residing in this country who are not citizens—cannot vote or run for office. Nevertheless, they must pay taxes just as if they were citizens. And they are entitled to many constitutional rights, even if they are in this country illegally. This is because most of the rights mentioned in the Constitution refer to "people" or "persons," not to "citizens." For example, the Fourteenth Amendment bars a state from depriving "*any person* of life, liberty, or property, without due process of law" or from denying "to *any person* within its jurisdiction the equal protection of the laws" [italics added]. As a result, the courts have held that:

- The children of illegal aliens cannot be excluded from the public school system.[1]
- Legally admitted aliens are entitled to welfare benefits.[2]
- Illegal aliens cannot be the object of reprisals if they attempt to form a labor union where they work.[3]

- The First Amendment rights of free speech, religion, press, and assembly and the Fourth Amendment protections against arbitrary arrest and prosecution extend to aliens as well as to citizens.[4]
- Aliens are entitled to own property.

The government can make rules that apply to aliens only, but they must justify the reasonableness of the rules. For example:

- The Immigration and Naturalization Service has broader powers to arrest and search illegal aliens than police departments have to arrest and search citizens.[5]
- States can limit certain jobs, such as police officer and schoolteacher, to citizens.[6]
- The president or Congress can bar the employment of aliens by the federal government.[7]
- States can bar aliens from serving on a jury.[8]
- Illegal aliens are not entitled to obtain a Social Security card.

[1]*Plyler v. Doe*, 457 U.S. 202 (1982).

[2]*Graham v. Richardson*, 403 U.S. 365 (1971).

[3]*Sure-Tan v. National Labor Relations Board*, 467 U.S. 883 (1984).

[4]*Chew v. Colding*, 344 U.S. 590 (1953).

[5]*U.S. v. Brignoni-Ponce*, 422 U.S. 873 (1975); *INS v. Delgado*, 466 U.S. 210 (1984); *INS v. Lopez-Mendoza*, 486 U.S. 1032 (1984).

[6]*Cabell v. Chavez-Salido*, 454 U.S. 432 (1982); *Foley v. Connelie*, 435 U.S. 291 (1978); *Amblach v. Norwick*, 441 U.S. 68 (1979).

[7]*Hampton v. Mow Sun Wong*, 436 U.S. 67 (1976).

[8]*Schneider v. New Jersey*, 308 U.S. 147 (1939).

results might agree that there is something odd about a factory or university that hires no African Americans or women, and both might press it to prove that its hiring policy is fair. Affirmative action in this case can mean *either* looking hard for qualified women and minorities and giving them a fair shot at jobs *or* setting a numerical goal for the number of women and minorities that should be hired and insisting that that goal be met. Persons who defend the second course of action call these goals "targets"; persons who criticize that course call them "quotas."

The issue has largely been fought out in the courts. Between 1978 and 1990 about a dozen major cases involving affirmative action were decided by the Supreme Court; in about half it was upheld, and in the other half it was overturned. The different out-

★ **HOW THINGS WORK** ★

The Rights of the Disabled

In 1990 the federal government passed the Americans with Disabilities Act (ADA), a sweeping law that extended many of the protections enjoyed by women and racial minorities to disabled persons.

Who Is a Disabled Person?

Anyone who *has* a physical or mental impairment that substantially limits one or more major life activities (for example, holding a job), anyone who has a *record* of such impairment, or anyone who is *regarded* as having such an impairment is considered disabled.

What Rights Do Disabled Persons Have?

Employment Disabled persons may not be denied employment or promotion if, with "reasonable accommodation," they can perform the duties of that job. (Excluded from this protection are people who currently use illegal drugs, gamble compulsively, or are homosexual or bisexual.) Reasonable accommodation need not be made if this would cause "undue hardship" on the employer.

Government Programs and Transportation Disabled persons may not be denied access to government programs or benefits. New buses, taxis, and trains must be accessible to disabled persons, including those in wheelchairs.

Public Accommodations Disabled persons must enjoy "full and equal" access to hotels, restaurants, stores, schools, parks, museums, auditoriums, and the like. To achieve equal access, owners of existing facilities must alter them "to the maximum extent feasible"; builders of new facilities must ensure that they are readily accessible to disabled persons, unless this is structurally impossible.

Telephones The ADA directs the Federal Communications Commission to issue regulations to ensure that telecommunications devices for hearing- and speech-impaired people are available "to the extent possible and in the most efficient manner."

Congress The rights under this law apply to employees of Congress.

Rights Compared The ADA does not enforce the rights of disabled persons in the same way as the Civil Rights Act enforces the rights of African Americans and women. Racial or gender discrimination must end *regardless of cost*; denial of access to disabled persons must end unless "undue hardship" or excessive costs would result.

---

comes reflect two things—the differences in the facts of the cases and the arrival on the Court of three justices (Kennedy, O'Connor, and Scalia) appointed by a president, Ronald Reagan, who was opposed to at least the broader interpretation of affirmative action. As a result of these decisions, the law governing affirmative action is now complex and confusing.

Consider one issue: should the government be allowed to use a quota system to select workers, enroll students, award contracts, or grant licenses? In the *Bakke* decision in 1978, the Court said that the medical school of the University of California at Davis could not use an explicit numerical quota in admitting minority students but could "take race into account."[56] So no numerical quotas, right? Wrong. Two years later the Court upheld a federal rule that set aside 10 percent of all federal construction contracts for minority-owned firms.[57] All right, maybe quotas can't be used in medical schools, but they can be used in the construction industry. Not exactly. In 1989 the Court overturned a Richmond, Virginia, law that set aside 30 percent of its construction contracts for minority-owned firms.[58] Well, maybe the Court just changed its mind between 1980 and 1989. No. One year later it upheld a federal rule that gave preference to minority-owned firms in the awarding of broadcast licenses.[59] Then in 1993 it upheld the right of white contractors to challenge minority set-aside laws in Jacksonville, Florida.[60]

It is too early to try to make sense of these twists and turns, especially since a deeply divided Court is still wrestling with these issues and Congress (as with the Civil Rights Act of 1991) is modifying or superseding some earlier Court decisions. But a few

The federal government subsidizes some job training programs, such as for these medical assistants.

general standards seem to be emerging. In simplified form, they are as follows:

- The courts will subject any quota system created by state or local governments to "strict scrutiny" and will look for a "compelling" justification for it.
- Quotas or preference systems cannot be used by state or local governments without first showing that such rules are needed to correct an actual past or present pattern of discrimination.[61]
- In proving that there has been discrimination, it is not enough to show that African Americans (or other minorities) are statistically underrepresented among employees, contractors, or union members; you must identify the actual practices that have had this discriminatory impact.[62]
- Quotas or preference systems that are created by *federal* law will be given greater deference, in part because Section 5 of the Fourteenth Amendment gives to Congress powers not given to the states to correct the effects of racial discrimination.[63]
- It may be easier to justify in court a voluntary preference system (for example, one agreed to in a labor-management contract) than one that is required by law.[64]
- Even when you can justify special preferences in *hiring* workers, the Supreme Court is not likely to allow racial preferences to govern who gets *laid off*. A worker laid off to make room for a minority worker loses more than does a worker not hired in preference to a minority applicant.[65]

Complex as they are, these rulings still generate a great deal of passion. Supporters of the decisions barring certain affirmative action plans hail these decisions as steps back from an emerging pattern of reverse discrimination. In contrast, civil rights organizations have denounced those decisions that have overturned affirmative action programs. In 1990 their congressional allies introduced legislation that would reverse several decisions. In particular this legislation would put the burden of proof on the employer, not the employee, to show that the underrepresentation of minorities in the firm's work force was the result of legitimate and necessary business decisions and not the result of discrimination. If the employer could not prove this, the aggrieved employee would be able to collect large damage awards. (In the past, he or she could collect only back pay.) In 1991 the bill was passed and was signed by President Bush.

In thinking about these matters, most Americans distinguish between compensatory action and preferential treatment. They define *compensatory action* as "helping disadvantaged people catch up, usually by giving them extra education, training, or services." A majority of the public supports this. They define preferential treatment as "giving minorities preference in hiring, promotions, college admissions, and contracts." Large majorities oppose this.[66] These views reflect an enduring element in American political culture—a strong commitment to individualism ("nobody should get something without deserving it") coupled with support for help for the disadvantaged ("somebody who is suffering through no fault of his or her own deserves a helping hand").

Where does affirmative action fit into this culture? Polls suggest that if affirmative action is defined as "helping," people will support it, but if it is defined as "using quotas," they will oppose it. On this matter blacks and whites see things differently. Blacks think that they should receive preferences in employment to create a more diverse work force and to make up for past discrimination; whites oppose using goals to create diversity or to remedy past ills. In sum the controversy over affirmative action depends on what you mean by it and on what your racial identity is.[67]

A small construction company named Adarand tried to get a contract to build guardrails along a highway in Colorado. Though it was the low bidder, it lost the contract because of a government policy that favors small businesses owned by "socially and economically disadvantaged individuals"—that is, by racial and ethnic minorities. In a five-to-four decision the Court agreed with Adarand and sent the case back to Colorado for a new trial.

LANDMARK CASES

Affirmative Action

- *United Steelworkers v. Weber* **(1979):** Despite the ban on racial classifications in the 1964 Civil Rights Act, this case upheld the use of race in an employment agreement between the steelworkers union and steel plant.
- *Regents of the University of California v. Bakke* **(1978):** In a confused set of rival opinions, the decisive vote was cast by Justice Powell, who said that a quotalike ban on Bakke's admission was unconstitutional but that "diversity" was a legitimate goal that could be pursued by taking race into account.
- *Richmond v. Croson* **(1989):** Affirmative action plans must be judged by the strict scrutiny standard that requires any race-conscious plan to be narrowly tailored to serve a compelling interest.
- *Grutter v. Bollinger and Gratz v. Bollinger* **(2003):** Numerical benefits cannot be used to admit minorities into college, but race can be a "plus factor" in making those decisions.

The essence of its decision was that *any* discrimination based on race must be subject to strict scrutiny, even if its purpose is to help, not hurt, a racial minority. Strict scrutiny means two things:

- Any racial preference must serve a "compelling government interest."
- The preference must be "narrowly tailored" to serve that interest.[68]

To serve a compelling governmental interest, it is likely that any racial preference will have to remedy a clear pattern of past discrimination. No such pattern had been shown in Colorado.

This decision prompted a good deal of political debate about affirmative action. In California an initiative was put on the 1996 ballot to prevent state authorities from using "race, sex, color, ethnicity, or national origin as a criterion for either discriminating against, or granting preferential treatment to, any individual or group" in public employment, public education, or public contracting. When the votes were counted, it passed. Washington has also adopted a similar measure, and other states are debating it.

But the *Adarand* case and the passage of the California initiative did not mean that affirmative action was dead. Though the federal Court of Appeals for the Fifth Circuit had rejected the affirmative action program of the University of Texas Law School,[69] the Supreme Court did not take up that case. It waited for

several more years to rule on a similar matter arising from the University of Michigan. In 2003 the Supreme Court overturned the admissions policy of the University of Michigan that had given to every African American, Hispanic, and Native American applicant a bonus of 20 points out of the 100 needed to guarantee admission to the University's undergraduate program.[70] This policy was not "narrowly tailored." In rejecting the bonus system, the Court reaffirmed its decision in the *Bakke* case made in 1978 in which it had rejected a university using a "fixed quota" or an exact numerical advantage to the exclusion of "individual" considerations.

But that same day, the Court upheld the policy of the University of Michigan Law School that used race as a "plus factor" but not as a numerical quota.[71] It did so even though using race as a plus factor increased by threefold the proportion of minority applicants who were admitted. In short, admitting more minorities serves a "compelling state interest" and doing so by using race as a plus factor is "narrowly tailored" to achieve that goal.

☆ Gays and the Constitution

At first, the Supreme Court was willing to let states decide how many rights homosexuals should have. Georgia, for example, passed a law banning sodomy

---

LANDMARK CASES

Gay Rights

- *Lawrence v. Texas* **(2003):** State law may not ban sexual relations between same-sex partners.
- *Boy Scouts of America v. Dale* **(2000):** A private organization may ban gays from its membership.

(that is, any sexual contact involving the sex organs of one person and the mouth or anus of another). Though the law applied to all persons, homosexuals sued to overturn it. In *Bowers v. Hardwick,* the Supreme Court decided, by a five-to-four majority, that there was no reason in the Constitution to prevent a state from having such a law. There was a right to privacy, but it was designed simply to protect "family, marriage, or procreation."[72]

But ten years later the Court seemed to take a different position. The voters in Colorado had adopted a state constitutional amendment that made it illegal to pass any law to protect persons based on their "homosexual, lesbian, or bisexual orientation." The law did not penalize gays and lesbians; instead it said that they could not become the object of specific legal protection of the sort that had traditionally been given to racial or ethnic minorities. (Ordinances to give specific protection to homosexuals had been adopted in some Colorado cities.) The Supreme Court struck down the Colorado constitutional amendment because it violated the equal protection clause of the federal Constitution.[73]

Now we faced a puzzle: a state can pass a law banning homosexual sex, as Georgia had, but a state cannot adopt a rule preventing cities from protecting homosexuals, as Colorado had. The matter was finally put to rest in 2003. In *Lawrence v. Texas,* the Court, again by a five-to-four vote, overturned a Texas law that banned sexual contact between persons of the same sex. The Court repeated the language it had used earlier in cases involving contraception and abortion. If "the right to privacy means anything, it is the right of the individual, married or single, to be free from unwanted governmental intrusion" into sexual matters. The right of privacy means the "right to define one's own concept of

existence, of meaning, of the universe, and of the mystery of human life." It specifically overruled *Bowers v. Hardwick.*[74]

The *Lawrence* decision had a benefit and a cost. The benefit was to strike down a law that was rarely enforced and if introduced today probably could not be passed. The cost was to create the possibility that the Court, and not Congress or state legislatures, might decide whether same-sex marriages were legal.

That same year, the Massachusetts Supreme Judicial Court decided, by a four-to-three vote, that gays and lesbians must be allowed to be married in the

Proponents and opponents of gay marriage confront one another in front of the Massachusetts Statehouse.

state.[75] The Massachusetts legislature responded by passing a bill that, if it becomes a state constitutional amendment, will reverse the state court's decision. But for that to happen, the legislature must vote again on this matter and so the amendment could not take effect until 2006,

The mayor of San Francisco, Gavin Newsom, in apparent defiance of state law, began issuing marriage licenses to gay and lesbian couples. In August 2004 the California Supreme Court struck down his actions as inconsistent with existing law.

Public opinion polls suggest that many voters are opposed to same-sex marriages but would allow "civil unions" among same-sex couples of the sort now approved in Vermont. Many states have passed laws banning same-sex marriages, and in 1996 Congress enacted a bill, signed by President Clinton, called the Defense of Marriage Act. Under it, no state would have to give legal status to a same-sex marriage performed in another state, and it would define marriage as a lawful union of husband and wife. But state and federal laws on this matter could be overturned if the Supreme Court should decide in favor of same-sex marriage, using language that appears in the *Lawrence* case. That could be prevented by an amendment to the Constitution, but Congress is not willing to propose one and, if proposed, it is not clear the states would ratify it.

Private groups, however, can exclude homosexuals from their membership. In another five-to-four decision, the Supreme Court decided that the Boy Scouts of America could exclude gay men and boys because that group had a right to determine its own membership.[76]

☆ SUMMARY

*T*he civil rights movement in the courts and in Congress profoundly changed the nature of African American participation in politics by bringing southern blacks into the political system so that they could become an effective interest group. The decisive move was to enlist northern opinion in this cause, a job made easier by the northern perception that civil rights involved simply an unfair contest between two minorities—southern whites and southern blacks. That perception changed when it became evident that the court rulings and legislative decisions would apply to the North as well as the South, leading to the emergence of northern opposition to court-ordered busing and affirmative action programs.

By the time this reaction developed, the legal and political system had been changed sufficiently to make it difficult if not impossible to limit the application of civil rights laws to the special circumstances of the South or to alter by legislative means the decisions of federal courts. Though the courts can accomplish little when they have no political allies (as revealed by the massive resistance to early school-desegregation decisions), they can accomplish a great deal, even in the face of adverse public opinion, when they have some organized allies (as revealed by their ability to withstand antibusing moves).

The feminist movement has paralleled in organization and tactics many aspects of the black civil rights movement, but with important differences. Women sought to repeal or reverse laws and court rulings that in many cases were ostensibly designed to protect rather than subjugate them. The conflict between protection and liberation was sufficiently intense to defeat the effort to ratify the Equal Rights Amendment.

The most divisive civil rights issues in American politics are abortion and affirmative action. From 1973 to 1989 the Supreme Court seemed committed to giving constitutional protection to all abortions within the first trimester; since 1989 it has approved various state restrictions on the circumstances under which abortions can be obtained.

There has been a similar shift in the Court's view of affirmative action. Though it will still approve some quota plans, it now insists that they pass strict scrutiny to ensure that they are used only to correct a proven history of discrimination, that they place the burden of proof on the party alleging discrimination, and that they be limited to hiring and not extended to layoffs. Congress has modified some of these rulings with new civil rights legislation.

RECONSIDERING WHO GOVERNS?

1. *Since Congress enacts our laws, why has it not made certain that all groups have the same rights?*

Congress responds to public demands. During much of our history, people have expected women, African Americans, Native Americans, and many other groups to be treated differently than are others. The Bill of Rights is a check on congressional and state authority; to be effective, it must be enforced by independent courts.

2. *After the Supreme Court ended racial segregation in the schools, what did the president and Congress do?*

For a while, not much. But in time these institutions began spending federal money and using federal troops and law enforcement officials in ways that greatly increased the rate of integration.

RECONSIDERING TO WHAT ENDS?

1. *If the law supports equality of opportunity, why has affirmative action become so important?*

There are several reasons. If there has been active discrimination in the past, affirmative action can be a way to help disadvantaged groups catch up. But the Supreme Court has also held, though by narrow majorities, that even when there has not been a legacy of discrimination, pursuing "diversity" is a "compelling" interest. The real issue is what diversity means and how best to achieve it.

2. *Under what circumstances can men and women be treated differently?*

A difference in treatment can be justified constitutionally if the difference is fair, reasonable, and not arbitrary. Sex differences need not meet the "strict scrutiny" test. It is permissible to punish men for statutory rape and to bar them from hospital delivery rooms; men are different from women in these respects. Congress may draft men without drafting women.

WORLD WIDE WEB RESOURCES

Court cases: **www.law.cornell.edu**

Department of Justice: **www.usdoj.gov**

Civil rights organizations:
National Association for the Advancement of Colored People: **www.naacp.org**

National Organization for Women: **www.now.org**

National Gay and Lesbian Task Force:
www.thetaskforce.org

National Council of La Raza: **www.nclr.org**

American Arab Anti-Discrimination Committee:
www.adc.org

Anti-Defamation League: **www.adl.org**

SUGGESTED READINGS

Branch, Taylor. *Parting the Waters: America in the King Years*. New York: Simon and Schuster, 1988. A vivid account of the civil rights struggle.

Flexner, Eleanor. *Century of Struggle: The Women's Rights Movement in the United States*. Rev. ed. Cambridge: Harvard University Press, 1975. A historical account of the feminist movement and its political strategies.

Friedan, Betty. *The Feminine Mystique*. New York: Norton, 1963. Tenth anniversary edition, 1974. A well-known call for women to become socially and culturally independent.

Foreman, Christopher A. *The African-American Predicament*. Washington, D.C.: Brookings Institution, 1999. Thoughtful essays on problems faced by African Americans today.

Franklin, John Hope. *From Slavery to Freedom*. 5th ed. New York: Knopf, 1980. A survey of black history in the United States.

Kluger, Richard. *Simple Justice*. New York: Random House/Vintage Books, 1977. Detailed and absorbing account of the school-desegregation issue, from the Fourteenth Amendment to the *Brown* case.

Kull, Andrew. *The Color-Blind Constitution*. Cambridge: Harvard University Press, 1992. A history of efforts, none yet successful, to make the Constitution color-blind.

Mansbridge, Jane J. *Why We Lost the ERA*. Chicago: University of Chicago Press, 1986. Explains why the Equal Rights Amendment did not become part of the Constitution.

Thernstrom, Stephan, and Abigail Thernstrom. *America in Black and White*. New York: Simon and Schuster, 1997. Detailed history and portrait of African Americans.

Wilhoit, Francis M. *The Politics of Massive Resistance*. New York: George Braziller, 1973. The methods—and ultimate collapse—of all-out southern resistance to school desegregation.

Woodward, C. Vann. *The Strange Career of Jim Crow*. New York: Oxford University Press, 1957. Brief, lucid account of the evolution of Jim Crow practices in the South.

PART II

Opinions, Interests, and Organizations

The latent causes of faction are thus sown in the nature of man; and we see them everywhere brought into different degrees of activity, according to the different circumstances of civil society.

FEDERALIST No. 10

CHAPTER 7

Public Opinion

What Is Public Opinion?
How Polling Works ● How Opinions Differ

Political Socialization: The Family
Religion ● The Gender Gap ● Schooling and Information

Cleavages in Public Opinion
Social Class ● Race and Ethnicity ● Region

Political Ideology
Consistent Attitudes ● What Do Liberalism and Conservatism Mean? ● Various Categories ● Analyzing Consistency ● Political Elites

Political Elites, Public Opinion, and Public Policy

WHO GOVERNS?

1. How does public opinion in America today vary by race, gender, and other differences?
2. What is political ideology, and how does it affect political behavior and influence public policy?

TO WHAT ENDS?

1. What role did the Framers of the Constitution think public opinion should play in American democracy?
2. When, if ever, should public policies mirror majority opinion?

*I*n the Gettysburg Address Abraham Lincoln said that the United States has a government "of the people, by the people, and for the people." That suggests that the government should do what the people want. If that is the case, it is puzzling that:

- The federal government has often had a large budget deficit, but the people want a balanced budget.
- Courts have ordered that children be bused in order to balance the schools racially, but the people opposed busing.
- The Equal Rights Amendment to the Constitution was not ratified, but polls showed that most people supported it.
- The House of Representatives voted to impeach President Bill Clinton even though most Americans opposed this.
- Most people believe that there should be a limit on the number of terms to which U.S. senators and members of the U.S. House of Representatives can be elected, but Congress has not approved term limits.

Some people, reflecting on the many gaps between what the government does and what the people want, may become cynical and think our system is democratic in name only. That would be a mistake. There are several very good reasons why government policy will often appear to be at odds with public opinion.

First, the Framers of the Constitution did not try to create a government that would do from day to day "what the people want." They created a government for the purpose of achieving certain substantive goals. The preamble to the Constitution lists six of these: "to form a more perfect Union, establish Justice, ensure domestic Tranquility, provide for the common defense, promote the general Welfare, and secure the Blessings of Liberty."

One means of achieving these goals was popular rule, as provided for by the right of the people to vote for members of the House of Representatives (and later for senators and presidential electors). But other means were provided as well: representative government, federalism, the separation of powers, a Bill of Rights, and an independent judiciary. These were all intended to be checks on public opinion. In addition the Framers knew that in a nation as large and diverse as the United States there would rarely be any such thing as "public opinion"; rather there would be many "publics" (that is, factions) holding many opinions. The Framers hoped that the struggle among these many publics would protect liberty (no one "public"

155

American politics is intensely local, as when Rep. Loretta Sanchez shakes hands with a voter in her California district.

would dominate) while at the same time permitting the adoption of reasonable policies that commanded the support of many factions.

Second, it is not as easy as one may suppose to know what the public thinks. We are so inundated these days with public opinion polls that we may imagine that they tell us what the public believes. That may be true on a few rather simple, clear-cut, and widely discussed issues, but it is not true with respect to most matters on which the government must act. The best pollsters know the limits of their methods, and the citizen should know them as well.

In this chapter we take a close look at what "public opinion" is, how it is formed and how opinions differ. In later chapters we examine the workings of political parties, interest groups, and government institutions and consider what impact they have on whether public opinion affects government policy.

☆ What Is Public Opinion?

Some years ago researchers at the University of Cincinnati asked twelve hundred local residents whether they favored passage of the Monetary Control Bill. About 21 percent said that they favored the bill, 25 percent said that they opposed it, and the rest

---

public opinion   How people think or feel about particular things.

---

said that they hadn't thought much about the matter or didn't know. But there was no such thing as the Monetary Control Bill. The researchers made it up. About 26 percent of the people questioned in a national survey also expressed opinions on the same nonexistent piece of legislation.[1] In many surveys, wide majorities favor expanding most government programs *and* paying less in taxes. On some issues, the majority in favor one month gives way to the majority opposed the next, often with no obvious basis for the shift.

How much confidence should we place in surveys that presumably tell us "what the American people think" about legislation and other issues, and how should we assess "public opinion"?

Defined simply, **public opinion** refers to how people think or feel about particular things. For businesses, understanding public opinion—for example, knowing whether consumers are likely to want a new product or be willing to pay more for an old one—can spell the difference between profit and loss. In the early twentieth century, corporations and marketing firms pioneered attempts to systematically measure public views. But political scientists were not far behind them.

The first major academic studies of public opinion and voting, published in the 1940s, painted a distressing picture of American democracy. The studies found that, while a small group of citizens knew lots about government and had definite ideas on many issues, the vast majority knew next to nothing about government and had only vague notions even on much-publicized public policy matters that affected them directly.[2] In the ensuing decades, however, other studies painted a somewhat more reassuring picture. These studies suggested that, while most citizens are poorly informed about government and care little about most public policy issues, they are nonetheless pretty good at using limited information (or cues) to figure out what policies, parties, or candidates most nearly reflect their values or favor their interests, and then acting (or voting) accordingly.[3]

The closer scholars have studied public opinion on particular issues, the less uniformed, indifferent, or fickle it has appeared to be. For example, a 2001 study by political scientist Terry M. Moe analyzed public opinion concerning whether the government should provide parents with publicly funded grants, or vouchers, that they can apply toward tuition at private schools. He found that although most people are unfamiliar with the voucher issue, "they do a much better job of formulating their opinions than skeptics would lead us to expect."[4] When supplied with basic information, average citizens adopt "their positions for good substantive reasons, just as the informed do."[5]

How Polling Works

If properly conducted, a survey of public opinion—popularly called a **poll**—can capture the opinions of 250 million citizens by interviewing as few as 1,500 of them. There are many keys to good polling: posing comprehensible questions (asking people about things they have some basis for forming an opinion about); wording questions fairly (not using "loaded" or "emotional" words or indicating what the "right" answer is); and others.

But no poll, whatever it asks and however worded, can provide us with a reasonably accurate measure of how people think or feel unless the persons polled are a **random sample** of the entire population, meaning that any given voter or adult has an equal chance of being interviewed. Through a process called stratified or multistage area sampling, the pollster makes a list of all the geographical units in the country—say all the counties—and groups (or "stratifies") them by size of their population. The pollster then selects at random units from each group or stratum in proportion to its total population. Within each selected county smaller and smaller geographical units (down to particular blocks or streets) are chosen, and then, within the smallest unit, individuals are selected at random (by, for example, choosing the occupant of every fifth house). Repeat the process using equally randomized methods, and the pollster might get slightly different results. The difference between the results of two surveys or samples is called **sampling error.** For example, if one random sample shows that 70 percent of all Americans approve of the way the president is handling his job, and another random sample taken at the same time shows that 65 percent do, the sampling error is 5 percent.

Even if properly conducted, polls are hardly infallible. Since 1952 every major poll has in fact picked the winner of the presidential election. Likewise, **exit polls,** interviews with randomly selected voters conducted at polling places on election day in a representative sample of voting districts, have proven quite

accurate. But as a result of sampling error and for other reasons, it is very hard for pollsters to predict the winner in a close election.

For any population over 500,000, pollsters need to make about 15,000 telephone calls to reach a number of respondents (technically, the number computes to 1,065) sufficient to ensure that the opinions of the sample differ only slightly (by a 3 percent plus or minus margin) from what the results would have been had they interviewed the entire population from which the sample was drawn. That can be very expensive to do, and with more people trying to avoid telemarketers (who sometimes pose as pollsters) and using call-screening devices, pollsters are finding it harder than ever to get people to answer their calls.[6] Low response rates can harm a poll's reliability.

How Opinions Differ

Nobody fully understands how public opinion influences everything from who wins an election to what gets politicians' attention to whether given bills become law, but a few things are clear: some people care more about certain issues than other people do (*opinion saliency*); on some issues or choices, opinions are pretty steady, while on others they tend to be more volatile (*opinion stability*); and, on some issues government seems largely in sync with popular views or majority sentiments, while on other issues it seems significantly out of sync (*opinion-policy congruence*). For example, most Americans have an opinion on U.S. involvement in Iraq, but some feel more strongly about it than others do, and opinions have changed in response to news of positive or negative developments. In mid-2004, for example, much news on the situation in Iraq was negative, and mass public support for U.S. involvement fell.

---

poll A survey of public opinion.

random sample Method of selecting from a population in which each person has an equal probability of being selected.

sampling error The difference between the results of random samples taken at the same time.

exit polls Polls based on interviews conducted on Election Day with randomly selected voters.

Children grow up learning, but not always following, their parents' political views.

Studies also tell us that people with certain characteristics in common sometimes hold certain political beliefs in common. By no means do people with similar or even virtually identical family histories, religious affiliations, formal educations, or job experiences think or vote exactly the same way on all or most issues. But **political socialization**—the process by which personal and other background traits influence one's views about politics and government—matters. It is behind the fact, to be discussed in the next section, that children tend to share their parents' political orientations and party affiliations; and it helps to explain why, as we shall see, opinions seem to vary in interesting ways asso-ciated with class, race, religion, gender, and other characteristics.

Research has also made clear that mass and elite opinion differ. By "elite" we do not mean people who are "better" than others. Rather, as we discussed in Chapter 1, **elite** is a term used by social scientists to refer to people who have a disproportionate amount of some valued resource—money, schooling, prestige, political power, or whatever. Not only do political elites *know more* about politics than the rest of us, they *think differently* about it—they have different views and beliefs. As we explain later in this chapter, they are more likely than average citizens to hold a

> **political socialization** Process by which background traits influence one's political views.
>
> **elite** People who have a disproportionate amount of some valued resource.

more or less consistent set of opinions as to the policies government ought to pursue. The government attends more to the elite views than to popular views, at least on many matters.

☆ Political Socialization: The Family

The best-studied (though not necessarily the most important) case of opinion formation is that of party identification. The majority of young people identify with their parents' political party. A study of high school seniors showed that, of these young men and women, almost all (91 percent) knew accurately the presidential preference of their parents, the great majority (71 percent) knew accurately their parents' party identification, and most shared that identification (only 9 percent identified with the party opposite to that of their parents). This process begins fairly early in life: by the time they are in the fifth grade (age eleven), over half of all schoolchildren identify with one party or the other, and another fifth claim to be independents.[7]

Naturally, as people grow older, they become more independent of their parents in many ways, including politically, but there nonetheless remains a great deal of continuity between youthful partisanship, learned from one's parents, and adult partisanship. One study of adults found that around 60 percent still had the party identification—Democrat, Republican, or independent—of their parents. Of those who differed with their parents, the overwhelming majority did so not by identifying with the opposite party but by describing themselves as "independents."[8]

The ability of the family to inculcate a strong sense of party identification has declined in recent years. The proportion of citizens who say they consider themselves to be Democrats or Republicans has become steadily smaller since the early 1950s. Accompanying this decline in partisanship has been a sharp rise in the proportion of citizens describing themselves as independents.

Part of this change results from the fact that young voters have always had a weaker sense of partisanship than older ones. But the youthfulness of the population cannot explain all the changes, for the decline in partisanship has occurred at all age levels. Moreover, those who reached voting age in the 1960s were less apt than those who matured in the 1950s to keep the party identification of their parents.[9]

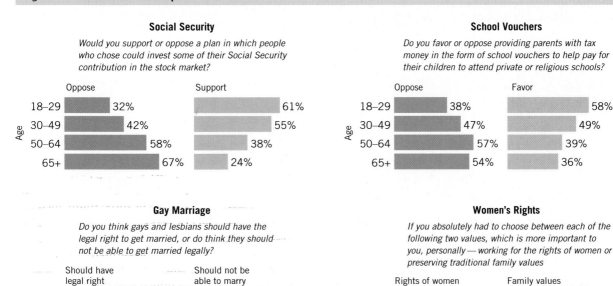

Figure 7.1   Generational Gaps on the Issues

Source: Survey by *Washington Post*/Henry J. Kaiser Family Foundation/Harvard University, August 2–September 1, 2002, as reported in Elizabeth Hamel et al., "Younger Voters," *Public Perspective,* May/June 2003, p. 11.

Though we still tend to acquire some measure of partisanship from our parents, the meaning of that identification is far from clear. There are, after all, liberal and conservative Democrats, as well as liberal and conservative Republicans. So far the evidence suggests that children are more independent of their parents in policy preferences than in party identification. As Figure 7.1 summarizes, there are sizable age-related differences in opinions on several issues.

In most families, the family dinner table is not a seminar in political philosophy but a place where people discuss school, jobs, dates, and chores. In some families, however, the dinner table is a political classroom. Fairly clear political ideologies (a term we shall define in a later section) seem to be communicated to that small proportion of children raised in families where politics is a dominant topic of conversation and political views are strongly held. Studies of the participants in various student radical movements in the 1960s suggested that college radicals were often the sons and daughters of people who had themselves been young radicals; some commentators dubbed them the "red-diaper babies." Presumably, deeply conservative people come disproportionately from families that were also deeply conservative. This transfer of political beliefs from one generation to the next does not appear in large national studies, because such a small proportion of the population is at either the far left or the far right of the political spectrum.

Religion

One way in which the family forms and transmits political beliefs is by its religious tradition. Religious differences make for political differences, but the differences are generally more complicated than first meets the eye. For example, opinions on school prayer and other issues differ by religion. Table 7.1 shows that Catholics basically mirror the general public in the extent to which they see school prayer as an effective way to shape young people's values and behavior, while Evangelicals differ widely with Jews and the nonreligious both on that question and

Table 7.1 Opinion on School Prayer, By Religion					
	General Public	Catholic	Evangelical	Jewish	Nonreligious
	Agree Strongly % / Disagree Strongly %				
School prayer is . . .					
an especially effective way to improve the values and behavior of today's young people	37/24	37/21	55/10	11/61	6/66
violates the Constitution	21/38	20/33	10/56	62/10	58/11
	Agree %				
Public schools should . . .					
have a moment of silence	53	57	53	30	36
say prayers that refer to God but to no particular religion	20	22	26	9	7
say a prayer that refers to Jesus	6	4	12	2	1

Source: Adapted from *For Goodness Sake: Why So Many Want Religion to Play a Greater Role in American Life* (New York: the Public Agenda Foundation, 2001), tables 5 and 7.

whether school prayer violates the Constitution. But scroll down the table and you see that no group, regardless of religion, harbors majorities favoring school prayers that refer to a particular religion.

Most studies have found that, whatever the faith in question, religious influences on public opinion are most pronounced with respect to social issues and less evident on others. For example, as Table 7.2 shows, only one in ten people rank religious beliefs as the biggest influence in their thinking about Iraq, while 40 percent deem religious beliefs the biggest influence on their thinking about gay marriage.

The Gender Gap

Journalists often point out that women have "deserted" Republican candidates to favor Democratic ones. In some cases that is true. But it would be more correct to say that men have "deserted" Democratic candidates for Republican ones. The **gender gap** is the difference in political views between men and women. That gap has existed for a long time, and it is a problem for both political parties.

Men have become increasingly Republican since the mid-1960s, while the voting behavior of women

---

gender gap Difference in political views between men and women.

---

has remained unchanged. In 1952 men and women identified with the Democratic party at about the same level, around 58 or 59 percent. In 1996 women still identified with the Democrats at about the same level, while men had abandoned the Democratic party and identified more with the Republicans.[10] In the 2004 presidential election, women voted for Democrat John Kerry by a margin of 51 percent to 48 percent, while men voted for Republican George W. Bush by a margin of 55 percent to 44 percent.

The biggest reason for this gap seems to involve attitudes about the size of government, gun control, spending programs aimed at the poor, and gay rights. Men have always been more conservative than women in their views on these social issues, but by the late 1960s and early 1970s men had changed their party loyalty to match their policy preferences. As Table 7.3 shows, men and women are similar in their views on abortion but quite different in their opinions about welfare, spending money to help the homeless or to increase military defense, and sexual harassment in the workplace.

It would be a mistake, however, to suppose that the gender gap is unchanging, matters the same in all elections, or applies equally to all groups or subgroups. The gender gap has been less evident in midterm congressional elections than it has been in presidential elections. In the 2002 midterm House elections the gap between how men and women vote

Table 7.2	Religious Influence on Public Opinion, By Issue			
Biggest influence on your thinking about . . .	**Iraq %**	**Death Penalty %**	**Abortion %**	**Gay Marriage %**
Media	41	25	7	9
Personal experience	16	12	18	12
Education	11	14	22	12
Religious beliefs	**10**	**28**	**28**	**40**
Friends and family	7	5	7	8
Other	11	17	16	15
Don't know	4	4	2	4

Source: Adapted from *Different Faiths, Different Messages* (Washington, D.C.: Pew Forum on Religion and Public Life, March 2003), p. 3.

(four points, with women splitting their vote evenly between Republican and Democratic candidates) was the lowest since the 1994 midterm House elections (when it was eleven points).[12] Because there are not as yet sufficient (or sufficiently reliable) polling data, it is unclear whether the gap is as large for Hispanics as it is for African Americans or whites. Moreover, marriage matters as much as gender: in 2004 married women supported Bush while unmarried ones supported Kerry.

Schooling and Information

Americans born from the mid-1920s through the mid-1960s (the World War II generation and their baby-boomer children) went to college in record numbers. Much research has shown that attending college had a big impact on their political attitudes, usually making them more liberal.[13] This proved especially true for those who attended the most prestigious colleges. Related studies showed that increased schooling led to significant increases in voting and other political activity.[14] During the 1960s, many antiwar and other protest movements drew their members largely from college students who majored in liberal arts subjects.[15]

These generalizations apply less well to today's college students. Although more research is needed, there is evidence to suggest that while college students today are somewhat more conservative than students were two decades ago, their opinions are complicated in ways that defy simple categorization. For example, many surveys find today's eighteen- to twenty-four-year-olds to be quite favorably disposed toward the private sector even though they are not consistently for smaller government. Likewise, polls find most young people to be in favor of school vouchers (generally regarded as the conservative position on that issue) but also in favor of legally sanctioning gay marriage (generally regarded as the liberal position on that issue). Belief in the idea of individual choice—that parents should be free to use vouchers to send their children to whatever school they choose, that gays should have the choice to get married, and so forth—may well be present-day college-age Americans' core political opinion.[16]

Table 7.3	The Gender Gap: Differences in Political Views of Men and Women	
Issue	**Men**	**Women**
Federal spending for welfare programs should be increased.	8%	14%
Abortion should be permitted by law.	57	60
Sexual harassment is a very serious problem in the workplace.	24	38
This country would be better off if we just stayed home and did not concern ourselves with problems in other parts of the world.	24	29
Generally speaking, I think of myself as a Democrat.	32	44
The United States should increase defense spending.	37	26
The United States should increase spending on solving the problems of the homeless.	51	63
Ban all handguns except for the police.	33	58

Source: ICPSR American National Election Survey, 1996. Pre- and Post-Election Surveys.

A teen volunteer talks to boys in a gym.

Since the 1960s the number of college students in the social sciences and humanities has plummeted relative to the number in business, preprofessional schools, hotel management, nursing, justice administration, computer science, and other nonliberal arts fields.[17] Whatever the reason, over the past generation, increased schooling has not been associated with increased political activity; in fact, by many measures, political participation among college students has declined.[18] Many contemporary college students believe that volunteering is a more significant civic act than voting, and that community service is more worthwhile than political engagement.[19] Since the mid-1980s even elite colleges that have few conservative faculty members have been affected by concerns about "political correctness," and most now have (often small but vocal) conservative student groups on campus. Also, after decades of decline, many religious colleges and universities have increased their enrollments while reinforcing their traditional religious identities.

The politically liberalizing effects of college, at least among older Americans, were probably attributable in part to the fact that, compared to high school graduates, yesteryear's college graduates read newspapers and newsmagazines. Evidence collected by political scientist John Zaller shows that the level of political information one has is the best single predictor of being liberal on some kinds of issues, such as civil liberties and civil rights.[20] Information on these matters, he suggests, is today produced by a predominantly liberal elite.

But surveys also find that today's college students seem much less apt to read newspapers and newsmagazines than previous generations of college students were.[21] With the Internet, all-day cable news channels, talk radio, and television programs that emphasize political themes, researchers are far from being able to measure precisely how much political information of given types college students or other citizens get, from what sources, embodying which biases, and with what (if any) short- or long-term effects on opinions; we will return to this topic when we discuss the media in Chapter 12.

☆ Cleavages in Public Opinion

The way in which political opinions are formed helps explain the cleavages that exist among these opinions and why these cleavages do not follow any single political principle but instead overlap and crosscut in bewildering complexity. If, for example, the United States lacked regional differences and was composed almost entirely of white Protestants who had never attended college, there would still be plenty of political conflict—the rich would have different views from the poor; workers would have different views from farmers—but that conflict would be much simpler to describe and explain. It might even lead to political parties that were more clearly aligned with competing political philosophies than those we now have. In fact some democratic nations in the world today do have a population very much like the one we have asked you to imagine, and the United States itself, during the first half of the nineteenth century, was overwhelmingly white, Protestant, and without much formal schooling.

Today, however, there are crosscutting cleavages based on race, ethnicity, religion, region, and education, in addition to those created by income and occupation. To the extent that politics is sensitive to public opinion, it is sensitive to a variety of different and even competing publics. Not all these publics have influence proportionate to their numbers or even to their numbers adjusted for the intensity of their feelings. As will be described later, a filtering process occurs that makes the opinions of some publics more influential than those of others.

Whatever this state of affairs may mean for democracy, it creates a messy situation for political scientists. It would be so much easier if everyone's opinion on political affairs reflected some single feature of his or her life, such as income, occupation, age, race, or sex. Of course, some writers have argued that political opinion is a reflection of one such feature, social class, usually defined in terms of income or occupation, but that view, though containing some truth, is beset with inconsistencies: poor blacks and poor whites disagree sharply on many issues involving race; well-to-do Jews and well-to-do Protestants often have opposing opinions on social welfare policy; and low-income elderly people are much more worried about crime than are low-income graduate students. Plumbers and professors may have similar incomes, but they rarely have similar views, and business people in New York City often take a very different view of government than business people in Houston or Birmingham.

In some other democracies a single factor such as class may explain more of the differences in political attitudes than it does in the more socially heterogeneous United States. Most blue-collar workers in America think of themselves as being "middle-class," whereas most such workers in Britain and France describe themselves as "working-class." In England the working class prefers the Labour party by a margin of three to one, while in the United States workers prefer the Democratic party by less than two to one.[22]

Social Class

Americans speak of "social class" with embarrassment. The norm of equality tugs at our consciences, urging us to judge people as individuals, not as parts of some social group (such as "the lower class"). Social scientists speak of "class" with confusion. They know it exists but quarrel constantly about how to define it: by income? occupation? wealth? schooling? prestige? personality?

Let's face up to the embarrassment and skip over the confusion. Truck drivers and investment bankers look different, talk differently, and vote differently. There is nothing wrong with saying that the first group consists of "working-class" (or "blue-collar") people and the latter of "upper-class" (or "management") people. Moreover, though different definitions of class produce slightly different groupings of people, most definitions overlap to such an extent that it does not matter too much which we use.

Union members protest against President Bush outside the 2004 Republican National Convention in New York City.

However defined, public opinion and voting have been less determined by class in the United States than in Europe, and the extent of class cleavage has declined in the last few decades in both the United States and Europe. In the 1950s V. O. Key, Jr., found that differences in political opinion were closely associated with occupation. He noted that people holding managerial or professional jobs had distinctly more conservative views on social welfare policy and more internationalist views on foreign policy than did manual workers.[23]

During the next decade this pattern changed greatly. Opinion surveys done in the late 1960s showed that business and professional people had views quite similar to those of manual workers on matters such as the poverty program, health insurance, American policy in Vietnam, and government efforts to create jobs.[24]

The voting patterns of different social classes have also become somewhat more similar. Class voting has declined sharply since the late 1940s in the United States, France, Great Britain, and West Germany and declined moderately in Sweden.

Class differences remain, of course. Unskilled workers are more likely than affluent white-collar workers to be Democrats and to have liberal views on economic policy. And when economic issues pinch—for example, when farmers are hurting or steelworkers are being laid off—the importance of economic interests in differentiating the opinions of various groups rises sharply.

Table 7.4 African American and White Opinion	African American	White
Favor expanding affirmative action programs[a]	53%	22%
Believe the justice system is racially biased against blacks[a]	72	44
Favor harsher treatment of criminals by the courts[b]	78	76
Favor more spending on national defense[c]	13	18
Favor national health insurance by government[c]	39	23
Believe the U.S. Census Bureau should stop collecting information on race and ethnicity[d]	48	47
Believe abortion should be legal in all cases[e]	24	28
Approve of black/white marriages[a]	77	61
Willing to vote for a black person for president[a]	93	91
Believe that too much is made of the differences between blacks and whites and not enough of what they have in common[f]	89	92

Sources: (a) *Black/White Perspectives in the United States* (Princeton, N.J.: The Gallup Organization, June 1997), 14, 16, 23, 24; (b) Gallup Polls, 1993 and 1994; (c) American National Election Survey, 1996; (d) "The Newsweek Poll," *Newsweek* (February 13, 1995): 65; (e) *The Public Perspective* (May 1995): 19; (f) *The American Enterprise* (November/December 1998): 92, reporting results of a March–April 1998 Public Agenda survey of white and black parents or guardians of children in kindergarten through twelfth grade.

Still, many of the issues that now lead us to choose which party to support and that determine whether we think of ourselves as liberals or conservatives are noneconomic issues. In recent years our political posture has been shaped by the positions we take on race relations, abortion, school prayer, environmentalism, and terrorism, issues that do not clearly affect the rich differently than the poor (or at least do not affect them as differently as do the union movement, the minimum wage, and unemployment). Moral, symbolic, and foreign policy matters do not divide rich and poor in the same way as economic ones. Thus we have many well-off people who think of themselves as liberals because they take liberal positions on these noneconomic matters, and many not-so-well-off people who think of themselves as conservatives because that is the position they take on these issues.

Race and Ethnicity

Social class clearly has become a less clear-cut source of political cleavage, but it is harder to know what to make of race and ethnicity. In some ways racial differences are of central importance. African Americans are overwhelming Democrats, while whites are much more likely to be Republicans. African Americans thought that O. J. Simpson was innocent of killing his wife, but white Americans thought that he was guilty. Blacks believe that the criminal justice system is biased against them; whites disagree. Blacks favor a stronger affirmative action program; whites are opposed to it (see Table 7.4).

But in other respects the opinions of whites and blacks are similar. Majorities of both groups oppose the use of racial quotas, want the courts to get tougher on criminals, oppose making abortion legal in all cases, and nearly identical percentages wish that the Census Bureau would stop collecting data on race and ethnicity. Huge majorities in both groups think that too much is made of racial differences and would be willing to vote for an African American presidential candidate.

There is some evidence that the differences between white and black Americans may be narrowing. About 26 percent of African Americans ages twenty-six to thirty-five (as opposed to only 3 percent of those ages fifty-one to sixty-four) identify themselves as Republicans.[25] Likewise, African American teenagers are only half as likely as African American adults to think that the social and economic differences between whites and blacks are mainly due to racial discrimination.[26] Other hints of a decline in differences in black-white opinions can be seen in Table 7.5, which shows that majorities or pluralities in each group believe their incomes will rise, and that race relations will improve, over the next decade. A 2001 study examined gaps in opinion between younger and older blacks with regard to criminal justice, education, the environ-

Table 7.5 Opinions About the Next Decade, By Race

Ten years from now, my family income will be . . .	Better %	About the same %	Worse %
Whites	59	28	8
Blacks	71	16	8
Ten years from now, race relations will be . . .	Better %	About the same %	Worse %
Whites	47	40	9
Blacks	42	37	14

Source: Adapted from *The American Enterprise,* April/May 2002, p. 61.

ment, voting, and other issues.[27] Among other significant differences, black young adults (ages eighteen to twenty-five) were far more likely than those ages fifty-one to sixty-four to say that it is okay not to vote if you do not like any of the candidates and were far more receptive than their elders to arguments in favor of school vouchers. It remains to be seen, however, whether this generation gap between younger and older African Americans will persist or have any important political effects.

There is evidence of an opinion gap between the leaders of African American organizations and African Americans in general, with leaders more likely than the rank and file to favor abortion, support affirmative action, and doubt that blacks are making progress.[28] This cleavage should not surprise us; as we shall see, there is a similar cleavage between white leaders and white citizens. But in 2004 some division of opinion between the leaders of African American organizations came to public view when President George W. Bush, who had refused invitations to speak before the National Association for the Advancement of Colored People (NAACP), accepted an invitation to speak before the National Urban League, another historic civil rights organization led by African Americans. The NAACP's leaders had criticized Bush strongly, while the National Urban League's leaders had been more moderate in their criticism of him.

America is now home to over 30 million Latinos. But the literature on Latino public opinion has been called "small, disproportionately oriented toward immigration, and relatively silent on the influence of gender" and other possible intragroup opinion cleavages.[29] Likewise, despite the country's growing Asian population, there is as yet also virtually no literature on Asian public opinion. However, an early survey of ethnic groups in California, a state where fully one-third of all recent immigrants to this country live, gives us some hint of how Latinos and Asian Americans feel about political parties and issues. Latinos identify themselves as Democrats, but much less so than do blacks, and Asian Americans are even more identified with the Republican party than Anglo whites. On issues such as spending on the military and welfare programs, prayer in public schools, and the imposition of the death penalty for murder, Asian American views are much more like those of Anglo whites than those of either blacks or Hispanics. Latinos are somewhat more liberal than Anglos or Asian Americans, but much less liberal than blacks, except with respect to bilingual education programs.[30]

These figures conceal important differences within these ethnic groups. For example, Japanese Americans are among the more conservative Asian Americans, whereas Korean Americans (perhaps because they are among the most recent immigrants) are more liberal. Similarly, Latinos, the fastest-growing ethnic group in the United States, are a diverse mix of Cuban Americans, Mexican Americans, Central Americans, and Puerto Ricans, each with distinct political views. A study of Latino voting in the 1988 presidential election found that Mexican Americans were the most Democratic, Cuban Americans were the most Republican, and Puerto Ricans were in between the other two groups.[31] But no group of Latino voters has become predictably partisan. In 1998, 78 percent of California's Latino (predominantly Mexican American) vote went to Democrat Gray Davis in the governor's race, but in Texas half of the Latino (also predominantly Mexican American) vote went to reelect Republican governor George W. Bush.[32]

A 2003 survey furnished a reasonably comprehensive look at Hispanic political opinion. As Figure 7.2 shows, Hispanic majorities seem to favor bigger

Figure 7.2   Hispanic Opinions on U.S. Politics

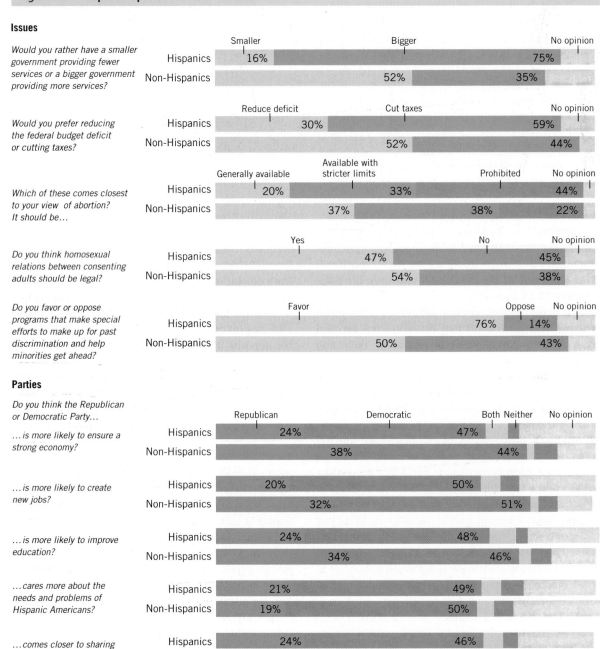

Issues

Would you rather have a smaller government providing fewer services or a bigger government providing more services?

	Smaller	Bigger	No opinion
Hispanics	16%	75%	
Non-Hispanics	52%	35%	

Would you prefer reducing the federal budget deficit or cutting taxes?

	Reduce deficit	Cut taxes	No opinion
Hispanics	30%	59%	
Non-Hispanics	52%	44%	

Which of these comes closest to your view of abortion? It should be…

	Generally available	Available with stricter limits	Prohibited	No opinion
Hispanics	20%	33%	44%	
Non-Hispanics	37%	38%	22%	

Do you think homosexual relations between consenting adults should be legal?

	Yes	No	No opinion
Hispanics	47%	45%	
Non-Hispanics	54%	38%	

Do you favor or oppose programs that make special efforts to make up for past discrimination and help minorities get ahead?

	Favor	Oppose	No opinion
Hispanics	76%	14%	
Non-Hispanics	50%	43%	

Parties

Do you think the Republican or Democratic Party…

…is more likely to ensure a strong economy?

	Republican	Democratic	Both	Neither	No opinion
Hispanics	24%	47%			
Non-Hispanics	38%	44%			

…is more likely to create new jobs?

	Republican	Democratic	Both	Neither	No opinion
Hispanics	20%	50%			
Non-Hispanics	32%	51%			

…is more likely to improve education?

	Republican	Democratic	Both	Neither	No opinion
Hispanics	24%	48%			
Non-Hispanics	34%	46%			

…cares more about the needs and problems of Hispanic Americans?

	Republican	Democratic	Both	Neither	No opinion
Hispanics	21%	49%			
Non-Hispanics	19%	50%			

…comes closer to sharing your moral values?

	Republican	Democratic	Both	Neither	No opinion
Hispanics	24%	46%			
Non-Hispanics	41%	42%			

Source: New York Times/CBS News Poll, as reported in New York Times, August 3, 2003, p. 14.

government, oppose making abortions generally available, and think that the Democratic party cares more about them and is better able to handle economic and other issues. Whether this opinion snapshot will change over time remains to be seen.

Region

It is widely believed that geographic region affects political attitudes and in particular that southerners and northerners disagree significantly on many policy questions. At one time white southerners were conspicuously less liberal than easterners, midwesterners, or westerners on questions such as aid to minorities, legalizing marijuana, school busing, and enlarging the rights of those accused of crimes. Although more conservative on these issues, they held views on economic issues similar to those of whites in other regions of the country. This helps to explain why the South was for so long a part of the Democratic party coalition: on national economic and social welfare policies, southerners expressed views not very different from those of northerners. That coalition was always threatened, however, by the divisiveness produced by issues of race and liberty.

The southern lifestyle is in fact different from that of other regions of the country. The South has, on the whole, been more accommodating to business enterprise and less so to organized labor than, for example, the Northeast; it gave greater support to the third-party candidacy of George Wallace in 1968, which was a protest against big government and the growth of national political power as well as against civil rights; and it was in the South that the greatest opposition arose to income-redistribution plans such as the Family Assistance Plan of 1969. Moreover, there is some evidence that white southerners became by the 1970s more conservative than they had been in the 1950s, at least when compared to white northerners.[33] Finally, white southerners have become less attached to the Democratic party: whereas over three-fourths described themselves as Democrats in 1952, only a third did by 1996.[34]

These changes in the South can have great significance, as we shall see in the next three chapters when we consider how elections are fought. It is enough for now to remember that, without the votes of the southern states, no Democrat except Lyndon Johnson in 1964 would have been elected president from 1940 through 1976. (Without the South, Roosevelt would have lost in 1944, Truman in 1948, Kennedy in 1960, and Carter in 1976. And even though Carter carried the South, he did not win a majority of white southern votes.) Clinton won in 1992 and 1996 without carrying the South, but those were three-man races.

☆ Political Ideology

Up to now the words *liberal* and *conservative* have been used here as if everyone agreed on what they meant and as if they accurately described general sets of political beliefs held by large segments of the population. Neither of these assumptions is correct. Like many useful words—*love, justice, happiness*—they are as vague as they are indispensable.

When we refer to people as liberals, conservatives, socialists, or radicals, we are implying that they have a patterned set of beliefs about how government and other important institutions in fact operate and how they ought to operate, and in particular about what kinds of policies government ought to pursue. They are said to display to some degree a **political ideology**—that is, a more or less consistent set of beliefs about what policies government ought to pursue. Political scientists measure the extent to which people have a political ideology in two ways: first, by seeing how frequently people use broad political categories (such as "liberal," "conservative," "radical") to describe their own views or to justify their preferences for various candidates and policies, and second, by seeing to what extent the policy preferences of a citizen are consistent over time or are based at any one time on consistent principles.

This second method involves a simple mathematical procedure: measuring how accurately one can predict a person's view on a subject at one time based on his or her view on that subject at an earlier time, or measuring how accurately one can predict a person's view on one issue based on his or her view on a different issue. The higher the accuracy of such predictions (or correlations), the more we say a person's political opinions display "constraint," or

political ideology A more or less consistent set of beliefs about what policies government ought to pursue.

Figure 7.3   **Ideological Self-Identification**

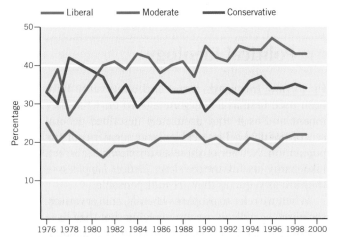

QUESTION

How would you describe your views on most political matters? Generally, do you think of yourself as a liberal, moderate, or conservative?

Source: The American Enterprise (March/April 1993): 84, Robert S. Erikson and Kent L. Tedin, *American Public Opinion* (New York: Longman, 2001), 101, citing surveys by CBS/*New York Times*.

ideology. Despite annual fluctuations, ideological self-identification surveys typically find that moderates are the largest group among American voters, conservatives the second largest, and liberals the smallest (see Figure 7.3). This pattern held throughout the 1990s. In 1998 one-fifth of voters described themselves as liberal, one-third described themselves as conservative, and a plurality called themselves moderate.[35]

Except when asked by pollsters, most Americans do not actually employ the words *liberal* or *conservative* in explaining or justifying their preferences for candidates or policies, and not many more than half can give plausible definitions of these terms. Furthermore, there are relatively low correlations among the answers to similar questions asked by pollsters at different times and to comparable questions asked at the same time. From this, many scholars have concluded that the great majority of Americans do not think about politics in an ideological or even in a very coherent manner and that they make little use of such concepts, so dear to political commentators and professors alike, as "liberal" and "conservative."[36]

Consistent Attitudes

This does not settle the question entirely, however. Critics of the view that Americans are nonideological have argued that people can have general, and strongly felt, political predispositions even though they are not able to use terms such as *liberal* correctly. Moreover, public opinion polls must of necessity ask rather simple questions, and the apparent "inconsistency" in the answers people give at different times may mean only that the nature of the problem and the wording of the question have changed in ways not obvious to the people analyzing the surveys.[37]

People can have an ideology without using the words *liberal* or *conservative* and without having beliefs that line up neatly along the conventional liberal-versus-conservative dimension. We saw in Chapter 4 that most Americans share a distinctive political culture—a belief in freedom, equality (of political condition and economic opportunity), and civic duty. They also attach a great deal of importance to "Americanism." Though these words may be vague, they are not trivial—at some level they are an ideology.

Scholars regularly discover that people have what some would consider "inconsistent" opinions. For example, a voter may want the government to spend more on education and the environment and at the same time favor a bigger military budget and a tough posture toward unfriendly nations. These views are "inconsistent" only in the sense that they violate a political rule of thumb, common in the media and in national policy debates, that expects people who favor a bigger welfare state to favor a smaller military establishment as well. That is the conventional "liberal" view. Similarly, the rule of thumb in the media is that people who support a strong military posture are also going to favor prayer in the schools and oppose abortion on demand. That is the conventional "conservative" position. But of course many citizens violate these rules of thumb, picking and choosing their positions without regard to the conventional definitions of liberalism and conservatism.

What Do Liberalism and Conservatism Mean?

Just because most people are not consistent liberals or consistent conservatives does not prove that these terms are meaningless. As we shall see, they are very meaningful for political elites. And they even have meaning for ordinary citizens, but this meaning is a complicated one that requires careful analysis.

The definition of these words has changed since they first came into use in the early nineteenth century. At that time a liberal was a person who favored personal and economic liberty—that is, freedom from the controls and powers of the state. An economic liberal, for example, supported the free market and opposed government regulation of trade. A conservative was originally a person who opposed the excesses of the French Revolution and its emphasis on personal freedom and favored instead a restoration of the power of the state, the church, and the aristocracy.

Beginning around the time of Franklin Roosevelt and the New Deal, the meaning of these terms began to change. Roosevelt used the term *liberal* to refer to his political program—one that called for an active national government that would intervene in the economy, create social welfare programs, and help certain groups (such as organized labor) acquire greater bargaining power. In time the opponents of an activist national government began using the term *conservative* to describe themselves. (Barry Goldwater, in 1964, was the first major U.S. politician to proclaim himself a conservative.) In general a conservative favored a free market rather than a regulated one, states' rights over national supremacy, and greater reliance on individual choice in economic affairs.

Though the meaning of these terms changed, it did not in the process become more precise. Two persons may describe themselves as liberals even though the first favors both the welfare state and a strong national defense and the second favors the welfare state but wants a sharp reduction in military spending. Similarly, one conservative may favor enforcement of laws against drug abuse, and another may believe that the government should let people decide for themselves what drugs to take. Once liberals favored laws guaranteeing equality of opportunity among the races; now some liberals favor "affirmative action" plans involving racial quotas or goals. Once conservatives opposed American intervention abroad; today many conservatives believe the United States should play an active role in foreign affairs.

In view of this confusion one is tempted to throw up one's hands in disgust and consign words like *liberal* and *conservative* to the garbage can. While understandable, such a reaction would be a mistake, because in spite of their ambiguities, these words remain in general use, convey some significant

meaning, and point to real differences between, for example, the liberal and conservative wings of the Democratic and Republican parties. Our task is to clarify these differences by showing the particular meanings these words have. One way to do this is by considering how self-described liberals and conservatives differ in their opinions on prominent issues, such as those listed in Table 7.6.

Various Categories

We can imagine certain broad categories of opinion to which different people subscribe. These categories are found by analyzing the answers people give to dozens of questions about political issues. Different analysts come up with slightly different categories, but on the whole there is a substantial amount of agreement. Three categories in particular have proved useful.

The first category involves questions about government policy with regard to the *economy*. We will describe as liberal those persons who favor government efforts to ensure that everyone has a job, to spend more money on medical and educational programs, and to increase rates of taxation for well-to-do persons.

The second involves questions about *civil rights* and race relations. We will describe as liberal those who favor strong federal action to desegregate schools, to increase hiring opportunities for minorities, to provide compensatory programs for minorities, and to enforce civil rights laws strictly.

The third involves questions about public and political *conduct*. We will describe as liberal those who are tolerant of protest demonstrations, who favor legalizing marijuana and in other ways wish to "decriminalize" so-called victimless crimes, who emphasize protecting the rights of the accused over punishing criminals, and who see the solution to crime in eliminating its causes rather than in getting tough with offenders.

Analyzing Consistency

Now it is obvious that people can take a liberal position on one of these issues and a conservative position on another without feeling in the slightest degree "inconsistent." Several studies, such as those by Seymour Martin Lipset and Earl Raab and by Herbert McClosky and John Zaller, show that this is exactly what most people do.[38]

This fact does not mean that people are unideological but that we need more than two labels to describe their ideology. If we considered all possible

Table 7.6   How Liberals and Conservatives Differ

Belief	Support Among Self-Declared Liberals	Support Among Self-Declared Conservatives
The government should provide "more services even if it means an increase in spending."	73%	32%
The government should guarantee "that every person has a job and a good standard of living."	55	21
Favor "government insurance plan which would cover all medical and hospital expenses for everyone."	82	27
The government "should make every effort to improve the social and economic position of blacks."	55	18
The U.S. "should spend less on defense."	85	65
"Aid to [Russia] should be increased."	36	32
"Women should have an equal role in running business, industry, and government."	96	81
The United States should always permit abortion "as a matter of personal choice."	72	36
"Homosexuals should be allowed to serve in U.S. Armed Forces."	70	45
"Oppose death penalty for persons convicted of murder."	35	15

Source: Robert S. Erikson and Kent L. Tedin, *American Public Opinion,* 5th ed. (Boston: Allyn and Bacon, 1995), 69. Copyright © 1995 by Addison-Wesley-Longman. Reprinted with permission.

combinations of the three sets of views described above, we would have nine categories of opinion; if people always stuck with whichever category they were in, we would need nine different ideological labels to describe those people.

To invent those labels and describe the people who have those views would take countless pages and bore readers to tears. To avoid all that pain and suffering, let's use just two sets of views—those on economic policy and those on personal conduct—and describe the kinds of people who have each of the four combinations (liberal or conservative on each set).[39]

1. *Pure liberals*   These people are liberal on both economic policy and personal conduct. They want the government to reduce economic inequality, regulate business, tax the rich heavily, cure the (presumably) economic causes of crime, allow abortions, protect the rights of the accused, and guarantee the broadest possible freedoms of speech and press.
   Traits: Pure liberals are more likely than the average citizen to be young, college-educated, and nonreligious.

2. *Pure conservatives*   These people are conservative on both economic and conduct issues. They

want the government to cut back on the welfare state, allow the market to allocate goods and services, keep taxes low, lock up criminals, and curb forms of conduct they regard as antisocial.
   Traits: Pure conservatives are more likely than the average citizen to be older, to have higher incomes, to be white, and to live in the Midwest.

3. *Libertarians*   These people are conservative on economic matters and liberal on social ones. The common theme is that they want a small, weak government—one that has little control over either the economy or the personal lives of citizens.
   Traits: Libertarians are more likely than the average citizen to be young, college-educated, and white, to have higher incomes and no religion, and to live in the West.

4. *Populists*   These people are liberal on economic matters and conservative on social ones. They want a government that will reduce economic inequality and control business, but they also want it to regulate personal conduct, lock up criminals, and permit school prayer.
   Traits: Populists are more likely than the average citizen to be older, poorly educated, low-income, religious, and female and to live in the South or Midwest.

Obviously this classification is an oversimplification. There are many exceptions, and the number of people in each category changes from time to time. Moreover, this categorization leaves out about one-seventh of the population—their views do not fit any of these categories. Nonetheless, it is a useful way to explain how complex are the political ideologies in this country and why terms such as *liberal* and *conservative*, in their "pure" form, describe the views of relatively few people.

Political Elites

There is one group that can be classified as liberals and conservatives in a pure sense, and it is made up of people who are in the political elite. Every society has an elite, because in every society government officials will have more power than ordinary folk, some persons will make more money than others, and some people will be more popular than others. In the former Soviet Union they even had an official name for the political elite—the *nomenklatura*. But, in America, we often refer to **political elites** more casually as "activists"— people who hold office, run for office, work in campaigns or on newspapers, lead interest groups and social movements, and speak out on public issues. Being an activist is not an all-or-nothing proposition: people display differing degrees of activism, from full-time politicians to persons who occasionally get involved in a campaign (see Chapter 8). But the more a person is an activist, the more likely it is that he or she will display ideological consistency on the conventional liberal-conservative spectrum.

The reasons for this greater consistency seem to be information and peers. First, information: in general, the better informed people are about politics and the more interest they take in politics, the more likely they are to have consistently liberal or conservative views.[40] This higher level of information and interest may lead them to find relationships among issues that others don't see and to learn from the media and elsewhere what are the "right" things to believe. This does not mean that there are no differences within liberal elites (or within conservative ones), only that the differences occur within a liberal (or conservative) consensus that is more well defined, more consistent, and more important to those who share it than would be the case among ordinary citizens.

Second, peers: politics does not make strange bedfellows. On the contrary, politics is a process of likes attracting likes. The more active you are in politics,

Table 7.7	Policy Preferences of Democratic and Republican Voters		

		Preferences	
Issue		**Democrats**	**Republicans**
Should allow people to invest part of Social Security taxes on their own.		44%	61%
For murder, penalty should be death.		46	55
Unfavorable opinion of National Rifle Association.		44	20
Abortion should be available to those who want it.		48	25
Must protect environment even if jobs are lost.		72	57
Parents should get tax-paid vouchers to help pay for children attending private schools.		41	53

Source: Adapted from *New York Times*/CBS News poll, *New York Times*, (August 14, 2000), A17. Copyright © 2000 *The New York Times*.

the more you will associate with people who agree with you on some issues; and the more time you spend with those people, the more your other views will shift to match theirs.

The greater ideological consistency of political elites can be seen in Congress. As we shall note in Chapter 13, Democratic members of Congress tend to be consistently liberal, and Republican members of Congress tend to be consistently conservative— *far more* consistently than Democratic voters and Republican voters. By the same token we shall see in Chapter 9 that the delegates to presidential nominating conventions are far more ideological (liberal in the Democratic convention, conservative in the Republican one) than is true of voters who identify with the Democratic or Republican party.

Still, on a large number of issues, the policy preferences of average Republican and Democratic voters do differ significantly from one another (see Table 7.7). Some political scientists argue that Republican and Democratic leaders in Congress are more polarized because voters are more polarized. For example, in

political elites Persons with a disproportionate share of political power.

After Saddam Hussein's government was overthrown by American and other troops, his statue was pulled down in Baghdad.

1970 only 30 percent of voters who opposed abortion under all circumstances identified themselves as Republicans; by 1998, 71 percent did so.[41] Since the 1980s partisan voting has become more common, while the share of those who are independent has shrunk.[42]

Other political scientists, however, analyze the available polling and election data differently. They find that ideological changes among voters have been "marginal at best," while public opinion among Democrats voting in districts represented by Democrats and among Republicans voting in districts represented by Republicans has been remarkably stable.[43] Which side is right? We have no data that will allow us to compare in each district what voters think and how their representatives behave. To amass such data would require polls of perhaps five hundred voters in each congressional district taken several years apart. Nobody thinks it is worth spending millions of dollars to interview over ten thousand voters at different times just to answer this one academic puzzle.

☆ Political Elites, Public Opinion, and Public Policy

Though the elites and the public see politics in very different ways, and though there are often intense antagonisms between the two groups, the elites influence public opinion in at least two important ways.

First, elites, especially those in or having access to the media (see Chapter 12), raise and frame political issues. At one time environmentalism was not on the political agenda; at a later time not only was it on the agenda, it was up near the top of government concerns. At some times the government had little interest in what it should do in South Africa or Central America; at other times the government was preoccupied with these matters. Though world events help

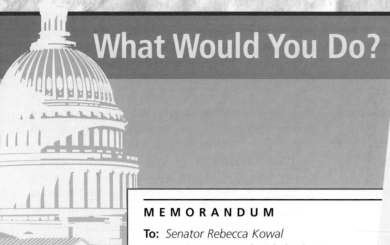

What Would You Do?

U.S. Senate to Debate New Curbs on Legal Immigration

May 22
WASHINGTON

Legal immigration to the United States has reached record highs. From 1991 to 2000 more than 9 million people, or about 300,000 more than entered the country during the first decade of the twentieth century, came to America. Next week the Senate begins debate on several bills that would slow or stop the flow of legal immigrants . . .

MEMORANDUM

To: *Senator Rebecca Kowal*
From: *Lia Fantuzzo, legislative intern*
Subject: *Reducing legal immigration*

Your constituents are evenly divided over restrictions. Having declared yourself "neutral pending further study and debate," you are nonetheless being urged by valued colleagues on both sides of the issue and by the press to take a position on cutting legal immigration.

Arguments for:

1. Since Congress liberalized U.S. immigration laws in 1965, nearly 25 million legal immigrants have settled in America, and the percentage of foreign-born U.S. residents has risen to 10 percent. At this rate, by 2050 the total U.S. population will rise by about 125 million, to nearly 400 million. Two-thirds of the increase will be due to legal immigration.
2. For every ten legal immigrants, about three undocumented aliens enter the country. Together they take jobs away from native-born Americans.
3. Most immigrants settle in one of four states (California, Florida, New York, and Texas), placing an undue burden on those states to pay for services such as health care and welfare for immigrants.

Arguments against:

1. From 1860 to 1930 over 10 percent of U.S. residents were foreign born. Without immigration the U.S. population will reach 310 million by 2035 and then decline. Immigrants not only consume public services but also pay taxes and provide a younger, more vital labor pool.
2. All told only about 5 million noncitizens are living unlawfully in the United States. Legal immigrants include people with advanced degrees and highly marketable skills. Low-skilled immigrants often take menial jobs that nobody else wants.
3. Immigrants have always tended to settle in a few areas. In the first half of the twentieth century, most settled in a half dozen big cities. Today the federal government provides funds to the states to pay for at least some of the costs of social services for residents, including immigrants.

Your decision:

Favor curbs _____
Oppose curbs _____

shape the political agenda, so also do political elites. A path-breaking study by John Zaller shows in fact that elite views shape mass views by influencing both what issues capture the public's attention and how those issues are debated and decided.[44] Contrary to the myth of the pandering politician, recent evidence suggests that what scholars of the subject call opinion-policy congruence (essentially the rate at which governments adopt crime, health, trade, and other policies supported by majorities in polls) has been declining, not rising, since 1980, a trend that may reflect greater elite influence over how policy options are presented to the public.[45]

Second, elites state the norms by which issues should be settled. (A **norm** is a standard of right or proper conduct.) By doing this they help determine the range of acceptable and unacceptable policy options. For example, elites have for a long time emphasized that racism is wrong. Of late they have emphasized that sexism is wrong. Over a long period the steady repetition of views condemning racism and sexism will at least intimidate, and perhaps convince, those of us who are racist and sexist.

A recent example of this process has been the public discussion of AIDS and its relationship to homosexuality. The initial public reaction to AIDS was one of fear and loathing. But efforts to quarantine people infected with AIDS were met with firm resistance from the medical community and from other policy elites. The elites even managed to persuade some legislatures to bar insurance companies from testing insurance applicants for the disease.

There are limits to how much influence elites can have on the public. For instance, elites do not define economic problems—people can see for themselves that there is or is not unemployment, that there is or is not raging inflation, that there are or are not high interest rates. Elite opinion may shape the policies, but it does not define the problem. Similarly, elite opinion has little influence on whether we think there is a crime or drug problem; it is, after all, *our* purses being snatched, cars being stolen, and children being drugged. On the other hand, elite opinion does define the problem as well as the policy options with respect to most aspects of foreign affairs; the public has little firsthand experience with which to judge what is going on in Iraq.

Because elites affect how we see some issues and determine how other issues get resolved, it is important to study the differences between elite and public opinion. But it is wrong to suppose that there is one elite, unified in its interests and opinions. Just as there are many publics, and hence many public opinions, there are many elites, and hence many different elite opinions. Whether there is enough variety of opinion and influence among elites to justify calling our politics "pluralist" is one of the central issues confronting any student of government.

☆ SUMMARY

"*P*ublic opinion" is a slippery notion, partly because there are many publics, with many different opinions, and partly because opinion on all but relatively simple matters tends to be uninformed, unstable, and sensitive to different ways of asking poll questions. Polling is a difficult and expensive art, not an exact science.

Political attitudes are shaped by family, schooling, and other experiences. Opinions vary in America according to class, gender, and other characteristics. Americans are also divided by their political ideologies but not along a single liberal-conservative dimension.

There are several kinds of issues on which people may take "liberal" or "conservative" positions, and they often do not take the same position on all issues. Just using two kinds of issues—economic and social—it is possible to define four kinds of ideologies: pure liberal, pure conservative, libertarian, and populist.

Political elites are much more likely to display a consistently liberal or consistently conservative ideology. Elites are important because they have a disproportionate influence on public policy and even an influence on mass opinion (through the dissemination of information and the evocation of political norms).

norm   A standard of right or proper conduct.

RECONSIDERING WHO GOVERNS?

1. How does public opinion in America today vary by race, gender, and other differences?

There are cleavages in American public opinion, but they change over time, and it is hard to generalize meaningfully about how they affect politics and government. For example, on some issues, the opinions of whites and blacks are similar or narrowing, but on other issues, wide opinion gaps remain between whites and blacks. Surprisingly, little major research exists on the opinions and partisan preferences of the country's over 30 million Latinos. People who attend worship services regularly are more conservative and far more likely to vote Republican in presidential elections than people who attend worship services rarely if ever. Women are far more sympathetic to liberal causes and Democratic candidates than men, but these so-called gender gaps in opinion and voting behavior are more pronounced in some elections than in others.

2. What is political ideology, and how does it affect political behavior and influence public policy?

Political ideology is a more or less consistent set of beliefs about the policies government ought to pursue. Political scientists measure the extent to which people have a political ideology by seeing how frequently people use broad political categories (such as "liberal" and "conservative") to describe their own views or to justify their preferences for candidates and policies. They also measure it by seeing to what extent the policy preferences of a citizen are consistent over time or are based at any one time on consistent principles. Many scholars believe that Americans are becoming more ideological. On many issues, for example, the policy preferences of average Republican and Democratic voters now differ significantly from one another. There is clear evidence that political elites are more ideological today than they were just a generation or two ago. The government attends more to the elite views than to popular views, at least on many matters.

RECONSIDERING TO WHAT ENDS?

1. What role did the Framers of the Constitution think public opinion should play in American democracy?

Basically, a rather limited role. Turn to the Appendix and read *Federalist* No. 10 by James Madison. In it, Madison makes plain his view that the public interest is not always, or even often, the same as what most people demand from the government. Instead members of Congress are to be "proper guardians of the public weal," representatives who serve "the permanent and aggregate interests" of the country. He holds that "the regulation of these various and interfering interests" is the "principal task" of representatives.

2. When, if ever, should public policies mirror majority opinion?

For most of us, the answer depends on the issue in question. (Which, if any, of the gaps between majority opinion and public policy mentioned on the first page of this chapter would you wish to see closed?) When it comes to civil rights and civil liberties (see Chapters 5 and 6), few of us would be willing, strictly speaking, to trust our freedoms to a popular vote. On the other hand, few of us would consider our system truly democratic if government only rarely did pretty much what most people wanted. The Framers of the Constitution offer one principled answer. They believed temporary or transient popular majorities should carry little weight with representatives, but persistent popular majorities—for example, ones that persist over the staggered terms of House and Senate and over more than a single presidential term—should be heard and in many, though not in all, cases heeded.

WORLD WIDE WEB RESOURCES

Roper Center for Public Opinion Research:
www.lib.uconn.edu/RoperCenter
CBS News poll: **cbsnews.cbs.com**
Gallup opinion poll: **www.gallup.com**
Los Angeles Times poll:
www.latimes.com/news/custom/timespoll

The Pew Research Center for the People & the Press:
www.people-press.org
Zogby International: **www.zogby.com**

SUGGESTED READINGS

Converse, Philip E. "The Nature of Belief Systems in Mass Publics." In *Ideology and Discontent*, edited by David Apter. Glencoe, Ill.: Free Press, 1964. The classic discussion of inconsistencies in public opinion.

Erikson, Robert S., and Kent L. Tedin. *American Public Opinion.* 5th ed. Boston: Allyn and Bacon, 1995. An excellent summary of how opinion is measured, what it shows, and how it affects politics.

Jennings, M. Kent, and Richard G. Niemi. *Generations and Politics.* Princeton, N.J.: Princeton University Press, 1981. A study of persistence and change in the political views of young adults and their parents.

————.*The Political Character of Adolescence: The Influence of Families and Schools.* Princeton, N.J.: Princeton University Press, 1974. A study of political attitudes among high school students.

Key, V. O., Jr. *The Responsible Electorate.* Cambridge: Harvard University Press, 1966. An argument, with evidence, that American voters are not fools.

Lipset, Seymour Martin. *Political Man: The Social Bases of Politics.* Garden City, N.Y.: Doubleday, 1959. An exploration of the relationship between society, opinion, and democracy in America and abroad.

Moe, Terry M. *Schools, Vouchers, and the American Public.* Washington, D.C.: Brookings Institution Press, 2001. A masterful study of how public opinion matters to education policy, suggesting that most people, with only slight information, form reasonable views.

Nie, Norman H., Sidney Verba, and John R. Petrocik. *The Changing American Voter.* Cambridge: Harvard University Press, 1976. Traces shifts in American voter attitudes since 1960.

Weissberg, Robert. *Polling, Policy, and Public Opinion.* New York: Palgrave Macmillan, 2002. A critique of what we think we know from opinion polling, showing the many ways in which polls can give us misleading answers.

Zaller, John. *The Nature and Origins of Mass Opinion.* Cambridge, England: Cambridge University Press, 1992. A path-breaking study of how the public forms an opinion, illustrating the ways in which elite views help shape mass views.

Political Participation

A Closer Look at Nonvoting

The Rise of the American Electorate
From State to Federal Control ●
Voter Turnout

Who Participates in Politics?
Forms of Participation ● The Causes
of Participation ● The Meaning of
Participation Rates

WHO GOVERNS?

1. Who votes, who doesn't?
2. Why do some people participate in politics at higher rates than others?

TO WHAT ENDS?

1. How did the Framers of the Constitution think average citizens should participate in America's representative democracy?
2. Should today's college-age citizens participate more in politics?

*A*mericans are often embarrassed by their low rate of participation in national elections. Data such as those shown in Table 8.1 are frequently used to make the point: whereas well over 80 percent of the people vote in many European elections, only about half of the people vote in American presidential elections (and a much smaller percentage vote in congressional contests). Many observers blame this low turnout on voter apathy and urge the government and private groups to mount campaigns to get out the vote.

There are only three things wrong with this view. First, it is a misleading description of the problem; second, it is an incorrect explanation of the problem; and third, it proposes a remedy that probably won't work.

☆ A Closer Look at Nonvoting

First, let's look at how best to describe the problem. The conventional data on voter turnout here and abroad are misleading because they compute participation rates by two different measures. In this country only two-thirds of the voting-age population is registered to vote. To understand what this means, look at Table 8.1. In column A are several countries ranked in terms of the percentage of the **voting-age population** that voted in 1996–2001 national elections. As you can see, the United States, where 47.2 percent voted, ranked near the bottom; only Switzerland was lower. Now look at column B, where the same countries are ranked in terms of the percentage of **registered voters** who participated in these national elections. The United States, where 63.4 percent of registered voters turned out at the polls, is now fifth from the bottom.[1]

Second, let's consider a better explanation for the problem. Apathy on election day is clearly not the source of the problem. Of those who are registered, the overwhelming majority vote. The real source of the participation problem in the United States is that a relatively low percentage of the adult population is registered to vote.

Third, let's look at how to cure the problem. Mounting a get-out-the-vote drive probably wouldn't make much difference. In a study published in 2004, political scientists Donald P. Green and Alan S. Gerber analyzed evidence on a wide variety of voter mobilization strategies: door-to-door canvassing, leaflets, direct mail, phone banks, and electronic mail.[2] In most cases, the effects on voter turnout were small or nil. Neither reminding voters that election day is near nor supplying them with information seems to make much difference. But in low-turnout elections (for example, midterm congressional elections), people who normally vote anyway "are especially receptive to get-out-the-vote appeals, particularly when contacted face-to-face."[3]

Still, it's not frequent voters, but nonregistered voters, who must be mobilized if turnout rates are to rise significantly. What might make a difference is a plan that would get more people to register to vote. But doing that does not necessarily involve overcoming the "apathy" of unregistered voters. Some people may not register because they don't care about politics or their duty as citizens. But there are other explanations for being unregistered. In this country the entire burden of registering to vote falls on the individual voters. They must learn how and when and where to register; they must take the time and trouble to go someplace and fill out a registration form; and they must reregister in a new county or state if they happen to move. In most European nations registration is done for you, automatically, by the government. Since it is costly to register in this country and costless to register in other countries, it should not be surprising that fewer people are registered here than abroad.

In 1993 Congress passed a law designed to make it easier to register to vote. Known as the motor-voter law, the law requires states to allow people to register to vote when applying for driver's licenses and to provide registration through the mail and at some state offices that serve the disabled or provide public assistance (such as welfare checks). The motor-voter law took effect in 1995. In just two months, 630,000 new voters signed up in twenty-seven states. Even so, the results of the law so far have been mixed. By 1999, registration in motor vehicle offices accounted for a third of all voter registration applications, and in 2001–2002 over 16 million people, representing over 40 percent of all voter applications, registered in motor-vehicle offices (see Figure 8.1). Still, there is scant evidence that the motor-voter law has had much of an impact on either voter turnout or election outcomes. A 2001 study found that turnout of motor-voter registrants was lower than that of other new registrants and concluded "that those who register when the process is costless are less likely to vote."[4]

A final point: voting is only one way of participating in politics. It is important (we could hardly be considered a democracy if nobody voted), but it is not

Table 8.1	Two Ways of Calculating Voter Turnout, 1996–2001 Elections, Selected Countries	
A Turnout as Percentage of Voting-Age Population		**B** Turnout as Percentage of Registered Voters
Belgium	83.2%	Australia	95.2%
Denmark	83.1	Belgium	90.6
Australia	81.8	Denmark	86.0
Sweden	77.7	New Zealand	83.1
Finland	76.8	Germany	82.2
Germany	75.3	Sweden	81.4
New Zealand	74.6	Austria	80.4
Norway	73.0	France	79.7
Austria	72.6	Finland	76.8
France	72.3	Norway	75.0
Netherlands	70.1	Netherlands	73.2
Japan	59.0	UNITED STATES	63.4
United Kingdom	57.6	Japan	62.0
Canada	54.6	Canada	61.2
UNITED STATES	47.2	United Kingdom	59.4
Switzerland	34.9	Switzerland	43.2

Source: From the International Institute for Democracy and Electoral Assistance (IDEA), *Voter Turnout: A Global Survey* (Stockholm, Sweden, 2001). Reprinted with the permission of Cambridge University Press.

all-important. Joining civic associations, supporting social movements, writing to legislators, fighting city hall—all these and other activities are ways of participating in politics. It is possible that, by these measures, Americans participate in politics *more* than most Europeans—or anybody else, for that matter. Moreover, it is possible that low rates of registration indicate that people are reasonably well satisfied with how the country is governed. If 100 percent of all adult Americans registered and voted (especially under a system that makes registering relatively difficult), it could mean that people were deeply upset about how things were run. In short, it is not at all clear whether low voter turnout is a symptom of political disease or a sign of political good health.

The important question about participation is not how much participation there is but how different

voting-age population Citizens who are eligible to vote after reaching the minimum age requirement.

registered voters People who are registered to vote.

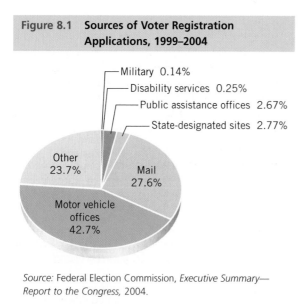

Figure 8.1   Sources of Voter Registration Applications, 1999–2004

- Military 0.14%
- Disability services 0.25%
- Public assistance offices 2.67%
- State-designated sites 2.77%

Other 23.7%

Mail 27.6%

Motor vehicle offices 42.7%

Source: Federal Election Commission, *Executive Summary— Report to the Congress,* 2004.

it also requires us to look at the composition and activities of political parties, interest groups, and the media (the subjects of later chapters).

Nonetheless, voting is important. To understand why participation in American elections takes the form that it does, we must first understand how laws have determined who shall vote and under what circumstances.

☆ The Rise of the American Electorate

It is ironic that relatively few citizens vote in American elections, since it was in this country that the mass of people first became eligible to vote. At the time the Constitution was ratified, the vote was limited to property owners or taxpayers, but by the administration of Andrew Jackson (1829–1837) it had been broadened to include virtually all white male adults. Only in a few states did property restrictions persist: they were not abolished in New Jersey until 1844 or in North Carolina until 1856. And, of course, African American males could not vote in

kinds of participation affect the kind of government we get. This question cannot be answered just by looking at voter turnout, the subject of this chapter;

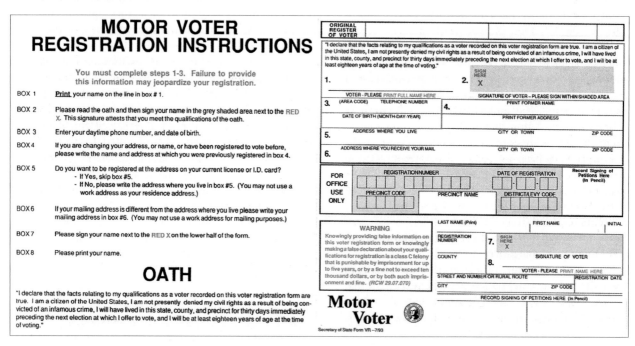

When you apply for a driver's license in the state of Washington, you are given this form so that you can register to vote at the same time. This "motor-voter" idea became the basis of a federal law passed in 1993.

many states, in the North as well as the South, even if they were not slaves. Women could not vote in most states until the twentieth century; Chinese Americans were widely denied the vote; and being in prison is grounds for losing the franchise even today. Aliens, on the other hand, were often allowed to vote if they had at least begun the process of becoming citizens. By 1880 only an estimated 14 percent of all adult males in the United States could not vote; in England in the same period about 40 percent of adult males were disfranchised.[5]

From State to Federal Control

Initially it was left entirely to the states to decide who could vote and for what offices. The Constitution gave Congress the right to pick the day on which presidential electors would gather and to alter state regulations regarding congressional elections. The only provision of the Constitution requiring a popular election was the clause in Article I stating that members of the House of Representatives be chosen by the "people of the several states."

Because of this permissiveness, early federal elections varied greatly. Several states picked their members of the House at large (that is, statewide) rather than by district; others used districts but elected more than one representative from each. Still others had their elections in odd-numbered years, and some even required that a congressional candidate win a majority, rather than simply a plurality, of votes to be elected (when that requirement was in effect, runoff elections—in one case as many as twelve—were necessary). Furthermore, presidential electors were at first picked by state legislatures rather than by the voters directly.

Congress, by law and constitutional amendment, has steadily reduced state prerogatives in these matters. In 1842 a federal law required that all members of the House be elected by districts; other laws over the years required that all federal elections be held in even-numbered years on the Tuesday following the first Monday in November.

The most important changes in elections have been those that extended the suffrage to women, African Americans, and eighteen-year-olds and made mandatory the direct popular election of U.S. senators. The Fifteenth Amendment, adopted in 1870, said that the "right of citizens of the United States to vote shall not be denied or abridged by the United States or by any state on account of race,

color, or previous condition of servitude." Reading those words today, one would assume that they gave African Americans the right to vote. That is not what the Supreme Court during the 1870s thought they meant. By a series of decisions, it held that the Fifteenth Amendment did not necessarily confer the right to vote on anybody; it merely asserted that if someone was denied that right, the denial could not be explicitly on the grounds of race. And the burden of proving that it was race that led to the denial fell on the black who was turned away at the polls.[6]

This interpretation opened the door to all manner of state stratagems to keep blacks from voting. One was a **literacy test** (a large proportion of former slaves were illiterate); another was a requirement that a **poll tax** be paid (most former slaves were poor); a third was the practice of keeping blacks from voting in primary elections (in the one-party South the only meaningful election was the Democratic primary). To allow whites who were illiterate or poor to vote, a **grandfather clause** was added to the law, saying that a person could vote, even if he did not meet the legal requirements, if he or his ancestors voted before 1867 (blacks, of course, could not vote before 1867). When all else failed, blacks were intimidated, threatened, or harassed if they showed up at the polls.

There began a long, slow legal process of challenging in court each of these restrictions in turn. One by one the Supreme Court set most of them aside. The grandfather clause was declared unconstitutional in 1915,[7] and the **white primary** finally fell in 1944.[8] Some of the more blatantly discriminatory literacy tests were also overturned.[9] The practical result of these rulings was slight: only a small proportion of voting-age blacks were able to register

literacy test   A requirement that citizens pass a literacy test in order to register to vote.

poll tax   A requirement that citizens pay a tax in order to register to vote.

grandfather clause   A clause in registration laws allowing people who do not meet registration requirements to vote if they or their ancestors had voted before 1867.

white primary   The practice of keeping blacks from voting in the southern states' primaries through arbitrary use of registration requirements and intimidation.

WHITE SUPREMACY!

Attention, White Men!

Grand Torch-Light Procession

At JACKSON,

On the Night of the

Fourth of January, 1890.

**The Final Settlement of Democratic Rule
and White Supremacy in Mississippi.**

GRAND PYROTECHNIC DISPLAY!
Transparencies and Torches Free for all.

**All in Sympathy with the Grand Cause
are Cordially and Earnestly Invited to be
on hand, to aid in the Final Overthrow of
Radical Rule in our State.**

Come on foot or on horse-back; come any way, but
be sure to get there.
Brass Bands, Cannon, Flambeau Torches, Transparencies, Sky-rockets, Etc.

A GRAND DISPLAY FOR A GRAND CAUSE.

*After Reconstruction ended in 1876, black voting shrank
under the attack of white supremacists.*

*After the Civil Rights Act of 1964 was passed, blacks and
whites voted together in a small Alabama town.*

and vote in the South, and they were found mostly in the larger cities. A dramatic change did not begin until 1965, with the passage of the Voting Rights Act. This act suspended the use of literacy tests and authorized the appointment of federal examiners who could order the registration of blacks in states and counties (mostly in the South) where fewer than 50 percent of the voting-age population were registered or had voted in the last presidential election. It also provided criminal penalties for interfering with the right to vote.

Though implementation in some places was slow, the number of African Americans voting rose sharply throughout the South. For example, in Mississippi the proportion of voting-age blacks who registered rose from 5 percent to over 70 percent in just ten years (see Table 8.2). These changes had a profound effect on the behavior of many white southern

politicians: Governor George Wallace stopped making prosegregation speeches and began courting the black vote.

Women were kept from the polls by law more than by intimidation, and when the laws changed, women almost immediately began to vote in large numbers. By 1915 several states, mostly in the West, had begun to permit women to vote. But it was not until the Nineteenth Amendment to the Constitution was ratified in 1920, after a struggle lasting many decades, that women generally were allowed to vote. At one stroke the size of the eligible voting population almost doubled. Contrary to the hopes of some and the fears of others, no dramatic changes occurred in the conduct of elections, the identity of the winners, or the substance of public policy. Initially, at least, women voted more or less in the same manner as men, though not quite as frequently.

| Table 8.2 | Voter Registration in the South |

		Percentage of Voting-Age Population That Is Registered											
		Ala.	Ark.	Fla.	Ga.	La.	Miss.	N.C.	S.C.	Tenn.	Tex.	Va.	Total
1960	White	63.6%	60.9%	69.3%	56.8%	76.9%	63.9%	92.1%	57.1%	73.0%	42.5%	46.1%	61.1%
	Black*	13.7	38.0	39.4	29.3	31.1	5.2	39.1	13.7	59.1	35.5	23.1	29.1
1970	White	85.0	74.1	65.5	71.7	77.0	82.1	68.1	62.3	78.5	62.0	64.5	62.9
	Black	66.0	82.3	55.3	57.2	57.4	71.0	51.3	56.1	71.6	72.6	57.0	62.0
1986	White	77.5	67.2	66.9	62.3	67.8	91.6	67.4	53.4	70.0	79.0	60.3	69.9
	Black	68.9	57.9	58.2	52.8	60.6	70.8	58.4	52.5	65.3	68.0	56.2	60.8
1996	White	75.8	64.5	63.7	67.8	74.5	75.0	70.4	69.7	66.3	62.7	68.4	69.0
	Black	69.2	65.8	53.1	64.6	71.9	67.4	65.5	64.3	65.7	63.2	64.0	65.0
2002	White	73.7	62.9	60.7	62.7	74.2	70.7	63.1	66.2	62.3	57.7	64.1	62.6
	Black	67.7	62.0	47.9	61.7	73.5	67.9	58.2	68.3	54.1	65.1	47.5	60.2

*Includes other minority races.

Source: Voter Education Project, Inc., of Atlanta, Georgia, as reported in *Statistical Abstract of the United States, 1990 and 1996*. Figures for 2002 compiled from U.S. Bureau of Census data by Marc Siegal.

The political impact of the youth vote was also less than expected. The Voting Rights Act of 1970 gave eighteen-year-olds the right to vote in federal elections beginning January 1, 1971. It also contained a provision lowering the voting age to eighteen in state elections, but the Supreme Court declared this unconstitutional. As a result a constitutional amendment, the Twenty-sixth, was proposed by Congress and ratified by the states in 1971. The 1972 elections became the first in which all people between the ages of eighteen and twenty-one could cast ballots (before then, four states had allowed those under twenty-one to vote). About 25 million people suddenly became eligible to participate in elections, but their turnout (42 percent) was lower than for the population as a whole, and they did not flock to any particular party or candidate. Since then voter turnout by eighteen- to twenty-four-year-olds has fallen both in absolute terms and relative to rates among senior citizens. For instance, 22 percent of eighteen- to twenty-four-year-olds, versus three-fifths of citizens older than sixty-five, voted in the midterm congressional elections of 1986, and just 17 percent of them voted, versus the same three-fifths of citizens older than sixty-five, in the midterm congressional elections of 1998.[10] In the 1996 presidential election turnout among eighteen- to twenty-four-year-olds was about 30 percent, rising to about 38 percent in the 2000 presidential election, then dipping slightly below 20 percent in the

2002 midterm congressional elections.[11] At the same time, however, young Americans' rates of participation in civic activities such as community service have hit all-time highs. Several studies find that both the fraction of adults under thirty who volunteer and the average number of hours they volunteer per year have increased significantly over the past generation.[12] The late Senator Paul Wellstone of Minnesota, a liberal Democrat who taught political science and who was a campus political protester during the 1970s and 1980s, believed that among young people today, "community service is viewed as good, and political service is viewed as disreputable."[13] Systematic studies of the subject are few, but the senator was probably right.[14]

National standards now govern almost every aspect of voter eligibility. All persons eighteen years of age and older may vote; there may be no literacy test or poll tax; states may not require residency of more than thirty days in that state before a person may vote; areas with significant numbers of citizens not speaking English must give those people ballots written in their own language; and federal voter registrars and poll watchers may be sent into areas where less than 50 percent of the voting-age population participates in a presidential election. Before 1961 residents of the District of Columbia could not vote in presidential elections; the Twenty-third Amendment to the Constitution gave them this right.

The campaign to win the vote for women nationwide succeeded with the adoption of the Nineteenth Amendment in 1920.

Voter Turnout

Given all these legal safeguards, one might expect that participation in elections would have risen sharply. In fact the proportion of the voting-age population that has gone to the polls in presidential elections has remained about the same—between 50 and 60 percent of those eligible—at least since 1928 and appears today to be much smaller than it was in the latter part of the nineteenth century (see Figure 8.2). In every presidential election between 1860 and 1900, at least 70 percent of the eligible population apparently went to the polls, and in some years (1860 and 1876) almost 80 percent seem to have voted. Since 1900 not a single presidential election turnout has reached 70 percent, and on two occasions (1920 and 1924) it did not even reach 50 percent.[15] Even outside the South, where efforts to disfranchise African Americans make data on voter turnout especially hard to interpret, turnout seems to have declined: over 84 percent of the voting-age population participated in presidential elections in nonsouthern states between 1884 and 1900, but only 68 percent participated between 1936 and 1960, and even fewer have done so since 1960.[16]

Scholars have vigorously debated the meaning of these figures. One view is that this decline in turnout, even allowing for the shaky data on which the estimates are based, has been real and is the result of a decline of popular interest in elections and a weaken-

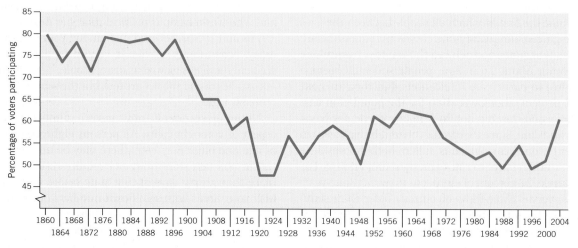

Figure 8.2   Voter Participation in Presidential Elections, 1860–2004

Note: Several southern states did not participate in the 1864 and 1868 elections.
Sources: For 1860–1928: Bureau of the Census, *Historical Statistics of the United States, Colonial Times to 1970,* part 2, 1071; 1932–1944: *Statistical Abstract of the United States, 1992,* 517; 1948–2000: Michael P. McDonald and Samuel L. Popkin, "The Myth of the Vanishing Voter," *American Political Science Review* 95 (December 2001): table 1, 966.

ing of the competitiveness of the two major parties. During the nineteenth century, according to this theory, the parties fought hard, worked strenuously to get as many voters as possible to the polls, afforded the mass of voters a chance to participate in party politics through caucuses and conventions, kept the legal barriers to participation (such as complex registration procedures) low, and looked forward to close, exciting elections. After 1896, by which time the South had become a one-party Democratic region and the North heavily Republican, both parties became more conservative, national elections usually resulted in lopsided victories for the Republicans, and citizens began to lose interest in politics because it no longer seemed relevant to their needs. The parties ceased functioning as organizations to mobilize the mass of voters and fell under the control of leaders, mostly conservative, who resisted mass participation.[17]

There is another view, however. It argues that the decline in voter turnout has been more apparent than real. Though elections were certainly more of a popular sport in the nineteenth century than they are today, the parties were no more democratic then than now, and voters then may have been more easily manipulated. Until around the beginning of the twentieth century, voting fraud was commonplace, because it was easy to pull off. The political parties, not the government, printed the ballots; they were often cast in public, not private, voting booths; there were few serious efforts to decide who was eligible to vote, and the rules that did operate were easily evaded.

Under these circumstances it was easy for a person to vote more than once, and the party machines made heavy use of these "floaters," or repeaters. "Vote early and often" was not a joke but a fact. The parties often controlled the counting of votes, padding the totals whenever they feared losing. As a result of these machinations, the number of votes counted was often larger than the number cast, and the number cast was in turn often larger than the number of individuals eligible to vote.

Around 1890 the states began adopting the **Australian ballot**. This was a government-printed ballot of uniform size and shape that was cast in secret, created to replace the old party-printed ballots cast in public. By 1910 only three states were without the Australian ballot. Its use cut back on (but certainly did not eliminate) vote buying and fraudulent vote counts.

In short, if votes had been legally cast and honestly counted in the nineteenth century, the statistics on

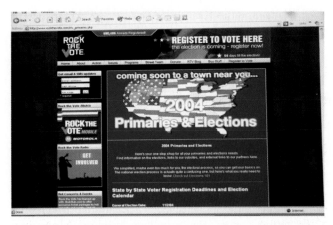

A "Rock the Vote" web site during the 2004 presidential election.

election turnout might well be much lower than the inflated figures we now have.[18] To the extent that this is true, we may not have had a decline in voter participation as great as some have suggested. Nevertheless, most scholars believe that turnout probably did actually decline somewhat after the 1890s. One reason was that voter-registration regulations became more burdensome: there were longer residency requirements; aliens who had begun but not completed the process of becoming citizens could no longer vote in most states; it became harder for African Americans to vote; educational qualifications for voting were adopted by several states; and voters had to register long in advance of the elections. These changes, designed to purify the electoral process, were aspects of the progressive reform impulse (described in Chapter 9) and served to cut back on the number of people who could participate in elections.

Strict voter-registration procedures tended, like most reforms in American politics, to have unintended as well as intended consequences. These changes not only reduced fraudulent voting but also reduced voting generally, because they made it more difficult for certain groups of perfectly honest voters—those with little education, for example, or those who had

---

Australian ballot   A government-printed ballot of uniform dimensions to be cast in secret that many states adopted around 1890 to reduce voting fraud associated with party-printed ballots cast in public.

recently moved—to register and vote. This was not the first time, and it will not be the last, that a reform designed to cure one problem created another.

Following the controversy over Florida's vote count in the 2000 presidential election, many proposals were made to overhaul the nation's voting system. In 2002, Congress passed a measure that for the first time requires each state to have in place a system for counting the disputed ballots of voters whose names were left off official registration lists. In addition, the law provides federal funds for upgrading voting equipment and procedures and for training election officials. But it stops short of creating a uniform national voting system. Paper ballots, lever machines, and punch-card voting systems will still be used in some places, while optical scan and direct recording electronic equipment will still be used in others. Following the 2004 national elections, however, calls to overhaul the nation's voting system were more muted, partly because the popular vote for president was not terribly close (President Bush received 51 percent, John Kerry received 48 percent), and partly because in most states there were few reported problems.

Even after all the legal changes are taken into account, there seems to have been a decline in citizen participation in elections. Between 1960 and 1980 the proportion of voting-age people casting a ballot in presidential elections fell by about 10 percentage points, a drop that cannot be explained by how ballots were printed or how registration rules were rewritten. Nor can these factors explain why 1996 witnessed not only the lowest level of turnout (49 percent) in a presidential election since 1924 but also the single steepest four-year decline (from 55 percent in 1992) since 1920.

There is, however, one alternative theory: voter turnout has not, in fact, been going down. As we saw earlier in this chapter (refer back to Table 8.1), there are different ways of calculating voter turnout. Turnout means the percentage of the voting-age population that votes; an accurate measure of turnout means having an accurate count of both how many people voted and how many people could have voted. In fact, we do not have very good measures of either number. Eligible voters are derived from census reports that tell us what the voting-age population (VAP) is—that is, how many people exist who are age eighteen and over (or before younger people were allowed to vote, the number age twenty-one and over). But within the VAP are a lot of people who cannot vote, such as prisoners, felons, and aliens.

Table 8.3	Two Methods of Calculating Turnout in Presidential Elections, 1948–2000	
Year	Voting Age Population (VAP)	Voting Eligible Population (VEP)
1948	51.1%	52.2%
1952	61.6	62.3
1956	59.3	60.2
1960	62.8	63.8
1964	61.9	62.8
1968	60.9	61.5
1972	55.2	56.2
1976	53.5	54.8
1980	52.8	54.7
1984	53.3	57.2
1988	50.3	54.2
1992	55.0	60.6
1996	48.9	52.6
2000	51.2	55.6

Source: Adapted from Michael P. McDonald and Samuel L. Popkin, "The Myth of the Vanishing Voter," *American Political Science Review* 95 (December 2001): table 1, 966. Reprinted with permission of Cambridge University Press.

Political scientists Michael P. McDonald and Samuel L. Popkin have adjusted the VAP to take into account these differences.[19] They call their alternate measure of turnout the voting eligible population (VEP). Tables 8.3 and 8.4 show how turnout percentages differ depending on which measure, VAP or VEP, is used. Calculated by the VEP, national voter turnout in presidential elections has *not* fallen since the early 1970s. Calculated by

Table 8.4	Two Methods of Calculating Voter Turnout in Selected States, 2000	
State	Voting Age Population (VAP)	Voting Eligible Population (VEP)
California	44.09%	55.78%
Florida	50.65	59.75
New York	49.42	57.72
Texas	43.14	50.33
New Jersey	51.04	58.24
Connecticut	58.35	64.25
Arizona	42.26	48.48
Nevada	43.81	49.86
Oregon	60.50	66.60
D.C.	48.99	54.61

Source: Data from Michael McDonald as reported in Louis Jacobson, "Recalibrating Voter Turnout Gauges," *National Journal* (January 1, 2002).

the VAP, California's turnout rate in the 2000 presidential election was 44 percent, but calculated by the VEP, it was nearly 56 percent. Whichever measure one uses, however, two things are the same: the days when turnout routinely exceeded 60 percent (1952–1968) in presidential elections are gone, and post-1970 turnout in midterm congressional elections has been anemic, averaging only 38 to 40 percent, however it is calculated.[20]

Actual trends in turnout aside, what if they gave an election and everyone came? Would universal turnout change national election outcomes and the content of public policy? It has long been argued that because the poor, less educated, and minorities are overrepresented among nonvoters, universal turnout would strongly benefit Democratic candidates and liberal causes. But a careful study of this question found that the "party of nonvoters" largely mirrors the demographically diverse and ideologically divided population that goes to the polls.[21] In 1992 and 1996, for example, the two most common demographic features of nonvoters were residential mobility and youth: "fully 43 percent of nonvoters had moved within two years of the election and one third were under the age of thirty."[22] If everyone who was eligible had voted in those elections, Bill Clinton's winning margin over George Bush the elder and Bob Dole, respectively, would have been a bit wider, but there would have been "no Mother Lode of votes for Democratic candidates or pressure for liberal causes."[23]

☆ Who Participates in Politics?

To understand better why voter turnout declined and what, if anything, that decline may mean, we must first look at who participates in politics.

Forms of Participation

Voting is by far the most common form of political participation, while giving money to a candidate and being a member of a political organization are the least common. Many Americans exaggerate how frequently they vote or how active they are in politics. In a study by Sidney Verba and Norman Nie, 72 percent of those interviewed said that they voted "regularly" in presidential elections.[24] Yet we know that since 1960, on average only 56 percent of the voting-age population has actually cast presidential ballots. Careful studies of this discrepancy suggest that 8 to

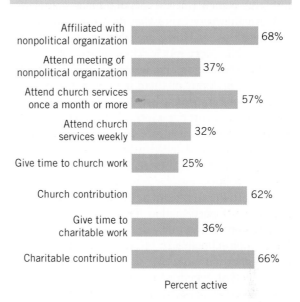

Figure 8.3   Nonpolitical Voluntary Activity Among Citizens

Activity	Percent active
Affiliated with nonpolitical organization	68%
Attend meeting of nonpolitical organization	37%
Attend church services once a month or more	57%
Attend church services weekly	32%
Give time to church work	25%
Church contribution	62%
Give time to charitable work	36%
Charitable contribution	66%

Source: Sidney Verba et al., *Voice and Equality: Civic Voluntarism in American Politics* (Cambridge: Harvard University Press, 1995), 77–79.

10 percent of Americans interviewed misreport their voting habits: they claim to have voted when in fact they have not. Young, low-income, less-educated, and nonwhite people are more likely to misreport than others.[25] If people misreport their voting behavior, it is likely that they also misreport—that is, exaggerate—the extent to which they participate in other ways.

Indeed, most research shows that "politics is not at the heart of the day-to-day life of the American people."[26] Work, family, church, and other voluntary activities come first, both in terms of how Americans spend their time and in terms of the money they donate. For example, a study by Verba and others found that a higher proportion of citizens take part in nonpolitical than political activities: "More citizens reported giving time to church-related or charitable activities than indicated contacting a government official or working informally on a community problem, two of the most frequent forms of political participation beyond the vote"[27] (see Figure 8.3).

In an earlier study Verba and Nie analyzed the ways in which people participate in politics and came up with six forms of participation that are characteristic of six different kinds of U.S. citizens. About one-fifth (22 percent) of the population is completely inactive: they rarely vote, they do not get involved in organizations, and they probably do not even talk about politics very much. These inactives typically have little education and low incomes and are relatively young. Many of them are African American. At the opposite extreme are the complete **activists,** constituting about one-ninth of the population (11 percent). These people are highly educated, have high incomes, and tend to be middle-aged rather than young or old. They tend to participate in all forms of politics.

Between these extremes are four categories of limited forms of participation. The *voting specialists* are people who vote but do little else; they tend not to have much schooling or income and to be substantially older than the average person. *Campaigners* not only vote but also like to get involved in campaign activities. They are better educated than the average voter, but what seems to distinguish them most is their interest in the conflicts, passions, and struggle of politics; their clear identification with a political party; and their willingness to take strong positions. *Communalists* are much like campaigners in social background but have a very different temperament: they do not like the conflict and tension of partisan campaigns. They tend to reserve their energy for community activities of a more nonpartisan nature—forming and joining organizations to deal with local problems and contacting local officials about these problems. Finally, there are some *parochial participants*, who do not vote and stay out of election campaigns and civic associations but are willing to contact local officials about specific, often personal, problems.[28]

The Causes of Participation

Whether participation takes the form of voting or being a complete activist, it is higher among people who have gone to college than among those who have not and higher among people who are over forty-four years of age than among those who are under thirty-five. (The differences in voting rates for these groups are shown in Figure 8.4.) Even after controlling for differences in income and occupation, the more schooling one has, the more likely one is to vote. Of course, it may not be schooling itself that causes participation but something that is strongly correlated with schooling, such as high levels of political information.[29]

In fact the differences in participation that are associated with schooling (or its correlates) are probably even greater than reported in this figure, since we have already seen that less-educated people exaggerate how frequently they vote. An excellent study of turnout concludes that people are more likely to vote when they have those personal qualities that "make learning about politics easier and more gratifying."[30]

Religious involvement also increases political participation. If you are a regular churchgoer who takes your faith seriously, the chances are that you will be more likely to vote and otherwise take part in politics than if you are a person of the same age, sex, income, and educational level who does not go to church. Church involvement leads to social connectedness, teaches organizational skills, increases one's awareness of larger issues, and puts one in contact with like-minded people.[31]

Men and women vote at about the same rate, but blacks and whites do not. Although at one time that difference was largely the result of discrimination, today it can be explained mostly by differences in social class—blacks are poorer and have less schooling, on average, than whites. However, among people of the same socioeconomic status—that is, having roughly the same level of income and schooling—blacks tend to participate *more* than whites.[32]

Because the population has become younger (due to the baby boom of the 1960s and 1970s) and because blacks have increased in numbers faster than whites, one might suppose that these demographic changes would explain why the turnout in presidential elections has gone down a bit since the early 1960s. And they do—up to a point. But there is another factor that ought to make turnout go *up*—schooling. Since college graduates are much more likely to vote than those with less educational experience, and since the college-graduate proportion of the population has gone up sharply, turnout should have risen. But it has not. What is going on here?

---

activists   People who tend to participate in all forms of politics.

Figure 8.4   **Voter Turnout in Presidential Elections, by Age, Schooling, and Race, 1964–2000**

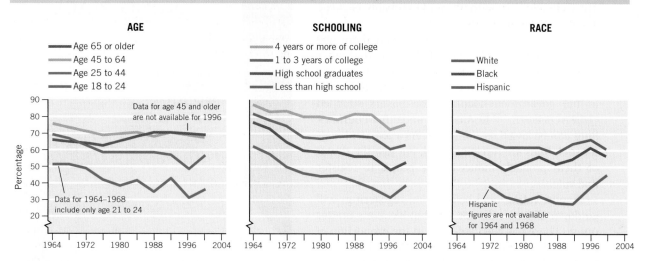

Sources: Updated from Gary R. Orren, "The Linkage of Policy to Participation," in *Presidential Selection,* eds. Alexander Heard and Michael Nelson (Durham, N.C.: Duke University Press, 1987). Data for 1996 are from *Statistical Abstract of the United States 1998,* 296, as supplied by Christopher Blunt. Data for 2000 are from *Statistical Abstract of the United States 2002,* 6, as supplied by Marc Siegal.

Perhaps turnout has declined despite the higher levels of schooling because of the rising level of distrust of government. We saw in Chapter 4 that, well into the 1990s, more and more people were telling pollsters that they lacked confidence in political leaders. Rising distrust seems a plausible explanation for declining turnout, until one looks at the facts. The data show that there is *no correlation* between expressing distrust of political leaders and not voting.[33] People who are cynical about our leaders are just as likely to vote as people who are not.

As we have seen, turnout is powerfully affected by the number of people who have registered to vote; perhaps in recent years it has become harder to register. But in fact exactly the opposite is true. Since 1970 federal law has prohibited residency requirements longer than thirty days for presidential elections, and a Supreme Court decision in 1972 held that requirements much in excess of this were invalid for state and local elections.[34] By 1982 twenty-one states and the District of Columbia, containing about half the nation's population, had adopted laws permitting voters to register by mail. In four states—Maine, Minnesota, Oregon, and Wisconsin—voters can register and vote on the same day, all at once.

What is left? Several small things. First, the greater youthfulness of the population, together with the presence of growing numbers of African Americans and other minorities, has pushed down the percentage of voters who are registered and vote.

Second, political parties today are no longer as effective as they once were in mobilizing voters, ensuring that they are registered, and getting them to the polls. As we shall see in Chapter 9, the parties once were grassroots organizations with which many people strongly identified. Today the parties are somewhat distant, national bureaucracies with which most of us do not identify very strongly.

Third, the remaining impediments to registration exert some influence. One study estimated that if every state had registration requirements as easy as the most permissive states, turnout in a presidential election would be about 9 percent higher.[35] The experience of the four states where you can register and vote on the same day is consistent with this: in 1976, when same-day registration first went into effect, three of the four states that had it saw their turnout go up by 3 or 4 percent, while those states that did not have it saw their turnout go down.[36] If an even bolder plan were adopted, such as the Canadian system of universal enrollment, whereby the government automatically puts on the voter list every eligible citizen, there would probably be some additional gain in turnout.[37]

Fourth, if *not* voting is costless, then there will be more nonvoting. Several nations with higher turnouts than ours make voting compulsory. For example, in Italy a person who does not vote has his or her government identification papers stamped "*DID NOT VOTE.*"[38] In Australia and other countries fines can be levied on nonvoters. As a practical matter such fines are rarely imposed, but just the threat of them probably induces more people to register and vote.

Finally, voting (and before that, registering) will go down if people do not feel that elections matter much. There has been a decline in the proportion of people who feel that elections matter a lot, corresponding to the decrease in those who do participate in elections.

In short, there are a number of reasons why we register and vote less frequently in the United States than do citizens of other countries. Two careful studies of all these factors found that almost all of the differences in turnout among twenty-four democratic nations, including the United States, could be explained by party strength, automatic registration, and compulsory voting laws.[39]

The presence of these reasons does not necessarily mean that somebody ought to do something about

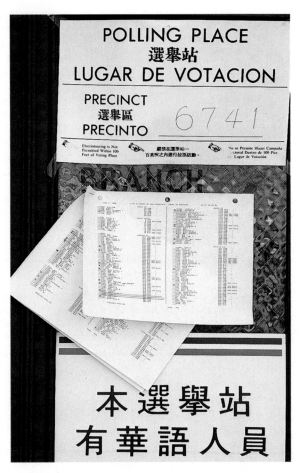

In San Francisco, voting instructions are printed in English, Spanish, and Chinese.

them. We could make registration automatic—but that might open the way to voter fraud, since people move around and change names often enough to enable some of them, if they wanted to, to vote more than once. We could make voting compulsory, but Americans have an aversion to government compulsion in any form and probably would object strenuously to any plan for making citizens carry identification papers that the government would stamp.

Democrats and Republicans fight over various measures designed to increase registration and voting because one party (usually the Democrats) thinks that higher turnout will help them and the other (usually the Republicans) fears that higher turnout will hurt them. In fact no one really knows

Demonstrations are almost as important as elections in shaping public policy.

Table 8.5	How Citizens Participate		
Specific Activity	Percentage Engaging in Fourteen Acts of Participation, 1967 and 1987		
	1967	**1987**	**Absolute Change**
Voting			
Regularly vote in presidential elections	66%	58%	−8%
Always vote in local elections	47	35	−12
Campaigning			
Persuade others how to vote	28	32	+4
Actively work for party or candidate	26	27	+1
Attend political meetings or rallies	19	19	0
Contribute money to a party or candidate	13	23	+10
Participate in a political club	8	4	−4
Contacting Government			
Contact local officials: issue-based	14	24	+10
Contact state or national officials: issue-based	11	22	+11
Contact local officials: particularized	7	10	+3
Contact state or national officials: particularized	6	7	+1
Taking Action in the Community			
Work with others on a local problem	30	34	+4
Actively participate in community problem-solving organization	31	34	+3
Form group to help solve local problem	14	17	+3

Source: Reprinted by permission of the publisher from *Voice and Equality: Civic Voluntarism in American Politics* by Sidney Verba, Kay Lehman Schlozman, and Henry A. Brady, Cambridge, Mass.: Harvard University Press, Copyright © 1995 by the Presidents and Fellows of Harvard College. Data from p. 72.

whether either party would be helped or hurt by higher voter turnout.

Nonvoters are more likely than voters to be poor, black or Hispanic, or uneducated. However, the proportion of nonvoters with some college education rose from 7 percent in 1960 to 39 percent in 1996. In addition the percentage of nonvoters who held white-collar jobs rose from 33 percent to 50 percent in the same period. Many of these better-off nonvoters might well have voted Republican had they gone to the polls. And even if the turnout rates only of blacks and Hispanics had increased, there would not have been enough votes added to the Democratic column to affect the outcome of the 1984 or 1988 presidential elections.[40]

Both political parties try to get a larger turnout among voters likely to be sympathetic to them, but it is hard to be sure that these efforts will produce real gains. If one party works hard to get its nonvoters to the polls, the other party will work just as hard to get its people there. For example, when Jesse Jackson ran for the presidency in 1984, registration of southern blacks increased, but registration of southern whites increased even more.

The Meaning of Participation Rates

Americans may be voting less, but there is evidence that they are participating more. As Table 8.5 shows, between 1967 and 1987 the percentage of Americans who voted regularly in presidential and local elections dropped, but the percentage who participated in ten out of twelve other political activities increased, steeply in some cases. Thus, although Americans are going to the polls less, they are campaigning, contacting government officials, and working on community issues more. And while the proportion of the population that votes is lower in the United States than in

Table 8.6 Participation Beyond Voting in Fourteen Democracies

Percentage of adult population who engaged in some form of political participation beyond voting in 1990.

Britain	77%	Italy	56%
Sweden	74	Iceland	55
Norway	68	Netherlands	54
UNITED STATES	66	Belgium	51
Denmark	59	Ireland	46
France	57	Finland	38
West Germany	57	Spain	32

Sources: U.S. percentage calculated from Sidney Verba et al., *Voice and Equality: Civic Voluntarism in American Politics* (Cambridge: Harvard University Press, 1995), 83; other percentages calculated from Max Kaase and Kenneth Newton, *Beliefs in Government*, vol. 5 (New York: Oxford University Press, 1995), 51.

many other democracies, the percentage of Americans who engage in one or more political activities beyond voting is higher (see Table 8.6).

Public demonstrations such as sit-ins and protest marches have become much more common in recent decades than they once were. By one count there were only 6 demonstrations per year between 1950 and 1959, but over 140 per year between 1960 and 1967. Though the demonstrations of the 1960s began with civil rights and antiwar activists, public protests were later employed by farmers demanding government aid, truckers denouncing the national speed limit, people with disabilities seeking to dramatize their needs, parents objecting to busing to achieve racial balance in the schools, conservationists hoping to block nuclear power plants, and construction workers urging that nuclear power *not* be blocked.[41]

Although we vote at lower rates here than people do abroad, the meaning of our voting is different. For one thing we elect far more public officials than do the citizens of any other nation. One scholar has estimated that there are over a half million elective offices in the United States and that almost every week of the year there is an election going on somewhere in this country.[42]

A citizen of Massachusetts, for example, votes not only for the U.S. president but also for two senators, the state governor, the member of the House of Representatives for his or her district, a state representa-

tive, a state senator, the state attorney general, the state auditor, the state treasurer, the secretary of state, a county commissioner, a sheriff, and clerks of various courts, as well as (in the cities) for the mayor, the city councillor, and school committee members and (in towns) for selectmen, town-meeting members, a town moderator, library trustees, health board members, assessors, water commissioners, the town clerk, housing authority members, the tree warden, and the commissioner of the public burial ground. (There are probably others that we have forgotten.)

In many European nations, by contrast, the voters get to make just one choice once every four or five years: they can vote for or against a member of parliament. When there is only one election for one office every several years, that election is bound to assume more importance to voters than many elections for scores of offices. But one election for one office probably has less effect on how the nation is governed than many elections for thousands of offices. Americans may not vote at high rates, but voting affects a far greater part of the political system here than abroad.

The kinds of people who vote here are also different from those who vote abroad. Since almost everybody votes in many other democracies, the votes cast there mirror almost exactly the social composition of those nations. Since only slightly over half of the voting-age population turns out even for presidential elections here, the votes cast in the United States may not truly reflect the country.

That is in fact the case. The proportion of each major occupational group—or if you prefer, social class—votes at about the same rate in Japan and Sweden. But in the United States the turnout is heavily skewed toward higher-status persons: those in professional, managerial, and other white-collar occupations are overrepresented among the voters.[43]

Although nonwhites and Latinos are the fastest-growing segment of the U.S. population, they tend to be the most underrepresented groups among American voters. Little is known about the relationship between political participation and variables such as command of the language and involvement in nonpolitical institutions that provide information or impart skills relevant to politics (such as workplaces and voluntary associations). However, such factors could be quite important in explaining differences in

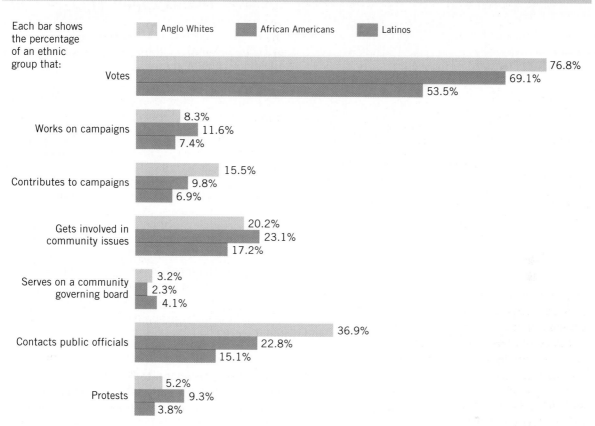

Figure 8.5   Electoral and Nonelectoral Political Participation Among Anglo Whites, African Americans, and Latinos

Each bar shows the percentage of an ethnic group that:

Anglo Whites   African Americans   Latinos

Votes
76.8%
69.1%
53.5%

Works on campaigns
8.3%
11.6%
7.4%

Contributes to campaigns
15.5%
9.8%
6.9%

Gets involved in community issues
20.2%
23.1%
17.2%

Serves on a community governing board
3.2%
2.3%
4.1%

Contacts public officials
36.9%
22.8%
15.1%

Protests
5.2%
9.3%
3.8%

Source: Adapted from Sidney Verba, Kay Lehman Schlozman, Henry Brady, and Norman H. Nie, *Voice and Equality: Civic Voluntarism in American Politics,* (Cambridge: Harvard University Press, 1995).

political participation rates among poor and minority citizens. As we can see in Figure 8.5, blacks, though less involved than whites, participate in voting and political activities at higher rates than do Latinos. One excellent study suggests that these differences are due in part to the fact that blacks are more likely than Latinos to be members of churches that stimulate political interest, activity, and mobilization.[44] Language barriers also make it harder for many Latinos to get in touch with a public official, serve on local governing boards, and engage in other forms of political participation in which command of

English is an asset. The lower participation rates of minority citizens are likely compounded by their being disproportionately of low socioeconomic status compared to white Americans.

Exactly what these differences in participation mean in terms of how the government is run is not entirely clear. But since we know from evidence presented in the last chapter that upper-status persons are more likely to have an ideological view of politics, it may suggest that governance here is a bit more sensitive not only to the interests of upper-status white people but also to their (conflicting) ideologies.

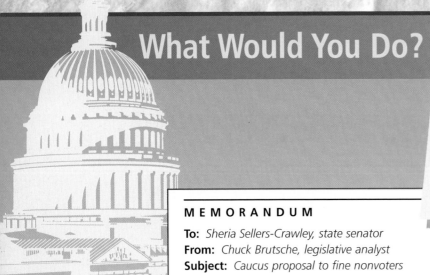

What Would You Do?

Caucus Declares "Saving Democracy" Means Fining Nonvoters

May 30
SACRAMENTO, CA

Voting has never been America's favorite pastime, but a report issued by the state senate's Democracy Caucus declares that "nonvoting is now a civic epidemic" that "can best be cured by fining nonvoters as they do in some other democracies"...

MEMORANDUM

To: *Sheria Sellers-Crawley, state senator*
From: *Chuck Brutsche, legislative analyst*
Subject: *Caucus proposal to fine nonvoters*

In the 1990s barely half of the electorate voted for president, and only a third or so cast ballots for the U.S. House of Representatives. In a few recent presidential primaries and statewide special elections, turnout has run 10 percent or below. In the mid-1960s, 47 percent of people who did not finish high school and one-third of people in their early twenties voted in the most recent election, but by the mid-1990s only one-quarter of the former group and one-fifth of the latter group did so. Does fining nonvoters make good sense, and would it work?

Arguments for:

1. Australia instituted compulsory voting after its turnout rate fell below 60 percent in 1922. Italy did the same after World War II. Since the early 1920s Australia's turnout has never fallen below 90 percent, and since the early 1950s Italy's has averaged between 85 and 90 percent.
2. The usual fine for nonvoting in these countries is under fifty dollars. Judges or other officials excuse people who are too sick to vote or have other valid excuses.
3. The law sends a moral message that voting is a civic duty in a democracy. More citizens will feel morally obliged to vote if all citizens are legally obliged to vote.

Arguments against:

1. Americans vote in more elections and participate in more political activities beyond voting than other democratic peoples do. Other reforms—streamlining voter registration requirements, holding elections on weekends, making election day a national holiday, increasing get-out-the-vote public service ads—are worth trying instead.
2. Most Americans would probably assert that they have a right not to vote, and many would simply refuse to pay even a small fine for not voting. What then, jail them?
3. Compelling people with limited or no political knowledge to vote leads to what Australians aptly call the "donkey vote." It is both unwise and undemocratic to legally oblige people to vote.

Your decision:

Favor proposal _____
Oppose proposal _____

☆ SUMMARY

*T*he popular view that Americans don't vote as a result of apathy is not quite right. It is nearer to the truth to say that we don't all register to vote and don't always vote even when registered. There are many factors having nothing to do with apathy that shape our participation rates—age, race, party organization, the barriers to registration, and popular views about the significance of elections.

Compared to other nations, Americans vote at lower rates but more frequently and for many more offices, so elections make a bigger difference in the conduct of public affairs here than abroad. We also engage somewhat more frequently than do people abroad in various nonelectoral forms of participation.

RECONSIDERING WHO GOVERNS?

1. Who votes, who doesn't?

The most powerful determinants of voting are age (older people vote more than younger people) and education (college graduates vote more than high school graduates). Race makes a difference, but black participation rates approximate white rates once you control for socioeconomic status.

2. Why do some people participate in politics at higher rates than others?

Older people and college graduates have learned to have a greater interest in politics, in part because they see ways in which government policies will affect them, in part because they may have acquired a political ideology that makes politics intrinsically interesting. As we have seen, Americans vote less than people in most other democratic nations. That gap is in part the result of the failure of many Americans to register to vote; efforts to increase registration, such as the motor-voter law, have got more names onto the voting rolls, but these new additions often do not vote as often as do other registered voters.

RECONSIDERING TO WHAT ENDS?

1. How did the Framers of the Constitution think average citizens should participate in America's representative democracy?

The Framers believed that citizens should play an important but not the decisive role in the American Republic. They elect the House, but until the Constitution was amended in 1913, they did not elect the Senate; the president and senators, not ordinary people, select federal judges; and the president is chosen by electors. Over time the system has become much more responsive to public opinion. Voters now help pick party candidates through party primaries, and their views are regularly solicited by opinion polls.

2. Should today's college-age citizens participate more in politics?

We would say yes, but the fact is that many young adults seem less disposed to traditional forms of political activity, including voting, than they are toward other types of civic engagement, such as community service or volunteer work. One forecast to ponder: unless youth voting rates increase relative to those of senior citizens, then, on Election Day 2020, persons age sixty-five and older (about 22 percent of the general population) will cast a quarter of all ballots, while persons ages eighteen to twenty-nine (about 21 percent of the general population) will account for less than an eighth of the voting electorate.

WORLD WIDE WEB RESOURCES

Information for voters

DemocracyNet:
http://www.congress.org/congressorg/e4/
League of Women Voters: **http://www.lwv.org/**
Voter Information Services: **http://www.vis.org/**
Women's Voting Guide:
http://www.womenvote.org/resources

National Mail Voter Registration Form:
http://www.fec.gov/votregis/vr.shtml
The Vanishing Voter:
http://www.vanishingvoter.org/
Voter turnout statistics:
http://www.fec.gov/pages/electpg.htm

SUGGESTED READINGS

Burnham, Walter Dean. *Critical Elections and the Mainsprings of American Politics*. New York: Norton, 1970. An argument about the decline of voter participation, linking it to changes in the economic system.

Conway, M. Margaret. *Political Participation in the United States*. 2d ed. Washington, D.C.: Congressional Quarterly Press, 1991. Good brief summary of what we need to know about who participates in politics and why.

Green, Donald P., and Alan S. Gerbec. *Get Out the Vote!: How to Increase Voter Turnout*. Washington, D.C.: Brookings Institution Press, 2004. Excellent review of the evidence on what works—and what doesn't—to get more people to the polls.

Eisner, Jane. *Taking Back the Vote: Getting American Youth Involved in Our Democracy*. Boston: Beacon Press, 2004. Highly readable account of why today's college-age Americans volunteer lots but vote little, with recommendations for getting young people more interested in politics.

Verba, Sidney, et al. *Voice and Equality: Civic Voluntarism in American Politics*. Cambridge: Harvard University Press, 1995.

Verba, Sidney, Norman H. Nie, and Jae-on Kim. *Participation and Political Equality*. Cambridge: Cambridge University Press, 1978. Comparative study of political participation in seven nations.

Wolfinger, Raymond E., and Steven R. Rosenstone. *Who Votes?* New Haven, Conn.: Yale University Press, 1980. Excellent analysis of what factors determine turnout.

CHAPTER 9

Political Parties

Parties—Here and Abroad
  Political Culture

The Rise and Decline of the Political Party
  The Founding ● The Jacksonians ● The Civil War and Sectionalism ● The Era of Reform ● Party Realignments ● Party Decline

The National Party Structure Today
  National Conventions

State and Local Parties
  The Machine ● Ideological Parties ● Solidary Groups ● Sponsored Parties ● Personal Following

The Two-Party System

Minor Parties

Nominating a President
  Are the Delegates Representative of the Voters? ● Who Votes in Primaries? ● Who Are the New Delegates?

Parties Versus Voters

WHO GOVERNS?

1. How has America's two-party system changed, and how does it differ from the party systems of other representative democracies?
2. How much do parties affect how Americans vote?

TO WHAT ENDS?

1. Did the Founding Fathers think that political parties were a good idea?
2. How, if at all, should America's two-party system be reformed?

*O*ne of the reasons why voter turnout is higher abroad than in this country is that political parties in other democratic nations are more effective at mobilizing voters than are those here. The sense of being a party member and the inclination to vote the party ticket are greater in France, Italy, and Sweden than in the United States. From this fact you might suppose that political parties here are recent inventions with little experience at organizing and no history of attracting voter identification.

Quite the contrary. American political parties are the oldest in the world, and at one time being a Democrat or a Republican was a serious commitment that people did not make lightly or abandon easily. In those days it would have been hard to find anything in Europe that could match the vote-getting power of such party organizations as those in Chicago, New York, and Philadelphia.

Parties in the United States are relatively weak today, not because they are old but because the laws and rules under which they operate have taken away much of their power at the same time that many voters have lost their sense of commitment to party identification. This weakening has proceeded unevenly, however, because our constitutional system has produced a decentralized party system just as it has produced a decentralized governmental system, with the result that parties in some places are strong and in other places almost nonexistent.

☆ Parties—Here and Abroad

A **political party** is a group that seeks to elect candidates to public office by supplying them with a label—a "party identification"—by which they are known to the electorate.[1] This definition is purposefully broad so that it will include both familiar parties (Democratic, Republican) and unfamiliar ones (Whig, Libertarian, Socialist Workers) and will cover periods in which a party is very strong (having an elaborate and well-disciplined organization that provides money and workers to its candidates) as well as periods in which it is quite weak (supplying nothing but the label to candidates). The label by which a candidate is known may or may not actually be printed on the ballot opposite the candidate's name: in the United States it does appear on the ballot in all national elections but in only a minority of municipal ones; in Australia and Israel (and in Great Britain before 1969) it never appears on the ballot at all.

Figure 9.1   Decline in Party Identification, 1952–2002

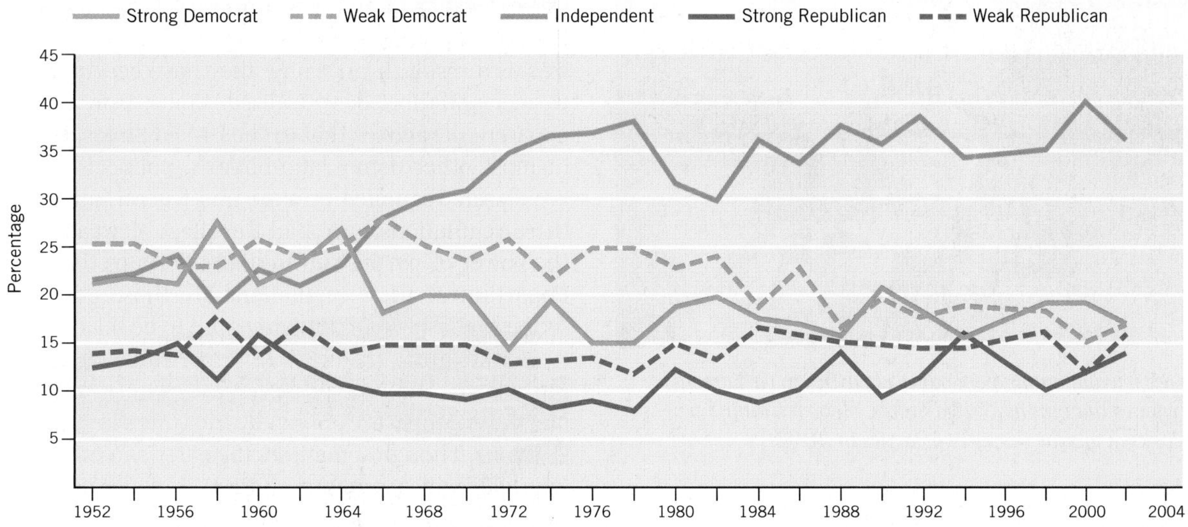

—— Strong Democrat   - - - Weak Democrat   —— Independent   —— Strong Republican   ▪▪▪ Weak Republican

Source: National Election Studies, *The NES Guide to Public Opinion and Electoral Behavior, 1952–2000*, table 20.1, and data for 2002 updated by Marc Siegal.

This definition suggests the three political arenas within which parties may be found. A party exists as a *label* in the minds of the voters, as an *organization* that recruits and campaigns for candidates, and as a *set of leaders* who try to organize and control the legislative and executive branches of government. A powerful party is one whose label has a strong appeal for the voters, whose organization can decide who will be candidates and how their campaigns will be managed, and whose leaders can dominate one or all branches of government.

American parties have become weaker in all three arenas. As a *label* with which voters identify, the parties are probably much weaker than they were in the nineteenth century but only somewhat weaker than they were forty years ago (see Figure 9.1). In 1952, a total of 36 percent of the electorate identified strongly as Democrats (22 percent) or Republicans (14 percent), while a total of 23 percent of the electorate identified as independents. By 2002, total strong party identifiers had dropped to 33 percent of the electorate, while all independents had risen to 36 percent of the electorate. But the best evidence of weakening party identification is what voters *do*. As we shall see in the next chapter, in some elections many people vote split tickets—that is, supporting a

president from one party and members of Congress from the other.

As a *set of leaders* who organize government, especially Congress, political parties remain somewhat strong in ways that will be described in Chapter 13. As *organizations* that nominate and elect candidates, parties have become dramatically weaker since the 1960s. In most states parties have very little control over who gets nominated to office. The causes and consequences of that change are the subject of this chapter.

In Europe things are very different. Almost the only way a person can become a candidate for elective office is to be nominated by party leaders. Campaigns are run by the party, using party funds and workers, not by the candidate. Once in office the elected officials are expected to vote and act together with other members of their party. The principal criterion by which voters choose among candidates is their party identification or label. This has been changing somewhat of late: European parties, like

political party   A group that seeks to elect candidates to public office.

There are usually many more political parties in parliamentary regimes than in the United States. Here, a Ukrainian voter looks at ads for thirty-two parties in 2002.

American ones, have not been able to count as heavily as in the past on party loyalty among the voters.

Several factors explain the striking differences between American and European political parties. First, the federal system of government in the United States decentralizes political authority and thus decentralizes political party organizations. For nearly two centuries most of the important governmental decisions were made at the state and local levels—decisions regarding education, land use, business regulation, and public welfare—and thus it was at the state and local levels that the important struggles over power and policy occurred. Moreover, most people with political jobs—either elective or appointive—worked for state and local government, and thus a party's interest in obtaining these jobs for its followers meant that it had to focus attention on who controlled city hall, the county courthouse, and the state capitol. Federalism, in short, meant that political parties would acquire jobs and money from local sources and fight local contests. This, in turn, meant that the national political parties would be coalitions of local parties, and though these coalitions would have a keen interest in capturing the presidency (with it, after all, went control of large numbers of federal jobs), the national party leaders rarely had as much power as the local ones. The Republican leader of Cuyahoga County, Ohio, for example, could often ignore the decisions of the Republican national chairman and even of the Ohio state chairman.

Political authority in the United States has of late come to be far more centralized: the federal government now makes decisions affecting almost all aspects of our lives, including those—such as schooling and welfare—once left entirely in local hands. Yet the political parties have not become more centralized as a result. If anything, they have become even weaker and more decentralized. One reason for this apparent paradox is that in the United States, unlike in most other democratic nations, political parties are closely regulated by state and federal laws, and these regulations have had the effect of weakening the power of parties substantially. Perhaps the most important of these regulations are those that prescribe how a party's candidates are to be selected.

In the great majority of American states, the party leaders do not select people to run for office; by law those people are chosen by the voters in primary elections. Though sometimes the party can influence who will win a primary contest, in general people running for state or national office in this country owe little to party leaders. In Europe, by contrast, there is no such thing as a primary election—the only way to become a candidate for office is to persuade party leaders to put your name on the ballot. In a later section of this chapter, the impact of the direct primary will be discussed in more detail; for now, it is enough to note that its use removes from the hands of the party leadership its most important source of power over officeholders.

Furthermore, if an American political party wins control of Congress, it does not—as in most European nations with a parliamentary system of government—also win the right to select the chief executive of the government. The American president, as we have seen, is independently elected, and this means that he will choose his principal subordinates not from among members of Congress but from among persons out of Congress. Should he pick a representative or senator for his cabinet, the Constitution requires that person to resign from Congress in order to accept the job. Thus an opportunity to be a cabinet secretary is not an important reward for members of Congress, and so the president cannot use the prospect of that reward as a way of controlling congressional action. All this weakens the significance and power of parties in terms of organizing the government and conducting its business.

Political Culture

The attitudes and traditions of American voters reinforce the institutional and legal factors that make

American parties relatively weak. Political parties in this country have rarely played an important part in the life of the average citizen; indeed, one does not usually "join" a party here except by voting for its candidates. In many European nations, on the other hand, large numbers of citizens will join a party, pay dues, and attend regular meetings. Furthermore, in countries such as France, Austria, and Italy, the political parties sponsor a wide range of activities and dominate a variety of associations to which a person may belong—labor unions, youth groups, educational programs, even chess clubs.

In the United States we tend to keep parties separate from other aspects of our lives. As Democrats or Republicans, we may become excited by a presidential campaign, and a few of us may even participate in helping elect a member of Congress or state senator. Our social, business, working, and cultural lives, however, are almost entirely nonpartisan. Indeed, most Americans, unlike many Europeans, would resent partisanship's becoming a conspicuous feature of other organizations to which they belong. All this is a way of saying that American parties play a segmental, rather than a comprehensive, role in our lives and that even this role is diminishing as more and more of us proclaim ourselves to be "independents."

☆ The Rise and Decline of the Political Party

Our nation began without parties, and today's parties, though far from extinct, are about as weak as at any time in our history. In between the Founding and the present, however, parties arose and became powerful. We can see this process in four broad periods of party history: when political parties were created (roughly from the Founding to the 1820s); when the more or less stable two-party system emerged (roughly from the time of President Jackson to the Civil War); when parties developed a comprehensive organizational form and appeal (roughly from the Civil War to the 1930s); and finally when party "reform" began to alter the party system (beginning in the early 1900s but taking effect chiefly since the New Deal).

The Founding

The Founders disliked parties, thinking of them as "factions" motivated by ambition and self-interest.

George Washington, dismayed by the quarreling between Hamilton and Jefferson in his cabinet, devoted much of his Farewell Address to condemning parties. This hostility toward parties was understandable: the legitimacy and success of the newly created federal government were still very much in doubt. When Jefferson organized his followers to oppose Hamilton's policies, it seemed to Hamilton and *his* followers that Jefferson was opposing not just a policy or a leader but also the very concept of a national government. Jefferson, for his part, thought that Hamilton was not simply pursuing bad policies but was subverting the Constitution itself. Before political parties could become legitimate, it was necessary for people to be able to separate in their minds quarrels over policies and elections from disputes over the legitimacy of the new government itself. The ability to make that distinction was slow in coming, and thus parties were objects of profound suspicion, defended, at first, only as temporary expedients.

The first organized political party in American history was made up of the followers of Jefferson, who, beginning in the 1790s, called themselves *Republicans* (hoping to suggest thereby that their opponents were secret monarchists).* The followers of Hamilton kept the label *Federalist,* which once had been used to refer to all supporters of the new Constitution (hoping to imply that their opponents were "Antifederalists," or enemies of the Constitution).

These parties were loose caucuses of political notables in various localities, with New England being strongly Federalist and much of the South passionately Republican. Jefferson and his ally James Madison thought that their Republican party was a temporary arrangement designed to defeat John Adams, a Federalist, in his bid to succeed Washington in 1796. (Adams narrowly defeated Jefferson, who, under the system then in effect, became vice president because he had the second most electoral votes.) In 1800 Adams's bid to succeed himself intensified party activity even more, but this time Jefferson won and the Republicans assumed office. The Federalists feared that Jefferson would dismantle the Constitution, but Jefferson adopted a conciliatory posture, saying in his inaugural address that "we are

---

*The Jeffersonian Republicans were not the party that today we call Republican. In fact, present-day Democrats consider Jefferson to be the founder of their party.

When Andrew Jackson ran for president in 1828, over a million votes were cast for the first time in American history. This poster, from the 1832 election, was part of the emergence of truly mass political participation.

all Republicans, we are all Federalists."[2] It was not true, of course: the Federalists detested Jefferson, and some were planning to have New England secede from the Union. But it was good politics, expressive of the need that every president has to persuade the public that, despite partisan politics, the presidency exists to serve all the people.

So successful were the Republicans that the Federalists virtually ceased to exist as a party. Jefferson was reelected in 1804 with almost no opposition; Madison easily won two terms; James Monroe carried sixteen out of nineteen states in 1816 and was reelected without opposition in 1820. Political parties had seemingly disappeared, just as Jefferson had hoped. The weakness of this so-called first party system can be explained by the fact that it was the first: nobody had been born a Federalist or a Republican; there was no ancestral party loyalty to defend; the earliest political leaders did not think of themselves as professional politicians; and the Federalist party had such a limited sectional and class base that it could not compete effectively in national elections.

The parties that existed in these early years were essentially small groups of local notables. Political participation was limited, and nominations for most local offices were arranged rather casually.

Even in this early period, the parties, though they had very different views on economic policy and somewhat different class bases, did not represent clear, homogeneous economic interests. Farmers in Virginia were Republicans, but farmers in Delaware were Federalists; the commercial interests of Boston were firmly Federalist, but commercial leaders in urban Connecticut were most likely to be Republican.

From the beginning to the present elections have created heterogeneous coalitions, as Madison anticipated.

The Jacksonians

What is often called the second party system emerged around 1824 with Andrew Jackson's first run for the presidency and lasted until the Civil War became inevitable. Its distinctive feature was that political participation became a mass phenomenon. For one thing, the number of voters to be reached had become quite large. Only about 365,000 popular votes were cast in 1824. But as a result of laws that enlarged the number of people eligible to vote and of an increase in the population, by 1828 well over a million votes were tallied. By 1840 the figure was well over 2 million. (In England at this time there were only 650,000 eligible voters.) In addition, by 1832 presidential electors were selected by popular vote in virtually every state. (As late as 1816 electors were chosen by the state legislatures, rather than by the people, in about half the states.) Presidential politics had become a truly national, genuinely popular activity; indeed, in many communities election campaigns had become the principal public spectacle.

The party system of the Jacksonian era was built from the bottom up rather than—as during the period of the Founding—from the top down. No change better illustrates this transformation than the abandonment of the system of having caucuses composed of members of Congress nominate presidential candidates. The caucus system was an effort to unite the legislative and executive branches by giving the former some degree of control over who would have a chance to capture the latter. The caucus system became unpopular when the caucus candidate for president in 1824 ran third in a field of four in the general election, and it was completely discredited that same year when Congress denied the presidency to Jackson, the candidate with the greatest share of the popular vote.

To replace the caucus, the party convention was invented. The first convention in American history was that of the Anti-Masonic party in 1831; the first convention of a major political party was that of the anti-Jackson Republicans later that year (it nominated Henry Clay for president). The Democrats held a convention in 1832 that ratified Jackson's nomination for reelection and picked Martin Van Buren as his running mate. The first convention to select a man who would be elected president and who was not already the incumbent president was held by the Democrats in 1836; it chose Van Buren.

Considering the many efforts made in recent years to curtail or even abolish the national nominating convention, it is worth remembering that the convention system was first developed in part as a reform—a way of allowing for some measure of local control over the nominating process. Virtually no other nation adopted this method, just as no other nation was later to adopt the direct primary after the convention system became the object of criticism. It is interesting, but perhaps futile, to speculate on how American government would have evolved if the legislative caucus had remained the method for nominating presidents.

The Civil War and Sectionalism

Though the party system created in the Jacksonian period was the first truly national system, with Democrats (followers of Jackson) and Whigs (opponents of Jackson) fairly evenly balanced in most regions, it could not withstand the deep split in opinion created by the agitation over slavery. Both parties tried, naturally, to straddle the issue, since neither wanted to divide its followers and thus lose the election to its rival. But slavery and sectionalism were issues that could not be straddled. The old parties divided and new ones emerged. The modern Republican party (not the old Democratic-Republican party of Thomas Jefferson) began as a third party. As a result of the Civil War it came to be a major party (the only third party ever to gain major-party status) and to dominate national politics, with only occasional interruptions, for three-quarters of a century.

Republican control of the White House, and to a lesser extent of Congress, was in large measure the result of two events that gave to Republicans a marked advantage in the competition for the loyalties of voters. The first of these was the Civil War. This bitter, searing crisis deeply polarized popular attitudes. Those who supported the Union side became, for generations, Republicans; those who supported the Confederacy, or who had opposed the war, became Democrats.

As it turned out, this partisan division was, for a while, nearly even: though the Republicans usually won the presidency and the Senate, they often lost control of the House. There were many northern Democrats. In 1896, however, another event—the presidential candidacy of William Jennings Bryan—further strengthened the Republican party. Bryan, a Democrat, alienated many voters in the populous northeastern states while attracting voters in the South and Midwest. The result was to confirm and deepen the split in the country, especially North versus South, begun by the Civil War. From 1896 to the 1930s, with rare exceptions northern states were solidly Republican, southern ones solidly Democratic.

This split had a profound effect on the organization of political parties, for it meant that most states were now one-party states. As a result, competition for office at the state level had to go on *within* a single dominant party (the Republican party in Massachusetts, New York, Pennsylvania, Wisconsin, and elsewhere; the Democratic party in Georgia, Mississippi, South Carolina, and elsewhere). Consequently there emerged two major factions within each party, but especially within the Republican party. One was composed of the party regulars—the professional politicians, the "stalwarts," the Old Guard. They were preoccupied with building up the party machinery, developing party loyalty, and acquiring and dispensing patronage—jobs and other favors—for themselves and their faithful followers. Their great skills were in organization, negotiation, bargaining, and compromise; their great interest was in winning.

The other faction, variously called **mugwumps** or **progressives** (or "reformers"), was opposed to the heavy emphasis on patronage; disliked the party machinery, because it permitted only bland candidates to rise to the top; was fearful of the heavy influx

---

mugwumps or **progressives**   Republican party faction of the 1890s to the 1910s, composed of reformers who opposed patronage.

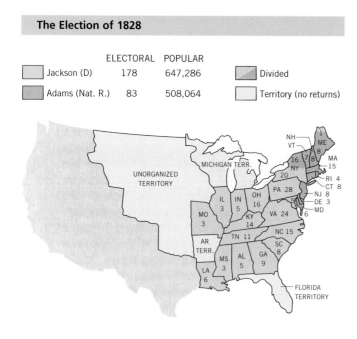

The Election of 1828

	ELECTORAL	POPULAR
Jackson (D)	178	647,286
Adams (Nat. R.)	83	508,064

Divided

Territory (no returns)

The Election of 1860

	ELECTORAL	POPULAR
Lincoln (R)	180	1,866,452
Douglas (No. D)	12	1,375,157
Breckenridge (So. D)	76	847,953
Bell (Const. Union)	39	590,631

Divided

Territory (no returns)

of immigrants into American cities and of the ability of the party regulars to organize them into "machines"; and wanted to see the party take unpopular positions on certain issues (such as free trade). Their great skills lay in the areas of advocacy and articulation; their great interest was in principle.

At first the mugwumps tried to play a balance-of-power role, sometimes siding with the Republican party of which they were members, at other times defecting to the Democrats (as when they bolted the Republican party to support Grover Cleveland, the Democratic nominee, in 1884). But later, as the Republican strength in the nation grew, progressives within that party became less and less able to play a balance-of-power role, especially at the state level. Wisconsin, Michigan, Ohio, and Iowa were solidly Republican; Georgia, the Carolinas, and the rest of the Old South had by 1880 become so heavily Democratic that the Republican party in many areas had virtually ceased to exist. If the progressives were to have any power, it would require, they came to believe, an attack on the very concept of partisanship itself.

The Era of Reform

Progressives began to espouse measures to curtail or even abolish political parties. They favored primary elections to replace nominating conventions, because the latter were viewed as being manipulated by party bosses; they favored nonpartisan elections at the city level and in some cases at the state level as well; they argued against corrupt alliances between parties and businesses. They wanted strict voter-registration requirements that would reduce voting fraud (but would also, as it turned out, keep ordinary citizens who found the requirements cumbersome from voting); they pressed for civil service reform to eliminate patronage; and they made heavy use of the mass media as a way of attacking the abuses of partisanship and of promoting their own ideas and candidacies.

The progressives were more successful in some places than in others. In California, for example, progressives led by Governor Hiram Johnson in 1910–1911 were able to institute the direct primary and to adopt procedures—called the *initiative* and the *referendum*—so that citizens could vote directly on proposed legislation, thereby bypassing the state legislature. Governor Robert La Follette brought about similar changes in Wisconsin.

The effect of these changes was to reduce substantially the worst forms of political corruption and ultimately to make boss rule in politics difficult if not impossible. But they also had the effect of making political parties, whether led by bosses or by statesmen, weaker, less able to hold officeholders accountable, and less able to assemble the power necessary for governing the fragmented political institutions created by the Constitution. In Congress party lines began to grow fainter, as did the power of congressional leadership. Above all, the progressives did not have an answer to the problem first faced by Jefferson: if there is not a strong political party, by what other means will candidates for office be found, recruited, and supported?

Party Realignments

There have clearly been important turning points in the strength of the major parties, especially in the twentieth century, when for long periods we have not so much had close competition between two parties as we have had an alternation of dominance by one party and then the other. To help explain these major shifts in the tides of politics, scholars have developed the theory of **critical** or **realigning periods.** During such periods a sharp, lasting shift occurs in the popular coalition supporting one or both parties. The issues that separate the two parties change, and so the kinds of voters supporting each party change. This shift may occur at the time of the election or just after, as the new administration draws in new supporters.[3] There seem to have been five realignments so far, during or just after these elections: 1800 (when the Jeffersonian Republicans defeated the Federalists), 1828 (when the Jacksonian Democrats came to power), 1860 (when the Whig party collapsed and the Republicans under Lincoln came to power), 1896 (when the Republicans defeated William Jennings Bryan), and 1932 (when the Democrats under Roosevelt came into office).

There are at least two kinds of realignments—one in which a major party is so badly defeated that it disappears and a new party emerges to take its place (this happened to the Federalists in 1800 and to the Whigs in 1856–1860), and another in which the two existing parties continue but voters shift their support from one to the other (this happened in 1896 and 1932).

The three clearest cases seem to be 1860, 1896, and 1932. By 1860 the existing parties could no longer straddle the fence on the slavery issue. The Republican party was formed in 1856 on the basis of clear-cut opposition to slavery; the Democratic party split in half in 1860, with one part (led by Stephen A. Douglas and based in the North) trying to waffle on the issue and the other (led by John C. Breckinridge and drawing its support from the South) categorically denying that any government had any right to

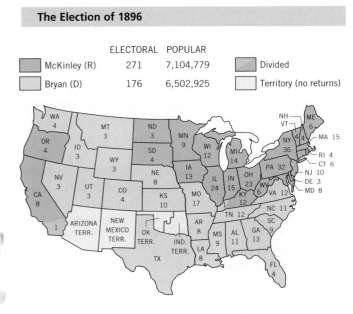

The Election of 1896

	ELECTORAL	POPULAR
McKinley (R)	271	7,104,779
Bryan (D)	176	6,502,925
Divided		
Territory (no returns)		

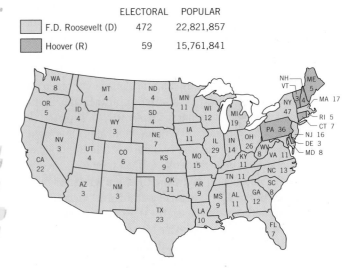

The Election of 1932

	ELECTORAL	POPULAR
F.D. Roosevelt (D)	472	22,821,857
Hoover (R)	59	15,761,841

outlaw slavery. The remnants of the Whig party, renamed the Constitutional Union party, tried to unite the nation by writing no platform at all, thus

---

critical or **realignment period**   Periods when a major, lasting shift occurs in the popular coalition supporting one or both parties.

remaining silent on slavery. Lincoln and the antislavery Republicans won in 1860; Breckinridge and the proslavery Southern Democrats came in second. From that moment on, the two major political parties acquired different sources of support and stood (at least for a decade) for different principles. The parties that had tried to straddle the fence were eliminated. The Civil War fixed these new party loyalties deep in the popular mind, and the structure of party competition was set for nearly forty years.

In 1896 a different kind of realignment occurred. Economics rather than slavery was at issue. A series of depressions during the 1880s and 1890s fell especially hard on farmers in the Midwest and parts of the South. The prices paid to farmers for their commodities had been falling more or less steadily since the Civil War, making it increasingly difficult for them to pay their bills. A bitter reaction against the two major parties, which were straddling this issue as they had straddled slavery, spread like a prairie fire, leading to the formation of parties of economic protest—the Greenbackers and the Populists. Reinforcing the economic cleavages were cultural ones: Populists tended to be fundamentalist Protestants; urban voters were increasingly Catholic. Matters came to a head in 1896 when William Jennings Bryan captured the Democratic nomination for president and saw to it that the party adopted a Populist platform. The existing Populist party endorsed the Bryan candidacy. In the election anti-Bryan Democrats deserted the party in droves to support the Republican candidate, William McKinley. Once again a real issue divided the two parties: the Republicans stood for industry, business, hard money, protective tariffs, and urban interests; the Democrats for farmers, small towns, low tariffs, and rural interests. The Republicans won, carrying the cities, workers and business people alike; the Democrats lost, carrying most of the southern and midwestern farm states. The old split between North and South that resulted from the Civil War was now replaced in part by an East versus West, city versus farm split.[4] It was not, however, only an economic cleavage—the Republicans had been able to appeal to Catholics and Lutherans, who disliked fundamentalism and its hostility toward liquor and immigrants.

This alignment persisted until 1932. Again change was triggered by an economic depression; again more than economic issues were involved. The

New Deal coalition that emerged was based on bringing together into the Democratic party urban workers, northern blacks, southern whites, and Jewish voters. Unlike in 1860 and 1896, it was not preceded by any third-party movement; it occurred suddenly (though some groups had begun to shift their allegiance in 1928) and gathered momentum throughout the 1930s. The Democrats, isolated since 1896 as a southern and midwestern sectional party, had now become the majority party by finding a candidate and a cause that could lure urban workers, blacks, and Jews away from the Republican party, where they had been for decades. It was obviously a delicate coalition—blacks and southern whites disagreed on practically everything except their liking for Roosevelt; Jews and the Irish bosses of the big-city machines also had little in common. But the federal government under Roosevelt was able to supply enough benefits to each of these disparate groups to keep them loyal members of the coalition and to provide a new basis for party identification.

These critical elections may have involved not converting existing voters to new party loyalties but recruiting into the dominant party new voters—young people just coming of voting age, immigrants just receiving their citizenship papers, and blacks just receiving, in some places, the right to vote. But there were also genuine conversions—northern blacks, for example, had been heavily Republican before Roosevelt but became heavily Democratic after his election.

In short, an electoral realignment occurs when a new issue of utmost importance to the voters (slavery, the economy) cuts across existing party divisions and replaces old issues that were formerly the basis of party identification.

Some people wondered whether the election of 1980, since it brought into power the most conservative administration in half a century, signaled a new realignment. Many of President Reagan's supporters began talking of their having a "mandate" to adopt major new policies in keeping with the views of the "new majority." But Reagan won in 1980 less because of what he stood for than because he was not Jimmy Carter, and he was reelected in 1984 primarily because people were satisfied with how the country was doing, especially economically.[5]

Just because we have had periods of one-party dominance in the past does not mean that we will have them in the future. Reagan's election could not have been a traditional realignment, because it left Congress in the hands of the Democratic party. Moreover, some scholars are beginning to question the theory of critical elections, or at least the theory that they occur with some regularity.

Nevertheless, one major change has occurred of late—the shift in the presidential voting patterns of the South. From 1972 through 2004 the South was more Republican than the nation as a whole. The proportion of white southerners describing themselves to pollsters as "strongly Democratic" fell from more than one-third in 1952 to about one-seventh in 1984. There has been a corresponding increase in "independents." As it turns out, southern white independents have voted overwhelmingly Republican in recent presidential elections.[6] If you lump independents together with the parties for which they actually vote, the party alignment among white southerners has gone from six-to-one Democratic in 1952 to about fifty-fifty Democrats and Republicans. If this continues, it will constitute a major realignment in a region of the country that is growing rapidly in population and political clout.

In general, however, the kind of dramatic realignment that occurred in the 1860s or after 1932 may not occur again, because party labels have lost their meaning for a growing number of voters. For these people politics may *de*align rather than *re*align.

Party Decline

The evidence that the parties are decaying, not realigning, is of several sorts. We have already noted that the proportion of people identifying with one or the other party declined between 1960 and 1980. Simultaneously, the proportion of those voting a **split ticket** (as opposed to a **straight ticket**) increased. Figure 9.2, for example, shows the steep increase in the percentage of congressional districts carried by one party for the presidency and by the other for Congress. Whereas in the 1940s one party would carry a given district for both its presidential and congressional candidates, today about a fifth of the districts split their votes between one party's presidential candidate and the other's congressional candidate.

In 1988 more than *half* of all House Democrats were elected in districts that voted for Republican George Bush as president. This ticket splitting was greatest in the South, but it was common everywhere. If every district that voted for Bush had also

elected a Republican to Congress, the Republican party would have held a two-to-one majority in the House of Representatives. Ticket splitting creates divided government—the White House and Congress are controlled by different parties (see Chapter 14). Ticket splitting helped the Democrats keep control of the House of Representatives from 1954 to 1994.

Ticket splitting was almost unheard-of in the nineteenth century, and for a very good reason. In those days the voter was either given a ballot by the party of his choice and he dropped it, intact, into the ballot box (thereby voting for everybody listed on the ballot), or he was given a government-printed ballot that listed in columns all the candidates of each party. All the voter had to do was mark the top of one column in order to vote for every candidate in that column. (When voting machines came along, they provided a single lever that, when pulled, cast votes for all the candidates of a particular party.) Progressives around the turn of the century began to persuade states to adopt the **office-bloc** (or "Massachusetts") **ballot** in place of the **party-column** (or "Indiana") **ballot.** The office-bloc ballot lists all candidates by office; there is no way to vote a straight party ticket by making one mark. Not surprisingly, states using the office-bloc ballot show much more ticket splitting than those without it.[7]

☆ The National Party Structure Today

It would be a mistake, however, to conclude that parties have declined simply because many voters now split tickets in national elections. Despite many changes and challenges (see Figure 9.3), America's

---

split ticket Voting for candidates of different parties for various offices in the same election.

straight ticket Voting for candidates who are all of the same party.

office-bloc ballot A ballot listing all candidates of a given office under the name of that office; also called a "Massachusetts" ballot.

party-column ballot A ballot listing all candidates of a given party together under the name of that party; also called an "Indiana" ballot.

Figure 9.2   **Trends in Split-Ticket Voting for President and Congress, 1920–2000**

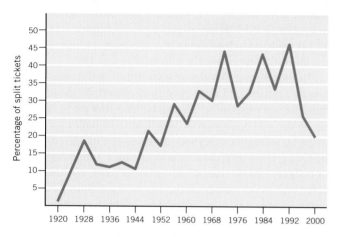

Note: The figure is the percentage of congressional districts carried by presidential and congressional candidates of different parties in each election year.

two-party system remains strong. In most elections—national, state, and local—voters registered as Democrats still vote for Democratic candidates, and voters registered as Republicans still vote for Republican candidates. In Congress, state legislatures, and city councils, members still normally vote along party lines. Local political machines have died, but, as we shall now explain, national party structures remain alive and well.

Since political parties exist at the national, state, and local levels, you might suppose that they are arranged like a big corporation, with a national board of directors giving orders to state managers, who in turn direct the activities of rank-and-file workers at the county and city level.

> **national convention**   A meeting of party delegates held every four years.
>
> **national committee**   Delegates who run party affairs between national conventions.
>
> **congressional campaign committee**   A party committee in Congress that provides funds to members and would-be members.
>
> **national chairman**   Day-to-day party manager elected by the national committee.

Nothing could be further from the truth. At each level a separate and almost entirely independent organization exists that does pretty much what it wants, and in many counties and cities there is virtually no organization at all.

On paper the national Democratic and Republican parties look quite similar. In both parties ultimate authority is in the hands of the **national convention** that meets every four years to nominate a presidential candidate. Between these conventions party affairs are managed by a **national committee**, made up of delegates from each state and territory. In Congress each party has a **congressional campaign committee** that helps members of Congress who are running for reelection or would-be members running for an open seat or challenging a candidate from the opposition party. The day-to-day work of the party is managed by a full-time, paid **national chairman,** who is elected by the committee.

For a long time the two national parties were alike in behavior as well as description. The national chairman, if his party held the White House, would help decide who among the party faithful would get federal jobs. Otherwise the parties did very little.

But beginning in the late 1960s and early 1970s, the Republicans began to convert their national party into a well-financed, highly staffed organization devoted to finding and electing Republican candidates, especially to Congress. At about the same time, the Democrats began changing the rules governing how presidential candidates are nominated in ways that profoundly altered the distribution of power within the party. As a consequence the Republicans became a bureaucratized party and the Democrats became a factionalized one. After the Republicans won four out of five presidential elections from 1968 to 1984 and briefly took control of the Senate, the Democrats began to suspect that maybe an efficient bureaucracy was better than a collection of warring factions, and so they made an effort to emulate the Republicans.

What the Republicans had done was to take advantage of a new bit of technology—computerized mailings. They built up a huge file of names of people who had given or might give money to the party, usually in small amounts, and used that list to raise a big budget for the national party. The RNC used this money to run, in effect, a national political consulting firm. Money went to recruit and train

Republican candidates, give them legal and financial advice, study issues and analyze voting trends, and conduct national advertising campaigns on behalf of the party as a whole.

When the Democratic National Committee (DNC) decided to play catch-up, it followed the RNC strategy. Using the same computerized direct-mail techniques, the Democratic party committees—the National Committee, Senatorial Committee, and Congressional Committee—raised more money than they had ever raised before, though not as much as the Republicans. In 2004 the Democrats and their allies outspent the Republicans. The Democrats, like the Republicans, ship a lot of their national party money to state organizations to finance television ads supporting their parties.

Despite the recent enactment of campaign finance laws intended to check the influence of money on national elections, in 2004 both Democrats and Republicans redoubled efforts to raise what is called *soft money*—that is, funds to aid parties (and their ads and polls). In the Democrat presidential primary, Howard Dean alone raised $30 million over the Internet with average contributions under $100.

National Conventions

The national committee selects the time and place of the next national convention and issues a "call" for the convention that sets forth the number of delegates each state and territory is to have and also the rules under which delegates must be chosen. The number of delegates and their manner of selection can significantly influence the chances of various presidential candidates, and considerable attention is thus devoted to these matters. In the Democratic party, for example, a long struggle took place between those who wished to see southern states receive a large share of delegates to the convention, in recognition of their firm support of Democratic candidates in presidential elections, and those who preferred to see a larger share of delegates allotted to northern and western states, which, though less solidly Democratic, were larger or more liberal. A similar conflict within the Republican party has pitted conservative Republican leaders in the Midwest against liberal ones in the East.

A compromise formula is usually chosen; nevertheless, over the years these formulas have gradually changed, shifting voting strength in the Democratic

Figure 9.3 Cleavages and Continuity in the Two-Party System

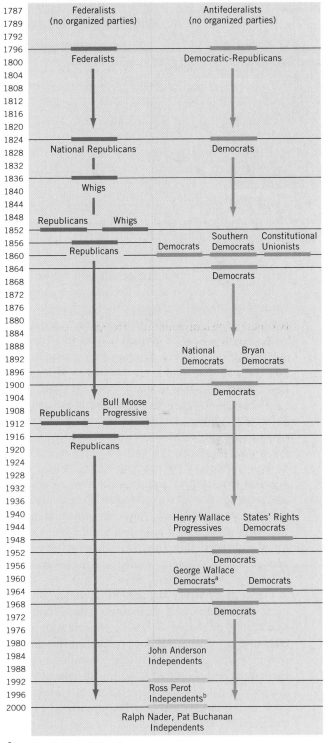

[a] American Independent party.
[b] United We Stand America or Reform Party.

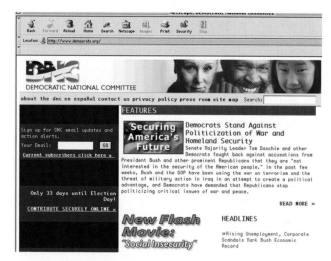

The Internet is the latest means through which people are becoming politically informed and active. It has also become an important way to raise money for candidates and parties.

convention away from the South and toward the North and West and in the Republican convention away from the East and toward the South and Southwest. These delegate allocation formulas are but one sign (others will be mentioned later in this chapter) of the tendency of the two parties' conventions to move in opposite ideological directions—Democrats more to the left, Republicans more to the right.

The exact formula for apportioning delegates is extremely complex. For the Democrats it takes into account the vote each state cast for Democratic candidates in past elections and the number of electoral votes of each state; for the Republicans it takes into account the number of representatives in Congress and whether the state in past elections cast its electoral votes for the Republican presidential candidate and elected Republicans to the Senate, the House, and the governorship. Thus the Democrats give extra delegates to large states, while the Republicans give extra ones to loyal states.

The way in which delegates are chosen can be even more important than their allocation. The Democrats, beginning in 1972, have developed an elaborate set of rules designed to weaken the control over delegates by local party leaders and to increase the proportion of women, young people, African Americans, and Native Americans attending the convention. These rules were first drafted by a party commission chaired by Senator George McGovern (who was later to make skillful use of these new pro-

cedures in his successful bid for the Democratic presidential nomination). They were revised in 1974 by another commission, chaired by Barbara Mikulski, whose decisions were ratified by the 1974 midterm convention. After the 1976 election yet a third commission, chaired by Morley Winograd, produced still another revision of the rules, which took effect in 1980. Then a fourth commission, chaired by North Carolina governor James B. Hunt, recommended in 1981 yet another set of rules, which became effective with the 1984 convention.

The general thrust of the work of the first three rules commissions was to broaden the antiparty changes started by the progressives at the beginning of this century. Whereas the earlier reformers had tried to minimize the role of parties in the election process, those of the 1970s sought to weaken the influence of leaders within the party. In short, the newer reforms were aimed at creating *intra*party democracy as well as *inter*party democracy. This was done by rules that, for the 1980 convention, required:

- Equal division of delegates between men and women
- Establishment of "goals" for the representation of African Americans, Hispanics, and other groups in proportion to their presence in a state's Democratic electorate
- Open delegate selection procedures, with advance publicity and written rules
- Selection of 75 percent of the delegates at the level of the congressional district or lower
- No "unit rule" that would require all delegates to vote with the majority of their state delegation
- Restrictions on the number of party leaders and elected officials who could vote at the convention
- A requirement that all delegates pledged to a candidate vote for that candidate

In 1981 the Hunt Commission changed some of these rules—in particular, the last two—in order to increase the influence of elected officials and to make the convention a somewhat more deliberative body. The commission reserved about 14 percent of the delegate seats for party leaders and elected officials, who would not have to commit themselves in advance to a presidential candidate, and it repealed the rule requiring that delegates pledged to a candidate vote for that candidate.

Rules have consequences. Walter Mondale was the chief beneficiary of the delegate selection rules.

National party conventions no longer make important decisions, but they generate enthusiasm as among Republicans who unanimously nominated George W. Bush in 2004.

He won the support of the overwhelming majority of elected officials—the so-called **superdelegates**—and he did especially well in those states that held winner-take-all primaries.

But the "reform" of the parties, especially the Democratic party, has had far more profound consequences than merely helping one candidate or another. Before 1968 the Republican party represented, essentially, white-collar voters and the Democratic party represented blue-collar ones. After a decade of "reform" the Republican and the Democratic parties each represented two ideologically different sets of upper-middle-class voters (see Table 9.1). In the terminology of Chapter 7, the Republicans came to represent the more conservative wing of the traditional middle class and the Democrats the more leftist wing of the liberal middle class.

This was more troubling to the Democrats than to the Republicans, because the traditional middle class is somewhat closer to the opinions of most citizens than is the liberal middle class (and thus the Republican national convention more closely reflected public opinion than did the Democratic national convention). And for whatever reason, the Republicans won five out of six presidential races between 1968 and 1988.

Before the 1988 convention the Democrats took a long, hard look at their party procedures. Under the leadership of DNC chairman Paul Kirk, they decided against making any major changes, especially ones that would increase the power of grassroots activists at the expense of elected officials and party leaders. The number of such officials (or superdelegates) to be given delegate seats was increased. For example, 80 percent of the Democratic members of Congress and all Democratic governors were automatically made convention delegates in 1988. The official status of some special-interest caucuses (such as those organized to represent African Americans, homosexuals, and various ethnic groups) was reduced in order to lessen the perception that the Democrats were simply a party of factions.

The surface harmony was a bit misleading, however, as some activists, notably supporters of Jesse Jackson, protested that the rules made it harder for candidates like Jackson to win delegates in proportion to their share of the primary vote. (In 1984 Jackson got 18 percent of the primary vote but only 12 percent of the delegates.) The DNC responded by

superdelegates　Party leaders and elected officials who become delegates to the national convention without having to run in primaries or caucuses.

T·R·I·V·I·A

Political Parties

First national political convention	Anti-Masonic party, 1831, in Baltimore
First-time incumbent governors were nominated for president	Rutherford B. Hayes of Ohio, by Republicans in 1876 Samuel J. Tilden of New York, by Democrats in 1876
First African American to receive a vote at a national party convention	Frederick Douglass, at Republican convention in 1888
First year in which women attended conventions as delegates	1900 (one woman at both Democratic and Republican conventions)
Most ballots needed to choose a presidential nominee	103, by Democrats in 1924 to select John W. Davis
Closest vote in convention history	$543\frac{1}{20}$ to $542\frac{7}{20}$, defeating a motion to condemn the Ku Klux Klan at 1924 Democratic convention
First Catholic nominated for president by a major party	Al Smith, by Democrats in 1928
Only person nominated for president four times by a major political party	Franklin D. Roosevelt, by Democrats in 1932, 1936, 1940, and 1944
First presidential nominee to make an acceptance speech at the party convention	Franklin D. Roosevelt

Table 9.1   Who Are the Party Delegates?

Characteristics of delegates to Democratic and Republican national conventions in 2004.

	Democrats	Republicans
Sex and Race		
Women	50%	43%
Blacks	18	6
Religion		
Protestant	43	65
Catholic	32	—
Jewish	8	—
Education		
College degree and beyond	77	73
Post graduate	53	44
Family Income		
Under $50,000	15	8
$100,000 and over	42	44
Belong to union	25	8
Born-again Christian	13	33
Gun owner in household	22	45

Sources: New York Times (August 29, 2004); CBSNEWS.COM, July 24, 2004; Boston Globe, August 31, 2004.

changing the rules for the 1992 campaign. Former DNC chairman Ronald H. Brown (later President Clinton's secretary of commerce) won approval for three important requirements:

- The winner-reward systems of delegate distribution, which gave the winner of a primary or caucus extra delegates, were banned. (In 1988 fifteen states used winner-reward systems, including such vote-rich states as Florida, Illinois, New Jersey, and Pennsylvania.)

- The proportional representation system was put into use. This system divides a state's publicly elected delegates among candidates who receive at least 15 percent of the vote.

- States that violate the rules are now penalized with the loss of 25 percent of their national convention delegates.

Even though the Democrats have retreated a bit from the reforms of the 1960s and 1970s, the conventions of both parties have changed fundamentally, and probably permanently. Delegates once selected by party leaders are now chosen by primary elections and grassroots caucuses. As a result the national party conventions are no longer places where party leaders meet to bargain over the selection of their presidential candidates; they are instead places where delegates come together to ratify choices already made by party activists and primary voters.

Most Americans dislike bosses, deals, and manipulation and prefer democracy, reform, and openness. These are commendable instincts. But such instincts, unless carefully tested against practice, may mislead us into supposing that anything carried out in the name of reform is a good idea. Rules must be judged by their practical results as well as by their conformity to some principle of fairness. Rules affect the distribution of power: they help some people win and others lose. Later in this chapter we shall try to assess delegate selection rules by looking more closely at how they affect who attends conventions and which presidential candidates are selected there.

☆ State and Local Parties

While the national party structures have changed, the grassroots organizations have withered. In between, state party systems have struggled to redefine their roles.

In every state there is a Democratic and a Republican state party organized under state law. Typically each consists of a state central committee, below which are found county committees and sometimes city, town, or even precinct committees. The members of these committees are chosen in a variety of ways—sometimes in primary elections, sometimes by conventions, sometimes by a building-block process whereby people elected to serve on precinct or town committees choose the members of county committees, who in turn choose state committee members.

Knowing these formal arrangements is much less helpful than knowing the actual distribution of power in each state party. In a few places strong party bosses handpick the members of these committees; in other places powerful elected officials—key state legislators, county sheriffs, or judges—control the committees. And in many places no one is in charge, so that either the party structure is largely meaningless or it is made up of the representatives of various local factions.

To understand how power is distributed in a party, we must first know what *incentives* motivate people in a particular state or locality to become active in a party organization. Different incentives lead to different ways of organizing parties.

The Machine

A **political machine** is a party organization that recruits its members by the use of tangible incentives—money, political jobs, an opportunity to get favors from government—and that is characterized

by a high degree of leadership control over member activity. At one time many local party organizations were machines, and the struggle over political jobs—patronage—was the chief concern of their members. Though Tammany Hall in New York City began as a caucus of well-to-do notables in the local Democratic party, by the late nineteenth century it had become a machine organized on the basis of political clubs in each assembly district. These clubs were composed of party workers whose job it was to get out the straight party vote in their election districts and who hoped for a tangible reward if they were successful.

And there were abundant rewards to hope for. During the 1870s it was estimated that one out of every eight voters in New York City had a federal, state, or city job.[8] The federal bureaucracy was one important source of those jobs. The New York Customhouse alone employed thousands of people, virtually all of whom were replaced if their party lost the presidential election. The postal system was another source, and it was frankly recognized as such. When James N. Tyner became postmaster general in 1876, he was "appointed not to see that the mails were carried, but to see that Indiana was carried."[9] Elections and conventions were so frequent and the intensity of party competition so great that being a party worker was for many a full-time paid occupation.

Well before the arrival of vast numbers of poor immigrants from Ireland, Italy, and elsewhere, old-stock Americans had perfected the machine, run up the cost of government, and systematized voting fraud. Kickbacks on contracts, payments extracted from officeholders, and funds raised from business people made some politicians rich but also paid the huge bills of the elaborate party organization. When the immigrants began flooding the eastern cities, the party machines were there to provide them with all manner of services in exchange for their support at the polls: the machines were a vast welfare organization operating before the creation of the welfare state.

The abuses of the machine were well known and gradually curtailed. Stricter voter registration laws reduced fraud, civil service reforms cut down the

> **political machine**   A party organization that recruits members by dispensing patronage.

Ex-senator George Washington Plunkitt of Tammany Hall explains machine politics from atop the bootblack stand in front of the New York County Courthouse around 1905.

number of patronage jobs, and competitive-bidding laws made it harder to award overpriced contracts to favored businesses. The Hatch Act (passed by Congress in 1939) made it illegal for federal civil service employees to take an active part in political management or political campaigns by serving as party officers, soliciting campaign funds, running for partisan office, working in a partisan campaign, endorsing partisan candidates, taking voters to the polls, counting ballots, circulating nominating petitions, or being delegates to a party convention. (They may still vote and make campaign contributions.)

These restrictions gradually took federal employees out of machine politics, but they did not end the machines. In many cities—Chicago, Philadelphia, and Albany—ways were found to maintain the machines even though city employees were technically under the civil service. Far more important than the various progressive reforms that weakened the machines were changes among voters. As voters grew in education, income, and sophistication, they depended less and less on the advice and leadership of local party officials. And as the federal government created a bureaucratic welfare system, the parties' welfare systems declined in value.

It is easy either to scorn the political party machine as a venal and self-serving organization or to romanticize it as an informal welfare system. In truth it was a little of both. Above all it was a frank recognition of the fact that politics requires organization; the machine was the supreme expression of the value of organization. Even allowing for voting fraud, in elections where party machines were active, voter turnout was huge: more people participated in politics when mobilized by a party machine than when appealed to by television or good-government associations.[10] Moreover, because the party machines were interested in winning, they would subordinate any other consideration to that end. This has meant that the machines were usually willing to support the presidential candidate with the best chance of winning, regardless of his policy views (provided, of course, that he was not determined to wreck the machines once in office). Republican machines helped elect Abraham Lincoln as well as Warren G. Harding; Democratic machines were of crucial importance in electing Franklin D. Roosevelt and John F. Kennedy.

The old-style machine is almost extinct, though important examples still can be found in the Democratic organization in Cook County (Chicago) and the Republican organization in Nassau County (New York). But a new-style machine has emerged in a few places. It is a machine in the sense that it uses money to knit together many politicians, but it is new in that the money comes not from patronage and contracts but from campaign contributions supplied by wealthy individuals and the proceeds of direct-mail campaigns.

The political organization headed by Democratic congressmen Henry A. Waxman and Howard L. Berman on the west side of Los Angeles is one such new-style machine. By the astute use of campaign funds, the "Waxman-Berman organization" builds loyalties to it among a variety of elected officials at all levels of government. Moreover, this new-style machine, unlike the old ones, has a strong interest in issues, especially at the national level. In this sense it is not a machine at all, but a cross between a machine and an ideological party.

Ideological Parties

At the opposite extreme from the machine is the **ideological party.** Where the machine values winning above all else, the ideological party values principle above all else. Where the former depends on money incentives, the latter spurns them. Where the former is hierarchical and disciplined, the latter is usually contentious and factionalized.

The most firmly ideological parties have been independent "third parties," such as the Socialist, Socialist Workers, Libertarian, and Right-to-Life parties. But there have been ideological factions within the Democratic and Republican parties as well, and in some places these ideological groups have taken over the regular parties.

In the 1950s and 1960s these ideological groups were "reform clubs" within local Democratic and Republican parties. In Los Angeles, New York, and many parts of Wisconsin and Minnesota, issue-oriented activists fought to take over the party from election-oriented regulars. Democratic reform clubs managed to defeat the head of Tammany Hall in Manhattan; similar activist groups became the dominant force in California state politics.[11] Democratic club leaders were more liberal than rank-and-file Democrats, and Republican club leaders were often more conservative than rank-and-file Republicans.

The 1960s and 1970s saw these "reform" movements replaced by more focused social movements. The "reform" movement was based on a generalized sense of liberalism (among Democrats) or conservatism (among Republicans). With the advent of social movements concerned with civil rights, peace,

feminism, environmentalism, libertarianism, and abortion, the generalized ideology of the clubs was replaced by the specific ideological demands of single-issue activists.

The result is that in many places the party has become a collection of people drawn from various social movements. For a candidate to win the party's support, he or she often has to satisfy the "litmus test" demands of the ideological activists in the party. Democratic senator Barbara Mikulski put it this way: "The social movements are now our farm clubs."

With social movements as their farm clubs, the big-league teams—the Democrats and Republicans at the state level—behave very differently than they did when political machines were the farm clubs. Internal factionalism is more intense, and the freedom of action of the party leader (say, the chairperson of the state committee) has been greatly reduced. A leader who demands too little or gives up too much, or who says the wrong thing on a key issue, is quickly accused of having "sold out." Under these circumstances many "leaders" are that in name only.

Solidary Groups

Many people who participate in state and local politics do so not in order to earn money or vindicate some cause, but simply because they find it fun. They enjoy the game, they meet interesting people, and they like the sense of being "in the know" and rubbing shoulders with the powerful. When people get together out of gregarious or game-loving instincts, we say that they are responding to **solidary incentives;** if they form an organization, it is a solidary association.

Some of these associations were once machines. When a machine loses its patronage, some of its members—especially the older ones—may continue to serve in the organization out of a desire for camaraderie. In other cases precinct, ward, and district committees are built up on the basis of friendship networks. One study of political activists in Detroit found that most of them mentioned friendships and

ideological party A party that values principled stands on issues above all else.
solidary incentives The social rewards (sense of pleasure, status, or companionship) that lead people to join political organizations.

The personal following of former President George Bush was passed on to his sons, George W. (left) and Jeb (right), both of whom became governors of large states, and the former of whom is now president.

a liking for politics, rather than an interest in issues, as their reasons for joining the party organization.[12] Members of ward and town organizations in St. Louis County gave the same answers when asked why they joined.[13] Since patronage has declined in value and since the appeals of ideology are limited to a minority of citizens, the motivations for participating in politics have become very much like those for joining a bowling league or a bridge club.

The advantage of such groups is that they are neither corrupt nor inflexible; the disadvantage is that they often do not work very hard. Knocking on doors on a rainy November evening to try to talk people into voting for your candidate is a chore under the best of circumstances; it is especially unappealing if you joined the party primarily because you like to attend meetings or drink coffee with your friends.[14]

Sponsored Parties

Sometimes a relatively strong party organization can be created among volunteers without heavy reliance on money or ideology and without depending entirely on people's finding the work fun. This type of

---

sponsored party   A local or state political party that is largely supported by another organization in the community.

personal following   The political support provided to a candidate on the basis of personal popularity and networks.

---

sponsored party occurs when another organization exists in the community that can create, or at least sponsor, a local party structure. The clearest example of this is the Democratic party in and around Detroit, which has been developed, led, and to a degree financed by the political-action arm of the United Auto Workers union. The UAW has had a long tradition of rank-and-file activism, stemming from its formative struggles in the 1930s, and since the city is virtually a one-industry town, it was not hard to transfer some of this activism from union organizing to voter organizing.

By the mid-1950s union members and leaders made up over three-fourths of all the Democratic party district leaders within the city.[15] On election day union funds were available for paying workers to canvass voters; between elections political work on an unpaid basis was expected of union leaders. Though the UAW-Democratic party alliance in Detroit has not always been successful in city elections (the city is nonpartisan), it has been quite successful in carrying the city for the Democratic party in state and national elections.

Not many areas have organizations as effective or as dominant as the UAW that can bolster, sponsor, or even take over the weak formal party structure. Thus sponsored local parties are not common in the United States.

Personal Following

Because most candidates can no longer count on the backing of a machine, because sponsored parties are limited to a few unionized areas, and because solidary groups are not always productive, a person wanting to get elected will often try to form a **personal following** that will work for him or her during a campaign and then disband until the next election rolls around. Sometimes a candidate tries to meld a personal following with an ideological group, especially during the primary election campaign, when candidates need the kind of financial backing and hard work that only highly motivated activists are likely to supply.

To form a personal following, the candidate must have an appealing personality, a lot of friends, or a big bank account. The Kennedy family has all three, and the electoral success of the personal followings of John F. Kennedy, Edward M. Kennedy, Robert Kennedy, and Joseph P. Kennedy II are legendary. President George H.W. Bush also established such a following. After he left office, one son (Jeb) became governor of Florida and another one (George W.) became governor of Texas and forty-third president of the United States.

Southern politicians who have to operate in one-party states with few, if any, machines have become grand masters at building personal followings, such as those of the Talmadge family in Georgia, the Long family in Louisiana, and the Byrd family in Virginia. But the strategy is increasingly followed wherever party organization is weak. The key asset is to have a known political name. That has helped the electoral victories of the son of Hubert Humphrey in Minnesota, the son and daughter of Pat Brown in California, the son of Birch Bayh in Indiana, the son of George Wallace in Alabama, and the son and grandson of Robert La Follette in Wisconsin.

The traditional party organization—one that is hierarchical, lasting, based on material incentives, and capable of influencing who gets nominated for office—exists today, according to political scientist David Mayhew, in only about eight states, mostly the older states of the Northeast. Another five states, he feels, have faction-ridden versions of the traditional party organization.[16] The states in the rest of the country display the weak party system of solidary clubs, personal followings, ideological groups, and sponsored parties. What that means can be seen in the composition of Democratic national conventions. More than half of the delegates have been drawn from the ranks of the AFL-CIO, the National Education Association, and the National Organization for Women.[17]

☆ The Two-Party System

With so many different varieties of local party organizations (or nonorganizations), and with such a great range of opinion found within each party, it is remarkable that we have had only two major political parties for most of our history. In the world at large a **two-party system** is a rarity; by one estimate only fifteen nations have one.[18] Most European democracies are multiparty systems. We have only two parties with any chance of winning nationally, and these parties have been, over time, rather evenly balanced—between 1888 and 2000, the Republicans won sixteen presidential elections and the Democrats thirteen. Furthermore, whenever one party has achieved a temporary ascendancy and its rival has been pronounced dead (as were the Democrats in the first third of this century and the Republicans during the 1930s and the 1960s), the "dead" party has displayed remarkable powers of recuperation, coming back to win important victories.

At the state and congressional district levels, however, the parties are not evenly balanced. For a long time the South was so heavily Democratic at all levels of government as to be a one-party area, while upper New England and the Dakotas were strongly Republican. All regions are more competitive today than once was the case, but even now one party tends to enjoy a substantial advantage in at least half the states and in perhaps two-thirds of the congressional districts. Nevertheless, though the parties are not as competitive in state elections as they are in presidential ones, states have rarely had, at least for any extended period, political parties other than the Democratic and Republican (see Table 9.2).

Scholars do not entirely agree on why the two-party system should be so permanent a feature of American political life, but two explanations are of major importance. The first has to do with the system of elections, the second with the distribution of public opinion.

Elections at every level of government are based on the plurality, winner-take-all method. The **plurality system** means that in all elections for representative, senator, governor, or president, and in almost all elections for state legislator, mayor, or city councillor, the winner is that person who gets the *most* votes, even if he or she does not get a *majority* of all votes cast. We are so familiar with this system that we sometimes forget that there are other ways of running an election. For example, one could require that the winner get a majority of the votes, thus producing runoff elections if nobody got a majority on the first try. France does this in choosing its national legislature. In the first election candidates

---

two-party system   An electoral system with two dominant parties that compete in national elections.

plurality system   An electoral system in which the winner is the person who gets the most votes, even if he or she does not receive a majority; used in almost all American elections.

Table 9.2	The Rise of Republican Politics in the South, 1956–2004						
	Number of Representatives		Number of Senators		Number of Governors		Number of States Voting for Presidential Nominee
Year	Dem.	Rep.	Dem.	Rep.	Dem.	Rep.	Dem.	Rep.
1956	99	7	22	0	11	0	6	5
1958	99	7	22	0	11	0	—	—
1960	99	7	22	0	11	0	8[a]	2
1962	95	11	21	1	11	0	—	—
1964	89	17	21	1	11	0	6	5
1966	83	23	19	3	9	2	—	—
1968	80	26	18	4	9	2	1	5[b]
1970	79	27	16 (1)[c]	5	9	2	—	—
1972	74	34	14 (1)[c]	7	8	3	0	11
1974	81	27	15 (1)[c]	6	8	3	—	—
1976	82	26	16 (1)[c]	5	9	2	10	1
1978	77	31	15 (1)[c]	6	8	3	—	—
1980	55	53	11 (1)[c]	10	6	5	1	10
1982	80	33	11	11	11	0	—	—
1984	72	41	11	11	10	1	0	11
1986	77	39	16	6	6	5	—	—
1988	80	36	15	7	6	5	0	11
1990	77	39	15	7	8	3	—	—
1992	82	43	14	8	8	3	4	7
1994	61	64	9	13	5	6	—	—
1996	54	71	9	13	4	7	4	7
1998	54	71	8	14	4	7	—	—
2000	54	71	7	15	6	5	0	11
2002	67	64	8	14	6	5	—	—
2004	48	83	4	18	4	7	0	11

[a]Eight Mississippi electors voted for Harry Byrd.

[b]George Wallace won five states on the American Independent ticket.

[c]Harry Byrd, Jr., was elected in Virginia in 1970 and 1976 as an independent.

[d]Virgil H. Goode, Jr., was elected in Virginia in 1996 as an independent.

for parliament who win an absolute majority of the votes cast are declared elected. A week later remaining candidates who received at least one-eighth, but less than one-half of the vote, go into a runoff election; those who then win an absolute majority are also declared elected.

The French method encourages many political parties to form, each hoping to win at least one-eighth of the vote in the first election and then to enter into an alliance with its ideologically nearest rival in order to win the runoff. In the United States the plurality system means that a party must make all the alliances it can before the first election—there is no second chance. Hence every party must be as broadly based as possible; a narrow, minor party has no hope of winning.

The winner-take-all feature of American elections has the same effect. Only one member of Congress is elected from each district. In many European countries the elections are based on proportional representation. Each party submits a list of candidates for parliament, ranked in order of preference by the party leaders. The nation votes. A party winning 37 percent of the vote gets 37 percent of the seats in parliament; a party winning 2 percent of the vote gets 2 percent of the seats. Since even the smallest parties have a chance of winning something, minor parties have an incentive to organize.

The most dramatic example of the winner-take-all principle is the electoral college (see Chapter 14). In every state but Maine and Nebraska, the candidate who wins the most popular votes in a state wins *all* of that state's electoral votes. In 1992, for example, Bill Clinton won only 45 percent of the popular vote in Missouri, but he got all of Missouri's eleven electoral votes because his two rivals (George Bush and Ross Perot) each got fewer popular votes. Minor parties cannot compete under this system. Voters are often reluctant to "waste" their votes on a minor-party candidate who cannot win.

The United States has experimented with other electoral systems. Proportional representation was used for municipal elections in New York City at one time and is still in use for that purpose in Cambridge, Massachusetts. Many states have elected more than one state legislator from each district. In Illinois, for example, three legislators have been elected from each district, with each voter allowed to cast two votes, thus virtually guaranteeing that the minority party will be able to win one of the three seats. But none of these experiments has altered the national two-party system, probably because of the existence of a directly elected president chosen by a winner-take-all electoral college.

The presidency is the great prize of American politics; to win it you must form a party with as broad appeal as possible. As a practical matter that means there will be, in most cases, only two serious parties—one made up of those who support the party already in power, and the other made up of everybody else. Only one third party ever won the presidency—the Republicans in 1860—and it had by then pretty much supplanted the Whig party. No third party is likely to win, or even come close to winning, the presidency anytime soon. Despite the decline in mass party attachment, among Americans who actually vote in presidential elections, party voting is almost as strong today as it was in the early 1950s. As Table 9.3 shows, in the presidential elections of 1984 through 2004,

the vast majority of Democrats voted for the Democrat, and the vast majority of Republicans voted for the Republican. Meanwhile, most independents voted for the winning Republican in 1984, 1988, and 2000, and pluralities of independents voted for the winning Democrat in 1992 and 1996. In the 2004 presidential election, Independents voted for Democrat John Kerry by a margin of 49 percent to 48 percent, but Republican George W. Bush still won the national popular vote by a margin of 51 to 48 percent.

The second explanation for the persistence of the two-party system is to be found in the opinions of the voters. There remains a kind of rough parity between the two parties regarding which of them most citizens think is likely to govern best on given issues. For example, in public opinion surveys conducted in 1997 and 1998, respondents favored the Republicans over the Democrats on national defense and crime, favored the Democrats over the Republicans on poverty and the environment, and were split evenly between the two parties on taxes and economic prosperity (see Table 9.4).

Though there have been periods of bitter dissent, most of the time most citizens have agreed enough to permit them to come together into two broad coalitions. There has not been a massive and persistent body of opinion that has rejected the prevailing economic system (and thus we have not had a Marxist party with mass appeal); there has not been in our history an aristocracy or monarchy (and thus there has been no party that has sought to restore aristocrats or monarchs to power). Churches and religion have almost always been regarded as matters of private choice that lie outside politics (and thus there has not been a party seeking to create or abolish special government privileges for one church or another). In some European nations the organization of

Party Affiliation of Voter	1988 Dem.	Rep.	1992 Dem.	Rep.	Ind.	1996 Dem.	Rep.	Ind.	2000 Dem.	Rep.	Ind.	2004 Dem.	Rep.	Ind.
Democrat	85%	15%	82%	8%	10%	84%	10%	5%	85%	10%	3%	89%	11%	0%
Republican	7	93	7	77	16	13	80	6	7	91	1	6	93	0
Independent	43	57	39	30	31	43	35	17	37	42	9	49	48	1

Table 9.3 Party Voting in Presidential Elections

Source: Data from CNN exit polls for each year.

Table 9.4   The Public Rates the Two Parties

Question
Do you think the Republican party or the Democratic party would do a better job of dealing with each of the following issues and problems?

	Democrats	Republicans
Advantage Republicans		
National defense*	37%	53%
Foreign trade	35	48
Crime	36	43
Campaign finance reform	31	37
Split Between the Parties		
Economic prosperity	44	42
Taxes	43	42
Advantage Democrats		
Poverty*	61	27
Environment	54	31
Health care	51	34
Social Security	46	35

*Question on this item asked as "Which party, the Democrats or the Republicans, do you trust to do a better job on . . . ?"

Source: The Public Perspective (April/May 1998): 13, reporting the results of a survey by the Gallup Organization for CNN/USA Today, October 27–28, 1997, and a survey by ABC News/Washington Post, January 15–19, 1998.

the economy, the prerogatives of the monarchy, and the role of the church have been major issues with long and bloody histories. So divisive have these issues been that they have helped prevent the formation of broad coalition parties.

But Americans have had other deep divisions—between white and black, for example, and between North and South—and yet the two-party system has endured. This suggests that our electoral procedures are of great importance—the winner-take-all, plurality election rules have made it useless for anyone to attempt to create an all-white or an all-black national party except as an act of momentary defiance or in the hope of taking enough votes away from the two major parties to force the presidential election into the House of Representatives. (That may have been George Wallace's strategy in 1968.)

For many years there was an additional reason for the two-party system: the laws of many states made it difficult, if not impossible, for third parties to get on the ballot. In 1968, for example, the American Independent party of George Wallace found that it would have to collect 433,000 signatures (15 percent of the votes cast in the last statewide election) in order to get on the presidential ballot in Ohio. Wallace took the issue to the Supreme Court, which ruled, six to three, that such a restriction was an unconstitutional violation of the equal-protection clause of the Fourteenth Amendment.[19] Wallace got on the ballot. In 1980 John Anderson, running as an independent, was able to get on the ballot in all fifty states; in 1992 Ross Perot did the same. But for the reasons already indicated, the two-party system will probably persist even without the aid of legal restrictions.

☆ Minor Parties

The electoral system may prevent minor parties from winning, but it does not prevent them from forming. Minor parties—usually called, erroneously, "third parties"—have been a permanent feature of American political life. Four major kinds of minor parties, with examples of each, are described in the box on page 221.

The minor parties that have endured have been the ideological ones. Their members feel themselves to be outside the mainstream of American political life and sometimes, as in the case of various Marxist parties, look forward to a time when a revolution or some other dramatic change in the political system will vindicate them. They are usually not interested in immediate electoral success and thus persist despite their poor showing at the polls. One such party, however, the Socialist party of Eugene Debs, won nearly 6 percent of the popular vote in the 1912 presidential election and during its heyday elected some twelve hundred candidates to local offices, including seventy-nine mayors. Part of the Socialist appeal arose from its opposition to municipal corruption, part from its opposition to American entry into World War I, and part from its critique of American society. No ideological party has ever carried a state in a presidential election.

Apart from the Republicans, who quickly became a major party, the only minor parties to carry states and thus win electoral votes were one party of economic protest (the Populists, who carried five states in 1892) and several factional parties (most recently, the States' Rights Democrats in 1948 and the Amer-

★ HOW THINGS WORK ★

Types of Minor Parties

Ideological parties: Parties professing a comprehensive view of American society and government that is radically different from that of the established parties. Most have been Marxist in outlook, but some are quite the opposite, such as the Libertarian party.

Examples:
Socialist party (1901 to 1960s)
Socialist Labor party (1888 to present)
Socialist Workers party (1938 to present)
Communist party (1920s to present)
Libertarian party (1972 to present)
Green party (1984 to present)

One-issue parties: Parties seeking a single policy, usually revealed by their names, and avoiding other issues.

Examples:
Free-Soil party—to prevent the spread of slavery (1848–1852)
American or "Know-Nothing" party—to oppose immigration and Catholics (1856)
Prohibition party—to ban the sale of liquor (1869 to present)
Woman's party—to obtain the right to vote for women (1913–1920)

Economic-protest parties: Parties, usually based in a particular region, especially involving farmers, that protest against depressed economic conditions. These tend to disappear as conditions improve.

Examples:
Greenback party (1876–1884)
Populist party (1892–1908)

Factional parties: Parties that are created by a split in a major party, usually over the identity and philosophy of the major party's presidential candidate.

Examples:
Split off from the Republican party:
 "Bull Moose" Progressive party (1912)
 La Follette Progressive party (1924)
Split off from the Democratic party:
 States' Rights ("Dixiecrat") party (1948)
 Henry Wallace Progressive party (1948)
 American Independent (George Wallace) party (1968)
Split off from both Democrats and Republicans:
 Reform party (Ross Perot)

---

ican Independent party of George Wallace in 1968). Though factional parties may hope to cause the defeat of the party from which they split, they have not always been able to achieve this. Harry Truman was elected in 1948 despite the defections of both the leftist progressives, led by Henry Wallace, and the right-wing Dixiecrats, led by J. Strom Thurmond. In 1968 it seems likely that Hubert Humphrey would have lost even if George Wallace had not been in the race (Wallace voters would probably have switched to Nixon rather than to Humphrey, though of course one cannot be certain). It is quite possible, on the other hand, that a Republican might have beaten Woodrow Wilson in 1912 if the Republican party had not split in two (the regulars supporting William

Howard Taft, the progressives supporting Theodore Roosevelt).

What is striking is not that we have had so many minor parties but that we have not had more. There have been several major political movements that did not produce a significant third party: the civil rights movement of the 1960s, the antiwar movement of the same decade, and, most important, the labor movement of the twentieth century. African Americans were part of the Republican party after the Civil War and part of the Democratic party after the New Deal (even though the southern wing of that party for a long time kept them from voting). The antiwar movement found candidates with whom it could identify within the Democratic party (Eugene

The Socialist party and the Progressive party were both minor parties, but their origins were different. The Socialist party was an ideological party; the "Bull Moose" Progressive party split off from the Republicans to support Theodore Roosevelt.

McCarthy, Robert F. Kennedy, George McGovern), even though it was a Democratic president, Lyndon B. Johnson, who was chiefly responsible for the U.S. commitment in Vietnam. After Johnson only narrowly won the 1968 New Hampshire primary, he withdrew from the race. Unions have not tried to create a labor party—indeed, they were for a long time opposed to almost any kind of national political activity. Since labor became a major political force in the 1930s, the largest industrial unions have been content to operate as a part (a very large part) of the Democratic party.

One reason why some potential sources of minor parties never formed such parties, in addition to the dim chance of success, is that the direct primary and the national convention have made it possible for dissident elements of a major party, unless they become completely disaffected, to remain in the party and influence the choice of candidates and policies. The antiwar movement had a profound effect on the Democratic conventions of 1968 and 1972; African Americans have played a growing role in the Democratic party, especially with the candidacy of Jesse Jackson in 1984 and 1988; only in 1972 did the unions feel that the Democrats nominated a presidential candidate (McGovern) unacceptable to them.

The impact of minor parties on American politics is hard to judge. One bit of conventional wisdom holds that minor parties develop ideas that the major parties later come to adopt. The Socialist party, for example, is supposed to have called for major social and economic policies that the Democrats under Roosevelt later embraced and termed the New Deal. It is possible that the Democrats did steal the thunder of the Socialists, but it hardly seems likely that they did it because the Socialists had proposed these

Robert M. La Follette campaigned for the presidency as the candidate of the Progressive Party in 1924. He won 17 percent of the vote.

things or proved them popular. (In 1932 the Socialists got only 2 percent of the vote and in 1936 less than one-half of 1 percent.) Roosevelt probably adopted the policies he did in part because he thought them correct and in part because dissident elements within his *own* party—leaders such as Huey Long of Louisiana—were threatening to bolt the Democratic party if it did not move to the left. Even Prohibition was adopted more as a result of the efforts of interest groups such as the Anti-Saloon League than as the consequence of its endorsement by the Prohibition party.

The minor parties that have probably had the greatest influence on public policy have been the factional parties. Mugwumps and liberal Republicans, by bolting the regular party, may have made that party more sensitive to the issue of civil service reform; the Bull Moose and La Follette Progressive parties probably helped encourage the major parties to pay more attention to issues of business regulation and party reform; the Dixiecrat and Wallace movements probably strengthened the hands of those who

wished to go slow on desegregation. The threat of a factional split is a risk that both major parties must face, and it is in the efforts that each makes to avoid such splits that one finds the greatest impact, at least in this century, of minor parties.

In 1992 and again in 1996, Ross Perot led the most successful recent third-party movement. It began as United We Stand America and was later renamed the Reform party. Perot's appeal seemed to reflect a growing American dissatisfaction with the existing political parties and a heightened demand for bringing in a leader who would "run the government without politics." Of course it is no more possible to take politics out of governing than it is to take churches out of religion. Though unrealistic, people seem to want policies without bargaining.

☆ Nominating a President

The major parties face, as we have seen, two contrary forces: one, generated by the desire to win the presidency, pushes them in the direction of nominating a candidate who can appeal to the majority of voters and who will thus have essentially middle-of-the-road views. The other, produced by the need to keep dissident elements in the party from bolting and forming a third party, leads them to compromise with dissidents or extremists in ways that may damage the party's standing with the voters.

The Democrats and Republicans have always faced these conflicting pressures, but of late they have become especially acute. When the presidential nomination was made by a party convention that was heavily influenced, if not controlled, by party leaders and elected officials, it was relatively easy to ignore dissident factions and pick candidates on the basis of who could win. The *electoral* objectives of the party were predominant. The result was that often a faction left the party and ran a separate ticket—as in 1912, 1924, 1948, 1968, and 1980. Today the power of party leaders and elected officials within the parties is greatly diminished, with most delegates now selected by primary elections. A larger proportion of the delegates is likely to be more interested in issues and to be less amenable to compromise over those issues than formerly. In these circumstances the *policy* interests of the party activists are likely to be important.

Are the Delegates Representative of the Voters?

There would be no conflict between the electoral and policy interests of a political party if the delegates to its nominating convention had the same policy views as most voters, or at least as most party supporters. In fact this is not the case: in parties, as in many organizations, the activists and leaders tend to have views different from those of the rank and file.[20] In American political parties in recent years this difference has become very great.

In 1964 the Republican party nominated the highly conservative Barry Goldwater for president. We have no opinion data for delegates to that convention as detailed and comprehensive as those available for subsequent conventions, but it seems clear that the Republican delegates selected as their nominee a person who was not the most popular candidate among voters at large and thus not the candidate most likely to win.

At every Democratic national convention since 1972 the delegates have had views on a variety of important issues that were vastly different from those of rank-and-file Democrats. On welfare, military policy, school desegregation, crime, and abortion, Democratic delegates expressed opinions almost diametrically opposed to those of most Democrats. The delegates to the 1980, 1984, and (to a lesser extent) 1988, 1992, 1996, and 2000 conventions were ideologically very different from the voters at large. The Democratic delegates were more liberal than the Democratic voters, and the Republican delegates were more conservative than the Republican voters (see Table 9.5).[21]

What accounts for the sharp disparity between delegate opinion (and often delegate candidate preference) and voter attitudes? Some blame the discrepancy on the rules, described earlier in this chapter, under which Democratic delegates are chosen, especially those that require increased representation for women, minorities, and the young. Close examination suggests that this is not a complete explanation. For one thing, it does not explain why the Republicans nominated Goldwater in 1964 (and almost nominated Ronald Reagan instead of Gerald Ford in 1976). For another, women, minorities, and youth have among them all shades of opinions: there are many middle-of-the-road women and young people, as well as very liberal or very conservative ones. (There are not many very conservative African Americans, at least on race issues, but there are certainly plenty who are moderate on race and conservative on other issues.) The question is why only *certain* elements of these groups are heavily represented at the conventions.

Who Votes in Primaries?

Maybe delegates are unrepresentative of the party rank and file because they are chosen in caucuses and primary elections whose participants are unrepresentative. Before 1972 most delegates were picked by party leaders; primaries were relatively unimportant, and voter caucuses were almost unheard-of. Adlai Stevenson in 1952 and Hubert Humphrey in 1968 won the Democratic presidential nominations without even entering a primary. Harry Truman once described primaries as "eyewash."[22]

After 1972 they were no longer eyewash. The vast majority of delegates were selected in primaries and caucuses. In 1992 forty states and territories held primaries, and twenty held caucuses (some places had both primaries and caucuses).

Only about half as many people vote in primaries as in general elections. If these primary voters have more extreme political views than do the rank-and-file party followers, then they might support presidential delegates who also have extreme views.

Liberal Ideology	1984	1988	1992	1996	2000
Democrats					
Delegates	66%	39%	47%	43%	41%
Voters	31	25	28	27	34
Republicans					
Delegates	2	1	1	0	1
Voters	15	12	12	7	8

Table 9.5 How Party Delegates and Party Voters Differ in Liberal Ideology

Sources: For 1984: Los Angeles Times (August 19, 1984); for 1988: New York Times/CBS News poll, in New York Times (August 14, 1988); for 1992: New York Times (July 13 and August 17, 1992) and unpublished CBS News poll, "The 1992 Republican Convention Delegates"; for 1996: New York Times (August 12 and 26, 1996); for 2000, New York Times (August 29, 2004).

However, there is not much evidence that such is the case. Studies comparing the ideological orientations of primary voters with those of rank-and-file party voters show few strong differences.[23]

When it comes to presidential primaries, a good fight draws a crowd. For example, in twelve of the first eighteen Republican presidential primaries in 2000, voter turnout hit record highs as Governor George W. Bush battled state by state to stay ahead of Senator John McCain. But the "crowd" represented only 13.6 percent of the voting-age population, up 4.3 percent from the 1996 turnout, and the highest since Senator Barry Goldwater's campaign for the nomination divided Republicans in 1964.[24] In the states that voted after Bush had the nomination all but won, turnout was considerably lower. Likewise, the contest between Vice President Al Gore and Senator Bill Bradley resulted in the second-lowest Democratic presidential primary turnout since 1960.

Primaries differ from caucuses. A **caucus** is a meeting of party followers, often lasting for hours and held in the dead of winter in a schoolhouse miles from home, in which party delegates are picked. Only the most dedicated partisans attend. For the Democrats these have been liberals; for the Republicans, conservatives. In 1988 the most liberal Democratic candidate, Jesse Jackson, got more delegates in the Alaska, Delaware, Michigan, and Vermont caucuses than did Michael Dukakis, the eventual nominee. Republican evangelist Pat Robertson did not win any primary, but he won the caucuses in Alaska, Hawaii, and Washington.

Who Are the New Delegates?

However delegates are chosen, they are a different breed today than they once were. Whether picked by caucuses or primaries, and whatever their sex and race, a far larger proportion of convention delegates, both Republican and Democratic, are issue-oriented activists—people with an "amateur" or "purist" view of politics. Far fewer delegates are in it for the money (there is no longer much patronage to pass around) or to help their own reelection prospects. For example, in 1980 only 14 percent of the Democratic senators and 15 percent of the Democratic members of the House were delegates to the national convention. In 1956, by contrast, 90 percent of the senators and 33 percent of the representatives were delegates.[25] Party activists, especially those who work without

pay and who are in politics out of an interest in issues, are not likely to resemble the average citizen, for whom politics is merely an object of observation, discussion, and occasional voting.

The changing incentives for participation in party work, in addition to the effects of the primary system, have contributed to the development of a national presidential nominating system different from that which once existed. The advantage of the new system is that it increases the opportunity for those with strong policy preferences to play a role in the party and thus reduces the chance that they will bolt the party and form a factional minor party. The disadvantage of the system is that it increases the chances that one or both parties may nominate presidential candidates who are not appealing to the average voter or even to a party's rank and file.

In sum, presidential nominating conventions are now heavily influenced by ideologically motivated activists. Democratic conventions have heavy representation from organized feminists, unionized schoolteachers, and abortion rights activists; Republican conventions have large numbers of antiabortion activists, Christian conservatives, and small-government libertarians. As a result the presidential nominating system is now fundamentally different from what it was as late as the mid-1960s.

★ Parties Versus Voters

Since 1968 the Democratic party has had no trouble winning congressional elections but great difficulty winning presidential contests. Except for 1980–1986 and since 1994, the Democrats have controlled both houses of Congress; except for 1976, 1992, and 1996, they have lost every presidential election. The Republican party has had the opposite problem: though it won five out of seven presidential elections between 1968 and 1992, it did not control Congress for the forty years preceding its big win in 1994.

There are many reasons for this odd state of affairs, most of which will be discussed later. But one

---

caucus A meeting of party members to select delegates backing one or another primary candidate.

requires attention here. The difficulty the Democrats have had in competing for the presidency is in part because their candidates for the presidency have had, on certain issues—chiefly social and taxation issues—views very different from those of the average voter. That disparity to a large degree mirrors (and may be caused by) the gulf that separates the opinions of delegates to Democratic nominating conventions from the opinions of most citizens.

The Republicans have not been immune to this problem. In 1964 they nominated a candidate, Barry Goldwater, whose beliefs placed him well to the right of most voters. Not surprisingly, he lost. And the delegates to recent Republican conventions have held opinions on some matters that continue to be very different from most people's. Still, the problem has been somewhat more acute for the Democrats.

The problem can be seen in Table 9.6. A lot of information is shown there; to understand it, study the table step by step. First, look at the middle column, which summarizes the views of voters in 2004. (Because there are about the same number of Democratic and Republican voters, the opinion of the average voter is about halfway between those of the followers of the two parties.) Now look at the columns on the far left and the far right. These show the views of delegates to the 2004 Democratic and Republican conventions. On almost every issue the delegates are in sharp disagreement. There were hardly any conservatives at the Democratic convention or liberals at the Republican convention. On each and every issue, the delegates were at opposite ends of the spectrum.

Still, either party can win if its delegates nominate a candidate whose views put him or her closer to the average citizen than to the average delegate or if the campaign is fought out over issues on which the delegates and the voters agree. For example, if the election turned on what to do about an economic recession, the delegates, the voters, and the candidate would probably all agree: do whatever is necessary to end the recession. Exactly that happened in 1992, and the Democrats won.

Of course, even without a scandal, recession, or some other unifying issue, the need to win an election will lead all candidates to move toward the middle of the road. That is where the votes are. But this creates a dilemma for a candidate of either party. The stance one takes to win support from party activists in the caucuses and primaries will often be quite different from the stance one should take to win votes from the general public. In the next chapter we shall look more closely at how politicians try to cope with that dilemma.

Table 9.6   Political Opinions of Delegates and Voters, 2004

	Democratic Delegates	Voters	Republican Delegates
Who They Are			
Male	50%	49%	57%
Female	50	51	43
African American	18	14	6
Income over $75,000	61	28	58
What They Think			
Government should do more to solve national problems.	79	42	9
Abortion should be generally available.	75	34	13
Religion is extremely important in daily life.	21	28	39
Government's antiterrorism laws restrict civil liberties.	77	43	15
The penalty for murder should be death, not life in prison.	19	50	57
Protect the environment even if jobs are lost because of it.	62	52	25
There should be no legal recognition of a gay couple's relationship.	5	39	49

Source: New York Times/CBS News polls as reported in Katharine Q. Seeley and Marjorie Connelly, "The Conventioneers; Delegates Leaning to the Right of G.O.P. and the Nation," *New York Times*, August 29, 2004.

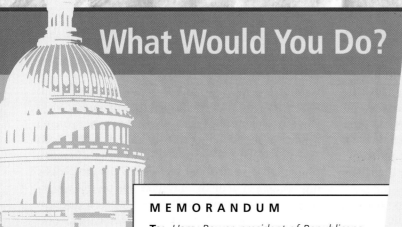

What Would You Do?

Pro-Life Group Threatens to Bolt GOP

February 1
HARRISBURG, PA

At a televised press conference last week several top Republican officials called for "moderating" their party's pro-life platform. Yesterday a leading antiabortion political action committee responded by running full-page newspaper ads calling for "independent candidates and a third party to represent the views of pro-life Republicans and Democrats alike" . . .

MEMORANDUM

To: *Harry Bower, president of Republicans for Life*

From: *Patricia Nucanon, political consultant*

Subject: *Forming a third party*

Without regard to your organization's particular cause or issue, I have been employed to brief you on the general pros and cons of backing independent candidates and forming a third party.

Arguments for:

1. Independent and third-party candidates can garner votes and even win. In 1992 independent candidate Ross Perot won nearly a fifth of the vote for president. In 1998 the Reform party candidate Jesse Ventura became governor of Minnesota.
2. Even losing independent candidates (Eugene Debs, Robert La Follette, and George Wallace, to name just three) have made real marks on American politics. "Unsuccessful" third parties were the first to advocate policy positions later championed by the two main parties: abolishing slavery (Free-Soil party), giving women the vote (Woman's party), the direct election of senators (Progressive party), and many others.
3. Splitting off from a major party courts public attention and eventually gets policy results.

Arguments against:

1. The two-party system is supported by more than 150 years of political tradition featuring winner-take-all, single-member election districts. Since the 1850s, more than 100 third parties and thousands of independent candidates have come, gone, and been forgotten by all except historians.
2. Usually the two main parties adapt and co-opt, not adopt, third-party ideas and positions. In the 1930s the Democrats watered down the Socialist party's plan and gave birth to the Social Security system. In the 1980s the Republican position on tax relief was but a faint echo of the Libertarian party's.
3. Splitting off from a major party courts political oblivion and reduces the chances that the issue or cause will be raised or represented even halfheartedly by either main party.

Your decision:

Favor a third party _____

Oppose third party _____

★ SUMMARY

A political party exists in three arenas: among the voters who psychologically identify with it, as a grassroots organization staffed and led by activists, and as a group of elected officials who follow its lead in lawmaking. In this chapter we have looked at the party primarily as an organization and seen the various forms it takes at the local level—the machine, the ideological party, the solidary group, the sponsored party, and the personal following.

The spread of the direct primary has made it harder for parties to control who is nominated for elective office, thus making it harder for the parties to influence the behavior of these people once elected. Delegate selection rules, especially in the Democratic party, have helped shift the center of power in the national nominating convention. Because of the changes in rules, power has moved away from officeholders and party regulars and toward the more ideological wings of the parties.

Minor parties have arisen from time to time, but the only ones that have affected the outcome of presidential elections have been those that represented a splinter group within one of the major parties (such as the Bull Moose progressives). The two-party system is maintained, and minor parties are discouraged, by an election system (winner-take-all, plurality elections) that makes voters reluctant to waste a vote on a minor party and by the ability of potential minor parties to wield influence within a major party by means of the primary system.

In the next chapter we shall look at the role of parties in shaping voter attitudes, and in Chapter 13 we shall look at the role of parties in Congress. In each of these areas we will find more evidence of party decay.

RECONSIDERING WHO GOVERNS?

1. How has America's two-party system changed, and how does it differ from the party systems of other representative democracies?

American parties during the nineteenth century and the first half of the twentieth century were strong organizations that picked their candidates for office. Parties in European democracies still do that, but America has changed. Now, candidates are usually picked by direct primary elections as the American voters' loyalty to parties has weakened.

2. How much do parties affect how Americans vote?

Registered Democrats are more likely to vote for Democratic candidates, and registered Republicans are more likely to vote for Republican candidates, but more voters now register as independents, the proportion of people identifying with one or the other party has declined, and split-ticket voting has been common in the American electorate. The declining attachment of voters to parties and their weaknesses as organizations have led many candidates for president and other offices to run more as individuals than as party members.

RECONSIDERING TO WHAT ENDS?

1. Did the Founding Fathers think that political parties were a good idea?

No. For example, George Washington denounced parties as "factions." But as soon as it was time to select his replacement, the republic's first leaders realized they had to organize their followers to win the election, and parties were born. It was not, however, until well into the nineteenth century that the idea of a permanent two-party system was considered legitimate by virtually all of the country's political leaders.

2. How, if at all, should America's two-party system be reformed?

Any answer should depend, at least in part, on how one evaluates the many reforms that already have been made. For instance, some argue that the parties should become more open to popular influences. To a large extent, however, that has already happened. Whereas once presidential candidates were selected by party leaders, today they are selected by primaries. Others maintain that there is little real difference between the two parties. That opinion, however, is at variance with the wide differences on many important issues one finds in party platforms, as well as with the fact that delegates to the Republican National Convention and delegates to the Democratic National Convention differ widely on the issues. Still others contend that the plurality system in which the winner is the candidate who gets the most votes, even if he or she does not receive a majority, is unfair to minor or third-party candidates. Perhaps, but Bill Clinton was twice (1992 and 1996) a popular plurality president. Besides, America has had little experience with other voting or party systems, and democracies that have proportional voting or multiparty systems have other shortcomings (such as unduly empowering small parties with extreme views).

WORLD WIDE WEB RESOURCES

Democratic National Committee: **www.democrats.org**

Republican National Committee: **www.rnc.org**

Green party: **www.greens.org**

Libertarian party: **www.lp.org**

Reform party: **www.reformparty.org**

SUGGESTED READINGS

Chambers, William Nisbet, and Walter Dean Burnham, eds. *The American Party Systems: Stages of Political Development.* 2nd ed. New York: Oxford University Press, 1975. Essays tracing the rise of the party system since the Founding.

Goldwin, Robert A., ed. *Political Parties in the Eighties.* Washington, D.C.: American Enterprise Institute, 1980. Essays evaluating parties and efforts at reform.

Key, V. O., Jr. *Southern Politics.* New York: Knopf, 1949. A classic account of the one-party South.

Mayhew, David R. *Placing Parties in American Politics.* Princeton, N.J.: Princeton University Press, 1986. A state-by-state description of state party organizations.

Nader, Ralph. *Crashing the Party: Taking on the Corporate Government in an Age of Surrender.* New York: St. Martin's Press, 2002. An impassioned attack on the two-party system by a well-known activist who ran for president as a minor-party candidate in 2000 and 2004.

Polsby, Nelson W. *Consequences of Party Reform.* New York: Oxford University Press, 1983. Fine analysis of how changed party rules have affected the parties and the government.

Ranney, Austin. *Curing the Mischiefs of Faction: Party Reform in America.* Berkeley: University of California Press, 1975. History and analysis of party "reforms," with special attention to the 1972 changes in the Democratic party rules.

Riordan, William L. *Plunkitt of Tammany Hall.* New York: Knopf, 1948. (First published in 1905.) Insightful account of how an old-style party boss operated.

Schattschneider, E. E. *Party Government.* New York: Holt, Rinehart and Winston, 1942. An argument for a more disciplined and centralized two-party system.

Shafer, Byron E. *Quiet Revolution: The Struggle for the Democratic Party and the Shaping of Post-Reform Politics.* New York: Russell Sage Foundation, 1983. Detailed, insightful history of how the Democratic party came to be reformed.

Sundquist, James L. *Dynamics of the Party System.* Rev. ed. Washington, D.C.: Brookings Institution, 1983. History of the party system, emphasizing the impact of issues on voting.

Wilson, James Q. *The Amateur Democrat.* Chicago: University of Chicago Press, 1962. Analysis of the issue-oriented political clubs that rose in the 1950s and 1960s.

CHAPTER 10

Elections and Campaigns

Presidential Versus Congressional Campaigns
Running for President ● Getting Elected to Congress

Primary Versus General Campaigns
Two Kinds of Campaign Issues ● Television, Debates, and Direct Mail

Money
The Sources of Campaign Money ● Campaign Finance Rules ● A Second Campaign Finance Law ● New Sources of Money ● Money and Winning

What Decides the Election?
Party ● Issues, Especially the Economy ● The Campaign ● Finding a Winning Coalition

The Effects of Elections on Policy

WHO GOVERNS?

1. How do American elections determine the kind of people who govern us?
2. What matters most in deciding who wins presidential and congressional elections?

TO WHAT ENDS?

1. Do elections make a real difference in what laws get passed?

*I*f you want to be elected to Congress or to the presidency, you must develop a game plan that is in tune with the unique legal, political, and financial realities of American politics. A plan that will work here would be useless in almost any other democratic nation; one that would work abroad would be useless here.

Elections have two crucial phases—getting nominated and getting elected. Getting nominated means getting your name on the ballot. In the great majority of states, winning your party's nomination for either the presidency or Congress requires an *individual* effort—*you* decide to run, *you* raise money, *you* and your friends collect signatures to get your name on the ballot, and *you* appeal to voters in primary elections on the basis of your personality and your definition of the issues. In most European nations winning your party's nomination for parliament involves an *organizational* decision—*the party* looks you over, *the party* decides whether to allow you to run, and *the party* puts your name on its list of candidates.

American political parties do play a role in determining the outcome of the final election, but even that role involves parties more as labels in the voters' minds than as organizations that get out the vote. By contrast, many other democratic nations conduct campaigns that are almost entirely a contest between parties as organizations. In Israel and the Netherlands the names of the candidates for the legislature do not even appear on the ballot; only the party names are listed there. And even where candidate names are listed, as in Great Britain, the voters tend to vote "Conservative" or "Labour" more than they vote for Smith or Jones. European nations (except France) do not have a directly elected president; instead the head of the government—the prime minister—is selected by the party that has won the most seats in parliament.

At one time parties played a much larger role in elections in the United States than they do now. Until well into this century they determined, or powerfully influenced, who got nominated. In the early nineteenth century the members of Congress from a given party would meet in a caucus to pick their presidential candidate. After these caucuses were replaced by national nominating conventions, the real power over presidential nominations was wielded by local party leaders, who came together (sometimes in the legendary "smoke-filled rooms") to choose the candidate, whom the rest of the delegates would then endorse.

231

Congressional candidates were often handpicked by powerful local party bosses. In the past people were much more likely to vote a straight party ticket than they are today.

Chapter 9 described the factors that weakened the parties' ability to control nominations. There is little chance that they will ever regain that control. Thus candidates are now pretty much on their own. So if you want to be a candidate, what do you do?

☆ Presidential Versus Congressional Campaigns

Presidential and congressional races differ in important ways. The most obvious, of course, is size: more voters participate in the former than the latter contests, and so presidential candidates must work harder and spend more. But there are some less obvious differences that are equally important.

First, presidential races are more competitive than those for the House of Representatives. In the thirty-five elections from 1932 to 2000 the Republicans won control of the House only six times (17 percent of the time); in the eighteen presidential elections during the same period the Republicans won the White House on eight occasions (44.5 percent of the time). In the typical presidential race the winner gets less than 55 percent of the two-party vote; in the typical House race, the **incumbent** wins with over 60 percent of the vote.

Second, a much smaller proportion of people vote in congressional races during off years (that is, when there is no presidential contest) than vote for president. This lower turnout (around 36 percent of the voting-age population) means that candidates in congressional races must be appealing to the more motivated and partisan voter.

Third, members of Congress can do things for their constituents that a president cannot. They take credit—sometimes deserved, sometimes not—for every grant, contract, bridge, canal, and highway

---

incumbent   The person already holding an elective office.

coattails   The alleged tendency of candidates to win more votes in an election because of the presence at the top of the ticket of a better-known candidate, such as the president.

---

that the federal government provides the district or state. They send letters (at the government's expense) to large fractions of their constituents and visit their districts every weekend. Presidents get little credit for district improvements and must rely on the mass media to communicate with voters.

Fourth, a candidate for Congress can deny that he or she is responsible for "the mess in Washington," even when the candidate is an incumbent. Incumbents tend to run as individuals, even to the point of denouncing the very Congress of which they are a part. An incumbent president can't get away with this; rightly or wrongly, he is often held responsible for whatever has gone wrong, not only in the government but in the nation as a whole.

These last three factors—low voter turnout, services to constituents, and the ability to duck responsibility—probably help explain why so high a percentage of congressional incumbents get reelected.

But they do not enjoy a completely free ride. Members of Congress who belong to the same party as the president often feel voters' anger about national affairs, particularly economic conditions. When the economy turns sour and a Republican is in the White House, Republican congressional candidates lose votes; if a Democrat is in the White House, Democratic congressional candidates lose votes.

At one time the **coattails** of a popular presidential candidate could help congressional candidates in his own party. But there has been a sharp decline in the value of presidential coattails; indeed, some scholars doubt that they still exist.

The net effect of all these factors is that, to a substantial degree, congressional elections have become independent of presidential ones. Though economic factors may still link the fate of a president and some members of his party, by and large the incumbent members of Congress enjoy enough of a cushion to protect them against whatever political storms engulf an unpopular president. This fact further reduces the meaning of party—members of Congress can get reelected even though their party's "leader" in the White House has lost popular support, and nonincumbent candidates for Congress may lose despite the fact that a very popular president from their party is in the White House.

Running for President

The first task facing anyone who wishes to be president is to get "mentioned" as someone who is of "presidential caliber." No one is quite sure why some people are mentioned and others are not. The journalist David Broder has suggested that somewhere there is "The Great Mentioner" who announces from time to time who is of presidential caliber (and only The Great Mentioner knows how big that caliber is).

But if The Great Mentioner turns out to be as unreal as the Easter Bunny, you have to figure out for yourself how to get mentioned. One way is to let it be known to reporters, "off the record," that you are thinking about running for president. Another is to travel around the country making speeches (Ronald Reagan, while working for General Electric, made a dozen or more speeches *a day* to audiences all over the country). Another way is to already have a famous name (John Glenn, the former astronaut, was in the public eye long before he declared for the presidency in 1984). Another way to get mentioned is to be identified with a major piece of legislation. Former Senator Bill Bradley of New Jersey was known as an architect of the Tax Reform Act of 1986; Representative Richard Gephardt of Missouri was known as an author of a bill designed to reduce foreign imports. Still another way is to be the governor of a big state. Former New York governors, such as Mario Cuomo, are often viewed as presidential prospects, partly because New York City is the headquarters of the television and publishing industries.

Once you are mentioned, it is wise to set aside a lot of time to run, especially if you are only "mentioned" as opposed to being really well known. Ronald Reagan devoted the better part of six years to running; Walter Mondale spent four years campaigning; Howard Baker resigned from the Senate in 1984 to prepare to run in 1988 (he finally dropped out of the race). However, most post-1988 candidates—senators Bob Dole, Tom Harkin, Bob Kerrey, Paul Simon, and John Kerry; governors Michael Dukakis, Bill Clinton, and George W. Bush; vice presidents George Bush and Al Gore; and House members Richard Gephardt and Jack Kemp—made the run while holding elective office.

Though presidential candidates come from various backgrounds, in general the voters tend to prefer those with experience as governors or military leaders rather than those who come immediately from Congress. Some candidates, such as John F. Kennedy, have been elected president directly after being a senator, but most are either war heroes (Dwight Eisenhower), former governors (George W. Bush, Bill Clinton, Ronald Reagan, Jimmy Carter, and Franklin

Political campaigns are hard work, even when you get to fly on the vice president's airplane.

D. Roosevelt) or former members of Congress who have already had experience as vice presidents (Gerald Ford, Richard Nixon, Lyndon Johnson, and Harry Truman).

■ **Money**   One reason why running takes so much time is that it takes so long to raise the necessary money and build up an organization of personal followers. As we shall see later in this chapter, federal law restricts the amount that any single individual can give a candidate to $2,000 in each election. (A **political action committee,** or PAC, which is a committee set up by and representing a corporation, labor union, or other special-interest group, can give up to $5,000.) Moreover, to be eligible for federal matching grants to pay for your primary campaign, you must first raise at least $5,000, in individual contributions of $250 or less, in each of twenty states.

■ **Organization**   Raising and accounting for this money requires a staff of fund-raisers, lawyers, and accountants. You also need a press secretary, a travel scheduler, an advertising specialist, a direct-mail company, and a pollster, all of whom must be paid, plus a

---

political action committee (PAC)   A committee set up by a corporation, labor union, or interest group that raises and spends campaign money from voluntary donations.

large number of volunteers in at least those states that hold early primary elections or party caucuses. These volunteers will brief you on the facts of each state, try to line up endorsements from local politicians and celebrities, and put together a group of people who will knock on doors, make telephone calls, organize receptions and meetings, and try to keep you from mispronouncing the name of the town in which you are speaking. Finally, you have to assemble advisers on the issues. These advisers will write "position papers" for you on all sorts of things that you are supposed to know about (but probably don't). Because a campaign is usually waged around a few broad themes, these position papers rarely get used or even read. The papers exist so that you can show important interest groups that you have taken "sound" positions, so that you can be prepared to answer tough questions, and so that journalists can look up your views on matters that may become topical.

■ **Strategy and Themes**   Every candidate picks a strategy for the campaign. In choosing one, much

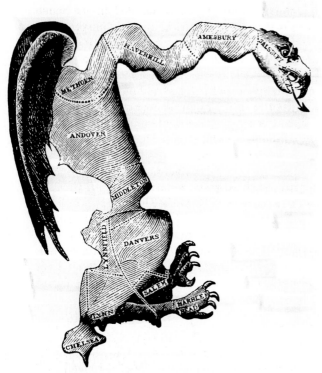

The original Gerrymander: Elbridge Gerry had this Massachusetts district drawn to ensure the election of a Republican. Cartoonist Elkanah Tinsdale in 1812 compared the district to a salamander and termed it a "Gerry-Mander."

depends on whether you are the incumbent. Incumbents must defend their records, like it or not. (An incumbent ran for president in 1964, 1972, 1976, 1980, 1984, 1992, 1996, and 2004.) The challenger attacks the incumbent. When there is no incumbent (as in 1960, 1968, 1988, and 2000), both candidates can announce their own programs; however, the candidate from the party that holds the White House must take, whether he thinks he deserves it or not, some of the blame for whatever has gone wrong in the preceding four years. Within these limits a strategy consists of the answers to questions about tone, theme, timing, and targets:

- What *tone* should the campaign have? Should it be a positive (build-me-up) or negative (attack-the-opponent) campaign? In 1988 George H.W. Bush began with a negative campaign; Michael Dukakis followed suit.
- What *theme* can I develop? A theme is a simple, appealing idea that can be repeated over and over again. For Jimmy Carter in 1976 it was "trust"; for Ronald Reagan in 1980 it was "competence" and in 1984 it was "it's morning again in America"; for Bush in 1988 it was "stay the course"; for Clinton in 1992 it was "we need to change;" for George W. Bush in 2000 it was "compassionate conservatism."
- What should be the *timing* of the campaign? If you are relatively unknown, you will have to put everything into the early primaries and caucuses, try to emerge a front-runner, and then hope for the best. If you are already the front-runner, you may either go for broke early (and try to drive out all your opponents) or hold back some reserves for a long fight.
- Whom should you *target*? Only a small percentage of voters change their vote from one election to the next. Who is likely to change this time—unemployed steelworkers? Unhappy farmers? People upset by inflation?

Getting Elected to Congress

A president cannot serve more than two terms, so at least once every eight years you have a chance of running against a nonincumbent; members of Congress can serve for an unlimited number of terms, and so chances are you will run against an incumbent. If you decide to run for the House, the odds are very much against you. Since 1962, over 90 percent of the House incumbents who sought reelection won it. In 2000, 394 reelection-seeking incumbents won, and only 9 lost.

But the incredible incumbency advantage enjoyed by modern-day House members is hardly the whole story of getting elected to Congress. Who serves in Congress, and what interests are represented there, is affected by how its members are elected. Each state is entitled to two senators, who serve six-year terms, and at least one representative, who serves a two-year term. How many more representatives a state has depends on its population; what local groups these representatives speak for depends in part on how the district lines are drawn.

The Constitution says very little about how representatives will be selected except to require that they be inhabitants of the states from which they are chosen. It says nothing about districts and originally left it up to the states to decide who would be eligible to vote for representatives. The size of the first House was set by the Constitution at sixty-five members, and the apportionment of the seats among the states was spelled out in Article I, section 2. From that point on, it has been up to Congress to decide how many representatives each state would have (provided that each had at least one).

Initially some states did not create congressional districts; all their representatives were elected at large. In other states representatives were elected from multimember as well as single-member districts. In time all states with more than one representative elected each from a single-member district. How those district boundaries were drawn, however, could profoundly affect the outcomes of elections. There were two problems. One was **malapportionment,** which results from having districts of very unequal size. If one district is twice as populous as another, twice as many votes are needed in the larger district to elect a representative. Thus a citizen's vote in the smaller district is worth twice as much as a vote in the larger.

The other problem was **gerrymandering**, which means drawing a district boundary in some bizarre or unusual shape to make it easy for the candidate of one party to win election in that district. In a state entitled to ten representatives, where half the voters are Democrats and half are Republicans, district lines could be drawn so that eight districts would have a slight majority of citizens from one party and two districts would have lopsided majorities from the other. Thus it can be made easy for one party to win eight of the ten seats.

Malapportionment and gerrymandering have been conspicuous features of American congressional politics. In 1962, for example, one district in Texas had nearly a million residents, while another had less than a quarter million. In California Democrats in control of the state legislature drew district lines in the early 1960s, so that two pockets of Republican strength in Los Angeles separated by many miles were connected by a thin strip of coastline. In this way most Republican voters were thrown into one district, while Democratic voters were spread more evenly over several.

Hence there are four problems to solve in deciding who gets represented in the House:

1. Establishing the total size of the House
2. Allocating seats in the House among the states
3. Determining the size of congressional districts within states
4. Determining the shape of those districts

By and large Congress has decided the first two questions, and the states have decided the last two—but under some rather strict Supreme Court rules.

In 1911 Congress decided that the House had become large enough and voted to fix its size at 435 members. There it has remained ever since (except for a brief period when it had 437 members owing to the admission of Alaska and Hawaii to the Union in 1959). Once the size was decided upon, it was necessary to find a formula for performing the painful task of apportioning seats among the states as they gained and lost population. The Constitution requires such reapportionment every ten years. A more or less automatic method was selected in 1929 based on a complex statistical system that has withstood decades of political and scientific testing. Under this system, since 1990 eighteen states have lost representation in the House and eleven have gained it. Florida and California posted the biggest

---

malapportionment   Drawing the boundaries of legislative districts so that they are unequal in population.

gerrymandering   Drawing the boundaries of legislative districts in bizarre or unusual shapes to favor one party.

Table 10.1   Changes in State Representation in the House of Representatives

States	Number of Seats			
	Before 1990 Census	After 1990 Census	After 2000 Census	Change
Gained Seats				
After Both 1990 and 2000 Census				
Arizona	6	8	10	+4
California	45	52	53	+8
Florida	15	23	25	+10
Georgia	10	11	13	+3
North Carolina	11	12	13	+2
Texas	27	30	32	+5
Lost Seats				
After Both 1990 and 2000 Census				
Illinois	22	20	19	−3
Michigan	18	16	15	−3
New York	34	31	29	−5
Ohio	21	19	18	−3
Pennsylvania	23	21	19	−4

Source: U.S. Bureau of the Census.

gains, while New York and Pennsylvania suffered the largest losses (see Table 10.1).

The states did little about malapportionment and gerrymandering until ordered to do so by the Supreme Court. In 1964 the Court ruled that the Constitution requires that districts be drawn so that, as nearly as possible, one person's vote would be worth as much as another's.[1] The Court rule, "one person, one vote," seems clear but in fact leaves a host of questions unanswered. How much deviation from equal size is allowable? Should other factors be considered besides population? (For example, a state legislature might want to draw district lines to make it easier for African Americans, Italian Americans, farmers, or some other group with a distinct interest to elect a representative; the requirement of exactly equal districts might make this impossible.) And the gerrymandering problem remains: districts of the

sophomore surge   An increase in the votes congressional candidates usually get when they first run for reelection.

same size can be drawn to favor one party or another. The courts have struggled to find answers to these questions, but they remain far from settled.

■ **Winning the Primary**   However the district lines are drawn, getting elected to Congress first requires getting one's name on the ballot. At one time the political parties nominated candidates and even printed ballots with the party slates listed on them. All the voter had to do was take the ballot of the preferred party and put it in the ballot box. Today, with rare exceptions, a candidate wins a party's nomination by gathering enough voter signatures to get on the ballot in a primary election, the outcome of which is often beyond the ability of political parties to influence. Candidates tend to form organizations of personal followings and win "their party's" nomination simply by getting more primary votes than the next candidate. It is quite unusual for an incumbent to lose a primary: from 1990 through 2002 only 10 percent of incumbent senators and fewer than 5 percent of incumbent representatives seeking reelection failed to win renomination in primaries. These statistics suggest how little opportunity parties have to control or punish their congressional members.

Most newly elected members become strong in their districts very quickly; this is called the **sophomore surge.** It is the difference between the votes candidates get the first time they are elected (and thus become freshman members) and the votes they get when they run for reelection (in hopes of becoming sophomore members). Before the 1960s House candidates did not do much better the second time they ran than the first. Beginning then, however, the sophomore surge kicked in, so that today freshman candidates running for reelection will get 8 to 10 percent more votes than when they were first elected. Senate candidates also benefit now from a sophomore surge, though to a lesser degree.

The reason for this surge is that members of Congress have figured out how to use their offices to run *personal* rather than party campaigns. They make use of free ("franked") mail, frequent trips home, radio and television broadcasts, and the distribution of services to their districts to develop among their constituents a good opinion of themselves, not their party. They also cater to their constituents' distrust of the federal government by promising to "clean things up" if reelected. They run *for* Congress by running *against* it.[2]

To the extent that they succeed, they enjoy great freedom in voting on particular issues and have less need to explain away votes that their constituents might not like. If, however, any single-issue groups are actively working in their districts for or against abortion, gun control, nuclear energy, or tax cuts, muting the candidates' voting record may not be possible.

■ **Staying in Office**   The way people get elected to Congress has two important effects. First, it produces legislators who are closely tied to local concerns (their districts, their states), and second, it ensures that party leaders will have relatively weak influence over them (because those leaders cannot determine who gets nominated for office).

The local orientation of legislators has some important effects on how policy is made. For example:

- Every member of Congress organizes his or her office to do as much as possible for people back home.
- If your representative serves on the House Transportation and Infrastructure Committee, your state has a much better chance of getting a new bridge or canal than if you do not have a representative on this committee.[3]
- If your representative serves on the House Appropriations Committee, your district is more likely to get approval for a federal grant to improve your water and sewage-treatment programs than if your representative does not serve on that committee.[4]

Former House Speaker Thomas P. "Tip" O'Neill had this in mind when he said, "All politics is local." Some people think that this localism is wrong; in their view members of Congress should do what is best for "the nation as a whole." This argument is about the role of legislators: are they supposed to be *delegates* who do what their district wants or *trustees* who use their best judgment on issues without regard to the preferences of their district?

Naturally most members are some combination of delegate and trustee, with the exact mix depending on the nature of the issue. But some, as we shall see, definitely lean one way or the other. All members want to be reelected, but "delegates" tend to value this over every other consideration and so seek out committee assignments and projects that will produce benefits for their districts. On the other hand, "trustees" will seek out committee assignments that give them a chance to address large questions, such as foreign affairs, that may have no implications at all for their districts.

☆ Primary Versus General Campaigns

When you run for federal office, you must run in two elections, not just one. The first consists of primary elections designed to choose each party's nominee, the second is the general election that picks the winner who will hold office. If you are running for president, some states, such as Iowa, hold caucuses instead of primary elections. A caucus is a meeting of people, often in an auditorium or church basement, where they vote on who they would like their party's nominee to be.

Each election or caucus attracts a different mix of voters. What may help you win a primary or a caucus may be very different from what will help you win the general election. To win a primary or a caucus you must mobilize political activists who will give money, do volunteer work, and attend local caucuses. As we saw in Chapters 7 and 8, activists are more ideologically stringent than the voters at large. To motivate these activists you must be more liberal (if you are a Democrat) in your tone and theme than are rank-and-file Democrats, or more conservative (if you are a Republican) than are rank-and-file Republicans.

Consider the caucuses held in Iowa in early February of a presidential election year. This is the first real test of the candidates vying for the nomination. Anyone who does poorly here is at a disadvantage, in terms of media attention and contributor interest, for the rest of the campaign.

The several thousand Iowans who participate in their parties' caucuses are not representative of the followers of their party in the state, much less nationally. In 1988 Senator Robert Dole came in first and evangelist Pat Robertson came in second in the Iowa Republican caucus, with Vice President George Bush finishing third. As it turned out, there was little support for Dole or Robertson in the rest of the country.

Democrats who participate in the Iowa caucus tend to be more liberal than Democrats generally.[5] Moreover, the way the caucuses are run is a far cry from how most elections are held. To vote in the Republican caucus, you need not prove you are a

★ HOW THINGS WORK ★

Qualifications for Entering Congress and Privileges of Being in Congress

Qualifications

Representative

- Must be twenty-five years of age (when seated, not when elected)
- Must have been a citizen of the United States for seven years
- Must be an inhabitant of the state from which elected (*Note*: Custom, but *not* the Constitution, requires that a representative live in the district that he or she represents.)

Senator

- Must be thirty years of age (when seated, not when elected)
- Must have been a citizen of the United States for nine years
- Must be an inhabitant of the state from which elected

Judging Qualifications

Each house is the judge of the "elections, returns, and qualifications" of its members. Thus Congress alone can decide disputed congressional elections. On occasion it has excluded a person from taking a seat on the grounds that the election was improper.

Either house can punish a member—by reprimand, for example—or, by a two-thirds vote, expel a member.

Privileges

Members of Congress have certain privileges, the most important of which, conferred by the Constitution, is that "for any speech or debate in either house they shall not be questioned in any other place." This doctrine of "privileged speech" has been interpreted by the Supreme Court to mean that members of Congress cannot be sued or prosecuted for anything that they say or write in connection with their legislative duties.

When Senator Mike Gravel read the Pentagon Papers—some then-secret government documents about the Vietnam War—into the *Congressional Record* in defiance of a court order restraining their publication, the Court held that this was "privileged speech" and beyond challenge [*Gravel v. United States*, 408 U.S. 606 (1972)]. But when Senator William Proxmire issued a press release critical of a scientist doing research on monkeys, the Court decided that the scientist could sue him for libel because a press release was not part of the legislative process [*Hutchinson v. Proxmire*, 443, U.S. 111 (1979)].

Republican or even a voter. The Democratic caucus is not an election at all; instead a person supporting a certain candidate stands in one corner of the room with people who also support him, while those supporting other candidates stand in other corners with other groups. There is a lot of calling back and forth, intended to persuade people to leave one group and join another. No group with fewer than 15 percent of the people in attendance gets to choose any delegates, so people in these small groups then go to other, larger ones. It is a cross between musical chairs and fraternity pledge week.

Suppose you are a Democrat running for president and you do well in the Iowa caucus. Suppose you go on to win your party's nomination. Now you have to go back to Iowa to campaign for votes in the general election. Between 1940 and 2004 Iowa has voted Republican in every presidential election but six (1948, 1964, 1988, 1992, 1996, and 2000). Your Republican opponent is not going to let you forget all of the liberal slogans you uttered nine months before. The Republican candidate faces the mirror image of this problem—sounding very conservative to get support from Republican activists in states such as Massachusetts and New York and then having to defend those speeches when running against his Democratic opponent in those states.

The problem is not limited to Iowa but exists in every state where activists are more ideologically polarized than the average voter. To get activist support for the nomination, candidates move to the ideological extremes; to win the general election, they try to move back to the ideological center. The typical voter looks at the results and often decides that neither candidate appeals to him or her very much, and so casts a "clothespin vote" (see the box on this page).

Early in the 2004 presidential caucuses and primaries, John Kerry claimed that he was an opponent of the American invasion of Iraq in order to defeat Howard Dean, the Vermont governor who seemed to be capturing the antiwar vote among Democrats. But after he won his party's nomination, Kerry backed away from an antiwar stance in order to be more attractive to centrist voters. He had learned a lesson that George McGovern did not understand in 1972. McGovern maintained his liberal views on the war in Vietnam, decriminalizing marijuana, and providing amnesty for draft dodgers.[6] His opponent, Richard Nixon, defeated him easily by taking more centrist positions.

Two Kinds of Campaign Issues

In election campaigns there are two different kinds of issues.[7] A **position issue** is one in which the rival candidates have opposing views on a question that also divides the voters. For example, in the 2004 election George W. Bush wanted to let people put some of their Social Security money into private savings accounts; John Kerry opposed this.

Since 1860 many of the great party realignments have been based on differing position issues. After the Civil War the question was whether African Americans should be slaves or free. In the 1890s it was whether tariffs should be high or low and whether the dollar should be made cheaper. In the 1960s it was whether broad new civil rights legislation was needed.

But sometimes voters are not divided on important issues. Instead the question is whether a candidate fully supports the public's view on a matter about which nearly everyone agrees. These are called **valence issues.** For example, everybody wants a strong economy and low crime rates, and so no candidate favors high unemployment or more crime. What voters look for on valence issues is which candidate seems most closely linked to a universally shared view.

Valence issues are quite common. In 1968 Richard Nixon seemed to be more supportive of anticrime measures than his rival; in 1976 Jimmy Carter seemed more likely to favor honesty in government

☆ POLITICALLY SPEAKING ☆

Clothespin Vote

The vote cast by a person who does not like either candidate and so votes for the less objectionable of the two, putting a clothespin over his or her nose to keep out the unpleasant stench.

than his opponent; in 1984 Ronald Reagan seemed more closely identified with a strong economy than his opponent; in 1988 George H.W. Bush seemed more closely linked to patriotism than his opponent. Notice that we have said "seemed." This is how voters perceived the winners; it does not mean that the opponents favored crime, corruption, unemployment, or anti-Americanism.

In 1992 Bill Clinton was beset with charges that he was guilty of dodging the draft, marital infidelity, and smoking pot. But his strategists decided to focus the campaign on the valence issue of the economy, and they went about rescuing Clinton from the other criticisms. One observer later reported, "Retooling the image of a couple who had already been in the public eye for five battering months required a campaign of

position issues An issue about which the public is divided and rival candidates or political parties adopt different policy positions.

valence issue An issue about which the public is united and rival candidates or political parties adopt similar positions in hopes that each will be thought to best represent those widely shared beliefs.

T·R·I·V·I·A
....

Elections

Only two men to have been elected president by the House of Representatives after failing to win a majority in the electoral college	Thomas Jefferson (1800) and John Quincy Adams (1824)
Only Democratic senator to be the running mate of a Republican presidential candidate	Andrew Johnson (1864)
Candidates for president who received more popular votes than their opponents but were not elected	Grover Cleveland and Al Gore got more popular votes but fewer electoral votes than their opponents
President who won the largest percentage of the popular vote	Lyndon B. Johnson, 61.7 percent (1964)
Only person to serve as vice president and president without having been elected to either post	Gerald Ford (1973–1976)
President who won the most electoral votes	Ronald Reagan (525 in 1984)
First woman to run for national office on a major-party ticket	Geraldine Ferraro (Democratic candidate for vice president, 1984)

behavior modification and media manipulation so elaborate that its outline ran to fourteen single-spaced pages."[8] Bill Clinton and his wife, Hillary, made joint appearances on television during which they demonstrated their affection for each other. The plan even called for staging an event where Bill Clinton and his daughter would surprise Hillary Clinton on Mother's Day.[9]

The 2004 campaign relied on both valence issues (Bush and Kerry supported military defense while differing on how to recruit allies) and position issues (Bush supported his tax cuts while Kerry favored repealing them for people earning over $200,000 a year).

Campaigns have usually combined both position and valence questions, but the latter have increased in importance in recent years. This has happened in part because presidential campaigns are now conducted largely on television, where it is important to project popular symbols and manipulate widely admired images. Candidates try to show that they are likable, and they rely on televised portraits of their similarity to ordinary people.

Television, Debates, and Direct Mail

Once campaigns mostly involved parades, big rallies, "whistle-stop" train tours, and shaking hands outside factory gates and near shopping centers. All of this still goes on, but increasingly presidential and senatorial candidates (and those House candidates with television stations in their districts) use broadcasting.

There are two ways to use television—by running paid advertisements and by getting on the nightly news broadcasts. In the language of campaigners, short television ads are called *spots,* and a campaign activity that appears on a news broadcast is called a *visual.* Much has been written about the preparation of spots, usually under titles such as "the selling of the president" or "packaging the candidate" (and mostly by advertising executives, who are not especially known for underestimating their own influence). No doubt spots can have an important effect in some cases. A little-known candidate can increase his or her visibility by frequent use of spots (this is what Jimmy Carter did in the 1976 presidential primaries).

The effect of television advertising on general elections is probably a good deal less than its effect on primaries; indeed, as we shall see in Chapter 12, most scientific studies of television's influence on voting decisions have shown that either it has no effect or the effect is subtle and hard to detect. Nor is it surprising that this should be the case. In a general election, especially one for a high-visibility office (such as president or governor), the average voter has many sources of information—his or her own party or ideological preference, various kinds of advertising, the opinions of friends and family, and newspaper and magazine stories. Furthermore, both sides will use TV spots; if well done, they are likely to cancel each other out. In short, it is not yet clear that a gullible public is being sold a bill of goods by slick Madison Avenue advertisers, whether the goods are automobiles or politicians.

Visuals are a vital part of any major campaign effort because, unlike spots, they cost the campaign little and, as "news," they may have greater credibility with the viewer. A visual is a brief, filmed episode

☆ HOW THINGS WORK ☆

Kinds of Elections

There are two kinds of elections in the United States: general and primary. A **general election** is used to fill an elective office. A **primary election** is used to select a party's candidates for an elective office, though in fact those who vote in a primary election may not consider themselves party members. Some primaries are closed. In a **closed primary** you must declare in advance (sometimes several weeks in advance) that you are a registered member of the political party in whose primary you wish to vote. About forty states have closed primaries.

Other primaries are open. In an **open primary** you can decide when you enter the voting booth which party's primary you wish to participate in. You are given every party's ballot; you may vote on one. Idaho, Michigan, Minnesota, Montana, North Dakota, Utah, Vermont, and Wisconsin have open primaries. A variant on the open primary is the **blanket** (or "free love") **primary**—in the voting booth you mark a ballot that lists the candidates of all the parties, and thus you can help select the Democratic candidate for one office and the Republican candidate for another. Alaska and Washington have blanket primaries.

The differences among these kinds of primaries should not be exaggerated, for even the closed primary does not create any great barrier for a voter who wishes to vote in the Democratic primary in one election and the Republican in another. Some states also have a **runoff primary**: if no candidate gets a majority of the votes, there is a runoff between the two with the most votes. Runoff primaries are common in the South.

A special kind of primary, a presidential primary, is that used to pick delegates to the presidential nominating conventions of the major parties. Presidential primaries come in a bewildering variety. A simplified list looks like this:

- **Delegate selection only** Only the names of prospective delegates to the convention appear on the ballot. They may or may not indicate their presidential preferences.
- **Delegate selection with advisory presidential preference** Voters pick delegates and indicate their preferences among presidential candidates. The delegates are not legally bound to observe these preferences.
- **Binding presidential preference** Voters indicate their preferred presidential candidates. Delegates must observe these preferences, at least for a certain number of convention ballots. The delegates may be chosen in the primary or by a party convention.

In 1981 the Supreme Court ruled that political parties, not state legislatures, have the right to decide how delegates to national conventions are selected. Thus Wisconsin could not retain an open primary if the national Democratic party objected (*Democratic Party v. La Follette,* 101 Sup. Ct. 1010, 1981). Now the parties can insist that only voters who declare themselves Democrats or Republicans can vote in presidential primaries. The Supreme Court's ruling may have relatively little practical effect, however, since the "declaration" might occur only an hour or a day before the election.

general election An election held to choose which candidate will hold office.

primary election An election held to choose candidates for office.

closed primary A primary election in which voting is limited to already registered party members.

open primary A primary election in which voters may choose in which party to vote as they enter the polling place.

blanket primary A primary election in which each voter may vote for candidates from both parties.

runoff primary A second primary election held when no candidate wins a majority of the votes in the first primary.

showing the candidate doing something that a reporter thinks is newsworthy. Simply making a speech, unless the speech contains important new facts or charges, is often thought by TV editors to be uninteresting: television viewers are not attracted by pictures of "talking heads," and in the highly competitive world of TV, audience reactions are all-important determinants of what gets on the air. Knowing this, campaign managers will strive to have their candidates do something visually interesting every day, no later than 3:00 P.M. (if the visual is to be on the 6:00 P.M. news)—talk to elderly folks in a nursing home, shake hands with people waiting in an unemployment line, or sniff the waters of a polluted lake. Obviously all these efforts are for naught if a TV camera crew is not around; great pains are therefore taken to schedule these visuals at times and in places that make it easy for the photographers to be present.

Ironically, visuals—and television newscasts generally—may give the viewer less information than commercial spots. This, of course, is the exact opposite of what many people believe. It is commonplace to deplore political advertising, especially the short spot, on the grounds that it is either devoid of information or manipulative, and to praise television news programs, especially longer debates and interviews, because they are informative and balanced. In fact the best research we have so far suggests that the reverse is true: news programs covering elections tend to convey very little information (they often show scenes of crowds cheering or candidates shouting slogans) and make little or no impression on viewers, if indeed they are watched at all. Paid commercials, on the other hand, especially the shorter spots, often contain a good deal of information that is seen, remembered, and evaluated by a public that is quite capable of distinguishing between fact and humbug.[10]

A special kind of television campaigning is the campaign debate. Incumbents or well-known candidates have little incentive to debate their opponents; by so doing, they only give more publicity to lesser-known rivals. Despite the general rule among politicians never to help an opponent, Vice President Nixon debated the less-well-known John Kennedy in 1960, and President Gerald Ford debated the less-well-known Jimmy Carter in 1976. Nixon and Ford lost. Lyndon Johnson would not debate Barry Goldwater in 1964, nor would Nixon debate Humphrey in 1968 or McGovern in 1972. Johnson and Nixon won. Carter debated the equally well-known Reagan in 1980 (but refused to join in a three-way debate

with Reagan and John Anderson). Carter lost. It is hard to know what effect TV debates have on election outcomes, but poll data suggest that in 1980 voters who watched the debates were reassured by Reagan's performance; after the second debate with Carter, he took a lead in the polls that he never relinquished.[11] In 1984 most people thought that Mondale did better than Reagan in the first debate, but there is little evidence that the debate affected the outcome of the election. In 1992 and 1996 Clinton was probably the better debater, but he most likely would have won even if he had stumbled.

In 2004 George W. Bush and John F. Kerry held three televised debates. Opinions differ as to who did better, but there is little evidence that these encounters affected the election results.

Though TV visuals and debates are free, they are also risky. The risk is the slip of the tongue. You may have spent thirty years of your life in unblemished public service, you may have thought through your position on the issues with great care, you may have rehearsed your speeches until your dog starts to howl, but just make one verbal blunder and suddenly the whole campaign focuses on your misstep. In 1976 President Ford erroneously implied that Poland was not part of the Soviet bloc. For days the press dwelt on this slip. His opponent, Jimmy Carter, admitted in a *Playboy* interview that he had sometimes had lust in his heart. It is hard to imagine anyone who has not, but apparently presidents are supposed to be above that sort of thing. In 1980 Ronald Reagan said that trees cause pollution—oops, here we go again.

Because of the fear of a slip, because the voters do not want to hear long, fact-filled speeches about complex issues, and because general-election campaigns are fights to attract the centrist voter, the candidates will rely on a stock speech that sets out the campaign theme as well as on their ability to string together several proven applause-getting lines. For reporters covering the candidate every day, it can be a mind-numbing experience. Nelson Rockefeller spoke so often of the "brotherhood of man and the fatherhood of God" that the reporters started referring to it as his BOMFOG speech. Occasionally this pattern is interrupted by a "major" address—that is, a carefully composed talk on some critical issue, usually delivered before a live audience and designed to provide issue-related stories for the reporters to write.

If you dislike campaign oratory, put yourself in the candidate's shoes for a moment. Every word you say will be scrutinized, especially for slips of the tongue. Interest group leaders and party activists will react sharply to any phrase that departs from their preferred policies. Your opponent stands ready to pounce on any error of fact or judgment. You must give countless speeches every day. The rational reaction to this state of affairs is to avoid controversy, stick to prepared texts and tested phrases, and shun anything that sounds original (and hence untested). You therefore wind up trying to sell yourself as much as or more than your ideas. Voters may *say* that they admire a blunt, outspoken person, but in a tough political campaign they would probably find such bluntness a little unnerving.

Television is the most visible example of modern technology's effect on campaigns. Since 1960 presidential elections have been contested largely through television. Without television the campaign waged in 1992 by independent candidate Ross Perot might not have happened at all. Perot launched his candidacy with successive appearances on Cable News Network's call-in program "Larry King Live," and he bought several half-hour chunks of television time to air his views on the federal budget deficit. In early October, before the first of three televised debates featuring Perot, Republican incumbent George H.W. Bush, and Democratic challenger Bill Clinton, most national polls showed Perot with only 10 percent of the vote. But after the debates Perot's support in the polls doubled, and he ended up with about 19 percent of the votes cast on election day.

In 1996 the big television networks agreed to make some free television time available to the major presidential candidates. The Federal Communications Commission approved the plan to limit the free TV to "major" candidates, thus denying it to minor third-party nominees.

Less visible than television but perhaps just as important is the Internet. The computer makes possible sophisticated direct-mail campaigning, and this in turn makes it possible for a candidate to address specific appeals to particular voters easily and rapidly solicit campaign contributions. In the 2004 presidential campaign Vermont Governor Howard Dean, at first a largely unknown person, raised a huge amount of money from Internet appeals in which he emphasized his opposition to our war in Iraq. Other candidates will no doubt do the same. However, the Internet lends itself to ideological appeals that motivate small contributions, and not every candidate will want to make such arguments.

In the 1888 presidential campaign, supporters of Benjamin Harrison rolled a huge ball covered with campaign slogans across the country. The gimmick, first used in 1840, gave rise to the phrase "keep the ball rolling."

Whereas television is heard by everybody—and thus leads the candidate using it to speak in generalities to avoid offending anyone—direct mail is aimed at particular groups (college students, Native Americans, bankers, autoworkers), to whom specific views can be

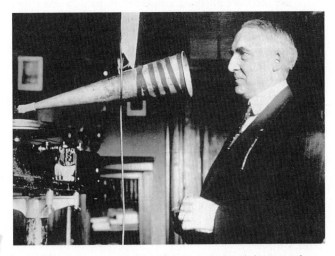

Candidates first made phonographic recordings of their speeches in 1908. Warren G. Harding is shown here recording a speech during the 1920 campaign.

John F. Kennedy and Richard Nixon debate during the 1960 presidential campaign.

expressed with much less risk of offending someone. So important are the lists of names of potential contributors to whom a computer may send appeals that a prized resource of any candidate, guarded as if it were a military secret, is "The List." Novices in politics must slowly develop their own lists or beg sympathetic incumbents for a peek at theirs.

The chief consequence of the new style of campaigning is not, as some think, that it is more manipulative than old-style campaigning (picnics with free beer and $5 bills handed to voters can be just as manipulative as TV ads); rather it is that running campaigns has become divorced from the process of governing. Previously the party leaders who ran the campaigns would take part in the government once it was elected, and since they were *party* leaders, they had to worry about getting their candidate *re*elected. Modern political consultants take no responsibility for governing, and by the time the next election rolls around, they may be working for someone else.

☆ Money

All these consultants, TV ads, and computerized mailings cost money—lots of it. A powerful California politician once observed that "money is the mother's milk of politics," and many people think

that our democracy is drowning in it. In 2002 winning House and Senate candidates spent a combined total of over half a billion dollars (see Figure 10.1). When that kind of money is spent, many people will cynically conclude that elections are being bought and sold. Clever television producers are being paid huge sums, so the theory goes, to put on TV ads that sell candidates as if they were boxes of soap.

But matters are a good deal more complicated and less sinister than the popular theory supposes. Money is important in politics as in everything else, but it is not obvious that the candidates with the most money always win or that the donors of the money buy big favors in exchange for their big bucks. In Chapter 11 we will consider what, if anything, interest groups get for the money they give to politicians, and in Chapter 12 we shall summarize what we know about the effects of television advertising on elections. Here let us try to answer four questions: Where does campaign money come from? What rules govern how it is raised and spent? What has been the effect of campaign finance reform? What does campaign spending buy?

The Sources of Campaign Money

Presidential candidates get part of their money from private donors and part from the federal government; congressional candidates get all of their money from

Figure 10.1   The Cost of Winning

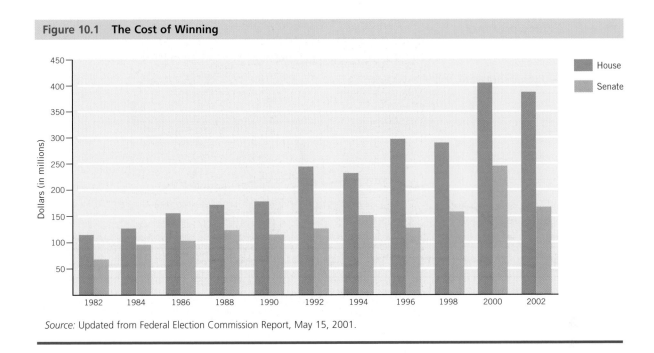

Source: Updated from Federal Election Commission Report, May 15, 2001.

private sources. In the presidential primaries, candidates raise money from private citizens and interest groups. The federal government will provide matching funds, dollar for dollar, for all monies raised from individual donors who contribute no more than $250. Since every candidate wants as much of this "free" federal money as possible, each has an incentive to raise money from small, individual givers. (To prove they are serious candidates, they must first raise $5,000 in each of twenty states from such small contributors.) The government also gives a lump-sum grant to each political party to help pay the costs of its nominating convention. In the gener-

al election the government pays all the costs of each candidate, up to a limit set by law (in 2004 that limit was $74.4 million for each major candidate).

Congressional candidates get no government funds; all their money must come out of their own pockets or be raised from individuals, interest groups (PACs), or the political parties. Contrary to what many people think, most of that money comes—and has always come—from individual donors (see Table 10.2). Because the rules sharply limit how much any individual can give, these donors tend not to be fat cats but people of modest means who contribute $100 or $200 per person.

Table 10.2   Sources of Campaign Funds for All House and Senate Candidates in 2001–2002, by Party (in Millions)

Sources	Incumbents	Challengers	Open Seats
Individuals			
Democrats	$132.7	$47.1	$40.2
Republicans	125.5	44.1	55.8
PACs			
Democrats	93.2	13.6	14.5
Republicans	100.1	8.8	20.0

Source: Calculated from Harold W. Stanley and Richard G. Niemi, *Vital Statistics on American Politics, 2003–2004* (Washington, D.C.: Congressional Quarterly Press, 2003), Table 2.6.

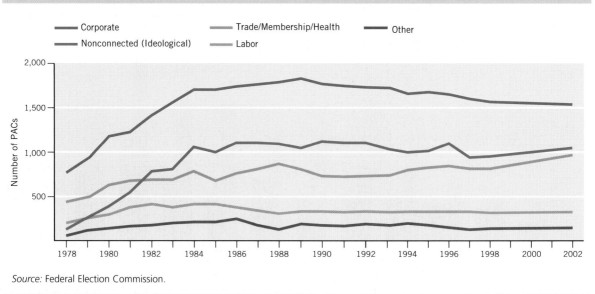

Figure 10.2   Growth of PACs

Source: Federal Election Commission.

Since the typical individual contribution is very small (and in no case larger than $2,000), some candidates have turned to rock bands and movie stars to put on benefit performances. If five thousand people will each pay $75 for a performance by U2, a lot of money can be raised in a hurry.

The most a PAC can give a candidate in any election is $5,000, but the typical PAC does not donate anything approaching the maximum amount; usually it gives a few hundred dollars to each candidate it supports.

These figures conceal some important differences among kinds of candidates, however. As Table 10.2 shows, incumbent members of Congress running for reelection get over half of their money from PACs and spend next to nothing from loans. Their challengers, by contrast, spend only half as much and are able to get only one-eighth of that from PACs. Challengers have to borrow much more money. As we shall see in the next section, these money problems weaken the ability of challengers to mount effective campaigns. Three states, Arizona, Maine, and Vermont, now fund campaigns with public money, but there is as yet no solid evidence about what difference it makes, or how.

Campaign Finance Rules

During the 1972 presidential election, men hired by President Nixon's campaign staff broke into the headquarters of the Democratic National Committee in the Watergate office building. They were caught by an alert security guard. The subsequent investigation disclosed that the Nixon people had engaged in dubious or illegal money-raising schemes, including taking large sums from wealthy contributors in exchange for appointing them to ambassadorships. Many individuals and corporations were indicted for making illegal donations (since 1925 it had been against the law for corporations or labor unions to contribute money to candidates, but the law had been unenforceable). Some of the accused had given money to Democratic candidates as well as to Nixon.

When the break-in was discovered, the Watergate scandal unfolded. It had two political results: President Nixon was forced to resign, and a new campaign finance law was passed.

Under the new law, individuals could not contribute more than $1,000 to a candidate during any single election. Corporations and labor unions had for many decades been prohibited from spending money on campaigns, but the new law created a substitute: political action committees (PACs). A PAC must have at least fifty members (all of whom enroll voluntarily), give to at least five federal candidates, and must not give more than $5,000 to any candidate in any election or more than $15,000 per year to any political party.

In addition, the law made federal tax money available to help pay for presidential primary campaigns

★ HOW THINGS WORK ★

Major Federal Campaign Finance Rules

General

- All federal election contributions and expenditures are reported to a Federal Election Commission.
- All contributions over $100 must be disclosed, with name, address, and occupation of contributor.
- No *cash* contributions over $100 or foreign contributions.
- No ceiling on how much candidates may spend out of their own money (unless they accept federal funding for a presidential race).

Individual Contributions

- An individual may not give more than $2,000 to any candidate in any election.
- An individual may not make federal political gifts exceeding $95,000 every two years, of which only $37,500 may go to candidates.

Political Action Committees (PACs)

- Each corporation, union, or association may establish one.
- A PAC must register six months in advance, have at least fifty contributors, and give to at least five candidates.
- PAC contributions may not exceed $5,000 per candidate per election, or $15,000 to a national political party.

Ban on Soft Money

- No corporation or union may give money from its own treasury to any national political party.

Independent Expenditures

- Corporations, unions, and associations may not use their own money to fund "electioneering communications" that refer to clearly identified candidates sixty days before a general election or thirty days before a primary contest.
- PACs may fund electioneering communications up to their expenditure limits.

Presidential Primaries

- Federal matching funds can be given to match individual contributions of $250 or less.
- To be eligible, a candidate must raise $5,000 in each of twenty states in contributions of $250 or less.

Presidential Election

- The federal government will pay all campaign costs (up to a legal limit) of major-party candidates and part of the cost of minor-party candidates (those winning between 5 and 25 percent of the vote).

---

and for paying all of the campaign costs of a major-party candidate and a fraction of the costs of a minor-party candidate in a presidential general election.

The new law helped increase the amount of money spent on elections and, in time, changed the way money was spent. There are now more than four thousand PACs (see Figure 10.2). In 2002 they gave over $250 million to congressional candidates. But PACs are not a dominant influence on candidates because they in fact give rather little (often no more than $500). A small contribution is enough to ensure that a phone call to a member of Congress from a PAC sponsor will be returned but not enough,

in most cases, to guarantee that the member will act as the PAC wishes.

Moreover, most money for congressional candidates still comes from individuals. But since the limit until 2002 was $1,000 per election (a limit set in the early 1970s), candidates had to devise clever ways of reaching a lot of individuals in order to raise the amount of money they needed. This usually meant direct mail and telephone solicitations. If you are bothered by constant appeals for campaign funds, remember—that's what the law requires.

By contrast, when George McGovern ran against Richard Nixon in 1972, he was chiefly supported by

The 2004 Election

The 2004 election revealed an electorate as deeply divided as it was in 2000. But unlike 2000, when Bush won fewer popular votes than Al Gore and the contest did not end until after a long recount in Florida and a major Supreme Court decision, Bush in 2004 won many more popular votes than did John Kerry, carried Florida without any chance of a recount, and obtained 286 electoral votes.

With only a few exceptions, Bush and Kerry in 2004 won the same states that Bush and Gore had won in 2000. There were three differences: Kerry won New Hampshire and Bush carried Iowa and New Mexico. The similarity between the two elections has led people to refer to "Red states" that Republicans carry and "Blue states" that the Democrats win. In the map on page 249, we show the split between Red and Blue *counties* rather than states because in many Red and Blue states the opponent won several counties. The Democrats dominate New England, the bigger cities in the Midwest, and the coastal areas on California, Oregon, and Washington; the Republicans carried almost everything else.

Bush was helped by the assignment of electoral votes to the states following the 2000 Census. In 2004 he gained seven more electoral votes by carrying the same states he had won in 2000.

In 2004 we were at war in Iraq. Though we had easily conquered the country from the Saddam Hussein dictatorship, dissident elements in Iraq kept relentlessly attacking American troops as well as other foreigners and members of the new Iraq government. American experience over many decades has shown that though the public will support a war, that backing weakens when we seem stalemated. Moreover, many Kerry supporters never wanted us to fight in Iraq at all and deeply distrusted Bush because they thought him to be "too religious."

John Kerry had his own troubles. Not only was he trying to unseat a president during wartime, his own experiences as a naval officer in Vietnam became controversial. A group of naval veterans (the "Swift Boat Veterans for Truth") with experience in Vietnam attacked him for not having won his medals fairly and for his having bitterly criticized the American military in testimony he gave to the Congress after his return. For many weeks, the only campaign issue seemed to be whether Kerry had behaved honorably.

The campaign was especially intense, leading to a very high turnout. Almost 60 percent of the voting-age population cast ballots, the highest since 1968. The big increase in the number of registered voters and the massive get-out-the-vote drives probably helped Bush more than Kerry. In every state but two (South Dakota and Vermont), Bush increased his share of the vote over what he had received four years earlier.

Bush won the votes of men, whites, conservatives, Protestants, married couples, the especially religious, military veterans, gun owners, strong critics of abortion, voters deeply concerned about the war against terrorism, opponents of same-sex marriages, and people worried about taxes and moral values and who approved of Bush's tax cuts. Kerry won a majority of the votes of women, blacks, liberals, union members, Jews, unmarried voters, secularists, gays, people favoring same-sex marriages, strong supporters of abortion, opponents of our war in Iraq, and people who worried about education and the economy and were critics of the tax cuts.

If there was any one decisive issue, it was voters' concerns about terrorism and national security. Opponents of the war in Iraq supported Kerry, but for people who worried about terrorism, the overwhelming majority supported Bush.

In the struggle to control Congress, the Republicans did better than the Democrats, increasing their majority in the House by at least three seats and in the Senate by four seats. In the Senate campaigns, the Republicans increased their hold on the South by winning seats in Louisiana, Georgia, and North and South Carolina. Perhaps the Republicans' most dramatic win was the defeat of Senate minority leader Tom Daschle of South Dakota. He had served in Congress for over a quarter of a century, but lost to John Thune.

People paid a great deal of attention to the 2004 election. When pollsters asked the voters if they were "very interested" in the election, a higher percentage said "yes" than in any election since at least 1996. In 1996 and 2000, 17 percent of the voters made up their minds just a few days before the election; in 2004, only 6 percent waited that long.[12]

The Election of 2004, by County

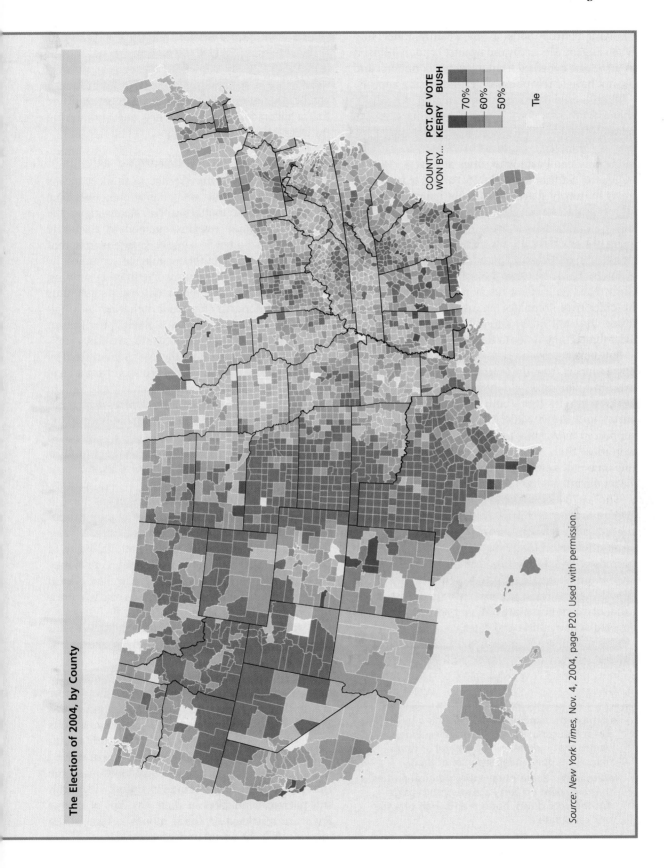

Source: New York Times, Nov. 4, 2004, page P20. Used with permission.

the large contributions of one wealthy donor, and when Eugene McCarthy ran against Lyndon Johnson in 1968, he benefited from a few big donations and did not have to rely on massive fund-raising appeals.

Presidential candidates are treated differently than congressional candidates. The former may get money directly from the federal government. In the primary campaign, candidates can receive *matching funds.* Any candidate who raises at least $5,000 in individual contributions of $250 or less from people living in twenty states is eligible for matching funds. Once eligible, a candidate gets federal money to match, dollar for dollar, what he or she has raised in contributions of $250 or less. But a presidential candidate can decide to forgo federal primary funding and raise his or her own money. In 2000 George W. Bush relied entirely on his own fund-raising, while his chief rival, John McCain, used federal matching funds. In 2004 Bush, Kerry, and Dean all declined federal matching funds in the primary elections.

If you are a minor-party candidate, you can get some support from the federal government provided you have won at least 5 percent of the vote in the last election. In 2000, both Pat Buchanan (Reform party) and Ralph Nader (Green party) got partial support from Washington because their parties had won more than 5 percent of the vote in 1996. But this time out, neither party won that much, and so Nader did not get federal support in 2004.

The 1973 campaign finance law produced two problems. The first was **independent expenditures.** A PAC, a corporation, or a labor union could spend whatever it wanted supporting or opposing a candidate, so long as this spending was "independent," that is, not coordinated with or made at the direction of the candidate's wishes. Simply put, independent expenditures are ordinary advertising that is directed at or against candidates.

The second was **soft money.** Under the law, individuals, corporations, labor unions, and other groups could give unlimited amounts of money to political parties provided the money was not used to back candidates by name. But the money could be used in ways that helped candidates by financing voter-registration and get-out-the-vote drives. Over half a billion dollars in soft money was spent during the 2000 presidential campaign.

A Second Campaign Finance Law

Reform is a tricky word. We like to think it means fixing something that has gone wrong. But some reforms can make matters worse. For example, the campaign finance reforms enacted in the early 1970s helped matters in some ways by ensuring that all campaign contributors would be identified by name. But they made things worse in other ways by, for example, requiring candidates to raise small sums from many donors. This made it harder for challengers to run (incumbents are much better known and raise more money) and easier for wealthy candidates to run because, under the law as interpreted by the Supreme Court, candidates can spend as much of their own money as they want.

After the 2000 campaign, a strong movement developed in Congress to reform the reforms of the 1970s. The result was the Bipartisan Campaign Finance Reform Act of 2002, which passed easily in the House and Senate and was signed by President Bush.

The law made three important changes. First, it banned "soft money" contributions to national political parties from corporations and unions. After the federal elections in 2002, no national party or party committee can accept soft money. Any money the national parties get must come from "hard money"—that is, individual donations or PAC contributions as limited by federal law.

Second, the limit on individual contributions was raised from $1,000 per candidate per election to $2,000.

Third, "independent expenditures" by corporations, labor unions, trade associations, and (under certain circumstances) nonprofit organizations are sharply restricted. Now none of these organizations can use their own money to refer to a clearly identified federal candidate in any advertisement during the sixty days preceding a general election or the thirty days preceding a primary contest. (PACs can still refer to candidates in their ads, but of course PACs are restricted to "hard money"—that is, the amount they can spend under federal law.)

---

independent expenditures   Spending by political action committees, corporations, or labor unions that is done to help a party or candidate but is done independently of them.

soft money   Funds obtained by political parties that are spent on party activities, such as get-out-the-vote drives, but not on behalf of a specific candidate.

The Florida Vote-Count Controversy

The presidential election of 2000 was decided in favor of George W. Bush on December 12, 2000, when the U.S. Supreme Court suspended the counting of disputed ballots in Florida as ordered by the Florida Supreme Court. When the recounting was halted, Bush was ahead by 537 votes. But would Bush have won Florida and the election anyway?

According to an exhaustive nine-month analysis of 175,010 Florida ballots conducted by eight media organizations in 2001 with the help of the National Opinion Research Center (NORC) at the University of Chicago, the answer is yes. The analysis suggested that if the U.S. Supreme Court had allowed the vote counting ordered by the Florida Supreme Court to continue, Bush still would have won Florida by 493 votes, rather than by 537 votes. Likewise, the analysis suggested that if Al Gore had won his original request for hand counts in just four heavily Democratic Florida counties, Bush would have won by 225 votes.

But the controversy was hardly settled by these results. For one thing, the NORC study also suggested that a majority of Florida voters who went to the polls on November 7, 2000, went intending to vote for Gore, but thousands more Gore than Bush voters failed to cast their ballots for their favorite candidate because of mistakes engendered by confusing ballots. For another, the NORC study's findings further indicated that, had the ballots been recounted using the exacting "equal protection" standard that the U.S. Supreme Court ruled was constitutionally necessary but that was impossible to complete given legal time limits, Gore probably would have won.

The U.S. Supreme Court's five-to-four decision in *Bush v. Gore* was hotly debated at the time it was announced, and it has only grown more controversial since. Even some conservative Republicans who wanted Bush to win have criticized not only the Florida Supreme Court for extending the recounts, but the U.S. Supreme Court's majority for deciding the issue as it did. They would have preferred the Florida Supreme Court to do nothing except uphold the state's vote recount law and, failing that, the U.S. Supreme Court to allow Congress to decide the matter as the Constitution seems to require.

Sources: Jackie Calmes and Edward P. Foldessy, "Florida Revisited: Bush Wins Without Supreme Court Help," *Wall Street Journal* (November 2001); E.J. Dionne and William J. Kristol, eds., *Bush v. Gore* (Washington, D.C.: Brookings Institution, 2001).

Immediately after the law was signed, critics filed suit in federal court claiming that it was unconstitutional. The suit brought together a number of organizations that rarely work together, such as the American Civil Liberties Union and the National Right to Life Committee.

The suit's central arguments are that the ban on independent spending that "refers to" clearly identified candidates sixty days before an election is unconstitutional because it is an abridgement of the right of free speech. Under the law, an organization need not even endorse or oppose a candidate; it is enough that it mention a politician. This means that an organization, sixty days before an election, cannot say that it "supports (or opposes) a bill proposed by Congressman Hastert."

Newspapers, magazines, and radio and television stations are not affected by the law, so that they can say whatever they want for or against a candidate. One way of evaluating the law is to observe that it shifts influence away from businesses and unions and toward the media.

The Supreme Court decided to uphold almost all of the law. As we saw in Chapter 5, it rejected the argument of those who claimed that speech requires money and decided it was no violation of the free speech provisions of the First Amendment to eliminate the ability of corporations and labor unions (and the organizations that use their money) to even *mention* a candidate for federal office for sixty days before the national election.

New Sources of Money

If money is, indeed, the mother's milk of politics, efforts to make the money go away are not likely to work. The Bipartisan Campaign Reform Act, once

Senators John McCain and Russell Feingold wrote the campaign finance reform act that passed in 2002.

enforced, immediately stimulated people to find other ways to spend political money.

The most common were **527 organizations.** These groups, named after a provision of the Internal Revenue Code, are designed to permit the kind of soft money expenditures once made by political parties. In 2004 the Democrats created the Media Fund, America Coming Together, America Votes, and many other groups. George Soros, the wealthy businessman, gave over $23 million to organizations pledged to defeat George Bush. The Republicans responded by creating Progress for America, The Leadership Forum, America for Job Security, and other groups.

---

527 organizations Organizations that, under section 527 of the Internal Revenue Code, raise and spend money to advance political causes.

Under the law, as it is now interpreted, 527 organizations can spend their money on politics so long as they do not coordinate with a candidate or lobby directly for that person. In 2004, 527 organizations raised and spent over one-third of a billion dollars. So far the lesson seems to be this: campaign finance laws are not likely to take money out of politics.

Money and Winning

In the general election for president, money does not make much difference, because both major-party candidates have the same amount, contributed by the federal government. During peacetime, presidential elections are usually decided by three things: political party affiliation, the state of the economy, and the character of the candidates.

For all the talk about voting for "the person, not the party," history teaches that at least 80 percent of the presidential vote will go to the candidates of the two main parties. This means that a presidential election will normally be decided by the 20 percent of voters who cannot be counted on to vote either Democratic or Republican.

In good economic times the party holding the White House normally does well; in poor times it does badly. This is sometimes called the "pocketbook vote." But it is not clear whose pocketbook determines how a person will vote. Many people who are doing well financially will vote against the party in power if the country as a whole is not doing well. A person who is doing well may have friends or family members who are doing poorly. Or the well-off voter may think that if the country is doing poorly, he or she will soon feel the pinch by losing a job or losing customers.

Voters also care about character, and so some money from presidential campaign coffers goes to fund "character ads." *Character* here means several things: Is the candidate honest and reliable? Does the candidate think as the voter thinks about social issues such as crime, abortion, and school prayer? Does the candidate act presidential? Acting presidential seems to mean being an effective speaker, displaying dignity and compassion, sounding like someone who can take charge and get things done, and coming across consistently as a reasonable, likable person. Rash, disagreeable extremists need not apply.

Since both major candidates get the same amount of federal money for the general-election campaign, money does not make much of a difference in deter-

Table 10.3	The Incumbency Advantage in Congressional Campaign Spending (constant 1992 dollars)				
Year	Average Incumbent Spending	Average Challenger Spending	Number of Races	Incumbent-to-Challenger Spending Ratio	Median Ratio
1978	$284,577	$202,863	235*	1.40	1.93
1980	$298,510	$174,031	338	1.72	3.82
1982	$400,630	$202,689	315	1.98	3.24
1984	$417,815	$192,433	338	2.17	4.47
1986	$488,447	$175,418	319	2.78	5.39
1988	$496,894	$148,723	328	3.34	7.08
1990	$479,969	$124,899	321	3.84	10.02
1992	$609,060	$172,802	307	3.52	5.35
1994	$573,374	$223,664	328	2.56	4.68
1996	$630,852	$254,964	357	2.47	5.11
Total	$473,421	$187,587	3,186	2.52	4.66

*Number of cases is small due to nonfilers.

Source: Stephen Ansolabehere and James Snyder, "The Sources of the Incumbency Advantage in Congressional Campaign Finance," Department of Political Science, Massachusetts Institute of Technology, June 1997, 29.

mining the winner. Other factors that also do not make much of a difference include the following:

- *Vice-presidential nominee:* There has rarely been an election in which his or her identity has made a difference.
- *Political reporting:* It may make a difference in some elections, but not in presidential ones.
- *Religion:* Being a Catholic was once a barrier, but since John F. Kennedy was elected president in 1960, this is no longer true.
- *Abortion:* This probably affects who gets a party's nomination, but in the general election ardent supporters and ardent opponents are about evenly balanced.

In congressional races, however, in general it seems that money does make a decisive difference. Scholars are not entirely agreed on the facts, but there is strong evidence that how much the challenger spends is most important, because the challenger usually must become known to the public. Buying name recognition is expensive. Gary Jacobson has shown that, other things being equal, in every congressional election from 1972 to the mid-1980s, challengers who spent more money did better than those who spent less.[13] Jacobson also suggested that how much the incumbents spent was not very important, presumably because they already had all the name recognition they needed (as well as the other benefits of holding office, such as free mail and travel). Other scholars, applying different statistical methods to the same facts, have come to different conclusions. It now seems that, other things being equal, high-spending incumbents do better than low-spending ones.[14] It also now seems that ever higher spending by incumbents, both in absolute dollars and relative to what challengers spend, has become the congressional campaign norm. As Table 10.3 shows, in 1978 average incumbent spending in congressional races was $284,577, average challenger spending was $202,863, and the incumbent-to-challenger spending ratio was 1.40. By 1996 the average for incumbents had soared to $630,852, the average for challengers had grown to $254,964, and the incumbency spending advantage was 2.47.

Incumbents find it easier to raise money than do challengers; incumbents provide services to their districts that challengers cannot; incumbents regularly send free ("franked") mail to their constituents, while challengers must pay for their mailings; incumbents can get free publicity by sponsoring legislation or conducting an investigation. Thus it is hardly surprising that incumbents who run for reelection win in the overwhelming majority of races.

☆ What Decides the Election?

To the voter it all seems quite simple—he or she votes for "the best person" or maybe "the least-bad person." To scholars it is all a bit mysterious. How do voters decide who the best person is? What does "best" mean, anyway?

Party

One answer to these questions is party identification. People may say that they are voting for the "best person," but for many people the best person is always a Democrat or a Republican. Moreover, we have seen in Chapter 7 that many people know rather little about the details of political issues. They may not even know what position their favored candidate has taken on issues that the voters care about. Given these facts, many scholars have argued that party identification is the principal determinant of how people vote.[15]

If it were only a matter of party identification, though, the Democrats would always win the presidency, since usually more people identify with the Democratic than the Republican party. But we know

that the Democrats lost six of the nine presidential elections between 1968 and 2000. Here are three reasons for this.

First, those people who consider themselves Democrats are less firmly wedded to their party than are Republicans. Table 10.4 shows how people identifying themselves as Democrats, Republicans, or independents voted in presidential elections from 1960 to 2004. In every election except 1992, at least 80 percent of Republican voters supported the Republican candidate in each election. By contrast, there have been more defections among Democratic voters—in 1972 a third of Democrats supported Nixon, and in 1984 some 26 percent supported Reagan.

The second reason, also clear from Table 10.4, is that the Republicans do much better than the

Table 10.4 Percentage of Popular Vote by Groups in Presidential Elections, 1960–2004

		National	Republicans	Democrats	Independents
1960	Kennedy	50%	5%	84%	43%
	Nixon	50	95	16	57
1964	Johnson	61	20	87	56
	Goldwater	39	80	13	44
1968	Humphrey	43	9	74	31
	Nixon	43	86	12	44
	Wallace	14	5	14	25
1972	McGovern	38	5	67	31
	Nixon	62	95	33	69
1976	Carter	51	11	80	48
	Ford	49	89	20	52
1980[a]	Carter	41	11	66	30
	Reagan	51	84	26	54
	Anderson	7	4	6	12
1984	Mondale	41	7	73	35
	Reagan	59	92	26	63
1988	Dukakis	46	8	82	43
	Bush	54	91	17	55
1992	Clinton	43	10	77	38
	Bush	38	73	10	32
	Perot	19	17	13	30
1996	Clinton	49	13	84	43
	Dole	41	80	10	35
	Perot	8	6	5	17
2000	Gore	49	8	86	45
	Bush	48	91	11	47
2004	Kerry	49	6	89	49
	Bush	51	93	11	48

[a]The figures for 1980, 1984, 1988, and 1996 fail to add up to 100 percent because of missing data.

Sources: Updated from Gallup poll data, compiled by Robert D. Cantor, *Voting Behavior and Presidential Elections* (Itasca, Ill.: F. E. Peacock, 1975), 35; Gerald M. Pomper, *The Election of 1976* (New York: David McKay, 1977), 61; Gerald M. Pomper et al., *The Election of 1980* (Chatham, N.J.: Chatham House, 1981), 71; *New York Times*/CBS Poll, November 5, 1992.

Democrats among the self-described "independent" voters. In every election since 1960 (except 1964, 1992, 1996, and 2004), the Republican candidate has won a larger percentage of the independent vote than the Democratic nominee; in fact the Republicans usually got a majority of the independents, who tend to be younger whites.

Finally, a higher percentage of Republicans than Democrats vote in elections. In every presidential contest in the past thirty years, those describing themselves as "strongly Republican" have been much more likely to vote than those describing themselves as "strongly Democratic."

Issues, Especially the Economy

Even though voters may not know a lot about the issues, that does not mean that issues play no role in elections or that voters respond irrationally to them. For example, V. O. Key, Jr., looked at those voters who switched from one party to another between elections and found that most of them switched in a direction consistent with their own interests. As Key put it, the voters are not fools.[16]

Moreover, voters may know a lot more than we suppose about issues that really matter to them. They may have hazy, even erroneous, views about monetary policy, business regulation, and the trade deficit, but they are likely to have a very good idea about whether unemployment is up or down, prices at the supermarket are stable or rising, or crime is a problem in their neighborhoods. And on some issues—such as abortion, school prayer, and race relations—they are likely to have some strong principles that they want to see politicians obey.

Contrary to what we learn in our civics classes, representative government does not require voters to be well informed on the issues. If it were our duty as citizens to have accurate facts and sensible ideas about how best to negotiate with foreign adversaries, stabilize the value of the dollar, revitalize failing industries, and keep farmers prosperous, we might as well forget about citizenship and head for the beach. It would be a full-time job, and then some, to be a citizen. Politics would take on far more importance in our lives than most of us would want, given our need to earn a living and our belief in the virtues of limited government.

To see why our system can function without well-informed citizens, we must understand the differences between two ways in which issues can affect elections.

■ **Prospective Voting** *Prospective* means "forward-looking"; we vote prospectively when we examine the views that the rival candidates have on the issues of the day and then cast our ballots for the person we think has the best ideas for handling these matters. **Prospective voting** requires a lot of information about issues and candidates. Some of us do vote prospectively. Those who do tend to be political junkies. They are either willing to spend a lot of time learning about issues or are so concerned about some big issue (abortion, school busing, nuclear energy) that all they care about is how a candidate stands on that question.

Prospective voting is more common among people who are political activists, have a political ideology that governs their voting decision, or are involved in interest groups with a big stake in the election. They are a minority of all voters, but (as we saw in Chapters 7 and 8) they are more influential than their numbers would suggest. Some prospective voters (by no means all) are organized into single-issue groups, to be discussed in the next section.

■ **Retrospective Voting** *Retrospective* means "backward-looking"; **retrospective voting** involves looking at how things have gone in the recent past and then voting for the party that controls the White House if we like what has happened and voting against that party if we don't like what has happened. Retrospective voting does not require us to have a lot of information—all we need to know is whether things have, in our view, gotten better or worse.

Elections are decided by retrospective voters.[17] In 1980 they decided to vote against Jimmy Carter because inflation was rampant, interest rates were high, and we seemed to be getting the worst of things overseas. The evidence suggests rather clearly that they did not vote *for* Ronald Reagan; they voted for *an alternative to* Jimmy Carter. (Some people did vote for Reagan and his philosophy; they were voting prospectively, but they were in the minority.) In 1984

prospective voting Voting for a candidate because you favor his or her ideas for handling issues.

retrospective voting Voting for a candidate because you like his or her past actions in office.

people voted for Ronald Reagan because unemployment, inflation, and interest rates were down and because we no longer seemed to be getting pushed around overseas. In 1980 retrospective voters wanted change; in 1984 they wanted continuity. In 1988 there was no incumbent running, but George H.W. Bush portrayed himself as the candidate who would continue the policies that had led to prosperity and depicted Michael Dukakis as a "closet liberal" who would change those policies. In 1992 the economy had once again turned sour, and so voters turned away from Bush and toward his rivals, Bill Clinton and Ross Perot.

Though most incumbent members of Congress get reelected, those who lose do so, it appears, largely because they are the victims of retrospective voting. After Reagan was first elected, the economy went into a recession in 1981–1982. As a result Republican members of Congress were penalized by the voters, and Democratic challengers were helped. But it is not just the economy that can hurt congressional candidates. In most midterm elections the party holding the White House has lost seats in Congress. Just why this should be is not entirely clear, but it probably has something to do with the tendency of some voters to change their opinions of the presidential party once that party has had a chance to govern—which is to say, a chance to make some mistakes, disappoint some supporters, and irritate some interests.

Some scholars believe that retrospective voting is based largely on economic conditions. Figure 10.3 certainly provides support for this view. Each dot represents a presidential election (fifteen of them, from 1948 to 2004). The horizontal axis is the percentage increase or decrease in per capita disposable income (adjusted for inflation) during the election year. The vertical axis is the percentage of the two-party vote won by the party already occupying the White House. You can see that, as per capita income goes up (as you move to the right on the horizontal axis), the incumbent political party tends to win a bigger share of the vote.

Other scholars feel that matters are more complicated than this. As a result a small industry has grown up consisting of people who use different techniques to forecast the outcome of elections. If you know how the president stands in the opinion polls several months before the election and how well the economy is performing, you can make a pretty

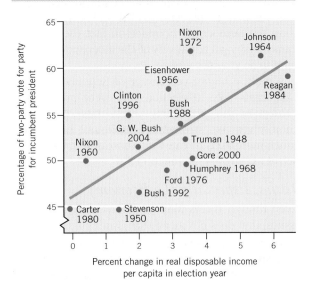

Figure 10.3   **The Economy and Vote for President, 1948–2004**

Notes: (1) Each dot represents a presidential election, showing the popular vote received by the incumbent president's party. (2) 1992 data do not include votes for independent candidate H. Ross Perot. (3) 2004 value on RDI is projection from data available in December 2004.

Source: From *American Public Opinion,* 5th ed., by Robert S. Erikson and Kent L. Tedin. Copyright © 1995 by Addison-Wesley Educational Publishers, Inc. Reprinted by permission of Pearson Education, Inc.

good guess as to who is going to win the presidency. For congressional races predicting the result is a lot tougher, because so many local factors affect these contests. Election forecasting remains an inexact science. As one study of the performance of presidential election forecasting models and the 1992 election concluded, "Models may be no improvement over pundits."[18]

The Campaign

If party loyalty and national economic conditions play so large a role in elections, is the campaign just sound and fury, signifying nothing?

No. Campaigns can make a difference in three ways. First, they reawaken the partisan loyalties of voters. Right after a party's nominating convention selects a presidential candidate, that person's standing with voters of both parties goes way up in the polls. The reason is that the just-nominated candidate has received a lot of media attention during the summer months, when not much else is happening. When the campaign gets under way, however, both candidates get publicity, and voters return to their normal Democratic or Republican affiliations.

Second, campaigns give voters a chance to watch how the candidates handle pressure, and they give candidates a chance to apply that pressure. The two rivals, after promising to conduct a campaign "on the issues" without mudslinging, immediately start searching each other's personal histories and records to find acts, statements, or congressional votes that can be shown in the worst possible light in newspaper or television ads. Many voters don't like these "negative ads"—but they work. Careful statistical studies based on actual campaigns (as opposed to voter surveys or laboratory-like focus group studies) suggest that negative ads work by stimulating voter turnout.[19] As a result every politician constantly worries about how an opponent might portray his or her record, a fact that helps explain why so many politicians never do or say anything that can't be explained in a thirty-second television spot.

Third, campaigns allow voters an opportunity to judge the character and core values of the candidates. Most voters don't study in detail a candidate's positions on issues; even if they had the time, they know that you can't predict how politicians will behave just from knowing what a campaign manager has written in a position paper. The voters want some guidance as to how a candidate will behave once elected. They get that guidance by listening not to the details of what a candidate says but to the themes and tone of those statements. Is the candidate tough on crime and drugs? Are his or her statements about the environment sincere or perfunctory? Does the candidate favor having a strong military? Does the candidate care more about not raising taxes or more about helping the homeless?

The desire of voters to discern character, combined with the mechanics of modern campaigning— short radio and television ads and computer-targeted direct mail—lend themselves to an emphasis on themes at the expense of details. This tendency is reinforced by the expectations of ideological party activists and single-issue groups.

Thematic campaigning, negative ads, and the demands of single-issue groups are not new; they are as old as the republic. In the nineteenth century the theme was slavery and the single-issue groups were

Union members were once heavily Democratic, but since Ronald Reagan began winning white union votes in 1980, these votes have been up for grabs.

abolitionists and their opponents; their negative ads make the ones we have today sound like Sunday school sermons. At the turn of the century the themes were temperance and the vote for women; both issues led to no-holds-barred, rough-and-tumble campaigning. In the 1970s and 1980s new themes were advanced by fundamentalist Christians and by pro- and antiabortion groups.

What has changed is not the tone of campaigning but the advent of primary elections. Once, political parties picked candidates out of a desire to win elections. Today activists and single-issue groups influence the selection of candidates, sometimes out of a belief that it is better to lose with the "right" candidate than to win with the wrong one. In a five-candidate primary, only 21 percent of the voters can pick the winner. Single-issue groups can make a big difference under these conditions, even though they may not have much influence in the general election.

Finding a Winning Coalition

Putting together a winning electoral coalition means holding on to your base among committed partisans and attracting the swing voters who cast their ballots in response to issues (retrospectively or prospectively) and personalities.

There are two ways to examine the nature of the parties' voting coalitions. One is to ask what percentage of various identifiable groups in the population supported the Democratic or Republican candidate for president. The other is to ask what proportion of a party's total vote came from each of these groups. The answer to the first question tells us how *loyal* African Americans, farmers, union members, and others are to the Democratic or Republican party or candidate; the answer to the second question tells us how *important* each group is to a candidate or party.

For the Democratic coalition African Americans are the most loyal voters. In every election but one since 1952, two-thirds or more of all African Americans voted Democratic; since 1964 four-fifths have gone Democratic. Usually, Jewish voters are almost as solidly Democratic. Most Hispanics have been Democrats, though the label "Hispanic" conceals differences among Cuban Americans (who often vote Republican) and Mexican Americans and Puerto Ricans (who are strongly Democratic). The turnout among most Hispanic groups has been quite low

(many are not yet citizens), so their political power is not equivalent to their numbers.

The Democrats have lost their once strong hold on Catholics, southerners, and union members. In 1960 Catholics supported John F. Kennedy (a Democrat and fellow Catholic), but they also voted for Eisenhower, Nixon, and Reagan, all Republicans. Union members deserted the Democrats in 1968 and 1972, came back in 1980 and 1988, and divided about evenly between the two parties in 1952, 1956, and 1980. White southerners have voted Republican in national elections but Democratic in many local ones (see Table 10.5).

The Republican party is often described as the party of business and professional people. The loyalty of these groups to Republicans is in fact strong: only in 1964 did they desert the Republican candidate to support Lyndon Johnson. Farmers have usually been Republican, but they are a volatile group,

Table 10.5   Who Likes the Democrats?

Percentage of various groups saying that they voted for the Democratic presidential candidate, 1964–2004.

	1968[a]	1972	1976	1980[c]	1984	1988	1992[d]	1996	2000	2004
Sex										
Men	41%	37%	53%	37%	37%	41%	41%	43%	42%	45%
Women	45	38	48	45	42	49	46	54	54	52
Race										
White	38	32	46	36	34	40	39	43	42	42
Nonwhite	85	87	85	82	90	86	82	84	90	89
Education										
College	37	37	42	35	40	43	44	47	45	47
Grad school	52	49	58	43	49	56	55	52	52	55
Age										
Under 30	47	48	53	43	41	47	44	53	48	54
50 and over	41	36	52	41[e]	39	49	50	48[g]	48	49
Religion										
Protestant	35	30	46	NA	NA	33[f]	33	36	42	41
Catholic	59	48	57	40	44	47	44	53	50	48
Jewish[b]	85	66	68	45	66	64	78	78	79	76
Southerners	31	29	54	47	36	41	42	46	NA	41

[a]1968 election had three major candidates (Humphrey, Nixon, and Wallace). [b]Jewish vote estimated from various sources; since the number of Jewish persons interviewed is often less than 100, the error in this figure, as well as that for nonwhites, may be large. [c]1980 election had three major candidates (Carter, Reagan, and Anderson). [d]1992 election had three major candidates (Clinton, Bush, and Perot). [e]For 1980–1992, refers to age 60 and over. [f]For 1988, white Protestants only. [g]For 1996, refers to age 45 and over.

Sources: For 1964–1976: Gallup poll data, as tabulated in Jeane J. Kirkpatrick, "Changing Patterns of Electoral Competition," in *The New American Political System*, ed. Anthony King (Washington, D.C.: American Enterprise Institute, 1978), 264–256. For 1980–1992: Data from *New York Times*/CBS News exit polls. For 1996: *Congressional Quarterly Weekly Report*, 1997, p. 188; For 2000: Exit polls supplied by ABC News. For 2004, CNN exit polls.

highly sensitive to the level of farm prices—and thus quick to change parties. Contrary to popular wisdom, the Republican party usually wins a majority of the votes of poor people (defined as those earning less than roughly $5,000 a year). Only in 1964 did most poor people support the Democratic candidate. This can be explained by the fact that the poor include quite different elements—low-income blacks (who are Democrats) and many elderly, retired persons (who usually vote Republican).

In sum, the loyalty of most identifiable groups of voters to either party is not overwhelming. Only African Americans, business people, and Jews usually give two-thirds or more of their votes to one party or the other; other groups display tendencies, but none that cannot be overcome.

The contribution that each of these groups makes to the party coalitions is a different matter. Though African Americans are overwhelmingly and persistently Democratic, they make up so small a portion of the total electorate that they have never accounted for more than a quarter of the total Democratic vote. The groups that make up the largest part of the Democratic vote—Catholics, union members, southerners—are also the least dependable parts of that coalition.[20]

When representatives of various segments of society make demands on party leaders and presidential candidates, they usually stress their numbers or their loyalty, but rarely both. African American leaders, for example, sometimes describe the black vote as being of decisive importance to Democrats and thus deserving of special consideration from a Democratic president. But African Americans are so loyal that a Democratic candidate can almost take their votes for granted, and in any event they are not as numerous as other groups. Union leaders emphasize how many union voters there are, but a president will know that union leaders cannot "deliver" the union vote and that this vote may go to the president's opponent, whatever the leaders say. For any presidential candidate a winning coalition must be put together anew for each election. Only a few voters can be taken for granted or written off as a lost cause.

☆ The Effects of Elections on Policy

To the candidates, and perhaps to the voters, the only interesting outcome of an election is who won. To a political scientist the interesting outcomes are the broad trends in winning and losing and what they imply about the attitudes of voters, the operation of the electoral system, the fate of political parties, and the direction of public policy.

Figure 10.4 shows the trend in the popular vote for president since before the Civil War. From 1876 to 1896 the Democrats and Republicans were hotly competitive. The Republicans won three times, the Democrats twice in close contests. Beginning in 1896 the Republicans became the dominant party, and except for 1912 and 1916, when Woodrow Wilson, a Democrat, was able to win owing to a split in the Republican party, the Republicans carried every presidential election until 1932. Then Franklin Roosevelt put together what has since become known as the "New Deal coalition," and the Democrats became the dominant party. They won every election until 1952, when Eisenhower, a Republican and a popular military hero, was elected for the first of his two terms. In the presidential elections since 1952, power has switched hands between the parties frequently.

Still, cynics complain that elections are meaningless: no matter who wins, crooks, incompetents, or self-serving politicians still hold office. The more charitable argue that elected officials are usually decent enough, but that public policy remains more or less the same no matter which official or party is in office.

There is no brief and simple response to this latter view. Much depends on which office or policy you examine. One reason it is so hard to generalize about the policy effects of elections is that the offices to be filled by the voters are so numerous and the ability of the political parties to unite these officeholders behind a common policy is so weak that any policy proposal must run a gauntlet of potential opponents. Though we have but two major parties, and though only one party can win the presidency, each party is a weak coalition of diverse elements that reflect the many divisions in public opinion. The proponents of a new law must put together a majority coalition almost from scratch, and a winning coalition on one issue tends to be somewhat different—quite often dramatically different—from a winning coalition on another issue.

In a parliamentary system with strong parties, such as that in Great Britain, an election can often have a major effect on public policy. When the Labour party won office in 1945, it put several major industries under public ownership and launched a comprehensive set of social services, including a

Figure 10.4   Partisan Division of the Presidential Vote in the Nation, 1856–2004

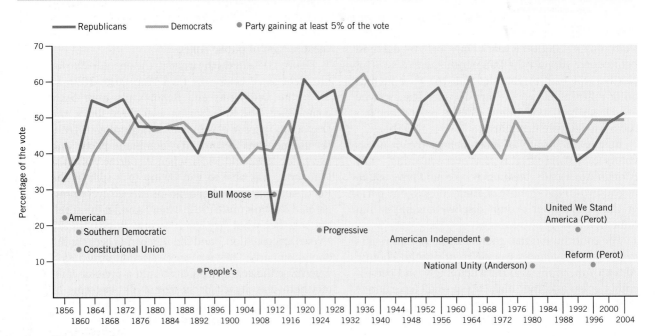

Sources: Updated from Historical Data Archive, Inter-University Consortium for Political Research, as reported in William H. Flanigan and Nancy H. Zingale, *Political Behavior of the American Electorate*, 3rd ed., 32.

nationalized health care plan. Its ambitious and controversial campaign platform was converted, almost item by item, into law. When the Conservative party returned to power in 1951, it accepted some of these changes but rejected others (for example, it denationalized the steel industry).

American elections, unless accompanied by a national crisis such as a war or a depression, rarely produce changes of the magnitude of those that occurred in Britain in 1945. The constitutional system within which our elections take place was designed to moderate the pace of change—to make it neither easy nor impossible to adopt radical proposals. But the fact that the system is intended to moderate the rate of change does not mean that it will always work that way.

The election of 1860 brought to national power a party committed to opposing the extension of slavery and southern secession; it took a bloody war to vindicate that policy. The election of 1896 led to the dominance of a party committed to high tariffs, a strong currency, urban growth, and business prosperity—a commitment that was not significantly altered until

1932. The election of that year led to the New Deal, which produced the greatest single enlargement of federal authority since 1860. The election of 1964 gave the Democrats such a large majority in Congress (as well as control of the presidency) that there began to issue forth an extraordinary number of new policies of sweeping significance—Medicare and Medicaid, federal aid to education and to local law enforcement, two dozen environmental and consumer protection laws, the Voting Rights Act of 1965, a revision of the immigration laws, and a new cabinet-level Department of Housing and Urban Development.

The election of 1980 brought into office an administration determined to reverse the direction of policy over the preceding half century. Reagan's administration succeeded in obtaining large tax cuts, significant reductions in spending (or in the rate of increase of spending) on some domestic programs, and changes in the policies of some regulatory agencies. The election of 1982, in which the Democrats made gains in the House of Representatives, stiffened congressional resistance to further spending cuts

What Would You Do?

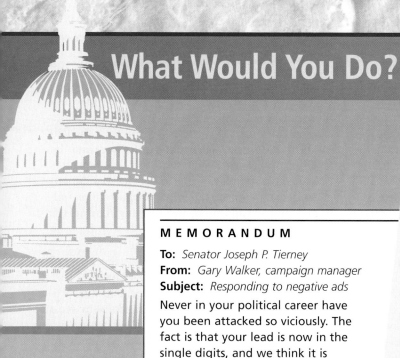

U.S. Senate Challenger Launches Blistering Media Attack

TV and Radio Ads Call Incumbent "Callous" Puppet of Big Money

October 20
PHOENIX, AZ

Until last week every statewide poll showed U.S. senator Joseph P. Tierney coasting to a comfortable reelection victory. Today, however, the Tierney campaign is reeling. Polls show the race tightening fast, thanks to thirty-second negative ads depicting the senator's votes against certain gun control bills and prescription drug price control plans as evidence of his "heartless approach to public safety and callous disregard for the lives of the medically needy." The ads call Tierney's votes "political payoffs to the gun makers and big drug companies who have owned him" for years . . .

MEMORANDUM

To: *Senator Joseph P. Tierney*
From: *Gary Walker, campaign manager*
Subject: *Responding to negative ads*

Never in your political career have you been attacked so viciously. The fact is that your lead is now in the single digits, and we think it is because of the negative ads. With only a few weeks left until election day, you need to decide whether you want us to fight fire with fire.

Arguments for:

1. Negative ads work. In particular some studies, and lots of political lore, suggest that "going negative" helps lesser-known, less-well-financed challengers against better-known, better-financed incumbents who fail to respond in kind and in time.
2. In the age of the political sound bite, it is much easier to dish dirt on an opponent's personal history and official record than it is to explain the complexities behind one's own past votes or to put one's past public statements back into context.
3. If you don't sling the mud back, it will stick to you, and people will question not only your integrity but also your toughness.

Arguments against:

1. Negative ads can backfire. People don't like them, especially when the charges are harshly personal or otherwise over the top.
2. A tit-for-tat sound bite volley can be positive: "I am a person of integrity. I vote my conscience. I live to serve."
3. If you stay positive and "wrap yourself in the flag," the mud will melt away and people will question your opponent's decency and character.

Your decision:

Go negative _____
Stay positive _____

and stimulated renewed interest in tax increases as a way of reducing the deficit. Following the election of 1984 a major tax reform plan was passed. After the 1996 election Clinton and Republican congressional leaders agreed on a plan to balance the budget.

In view of all these developments it is hard to argue that the pace of change in our government is always slow or that elections never make a difference. Studies by scholars confirm that elections are often significant, despite the difficulty of getting laws passed. One analysis of about fourteen hundred promises made between 1944 and 1964 in the platforms of the two major parties revealed that 72 percent were put into effect.[21]

Another study examined the party platforms of the Democrats and Republicans from 1844 to 1968 and all the laws passed by Congress between 1789 and 1968. By a complex statistical method, the author of the study was able to show that during certain periods the differences between the platforms of the two parties were especially large (1856, 1880, 1896, 1932) and that there was at about the same time a high rate of change in the kinds of laws being passed.[22] This study supports the general impression conveyed by history that elections can often be central to important policy changes.

Why then do we so often think that elections make little difference? It is because public opinion and the political parties enter a phase of consolidation and continuity between periods of rapid change. During this phase the changes are, so to speak, digested, and party leaders adjust to the new popular consensus, which may (or may not) evolve around the merits of these changes. During the 1870s and 1880s Democratic politicians had to come to terms with the failure of the southern secessionist movement and the abolition of slavery; during the 1900s the Democrats had to adjust again, this time to the fact that national economic policy was going to support industrialization and urbanization, not farming; during the 1940s and 1950s the Republicans had to learn to accept the popularity of the New Deal.

Elections in ordinary times are not "critical"—they do not produce any major party realignment, they are not fought out over a dominant issue, and they provide the winners with no clear mandate. In most cases an election is little more than a retrospective judgment on the record of the incumbent president and the existing congressional majority. If times are good, incumbents win easily; if times are bad, incumbents may lose even though their opponents may have no clear plans for change. But even a "normal" election can produce dramatic results if the winner is a person such as Ronald Reagan, who helped give his party a distinctive political philosophy.

☆ SUMMARY

*T*oday's political candidates face the problem of creating a temporary organization that can raise money from large numbers of small donors, mobilize enthusiastic supporters, and win a nomination in a way that will not harm their ability to appeal to a broader, more diverse constituency in the general election. Campaigning has an uncertain effect on election outcomes, but election outcomes can have important effects on public policy, especially at those times—during critical or "realigning" elections—when new voters are coming into the electorate in large numbers, old party loyalties are weakening, or a major issue is splitting the majority party. Most people vote retrospectively rather than prospectively.

RECONSIDERING WHO GOVERNS?

1. *How do American elections determine the kind of people who govern us?*

American democracy rewards candidates who have personal appeal rather than party endorsements. Politics here produces individualists who usually have a strong ideological orientation toward liberal or conservative causes, but only a weak sense of loyalty to the political parties who endorse those ideologies.

2. *What matters most in deciding who wins presidential and congressional elections?*

The party identification of the voters matters the most. Only 10 to 20 percent of the voters are available to have their votes changed. For them, the state of the economy, and in wartime the success or failures we have while fighting abroad, make the most difference. Closely allied with those issues, at least for presidential candidates, is the voters' assessment of their character.

RECONSIDERING TO WHAT ENDS?

1. *Do elections make a real difference in what laws get passed?*

Yes. During campaigns parties may try to sound alike, in order to attract centrist voters, but when in office they differ greatly in the policies they put into law.

WORLD WIDE WEB RESOURCES

Federal Election Commission: **www.fec.gov**

Project Vote Smart: **www.vote-smart.org**

Election history: **clerkweb.house.gov**

Electoral college: **www.fec.gov/pages/ecmenu2**

Campaign finance: **www.opensecrets.org**

SUGGESTED READINGS

Asher, Herbert. *Presidential Elections and American Politics.* 5th ed. Pacific Grove, Calif.: Brooks/Cole, 1992. A useful, brief analysis of how Americans have voted.

Burnham, Walter Dean. *Critical Elections and the Mainsprings of American Politics.* New York: Norton, 1970. An argument about the decline in voting participation and the significance of the realigning election of 1896.

Dionne, E. J., and William Kristol, eds. *Bush v. Gore.* Washington, D.C.: Brookings Institution, 2001. Excellent collection of readings and court cases on the disputed Florida vote count in 2000.

Jacobson, Gary C. *The Politics of Congressional Elections.* 4th ed. Boston: Little, Brown, 1997. Careful analysis of how people get elected to Congress.

Kayden, Xandra. *Campaign Organization.* Lexington, Mass.: D. C. Heath, 1978. A close look at how political campaigns are organized, staffed, and led at the state level.

Page, Benjamin I. *Choices and Echoes in Presidential Elections.* Chicago: University of Chicago Press, 1978. Analyzes the interaction between the behavior of candidates and of voters in American elections.

Sundquist, James L. *Dynamics of the Party System: Alignment and Realignment of Political Parties in the United States.* Rev. ed. Washington, D.C.: Brookings Institution, 1983. Historical analysis of realigning elections from 1860 to the nonrealignment of 1980.

CHAPTER

11

Interest Groups

Explaining Proliferation

The Birth of Interest Groups

Kinds of Organizations
Institutional Interests ● Membership
Interests ● Incentives to Join ● The
Influence of the Staff

**Interest Groups and Social
Movements**
The Environmental Movement ● The
Feminist Movement ● The Union
Movement

Funds for Interest Groups
Foundation Grants ● Federal Grants
and Contracts ● Direct Mail

The Problem of Bias

The Activities of Interest Groups
Information ● Public Support: The Rise
of the New Politics ● Money and PACs
● The "Revolving Door" ● Trouble

Regulating Interest Groups

WHO GOVERNS?

1. Do interest groups dominate government, and is any particular lobby politically unbeatable?
2. Why do people join interest groups?

TO WHAT ENDS?

1. Is the proliferation of political action committees (PACs) and other groups good or bad for America's representative democracy?
2. Should interest groups' political activities be restricted by law?

*A*lmost every tourist arriving in Washington visits the White House and the Capitol. Many look at the Supreme Court building. But hardly any walk down K Street, where much of the political life of the country occurs.

K Street? From the sidewalk it is just a row of office buildings, no different from what one might find in downtown Seattle or Kansas City. What's to see? But in these buildings, and in similar ones lining nearby streets, are the offices of the nearly seven thousand organizations that are represented in Washington.

It is doubtful whether there is any other nation in which so many organizations are represented in its capital. They are there to participate in politics. They are interest groups, or, if you prefer, lobbies.

☆ Explaining Proliferation

There are at least three reasons why interest groups are so common in this country. First, the more cleavages there are in a society, the greater the variety of interests that will exist. In addition to divisions along lines of income and occupation found in any society, America is a nation of countless immigrants and many races. There are at least seventy-two religions that claim sixty-five thousand members or more. Americans are scattered over a vast land made up of many regions with distinctive traditions and cultures. These social facts make for a great variety of interests and opinions. As James Madison said in *Federalist* No. 10, "The latent causes of faction are thus sown in the nature of man."

Second, the American constitutional system contributes to the number of interest groups by multiplying the points at which such groups can gain access to the government. In a nation such as Great Britain, where most political authority is lodged in a single official such as the prime minister, there are only a few places where important decisions are made—and thus only a few opportunities for affecting those decisions. But when political authority is shared by the president, the courts, and Congress (and within Congress among two houses and countless committees and subcommittees), there are plenty of places where one can argue one's case. And the more chances there are to influence policy, the more organizations there will be that seek to exercise that influence.

This fact helps explain why in Great Britain there is often only one organization representing a given interest, whereas in the United States there are

265

several. In London only one major association represents farmers, one represents industry, one represents veterans, and one represents doctors. In the United States, by contrast, at least three organizations represent farmers (the American Farm Bureau Federation, the National Farmers' Union, and the Grange), and each of these is made up of state and county branches, many of which act quite independently of national headquarters. Though there is one major American labor organization, the AFL-CIO, it is in fact a loose coalition of independent unions (plumbers, steelworkers, coal miners), and some large unions, such as the Teamsters, were for many years not part of the AFL-CIO at all.

Third, the weakness of political parties in this country may help explain the number and strength of our interest groups. Where parties are strong, interests work through the parties; where parties are weak, interests operate directly on the government. That at least is the theory. Though scholars are not certain of its validity, it is a plausible theory and can be illustrated by differences among American cities. In cities such as Chicago where a party (in this case, the Democrats) has historically been very strong, labor unions, business associations, and citizens groups have had to work with the party and on its terms. But in cities such as Boston and Los Angeles where the parties are very weak, interest groups proliferate and play a large role in making policy.[1]

In Austria, France, and Italy many if not most interest groups are closely linked to one or another political party. In Italy, for example, each party—Socialist, Communist, and Christian Democrat—has a cluster of labor unions, professional associations, and social clubs allied with it.[2] Though American interest groups often support one party (the AFL-CIO, for example, almost always backs Democratic candidates for office), the relationship between party and interest group here is not as close as it is in Europe.

★ The Birth of Interest Groups

The number of interest groups has grown rapidly since 1960. A study of Washington-based political associations revealed that roughly 70 percent of them established their Washington offices after 1960, and nearly half opened their doors after 1970.[3]

The 1960s and 1970s were boom years for interest groups, but there have been other periods in our history when political associations were created in especially large numbers. During the 1770s many groups arose to agitate for American independence; during the 1830s and 1840s the number of religious associations increased sharply, and the antislavery movement began. In the 1860s trade unions based on crafts emerged in significant numbers, farmers

The greater the activity of government—for example, in regulating the timber industry—the greater the number of interest groups.

formed the Grange, and various fraternal organizations were born. In the 1880s and 1890s business associations proliferated. The great era of organization building, however, was in the first two decades of the twentieth century. Within this twenty-year period many of the best-known and largest associations with an interest in national politics were formed: the Chamber of Commerce, the National Association of Manufacturers, the American Medical Association, the National Association for the Advancement of Colored People (NAACP), the Urban League, the American Farm Bureau Federation, the Farmers' Union, the National Catholic Welfare Conference, the American Jewish Committee, and the Anti-Defamation League. The wave of interest group formation that occurred in the 1960s led to the emergence of environmental, consumer, and political reform organizations such as those sponsored by consumer activist Ralph Nader.

The fact that associations in general, and political interest groups in particular, are created more rapidly in some periods than in others suggests that these groups do not arise inevitably out of natural social processes. There have always been farmers in this country, but there were no national farm organizations until the latter part of the nineteenth century. Blacks had been victimized by various white-supremacy policies from the end of the Civil War on, but the NAACP did not emerge until 1910. Men and women worked in factories for decades before industrial unions were formed.

At least four factors help explain the rise of interest groups. The first consists of broad economic developments that create new interests and redefine old ones. Farmers had little reason to become organized for political activity so long as most of them consumed what they produced. The importance of regular political activity became evident only after most farmers began to produce cash crops for sale in markets that were unstable or affected by forces (the weather, the railroads, foreign competition) that farmers could not control. Similarly, for many decades most workers were craftspeople working alone or in small groups. Such unions as existed were little more than craft guilds interested in protecting members' jobs and in training apprentices. The reason for large, mass-membership unions did not exist until there arose mass-production industry operated by large corporations.

Second, government policy itself helped create interest groups. Wars create veterans, who in turn demand pensions and other benefits. The first large veterans organization, the Grand Army of the Republic, was made up of Union veterans of the Civil War. By the 1920s these men were receiving about a quarter of a billion dollars a year from the government, and naturally they created organizations to watch over the distribution of this money. The federal government encouraged the formation of the American Farm Bureau Federation (AFBF) by paying for county agents who would serve the needs of farmers under the supervision of local farm organizations; these county bureaus eventually came together as the AFBF. The Chamber of Commerce was launched at a conference attended by President William Howard Taft.

Professional societies, such as those made up of lawyers and doctors, became important in part because state governments gave to such groups the authority to decide who was qualified to become a lawyer or a doctor. Workers had a difficult time organizing so long as the government, by the use of injunctions enforced by the police and the army, prevented strikes. Unions, especially those in mass-production industries, began to flourish after Congress passed laws in the 1930s that prohibited the use of injunctions in private labor disputes, that required employers to bargain with unions, and that allowed a union representing a majority of the workers in a plant to require all workers to join it.[4]

Third, political organizations do not emerge automatically, even when government policy permits them and social circumstances seem to require them. Somebody must exercise leadership, often at substantial personal cost. These organizational entrepreneurs are found in greater numbers at certain times than at others. They are often young, caught up in a social movement, drawn to the need for change, and inspired by some political or religious doctrine. Antislavery organizations were created in the 1830s and 1840s by enthusiastic young people influenced by a religious revival then sweeping the country. The period from 1890 to 1920, when so many national organizations were created, was a time when the college-educated middle class was growing rapidly. (The number of men and women who received college degrees each year tripled between 1890 and 1920.)[5] During this era natural

Table 11.1   Dates of Founding of Organizations Having Washington Offices

Organization	Percentage Founded	
	After 1960	After 1970
Corporations	14%	6%
Unions	21	14
Professional	30	14
Trade	38	23
Civil rights	56	46
Women/elderly/disabled	56	46
"Public interest"	76	57
Social welfare	79	51

Source: Kay Lehman Schlozman and John T. Tierney, *Organized Interests and American Democracy* (New York: Harper & Row, 1986), 76. Copyright © 1986 by Kay Lehman Schlozman and John T. Tierney. Reprinted by permission of Addison-Wesley Educational Publishers, Inc.

science and fundamentalist Christianity were locked in a bitter contest, with the Gospels and Darwinism offering competing ideas about personal salvation and social progress. The 1960s, when many new organizations were born, was a decade in which young people were powerfully influenced by the civil rights and antiwar movements and when college enrollments more than doubled.

Finally, the more activities government undertakes, the more organized groups there will be that are interested in those activities. As can be seen from Table 11.1, most Washington offices representing corporations, labor unions, and trade and professional associations were established before 1960—in some cases many decades before—because it was during the 1930s or even earlier that the government began making policies important to business and labor. The great majority of "public-interest" lobbies (those concerned with the environment or consumer protection), social welfare associations, and organizations concerned with civil rights, the elderly, and the handicapped established offices in Washington after 1960. Policies of interest to these groups, such as the major civil rights and environmental laws, were adopted after that date. In fact

interest group   An organization of people sharing a common interest or goal that seeks to influence the making of public policy.

over half the public-interest lobbies opened their doors after 1970.

 # Kinds of Organizations

An **interest group** is any organization that seeks to influence public policy. When we think of an organization, we usually think of something like the Boy Scouts or the League of Women Voters—a group consisting of individual members. In Washington, however, many organizations do not have individual members at all but are offices—corporations, law firms, public relations firms, or "letterhead" organizations that get most of their money from foundations or from the government—out of which a staff operates. It is important to understand the differences between the two kinds of interest groups—institutional and membership interests.[6]

Institutional Interests

Institutional interests are individuals or organizations representing other organizations. General Motors, for example, has a Washington representative. Over five hundred firms have such representatives in the capital, most of whom have opened their offices since 1970.[7] Firms that do not want to place their own full-time representative in Washington can hire a Washington lawyer or public relations expert on a part-time basis. Between 1970 and 1980 the number of lawyers in Washington more than tripled; Washington now has more lawyers (over 38,000) than Los Angeles, a city three times its size.[8] Another kind of institutional interest is the trade or governmental association, such as the National Independent Retail Jewelers or the National Association of Counties.

Individuals or organizations that represent other organizations tend to be interested in bread-and-butter issues of vital concern to their clients. Some of the people who specialize in this work can earn very large fees. Top public relations experts and Washington lawyers can charge $400 an hour or more for their time. Since they earn a lot, they are expected to deliver a lot.

Just what they are expected to deliver, however, varies with the diversity of the groups making up the organization. The American Cotton Manufacturers Institute represents southern textile mills. Those mills are few enough in number and similar enough in outlook to allow the institute to carry out clear policies squarely based on the business interests of its clients. For example, the institute works hard to get the federal government to adopt laws and rules that will keep foreign-made textiles from competing too easily with American-made goods. Sometimes the institute is successful, sometimes not, but it is never hard to explain what it is doing.

By contrast, the U.S. Chamber of Commerce represents thousands of different businesses in hundreds of different communities. Its membership is so large and diverse that the Chamber in Washington can speak out clearly and forcefully on only those relatively few matters in which all, or most, businesses take the same position. Since all businesses would like lower taxes, the Chamber favors that. On the other hand, since some businesses (those that import goods) want low tariffs and other businesses (those that face competition from imported goods) want higher tariffs, the Chamber says little or nothing about tariffs.

Institutional interests do not just represent business firms; they also represent governments, foundations, and universities. For example, the American Council on Education claims to speak for most institutions of higher education, the American Public Transit Association represents local mass-transit systems, and the National Association of Counties argues on behalf of county governments.

Membership Interests

It is often said that Americans are a nation of joiners, and so we take for granted the many organizations around us supported by the activities and contributions of individual citizens. But we should not take this multiplicity of organizations for granted; in fact their existence is something of a puzzle.

Americans join only certain kinds of organizations more frequently than do citizens of other democratic countries. We are no more likely than the British, for example, to join social, business, professional, veterans, or charitable organizations, and we are *less* likely to join labor unions. Our reputation as a nation of joiners arises chiefly out of our unusually high tendency to join religious and civic or political associations. About three times as many Americans as Britons say that they are members of a civic or political organization.[9]

This proclivity of Americans to get together with other citizens to engage in civic or political action reflects, apparently, a greater sense of political efficacy and a stronger sense of civic duty in this country. When Gabriel Almond and Sidney Verba asked citizens of five nations what they would do to protest an unjust local regulation, 56 percent of the Americans—but only 34 percent of the British and 13 percent of the Germans—said that they would try to organize their neighbors to write letters, sign petitions, or otherwise act in concert.[10] Americans are also more likely than Europeans to think that organized activity is an effective way to influence the national government, remote as that institution may seem. And this willingness to form civic or political groups is not a product of higher levels of education in this country; Americans of every level of schooling are political joiners.[11]

But explaining the American willingness to join politically active groups by saying that Americans feel a "sense of political efficacy" is not much of an explanation; we might as well say that people vote because they think that their vote makes a difference. But one vote clearly makes no difference at all in almost any election; similarly, one member, more or less, in the Sierra Club, the National Rifle Association, or the NAACP clearly will make no difference in the success of those organizations.

And in fact most people who are sympathetic to the aims of a mass-membership interest group do not join it. The NAACP, for example, enrolls as members only a tiny fraction of all African Americans. This is not because people are selfish or apathetic but because they are rational and numerous. A single African American, for example, knows that he or she

W.E.B. Du Bois (center) was one of the founders of the NAACP in 1910 and the editor of its magazine, The Crisis.

The largest interest group in America is the AARP, the American Association of Retired Persons.

can make no difference in the success of the NAACP, just as a single nature enthusiast knows that he or she cannot enhance the power of the Sierra Club. Moreover, if the NAACP or the Sierra Club succeeds, African Americans and nature lovers will benefit even if they are not members. Therefore rational people who value their time and money would no more join such organizations than they would attempt to

---

> **incentive**   Something of value one cannot get without joining an organization.
>
> **solidary incentives**   The social rewards (sense of pleasure, status, or companionship) that lead people to join political organizations.
>
> **material incentives**   Money or things valued in monetary terms.

---

empty a lake with a cup—unless they got something out of joining.

Incentives to Join

To get people to join mass-membership organizations, they must be offered an **incentive**—something of value they cannot get without joining. There are three kinds of incentives.

Solidary incentives are the sense of pleasure, status, or companionship that arises out of meeting together in small groups. Such rewards are extremely important, but because they tend to be available only from face-to-face contact, national interest groups offering them often have to organize themselves as coalitions of small local units. For example, the League of Women Voters, the Parent Teacher Association (PTA), the NAACP, the Rotary Club, and the American Legion all consist of small local chapters that support a national staff. It is the task of the local chapters to lure members and obtain funds from them; the state or national staff can then pursue political objectives by using these funds. Forming organizations made up of small local chapters is probably easier in the United States than in Europe because of the great importance of local government in our federal system. There is plenty for a PTA, an NAACP, or a League of Women Voters to do in its own community, and so its members can be kept busy with local affairs while the national staff pursues larger goals.

A second kind of incentive consists of **material incentives**—that is, money, or things and services readily valued in monetary terms. Farm organizations have recruited many members by offering a wide range of services. The Illinois Farm Bureau, for example, offers to its members—and *only* to its members—a chance to buy farm supplies at discount prices, to market their products through cooperatives, and to purchase low-cost insurance. These material incentives help explain why the Illinois Farm Bureau has been able to enroll nearly every farmer in the state as well as many nonfarmers who also value these rewards.[12]

Similarly, the American Association of Retired Persons (AARP) has recruited over 30 million members by supplying them with everything from low-cost life insurance and mail-order discount drugs to tax advice and group travel plans. About 45 percent of the nation's population that is fifty and older—one out of every four registered voters—belongs to the AARP. With an annual operating budget of over

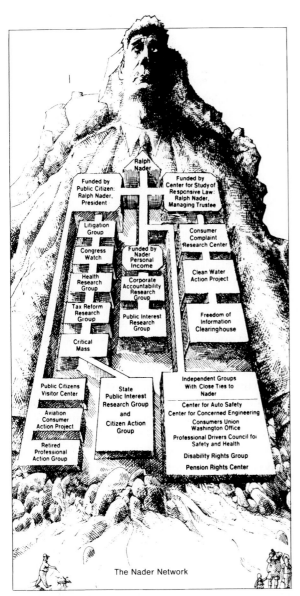

The Nader Network

Since the mid-1960s consumer activist Ralph Nader has spawned more than a dozen interest groups. In 2000 Nader ran for president as a Green party candidate.

$200 million and a cash flow estimated at a whopping $10 billion, the AARP seeks to influence public policy in many areas, from health and housing to taxes and transportation. To gain additional benefits for members, interest groups like the AARP also seek to influence how public laws are administered and who gets government grants. For example, the Environmental Protection Agency funds the AARP to hire senior citizens as temporary workers for various environmental projects.[13]

The third—and most difficult—kind of incentive is the *purpose* of the organization. Many associations rely chiefly on this **purposive incentive**—the appeal of their stated goals—to recruit members. If the attainment of those goals will also benefit people who do not join, individuals who do join will have to be those who feel passionately about the goal, who have a strong sense of duty (or who cannot say no to a friend who asks them to join), or for whom the cost of joining is so small that they are indifferent to joining or not. Organizations that attract members by appealing to their interest in a coherent set of (usually) controversial principles are sometimes called **ideological interest groups.**

When the purpose of the organization, if attained, will principally benefit nonmembers, it is customary to call the group a **public-interest lobby.** (Whether the public at large will really benefit, of course, is a matter of opinion, but at least the group members think that they are working selflessly for the common good.)

Though some public-interest lobbies may pursue relatively noncontroversial goals (for example, persuading people to vote or raising money to house orphans), the most visible of these organizations are highly controversial. It is precisely the controversy that attracts the members, or at least those members who support one side of the issue. Many of these groups can be described as markedly liberal or decidedly conservative in outlook.

Perhaps the best known of the liberal public-interest groups are those founded by or associated with Ralph Nader. Nader became a popular figure in the mid-1960s after General Motors made a clumsy attempt to investigate and discredit his background at a time when he was testifying in favor of an auto-safety bill. Nader won a large out-of-court settlement against General Motors, his books began to earn royalties, and he was able to command substantial lecture fees. Most of this money was turned over to various organizations he created that dealt with matters of interest to

purposive incentive A benefit that comes from serving a cause or principle.
ideological interest groups Political organizations that attract members by appealing to their political convictions or principles.
public-interest lobby A political organization whose goals will principally benefit nonmembers.

Public-Interest Law Firms

A special kind of public-interest lobby is an organization that advances its cause by bringing lawsuits to challenge existing practices or proposed regulations. A public-interest law firm will act in one of two ways: First, it will find someone who has been harmed by some public or private policy and bring suit on his or her behalf. Second, it will file a brief with a court supporting somebody else's lawsuit (this is called an amicus curiae brief; it is explained in Chapter 16).

Here are some examples of liberal and conservative public-interest law firms:

Liberal	*Conservative*
American Civil Liberties Union	Atlantic Legal Foundation
Asian American Legal Defense Fund	The Center for Individual Rights
Lawyers' Committee for Civil Rights	Criminal Justice Legal Foundation
Mexican American Legal Defense Fund	Landmark Legal Foundation
NAACP Legal Defense and Education Fund	Mountain States Legal Foundation
Natural Resources Defense Council	Pacific Legal Foundation
Women's Legal Defense Fund	Washington Legal Foundation

consumers. In addition he founded a group called Public Citizen that raised money by direct-mail solicitation from thousands of small contributors and sought foundation grants. Finally, he helped create Public Interest Research Groups (PIRGs) in a number of states, supported by donations from college students (voluntary at some colleges, a compulsory assessment levied on all students at others) and concerned with organizing student activists to work on local projects.

Recently cracks have begun to appear in the Nader movement. When Hawaii and California considered plans to develop no-fault automobile insurance, some former allies of Nader led the effort to reduce auto insurance prices by adopting a no-fault system. Nader denounced this effort and urged Hawaii's governor to veto the no-fault bill. Each side criticized the other.

Conservatives, though slow to get started, have also adopted the public-interest organizational strategy. As with such associations run by liberals, they are of two kinds: those that engage in research and lobbying and those that bring lawsuits designed to advance their cause. The boxes on pages 272 and 273 list some examples of public-interest organizations that support liberal or conservative causes.

Membership organizations that rely on purposive incentives, especially appeals to deeply controversial purposes, tend to be shaped by the mood of the times. When an issue is hot—in the media or with the pub-

lic—such organizations can grow rapidly. When the spotlight fades, the organization may lose support. Thus such organizations have a powerful motive to stay in the public eye. To remain visible, public-interest lobbies devote a lot of attention to generating publicity by developing good contacts with the media and issuing dramatic press releases about crises and scandals.

Because of their need to take advantage of a crisis atmosphere, public-interest lobbies often do best when the government is in the hands of an administration that is *hostile*, not sympathetic, to their views. Environmentalist organizations could mobilize more resources when James Watt, an opponent of much of the environmental movement, was secretary of the interior than they could when Cecil D. Andrus, his proenvironment predecessor, was in office. By the same token many conservative interest groups were able to raise more money with the relatively liberal Jimmy Carter or Bill Clinton in the White House than with the conservative Ronald Reagan or George W. Bush.

The Influence of the Staff

We often make the mistake of assuming that what an interest group does politically is simply to exert influence on behalf of its members. That is indeed the case when all the members have a clear and similar stake in an issue. But many issues affect different members differently. In fact, if the members joined to obtain solidary or material benefits, they may not

Think Tanks in Washington

Think tanks are public-interest organizations that do research on policy questions and disseminate their findings in books, articles, conferences, op-ed essays for newspapers, and (occasionally) testimony before Congress. Some are nonpartisan and ideologically more or less neutral, but others—and many of the most important ones—are aligned with liberal or conservative causes. Here are some examples of each:

Liberal	*Conservative*
Center on Budget and Policy Priorities	American Enterprise Institute
Center for Defense Information	Cato Institute
Children's Defense Fund	Center for Strategic and
Economic Policy Institute	International Studies
Institute for Policy Studies	Competitive Enterprise Institute
Joint Center for Political and	Ethics and Public Policy Center
Economic Studies	Free Congress Foundation
Progressive Policy Institute	Heritage Foundation

Note that the labels "liberal" and "conservative," while generally accurate, conceal important differences among the think tanks in each list.

care at all about many of the issues with which the organization gets involved. In such cases what the interest group does may reflect more what the staff wants than what the members believe.

For example, a survey of the white members of a large labor union showed that one-third of them believed that the desegregation of schools, housing, and job opportunities had gone too fast; only one-fifth thought that it had gone too slowly. But among the staff members of the union, *none* thought that desegregation had gone too fast, and over two-thirds thought that it had gone too slowly.[14] As a result the union staff aggressively lobbied Congress for the passage of tougher civil rights laws, even though most of the union's members did not feel that they were needed. The members stayed in the union for reasons unrelated to civil rights, giving the staff the freedom to pursue its own goals.

☆ Interest Groups and Social Movements

Because it is difficult to attract people with purposive incentives, interest groups employing them tend to arise out of social movements. A **social movement** is a widely shared demand for change in some aspect of the social or political order. The civil rights movement of the 1960s was such an event, as was the environmentalist movement of the 1970s. A social movement need not have liberal goals. In the nineteenth century, for example, there were various nativist movements that sought to reduce immigration to this country or to keep Catholics or Masons out of public office. Broad-based religious revivals are social movements.

No one is quite certain why social movements arise. At one moment people are largely indifferent to some issue; at another moment many of these same people care passionately about religion, civil rights, immigration, or conservation. A social movement may be triggered by a scandal (an oil spill on the Santa Barbara beaches helped launch the environmental movement), the dramatic and widely publicized activities of a few leaders (lunch counter sit-ins helped stimulate the civil rights movement), or the coming of age of a new generation that takes up a cause advocated by eloquent writers, teachers, or evangelists.

social movement A widely shared demand for change in some aspect of the social or political order.

The Million Moms March in 2004 demanded a federal ban on assault weapons.

The Environmental Movement

Whatever its origin, the effect of a social movement is to increase the value some people attach to purposive incentives. As a consequence new interest groups are formed that rely on these incentives. In the 1890s, as a result of the emergence of conservation as a major issue, the Sierra Club was organized. In the 1930s conservation once again became popular, and the Wilderness Society and the National Wildlife Federation took form. In the 1960s and 1970s environmental issues again came to the fore, and we saw the emergence of the Environmental Defense Fund and Environmental Action.

The smallest of these organizations (Environmental Action and the Environmental Defense Fund) tend to have the most liberal members. This is often the case with social movements. A movement will spawn many organizations. The most passionately aroused people will be the fewest in number, and they will gravitate toward the organizations that take the most extreme positions; as a result these organizations are small but vociferous. The more numerous and less passionate people will gravitate toward more moderate, less vociferous organizations, which will tend to be larger.

The Feminist Movement

There have been several feminist social movements in this country's history—in the 1830s, in the 1890s, in the 1920s, and in the 1960s. Each period has brought into being new organizations, some of which have endured to the present. For example, the League of Women Voters was founded in 1920 to educate and organize women for the purpose of using effectively their newly won right to vote.

Though a strong sense of purpose may lead to the creation of organizations, each will strive to find some incentive that will sustain it over the long haul. These permanent incentives will affect how the organization participates in politics.

There are at least three kinds of feminist organizations. First, there are those that rely chiefly on solidary incentives, enroll middle-class women with relatively high levels of schooling, and tend to support those causes that command the widest support among women generally. The League of Women Voters and the Federation of Business and Professional Women are examples. Both supported the campaign to ratify the Equal Rights Amendment (ERA), but as Jane Mansbridge has observed in her history of the ERA, they were uneasy with the kind of intense, partisan fighting displayed by some other women's organizations and with the tendency of more militant groups to link the ERA to other issues, such as abortion. The reason for their uneasiness is clear: to the extent they relied on solidary incentives, they had a stake in avoiding issues and tactics that would divide their membership or reduce the extent to which membership provided camaraderie and professional contacts.[15]

Second, there are women's organizations that attract members with purposive incentives. The National Organization for Women (NOW) and the National Abortion Rights Action League (NARAL) are two of the largest such groups, though there are many smaller ones. Because they rely on purposes, these organizations must take strong positions, tackle divisive issues, and employ militant tactics. Anything less would turn off the committed feminists who make up the rank and file and contribute the funds. But because these groups take controversial stands, they are constantly embroiled in internal quarrels between those who think that they have gone too far and those who think that they have not gone far enough, between women who want NOW or NARAL to join with lesbian and socialist organizations and those who want them to steer clear. Moreover, as Mansbridge showed, purposive organizations often cannot make their decisions stick on the local level (local chapters will do pretty much as they please).[16]

Figure 11.1   The Decline in Union Membership

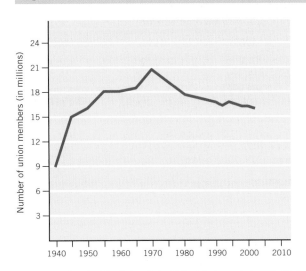

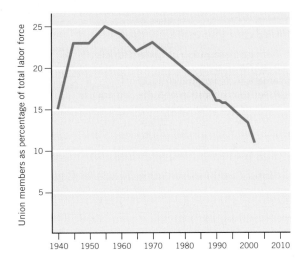

Sources: *Historical Statistics of the United States*, vol. 1, 178; *Statistical Abstract of the United States*, *1998*, 444; U.S. Census Bureau; *Statistical Abstract of the United States*, 2003, 432, 433.

The third kind of women's organization is the caucus that takes on specific issues that have some material benefit to women. The Women's Equity Action League (WEAL) is one such group. Rather than relying on membership dues for financial support, it obtains grants from foundations and government agencies. Freed of the necessity of satisfying a large rank-and-file membership, WEAL has concentrated its efforts on bringing lawsuits aimed at enforcing or enlarging the legal rights of women in higher education and other institutions. In electoral politics the National Women's Political Caucus (officially nonpartisan, but generally liberal and Democratic) and the National Federation of Republican Women (openly supportive of the Republican party) work to get more women active in politics and more women elected or appointed to office.

The feminist movement has, of course, spawned an antifeminist movement, and thus feminist organizations have their antifeminist counterparts. The campaign by NOW for the ERA was attacked by a women's group called STOP ERA; the proabortion position of NARAL has been challenged by the various organizations associated with the right-to-life movement. These opposition groups have their own tactical problems, which arise in large part from their reliance on different kinds of incentives. In the chapter on civil rights we shall see how the conflict between these opposing groups shaped the debate over the ERA.

The Union Movement

When social movements run out of steam, they leave behind organizations that continue the fight. But with the movement dead or dormant, the organizations often must struggle to stay alive. This has happened to labor unions.

The major union movement in this country occurred in the 1930s, when the Great Depression, popular support, and a sympathetic administration in Washington led to a rapid growth in union membership. In 1945 union membership peaked; at that time nearly 36 percent of all nonfarm workers were union members.

Since then union membership has fallen more or less steadily, so that by 2002 only 11 percent of all workers were unionized (see Figure 11.1). This decline has been caused by several factors. There has been a shift in the nation's economic life away from industrial production (where unions have traditionally been concentrated) and toward service delivery (where unions have usually been weak). But accompanying this decline, and perhaps contributing to it, has been a decline in popular approval of unions.

	Number of Members			
Union	1979	1983	1993	2002
National Association of Letter Carriers	151,000	201,000	210,000	302,000
Postal Workers	245,000	213,999	249,000	332,000
American Federation of Teachers	423,000	544,000	574,000	1.3 million
American Federation of State and County Municipal Employees	889,000	1 million	1.16 million	1.4 million

Table 11.2   The Rise in Four Government Employee Unions

Four-Union Total 1979: 1.71 million
Four-Union Total 2002: 3.33 million
Percent Change, 1979–2002: +94%

Sources: Statistical Abstract of the United States, 1994, table 696, 443; post-1998 press releases and fact sheets by each organization.

Approval has moved down side by side with a decline in membership and declines in union victories in elections held to see whether workers in a plant want to join a union. The social movement that supported unionism has faded.

But unions will persist, because most can rely on incentives other than purposive ones to keep them going. In many industries they can require workers to join if they wish to keep their jobs, and in other industries workers believe that they get sufficient benefits from the union to make even voluntary membership worthwhile. And in a few industries, such as teaching and government, there has been a growth in membership, as some white-collar workers have turned to unions to advance their interests.

Unions composed of government workers are becoming the most important part of the union movement. They are almost the only part that is growing in size. For example, from 1983 to 1999 the number of private sector union members fell from 11.9 million to 9.4 million, a 21 percent drop. Over the same period, however, the number of public sector union members rose from 5.7 million to 7 million, a 22 percent increase.[17] Especially significant has been the membership growth in certain government employee unions (see Table 11.2). These unions have gained new members and political clout at a time when almost every industrial union was losing both.

☆ Funds for Interest Groups

All interest groups have some trouble raising money, but membership organizations have more trouble than most, especially membership organizations relying on appeals to purpose—to accomplishing stated goals. As a result the Washington office of a public-interest lobbying group is likely to be small, stark, and crowded, whereas that of an institutional lobby, such as the AFL-CIO or the American Council on Education, will be rather lavish.

To raise more money than members supply in dues, lobbying organizations have turned to three sources that have become important in recent years: foundation grants, government grants, and direct-mail solicitation.

Foundation Grants

One study of eighty-three (primarily liberal) public-interest lobbying groups found that one-third of them received half or more of all their funds from foundation grants; one-tenth received over 90 percent from such sources.[18] In one ten-year period the Ford Foundation alone contributed about $21 million to liberal public-interest groups. Many of these organizations were law firms that, other than the staff lawyers, really had no members at all. The Environmental Defense Fund is supported almost entirely by grants from foundations such as the Rockefeller Family Fund. The more conservative Scaife foundations gave $1.8 million to a conservative public-interest group, the National Legal Center for the Public Interest.[19]

Federal Grants and Contracts

The expansion of federal grants during the 1960s and 1970s benefited interest groups as well as cities and states; the cutbacks in those grants during the early 1980s hurt interest groups even more than they hurt local governments. Of course the federal government usually does not give the money to support lobbying itself; it is given instead to support some project that the organization has undertaken.

For example, many large national for-profit firms with trade representatives or other lobbyists in Washington (sometimes unflatteringly referred to as "beltway bandits") do most or all of their business by winning federal grants and contracts. Even large national religious nonprofit organizations such as Lutheran Social Services, Catholic Charities, the Salvation Army, and the Jewish Federations have received millions of dollars in government grants to provide diverse social services and run various community projects. But money for a service or project helps support the organization as a whole and thus enables the organization to press Congress for policies it favors (including, of course, policies that will supply it with more grants and contracts).

Nobody really knows whether the groups that win federal grants and contracts are doing a good job or not. The nonprofit and other organizations that receive the lion's share of federal grants and contracts are rarely, if ever, subjected to government performance audits or independent research evaluations.[20] A White House report on grant-making across five federal agencies found that each agency's top ten discretionary grant recipients changed little over the course of a decade.[21] Due in part to the interest-group politics of federal grants and contracts, the "organizations that administer social services funded by Washington are typically large and entrenched, in an almost monopolistic fashion."[22]

In the 1980s the Reagan administration attempted to cut back on federal funds going to nonprofit groups that conservatives claimed also lobbied for liberal causes. Some writers called this an effort to "de-fund the left." In 2001 the Bush administration attempted to increase federal funds going to faith-based organizations. Some writers construed this an effort to "fund the religious right." Neither effort, however, made a significant difference either in which organizations won or lost federal grants and contracts, or in how much federal money was available overall.

Direct Mail

If there is any one technique that is unique to the modern interest group, it is the sophistication with which mailings are used both to raise money and to

Many large religious nonprofit organizations, like the Salvation Army, receive some government funding.

mobilize supporters. By using computers, membership interest groups can mail directly to specialized audiences identified from lists developed by the staff or purchased from other organizations. Letters can be tailor-made, for example, to appeal to upper-income residents of Oregon who belong to the Sierra Club, live near the Columbia River, own four-wheel-drive vehicles, and thus might be interested in maintaining a local wilderness area.

A classic example of an interest group that was created and maintained by direct-mail solicitation is Common Cause, a liberal organization founded in 1970. Its creator, John Gardner, sent letters to tens of thousands of people selected from mailing lists it had acquired, urging them to join the organization and to send in money. Over two hundred thousand members were obtained in this way, each of whom mailed in dues (initially $15 a year) in return for nothing more than the satisfaction of belonging.

But raising money by mail costs money—lots of money. To bring in more money than it spends, the interest group must write a letter that will galvanize enough readers to send in a check. "Enough" usually amounts to at least 2 percent of the names on the list. Techniques include the following:

- Put a "teaser" on the outside of the envelope so that it won't be thrown out as "junk mail." If the letter is going to African Americans, put a picture of Reverend Martin Luther King, Jr. on the envelope.
- Arouse emotions, preferably by portraying the threat posed by some "devil." To environmentalists, a typical devil would be former secretary of

the interior James Watt; to civil libertarians, former Moral Majority leader Jerry Falwell; to conservatives, Senator Ted Kennedy.

- Have the endorsement of a famous name. For liberals it is often Senator Kennedy; for conservatives it may be House leader Tom DeLay.
- Personalize the letter by instructing the computer to insert the recipient's name into the text of the letter to create the impression that it was written personally to him or her.

☆ The Problem of Bias

Many observers believe that the interest groups active in Washington reflect an upper-class bias. There are two reasons for this belief: first, well-off people are more likely than poor people to join and be active in interest groups, and second, interest groups representing business and the professions are much more numerous and better financed than organizations representing minorities, consumers, or the disadvantaged.

Doubtless both these facts are true. Many scholars have shown that people with higher incomes, those whose schooling went through college or beyond, and those in professional or technical jobs were much more likely to belong to a voluntary association than people with the opposite characteristics. Just as we would expect, higher-income people can afford more organizational memberships than lower-income ones; people in business and the professions find it both easier to attend meetings (they have more control over their own work schedules) and more necessary to do so than people in blue-collar jobs; and people with college degrees often have a wider range of interests than those without. One study found that over half of the many thousand groups represented in Washington were corporations, and another third were professional and trade associations. Only 4 percent were public-interest groups; fewer than 2 percent were civil rights or minority groups.[23] About 170 organizations represented in Washington were concerned just with the oil industry.

But the question of an upper-class bias cannot be settled by these two facts taken alone. In the first place, they describe only certain *inputs* into the political system; they say nothing about the *outputs*—that is, who wins and who loses on particular issues. Even if 170 interest groups are trying to protect the oil industry,

this is important only if the oil industry in fact gets protected. Sometimes it does; sometimes it does not. At one time, when oil prices were low, oil companies were able to get Congress to pass a law that sharply restricted the importation of foreign oil. A few years later, after oil prices had risen and people were worried about energy issues, these restrictions were ended.

In the second place, business-oriented interest groups are often divided among themselves. Take one kind of business: farming. Once, farm organizations seemed so powerful in Washington that scholars spoke of an irresistible "farm bloc" in Congress that could get its way on almost anything. Today dozens of agricultural organizations operate in the capital, with some (such as the Farm Bureau) attempting to speak for all farmers and others (such as the Tobacco Institute and Mid-America Dairymen) representing particular commodities and regions.

Farmers still have a great deal of influence, especially when it comes to blocking a bill that they oppose. But it is proving difficult for them to get Congress to approve a bill that they want passed. In part this political weakness reflects the decline in the number of farmers and thus in the number of legislators who must take their interests into account. In part their political weakness reflects splits among the farmers themselves, with southern cotton growers often seeing things differently from midwestern wheat growers or New England dairy farmers. And to some extent it reflects the context within which interest group politics must operate. In the 1950s few people thought that providing subsidies for farmers was too expensive—if indeed they knew of such programs at all. But by the 1980s consumers were acutely aware of food prices, and their legislators were keenly aware of the cost of farm-support programs.[24]

Whenever American politics is described as having an upper-class bias, it is important to ask exactly what this bias is. Most of the major conflicts in American politics—over foreign policy, economic affairs, environmental protection, or equal rights for women—are conflicts *within* the upper middle class; they are conflicts, that is, among politically active elites. As we saw in Chapter 7, there are profound cleavages of opinion among these elites. Interest group activity reflects these cleavages.

Nonetheless, it would be a mistake to ignore the overrepresentation of business in Washington. A student of politics should always take differences in the

Farmers once had great influence in Congress and could get their way with a few telephone calls. Today they often must use mass protest methods.

availability of political resources as an important clue to possible differences in the outcomes of political conflicts. But they are only clues, not conclusions.

☆ The Activities of Interest Groups

Size and wealth are no longer entirely accurate measures of an interest group's influence—if indeed they ever were. Depending on the issue, the key to political influence may be the ability to generate a dramatic newspaper headline, mobilize a big letter-writing campaign, stage a protest demonstration, file a suit in federal court to block (or compel) some government action, or quietly supply information to key legislators. All of these things require organization, but only some of them require big or expensive organizations.

Information

Of all these tactics, the single most important one—in the eyes of virtually every lobbyist and every academic student of lobbying—is supplying credible information. The reason why information is so valuable is

that, to busy legislators and bureaucrats, information is in short supply. Legislators in particular must take positions on a staggering number of issues about which they cannot possibly become experts.

Though there are nonpolitical sources of information, such as encyclopedias, they often do not provide the kind of detailed, specific, up-to-date information that politicians need. This kind of information will ordinarily be gathered only by a group that has a strong interest in some issue. Lobbyists, for the most part, are not flamboyant, party-giving arm-twisters; they are specialists who gather information (favorable to their clients, naturally) and present it in as organized, persuasive, and factual a manner as possible. All lobbyists no doubt exaggerate, but few can afford to misrepresent the facts or mislead a legislator, and for a very simple reason: almost every lobbyist must develop and maintain the confidence of a legislator over the long term, with an eye on tomorrow's issues as well as today's. Misrepresentation or bad advice can embarrass a legislator who accepts it or repel one who detects it, leading to distrust of the lobbyist. Maintaining contacts and channels of communication is vital; to that end, maintaining trust is essential.

The value of the information provided by a lobbyist is often greatest when the issue is fairly narrow, involving only a few interest groups or a complex economic or technical problem. The value of information, and thus the power of the lobbyist, is likely to be least when the issue is one of broad and highly visible national policy.

Sometimes the nature of an issue or the governmental process by which an issue is resolved gives a great advantage to the suppliers of certain information and imposes a great burden on would-be suppliers of contrary information. This is an example of what is called "client politics." For example, the Civil Aeronautics Board (CAB) once set airline fares and decided what airlines would fly to what cities. Historically the only organizations with any incentive to appear before the CAB and supply the necessary information were, naturally, the airlines. Until the CAB began to deregulate civil aviation, CAB decisions often tended to favor the established airlines.

For a long time only radio and television broadcasters had any incentive (or could afford) to appear before the Federal Communications Commission (FCC), which decides which broadcasters shall be licensed and on what terms. Owing to changes in the industry (such as the rise of cable and satellite television) and to the growth of consumer groups, FCC hearings are now often hotly contested. When the Federal Energy Administration (FEA) was trying to allocate scarce oil and gasoline supplies among competing users, it discovered that the information it needed was possessed only by the oil companies. (It later took steps to develop its own sources of data.)

Public officials not only want technical information; they also want political cues. A **political cue** is a signal telling the official what values are at stake in an issue—who is for, who against a proposal—and how that issue fits into his or her own set of political beliefs. Some legislators feel comfortable when they are on the liberal side of an issue, and others feel comfortable when they are on the conservative side, especially when they are not familiar with the details of the issue. A liberal legislator will look to see

whether the AFL-CIO, the NAACP, the Americans for Democratic Action, the Farmers' Union, and various consumer organizations favor a proposal; if so, that is often all he or she has to know. If these liberal groups are split, then the legislator will worry about the matter and try to look into it more closely. Similarly, a conservative legislator will feel comfortable taking a stand on an issue if the Chamber of Commerce, the National Rifle Association, the American Medical Association, various business associations, and Americans for Constitutional Action are in agreement about it; he or she will feel less comfortable if such conservative groups are divided. As a result of this process lobbyists often work together in informal coalitions based on general political ideology.

One important way in which these cues are made known is by **ratings** that interest groups make of legislators. These are regularly compiled by the AFL-CIO (on who is prolabor), by the Americans for Democratic Action (on who is liberal), by the Americans for Constitutional Action (on who is conservative), by the Consumer Federation of America (on who is proconsumer), and by the League of Conservation Voters (on who is pro-environment). These ratings are designed to generate public support for (or opposition to) various legislators. They can be helpful sources of information, but they are sometimes biased by the arbitrary determination of what constitutes a liberal, proconsumer, or conservative vote.

Both political information and political cues now arrive in the offices of politicians at a faster rate than ever before, thanks to fax machines and the Internet. Many interest groups and political activists have banks of computer-operated fax machines that can get a short, snappy document into the hands of every legislator within minutes. William Kristol, a Republican activist, used this technique to good effect in 1993 when he bombarded Republican members of Congress with arguments concerning why they should oppose President Clinton's health care plan. Many believe he played a major role in the defeat of that plan.

Public Support: The Rise of the New Politics

Once upon a time, when the government was small, Congress was less individualistic, and television was nonexistent, lobbyists mainly used an *insider strategy:* they worked closely with a few key members of

---

political cue   A signal telling a legislator what values are at stake in a vote, and how that issue fits into his or her own political views on party agenda.

ratings   Assessments of a representative's voting record on issues important to an interest group.

Congress, meeting them privately to exchange information and (sometimes) favors. Matters of mutual interest could be discussed at a leisurely pace, over dinner or while playing golf. Public opinion was important on some highly visible issues, but there were not many of these.

Following an insider strategy is still valuable, but increasingly interest groups have turned to an *outsider strategy*. The newly individualistic nature of Congress has made this tactic useful, and modern technology has made it possible. Radio, fax machines, and the Internet can now get news out almost immediately. Satellite television can be used to link interested citizens in various locations across the country. Toll-free phone numbers can be publicized, enabling voters to call the offices of their members of Congress without charge. Public opinion polls can be done by telephone, virtually overnight, to measure (and help generate) support for or opposition to proposed legislation. Mail can be directed by computers to people already known to have an interest in a particular matter.

This kind of *grassroots lobbying* is central to the outsider strategy. It is designed to generate public pressure directly on government officials. The "public" that exerts this pressure is not every voter or even most voters; it is that part of the public (sometimes called an *issue public*) that is directly affected by or deeply concerned with a government policy. What modern technology has made possible is the overnight mobilization of specific issue publics.

Not every issue lends itself to an outsider strategy: it is hard to get many people excited about, for example, complex tax legislation affecting only a few firms. But as the government does more and more, its policies affect more and more people, and so more and more will join in grassroots lobbying efforts over matters such as abortion, Medicare, Social Security, environmental protection, and affirmative action.

Undoubtedly the new politics creates new conflicts. Since conflict is the essence of politics, it may seem strange that politicians dislike controversy. But they do, and for perfectly human reasons: no one enjoys dealing with people who are upset or who find one's viewpoint objectionable or unworthy. Consequently, most legislators tend to hear what they want to hear and to deal with interest groups that agree with them.[25] Two senators from the same state may choose to listen to very different constituencies in that state and to take very different policy positions.

Neither senator may feel "pressured" or "lobbied," because each has heard mostly from groups or persons who share his or her views. (Politicians define "pressure" as arguments and inducements supplied by somebody with whom they disagree.)

Members of an interest group will also tend to work primarily with legislators with whom they agree; lobbyists do not like to argue with people who are suspicious of them or who are unlikely to change their minds no matter what is said. For the lobbyist the key target is the undecided or wavering legislator or bureaucrat. Sometimes lobbyists will make a major effort to persuade an undecided legislator that public opinion is strongly inclined in one direction. A lobbyist will do this by commissioning public opinion polls, stimulating local citizens to write letters or send telegrams, arranging for constituents to pay personal visits to the legislator, or getting newspapers to run editorials supporting the lobbyist's position.

Though most lobbying organizations cultivate the goodwill of government officials, there are important exceptions. Some groups, especially those that use an ideological appeal to attract supporters or that depend for their maintenance and influence on media publicity, will deliberately attack actual or potential allies in government in order to embarrass them. Ralph Nader is as likely to denounce as to praise those officials who tend to agree with him, if their agreement is not sufficiently close or public. He did this with Senator Edmund Muskie, the author of the Clean Air Act, and with William Haddon, Jr., an early administrator of the National Highway Traffic Safety Administration. The head of the Fund for Animals is not reluctant to attack those officials in the Forest Service and the Interior Department on whose cooperation the fund must rely if it is to achieve its goals.[26] Sometimes, as we shall see later in this chapter, the use of threats instead of rewards extends to physical confrontations.

It is not clear how often public pressure works. Members of Congress are skilled at recognizing and discounting organized mail campaigns and feel that they can occasionally afford to go against even legitimate expressions of hostile public opinion. Only a few issues of great symbolic significance and high visibility are so important that a member of Congress would think that to ignore public opinion would mean losing the next election. In 1978 the proposed Panama Canal treaties were one such case; since the 1980s abortion has been another. Issues such as these can make or break a member of Congress.

Of late, interest groups have placed great emphasis on developing grassroots support. Sometimes it is impossible to develop such support, as when a complicated tax regulation of interest to only a few firms is being changed. But sometimes a proposed bill touches a public nerve such that even businesses can help generate an outpouring of mail: when the Food and Drug Administration announced it was going to ban saccharin on the grounds that it caused cancer in laboratory animals, the Calorie Control Council (closely tied to the Coca-Cola Company, a big user of saccharin in soft drinks such as Tab) ran newspaper ads denouncing the policy. The public, worried about losing access to an artificial sweetener important to dieters, responded with an avalanche of mail to Congress, which promptly passed a law reversing the ban.

Usually, however, the public at large doesn't care that much about an issue, and so interest groups will try by direct-mail campaigns to arouse a small but passionate group to write letters or vote (or not vote) for specified candidates. Beginning in 1970 Environmental Action designated certain members of the House of Representatives as the "Dirty Dozen" because of their votes against bills that the lobbying group claimed were necessary to protect the environment. Of the thirty-one members of Congress so listed in various elections, only seven survived in office. Many members of Congress believe that the "Dirty Dozen" label hurts them with pro-environment voters in their districts, and though they are angry over what they feel is the unfair use of that label, they strive to avoid it if at all possible.

The press sometimes depicts certain large, well-funded interest groups as all-powerful, but few are. Take, for example, the National Rifle Association (NRA). Founded in 1871 as a group dedicated to shooting instruction, the NRA in the 1960s and 1970s became a lobby opposing policies that would restrict citizens' rights to own and use firearms for sporting and other legal purposes. By the 1980s the NRA's dues-paying membership had increased from 1 million to nearly 3 million. Its members receive magazines, decals, and other direct benefits. From 1983 to 1992 the NRA spent $8 million on congressional races both in direct contributions to their favored candidates and in independent expenditures supporting or opposing various candidates. Still, in the mid-1990s the NRA lost a major battle to repeal New Jersey's ban on certain types of semiautomatic weapons and lost similar battles in Connecticut, Vir-

ginia, and other states. In 1993, over fierce opposition from the NRA, Congress passed the Brady bill, a major piece of gun control legislation named after Jim Brady, the press secretary who was shot and permanently disabled during an attempt to assassinate President Reagan. By the late 1990s the NRA had a negative image even among most gun owners, and the organization found itself constantly in the political cross hairs of small but media-savvy pro–gun control lobbies such as Handgun Control, Inc. As the NRA's recent history teaches, in American politics no interest group, no matter how big its budget or mammoth its membership, is a lobby that cannot be beat.

Money and PACs

Contrary to popular suspicions, money is probably one of the less effective ways by which interest groups advance their causes. That was not always the case. Only a few decades ago powerful interests used their bulging wallets to buy influence in Congress. The passage of the campaign finance reform law in 1973 changed that. The law had two effects. First, it sharply restricted the amount that any interest could give to a candidate for federal office (see Chapter 10). Second, it made it legal for corporations and labor unions to form political action committees (PACs) that could make political contributions.

The effect of the second change was to encourage the rapid growth of PACs. By 1993 some 4,200 PACs existed, over six times the number that existed in 1975. In 1999–2000 they gave nearly $260 million to congressional candidates. Some people worry that the existence of all this political money has resulted in our having, as Senator Edward Kennedy put it, "the finest Congress that money can buy." More likely the increase in the number of PACs has had just the opposite effect. The reason is simple: with PACs so numerous and so easy to form, it is now probable that there will be money available on every side of almost every conceivable issue. As a result members of Congress can take money and still decide for themselves how to vote. As we shall see, there is not much scholarly evidence that money buys votes in Congress.

Indeed, some members of Congress tell PACs what to do rather than take orders from them. Members will frequently inform PACs that they "expect" money from them; grumbling PAC officials feel that they have no choice but to contribute for fear of alienating the members. Moreover, some members have created their *own* PACs—organizations set up to raise money from individual donors that is then given to favored political allies in and out of Congress or used to advance the members' own political ambitions. When Charles Rangel, congressman from New York, was hoping to be elected whip of the Democratic party in the House, he set up a PAC that made campaign contributions to fellow representatives in hopes that they might vote for him as whip. There are many other examples from both sides of the aisle. An ironic consequence of this is that a conservative Republican may give money to a PAC set up by a moderate Democrat, who then gives the money to a liberal Democrat (or vice versa), with the result that the original donor winds up having his or her money go to somebody that he or she profoundly dislikes.

Almost any kind of organization—corporation, labor union, trade association, public-interest lobby, citizens group—can form a PAC. Over half of all PACs are sponsored by corporations, about a tenth by labor unions, and the rest by various groups, including ideological ones.

The rise of ideological PACs has been the most remarkable development in interest group activity in recent years. They have increased in number at a faster rate than business or labor PACs, and in several elections they raised more money than either business or labor. One study calculated that there were more than one thousand ideological PACs; about one-third were liberal, about two-thirds conservative.[27]

Though the ideological PACs raised more money than business or labor ones, they spent less on campaigns and gave less to candidates. The reason for this anomaly is that an ideological PAC usually has to raise its money by means of massive direct-mail solicitations, expensive efforts that can consume all the money raised, and more. By contrast, a typical business or labor PAC solicits money from within a single corporation or union. Even a well-run ideological PAC must spend fifty cents to raise a dollar; some spend much more than that.[28]

As Table 11.3 shows, of the ten PACs that gave the most money to candidates in the 2004 election, most were labor unions, business organizations, and groups that represented doctors, lawyers, realtors, and government employees.

Table 11.4 shows that, as we learned in Chapter 10, incumbents received more PAC money than challengers and that, whereas labor PACs gave almost exclusively to Democrats, business PACs favored Republicans.

Table 11.3 Spending by Political Action Committees (PACs), 2003–2004*

Committee	Contribution
National Association of Realtors	$2,106,733
National Beer Wholesalers Association	1,994,500
International Brotherhood of Electrical Workers	1,714,900
National Association of Homebuilders	1,700,700
Association of Trial Lawyers of America	1,668,499
United Parcel Service, Inc.	1,592,160
National Automobile Dealers Association	1,547,100
Wal-Mart Stores, Inc.	1,484,000
Credit Union Legislative Action Council	1,428,705
Service Employees International Union	1,411,500

*January 1, 2003, through June 30, 2004.
Source: Federal Election Commission.

Both parties have become dependent on PAC money. Still, the popular image of rich PACs stuffing huge sums into political campaigns and thereby buying the attention and possibly the favors of the grateful candidates is a bit overdrawn. For one thing, the typical PAC contribution is rather small. The average PAC donation to a House candidate is only a few hundred dollars and accounts for less than 1 percent of the candidate's total receipts. Most PACs spread small sums of money over many candidates, and despite their great growth in numbers and expenditures, PACs still provide only about one-third of all the money spent by candidates for the House.[29]

Moreover, scholars have yet to find systematic evidence that PAC contributions generally affect how members of Congress vote. On most issues how legislators vote can be explained primarily by their general ideological outlooks and the characteristics of their constituents; how much PAC money they have received turns out to be a small factor. On the other hand, when an issue arises in which most of their constituents have no interest and ideology provides little guidance, there is a slight statistical correlation between PAC contributions and votes. But even here the correlation may be misleading. The same groups that give money also wage intensive lobbying campaigns, flooding representatives with information, press releases, and letters from interested constituents. What these studies may be measuring is the effect of persuasive arguments, not dollars; no one can be certain.[30]

Table 11.4   How PACs Spent Their Money in 2003–2004* (in millions of dollars)

PAC Sponsor	House					Senate				
	Dem.	Rep.	Incumbent	Challenger	Open	Dem.	Rep.	Incumbent	Challenger	Open
Corporate	$18.1	$38.0	$53.5	$.83	$1.7	$8.6	$14.1	$18.5	$1.3	$2.9
Trade/professional	15.6	26.9	39.3	1.1	2.1	4.9	6.8	9.3	0.9	1.5
Labor	25.2	4.0	25.0	2.2	2.0	5.3	0.75	4.2	0.64	1.3
Nonconnected	6.0	13.7	14.7	2.3	2.6	4.5	5.2	6.0	1.5	2.2

*January 1, 2003 to June 30, 2004.
Source: Federal Election Commission.

It is possible that money affects legislative behavior in ways that will never appear in studies of roll-call votes in Congress. Members of Congress may be more willing to set aside time in their busy schedules for a group that has given money than for a group that has not. What the money has bought is access: it has helped open the door. Or contributions might influence how legislators behave on the committees on which they serve, subtly shaping the way in which they respond to arguments and the facts on which they rely. No one knows, because the research has not been done.

In any event, if interest group money makes a difference at all, it probably makes it on certain kinds of issues more than others. In the chapter on policy-making we define the kind of issues—we call them "client politics"—on which a given interest group is likely to be especially influential, whether by means of arguments, money, or both. After reading that chapter and considering the examples given there, it will be easier to put the present discussion of PAC money into context.

The "Revolving Door"

Every year, hundreds of people leave important jobs in the federal government to take more lucrative positions in private industry. Some go to work as lobbyists, others as consultants to business, still others as key executives in corporations, foundations, and universities. Many people worry that this "revolving door" may give private interests a way of improperly influencing government decisions. If a federal official uses his or her government position to do something for a corporation in exchange for a cushy job after leaving government, or if a person who has left government uses his or her personal contacts in Washington to get favors for private parties, then the public interest may suffer.

From time to time there are incidents that seem to confirm these fears. Michael K. Deaver, once the deputy chief of staff in the Reagan White House, was convicted of perjury in connection with a grand jury investigation of his having used his former government contacts to help the clients of his public relations firm. Lyn Nofziger, a former Reagan White House aide, was convicted of violating the Ethics in Government Act by lobbying the White House, soon after he left it, on behalf of various businesses and labor unions.

In 1988 federal investigators revealed evidence of corrupt dealings between some Defense Department officials and industry executives. Contractors and their consultants, many of whom were former Pentagon personnel, obtained favors from procurement officials, gaining an edge on their competitors.

How systematic is this pattern of abuse? We don't know. Studies of the revolving door in federal regulatory agencies have found no clear pattern of officials' tilting their decisions in hopes of landing a lucrative business job.[31]

Agencies differ in their vulnerability to outside influences. If the Food and Drug Administration is not vigilant, people in that agency who help decide whether a new drug should be placed on the market may have their judgment affected somewhat by the possibility that, if they approve the drug, the pharmaceutical company that makes it will later offer them a lucrative position.

On the other hand, lawyers in the Federal Trade Commission who prosecute businesses that violate the antitrust laws may decide that their chances for getting a good job with a private law firm later on will increase

★ HOW THINGS WORK ★

Conflict of Interest

In 1978 a new federal law, the Ethics in Government Act, codified and broadened the rules governing possible conflicts of interest among senior members of the executive branch. The key provisions were as follows.

The president, vice president, and top-ranking (GS-16 and above) executive branch employees must each year file a public financial disclosure report that lists:

- The source and amount of all earned income as well as income from stocks, bonds, and property; the worth of any investments or large debts; and the source of a spouse's income, if any
- Any position held in business, labor, or certain nonprofit organizations

Employment after government service is restricted. Former executive branch employees may *not:*

- Represent anyone before their former agencies in connection with any matter that the former employees had been involved in before leaving the government

- Appear before an agency, for two years after leaving government service, on matters that came within the former employees' official sphere of responsibility, even if they were not personally involved in the matter
- Represent anyone on any matter before their former agencies, for one year after leaving them, even if the former employees had no connection with the matter while in the government

In addition, another law prohibits bribery. It is illegal to ask for, solicit, or receive anything of value in return for being influenced in the performance of one's duties.

Finally, an executive order forbids outside employment. An official may not hold a job or take a fee, even for lecturing or writing, if such employment or income might create a conflict of interest or an apparent conflict of interest.

Sources: National Journal (November 19, 1977): 1796–1803; *Congressional Quarterly Weekly Report* (October 28, 1978): 3121–3127.

if they are particularly vigorous and effective prosecutors. The firm, after all, wants to hire competent people, and winning a case is a good test of competence.[32]

Trouble

Public displays and disruptive tactics—protest marches, sit-ins, picketing, and violence—have always been a part of American politics. Indeed, they were among the favorite tactics of the American colonists seeking independence in 1776.

Both ends of the political spectrum have used display, disruption, and violence. On the left feminists, antislavery agitators, coal miners, autoworkers, welfare mothers, African Americans, antinuclear power groups, public housing tenants, the American Indian Movement, the Students for a Democratic Society, and the Weather Underground have created "trouble" ranging from peaceful sit-ins at segregated

lunch counters to bombings and shootings. On the right the Ku Klux Klan has used terror, intimidation, and murder; parents opposed to forced busing of schoolchildren have demonstrated; business firms have used strong-arm squads against workers; right-to-life groups have blockaded abortion clinics; and an endless array of "anti-" groups (anti-Catholics, anti-Masons, anti-Jews, anti-immigrants, antisaloons, antiblacks, antiprotesters, and probably even anti-antis) have taken their disruptive turns on stage. These various activities are not morally the same—a sit-in demonstration is quite different from a lynching—but politically they constitute a similar problem for a government official.

An explanation of why and under what circumstances disruption occurs is beyond the scope of this book. To understand interest group politics, however, it is important to remember that making trouble has,

Lawsuits, such as this one arguing that Massachusetts allow marriages among gay and lesbian couples, are often more effective than protest demonstrations in changing policies.

since the 1960s, become a quite conventional political resource and is no longer simply the last resort of extremist groups. Making trouble is now an accepted political tactic of ordinary middle-class citizens as well as the disadvantaged or disreputable.

There is of course a long history of the use of disruptive methods by "proper" people. In a movement that began in England at the turn of the century and then spread here, feminists would chain themselves to lampposts or engage in what we now call "sit-ins" as part of a campaign to win the vote for women. The object then was much the same as the object of similar tactics today: to disrupt the working of some institution so that it is forced to negotiate with you, or, failing that, to enlist the sympathies of third parties (the media, other interest groups) who will come to your aid and press your target to negotiate with you, or, failing that, to goad the police into making attacks and arrests so that martyrs are created.

The civil rights and antiwar movements of the 1960s gave experience in these methods to thousands of young people and persuaded others of the effectiveness of such methods under certain conditions. Though these movements have abated or disappeared, their veterans and emulators have put such tactics to new uses—trying to block the construction of a nuclear power plant, for example, or occupying the office of a cabinet secretary to obtain concessions for a particular group.

Government officials dread this kind of trouble. They usually find themselves in a no-win situation. If they ignore the disruption, they are accused of being "insensitive," "unresponsive," or "arrogant." If they give in to the demonstrators, they encourage more demonstrations by proving that this is a useful tactic. If they call the police, they run the risk of violence and injuries, followed not only by bad publicity but by lawsuits.

☆ Regulating Interest Groups

Interest group activity is a form of political speech protected by the First Amendment to the Constitution: it cannot lawfully be abolished or even much curtailed. In 1946 Congress passed the Federal Regulation of Lobbying Act, which requires groups and individuals seeking to influence legislation to register with the secretary of the Senate and the clerk of the House and to file quarterly financial reports. The Supreme Court upheld the law but restricted its application to lobbying efforts involving direct contacts with members of Congress.[33] More general "grassroots" interest group activity may not be restricted by the government. The 1946 law had little practical effect. Not all lobbyists took the trouble to register, and there was no guarantee that the financial statements were accurate. There was no staff in charge of enforcing the law.

After years of growing popular dissatisfaction with Congress, prompted in large measure by the (exaggerated) view that legislators were the pawns of powerful special interests, Congress in late 1995 unanimously passed a bill that tightened up the registration and disclosure requirements. Signed by the president, the law restates the obligation of lobbyists to register with the House and Senate, but it broadens the definition of a lobbyist to include the following:

- People who spend at least 20 percent of their time lobbying
- People who are paid at least $5,000 in any six-month period to lobby
- Corporations and other groups that spend more than $20,000 in any six-month period on their own lobbying staffs

The law covers people and groups who lobby the executive branch and congressional staffers as well as elected members of Congress, and it includes law firms that represent clients before the government. Twice a year, all registered lobbyists must report the following:

- The names of their clients
- Their income and expenditures
- The issues on which they worked

The registration and reporting requirements do not, however, extend to so-called grassroots organizations—that is, campaigns (sometimes led by volunteers, sometimes by hired professionals) to mobilize citizens to write or call the government about some issue. Nor was any new enforcement organization created, although congressional officials may refer violations to the Justice Department for investigation. Fines for breaking the law could amount to $50,000. In addition, the law bars tax-exempt, nonprofit advocacy groups that lobby from getting federal grants, a provision aimed at organizations such as the American Association of Retired Persons (AARP).

The most significant legal constraints on interest groups come not from the current federal lobbying law (though that may change) but from the tax code and the campaign finance laws. A nonprofit organization—which includes not only charitable groups but almost all voluntary associations that have an interest in politics—need not pay income taxes, and financial contributions to it can be deducted on the donor's income tax return, provided that the organization does not devote a "substantial part" of its activities to "attempting to influence legislation."[34] Many tax-exempt organizations do take public positions on political questions and testify before congressional committees. If the organization does any serious lobbying, however, it will lose its tax-exempt status (and thus find it harder to solicit donations and more expensive to operate). Exactly this happened to the Sierra Club in 1968 when the Internal Revenue Service revoked its tax-exempt status because of its extensive lobbying activities. Some voluntary associations try to deal with this problem by setting up separate organizations to collect tax-exempt money—for example, the NAACP, which lobbies, must pay taxes, but the NAACP Legal Defense and Education Fund, which does not lobby, is tax-exempt.

Finally, the campaign finance laws, described in detail in Chapter 10, limit to $5,000 the amount any political action committee can spend on a given candidate in a given election. These laws have sharply curtailed the extent to which any *single* group can give money, though they have increased the *total* amount that different groups are providing.

Beyond making bribery or other manifestly corrupt forms of behavior illegal and restricting the sums that campaign contributors can donate, there is probably no system for controlling interest groups that would both make a useful difference and leave important constitutional and political rights unimpaired. Ultimately the only remedy for imbalances or inadequacies in interest group representation is to devise and sustain a political system that gives all affected parties a reasonable chance to be heard on matters of public policy. That, of course, is exactly what the Founders thought they were doing. Whether they succeeded or not is a question to which we shall return at the end of this book.

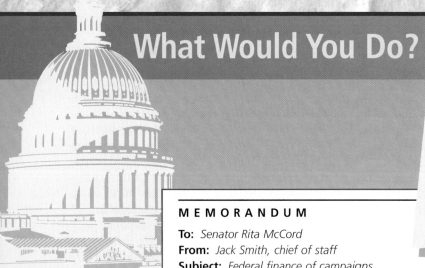

U.S. Senator Wants Feds to Foot the Bill for Political Campaigns

September 4
WASHINGTON

Calling the country's campaign finance system "corrupt and complicated beyond comprehension," an ex-presidential contender and sitting senator is corralling congressional cosponsors for a new law that would have the federal government pay the entire cost of presidential races and lead to full federal funding for congressional campaigns as well . . .

M E M O R A N D U M

To: *Senator Rita McCord*
From: *Jack Smith, chief of staff*
Subject: *Federal finance of campaigns*

Every presidential election since 1976 has been financed in part by federal funds, but the proposal in question would start by limiting major presidential candidates to federal financing.

Arguments for:

1. The legal precedents are promising. Federal matching funds already go to presidential-primary candidates who have raised at least a total of $5,000, in contributions of $250 or less, in each of twenty states, and each major party nominee is already eligible for federal grants if he or she agrees to spend no more than the grant amount.
2. The sums required would be small. The hard money spent on presidential campaigns totaled less than $1 billion—hardly a fiscal drain were it paid out of a nearly $2 trillion annual federal budget.
3. The effects would be pervasive. Candidates and party leaders would stop covertly courting soft-money suppliers, stop compromising themselves with big-money donors (phone calls, luncheons, personal visits), and start focusing on the needs of average citizens.

Arguments against:

1. The constitutional precedents are prohibitive. The Supreme Court's *Buckley v. Valeo* (1976) decision upheld legal limits on campaign contributions but defined spending money for political purposes as a form of political expression protected by the First Amendment.
2. The sums spent would soon spiral. The federal government would be unable to restrict spending by individuals or organizations working independently, and federal funds would supplement, not supplant, new private money.
3. The effects would be perverse. Candidates would rely less on party leaders, which would further weaken the political parties. Many average citizens (most of whom have not opted to help pay for campaigns through voluntary federal income tax checkoffs) and nonvoters would feel as if they were being bullied into bankrolling a process that serves the politicians, not the people.

Your decision:

Favor proposal _____ Oppose proposal _____

☆ SUMMARY

*I*nterest groups in the United States are more numerous and more fragmented than those in nations such as Great Britain, where the political system is more centralized. The goals and tactics of interest groups reflect not only the interests of their members but also the size of the groups, the incentives with which they attract supporters, and the role of their professional staffs. The chief source of interest group influence is information; public support, money, and the ability to create "trouble" are also important. The right to lobby is protected by the Constitution, but the tax and campaign finance laws impose significant restrictions on how money may be used.

RECONSIDERING WHO GOVERNS?

1. Do interest groups dominate government, and is any particular lobby politically unbeatable?

The answers are "not really" and "no," respectively. There are so many governmental institutions in which power may be exercised that no single group can dominate most public policy decisions. What the government does is often the outcome of a complex pattern of political haggling, innumerable compromises, and shifting alliances among and between different groups and their leaders. Even supposedly all-powerful lobbies (like the National Rifle Association [NRA] on gun control, or the American Association of Retired Persons [AARP] on senior citizens' health care benefits) sometimes find themselves on the losing side of legislative decisions and court opinions.

2. Why do people join interest groups?

Pretty much for the same basic reasons that people join any organization. There are three kinds of incentives: solidary, material, and purposive. Organizations, including interest groups, can attract members through one, two, or all three incentives. Some interest groups rely mainly on one incentive. For example, ideological political action committees (PACs) rely largely on purposive incentives, attracting members by appealing to their beliefs in a coherent set of principles or their passions on a particular set of issues. Even these groups, however, normally provide their members with certain tangible, members-only benefits (for example, magazines or special discounts on various products). Organizations that principally benefit nonmembers are sometimes called public-interest lobbies.

RECONSIDERING TO WHAT ENDS?

1. Is the proliferation of political action committees (PACs) and other groups good or bad for America's representative democracy?

What would James Madison say? Go back to the Appendix and *Federalist* No. 10. Madison recognized that freedom begat factions, but he hoped that the government proposed under the Constitution would succeed in "regulating these various and interfering interests" in ways that secured the "public good." The mere proliferation of interest groups in our time does not justify a negative answer to that question. Rather, one would also have to believe that the political process is dominated by groups that seek to serve their members with little or no regard for the well-being and rights of other citizens. To some prochoice voters, certain pro-life groups may appear as factions, and to some pro-life citizens, certain prochoice groups may appear as factions. Both these and other ideological groups have proliferated in recent decades. Whether this is good or bad for American's representative democracy is a question on which reasonable minds can and do differ. But this much is clear: in contemporary American politics, one citizen's special-interest group is often another citizen's public-interest lobby.

2. Should interest groups' political activities be restricted by law?

The first thing to notice is that there are already literally scores of such laws on the books. For example, Washington lobbyists must register with the House or Senate. All registered lobbyists must publicly divulge their client list and expenditures. There are legal limits on PAC contributions. Every new wave of campaign finance laws (see Chapter 10) has resulted in more rules regulating interest groups. The Internal

Revenue Service (IRS) has tightly restricted political activity by religious groups, private schools, and other organizations as a condition for their exemption from federal income tax. The courts have consistently upheld such restrictions and ruled that they do not, under most circumstances, violate freedom of speech or other constitutional protections. On the other hand, the courts have effectively afforded even tax-exempt groups ways of legally, but indirectly, engaging in political activity. Finally, states and cities have their own laws regulating interest groups, and some places are more restrictive than others.

WORLD WIDE WEB RESOURCES

Conservative interest groups
American Conservative Union: **www.conservative.org**
Christian Coalition: **www.cc.org**
Liberal interest groups
American Civil Liberties Union: **www.aclu.org**
Americans for Democratic Action: **www.adaction.org**
Environmental groups
Environmental Defense: **www.environmentaldefense.org**

National Resources Defense Council: **www.nrdc.org**
Civil rights groups
NAACP: **www.naacp.org**
Center for Equal Opportunity: **www.ceousa.org**
Feminist group
National Organization for Women: **www.now.org**

SUGGESTED READINGS

Bauer, Raymond A., Ithiel de Sola Pool, and Lewis A. Dexter. *American Business and Public Policy*. New York: Atherton, 1963. A classic study of how business groups tried to shape foreign-trade legislation, set in a broad analysis of pressure groups and Congress.

Berry, Jeffrey M. *Lobbying for the People*. Princeton, N.J.: Princeton University Press, 1977. Analyzes more than eighty "public-interest" lobbies, with a detailed discussion of two.

Cigler, Allan J., and Burdett A. Loomis, eds. *Interest Group Politics*. 4th ed. Washington, D.C.: Congressional Quarterly Press, 1995. Essays on several interest groups active in Washington.

Lowi, Theodore J. *The End of Liberalism*. New York: Norton, 1969. A critique of the role of interest groups in American government.

Malbin, Michael J., ed. *Money and Politics in the United States*. Chatham, N.J.: Chatham House, 1984. Excellent studies of PACs and of the influence of money in elections.

Mansbridge, Jane J. *Why We Lost the ERA*. Chicago: University of Chicago Press, 1986. Insightful analysis of the relationship between organizational incentives and tactics in the ERA campaign.

Olson, Mancur. *The Logic of Collective Action*. Cambridge: Harvard University Press, 1965. An economic analysis of interest groups, especially the "free-rider" problem.

Sabato, Larry. *PAC Power*. New York: Norton, 1985. A full discussion of the nature and activities of political action committees.

Schlozman, Kay Lehman, and John T. Tierney. *Organized Interests and American Democracy*. New York: Harper and Row, 1985. Comprehensive treatise on interest groups based on original research.

Truman, David B. *The Governmental Process*. 2d ed. New York: Knopf, 1971. First published in 1951, this was the classic analysis—and defense—of interest group pluralism.

Wilson, James Q. *Political Organizations*. Rev. ed. Princeton, N.J.: Princeton University Press, 1995. A theory of interest groups emphasizing the incentives they use to attract members.

The Media

Journalism in American Political History

The Party Press • The Popular Press • Magazines of Opinion • Electronic Journalism • The Internet

The Structure of the Media

Degree of Competition • The National Media

Rules Governing the Media

Confidentiality of Sources • Regulating Broadcasting • Campaigning

Are the National Media Biased?

Government and the News

Prominence of the President • Coverage of Congress • Why Do We Have So Many News Leaks? • Sensationalism in the Media • Government Restraints on Journalists

WHO GOVERNS?

1. How much power do the media have?
2. Can we trust the media to be fair?

TO WHAT ENDS?

1. What public policies will the media support?

Much of what you know about politics comes from what you read in newspapers, watch on television, or listen to on the radio. And if you like using the computer, a lot more can be learned from World Wide Web pages and the various chatrooms and web logs (or **blogs**) that you can find there. Blogs have become so important that many people now consider them the New Media that is challenging the Old Media (newspapers and television stations) by providing immediate checks on what the latter says. In 2004, *60 Minutes,* a CBS television news program, ran a story claiming that documents it had proved that President Bush had performed poorly during his service in the Air National Guard. Within hours bloggers were showing evidence that the documents were forgeries, a fact that CBS later admitted was true. Somebody gave the forgeries to CBS; the Web discovered that fact.

The mass media and the Internet are essentially unregulated ventures, accountable for their content chiefly to themselves and their users. But if the media regulate themselves, will they be honest and fair? And how will politicians deal with them?

All public officials have a love-hate relationship with newspapers, television, and the other media of mass communication. They depend on the media for the advancement of their careers and policies but fear the media's power to criticize, expose, and destroy. As political parties have declined—especially, strong local party organizations—politicians have become increasingly dependent on the media. Their efforts to woo the press have become ever greater, and their expressions of rage and dismay when that courtship is spurned, ever stronger. At the same time, the media have been changing, especially in regard to the kinds of people who have been attracted to leading positions in journalism and the attitudes they have brought with them. There has always been an adversarial relationship between those who govern and those who write, but events of recent decades have, as we shall see, made that conflict especially keen.

The relationships between government and the media in this country are shaped by laws and understandings that accord the media a degree of freedom greater than that found in almost any other nation. Though many public officials secretly might like to control the media, and though no medium of communication in the United States or elsewhere is totally free of government influence, the press in this country is among the freest in the world. A study of 193 countries found that in about one-third the press enjoyed a high degree of freedom: the United States and most nations in Europe are among these places.[1] But even in some democratic nations with a free press there are restrictions that would be unfamiliar to Americans. For example, the laws

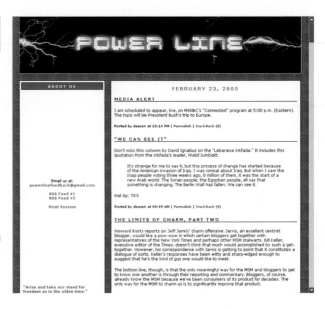

Blogs, both liberal and conservative, have become a major source of news and politics.

governing libel are much stricter in Great Britain than in the United States. As a result, it is easier in the former country for politicians to sue newspapers for publishing articles that defame or ridicule them. In this country the libel laws make it almost impossible to prevent press criticisms of public figures. Moreover, England has an Official Secrets Act that can be used to punish any past or present public officials who leak information to the press.[2] In this country, leaking information occurs all of the time and our Freedom of Information Act makes it relatively easy for the press to extract documents from the government.

In Italy the prime minister owns a large media empire that he can use to build support for him and his party. In France it has been possible in the recent past to punish a newspaper for being excessively critical of the French president.[3]

America has a long tradition of privately owned media. By contrast, private ownership of television has come only recently to France. And the Internet is not owned by anybody: here and in many nations, people can say or read whatever they want by means of their computers.

Newspapers in this country require no government permission to operate, but radio and television stations do need licenses that are granted by the Federal Communications Commission (FCC). These licenses must be renewed periodically. On occasion the White House has made efforts to use license renewals as a way of influencing station owners who were out of political favor, but of late the level of FCC control over what is broadcast has lessened.

There are two potential limits to the freedom of privately owned newspapers and broadcast stations. The first is the fact that they must make a profit. Some critics believe that the need for profit will lead media outlets to distort the news in order to satisfy advertisers or to build an audience. Though there is some truth to this argument, it is too simple. Every media outlet must satisfy a variety of people—advertisers, subscribers, listeners, reporters, and editors—and balancing those demands is complicated and will be done differently by different owners.

The second problem is media bias. If most of the reporters and editors have similar views about politics and if they act on those views, then the media will give us only one side of many stories. Later in this chapter we shall take a close look at this possibility.

☆ Journalism in American Political History

Important changes in the nature of American politics have gone hand in hand with major changes in the organization and technology of the press. It is the nature of politics, being essentially a form of communication, to respond to changes in how communications

blog series, or log, of discussion items on a page of the World Wide Web.

The National Gazette, *edited by Philip Freneau, supported the Thomas Jefferson faction in national politics. Jefferson, as secretary of state, helped Freneau by giving him a job in the State Department. The* Gazette of the United States, *published by John Fenno, supported Jefferson's rival, Alexander Hamilton.*

are carried on. This can be seen by considering four important periods in journalistic history.

The Party Press

In the early years of the Republic, politicians of various factions and parties created, sponsored, and controlled newspapers to further their interests. This was possible because circulation was of necessity small (newspapers could not easily be distributed to large audiences, owing to poor transportation) and newspapers were expensive (the type was set by hand and the presses printed copies slowly). Furthermore, there were few large advertisers to pay the bills. These newspapers circulated chiefly among the political and commercial elites, who could afford the high subscription prices. Even with high prices, the news-

papers, to exist, often required subsidies. That money frequently came from the government or from a political party.

During the Washington administration the Federalists, led by Alexander Hamilton, created the *Gazette of the United States.* The Republicans, led by Thomas Jefferson, retaliated by creating the *National Gazette* and made its editor, Philip Freneau, "clerk for foreign languages" in the State Department at $250 a year to help support him. After Jefferson became president, he induced another publisher, Samuel Harrison Smith, to start the *National Intelligencer,* subsidizing him by giving him a contract to print government documents. Andrew Jackson, when he became president, aided in the creation of the *Washington Globe.* By some estimates there were over fifty journalists on the government payroll during this era.[4] Naturally these newspapers were relentlessly partisan in their views. Citizens could choose among different party papers, but only rarely could they find a paper that presented both sides of an issue.

The Popular Press

Changes in society and technology made possible the rise of a self-supporting, mass-readership daily newspaper. The development of the high-speed rotary press enabled publishers to print thousands of copies of a newspaper cheaply and quickly. The invention of the telegraph in the 1840s meant that news from Washington could be flashed almost immediately to New York, Boston, Philadelphia, and Charleston, thus providing local papers with access to information that once only the Washington papers enjoyed. The creation in 1848 of the Associated Press allowed telegraphic dissemination of information to newspaper editors on a systematic basis. Since the AP provided stories that had to be brief and that went to newspapers of every political hue, it could not afford to be partisan or biased; to attract as many subscribers as possible, it had to present the facts objectively. Meanwhile the nation was becoming more urbanized, with large numbers of people brought together in densely settled areas. These people could support a daily newspaper by paying only a penny per copy and by patronizing merchants who advertised in its pages. Newspapers no longer needed political patronage to prosper, and soon such subsidies began to dry up. In 1860 the Government Printing Office was established, thereby putting an end to most of the printing contracts that Washington newspapers had once enjoyed.

The mass-readership newspaper was scarcely nonpartisan, but the partisanship it displayed arose from the convictions of its publishers and editors rather than from the influence of its party sponsors. And these convictions blended political beliefs with economic interest. The way to attract a large readership was with sensationalism: violence, romance, and patriotism, coupled with exposés of government, politics, business, and society. As practiced by Joseph Pulitzer and William Randolph Hearst, founders of large newspaper empires, this editorial policy had great appeal for the average citizen and especially for the immigrants flooding into the large cities.

Strong-willed publishers could often become powerful political forces. Hearst used his papers to agitate for war with Spain when the Cubans rebelled against Spanish rule. Conservative Republican political leaders were opposed to the war, but a steady diet of newspaper stories about real and imagined Spanish brutalities whipped up public opinion in favor of intervention. At one point Hearst sent the noted artist Frederic Remington to Cuba to supply paintings of the conflict. Remington cabled back: "Everything is quiet.... There will be no war." Hearst supposedly replied: "Please remain. You furnish the pictures and I'll furnish the war."[5] When the battleship USS *Maine* blew up in Havana harbor, President William McKinley felt helpless to resist popular pressure, and war was declared in 1898.

For all their excesses, the mass-readership newspapers began to create a common national culture, to establish the feasibility of a press free of government control or subsidy, and to demonstrate how exciting (and profitable) could be the criticism of public policy and the revelation of public scandal.

Magazines of Opinion

The growing middle class was often repelled by what it called "yellow journalism" and was developing, around the turn of the century, a taste for political reform and a belief in the doctrines of the progressive movement. To satisfy this market, a variety of national magazines appeared that, unlike those devoted to manners and literature, discussed issues of public policy. Among the first of these were the *Nation*, the *Atlantic Monthly*, and *Harper's*, founded in the 1850s and 1860s; later there came the more broadly based mass-circulation magazines such as *McClure's*, *Scribner's*, and *Cosmopolitan*. They provided the means for developing a national constituency for certain issues, such as regulating business (or in the language of the times, "trustbusting"), purifying municipal politics, and reforming the civil service system. Lincoln Steffens and other so-called muckrakers were frequent contributors to the magazines, setting a pattern for what we now call "investigative reporting."

The national magazines of opinion provided an opportunity for individual writers to gain a nationwide following. The popular press, though initially under the heavy influence of founder-publishers, made the names of certain reporters and columnists household words. In time the great circulation wars between the big-city daily newspapers started to wane, as the more successful papers bought up or otherwise eliminated their competition. This reduced the need for the more extreme forms of sensationalism, a change that was reinforced by the growing sophistication and education of America's readers.

Before television and the Internet, news came by radio, as here in 1939.

And the founding publishers were gradually replaced by less flamboyant managers. All of these changes—in circulation needs, in audience interests, in managerial style, in the emergence of nationally known writers—helped increase the power of editors and reporters and make them a force to be reckoned with.

Although politics dominated the pages of most national magazines in the late nineteenth century, today national magazines that focus mainly on politics and government affairs account for only a small and declining portion of the national magazine market. Among all magazines in circulation today, only a fraction focus on politics—the majority of today's magazines focus on popular entertainment and leisure activities.

Electronic Journalism

Radio came on the national scene in the 1920s, television in the late 1940s. They represented a major change in the way news was gathered and disseminated, though few politicians at first understood the importance of this change. A broadcast permits public officials to speak directly to audiences without their remarks being filtered through editors and reporters. This was obviously an advantage to politicians, provided they were skilled enough to use it: they could in theory reach the voters directly on a

sound bite   A radio or video clip of someone speaking.

national scale without the services of political parties, interest groups, or friendly editors.

But there was an offsetting disadvantage—people could easily ignore a speech broadcast on a radio or television station, either by not listening at all or by tuning to a different station. By contrast, the views of at least some public figures would receive prominent and often unavoidable display in newspapers, and in a growing number of cities there was only one daily paper. Moreover, space in a newspaper is cheap compared to time on a television broadcast. Adding one more story, or one more name to an existing story, costs the newspaper little. By contrast, less news can be carried on radio or television, and each news segment must be quite brief to avoid boring the audience. As a result, the number of political personalities that can be covered by radio and television news is much smaller than is the case with newspapers, and the cost (to the station) of making a news item or broadcast longer is often prohibitively large.

Thus, to obtain the advantages of electronic media coverage, public officials must do something sufficiently bold or colorful to gain free access to radio and television news—or they must find the money to purchase radio and television time. The president of the United States, of course, is routinely covered by radio and television and can ordinarily get free time to speak to the nation on matters of importance. All other officials must struggle for access to the electronic media by making controversial statements, acquiring a national reputation, or purchasing expensive time.

The rise of the talk show as a political forum has increased politicians' access to the electronic media, as has the televised "town meeting." But such developments need to be understood as part of a larger story.

Until the 1990s, the "big three" television networks (ABC, CBS, and NBC) together claimed 80 percent or more of all viewers (see Table 12.1). Their evening newscasts dominated electronic media coverage of politics and government affairs. When it came to presidential campaigns, for example, the three networks were the only television games in town—they reported on the primaries, broadcast the party conventions, and covered the general election campaigns, including any presidential debates. But over the last few decades, the networks' evening newscasts have changed in ways that have made it harder for candidates to use them to get their messages across. For instance, the average **sound bite**—a video clip of a presidential contender speaking—

Table 12.1	Decline in Viewership of the Television Networks

"Big Three" Networks: Average Shares of Prime-Time Viewing Audience

Year	Share
1961	94%
1971	91
1981	83
1991	41
1997	33
2002	29

Source: Updated from *The Public Perspective* (September/October 1992): 6, reporting data provided by Nielsen Media Research and NBC. Used by permission of *The Public Perspective,* a publication of the Roper Center for Public Opinion Research, University of Connecticut; Cabletelevision Advertising Bureau analysis of Nielsen data, April 25, 2002–May 21, 2002.

dropped from about forty-two seconds in 1968 to 7.3 seconds in 2000.[6]

Today politicians have sources other than the network news for sustained and personalized television exposure. Cable television, early-morning news and entertainment programs, and prime-time "news-magazine" shows have greatly increased and diversified politicians' access to the electronic media. One of the most memorable moments of the 1992 presidential campaign—Ross Perot's declaring his willingness to run for president on CNN's "Larry King Live"—occurred on cable television. In 2003 Arnold Schwarzenegger announced that he would run for governor of California on "The Tonight Show with Jay Leno." And while the networks' evening news programs feature only small sound bites, their early-morning programs and newsmagazine shows feature lengthy interviews with candidates.

Naturally many politicians favor the call-in format, town-meeting setups, lengthy human interest interviews, and casual appearances on entertainment shows to televised confrontations on policy issues with seasoned network journalists who push, probe, and criticize. And naturally they favor being a part of visually interesting programs rather than traditional "talking heads" news shows. But what is preferable to candidates is not necessarily helpful to the selection process that voters must go through in choosing a candidate. No one has yet systematically analyzed what, if any, positive or negative consequences these recent changes in politicians' access to

the electronic media hold for campaigns, elections, or governance. Nor, for that matter, is there yet any significant research on the broader societal consequences of so-called narrowcasting—the proliferation of television and radio stations that target highly segmented listening and viewing audiences, and the relative decline of electronic and print media that reach large and heterogeneous populations.

One thing is clear: most politicians crave the media spotlight, both on the campaign trail and in office. The efforts made by political candidates to get "visuals"—filmed stories—on television continue after they are elected. Since the president is always news, a politician wishing to make news is well advised to attack the president. Even better, attack him with the aid of a photogenic prop: when the late Senator John Heinz III of Pennsylvania wanted to criticize a president's bridge-repair program, Heinz had himself filmed making the attack not in his office but standing on a bridge.

The Internet

The newest electronic source of news is the Internet. In 2000 over half of all American households had at least one computer, and in four out of every ten households someone used the Internet.[7] The political news that is found there ranges from summaries of stories from newspapers and magazines to political rumors and hot gossip. Many web logs, or blogs, exist on which viewers can scan political ideas posted there; many blogs specialize in offering liberal, conservative, or libertarian perspectives. The Internet is the ultimate free market in political news: no one can ban, control, or regulate it, and no one can keep facts, opinions, or nonsense off of it.

The Internet is beginning to play a big role in politics. When Howard Dean ran for the Democratic presidential nomination in 2004, he raised most of his money from Internet appeals. When John Kerry, who won the nomination, was campaigning, the Internet and the blogs on it were a major source of discussion of the criticisms made of him by former Vietnam war veterans. Now every candidate for important offices has a web site.

The rise of the Internet has completed a remarkable transformation in American journalism. In the days of the party press only a few people read newspapers. When mass-circulation newspapers arose, there also arose mass politics. When magazines of opinion developed, there also developed interest groups. When radio and television became dominant, politicians could build their own bridges to voters without party or interest group influence. And now, with the Internet, voters and political activists can talk to each other.

☆ The Structure of the Media

The relationship between journalism and politics is a two-way street: though politicians take advantage as best they can of the communications media available to them, these media in turn attempt to use politics and politicians as a way of both entertaining and informing their audiences. The mass media, whatever their disclaimers, are not simply a mirror held up to reality or a messenger that carries the news. There is inevitably a process of selection, of editing, and of emphasis, and this process reflects, to some degree, the way in which the media are organized, the kinds of audiences they seek to serve, and the preferences and opinions of the members of the media.

Figure 12.1   Young People Have Become Less Interested in Political News

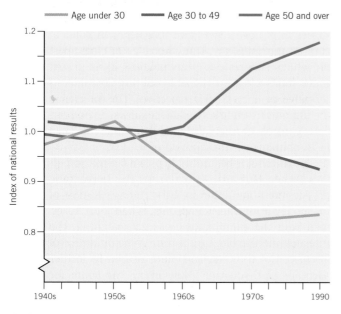

The three lines show how attentive people of different ages were to news stories during the 1940s, 1950s, 1960s, and 1990. The tan line represents those under age 30, the blue line those 30–49, and the red line those 50 and older.

Source: Los Angeles Times, Times Mirror Center for the People and the Press (June 28, 1990).

Degree of Competition

There has been a large decline in the numbers of daily newspapers that serve large communities. There were competing papers in 60 percent of American cities in 1900 but in only 4 percent in 1972. Several large cities—Boston, Chicago, Detroit, Los Angeles, New York, Philadelphia, and Washington, D.C.—have more than one paper, but in some of these the same business owns both papers. This ownership pattern is called a *joint operating agreement,* or JOA. Supposedly a JOA allows the business side to merge while preserving editorial independence, but sometimes that independence is not very large. JOAs control the papers in Denver, Detroit, Cincinnati, Seattle, and a few other cities. And newspaper circulation has fallen in recent years, with more and more people getting their news from radio and television. Young people especially have turned away from political news, as one can see in Figure 12.1.

Unlike newspapers, radio and television are intensely competitive. Almost every American home has a radio and a television set. Though there are only five major television networks, there are over one thousand television stations, each of which has its own news programs. Local stations affiliated with a network are free to accept or reject network programs. There are more than eleven thousand cable TV systems, serving over 50 million people (and a typical cable can carry dozens of channels). In addition there are nearly ten thousand radio stations; some broadcast nothing but news, and others develop a specialized following among blacks, Hispanics, or other minorities. Magazines exist for every conceivable interest. The number of news sources available to an American is vast—more than even dedicated readers and viewers can keep up with.

To a degree that would astonish most foreigners, the American press—radio, television, and newspapers—is made up of locally owned and managed enterprises. In Britain, France, Germany, Japan, Sweden, and elsewhere, the media are owned and operated with a national audience in mind. The *Times* of London may be published in that city, but it is read throughout Great Britain, as are the *Guardian,* the *Daily Telegraph,* and the *Daily Mirror.* Radio and television broadcasts are centrally planned and nationally aired.

The American newspaper, however, is primarily oriented to its local market and local audience, and there is typically more local than national news in it.

Radio and television stations accept network programming, but the early- and late-evening news programs provide a heavy diet of local political, social, and sports news. Government regulations developed by the Federal Communications Commission (FCC) are in part responsible for this. Until the mid-1990s, no one could own and operate more than one newspaper, one AM radio station, one FM radio station, or one television station in a given market. The networks still today may not compel a local affiliate to accept any particular broadcast. (In fact almost all network news programs are carried by the affiliates.) The result has been the development of a decentralized broadcast industry.

The National Media

The local orientation of much of the American communications media is partially offset, however, by the emergence of certain publications and broadcast services that constitute a kind of national press. The wire services—the Associated Press and United Press International—supply most of the national news that local papers publish. Certain newsmagazines—*Time, Newsweek, U.S. News & World Report*—have a national readership. The network evening news broadcasts produced by ABC, CBS, and NBC are carried by most television stations with a network affiliation. Both CNN (Cable News Network) and Fox News broadcast news around the clock and have large audiences, as does MSNBC. Though most newspapers have only local audiences, several have acquired national influence. The *New York Times* and the *Wall Street Journal* are printed in several locations and can be delivered to many homes early in the morning. *USA Today* was created as a national newspaper and is distributed everywhere, aimed especially at people who travel a lot.

These newspapers have national standing for several reasons. First, they distribute a lot of copies: over 1 million each day for the *Times* and the *Journal,* and over 2 million a day for *USA Today.* Second, these papers, as well as the *Washington Post,* are carefully followed by political elites. Unlike most people, the elites even read the editorials. By contrast, local newspapers and radio stations may be invisible to Washington politicians. Third, radio and television stations often decide what to broadcast by looking at the front pages of the *Times* and the *Post.* One study showed that the front page of the *Times* was a model for each network's evening news broadcast.[8] Finally, the editors and reporters for the national press tend to be better educated and more generously paid than their counterparts in local outlets. And as we shall

To help reach voters directly without going through reporters, political leaders, such as Vice President Dick Cheney, appear on television programs such as Meet the Press.

see, the writers for the national press tend to have distinctly liberal political views. Above all they seek—and frequently obtain—the opportunity to write stories that are not accounts of a particular news event but "background," investigative, or interpretive stories about issues and policies.

The national press plays the role of gatekeeper, scorekeeper, and watchdog for the federal government.

■ **Gatekeeper** As gatekeeper it can influence what subjects become national political issues and for how long. Automobile safety, water pollution, and the quality of prescription drugs were not major political issues before the national press began giving substantial attention to these matters and thus helped place them on the political agenda. When crime rates rose in the early 1960s, the subject was given little political attention in Washington, in part because the media did not cover it extensively. Media attention to crime increased in the late 1960s and early 1970s, slackened in the late 1970s, and rose again in the 1980s and early 1990s. Throughout most of these years crime went up. In short, *reality* did not change during this time; only the focus of media and political attention shifted. Elite opinion about the war in Vietnam also changed significantly as the attitude toward the war expressed by the national media changed.

■ **Scorekeeper** As scorekeepers the national media keep track of and help make political reputations, note who is being "mentioned" as a presidential candidate, and help decide who is winning and losing in Washington politics. When Jimmy Carter, a virtually unknown former governor of Georgia, was planning his campaign to get the Democratic nomination for president, he understood clearly the importance of being "mentioned." So successful was he in cultivating members of the national press that, before the first primary election was held, he was the subject of more stories in the *New York Times,* the *Washington Post,* and the *Columbus Dispatch* than any other potential Democratic presidential candidate.

The scorekeeper role of the media often leads the press to cover presidential elections as if they were horse races rather than choices among policies. Consider the enormous attention the media give to the Iowa caucus and the New Hampshire primary election, despite the fact that these states produce only a tiny fraction of the delegates to either party's nominating convention and that neither state is representative of the nation as a whole. The results of the Iowa caucus, the first in the nation, are given great importance by the press. Consequently the coverage received by a candidate who does well in Iowa constitutes a tremendous amount of free publicity that can help him or her in the New Hampshire primary election. Doing well in that primary results in even more media attention, thus boosting the candidate for the next primaries, and so on.

■ **Watchdog**   Once the scorekeepers decide that you are the person to watch, they adopt their watchdog role. When Gary Hart was the front-runner for the 1988 Democratic presidential nomination, the press played its watchdog role right from the start. When rumors circulated that he was unfaithful to his wife, the *Miami Herald* staked out his apartment in Washington, D.C., and discovered that he had spent several evening hours there with an attractive young woman, Donna Rice. Soon there appeared other stories about his having taken Ms. Rice on a boat trip to Bimini. Not long thereafter Hart dropped out of the presidential race, accusing the press of unfair treatment.

This close scrutiny is natural. The media have an instinctive—and profitable—desire to investigate personalities and expose scandals. To some degree all reporters probably share the belief that the role of the press is to "comfort the afflicted and afflict the comfortable." They tend to be tolerant of underdogs, tough on front-runners. Though some reporters develop close relations with powerful personages, many—especially

younger ones—find the discovery of wrongdoing both more absorbing and more lucrative. Bob Woodward and Carl Bernstein, who wrote most of the Watergate stories for the *Washington Post,* simultaneously performed an important public service, received the accolades of their colleagues, and earned a lot of money.

Newspapers and television stations play these three roles in somewhat different ways. A newspaper can cover more stories in greater depth than a TV station and faces less competition from other papers than TV stations face from other broadcasters. A TV station faces brutal competition, must select its programs in part for their visual impact, and must keep its stories short and punchy. As a result newspaper reporters have more freedom to develop their own stories, but they earn less money than television news broadcasters. The latter have little freedom (the fear of losing their audience is keen), but they can make a lot of money (if they are attractive personalities who photograph well).

☆ Rules Governing the Media

Ironically, the least competitive media outlets—the big-city newspapers—are almost entirely free from government regulation, while the most competitive ones—radio and television stations—must have a government license to operate and must adhere to a variety of government regulations.

Newspapers and magazines need no license to publish, their freedom to publish may not be restrained in advance, and they are liable for punishment for what they do publish only under certain highly restricted circumstances. The First Amendment to the Constitution has been interpreted as meaning that no government, federal or state, can place "prior restraints" (that is, censorship) on the press except under very narrowly defined circumstances.[9] When the federal government sought to prevent the *New York Times* from publishing the Pentagon Papers, a set of secret government documents stolen by an antiwar activist, the Court held that the paper was free to publish them.[10]

Once something is published, a newspaper or magazine may be sued or prosecuted if the material is libelous or obscene or if it incites someone to commit an illegal act. But these are usually not very serious restrictions, because the courts have defined *libelous, obscene,* and *incitement* so narrowly as to make it more difficult here than in any other nation to find the press guilty of such conduct. For example, for a paper to be found guilty of libeling a public official or other prominent person, the person must not only show that what was printed was wrong and damaging but must also show, with "clear and convincing evidence," that it was printed maliciously—that is, with "reckless disregard" for its truth or falsity.[11] When in 1984 Israeli General Ariel Sharon sued *Time* magazine for libel, the jury decided that the story that *Time* had printed was false and defamatory but that *Time* had not published it as the result of malice, and so Sharon did not collect any damages.

There are also laws intended to protect the privacy of citizens, but they do not really inhibit newspapers. In general, your name and picture can be printed without your consent if they are part of a news story of some conceivable public interest. And if a paper attacks you in print, the paper has no legal obligation to give you space for a reply.[12]

It is illegal to use printed words to advocate the violent overthrow of the government if by your advocacy you incite others to action, but this rule has been applied to newspapers only rarely.[13]

Confidentiality of Sources

Reporters believe that they should have the right to keep confidential the sources of their stories. Some states agree and have passed laws to that effect. Most states and the federal government do not agree, so the courts must decide in each case whether the need of a journalist to protect confidential sources does or does not outweigh the interest of the government in gathering evidence in a criminal investigation. In general the Supreme Court has upheld the right of the government to compel reporters to divulge information as part of a properly conducted criminal investigation, if it bears on the commission of a crime.[14]

This conflict arises not only between reporters and law enforcement agencies but also between reporters and persons accused of committing a crime. Myron Farber, a reporter for the *New York Times,* wrote a series of stories that led to the indictment and trial of a physician on charges that he had murdered five patients. The judge ordered Farber to show him his notes to determine whether they should be given to the defense lawyers. Farber refused, arguing that revealing his notes would infringe upon the confidentiality that he had promised to his sources. Farber was sent to jail for contempt of court. On appeal the New Jersey Supreme Court and the U.S. Supreme Court decided against Farber, holding that the accused person's right to a fair trial includes the right to compel the production of evidence, even from reporters.

In another case the Supreme Court upheld the right of the police to search newspaper offices, so long as they have a warrant. But Congress then passed a law forbidding such searches (except in special cases), requiring instead that the police subpoena the desired documents.[15]

Regulating Broadcasting

Although newspapers and magazines by and large are not regulated, broadcasting is regulated by the government. No one may operate a radio or television station without a license from the Federal Communications Commission, renewable every seven years for radio and every five for television stations. An application for renewal is rarely refused, but until recently the FCC required the broadcaster to submit detailed information about its programming and how it planned to serve "community needs" in order to get a renewal. Based on this information or on the complaints of some group, the FCC could use its powers of renewal to influence what the station put on the air. For example, it could induce stations to reduce the amount of violence shown, increase the proportion of "public service" programs on the air, or alter the way it portrayed various ethnic groups.

Of late a movement has arisen to deregulate broadcasting, on the grounds that so many stations are now on the air that competition should be allowed to determine how each station defines and serves community needs. In this view citizens can choose what they want to hear or see without the government's shaping the content of each station's programming. For example, since the early 1980s a station can simply submit a postcard requesting that its license be renewed, a request automatically granted unless some group formally opposes the renewal. In that case the FCC holds a hearing. As a result some of the old rules—for instance, that each hour on TV could contain only sixteen minutes of commercials—are no longer rigidly enforced.

Radio broadcasting has been deregulated the most. Before 1992 one company could own one AM and one FM station in each market. In 1992 this number was doubled. And in 1996 the Telecommunications Act allowed one company to own as many as eight stations in large markets (five in smaller ones) and as many as it wished nationally. This trend has had two results. First, a few large companies now

LANDMARK CASES

The Rights of the Media

- ***Near v. Minnesota* (1931):** Freedom of the press applies to state governments, so that they cannot impose prior restraint on newspapers.
- ***New York Times v. Sullivan* (1964):** Public officials may not win a libel suit unless they can prove that the statement was made knowing it to be false or with reckless disregard of its truth.
- ***Miami Herald v. Tornillo* (1974):** A newspaper cannot be required to give someone a right to reply to one of its stories.

own most of the big-market radio stations. Second, the looser editorial restrictions that accompanied deregulation mean that a greater variety of opinions and shows can be found on radio. There are many more radio talk shows than would have been heard when content was more tightly controlled.

Deregulation has also lessened the extent to which the federal government shapes the content of broadcasting. At one time, for example, there was a Fairness Doctrine that required broadcasters that air one side of a story to give time to opposing points of view. But there are now so many radio and television stations that the FCC relies on competition to manage differences of opinion. The abandonment of the Fairness Doctrine permitted the rise of controversial talk radio shows. If the doctrine had stayed in place, there would be no Rush Limbaugh. The FCC decided that competition among news outlets protected people by giving them many different sources of news.

There still exists an **equal time rule** that obliges stations that sell advertising time to one political candidate to sell equal time to that person's opponents.

Campaigning

When candidates wish to campaign on radio or television, the equal time rule applies. A broadcaster must provide equal access to candidates for office and charge them rates no higher than the cheapest rate applicable to commercial advertisers for comparable time.

---

equal time rule An FCC rule that if a broadcaster sells time to one candidate, it must sell equal time to other candidates.

At one time this rule meant that a station or network could not broadcast a debate between the Democratic and Republican candidates for an office without inviting all other candidates as well—Libertarian, Prohibitionist, or whatever. Thus a presidential debate in 1980 could be limited to the major candidates, Reagan and Carter (or Reagan and Anderson), only by having the League of Women Voters sponsor it and then allowing radio and TV to cover it as a "news event." Now stations and networks can themselves sponsor debates limited to major candidates.

Though laws guarantee that candidates can buy time at favorable rates on television, not all candidates take advantage of this. The reason is that television is not always an efficient way to reach voters. A television message is literally "broad cast"—spread out to a mass audience without regard to the boundaries of the district in which a candidate is running. Presidential candidates, of course, always use television, because their constituency is the whole nation. Candidates for senator or representative, however, may or may not use television, depending on whether the boundaries of their state or district conform well to the boundaries of a television market.

A *market* is an area easily reached by a television signal; there are about two hundred such markets in the country. If you are a member of Congress from South Bend, Indiana, you come from a television market based there. You can buy ads on the TV stations in South Bend at a reasonable fee. But if you are a member of Congress from northern New Jersey, the only television stations are in nearby New York City. In that market, the costs of a TV ad are very high because they reach a lot of people, most of whom are not in your district and so cannot vote for you. Buying a TV ad is a waste of money. As a result, a much higher percentage of Senate than of House candidates use television ads.

☆ Are the National Media Biased?

Everyone believes that the media have a profound effect, for better or for worse, on politics. Many think that the political opinions of writers and editors influence that effect. To decide whether these statements are true, we must answer three questions:

1. Do members of the media have a distinctive political attitude?
2. Does that attitude affect what they write or say?
3. Does what they write or say affect what citizens believe?

The answers to these questions, to be discussed below, are yes, yes, and probably.

1. What are the views of members of the national media? The great majority is liberal. There have been many studies of this that date back to the early 1980s, and they all come to the same conclusion: members of the national press are more liberal than the average citizen. Table 12.2 provides one glimpse of this, but other studies confirm it.[16] In 1992, 91 percent of the media members who were interviewed said that they had voted for the Democratic candidate for president. By contrast, only 43 percent of the public voted that way.[17]

Not only are they more liberal, they tend to be more secular. About 70 percent say they never or only a few times a year attend a religious service. And in recent years the surveys suggest that they have become more liberal. For example, between 1980 and 1995 the proportion of media members who believe that the government should guarantee jobs to people rose, and the proportion who think that government should reduce the regulation of business fell.[18]

The public certainly believes that members of the media are liberals. A Gallup Poll done in 2003 found that 45 percent of Americans believe that the media are "too liberal" (15 percent thought they were "too conservative"). In another study, even Democrats agreed with this view.[19]

There are conservative media outlets, and they have become more visible in recent years. Radio talk shows, such as those managed by Rush Limbaugh and Sean Hannity, are conservative, as is some of the reporting

Spanish-speaking voters have become so important that candidates (such as George W. Bush here) run Spanish-language web sites.

broadcast on Fox News television, such as the "O'Reilly Factor." Limbaugh and Hannity have large audiences, and Fox News has grown in popularity.

One-fifth of all Americans listen to radio talk shows every day and another tenth listen several times a week. A puzzling fact is that talk radio, which

Table 12.2	Journalist Opinion Versus Public Opinion	
	Journalists	**The Public**
Self-described ideology:		
Liberal	55%	23%
Conservative	17	29
Favor government regulation of business	49	22
U.S. should withdraw investments from South Africa	62	31
Allow women to have abortions	82	49
Allow prayer in public schools	25	74
Favor "affirmative action"	81	56
Favor death penalty for murder	47	75
Want stricter controls on handguns	78	50
Increase defense budget	15	38
Favor hiring homosexuals	89	55

Sources: Los Angeles Times poll of about 3,000 citizens and 2,700 journalists nationwide, as reported in William Schneider and I. A. Lewis, "Views on the News," *Public Opinion* (August/September 1985): 7. Reprinted with permission of American Enterprise Institute for Public Policy Research.

How to Read a Newspaper

Newspapers don't simply report the news; they report somebody's idea of what is news, written in language intended to persuade as well as inform. To read a newspaper intelligently, look for three things: what is covered, who are the sources, and how language is used.

Coverage

Every newspaper will cover a big story, such as a flood, fire, or presidential trip, but newspapers can pick and choose among lesser stories. One paper will select stories about the environment, business fraud, and civil rights; another will prefer stories about crime, drug dealers, and "welfare cheats." What do these choices tell you about the beliefs of the editors and reporters working for these two papers? What do these people want you to believe are the important issues?

Sources

For some stories, the source is obvious: "The Supreme Court decided . . . ," "Congress voted . . . ," or "The president said. . . ." For others, the source is not so obvious. There are two kinds of sources you should beware of. The first is an anonymous source. When you read phrases such as "a high official said today . . . " or "White House sources revealed that . . . " always ask yourself this question: Why does the source want me to know this? The answer usually will be this: because if I believe what he or she said, it will advance his or her interests. This can happen in one of three ways. First, the source may support a policy or appointment and want to test public reaction to it. This is called floating a **trial balloon.** Second, the source may oppose a policy or appointment and hope that by leaking word of it, the idea will be killed. Third, the source may want to take credit for something good that happened or shift blame onto somebody else for something bad that happened. When you read a story that is based on anonymous sources, ask yourself these questions: Judging from the tone of the story, is this leak designed to support or kill an idea? Is it designed to take credit or shift blame? In whose interest is it to accomplish these things? By asking these questions, you often can make a pretty good guess as to the identity of the anonymous source.

Some stories depend on the reader's believing a key fact, previously unknown. For example: "The world's climate is getting hotter because of man-made pollution," "drug abuse is soaring," "the death penalty will prevent murder," "husbands are more likely to beat up on their wives on Super Bowl Sunday." Each of these "facts" is either wrong, grossly exaggerated, or stated with excessive confidence. But each comes from an advocate organization that wants you to believe it, because if you do, you will take that organization's solution more seriously. Be skeptical of key facts if they come from an advocacy source. Don't be misled by the tendency of many advocacy organizations to take neutral or scholarly names like "Center for the Public Interest" or "Institute for Policy Research." Some of these really are neutral or scholarly, but many aren't.

Language

Everybody uses words to persuade people of something without actually making a clear argument for it. This is called using **loaded language.** For example: if you like a politician, call him "Senator Smith"; if you don't like him, refer to him as "right-wing (or left-wing) senators such as Smith." If you like an idea proposed by a professor, call her "respected"; if you don't like the idea, call her "controversial." If you favor abortion, call somebody who agrees with you "pro-choice" ("choice" is valued by most people); if you oppose abortion, call those who agree with you "pro-life" ("life," like "choice," is a good thing). Recognizing loaded language in a newspaper article can give you important clues to the writer's own point of view.

has grown rapidly in importance, should be predominately conservative. Almost half of the twenty-eight largest talk shows were hosted by outspoken conservatives.

None of this dominance is the result of radio station owners plotting to put conservatives on the air. Media owners are interested in ratings—that is, in measures of how big their audiences are. Liberal talk show hosts have had big corporate sponsors, but they dropped away when the show did not get good ratings. If Fidel Castro got high ratings by playing the harmonica, Castro would be on the air.

William G. Mayer, a political scientist, has speculated as to why conservative talk shows are so common. First, there are more self-described conservatives than liberals in this country. Second, conservative listeners do not think their views are reflected in what big-city newspapers, the major television networks, and the leading news magazines display. Liberals, by contrast, think their views are encouraged by newspapers and television stations. Third, much of the liberal audience is broken up into distinctive racial and ethnic groups that have their own radio outlets. Many Hispanics listen to stations that broadcast in Spanish; many African Americans prefer stations that have black hosts and focus on black community issues.[20]

2. Do the beliefs of the national media affect how they report the news? That is a harder question to answer. In the United States, the journalistic philosophy in many media documents is that the press, when it reports the news (though not in editorial pages), should be neutral and objective. That view, of course, does not cover radio talk shows, but it is supposed to cover newspapers. A different view can be found in France or Great Britain where newspapers often clearly identify with one party or another.

But it is hard to measure whether the American commitment to objectivity is actually achieved. One would have to take into account not only how much space a politician or policy receives, but the tone in which it is handled and the adjectives used to describe people who are part of those stories.

New stories differ significantly in the opportunity for bias. **Routine stories** cover major political events that will be covered by many reporters and that involve relatively simple matters. For example: the president takes a trip, the Congress passes a major bill, or the Supreme Court issues a ruling. **Feature stories** cover events that, though public, a reporter has to seek out because they are not routinely covered by the press. The reporter has to find the story and persuade an editor to publish it. For example: an interest group works hard to get a bill passed, a government agency adopts a new ruling, or a member of Congress conducts an unusual investigation. **Insider stories** cover things that are often secret. Investigative reporters are often credited with uncovering these stories, though it is often the case that some government insider leaked the story to the press. Which leak a reporter picks up

on may be influenced by the reporter's view as to what is important to him or her.

Routine stories are often covered in much the same way by reporters. The space given to the story and the headline attached to it may reflect the political views of the editor, but the story itself is often written about the same way by every reporter. Feature and insider stories, by contrast, may more easily reflect the political views of reporters and editors. On these stories, journalists have to make choices.

Early in American history, newspapers had virtually no routine stories; almost everything they printed was an expression of opinion. By the twentieth century, with the advent of telephone and telegraph lines that made it easy for news organizations such as the Associated Press to send the same story to almost every newspaper, routine stories became commonplace. But with the advent of radio and television and the rise of around-the-clock news broadcasting, feature and insider stories became much more important to newspapers. If people got their routine news from radio and television, newspapers had to sell something different; what was different were feature and insider stories.

A conservative newspaper might print feature or insider stories about crime, drug abuse, or welfare cheats, while a liberal newspaper might run ones on feminism, the environment, or civil rights. There are, however, very few conservative newspapers with a national audience.

A key question is whether there are facts to back up these generalizations. There are no definitive answers; here we can take a look at a few of the better studies.

One looked at twelve years, worth of political stories published in the *New York Times* and the *Washington Post*. It asked how these papers described the ten most liberal and the ten most conservative senators. The authors found that conservative senators

trial balloon Information leaked to the media to test public reaction to a possible policy.

loaded language Words that imply a value judgment, used to persuade a reader without having made a serious argument.

routine stories Media stories about events that are regularly covered by reporters.

feature stories Media stories about events that, though public, are not regularly covered by reporters.

insider stories Media stories about events that are not usually made public.

were about three times more likely to be called conservative than liberal senators were to be called liberal.[21] The difference in the use of adjectives may influence how readers feel about the story. Politically independent readers might (no one knows) take more seriously the views of senators that are given no ideological labels than they will of those to which such labels have been attached.

There have been efforts to see how newspapers and magazines cover specific issues. When *Time* and *Newsweek* ran stories about nuclear power, scholars found they tended to avoid quoting scientists and engineers working in this field because these specialists were in favor of nuclear power at a time when the magazines were opposed to it.[22]

Another study looked at how the top ten newspapers and the Associated Press cover economic news when there is either a Democratic or Republican president in office. The news was based on government reports about sales, unemployment, and economic growth over a thirteen-year period. The authors decided whether a newspaper's headline covering that news (on the day it was released) was either positive, negative, or neutral. In general, these headlines gave a more positive spin when there was a Democrat in the White House and a more negative one when there was a Republican there.[23]

But perhaps the easiest evidence to understand comes from reporters themselves. The *New York Times* has a "public editor," that is, a person charged with receiving complaints from the public. When asked, "Is the *New York Times* a liberal newspaper?" he answered, in print, very simply: "Of course it is." On "gay rights, gun control, abortion, and environmental regulation, among others" the *Times* does not play it "down the middle."[24]

Public distrust of the media has grown. As can be see in Figure 12.2, the proportion of people saying that news stories are often inaccurate has grown significantly since 1985.

3. Does what the media write or say influence how their readers and viewers think? This is the hardest question to answer. Some people will be influenced by what they read or hear, but others will not. There is a well-known psychological process

called **selective attention.** It means that people remember or believe only what they want to. If they see or hear statements that are inconsistent with their existing beliefs, they will tune out these message.[25]

To identify who, if anyone, is influenced by what the press says or broadcasts, one would have to study how people think about political candidates and public policy issues in ways that take into account what they read or hear. That is very hard to do. There have been some efforts along these lines, however.

After the 1964 presidential election, one study suggested that in the northern part of the United States a newspaper endorsement favoring Democratic candidate Lyndon Johnson added about five percentage points to the vote he received.[26]

Another study examined the vote in more than sixty contests for the U.S. Senate held over a five-year period. Newspaper stories about the rival candidates were scored as positive, negative, or neutral. How voters felt about the candidates were learned from public opinion polls. Obviously, many things other than newspaper stories will affect how voters feel, and so the authors of this study tried to control for these factors. They held constant the seniority of incumbent candidates, the level of political experience of challengers, the amount of campaign spending, how close each race was, and the political ideology and party identification of voters. After doing all of this, they discovered two things. First, newspapers that endorsed incumbents on their editorial pages gave more positive news coverage to them than did newspapers that did not endorse them. Second, the voters had more positive feelings about endorsed incumbents than they did about nonendorsed ones. In short, editorial views affect news coverage, and news coverage affects public attitudes.[27]

What the press covers affects the policy issues that people think are important. Experiments conducted in New Haven, Connecticut, and a study done in North Carolina show that what citizens believe about some policy questions reflects what newspapers and television stations say about them.[28]

But there are limits to media influence. If people are unemployed, the victims of crime, or worried about high gasoline prices, they do not have to be told these things by the media.[29] They learn them by themselves. But most people have no personal knowledge of highway fatalities, the condition of the environment, or American foreign policy in Europe. On these matters, the media are likely to have much more influence.

But the best evidence of how important the media are comes from the behavior of people trying to get

---

selective attention   Paying attention only to those news stories with which one already agrees.

W. Mark Felt, once the second in command at the FBI, was the "Deep Throat" who leaked information to the Wash-ington Post about President Nixon's involvement in the Watergate scandal.

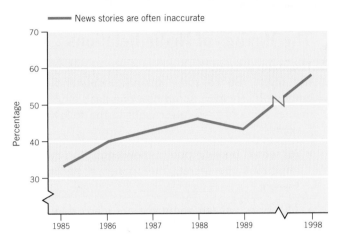

Figure 12.2   Public Perception of Accuracy in the Media

— News stories are often inaccurate

Source: Pew Research Center, "The People and the Press" (February 1999), 13.

elected. In 1950 Estes Kefauver was a little-known senator from Tennessee. Then he chaired a Senate committee investigating organized crime. When these dramatic hearings were televised, Kefauver became a household name. In 1952 he ran for the Democratic nomination for president and won a lot of primary votes before losing to Adlai Stevenson.

From that time on, developing a strong media presence became a top priority for political candidates. Sometimes it backfires. In 2004 Howard Dean, then a candidate for the Democratic presidential nomination, saw his campaign start to sputter after television carried a speech he gave to his supporters that seemed to end in a kind of anguished scream. And every White House staffer spends a lot of time worrying about how to get the press, especially television, to cover the president. Studies show that television commentary about presidents affects their popularity.[30] President Lyndon Johnson reportedly concluded that the war he was supporting in Vietnam was a hopeless cause after Walter Cronkite, then the star of the popular CBS News program, turned against the war.

☆ Government and the News

Every government agency, every public official, spends a great deal of time trying to shape public opinion. From time to time somebody publishes an exposé of the efforts of the Pentagon, the White House, or some bureau to "sell" itself to the people, but in a government of separated powers, weak parties, and a decentralized legislature, any government agency that fails to cultivate public opinion will sooner or later find itself weak, without allies, and in trouble.

Prominence of the President

Theodore Roosevelt was the first president to raise the systematic cultivation of the press to an art form. From the day he took office, he made it clear that he would give inside stories to friendly reporters and withhold them from hostile ones. He made sure that scarcely a day passed without his doing something newsworthy. In 1902 he built the West Wing of the White House and included in it, for the first time, a special room for reporters near his office, and he invited the press to become fascinated by the antics of his children. In return the reporters adored him. Teddy's nephew Franklin Roosevelt institutionalized this system by making his press secretary (a job created by Herbert Hoover) a major instrument for cultivating and managing, as well as informing, the press.[31]

The "Rules" of Politics

The Maxims of Media Relations

The importance of the national media to politicians has given rise to some shared understandings among officeholders about how one deals with the media. Some of these are caught in the following maxims:

- All secrets become public knowledge. The more important the secret, the sooner it becomes known.

- All stories written about me are inaccurate; all stories written about you are entirely accurate.

- The rosier the news, the higher ranking the official who announces it.

- Always release bad news on Saturday night. Fewer people notice it.

- Never argue with a person who buys ink by the barrel.

Today the press secretary heads a large staff that meets with reporters, briefs the president on questions he is likely to be asked, attempts to control the flow of news from cabinet departments to the press, and arranges briefings for out-of-town editors (to bypass what many presidents think are the biases of the White House press corps).

All this effort is directed primarily at the White House press corps, a group of men and women who have a lounge in the White House itself where they wait for a story to break, attend the daily press briefing, or take advantage of a "photo op"—an opportunity to photograph the president with some newsworthy person.

No other nation in the world has brought the press into such close physical proximity to the head of its government. The result is that the actions of our government are personalized to a degree not found in most other democracies. Whether the president rides a horse, comes down with a cold, greets a Boy Scout, or takes a trip in his airplane, the press is there. The prime minister of Great Britain does not share his home with the press or expect to have his every sneeze recorded for posterity.

Coverage of Congress

Congress has watched all this with irritation and envy. It resents the attention given the president, but it is not certain how it can compete. The 435 members of the House are so numerous and play such specialized roles that they do not get much individualized press attention. In the past the House was quite restrictive about television or radio coverage of its proceedings. Until 1978 it prohibited television cameras on the floor except on purely ceremonial occasions (such as the annual State of the Union message delivered by the president). From 1952 to 1970 the House would not even allow electronic coverage of its committee hearings (except for a few occasions during those periods when the Republicans were in the majority). Significant live coverage of committee hearings began in 1974 when the House Judiciary Committee was discussing the possible impeachment of President Nixon.[32] Since 1979 cable TV (C-SPAN) has provided gavel-to-gavel coverage of speeches on the House floor.

The Senate has used television much more fully, heightening the already substantial advantage that senators have over representatives in getting the public eye. Although radio and television coverage of the Senate floor was not allowed until 1978 (when the debates on the Panama Canal treaties were broadcast live), Senate committee hearings have frequently been televised for either news films or live broadcasts ever since Estes Kefauver demonstrated the power of this medium in 1950. Since 1986 the Senate has allowed live C-SPAN coverage of its sessions.

Senatorial use of televised committee hearings has helped turn the Senate into the incubator for presidential candidates. At least in most states, if you are a governor, you are located far from network television news cameras; the best you can hope for is that some disaster—a flood or a blizzard—will bring the cameras to you and focus them on your leadership. But senators all work in Washington, a city filled with cameras. No disaster is necessary to get on the air; only an investigation, a scandal, a major political conflict, or an articulate and telegenic personality is needed.

Why Do We Have So Many News Leaks?

American government is the leakiest in the world. The bureaucracy, members of Congress, and the White House staff regularly leak stories favorable to their interests. Of late the leaks have become geysers, gushing forth torrents of insider stories. Many people in and out of government find it depressing that our government seems unable to keep anything secret for long. Others think that the public has a right to know even more and that there are still too many secrets.

However you view leaks, you should understand why we have so many. The answer is found in the Constitution. Because we have separate institutions that must share power, each branch of government competes with the others to get power. One way to compete is to try to use the press to advance your pet projects and to make the other side look bad. There are far fewer leaks in other democratic nations in part because power is centralized in the hands of a prime minister, who does not need to leak in order to get the upper hand over the legislature, and because the legislature has too little information to be a good source of leaks. In addition we have no Official Secrets Act of the kind that exists in England; except for a few matters, it is not against the law for the press to receive and print government secrets.

Even if the press and the politicians loved each other, the competition between the various branches of government would guarantee plenty of news leaks. But since the Vietnam War, the Watergate scandal, and the Iran-contra affair, the press and the politicians have come to distrust one another. As a result, journalists today are far less willing to accept at face value the statements of elected officials and are far more likely to try to find somebody who will leak "the real story." We have come, in short, to have an **adversarial press**—that is, one that (at least at the national level) is suspicious of officialdom and eager to break an embarrassing story that will win for its author honor, prestige, and (in some cases) a lot of money.

This cynicism and distrust of government and elected officials have led to an era of attack journalism—seizing upon any bit of information or rumor that might call into question the qualifications or character of a public official. Media coverage of gaffes—misspoken words, misstated ideas, clumsy moves—has become a staple of political journalism. At one time, such "events" as President Ford slipping down some stairs, Governor Dukakis dropping the ball while playing catch with a Boston Red Sox player, or Vice President Quayle misspelling the word *potato* would have been ignored, but now they are hot news items. Attacking public figures has become a professional norm, where once it was a professional taboo.

During the 1992 election, most of the national press clearly supported Bill Clinton. The love affair between Clinton and reporters lasted for several months after his inauguration. But when stories

When President Theodore Roosevelt cultivated the media, reporters were usually unknown and poorly paid.

began to appear about Whitewater (an Arkansas real estate deal in which the Clintons were once involved), Clinton's alleged sexual escapades, and Hillary Rodham Clinton's profits in commodities trading, the press went into a feeding frenzy. The Clintons learned the hard way the truth of an old adage: if you want a friend in Washington, buy a dog.

Many people do not like this type of journalism, and the media's rising cynicism about the government is mirrored by the public's increasing cynicism about the media. In a national survey of registered voters conducted shortly before the 2000 presidential election, 89 percent of respondents agreed that the media's "political views influence coverage" often (57 percent) or sometimes (32 percent); 47 percent believed that "most journalists" were "pulling for" Gore to win; and 23 percent believed that most journalists were partial to Bush.[33] Most Americans really dislike biased journalism (or journalism they perceive as biased): 53 percent say they would require a license to practice journalism, and 70 percent favor court-imposed fines for inaccurate or biased reporting.[34]

Furthermore, the public's confidence in big business has eroded along with its confidence in government, and the media are increasingly big business. As

---

adversarial press   The tendency of the national media to be suspicious of officials and eager to reveal unflattering stories about them.

In 1933 White House press conferences were informal affairs, as when reporters gathered around Franklin Roosevelt's desk in the Oval Office. Today they are huge gatherings held in a special conference room, as on the right.

noted earlier in this chapter, network television has become a highly competitive industry. Under these circumstances, every contribution to "market share" is vitally important, and the newsroom is no exception. In a highly competitive environment that is rich in information, those who aspire to reach a mass market must find a mass theme into which they can tap with visually dramatic, quick-tempo messages. In politics the theme is obvious: politics is a corrupt, self-serving enterprise. Many people include the profit-driven press in their antipolitical sentiments.

Given their experiences with Watergate and Irangate, given the highly competitive nature of national newsgathering, and given their political ideology (which tends to put them to the left of the administration in power), American editors and reporters, at least at the national level, are likely to have an adversarial relationship with government for a long time to come. Given our constitutional system, there will always be plenty of people in government eager to help them with leaks hostile to one faction or another.

One side effect of the increasingly adversarial nature of the press is the increased prevalence of negative campaign advertising—that is, of ads that lambaste opponents and attack them on a personal level. Adversarial media coverage has helped make these types of ads more socially acceptable. The reason candidates use attack ads is simple: they work. A good negative ad will change the preferences of some voters. But this change is purchased at a price.

Research shows that a negative ad not only changes voter preferences, it reduces voter turnout. Negative advertising may help a candidate win, but only by turning other people against elections.

Sensationalism in the Media

Back in the 1930s newspaper reporters knew that President Franklin Roosevelt had a romantic affair with a woman other than his wife. They did not report it. In the early 1960s many reporters knew that President John Kennedy had many sexual affairs outside his marriage. They did not report this. In 1964 the director of the Federal Bureau of Investigation played for reporters secret tape recordings of the Reverend Martin Luther King, Jr., having sex with women other than his wife. They did not report it.

By the 1980s sex and politics were extensively covered. When presidential candidate Gary Hart was caught in adultery and when President Bill Clinton was accused of adultery by Gennifer Flowers, of asking for sexual favors by Paula Jones, and of having sex with Monica Lewinsky in the Oval Office, these were headline news stories.

What had changed? Not politics: all of the people whom the press protected or reported on were Democrats. The big change was in the economics of journalism and the ideas of reporters.

Until the 1970s Americans gathered their political news from one of three networks—ABC, CBS, or NBC. For a long time these networks had only one half-hour news show a day. Today, however, viewers have the same three networks plus three cable news networks, two sports networks, ten weekly news-magazine shows, countless radio talk shows, and the Internet. Many of the cable networks, such as CNN, carry news 24 hours a day. The result of this intense competition is that each radio or television network has a small share of the audience. Today less than half the public watches the evening network news shows. Dozens of news programs are trying to reach a shrinking audience, with the result that the audience share of each program is small. To attract any audience at all, each program has a big incentive to rely on sensational news stories—sex, violence, and intrigue. Reinforcing this desire to go with sensationalism is the fact that covering such stories is cheaper than investigating foreign policy or analyzing the tax code. During its first month, the Lewinsky story consumed more than one-third of the on-air time of the news networks—more than the U.S. showdown with Iran, the Winter Olympics, the pope's visit to Cuba, and the El Niño weather pattern combined.

Since the days of Vietnam and Watergate, journalists have become adversaries of the government. They instinctively distrust people in government. But to that attitude change can be added an economic one: in their desperate effort to reclaim market share, journalists are much more likely to rely on unnamed sources than once was the case. When the *Washington Post* broke the Watergate story in the 1970s, it required the reporters to have at least two sources for their stories. Now many reporters break stories that have only one unnamed source, and often not a source at all but a rumor posted on the Internet.

As a result, reporters are more easily manipulated by sources than once was the case. Spokesmen for President Clinton tried to "spin" the news about his affairs, usually by attacking his critics. Gennifer Flowers, Paula Jones, and Monica Lewinsky were portrayed as bimbos, liars, or stalkers. Much of the press used the spin. To see how successful spin can be, compare independent counsel Lawrence Walsh's investigation of aides to President Ronald Reagan over the sale of arms to Iran with independent counsel Kenneth Starr's investigation of the Clinton administration. Walsh's inquiry got full press support, while Starr was regularly attacked by the press.

Since the terrorist attack on the United States on September 11, 2001, there has been scattered evidence to suggest that sensationalism in the media has declined a bit, while public interest in national news

"*Those are the headlines, and we'll be back in a moment to blow them out of proportion.*"

and trust of news organizations have increased somewhat. The big stories of the preceding years were the sexual conduct of President Clinton and the connection between California representative Gary Condit and a missing young woman. After September 11, the press focused on a more important matter—defeating terrorism at home and abroad. By early 2002, surveys indicated that the number of people who said they followed national news closely had increased slightly from 48 percent to 53 percent; the number who said the media usually get the facts straight rose from 35 percent to 46 percent (the best public grade for accuracy in a decade); and the number who rated the media's coverage of the war on terrorism as good or excellent never fell below three-quarters.[35] But the television networks do not seem to be gaining any viewers back as a result of the crisis: fully 53 percent cited cable as their primary source for news on terrorism, versus 18 percent for local television and 17 percent for national networks.[36]

Government Constraints on Journalists

An important factor works against the influence of ideology and antiofficial attitudes on reporters—the need every reporter has for access to key officials. A reporter is only as good as his or her sources, and it is difficult to cultivate good sources if you regularly antagonize them. Thus Washington reporters must constantly strike a balance between expressing their own views (and risk losing a valuable source) and keeping a source (and risk becoming its mouthpiece).

The great increase in the number of congressional staff members has made striking this balance easier than it once was. Since it is almost impossible to keep anything secret from Congress, the existence of fifteen thousand to twenty thousand congressional staffers

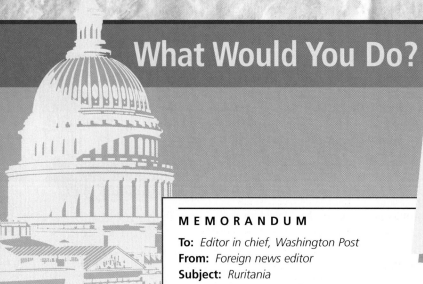

What Would You Do?

Tensions Mount Between U.S. and Ruritania

U.S. 6th Fleet Maneuvering near African Nation

February 23
WASHINGTON

The State Department today denied Ruritanian claims that the United States is planning military action against Ruritania in the wake of Ruritanian-sponsored terrorist actions . . .

MEMORANDUM

To: *Editor in chief, Washington Post*
From: *Foreign news editor*
Subject: *Ruritania*

One of our best reporters has information that the United States plans to invade Ruritania three days from now. His source is a top military official who has been reliable in the past. As of now we do not think that any other newspaper has this story. As you know, opinion in the government is deeply divided over the wisdom of any action against Ruritania. So far all official sources in the White House and the State Department have denied that anything is afoot. But we all know that the president is deeply upset by the continuation of Ruritanian-sponsored terrorism against U.S. personnel overseas. Your options are:

1. Print the story in tomorrow's edition.

Advantages: (a) This is important news, and we have an obligation to publish news. (b) We get a major scoop that no other newspaper can match. (c) In our editorials we have said that we think an invasion of Ruritania would be a mistake. This story, if printed now, may lead to a cancellation of the military action.

Disadvantages: (a) There is a small chance that we could be wrong and no invasion is planned. (b) We will be criticized for leaking military secrets. (c) If the invasion takes place despite our story, the United States may lose the element of surprise, and this may affect the outcome and cause additional casualties.

2. Do not print the story.

Advantages: (a) We avoid charges that we are leaking military secrets. (b) If an invasion occurs, we will not have alerted the enemy.

Disadvantages: (a) There is the possibility that another newspaper may learn of this story in the next two days; if we don't publish now, they may publish later and we will look foolish. (b) We will be failing in our duty to inform the people about the activities of their government. (c) The Ruritanians may already know of the planned invasion, and so our story will not have alerted them.

Your decision:

Option 1 _____
Option 2 _____

means that there is a potential source for every conceivable issue and cause. Congress has become a gold mine for reporters. If a story annoys one congressional source, another source can easily be found.

The government is not without means to fight back. The number of press officers on the payroll of the White House, Congress, and the executive agencies has grown sharply in recent decades. Obviously these people have a stake in putting out news stories that reflect favorably on their elected superiors. They can try to do this with press releases, but adversarial journalists are suspicious of "canned news" (although they use it nonetheless). Or the press officers can try to win journalistic friends by offering leaks and supplying background stories to favored reporters.

There are four ways in which reporters and public officials, or their press officers, can communicate:

- On the record: The reporter can quote the official by name.
- Off the record: What the official says cannot be used.
- On **background:** What the official says can be used but may not be attributed to him or her by name. Reporters often call these anonymous source "a high-ranking official" or "a knowledgeable member of Congress."
- On deep background: What the official says can be used but not attributed to anybody, even an anonymous source.

To get around the national press, public officials and their press officers can try to reach the local media directly by giving interviews or appearing on radio talk shows. The local media are a bit less likely than the national media to have an adversarial attitude toward the national government, and one can select talk-show hosts on the basis of their known ideology.

The ultimate weapon in the government's effort to shape the press to its liking is the president's rewarding of reporters and editors who treat him well and his punishing of those who treat him badly. President Kennedy regularly called in offending reporters for brutal tongue-lashings and favored friendly reporters with tips and inside stories. Johnson did the same, with special attention to television reporters. Nixon made the mistake of attacking the press publicly, thereby allowing it to defend itself with appeals to the First Amendment. (Kennedy's and Johnson's manipulative skills were used privately.) Probably every president tries to use the press with whatever means are at his disposal, but in the long run it is the press, not the president, who wins. Johnson decided not to run again in 1968 in part because of press hostility to him; Nixon was exposed by the press; Carter and Bush came to be disliked by national reporters. The press and the president need but do not trust one another; it is inevitably a stormy relationship.

☆ SUMMARY

*C*hanges in the nature of American politics have been accompanied by—and influenced by— changes in the nature of the mass media. The rise of strong national political party organizations was facilitated by the emergence of mass-circulation daily newspapers. Political reform movements depended in part on the development of national magazines catering to middle-class opinion. The weakening of political parties was accelerated by the ability of candidates to speak directly to constituents by radio and television.

The role of journalists in a democratic society poses an inevitable dilemma: if they are to serve well their functions as information gatherer, gatekeeper, scorekeeper, and watchdog, they must be free of government controls. But to the extent that they are free of such controls, they are also free to act in their own interests, whether political or economic. In the United States a competitive press largely free of government controls (except in the area of broadcast licenses) has produced both a substantial diversity of opinion and a general (though not unanimous) commitment to the goal of fairness in news reporting. The national media are in general more liberal than the local media, but the extent to which a reporter's beliefs affect reporting varies greatly with the kind of story—routine, feature, or insider.

background A public official's statement to a reporter that is given on condition that the official not be named.

RECONSIDERING WHO GOVERNS?

1. How much power do the media have?

A lot, but it is limited by selective attention and personal knowledge. Selective attention means that people tend to believe only those arguments that are consistent with their own beliefs. Personal knowledge means that people know a lot based on their own experiences regardless of what the press says. Politicians in and out of office spend a great deal of time cultivating the media, but in many campaigns it is clear that the press is more likely to favor some people than others.

2. Can we trust the media to be fair?

The public does not believe that we can trust the press, and that hostility has increased in recent years. Members of the national media are disproportionately liberal and secular, and there is some evidence that these liberal views affect what they say or write. The extent of that political influence will differ, however, depending on whether a story is a routine, feature, or insider account.

RECONSIDERING TO WHAT ENDS?

1. What public policies will the media support?

The media will lead the public to think about issues that are remote from their personal experiences, such as foreign policy. But the press can take up or drop issues, not because the issue has changed, but because the issue has become, to journalists, stale.

Crime and drug abuse may be big topics some years and minor ones in other years. Liberal newspapers, such as the New York Times, will be much more interested in gay rights, gun control, and the environment than will conservative newspapers or even than the public generally.

WORLD WIDE WEB RESOURCES

To search many newspapers: **www.ipl.org**

To get analyses of the press
Nonpartisan view: **www.cmpa.org**
A liberal view: **www.fair.org**
A conservative view: **www.mrc.org**

Public opinion about the press
Pew Research Center: **people-press.org**

National media:
New York Times: **www.nytimes.com**
Wall Street Journal: **www. wsj.com**
Washington Post: **www.washingtonpost.com**

SUGGESTED READINGS

Crouse, Timothy. *The Boys on the Bus.* New York: Random House, 1973. A lively, irreverent account by a participant of how reporters cover a presidential campaign.

Epstein, Edward J. *Between Fact and Fiction: The Problem of Journalism.* New York: Random House, 1975. Essays by a perceptive student of the press on media coverage of Watergate, the Pentagon Papers, the deaths of Black Panthers, and other major stories.

———. *News from Nowhere.* New York: Random House, 1973. Analysis of how television network news programs are produced and shaped.

Garment, Suzanne. *Scandal.* New York: Random House, 1991. A careful look at the role of the media (and others) in fostering the "culture of mistrust."

Graber, Doris A. *Mass Media and American Politics.* 6th ed. Washington, D.C.: Congressional Quarterly Press, 2002. A good summary of what we know about the press and politics.

Iyengar, Shanto, and Donald R. Kinder. *News That Matters.* Chicago: University of Chicago Press, 1987. The report of experiments testing the effect of television news on public perceptions of politics.

Kurtz, Howard. *Spin Cycle: Inside the Clinton Propaganda Machine.* New York: Free Press, 1998. A journalistic account of how one president's staff tried to influence the media.

Lichter, S. Robert, Stanley Rothman, and Linda S. Lichter. *The Media Elite.* Bethesda, Md.: Adler and Adler, 1986. A study of the political beliefs of "elite" journalists and how those beliefs influence what we read and hear.

McGowan, William. *Coloring the News.* San Francisco: Encounter Books, 2001. An argument about the harmful effects of affirmative action and "identity politics" on news coverage.

Robinson, Michael J., and Margaret A. Sheehan. *Over the Wire and on TV.* New York: Russell Sage Foundation, 1983. Analyzes how CBS News and United Press International covered the 1980 election.

Sabato, Larry J. *Feeding Frenzy.* New York: Free Press, 1991. Explains the press focus on political misconduct.

PART III

Institutions of Government

But the great security against a gradual concentration of the several powers in the same department consists in giving to those who administer each department the necessary constitutional means and personal motives to resist encroachments of the others.

FEDERALIST No. 51

Congress

Congress Versus Parliament

The Evolution of Congress

Who Is in Congress?
Sex and Race ● Incumbency ● Party

Do Members Represent Their Voters?
Representational View ●
Organizational View ● Attitudinal
View

Ideology and Civility in Congress

**The Organization of Congress: Parties
and Caucuses**
Party Organization of the Senate ●
Party Structure in the House ● The
Strength of Party Structures ● Party
Unity ● Caucuses

**The Organization of Congress:
Committees**

**The Organization of Congress: Staffs
and Specialized Offices**
Tasks of Staff Members ● Staff
Agencies

How a Bill Becomes Law
Introducing a Bill ● Study by
Committees ● Floor Debate—The
House ● Floor Debate—The Senate ●
Methods of Voting

Reducing Power and Perks

The Post-9/11 Congress

WHO GOVERNS?

1. Are members of Congress representative of the American people?
2. Does Congress normally do what most citizens want it to do?

TO WHAT ENDS?

1. Should Congress run under strong leadership?
2. Should Congress act more quickly?

The bipartisan Continuity of Government Commission was formed after September 11, 2001, to help ensure that America's three branches of national government would be able to function after a catastrophic attack that killed or incapacitated large numbers of the nation's legislators, executive branch officials, or judges. In its May 2003 report, the Commission focused first and foremost on the United States Congress.[1] This should not be surprising. Both in the minds of the Federalists (see Chapter 2) and in terms of its present-day constitutional powers and prerogatives, Congress was and remains America's "first branch of government." As we shall explain, it has the ultimate power of the purse, can pass a law even if the president vetoes it, and can alter, profoundly at times, how existing laws are administered through its oversight of executive agencies. Congress can likewise expand or contract the appellate jurisdiction of the U.S. Supreme Court. It may use these powers only rarely, but it has them, and myriad others, in reserve.

However, Congress is now considered by many to be the system's broken branch, badly in need of fixing. It has probably been the object of more mass public mistrust and more elite reform proposals than either the presidency or the federal judiciary combined. This is true even though most incumbent members of Congress who seek reelection win it, and even though Congress as a whole has pretty consistently expanded the programs and adopted the reforms that most citizens favor.

Once you master its basics, Congress is full of supremely interesting political puzzles. Its diverse membership, its daily workings, and its legislative decisions arguably reveal more about America's representative democracy, past and present, warts and all, than is revealed by any other institution. It would be only a slight exaggeration to say that he or she who really knows Congress knows more about American politics than he or she who knows virtually everything else about the system but not much about Congress. There is no one key to understanding who governs and to what ends in America, but if we had to nominate a single candidate, we would nominate Congress.

The late senator Daniel Patrick Moynihan of New York once remarked that the United States is the only democratic government that has a legislative branch. Of course, lots of democracies have parliaments that can pass laws. What he meant is that among the large democracies of the world, only the U.S. Congress has great powers that it can exercise independently

317

Senator Bill Frist and colleagues voted for a huge expansion in Medicare by approving a program to provide prescription drugs.

of the executive branch. To see why this is so, we must understand the difference between a congress and a parliament.

☆ Congress Versus Parliament

The United States (along with many Latin American nations) has a congress; Great Britain (along with most Western European nations) has a parliament. A hint as to the difference between the two kinds of legislatures can be found in the original meanings of the words: *Congress* derives from a Latin term that means "a coming together," a meeting, as of representatives from various places. *Parliament* comes from a French word, *parler,* that means "to talk."

There is of course plenty of talking—some critics say that there is nothing *but* talking—in the U.S. Congress, and certainly members of a parliament represent to a degree their local districts. But the differences implied by the names of the lawmaking groups are real ones, with profound significance for how laws are made and how the government is run. These differences affect two important aspects of lawmaking bodies: how one becomes a member and what one does as a member.

Ordinarily a person becomes a member of a parliament (such as the British House of Commons) by persuading a political party to put his or her name on the ballot. Though usually a local party committee selects a person to be its candidate, that committee often takes suggestions from national party headquarters. In any case the local group selects as its candidate someone willing to support the national party program and leadership. In the election voters in the district choose not between two or three personalities running for office, but between two or three national parties.

By contrast, a person becomes a candidate for representative or senator in the U.S. Congress by running in a primary election. Except in a very few places, political parties exercise little control over the choice of who is nominated to run for congressional office. (This is the case even though the person who wins the primary will describe himself or herself in the general election as a Democrat or a Republican.) Voters select candidates in the primaries because of their personalities, positions on issues, or overall reputation. Even in the general election, where the party label affects who votes for whom, many citizens vote "for the man" (or for the woman), not for the party. As a result of these different systems, a parliament tends to be made up of people loyal to the national party leadership who meet to debate and vote on party issues. A congress, on the other hand, tends to be made up of people who think of themselves as independent representatives of their districts or states and who, while willing to support their party on many matters, expect to vote as their (or their constituents') beliefs and interests require.

Once they are in the legislature, members of a parliament discover that they can make only one important decision—whether or not to support the government. The government in a parliamentary system such as Britain's consists of a prime minister and various cabinet officers selected from the party that has the most seats in parliament. As long as the members of that party vote together, that government will remain in power (until the next election). Should members of a party in power in parliament decide to vote against their leaders, the leaders lose office, and a new government must be formed. With so much at stake, the leaders of a party in parliament have a powerful incentive to keep their followers in line. They insist that all members of the party vote together on almost all issues. If someone refuses, the penalty is often drastic: the party does not renominate the offending member in the next election.

Members of the U.S. Congress do not select the head of the executive branch of government—that is done by the voters when they choose a president. Far from making members of Congress less powerful, this makes them more powerful. Representatives and senators can vote on proposed laws without worrying that their votes will cause the government to collapse and without fearing that a failure to support their party will lead to their removal from the ballot in the next election. Congress has independent powers, defined by the Constitution, that it can exercise without regard to presidential preferences. Political parties do not control nominations for office, and thus they cannot discipline members of Congress who fail to support the party leadership. Because Congress is constitutionally independent of the president, and because its members are not tightly disciplined by a party leadership, individual members of Congress are free to express their views and vote as they wish. They are also free to become involved in the most minute details of lawmaking, budget making, and supervision of the administration of laws. They do this through an elaborate set of committees and subcommittees.

A real parliament, such as that in Britain, is an assembly of party representatives who choose a government and discuss major national issues. The principal daily work of a parliament is debate. A congress, such as that in the United States, is a meeting place of the representatives of local constituencies—districts and states. Members of the U.S. Congress can initiate, modify, approve, or reject laws, and they share with the president supervision of the administrative agencies of the government. The prin-

Illinois Senator Barack Obama spoke to the Democratic National Convention in 2004.

cipal work of a congress is representation and action, most of which takes place in committees.

What this means in practical terms to the typical legislator is easy to see. Since members of the British House of Commons have little independent power, they get rather little in return. They are poorly paid, may have no offices of their own and virtually no staff, are allowed only small sums to buy stationery, and can make a few free local telephone calls. Each is given a desk, a filing cabinet, and a telephone, but not always in the same place.

By contrast, a member of the U.S. House of Representatives, even a junior one, has power and is rewarded accordingly. For example, in 2004 each member earned a substantial salary ($150,000) and was entitled to a large office (or "clerk-hire") allowance, to pay for as many as twenty-two staffers. Each member also received individual allowances for travel, computer services, and the like. In addition, each member could mail newsletters and certain other documents to constituents for free using the "franking privilege." Senators, and representatives with seniority, received even

★ **HOW THINGS WORK** ★

The Powers of Congress

The powers of Congress are found in Article I, section 8, of the Constitution.

- To lay and collect taxes, duties, imposts, and excises
- To borrow money
- To regulate commerce with foreign nations and among the states
- To establish rules for naturalization (that is, becoming a citizen) and bankruptcy
- To coin money, set its value, and punish counterfeiting
- To fix the standard of weights and measures
- To establish a post office and post roads
- To issue patents and copyrights by inventors and authors
- To create courts inferior to (that is, below) the Supreme Court
- To define and punish piracies, felonies on the high seas, and crimes against the law of nations

- To declare war
- To raise and support an army and navy and make rules for their governance
- To provide for a militia (reserving to the states the right to appoint militia officers and to train the militia under congressional rules)
- To exercise exclusive legislative powers over the seat of government (that is, the District of Columbia) and other places purchased to be federal facilities (forts, arsenals, dockyards, and "other needful buildings")
- To "make all laws which shall be necessary and proper for carrying into execution the foregoing powers, and all other powers vested by this Constitution in the government of the United States" (*Note*: This "necessary and proper," or "elastic," clause has been generously interpreted by the Supreme Court, as explained in Chapter 16.)

larger benefits. Each senator was entitled to a generous office budget and legislative assistance allowance and was free to hire as many staff members as he or she wished with the money. These examples are not given to suggest that members of Congress are overrewarded, but only that their importance, as individuals, in our political system can be inferred from the resources that they command.

Because the United States has a congress made up of people chosen to represent their states and districts, rather than a parliament made up to represent competing political parties, no one should be surprised to learn that members of the U.S. Congress are more concerned with their own constituencies and careers than with the interests of any organized party or program of action. And since Congress does not choose the president, members of Congress know that worrying about the voters they represent is much more important than worrying about whether the president succeeds with his programs. These two factors taken together mean that Congress tends to be a decentralized institution, with each

member more interested in his or her own views and those of his or her voters than with the programs proposed by the president.

Indeed, Congress was designed by the Founders in ways that almost inevitably make it unpopular with voters. Americans want government to take action, follow a clear course of action, and respond to strong leaders. Americans dislike political arguments, the activities of special-interest groups, and the endless pulling and hauling that often precede any congressional decision. But the people who feel this way are deeply divided about what government should do: Be liberal? Be conservative? Spend money? Cut taxes? Support abortions? Stop abortions? Since they are divided, and since members of Congress must worry about how voters feel, it is inevitable that on controversial issues Congress will engage in endless arguments, worry about what interest groups (who represent different groups of voters) think, and work out compromise decisions. When it does those things, however, many people feel let down and say that they have a low opinion of Congress.

Three powerful Speakers of the House: Thomas B. Reed (1889–1891, 1895–1899) (left), Joseph G. Cannon (1903–1911) (center), and Sam Rayburn (1941–1947, 1949–1953, 1955–1961) (right). Reed put an end to a filibuster in the House by refusing to allow dilatory motions and by counting as "present"—for purposes of a quorum—members in the House even though they were not voting. Cannon further enlarged the Speaker's power by refusing to recognize members who wished to speak without Cannon's approval and by increasing the power of the Rules Committee, over which he presided. Cannon was stripped of much of his power in 1910. Rayburn's influence rested more on his ability to persuade than on his formal powers.

Of course, a member of Congress might explain all these constitutional facts to the people, but not many members are eager to tell their voters that they do not really understand how Congress was created and organized. Instead they run for reelection by promising voters that they will go back to Washington and "clean up that mess."

☆ The Evolution of Congress

The Framers chose to place legislative powers in the hands of a congress rather than a parliament for philosophical and practical reasons. They did not want to have all powers concentrated in a single governmental institution, even one that was popularly elected, because they feared that such a concentration could lead to rule by an oppressive or impassioned majority. At the same time, they knew that the states were jealous of their independence and would never consent to a national constitution if it did not protect their interests and strike a reasonable

balance between large and small states. Hence they created a **bicameral** (two-chamber) **legislature**—with a House of Representatives, to be elected directly by the people, and a Senate, consisting of two members from each state, to be chosen by the legislatures of each state. Though "all legislative powers" were to be vested in Congress, those powers would be shared with the president (who could veto acts of Congress), limited to powers explicitly conferred on the federal government, and, as it turned out, subject to the power of the Supreme Court to declare acts of Congress unconstitutional.

For decades, critics of Congress have complained that the body cannot plan or act quickly. They are right, but two competing values are at stake: centralization versus decentralization. If Congress were to act quickly and decisively as a body, then there would

bicameral legislature   A lawmaking body made up of two chambers or parts.

House History: Six Phases

One of the most powerful Speakers of the House, Henry Clay, is shown here addressing the U.S. Senate around 1850.

Phase One: The Powerful House

During the first three administrations—of George Washington, John Adams, and Thomas Jefferson—leadership in Congress was often supplied by the president or his cabinet officers. Rather quickly, however, Congress began to assert its independence. The House of Representatives was the preeminent institution, overshadowing the Senate.

Phase Two: The Divided House

In the late 1820s the preeminence of the House began to wane. Andrew Jackson asserted the power of the presidency by vetoing legislation that he did not like. The party unity necessary for a Speaker, or any leader, to control the House was shattered by the issue of slavery. Of course, representatives from the South did not attend during the Civil War, and their seats remained vacant for several years after it ended. A group called the Radical Republicans, led by men such as Thaddeus Stevens of Pennsylvania, produced strong majorities for measures aimed at punishing the defeated South. But as time passed, the hot passions the war had generated began to cool, and it became clear that the leadership of the House remained weak.

Phase Three: The Speaker Rules

Toward the end of the nineteenth century the Speaker of the House gained power. When Thomas B. Reed of Maine became Speaker in 1889, he obtained by vote of the Republican majority more authority than any of his predecessors, including the right to select the chairmen and members of all committees. He chaired the Rules Committee and decided what business would come up for a vote,

have to be strong central leadership, restrictions on debate, few opportunities for stalling tactics, and minimal committee interference. If, on the other hand, the interests of individual members—and the constituencies that they represent—were to be protected or enhanced, then there would have to be weak leadership, rules allowing for delay and discussion, and many opportunities for committee activity.

Though there have been periods of strong central leadership in Congress, the general trend, especially since the mid-twentieth century, has been toward decentralizing decision-making and enhancing the power of the individual member at the expense of the congressional leadership. This decentralization may not have been inevitable. Most American states have constitutional systems quite similar to the federal one, yet in many state legislatures, such as those in New York, Massachusetts, and Indiana, the leadership is quite powerful. In part the position of these strong state legislative leaders may be the result of the greater strength of political parties in some states than in the nation as a whole. In large measure, however, it is a consequence of permitting state legislative leaders to decide who shall chair what committee and who shall receive what favors.

The House of Representatives, though always powerful, has often changed the way in which it is organized and led. In some periods it has given its leader, the Speaker, a lot of power; in other periods it has given much of that power to the chairmen of the House committees; and in still other periods it has allowed individual members to acquire great influence. To simplify a complicated story, the box above outlines six different periods in the history of the House.

what the limitations on debate would be, and who would be allowed to speak and who would not. In 1903, Joseph G. Cannon of Illinois became Speaker. He tried to maintain Reed's tradition, but he had many enemies within his Republican ranks.

Phase Four: The House Revolts

In 1910–1911 the House revolted against "Czar" Cannon, voting to strip the Speaker of his right to appoint committee chairmen and to remove him from the Rules Committee. The powers lost by the Speaker flowed to the party caucus, the Rules Committee, and the chairmen of the standing committees. It was not, however, until the 1960s and 1970s that House members struck out against all forms of leadership.

Phase Five: The Members Rule

Newly elected Democrats could not get the House to vote on a meaningful civil rights bill until 1965 because powerful committee chairmen, most of them from the South, kept such legislation bottled up. In response, Democrats changed their rules so that chairmen lost much of their authority. Beginning in the 1970s committee chairmen would no longer be selected simply on the basis of seniority: they had to be elected by the members of the majority party. Chairmen could no longer refuse to call committee meetings, and most meetings had to be public. Committees without subcommittees had to create them and allow their members to choose subcommittee chairmen. Individual members' staffs were greatly enlarged, and half of all majority-party members were chairmen of at least one committee or subcommittee.

Phase Six: The Leadership Returns

Since every member had power, it was harder for the House to get anything done. By slow steps, culminating in some sweeping changes made in 1995, there were efforts to restore some of the power the Speaker had once had. The number of committees and subcommittees was reduced. Republican Speaker Newt Gingrich dominated the choice of committee chairmen, often passing over more senior members for more agreeable junior ones. But Gingrich's demise was as quick as his rise. His decision not to pass some appropriations bills forced many government offices to close for a short period, he had to pay a fine for using tax-exempt funds for political purposes, and then the Republicans lost a number of seats in the 1998 election. Gingrich resigned as Speaker and as a member of the House and was replaced by a more moderate Speaker, Dennis Hastert of Illinois, with a penchant for accommodating his colleagues. As the 109th Congress began in 2005, Hastert was widely regarded as a powerful speaker.

The House faces fundamental problems: it wants to be both big (it has 435 members) and powerful, and its members want to be powerful both as individuals and as a group. But being big makes it hard for the House to be powerful unless some small group is given the authority to run it. If a group runs the place, however, the individual members lack much power. Individuals can gain power, but only at the price of making the House harder to run and thus reducing its collective power in government. There is no lasting solution to these dilemmas, and so the House will always be undergoing changes.

The Senate does not face any of these problems. It is small enough (100 members) that it can be run without giving much authority to any small group of leaders. In addition, it has escaped some of the problems the House once faced. During the period leading up to the Civil War it was carefully balanced so that the number of senators from slaveowning states exactly equaled the number from free states. Hence fights over slavery rarely arose in the Senate.

From the first the Senate was small enough that no time limits had to be placed on how long a senator could speak. This meant that there never was anything like a Rules Committee that controlled the amount of debate.

Finally, senators were not elected by the voters until this century. Prior to that they were picked instead by state legislatures. Thus senators were often the leaders of local party organizations, with an interest in funneling jobs and contracts back to their states.

The big changes in the Senate came not from any fight about how to run it (nobody ever really ran it), but from a dispute over how its members should be chosen. For more than a century after, the Founding

Filibuster

A filibuster is a technique by which a small number of senators attempt to defeat a measure by talking it to death—that is, by speaking continuously and at such length as to induce the supporters of the measure to drop it in order to get on with the Senate's business.

The right to filibuster is governed by the Senate's Rule 22, which allows for unlimited debate unless at least sixty senators agree to a motion to cut it off.

Originally *filibusterers* were sixteenth-century English and French pirates and buccaneers who raided Spanish treasure ships. The term came from a Dutch word, *vrijbuiter,* meaning "freebooter," which was converted into the English word *filibuster.*

The word came into use in America as a term for "continuous talking" in the mid-nineteenth century. One of its first appearances was in 1854, when a group of senators tried to talk to death the Kansas-Nebraska Act.

Source: From *Safire's Political Dictionary* by William Safire. Copyright © 1968, 1972, 1978 by William Safire. Reprinted by permission of Random House, Inc. and the author.

the end of the nineteenth century the Senate was known as the Millionaires' Club because of the number of wealthy party leaders and businessmen in it. There arose a demand for the direct, popular election of senators.

Naturally the Senate resisted, and without its approval the necessary constitutional amendment could not pass Congress. When some states threatened to demand a new constitutional convention, the Senate feared that such a convention would change more than just the way in which senators were chosen. A protracted struggle ensued, during which many state legislatures devised ways to ensure that the senators they picked would already have won a popular election. The Senate finally agreed to a constitutional amendment that required the popular election of its members, and in 1913 the Seventeenth Amendment was approved by the necessary three-fourths of the states. Ironically, given the intensity of the struggle over this question, no great change in the composition of the Senate resulted; most of those members who had first been chosen by state legislatures managed to win reelection by popular vote.

THE WAY WE BECOME SENATOR NOWADAYS.

A cartoon from Puck *in 1890 expressed popular resentment over the "Millionaires' Club," as the Senate had become known.*

members of the Senate were chosen by state legislatures. Though often these legislatures picked popular local figures to be senators, just as often there was intense political maneuvering among the leaders of various factions, each struggling to win (and sometimes buy) the votes necessary to become senator. By

Table 13.1	Blacks, Hispanics, and Women in Congress, 1971–2006					
	Senate			House		
Congress	Blacks	Hispanics	Women	Blacks	Hispanics	Women
109th (2005–2006)	1	0	14	37	23	59
108th	0	0	13	39	23	62
107th	0	0	13	36	19	59
106th	0	0	9	39	19	58
105th	1	1	9	37	18	51
104th	1	0	8	38	18	48
103rd	1	0	6	38	17	47
102nd	0	0	2	26	10	29
101st	0	0	2	24	11	25
100th	0	0	2	23	11	23
99th	0	0	2	20	11	22
98th	0	0	2	21	10	22
97th	0	0	2	17	6	19
96th	0	0	1	16	6	16
95th	1	0	2	16	5	18
94th	1	1	0	15	5	19
93rd	1	1	0	15	5	14
92nd (1971–1972)	1	1	2	12	5	13

Source: Congressional Quarterly Almanac, various years.

The other major issue in the development of the Senate was the filibuster. A **filibuster** is a prolonged speech, or series of speeches, made to delay action in a legislative assembly. It had become a common—and unpopular—feature of Senate life by the end of the nineteenth century. It was used by liberals and conservatives alike and for lofty as well as self-serving purposes. The first serious effort to restrict the filibuster came in 1917, after an important foreign policy measure submitted by President Wilson had been talked to death by, as Wilson put it, "eleven willful men." Rule 22 was adopted by a Senate fearful of tying a president's hands during a wartime crisis. The rule provided that debate could be cut off if two-thirds of the senators present and voting agreed to a "cloture" motion (it has since been revised to allow sixty senators to cut off debate). Two years later it was first invoked successfully when the Senate voted cloture to end, after fifty-five days, the debate over the Treaty of Versailles. Despite the existence of Rule 22, the tradition of unlimited debate remains strong in the Senate.

☆ Who Is in Congress?

With power so decentralized in Congress, the kind of person elected to it is especially important. Since each member exercises some influence, the beliefs and interests of each individual affect policy. Viewed simplistically, most members of Congress seem the same: the typical representative or senator is a middle-aged white Protestant male lawyer. If all such persons usually thought and voted alike, that would be an interesting fact, but they do not, and so it is necessary to explore the great diversity of views among seemingly similar people.

Sex and Race

Congress has gradually become less male and less white. Between 1950 and 2005 the number of women in the House increased from nine to fifty-nine and the number of African Americans from two to thirty-seven. There are also twenty-three Hispanic members.

Until recently the Senate changed much more slowly (see Table 13.1). Before the 1992 election there were no African Americans and only two women in the Senate. But in 1992 four more women, including one black woman, Carol Mosely Braun of

filibuster   An attempt to defeat a bill in the Senate by talking indefinitely, thus preventing the Senate from taking action to the bill.

Illinois, were elected. Two more were elected in 1994, when a Native American, Ben Nighthorse Campbell of Colorado, also became a senator. By 2004, there was one African American and fourteen women in the Senate.

The relatively small number of African Americans and Hispanics in the House understates their influence, at least when the Democrats are in the majority. In 1994 four House committees were chaired by blacks and three by Hispanics. In the same year, however, no woman chaired a committee. The reason for this difference in power is that the former tend to come from safe districts (see page 327) and thus to have more seniority than the latter. Since 1995, Republican control of the House has reduced minority influence.

Incumbency

The most important change that has occurred in the composition of Congress has been so gradual that

most people have not noticed it. In the nineteenth century a large fraction—often a majority—of congressmen served only one term. In 1869, for example, more than half the members of the House were serving their first term in Congress. Being a congressman in those days was not regarded as a career. This was in part because the federal government was not very important (most of the interesting political decisions were made by the states); in part because travel to Washington, D.C., was difficult and the city was not a pleasant place in which to live; and in part because being a congressman did not pay well. Furthermore, many congressional districts were highly competitive, with the two political parties fairly evenly balanced in each.

By the 1950s, however, serving in Congress had become a career. Between 1863 and 1969 the proportion of first-termers in the House fell from 58 percent to 8 percent (see Figure 13.1).[2] As the public

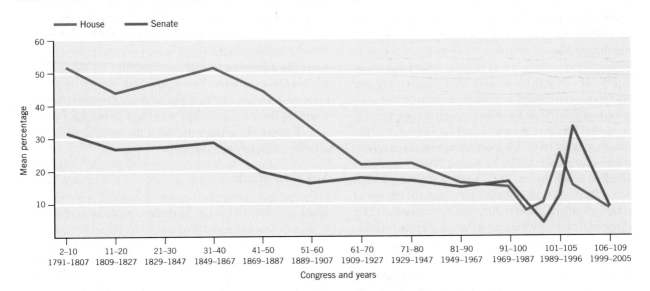

Figure 13.1   Changing Percentage of First-Term Members in Congress

Notes: The 1989 freshman class in the House was the smallest in history. The 1993 freshman class in the House was the largest since 1949.

Sources: Data for 90th through 103rd congresses are from *Congressional Quarterly Weekly Reports.* Data for 69th through 89th congresses are adapted from Nelson W. Polsby, "The Institutionalization of the U.S. House of Representatives," *American Political Science Review* (March 1968): 146. Data for 1st through 68th congresses are from Stuart A. Rice, *Quantitative Methods in Politics* (New York: Knopf, 1928), 296–297, as reported in Polsby, 146. Data for Senate are from N. J. Ornstein, T. J. Mann, and M. J. Malbin, *Vital Statistics on Congress, 1989–1990* (Washington, D.C.: Congressional Quarterly Press, 1990), 56–57, 59–60; and Stanley Harold and Richard Niemi, *Vital Statistics on American Politics* (Washington, D.C.: Congressional Quarterly Press, 2001).

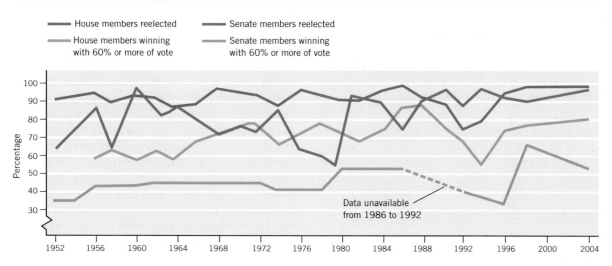

Figure 13.2   Percentage of Incumbents Reelected to Congress

House members reelected
House members winning with 60% or more of vote
Senate members reelected
Senate members winning with 60% or more of vote

Data unavailable from 1986 to 1992

Source: Harold W. Stanley and Richard G. Niemi, *Vital Statistics on American Politics, 1999–2000* (Washington, D.C.: Congressional Quarterly Press, 2000), table 1-18; 2004 update by Marc Siegal.

took note of this shift, people began to complain about "professional politicians" being "out of touch with the people." A movement to impose term limits was started. In 1995 the House approved a constitutional amendment to do just that, but it died in the Senate. Then the Supreme Court struck down an effort by a state to impose term limits on its own members of Congress.

As it turned out, natural political forces were already doing what the term limits amendment was supposed to do. The 1992 and 1994 elections brought scores of new members to the House, with the result that by 1995 the proportion of members who were serving their first or second terms had risen sharply. Three things were responsible for this change. First, when congressional district lines were redrawn after the 1990 census, a lot of incumbents found themselves running in new districts that they couldn't carry. Second, voter disgust at a variety of Washington political scandals made them receptive to appeals from candidates who could describe themselves as "outsiders." And third, the Republican victory in 1994—made possible in part by the conversion of the South from a Democratic bastion to a Republican stronghold—brought a lot of new faces to the Capitol.

This influx of freshman members should not obscure the fact that incumbents still enjoy enormous

advantages in congressional elections.[3] Even in 1994, when thirty-five incumbent Democrats lost to Republicans, over 90 percent of all House members who ran for reelection were reelected. In the Senate 92 percent of incumbents who ran again were reelected. In 2004, one of the most hotly contested elections in recent history, only ten of the four hundred House incumbents who ran for reelection lost.

The arrival of scores of new faces in the 1990s should not obscure the fact that most House members still win big in their districts. Political scientists call districts that have close elections (when the winner gets less than 55 percent of the vote) **marginal districts** and districts where incumbents win by wide margins (55 percent or more) **safe districts.** The proportion of House incumbents who have won reelection with at least 60 percent of the vote increased from about three-fifths in the 1950s and early 1960s to three-quarters in the 1970s and almost nine-tenths in the late 1980s (see Figure 13.2). Even as this trend began

marginal districts   Political districts in which candidates elected to the House of Representatives win in close elections, typically by less than 55 percent of the vote.

safe districts   Districts in which incumbents win by margins of 55 percent or more.

Table 13.2	Incumbents in Congress Reelected by 60 Percent or More

House, 1956–2004

Year	Number of Incumbents Running in General Election	Percentage of Incumbents Reelected with at Least 60 Percent of the Vote
1956	403	59.1%
1958	390	63.1
1960	400	58.9
1962	376	63.6
1964	388	58.5
1966	401	67.7
1968	397	72.2
1970	389	77.3
1972	373	77.8
1974	383	66.4
1976	381	71.9
1978	377	78.0
1980	392	72.9
1982	383	68.9
1984	406	74.6
1986	391	86.4
1988	407	88.5
1990	406	76.4
1992	349	65.6
1994	383	64.5
1996	383	73.6
1998	400	77.2
2000	403	81.1
2002	394	83.5
2004	405	82.2

Senate, 1944–2004

Election Period	Number of Incumbents Running in General Election	Percentage of Incumbents Reelected with at Least 60 Percent of the Vote
1944–1948	61	39.3%
1950–1954	76	35.5
1956–1960	84	42.9
1962–1966	86	44.2
1968–1972	74	44.6
1974–1978	70	41.4
1980–1984	84	54.1
1986–1990	87	57.5
1992–1994	53	43.4
1996–1998	49	57.1
1998–2000	29	65.5
2000–2002	29	69.0
2002–2004	27	55.6

Source: Harold W. Stanley and Richard G. Niemi, *Vital Statistics on American Politics, 2001–2002* (Washington, D.C.: Congressional Quarterly Press, 2001), table 1-18; 2002–2004 update by Marc Siegal.

to change in 1990, most House districts remained safe. Senators remained less secure: the rule, to which the period 1980–1990 and the year 1998 are the exceptions, is that fewer than half of Senate incumbents win with as much as 60 percent of the vote (see Table 13.2).

Why congressional seats have become less marginal—that is, safer—is a matter on which scholars do not agree. Some feel that it is the result of television and other media. But challengers can go on television, too, so why should this benefit incumbents? Another possibility is that voters are becoming less and less likely to automatically support whatever candidate wins the nomination of their own party. They are more likely, in short, to vote for the person rather than the party. And they are more likely to have heard of a person who is an incumbent: incumbents can deluge the voter with free mailings, they can travel frequently (and at public expense) to meet constituents, and they can get their names in the newspaper by sponsoring bills or conducting investigations. Simply having a familiar name is important in getting elected, and incumbents find it easier than challengers to make their names known.

Finally, some scholars argue that incumbents can use their power to get programs passed or funds spent to benefit their districts—and thereby to benefit themselves. They can help keep an army base open, support the building of a new highway (or block the building of an unpopular one), take credit for federal grants to local schools and hospitals, make certain that a particular industry or labor union is protected by tariffs against foreign competition, and so on.[4]

Probably all of these factors make some difference. Whatever the explanation, the tendency of voters to return incumbents to office means that in ordinary times no one should expect any dramatic changes in the composition of Congress.

Party

From 1933 to 2004 thirty-six Congresses convened (a new Congress convenes every two years). The Democrats controlled both houses in twenty-five of these Congresses and at least one house in twenty-nine of them. Scholars differ in their explanations of why the Democrats have so thoroughly dominated Congress. Most of the research on the subject has focused on the reasons for Democratic control of the House.

As Table 13.3 shows, in every election from 1968 to 1992 the percentage of the popular vote for Republican candidates to the House was higher than the percentage of House seats that actually went to

Table 13.3	Republican Vote-Seat Gap, 1968–2002	
Year	Percentage of Popular Vote for Republican House Candidates	Percentage of House Seats Held by Republicans
1968	48.2%	44.1%
1970	44.5	41.4
1972	46.4	44.2
1974	40.5	33.1
1976	42.1	32.9
1978	44.7	36.3
1980	48.0	44.1
1982	43.3	38.2
1984	47.0	41.8
1986	44.6	40.7
1988	45.5	40.2
1990	45.0	38.4
1992	45.6	40.5
1994	52.4	52.9
1996	48.9	52.2
1998	48.7	51.3
2000	48.7	50.8
2002	53.4	52.4

Source: Harold W. Stanley and Richard G. Niemi, *Vital Statistics on American Politics, 2001–2002* (Washington, D.C.: Congressional Quarterly Press, 2001), table 1–12.

Republicans. For example, in 1976 the Republicans won 42.1 percent of the vote but received only 32.9 percent of the seats. Some have argued that this gap between votes and seats has occurred because Democratic-controlled state legislatures have redrawn congressional district maps in ways that make it hard for Republicans to win House seats. There is some striking anecdotal evidence to support this conclusion. For example, following the 1990 census, the Democratic-controlled Texas legislature crafted a new congressional district map clearly designed to benefit Democrats. In 1992 Republicans won 48 percent of the House vote in Texas but received only 30 percent of the seats. Similarly, in 1984 Democrats in California won nine more congressional seats than did Republicans, even though the latter received about one hundred thousand more votes statewide. After 1990 California's congressional map was redrawn by a state court, and in 1992 Republican House candidates won 41 percent of the statewide vote and 42 percent of the seats.[5] Only in 1994, with the historic election of the first Republican majorities in Congress in four decades, did the gap close and begin to work slightly in Republicans' favor.

Partisan tinkering with district maps and other structural features of House elections is not a sufficient explanation of why Democrats dominated the House until 1994. As one study concluded, "Virtually all the political science evidence to date indicates that the electoral system has little or no partisan bias, and that the net gains nationally from redistricting for one party over another are very small."[6] To control the redistricting process, one party must control both houses of the legislature, the governor's office, and, where necessary, the state courts. These conditions simply do not exist in most states. And even if district lines were consistently drawn with scrupulous fairness, the Democrats would still win control of the House, because they win more votes. The pre-1994 Republican vote-seat gap is accounted for in part by the fact that the Democrats tend to do exceptionally well in low-turnout districts such as minority-dominated inner cities, while the Republicans tend to do well in high-turnout districts such as affluent white suburbs.

In 1994, however, the year the gap closed, Republican candidates for the House ran especially strong in the roughly half of all districts that have predominantly suburban constituencies. Thus even though only 19 percent of eligible voters cast a vote for a Republican, it was enough to best the Democrats, who won the votes of only 16.6 percent of all eligible voters.

Congressional incumbents have come to enjoy certain built-in electoral advantages over challengers. Democrats were in the majority as the advantages of incumbency grew, but Republicans have enjoyed the same or greater advantages since 1994. Studies suggest that the incumbency advantage was worth about two percentage points prior to the 1960s but has grown to six to eight points today.

By 2004, the Republican share of House seats had risen from 176 in 1992 to 232, a 31 percent increase. The closing of the GOP vote-seat gap in the House was accompanied by a rise in the number of Republican senators (55 in 2005, the most senate seats held by Republicans since 1949, and including five new Republican senators in the South), state legislators (from 3,031 in 1992 to 3,650 in 2005), and governorships (from 18 in 1992 to 28 in 2005). This has led some leading academic experts, including Walter Dean Burnham, to speculate that the sudden shift to Republican control of the House that occurred in 1994 has now been succeeded by "a stable pattern of Republican rule" at the federal level and in most states.[7]

While scholars debate whether, in fact, the historic 1994 House elections had by 2004 ushered in a Republican-dominated critical or realigning period (see Chapter 9) in American politics, it is important to remember that from time to time major electoral convulsions do alter the membership of Congress. For example, in the election of 1938 the Democrats lost seventy seats in the House; in 1942 they lost fifty; in 1950 they lost twenty-nine; and in 1966 they lost forty-eight. Despite these big losses, the Democrats retained a majority in the House in each of these years. Not so, however, in 1994, when the Democrats lost fifty-two House seats (the largest loss by either party since the Republicans lost seventy-five seats in 1948), and Republicans gained majorities in both the House and the Senate.

Just as it is not easy to explain why Democrats dominated Congress for half a century, so it is not easy to explain why that domination ended when and as it did. Several reasons, however, stand out. By the 1990s the advantages of incumbency had turned into disadvantages: voters increasingly came to dislike "professional politicians," whom they held responsible for "the mess in Washington." Just what "the mess" was varied according to which voter you asked, but it included chronic budget deficits, the congressional habit of exempting itself from laws that affected everybody else, constant bickering between Congress and the White House, and various congressional scandals. During the 1980s about forty members of Congress were charged with misconduct ranging from having sex with minors to accepting illegal gifts. When it was disclosed that the House had its own bank that would cash checks even for members who (temporarily) had no funds in their accounts, public indignation exploded, even though almost no taxpayer money was lost. Public respect for Congress, as measured by the polls, plummeted.

The Democrats had the misfortune of being the majority party in Congress when all of this happened. The anti-incumbent mood, coupled with the effects of redistricting after the 1990 census and the shift of the South to the Republican party, brought the Republicans into power in the House and Senate in the 1994 elections.

In the past the Democratic party was more deeply divided than the Republicans, because of the presence in Congress of conservative Democrats from the South. Often these southern Democrats would vote with the Republicans in the House or Senate, thereby forming what came to be called the **conservative coalition.** During the 1960s and 1970s that coalition came together in about one-fifth of all roll-call votes. When it did, it usually won, defeating northern Democrats. But since the 1980s, and especially since the watershed election of 1994, the conservative coalition has become much less important. The reason is simple: many southern Democrats in Congress have been replaced by southern Republicans, and the southern Democrats who remain (many of them African Americans) are as liberal as northern Democrats. The effect of this change is to make Congress, and especially the House, more ideologically partisan—Democrats are liberals, Republicans are conservatives—and this in turn helps explain why there is more party unity in voting.

☆ Do Members Represent Their Voters?

In a decentralized, individualistic institution such as Congress, it is not obvious how its members will behave. They could be devoted to doing whatever their constituents want or, since most voters are not aware of what their representatives do, act in accordance with their own beliefs, the demands of pressure groups, or the expectations of congressional leaders. You may think it would be easy to figure out whether members are devoted to their constituents by analyzing how they vote, but that is not quite right. Members can influence legislation in many ways other than by voting: they can conduct hearings, help mark up bills in committee meetings, and offer amendments to the bills proposed by others. A member's final vote on a bill may conceal as much as it reveals: some members may vote for a bill that contains many things they dislike because it also contains a few things they value.

There are at least three theories about how members of Congress behave: representational, organizational, and attitudinal.

conservative coalition   An alliance between Republican and conservative Democrats.

The *representational* explanation is based on the reasonable assumption that members want to get reelected, and therefore they vote to please their constituents. The *organizational* explanation is based on the equally reasonable assumption that since most constituents do not know how their legislator has voted, it is not essential to please them. But it is important to please fellow members of Congress, whose goodwill is valuable in getting things done and in acquiring status and power in Congress. The *attitudinal* explanation is based on the assumption that there are so many conflicting pressures on members of Congress that they cancel one another out, leaving them virtually free to vote on the basis of their own beliefs.

Political scientists have studied, tested, and argued about these (and other) explanations for decades, and nothing like a consensus has emerged. Some facts have been established, however.

Representational View

The representational view has some merit under certain circumstances—namely, when constituents have a clear view on some issue and a legislator's vote on that issue is likely to attract their attention. Such is often the case for civil rights laws: representatives with significant numbers of black voters in their districts are not likely to oppose civil rights bills; representatives with few African Americans in their districts are comparatively free to oppose such bills. (Until the late 1960s many southern representatives were able to oppose civil rights measures because the African Americans in their districts were prevented from voting. On the other hand, many representatives without black constituents have supported civil rights bills, partly out of personal belief and partly, perhaps, because certain white groups in their districts—organized liberals, for example—have insisted on such support.)

One study of congressional roll-call votes and constituency opinion showed that the correlation between the two was quite strong on civil rights bills. There was also a positive (though not as strong) correlation between roll-call votes and constituency opinion on social welfare measures. Scarcely any correlation, however, was found between congressional votes and hometown opinion on foreign policy measures.[8] Foreign policy is generally remote from the daily interests of most Americans, and public opinion about such matters can change rapidly. It is

Political issues may be national, but campaigning for office is intensely local, as when Dennis Hastert (middle) talks to factory employees in his Illinois district.

not surprising, therefore, that congressional votes and constituent opinion should be different on such questions.

From time to time an issue arouses deep passions among the voters, and legislators cannot escape the need either to vote as their constituents want, whatever their personal views, or to anguish at length about which side of a divided constituency to support. Gun control has been one such question, the use of federal money to pay for abortions has been another, and the effort to impeach President Clinton was a third. Some fortunate members of Congress get unambiguous cues from their constituents on these matters, and no hard decision is necessary. Others get conflicting views, and they know that whichever way they vote, it may cost them dearly in the next election. Occasionally members of Congress in this fix will try to be out of town when the matter comes up for a vote. One careful study found that constituency influences were an important factor in Senate votes,[9] but no comparable study has been done for the House.

You might think that members of Congress who won a close race in the last election—who come from a "marginal" district—would be especially eager to vote the way that their constituents want. Research so far has shown that is not generally the case. There seem to be about as many independent-minded members of Congress from marginal as from safe districts.

Perhaps it is because opinion is so divided in a marginal seat that one cannot please everybody; as a result the representative votes on other grounds.

In general, the problem with the representational explanation is that public opinion is not strong and clear on most measures on which Congress must vote. Many representatives and senators face constituencies that are divided on key issues. Some constituents go to special pains to make their views known (these interest groups were discussed in Chapter 11). But as we indicated, the power of interest groups to affect congressional votes depends, among other things, on whether a legislator sees them as united and powerful or as disorganized and marginal.

This does not mean that constituents rarely have a direct influence on voting. The influence that they have probably comes from the fact that legislators risk defeat should they steadfastly vote in ways that can be held against them by a rival in the next election. Though most congressional votes are not known to most citizens, blunders (real or alleged) quickly become known when an electoral opponent exploits them.

Still, any member of Congress can choose the positions that he or she takes on most roll-call votes (and on all voice or standing votes, where names are not recorded). And even a series of recorded votes that are against constituency opinion need not be fatal: a member of Congress can win votes in other ways—for example, by doing services for constituents or by appealing to the party loyalty of the voters.

Organizational View

When voting on matters where constituency interests or opinions are not vitally at stake, members of Congress respond primarily to cues provided by their colleagues. This is the organizational explanation of their votes. The principal cue is party; as already noted, what party a member of Congress belongs to explains more about his or her voting record than any other single factor. Additional organizational cues come from the opinions of colleagues with whom the member of Congress feels a close ideological affinity: for liberals in the House it is the Democratic Study Group; for conservatives it has often been the Republican Study Committee or the Wednesday Club. But party and other organizations do not have clear positions on all matters. For the scores of votes that do not involve the "big questions," a representative or senator is especially likely to be influenced by

the members of his or her party on the sponsoring committee.

It is easy to understand why. Suppose you are a Democratic representative from Michigan who is summoned to the floor of the House to vote on a bill to authorize a new weapons system. You haven't the faintest idea what issues might be at stake. There is no obvious liberal or conservative position on this matter. How do you vote? Simple. You take your cue from several Democrats on the House Armed Services Committee that handled the bill. Some are liberal; others are conservative. If both liberals and conservatives support the bill, you vote for it unhesitatingly. If they disagree, you vote with whichever Democrat is generally closest to your own political ideology. If the matter is one that affects your state, you can take your cue from members of your state's delegation to Congress.

Attitudinal View

Finally, there is evidence that the ideology of a member of Congress affects how he or she votes. We have seen that Democratic and Republican legislators differ sharply on a liberal-versus-conservative scale. On both domestic and foreign policy issues many tend to be consistently liberal or conservative.[10]

This consistency isn't surprising. As we saw in Chapter 7, political elites think more ideologically than the public generally.

On many issues the average member of the House has opinions close to those of the average voter. Senators, by contrast, are often less in tune with public opinion. In the 1970s they were much more liberal than voters; in the early 1980s more conservative. Two senators from the same state often mobilize quite different bases of support. The result is that many states, such as California, Delaware, and New York, have been represented by senators with almost diametrically opposed views.

Of late, the Senate has gone through three phases. In the first, during the 1950s and early 1960s, it was a cautious, conservative institution dominated by southern senators and displaying many of the features of a "club" that welcomed members into its inner circle only after they had displayed loyalty to its gentlemanly (and, in effect, conservative) customs. This was the era when the Senate was the graveyard of civil rights bills.

The second period began in the mid-1960s as liberal senators rose steadily in number, seniority, and influence, helped along by the Johnson reforms, which made it easier for junior senators to gain chairmanships. The decentralization of the Senate gave more power to individual senators, including liberals. In 1972 there were about twenty-four liberal senators, but among them they held forty subcommittee chairmanships.[11]

The third period began in the late 1970s and became most visible after the 1980 elections, when many liberals lost their seats to conservative Republicans. The conservatism of the present Senate is based more on ideology than on the rules of the southern "club" that characterized it in the 1950s.

The Democratic party is more deeply divided than the Republican. There are only a few liberal Republicans, but there have been many more conservative Democrats from the South and West. Southern Democrats often teamed up with Republicans to form a conservative coalition. In a typical year a majority of Republicans and southern Democrats would vote together against a majority of northern Democrats about 20 to 25 percent of the time. When the conservative coalition did form, it usually won: between 1970 and 1982 it won about two-thirds of the votes on which it held together. After the Reagan victory and the Republican gain of thirty seats in the House in 1981, the conservative coalition became even more effective, dominating key votes on the Reagan budget and tax plans.

But the conservative coalition was important only when there were a lot of conservative southern Democrats. Many of these have now been replaced with southern Republicans. As a result almost all of the conservatives are now in the Republican party, so there is not much of a coalition left to form. In 1998 this coalition—that is, a majority of Republicans and southern Democrats voting against a majority of northern Democrats—existed in only 6 percent of all congressional votes. In the 1970s, by contrast, it appeared in about one-quarter of all votes.

☆ Ideology and Civility in Congress

Congress has become an increasingly ideological organization. By that we mean its members are more sharply divided by political ideology than they once were and certainly more divided than are American voters. In short, the attitudinal explanation of how members vote has increased in importance, while the organizational explanation has declined. All of Congress's most liberal members are Democrats, and all of its most conservative ones are Republicans. That is not what you would find among ordinary voters. A lot of us split our tickets, voting for one party's presidential nominee and a different party's congressional candidate.

This higher level of congressional ideology does not mean that its existing members have changed how they think. Rather it means that new kinds of members have been elected, bringing to Congress a more ideological perspective.[12] In 1974 (the election right after Watergate) a large number of more ideological Democrats entered Congress. In 1994 there was a large influx of more ideological Republicans.

Congress has become more polarized than voters in terms of political beliefs. Among voters the average Democrat and the average Republican, though they surely disagree, nonetheless have views that put them close to the center of the political spectrum. But among members of Congress the average Democrat is very liberal and the average Republican very conservative, a fact that keeps them far from the political center. There are, of course, some conservative Democrats and some liberal Republicans, but their numbers have been getting smaller and smaller.

One result of this polarization is that members of Congress, especially those in the House, do not get along as well as they once did with members who disagree with them, and they are more likely to challenge, investigate, and denounce one another. Two Speakers of the House, Jim Wright and Newt Gingrich, were investigated and resigned. Many presidential nominees have been subjected to withering investigations, some based on ideological differences and some on charges of ethical violations, many of which were dubious. President Clinton was impeached on a nearly party-line vote. Members regularly accuse one another of misconduct. When they run for reelection, they often use negative ads of the sort discussed in Chapter 10. The mass media feed on and aggravate this tendency because of their interest in scandal.

The result is that the public—already puzzled by the constitutional need members have to discuss policy matters for long periods, listen to interest groups, and reach compromise settlements—are now put off even more by the political disposition members have

★ POLITICALLY SPEAKING ★

Whip

A whip is a party leader who makes certain that party members are present for a vote and vote the way the party wishes. In the British House of Commons the whips produce strong party votes; in the U.S. Congress whips are a lot less successful.

The word comes from *whipper-in,* a term from fox hunting denoting the person whose job it is to keep the hounds from straying off the trail. It became a political term in England in the eighteenth century, and from there came to the United States.

Source: From *Safire's Political Dictionary* by William Safire. Copyright © 1968, 1972, 1978 by William Safire. Reprinted by permission of Random House, Inc. and the author.

to attack one another. At one time the constitutional need to negotiate was facilitated by reasonably good relationships between Democrats and Republicans, most of whom treated one another with politeness and socialized together after hours. This congenial social relationship no longer exists in most cases, and the public has noticed.

> **majority leader**   The legislative leader elected by party members holding the majority of seats in the House or the Senate.
>
> **minority leader**   The legislative leader elected by party members holding a minority of seats in the House or the Senate.

☆ The Organization of Congress: Parties and Caucuses

Congress is not a single organization; it is a vast and complex collection of organizations by which the business of the legislative branch is carried on and through which its members form alliances. If we were to look inside the British House of Commons, we would find only one kind of organization of any importance—the political party. Though party organization is important in the U.S. Congress, it is only one of many important elements. In fact other organizations have grown in number as the influence of the parties has declined.

The Democrats and Republicans in the House and the Senate are organized by party leaders. The key leaders in turn are elected by the full party membership within the House and Senate. The description that follows is confined to the essential positions.

Party Organization of the Senate

The majority party chooses one of its members—usually the person with the greatest seniority—to be president pro tempore of the Senate. It is largely an honorific position, required by the Constitution so that the Senate will have a presiding officer in the absence of the vice president of the United States (who is also, according to the Constitution, the president of the Senate). In fact, presiding over the Senate is a tedious chore that neither the vice president nor the president pro tem relishes, and so the actual task of presiding is usually assigned to some junior senator.

The real leadership is in the hands of the **majority leader** (chosen by the senators of the majority party) and the **minority leader** (chosen by the senators of the other party). In addition, the senators of each party elect a whip. The principal task of the majority leader is to schedule the business of the Senate, usually in consultation with the minority leader. The majority leader has the right to be recognized first in any floor debate. A majority leader with a strong personality who is skilled at political bargaining may do much more. Lyndon Johnson, who was Senate majority leader for the Democrats during much of the 1950s, used his prodigious ability to serve the needs of fellow senators. He helped them with everything from obtaining extra office space to getting choice committee assignments, and in this way he acquired substantial influence over the substance as well as the schedule of Senate business. Johnson's successor, Mike Mansfield, was a less assertive majority leader and had less influence.

The **whip** is a senator who helps the party leader stay informed about what party members are thinking, rounds up members when important votes are to be taken, and attempts to keep a nose count on how the voting on a controversial issue is likely to go. The whip has several senators who assist him or her in this task.

Each party in the Senate also chooses a Policy Committee composed of a dozen or so senators who help the party leader schedule Senate business, choosing what bills are to be given major attention and in what order.

From the point of view of individual senators, however, the key party organization is the group that assigns senators to the standing committees of the Senate. The Democrats have a Steering Committee that does this; the Republicans have a Committee on Committees. These assignments are especially important for newly elected senators: their political careers, their opportunities for favorable publicity, and their chances for helping their states and their supporters depend in great part on the committees to which they are assigned.

Party control of the Senate has changed frequently. When George W. Bush took office in 2001, the Republicans briefly retained control by having 50 seats plus a tie-breaking vote cast by Vice President Cheney. But then Senator James Jeffords, a Republican, became an independent and voted to let the Democrats control it, 51 to 49. But that ended when the Republicans won enough seats in the 2002 election to regain control. Having a tiny majority in the Senate does not affect most important votes since the other side can filibuster, but having your own party control the chairmanships is very important because it helps determine what issues will get to the floor for a vote.

The key—and delicate—aspect of selecting party leaders, of making up the important party committees, and of assigning freshman senators to Senate committees is achieving ideological and regional balance. Liberals and conservatives in each party will fight over the choice of majority and minority leader, but factors in addition to ideology play a part in the choice. These include personal popularity, the ability of the leader to make an effective television appearance, and who owes whom what favors.

Minority leader Nancy Pelosi, the first woman to hold a party leadership role in Congress.

Party Structure in the House

Though the titles of various posts are different, the party structure is essentially the same in the House as in the Senate. Leadership carries more power in the House than in the Senate because of the House rules. Being so large (435 members), the House must restrict debate and schedule its business with great care; thus leaders who do the scheduling and who determine how the rules shall be applied usually have substantial influence.

The Speaker is the most important person in the House. He is elected by whichever party has a majority, and he presides over all House meetings. Unlike

---

whip A senator or representative who helps the party leader stay informed about what party members are thinking.

★ HOW THINGS WORK ★

Party Leadership Structure in 2005

SENATE
President Pro Tempore   Selected by majority party

Democrats

Minority Leader   Leads the party
Minority Whip   Assists the leader, rounds up votes, heads group of deputy whips
Chairman of the Conference   Presides over meetings of all Senate Democrats
Policy Committee   Schedules legislation
Steering Committee   Assigns Democratic senators to committees
Democratic Senatorial Campaign Committee   Provides funds, assistance to Democratic candidates for the Senate

Republicans

Majority Leader   Leads the party
Assistant Majority Leader   Assists the leader, rounds up votes
Chairman of the Conference   Presides over meetings of all Senate Republicans
Policy Committee   Makes recommendations on party policy
Committee on Committees   Assigns Republican senators to committees
Republican Senatorial Committee   Provides funds, advice to Republican candidates for the Senate

HOUSE
Speaker of the House   Selected by majority party

Democrats

Minority Leader   Leads the party
Minority Whip   Assists the leader, rounds up votes, heads group of deputy and assistant whips
Chairman of the Caucus   Presides over meetings of all House Democrats
Steering and Policy Committee   Schedules legislation, assigns Democratic representatives to committees
Democratic Congressional Campaign Committee   Provides funds, advice to Democratic candidates for the House

Republicans

Majority Leader   Leads the party
Majority Whip   Assists the leader, rounds up votes, heads large group of deputy and assistant whips
Chairman of the Conference   Presides over meetings of all House Republicans
Committee on Committees   Assigns Republican representatives to committees
Policy Committee   Advises on party policy
National Republican Congressional Committee   Provides funds, advice to Republican candidates for the House
Research Committee   On request, provides information about issues

the president pro tem of the Senate, however, his position is anything but honorific. He is the principal leader of the majority party as well as the presiding officer of the entire House. Though Speakers-as-presiders are expected to be fair, Speakers-as-party-leaders are expected to use their powers to help pass legislation favored by their party.

In helping his party, the Speaker has some important formal powers at his disposal: he decides who shall be recognized to speak on the floor of the House; he rules whether a motion is relevant and germane to the business at hand; and he decides (subject to certain rules) the committees to which new bills shall be assigned. He influences what bills are brought up for a vote and appoints the members of special and select committees (to be explained on pages 341–345). Since 1975 the Speaker has been able to nominate the majority-party members of the Rules Committee. He also has some informal powers: he controls some patronage jobs in the Capitol building and the assignment of extra office space. Even though he is far less powerful than in the days of Clay, Reed, and Cannon, the Speaker is still an important person to have on one's side. Sam Rayburn of

Figure 13.3   The U.S. Congress

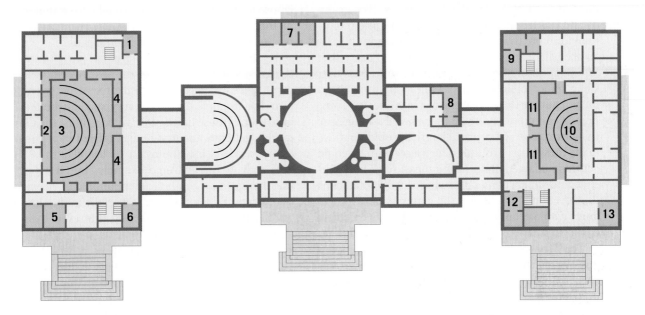

HOUSE OF REPRESENTATIVES
1. House Minority Whip
2. Lobby
3. House chamber
4. Cloakrooms
5. Speaker of the House
6. Ways and Means Committee
7. House Minority Leader

SENATE
8. Senate Minority Leader
9. Office of the Secretary
10. Senate chamber
11. Cloakrooms
12. Senate Majority Leader
13. Vice President

The House and Senate meet at opposite ends of the Capitol building. When there is a joint session of Congress—for example, to hear the president's State of the Union address—the senators sit with the representatives in the House chamber. Though the most important work of Congress goes on in committee meetings, which are held in office buildings behind the Capitol, some important political negotiations occur in the offices surrounding the chambers—especially in the cloakrooms (actually, lounges) and the offices of the majority and minority leaders, the Speaker and the vice president, and the secretary of the Senate.

Texas exercised great influence as Speaker, and Tip O'Neill, Jim Wright, Tom Foley, and Newt Gingrich tried to do the same.

In the House, as in the Senate, the majority party elects a floor leader, called the majority leader. The other party also chooses a leader—the minority leader. Traditionally the majority leader becomes Speaker when the person in that position dies or retires—provided, of course, that the departing Speaker's party is still in the majority. Each party also has a whip, with several assistant whips in charge of rounding up votes from various state delegations. Committee assignments are made and the scheduling of legislation is discussed, by the Democrats, in a

Steering and Policy Committee, chaired by the Speaker. The Republicans have divided committee assignments and policy discussions, with the former task assigned to a Committee on Committees and the latter to a Policy Committee. Each party also has a congressional campaign committee to provide funds and other assistance to party members running for election or reelection to the House.

The Strength of Party Structures

One important measure of the strength of the parties in Congress is the ability of party leaders to get their members to vote together on the rules and structure of Congress. When Newt Gingrich became Speaker of the Republican-controlled House in 1995, he proposed sweeping changes in House rules, many not popular with some Republican members. For example, he wanted no one to serve as a committee chairman for more than six years, for three committees to be abolished, and for other committees to lose either functions or members. He also wanted to pass over some senior members in picking committee chairmen. Though these moves adversely affected some Republican representatives, they all voted in favor of the new rules.[13] Of course, Gingrich would not have made these proposals unless he was certain he could get them adopted. But it was a measure of his influence and support among newly elected Republicans that even major changes in congressional procedures would get unanimous party support.[14] Getting support on proposed legislation is a harder task.

The Senate is another matter. As Barbara Sinclair has argued, in the last few decades the Senate has been transformed by changes in norms (informal understandings governing how members ought to behave toward their colleagues), without any far-reaching changes in the written Senate rules.[15] Compared to the Senate of the 1950s and 1960s, today's Senate is less party-centered, less leader-oriented, more hospitable to freshmen (who no longer have to "pay their dues" before assuming major roles as legislators), more heavily staffed, and more subcommittee-oriented.

Party Unity

The strength of Congress's elaborate party machinery can also be measured by the extent to which members of a party vote together in the House and Senate. **Party polarization** is defined as a vote in which a majority of voting Democrats oppose a majority of voting Republicans. In seven of the thirteen years from 1953 to 1965, at least half of all House votes pitted a majority of voting Democrats against a majority of voting Republicans (see Table 13.4). But in 1966 the number dropped to 41 percent, and it was not until 1983 that voting in the House once again took on a distinctively partisan cast. By the 1990s party unity voting was the norm in both the House and the Senate. A kindred measure of party strength is the cohesion of the parties on

---

party polarization   A vote in which a majority of Democratic legislators oppose a majority of Republican legislators.

---

votes that elicit a party split. By this measure, between 1991 and 1994 over 80 percent of all House and Senate Democrats voted with a majority of their party on party unity votes, as did over 80 percent of House and Senate Republicans.

As these recent trends make plain, party unity in Congress is hardly a thing of the past. Specific issues can trigger an extraordinary degree of party cohesion. For example, in 1993 every single Republican in both the House and Senate voted against the Clinton budget plan, the first budget offered by a Democratic president since Jimmy Carter left office in 1980. This may be an extreme example, but it reflects the increasingly adversarial relationship between Democrats and Republicans, especially in the House.

Still, it is worth remembering that even today's Congress is less divided along party lines than many of its predecessors were. During the years 1890–1910, for example, two-thirds of all votes evoked a party split, and in several sessions more than half the roll calls found 90 percent of each party's members opposing the other party.[16] Whereas the party splits of the past often reflected the routine operations of highly disciplined parties interested mainly in winning elections, dispensing patronage, and keeping power, today's party splits often reflect sharp ideological differences between the parties (or at least between their respective leaders).

The sharp increase in party votes among members of Congress since 1970 is remarkable, since it is not obvious that the Americans who vote for these members are as deeply divided by party. When social scientists describe a trait among people—say, their height—they usually note that there are a few very short ones and a few very tall ones, but that most people are in the middle. They call this distribution "unimodal." But when one describes voting in Congress, except on matters of national urgency, the votes are "bimodal"—that is, almost all of the Democrats vote one way and almost all of the Republicans vote a different way.

For example, when President Clinton was impeached, 98 percent of the House Republicans voted for at least one of the four impeachment articles and 98 percent of the House Democrats voted against all four, and this happened despite the fact that most Americans did not want to have the president impeached. In fact, the Republican vote did not even match how people felt who lived in districts represented by Republicans. On abortion, most Americans favor it but with some important limitations,

Table 13.4 Party Polarization in Congressional Voting, 1953–2002 (percentage of all votes)

Year	House	Senate	Year	House	Senate
1953	52%	N.A.	1978	33%	45%
1954	38	47%	1979	47	47
1955	41	30	1980	38	46
1956	44	53	1981	37	48
1957	59	36	1982	36	43
1958	40	44	1983	56	44
1959	55	48	1984	47	40
1960	53	37	1985	61	50
1961	50	62	1986	57	52
1962	46	41	1987	64	41
1963	49	47	1988	47	42
1964	55	36	1989	55	35
1965	52	42	1990	49	54
1966	41	50	1991	55	49
1967	36	35	1992	64	53
1968	35	32	1993	65	67
1969	31	36	1994	62	52
1970	27	35	1995	73	69
1971	38	42	1996	56	62
1972	27	36	1997	50	50
1973	42	40	1998	56	56
1974	29	44	1999	47	63
1975	48	48	2000	43	49
1976	36	37	2001	40	55
1977	42	42	2002	43	45

Source: Harold W. Stanley and Richard G. Niemi, *Vital Statistics on American Politics, 2003–2004* (Washington, D.C.: Congressional Quarterly Press, 2003), table 5.7.

but in Congress Democrats almost always support it with no restrictions and Republicans usually want to put on lots of restrictions. Votes on less emotional matters, like the tax bills, often show the same pattern of Democrats and Republicans at loggerheads.

How could these things happen in a democratic nation? If the American people are usually in the center on political issues, why are congressional Democrats almost always liberal and congressional Republicans almost always conservative?

There is no simple or agreed-upon answer to this question. Some scholars have argued that in the last thirty years or so voters have in fact become more partisan. "More partisan" means that they see important differences between the two parties, they identify themselves as either conservatives or liberals, and they favor parties that share their ideological preferences.[17]

One reason this has happened has been the way congressional districts are drawn for House members. The vast majority are drawn so as to protect one party or the other. This means that if you are a Republican living in a pro-Democratic district (or a Democrat living in a pro-Republican one), your votes don't make much difference in an election. Most House districts are not competitive, meaning that in them the only election that counts is the primary used to pick a candidate. In primaries voter turnout is lower, so that the most motivated (and thus most ideological) voters play a disproportionate role in choosing candidates.

A second possibility is that the voters have become more partisan as a result of Congress having become more partisan. When House Democrats vote liberal and House Republicans vote conservative, a lot of voters follow this cue and take positions based on a similar ideology.[18] People who don't see the world this way have either become less numerous or vote less often.

And a third is the role of seniority. Even though the so-called seniority rule is no longer strictly followed, the chairmen of committees are typically the members who have been on those committees the longest, and they will, of course, be ones from the safest districts. Since the chairmen have a lot of influence over how bills are written, their views—which have been shaped by a lifetime of dedication to Democratic or Republican causes—will be very important.

Still, just how much congressmen are influenced by committee chairmen and other party leaders is hard to know. In several sophisticated studies, political scientists Keith T. Poole and Howard Rosenthal have suggested that, while parties and their leaders matter, individual members' ideological views (see Chapter 7) probably matter as much or more than party discipline does in explaining how Congress works and how congressmen behave. "Members of Congress," they find, "come to Washington with a staked-out position on the (liberal-conservative) continuum, and then, largely 'die with their ideological boots on.'"[19] Everything from which "ideological boots" a given member chooses to wear in the first place to how he or she votes on a particular issue "may result as much from external pressures of campaign donors and primary voters as from the internal pressures of the congressional party."[20]

In short, party *does* make a difference in Congress—not as much as it once did, and not nearly as much as it does in a parliamentary system, but enough so that party affiliation is still the most important thing to know about a member of Congress. Knowing whether a member is a Democrat or a Republican will not tell you everything about the member, but it will tell you more than any other single fact.

Caucuses

Congressional caucuses are a growing rival to the parties as a source of policy leadership. A **caucus** is an association of members of Congress created to advocate a political ideology or a regional or economic interest. In 1959 there were only four caucuses; by the late 1980s there were over one hundred.

As Congress expert Susan Webb Hammond has observed, "The pace of caucus formation accelerated rapidly during the 1970s as members, operating

---

caucus   An association of Congress members created to advance a political ideology or a regional, ethnic, or economic interest.

---

with increased and more equitably distributed resources within a decentralized institution, sought to respond to increased external demands. . . . Members derive benefits—gaining information, being identified as a 'leader,' symbolically showing that they care about an issue of importance to constituents—from caucus activities."[21] In January 1995, at the beginning of the Republican-led 104th Congress, it was widely reported that the House of Representatives would "abolish" congressional caucuses. Yet as of January 1996 there were 129 congressional caucuses—111 from the 103rd Congress and 18 new ones established by the 104th. What the Republicans did do was to adopt a rule making the operation of caucuses more difficult. All aides working on caucus matters must be housed in members' offices. Therefore, aides are often scattered among several offices, and coordination becomes more difficult. Some caucuses responded by spinning off informational functions to new outside groups. Clearly the death of the caucuses was greatly exaggerated.

The caucuses are alive, well, and changing. Hammond has identified six types, four of which are constituency-based (see Table 13.5). Intraparty caucuses are formed by groups whose members share a similar ideology; for example, the Democratic Study Group was established by liberal Democrats. Personal-interest caucuses form around a common interest in an issue—for example, the environment, the arts, or human rights. Constituency caucuses are established to represent certain groups (African Americans, women, Vietnam veterans), regions (New England, the western states), or both (in states or congressional districts with diffuse constituents, such as different ethnic populations or family and corporate farms).

One long-established national constituency caucus is the Congressional Black Caucus (CBC). Founded in 1970, its membership increased from nine members that year to forty in the 104th Congress. Most CBC members have been liberal House Democrats. J. C. Watts, a black Republican from Oklahoma, was elected in 1994 but refused to join the CBC. In the Democratic-controlled 103rd Congress, CBC members chaired three standing committees and eighteen subcommittees.

But in the Republican-controlled 104th Congress, CBC committee leaders became ranking minority members, and some caucus Democrats lost their seats on major House committees—Appropriations, Ways and Means, and Rules. Moreover, the CBC grew

Table 13.5	Congressional Caucuses
Type	**Typical Examples**
Intraparty	Class Clubs The Coalition Conservative Opportunity Society Democratic Study Group Tuesday Lunch Bunch Wednesday Groups
Personal interest	Arts Caucuses Constitutional Caucus Constitutional Forum Congressional Family Caucus Human Rights Caucuses Military Reform Caucus Population and Development Coalition Senate Children's Caucus
Constituency concerns, national	Congressional Black Caucus Congressional Caucus for Women's Issues Congressional Hispanic Caucus Vietnam Veterans Caucus
Constituency concerns, regional	Congressional Border Caucus Congressional Sunbelt Council Northeast-Midwest Congressional Coalition Tennessee Valley Authority Caucus Western Caucus Western States Senate Coalition

Constituency
concerns,
state/district
	Congressional Caucus on
	   American Issues
	Export Caucus
	Irish Caucuses
	Rural Caucus
	Suburban Caucus
	Task Force on Industrial
	   Innovation and Productivity

Constituency concerns, industry	Automotive Caucus Boating Caucus Depot Caucus Steel Caucuses Textile Caucus Travel and Tourism Caucus

Source: Lawrence C. Dodd and Bruce I. Oppenheimer, eds., *Congress Reconsidered*, 6th ed. Washington, D.C.: Congressional Quarterly Press, 1997), table 12-1 by Susan Hammond.

Swearing-in ceremony for incoming chairman of the Congressional Black Caucus, Melvin Watt (D-NC) (center) and incoming vice-chair, Corrine Brown (D-FL). Outgoing chairman Elijah Cummings (D-MD) is on the left (January 4, 2004, 109th Congress).

less unified as liberal Democratic members from northern districts were forced to share power with more centrist members representing southern rural and suburban districts.

By contrast, other caucuses (and not only Republican ones), have fared better in recent years. For example, an intraparty caucus of "Blue Dog Democrats" known as the Coalition was born in February 1995. The Coalition's two dozen moderate-to-conservative members favor "middle-of-the-road" policies, especially on welfare and budget issues. For example, in 1995 the Coalition introduced its own welfare and budget bills, and although neither proposal was enacted, certain provisions of each strongly influenced final House deliberations. As Hammond has concluded, although the political fortunes of the CBC, the Coalition, and other caucuses may change from year to year, caucuses will continue and thrive as congressional institutions "because they help members to achieve personal goals of policy, representation, or power."[22]

☆ The Organization of Congress: Committees

The most important organizational feature of Congress is the set of legislative committees of the House and Senate. It is there that the real work of Congress is done, and it is in the chairmanships of these committees and their subcommittees that most of the power in Congress is found. The number and jurisdiction of these committees are of the greatest interest to members of Congress, since decisions on these subjects determine what group of members, with what political views, will pass on legislative proposals, oversee the workings of agencies in the executive branch, and conduct investigations.

There are three kinds of committees: **standing committees** (more or less permanent bodies with specified legislative responsibilities), **select committees** (groups appointed for a limited purpose and usually lasting for only a few congresses), and **joint committees** (those on which both representatives and senators serve). An especially important kind of joint committee is the **conference committee,** made up of representatives and senators appointed to resolve differences in the Senate and House versions of the same piece of legislation before final passage.

In the 104th Congress (1995–1996) the new Republican majority reduced the number of committees as part of its larger plan to reform House operations. Similar efforts were made in the Senate. When the dust settled on Capitol Hill, the total number of House and Senate committees had fallen from 252 in the previous Congress to 198, a smaller total even than the 242 committees of the 84th Congress (1955–1956). The House went from 22 to 19 standing committees and from 115 to 84 subcommittees of standing committees. The Senate maintained 17 committees but reduced the number of subcommittees of standing committees from 86 to 68. By 2004 the number of House subcommittees had risen slightly to 88.

Though members of the majority party could, in theory, occupy all of the seats on all of the committees, in practice they take the majority of seats on each committee, name the chairman, and allow the

minority party to have the other seats. Usually the ratio of Democrats to Republicans on a committee roughly corresponds to their ratio in that house of Congress, but on occasion the majority party will try to take extra seats on some key panels, such as the House Appropriations or Ways and Means Committees. Then the minority party complains, as the Republicans did in 1981 and the Democrats did in 1999, usually with little effect. In 2001, with the Senate evenly divided between Democrats and Republicans, each committee had the same number of members from each party with Republicans serving as chairmen.

Standing committees are the important ones, because, with a few exceptions, they are the only ones that can propose legislation by reporting a bill out to the full House or Senate. Each member of the House usually serves on two standing committees, unless he or she is on an "exclusive" committee—Appropriations, Rules, or Ways and Means. In such a case the representative is limited to one. Each senator may serve on two "major" committees and one "minor" committee.

When party leaders were strong, as under Speakers Reed and Cannon, committee chairmen were picked on the basis of loyalty to the leader. Now that this leadership has been weakened, seniority on the committee governs the selection of chairmen. Of late, however, even seniority has been under attack. In 1971 House Democrats decided in their caucus to elect committee chairmen by secret ballot. From then through 1991 they used that procedure to remove six committee chairmen. When the Republicans took control of the House in 1995, they could have returned to the strict seniority rule, but they did not. House Speaker Gingrich passed over three senior representatives in favor of more junior ones as committee chairmen. The Republicans imposed six-year term limits on House chairmen, so in 2001, when they organized the House, many veteran chairmen were replaced with new leaders. For example, Henry Hyde was replaced as chairman of the Judiciary Committee by James Sensenbrenner.

Traditionally the committees of Congress were dominated by the chairmen. They often did their most important work behind closed doors (though their hearings and reports were almost always published in full). In the early 1970s Congress further decentralized and democratized its operations by a series of

standing committees Permanently established legislative committees that consider and are responsible for legislation within a certain subject area.

select committees Congressional committees appointed for a limited time and purpose.

joint committees Committees on which both senators and representatives serve.

conference committees A joint committee appointed to resolve differences in the Senate and House versions of the same bill.

changes that some members regarded as a "bill of rights" for representatives and senators, especially those with relatively little seniority. These changes were by and large made by the Democratic Caucus, but since the Democrats were in the majority, the changes, in effect, became the rules of Congress. The more important ones were as follows.

House

- Committee chairmen to be elected by secret ballot in party caucus
- No member to chair more than one committee
- All committees with more than twenty members to have at least four subcommittees (at the time, Ways and Means had no subcommittees)
- Committee and personal staffs to be increased in size
- Committee meetings to be public unless members vote to close them

Senate

- Committee meetings to be public unless members vote to close them
- Committee chairmen to be selected by secret ballot at the request of one-fifth of the party caucus
- Committees to have larger staffs
- No senator to chair more than one committee

The effect of these changes, especially in the House, was to give greater power to individual members and to lessen the power of party leaders and committee chairmen. The decentralization of the House meant that it was much harder for chairmen to block legislation they did not like or to discourage junior members from playing a large role. House members were quick to take advantage of these enlarged opportunities. In the 1980s they proposed three times as many amendments to bills as they had in the 1950s.[23]

There was a cost to be paid, however, for this empowerment of the membership. The 435 members of the House could not get much done if they all talked as much as they liked and introduced as many amendments as they wished. And with the big increase in the number of subcommittees, many subcommittee meetings were attended by (and thus controlled by) only one person, the chairman. To deal with this, the Democratic leaders began reclaim-

★ POLITICALLY SPEAKING ★

Caucus

A *caucus* is a closed meeting of the members of a political party either to select a candidate for office or to agree on a legislative position.

The term is from an American Indian word meaning "elder" or "counselor." It quickly entered political usage in the United States, there being a Caucus Club in Boston as early as 1763.

The first national political caucuses were in Congress, where legislators would gather to select their party's candidate for president. Persons who did not get a caucus endorsement soon began denouncing the entire procedure, referring contemptuously to the "decrees of King Caucus." Popular resentment led in the 1830s to the creation of the nominating convention as a way of choosing presidential candidates.

Today congressional caucuses are organizations of legislators from a single party (Democrats or Republicans), with a common background (for example, women, African Americans, Hispanics), sharing a particular ideology (liberals or conservatives), or having an interest in a single issue (such as mushrooms, steel mills, or the environment).

Source: From *Safire's Political Dictionary* by William Safire. Copyright © 1968, 1972, 1978 by William Safire. Reprinted by permission of Random House, Inc. and the author.

ing some of their lost power. They made greater use of restrictive rules that sharply limited debate and the introduction of amendments. Committee

⋆ **HOW THINGS WORK** ⋆

Standing Committees of the Senate

Major Committees

No senator is supposed to serve on more than two (but some do).

Agriculture, Nutrition, and Forestry
Appropriations
Armed Services
Banking, Housing, and Urban Affairs
Budget
Commerce, Science, and Transportation
Energy and Natural Resources
Environment and Public Works
Finance
Foreign Relations
Governmental Affairs
Health, Education, Labor, and Pensions
Judiciary

Minor Committees

No senator is supposed to serve on more than one (but some do).

Rules and Administration
Small Business
Veterans' Affairs

Select Committees

Aging
Ethics
Indian Affairs
Intelligence

chairmen began casting proxy votes. (A proxy is a written authorization to cast another person's vote.) In this way a chairman could control the results of committee deliberations by casting the proxies of absent members.

Republican House members were angered by all of this. They suspected that restrictive rules and proxy voting were designed to keep them from having any voice in House affairs. When they took control of the House in 1995, they announced some changes:

* They banned proxy voting.
* They limited committee and subcommittee chairmen's tenures to three terms (six years) and the Speaker's to four terms (eight years).
* They allowed more frequent floor debate under open rules.
* They reduced the number of committees and subcommittees.
* They authorized committee chairmen to hire subcommittee staffs.

The endless arguments about rules illustrate a fundamental problem that the House faces. Closed rules, proxy voting, powerful committee chairmen, and strong Speakers make it easier for business to get done; they put the House in a good bargaining position with the president and the Senate; and they make it easier to reduce the number of special-interest groups with legislative power. But this system also keeps individual members weak. The opposite arrangements—open rules, weak chairmen, many subcommittees, meetings open to the public—help individual members be heard and increase the amount of daylight shining on congressional processes. But if everyone is heard, no one is heard, because the noise is deafening and the speeches endless. And though open meetings and easy amending processes may be intended to open up the system to "the people," the real beneficiaries are the lobbyists.

The House Republican rules of 1995 gave back some power to the chairmen (for example, by letting them pick all staff members) but further reduced it in other ways (for example, by imposing term limits and banning proxy voting). The commitment to public meetings remained.

⭐ HOW THINGS WORK ⭐

Standing Committees of the House

Exclusive Committees

Members may not serve on any other committee except Budget.

Appropriations
Rules
Ways and Means

Major Committees

Members may serve on only one major committee.

Agriculture
Armed Services
Education and the Workforce
Energy and Commerce
Financial Services
International Relations
Judiciary
Transportation and Infrastructure

Nonmajor Committees

Members may serve on one major and one nonmajor committee, or on two nonmajor committees.

Budget
Government Reform
House Administration
Resources
Science
Small Business
Standards of Official Conduct
Veterans' Affairs

Note: In 1995 the House Republican majority abolished three committees—District of Columbia, Post Office and Civil Service, and Merchant Marine and Fisheries—and gave their duties to other standing committees.

In the Senate there have been fewer changes, in part because individual members of the Senate have always had more power than their counterparts in the House. Two important changes were made by the Republicans in 1995:

- A six-year term limit on all committee chairmen (no limit on the majority leader's term)
- A requirement that committee members select their chairmen by secret ballot

Despite these new rules, the committees remain the place where the real work of Congress is done. The different types of committees tend to attract different kinds of members. Some, such as the committees that draft tax legislation (the Senate Finance Committee and the House Ways and Means Committee) or that oversee foreign affairs (the Senate Foreign Relations Committee and the House International Relations Committee) are attractive to members who want to shape public policy, become experts on important issues, or have influence with their colleagues. Others, such as the House and Senate committees dealing with public lands, small business, and veterans' affairs, are attractive to members who want to serve particular constituents.[24]

⭐ The Organization of Congress: Staffs and Specialized Offices

In 1900 representatives had no personal staffs, and senators averaged fewer than one staff member each. As recently as 1935 the typical representative had but two aides. By 1998 the average representative had seventeen assistants and the average senator over forty. To the more than ten thousand individuals who served on the personal staffs of members of the 103rd Congress must be added three thousand more who worked for congressional committees and yet another three thousand employed by various congressional research agencies. Until the 1990s Congress had the most rapidly growing bureaucracy in Washington—the personal staffs of legislators increased more than fivefold from 1947 to 1991,

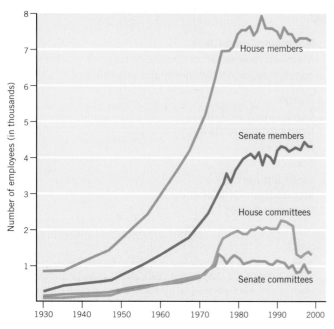

Figure 13.4 The Growth in Staffs of Members and Committees in Congress, 1930–2002

Source: From Harold Stanley and Richard Niemi, *Vital Statistics on American Politics 2001–2002* (Washington, D.C.: Congressional Quarterly Press, 2001). Reprinted with permission.

then leveled off and declined slightly (see Figure 13.4). Though some staffers perform routine chores, many help draft legislation, handle constituents, and otherwise shape policy and politics.

Tasks of Staff Members

Staff members assigned to a senator or representative spend most of their time servicing requests from constituents—answering mail, handling problems, sending out newsletters, and meeting with voters. In short, a major function of a member of Congress's staff is to help constituents solve problems and thereby help that member get reelected. Indeed, over the last two decades a larger and larger portion of congressional staffs—now about one-third—work in the local (district or state) office of the member of Congress rather than in Washington. Almost all members of Congress have such offices on a full-time basis; about half maintain two or more offices in their constituencies. Some scholars believe that this

growth in constituency-serving staffs helps explain why it is so hard to defeat an incumbent representative or senator.

The legislative function of congressional staff members is also important. With each senator serving on an average of more than two committees and seven subcommittees and each representative serving on an average of six committees and subcommittees, it is virtually impossible for members of Congress to become familiar in detail with all the proposals that come before them or to write all the bills that they feel ought to be introduced. As the workload of Congress has grown (over six thousand bills are introduced, about six hundred public laws are passed, and uncounted hearings and meetings are held during a typical Congress), the role of staff members in devising proposals, negotiating agreements, organizing hearings, writing questions for members of Congress to ask of witnesses, drafting reports, and meeting with lobbyists and administrators has grown correspondingly.

Those who work for individual members of Congress, as opposed to committees, see themselves entirely as advocates for their bosses. As the mass media have supplanted political parties as ways of communicating with voters, the advocacy role of staff members has led them to find and promote legislation for which a representative or senator can take credit. This is the entrepreneurial function of the staff. While it is sometimes performed under the close supervision of the member of Congress, just as often a staff member takes the initiative, finds a policy, and then "sells" it to his or her employer. Lobbyists and reporters understand this completely and therefore spend a lot of time cultivating congressional staffers, both as sources of information and as consumers of ideas.

One reason for the rapid growth in the size and importance of congressional staffs is that a large staff creates conditions that seem to require an even larger staff. As the staff grows in size, it generates more legislative work. Subcommittees proliferate to handle all the issues with which legislators are concerned. But as the workload increases, legislators complain that they cannot keep up and need more help.

The increased reliance on staff has changed Congress, not because staffers do things against the wishes of their elected masters but because the staff has altered the environment within which Congress does its work. In addition to their role as entrepreneurs promoting new policies, staffers act as negotiators. As a result members of Congress are more likely to deal with one another through staff intermediaries than personally. Congress has thereby become less collegial, more individualistic, and less of a deliberative body.[25]

Staff Agencies

In addition to increasing the number of staff members, Congress has also created a set of staff agencies that work for Congress as a whole. These staff agencies have come into being in large part to give Congress specialized knowledge equivalent to what the president has by virtue of his position as chief of the executive branch.

■ **Congressional Research Service (CRS)**   Formerly the Legislative Reference Service, the CRS is part of the Library of Congress. Since 1914 it has responded to congressional requests for information and now employs nearly nine hundred people, many with advanced academic training, to respond to more than a quarter of a million questions each year. As a politically neutral body, it does not recommend policy, but it will look up facts and indicate the arguments for and against a proposed policy. CRS also keeps track of the status of every major bill before Congress and produces a summary of each bill introduced. This information is instantly available to legislators via computer terminals located in almost all Senate and most House offices.

■ **General Accounting Office (GAO)**   Created in 1921, this agency once performed primarily routine financial audits of the money spent by executive-branch departments. Today it also investigates agencies and policies and makes recommendations on almost every aspect of government—defense contracting, drug enforcement policies, the domestic security investigations of the FBI, Medicare and Medicaid programs, water pollution programs, and so forth. Though the head of the GAO—the comptroller general—is appointed by the president (with the consent of the Senate), he or she serves for a fifteen-year term and is very much the servant of Congress rather than of the president. The GAO employs about five thousand people, many of whom are permanently assigned to work with various congressional committees.

■ **Office of Technology Assessment (OTA)**   Established in 1972 to study and evaluate policies and programs with a significant use of or impact on technology, the OTA had a staff of more than one hundred. Staff members looked into matters such as a plan to build a pipeline to transport coal slurry. The agency had little impact and was abolished in 1995.

■ **Congressional Budget Office (CBO)**   Created in 1974, the CBO advises Congress on the likely economic effects of different spending programs and provides information on the costs of proposed policies. This latter task has been more useful to Congress than the more difficult job of estimating future economic trends. The CBO prepares analyses of the president's budget and economic projections that often come to conclusions different from those of the administration, thus giving members of Congress arguments to use in the budget debates.

☆ How a Bill Becomes Law

Some bills zip through Congress; others make their way slowly and painfully. Congress, an English observer once remarked, is like a crowd, moving either sluggishly or with great speed.

Bills that have sped through on the fast track include ones to reduce drug abuse, reform Defense Department procurement procedures, end the mandatory retirement age, and help the disabled. Those that have plodded through on the slow track include ones dealing with health care, tax laws, energy conservation, and foreign trade, as well as several appropriations bills.

Why the difference? Studying the list above gives some clues. Bills to spend a lot of money move slowly, especially during times (such as the 1980s and early 2000s) when the government is running up big deficits. Bills to tax or regulate businesses move slowly because so many different interests have to be heard and accommodated. On the other hand, bills that seem to embody a clear, appealing idea ("stop drugs," "help old folks," "end scandal") gather momentum quickly, especially if the government doesn't have to spend a lot of its money (as opposed to requiring other people to spend their money) on the idea.

In the following account of how a bill becomes law, keep in mind the central fact that the complexity of

★ HOW THINGS WORK ★

How a Bill Becomes Law

INTRODUCTION

Draft and Introduce You do not need to be a member of Congress to draft a bill; lobbyists, congressional staff, and others draft legislation all the time. But you do need to be a member of Congress to introduce legislation. The bill or resolution gets a number preceded by *H.R.* for House bills and *S.* for Senate bills.

Refer to Committee Numbered bills get referred to standing committees depending on their content and in accordance with detailed rules and procedures that differ somewhat between the House and the Senate. Once referred, the bill gets on the committee's calendar for review by a subcommittee or by the full committee.

COMMITTEE ACTION

Get Committee Action Not every bill on the calendar gets action. Many bills get referred to subcommittees for staff analysis and hearings held in public. But getting a hearing is not the same thing as getting action. Even after study, hearings, and other consideration of the bill, if the committee fails to act, the bill is dead.

Go to Mark Up If, however, the committee so chooses, the bill then goes to "mark up," a process that normally works by subcommittee members and staff editing or amending the bill, often extensively. But even after "the mark," the subcommittee may decide not to recommend the bill to the full committee, and the bill dies there.

Order the Bill Once the full committee gets the bill, it may or may not conduct more analysis and hold more hearings on the legislation, consider amendments thereto, and vote its recommendation to the House or Senate (a procedure called "ordering the bill" or "ordering the bill reported"). If the bill is ordered, it still has a chance; if not, it is dead.

Publish a Report The committee chairman orders a public report on the bill. Most such reports are prepared by committee staff and describe the nature and purpose of the bill; what various experts have said or testified concerning it; what, if any, position

the president has taken on it; what, if any, public comments the relevant cabinet agencies or other executive branch units have offered on it; and what dissenting members of the committee have to say about it.

FLOOR ACTION AND CONFERENCE ACTION

Get a Date The bill goes back to the chamber that originated it and is scheduled for floor debate and a vote. The House has many different scheduling procedures or "calendars," while the Senate has but one. Even having come this far, the bill might or might not get a date, or come up in an order that makes it likely to keep going.

Win Two Chambers The debate over the bill and any amendments having concluded, the members vote. If the bill is defeated, it is dead. If the bill is approved, it next goes to the other chamber, which begins the process again, starting with the bill being referred to committee. Anything can happen. The second chamber can accept the bill as is, change it, or never even consider it. The bill can go back to the first chamber with few or no changes, go to a "conference committee" to reconcile any significant differences between the two versions of the bill, or go nowhere. If the two chambers agree, a conference report on the final bill is prepared. Only if the two chambers approve exactly the same final bill with identical language does the bill get sent to the president for consideration.

PRESIDENT

Get President's Signature If the president signs the bill, it becomes law. If the president takes no action for ten days after receiving the bill, and Congress is still in session, the bill becomes law. If the president takes no action after the Congress has adjourned, the bill dies from his "pocket veto." Or, the president can veto the bill outright, in which case it goes back to Congress.

Override President's Veto If the president vetoes a bill, Congress can still turn it into law, but that requires a two-thirds vote of the members, and there must be enough members present to form a quorum.

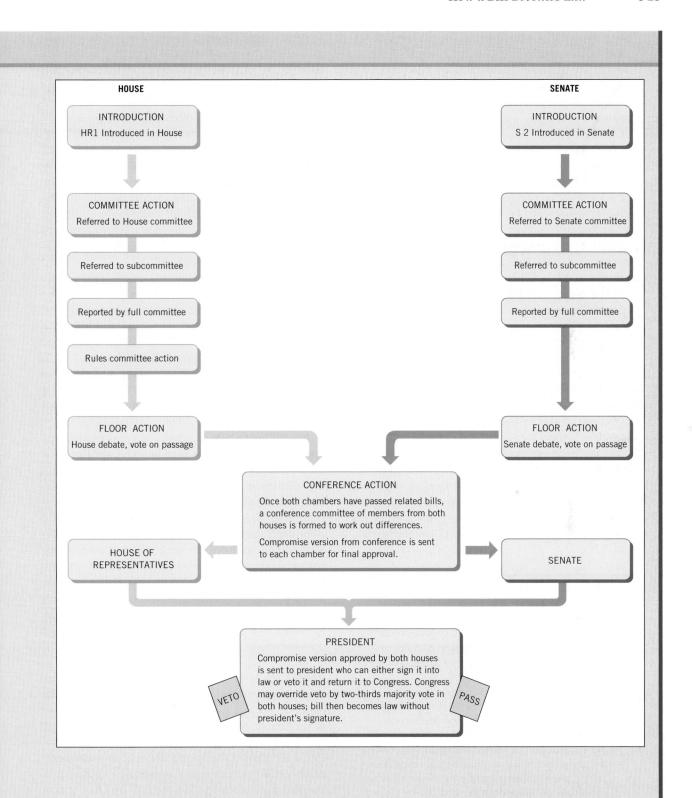

these procedures ordinarily gives a powerful advantage to the opposition. There are many points at which action can be blocked. This does not mean that nothing gets done but that, to get something done, a member of Congress must *either* assemble a majority coalition slowly and painstakingly *or* take advantage of temporary enthusiasm for some new cause that sweeps away the normal obstacles.

Introducing a Bill

Any member of Congress may introduce a bill—in the House simply by handing it to a clerk or dropping it in a box (the "hopper"), in the Senate by being recognized by the presiding officer and announcing the bill's introduction. Bills are numbered and sent to the printer: a House bill bears the prefix *H.R.*, a Senate bill the prefix S. A bill can be either a **public bill** (pertaining to public affairs generally) or a **private bill** (pertaining to a particular individual, such as a person pressing a financial claim against the government or seeking special permission to become a naturalized citizen). Private bills were once very numerous; today many such matters have been delegated to administrative agencies or the courts. If a bill is not passed by both houses and signed by the president within the life of one Congress, it is dead and must be reintroduced during the next Congress. Pending legislation does not carry over from one Congress to the next. (A new Congress is organized every two years.)

We often hear that legislation is initiated by the president and enacted by Congress—the former pro-

poses, the latter disposes. The reality is more complicated. Congress frequently initiates legislation; in fact most of the consumer and environmental protection legislation passed since 1966 began in Congress, not in the executive branch. And even laws formally proposed by the president often represent presidential versions of proposals that have incubated in Congress. This was the case, for example, with some civil rights laws and with the proposal that eventually became Medicare. Even when the president is the principal author of a bill, he usually submits it (if he is prudent) only after careful consultation with key congressional leaders. In any case the president cannot himself introduce legislation; he must get a member of Congress to do it for him.

One study showed that of ninety major laws passed between 1880 and 1945, seventy-seven were introduced without presidential sponsorship. In shaping the final contents, congressional influence dominated in thirty-five cases, presidential influence dominated in nineteen, and influence was mixed in the remaining thirty-six. Another study, covering the period 1940 to 1967, found that Congress was the major contributor to the contents of about half of all laws passed.[26]

In addition to bills, Congress can pass resolutions. A **simple resolution** (passed by either the House or the Senate) is used for matters such as establishing the rules under which each body will operate. A **concurrent resolution** settles housekeeping and procedural matters that affect both houses. Simple and concurrent resolutions are not signed by the president and do not have the force of law. A **joint resolution** requires the approval of both houses and the signature of the president; it is essentially the same as a law. A joint resolution is also used to propose a constitutional amendment; in this case it must be approved by a two-thirds vote of both houses, but it does not require the signature of the president.

Study by Committees

A bill is referred to a committee for consideration by either the Speaker of the House or the presiding officer of the Senate. Rules govern which committee will get which bill, but sometimes a choice is possible. In the House the right of the Speaker to make such choices is an important component of his powers. (His decisions can be appealed to the full House.) In 1963 a civil rights bill was referred by the presiding officer of the Senate to the Commerce Committee in order to keep it

public bill   A legislative bill that deals with matters of general concern.

private bill   A legislative bill that deals only with specific, private, personal, or local matters.

simple resolution   An expression of opinion either in the House or Senate to settle procedural matters in either body.

concurrent resolution   An expression of opinion without the force of law that requires the approval of both the House and the Senate, but not the president.

joint resolution   A formal expression of congressional opinion that must be approved by both houses of Congress and by the president; constitutional amendments need not be signed by the president.

H.R.1661

Children's Health Insurance Accountability Act of 1999 (Introduced in the House)

HR 1661 IH

106th CONGRESS

1st Session

H. R. 1661

To amend title XXVII of the Public Health Service Act and part 7 of subtitle B of title I of the Employee Retirement Income Security Act of 1974 to establish standards for the health quality improvement of children in managed care plans and other health plans.

IN THE HOUSE OF REPRESENTATIVES

May 4, 1999

Mrs. MORELLA (for herself, Mr. BALDACCI, Mr. SAWYER, and Mr. HILLIARD) introduced the following bill; which was referred to the Committee on Commerce, and in addition to the Committee on Education and the Workforce, for a period to be subsequently determined by the Speaker, in each case for consideration of such provisions as fall within the jurisdiction of the committee concerned

---

A BILL

To amend title XXVII of the Public Health Service Act and part 7 of subtitle B of title I of the Employee Retirement Income Security Act of 1974 to establish standards for the health quality improvement of children in managed care plans and other health plans.

Be it enacted by the Senate and House of Representatives of the United States of America in Congress assembled,

---

A bill (H.R. 1661) as it looks when introduced in the House.

out of the hands of the chairman of the Judiciary Committee, who was hostile to the bill. In the House the same piece of legislation was referred by the Speaker to the Judiciary Committee in order to keep it out of the grasp of the hostile chairman of the Interstate and Foreign Commerce Committee.

The Constitution requires that "all bills for raising revenue shall originate in the House of Representatives." The Senate can and does amend such bills, but only after the House has acted first. Bills that are not for raising revenue—that is, bills that do not change the tax laws—can originate in either house. In practice the House also originates appropriations bills—that is, bills directing how money shall be spent. Because of the House's special position in relation to revenue legislation, the committee that handles those bills—the Ways and Means Committee—is particularly powerful.

Most bills die in committee. They are often introduced only to get publicity for the member of Congress or to enable the member to say to constituents or pressure groups that he or she "did something" on a matter concerning them. Bills of general interest—many of which are drafted in the executive branch but introduced by a member of Congress—are assigned to a subcommittee for a hearing, where witnesses appear, evidence is taken, and questions are asked. These hearings are used to inform members of Congress, to permit interest groups to speak out (whether or not they have anything helpful to say),

and to build public support for a measure favored by the majority of the committee.

Though committee hearings are necessary and valuable, they also fragment the process of considering bills dealing with complex matters. Both power and information are dispersed in Congress, and thus it is difficult to take a comprehensive view of matters cutting across committee boundaries.

To deal with this problem Congress has established a process whereby a bill may now be referred to several committees that simultaneously consider it in whole or in part. This process, called **multiple referral,** was used in 1977 to send President Carter's energy proposals to six different committees in both the House and Senate. An even bigger multiple referral was used for the 1988 trade bill, which was considered by fourteen committees in the House and nine in the Senate. The advantage of this procedure is that all views have a chance to be heard; the disadvantage is that it takes a lot of time and gives opponents a greater chance to kill or modify the bill. And if the different committees disagree about the bill, their members have to come together in a gargantuan joint meeting to iron out their differences.

---

multiple referral   A congressional process whereby a bill may be referred to several committees.

⋆ HOW THINGS WORK ⋆

Congressional Calendars

House

Union Calendar   Bills to raise revenue or spend money
   Example: an appropriations bill

House Calendar   Nonmoney bills of major importance
   Example: a civil rights bill

Private Calendar   Private bills
   Example: a bill to waive the immigration laws so that a Philadelphia woman could be joined by her Italian husband

Consent Calendar   Noncontroversial bills
   Example: a resolution creating National Stenographers Week

Discharge Calendar   Discharge petitions

Senate

Executive Calendar   Presidential nominations, proposed treaties

Calendar of Business   All legislation

In these cases the advantages of the committee system—providing expert knowledge and careful deliberation—are often lost. Before the practice was abolished in 1995, about a quarter of all House bills and resolutions went through multiple referrals. Under the new rules, the Speaker is allowed to send a bill to a second committee after the first is finished acting, or he may refer parts of a bill to separate committees. This process, called **sequential referral,** has not noticeably slowed down the pace of legislative activity in Congress. In the 108th Congress, House rules were changed to give the Speaker, "under exceptional circumstances the right to not designate a primary committee." It is still too soon to know what, if any, difference this change will make.

After the hearings the committee or subcommittee will "mark up" the bill—that is, make revisions and additions, some of which are extensive. These changes do not become part of the bill unless they are approved by the house of which the committee is a part. If a majority of the committee votes to report a bill out to the House or Senate, it goes forward. It is accompanied by a report that explains why the committee favors the bill and why it wishes to see its amendments, if any, adopted. Committee members who oppose the bill have an opportunity to include their dissenting opinions in the report.

If the committee does not report the bill out favorably, that ordinarily kills it. There is a procedure whereby the full House or Senate can get a bill that is stalled in committee out and onto the floor, but it is rarely used. In the House a **discharge petition** must be signed by 218 members; if the petition is approved by a vote of the House, the bill comes before it directly. In the Senate a member can move to discharge a committee of any bill, and if the motion passes, the bill comes before the Senate. During the last century there have been over eight hundred efforts in the House to use discharge petitions; only two dozen have succeeded. Discharge is rarely tried in the Senate, in part because Senate rules permit almost any proposal to get to the floor as an amendment to another bill.

For a bill to come before either house, it must first be placed on a calendar. There are five such calendars in the House and two in the Senate (see the box above).

Though the bill goes onto a calendar, it is not necessarily considered in chronological order or even considered at all. In the House, the Rules Committee reviews most bills and adopts a rule that governs the procedures under which they will be considered by the House. A **closed rule** sets a strict time limit on debate

---

sequential referral   A congressional process by which a Speaker may send a bill to a second committee after the first is finished acting.

discharge petition   A device by which any member of the House, after a committee has had the bill for thirty days, may petition to have it brought to the floor.

closed rule   An order from the House Rules Committee that sets a time limit on debate; forbids a bill from being amended on the floor.

and forbids the introduction of any amendments from the floor, or forbids amendments except those offered by the sponsoring committee. Obviously such a rule can make it very difficult for opponents to do anything but vote yes or no on the measure. An **open rule** permits amendments from the floor. A **restrictive rule** permits some amendments but not others.

In the early 1970s most bills were debated under open rules. In the 1980s the Rules Committee—which is controlled by the Speaker—increasingly introduced bills for consideration under closed or restrictive rules in an effort to reduce the number of amendments from the floor (and, the Republicans argued, to reduce Republican influence). By the end of the 1980s roughly half of all bills, and nearly three-fourths of all important ones, were debated under restrictive or closed rules. In 1992 only one-third of all bills were considered under an open rule.[27] In 1995 the Republicans allowed more debate under open rules.

The House has at least three ways of bypassing the Rules Committee: (1) a member can move that the rules be suspended, which requires a two-thirds vote; (2) a discharge petition, as explained above, can be filed; or (3) the House can use the "Calendar Wednesday" procedure.* These methods are not used very often, but they are available if the Rules Committee departs too far from the sentiments of the House.

In theory, few such barriers to floor consideration exist in the Senate. There bills may be considered in any order at any time whenever a majority of the Senate chooses. The majority leader, in consultation with the minority leader, schedules bills for consideration. In practice, however, getting proposals to the Senate floor is far more complicated. Whereas the House normally plows through its legislative schedule, ignoring individual members' complaints in favor of getting its work done, the Senate majority leader must accommodate the interests of individual senators before proceeding with the Senate's business.

---

*On Wednesdays the list of committees of the House is called more or less in alphabetical order, and any committee can bring up for action a bill of its own already on a calendar. Action on a bill brought to the floor on Calendar Wednesday must be completed that day, or the bill goes back to committee. Since major bills rarely can be voted on in one day, this procedure is not often used.

Floor Debate—The House

Once on the floor, the bills are debated. In the House all revenue and most other bills are discussed by the "Committee of the Whole," which is nothing more than whoever happens to be on the floor at the time. The **quorum,** or minimum number of members who must be present for business to be conducted, is only 100 members for the Committee of the Whole. Obviously this number is easier to assemble than a quorum for the House itself, which the Constitution specifies as a majority, or 218 members. The Speaker does not preside but chooses another person to wield the gavel. The Committee of the Whole debates, amends, and generally decides the final shape of the bill, but technically cannot pass it. To do that the Committee of the Whole reports the bill back to the House (that is, to itself), which takes final action. During the debate in the Committee of the Whole, the committee sponsoring the bill guides the discussion, divides the time equally between proponents and opponents, and decides how long each member will be permitted to speak. If amendments are allowed under the rule, they must be germane to the purpose of the bill—extraneous matters (riders) are not allowed—and no one may speak for more than five minutes on an amendment. During this process people wishing to take time out to huddle about strategy or to delay action can demand a **quorum call**—a calling of the roll to find out whether the necessary minimum number of members are present. If a quorum is not present, the House must either adjourn or dispatch the sergeant at arms to round up missing

---

open rule   An order from the House Rules Committee that permits a bill to be amended on the floor.

restrictive rule   An order from the House Rules Committee that permits certain kinds of amendments but not others to be made into a bill on the floor.

quorum   The minimum number of members who must be present for business to be conducted in Congress.

quorum call   A roll call in either house of Congress to see whether the minimum number of representatives required to conduct business is present.

★ POLITICALLY SPEAKING ★

Riders and Christmas Trees

A **rider** is a provision added to a piece of legislation that is not germane to the bill's purpose. The goal is usually to achieve one of two outcomes: either to get the president (or governor) to sign an otherwise objectionable bill by attaching to it, as an amendment, a provision that the chief executive desperately wants to see enacted, or to get the president to veto a bill that he would otherwise sign by attaching to it, as an amendment, a provision that the chief executive strongly dislikes.

A rider is a convenient way for a legislator to get a pet project approved that might not be approved if it had to be voted on by itself. The term can be traced back to seventeenth-century England.

When a bill has lots of riders, it becomes a **Christmas tree bill.** In 1966, for example, the Foreign Investors Act, a bill designed to solve the balance-of-payments problem, had added to it riders giving assistance to hearse owners, the mineral ore business, importers of scotch whiskey, and presidential candidates.

Source: From *Safire's Political Dictionary* by William Safire. Copyright © 1968, 1972, 1978 by William Safire. Reprinted by permission of Random House, Inc. and the author.

---

cloture rule   A rule used by the Senate to end or limit debate.

---

members. The sponsoring committee almost always wins; its bill, as amended by it, usually is the version that the House passes.

Floor Debate—The Senate

Things are a good deal more casual in the Senate. Short of cloture (discussed below), there is no rule limiting debate, and members can speak for as long as they can stay on their feet. A senator's remarks need not be relevant to the matter under consideration (some senators have read aloud from the Washington telephone directory), and anyone can offer an amendment at any time. There is no Committee of the Whole. Amendments need not be germane to the purpose of the bill, and thus the Senate often attaches riders to bills.

In fact, the opportunity to offer nongermane amendments gives a senator a chance to get a bill onto the floor without regard to the calendar or the schedule of the majority leader: he or she need only offer a pet bill as an "amendment" to a bill already under discussion. (This cannot be done to an appropriations bill.) Indeed, the entire committee hearing process can be bypassed in the Senate if the House has already passed the bill. In that case a senator can get the House-passed measure put directly onto the Senate calendar without committee action. In 1957 and again in 1964 this was done with House-passed civil rights bills to make certain that they would not be bottled up in the conservative Senate Judiciary Committee.

A Senate filibuster is difficult to break. The current **cloture rule** requires that sixteen senators sign a petition to move cloture. The motion is voted on two days after the petition is introduced; to pass, three-fifths of the entire Senate membership (sixty senators if there are no vacancies) must vote for it. If it passes, each senator is thereafter limited to one hour of debate on the bill under consideration. The total debate, including roll calls and the introduction of amendments, cannot exceed one hundred hours.

In recent years both filibusters and cloture votes have become more common. The filibuster occurs more frequently because it is now easier to stage one. Often it consists not of a senator's making a long speech but of endless requests for the clerk to call the roll. More filibusters means more cloture votes, which are now easier to win since the 1975 change lowering the required number of supporters from two-thirds to three-fifths of all senators. During the 100th Congress (1987–1988) there were almost as many cloture votes—forty-three—as there had been in the half century after the procedure was invented. Since 1975 about 40 percent of all cloture votes have succeeded in cutting off debate.

Conservatives have used the filibuster to try to block civil rights laws; liberals have used it to try to block decontrol of gas prices. Since both factions have found the filibuster useful, it seems most unlikely that it will ever be abolished, though it has been somewhat curtailed. One way to keep the Senate going during a filibuster is through **double-tracking,** whereby the disputed bill is shelved temporarily so that the Senate can get on with other business. Because double-tracking permits the Senate to discuss and vote on matters other than the bill that is being filibustered, it is less costly to individual senators to stage a filibuster. In the past, before double-tracking, a senator and his allies had to keep talking around the clock to keep their filibuster alive. If they stopped talking, the Senate was free to take up other business. Opponents of the filibuster would bring cots and blankets to the Senate so that they could sleep and eat there, ready to take the floor the moment the filibuster faltered. But with double-tracking other business can go on while the stalled bill is temporarily set aside. As a result the number of filibusters has skyrocketed. In the words of two expert Senate watchers, the "Senate has become increasingly unmanageable as filibusters have become virtually commonplace on both major and minor pieces of legislation, raising the standard for passage of even routine bills from fifty to sixty votes and resulting in frequent delays in scheduling, stop-and-go patterns of floor debate," and the use of other procedures "that make the institution hostage to the whims of individual senators."[28]

What the threat of a filibuster means in practice is this: neither political party can control the Senate unless it has at least sixty votes. Neither party has had that many Senate seats since 1979, and so for the Senate to act there must be a bipartisan majority.

Methods of Voting

Some observers of Congress make the mistake of deciding who was for and who was against a bill by the final vote. This can be misleading—often a member of Congress will vote for final passage of a bill after having supported amendments that, if they had passed, would have made the bill totally different. To keep track of various members' voting records, therefore, it is often more important to know how they voted on key amendments than to know how they voted on the bill itself.

Finding that out is not always easy, though it has become more so in recent years. There are four procedures for voting in the House. A **voice vote** consists of the members' shouting "yea" or "nay"; a **division** (or standing) **vote** involves the members' standing and being counted. In neither a voice nor a standing vote are the names of members recorded as having voted one way or the other.

To learn how an individual votes there must be either a recorded teller vote or a roll call. In a **teller vote** the members pass between two tellers, the yeas first and then the nays. Since 1971 a teller vote can be "recorded," which means that, at the request of twenty members, clerks write down the names of those favoring or opposing a bill as they pass the tellers. Since teller votes but not roll calls may be taken in the Committee of the Whole, the use of a recorded teller vote enables observers to find out how members voted in those important deliberations.

A **roll-call vote,** of course, consists of people answering "yea" or "nay" to their names. It can be done at the request of one-fifth of the representatives present in the House. When roll calls were handled orally, it was a time-consuming process, since the clerk had to drone through 435 names. Since 1973 an electronic voting system has been in operation that permits each member, by inserting a plastic card into

---

double-tracking A procedure to keep the Senate going during a filibuster in which the disputed bill is shelved temporarily so that the Senate can get on with other business.

voice vote A congressional voting procedure in which members shout "yea" in approval or "nay" in disapproval, permitting members to vote quickly or anonymously on bills.

division vote A congressional voting procedure in which members stand and are counted.

teller vote A congressional voting procedure in which members pass between two tellers, the "yeas" first and the "nays" second.

roll-call vote A congressional voting procedure that consists of members answering "yea" or "nay" to their names.

★ HOW THINGS WORK ★

House-Senate Differences: A Summary

House	Senate
435 members serve two-year terms.	100 members serve rotating six-year terms.
House members have only one major committee assignment, thus tend to be policy specialists.	Senators have two or more major committee assignments, thus tend to be policy generalists.
Speaker's referral of bills to committee is hard to challenge.	Referral decisions are easy to challenge.
Committees almost always consider legislation first.	Committee consideration is easily bypassed.
Scheduling and rules are controlled by the majority party.	Scheduling and rules are generally agreed to by majority and minority leaders.
Rules Committee is powerful; controls time of debate, admissibility of amendments.	Rules Committee is weak; few limits on debate or amendments.
Debate is usually limited to one hour.	Debate is unlimited unless shortened by unanimous consent or by invoking cloture.
Nongermane amendments may not be introduced from the floor.	Nongermane amendments may be introduced.

a slot, to record his or her own vote and to learn the total automatically. Owing to the use of recorded teller votes and the advent of electronic roll-call votes, the number of recorded votes has gone up sharply in the House. There were only seventy-three House roll calls in 1955; twenty years later there were over eight times that many. Voting in the Senate is much the same, only simpler: there is no such thing as a teller vote, and no electronic counters are used.

If a bill passes the House and Senate in different forms, the differences must be reconciled if the bill is to become law. If they are minor, the last house to act may simply refer the bill back to the other house, which then accepts the alterations. If the differences are major, it is often necessary to appoint a conference committee to iron them out. Only a minority of bills require a conference. Each house must vote to form such a committee. The members are picked by the chairmen of the House and Senate standing committees that have been handling the legislation, with representation given to the minority as well as the majority party. There are usually between three and fifteen members from each house. No decision can be made unless approved by a majority of both delegations.

Bargaining is long and hard; in the past it was also secret. Now some conference sessions are open to the public. Often—as with President Carter's energy bill—the legislation is substantially rewritten in conference. Complex bills can lead to enormous conference committees. The 1988 trade bill went before a conference committee of two hundred members. Theoretically the conferees are not supposed to change anything already agreed to by both the House and Senate, but in the inevitable give-and-take even matters already approved may be changed.

In most cases the conference reports tend to favor, slightly, the Senate version of the bill. Several studies

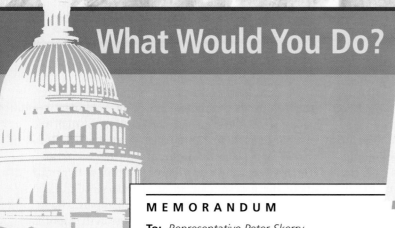

Should We Have a Bigger Congress?

November 15
WASHINGTON

A powerful citizens organization has demanded that the House of Representatives be made larger so that voters can feel closer to their members. Each representative now speaks for about 600,000 people—far too many, the group argues, to make it possible for all points of view to be heard. In its petition . . .

MEMORANDUM

To: *Representative Peter Skerry*
From: *Martha Bayles, legislative aide*
Subject: *The Size of the House of Representatives*

The House can decide how big it wishes to be. When it was created, there was one representative for every 30,000 people. Now there is one for every 600,000. In most other democracies each member of parliament represents far fewer than 600,000 people. Doubling the size of the House may be a way of avoiding term limits.

Arguments for:

1. Doubling the size of the House would reduce the huge demand for constituent services each member now faces.
2. A bigger House would represent more shades of opinion more fairly.
3. Each member could raise less campaign money because his or her campaign would be smaller.

Arguments against:

1. A bigger House would be twice as hard to manage, and it would take even longer to pass legislation.
2. Campaigns in districts of 300,000 people would cost as much as ones in districts with 600,000 people.
3. Interest groups do a better job of representing public opinion than would a House with more members.

Your decision:

Increase size of House _____
Do not increase size of House _____

have suggested that the Senate wins in 57 to 65 percent of cases.[29] Whoever wins (and both sides always claim that they got everything out of the bargaining that they possibly could have), conferees report their agreement back to their respective houses, which usually consider the report immediately. The report can be accepted or rejected; it cannot be amended. In the great majority of cases it is accepted: the alternative is to have no bill at all, at least for that Congress. The bill, now in final form, goes to the president for signature or veto. If a veto is cast, the bill returns to the house of origin. There an effort can be made to override the veto. This requires that two-thirds of those present (provided that there is a quorum) must vote to override; this vote must be a roll call. If both houses override in this manner, the bill becomes law without the president's approval.

☆ Reducing Power and Perks

While most citizens are only vaguely familiar with the rules and procedures under which Congress operates, they do care whether Congress as an institution serves the public interest and fulfills its mission as a democratic body. Over the last several decades, many proposals have been made to reform and improve Congress—term limitations, new ethics and campaign finance laws, and organizational changes intended to reduce the power and perks of members while making it easier for Congress to pass needed legislation in a timely fashion. Some of these proposals—for example, campaign finance reforms (see Chapter 10)—have recently become law.

Many would-be reformers share the view that Congress is overstaffed and self-indulgent. It is, they complain, quick to impose new laws on states, cities, businesses, and average citizens but slow to apply those same laws to itself and its members. It is quick to pass **pork-barrel legislation**—bills that give tangible benefits (highways, dams, post offices) to constituents in the hope of winning their votes in return—but slow to tackle complex and controversial questions of national policy. The reformers' image of Congress is unflattering, but is it wholly unwarranted?

No perk is more treasured by members of Congress than the frank. Members of Congress are allowed by law to send material through the mail free of charge by substituting their facsimile signature *(frank)* for postage. But rather than using this **franking privilege** to keep their constituents informed about the government, most members use franked newsletters and questionnaires as campaign literature. That is why use of the frank soars in the months before an election.

Thus the frank amounts to a taxpayer subsidy of members' campaigns, a perk that bolsters the electoral fortunes of incumbents. Some reformers do not believe that it is possible to fence in congressional use of the frank for public education or other legitimate purposes, and so they propose abolishing it outright. Other reformers argue that the frank can be fenced in by prohibiting mailings just before primaries and general elections.

For years Congress routinely exempted itself from many of the laws it passed. In defense of this practice members said that if members of Congress were subject to, for example, the minimum wage laws, the executive branch, charged with enforcing these laws, would acquire excessive power over Congress. This would violate the separation of powers. But as public criticism of Congress grew and confidence in government declined, more and more people demanded that Congress subject itself to the laws that applied to everybody else. In 1995 the 104th Congress did this by passing a bill that obliges Congress to obey eleven important laws governing things such as civil rights, occupational safety, fair labor standards, and family leave.

The bipartisan Congressional Accountability Act of 1995 had to solve a key problem: under the constitutional doctrine of separated powers, it would have been unwise and perhaps unconstitutional for the executive branch to enforce congressional compliance with executive-branch regulations. So Congress created the independent Office of Compliance and an employee grievance procedure to deal with implementation. Now Congress, too, must obey laws such as the Civil Rights Act, the Equal Pay Act, the Age Discrimination Act, and the Family and Medical Care Leave Act.

pork-barrel legislation   Legislation that gives tangible benefits to constituents in several districts or states in the hope of winning their votes in return.

franking privilege   The ability of members to mail letters to their constituents free of charge by substituting their facsimile signature for postage.

As already mentioned, bills containing money for local dams, bridges, roads, and monuments are referred to disparagingly as pork-barrel legislation. Reformers complain that when members act to "bring home the bacon," Congress misallocates tax dollars by supporting projects with trivial social benefits in order to bolster their reelection prospects.

No one can doubt the value of trimming unnecessary spending, but pork is not necessarily the villain it is made out to be. For example, the main cause of the budget deficit was the increase in spending on entitlement programs (like health care and interest on the national debt) without a corresponding increase in taxes. Spending on pork is a small fraction of spending on entitlements, and most categories of pork spending have decreased in the last ten or fifteen years. Furthermore, one person's pork is another person's necessity. No doubt some congressional districts get an unnecessary bridge or highway, but others get bridges and highways that are long overdue. The notion that every bridge or road a member of Congress gets for his or her district is wasteful pork is tantamount to saying that no member attaches any importance to merit.

Even if all pork were bad, it would still be necessary. Congress is an independent branch of government, and each member is, by constitutional design, the advocate of his or her district or state. No member's vote can be won by coercion, and few can be had by mere appeals to party loyalty or presidential needs. Pork is a way of obtaining consent. The only alternative is bribery, but bribery, besides being wrong, would benefit only the member, whereas pork usually benefits voters in the member's district. If you want to eliminate pork, you must eliminate Congress, by converting it into a parliament under the control of a powerful party leader or prime minister. In a tightly controlled parliament no votes need be bought; they can be commanded. But members of such a parliament can do little to help their constituents cope with government or to defend them against bureaucratic abuses, nor can they investigate the conduct of the executive branch. The price of a citizen-oriented Congress is a pork-oriented Congress.

☆ The Post-9/11 Congress

Critics of Congress sometimes complain that the body cannot plan, cannot act quickly, and cannot change how it is organized in order to meet new challenges.

☆ **POLITICALLY SPEAKING** ☆

Pork Barrel

Before the Civil War it was the custom to take salt pork from barrels and distribute it to the slaves. Often the eagerness of the slaves to get the food would result in a rush on the barrels, with each slave trying to get as much as possible.

By the 1870s members of Congress were using the term *pork* to refer to benefits for their districts and *pork barrel* to mean the piece of legislation containing those benefits.

Today the classic example of pork-barrel legislation is the rivers and harbors bill, which provides appropriations for countless dams, bridges, and canals to be built in congressional districts all over the country.

Source: From *Safire's Political Dictionary* by William Safire. Copyright © 1968, 1972, 1978 by William Safire. Reprinted by permission of Random House, Inc. and the author.

There is some truth to this line of criticism, but it is important to remember that the Framers purposely crafted Congress as an institution to favor deliberation over dispatch; to act boldly only when backed by a persistent popular majority, or a broad consensus among its leaders, or both; and to be slow to change its time-honored procedures and structures. Consider what has happened since September 11, 2001, concerning Congress and terrorism.

In its 2004 report, the bipartisan National Commission on Terrorist Attacks Upon the United States, better known as the 9/11 Commission, recommended that Congress consider making fundamental changes in how it oversees the Department of

★ HOW THINGS WORK ★

Rules on Congressional Ethics

Senate

Gifts: No gifts (in money, meals, or things) totaling $100 or more from anyone except a spouse or personal friend.

Lobbyists may not pay for gifts, official travel, legal defense funds, or charitable contributions to groups controlled by senators.

Fees: No fees for lectures or writing ("honoraria"), except that fees of up to $2,000 may go to a senator-designated charity.

Outside earned income may not exceed 15 percent of a senator's salary.

Ex-senators may not try to influence members of Congress for one year after leaving the Senate.

Mass mailings: No senator may receive more than $50,000 from the Senate to send out a mailing to constituents.

House

Gifts: No gifts (in money, meals, or things) totaling $100 or more from anyone except a spouse or personal friend.

Lobbyists may not offer gifts or pay for travel, even if lobbyist is a spouse or personal friend.

Travel: House members may travel at the expense of others if travel is for officially connected meetings.

Fees: No honoraria for House members.

Ex–House members may not lobby Congress for one year after leaving office.

Homeland Security and other federal agencies involved in intelligence-gathering and counter-terrorism activities.

Specifically, the 9/11 Commission warned that under "existing rules and resolutions the House and Senate intelligence committees lack the power, influence, and sustained capability to meet this challenge."[30] The "reforms we have suggested," the Commission concluded, "will not work if congressional oversight does not change too. Unity of effort in executive management can be lost if it is fractured by divided congressional oversight."[31] But the 9/11 Commission also frankly acknowledged that "few things are more difficult to change in Washington than congressional committee jurisdiction and prerogatives."[32]

Shortly after the November 2004 elections, those words seemed both timely and prophetic. Fresh from a reelection victory, with his own party leading both the House and the Senate, President George W. Bush urged Congress to pass a bill embodying key 9/11 Commission recommendations. Initially, the president's plan was opposed on Capitol Hill by many Republican leaders, as well as by senior Democrats whose committee jurisdiction and prerogatives seemed threatened by the president's proposals. Finally, however, Congress passed measures embodying many of the 9/11 Commission's proposals for reorganizing the federal government's intelligence-gathering and other counterterrorism activities.

Still, whatever additional antiterrorism bills, big or small, are passed or blocked before the presidential election in 2008, it will almost certainly take Congress the remainder of the present decade or longer to reorganize itself accordingly. Meanwhile, Congress faces the challenge mentioned at the very outset of this chapter: to ensure that "the first branch" can continue to function should a terrorist attack kill or incapacitate many or most of its members. In its May 2003 report, the bipartisan Continuity of Government Commission noted that, in the aftermath of the 9/11 attacks, "our government was able to function through normal constitutional channels."[33]

The 9/11 Commission, that reported on why Al Qaeda was able to attack America, held hearings in 2004.

But it could easily have been otherwise. Intelligence officials believe that the fourth plane involved in the 9/11 terrorist attacks, United Flight 93, was headed for the Capitol. But the plane took off late, and some passengers learned via cell phones that their flight was a suicide mission; they stormed the cockpit, bringing the plane down in Pennsylvania. The Continuity Commission urged members to recognize how close Congress had come to disaster on 9/11, look ahead, and think the unthinkable. "The greatest hole in our constitutional system is the possibility of an attack that would kill or injure many members of Congress":

Imagine a House of Representatives hit by an attack killing more than half the members and unable to reconstitute itself for months. Imagine any attack killing the president and vice president... Imagine a biological attack that prevented Congress from convening for months for fear of spreading infectious agents... (R)ecall that in the days after September 11th, Congress authorized the use of force in Afghanistan; appropriated funds for reconstruction of New York and for military preparations; and passed major legislation granting additional investigative powers and improving transportation security... In the event of a disaster that debilitated Congress, the vacuum could be filled by unilateral executive action—perhaps a benign form of martial law. The country might get by, but at a terrible cost to our democratic institutions.[34]

This "hole" in America's constitutional system is smaller with respect to the Senate than it is with respect to the House. Under the Seventeenth Amendment, governors can fill Senate vacancies within days by temporary appointment. The House, however, can fill vacancies only by special election (a process that, on average, takes states about four months to complete). In addition, the House's official interpretation of its quorum requirement makes it

---

☆ HOW THINGS WORK ☆

How Congress Raises Its Pay

For over two hundred years Congress has tried to find a politically painless way to raise its own pay. It has managed to vote itself a pay increase twenty-three times in those two centuries, but usually at the price of a hostile public reaction. Twice during the nineteenth century a pay raise led to a massacre of incumbents in the next election.

Knowing this, Congress has invented various ways to get a raise without actually appearing to vote for it. These have included the following:

- Voting for a tax deduction for expenses incurred as a result of living in Washington
- Creating a citizens commission that could recommend a pay increase that would take effect automatically, provided Congress did not vote *against* it
- Linking increases in pay to decreases in honoraria (that is, speaking fees)

In 1989 a commission recommended a congressional pay raise of over 50 percent (from $89,500 to $135,000) and a ban on honoraria. The House planned to let it take effect automatically. But the public wouldn't have it, demanding that Congress vote on the raise—and vote it down. It did.

Embarrassed by its maneuvering, Congress retreated. At the end of 1989 it voted itself (as well as most top executive and judicial branch members) a small pay increase (7.9 percent for representatives, 9.9 percent for senators) that also provided for automatic cost-of-living adjustments (up to 5 percent a year) in the future. But the automatic adjustments in congressional pay have been rejected every year in recorded roll-call votes. Apparently nobody in Congress wants to be accused of "getting rich" at the taxpayers' expense.

---

conceivable that, if only, say, 30 members were living and present, a group of 16 might proceed with business and elect a new Speaker who could, in the event that the president and vice president were also killed, become president.

Without providing details or proposing precise language, the Continuity Commission recommended a constitutional amendment that empowers governors, in the aftermath of a catastrophic attack, to appoint temporary representatives to fill seats in the House and in the Senate that are held by killed or incapacitated members. It urged Congress to draft and propose such an amendment as soon as possible, and expressed hope that the measure might be adopted within a two-year period.

In mid-2004, the House passed a bill mandating that if 100 or more members are killed, the speaker will issue a resolution calling for expedited special elections in vacant districts. But the bill fell far short of the Continuity Commission's proposed constitutional amendment, and several parts of the bill (for example, a provision to redefine a quorum after the fact to exclude incapacitated members) were widely believed to be unconstitutional. At the start of the 109th Congress in 2005, no major bills were proposed to enact the Continuity Commission's recommendations. Thus, while some important bills have been passed and some institutional changes have been made to combat terrorism, the post-9/11 Congress still closely resembles the pre-9/11 Congress.

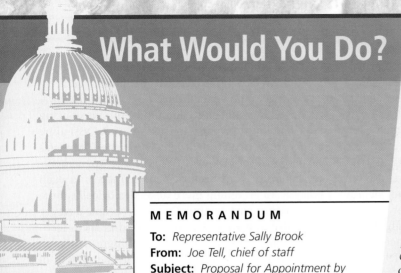

What Would You Do?

Nonpartisan Panel Proposes Letting Party Chiefs Pick Committee Chairs

February 14
WASHINGTON

Traditionally, there has been only one way to become a congressional committee chair: outlast everyone else. The so-called seniority system let the person with the longest tenure on a committee chair it. This eliminated fights over selection, and made it easier for legislators with unpopular views and for African Americans with tenure to become chairs. But, critics claim, it also sometimes landed incompetent people atop important committees, and made it harder for party leaders to move major legislation. Yesterday, a nonpartisan group of experts called for giving the seniority system "a decent but deep burial" and letting party leaders appoint committee chairs . . .

MEMORANDUM

To: *Representative Sally Brook*
From: *Joe Tell, chief of staff*
Subject: *Proposal for Appointment by Party Leaders*

You are on record as opposing the seniority system, but you have hitherto expressed no views in public about other methods by which committee chairs can be selected. One is election by party caucus. Letting party members elect committee chairs has some advantages: autocratic chairs can be ousted and committee chairs are likely to reflect the views of most party members. But it also has several disadvantages: it invites bruising fights for leadership posts that can divide party members and produce committee chairs who are not loyal to party leaders. Another method, now being debated around town and about which you might be asked at tomorrow's press briefing, is appointment by party leaders.

Arguments for:

1. Having the Speaker, majority leader, or minority leader choose chairs would increase party discipline and accountability.
2. Appointment by party leaders would make it easier for party programs to be enacted.

Arguments against:

1. Concentrating so much power in the hands of party leaders could corrupt even the best or most public-spirited of them.
2. Qualified and worthy members would be denied chairs just because they are out of favor with party leaders.

Your decision:

Favor proposal _____
Oppose proposal _____

★ SUMMARY

Over the last half century or so Congress, especially the House, has evolved through three stages.

During the first stage, lasting from the end of World War I until the early 1960s, the House was dominated by powerful committee chairmen who controlled the agenda, decided which members would get what services for their constituents, and tended to follow the leadership of the Speaker. Newer members were expected to be seen but not heard; power and prominence came only after a long apprenticeship. Congressional staffs were small, and so members dealt with each other face to face.

The second stage emerged in the early 1970s, in part as the result of trends already under way (for example, the steady growth in the number of staffers assigned to each member) and in part as a result of changes in procedures and organization brought about by younger, especially northern, members. Dissatisfied with southern resistance to civil rights bills and emboldened by a sharp increase in the number of liberals who had been elected in the Johnson landslide of 1964, the House Democratic caucus adopted rules that allowed the caucus to select committee chairmen without regard to seniority, dramatically increased the number and staffs of subcommittees (for the first time, the Ways and Means Committee was required to have subcommittees), authorized individual committee members (instead of the chairman) to choose the chairmen of these subcommittees, ended the ability of chairmen to refuse to call meetings, and made it much harder for those meetings to be closed to the public. The installation of electronic voting made it easier to require recorded votes, and so the number of times each member had to go on record rose sharply. The Rules Committee was instructed to issue more rules that would allow floor amendments.

At the same time, the number of southern Democrats in leadership positions began to decline, and the conservatism of the remaining ones began to lessen. (In 1990 southerners held only a quarter of committee chairmanships in the House and none of the major party leadership posts.) Moreover, northern and southern Democrats began to vote together a bit more frequently (though the conservative Boll Weevils remained a significant—and often swing—group).

These changes created a House ideally suited to serve the reelection needs of its members. Each representative could be an individual political entrepreneur, seeking publicity, claiming credit, introducing bills, holding subcommittee hearings, and assigning staffers to work on constituents' problems. There was no need to defer to powerful party leaders or committee chairmen. But because representatives in each party were becoming more alike ideologically, there was a rise in party voting. Congress became a career attractive to men and women skilled in these techniques, and these people entered Congress in large numbers. Their skill was manifest in the growth of the sophomore surge—the increase in their winning percentage during their first reelection campaign.

Even junior members could now make their mark on legislation. In the House more floor amendments were offered and passed; in the Senate filibusters became more commonplace. Owing to multiple referrals and overlapping subcommittee jurisdictions, more members could participate in writing bills and overseeing government agencies.

But lurking within the changes that defined the second stage were others, less noticed at the time, that created the beginnings of a new phase. The third stage was an effort in the House to strengthen and centralize party leadership. The Speaker acquired the power to appoint a majority of the members of the Rules Committee. That body, worried by the flood of floor amendments, began issuing more restrictive rules. By the mid-1980s this had reached the point where Republicans were complaining that they were being gagged. The Speaker also got control of the Democratic Steering and Policy Committee (it assigns new members to committees) and was given the power to refer bills to several committees simultaneously.

The evolution of the House remains an incomplete story; it is not yet clear whether it will remain in stage two or find some way of moving decisively into stage three. For now it has elements of both.

Meanwhile the Senate remains as individualistic and decentralized as ever—a place where it has always been difficult to exercise strong leadership.

Though its members may complain that Congress is collectively weak, to any visitor from abroad it seems extraordinarily powerful, probably the most powerful legislative body in the world. Congress has always been jealous of its constitutional independence and authority. Three compelling events led to Congress's reasserting its authority: the increasingly unpopular war in Vietnam; the Watergate scandals, which revealed a White House meddling illegally in the electoral process; and the advent of divided governments—with one party in control of the presidency and the other in control of Congress. It remains to be seen, however, whether Congress will function differently with the return of unified party government or in response to the threat of terrorism.

Claims that Congress became weak as the president grew stronger are a bit overdrawn. As we shall see in the next chapter, the view from the White House is quite different. Recent presidents have complained bitterly of their inability to get Congress even to act on, much less approve, many of their key proposals and have resented what they regard as congressional interference in the management of executive-branch agencies and the conduct of foreign affairs. If the past is prologue, the present era of unified party government will involve plenty of legislative-executive intraparty conflicts.

RECONSIDERING WHO GOVERNS?

1. Are members of Congress representative of the American people?

Demographically, no: most Americans are not middle-aged white males with law degrees or past political careers. Some groups (for example, women) are much less prevalent in Congress than they are in the nation as a whole, while other groups (for example, Catholics) constitute about the same fraction of Congress as they do of the American people. Ideologically, Republican members of Congress are more conservative than average Americans, and Democratic members of Congress are more liberal than average Americans.

2. Does Congress normally do what most citizens want it to do?

On most issues most of the time, Congress is in step with the public. But on some issues, most representatives' opinions are generally out of sync with mass public preferences. For example, most Americans have long favored protectionist trade policies, but most members of Congress have consistently voted for free trade policies. Likewise, most citizens are less solicitous of laws that reinforce civil liberties than the Congress has traditionally been. This, however, is much as the Framers of the Constitution had hoped and expected. They believed that representatives should refine, not reflect, public wishes, and mediate, not mirror, public views.

RECONSIDERING TO WHAT ENDS?

1. Should Congress run under strong leadership?

Congress has tried it both ways. Sometimes the House has had a strong Speaker, sometimes a weak one; sometimes committee chairmen were selected by seniority, sometimes by the Speaker, and sometimes by party vote. If we want a Congress that can act quickly and decisively as a body, then we should desire strong leadership, place restrictions on debate, provide few opportunities for stalling tactics, and brook only minimal committee interference. But if we want a Congress in which the interests of individual members and the people they represent are routinely protected or enhanced, then we must reject strong leadership, proliferate rules allowing for delay and discussion, and permit many opportunities for

committee activity. Unfortunately, the public often wants both systems to operate, the first for some issues and the second for others.

2. Should Congress act more quickly?

The Framers of the Constitution knew that Congress would normally proceed slowly and err in favor of deliberative, not decisive, action. Congress was intended to check and balance strong leaders in the executive branch, not automatically cede its authority to them, not even during a war or other national crisis. Today, the increased ideological and partisan polarization among members has arguably made Congress even less capable than it traditionally has been of planning ahead or swiftly adopting coherent changes in national policies. There is, however, only conflicting evidence concerning whether so-called policy gridlock has become more common than in decades past. Since September 11, 2001 terrorist attacks on the United States, Congress has passed a host of new laws intended to enhance America's homeland security. Still, Congress took its time with

several major proposals to reorganize the government around homeland security priorities. Some cite this as but the latest, and potentially the gravest, example of what's wrong with Congress. But others cite it as a salutary reminder that a Congress that could move swiftly to enact wise homeland security or other policies could also move swiftly to adopt unwise ones.

WORLD WIDE WEB RESOURCES

House of Representatives: **www.house.gov**

Senate: **www.senate.gov**

Library of Congress
thomas.loc.gov
lcweb.loc.gov/global/legislative/congress

For news about Congress
Roll Call magazine: **www.rollcall.com**
C-SPAN: **www.c-span.org**

SUGGESTED READINGS

Arnold, R. Douglas. *The Logic of Congressional Action.* New Haven and London: Yale University Press, 1990. Masterful analysis of how Congress sometimes passes bills that serve the general public, not just special interests.

Davidson, Roger H., and Walter J. Oleszek. *Congress and Its Members.* 7th ed. Washington, D.C.: Congressional Quarterly Press, 2000. Complete and authoritative account of who is in Congress and how it operates.

Fenno, Richard F., Jr. *Congressmen in Committees.* Boston: Little, Brown, 1973. Study of the styles of twelve standing committees.

Fiorina, Morris P. *Congress: Keystone of the Washington Establishment.* 2d ed. New Haven, Conn.: Yale University Press, 1989. Argues that congressional behavior is aimed at guaranteeing their chances for reelection.

Jacobson, Gary. *The Politics of Congressional Elections.* 4th ed. New York: Longman, 1997. Authoritative study of how members of Congress are elected.

Maass, Arthur. *Congress and the Common Good.* New York: Basic Books, 1983. Insightful account of congressional operations, especially those involving legislative-executive relations. Disputes Fiorina's argument that reelection needs explain congressional behavior.

Malbin, Michael J. *Unelected Representatives.* New York: Basic Books, 1980. Study of the influence of congressional staff members.

Mann, Thomas E., and Norman J. Ornstein. *Renewing Congress.* 2 vols. Washington, D.C.: Brookings Institution and American Enterprise Institute, 1993. Superb overview of what's really wrong with Congress and how to fix it.

Poole, Keith T., and Howard Rosenthal. *Congress: A Political-Economic History of Roll Call Voting.* New York: Oxford University Press, 1997. Sophisticated study of why members of Congress vote as they do and how relatively stable congressional voting patterns have been throughout American history.

Smith, Steven S., and Christopher J. Deering. *Committees in Congress.* Washington, D.C.: Congressional Quarterly, 1984. Analysis of how different kinds of congressional committees operate.

Sundquist, James L. *The Decline and Resurgence of Congress.* Washington, D.C.: Brookings Institution, 1981. A history of the fall and, after 1973, the rise of congressional power vis-à-vis the president.

The Presidency

Presidents and Prime Ministers

Divided Government
Does Gridlock Matter? ● Is Policy
Gridlock Bad?

The Evolution of the Presidency
Concerns of the Founders ● The
Electoral College ● The President's
Term of Office ● The First Presidents ●
The Jacksonians ● The Reemergence of
Congress

The Powers of the President

The Office of the President
The White House Office ● The
Executive Office of the President ●
The Cabinet ● Independent Agencies,
Commissions, and Judgeships

Who Gets Appointed

Presidential Character

The Power to Persuade
The Three Audiences ● Popularity and
Influence ● The Decline in Popularity

The Power to Say No
Veto ● Executive Privilege ●
Impoundment of Funds

The President's Program
Putting Together a Program ●
Attempts to Reorganize

Presidential Transition
The Vice President ● Problems of
Succession ● Impeachment

How Powerful Is the President?

WHO GOVERNS?

1. Did the Founders expect the presidency to be the most important political institution?
2. How important is the president's character in determining how he governs?

TO WHAT ENDS?

1. Should we abolish the electoral college?
2. Is it harder to govern when the presidency and the Congress are controlled by different political parties?

*P*rofessor Jones speaks to his political science class: "The president of the United States occupies one of the most powerful offices in the world. Presidents Kennedy and Johnson sent American troops to Vietnam, President Bush sent them to Saudi Arabia, and President Clinton sent them to Kosovo, all without war being declared by Congress. President Nixon imposed wage and price controls on the country. Between them, Presidents Carter and Reagan selected most of the federal judges now on the bench; thus the political philosophies of these two men were stamped on the courts. President George W. Bush created military tribunals to try captured terrorists and persuaded Congress to toughen antiterrorist laws. No wonder people talk about our having an 'imperial presidency.'"

A few doors down the hall, Professor Smith speaks to her class: "The president, compared to the prime ministers of other democratic nations, is one of the weakest chief executives anywhere. President Carter signed an arms-limitation treaty with the Soviets, but the Senate wouldn't ratify it. President Reagan was not allowed even to test antisatellite weapons, and in 1986 Congress rejected his budget before the ink was dry. President Clinton's health care plan was ignored, and the House voted to impeach him. Regularly, subordinates who are supposed to be loyal to the president leak his views to the press and undercut his programs before Congress. No wonder people call the U.S. president a 'pitiful, helpless giant.'"

Can Professors Jones and Smith be talking about the same office? Who is right? In fact they are both right. The American presidency is a unique office, with elements of great strength *and* profound weakness built into it by its constitutional origins.

☆ Presidents and Prime Ministers

The popularly elected president is an American invention. Of the roughly five dozen countries in which there is some degree of party competition and thus, presumably, some measure of free choice for the voters, only sixteen have a directly elected president, and thirteen of these are nations of North and South America. The democratic alternative is for the chief executive to be a prime minister, chosen by and responsible to the parliament. This system prevails in most Western European countries as well as in Israel and Japan. There is no nation with a purely presidential political system in

The first cabinet: left to right, Secretary of War Henry Knox, Secretary of State Thomas Jefferson, Attorney General Edmund Randolph, Secretary of the Treasury Alexander Hamilton, and President George Washington.

Europe; France combines a directly elected president with a prime minister and parliament.[1]

In a parliamentary system the prime minister is the chief executive. The prime minister is chosen not by the voters but by the legislature, and he or she in turn selects the other ministers from the members of parliament. If the parliament has only two major parties, the ministers will usually be chosen from the majority party; if there are many parties (as in Italy), several parties may participate in a coalition cabinet. The prime minister remains in power as long as his or her party has a majority of the seats in the legislature or as long as the coalition he or she has assembled holds together. The voters choose who is to be a member of parliament—usually by voting for one or another party—but cannot choose who is to be the chief executive officer.

Whether a nation has a presidential or a parliamentary system makes a big difference in the identity and powers of the chief executive.

■ **Presidents Are Often Outsiders**   People become president by winning elections, and sometimes winning is easier if you can show the voters that you are not part of "the mess in Washington." Prime ministers are selected from among people already in parliament, and so they are always insiders.

Jimmy Carter, Ronald Reagan, Bill Clinton, and George W. Bush did not hold national office before becoming president. Franklin Roosevelt had been assistant secretary of the navy, but his real political experience was as governor of New York. Dwight Eisenhower was a general, not a politician. John F. Kennedy, Lyndon Johnson, and Richard Nixon had been in Congress, but only Nixon had had top-level experience in the executive branch (he had been vice president). George H.W. Bush had had a great deal of executive experience in Washington—as vice president, director of the CIA, and representative to China, whereas Bill Clinton and George W. Bush both served as governors.

From 1828 through 2000, thirty-one different people were elected president. Of these, the great majority were governors, military leaders, or vice presidents; only 13 percent were legislators just before becoming president.

■ **Presidents Choose Cabinet Members from Outside Congress**   Under the Constitution, no sitting member of Congress can hold office in the executive branch. The persons chosen by a prime minister to be in the cabinet are almost always members of parliament.

Of the fifteen heads of cabinet-level departments in the first George W. Bush administration, only four had been members of Congress. The rest, as is customary with most presidents, were close personal friends or campaign aides, representatives of important constituencies (for example, farmers, blacks, or women), experts on various policy issues, or some combination of all three.

The prime minister of Great Britain, by contrast, picks all of his or her cabinet ministers from among members of Parliament. This is one way by which the prime minister exercises control over the legislature. If you were an ambitious member of Parliament, eager to become prime minister yourself someday, and if you knew that your main chance of realizing that ambition was to be appointed to a series of ever-more-important cabinet posts, then you would not be likely to antagonize the person doing the appointing.

■ **Presidents Have No Guaranteed Majority in the Legislature**   A prime minister's party (or coalition) always has a majority in parliament; if it did not, somebody else would be prime minister. A president's party often does not have a congressional majority; instead, Congress is often controlled by the opposite party, creating a divided government. Divided government means that cooperation between the two branches, hard to achieve under the best of circumstances, is often further reduced by partisan bickering.

Even when one party controls both the White House and Congress, the two branches often work at cross-purposes. The U.S. Constitution created a system of separate branches sharing powers. The authors of the document expected that there would be conflict between the branches, and they have not been disappointed.

When Kennedy was president, his party, the Democrats, held a big majority in the House and the Senate. Yet Kennedy was frustrated by his inability to get Congress to approve proposals to enlarge civil rights, supply federal aid for school construction, create a Department of Urban Affairs and Housing, or establish a program of subsidized medical care for the elderly. During his last year in office, Congress passed only about one-fourth of his proposals. Carter did not fare much better; even though the Democrats controlled Congress, many of his most important proposals were defeated or greatly modified. Only Franklin Roosevelt (1933–1945) and Lyndon Johnson (1963–1969) had even brief success in leading Congress, and for Roosevelt most of that success was confined to his first term or to wartime.

☆ Divided Government

In the forty-eight years between 1952 and 2000, there were twenty-four congressional or presidential elections. Sixteen of the twenty-four produced **divided government**—that is, a government in which

---

divided government   One party controls the White House and another party controls one or both houses of Congress.

unified government   The same party controls the White House and both houses of Congress.

British Prime Minister Tony Blair heads a parliamentary, rather than a presidential, government.

one party controls the White House and a different party controls one or both houses of Congress. When George W. Bush became president in 2001, it was only the third time since 1969 that the same party controlled the White House and Congress, creating a **unified government.** And it was only the first time since 1953 when the Republicans were in charge. But not long after the Senate convened, one Republican, James Jeffords of Vermont announced that he was an independent and voted with the Democrats. Divided government had returned until an additional Republican was elected to the Senate in 2002.

Americans say they don't like divided government. They, or at least the pundits who claim to speak for them, think divided government produces partisan bickering, political paralysis, and policy gridlock. During the 1990 battle between President Bush and a Democratic Congress, one magazine compared it to a movie featuring the Keystone Kops, characters from the silent movies who wildly chased each other around while accomplishing nothing.[2] In the 1992 campaign, Bush, Clinton, and Ross Perot bemoaned the "stalemate" that had developed in Washington. When Clinton was sworn in as president, many commentators spoke approvingly of the "end of gridlock."

There are two things wrong with these complaints. First, it is not clear that divided government produces a gridlock that is any worse than that which exists with unified government. Second, it is not clear that, even if **gridlock** does exist, it is always, or even usually, a bad thing for the country.

Does Gridlock Matter?

Despite the well-publicized stories about presidential budget proposals being ignored by Congress (Democrats used to describe Reagan's and Bush's budgets as being "dead on arrival"), it is not easy to tell whether divided governments produce fewer or worse policies than unified ones. The scholars who have looked closely at the matter have, in general, concluded that divided governments do about as well as unified ones in passing important laws, conducting important investigations, and ratifying significant treaties.[3] Political scientist David Mayhew studied 267 important laws that were enacted between 1946 and 1990. These laws were as likely to be passed when different parties controlled the White House and Congress as when the same party controlled both branches.[4] For example, divided governments produced the 1946 Marshall Plan to rebuild war-torn Europe and the 1986 Tax Reform Act.

Why do divided governments produce about as much important legislation as unified ones? The main reason is that "unified government" is something of a myth. Just because the Republicans control both the presidency and Congress does not mean that the Republican president and the Republican senators and representatives will see things the same way. For one thing, Republicans are themselves divided between conservatives (mainly from the South) and liberals (mainly from the Northeast and Midwest). They disagree about policy almost as much as Republicans and Democrats disagree. For another thing, the Constitution ensures that the president and Congress will be rivals for power and thus rivals in policy-making. That's what the separation of powers and checks and balances are all about.

As a result, periods of unified government often turn out not to be so unified. Democratic president Lyndon Johnson could not get many Democratic members of Congress to support his war policy in Vietnam. Democratic president Jimmy Carter could not get the Democratic-controlled Senate to ratify his strategic arms limitation treaty. Democratic president Bill Clinton could not get the Democratic Congress to go along with his policy on gays in the military or his health proposals; and when the heavily revised Clinton budget did pass in 1993, it was by just one vote.

The only time there really is a unified government is when not just the same party but the same *ideological wing* of that party is in effective control of both branches of government. This was true in 1933 when Franklin Roosevelt was president and change-oriented Democrats controlled Congress, and it was true again in 1965 when Lyndon Johnson and liberal Democrats dominated Congress. Both were periods when many major policy initiatives became law: Social Security, business regulations, Medicare, and civil rights legislation. But these periods of ideologically unified government are very rare.

Is Policy Gridlock Bad?

An American president has less ability to decide what laws get passed than does a British prime minister. If you think that the job of a president is to "lead the country," that weakness will worry you. The only cure for that weakness is either to change the Constitution so that our government resembles the parliamentary system in effect in Great Britain, or always to vote into office members of Congress who not only are of the same party as the president but also agree with him on policy issues.

We suspect that even Americans who hate gridlock and want more leadership aren't ready to make sweeping constitutional changes or to stop voting for presidents and members of Congress from different parties. This unwillingness suggests that they like the idea of somebody being able to block a policy they don't like. Since all of us don't like something, we all have an interest in some degree of gridlock.

And we seem to protect that interest. In a typical presidential election, about one-fourth of all voters

---

gridlock   The inability of the government to act because rival parties control different parts of the government.

will vote for one party's candidate for president and the other party's candidate for Congress. As a result, about one-fourth of all congressional districts will be represented in the House by a person who does not belong to the party of the president who carried that district. Some scholars believe that voters split tickets deliberately in order to create divided government and thus magnify the effects of the checks and balances built into our system, but the evidence supporting this belief is not conclusive.

Gridlock, to the extent that it exists, is a necessary consequence of a system of representative democracy. Such a system causes delays, intensifies deliberations, forces compromises, and requires the creation of broad-based coalitions to support most new policies. This system is the opposite of direct democracy. If you believe in direct democracy, you believe that what the people want on some issue should become law with as little fuss and bother as possible. Political gridlocks are like traffic gridlocks—people get overheated, things boil over, nothing moves, and nobody wins except journalists who write about the mess and lobbyists who charge big fees to steer their clients around the tie-up. In a direct democracy, the president would be a traffic cop with broad powers to decide in what direction the traffic should move and to make sure that it moves that way.

But if unified governments are not really unified—if in fact they are split by ideological differences within each party and by the institutional rivalries between the president and Congress—then this change is less important than it may seem. What *is* important is the relative power of the president and Congress. That has changed greatly.

☆ The Evolution of the Presidency

In 1787 few issues inspired as much debate or concern among the Framers as the problem of defining the chief executive. The delegates feared anarchy and monarchy in about equal measure. When the Constitutional Convention met, the existing state constitutions gave most, if not all, power to the legislatures. In eight states the governor was actually chosen by the legislature, and in ten states the governor could not serve more than one year. Only in New York, Massachusetts, and Connecticut did governors have much power or serve for any length of time.

Some of the Framers proposed a plural national executive (that is, several people would each hold the executive power in different areas, or they would exercise the power as a committee). Others wanted the executive power checked, as it was in Massachusetts, by a council that would have to approve many of the chief executive's actions. Alexander Hamilton strongly urged the exact opposite: in a five-hour speech he called for something very much like an elective monarchy, patterned in some respects after the British kind. No one paid much attention to this plan or even, at first, to the more modest (and ultimately successful) suggestion of James Wilson for a single, elected president.

In time, those who won out believed that the governing of a large nation, especially one threatened by foreign enemies, required a single president with significant powers. Their cause was aided, no doubt, by the fact that everybody assumed that George Washington would be the first president, and confidence in him—and in his sense of self-restraint—was widely shared. Even so, several delegates feared that the presidency would become, in the words of Edmund Randolph of Virginia, "the foetus of monarchy."

Concerns of the Founders

The delegates in Philadelphia, and later the critics of the new Constitution during the debate over its ratification, worried about aspects of the presidency that were quite different from those that concern us today. In 1787–1789 some Americans suspected that the president, by being able to command the state militia, would use the militia to overpower state governments. Others were worried that if the president were allowed to share treaty-making power with the Senate, he would be "directed by minions and favorites" and become a "tool of the Senate."

But the most frequent concern was over the possibility of presidential reelection: Americans in the late eighteenth century were sufficiently suspicious of human nature and sufficiently experienced in the arts of mischievous government to believe that a president, once elected, would arrange to stay in office in perpetuity by resorting to bribery, intrigue, and force. This might happen, for example, every time the presidential election was thrown into the House of Representatives because no candidate had received a majority of the votes in the electoral college, a situation that most people expected to happen frequently.

In retrospect, these concerns seem misplaced, even foolish. The power over the militia has had little significance; the election has gone to the House only twice (1800 and 1824); and though the Senate dominated the presidency off and on during the second half of the nineteenth century, it has not done so recently. The real sources of the expansion of presidential power—the president's role in foreign affairs, his ability to shape public opinion, his position as head of the executive branch, and his claims to have certain "inherent" powers by virtue of his office—were hardly predictable in 1787. And not surprisingly. There was nowhere in the world at that time, nor had there been at any time in history, an example of an American-style presidency. It was a unique and unprecedented institution, and the Framers and their critics can easily be forgiven for not predicting accurately how it would evolve. At a more general level, however, they understood the issue quite clearly. Gouverneur Morris of Pennsylvania put the problem of the presidency this way: "Make him too weak: the Legislature will usurp his powers. Make him too strong: he will usurp on the Legislature."

The Framers knew very well that the relations between the president and Congress and the manner in which the president is elected were of profound importance, and they debated both at great length. The first plan was for Congress to elect the president—in short, for the system to be quasi-parliamentary. But if that were done, some delegates pointed out, Congress could dominate an honest or lazy president, while a corrupt or scheming president might dominate Congress.

After much discussion it was decided that the president should be chosen directly by voters. But by which voters? The emerging nation was large and diverse. It seemed unlikely that every citizen would be familiar enough with the candidates to cast an informed vote for a president directly. Worse, a direct popular election would give inordinate weight to the large, populous states, and no plan with that outcome had any chance of adoption by the smaller states.

The Electoral College

Thus the **electoral college** was invented, whereby each of the states would select electors in whatever manner it wished. The electors would then meet in each state capital and vote for president and vice president. Many Framers expected that this proce-

dure would lead to each state's electors' voting for a favorite son, and thus no candidate would win a majority of the popular vote. In this event, it was decided, the House of Representatives should make the choice, with each state delegation casting one vote.

The plan seemed to meet every test: large states would have their say, but small states would be protected by having a minimum of three electoral votes no matter how tiny their population. The small states together could wield considerable influence in the House, where, it was widely expected, most presidential elections would ultimately be decided. Of course, it did not work out quite this way: the Framers did not foresee the role that political parties would play in producing nationwide support for a slate of national candidates.

Once the manner of electing the president was settled, the question of his powers was much easier to decide. After all, if you believe that the procedures are fair and balanced, then you are more confident in assigning larger powers to the president within this system. Accordingly, the right to make treaties and the right to appoint lesser officials, originally reserved for the Senate, were given to the president "with the advice and consent of the Senate."

The President's Term of Office

Another issue was put to rest soon thereafter. George Washington, the unanimous choice of the electoral college to be the first president, firmly limited himself to two terms in office (1789–1797), and no president until Franklin D. Roosevelt (1933–1945) dared to run for more (though Ulysses S. Grant tried). In 1951 the Twenty-second Amendment to the Constitution was ratified, formally limiting all subsequent presidents to two terms. The remaining issues concerning the nature of the presidency, and especially the relations between the president and Congress, have been the subject of continuing dispute. The pattern of relationships that we see today is the result of

> **electoral college**   The people chosen to cast each state's votes in a presidential election. Each state can cast one electoral vote for each senator and representative it has. The District of Columbia has three electoral votes, even though it cannot elect a representative or senator.

an evolutionary process that has extended over more than two centuries.

The first problem was to establish the legitimacy of the presidency itself: that is, to ensure, if possible, public acceptance of the office, its incumbent, and its powers and to establish an orderly transfer of power from one incumbent to the next.

Today we take this for granted. When George W. Bush was inaugurated in January 2001 as our forty-third president, Bill Clinton, the forty-second, quietly left the White House. In the world today such an uneventful succession is unusual. In many nations a new chief executive comes to power with the aid of military force or as a result of political intrigue; his predecessor often leaves office disgraced, exiled, or dead. At the time that the Constitution was written, the Founders could only hope that an orderly transfer of power from one president to the next would occur. France had just undergone a bloody revolution; England in the not-too-distant past had beheaded a king; and in Poland the ruler was elected by a process so manifestly corrupt and so open to intrigue that Thomas Jefferson, in what may be the first example of ethnic humor in American politics, was led to refer to the proposed American presidency as a "bad edition of a Polish king."

Yet by the time Abraham Lincoln found himself at the helm of a nation plunged into a bitter, bloody civil war, fifteen presidents had been elected, served their time, and left office without a hint of force being used to facilitate the process and with the people accepting the process—if not admiring all the presidents. This orderly transfer of authority occurred despite passionate opposition and deeply divisive elections (such as that which brought Jefferson to power). And it did not happen by accident.

The First Presidents

Those who first served as president were among the most prominent men in the new nation, all active either in the movement for independence or in the Founding or in both. Of the first five presidents, four (all but John Adams) served two full terms. Washington and Monroe were not even opposed. The first administration had at the highest levels the leading spokesmen for all of the major viewpoints: Alexander Hamilton was Washington's secretary of the treasury (and was sympathetic to the urban commercial interests), and Thomas Jefferson was secretary of state (and more inclined toward rural, small-town, and farming views). Washington spoke out strongly against political parties, and though parties soon emerged, there was a stigma attached to them: many people believed that it was wrong to take advantage of divisions in the country, to organize deliberately to acquire political office, or to make leg-

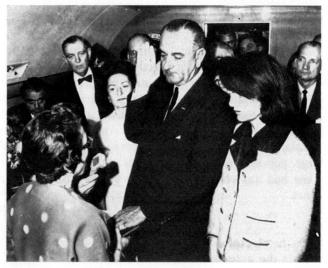

America has witnessed peaceful transfers of power not only between leaders of different parties (such as Woodrow Wilson and William Howard Taft in 1913), but also after a popular leader has been assassinated (Lyndon Johnson is sworn in after John F. Kennedy's death).

islation depend upon party advantage. As it turned out, this hostility to party (or "faction," as it was more commonly called) was unrealistic: parties are as natural to democracy as churches are to religion.

Establishing the legitimacy of the presidency in the early years was made easier by the fact that the national government had relatively little to do. It had, of course, to establish a sound currency and to settle the debt accrued during the Revolutionary War. The Treasury Department inevitably became the principal federal office, especially under the strong leadership of Hamilton. Relations with England and France were important—and difficult—but otherwise government took little time and few resources.

In appointing people to federal office, a general rule of "fitness" emerged: those appointed should have some standing in their communities and be well thought of by their neighbors. Appointments based on partisanship soon arose, but community stature could not be neglected.

The presidency was kept modest. Washington clearly had not sought the office and did not relish the exercise of its then modest powers. He traveled widely so that as many people as possible could see their new president. His efforts to establish a semiregal court etiquette were quickly rebuffed; the presidency was to be kept simple. Congress decided that not until after a president was dead might his likeness appear on a coin or on currency; no president until Eisenhower was given a pension on his retirement.

The president's relations with Congress were correct but not close. Washington appeared before the Senate to ask its advice on a proposed treaty with some Indian tribes. He got none and instead was politely told that the Senate would like to consider the matter in private. He declared that he would be "damned if he ever went there again," and he never did. Thus ended the responsibility of the Senate to "advise" the president. Vetoes were sometimes cast by the president, but sparingly, and only when the president believed that the law was not simply unwise but unconstitutional. Washington cast only two vetoes; Jefferson and Adams cast none.

The Jacksonians

At a time roughly corresponding to the presidency of Andrew Jackson (1829–1837), broad changes began to occur in American politics. These changes, together with the personality of Jackson himself,

President Andrew Jackson thought of himself as the "Tribune of the People," and he symbolized this by throwing a White House party that anyone could attend. Hundreds of people showed up and ate or carried away most of a 1,400-pound block of cheese.

altered the relations between president and Congress and the nature of presidential leadership. As so often happens, few people at the time Jackson took office had much sense of what his presidency would be like. Though he had been a member of the House of Representatives and of the Senate, he was elected as a military hero—and an apparently doddering one at that. Sixty-one years old and seemingly frail, he nonetheless used the powers of his office as no one before him had.

Jackson vetoed twelve acts of Congress, more than all his predecessors combined and more than any subsequent president until Andrew Johnson thirty years later. His vetoes were not simply on constitutional grounds but on policy ones: as the only official elected by the entire voting citizenry, he saw himself as the "Tribune of the People." None of his vetoes were overridden. He did not initiate many new policies, but he struck out against the ones that he did not like. He did so at a time when the size of the electorate was increasing rapidly, and new states, especially in the West, had entered the Union. (There were then twenty-four states in the Union, nearly twice the original number.)

Jackson demonstrated what could be done by a popular president. He did not shrink from conflict with Congress, and the tension between the two branches of government that was intended by the

HOW THINGS WORK

The Electoral College

Until November 2000, it was almost impossible to get a student interested in the electoral college. But in the 2000 presidential election Florida's electoral vote hung in the balance for weeks, with Bush finally winning it and (though he had fewer popular votes than Al Gore) the presidency.

Here are the essential facts: Each state gets electoral votes equal to the number of its senators and representatives (the District of Columbia also gets 3, even though it has no representatives in Congress). There are 538 electoral votes. To win, a candidate must receive at least half, or 270.

In all but two states, the candidate who wins the most popular votes wins all of the state's electoral votes. Maine and Nebraska have a different system. They allow electoral votes to be split by awarding some votes on the basis of a candidate's statewide total and some on the basis of how the candidate did in each congressional district.

The winning slates of electors assemble in their state capitals about six weeks after the election to cast their ballots. Ordinarily this is a pure formality. Occasionally, however, an elector will vote for a presidential candidate other than the one who carried the state. Such "faithless electors" have appeared in several elections since 1796. The state electoral ballots are opened and counted before a joint session of Congress during the first week of January. The candidate with a majority is declared elected.

If no candidate wins a majority, the House of Representatives chooses the president from among the three leading candidates, with each state casting one vote. By House rules, each state's vote is allotted to the candidate preferred by a majority of the state's House delegation. If there is a tie within a delegation, that state's vote is not counted.

The House has had to decide two presidential contests. In 1800 Thomas Jefferson and Aaron Burr tied in the electoral college because of a defect in the language of the Constitution—each state cast two electoral votes, without indicating which was for president and which for vice president. (Burr was supposed to be vice president, and after much maneuvering he was.) This problem was corrected by the Twelfth Amendment, ratified in 1804. The only House decision under the modern system was in 1824, when it chose John Quincy Adams over Andrew Jackson and William H. Crawford, even though Jackson had more electoral votes (and probably more popular votes) than his rivals.

Today the winner-take-all system in effect in forty-eight states makes it possible for a candidate to win at least 270 electoral votes without winning a majority of the popular votes. This happened in 2000, 1888, and 1876, and almost happened in 1960 and 1884. Today a candidate who carries the ten largest states wins 256 electoral votes, only 14 short of a presidential victory.

This means that the candidates have a strong incentive to campaign hard in big states they have a chance of winning. In 2000, Gore worked hard in California, New York, and Pennsylvania but pretty much ignored Texas, where Bush was a shoo-in. Bush campaigned hard in Florida, Illinois, and Ohio, but not so much in New York, where Gore was an easy winner.

But the electoral college can also help small states. South Dakota, for example, has 3 electoral votes (about 0.5 percent of the total), even though it casts only about 0.3 percent of the popular vote. South Dakota and other small states are thus overrepresented in the electoral college.

Most Americans would like to abolish the electoral college. But doing away with it entirely would have

Framers became intensified by the personalities of those in government: Jackson in the White House, and Henry Clay, Daniel Webster, and John Calhoun in Congress. These powerful figures walked the political stage at a time when bitter sectional conflicts— over slavery and commercial policies—were be-

ginning to split the country. Jackson, though he was opposed to a large and powerful federal government and wished to return somehow to the agrarian simplicities of Jefferson's time, was nonetheless a believer in a strong and independent presidency. This view, though obscured by nearly a century of subse-

Electoral Votes per State

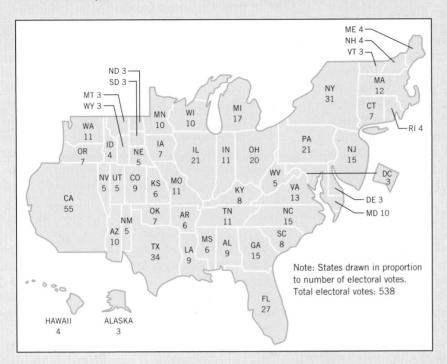

Note: States drawn in proportion to number of electoral votes. Total electoral votes: 538

some unforeseen effects. If we relied just on the popular vote, there would have to be a runoff election among the two leading candidates if neither got a majority because third-party candidates won a lot of votes. This would encourage the formation of third parties (we might have a Jesse Jackson party, a Pat Buchanan party, a Pat Robertson party, and a Ralph Nader party). Each third party would then be in a position to negotiate with one of the two major parties between the first election and the runoff about favors it wanted in return for its support. American presidential politics might come to look like the multiparty systems in France and Italy.

There are other changes that could be made. One is for each state to allocate its electoral votes proportional to the popular vote the candidates receive in that state. Voters in Colorado acted on that measure in November 2004, but that proposal failed. If every state did that, several past elections would have been decided in the House of Representatives because no candidate got a majority of the popular vote.

And the electoral college serves a larger purpose: it makes candidates worry about carrying states as well as popular votes, and so heightens the influence of states in national politics.

quent congressional dominance of national politics, was ultimately to triumph—for better or for worse.

The Reemergence of Congress

With the end of Jackson's second term, Congress quickly reestablished its power, and except for the

wartime presidency of Lincoln and brief flashes of presidential power under James Polk (1845–1849) and Grover Cleveland (1885–1889, 1893–1897), the presidency for a hundred years was the subordinate branch of the national government. Of the eight presidents who succeeded Jackson, two

(William H. Harrison and Zachary Taylor) died in office, and none of the others served more than one term. Schoolchildren, trying to memorize the list of American presidents, always stumble in this era of the "no-name" presidents. This is hardly a coincidence: Congress was the leading institution, struggling, unsuccessfully, with slavery and sectionalism.

It was also an intensely partisan era, a legacy of Jackson that lasted well into the twentieth century. Public opinion was closely divided. In nine of the seventeen presidential elections between the end of Jackson's term in 1837 and Theodore Roosevelt's election in 1904, the winning candidate received less than half the popular vote. Only two candidates (Lincoln in 1864 and Ulysses S. Grant in 1872) received more than 55 percent of the popular vote.

During this long period of congressional—and usually senatorial—dominance of national government, only Lincoln broke new ground for presidential power. Lincoln's expansive use of that power, like Jackson's, was totally unexpected. He was first elected in 1860 as a minority president, receiving less than 40 percent of the popular vote in a field of four candidates. Though a member of the new Republican party, he had been a member of the Whig party, a group that had stood for limiting presidential power. He had opposed America's entry into the Mexican War and had been critical of Jackson's use of executive authority. But as president during the Civil War, he made unprecedented use of the vague gift of powers in Article II of the Constitution, especially those that he felt were "implied" or "inherent" in the phrase "take care that the laws be faithfully executed" and in the express authorization for him to act as commander in chief. Lincoln raised an army, spent money, blockaded southern ports, temporarily suspended the writ of habeas corpus, and issued the Emancipation Proclamation to free the slaves—all without prior congressional approval. He justified this, as most Americans probably would have, by the emergency conditions created by civil war. In this he acted little differently from Thomas Jefferson, who while president waged undeclared war against various North African pirates.

After Lincoln, Congress reasserted its power and became, during Reconstruction and for many decades thereafter, the principal federal institution. But it had become abundantly clear that a national emergency could equip the president with great powers and that a popular and strong-willed president could expand his powers even without an emergency.

Except for the administrations of Theodore Roosevelt (1901–1909) and Woodrow Wilson (1913–1921), the president was, until the New Deal, at best a negative force—a source of opposition to Congress, not a source of initiative and leadership for it. Grover Cleveland was a strong personality, but for all his efforts he was able to do little more than veto bills that he did not like. He cast 414 vetoes—more than any other president until Franklin Roosevelt. A frequent target of his vetoes were bills to confer special pensions on Civil War veterans.

Today we are accustomed to thinking that the president formulates a legislative program to which Congress then responds, but until the 1930s the opposite was more the case. Congress ignored the initiatives of such presidents as Grover Cleveland, Rutherford Hayes, Chester Arthur, and Calvin Coolidge. Woodrow Wilson in 1913 was the first president since John Adams to deliver personally the State of the Union address, and he was one of the first to develop and argue for a presidential legislative program.

Our popular conception of the president as the central figure of national government, devising a legislative program and commanding a large staff of advisers, is very much a product of the modern era and of the enlarged role of government. In the past the presidency became powerful only during a national crisis (the Civil War, World War I) or because of an extraordinary personality (Andrew Jackson, Theodore Roosevelt, Woodrow Wilson). Since the 1930s, however, the presidency has been powerful no matter who occupied the office and whether or not there was a crisis. Because government now plays such an active role in our national life, the president is the natural focus of attention and the titular head of a huge federal administrative system (whether he is the real boss is another matter).

But the popular conception of the president as the central figure of national government belies the realities of present-day legislative-executive relations. During national policy-making from the Eisenhower years through the Reagan administration, Congress, not the president, often took the lead in setting the legislative agenda.[5] For example, the 1990 Clean Air Act, like the 1970 Clean Air Act before it, was born and bred mainly by congressional, not presidential, action. Indeed, administration officials played almost no role in the legislative process that culminated in these laws.[6] When President Bush signed the 1990 Clean Air Act or President Clinton signed the 1996

Welfare Reform Act, each took credit for it, but in fact both bills were designed by members of Congress, not by the president.[7] Likewise, although presidents dominated budget policy-making from the 1920s into the early 1970s, they no longer do. Instead, the "imperatives of the budgetary process have pushed congressional leaders to center stage."[8] Thus, as often as not, Congress proposes, the president disposes, and legislative-executive relations involve hard bargaining and struggle between these two branches of government.

☆ The Powers of the President

Though the president, unlike a prime minister, cannot command an automatic majority in the legislature, he does have some formidable, albeit vaguely defined, powers. These are mostly set forth in Article II of the Constitution and are of two sorts: those he can exercise in his own right without formal legislative approval, and those that require the consent of the Senate or of Congress as a whole.

■ Powers of the President Alone

- Serve as commander in chief of the armed forces
- Commission officers of the armed forces
- Grant reprieves and pardons for federal offenses (except impeachment)
- Convene Congress in special sessions
- Receive ambassadors
- Take care that the laws be faithfully executed
- Wield the "executive power"
- Appoint officials to lesser offices

■ Powers of the President That Are Shared with the Senate

- Make treaties
- Appoint ambassadors, judges, and high officials

■ Powers of the President That Are Shared with Congress as a Whole

- Approve legislation

Taken alone and interpreted narrowly, this list of powers is not very impressive. Obviously the president's authority as commander in chief is important, but literally construed, most of the other constitutional grants seem to provide for little more than a president who is chief clerk of the country. A hundred years after the Founding, that is about how matters appeared to even the most astute observers. In 1884 Woodrow Wilson wrote a book about American politics titled *Congressional Government*, in which he described the business of the president as "usually not much above routine," mostly "*mere* administration." The president might as well be an officer of the civil service. To succeed, he need only obey Congress and stay alive.[9]

But even as Wilson wrote, he was overlooking some examples of enormously powerful presidents, such as Lincoln, and was not sufficiently attentive to the potential for presidential power to be found in the more ambiguous clauses of the Constitution as well as in the political realities of American life. The president's authority as commander in chief has

A military officer carrying "the football," the briefcase containing the secret codes the president can use to launch a nuclear attack.

★ HOW THINGS WORK ★

The President: Qualifications and Benefits

Qualifications

- A natural-born citizen (can be born abroad of parents who are American citizens)
- Thirty-five years of age
- A resident of the United States for at least fourteen years (but not necessarily the fourteen years just preceding the election)

Benefits

- A nice house
- A salary of $400,000 per year (taxable)
- An expense account of $50,000 per year (tax-free)
- Travel expenses of $100,000 per year (tax-free)
- A pension, on retirement, equal to the pay of a cabinet member (taxable)
- Staff support and Secret Service protection on leaving the presidency
- A White House staff of 400 to 500 persons
- A place in the country—Camp David
- A personal airplane—Air Force One
- A fine chef

grown—especially, but not only, in wartime—to encompass not simply the direction of the military forces, but also the management of the economy and the direction of foreign affairs as well. A quietly dramatic reminder of the awesome implications of the president's military powers occurs at the precise instant that a new president assumes office. An army officer carrying a locked briefcase moves from the side of the outgoing president to the side of the new one. In the briefcase are the secret codes and orders that permit the president to authorize the launching of American nuclear weapons.

The president's duty to "take care that the laws be faithfully executed" has become one of the most elastic phrases in the Constitution. By interpreting this broadly, Grover Cleveland was able to use federal troops to break a labor strike in the 1890s, and Dwight Eisenhower was able to send troops to help integrate a public school in Little Rock, Arkansas, in 1957.

The greatest source of presidential power, however, is not found in the Constitution at all but in politics and public opinion. Increasingly since the 1930s, Congress has passed laws that confer on the executive branch broad grants of authority to achieve some general goals, leaving it up to the president and his deputies to define the regulations and programs that will actually be put into effect. In Chapter 15 we shall see how this delegation of legislative power to the president has contributed to the growth of the bureaucracy. Moreover, the American people—always in times of crisis, but increasingly as an everyday matter—look to the president for leadership and hold him responsible for a large and growing portion of our national affairs. The public thinks, wrongly, that the presidency is the "first branch" of government.

★ The Office of the President

It was not until 1857 that the president was allowed to have a private secretary paid for with public funds, and it was not until after the assassination of President McKinley in 1901 that the president was given a Secret Service bodyguard. He was not able to submit a single presidential budget until after 1921, when the Budget and Accounting Act was passed and the Bureau of the Budget (now called the Office of Management and Budget) was created. Grover Cleveland personally answered the White House telephone, and Abraham Lincoln often answered his own mail.

Today, of course, the president has hundreds of people assisting him, and the trappings of power—helicopters, guards, limousines—are plainly visible.

The White House staff has grown enormously. (Just how big the staff is, no one knows. Presidents like to pretend that the White House is not the large bureaucracy that it in fact has become.) Add to this the opportunities for presidential appointments to the cabinet, the courts, and various agencies, and the resources at the disposal of the president would appear to be awesome. That conclusion is partly true and partly false, or at least misleading, and for a simple reason. If the president was once helpless for lack of assistance, he now confronts an army of assistants so large that it constitutes a bureaucracy that he has difficulty controlling (see Figure 14.1).

The ability of a presidential assistant to affect the president is governed by the rule of propinquity: in general, power is wielded by people who are in the room when a decision is made. Presidential appointments can thus be classified in terms of their proximity, physical and political, to the president. There are three degrees of propinquity: the White House Office, the Executive Office, and the cabinet.

The White House Office

The president's closest assistants have offices in the White House, usually in the West Wing of that building. Their titles often do not reveal the functions that they actually perform: "counsel," "counselor," "assistant to the president," "special assistant," "special consultant," and so forth. The actual titles vary from one administration to another, but in general the men and women who hold them oversee the political and policy interests of the president. As part of the president's personal staff, these aides do not have to be confirmed by the Senate; the president can hire and fire them at will. In 2001 the Bush White House had four hundred staff members and a budget of $35.4 million.

There are essentially three ways in which a president can organize his personal staff—through the "pyramid," "circular," and "ad hoc" methods. In a **pyramid structure,** used by Eisenhower, Nixon, Reagan, Bush, and (after a while) Clinton, most assistants report through a hierarchy to a chief of staff, who then deals directly with the president. In a **circular structure,** used by Carter, cabinet secretaries and assistants report directly to the president. In an **ad hoc structure,** used for a while by President Clinton, task forces, committees, and informal groups of friends and advisers deal directly with the president. For example, the Clinton administration's health care

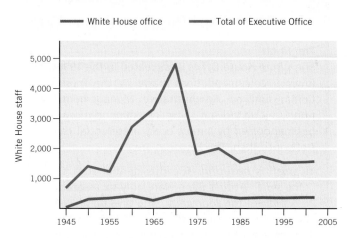

Figure 14.1 Growth of the White House Staff, 1945–2002

Note: Executive Office includes White House Office plus Office of Management and Budget, Council of Economic Advisers, National Security Council, Office of Science and Technology, Office of Administration, Special Representative for Trade Negotiations, and Domestic Council. *Source:* Harold W. Stanley and Richard G. Niemi, *Vital Statistics on American Politics, 2003–2004.* (Washington, D.C.: Congressional Quarterly Press, 2003), 254–255.

policy planning was spearheaded not by Health and Human Services secretary Donna E. Shalala, but by First Lady Hillary Rodham Clinton and a White House adviser, Ira Magaziner. Likewise, its initiative to reform the federal bureaucracy (the National Performance Review) was led not by Office of Management and Budget director Leon E. Panetta, but by an adviser to Vice President Gore, Elaine Kamarck.[10]

It is common for presidents to mix methods; for example, Franklin Roosevelt alternated between the circular and ad hoc methods in the conduct of his domestic policy and sometimes employed a pyramid

---

pyramid structure   A president's subordinates report to him through a clear chain of command headed by a chief of staff.

circular structure   Several of the president's assistants report directly to him.

ad hoc structure   Several subordinates, cabinet officers, and committees report directly to the president on different matters.

HOW THINGS WORK

The Myth and Reality of the White House Office

The Myth

The White House Office was created in the 1930s following recommendations made by the President's Commission on Administrative Management. The principles underlying those recommendations have been endorsed by almost every presidential chief of staff since then. The key ones are:

1. *Small is beautiful.* The presidential staff should be small. At first there were only six assistants.
2. *A passion for anonymity.* The president's personal assistants should stay out of the limelight.
3. *Honest brokers.* The presidential staff should not make decisions for the president; it should only coordinate the flow of information to the president.

The Reality

Increasingly the operations of the White House Office seem to reflect almost the exact opposite of these principles.

1. *Big is better.* The White House staff has grown enormously in size. Hundreds now work there.
2. *Get out front.* Key White House staffers have become household words—Henry Kissinger (under Nixon and Ford), H. R. Haldeman (under Nixon), Hamilton Jordan (under Carter), Howard Baker (under Reagan), George Stephanopoulos (under Clinton), and Karl Rove (under G.W. Bush).
3. *Be in charge.* Cabinet officers regularly complain that White House staffers are shutting them out and making all the important decisions. Congressional investigations have revealed the power of such White House aides as Haldeman, John Poindexter, and Lieutenant Colonel Oliver North.

Why the Gap Between Myth and Reality?

The answer is—the people and the government. The people expect much more from presidents today; no president can afford to say, "We're too busy here to worry about that." The government is much more complex, and so leadership requires more resources. Even conservatives such as Ronald Reagan have been activist presidents.

Source: Adapted from Samuel Kernell and Samuel L. Popkin, eds., *Chief of Staff* (Berkeley: University of California Press, 1986), 193–232.

structure when dealing with foreign affairs and military policy. Taken individually, each method of organization has advantages and disadvantages. A pyramid structure provides for an orderly flow of information and decisions, but does so at the risk of isolating or misinforming the president. The circular method has the virtue of giving the president a great deal of information, but at the price of confusion and conflict among cabinet secretaries and assistants. An ad hoc structure allows great flexibility, minimizes bureaucratic inertia, and generates ideas and information from disparate channels, but it risks cutting the president off from the government officials who are ultimately responsible for translating presidential decisions into policy proposals and administrative action.

All presidents claim that they are open to many sources of advice, and some presidents try to guarantee that openness by using the circular method of staff organization. President Carter liked to describe his office as a wheel with himself as the hub and his several assistants as spokes. But most presidents discover, as did Carter, that the difficulty of managing the large White House bureaucracy and of conserving their own limited supply of time and energy makes it necessary for them to rely heavily on one or two key subordinates. Carter, in July 1979, dramatically altered the White House staff organization by elevating Hamilton Jordan to the post of chief of staff, with the job of coordinating the work of the other staff assistants.

At first, President Reagan adopted a compromise between the circle and the pyramid, putting the White House under the direction of three key aides. At the beginning of his second term in 1985, however, the president shifted to a pyramid, placing all his assistants under a single chief of staff. Clinton began with an ad hoc system and then changed to one more like a pyramid. Each assistant has, of course, others working for him or her, sometimes a large number. There are, at a slightly lower level of status, "special assistants to the president" for various purposes. (Being "special" means, paradoxically, being less important.)

Typically senior White House staff members are drawn from the ranks of the president's campaign staff—longtime associates in whom he has confidence. A few members, however, will be experts brought in after the campaign: such was the case, for example, with Henry Kissinger, a former Harvard professor who became President Nixon's assistant for national security affairs. The offices that these men and women occupy are often small and crowded (Kissinger's was not much bigger than the one that he had while a professor at Harvard), but their occupants willingly put up with any discomfort in exchange for the privilege (and the power) of being *in* the White House. The arrangement of offices—their size, and especially their proximity to the president's Oval Office—is a good measure of the relative influence of the people in them.

To an outsider, the amount of jockeying among the top staff for access to the president may seem comical or even perverse. The staff attaches enormous significance to whose office is closest to the president's, who can see him on a daily as opposed to a weekly basis, who can get an appointment with the president and who cannot, and who has a right to see documents and memoranda just before they go to the Oval Office. To be sure, there is ample grist here for Washington political novels. But there is also something important at stake: it is not simply a question of power plays and ego trips. Who can see the president and who sees and "signs off" on memoranda going to the president affect in important ways who influences policy and thus whose goals and beliefs become embedded in policy.

For example, if a memo from a secretary of the treasury who believes in free trade can go directly to the president, the president may be more likely to support free trade (low tariffs). On the other hand, if

that memo must be routed through the office of the assistant to the president for political affairs, who is worried about the adverse effects of foreign competition on jobs in the American steel industry because the votes of steelworkers are important to the president's reelection campaign, then the president may be led to support higher tariffs.

The Executive Office of the President

Agencies in the Executive Office report directly to the president and perform staff services for him but are not located in the White House itself. Their members may or may not enjoy intimate contact with him; some agencies are rather large bureaucracies. The top positions in these organizations are filled by presidential appointment, but unlike the White House staff positions, these appointments must be confirmed by the Senate.

The principal agencies in the Executive Office are:

- Office of Management and Budget (OMB)
- Director of National Intelligence (DNI)
- Council of Economic Advisers (CEA)
- Office of Personnel Management (OPM)
- Office of the U.S. Trade Representative

Of all the agencies in the Executive Office of the President, perhaps the most important in terms of the president's need for assistance in administering the federal government is the Office of Management and Budget. First called the Bureau of the Budget when it was created in 1921, it became OMB in 1970 to reflect its broader responsibilities. Today it does considerably more than assemble and analyze the figures that go each year into the national budget that the president submits to Congress. It also studies the organization and operations of the executive branch, devises plans for reorganizing various departments and agencies, develops ways of getting better information about government programs, and reviews proposals that cabinet departments want included in the president's legislative program.

OMB has a staff of over five hundred people, almost all career civil servants, many of high professional skill and substantial experience. Traditionally OMB has been a nonpartisan agency—experts serving all presidents, without regard to party or ideology. In recent administrations, however, OMB has played a major role in advocating policies rather than merely analyzing them. David Stockman, President Reagan's OMB director, was the primary architect of the 1981 and 1985 budget cuts that were proposed by the president and enacted by Congress. Stockman's proposals were often adopted over the objections of the affected department heads.

The Cabinet

The **cabinet** is a product of tradition and hope. At one time the heads of the federal departments met regularly with the president to discuss matters, and some people, especially those critical of strong presidents, would like to see this kind of collegial decision-making reestablished. But in fact this role of the cabinet is largely a fiction. Indeed, the Constitution does not even mention the cabinet (though the Twenty-fifth Amendment implicitly defines it as consisting of "the principal offices of the executive departments"). When Washington tried to get his cabinet members to work together, its two strongest members—Alexander Hamilton and Thomas Jefferson—spent most of their time feuding. The cabinet, as a presidential committee, did not work any better for John Adams or Abraham Lincoln, for Franklin Roosevelt or John Kennedy. Dwight Eisenhower is almost the only modern president who came close to making the cabinet a truly deliberative body: he gave it a large staff, held regular meetings, and listened to opinions expressed there. But even under Eisenhower, the cabinet did not have much influence over presidential decisions, nor did it help him gain more power over the government.

By custom, cabinet officers are the heads of the fifteen major executive departments. These departments, together with the dates of their creation and the approximate number of their employees, are given in Table 14.1. The order of their creation is unimportant except in terms of protocol: where one sits at cabinet meetings is determined by the age of the department that one heads. Thus the secretary of state sits next to the president on one side and the secretary of the treasury next to him on the other. Down at the foot of the table are found the heads of the newer departments.

The president appoints or directly controls vastly more members of his cabinet departments than does the British prime minister (see Table 14.2). The rea-

---

cabinet The heads of the fifteen executive branch departments of the federal government.

Table 14.1 The Cabinet Departments

Department	Created	Approximate Employment (2000)
State	1789	27,000
Treasury	1789	142,700
Defense[a]	1947	673,500
Justice	1789	126,300
Interior	1849	68,000
Agriculture[b]	1889	99,300
Commerce	1913	45,000
Labor	1913	16,100
Health and Human Services[c]	1953	62,700
Housing and Urban Development	1965	10,300
Transportation	1966	63,900
Energy	1977	15,700
Education	1979	4,700
Veterans Affairs	1989	220,200
Homeland Security	2002	180,000

[a]Formerly the War Department, created in 1789. Figures are for civilians only.

[b]Agriculture Department created in 1862; made part of cabinet in 1889.

[c]Originally Health, Education and Welfare; reorganized in 1979.

Source: Statistical Abstract of the United States, 2003, Table 500, and data from the Department of Homeland Security.

---

son is simple: the president must struggle with Congress for control of these agencies, while the prime minister has no rival branch of government that seeks this power. Presidents get more appointments than do prime ministers to make up for what the separation of powers denies them.

This abundance of political appointments, however, does not give the president ample power over the departments. The secretary of Health and Human Services (HHS) reports to the president and has a few hundred political appointees to assist him or her in responding to the president's wishes. But the secretary of HHS heads an agency with over 65,000 employees, 11 operating divisions, hundreds of grant-making programs, and a budget of more than $460 billion. Likewise, the secretary of Housing and Urban Development (HUD) spends most of his or her time on departmental business and vastly less on talking to the president. It is hardly surprising that the secretary is largely a representative of HUD

Table 14.2	Number of Political Appointments in Cabinet Departments	
Department	**Political Appointees***
Agriculture	412
Commerce	221
Defense	601
Education	205
Energy	441
Health and Human Services	333
Housing and Urban Development	142
Interior	228
Justice	459
State	453
Transportation	248
Treasury	204
Veterans Affairs	319

Note: Department of Homeland Security is omitted for lack of data.

*All noncompetitive appointments.

Source: Committee on Governmental Affairs, United States Senate, *Policy and Supporting Positions,* November 8, 2000.

to the president than his representative to HUD. And no one should be surprised that the secretary of HUD rarely finds much to talk about with the secretary of defense at cabinet meetings.

Having the power to make these appointments does give the president one great advantage: he has a lot of opportunities to reward friends and political supporters. In the Education Department, for example, President Clinton found jobs for onetime mayors, senators, state legislators, and campaign aides.

Independent Agencies, Commissions, and Judgeships

The president also appoints people to four dozen or so agencies and commissions that are not considered part of the cabinet and that by law often have a quasi-independent status. The difference between an "executive" and an "independent" agency is not precise. In general, it means that the heads of executive agencies serve at the pleasure of the president and can be removed at his discretion. On the other hand, the heads of many independent agencies serve for fixed terms of office and can be removed only "for cause."

The president can also appoint federal judges, subject to the consent of the Senate. Judges serve for life unless they are removed by impeachment and conviction. The reason for the special barriers to the removal of judges is that they represent an independent branch of government as defined by the Constitution, and limits on presidential removal powers are necessary to preserve that independence.

One new feature of appointing top government officials is the increasing use of "acting" appointments. An acting appointee holds office until the Senate acts on his or her nomination. In 1998 acting officials held one-fifth of all of the Clinton administration's cabinet-level (or subcabinet-level)* jobs. Some were in office for many months. Many senators feel that this violates their right to consent to appointments and in particular violates the Vacancies Act passed in 1868. That law limits acting appointees to 120 days in office. If the Senate takes no action during those 120 days, the acting official may stay in office until he or she, or someone else, is confirmed for the post. Administration officials defend the practice as necessary given the slow pace of confirmations; senators attack it as an opportunity for a president to fill up his administration with unconfirmed officials.

☆ Who Gets Appointed

As we have seen, a president can make a lot of appointments, but he rarely knows more than a few of the people whom he does appoint.

Unlike cabinet members in a parliamentary system, the president's cabinet officers and their principal deputies usually have not served with the chief executive in the legislature. Instead they come from private business, universities, "think tanks," foundations, law firms, labor unions, and the ranks of former and present members of Congress as well as past state and local government officials. A president is fortunate if most cabinet members turn out to agree with him on major policy questions. President Reagan made a special effort to ensure that his cabinet members were ideologically in tune with him, but even so Secretary of State Alexander Haig soon got

---

Subcabinet refers to under secretary, deputy secretary, and assistant secretaries in each cabinet department.

★ HOW THINGS WORK ★

Federal Agencies

The following agencies are classified by whether the president has unlimited or limited right of removal.

"Executive" Agencies
Head can be removed at any time.

Action
Arms Control and Disarmament Agency
Commission on Civil Rights
Energy Research and Development Agency
Environmental Protection Agency
Federal Mediation and Conciliation Service
General Services Administration
National Aeronautics and Space Administration
Postal Service
Small Business Administration
All cabinet departments
Executive Office of the President

"Independent" or "Quasi-Independent" Agencies
Members serve for a fixed term.

Federal Reserve Board (14 years)
Consumer Product Safety Commission (6 years)
Equal Employment Opportunity Commission (5 years)
Federal Communications Commission (7 years)
Federal Deposit Insurance Corporation (6 years)
Federal Energy Regulatory Commission (5 years)
Federal Maritime Commission (5 years)
Federal Trade Commission (7 years)
National Labor Relations Board (5 years)
National Science Foundation (6 years)
Securities and Exchange Commission (5 years)
Tennessee Valley Authority (9 years)

---

into a series of quarrels with senior members of the White House staff and had to resign.

The men and women appointed to the cabinet and to the subcabinet will usually have had some prior federal experience. One study of over a thousand such appointments made by five presidents (Franklin Roosevelt through Lyndon Johnson) found that about 85 percent of the cabinet, subcabinet, and independent-agency appointees had some prior federal experience. In fact, most were in government service (at the federal, state, or local levels) just before they received their cabinet or subcabinet appointment.[11] Clearly the executive branch is not, in general, run by novices.

Many of these appointees are what Richard Neustadt has called "in-and-outers": people who alternate between jobs in the federal government and ones in the private sector, especially in law firms and in universities. Donald Rumsfeld, before becoming secretary of defense to President George W. Bush, had been secretary of defense and chief of staff under President Ford and before that a member of Congress. Between his Ford and Bush services, he

was an executive in a large pharmaceutical company. This pattern is quite different from that of parliamentary systems, where all the cabinet officers come from the legislature and are typically full-time career politicians.

At one time the cabinet had in it many people with strong political followings of their own—former senators and governors and powerful local party leaders. Under Franklin Roosevelt, Truman, and Kennedy, the postmaster general was the president's campaign manager. George Washington, Abraham Lincoln, and other presidents had to contend with cabinet members who were powerful figures in their own right: Alexander Hamilton and Thomas Jefferson worked with Washington; Simon Cameron (a Pennsylvania political boss) and Salmon P. Chase (formerly governor of Ohio) worked for—and against—Lincoln. Before 1824 the post of secretary of state was regarded as a steppingstone to the presidency; and after that at least ten persons ran for president who had been either secretary of state or ambassador to a foreign country.[12]

Of late, however, a tendency has developed for presidents to place in their cabinets people known for

Secretary of Labor Frances Perkins (left), appointed by President Franklin Roosevelt, was the first woman cabinet member. When Condoleezza Rice was made secretary of state by President Bush, she became the first African American woman to hold that key post.

their expertise or administrative experience rather than for their political following. This is in part because political parties are now so weak that party leaders can no longer demand a place in the cabinet and in part because presidents want (or think they want) "experts." A remarkable illustration of this is the number of people with Ph.D.'s who have entered the cabinet. President Nixon, who supposedly did not like Harvard professors, appointed two—Henry Kissinger and Daniel Patrick Moynihan—to important posts; Gerald Ford added a third, John Dunlop.

A president's desire to appoint experts who do not have independent political power is modified—but not supplanted—by his need to recognize various politically important groups, regions, and organizations. Since Robert Weaver became the first African American to serve in the cabinet (as secretary of HUD under President Johnson), it is clear that it would be quite costly for a president *not* to have one or more blacks in his cabinet. The secretary of labor must be acceptable to the AFL-CIO, the secretary of agriculture to at least some organized farmers. President George W. Bush, like President Clinton, appointed many women and minorities to his cabinet. Colin Powell became Bush's secretary of state and Con-

doleezza Rice, also an African American, his national security adviser and later, his secretary of state.

Because political considerations must be taken into account in making cabinet and agency appointments and because any head of a large organization will tend to adopt the perspective of that organization, there is an inevitable tension—even a rivalry—between the White House staff and the department heads. Staff members see themselves as extensions of the president's personality and policies; department heads see themselves as repositories of expert knowledge (often knowledge of why something will not work as the president hopes). White House staffers, many of them young men and women in their twenties or early thirties with little executive experience, will call department heads, often persons in their fifties with substantial executive experience, and tell them that "the president wants" this or that or that "the president asked me to tell you" one thing or another. Department heads try to conceal their irritation and then maneuver for some delay so that they can develop their own counterproposals. On the other hand, when department heads call a White House staff person and ask to see the president, unless they are one of the privileged few in whom the

Presidents

Only divorced president	Ronald Reagan
Only bachelor president	James Buchanan
Three presidents who died on the Fourth of July	Thomas Jefferson (1826) John Adams (1826) James Monroe (1831)
The shortest presidential term	William Henry Harrison (1 month)
The longest presidential term	Franklin D. Roosevelt (12 years and 1 month)
The youngest president when inaugurated	Theodore Roosevelt (42)
The oldest president when inaugurated	Ronald Reagan (69)
First president born in a hospital	Jimmy Carter
First presidential automobile	Owned by William Howard Taft
Only former presidents elected to Congress	John Quincy Adams (to House) and Andrew Johnson (to Senate)
Only president who never attended school	Andrew Johnson

president has special confidence, they are often told that "the president can't be bothered with that" or "the president doesn't have time to see you."

☆ Presidential Character

Every president brings to the White House a distinctive personality; the way the White House is organized and run will reflect that personality. Moreover, the public will judge the president not only in terms of what he accomplished, but also in terms of its perception of his character. Thus personality plays a more important role in explaining the presidency than it does in explaining Congress.

Dwight Eisenhower brought an orderly, military style to the White House. He was accustomed to delegating authority and to having careful and complete staff work done for him by trained specialists. Though critics often accused him of having a bumbling, incoherent manner of speaking, in fact much of that was a public disguise—a strategy for avoiding being pinned down in public on matters where he wished to retain freedom of action. His private papers reveal a very different Eisenhower—sharp, precise, deliberate.

John Kennedy brought a very different style to the presidency. He projected the image of a bold, articulate, and amusing leader who liked to surround himself with talented amateurs. Instead of clear, hierarchical lines of authority, there was a pattern of personal rule and an atmosphere of improvisation. Kennedy did not hesitate to call very junior subordinates directly and tell them what to do, bypassing the chain of command.

Lyndon Johnson was a master legislative strategist who had risen to be majority leader of the Senate on the strength of his ability to persuade other politicians in face-to-face encounters. He was a consummate deal maker who, having been in Washington for thirty years before becoming president, knew everybody and everything. As a result he tried to make every decision himself. But the style that served him well in political negotiations did not serve him well in speaking to the country at large, especially when trying to retain public support for the war in Vietnam.

Richard Nixon was a highly intelligent man with a deep knowledge of and interest in foreign policy, coupled with a deep suspicion of the media, his political rivals, and the federal bureaucracy. In contrast to Johnson, he disliked personal confrontations and tended to shield himself behind an elaborate staff system. Distrustful of the cabinet agencies, he tried first to centralize power in the White House and then to put into key cabinet posts former White House aides loyal to him. Like Johnson, his personality made it difficult for him to mobilize popular support. Eventually he was forced to resign under the threat of impeachment arising out of his role in the Watergate scandal.

Gerald Ford, before being appointed vice president, had spent his political life in Congress and was at home with the give-and-take, discussion-oriented procedures of that body. He was also a genial man who liked talking to people. Thus he preferred the circular to the pyramid system of White House organization. But this meant that many decisions were made in a disorganized fashion in which key people—and sometimes key problems—were not taken into account.

Jimmy Carter was an outsider to Washington and boasted of it. A former Georgia governor, he was determined not to be "captured" by Washington insiders. He also was a voracious reader with a wide range of interests and an appetite for detail. These dispositions led him to try to do many things and to do them personally. Like Ford, he began with a circular structure; unlike Ford, he based his decisions on reading countless memos and asking detailed questions. His advisers finally decided that he was trying to do too much in too great detail, and toward the end of his term he shifted to a pyramid structure.

Ronald Reagan was also an outsider, a former governor of California. But unlike Carter, he wanted to set the broad directions of his administration and leave the details to others. He gave wide latitude to subordinates and to cabinet officers, within the framework of an emphasis on lower taxes, less domestic spending, a military buildup, and a tough line with the Soviet Union. He was a superb leader of public opinion, earning the nickname "The Great Communicator."

George H.W. Bush lacked Reagan's speaking skills and was much more of a hands-on manager. Drawing on his extensive experience in the federal government (he had been vice president, director of the CIA, ambassador to the United Nations, representative to China, and a member of the House), Bush made decisions on the basis of personal contacts with key foreign leaders and Washington officials.

Bill Clinton, like Carter, paid a lot of attention to public policy and preferred informal, ad hoc arrangements for running his office. Unlike Carter, he was an effective speaker who could make almost any idea sound plausible. He was elected as a centrist Democrat but immediately pursued liberal policies such as comprehensive health insurance. When those failed and the Republicans won control of Congress in 1994, Clinton became a centrist again. His sexual affairs became the object of major investigations, and he was impeached by the House but acquitted by the Senate.

George W. Bush, the forty-third president, entered office as an outsider from Texas, but he was an outsider with a difference: his father had served as the forty-first president of the United States, his late

Three presidents—George H.W. Bush, Bill Clinton, and Jimmy Carter—at a summit to encourage volunteer activity.

paternal grandfather had served as a United States senator from Connecticut, and he won the presidency only after the U.S. Supreme Court halted a recount of ballots in Florida, where his brother was governor. During the campaign, he focused almost entirely on domestic issues, especially cutting taxes and reforming education. A deeply religious man, he talked openly about how he had stopped excessive drinking only after he had found God. He ran as a "compassionate conservative" concerned about America's needy children and families. Bush, who had earned an advanced degree in business administration from Harvard, ran a very tight White House ship, insisting that meetings run on time and that press contacts be strictly controlled. He turned back public doubts about his intellect through self-deprecating humor. Following the terrorist attack on America on September 11, 2001, his agenda shifted almost entirely to foreign and military affairs, the "war on terror," and the issue of homeland security.

★ The Power to Persuade

The sketchy constitutional powers given the president, combined with the lack of an assured legislative majority, mean that he must rely heavily on persuasion if he is to accomplish much. Here the Constitution gives him some advantages: he and the vice president are the only officials elected by the whole nation, and he is the ceremonial head of state as well as the chief executive of the government. The president can use his national constituency and ceremonial duties to enlarge his power, but he must do so quickly: the second half of his first term in office will be devoted to running for reelection, especially if he faces opposition for his own party's nomination (as was the case with Carter and Ford).

The Three Audiences

The president's persuasive powers are aimed at three audiences. The first, and often the most important, is his Washington, D.C., audience of fellow politicians and leaders. As Richard Neustadt points out in his book *Presidential Power*, a president's reputation among his Washington colleagues is of great importance in affecting how much deference his views receive and thus how much power he can wield.[13] If a president is thought to be "smart," "sure of himself," "cool," "on top of things," or "shrewd," and thus "effective," he *will* be effective. Franklin Roosevelt had that reputation, and so did Lyndon Johnson, at least for his first few years in office. Truman, Ford, and Carter often did not have that reputation, and they lost ground accordingly. Power, like beauty, exists largely in the eye of the beholder.

A second audience is composed of party activists and officeholders outside Washington—the partisan grassroots. These persons want the president to exemplify their principles, trumpet their slogans, appeal to their fears and hopes, and help them get reelected. Since, as we explained in Chapter 9, partisan activists increasingly have an ideological orientation toward national politics, these people will expect "their" president to make fire-and-brimstone

bully pulpit   The president's use of his prestige and visibility to guide or enthuse the American public.

speeches that confirm in them a shared sense of purpose and, incidentally, help them raise money from contributors to state and local campaigns.

The third audience is "the public." But of course that audience is really many publics, each with a different view or set of interests. A president on the campaign trail speaks boldly of what he will accomplish; a president in office speaks quietly of the problems that must be overcome. Citizens are often irritated at the apparent tendency of officeholders, including the president, to sound mealy-mouthed and equivocal. But it is easy to criticize the cooking when you haven't been the cook. A president learns quickly that his every utterance will be scrutinized closely by the media and by organized groups here and abroad, and his errors of fact, judgment, timing, or even inflection will be immediately and forcefully pointed out. Given the risks of saying too much, it is a wonder that presidents say anything at all.

Presidents have made fewer and fewer impromptu remarks in the years since Franklin Roosevelt held office and have instead relied more and more on prepared speeches from which political errors can be removed in advance. Hoover and Roosevelt held six or seven press conferences each month, but every president from Nixon through Clinton has held barely one a month. Instead modern presidents make formal speeches. A president's use of these speeches is often called the **bully pulpit,** a phrase that means taking advantage of the prestige and visibility of the presidency to try to guide or mobilize the American people.

Popularity and Influence

The object of all this talk is to convert personal popularity into congressional support for the president's legislative programs (and improved chances for reelection). It is not obvious, of course, why Congress should care about a president's popularity. After all, as we saw in Chapter 13, most members of Congress are secure in their seats, and few need fear any "party bosses" who might deny them renomination. Moreover, the president cannot ordinarily provide credible electoral rewards or penalties to members of Congress. By working for their defeat in the 1938 congressional election, President Roosevelt attempted to "purge" members of Congress who opposed his program, but he failed. Nor does presidential support help a particular member of Congress: most representatives win reelection anyway, and the few who

Year	President	Party	House	Senate

Table 14.3 Partisan Gains or Losses in Congress in Presidential Election Years

Gains or Losses of President's Party In:

Year	President	Party	House	Senate
1932	Roosevelt	Dem.	+90	+9
1936	Roosevelt	Dem.	+12	+7
1940	Roosevelt	Dem.	+7	−3
1944	Roosevelt	Dem.	+24	−2
1948	Truman	Dem.	+75	+9
1952	Eisenhower	Rep.	+22	+1
1956	Eisenhower	Rep.	−3	−1
1960	Kennedy	Dem.	−20	+1
1964	Johnson	Dem.	+37	+1
1968	Nixon	Rep.	+5	+7
1972	Nixon	Rep.	+12	−2
1976	Carter	Dem.	+1	+1
1980	Reagan	Rep.	+33	+12
1984	Reagan	Rep.	+16	−2
1988	Bush	Rep.	−3	−1
1992	Clinton	Dem.	−9	+1
1996	Clinton	Dem.	+9	−2
2000	Bush	Rep.	−3	−4
2004	Bush	Rep.	+4	+4

Sources: Updated from Congressional Quarterly, *Guide to U.S. Elections*, 928; and *Congress and the Nation*, vol. 4 (1973–1976), 28.

Careful studies of voter attitudes and of how presidential and congressional candidates fare in the same districts suggest that, whatever may once have been the influence of coattails, their effect has declined in recent years and is quite small today. The weakening of party loyalty and of party organizations, combined with the enhanced ability of members of Congress to build secure relations with their constituents, has tended to insulate congressional elections from presidential ones. When voters choose as members of Congress people of the same party as an incoming president, they probably do so out of desire for a general change and as an adverse judgment about the outgoing party's performance as a whole, not because they want to supply the new president with members of Congress favorable to him.[14] The big increase in Republican senators and representatives that accompanied the election of Ronald Reagan in 1980 was probably as much a result of the unpopularity of the outgoing president and the circumstances of various local races as it was of Reagan's coattails.

Nonetheless, a president's personal popularity may have a significant effect on how much of his program Congress passes, even if it does not affect the reelection chances of those members of Congress. Though they do not fear a president who threatens to campaign against them (or cherish one who promises to support them), members of Congress do have a sense that it is risky to oppose too adamantly the policies of a popular president. Politicians share a sense of a common fate: they tend to rise or fall together. Statistically a president's popularity, as measured by the Gallup poll (see Figure 14.2), is associated with the proportion of his legislative proposals that are approved by Congress (see Figure 14.3). Other things being equal, the more popular the president, the higher the proportion of his bills that Congress will pass.

But use these figures with caution. How successful a president is with Congress depends not just on the numbers reported here, but on a lot of other factors as well. First, he can be "successful" on a big bill or on a trivial one. If he is successful on a lot of small matters and never on a big one, the measure of presidential victories does not tell us much. Second, a president can keep his victory score high by not taking a position on any controversial measure. (President Carter made his views known on only 22 percent of the House votes, while President Eisenhower made his views known on 56 percent of those votes.) Third, a

are in trouble are rarely saved by presidential intervention. When President Reagan campaigned hard for Republican senatorial candidates in 1986, he, too, failed to have much impact.

For a while scholars thought that congressional candidates might benefit from the president's coattails: they might ride into office on the strength of the popularity of a president of their own party. It is true, as can be seen from Table 14.3, that a winning president will find that his party's strength in Congress increases.

But there are good reasons to doubt whether the pattern observed in Table 14.3 is the result of presidential coattails. For one thing, there are some exceptions. Eisenhower won 57.4 percent of the vote in 1956, but the Republicans lost seats in the House and Senate. Kennedy won in 1960, but the Democrats lost seats in the House and gained but one in the Senate. When Nixon was reelected in 1972 with one of the largest majorities in history, the Republicans lost seats in the Senate.

Figure 14.2   Presidential Popularity

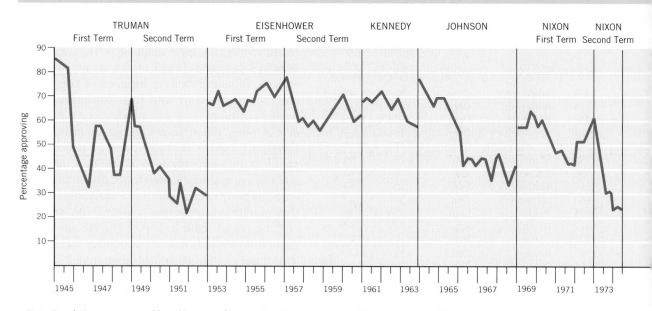

Note: Popularity was measured by asking every few months, "Do you approve of the way _____ is handling his job as president?"

Source: Thomas E. Cronin, *The State of the Presidency* (Boston: Little, Brown, 1975), 110–111. Copyright © 1975 by Little, Brown and Company, Inc. Reprinted by permission. Updated with Gallup poll data, 1976–2004. Reprinted by permission of the Gallup Poll News Service.

president can appear successful if a few bills he likes are passed, but most of his legislative program is bottled up in Congress and never comes to a vote. Given these problems, "presidential victories" are hard to measure accurately.

A fourth general caution: presidential popularity is hard to predict and can be greatly influenced by factors over which nobody, including the president, has much control. For example, when he took office in 2001, President George W. Bush's approval rating was 57 percent, nearly identical to what President Bill Clinton received in his initial rating (58 percent) in 1993. But Bush also had the highest initial *disap*proval rating (25 percent) of any president since polling began. This was undoubtedly partly due to his becoming president on the heels of the Florida vote-count controversy (see Chapter 10). Bush's approval ratings through his first six months were fairly typical for post-1960 presidents. But from the terrorist attack on the United States on September 11, 2001 through mid-2002, his approval ratings never dipped below 70 percent, and the approval rat-ings he received shortly after the attack (hovering around 90 percent) were the highest ever recorded.

The Decline in Popularity

Though presidential popularity is an asset, its value tends inexorably to decline. As can be seen from Figure 14.2, every president except Eisenhower, Reagan, and Clinton lost popular support between his inauguration and the time that he left office, except when his reelection gave him a brief burst of renewed popularity. Truman was hurt by improprieties among his subordinates and by the protracted Korean War; Johnson was crippled by the increasing unpopularity of the Vietnam War; Nixon was severely damaged by the Watergate scandal; Ford was hurt by having pardoned Nixon for his part in Watergate; Carter was weakened by continuing inflation, staff irregularities, and the Iranian kidnapping of American hostages; George H.W. Bush was harmed by an economic recession. Remarkably, Clinton's approval rating was not greatly harmed by his affair with Monica Lewinsky and his impeachment.

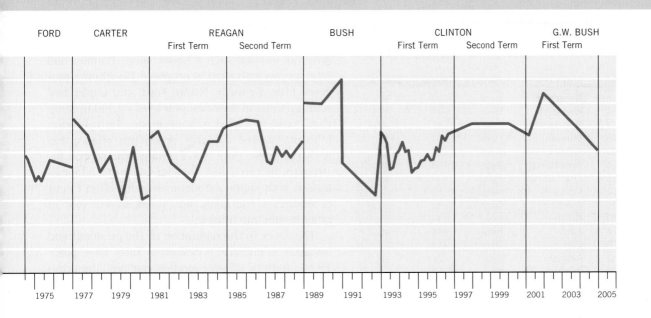

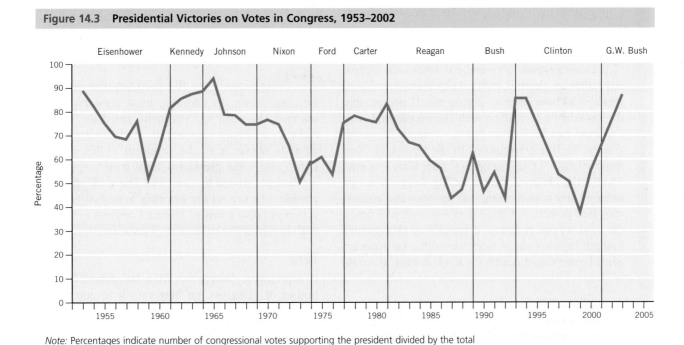

Figure 14.3   Presidential Victories on Votes in Congress, 1953–2002

Note: Percentages indicate number of congressional votes supporting the president divided by the total number of votes on which the president has taken a position.

Source: From Harold Stanley and Richard Niemi, *Vital Statistics on American Politics,* 2003–2004 (Washington, D.C.: Congressional Quarterly Press, 2003), Table 6–7.

Table 14.4	Partisan Gains or Losses in Congress in Off-Year Elections			
			Gains or Losses of President's Party In:	
Year	President	Party	House	Senate
1934	Roosevelt	Dem.	+9	+9
1938	Roosevelt	Dem.	−70	−7
1942	Roosevelt	Dem.	−50	−8
1946	Truman	Dem.	−54	−11
1950	Truman	Dem.	−29	−5
1954	Eisenhower	Rep.	−18	−1
1958	Eisenhower	Rep.	−47	−13
1962	Kennedy	Dem.	−5	+2
1966	Johnson	Dem.	−48	−4
1970	Nixon	Rep.	−12	+1
1974	Ford	Rep.	−48	−5
1978	Carter	Dem.	−12	−3
1982	Reagan	Rep.	−26	0
1986	Reagan	Rep.	−5	−8
1990	Bush	Rep.	−9	−1
1994	Clinton	Dem.	−52	−9
1998	Clinton	Dem.	+5	0
2002	G.W. Bush	Rep.	+8	+2

Source: Harold W. Stanley and Richard G. Niemi, *Vital Statistics on American Politics, 2002–2003* (Washington, D.C.: Congressional Quarterly, 2003), table 1–10.

Because a president's popularity tends to be highest right after an election, political commentators like to speak of a "honeymoon," during which, presumably, the president's love affair with the people and with Congress can be consummated. Certainly Roosevelt enjoyed such a honeymoon. In the legendary "first hundred days" of his presidency, from March to June 1933, FDR obtained from a willing Congress a vast array of new laws creating new agencies and authorizing new powers. But those were extraordinary times: the most serious economic depression of this century had put millions out of work, closed banks, impoverished farmers, and ruined the stock market. It would

veto message   A message from the president to Congress stating that he will not sign a bill it has passed. Must be produced within ten days of the bill's passage.

pocket veto   A bill fails to become law because the president did not sign it within ten days before Congress adjourns.

have been political suicide for Congress to have blocked, or even delayed, action on measures that appeared designed to help the nation out of the crisis.

Other presidents, serving in more normal times, have not enjoyed such a honeymoon. Truman had little success with what he proposed; Eisenhower proposed little. Kennedy, Nixon, Ford, and Carter had some victories in their first year in office, but nothing that could be called a honeymoon. Only Lyndon Johnson enjoyed a highly productive relationship with Congress; until the Vietnam War sapped his strength, he rarely lost. Reagan began his administration with important victories in his effort to cut expenditures and taxes, but in his second year in office he ran into trouble.

The decay in the reputation of the president and his party in midterm is evident in Table 14.4. Since 1934, in every off-year election but two, the president's party has lost seats in one or both houses of Congress. In 1998 the Democrats won five seats in the House and lost none in the Senate; in 2002 the Republicans gained eight House seats and two in the Senate. The ability of the president to persuade is important but limited. However, he also has a powerful bargaining chip to play: the ability to say no.

☆ The Power to Say No

The Constitution gives the president the power to veto legislation. In addition, most presidents have asserted the right of "executive privilege," or the right to withhold information that Congress may want to obtain from the president or his subordinates, and some presidents have tried to impound funds appropriated by Congress. These efforts by the president to say no are not only a way of blocking action but also a way of forcing Congress to bargain with him over the substance of policies.

Veto

If a president disapproves of a bill passed by both houses of Congress, he may veto it in one of two ways. One is by a **veto message.** This is a statement that the president sends to Congress accompanying the bill, within ten days (not counting Sundays) after the bill has been passed. In it he sets forth his reasons for not signing the bill. The other is the **pocket veto.** If the president does not sign the bill within ten days *and* Congress has adjourned within that time, then the bill will not become law. Obviously a pocket veto

Table 14.5	Presidential Vetoes, 1789–2004			
	Regular Vetoes	Pocket Vetoes	Total Vetoes	Vetoes Overridden
Washington	2	—	2	—
Madison	5	2	7	—
Monroe	1	—	1	—
Jackson	5	7	12	—
Tyler	6	3	9	1
Polk	2	1	3	—
Pierce	9	—	9	5
Buchanan	4	3	7	—
Lincoln	2	4	6	—
A. Johnson	21	8	29	15
Grant	45	49	94	4
Hayes	12	1	13	1
Arthur	4	8	12	1
Cleveland	304	109	413	2
Harrison	19	25	44	1
Cleveland	43	127	170	5
McKinley	6	36	42	—
T. Roosevelt	42	40	82	1
Taft	30	9	39	1
Wilson	33	11	44	6
Harding	5	1	6	—
Coolidge	20	30	50	4
Hoover	21	16	37	3
F. Roosevelt	372	263	635	9
Truman	180	70	250	12
Eisenhower	73	108	181	2
Kennedy	12	9	21	—
L. Johnson	16	14	30	—
Nixon	26	17	43	7
Ford	48	18	66	12
Carter	13	18	31	2
Reagan	39	39	78	9
Bush	29	15	44	1
Clinton	36	1	37	2
G.W. Bush	0	0	0	0

Source: Harold W. Stanley and Richard G. Niemi, *Vital Statistics on American Politics, 2003–2004* (Washington, D.C.: Congressional Quarterly, 2003), table 6-9.

can be used only during a certain time of the year—just before Congress adjourns at the end of its second session. At times, however, presidents have pocket-vetoed a bill just before Congress recessed for a summer vacation or to permit its members to campaign during an off-year election. In 1972 Senator Edward M. Kennedy of Massachusetts protested that this was unconstitutional, since a recess is not the same thing as an adjournment. In a case brought to federal court, Kennedy was upheld, and it is now understood that the pocket veto can be used only just before the life of a given Congress expires.

A bill that is not signed or vetoed within ten days while Congress is still in session becomes law automatically, without the president's approval. A bill that has been returned to Congress with a veto message can be passed over the president's objections if at least two-thirds of each house votes to override the veto. A bill that has received a pocket veto cannot be brought back to life by Congress (since Congress has adjourned), nor does such a bill carry over to the next session of Congress. If Congress wants to press the matter, it will have to start all over again by passing the bill anew in its next session, and then hope that the president will sign it or, if he does not, that they can override his veto.

The president must either accept or reject the entire bill. Presidents did not have the power, possessed by most governors, to exercise a **line-item veto,** with which the chief executive can approve some provisions of a bill and disapprove others. Congress could take advantage of this by putting items the president did not like into a bill he otherwise favored, forcing him to approve those provisions along with the rest of the bill or reject the whole thing. In 1996 Congress passed a bill, which the president signed into law, that gives the president the power of "enhanced rescission." This means the president could cancel parts of a spending bill passed by Congress without vetoing the entire bill. The president had five days after signing a bill to send a message to Congress rescinding some parts of what he had signed. These rescissions would take effect unless Congress, by a two-thirds vote, overturned them. Congress could choose which parts of the president's cancellations it wanted to overturn. But the Supreme Court has decided that this law is unconstitutional. The Constitution gives the president no such power to carve up a bill: he must either sign the whole bill, veto the whole bill, or allow it to become law without his signature.[15]

Nevertheless, the veto power is a substantial one, because Congress rarely has the votes to override it. From George Washington to Bill Clinton, over 2,500 presidential vetoes were cast; about 4 percent were overridden (see Table 14.5). Cleveland, Franklin Roosevelt, Truman, and Eisenhower made the most extensive use of vetoes, accounting for 65 percent of

line-item veto An executive's ability to block a particular provision in a bill passed by the legislature.

all vetoes ever cast. George W. Bush did not veto a single bill in his first term. Often the vetoed legislation is revised by Congress and passed in a form suitable to the president. There is no tally of how often this happens, but it is frequent enough so that both branches of government recognize that the veto, or even the threat of it, is part of an elaborate process of political negotiation in which the president has substantial powers.

Executive Privilege

The Constitution says nothing about whether the president is obliged to divulge private communications between himself and his principal advisers, but presidents have acted as if they do have that privilege of confidentiality. The presidential claim is based on two grounds. First, the doctrine of the separation of powers means that one branch of government does not have the right to inquire into the internal workings of another branch headed by constitutionally named officers. Second, the principles of statecraft and of prudent administration require that the president have the right to obtain confidential and candid advice from subordinates; such advice could not be obtained if it would quickly be exposed to public scrutiny.

For almost two hundred years there was no serious challenge to the claim of presidential confidentiality. The Supreme Court did not require the disclosure of confidential communications to or from the president.[16] Congress was never happy with this claim but until 1973 did not seriously dispute it. Indeed, in 1962 a Senate committee explicitly accepted a claim by President Kennedy that his secretary of defense, Robert S. McNamara, was not obliged to divulge the identity of Defense Department officials who had censored certain speeches by generals and admirals.

In 1973 the Supreme Court for the first time met the issue directly. A federal special prosecutor sought tape recordings of White House conversations between President Nixon and his advisers as part of his investigation of the Watergate scandal. In the case of *United States v. Nixon,* the Supreme Court, by a vote of eight to zero, held that while there may be a sound basis for the claim of executive privilege, especially where sensitive military or diplomatic matters are involved, there is no "absolute unqualified Presidential privilege of immunity from judicial process under all circumstances."[17] To admit otherwise

would be to block the constitutionally defined function of the federal courts to decide criminal cases.

Thus Nixon was ordered to hand over the disputed tapes and papers to a federal judge so that the judge could decide which were relevant to the case at hand and allow those to be introduced into evidence. In the future another president may well persuade the Court that a different set of records or papers is so sensitive as to require protection, especially if there is no allegation of criminal misconduct requiring the production of evidence in court. As a practical matter it seems likely that presidential advisers will be able, except in unusual cases such as Watergate, to continue to give private advice to the president.

In 1997 and 1998 President Clinton was sued while in office by a private person, Paula Jones, who claimed that he had solicited sex from her in ways that hurt her reputation. In defending himself against that and other matters, his lawyers attempted to claim executive privilege for Secret Service officers and government-paid lawyers who worked with him, but federal courts held that not only could a president be sued, but these other officials could not claim executive privilege.[18] One unhappy consequence of this episode is that the courts have greatly weakened the number of officials with whom the president can speak in confidence. It is not easy to run an organization when the courts can later compel your associates to testify about everything you said.

Impoundment of Funds

From time to time presidents have refused to spend money appropriated by Congress. Truman did not spend all that Congress wanted spent on the armed forces, and Johnson did not spend all that Congress made available for highway construction. Kennedy refused to spend money appropriated for new weapons systems that he did not like. Indeed, the precedent for impounding funds goes back at least to the administration of Thomas Jefferson.

But what has precedent is not thereby constitutional. The Constitution is silent on whether the president *must* spend the money that Congress appropriates; all it says is that the president cannot spend money that Congress has *not* appropriated. The major test of presidential power in this respect occurred during the Nixon administration. Nixon wished to reduce federal spending. He proposed in 1972 that Congress give him the power to reduce federal spending so that it would not exceed $250 billion for the coming year.

Congress, under Democratic control, refused. Nixon responded by pocket-vetoing twelve spending bills and then impounding funds appropriated under other laws that he had not vetoed.

Congress in turn responded by passing the Budget Reform Act of 1974, which, among other things, requires the president to spend all appropriated funds unless he first tells Congress what funds he wishes not to spend and Congress, within forty-five days, agrees to delete the items. If he wishes simply to delay spending the money, he need only inform Congress, but Congress then can refuse the delay by passing a resolution requiring the immediate release of the money. Federal courts have upheld the rule that the president must spend, without delay for policy reasons, money that Congress has appropriated.

☆ The President's Program

Imagine that you have just spent three or four years running for president, during which time you have given essentially the same speech over and over again. You have had no time to study the issues in any depth. To reach a large television audience, you have couched your ideas largely in rather simple—if not simple-minded—slogans. Your principal advisers are political aides, not legislative specialists.

You win. You are inaugurated. Now you must *be* a president instead of just talking about it. You must fill hundreds of appointive posts, but you know personally only a handful of the candidates. You must deliver a State of the Union message to Congress only two or three weeks after you are sworn in. It is quite possible that you have never read, much less written, such a message before. You must submit a new budget; the old one is hundreds of pages long, much of it comprehensible only to experts. Foreign governments, as well as the stock market, hang on your every word, interpreting many of your remarks in ways that totally surprise you. What will you do?

The Constitution is not much help. It directs you to report on the state of the union and to recommend "such measures" as you shall judge "necessary and expedient." Beyond that you are charged to "take care that the laws be faithfully executed."

At one time, of course, the demands placed on a newly elected president were not very great, because the president was not expected to do very much. The president, on assuming office, might speak of the tar-iff, or relations with England, or the value of veterans' pensions, or the need for civil service reform, but he was not expected to have something to say (and offer) to everybody. Today he is.

Putting Together a Program

To develop policies on short notice, a president will draw on several sources, each with particular strengths and weaknesses:

- **Interest groups**
  Strength: Will have specific plans and ideas.
  Weakness: Will have narrow view of the public interest.

- **Aides and campaign advisers**
  Strength: Will test new ideas for their political soundness.
  Weakness: Will not have many ideas to test, being inexperienced in government.

- **Federal bureaus and agencies**
  Strength: Will know what is feasible in terms of governmental realities.
  Weakness: Will propose plans that promote own agencies and will not have good information on whether plans will work.

- **Outside, academic, and other specialists and experts**
  Strength: Will have many general ideas and criticisms of existing programs.
  Weakness: Will not know the details of policy or have good judgment as to what is feasible.

There are essentially two ways for a president to develop a program. One, exemplified by Presidents Carter and Clinton, is to have a policy on almost everything. To do this they worked endless hours and studied countless documents, trying to learn something about, and then state their positions on, a large number of issues. The other method, illustrated by President Reagan, is to concentrate on three or four major initiatives or themes and leave everything else to subordinates.

But even when a president has a governing philosophy, as did Reagan, he cannot risk plunging ahead on his own. He must judge public and congressional reaction to this program before he commits himself fully to it. Therefore, he will often allow parts of his program to be "leaked" to the press, or to be "floated" as a trial balloon. Reagan's commitment to a 30 percent tax cut and larger military expenditures was so well known that it required no leaking, but he did have to float his ideas on Social Security and certain budget cuts to test popular reaction. His opponents in the bureaucracy did exactly the same thing, hoping for the opposite effect. They leaked controversial parts of the program in an effort to discredit the whole policy. This process of testing the winds by a president and his critics helps explain why so many news stories coming from Washington mention no person by name but only an anonymous "highly placed source."

In addition to the risks of adverse reaction, the president faces three other constraints on his ability to plan a program. One is the sheer limit of his time and attention span. Every president works harder than he has ever worked before. A ninety-hour week is typical. Even so, he has great difficulty keeping up with all the things that he is supposed to know and make decisions about. For example, Congress during an average year passes between four hundred and six hundred bills, each of which the president must sign, veto, or allow to take effect without his signature. Scores of people wish to see him. Hundreds of phone calls must be made to members of Congress and others in order to ask for help, to smooth ruffled feathers, or to get information. He must receive all newly appointed ambassadors and visiting heads of state and in addition have his picture taken with countless people, from a Nobel Prize winner to a child whose likeness will appear on the Easter Seal.

The second constraint is the unexpected crisis. Franklin Roosevelt obviously had to respond to a depression and to the mounting risks of world war. But most presidents get their crises when they least expect them. Consider these crises:

Kennedy

- Failure of Bay of Pigs invasion of Cuba
- Soviets put missiles in Cuba
- China invades India
- Federal troops sent to the South to protect blacks

Johnson

- Vietnam War
- Black riots in major cities
- War between India and Pakistan
- Civil war in Dominican Republic
- Arab-Israeli war
- Civil rights workers murdered in South

Nixon

- Watergate scandal
- Arab-Israeli war
- Value of dollar falls in foreign trade
- Arabs raise the price of oil

Carter

- OMB director Bert Lance accused of improprieties
- Lengthy coal strike
- Seizure of American hostages in Iran
- Soviet invasion of Afghanistan

Reagan

- Poland suppresses Solidarity movement
- U.S. troops sent to Lebanon
- U.S. hostages held in Lebanon
- Civil war in Nicaragua
- Iran-contra crisis

Bush (the elder)

- Soviet Union dissolves
- Iraq invades Kuwait

Clinton

- Civil war continues in Bosnia and other parts of the former Yugoslavia
- Investigation of possible wrongdoing of President and Mrs. Clinton in Whitewater real estate development
- Clinton impeached

Bush (the younger)

- Terrorist attacks on World Trade Center and Pentagon kill close to 3,000 people
- U.S.-led war against terrorists in Afghanistan and Iraq

The third constraint is the fact that the federal government and most federal programs, as well as the federal budget, can only be changed marginally, except in special circumstances. The vast bulk of federal expenditures are beyond control in any given year: the money must be spent whether the president likes it or not. Many federal programs have such strong congressional or public support that they must be left intact or modified only slightly. And this means that most federal employees can count on being secure in their jobs, whatever a president's views on reducing the bureaucracy.

The result of these constraints is that the president, at least in ordinary times, has to be selective about what he wants. He can be thought of as having a stock of influence and prestige the way that he might have a supply of money. If he wants to get the most "return" on his resources, he must "invest" that influence and prestige carefully in enterprises that promise substantial gains—in public benefits and political support—at reasonable costs. Each president tends to speak in terms of changing everything at once, calling his approach a "New Deal," a "New Frontier," a "Great Society," or the "New Federalism." But beneath the rhetoric he must identify a few specific proposals on which he wishes to bet his resources, mindful of the need to leave a substantial stock of resources in reserve to handle the inevitable crises and emergencies. In recent decades events have required every president to devote much of his time and resources to two key issues: the state of the economy and foreign affairs. What he manages to do beyond this will depend on his personal views and his sense of what the nation, as well as his reelection, requires.

And it will depend on one other thing: opinion polls. The last president who never used polls was Herbert Hoover. Franklin Roosevelt began making heavy use of them, and every president since has relied on them. Bill Clinton had voters polled about almost everything—where he should go on vacation (the West) and how to deal with Bosnia (no ground troops).

Once, when polls did not exist, politicians often believed that they should do what they thought the public interest required. Now that polls are commonplace, some politicians act on the basis of what their constituents want. Scholars call the first view the trustee approach: do what the public good requires, even if the voters are skeptical. The second view is the delegate model: do what your constituents want you to do.

But there is another way of looking at polls. They may be a device not for picking a policy, but for deciding what language to use in explaining that policy. Choose a policy that helps you get reelected or that satisfies an interest group, but then explain it with poll-tested words. President Clinton wanted to keep affirmative action (described in the chapter titled "Civil Rights") but knew that most voters disliked it. So he used a poll-tested phrase—"mend it but don't end it"—and then did nothing to mend it.

Finally, a president's program can be radically altered by a dramatic event or prolonged crisis. George W. Bush ran as a candidate interested in domestic issues and with little background in foreign affairs, but the terrorist attack of September 11, 2001, on the World Trade Center and the Pentagon dramatically changed his presidency into one preoccupied with foreign and military policy. He quickly launched a military attack on the Taliban regime in Afghanistan and assembled an international coalition to support it. His approval ratings rose to the highest level yet recorded, but a year later fell sharply.

Attempts to Reorganize

One item on the presidential agenda has been the same for almost every president since Herbert Hoover: reorganizing the executive branch of government. In the wake of the terrorist attack on the United States on September 11, 2001, the president, by executive order, created a new White House Office of Homeland Security, headed by his friend and former Pennsylvania governor, Tom Ridge. In the months that followed, it became clear to all, including the president, that he had given Ridge an impossible job. For one thing, despite its obvious importance, Ridge's office, like most units with the Executive Office of the President, had only a dozen or so full-time staff, little budgetary authority, and virtually no ability to make and enforce decisions regarding how cabinet agencies operated. Nobody could meaningfully coordinate the literally dozens of administrative units that the administration's new homeland security blueprint required Ridge's office to somehow manage.

To address this problem, President Bush called for a reorganization that would create the third-largest cabinet department encompassing twenty-two federal agencies, nearly 180,000 employees, and an annual budget of close to $40 billion. Among the federal agencies placed under the new Department of Homeland Security are the Coast Guard, the Customs Service, the Federal Emergency Management Agency, and the Immigration and Naturalization Service. A law authorizing the new Department of Homeland Security was enacted in November 2002, but it will take years and much effort for the new agency to become fully operational.

Important as it is, the ongoing attempt to reorganize the federal government around homeland security goals is neither the first, nor even the largest,

"15% LIKE YOU AS A CONSERVATIVE, 15% LIKE YOU LIBERAL, AND 70% DON'T CARE ... SO MY ADVICE IS TO REINVENT YOURSELF AS THE 'I DON'T CARE' CANDIDATE."

Polling dominates not only politics but also government, since some presidents rely on polls to decide how to discuss issues.

reorganization effort made by a sitting president. With few exceptions every president since 1928 has tried to change the structure of the staff, departments, and agencies that are theoretically subordinate to him. Every president has been appalled by the number of agencies that report to him and by the apparently helter-skelter manner in which they have grown up. But this is only one—and often not the most important—reason for wanting to reorganize. If a president wants to get something done, put new people in charge of a program, or recapture political support for a policy, it is often easier to do so by creating a new agency or reorganizing an old one than by abolishing a program, firing a subordinate, or passing a new law. Reorganization serves many objectives and thus is a recurring theme.

Legally the president can reorganize his personal White House staff anytime that he wishes. To reorganize in any important way the larger Executive Office of the President or any of the executive departments or agencies, however, Congress must first be consulted. For over forty years this consultation usually took the form of submitting to Congress a reorganization plan that would take effect provided that

neither the House nor the Senate passed, within sixty days, a concurrent resolution disapproving the plan (such a resolution was called a **legislative veto**). This procedure, first authorized by the Reorganization Act of 1939, could be used to change, but not create or abolish, an executive agency. In 1981 authority under that act expired, and Congress did not renew it. Two years later the Supreme Court declared that all legislative vetoes were unconstitutional (see Chapter 15), and so today any presidential reorganization plan would have to take the form of a regular law, passed by Congress and signed by the president.

What has been said so far may well give the reader the impression that the president is virtually helpless. That is not the case. The *actual* power of the president can only be measured in terms of what he can accomplish. What this chapter has described so far is the office as the president finds it—the burdens, restraints, demands, complexities, and resources that he encounters on entering the Oval Office for the first time. Every president since Truman has commented feelingly on how limited the powers of the president seem from the inside compared to what they appear to be from the outside. Franklin Roosevelt compared his struggles with the bureaucracy to punching a feather bed; Truman wrote that the power of the president was chiefly the power to persuade people to do what they ought to do anyway. After being in office a year or so, Kennedy spoke to interviewers about how much more complex the world appeared than he had first supposed. Johnson and Nixon were broken by the office and the events that happened there.

Yet Franklin Roosevelt helped create the modern presidency, with its vast organizational reach, and directed a massive war effort. Truman ordered two atomic bombs dropped on Japanese cities. Eisenhower sent American troops to Lebanon; Kennedy supported an effort to invade Cuba. Johnson sent troops to the Dominican Republic and to Vietnam; Nixon ordered an invasion of Cambodia; Reagan launched an invasion of Grenada and sponsored an antigovernment insurgent group in Nicaragua; Bush invaded Panama and sent troops to the Persian Gulf to fight Iraq; Clinton sent troops to Haiti and Bosnia. George W. Bush ordered a U.S. military operation in Afghanistan and Iraq. Obviously Europeans, Russians, Vietnamese, Cambodians, Dominicans, Panamanians, and Iraqis do not think of the American president as "helpless."

---

legislative veto   The authority of Congress to block a presidential action after it has taken place. The Supreme Court has held that Congress does not have this power.

☆ Presidential Transition

No president but Franklin Roosevelt has ever served more than two terms, and since the ratification of the Twenty-second Amendment in 1951, no president will ever again have the chance. But more than tradition or the Constitution escorts presidents from office. Only about one-third of the presidents since George Washington have been elected to a second term. Of the twenty-seven not reelected, four died in office during their first term. But the remainder either did not seek or (more usually) could not obtain reelection.

Of the eight presidents who died in office, four were assassinated: Lincoln, Garfield, McKinley, and Kennedy. At least six other presidents were the objects of unsuccessful assassination attempts: Jackson, Theodore Roosevelt, Franklin Roosevelt, Truman, Ford, and Reagan. (There may have been attempts on other presidents that never came to public notice; the attempts mentioned here involved public efforts to fire weapons at presidents.)

The presidents who served two or more terms fall into certain periods, such as the Founding (Washington, Jefferson, Madison, Monroe) or wartime (Lincoln, Wilson, Roosevelt), or they happened to be in office during especially tranquil times (Monroe, McKinley, Eisenhower, Clinton), or some combination of the above. When the country was deeply divided, as during the years just before the Civil War and during the period of Reconstruction after it, it was the rare president who was reelected.

The Vice President

Eight times a vice president has become president because of the death of his predecessor. It first happened to John Tyler, who became president in 1841 when William Henry Harrison died peacefully after only one month in office. The question for Tyler and for the country was substantial: was Tyler simply to be the acting president and a kind of caretaker until a new president was elected, or was he to be *president* in every sense of the word? Despite criticism and despite what might have been the contrary intention of the Framers of the Constitution, Tyler decided on the latter course and was confirmed in that opinion by a decision of Congress. Ever since, the vice president has automatically become president, in title and in powers, when the occupant of the White House has died or resigned.

But if vice presidents frequently acquire office because of death, they rarely acquire it by election. Since the earliest period of the Founding, when John Adams and Thomas Jefferson were each elected president after having first served as vice president under their predecessors, there have only been three occasions when a vice president was later able to win the presidency without his president's having died in office. One was in 1836, when Martin Van Buren was elected president after having served as Andrew Jackson's vice president; the second was in 1968, when Richard Nixon became president after having served as Dwight Eisenhower's vice president eight years earlier; the third was in 1988, when George Bush succeeded Ronald Reagan. Many vice presidents who entered the Oval Office because their predecessors died were subsequently elected to terms in their own right—Theodore Roosevelt, Calvin Coolidge, Harry Truman, and Lyndon Johnson. But no one who wishes to become president should assume that to become vice president first is the best way to get there.

The vice-presidency is just what so many vice presidents have complained about its being: a rather empty job. John Adams described it as "the most insignificant office that ever the invention of man contrived or his imagination conceived," and most of his successors would have agreed. Thomas Jefferson, almost alone, had a good word to say for it: "The second office of the government is honorable and easy, the first is but a splendid misery."[19] Daniel Webster rejected a vice-presidential nomination in 1848 with the phrase, "I do not choose to be buried until I am really dead."[20] (Had he taken the job, he would have become president after Zachary Taylor died in office, thereby achieving a remarkable secular resurrection.) For all the good and bad jokes about the vice-presidency, however, candidates still struggle mightily for it. John Nance Garner gave up the speakership of the House to become Franklin Roosevelt's vice president (a job he valued as "not worth a pitcher of warm spit"*), and Lyndon Johnson gave up the majority leadership of the Senate to become Kennedy's. Truman, Nixon, Humphrey, Mondale, and Gore all left reasonably secure Senate seats for the vice-presidency.

The only official task of the vice president is to preside over the Senate and to vote in case of a tie.

---

*The word he actually used was a good deal stronger than *spit,* but historians are decorous.

President Reagan, moments before he was shot on March 30, 1981, by a would-be assassin. The Twenty-fifth Amendment solves the problem of presidential disability by providing for an orderly transfer of power to the vice president.

Even this is scarcely time-consuming, as the Senate chooses from among its members a president pro tempore, as required by the Constitution, who (along with others) presides in the absence of the vice president. The vice president's leadership powers in the Senate are weak, especially when the vice president is of a different party from the majority of the senators. But on occasion the vice president can become very important. Right after the terrorists attacked the United States in 2001, President Bush was in his airplane while his advisers worried that he might be attacked next. Vice President Cheney was quickly hidden away in a secret, secure location so he could run the government if anything happened to President Bush. And for many months thereafter, Cheney stayed in this location in case he suddenly became president. But absent a crisis, the vice president is, at best, only an adviser to the president.

Problems of Succession

If the president should die in office, the right of the vice president to assume that office has been clear since the time of John Tyler. But two questions remain: What if the president falls seriously ill, but does not die? And if the vice president steps up, who then becomes the new vice president?

The first problem has arisen on a number of occasions. After President James A. Garfield was shot in 1881, he lingered through the summer before he died. President Woodrow Wilson collapsed from a stroke and was a virtual recluse for seven months in 1919 and an invalid for the rest of his term. Eisenhower had three serious illnesses while in office; Reagan was shot during his first term and hospitalized during his second.

The second problem has arisen on eight occasions when the vice president became president owing to the death of the incumbent. In these cases no elected person was available to succeed the new president, should he die in office. For many decades the problem was handled by law. The Succession Act of 1886, for example, designated the secretary of state as next in line for the presidency should the vice president die, followed by the other cabinet officers in order of seniority. But this meant that a vice president who became president could pick his own successor by choosing his own secretary of state. In 1947 the law was changed to make the Speaker of the House and then the president pro tempore of the Senate next in line for the presidency. But that created still other problems: a Speaker or a president pro tempore is likely to be chosen because of seniority, not executive skill, and in any event might well be of the party opposite to that occupying the White House.

Both problems were addressed in 1967 by the Twenty-fifth Amendment to the Constitution. It deals with the disability problem by allowing the vice president to serve as "acting president" whenever the president declares that he is unable to discharge the powers and duties of his office or whenever the vice president and a majority of the cabinet declare that the president is incapacitated. If the president disagrees with the opinion of his vice president and a majority of the cabinet, then Congress decides the issue. A two-thirds majority is necessary to confirm that the president is unable to serve.

The amendment deals with the succession problem by requiring a vice president who assumes the presidency (after a vacancy is created by death or resignation) to nominate a new vice president. This person takes office if the nomination is confirmed by a majority vote of both houses of Congress. When there is no vice president, then the 1947 law governs: next in line are the Speaker, the Senate president, and the fifteen cabinet officers, beginning with the secretary of state.

The disability problem has not arisen since the adoption of the amendment, but the succession problem has. In 1973 Vice President Spiro Agnew resigned, having pleaded no contest to criminal charges. President Nixon nominated Gerald Ford as vice president, and after extensive hearings he was confirmed by both houses of Congress and sworn in. Then on August 9, 1974, Nixon resigned the presidency—the first man to do so—and Ford became president. He nominated as his vice president Nelson Rockefeller, who was confirmed by both houses of Congress—again, after extensive hearings—and was sworn in on December 19, 1974. For the first time in history, the nation had as its two principal executive officers men who had not been elected to either the presidency or the vice-presidency. It is a measure of the legitimacy of the Constitution that this arrangement caused no crisis in public opinion.

Impeachment

There is one other way—besides death, disability, or resignation—by which a president can leave office before his term expires, and that is by impeachment. Not only the president and vice president, but also all "civil officers of the United States" can be removed by being impeached and convicted. As a practical matter civil officers—cabinet secretaries, bureau chiefs, and the like—are not subject to impeachment, because the president can remove them at any time and usually will if their behavior makes them a serious political liability. Federal judges, who serve during "good behavior"* and who are constitutionally independent of the president and Congress, have been the most frequent objects of impeachment.

An **impeachment** is like an indictment in a criminal trial: a set of charges against somebody, voted by (in this case) the House of Representatives. To be removed from office, the impeached officer must be convicted by a two-thirds vote of the Senate, which sits as a court, is presided over by the Chief Justice, hears the evidence, and makes its decision under whatever rules it wishes to adopt. Sixteen persons have been impeached by the House, and seven have been convicted by the Senate. The last conviction was in 1989, when two federal judges were removed from office.

Only two presidents have ever been impeached—Andrew Johnson in 1868 and Bill Clinton in 1998.

Representative Henry Hyde of Illinois (center, seated) chaired the House Judiciary Committee when it and the full House voted to impeach President Bill Clinton in 1998 for having lied under oath. The Senate did not convict Clinton.

Richard Nixon would surely have been impeached in 1974, had he not resigned after the House Judiciary Committee voted to recommend impeachment.

The Senate did not convict either Johnson or Clinton by the necessary two-thirds vote. The case against Johnson was entirely political—Radical Republicans, who wished to punish the South after the Civil War, were angry at Johnson, a southerner, who had a soft policy toward the South. The argument against him was flimsy.

The case against Clinton was more serious. The House Judiciary Committee, relying on the report of independent counsel Kenneth Starr, charged Clinton with perjury (lying under oath about his sexual affair with Monica Lewinsky), obstruction of justice (trying to block the Starr investigation), and abuse of power (making false written statements to the Judiciary Committee). The vote to impeach was passed by the House along party lines. A majority, but not two-thirds, of the Senate voted to convict.

Why did Clinton survive? There were many factors. The public disliked his private behavior, but did not think it amounted to an impeachable offense. (In

---

*"Good behavior" means a judge can stay in office until he retires or dies, unless he or she is impeached and convicted.

impeachment   Charges against a president approved by a majority of the House of Representatives.

★ POLITICALLY SPEAKING ★

Lame Duck

A **lame duck** is a politician whose power has diminished because he or she is about to leave office as a result of electoral defeat or statutory limitation (for example, the president can serve no more than two terms).

The expression was first used in eighteenth-century England, where it meant a "bankrupt businessman." Soon it was used to refer to "bankrupt" politicians. Perhaps they were called "lame ducks" because they had been shot on the wing and, though still alive, could no longer fly.

A lame duck is not to be confused with a "sitting duck" (somebody who is an easy target).

Source: From *Safire's Political Dictionary* by William Safire. Copyright © 1968, 1972, 1978 by William Safire. Reprinted by permission of Random House, Inc. and the author.

fact, right after Lewinsky revealed her sexual affair with him, his standing in opinion polls went up.) The economy was strong, and the nation was at peace. Clinton was a centrist Democrat who did not offend most voters.

The one casualty of the entire episode was the death of the law creating the office of the Independent Counsel. Passed in 1978 by a Congress that was upset by the Watergate crisis, the law directed the attorney general to ask a three-judge panel to appoint an independent counsel whenever a high

lame duck A person still in office after he or she has lost a bid for reelection.

official is charged with serious misconduct. (In 1993, when the 1978 law expired, President Clinton asked that it be passed again. It was.) Eighteen people were investigated by various independent counsels from 1978 to 1999. In about half the cases, no charges were brought to court.

For a long time Republicans disliked the law because the counsels were investigating them. After Clinton came to office, the counsels started investigating him and his associates, and so the Democrats began to oppose it. In 1999, when the law expired, it was not renewed.

A problem remains, however. How will any high official, including the president, be investigated when the attorney general, who does most investigations, is part of the president's team? One answer is to let Congress do it, but Congress may be controlled by the president's party. No one has yet solved this puzzle.

Some Founders may have thought that impeachment would be used frequently against presidents, but as a practical matter it is so complex and serious an undertaking that we can probably expect it to be reserved in the future only for the gravest forms of presidential misconduct. No one quite knows what a high crime or misdemeanor is, but most scholars agree that the charge must involve something illegal or unconstitutional, not just unpopular. Unless a president or vice president is first impeached and convicted, many experts believe that he is not liable to prosecution as would be an ordinary citizen. (No one is certain, because the question has never arisen.) President Ford's pardon of Richard Nixon meant that he could not be prosecuted under federal law for things that he may have done while in office.

Students may find the occasions of misconduct or disability remote and the details of succession or impeachment tedious. But the problem is not remote—succession has occurred nine times and disability at least twice—and what may appear tedious goes, in fact, to the heart of the presidency. The first and fundamental problem is to make the office legitimate. That was the great task George Washington set himself, and that was the substantial accomplishment of his successors. Despite bitter and sometimes violent partisan and sectional strife, beginning almost immediately after Washington stepped down, presidential succession has always occurred peacefully, without a military coup or a political plot. For centuries, in the bygone times of kings as well as in the present times of dictators and juntas, peaceful succession has been a rare event among the nations

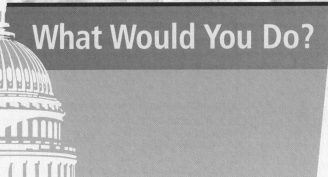

What Would You Do?

Six-Year Term for President

Delegates Divided on Big Issue

October 15
EUDORA, KS
  Here at the convention called to propose amendments to the United States Constitution, the major issue facing the delegates is the proposal to limit the president to a single six-year term. Proponents of the measure claim . . .

MEMORANDUM

To: *Delegate James Nagle*
From: *Robert Gilbert, legal staff*
Subject: *Six-year presidential term*

The proposal to give the president a single six-year term is perhaps the most popular amendment now before the convention. Polls suggest that it is supported by a sizable percentage of the American people.

Arguments for:

1. Today a president no sooner learns the ropes after being elected for the first time than he or she has to start preparing for the next election. A six-year term will give the president a chance to govern for several years after learning how to be president. This will lessen the extent to which political pressures dictate what the president does.
2. Limited to a single term, the president need not cater to special-interest groups or the media in deciding on policy. He or she can concentrate on what is good for the country.
3. Many states have limited their governors to a single term.

Arguments against:

1. It is the need to win reelection that keeps the president (like any politician) attentive to what the people want. A president unable to succeed himself or herself will be tempted to ignore public opinion.
2. Limiting a president to a single term will not free him or her from the need to play to the media or special-interest groups, since the formal powers of the presidency are too weak to permit the incumbent to govern without the aid of Congress and the press.
3. There is no evidence that presidents (such as Dwight Eisenhower) who served a second term knowing that they could not run for reelection did a better or less "political" job in the second term than in the first.

Your decision:

Favor amendment _____
Oppose amendment _____

of the world. Many of the critics of the Constitution believed in 1787 that peaceful succession would not happen in the United States either: somehow the president would connive to hold office for life or to handpick his successor. Their predictions were wrong, though their fears are understandable.

☆ How Powerful Is the President?

Just as members of Congress bemoan their loss of power, so presidents bemoan theirs. Can both be right?

In fact they can. If Congress is less able to control events than it once was, it does not mean that the president is thereby more able to exercise control. The federal government *as a whole* has become more constrained, so it is less able to act decisively. The chief source of this constraint is the greater complexity of the issues with which Washington must deal.

It was one thing to pass the Social Security Act in 1935; it is quite another thing to keep the Social Security system adequately funded. It was one thing for the nation to defend itself when attacked in 1941;

it is quite another to maintain a constant military preparedness while simultaneously exploring possibilities for arms control. It was not hard to give pensions to veterans; it seems almost impossible today to find the cure for drug abuse or juvenile crime.

In the face of modern problems, all branches of government, including the presidency, seem both big and ineffectual. Add to this the much closer and more critical scrutiny of the media and the proliferation of interest groups, and it is small wonder that both presidents and members of Congress feel that they have lost power.

Presidents have come to acquire certain rules of thumb for dealing with their political problems. Among them are these:

- *Move it or lose it.* A president who wants to get something done should do it early in his term, before his political influence erodes.
- *Avoid details.* President Carter's lieutenants regret having tried to do too much. Better to have three or four top priorities and forget the rest.
- *Cabinets don't get much accomplished; people do.* Find capable White House subordinates and give them well-defined responsibility; then watch them closely.[21]

☆ SUMMARY

A U.S. president, chosen by the people and with powers derived from a written constitution, has less power than does a British prime minister, even though the latter depends entirely on the support of his or her party in Parliament. The separation of powers between the executive and legislative branches, the distinguishing feature of the American system, means that the president must deal with a competitor—Congress—in setting policy and even in managing executive agencies.

Presidential power, though still sharply limited, has grown from its constitutional origins as a result of congressional delegation, the increased importance of foreign affairs, and public expectations. But if the president today has more power, more is also demanded of him. As a result how effective he is depends not on any general grant of authority, but on the nature of the issue that he confronts and the extent to which he can mobilize informal sources of power (public opinion, congressional support).

Though the president seemingly controls a vast executive-branch apparatus, in fact he appoints but a small portion of the officials, and the behavior of even these is often beyond his easy control. Moreover, public support, high at the beginning of any new presidency, usually declines as the term proceeds. Consequently each president must conserve his power (and his energy and time), concentrating these scarce resources to deal with a few matters of major importance. Virtually every president since Franklin Roosevelt has tried to enlarge his ability to manage the executive branch—by reorganization, by appointing White House aides, by creating specialized staff agencies—but no president has been satisfied with the results.

The extent to which a president will be weak or powerful will vary with the kind of issue and the circumstances of the moment. It is a mistake to speak of an "imperial presidency" or of an ineffectual one. A president's power is better assessed by considering how he behaves in regard to specific issues.

RECONSIDERING WHO GOVERNS?

1. *Did the Founders expect the presidency to be the most important political institution?*

Most did not. They worried about whether the presidency would be too strong or too weak, but designed a Constitution hoping that Congress would be the most important institution. And it was, with a few exceptions, until the twentieth century. Today the strength of the presidency depends chiefly on two things: the importance of military and foreign affairs, and the president's personal popularity.

2. *How important is the president's character in determining how he governs?*

Very important. Presidents with great personal skills, such as Franklin Roosevelt, Dwight Eisenhower, Ronald Reagan, and Bill Clinton can influence public opinion and that in turn influences Congress. But character is not the whole story. Having a majority of fellow believers in Congress, though rare, is important (as it was for Roosevelt and Lyndon Johnson), and so are unexpected events, such as wars and other crises.

RECONSIDERING TO WHAT ENDS?

1. *Should we abolish the electoral college?*

There are big risks in doing that. If no president were to win a majority of the popular vote (which happens quite often), there would either have to be a runoff election or the House would make the final decision. With an electoral college, small parties would play a bigger role and the United States could politically come to look like France or Italy. And without the college, a presidential campaign might be waged in just a few big states with the candidates ignoring most places.

2. *Is it harder to govern when the presidency and Congress are controlled by different parties?*

Not really. Both the Democratic and Republican parties have legislators who often vote with their party rivals. Unless the president has a big ideological majority in Congress, something that does not happen too often, he can easily lose legislative struggles. Gridlock does not in fact prevent major new pieces of legislation from being passed.

WORLD WIDE WEB RESOURCES

www.whitehouse.gov
www.ipl.org/ref/POTUS/
lcweb.loc.gov/global/executive/fed.html
www.interlink-cafe.com/uspresidents

SUGGESTED READINGS

General

Corwin, Edward S. *The President: Office and Powers.* 5th ed. New York: New York University Press, 1985. Historical, constitutional, and legal development of the office.

Jones, Charles O. *Passage to the Presidency* (Washington, D.C.: Brookings Institution, 1998). Insightful account of how four presidents—Nixon, Carter, Reagan, and Clinton—moved from the campaign to the presidency.

Neustadt, Richard E. *Presidential Power: The Politics of Leadership.* Rev. ed. New York: Wiley, 1976. How presidents try to acquire and hold political power in the competitive world of official Washington, by a man who has been both a scholar and an insider.

Peterson, Mark A. *Legislating Together: The White House and Congress from Eisenhower to Reagan.* Cambridge: Harvard University Press, 1990. Challenges the conventional view that "the president proposes, Congress disposes." Contains many excellent examples of bargaining and cooperation between Congress and the executive branch.

Polsby, Nelson W., and Aaron Wildavsky. *Presidential Elections.* 10th ed. New York: Chatham House, 2000. Excellent analysis of how campaigns and the electoral college shape the presidency.

On Franklin D. Roosevelt

Leuchtenberg, William E. *Franklin D. Roosevelt and the New Deal, 1932–1940.* New York: Harper & Row, 1963.

Maney, Richard J. *The Roosevelt Presence.* New York: Twayne, 1992.

On Harry S Truman

Hamby, A. L. *Beyond the New Deal: Harry S Truman and American Liberalism.* New York: Columbia University Press, 1973.

McCullough, David. *Truman.* New York: Simon and Schuster, 1984.

On Dwight D. Eisenhower

Ambrose, Stephen E. *Eisenhower.* New York: Simon and Schuster, 1984.

Greenstein, Fred I. *The Hidden-Hand Presidency: Eisenhower as Leader.* New York: Basic Books, 1982.

On John F. Kennedy

Paper, Lewis J. *The Promise and the Performance: The Leadership of John F. Kennedy.* New York: Crown, 1975.

Parmet, Herbert C. *Jack.* New York: Dial Press, 1980.

On Lyndon B. Johnson

Caro, Robert A. *The Years of Lyndon Johnson.* 3 vols. New York: Alfred Knopf, 1982–2002.

Dallek, Robert. *Lone Star Rising and Flawed Giant.* New York: Oxford University Press, 1991 and 1996.

Kearns, Doris. *Lyndon Johnson and the American Dream.* New York: Harper and Row, 1976.

On Richard M. Nixon

Ambrose, Stephen E. *Nixon.* 3 vols. New York: Simon and Schuster, 1987, 1989, 1991.

On Jimmy Carter

Bourne, Peter G. *Jimmy Carter.* New York: Scribner, 1997.

On Ronald Reagan

Cannon, Lou. *President Reagan.* New York: Simon and Schuster, 1991.

On George H.W. Bush

Parmet, Herbert C. *George Bush.* New York: Scribner, 1997.

The Bureaucracy

Distinctiveness of the American Bureaucracy

The Growth of the Bureaucracy
The Appointment of Officials ● A Service Role ● A Change in Role

The Federal Bureaucracy Today
Recruitment and Retention ● Personal Attributes ● Do Bureaucrats Sabotage Their Political Bosses? ● Culture and Careers ● Constraints ● Agency Allies

Congressional Oversight
The Appropriations Committee and Legislative Committees ● The Legislative Veto ● Congressional Investigations

Bureaucratic "Pathologies"

Reforming the Bureaucracy

WHO GOVERNS?

1. What happened to make the bureaucracy a "fourth branch" of American national government?
2. What are the actual size and scope of the federal bureaucracy?

TO WHAT ENDS?

1. What should be done to improve bureaucratic performance?
2. Is "red tape" all bad?

T here is probably not a man or woman in the United States who has not, at some time or other, complained about "the bureaucracy." Your letter was slow in getting to Aunt Minnie? The Internal Revenue Service took months to send you your tax refund? The Defense Department paid $400 for a hammer? The Occupational Safety and Health Administration told you that you installed the wrong kind of portable toilet for your farm workers? The "bureaucracy" is to blame.

For most people and politicians *bureaucracy* is a pejorative word implying waste, confusion, red tape, and rigidity. But for scholars—and for bureaucrats themselves—*bureaucracy* is a word with a neutral, technical meaning. A **bureaucracy** is a large, complex organization composed of appointed officials. By *complex* we mean that authority is divided among several managers; no one person is able to make all the decisions. A large corporation is a bureaucracy; so also are a big university and a government agency. With its sizable staff, even Congress has become, to some degree, a bureaucracy.

What is it about complex organizations in general, and government agencies in particular, that leads so many people to complain about them? In part the answer is to be found in their very size and complexity. But in large measure the answer is to be found in the political context within which such agencies must operate. If we examine that context carefully, we will discover that many of the problems that we blame on "the bureaucracy" are in fact the result of what Congress, the courts, and the president do.

☆ Distinctiveness of the American Bureaucracy

Bureaucratic government has become an obvious feature of all modern societies, democratic and nondemocratic. In the United States, however, three aspects of our constitutional system and political traditions give to the bureaucracy a distinctive character. First, political authority over the bureaucracy is not in one set of hands but is shared among several institutions. In a parliamentary regime, such as in Great Britain, the appointed officials of the national government work for the cabinet ministers, who are in turn dominated by the prime minister. In theory, and to a considerable extent in practice, British bureaucrats report to and take orders from the ministers in charge of their departments, do not deal directly with Parliament, and rarely give interviews to the press. In the United States the

Constitution permits both the president and Congress to exercise authority over the bureaucracy. Every senior appointed official has at least two masters: one in the executive branch and the other in the legislative. Often there are many more than two: Congress, after all, is not a single organization but a collection of committees, subcommittees, and individuals. This divided authority encourages bureaucrats to play one branch of government off against the other and to make heavy use of the media.

Second, most of the agencies of the federal government share their functions with related agencies in state and local government. Though some federal agencies deal directly with American citizens—the Internal Revenue Service collects taxes from them, the Federal Bureau of Investigation looks into crimes for them, the Postal Service delivers mail to them—many agencies work with other organizations at other levels of government. For example, the Department of Education gives money to local school systems; the Health Care Financing Administration in the Department of Health and Human Services reimburses states for money spent on health care for the poor; the Department of Housing and Urban Development gives grants to cities for community development; and the Employment and Training Administration in the Department of Labor supplies funds to local governments so that they can run job-training programs. In France, by contrast, government programs dealing with education, health, housing, and employment are centrally run, with little or no control exercised by local governments.

Third, the institutions and traditions of American life have contributed to the growth of what some writers have described as an "adversary culture," in which the definition and expansion of personal rights, and the defense of rights and claims through lawsuits as well as political action, are given central importance. A government agency in this country operates under closer public scrutiny and with a greater prospect of court challenges to its authority than in almost any other nation. Virtually every important decision of the Occupational Safety and Health Administration or of the Environmental Protection Agency is likely to be challenged in the courts or attacked by an affected party; in Sweden the decisions of similar agencies go largely uncontested.

The scope as well as the style of bureaucratic government differs. In most Western European nations the government owns and operates large parts of the economy: the French government operates the railroads and owns companies that make automobiles and cigarettes, and the Italian government owns many similar enterprises and also the nation's oil refineries. In just about every large nation except the United States, the telephone system is owned by the government. Publicly operated enterprises account for about 12 percent of all employment in France but less than 3 percent in the United States.[1] The U.S. government regulates privately owned enterprises to a degree not found in many other countries, however. Why we should have preferred regulation to ownership as the proper government role is an interesting question to which we shall return.

☆ The Growth of the Bureaucracy

The Constitution made scarcely any provision for an administrative system other than to allow the president to appoint, with the advice and consent of the Senate, "ambassadors, other public ministers and consuls, judges of the Supreme Court, and all other officers of the United States whose appointments are not herein otherwise provided for, and which shall be established by law."[2] Departments and bureaus were not mentioned.

In the first Congress, in 1789, James Madison introduced a bill to create a Department of State to assist the new secretary of state, Thomas Jefferson, in carrying out his duties. People appointed to this department were to be nominated by the president and approved by the Senate, but they were "to be removable by the president" alone. These six words, which would confer the right to fire government officials, occasioned six days of debate in the House. At stake was the locus of power over what was to become the bureaucracy. Madison's opponents argued that the Senate should consent to the removal of officials as well as their appointment. Madison responded that, without the unfettered right of removal, the president would not be able to control his subordinates, and without this control he would not be able to discharge his constitutional

bureaucracy   A large, complex organization composed of appointed officials.

obligation to "take care that the laws be faithfully executed."[3] Madison won, twenty-nine votes to twenty-two. When the issue went to the Senate, another debate resulted in a tie vote, broken in favor of the president by Vice President John Adams. The Department of State, and all cabinet departments subsequently created, would be run by people removable only by the president.

That decision did not resolve the question of who would really control the bureaucracy, however. Congress retained the right to appropriate money, to investigate the administration, and to shape the laws that would be executed by that administration—more than ample power to challenge any president who claimed to have sole authority over his subordinates. And many members of Congress expected that the cabinet departments, even though headed by people removable by the president, would report to Congress.

The government in Washington was at first minuscule. The State Department started with only nine employees; the War Department did not have eighty civilian employees until 1801. Only the Treasury Department, concerned with collecting taxes and finding ways to pay the public debt, had much power, and only the Post Office Department provided any significant service.

The Appointment of Officials

Small as the bureaucracy was, people struggled, often bitterly, over who would be appointed to it. From George Washington's day to modern times, presidents have found appointment to be one of their most important and difficult tasks. The officials that they select affect how the laws are interpreted (thus the political ideology of the job holders is important), what tone the administration will display (thus personal character is important), how effectively the public business is discharged (thus competence is important), and how strong the political party or faction in power will be (thus party affiliation is important). Presidents trying to balance the competing needs of ideology, character, fitness, and partisanship have rarely pleased most people. As John Adams remarked, every appointment creates one ingrate and ten enemies.

Because Congress, during most of the nineteenth and twentieth centuries, was the dominant branch of government, congressional preferences often controlled the appointment of officials. And since Congress was, in turn, a collection of people who represented local interests, appointments were made with an eye to rewarding the local supporters of members of Congress or building up local party organizations. These appointments made on the basis of political considerations—patronage—were later to become a major issue. They galvanized various reform efforts that sought to purify politics and to raise the level of competence of the public service. Many of the abuses that the reformers complained about were real enough, but patronage served some useful purposes as well. It gave the president a way to ensure that his subordinates were reasonably supportive of his policies; it provided a reward that the president could use to induce recalcitrant members of Congress to vote for his programs; and it enabled party organizations to be built up to perform the necessary functions of nominating candidates and getting out the vote.

Though at first there were not many jobs to fight over, by the middle of the nineteenth century there were a lot. From 1816 to 1861 the number of federal employees increased eightfold. This expansion was not, however, the result of the government's taking on new functions but simply a result of the increased demands on its traditional functions. The Post Office alone accounted for 86 percent of this growth.[4]

The Civil War was a great watershed in bureaucratic development. Fighting the war led, naturally, to hiring many new officials and creating many new offices. Just as important, the Civil War revealed the administrative weakness of the federal government and led to demands by the civil service reform movement for an improvement in the quality and organization of federal employees. And finally, the war was followed by a period of rapid industrialization and the emergence of a national economy. The effects of these developments could no longer be managed by state governments acting alone. With the creation of a nationwide network of railroads, commerce among the states became increasingly important. The constitutional powers of the federal government to regulate interstate commerce, long dormant for want of much commerce to regulate, now became an important source of controversy.

A Service Role

From 1861 to 1901 new agencies were created, many to deal with particular sectors of society and the economy. Over two hundred thousand new federal employees were added, with only about half of this increase in the Post Office. The rapidly growing Pension Office

The Hollerith machine (left), invented by Herman Hollerith, helped the government calculate census data in the early part of the twentieth century. Today, high-speed computers, such as those used by air traffic controllers, do the job at great speed.

began paying benefits to Civil War veterans; the Department of Agriculture was created in 1862 to help farmers; the Department of Labor was founded in 1882 to serve workers; and the Department of Commerce was organized in 1903 to assist business people. Many more specialized agencies, such as the National Bureau of Standards, also came into being.

These agencies had one thing in common: their role was primarily to serve, not to regulate. Most did research, gathered statistics, dispensed federal lands, or passed out benefits. Not until the Interstate Commerce Commission (ICC) was created in 1887 did the federal government begin to regulate the economy (other than by managing the currency) in any large way. Even the ICC had, at first, relatively few powers.

There were several reasons why federal officials primarily performed a service role. The values that had shaped the Constitution were still strong: these included a belief in limited government, the importance of states' rights, and the fear of concentrated discretionary power. The proper role of government in the economy was to promote, not to regulate, and a commitment to **laissez-faire**—a freely competitive economy—was strongly held. But just as important, the Constitution said nothing about giving any regulatory powers to bureaucrats. It gave to *Congress* the power to regulate commerce among the states. Now obviously Congress could not make the necessary day-to-day decisions to regulate, for example, the rates that interstate railroads charged to farmers and

other shippers. Some agency or commission composed of appointed officials and experts would have to be created to do that. For a long time, however, the prevailing interpretation of the Constitution was that no such agency could exercise such regulatory powers unless Congress first set down clear standards that would govern the agency's decisions. As late as 1935 the Supreme Court held that a regulatory agency could not make rules on its own; it could only apply the standards enacted by Congress.[5] The Court's view was that the legislature may not delegate its powers to the president or to an administrative agency.[6]

These restrictions on what administrators could do were set aside in wartime. During World War I, for example, President Woodrow Wilson was authorized by Congress to fix prices, operate the railroads, manage the communications system, and even control the distribution of food.[7] This kind of extraordinary grant of power usually ended with the war.

Some changes in the bureaucracy did not end with the war. During the Civil War, World War I, World War II, the Korean War, and the war in Vietnam, the number of civilian (as well as military)

---

laissez-faire   An economic theory that government should not regulate or interfere with commerce.

employees of the government rose sharply. These increases were not simply in the number of civilians needed to help serve the war effort; many of the additional people were hired by agencies, such as the Treasury Department, not obviously connected with the war. Furthermore, the number of federal officials did not return to prewar levels after each war. Though there was some reduction, each war left the number of federal employees larger than before.[8]

It is not hard to understand how this happens. During wartime almost every government agency argues that its activities have *some* relation to the war effort, and few legislators want to be caught voting against something that may help that effort. Hence in 1944 the Reindeer Service in Alaska, an agency of the Interior Department, asked for more employees because reindeer are "a valued asset in military planning."

A Change in Role

Today's bureaucracy is largely a product of two events: the depression of the 1930s (and the concomitant New Deal program of President Roosevelt) and World War II. Though many agencies have been added since then, the basic features of the bureaucracy were set mainly as a result of changes in public attitudes and in constitutional interpretation that occurred during these periods. The government was now expected to play an active role in dealing with economic and social problems. In the late 1930s the Supreme Court reversed its earlier decisions (see Chapter 16) on the question of delegating legislative powers to administrative agencies and upheld laws by which Congress merely instructs agencies to make decisions that serve "the public interest" in some area.[9] As a result it was possible for President Nixon to set up in 1971 a system of price and wage controls based on a statute that simply authorized the president "to issue such orders and regulations as he may deem appropriate to stabilize prices, rents, wages, and salaries."[10] The Cost of Living Council and other agencies that Nixon established to carry out this order were run by appointed officials who had the legal authority to make sweeping decisions based on general statutory language.

World War II was the first occasion during which the government made heavy use of federal income taxes—on individuals and corporations—to finance its activities. Between 1940 and 1945 total federal tax collections increased from about $5 billion to nearly $44 billion. The end of the war brought no substantial tax reduction: the country believed that a high level of military preparedness continued to be necessary and that various social programs begun before the war should enjoy the heavy funding made possible by wartime taxes. Tax receipts continued, by and large, to grow. Before 1913, when the Sixteenth Amendment to the Constitution was passed, the federal government could not collect income taxes at all (it financed itself largely from customs duties and excise taxes). From 1913 to 1940 income taxes were small (in 1940 the average American paid only $7 in federal income taxes). World War II created the first great financial boom for the government, permitting the sustained expansion of a wide variety of programs and thus entrenching a large number of administrators in Washington.[11]

Although it is still too soon to tell, a third event—the September 11, 2001, terrorist attacks on the United States—could affect bureaucracy as profoundly as the depression of the 1930s and World War II did. A law creating a massive new cabinet agency, the Department of Homeland Security (DHS), was passed in late 2002. Within two years of its creation, the DHS had consolidated under its authority some twenty-two smaller federal agencies with nearly 180,000 federal employees (third behind Defense and Veterans Affairs) and over $40 billion in budgets (fourth behind Defense, Health and Human Services, and Education). In addition, dozens of intergovernmental grant-making programs came under the authority of the DHS. In late 2004 Congress passed another law that promised, over time, to centralize under a single director of national intelligence the work of the over seventy federal agencies authorized to spend money on counterterrorist activities.

☆ The Federal Bureaucracy Today

No president wants to admit that he has increased the size of the bureaucracy. He can avoid saying this by pointing out that the number of civilians working for the federal government, excluding postal workers, has not increased significantly in recent years and is about the same today (2 million persons) as it was in 1960, and less than it was during World War II. This explanation is true but misleading, for it neglects the roughly 13 million people who work *indirectly* for Washington as employees of private firms and state

Figure 15.1 The Real "Washington" Bureaucracy

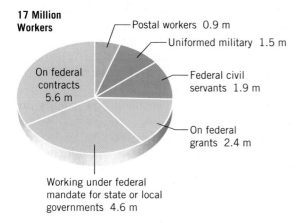

17 Million Workers

- Postal workers 0.9 m
- Uniformed military 1.5 m
- Federal civil servants 1.9 m
- On federal grants 2.4 m
- Working under federal mandate for state or local governments 4.6 m
- On federal contracts 5.6 m

Source: Paul C. Light, *The True Size of Government* (Washington, D.C.: Brookings Institution, 1999). Data for 1996.

or local agencies that are largely, if not entirely, supported by federal funds. As Figure 15.1 shows, there are nearly three persons earning their living indirectly from the federal government for every one earning it directly. While federal employment has remained quite stable, employment among federal contractors and consultants and in state and local governments has mushroomed. Indeed, most federal bureaucrats, like most other people who work for the federal government, live outside Washington, D.C. (see Figure 15.3 later in this chapter).

The power of the federal bureaucracy cannot be measured by the number of employees, however. A bureaucracy of five million persons would have little power if each employee did nothing but type letters or file documents, whereas a bureaucracy of only one hundred persons would have awesome power if each member were able to make arbitrary life-and-death decisions affecting the rest of us. The power of the bureaucracy depends on the extent to which appointed officials have **discretionary authority**—that is, the ability to choose courses of action and to make policies that are not spelled out in advance by laws. In Figure 15.2 we see how the volume of regulations issued and the amount of money spent have risen much faster than the number of federal employees who write the regulations and spend the money.

By this test the power of the federal bureaucracy has grown enormously. Congress has delegated substantial authority to administrative agencies in three areas: (1) paying subsidies to particular groups and organizations in society (farmers, veterans, scientists, schools, universities, hospitals); (2) transferring money from the federal government to state and local governments (the grant-in-aid programs described in Chapter 3); and (3) devising and enforcing regulations for various sectors of society and the economy. Some of these administrative functions, such as grants-in-aid to states, are closely monitored by Congress; others, such as the regulatory programs, usually operate with a greater degree of independence. These delegations of power, especially in the areas of paying subsidies and regulating the economy, did not become commonplace until the 1930s, and then only after the Supreme Court decided that such delegations were constitutional. Today, by contrast, appointed officials can decide, within rather broad limits, who shall own a television station, what safety features automobiles shall have, what kinds of scientific research shall be specially encouraged, what drugs shall appear on the market, which dissident groups shall be investigated, what fumes an industrial smokestack may emit, which corporate mergers shall be allowed, what use shall be made of national forests, and what prices crop and dairy farmers shall receive for their products.

If appointed officials have this kind of power, then how they use it is of paramount importance in understanding modern government. There are, broadly, four factors that may explain the behavior of these officials:

1. The manner in which they are recruited and rewarded
2. Their personal attributes, such as their socioeconomic backgrounds and their political attitudes
3. The nature of their jobs
4. The constraints that outside forces—political superiors, legislators, interest groups, journalists—impose on their agencies

Recruitment and Retention

The federal civil service system was designed to recruit qualified people on the basis of merit, not

discretionary authority The extent to which appointed bureaucrats can choose courses of action and make policies that are not spelled out in advance by laws.

Figure 15.2   Federal Government: Money, People, and Regulations

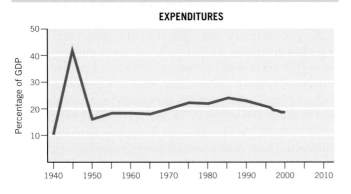

EXPENDITURES

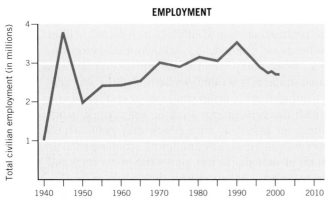

EMPLOYMENT

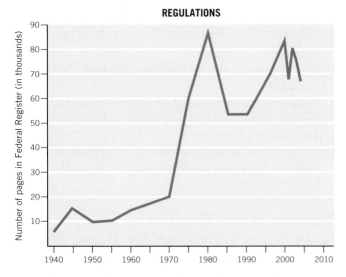

REGULATIONS

Sources: Expenditures and employment: *Statistical Abstract of the United States, 2000*, Nos. 483 and 582; regulations: Harold W. Stanley and Richard G. Niemi, *Vital Statistics on American Politics* (Washington, D.C.: Congressional Quarterly Press, 1998), tables 6-12, 6-14. Post-2000 data updated by Marc Siegel.

political patronage, and to retain and promote employees on the basis of performance, not political favoritism. Many appointed federal officials belong to the **competitive service.** This means that they are appointed only after they have passed a written examination administered by the Office of Personnel Management (OPM) or met certain selection criteria (such as training, educational attainments, or prior experience) devised by the hiring agency and approved by the OPM. Where competition for a job exists and candidates can be ranked by their scores or records, the agency must usually appoint one of the three top-ranking candidates.

In recent years the competitive service system has become decentralized, so that each agency now hires its own people without an OPM referral, and examinations have become less common. In 1952 more than 86 percent of all federal employees were civil servants hired by the competitive service; by 1996 that figure had fallen to less than 54 percent. This decentralization and the greater use of ways other than exams to hire employees were caused by three things. First, the old OPM system was cumbersome and often not relevant to the complex needs of departments. Second, these agencies had a need for more professionally trained employees—lawyers, biologists, engineers, and computer specialists—who could not be ranked on the basis of some standard exam. And third, civil rights groups pressed Washington to make the racial composition of the federal bureaucracy look more like the racial composition of the nation.

Thus it is wrong to suppose that a standardized, centralized system governs the federal service. As one recent study concluded, today much of the "real responsibility for recruiting, testing, and hiring has shifted to the agencies from OPM and its central system."[12]

Moreover, the kinds of workers being recruited into the federal civil service have changed. For example, blue-collar employment fell from 26 percent of the federal work force in 1973 to 16 percent in 1993. Meanwhile, the federal government's white-

competitive service   The government offices to which people are appointed on the basis of merit, as ascertained by a written exam or by applying certain selection criteria.

collar work force has become more diverse occupationally. As one writer on civil service reform has noted, the "need to recruit and retain physicists, biologists, oceanographers, nurses, statisticians, botanists, and epidemiologists, as well as large numbers of engineers, lawyers, and accountants, now preoccupies federal personnel managers."[13]

Employees hired outside the competitive service are part of the excepted service. They now make up almost half of all workers. Though not hired by the OPM, they still are typically hired in a nonpartisan fashion. Some are hired by agencies—such as the CIA, the FBI, and the Postal Service—that have their own selection procedures.

About 3 percent of the excepted employees are appointed on grounds other than or in addition to merit. These legal exceptions exist to permit the president to select, for policy-making and politically sensitive posts, people who are in agreement with his policy views. Such appointments are generally of three kinds:

1. Presidential appointments authorized by statute (cabinet and subcabinet officers, judges, U.S. marshals and U.S. attorneys, ambassadors, and members of various boards and commissions).
2. "Schedule C" appointments to jobs that are described as having a "confidential or policy-determining character" below the level of cabinet or subcabinet posts (including executive assistants, special aides, and confidential secretaries).
3. Noncareer executive assignments (NEAs) given to high-ranking members of the regular competitive civil service or to persons brought into the civil service at these high levels. These people are deeply involved in the advocacy of presidential programs or participate in policy-making.

These three groups of excepted appointments constitute the patronage available to a president and his administration. When President Kennedy took office in 1961, he had 451 political jobs to fill. When President George W. Bush took office in 2001, he had more than four times that number, including nearly four times the number of top cabinet posts. Scholars disagree over whether this proliferation of political appointees has improved or worsened Washington's performance, but one thing is clear: widespread presidential patronage is hardly unprecedented. In the nineteenth century practically every federal job was

Federal employees aren't just paper shufflers; many, such as this biologist, perform skilled professional tasks.

a patronage job. For example, when Grover Cleveland, a Democrat, became president in 1885, he replaced some forty thousand Republican postal employees with Democrats.

Ironically, two years earlier, in 1883, the passage of the Pendleton Act had begun a slow but steady transfer of federal jobs from the patronage to the merit system. It may seem strange that a political party in power (the Republicans) would be willing to relinquish its patronage in favor of a merit-based appointment system. Two factors made it possible for the Republicans to pass the Pendleton Act: (1) public outrage over the abuses of the spoils system, highlighted by the assassination of President James Garfield by a man always described in the history books as a "disappointed office seeker" (*lunatic* would be a more accurate term); and (2) the fear that if the Democrats came to power on a wave of antispoils

★ HOW THINGS WORK ★

A Day in the Life of a Bureaucrat

Here is how the commissioner of the Social Security Administration (SSA), a high-level bureaucrat, spent a typical day:

5:45 A.M.	Arise.
6:50 A.M.	Leave for the office.
7:30 A.M.	Read newspapers.
8:00 A.M.	Meet with deputy commissioner.
8:30 A.M.	Brief cabinet secretary on Social Security data.*
9:45 A.M.	Decide how to respond to press criticisms.
10:05 A.M.	Leave for meeting in another building.
11:30 A.M.	Meet with top staff.
1:00 P.M.	Meet with bureau chiefs on half a dozen issues.
2:45 P.M.	Meet with a deputy to discuss next year's budget.
3:30 P.M.	Meet with business executive about use of computers in SSA.
4:30 P.M.	Meet with deputy in charge of Medicare to discuss plan for national health insurance.
5:10 P.M.	Catch up on phone calls; meet with committee concerned with drug abuse.
6:10 P.M.	Leave for home. Get out of attending a dinner meeting in Washington.

As is obvious, high-level bureaucrats spend most of their time discussing things in meetings. It is in such meetings that government policy is made.

*SSA was part of the Department of Health and Human Services but no longer is.

Source: Adapted from "A Day in the Life of a Government Executive," in *Inside the System,* ed. Charles Peters and Nicholas Leamann, 4th ed. (New York: Holt, Rinehart and Winston, 1979), 205–213.

sentiment, existing Republican officeholders would be fired. (The Democrats won anyway.)

The merit system spread to encompass most of the federal bureaucracy, generally with presidential support. Though presidents may have liked in theory the idea of hiring and firing subordinates at will, most felt that the demands for patronage were impossible either to satisfy or to ignore. Furthermore, by increasing the coverage of the merit system a president could "blanket in" patronage appointees already holding office, thus making it difficult or impossible for the next administration to fire them.

■ **The Buddy System** The actual recruitment of civil servants, especially in middle- and upper-level jobs, is somewhat more complicated, and slightly more political, than the laws and rules might suggest. Though many people enter the federal bureaucracy by learn-

> **name-request job** A job that is filled by a person whom an agency has already identified.

ing of a job, filling out an application, perhaps taking a test, and being hired, many also enter on a "name-request" basis. A **name-request job** is one that is filled by a person whom an agency has already identified. In this respect the federal government is not so different from private business. A person learns of a job from somebody who already has one, or the head of a bureau decides in advance whom he or she wishes to hire. The agency must still send a form describing the job to the OPM, but it also names the person whom the agency wants to appoint. Sometimes the job is even described in such a way that the person named is the only one who can qualify for it. Occasionally this tailor-made, name-request job is offered to a person at the insistence of a member of Congress who wants a political supporter taken care of; more often it is made available because the bureaucracy itself knows whom it wishes to hire and wants to circumvent an elaborate search. This is the "buddy system."

The buddy system does not necessarily produce poor employees. Indeed, it is frequently a way of hiring people known to the agency as being capable of handling the position. It also opens up the possibility of hiring people whose policy views are congenial to those already in office. Such networking is based on shared policy views, not (as once was the case) on narrow partisan affiliations. For example, bureaucrats in consumer protection agencies recruit new staff from private groups with an interest in consumer protection, such as the various organizations associated with Ralph Nader, or from academics who have a proconsumer inclination.

There has always been an informal "old boys' network" among those who move in and out of high-level government posts; with the increasing appointment of women to these jobs, there has begun to emerge an old girls' network as well.[14] In a later section we will consider whether, or in what ways, these recruitment patterns make a difference.

■ **Firing a Bureaucrat** The great majority of bureaucrats who are part of the civil service and who do not hold presidential appointments have jobs that are, for all practical purposes, beyond reach. An executive must go through elaborate steps to fire,

demote, or suspend a civil servant. Realistically this means that no one is fired or demoted unless his or her superior is prepared to invest a great deal of time and effort in the attempt. In 1987 about 2,600 employees who had completed their probationary period were fired for misconduct or poor performance. That is about one-tenth of 1 percent of all federal employees. It is hard to believe that a large private company would fire only one-tenth of 1 percent of its workers in a given year. It's also impossible to believe that, as is often the case in Washington, it would take a year to fire anyone. To cope with this problem, federal executives have devised a number of stratagems for bypassing or forcing out civil servants with whom they cannot work—denying them promotions, transferring them to undesirable locations, or assigning them to meaningless work.

With the passage of the Civil Service Reform Act of 1978 Congress recognized that many high-level positions in the civil service have important policy-making responsibilities and that the president and his cabinet officers ought to have more flexibility in

One barrier to improving presidential control of the federal bureaucracy is that even the White House has become a large bureaucracy.

★ HOW THINGS WORK ★

Firing a Bureaucrat

To fire or demote a member of the competitive civil service, these procedures must be followed:

1. The employee must be given written notice at least thirty days in advance that he or she is to be fired or demoted for incompetence or misconduct.
2. The written notice must contain a statement of reasons, including specific examples of unacceptable performance.
3. The employee has the right to an attorney and to reply, orally or in writing, to the charges.
4. The employee has the right to appeal any adverse action to the Merit Systems Protection Board (MSPB), a three-person, bipartisan body appointed by the president with the consent of the Senate.
5. The MSPB must grant the employee a hearing, at which the employee has the right to have an attorney present.
6. The employee has the right to appeal the MSPB decision to a U.S. court of appeals, which can hold new hearings.

recruiting, assigning, and paying such people. Accordingly, the act created the Senior Executive Service (SES), about eight thousand top federal managers who can (in theory) be hired, fired, and transferred more easily than ordinary civil servants. Moreover, the act stipulated that members of the SES would be eligible for substantial cash bonuses if they performed their duties well. (To protect the rights of SES members, anyone who is removed from the SES is guaranteed a job elsewhere in the government.)

Things did not work out quite as the sponsors of the SES had hoped. Though most eligible civil servants joined it, there was only a modest increase in the proportion of higher-ranking positions in agencies that were filled by transfer from another agency; the cash bonuses did not prove to be an important incentive (perhaps because the base salaries of top bureaucrats did not keep up with inflation); and hardly any member of the SES was actually fired. Two years after the SES was created, less than one-half of 1 percent of its members had received an unsatisfactory rating, and none had been fired. Nor does the SES give the president a large opportunity to make political appointments: only 10 percent of the SES can be selected from outside the existing civil service. And no SES member can be transferred involuntarily.

■ **The Agency's Point of View**   When one realizes that most agencies are staffed by people who were recruited by those agencies, sometimes on a name-request basis, and who are virtually immune from dismissal, it becomes clear that the recruitment and retention policies of the civil service work to ensure that most bureaucrats will have an "agency" point of view. Even with the encouragement for transfers created by the SES, most government agencies are dominated by people who have not served in any other agency and who have been in government service most of their lives. This fact has some advantages: it means that most top-tier bureaucrats are experts in the procedures and policies of their agencies and that there will be a substantial degree of continuity in agency behavior no matter which political party happens to be in power.

But the agency point of view has its costs as well. A political executive entering an agency with responsibility for shaping its direction will discover that he or she must carefully win the support of career subordinates. A subordinate has an infinite capacity for discreet sabotage and can make life miserable for a political superior by delaying action, withholding information, following the rule book with literal exactness, or making an "end run" around a superior to mobilize members of Congress who are sympathetic to the bureaucrat's point of view. For instance, when one political executive wanted to downgrade a bureau in his department, he found, naturally, that the bureau chief was opposed. The bureau chief spoke to some friendly lobbyists and a key member of Congress. When the political executive asked the congressman whether he had any problem with the contemplated reorganization, the congressman replied, "No, you have the problem, because if you touch that bureau, I'll cut your job out of the budget."[15]

Personal Attributes

A second factor that might shape the way bureaucrats use their power is their personal attributes. These include their social class, education, and personal political beliefs. The federal civil service as a whole looks very much like a cross section of American society in the education, sex, race, and social origins of its members (see Figure 15.3). But as with many other employers, African Americans and other minorities are most likely to be heavily represented in the lowest grade levels and tend to be underrepresented at the executive level (see Table 15.1). At the higher-ranking levels, where the most power is found—say, in the supergrade ranks of GS 16

through GS 18—the typical civil servant is a middle-aged white male with a college degree whose father was somewhat more advantaged than the average citizen. In the great majority of cases this individual is in fact very different from the typical American in both background and personal beliefs.

Because political appointees and career bureaucrats are unrepresentative of the average American, and because of their supposed occupational self-interest, some critics have speculated that the people holding these jobs think about politics and government in ways very different from the public at large. The results of a 1998 survey would seem to prove them right: 57 percent of average citizens, versus 76 percent of career bureaucrats and 88 percent of Clinton administration appointees, described themselves as progovernment; 60 percent of all Americans, compared to just 4 percent of all career bureaucrats and

Figure 15.3   Characteristics of Federal Civilian Employees, 1960 and 1999

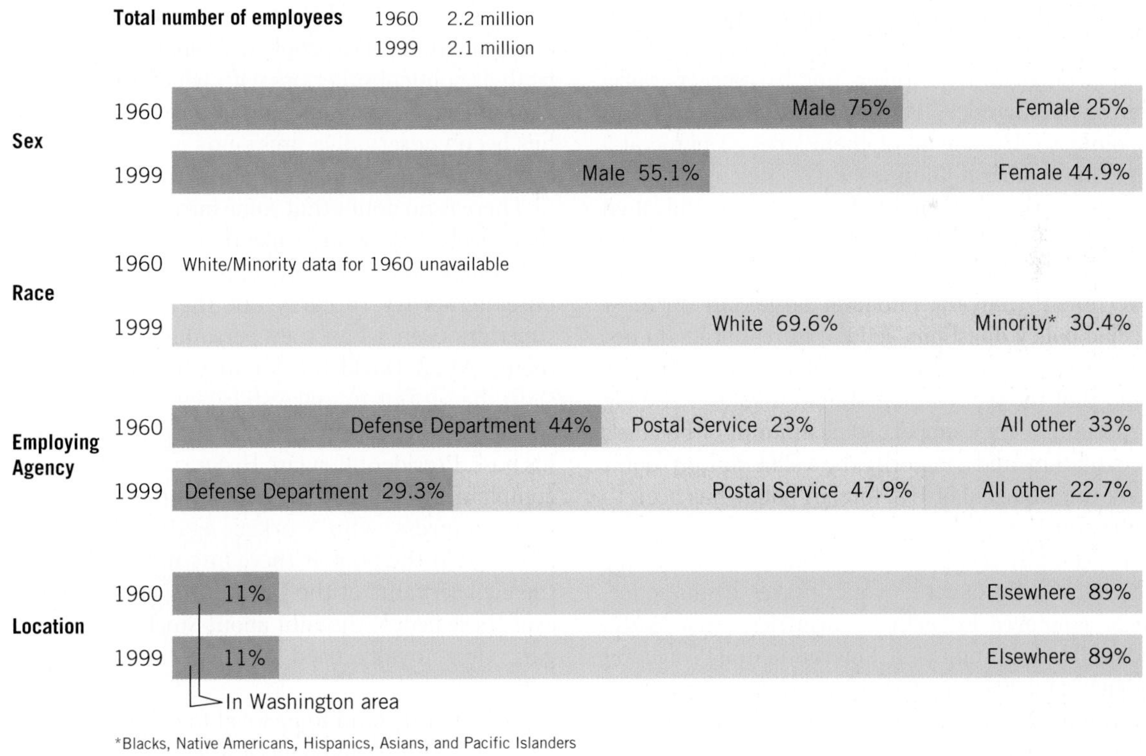

Total number of employees   1960   2.2 million
                             1999   2.1 million

Sex
1960   Male 75%   Female 25%
1999   Male 55.1%   Female 44.9%

Race
1960   White/Minority data for 1960 unavailable
1999   White 69.6%   Minority* 30.4%

Employing Agency
1960   Defense Department 44%   Postal Service 23%   All other 33%
1999   Defense Department 29.3%   Postal Service 47.9%   All other 22.7%

Location
1960   11%   Elsewhere 89%
1999   11%   Elsewhere 89%
        └─→ In Washington area

*Blacks, Native Americans, Hispanics, Asians, and Pacific Islanders

Sources: Statistical Abstract of the United States, 1961, 392–394; *Statistical Abstract of the United States, 2000,* Nos. 450, 482, 500, 595, 1118.

Table 15.1	Minority Employment in the Federal Bureaucracy by Rank, 2000				
				Percentage of Total	
Grade	Black	Hispanic		Black	Hispanic
GS 1–4	26,895	8,526		29.7%	9.4%
GS 5–8	99,937	31,703		27.0	8.6
GS 9–12	82,809	36,813		16.0	7.0
GS 13–15	31,494	12,869		10.3	4.2
SES	1,180	547		7.3	3.4
Total	298,701	115,247		17.0	6.7

Note: GS stands for "General Service." The higher the number, the higher the rank of people with that number.

Source: Statistical Abstract of the United States, 2001, 482.

Clinton appointees, agreed that most popular criticisms of the federal government were justified; about a third of the public, but under a fifth of the career and appointed public servants, described themselves as conservative; and only 13 or 14 percent of those in government agreed that the public knew enough about the issues to form wise opinions on policy.[16]

It is important, however, not to overgeneralize from such differences. For example, whereas Clinton appointees (virtually all of them strong Democrats) were more liberal than average citizens, Reagan appointees (virtually all of them loyal Republicans) were undoubtedly more conservative than average citizens. Likewise, career civil servants are more progovernment than the public at large, but on most specific policy questions, federal bureaucrats do not have extreme positions. They don't, for example, think that the government should take over the big corporations, they support some amount of business deregulation, and a majority (by a slim margin) don't think that the goal of U.S. foreign policy has been to protect business.[17]

We can also see, however, that the kind of agency for which a bureaucrat works makes a difference. Those employed in "activist" agencies, such as the Federal Trade Commission, Environmental Protection Agency, and Food and Drug Administration, have much more liberal views than those who work for the more "traditional" agencies, such as the departments of Agriculture, Commerce, and the Treasury.

This association between attitudes and kind of agency has been confirmed by other studies. Even when the bureaucrats come from roughly the same social backgrounds, their policy views seem to reflect the type of government work that they do. For example, people holding foreign service jobs in the State Department tended to be more liberal than those coming from similar family backgrounds and performing similar tasks (such as working on foreign affairs) in the Defense Department.[18] It is not clear whether these differences in attitudes were produced by the jobs that they held or whether certain jobs attract people with certain beliefs. Probably both forces were at work.

Whatever the mechanism involved, there seems little doubt that different agencies display different political ideologies. A study done in 1976 revealed that Democrats and people with liberal views tended to be overrepresented in social service agencies, whereas Republicans and people with conservative views tend to be overrepresented in defense agencies.[19]

Do Bureaucrats Sabotage Their Political Bosses?

Because it is so hard to fire career bureaucrats, it is often said that these people will sabotage any actions by their political superiors with which they disagree. And since civil servants tend to have liberal views, it has been conservative presidents and cabinet secretaries who have usually expressed this worry.

There is no doubt that some bureaucrats will drag their heels if they don't like their bosses, and a few will block actions they oppose. However, most bureaucrats try to carry out the policies of their superiors even when they personally disagree with them. When David Stockman was director of the OMB, he set out to make sharp cuts in government spending programs in accordance with the wishes of his boss, President Reagan. He later published a book complaining about all the people in the White House and Congress who worked against him.[20] But nowhere in the book is there any major criticism of the civil servants at the OMB. It appears that whatever these people thought about Stockman and Reagan, they loyally tried to carry out Stockman's policies.

Bureaucrats tend to be loyal to political superiors who deal with them cooperatively and constructively. An agency head who tries to ignore or discredit them can be in for a tough time, however. The powers of obstruction available to aggrieved bureaucrats are formidable. Such people can leak embarrassing stories to Congress or to the media, help interest groups mobilize against the agency head, and discover a thousand procedural reasons why a new course of action won't work.

The exercise of some of those bureaucratic powers is protected by the Whistle Blower Protection Act. Passed in 1989, the law created the Office of Special Counsel, charged with investigating complaints from bureaucrats that they were punished after reporting to Congress about waste, fraud, or abuse in their agencies.

It may seem odd that bureaucrats, who have great job security, would not always act in accordance with their personal beliefs instead of in accordance with the wishes of their bosses. Bureaucratic sabotage, in this view, ought to be very common. But bureaucratic cooperation with superiors is not odd, once you take into account the nature of a bureaucrat's job.

If you are a voter at the polls, your beliefs will clearly affect how you vote (see Chapter 7). But if you are the second baseman for the Boston Red Sox, your political beliefs, social background, and education will have nothing to do with how you field ground balls. Sociologists like to call the different things that people do in their lives "roles" and to distinguish between roles that are loosely structured (such as the role of voter) and those that are highly structured (such as that of second baseman). Personal attitudes greatly affect loosely structured roles and only slightly affect highly structured ones. Applied to the federal bureaucracy, this suggests that civil servants performing tasks that are routinized (such as filling out forms), tasks that are closely defined by laws and rules (such as issuing welfare checks), or tasks that are closely monitored by others (supervisors, special-interest groups, the media) will probably perform them in ways that can only partially be explained, if at all, by their personal attitudes. Civil servants performing complex, loosely defined tasks that are not closely monitored may carry out their work in ways powerfully influenced by their attitudes.

Among the loosely defined tasks are those performed by professionals, and so the values of these people may influence how they behave. An increasing number of lawyers, economists, engineers, and physicians are hired to work in federal agencies. These men and women have received extensive training that produces not only a set of skills, but also a set of attitudes as to what is important and valuable. For example, the Federal Trade Commission (FTC), charged with preventing unfair methods of competition among businesses, employs two kinds of professionals—lawyers, organized into a Bureau of Competition, and economists, organized into a Bureau of Economics. Lawyers are trained to draw up briefs and argue cases in court and are taught the legal standards by which they will know whether they have a chance of winning a case or not. Economists are trained to analyze how a competitive economy works and what costs consumers must bear if the goods and services are produced by a monopoly (one firm controlling the market) or an oligopoly (a small number of firms dominating the market).

Because of their training and attitudes, lawyers in the FTC prefer to bring cases against a business firm that has done something clearly illegal, such as attending secret meetings with competitors to rig the prices that will be charged to a purchaser. These cases appeal to lawyers because there is usually a victim (the purchaser or a rival company) who complains to the government, the illegal behavior can be proved in a court of law, and the case can be completed rather quickly.

Economists, on the other hand, are trained to measure the value of a case not by how quickly it can be proved in court, but by whether the illegal practice imposes large or small costs on the consumer. FTC economists often dislike the cases that appeal to lawyers. The economists feel that the amount of money that such cases save the consumer is often small and that the cases are a distraction from the major issues—such as whether IBM unfairly dominates the computer business or whether General Motors is too large to be efficient. Lawyers, in turn, are leery of big cases, because the facts are hard to prove and they may take forever to decide (one blockbuster case can drag through the courts for ten years). In many federal agencies divergent professional values such as these help explain how power is used.

Culture and Careers

Unlike the lawyers and economists working in the FTC, the government bureaucrats in a typical agency don't have a lot of freedom to choose a course of action. Their jobs are spelled out not only by the laws, rules, and routines of their agency, but also by the informal understandings among fellow employees as to how they are supposed to act. These understandings are the *culture* of the agency.[21]

If you belong to the air force, you can do a lot of things, but only one thing really counts: flying airplanes, especially advanced jet fighters and bombers. The culture of the air force is a pilots' culture. If you belong to the navy, you have more choices: fly jet aircraft or operate nuclear submarines. Both jobs provide status and a chance for promotion to the highest ranks. By contrast, sailing minesweepers or transport ships (or worse, having a desk job and not sailing anything at all) is not a very rewarding job. The culture of the CIA emphasizes working overseas as a clandestine agent; staying in Washington as a report writer is not as good for your career. The culture of the State Department rewards skill in political negotiations; being an expert on international economics or embassy security is much less rewarding.

You can usually tell what kind of culture an agency has by asking an employee, "If you want to get ahead here, what sort of jobs should you take?" The jobs that are career enhancing are part of the culture; the jobs that are not career enhancing (NCE in bureaucratic lingo) are not part of it.

Being part of a strong culture is good—up to a point. It motivates employees to work hard in order to win the respect of their coworkers as well as the approval of their bosses. But a strong culture also makes it hard to change an agency. FBI agents for many years resisted getting involved in civil rights or organized crime cases, and diplomats in the State Department didn't pay much attention to embassy security. These important jobs were not a career-enhancing part of the culture.

Constraints

The biggest difference between a government agency and a private organization is the vastly greater number of constraints on the agency. Unlike a business firm, the typical government bureau cannot hire, fire, build, or sell without going through procedures set down in laws. How much money it pays its members is determined by statute, not by the market. Not only the goals of an agency but often its exact procedures are spelled out by Congress.

At one time the Soil Conservation Service was required by law to employ at least 14,177 full-time workers. The State Department is forbidden by law from opening a diplomatic post in Antigua or Barbuda but forbidden from closing a post anywhere else. The Agency for International Development (which administers our foreign-aid program) has been given

by Congress 33 objectives and 75 priorities and must send to Congress 288 reports each year. When it buys military supplies, the Defense Department must give a "fair proportion" of its contracts to small businesses, especially those operated by "socially and economically disadvantaged individuals," and must buy from American firms even if, in some cases, buying abroad would be cheaper. Some of the more general constraints include the following:

- Administrative Procedure Act (1946). Before adopting a new rule or policy, an agency must give notice, solicit comments, and (often) hold hearings.
- Freedom of Information Act (1966). Citizens have the right to inspect all government records except those containing military, intelligence, or trade secrets or revealing private personnel actions.
- National Environmental Policy Act (1969). Before undertaking any major action affecting the environment, an agency must issue an environmental impact statement.
- Privacy Act (1974). Government files about individuals, such as Social Security and tax records, must be kept confidential.
- Open Meeting Law (1976). Every part of every agency meeting must be open to the public unless certain matters (for example, military or trade secrets) are being discussed.

One of the biggest constraints on bureaucratic action is that Congress rarely gives any job to a single agency. Stopping drug trafficking is the task of the Customs Service, the FBI, the Drug Enforcement Administration, the Border Patrol, and the Defense Department (among others). Disposing of the assets of failed savings-and-loan associations is the job of the Resolution Funding Corporation, Resolution Trust Corporation, Federal Housing Finance Board, Office of Thrift Supervision in the Treasury Department, Federal Deposit Insurance Corporation, Federal Reserve Board, and Justice Department (among others).

The effects of these constraints on agency behavior are not surprising.

- The government will often act slowly. (The more constraints that must be satisfied, the longer it will take to get anything done.)
- The government will sometimes act inconsistently. (What is done to meet one constraint—for example, freedom of information—may endanger another constraint—for example, privacy.)

The "Rules" of Politics

Learning Bureaucratese

A few simple rules, if remembered, will enable you to speak and write in the style of a government official.

- **Use nouns as if they were verbs.** Don't say, "We must set priorities"; say instead, "We must prioritize."

- **Use adjectives as if they were verbs.** Don't say, "We put the report in final form"; say instead, "We finalized the report."

- **Use several words where one word would do.** Don't say, "now"; say instead, "at this point in time."

- **Never use ordinary words where unusual ones can be found.** Don't say that you "made a choice"; say that you "selected an option."

- **No matter what subject you are discussing, employ the language of sports and war.** Never say, "progress"; say, "breakthrough." Never speak of a "compromise"; instead consider "adopting a fallback position."

- **Avoid active verbs.** Never say, "Study the problem"; say instead, "It is felt that the problem should be subjected to further study."

MISS WATSON, TURN SOME OF THESE NOUNS INTO VERBS FOR ME. I WANT THIS TO SOUND IMPORTANT.

© 1986 by NEA, Inc. THAVES 4-11

- It will be easier to block action than to take action. (The constraints ensure that lots of voices will be heard; the more voices that are heard, the more they may cancel each other out.)
- Lower-ranking employees will be reluctant to make decisions on their own. (Having many constraints means having many ways to get into trouble; to avoid trouble, let your boss make the decision.)
- Citizens will complain of red tape. (The more constraints to serve, the more forms to fill out.)

These constraints do not mean that government bureaucracy is powerless, only that, however great its power, it tends to be clumsy. That clumsiness arises not from the fact that the people who work for agencies are dull or incompetent, but from the complicated political environment in which that work must be done.

The moral of the story: the next time you get mad at a bureaucrat, ask yourself, Why would a rational, intelligent person behave that way? Chances are you will discover that there are good reasons for that action. You would probably behave the same way if you were working for the same organization.

■ **Why So Many Constraints?** Government agencies behave as they do in large part because of the many different goals they must pursue and the complex rules they must follow. Where does all this red tape come from?

From us. From us, the people.

Every goal, every constraint, every bit of red tape, was put in place by Congress, the courts, the White House, or the agency itself responding to the demands of some influential faction. Civil rights

The "Rules" of Politics

"Laws" of Bureaucratic Procedure

Acheson's Rule A memorandum is written not to inform the reader but to protect the writer.

Boren's Laws
When in doubt, mumble.
When in trouble, delegate.
When in charge, ponder.

Chapman's Rules of Committees
Never arrive on time, or you will be stamped a beginner.
Don't say anything until the meeting is half over; this stamps you as being wise.
Be as vague as possible; this prevents irritating others.
When in doubt, suggest that a subcommittee be appointed.

Meskimen's Law There's never time to do it right but always time to do it over.

Murphy's Law If anything can go wrong, it will.

O'Toole's Corollary to Murphy's Law Murphy was an optimist.

Parkinson's First Law Work expands to fill the time available for its completion.

Parkinson's Second Law Expenditure rises to meet income.

Peter Principle In every hierarchy, each employee tends to rise to his level of incompetence; thus, every post tends to be filled by an incompetent employee.

Robertson's Rule The more directives you issue to solve a problem, the worse it gets.

Smith's Principle Never do anything for the first time.

> **iron triangle**   A close relationship between an agency, a congressional committee, and an interest group.

---

groups want every agency to hire and buy from women and minorities. Environmental groups want every agency to file environmental impact statements. Industries being regulated want every new agency policy to be formulated only after a lengthy public hearing with lots of lawyers present. Labor unions also want those hearings so that they can argue against industry lawyers. Everybody who sells something to the government wants a "fair chance" to make the sale, and so everybody insists that government contracts be awarded only after complex procedures are followed. A lot of people don't trust the government, and so they insist that everything it does be done in the sunshine—no secrets, no closed meetings, no hidden files.

If we wanted agencies to pursue their main goal with more vigor and less encumbering red tape, we would have to ask Congress, the courts, or the White House to repeal some of these constraints. In other words, we would have to be willing to give up something we want in order to get something else we want even more. But politics does not encourage people to make these trade-offs; instead it encourages us to expect to get everything—efficiency, fairness, help for minorities—all at once.

Agency Allies

Despite these constraints, government bureaucracies are not powerless. In fact, some of them actively seek certain constraints. They do so because it is a way of cementing a useful relationship with a congressional committee or an interest group.

At one time scholars described the relationship between an agency, a committee, and an interest group as an **iron triangle.** For example, the Department of Veterans Affairs, the House and Senate committees on veterans' affairs, and veterans' organizations (such as the American Legion) would form a tight, mutually advantageous alliance. The department would do what the committees wanted and in return get political support and budget appropriations; the committee members would do what the veterans' groups wanted and in return get votes and campaign contributions. Iron triangles are examples of what are called *client politics*.

Many agencies still have important allies in Congress and the private sector, especially those bureaus that serve the needs of specific sectors of the economy or regions of the country. The Department of Agriculture works closely with farm organizations, the Department of the Interior with groups interested in obtaining low-cost irrigation or grazing rights, and the Department of Housing and Urban Development with mayors and real-estate developers.

Sometimes these allies are so strong that they can defeat a popular president. For years President Reagan tried to abolish the Small Business Administration (SBA), arguing that its program of loans to small firms was wasteful and ridden with favoritism. But Congress, reacting to pressures from small-business groups, rallied to the SBA's defense. As a result Reagan had to oversee an agency that he didn't want.

But iron triangles are much less common today than once was the case. Politics of late has become far more complicated. For one thing, the number and variety of interest groups have increased so much in recent years that there is scarcely any agency that is not subject to pressures from several competing interests instead of only from one powerful interest. For another, the growth of subcommittees in Congress has meant that most agencies are subject to control by many different legislative groups, often with very different concerns. Finally, the courts have made it much easier for all kinds of individuals and interests to intervene in agency affairs.

As a result, nowadays government agencies face a bewildering variety of competing groups and legislative subcommittees that constitute not a loyal group of allies, but a fiercely contentious collection of critics. The Environmental Protection Agency is caught between the demands of environmentalists and those of industry organizations, the Occupational Safety and Health Administration between the pressures of labor and those of business, and the Federal Communications Commission between the desires of broadcasters and those of cable television companies. Even the Department of Agriculture faces not a unified group of farmers, but many different farmers split into rival groups, depending on the crops they raise, the regions in which they live, and the attitudes they have toward the relative merits of farm subsidies or free markets.

Political scientist Hugh Heclo has described the typical government agency today as being embedded not in an iron triangle, but in an **issue network**.[22] These issue networks consist of people in Washington-based interest groups, on congressional staffs, in universities and think tanks, and in the mass media, who regularly debate government policy on a certain subject—say, health care or auto safety. The networks are contentious, split along political, ideologi-

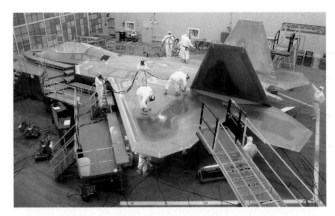

The real federal bureaucracy is bigger than just who works for the national government. Because defense contractors depend on government contracts, the bureaucracy includes people who work in these private firms.

cal, and economic lines. When a president takes office, he often recruits key agency officials from those members of the issue network who are most sympathetic to his views.

When Jimmy Carter, a Democrat, became president, he appointed to key posts in consumer agencies people who were from that part of the consumer issue network associated with Ralph Nader. Ronald Reagan, a conservative Republican, filled these same jobs with people who were from that part of the issue network holding free market or antiregulation views. When George Bush the elder, a more centrist Republican, took office, he filled these posts with more centrist members of the issue network. Bill Clinton brought back the consumer activists.

☆ Congressional Oversight

The main reason why some interest groups are important to agencies is that they are important to Congress. Not every interest group in the country has substantial access to Congress, but those that do and that are taken seriously by the relevant committees or subcommittees must also be taken seriously by the agency.

> **issue network** A network of people in Washington, D.C.–based interest groups, on congressional staffs, in universities and think tanks, and in the mass media, who regularly discuss and advocate public policies.

Furthermore, even apart from interest groups, members of Congress have constitutional powers over agencies and policy interests in how agencies function.

Congressional supervision of the bureaucracy takes several forms. First, no agency may exist (except for a few presidential offices and commissions) without congressional approval. Congress influences—and sometimes determines precisely—agency behavior by the statutes it enacts.

Second, no money may be spent unless it has first been authorized by Congress. **Authorization legislation** originates in a legislative committee (such as Agriculture, Education and Labor, or Public Works) and states the maximum amount of money that an agency may spend on a given program. This authorization may be permanent, it may be for a fixed number of years, or it may be annual (that is, it must be renewed each year, or the program or agency goes out of business).

Third, even funds that have been authorized by Congress cannot be spent unless (in most cases) they are also appropriated. Appropriations are usually made annually, and they originate not with the legislative committees but with the House Appropriations Committee and its various (and influential) subcommittees. An **appropriation** (money formally set aside for a specific use) may be, and often is, for less than the amount authorized. The Appropriations Committee's action thus tends to have a budget-cutting effect. There are some funds that can be spent without an appropriation, but in virtually every part of the bureaucracy each agency is keenly sensitive to congressional concerns at the time that the annual appropriations process is going on.

The Appropriations Committee and Legislative Committees

The fact that an agency budget must be both authorized and appropriated means that each agency serves not one congressional master but several, and that these masters may be in conflict. The real power over an agency's budget is exercised by the Appropriations Committee; the legislative committees are especially important when a substantive law is first passed or an agency is first created, or when an agency is subject to annual authorization.

In the past the power of the Appropriations Committee was rarely challenged: from 1947 through 1962, fully 90 percent of the House Appropriations Committee's recommendations on expenditures were approved by the full House without change.[23] Furthermore, the Appropriations Committee tends to recommend less money than an agency requests (though some specially favored agencies, such as the FBI, the Soil Conservation Service, and the Forest Service, have tended to get almost everything that they have asked for). Finally, the process of "marking up" (revising, amending, and approving) an agency's budget request gives to the Appropriations Committee, or one of its subcommittees, substantial influence over the policies that the agency follows.

Of late the appropriations committees have lost some of their great power over government agencies. This has happened in three ways:

First, Congress has created trust funds to pay for the benefits many people receive. The Social Security trust fund is the largest of these. In 1990 it took in about $260 billion in Social Security taxes and paid out about $220 billion in old-age benefits. There are several other trust funds as well. **Trust funds** operate outside the regular government budget, and the appropriations committees have no control over these expenditures. They are automatic.

Second, Congress has changed the authorization of many programs from permanent or multiyear to annual authorizations. This means that every year the legislative committees, as part of the reauthorization process, get to set limits on what these agencies can spend. This limits the ability of the appropriations committees to determine the spending limits. Before 1959 most authorizations were permanent or multiyear. Now a long list of agencies must be reauthorized every year—the State Department, NASA, military procurement programs of the Defense Department, the Justice Department, the Energy Department, and parts or all of many other agencies.

Third, the existence of huge budget deficits during the 1980s and early 2000s has meant that much of

authorization legislation   Legislative permission to begin or continue a government program or agency.

appropriation   A legislative grant of money to finance a government program or agency.

trust funds   Funds for government programs that are collected and spent outside the regular government budget.

Congress's time has been taken up with trying (usually not very successfully) to keep spending down. As a result there has rarely been much time to discuss the merits of various programs or how much ought to be spent on them; instead attention has been focused on meeting a target spending limit. In 1981 the budget resolution passed by Congress mandated cuts in several programs before the appropriations committees had even completed their work.[24]

In addition to the power of the purse, there are informal ways by which Congress can control the bureaucracy. An individual member of Congress can call an agency head on behalf of a constituent. Most such calls merely seek information, but some result in, or attempt to obtain, special privileges for particular people. Congressional committees may also obtain the right to pass on certain agency decisions. This is called **committee clearance,** and though it is usually not legally binding on the agency, few agency heads will ignore the expressed wish of a committee chair that he or she be consulted before certain actions (such as transferring funds) are taken.

The Legislative Veto

For many decades Congress made frequent use of the legislative veto to control bureaucratic or presidential actions. A **legislative veto** is a requirement that an executive decision must lie before Congress for a specified period (usually thirty or ninety days) before it takes effect. Congress could then veto the decision if a resolution of disapproval was passed by either house (a "one-house veto") or both houses (a "two-house veto"). Unlike laws, such resolutions were not signed by the president. Between 1932 and 1980 about two hundred laws were passed providing for a legislative veto, many of them involving presidential proposals to sell arms abroad.

But in June 1983 the Supreme Court declared the legislative veto to be unconstitutional. In the *Chadha* case the Court held that the Constitution clearly requires in Article I that "every order, resolution, or vote to which the concurrence of the Senate and House of Representatives may be necessary" (with certain minor exceptions) "shall be presented to the President of the United States," who must either approve it or return it with his veto attached. In short, Congress cannot take any action that has the force of law unless the president concurs in that action.[25] At a stroke of the pen parts of some two hundred laws suddenly became invalid.

At least that happened in theory. In fact since the *Chadha* decision Congress has passed a number of laws that contain legislative vetoes, despite the Supreme Court's having ruled against them! (Someone will have to go to court to test the constitutionality of these new provisions.)

Opponents of the legislative veto hope that future Congresses will have to pass laws that state much more clearly than before what an agency may or may not do. But it is just as likely that Congress will continue to pass laws stated in general terms and require that agencies implementing those laws report their plans to Congress, so that it will have a chance to enact and send to the president a regular bill disapproving the proposed action. Or Congress may rely on informal (but scarcely weak) means of persuasion, including threats to reduce the appropriations of an agency that does not abide by congressional preferences.

Congressional Investigations

Perhaps the most visible and dramatic form of congressional supervision of an agency is the investigation. Since 1792, when Congress investigated an army defeat by a Native American tribe, congressional investigations of the bureaucracy have been a regular feature—sometimes constructive, sometimes destructive—of legislative-executive relations. The investigative power is not mentioned in the Constitution, but has been inferred from the power to legislate. The Supreme Court has consistently upheld this interpretation, though it has also said that such investigations should not be solely for the purpose of exposing the purely personal affairs of private individuals and must not operate to deprive citizens of their basic rights.[26] Congress may compel a person to attend an investigation by issuing a subpoena; anyone who ignores the subpoena may be punished for contempt. Congress can vote to send the person to jail or can refer the matter to a court for further action. As explained in Chapter 14, the president and

committee clearance The ability of a congressional committee to review and approve certain agency decisions in advance and without passing a law.

legislative veto The authority of Congress to block a presidential action after it has taken place. The Supreme Court has held that Congress does not have this power.

his principal subordinates have refused to answer certain congressional inquiries on grounds of "executive privilege."

Although many areas of congressional oversight—budgetary review, personnel controls, investigations—are designed to control the exercise of bureaucratic discretion, other areas are intended to ensure the freedom of certain agencies from effective control, especially by the president. In dozens of cases Congress has authorized department heads and bureau chiefs to operate independent of presidential preferences. Congress has resisted, for example, presidential efforts to ensure that policies to regulate pollution do not impose excessive costs on the economy, and interest groups have brought suit to prevent presidential coordination of various regulatory agencies. If the bureaucracy sometimes works at cross-purposes, it is usually because Congress—or competing committees in Congress—wants it that way.

☆ Bureaucratic "Pathologies"

Everyone complains about bureaucracy in general (though rarely about bureaucratic agencies that everyone believes are desirable). This chapter should persuade you that it is difficult to say anything about bureaucracy "in general"; there are too many different kinds of agencies, kinds of bureaucrats, and kinds of programs to label the entire enterprise with some single adjective. Nevertheless, many people who recognize the enormous variety among government agencies still believe that they all have some general features in common and suffer from certain shared problems or pathologies.

This is true enough, but the reasons for it—and the solutions, if any—are not often understood. There are five major (or at least frequently mentioned) problems with bureaucracies: red tape, conflict, duplication, imperialism, and waste. **Red tape** refers to the complex rules and procedures that must be followed to get something done. *Conflict* exists because some agencies seem to be working at cross-purposes with other agencies. (For example, the

Agricultural Research Service tells farmers how to grow crops more efficiently, while the Agricultural Stabilization and Conservation Service pays farmers to grow fewer crops or to produce less.) *Duplication* (usually called "wasteful duplication") occurs when two government agencies seem to be doing the same thing, as when the Customs Service and the Drug Enforcement Administration both attempt to intercept illegal drugs being smuggled into the country. *Imperialism* refers to the tendency of agencies to grow without regard to the benefits that their programs confer or the costs that they entail. *Waste* means spending more than is necessary to buy some product or service.

These problems all exist, but they do not necessarily exist because bureaucrats are incompetent or power-hungry. Most exist because of the very nature of government itself. Take red tape: partly we encounter cumbersome rules and procedures because any large organization, governmental or not, must have some way of ensuring that one part of the organization does not operate out of step with another. Business corporations have red tape also; it is to a certain extent a consequence of bigness. But a great amount of governmental red tape is also the result of the need to satisfy legal and political requirements. Government agencies must hire on the basis of "merit," must observe strict accounting rules, must supply Congress with detailed information on their programs, and must allow for citizen access in countless ways. Meeting each need requires rules; enforcing the rules requires forms.

Or take conflict and duplication: they do not occur because bureaucrats enjoy conflict or duplication. (Quite the contrary!) They exist because Congress, in setting up agencies and programs, often wants to achieve a number of different, partially inconsistent goals or finds that it cannot decide which goal it values the most. Congress has 535 members and little strong leadership; it should not be surprising that 535 people will want different things and will sometimes succeed in getting them.

Imperialism results in large measure from government agencies' seeking goals that are so vague and so difficult to measure that it is hard to tell when they have been attained. When Congress is unclear as to exactly what an agency is supposed to do, the agency will often convert that legislative vagueness into bureaucratic imperialism by taking the largest possible view of its powers. It may do this on its own; more often it does so because interest groups and judges

---

red tape Complex bureaucratic rules and procedures that must be followed to get something done.

rush in to fill the vacuum left by Congress. As we saw in Chapter 3, the 1973 Rehabilitation Act was passed with a provision barring discrimination against people with disabilities in any program receiving federal aid. Under pressure from people with disabilities, that lofty but vague goal was converted by the Department of Transportation into a requirement that virtually every big-city bus have a device installed to lift people in wheelchairs on board.

Waste is probably the biggest criticism that people have of the bureaucracy. Everybody has heard stories of the Pentagon's paying $91 for screws that cost 3 cents in the hardware store. President Reagan's "Private Sector Survey on Cost Control," generally known as the Grace Commission (after its chairman, J. Peter Grace), publicized these and other tales in a 1984 report.

No doubt there is waste in government. After all, unlike a business firm worried about maximizing profits, in a government agency there are only weak incentives to keep costs down. If a business employee cuts costs, he or she often receives a bonus or raise, and the firm gets to add the savings to its profits. If a government official cuts costs, he or she receives no reward, and the agency cannot keep the savings—they go back to the Treasury.

But many of the horror stories are either exaggerations or unusual occurrences.[27] Most of the screws, hammers, and light bulbs purchased by the government are obtained at low cost by means of competitive bidding among several suppliers. When the government does pay outlandish amounts, the reason typically is that it is purchasing a new or one-of-a-kind item not available at your neighborhood hardware store—for example, a new bomber or missile.

Even when the government is not overcharged, it still may spend more money than a private firm in buying what it needs. The reason is red tape—the rules and procedures designed to ensure that when the government buys something, it will do so in a way that serves the interests of many groups. For example, it must often buy from American rather than foreign suppliers, even if the latter charge a lower price; it must make use of contractors that employ minorities; it must hire only union laborers and pay them the "prevailing" (that is, the highest) wage; it must allow public inspection of its records; it frequently is required to choose contractors favored by influential members of Congress; and so on. Pri-

These long lines of cars at the border between the United States and Mexico may be a symbol of "bureaucratic red tape" to some travelers, but they are a sign of "effective law enforcement" to people who want to cut off the flow of drugs and illegal immigrants.

vate firms do not have to comply with all these rules and thus can buy for less.

From this discussion it should be easy to see why these five basic bureaucratic problems are so hard to correct. To end conflicts and duplication Congress would have to make some policy choices and set some clear priorities, but with all the competing demands that it faces, Congress finds it difficult to do that. You make more friends by helping people than by hurting them, and so Congress is more inclined to add new programs than to cut old ones, whether or not the new programs are in conflict with existing ones. To check imperialism some way would have to be found to measure the benefits of government, but that is often impossible; government exists in part to achieve precisely those goals—such as national defense—that are least measurable. Furthermore, what might be done to remedy some problems would make other problems worse: if you simplify rules and procedures to cut red tape, you are also likely to reduce the coordination among agencies and thus to increase the extent to which there is duplication or conflict. If you want to reduce waste, you will have to have more rules and inspectors—in short, more red tape. The problem of bureaucracy is inseparable from the problem of government generally.

Just as people are likely to say that they dislike Congress but like their own member of Congress,

★ POLITICALLY SPEAKING ★

Red Tape

As early as the seventh century, legal and government documents in England were bound together with a tape of pinkish red color. In the 1850s historian Thomas Carlyle described a British politician as "little other than a red tape Talking Machine," and later the American writer Washington Irving said of an American figure that "his brain was little better than red tape and parchment."

Since then *red tape* has come to mean "bureaucratic delay or confusion," especially that accompanied by unnecessary paperwork.

Source: From *Safire's Political Dictionary* by William Safire. Copyright © 1968, 1972, 1978 by William Safire. Reprinted by permission of Random House, Inc. and the author.

---

they are inclined to express hostility toward "the bureaucracy" but goodwill for that part of the bureaucracy with which they have dealt personally. In 1973 a survey of Americans found that over half had had some contact with one or more kinds of government agencies, most of which were either run directly or funded indirectly by the federal government. The great majority of people were satisfied with these contacts and felt that they had been treated fairly and given useful assistance. When these people were asked their feelings about government officials in general, however, they expressed much less favorable attitudes. Whereas about 80 percent liked the officials with whom they had dealt, only 42 percent liked officials in general.[28] This finding helps explain why government agencies are rarely reduced in size or budget: whatever the popular feelings about

the bureaucracy, any given agency tends to have many friends.

★ Reforming the Bureaucracy

The history of American bureaucracy has been punctuated with countless efforts to make it work better and cost less. There were eleven major attempts in the twentieth century alone. The latest was the National Performance Review (NPR)—popularly called the plan to "reinvent government"—led by Vice President Al Gore.

The NPR differed from many of the preceding reform efforts in one important way. Most of the earlier ones suggested ways of increasing central (that is, presidential) control of government agencies: the Brownlow Commission (1936–1937) recommended giving the president more assistants, the First Hoover Commission (1947–1949) suggested ways of improving top-level management, and the Ash Council (1969–1971) called for consolidating existing agencies into a few big "super departments." The intent was to make it easier for the president and his cabinet secretaries to run the bureaucracy. The key ideas were efficiency, accountability, and consistent policies.

The NPR, by contrast, emphasized customer satisfaction (the "customers" in this case being the citizens who come into contact with federal agencies). To the authors of the NPR report, the main problem with the bureaucracy was that it had become too centralized, too rule-bound, too little concerned with making programs work, and too much concerned with avoiding scandal. The NPR report contained many horror stories about useless red tape, excessive regulations, and cumbersome procurement systems that make it next to impossible for agencies to do what they were created to do. (For example, before it could buy an ashtray, the General Services Administration issued a nine-page document that described an ashtray and specified how many pieces it must break into, should it be hit with a hammer.)[29] To solve these problems the NPR called for less centralized management and more employee initiative, fewer detailed rules and more emphasis on customer satisfaction. It sought to create a new kind of organizational culture in government agencies, one more like that found in the more innovative, quality-conscious American corporations. The NPR was reinforced legislatively by the Government Performance and Results Act (GPRA) of 1993, which required agencies "to set goals, measure performance, and report on the results."

Most bureaucrats are people we like, such as the letter carriers in the Postal Service.

But making these changes is easier said than done. Most of the rules and red tape that make it hard for agency heads to do a good job are the result either of the struggle between the White House and Congress for control over the agencies or of the agencies' desire to avoid irritating influential voters. Silly as the rules for ashtrays may sound, they were written so that the government could say it had an "objective" standard for buying ashtrays. If it simply went out and bought ashtrays at a department store the way ordinary people do, it would risk being accused by the Acme Ashtray Company of buying trays from its competitor, the A-1 Ashtray Company, because of political favoritism.

The rivalry between the president and Congress for control of the bureaucracy makes bureaucrats nervous about irritating either branch, and so they issue rules designed to avoid getting into trouble, even if these rules make it hard to do their job. Matters become even worse during periods of divided government when different parties control the White House and Congress. As we saw in Chapter 14, divided government may not have much effect on *making* policy, but it can have a big effect on *implementing* it. Presidents of one party have tried to increase political control over the bureaucracy ("executive micromanagement"), and Congresses of another party have responded by increasing the number of investigations and detailed rule-making ("legislative micromanagement"). Divided government intensifies the cross-fire between the executive and legislative branches, making bureaucrats dig into even deeper layers of red tape to avoid getting hurt.

This does not mean that reform is impossible, only that it is very difficult. For example, despite a lack of clear-cut successes in other areas, the NPR's procurement reforms stuck: government agencies can now buy things costing as much as $100,000 without following any complex regulations.

It might be easier to make desirable changes if the bureaucracy were accountable to only one master— say, the president—instead of to several. But that situation, which exists in many parliamentary democracies, creates its own problems. When the bureaucracy has but one master, it often ends up having none: it becomes so powerful that it controls the prime minister and no longer listens to citizen complaints. A weak, divided bureaucracy, such as exists in the United States, may strike us as inefficient, but that very inefficiency may help protect our liberties.

☆ SUMMARY

Bureaucracy is characteristic of almost all aspects of modern life, not simply the government. Government bureaucracies, however, pose special problems because they are subject to competing sources of political authority, must function in a constitutional system of divided powers and federalism, have vague goals, and lack incentive systems that will encourage efficiency. The power of a bureaucracy should be measured by its discretionary authority, not by the number of its employees or the size of its budget.

War and depression have been the principal sources of bureaucratic growth, aided by important changes in constitutional interpretation in the 1930s that permitted Congress to delegate broad grants of authority to administrative agencies. With only partial success Congress seeks to check or recover those grants by controlling budgets, personnel, and policy decisions and by the exercise of legislative vetoes. The uses to which bureaucrats put their authority can be explained in part by their recruitment and security (they have an agency

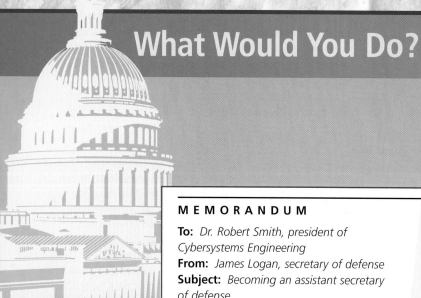

What Would You Do?

New Administration Struggling to Fill Top Posts

Cabinet Secretaries Say "The President Needs Help!"

May 20
WASHINGTON

Four months into the new administration, hundreds of assistant secretary and deputy assistant secretary positions remain unfilled. In 1960 the total number of presidential political appointees was just 450. Today the total is over 2,400, but sheer growth is not the whole story. Rather, say experts on federal bureaucracy, plum public service posts go unfilled because the jobs have become so unrewarding, even punishing . . .

MEMORANDUM

To: *Dr. Robert Smith, president of Cybersystems Engineering*
From: *James Logan, secretary of defense*
Subject: *Becoming an assistant secretary of defense*

As both secretary and a dear old college buddy of yours, I write again to express my hope that you will accept the president's call to service. We all desperately want you aboard. Yes, conflict-of-interest laws will require you to sell your stock in your present company and drop out of its generous pension plan. No, the government won't even pay moving costs. And once you leave office, you will be barred for life from lobbying the executive branch on matters in which you were directly involved while in office, and you will be barred for two years from lobbying on matters that were under your general official authority. Your other concerns have teeth, too, but let me help you weigh your options.

Arguments for:

1. I hate to preach, but it is one's duty to serve one's country when called. Your sacrifice would honor your family and benefit your fellow Americans for years to come.
2. As an accomplished professional and the head of a company that has done business with the government, you could help the president succeed in reforming the department so that it works better and costs less.
3. Despite the restrictions, you could resume your career once your public service was complete.

Arguments against:

1. Since you will have to be confirmed by the Senate, your life will be put under a microscope, and everything (even some of our old college mischief together) will be fair game for congressional staffers and reporters.
2. You will face hundreds of rules telling you what you can't do and scores of congressmen telling you what you should do. Old friends will get mad at you for not doing them favors. The president will demand loyalty. The press will pounce on your every mistake, real or imagined.
3. Given the federal limits on whom in the government you can deal with after you leave office, your job at Cybersystems may well suffer.

Your decision:

Accept position _____ Reject position _____

orientation), their personal political views, and the nature of the tasks that their agencies are performing.

Many of the popular solutions for the problems of bureaucratic rule—red tape, duplication, conflict, agency imperialism, and waste—fail to take into account that these problems are to a degree inherent in any government that serves competing goals and is supervised by rival elected officials. Nevertheless, some reform efforts have succeeded in making government work better and cost less to operate.

RECONSIDERING WHO GOVERNS?

1. What happened to make bureaucracy a "fourth branch" of American national government?

The Constitution made no provision for an administrative system other than to allow the president to appoint, with the advice and consent of the Senate, ambassadors, Supreme Court judges, and "all other officers . . . which shall be provided by law." By the early twentieth century, however, Washington's role in making, administering, and funding public policies had already grown far beyond what the Framers had contemplated. Two world wars, the New Deal, and the Great Society each left the government with expanded powers and requiring new batteries of administrative agencies to exercise them. Today, the federal bureaucracy is as vast as most people's expectations about Washington's responsibility for every public concern one can name. It is the appointed officials—the bureaucrats—not the elected officials or policymakers, who command the troops, deliver the mail, audit the tax returns, run the federal prisons, decide who qualifies for public assistance, and do countless other tasks. Unavoidably, many bureaucrats exercise discretion in deciding what public laws and regulations mean and how to apply them. Still, the president, cabinet secretaries, and thousands of political appointees are ultimately their bosses. Congress and the courts have ample, if imperfect, means of checking and balancing even the biggest bureaucracy, old or new.

2. What are the actual size and scope of the federal bureaucracy?

A few million civil servants work directly for the federal government, but over five times as many people work indirectly for Washington as employees of business firms or of nonprofit organizations that receive federal grants or contracts, or as state and local government employees working under federal mandates. For example, the U.S. Department of Health and Human Services (HHS) has about 65,000 employees, runs over 300 different programs, and makes over 60,000 grants a year. But millions more people work indirectly for the HHS—as state and local government employees whose entire jobs involve the administration of one or more HHS programs (for example, Medicaid), and as people who work for community-serving nonprofit organizations that receive HHS grants to administer social services.

RECONSIDERING TO WHAT ENDS?

1. What should be done to improve bureaucratic performance?

There have been numerous efforts to make the bureaucracy work better and cost less, including eleven presidential or other major commissions in the twentieth century. The latest was the National Performance Review (NPR), popularly called the plan to "reinvent government." Vice President Gore led the NPR during the two terms of the Clinton administration. The NPR was predicated on the view that bureaucracy had become too centralized, too rule-bound, too little concerned with program results, and too much concerned with avoiding scandal. In the end, the NPR produced certain money-saving changes in the federal procurement process (how government purchases goods and services from private contractors), and it also streamlined parts of the federal personnel process (how Washington hires career employees). Most experts, however, gave the NPR mixed grades and concluded that it had fallen far short of its ambitious goals of improving government performance.

2. Is "red tape" all bad?

No, not all. Red tape refers to the complex rules and procedures that must be followed to get something done. All large organizations, including business firms, have some red tape. Some red tape in government agencies is silly and wasteful (or worse), but try imagining government without any red tape at all.

Imagine no rules about hiring on the basis of merit, no strict financial accounting procedures, and no regulations concerning citizen access to information or public record keeping. As the Yale political scientist Herbert Kaufman once quipped, one citizen's "red tape" is often another's "treasured procedural safeguard."

WORLD WIDE WEB RESOURCES

For addresses and reports of various cabinet departments

> Web addresses: **www.whitehouse.gov/**

> Documents and bulletin boards: **www.fedworld.gov**

> National Performance Review: **www.npr.gov**

A few specific web sites of federal agencies

> Department of Defense: **www.defenselink.mil**

> Department of Education: **www.ed.gov**

> Department of Health and Human Services: **www.dhhs.gov**

> Department of State: **www.state.gov**

> Federal Bureau of Investigation: **www.fbi.gov**

> Department of Labor: **www.dol.gov**

SUGGESTED READINGS

Burke, John P. *Bureaucratic Responsibility*. Baltimore: Johns Hopkins University Press, 1986. Examines the problem of individual responsibility—for example, when to be a whistle blower—in government agencies.

DiIulio, John J., Gerald Garvey, and Donald F. Kettl. *Improving Government Performance: An Owner's Manual*. Washington, D.C.: Brookings Institution, 1993. A concise overview of the history of federal bureaucracy and ideas about how to reform it.

Downs, Anthony. *Inside Bureaucracy*. Boston: Little, Brown, 1967. An economist's explanation of why bureaucrats and bureaus behave as they do.

Halperin, Morton H. *Bureaucratic Politics and Foreign Policy*. Washington, D.C.: Brookings Institution, 1974. Insightful account of the strategies by which diplomatic and military bureaucracies defend their interests.

Heclo, Hugh. *A Government of Strangers*. Washington, D.C.: Brookings Institution, 1977. Analyzes how political appointees attempt to gain control of the Washington bureaucracy and how bureaucrats resist those efforts.

Johnson, Ronald L., and Gary Libecap. *The Federal Civil Service System and the Problem of Bureaucracy*. Chicago: University of Chicago Press, 1994. Two economists analyze how federal bureaucrats acquire positions and salaries.

Light, Paul C. *The True Size of Government*. Washington, D.C.: Brookings Institution, 1999. A revealing explanation of why the federal government is a lot bigger than is suggested by simply counting employees.

Moore, Mark H. *Creating Public Value: Strategic Management in Government*. Cambridge: Harvard University Press, 1995. A thoughtful account of how wise bureaucrats can make government work better.

Parkinson, C. Northcote. *Parkinson's Law*. Boston: Houghton Mifflin, 1957. Half-serious, half-joking explanation of why government agencies tend to grow.

Wilson, James Q. *Bureaucracy: What Government Agencies Do and Why They Do It*. New York: Basic Books, 1989. A comprehensive review of what we know about bureaucratic behavior in the United States.

The Judiciary

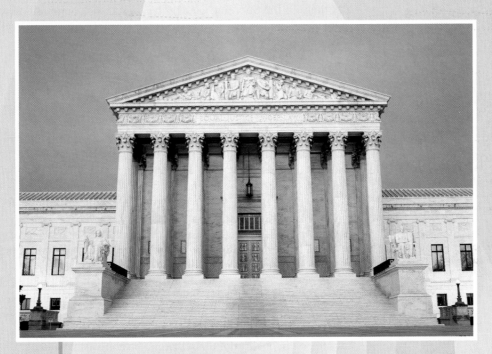

The Development of the Federal Courts
  National Supremacy and Slavery ●
  Government and the Economy ●
  Government and Political Liberty ●
  The Revival of State Sovereignty

The Structure of the Federal Courts
  Selecting Judges

The Jurisdiction of the Federal Courts

Getting to Court
  Fee Shifting ● Standing ●
  Class-Action Suits

The Supreme Court in Action

The Power of the Federal Courts
  The Power to Make Policy ● Views of
  Judicial Activism ● Legislation and the
  Courts

Checks on Judicial Power
  Congress and the Courts ● Public
  Opinion and the Courts

WHO GOVERNS?

1. Why should federal judges serve for life?

TO WHAT ENDS?

1. Why should federal courts be able to declare laws unconstitutional?
2. Should federal judges only interpret existing laws or should they be able to create new laws?

*H*ardly any American cares what people are picked to be federal district court judges. Can you name even one district court judge in your city? But Congress cares deeply about who is appointed to be federal judges, especially to the Supreme Court. The reason for congressional concern is that federal courts, even at the lowest level, make important decisions that affect all of us.

And as the power of the federal government has grown, so the power of federal courts has increased. At one time there was no federal policy about the environment, welfare, abortion, gun control, or civil rights; now there are policies on all of these matters, and so there are more and more court rulings that tell us what these policies mean.

When in 1991 President George H. W. Bush nominated Clarence Thomas to the Supreme Court, he was barely confirmed by a Senate vote that was the closest in over a century. When in 1987 Ronald Reagan nominated Robert Bork to a justice, he was not confirmed by the Senate. And when in 2003 George W. Bush nominated people to lower federal courts, some were blocked by a Democratic party filibuster.

Only in the United States would the selection of a judge produce so dramatic and bitter a conflict. The reason is simple: only in the United States do judges play so large a role in making public policy.

One aspect of this power is **judicial review**—the right of the federal courts to declare laws of Congress and acts of the executive branch void and unenforceable if they are judged to be in conflict with the Constitution. Since 1789 the Supreme Court has declared over one hundred sixty federal laws to be unconstitutional. In Britain, by contrast, Parliament is supreme, and no court may strike down a law that it passes. As the second earl of Pembroke is supposed to have said, "A parliament can do anything but make a man a woman and a woman a man." All that prevents Parliament from acting contrary to the (unwritten) constitution of Britain are the consciences of its members and the opinions of the citizens. About sixty nations do have something resembling judicial review, but in only a few cases does this power mean much in practice. Where it means something— in Australia, Canada, Germany, India, and some other nations—one finds a stable, federal system of government with a strong tradition of an independent judiciary.[1] (Some other nations—France, for example—have special councils, rather than courts, that can under certain circumstances decide that a law is not authorized by the constitution.)

Judicial review is the federal courts' chief weapon in the system of checks and balances on which the American government is based. Today few people would deny to the courts the right to decide that a legislative or executive act is unconstitutional, though once that right was controversial. What remains controversial is the method by which such review is conducted.

There are two competing views, each ardently pressed during the fight to confirm Clarence Thomas. The first holds that judges should only judge—that is, they should confine themselves to applying those rules that are stated in or clearly implied by the language of the Constitution. This is often called the **strict-constructionist approach.** The other argues that judges should discover the general principles underlying the Constitution and its often vague language, amplify those principles on the basis of some moral or economic philosophy, and apply them to cases. This is sometimes called the **activist approach.**

Note that the difference between activist and strict-constructionist judges is not necessarily the same as the difference between liberals and conservatives. Judges can be political liberals and still believe that they are bound by the language of the Constitution. A liberal justice, Hugo Black, once voted to uphold a state law banning birth control because nothing in the Constitution prohibited such a law. Or judges can be conservative and still think that they have a duty to use their best judgment in deciding what is good public policy. Rufus Peckham, one such conservative, voted to overturn a state law setting maximum hours of work because he believed that the Fourteenth Amendment guaranteed something called "freedom of contract," even though those words are not in the amendment.

Seventy years ago judicial activists tended to be conservatives and strict-constructionist judges tended to be liberals; today the opposite is usually the case.

☆ The Development of the Federal Courts

Most of the Founders probably expected the Supreme Court to have the power of judicial review (though they did not say that in so many words in the Constitution), but they did not expect federal courts to play

Table 16.1 Chief Justices of the United States		
Chief Justice	**Appointed By**	**Years of Service**
John Jay	Washington	1789–1795
Oliver Ellsworth	Washington	1796–1800
John Marshall	Adams	1801–1835
Roger B. Taney	Jackson	1836–1864
Salmon P. Chase	Lincoln	1864–1873
Morrison R. Waite	Grant	1874–1888
Melville W. Fuller	Cleveland	1888–1910
Edward D. White	Taft	1910–1921
William Howard Taft	Harding	1921–1930
Charles Evans Hughes	Hoover	1930–1941
Harlan Fiske Stone	F. Roosevelt	1941–1946
Fred M. Vinson	Truman	1946–1953
Earl Warren	Eisenhower	1953–1969
Warren E. Burger	Nixon	1969–1986
William H. Rehnquist	Reagan	1986–present

Note: Omitted is John Rutledge, who served for only a few months in 1795 and who was not confirmed by the Senate.

so large a role in making public policy. The traditional view of civil courts was that they judged disputes between people who had direct dealings with each other—they had entered into a contract, for example, or one had dropped a load of bricks on the other's toe—and decided which of the two parties was right. The court then supplied relief to the wronged party, usually by requiring the other person to pay him or her money ("damages").

This traditional understanding was based on the belief that judges would find and apply existing law. The purpose of a court case was not to learn what the judge believes but what the law requires. The later rise of judicial activism occurred when judges questioned this traditional view and argued instead that judges do not merely find the law, they make the law.

The view that judges interpret the law and do not make policy made it easy for the Founders to justify

---

judicial review The power of courts to declare laws unconstitutional.

strict-constructionist approach The view that judges should decide cases strictly on the basis of the language of the laws and the Constitution

activist approach The view that judges should discern the general principles underlying laws or the Constitution and apply them to modern circumstances.

Marbury v. Madison

The story of *Marbury v. Madison* is often told, but it deserves another telling because it illustrates so many features of the role of the Supreme Court—how apparently small cases can have large results, how the power of the Court depends not simply on its constitutional authority but also on its acting in ways that avoid a clear confrontation with other branches of government, and how the climate of opinion affects how the Court goes about its task.

When President John Adams lost his bid for reelection to Thomas Jefferson in 1800, he—and all members of his party, the Federalists—feared that Jefferson and the Republicans would weaken the federal government and turn its powers to what the Federalists believed were wrong ends (states' rights, an alliance with the French, hostility to business). Feverishly, as his hours in office came to an end, Adams worked to pack the judiciary with fifty-nine loyal Federalists by giving them so-called midnight appointments before Jefferson took office.

John Marshall, as Adams's secretary of state, had the task of certifying and delivering these new judicial commissions. In the press of business he delivered all but seventeen; these he left on his desk for the incoming secretary of state, James Madison, to send out. Jefferson and Madison, however, were furious at Adams's behavior and refused to deliver the seventeen. William Marbury and three other Federalists who had been promised these commissions hired a lawyer and brought suit against Madison to force him to produce the documents. The suit requested the Supreme Court to issue a writ of mandamus (from the Latin, "we command") ordering Madison to do his duty. The right to issue such writs had been given to the Court by the Judiciary Act of 1789.

Marshall, the man who had failed to deliver the commissions to Marbury and his friends in the first place, had become the chief justice and was now in a position to decide the case. These days a justice who had been involved in an issue before it came to the Court would probably disqualify himself or herself, but Marshall had no intention of letting others decide this question. He faced, however, not simply a partisan dispute over jobs but what was nearly a constitutional crisis. If he ordered the commission delivered, Madison might still refuse, and the Court had no way—if Madison was determined to resist—to compel him. The Court had no police force, whereas Madison had the support of the president of

the power of judicial review and led them to predict that the courts would play a relatively neutral, even passive, role in public affairs. Alexander Hamilton, writing in *Federalist* No. 78, described the judiciary as the branch "least dangerous" to political rights. The president is commander in chief and thus holds the "sword of the community"; Congress appropriates money and thus "commands the purse" as well as decides what laws shall govern. But the judiciary "has no influence over either the sword or the purse" and "can take no active resolution whatever." It has "neither force nor will but merely judgment," and thus is "beyond comparison the weakest of the three departments of power." As a result "liberty can have nothing to fear from the judiciary alone." Hamilton went on to state clearly that the Constitution intended to give to the courts the right to decide whether a law is contrary to the Constitution. But this authority, he explained, was designed not to enlarge the power of the courts but to confine that of the legislature.

Obviously things have changed since Hamilton's time. The evolution of the federal courts, especially the Supreme Court, toward the present level of activism and influence has been shaped by the political, economic, and ideological forces of three historical eras. From 1787 to 1865 nation building, the legitimacy of the federal government, and slavery were the great issues; from 1865 to 1937 the great issue was the relationship between the government and the economy; from 1938 to the present the major issues confronting the Court have involved personal liberty and social equality and the potential conflict between the two. In the first period the Court asserted the supremacy of the federal government; in the second it placed important restrictions on the powers of that government; and in the third it

the United States. And if the order were given, whether or not Madison complied, the Jeffersonian Republicans in Congress would probably try to impeach Marshall. On the other hand, if Marshall allowed Madison to do as he wished, the power of the Supreme Court would be seriously reduced.

Marshall's solution was ingenious. Speaking for a unanimous Court, he announced that Madison was wrong to withhold the commissions, that courts could issue writs to compel public officials to do their prescribed duty—*but* that the Supreme Court had no power to issue such writs in this case because the law (the Judiciary Act of 1789) giving it that power was unconstitutional. The law said that the Supreme Court could issue such writs as part of its "original jurisdiction"—that is, persons seeking such writs could go *directly* to the Supreme Court with their request (rather than go first to a lower federal court and then, if dissatisfied, appeal to the Supreme Court). Article III of the Constitution, Marshall pointed out, spelled out precisely the Supreme Court's original jurisdiction; it did not mention issuing writs of this sort and plainly indicated that on all matters not mentioned in the Constitution, the Court would have only appellate

John Adams   James Madison

jurisdiction. Congress may not change what the Constitution says; hence the part of the Judiciary Act attempting to do this was null and void.

The result was that a showdown with the Jeffersonians was avoided—Madison was not ordered to deliver the commissions—but the power of the Supreme Court was unmistakably clarified and enlarged. As Marshall wrote, "It is emphatically the province and duty of the judicial department to say what the law is." Furthermore, "a law repugnant to the Constitution is void."

enlarged the scope of personal freedom and narrowed that of economic freedom.

National Supremacy and Slavery

"From 1789 until the Civil War, the dominant interest of the Supreme Court was in that greatest of all the questions left unresolved by the Founders—the nation-state relationship."[2] The answer that the Court gave, under the leadership of Chief Justice John Marshall, was that national law was in all instances the dominant law, with state law having to give way, and that the Supreme Court had the power to decide what the Constitution meant. In two cases of enormous importance—*Marbury v. Madison* in 1803 and *McCulloch v. Maryland* in 1819—the Court, in decisions written by Marshall, held that the Supreme Court could declare an act of Congress unconstitutional; that the power granted by the Constitution to the federal government flows from the people and

thus should be generously construed (and thus any federal laws that are "necessary and proper" to the attainment of constitutional ends are permissible); and that federal law is supreme over state law, even to the point that a state may not tax an enterprise (such as a bank) created by the federal government.[3]

The supremacy of the federal government was reaffirmed by other decisions as well. In 1816 the Supreme Court rejected the claim of the Virginia courts that the Supreme Court could not review the decisions of state courts. The Virginia courts were ready to acknowledge the supremacy of the U.S. Constitution but believed that they had as much right as the U.S. Supreme Court to decide what the Constitution meant. The Supreme Court felt otherwise, and in this case and another like it the Court asserted its own broad powers to review any state court decision if that decision seemed to violate federal law or the federal Constitution.[4]

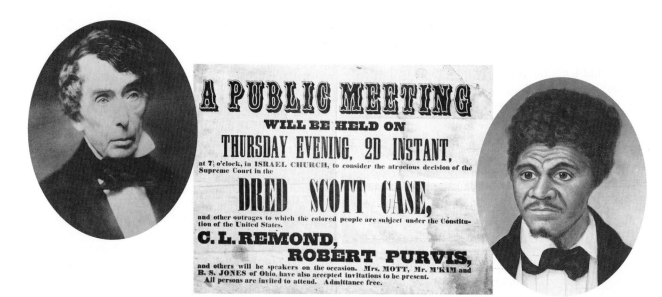

A PUBLIC MEETING

WILL BE HELD ON

THURSDAY EVENING, 2D INSTANT,

at 7½ o'clock, in ISRAEL CHURCH, to consider the atrocious decision of the Supreme Court in the

DRED SCOTT CASE,

and other outrages to which the colored people are subject under the Constitution of the United States.

C. L. REMOND,
ROBERT PURVIS,

and others will be speakers on the occasion. Mrs. MOTT, Mr. M'KIM and B. S. JONES of Ohio, have also accepted invitations to be present. All persons are invited to attend. Admittance free.

Roger B. Taney, chief justice from 1836 to 1864, wrote the Dred Scott *decision, which asserted that blacks were not citizens of the United States. Dred Scott claimed that when his master brought him north to a free state, he ceased to be a slave. The public outcry against the decision was intense, at least in the North, as is evident from this poster announcing a mass meeting "to consider the atrocious decision."*

The power of the federal government to regulate commerce among the states was also established. When New York gave to Robert Fulton, the inventor of the steamboat, the monopoly right to operate his steamboats on the rivers of that state, the Marshall Court overturned the license because the rivers connected New York and New Jersey and thus trade on those rivers would involve *inter*state commerce, and federal law in that area was supreme. Since there was a conflicting federal law on the books, the state law was void.[5]

All of this may sound rather obvious to us today, when the supremacy of the federal government is largely unquestioned. In the early nineteenth century, however, these were almost revolutionary decisions. The Jeffersonian Republicans were in power and had become increasingly devoted to states' rights; they were aghast at the Marshall decisions. President Andrew Jackson attacked the Court bitterly for defending the right of the federal government to create a national bank and for siding with the Cherokee Indians in a dispute with Georgia. In speaking of the latter case, Jackson is supposed to have remarked, "John Marshall has made his decision; now let him enforce it!"[6]

Though Marshall seemed to have secured the supremacy of the federal government over the state

governments, another even more divisive issue had arisen; that, of course, was slavery. Roger B. Taney succeeded Marshall as chief justice in 1836. He was deliberately chosen by President Jackson because he was an advocate of states' rights, and he began to chip away at federal supremacy, upholding state claims that Marshall would have set aside. But the decision for which he is famous—or infamous—came in 1857, when in the *Dred Scott* case he wrote perhaps the most disastrous judicial opinion ever issued. A slave, Dred Scott, had been taken by his owner to a territory (near what is now St. Paul, Minnesota) where slavery was illegal under federal law. Scott claimed that since he had resided in a free territory, he was now a free man. Taney held that Negroes were not citizens of the United States and could not become so, and that the federal law—the Missouri Compromise—prohibiting slavery in northern territories was unconstitutional.[7] The public outcry against this view was enormous, and the Court and Taney were discredited in the North, at least. The Civil War was ultimately fought over what the Court mistakenly had assumed was a purely legal question.

Government and the Economy

The supremacy of the federal government may have been established by John Marshall and the Civil War, but the scope of the powers of that government or even of the state governments was still to be defined. During the period from the end of the Civil War to the early years of the New Deal, the dominant issue the Supreme Court faced was deciding when the economy would be regulated by the states and when by the nation.

The Court revealed a strong though not inflexible attachment to private property. In fact that attachment had always been there: the Founders thought that political and property rights were inextricably linked, and Marshall certainly supported the sanctity of contracts. But now, with the muting of the federal supremacy issue and the rise of a national economy with important unanticipated effects, the property question became the dominant one. In general, the Court developed the view that the Fourteenth Amendment, adopted in 1868 primarily to protect African American claims to citizenship from hostile state action, also protected private property and the corporation from unreasonable state action. The crucial phrase was this: no state shall "deprive any person of life, liberty, or property, without due process of law." Once it became clear that a "person" could be a firm or a corporation as well as an individual, business and industry began to flood the courts with cases challenging various government regulations.

The Court quickly found itself in a thicket: it began ruling on the constitutionality of virtually every effort by any government to regulate any aspect of business or labor, and its workload rose sharply. Judicial activism was born in the 1880s and 1890s as the Court set itself up as the arbiter of what kind of regulation was permissible. In the first seventy-five years of this country's history, only 2 federal laws were held to be unconstitutional; in the next seventy-five years, 71 were.[8] Of the roughly 1,300 state laws held to be in conflict with the federal Constitution since 1789, about 1,200 were overturned after 1870. In one decade alone—the 1880s—5 federal and 48 state laws were declared unconstitutional.

Many of these decisions provided clear evidence of the Court's desire to protect private property: it upheld the use of injunctions to prevent labor strikes,[9] struck down the federal income tax,[10] sharply limited the reach of the antitrust law,[11] restricted the powers of the Interstate Commerce Commission to set railroad rates,[12] prohibited the federal government from eliminating child labor,[13] and prevented the states from setting maximum hours of work.[14] In 184 cases between 1899 and 1937, the Supreme Court struck down state laws for violating the Fourteenth Amendment, usually by economic regulation.[15]

But the Court also rendered decisions that authorized various kinds of regulation. It allowed states to regulate businesses "affected with a public interest,"[16] changed its mind about the Interstate Commerce Commission and allowed it to regulate railroad rates,[17] upheld rules requiring railroads to improve their safety,[18] approved state antiliquor laws,[19] approved state mine safety laws,[20] supported state workers' compensation laws,[21] allowed states to regulate fire-insurance rates,[22] and in time upheld a number of state laws regulating wages and hours. Indeed, between 1887 and 1910, in 558 cases involving the Fourteenth Amendment, the Supreme Court upheld state regulations over 80 percent of the time.[23]

To characterize the Court as probusiness or antiregulation is both simplistic and inexact. More accurate, perhaps, is to characterize it as supportive of the rights of private property but unsure how to draw the lines that distinguish "reasonable" from "unreasonable" regulation. Nothing in the Constitution clearly differentiates reasonable from unreasonable regulation, and the Court has been able to invent no consistent principle of its own to make this determination. For example, what kinds of businesses are "affected with a public interest"? Grain elevators and railroads are, but are bakeries? Sugar refiners? Saloons? And how much of commerce is "interstate"—anything that moves? Or only something that actually crosses a state line? The Court found itself trying to make detailed judgments that it was not always competent to make and to invent legal rules where no clear legal rules were possible.

In one area, however, the Supreme Court's judgments were clear: the Fourteenth and Fifteenth Amendments were construed so narrowly as to give African Americans only the most limited benefits of their provisions. In a long series of decisions the Court upheld segregation in schools and on railroad cars and permitted blacks to be excluded from voting in many states.

Government and Political Liberty

After 1936 the Supreme Court stopped imposing any serious restrictions on state or federal power to regulate the economy, leaving such matters in the hands of the legislatures. From 1937 to 1974 the Supreme Court did not overturn a single federal law designed to regulate business but did overturn thirty-six congressional enactments that violated personal political liberties. It voided as unconstitutional laws that restricted freedom of speech,[24] denied passports to communists,[25] permitted the government to revoke a person's citizenship,[26] withheld a person's mail,[27] or restricted the availability of government benefits.[28]

This new direction began when one justice changed his mind, and it continued as the composition of the Court changed. At the outset of the New Deal the Court was, by a narrow margin, dominated by justices who opposed the welfare state and federal regulation based on broad grants of discretionary authority to administrative agencies. President Franklin Roosevelt, who was determined to get just such legislation implemented, found himself powerless to alter the composition of the Court during his first term (1933–1937): because no justice died retired, he had no vacancies to fill. After his overwhelming reelection in 1936, he moved to remedy this problem by "packing" the Court.

Roosevelt proposed a bill that would have allowed him to appoint one new justice for each one over the age of seventy who refused to retire, up to a total membership of fifteen. Since there were six men in this category then on the Supreme Court, he would have been able to appoint six new justices, enough to ensure a comfortable majority supportive of his eco-

nomic policies. A bitter controversy ensued, but before the bill could be voted on, the Supreme Court, perhaps reacting to Roosevelt's big win in the 1936 election, changed its mind. Whereas it had been striking down several New Deal measures by votes of five to four, now it started approving them by the same vote. One justice, Owen Roberts, had switched his position. This was called the "switch in time that saved nine," but in fact Roberts had changed his mind *before* the FDR plan was announced.

The "Court-packing" bill was not passed, but it was no longer necessary. Justice Roberts had yielded before public opinion in a way that Chief Justice Taney a century earlier had not, thus forestalling an assault on the Court by the other branches of government. Shortly thereafter several justices stepped down, and Roosevelt was able to make his own appointments (he filled seven seats during his four terms in office). From then on the Court turned its attention to new issues— political liberties and, in time, civil rights.

With the arrival in office of Chief Justice Earl Warren in 1953, the Court began its most active period yet. Activism now arose to redefine the relationship of citizens to the government and especially to protect the rights and liberties of citizens from governmental trespass. Although the Court has always seen itself as protecting citizens from arbitrary government, before 1937 that protection was of a sort that

The "nine old men": The Supreme Court in 1937, not long after President Franklin D. Roosevelt tried, unsuccessfully, to "pack" it by appointing six additional justices who would have supported his New Deal legislation. Justice Owen J. Roberts (standing, second from the left) changed his vote on these matters, and the Court ceased to be a barrier to the delegation of power to the bureaucracy.

U.S. District and Appellate Courts

Note: Washington, D.C., is in a separate court. Puerto Rico is in the first circuit; the Virgin Islands are in the third; Guam and the Northern Mariana Islands are in the ninth.
Source: Administrative Office of the United States Courts (January 1983).

conservatives preferred; after 1937 it was of a kind that liberals preferred.

The Revival of State Sovereignty

For many decades the Supreme Court allowed Congress to pass almost any law authorized by the Constitution, no matter how it affected the states. As we saw in Chapter 3, the Court had long held that Congress could regulate almost any activity if it affected interstate commerce, and in the Court's opinion virtually every activity did affect it. The states were left with few rights to challenge federal power. But since around 1992 the Court has backed away from this view. By narrow majorities it has begun to restore the view that states have the right to resist some forms of federal action.

When Congress passed a bill that forbade anyone from carrying a gun near a school, the Court held that carrying guns did not affect interstate commerce, and so the law was invalid.[29] One year later it struck down a law that allowed Indian tribes to sue the states in federal courts, arguing that Congress lacks the power to ignore the "sovereign immunity" of states—that is, the right, protected by the Eleventh Amendment, not to be sued in federal court. (It has since upheld that view in two more cases.) And the next year it held that the Brady gun control law could not be used to require local law enforcement officers to do background checks on people trying to buy weapons.[30] These cases are all hints that there are some real limits to the supremacy of the federal government created by the existence and powers of the several states.

☆ The Structure of the Federal Courts

The only federal court that the Constitution requires is the Supreme Court, as specified in Article III. All other federal courts and their jurisdictions are creations of Congress. Nor does the Constitution indicate how many justices shall be on the Supreme Court (there were originally six, now there are nine) or what its appellate jurisdiction shall be.

Congress has created two kinds of lower federal courts to handle cases that need not be decided by the Supreme Court: constitutional and legislative courts. A **constitutional court** is one exercising the judicial powers found in Article III of the Constitution, and therefore its judges are given constitutional protection: they may not be fired (they serve during "good behavior"), nor may their salaries be reduced while they are in office. The most important of the constitutional courts are the **district courts** (a total of ninety-four, with at least one in each state, the District of Columbia, and the commonwealth of Puerto Rico) and the **courts of appeals** (one in each of eleven regions, or circuits, plus one in the District of Columbia). There are also certain specialized courts having constitutional status, such as the Court of International Trade, but we shall not be concerned with them.

A **legislative court** is one set up by Congress for some specialized purpose and staffed with people who have fixed terms of office and can be removed or have their salaries reduced. Legislative courts include the Court of Military Appeals and the territorial courts.

---

constitutional court A federal court authorized by Article III of the Constitution that keeps judges in office during good behavior and prevents their salaries from being reduced. They are the Supreme Court (created by the Constitution) and appellate and district courts created by Congress.

district courts The lowest federal courts; federal trials can be held only here.

courts of appeals Federal courts that hear appeals from district courts; no trials.

legislative courts Courts created by Congress for specialized purposes whose judges do not enjoy the protections of Article III of the Constitution.

Louis Brandeis, creator of the "Brandeis Brief" that developed court cases based on economic and social more than legal arguments, became the first Jewish Supreme Court justice. He served in the Court from 1916 until 1939.

Selecting Judges

Party background makes a difference in how judges behave. An analysis has been done of over eighty studies of the link between party and either liberalism or conservatism among state and federal judges in cases involving civil liberties, criminal justice, and economic regulation. It shows that judges who are Democrats are more likely to make liberal decisions and Republican judges are more likely to make conservative ones.* The party effect is not small.[31] We should not be surprised by this, since we have already seen that among political elites (and judges are certainly elites) party identification influences personal ideology.

---

*A "liberal" decision is one that favors a civil right, a criminal defendant, or an economic regulation; a "conservative" one opposes the right or the regulation or supports the criminal prosecutor.

But ideology does not entirely determine behavior. So many other things shape court decisions—the facts of the case, prior rulings by other courts, the arguments presented by lawyers—that there is no reliable way of predicting how judges will behave in all matters. Presidents often make the mistake of thinking that they know how their appointees will behave, only to be surprised by the facts. Theodore Roosevelt appointed Oliver Wendell Holmes to the Supreme Court, only to remark later, after Holmes had voted in a way that Roosevelt did not like, that "I could carve out of a banana a judge with more backbone than that!" Holmes, who had plenty of backbone, said that he did not "give a damn" what Roosevelt thought. Richard Nixon, an ardent foe of court-ordered school busing, appointed Warren Burger to be chief justice. Burger promptly sat down and wrote the opinion upholding busing. Another Nixon appointee, Harry Blackmun, wrote the opinion declaring the right to an abortion to be constitutionally protected.

■ **Senatorial Courtesy**   In theory the president nominates a "qualified" person to be a judge, and the Senate approves or rejects the nomination based on those "qualifications." In fact the tradition of *senatorial courtesy* gives heavy weight to the preferences of the senators from the state where a federal district judge is to serve. Ordinarily the Senate will not confirm a district court judge if the senior senator from the state where the district is located objects (if he is of the president's party). The senator can exercise this veto power by means of the "blue slip"—a blue piece of paper on which the senator is asked to record his or her views on the nominee. A negative opinion, or even failure to return the blue slip, usually kills the nomination. This means that as a practical matter the president nominates only persons recommended to him by that key senator. Someone once suggested that, at least with respect to district judges, the Constitution has been turned on its head. To reflect reality, he said, Article II, section 2, ought to read: "The senators shall nominate, and by and with the consent of the President, shall appoint" federal judges.

■ **The "Litmus Test"**   Of late, presidents have tried to exercise more influence on the selection of federal district and appellate court judges by getting the Justice Department to find candidates that not only are supported by their party's senators, but also reflect the political and judicial philosophy of the president.

Figure 16.1   Female and Minority Judicial Appointments, 1963–2003

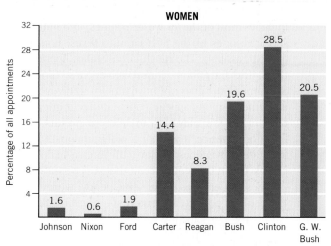

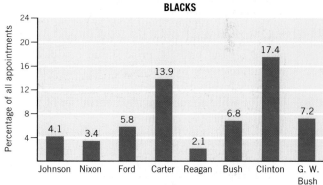

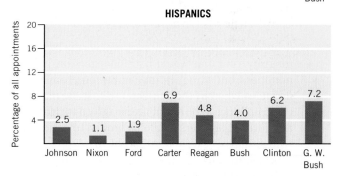

Source: Updated from Harold W. Stanley and Richard G. Niemi, *Vital Statistics on American Politics, 2003–2004* (Washington, D.C.: Congressional Quarterly, 2003), table 7.5.

Presidents Carter and Clinton sought out liberal, activist judges; President Reagan sought out conservative, strict-constructionist ones. The party membership of federal judges makes a difference in how they vote.[32]

Because different courts of appeals have different combinations of judges, some will be more liberal than others. For example, there are more liberal judges in the court of appeals for the ninth circuit (which includes most of the far western states) and more conservative ones in the fifth circuit (Texas, Louisiana, and Mississippi). The ninth circuit takes liberal positions, the fifth more conservative ones. Since the Supreme Court does not have time to settle every disagreement among appeals courts, different interpretations of the law may exist in different circuits. In the fifth, for instance, it was for a while unconstitutional for state universities to have affirmative action programs, but in the ninth circuit that was permitted.

These differences make some people worry about the use of a political **litmus test**—a test of ideological purity—in selecting judges. When conservatives are out of power, they complain about how liberal presidents use such a test; when liberals are out power, they complain about how conservative presidents use it. Many people would like to see judges picked on the basis of professional qualifications, without reference to ideology, but the courts are now so deeply involved in political issues that it is hard to imagine what an ideologically neutral set of professional qualifications might be.

The litmus test has grown in importance, with many senators now saying that it is important to take ideology into account. There are two issues: whether the Judiciary Committee will report out nominees and whether the nominee can withstand a filibuster on the Senate floor. In 2005, Senate Republican leaders threatened to pass a new rule by simple majority vote that would ban filibusters on judicial nominees, but at the last moment a compromise was arranged whereby the Democrats refused to filibuster three nominees, the Republicans agreed to drop two, and future filibusters would be limited to candidates who displayed "exceptional" problems.

The litmus test issue is of greatest importance in selecting Supreme Court justices. Here there is no tradition of senatorial courtesy. The president takes a keen personal interest in the choices and, of late, has sought to find nominees who share his philosophy. In the Reagan administration there were bruising fights in the Senate over the nomination of William Rehnquist to be chief justice (he won) and Robert Bork to be an associate justice (he lost), with liberals pitted against conservatives. When President George H.W. Bush nominated David Souter, there were lengthy hearings as liberal senators tried to pin down Souter's views on issues such as abortion. Souter refused to discuss matters on which he might later have to judge, however. Clarence Thomas, another Bush nominee, also tried to avoid the litmus test by saying that he had not formed an opinion on prominent abortion cases. In his case, however, the litmus test issue was overshadowed by sensational allegations from a former employee, Anita Hill, that Thomas had sexually harassed her.

Of the 145 Supreme Court nominees presented to it, the Senate has rejected 29. Only 5 of these were in the twentieth century. The reasons for rejecting a Supreme Court nominee are complex—each senator may have a different reason—but have involved such matters as the nominee's alleged hostility to civil rights, questionable personal financial dealings, a poor record as a lower-court judge, and Senate opposition to the nominee's political or legal philosophy. Nominations of district court judges are rarely defeated, because typically no nomination is made unless the key senators approve in advance.

☆ The Jurisdiction of the Federal Courts

We have a dual court system—one state, one federal—and this complicates enormously the task of describing what kinds of cases federal courts may hear and how cases beginning in the state courts may end up before the Supreme Court. The Constitution lists the kinds of cases over which federal courts have jurisdiction (in Article III and the Eleventh Amendment); by implication all other matters are left to state courts. Federal courts (see Figure 16.2) can hear all cases "arising under the Constitution, the laws of the United States, and treaties" (these are **federal-question cases**), and cases involving citizens of different states (called **diversity cases**).

---

litmus test   An examination of the political ideology of a nominated judge.

federal-question cases   Cases concerning the Constitution, federal laws, or treaties.

diversity cases   Cases involving citizens of different states who can bring suit in federal courts.

Figure 16.2   The Jurisdiction of the Federal Courts

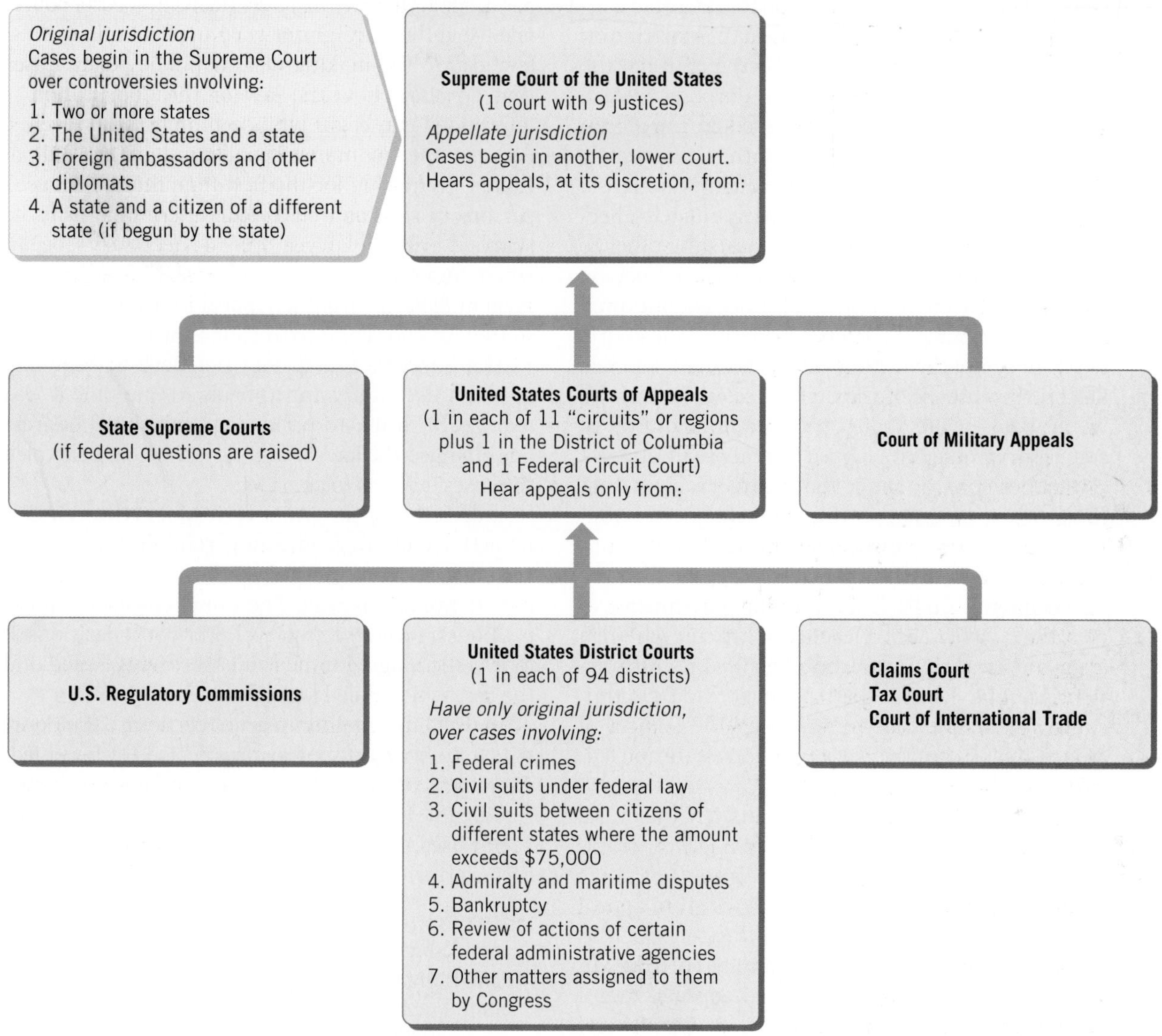

Original jurisdiction
Cases begin in the Supreme Court over controversies involving:

1. Two or more states
2. The United States and a state
3. Foreign ambassadors and other diplomats
4. A state and a citizen of a different state (if begun by the state)

Supreme Court of the United States
(1 court with 9 justices)
Appellate jurisdiction
Cases begin in another, lower court. Hears appeals, at its discretion, from:

State Supreme Courts
(if federal questions are raised)

United States Courts of Appeals
(1 in each of 11 "circuits" or regions plus 1 in the District of Columbia and 1 Federal Circuit Court)
Hear appeals only from:

Court of Military Appeals

U.S. Regulatory Commissions

United States District Courts
(1 in each of 94 districts)
Have only original jurisdiction, over cases involving:

1. Federal crimes
2. Civil suits under federal law
3. Civil suits between citizens of different states where the amount exceeds $75,000
4. Admiralty and maritime disputes
5. Bankruptcy
6. Review of actions of certain federal administrative agencies
7. Other matters assigned to them by Congress

**Claims Court
Tax Court
Court of International Trade**

Some kinds of cases can be heard in either federal or state courts. For example, if citizens of different states wish to sue one another and the matter involves more than $75,000, they can do so in either a federal or a state court. Similarly, if someone robs a federally insured bank, he or she has broken both state and federal law and thus can be prosecuted in state or federal courts, or both. Lawyers have become quite sophisticated in deciding whether, in a given civil case, their clients will get better treatment in a state or federal court. Prosecutors often send a person who has broken both federal and state law to whichever court system is likelier to give the toughest penalty.

Sometimes defendants may be tried in both state and federal courts for the same offense. In 1992 four Los Angeles police officers accused of beating Rodney King were tried in a California state court and acquitted of assault charges. They were then prosecuted in federal court for violating King's civil rights.

This time two of the four were convicted. Under the dual sovereignty doctrine, state and federal authorities can prosecute the same person for the same conduct. The Supreme Court has upheld this doctrine on two grounds: First, each level of government has the right to enact laws serving its own purposes.[33] As a result federal civil rights charges could have been brought against the officers even if they had already been convicted of assault in state court (though as a practical matter this would have been unlikely). Second, neither level of government wants the other to be able to block prosecution of an accused person who has the sympathy of the authorities at one level. For example, when certain southern state courts were in sympathy with whites who had lynched blacks, the absence of the dual sovereignty doctrine would have meant that a trumped-up acquittal in state court would have barred federal prosecution.

Furthermore, a matter that is exclusively within the province of a state court—for example, a criminal case in which the defendant is charged with violating only a state law—can be appealed to the U.S. Supreme Court under certain circumstances (described below). Thus federal judges can overturn state court rulings even when they had no jurisdiction over the original matter. Under what circumstances this should occur has been the subject of long-standing controversy between the state and federal courts.

Some matters, however, are exclusively under the jurisdiction of federal courts. When a federal criminal law is broken—but not a state one—the case is heard in federal district court. If you wish to appeal the decision of a federal regulatory agency, such as the Federal Communications Commission, you can do so only before a federal court of appeals. And if you wish to declare bankruptcy, you do so in federal court. If there is a controversy between two state governments—say, California and Arizona sue each other over which state is to use how much water from the Colorado River—the case can be heard only by the Supreme Court.

The vast majority of all cases heard by federal courts begin in the district courts. The volume of business there is huge. In 2002 the 650 or so district court judges received over 300,000 cases (about 500 per judge). Most of the cases heard in federal courts involve rather straightforward applications of law; few lead to the making of new public policy. Cases that do affect how the law or the Constitution is interpreted can begin with seemingly minor events. For example, a major broadening of the Bill of Rights—requiring for the first time that all accused persons in *state* as well as federal criminal trials be supplied with a lawyer, free if necessary—began when impoverished Clarence Earl Gideon, imprisoned in Florida, wrote an appeal in pencil on prison stationery and sent it to the Supreme Court.[34]

The Supreme Court does not have to hear any appeal it does not want to hear. At one time it was required to listen to certain appeals, but Congress has changed the law so that now the Court can pick the cases it wants to consider.

It does this by issuing a **writ of certiorari.** *Certiorari* is a Latin word meaning, roughly, "made more certain"; lawyers and judges have abbreviated it to *cert.* It works this way: The Court considers all the petitions it receives to review lower-court decisions. If four justices agree to hear a case, cert is issued and the case is scheduled for a hearing.

In deciding whether to grant certiorari, the Court tries to reserve its time for cases decided by lower federal courts or by the highest state courts in which a significant federal or constitutional question has been raised. For example, the Court will often grant certiorari when one or both of the following is true:

- Two or more federal circuit courts of appeals have decided the same issue in different ways.
- The highest court in a state has held a federal or state law to be in violation of the Constitution or has upheld a state law against the claim that it is in violation of the Constitution.

In a typical year the Court may consider over seven thousand petitions asking it to review decisions of lower or state courts. It rarely accepts more than about one hundred of them for full review.

In exercising its discretion in granting certiorari, the Supreme Court is on the horns of a dilemma. If it grants it frequently, it will be inundated with cases. As it is, the Court's workload has quintupled in the last fifty years. If, on the other hand, the Court grants certiorari only rarely, then the federal courts of appeals have the last word on the interpretation of

writ of certiorari   An order by a higher court directing a lower court to send up a case for review.

Clarence Earl Gideon studied law books while in prison so that he could write an appeal to the Supreme Court. His handwritten appeal asked that his conviction be set aside because he had not been provided with an attorney. His appeal was granted.

the Constitution and federal laws, and since there are twelve of these, staffed by about 167 judges, they may well be in disagreement. In fact this has already happened: because the Supreme Court reviews only about 1 or 2 percent of appeals court cases, applicable federal law may be different in different parts of the country.[35] One proposal to deal with this dilemma is to devote the Supreme Court's time entirely to major questions of constitutional interpretation and to create a national court of appeals that would ensure that the twelve circuit courts of appeals are producing uniform decisions.[36]

Because the Supreme Court has a heavy workload, the influence wielded by law clerks has grown. These clerks—recent graduates of law schools hired by the justices—play a big role in deciding which cases should be heard under a writ of *certiorari.* Indeed, some of the opinions written by the justices are drafted by the clerks. Since the reasons for a decision may be as important as the decision itself, and since these reasons are sometimes created by the clerks, the power of the clerks can be significant.

☆ Getting to Court

In theory the courts are the great equalizer in the federal government. To use the courts to settle a question, or even to alter fundamentally the accepted interpretation of the Constitution, one need not be elected to any office, have access to the mass media, be a member of an interest group, or be otherwise powerful or rich. Once the contending parties are before the courts, they are legally equal.

It is too easy to believe this theory uncritically or to dismiss it cynically. In fact it is hard to get before the Supreme Court: it rejects over 96 percent of the applications for *certiorari* that it receives. And the costs involved in getting to the Court can be high. To apply for *certiorari* costs only $300 (plus forty copies of the petition), but if *certiorari* is granted and the case is heard, the costs—for lawyers and for copies of the lower-court records in the case—can be very high. And by then one has already paid for the cost of the first hearing in the district court and probably one appeal to the circuit court of appeals. Furthermore, the time it takes to settle a matter in federal court can be quite long.

But there are ways to make these costs lower. If you are indigent—without funds—you can file and be heard as a pauper for nothing; about half the petitions arriving before the Supreme Court are **in forma pauperis** (such as the one from Gideon, described earlier). If your case began as a criminal trial in the district courts and you are poor, the government will supply you with a lawyer at no charge. If the matter is not a criminal case and you cannot afford to hire a lawyer, interest groups representing a wide spectrum of opinion sometimes are willing to take up the cause if the issue in the case seems sufficiently important. The American Civil Liberties Union (ACLU), a liberal group, represents some people who believe that their freedom of speech has been abridged or that their constitutional rights in criminal proceedings have been violated. The Center for Individual Rights, a conservative group, represents some people who feel that they have been victimized by racial quotas.

But interest groups do much more than just help people pay their bills. Many of the most important cases decided by the Court got there because an interest group organized the case, found the plaintiffs, chose the legal strategy, and mobilized legal allies. The NAACP has brought many key civil rights

in forma pauperis   A method whereby a poor person can have his or her case heard in federal court without charge.

cases on behalf of individuals. Although in the past most such cases were brought by liberal interest groups, of late conservative interest groups have entered the courtroom on behalf of individuals. One helped sue CBS for televising a program that allegedly libeled General William Westmoreland, once the American commander in Vietnam. (Westmoreland lost the case.) And many important issues are raised by attorneys representing state and local governments. Several price-fixing cases have been won by state attorneys general on behalf of consumers in their states.

Fee Shifting

Unlike what happens in most of Europe, each party to a lawsuit in this country must pay its own way. (In England, by contrast, if you sue someone and lose, you pay the winner's costs as well as your own.) But various laws have made it easier to get someone else to pay. **Fee shifting** enables the **plaintiff** (the party that initiates the suit) to collect its costs from the defendant if the defendant loses, at least in certain kinds of cases. For example, if a corporation is found to have violated the antitrust laws, it must pay the legal fees of the winner. If an environmentalist group sues the Environmental Protection Agency, it can get the EPA to pay the group's legal costs. Even more important to individuals, Section 1983 of Chapter 42 of the *United States Code* allows a citizen to sue a state or local government official—say, a police officer or a school superintendent—who has deprived the citizen of some constitutional right or withheld some benefit to which the citizen is entitled. If the citizen wins, he or she can collect money damages and lawyers' fees from the government. Citizens, more aware of their legal rights, have become more litigious, and a flood of such "Section 1983" suits has burdened the courts. The Supreme Court has restricted fee shifting to cases authorized by statute,[37] but it is clear that the drift of

policy has made it cheaper to go to court—at least for some cases.

Standing

There is, in addition, a nonfinancial restriction on getting into federal court. To sue, one must have **standing,** a legal concept that refers to who is entitled to bring a case. It is especially important in determining who can challenge the laws or actions of the government itself. A complex and changing set of rules governs standings; some of the more important ones are these:

- There must be an actual controversy between real adversaries. (You cannot bring a "friendly" suit against someone, hoping to lose in order to prove your friend right. You cannot ask a federal court for an opinion on a hypothetical or imaginary case or ask it to render an advisory opinion.)
- You must show that you have been harmed by the law or practice about which you are complaining. (It is not enough to dislike what the government or a corporation or a labor union does; you must show that you were actually harmed by that action.)
- Merely being a taxpayer does not ordinarily entitle you to challenge the constitutionality of a federal governmental action. (You may not want your tax money to be spent in certain ways, but your remedy is to vote against the politicians doing the spending; the federal courts will generally require that you show some other personal harm before you can sue.)

Congress and the courts have recently made it easier to acquire standing. It has always been the rule that a citizen could ask the courts to order federal officials to carry out some act that they were under a legal obligation to perform or to refrain from some action that was contrary to law. A citizen can also sue a government official personally in order to collect damages if the official acted contrary to law. For example, it was for long the case that if an FBI agent broke into your office without a search warrant, you could sue the agent and, if you won, collect money. However, you cannot sue the government itself without its consent. This is the doctrine of **sovereign immunity.** For instance, if the army accidentally kills your cow while testing a new cannon, you cannot sue the government to recover the cost of the cow unless the government agrees to be sued. (Since testing cannons is legal, you cannot sue the army

fee shifting   A rule that allows a plaintiff to recover costs from the defendant if the plaintiff wins.

plaintiff   The party that initiates a lawsuit.

standing   A legal rule stating who is authorized to start a lawsuit.

sovereign immunity   The rule that a citizen cannot sue the government without the government's consent.

officer who fired the cannon.) By statute Congress has given its consent for the government to be sued in many cases involving a dispute over a contract or damage done as a result of negligence (for example, the dead cow). Over the years these statutes have made it easier to take the government into court as a defendant.

Even some of the oldest rules defining standing have been liberalized. The rule that merely being a taxpayer does not entitle you to challenge in court a government decision has been relaxed where the citizen claims that a right guaranteed under the First Amendment is being violated. The Supreme Court allowed a taxpayer to challenge a federal law that would have given financial aid to parochial (or church-related) schools on the grounds that this aid violated the constitutional requirement of separation between church and state. On the other hand, another taxpayer suit to force the CIA to make public its budget failed because the Court decided that the taxpayer did not have standing in matters of this sort.[38]

Class-Action Suits

Under certain circumstances a citizen can benefit directly from a court decision, even though the citizen himself or herself has not gone into court. This can happen by means of a **class-action suit:** a case brought into court by a person on behalf not only of himself or herself, but of all other persons in similar circumstances. Among the most famous of these was the 1954 case in which the Supreme Court found that Linda Brown, a black girl attending the fifth grade in the Topeka, Kansas, public schools, was denied the equal protection of the laws (guaranteed under the Fourteenth Amendment) because the schools in Topeka were segregated. The Court did not limit its decision to Linda Brown's right to attend an unsegregated school but extended it—as Brown's lawyers from the NAACP had asked—to cover all "others similarly situated."[39] It was not easy to design a court order that would eliminate segregation in the schools, but the principle was clearly established in this class action.

Since the *Brown* case, many other groups have been quick to take advantage of the opportunity created by class-action suits. By this means the courts could be used to give relief not simply to a particular person but to all those represented in the suit. A landmark class-action case was that which challenged the malapportionment of state legislative

Linda Brown was refused admission to a white elementary school in Topeka, Kansas. On her behalf the NAACP brought a class-action suit that resulted in the 1954 landmark Supreme Court decision Brown v. Board of Education.

districts (see Chapter 13).[40] There are thousands of class-action suits in the federal courts involving civil rights, the rights of prisoners, antitrust suits against corporations, and other matters. These suits became more common partly because people were beginning to have new concerns that were not being met by Congress and partly because some class-action suits became quite profitable. The NAACP got no money from Linda Brown or from the Topeka Board of Education in compensation for its long and expensive labors, but beginning in the 1960s court rules were changed to make it financially attractive for lawyers to bring certain kinds of class-action suits.

---

class-action suit   A case brought by someone to help him or her and all others who are similarly situated.

Table 16.2   Supreme Court Justices in Order of Seniority, 2004

Name (Birth Date)	Home State	Prior Experience	Appointed By (Year)
William H. Rehnquist, Chief Justice (1924)	Arizona	Justice; assistant attorney general	Reagan (1986) as chief; Nixon (1971) as justice
John Paul Stevens (1916)	Illinois	Federal judge	Ford (1975)
Sandra Day O'Connor (1930)	Arizona	State judge	Reagan (1981)
Antonin Scalia (1936)	New York	Federal judge	Reagan (1986)
Anthony Kennedy (1936)	California	Federal judge	Reagan (1988)
David Souter (1939)	New Hampshire	State judge	Bush (1990)
Clarence Thomas (1948)	Georgia	Federal judge	Bush (1991)
Ruth Bader Ginsburg (1933)	New York	Federal judge	Clinton (1993)
Stephen Breyer (1938)	Massachusetts	Federal judge	Clinton (1994)

Suppose, for example, that you think your telephone company overcharged you by $75. You could try to hire a lawyer to get a refund, but not many lawyers would take the case, because there would be no money in it. Even if you were to win, the lawyer would stand to earn no more than perhaps one-third of the settlement, or $25. Now suppose that you bring a class action against the company on behalf of everybody who was overcharged. Millions of dollars might be at stake; lawyers would line up eagerly to take the case, because their share of the settlement, if they won, would be huge. The opportunity to win profitable class-action suits, combined with the possibility of having the loser pay the attorneys' fees, led to a proliferation of such cases.

In response to the increase in its workload, the Supreme Court decided in 1974 to tighten drastically the rules governing these suits. It held that it would no longer hear (except in certain cases defined by Congress, such as civil rights matters) class-action suits seeking monetary damages unless each and every ascertainable member of the class was individually notified of the case. To do this is often prohibitively expensive (imagine trying to find and send a letter to every customer that may have been overcharged by the telephone company!), and so the number of such cases declined and the number of lawyers seeking them out dropped.[41]

But it remains easy to bring a class-action suit in most state courts. State Farm automobile insurance company was told by a state judge in a small Illinois town that it must pay over $1 billion in damages on behalf of a "national" class, even though no one in this class had been notified. Big class-action suits powerfully affect how courts make public policy.

Such suits have forced into bankruptcy companies making asbestos and silicone breast implants and have threatened to put out of business tobacco companies and gun manufacturers. (Ironically, in some of these cases, such as the one involving breast implants, there was no scientific evidence showing that the product was harmful.) Some class-action suits, such as the one ending school segregation, are good, but others are frivolous efforts to get companies to pay large fees to the lawyers who file the suits.

In sum, getting into court depends on having standing and having resources. The rules governing standing are complex and changing, but generally they have been broadened to make it easier to enter the federal courts, especially for the purpose of challenging the actions of the government. Obtaining the resources is not easy but has become easier because laws in some cases now provide for fee shifting, private interest groups are willing to finance cases, and it is sometimes possible to bring a class-action suit that lawyers find lucrative.

★ The Supreme Court in Action

If your case should find its way to the Supreme Court—and of course the odds are that it will not—you will be able to participate in one of the more impressive, sometimes dramatic ceremonies of American public life. The Court is in session in its white marble building for thirty-six weeks out of each year, from early October until the end of June. The nine justices read briefs in their individual offices, hear oral arguments in the stately courtroom, and discuss their decisions with one another in a conference room where no outsider is ever allowed.

Most cases, as we have seen, come to the Court on a *writ of certiorari*. The lawyers for each side may then submit their briefs. A **brief** is a document that sets forth the facts of the case, summarizes the lower-court decision, gives the arguments for the side represented by the lawyer who wrote the brief, and discusses the other cases that the Court has decided bear on the issue. Then the lawyers are allowed to present their oral arguments in open court. They usually summarize their briefs or emphasize particular points in them, and they are strictly limited in time—usually to no more than a half hour. (The lawyer speaks from a lectern that has two lights on it. When the white light goes on, the attorney has five minutes remaining; when the red flashes, he or she must stop—instantly.) The oral arguments give the justices a chance to question the lawyers, sometimes searchingly.

Since the federal government is a party—as either plaintiff or defendant—to about half the cases that the Supreme Court hears, the government's top trial lawyer, the solicitor general of the United States, appears frequently before the Court. The solicitor general is the third-ranking officer of the Department of Justice, right after the attorney general and deputy attorney general. The solicitor general decides what cases the government will appeal from lower courts and personally approves every case the government presents to the Supreme Court. In recent years the solicitor general has often been selected from the ranks of distinguished law school professors.

In addition to the arguments made by lawyers for the two sides in a case, written briefs and even oral arguments may also be offered by "a friend of the court," or **amicus curiae.** An amicus brief is from an interested party not directly involved in the suit. For example, when Allan Bakke complained that he had been the victim of "reverse discrimination" when he was denied admission to a University of California medical school, fifty-eight amicus briefs were filed supporting or opposing his position. Before such briefs can be filed, both parties must agree or the Court must grant permission. Though these briefs sometimes offer new arguments, they are really a kind of polite lobbying of the Court that declare which interest groups are on which side. The ACLU, the NAACP, the AFL-CIO, and the U.S. government itself have been among the leading sources of such briefs.

These briefs are not the only source of influence on the justices' views. Legal periodicals such as the *Harvard Law Review* and the *Yale Law Journal* are frequently consulted, and citations to them often appear in the Court's decisions. Thus the outside world of lawyers and law professors can help shape, or at least supply arguments for, the conclusions of the justices.

The justices retire every Friday to their conference room, where in complete secrecy they debate the cases they have heard. The chief justice speaks first, followed by the other justices in order of seniority. After the arguments they vote, traditionally in reverse order of seniority: the newest justice votes first, the chief justice last. By this process an able chief justice can exercise considerable influence—in guiding or limiting debate, in setting forth the issues, and in handling sometimes temperamental personalities. In deciding a case, a majority of the justices must be in agreement: if there is a tie, the lower-court decision is left standing. (There can be a tie among nine justices if one is ill or disqualifies himself or herself because of prior involvement in the case.)

Though the vote is what counts, by tradition the Court usually issues a written opinion explaining its decision. Sometimes the opinion is brief and unsigned (called a **per curiam opinion**); sometimes it is quite long and signed by the justices agreeing with it. If the chief justice is in the majority, he will either write the opinion or assign the task to a justice who agrees with him. If he is in the minority, the senior justice on the winning side will decide who writes the Court's opinion. There are three kinds of opinions—an **opinion of the Court** (reflecting the majority's view), a **concurring opinion** (an opinion by one or more justices who agree with the

---

brief   A written statement by an attorney that summarizes a case and the laws and rulings that support it.

amicus curiae   A brief submitted by a "friend of the court."

per curiam opinion   A brief, unsigned court opinion.

opinion of the court   A signed opinion of a majority of the Supreme Court.

concurring opinion   A signed opinion in which one or more members agree with the majority view but for different reasons.

The members of the U.S. Supreme Court: from left to right, Antonin Scalia, Ruth Bader Ginsburg, John Paul Stevens, David Souter, William Rehnquist, Clarence Thomas, Sandra Day O'Connor, Stephen Breyer, Anthony Kennedy.

majority's conclusion but for different reasons that they wish to express), and a **dissenting opinion** (the opinion of the justices on the losing side). Each justice has three or four law clerks to help him or her review the many petitions the Court receives, study cases, and write opinions.

People like to think of the courts as expressing "liberal" or "conservative" opinions, and in many cases they seem to do just that. But that is far from the whole story. In many cases, perhaps two-fifths of those decided by the Supreme Court, the decisions are unanimous. Even two justices as different as Antonin Scalia and Ruth Bader Ginsburg vote the same way much of the time. The most important thing to remember is not the decision but the reasons

behind the decision. Many times judges will vote for a position that they don't personally like but feel obliged to support because that is how the law reads.

☆ The Power of the Federal Courts

The great majority of the cases heard in the federal courts have little or nothing to do with changes in public policy: people accused of bank robbery are tried, disputes over contracts are settled, personal-injury cases are heard, and the patent law is applied. In most instances the courts are simply applying a relatively settled body of law to a specific controversy.

The Power to Make Policy

The courts make policy whenever they reinterpret the law or the Constitution in significant ways, extend the reach of existing laws to cover matters not previously thought to be covered by them, or design

---

dissenting opinion   A signed opinion in which one or more justices disagree with the majority view.

remedies for problems that involve the judges' acting in administrative or legislative ways. By any of these tests the courts have become exceptionally powerful.

One measure of that power is the fact that more than 160 federal laws have been declared unconstitutional. And as we shall see, on matters where Congress feels strongly, it can often get its way by passing slightly revised versions of a voided law.

Another measure, and perhaps a more revealing one, is the frequency with which the Supreme Court changes its mind. An informal rule of judicial decision-making has been **stare decisis,** meaning "let the decision stand." It is the principle of precedent: a court case today should be settled in accordance with prior decisions on similar cases. (What constitutes a similar case is not always clear; lawyers are especially gifted at finding ways of showing that two cases are different in some relevant way.) There are two reasons why precedent is important. The practical reason should be obvious: if the meaning of the law continually changes, if the decisions of judges become wholly unpredictable, then human affairs affected by those laws and decisions become chaotic. A contract signed today might be invalid tomorrow. The other reason is at least as important: if the principle of equal justice means anything, it means that similar cases should be decided in a similar manner. On the other hand, times change, and the Court can make mistakes. As Justice Felix Frankfurter once said, "Wisdom too often never comes, and so one ought not to reject it merely because it comes late."[42]

However compelling the arguments for flexibility, the pace of change can become dizzying. By one count the Court has overruled its own previous decisions in over 260 cases since 1810.[43] In fact it may have done it more often, because sometimes the Court does not say that it is abandoning a precedent, claiming instead that it is merely distinguishing the present case from a previous one.

A third measure of judicial power is the degree to which courts are willing to handle matters once left to the legislature. For example, the Court refused for a long time to hear a case about the size of congressional districts, no matter how unequal their populations.[44] The determination of congressional district boundaries was regarded as a **political question**— that is, as a matter that the Constitution left entirely to another branch of government (in this case, Congress) to decide for itself. Then in 1962 the Court decided that it was competent after all to handle this matter, and the notion of a "political question"

became a much less important (but by no means absent) barrier to judicial power.[45]

By all odds the most powerful indicator of judicial power can be found in the kinds of remedies that the courts will impose. A **remedy** is a judicial order setting forth what must be done to correct a situation that a judge believes to be wrong. In ordinary cases, such as when one person sues another, the remedy is straightforward: the loser must pay the winner for some injury that he or she has caused, the loser must agree to abide by the terms of a contract he or she has broken, or the loser must promise not to do some unpleasant thing (such as dumping garbage on a neighbor's lawn). Today, however, judges design remedies that go far beyond what is required to do justice to the individual parties who actually appear in court. The remedies now imposed often apply to large groups and affect the circumstances under which thousands or even millions of people work, study, or live. For example, when a federal district judge in Alabama heard a case brought by a prison inmate in that state, he issued an order not simply to improve the lot of that prisoner but to revamp the administration of the entire prison system. The result was an improvement in the living conditions of many prisoners, at a cost to the state of an estimated $40 million a year. Similarly, a person who feels entitled to welfare payments that have been denied him or her may sue in court to get the money, and the court order will in all likelihood affect all welfare recipients. In one case certain court orders made an additional one hundred thousand people eligible for welfare.[46]

The basis for sweeping court orders can sometimes be found in the Constitution; the Alabama prison decision, for example, was based on the judge's interpretation of the Eighth Amendment, which prohibits "cruel and unusual punishments."[47] Others are based on court interpretations of federal laws. The Civil Rights Act of 1964 forbids discrimination on grounds of "race, color, or national origin" in any program receiving federal financial assistance. The Supreme Court

---

stare decisis   "Let the decision stand," or allowing prior rulings to control the current case.

political question   An issue the Supreme Court will allow the executive and legislative branches decide.

remedy   A judicial order enforcing a right or redressing a wrong.

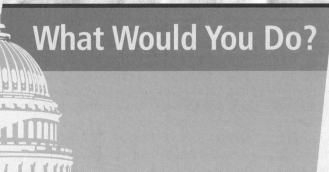

Supreme Court to Decide Constitutionality of Capital Punishment

March 20
WASHINGTON
    The Supreme Court has been asked to decide whether the death penalty is constitutional. A decision in this important case is expected by June . . .

MEMORANDUM

To: *Justice Robert Gilbert*
From: *David Wilson, law clerk*

Before I draft your opinion, I want to know how you feel about declaring the death penalty unconstitutional.

Arguments for:

1. As enforced, the death penalty tends to be discriminatory. Black convicts are, in some cases, more likely to be executed than white ones.
2. The death penalty is irrevocable. If an innocent man is executed, he cannot be brought back to life when his innocence becomes known.
3. The death penalty is "cruel and unusual punishment" that is banned by the Constitution.

Arguments against:

1. The Constitution does not ban the death penalty.
2. The death penalty existed when the Constitution and Bill of Rights were written. Their authors meant by "cruel and unusual punishment" the use of torture.
3. When a legislature decides to punish murder by death, its views are entitled to deference.
4. There is no strong evidence that the death penalty is imposed in a discriminatory manner.

Your decision:

Ban death penalty _____
Do not ban death penalty _____

interpreted that as meaning that the San Francisco school system was obliged to teach English to Chinese students unable to speak it.[48] Since a Supreme Court decision is the law of the land, the impact of that ruling was not limited to San Francisco. Local courts and legislatures elsewhere decided that that decision meant that classes must be taught in Spanish for Hispanic children. What Congress meant by the Civil Rights Act is not clear; it may or may not have believed that teaching Hispanic children in English rather than Spanish was a form of discrimination. What is important is that it was the Court, not Congress, that decided what Congress meant.

Views of Judicial Activism

Judicial activism has, of course, been controversial. Those who support it argue that the federal courts must correct injustices when the other branches of

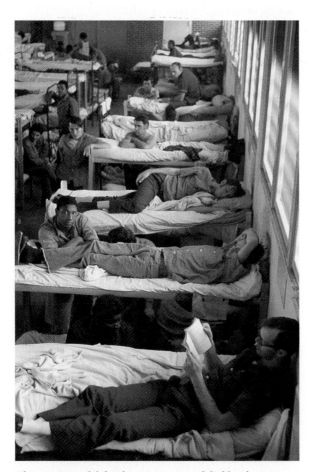

The activism of federal courts is exemplified by the sweeping orders they have issued to correct such problems as overcrowded prisons.

the federal government, or the states, refuse to do so. The courts are the institution of last resort for those without the votes or the influence to obtain new laws, and especially for the poor and powerless. After all, Congress and the state legislatures tolerated segregated public schools for decades. If the Supreme Court had not declared segregation unconstitutional in 1954, it might still be law today.

Those who criticize judicial activism rejoin that judges usually have no special expertise in matters of school administration, prison management, environmental protection, and so on; they are lawyers, expert in defining rights and duties but not in designing and managing complex institutions. Furthermore, however desirable court-declared rights and principles may be, implementing those principles means balancing the conflicting needs of various interest groups, raising and spending tax monies, and assessing the costs and benefits of complicated alternatives. Finally, federal judges are not elected; they are appointed and are thus immune to popular control. As a result, if they depart from their traditional role of making careful and cautious interpretations of what a law or the Constitution means and instead begin formulating wholly new policies, they become unelected legislators.

Some people think that we have activist courts because we have so many lawyers. The more we take matters to courts for resolution, the more likely it is that the courts will become powerful. It is true that we have more lawyers in proportion to our population than most other nations. There is one lawyer for every 325 Americans, but only one for every 970 Britons, every 1,220 Germans, and every 8,333 Japanese.[49] But that may well be a symptom, not a cause, of court activity. As we suggested in Chapter 4, we have an adversary culture based on an emphasis on individual rights and an implicit antagonism between the people and the government. Generally speaking, lawyers do not create cases; contending interests do, thereby generating a demand for lawyers.[50] Furthermore, we had more lawyers in relation to our population in 1900 than in 1970, yet the courts at the turn of the twentieth century were far less active in public affairs. In fact, in 1932 there were more court cases per 100,000 people than there were in 1972.

A more plausible reason for activist courts has been the developments discussed earlier in this chapter that have made it easier for people to get standing in the courts, to pay for the costs of litigation, and to bring class-action suits. The courts and Congress have gone a long way toward allowing private citizens to become "private attorneys general." Making it easier to get into court increases the number of cases being heard. For example, in 1961 civil rights cases, prisoners' rights cases, and cases under the Social Security laws were relatively uncommon in federal court. Between 1961 and 1990 the increase in the number of such matters was phenomenal: civil rights cases rose over sixtyfold and prisoners' petitions over fortyfold. Such matters are the fastest-growing portion of the courts' civil workload.

Legislation and the Courts

An increase in cases will not by itself lead to sweeping remedies. For that to occur, the law must be sufficiently vague to permit judges wide latitude in interpreting it, and the judges must want to exercise that opportunity fully. The Constitution is filled with words of seemingly ambiguous meaning—"due process of law," the "equal protection of the laws," the "privileges or immunities of citizens." Such phrases may have been clear to the Framers, but to the Supreme Court they have become equivocal or elastic. How the Court has chosen to interpret such phrases has changed greatly over the last two centuries in ways that can be explained in part by the personal political beliefs of the justices.

Increasingly Congress has passed laws that also contain vague language, thereby adding immeasurably to the courts' opportunities for designing remedies. Various civil rights acts outlaw discrimination but do not say how one is to know whether discrimination has occurred or what should be done to correct it if it does occur. That is left to the courts and the bureaucracy. Various regulatory laws empower administrative agencies to do what the "public interest" requires but say little about how the public interest is to be defined. Laws intended to alleviate poverty or rebuild neighborhoods speak of "citizen participation" or "maximum feasible participation" but do not explain who the citizens are that should participate, or how much power they should have.

In addition to laws that require interpretation, other laws induce litigation. Almost every agency that regulates business will make decisions that cause the agency to be challenged in court—by business firms if the regulations go too far, by consumer or labor organizations if they do not go far enough. One study showed that the federal courts of appeals heard over three thousand cases in which they had to review the decision of a regulatory agency. In two-thirds of them the agency's position was supported; in the other third the agency was overruled.[51] Perhaps one-fifth of these cases arose out of agencies or programs that did not even exist in 1960. The federal government today is much more likely to be on the defensive in court than it was twenty or thirty years ago.

Finally, the attitudes of the judges powerfully affect what they will do, especially when the law gives them wide latitude. Their decisions and opinions have been extensively analyzed—well enough, at least, to know that different judges often decide the same case in different ways. Conservative southern federal judges in the 1950s, for example, often resisted plans to desegregate public schools, while judges with a different background authorized bold plans.[52] Some of the greatest disparities in judicial behavior can be found in the area of sentencing criminals.[53]

★ Checks on Judicial Power

No institution of government, including the courts, operates without restraint. The fact that judges are not elected does not make them immune to public opinion or to the views of the other branches of government. How important these restraints are varies from case to case, but in the broad course of history they have been significant.

One restraint exists because of the very nature of courts. A judge has no police force or army; decisions that he or she makes can sometimes be resisted or ignored, *if* the person or organization resisting is not highly visible and is willing to run the risk of being caught and charged with contempt of court. For example, long after the Supreme Court had decided that praying and Bible reading could not take place in public schools,[54] schools all over the country were still allowing prayers and Bible reading.[55] Years after the Court declared segregated schools to be unconstitutional, scores of school systems remained segregated. On the other hand, when a failure to comply is easily detected and punished, the courts' power is usually unchallenged. When the Supreme Court declared the income tax to be unconstitutional in 1895, income tax collections promptly ceased. When the Court in 1952 declared illegal President Truman's effort to seize the steel mills in order to stop a strike, the management of the mills was immediately returned to their owners.

Congress and the Courts

Congress has a number of ways of checking the judiciary. It can gradually alter the composition of the judiciary by the kinds of appointments that the Senate is willing to confirm, or it can impeach judges that it does not like. Fifteen federal judges have been the object of impeachment proceedings in our history, and nine others have resigned when such proceedings seemed likely. Of the fifteen who were impeached, seven were acquitted, four were convicted, and one resigned. The most recent convictions were those of Alcee Hastings of Florida and Walter

TRIVIA

The Supreme Court

Supreme Court justice who served the longest	William O. Douglas: 36 years (1939–1975)
Only Supreme Court justice to run for president	Charles Evans Hughes (resigned from Court in 1916 to seek presidency; lost to Woodrow Wilson)
Only president to become Supreme Court justice	William Howard Taft (president, 1909–1913; chief justice, 1921–1930)
First Catholic Supreme Court justice	Roger B. Taney (1836–1864)
First Jewish Supreme Court justice	Louis Brandeis (1916–1939)
First black Supreme Court justice	Thurgood Marshall (1967–1991)
First woman Supreme Court justice	Sandra Day O'Connor (1981 to present)
Only Supreme Court justice to be impeached	Samuel Chase (impeached by House in 1804; acquitted by Senate)
Only Supreme Court justice whose grandson also served on the Court	John Harlan (1877–1911), whose grandson John Harlan served from 1954 to 1971

Nixon of Mississippi, both in 1989.[56] In practice, however, confirmation and impeachment proceedings do not make much of an impact on the federal courts because simple policy disagreements are not generally regarded as adequate grounds for voting against a judicial nominee or for starting an impeachment effort.

Congress can alter the number of judges, though, and by increasing the number sharply, it can give a president a chance to appoint judges to his liking. As described above, a "Court-packing" plan was proposed (unsuccessfully) by Franklin Roosevelt in 1937 specifically to change the political persuasion of the Supreme Court. In 1978 Congress passed a bill creating 152 new federal district and appellate judges to help ease the workload of the federal judiciary. This bill gave President Carter a chance to appoint over 40 percent of the federal bench. In 1984 an additional eighty-four judgeships were created; by 1988 President Reagan had appointed about half of all federal judges. In 1990 an additional seventy-two judges were authorized.

During and after the Civil War, Congress may have been trying to influence Supreme Court decisions when it changed the size of the Court three times in six years (raising it from nine to ten in 1863, lowering it again from ten to seven in 1866, and raising it again from seven to nine in 1869).

Congress and the states can also undo a Supreme Court decision interpreting the Constitution by amending that document. This happens, but rarely: the Eleventh Amendment was ratified to prevent a citizen from suing a state in federal court; the Thirteenth, Fourteenth, and Fifteenth were ratified to undo the *Dred Scott* decision regarding slavery; the Sixteenth was added to make it constitutional for Congress to pass an income tax; and the Twenty-sixth was added to give the vote to eighteen-year-olds in state elections.

On over thirty occasions Congress has merely repassed a law that the Court has declared unconstitutional. In one case a bill to aid farmers, voided in 1936, was accepted by the Court in slightly revised form three years later.[57] (In the meantime, of course, the Court had changed its collective mind about the New Deal.)

One of the most powerful potential sources of control over the federal courts, however, is the authority of Congress, given by the Constitution, to decide what the entire jurisdiction of the lower

Judicial Review in Canada and Europe

Courts outside the United States can declare laws to be unconstitutional, but most can do so in ways that are very different from that in the United States.

Canada: The highest court can declare a law unconstitutional, but not if the legislature has passed it with a special provision that says the law will survive judicial scrutiny notwithstanding the country's Charter of Rights. Such laws must be renewed every five years.

Europe: The European Court of Human Rights in Strasbourg can decide human rights cases that begin in any of the nations that make up the European Community.

France: Its Constitutional Council can declare a law unconstitutional, but only if asked to do so by government officials and only before (not after) the law goes into effect.

Germany: The Federal Constitutional Court can declare in an advisory opinion, before a case has emerged, that a law is unconstitutional, and it can judge the constitutionality of laws when asked to do so by a lower court (which itself cannot rule a law unconstitutional). The Federal Constitutional Court may hold an administrative or judicial action to be unjustified when a citizen, having exhausted all other remedies, files a petition.

courts and the appellate jurisdiction of the Supreme Court shall be. In theory Congress could prevent matters on which it did not want federal courts to act from ever coming before the courts. This happened in 1868. A Mississippi newspaper editor named McCar-

Thurgood Marshall became the first Black Supreme Court Justice. As chief council for the NAACP, Marshall argued the 1954 Brown v. Board of Education *case in front of the Supreme Court. He was appointed to the Court in 1967 and served until 1991.*

dle was jailed by federal military authorities who occupied the defeated South. McCardle asked the federal district court for a writ of habeas corpus to get him out of custody; when the district court rejected his plea, he appealed to the Supreme Court. Congress at that time was fearful that the Court might find the laws on which its Reconstruction policy was based (and under which McCardle was in jail) unconstitutional. To prevent that from happening, it passed a bill withdrawing from the Supreme Court appellate jurisdiction in cases of this sort. The Court conceded that Congress could do this and thus dismissed the case because it no longer had jurisdiction.[58]

Congress has threatened to withdraw jurisdiction on other occasions, and the mere existence of the threat may have influenced the nature of Court decisions. In the 1950s, for example, congressional opinion was hostile to Court decisions in the field of civil liberties and civil rights, and legislation was proposed that would have curtailed the Court's jurisdiction in these areas. It did not pass, but the Court may have allowed the threat to temper its decisions.[59] On the other hand, as congressional resistance to the Roosevelt Court-packing plan shows, the Supreme Court enjoys a good deal of prestige in the nation, even among people who disagree with some of its decisions, and so passing laws that would frontally attack it would not be easy except perhaps in times of national crisis.

Furthermore, laws narrowing jurisdiction or restricting the kinds of remedies that a court can impose are often blunt instruments that might not achieve the purposes of their proponents. Suppose that you, as a member of Congress, would like to prevent the federal courts from ordering schoolchildren to be bused for the purpose of achieving racial balance in the schools. If you denied the Supreme Court appellate jurisdiction in this matter, you would leave the lower federal courts and all state courts free to do as they wished, and many of them would go on ordering busing. If you wanted to attack that problem, you could propose a law that would deny to all federal courts the right to order busing as a remedy for racial imbalance. But the courts would still be free to order busing (and of course a lot of busing goes on even without court orders), provided that they did not say that it was for the purpose of achieving racial balance. (It could be for the purpose of "facilitating desegregation" or making possible "redistricting.") Naturally you could always make it illegal for children to enter a school bus for any reason, but then many children would not be able to get to school at all. Finally, the Supreme Court might well decide that if busing were essential to achieve a constitutional right, then any congressional law prohibiting such busing would itself be unconstitutional. Trying to think through how *that* dilemma would be resolved is like trying to visualize two kangaroos simultaneously jumping into each other's pouches.

Public Opinion and the Courts

Though they are not elected, judges read the same newspapers as members of Congress, and thus they, too, are aware of public opinion, especially elite opinion. Though it may be going too far to say that the Supreme Court follows the election returns, it is nonetheless true that the Court is sensitive to certain bodies of opinion, especially of those elites—liberal or conservative—to which its members happen to be attuned. The justices will keep in mind historical cases in which their predecessors, by blatantly disregarding public opinion, very nearly destroyed the legitimacy of the Court itself. This was the case with the *Dred Scott* decision, which infuriated the North and was widely disobeyed. No such crisis exists today, but it is altogether possible that changing political moods affect the kinds of remedies that judges will think appropriate.

Opinion not only restrains the courts; it may also energize them. The most activist periods in Supreme Court history have coincided with times when the political system was undergoing profound and lasting changes. The assertion by the Supreme Court,

under John Marshall's leadership, of the principles of national supremacy and judicial review occurred at the time when the Jeffersonian Republicans were coming to power and their opponents, the Federalists, were collapsing as an organized party. The proslavery decisions of the Taney Court came when the nation was so divided along sectional and ideological lines as to make almost any Court decision on this matter unpopular. Supreme Court review of economic regulation in the 1890s and 1900s came at a time when the political parties were realigning and the Republicans were acquiring dominance that would last for several decades. The Court decisions of the 1930s corresponded to another period of partisan realignment. (The meaning of a realigning election was discussed in Chapter 10.)

Pollsters have been measuring how much confidence the public has in the Supreme Court. The results are shown in Figure 16.3. The percentage of people saying that they had a "great deal of confidence" in the Court rose sharply from 1971 to 1974, fell again until 1976, seesawed up and down until 1989, took a sharp dip and then recovered from 1989 to 1991, and again seesawed before rising in 1996. These movements seem to reflect the public's reaction not only to what the Court does but also to what the government as a whole is doing. The upturn in the early 1970s was probably caused by the Watergate scandal, an episode that simultaneously discredited the presidency and boosted the stock of those institutions (such as the courts) that seemed to be checking the abuses of the White House. The gradual upturn in the 1980s may have reflected a general restoration of public confidence in government during that decade.[60]

Though popular support is now relatively low for the Supreme Court, this decline has so far not resulted in any legal checks being placed on it. In the 1970s and 1980s several bills were introduced in Congress that would have restricted the jurisdiction of federal courts over busing for purposes of racial integration or altered the Supreme Court's decisions regarding school prayer and abortion. None passed.

The changes that have occurred in the Court have been caused by changes in its personnel. Presidents Nixon and Reagan attempted to produce a less activist Court by appointing justices who were more inclined to be strict constructionists and conservatives. To some extent they succeeded: Justices Kennedy, O'Connor, Rehnquist, and Scalia were certainly less inclined than Justice Thurgood Marshall to find new rights in

Figure 16.3   **Patterns of Public Confidence in the Court, 1974–2003**

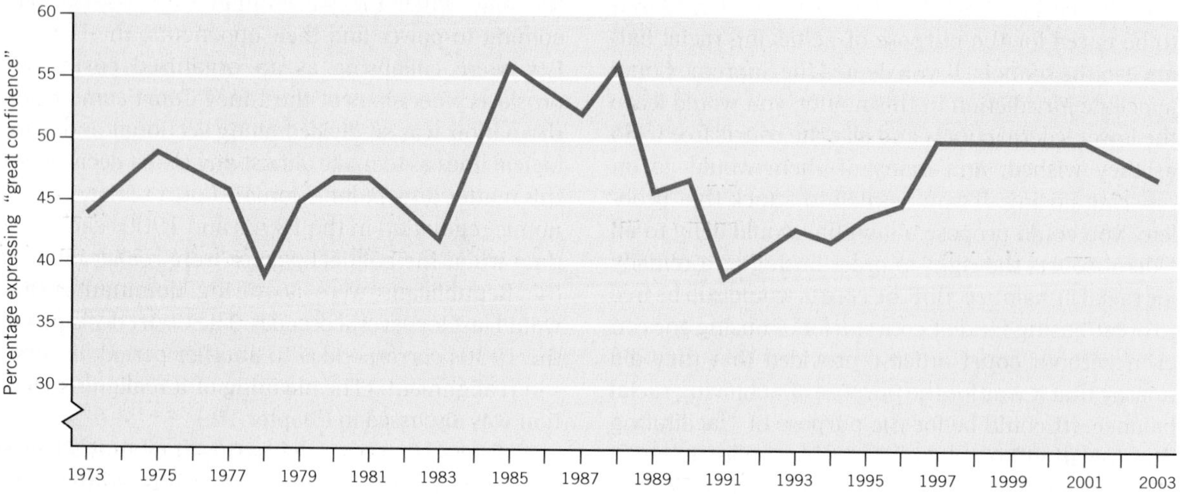

Source: The Gallup Poll.

the Constitution or to overturn the decisions of state legislatures. But as of yet there has been no wholesale retreat from the positions staked out by the Warren Court. As noted above, a Nixon appointee, Justice Blackmun, wrote the decision making antiabortion laws unconstitutional; and another Nixon appointee, Chief Justice Burger, wrote the opinion upholding court-ordered school busing to achieve racial integration. A Reagan appointee, Justice O'Connor, voted to uphold a right to an abortion. The Supreme Court has become somewhat less willing to impose restraints on police practices, and it has not blocked the use of the death penalty. But in general the major features of Court activism and liberalism during the Warren years—school integration, sharper limits on police practice, greater freedom of expression—have remained intact.

The reasons for the growth in court activism are clear. One is the sheer growth in the size and scope of

the government as a whole. The courts have come to play a larger role in our lives because Congress, the bureaucracy, and the president have come to play larger ones. In 1890 hardly anybody would have thought of asking Congress—much less the courts—to make rules governing the participation of women in college sports or the district boundaries of state legislatures. Today such rules are commonplace, and the courts are inevitably drawn into interpreting them. And when the Court decided how the vote in Florida would be counted during the 2000 presidential election, it created an opportunity in the future for scores of new lawsuits challenging election results.

The other reason for increased activism is the acceptance by a large number of judges, conservative as well as liberal, of the activist view of the function of the courts. If courts once existed solely to "settle disputes," today they also exist in the eyes of their members to "solve problems."

★ SUMMARY

*A*n independent judiciary with the power of judicial review—the right to decide the constitutionality of acts of Congress, the executive branch, and state governments—can be a potent political force in American life. That influence has been realized from

the earliest days of the nation, when Marshall and Taney put the Supreme Court at the center of the most important issues of the time. From 1787 to 1865 the Supreme Court was preoccupied with the establishment of national supremacy. From 1865 to

1937 it struggled with defining the scope of political power over the economy. In the present era it has sought to expand personal liberties.

The scope of the courts' political influence has increasingly widened as various groups and interests have acquired access to the courts, as the judges serving on them have developed a more activist stance, and as Congress has passed more laws containing vague or equivocal language. Whereas in other political arenas (the electorate, Congress, the bureaucracy) the influence of contending groups is largely dependent on their size, intensity, prestige, and political resources, the influence of contending groups before the courts depends chiefly on their arguments and the attitudes of the judges.

Though the Supreme Court is the pinnacle of the federal judiciary, most decisions, including many important ones, are made by the twelve courts of appeals and the ninety-four district courts. The Supreme Court can control its own workload by deciding when to grant *certiorari.* It has become easier for citizens and groups to gain access to the federal courts (through class-action suits, by *amicus curiae* briefs, by laws that require government agencies to pay legal fees, and because of the activities of private groups such as the NAACP and the ACLU).

At the same time, the courts have widened the reach of their decisions by issuing orders that cover whole classes of citizens or affect the management of major public and private institutions. However, the courts can overstep the bounds of their authority and bring upon themselves a counterattack from both the public and Congress. Congress has the right to control much of the courts' jurisdiction, but it rarely does so. As a result the ability of judges to make law is only infrequently challenged directly.

RECONSIDERING WHO GOVERNS?

1. Why should federal judges serve for life?

Strictly speaking, they serve during "good behavior," but that means they would have to be impeached and convicted in order to remove them. The reason for this protection is clear: The judiciary cannot be independent of the other two branches of government if judges could be easily removed by the president or Congress, and this independence ensures that they are a separate branch of government.

RECONSIDERING TO WHAT ENDS?

1. Why should federal courts be able to declare laws unconstitutional?

Though the Constitution does not explicitly give them that power, they have acquired it on the reasonable assumption that the Constitution would become meaningless if the president and Congress could ignore its provisions. The Constitution, after all, states that it shall be the "supreme law of the land."

2. Should federal judges only interpret existing laws or should they be able to create new laws?

The federal courts rarely think that their decisions create entirely new laws, but in fact their interpretations sometimes come close to just that. One reason is that many provisions of the Constitution are vague. What does the Constitution mean by "respecting an establishment of religion," the "equal protection of the law," or a "cruel and unusual punishment"? The courts must give concrete meaning to these phrases. But another reason is the personal ideology of judges. Some think that a free press is more important than laws governing campaign finance, while others think that a free press must give way to such laws. Some believe that the courts ought to use federal law to strike down discrimination, but others think that affirmative action programs must be put in place.

WORLD WIDE WEB RESOURCES

Federal Judicial Center: **www.fjc.gov**
Federal courts: **www.uscourts.gov**

Supreme Court decisions: **www.law.cornell.edu**
Finding laws and reports: **www.findlaw.com**

SUGGESTED READINGS

Abraham, Henry J. *The Judicial Process.* 7th ed. New York: Oxford University Press, 1998. An excellent, comprehensive survey of how the federal courts are organized and function.

Abraham, Henry J., and Barbara A. Perry. *Freedom of the Court.* 8th ed. Lawrence, KS: University of Kansas Press, 2003. Careful summary of civil liberties and civil rights cases.

Cardozo, Benjamin N. *The Nature of the Judicial Process.* New Haven, Conn.: Yale University Press, 1921. Important statement of how judges make decisions, by a former Supreme Court justice.

Ely, John Hart. *Democracy and Distrust.* Cambridge: Harvard University Press, 1980. Effort to create a theory of judicial review that is neither strict-constructionist nor activist.

Hall, Kermit L., ed. *The Oxford Companion to the Supreme Court of the United States.* New York: Oxford University Press, 1992. Everything you ever wanted to know about the Supreme Court, its justices, and its major decisions, arranged in more than one thousand alphabetical entries.

Lasser, William. *The Limits of Judicial Power.* Chapel Hill: University of North Carolina Press, 1988. Shows how the Court through history has withstood the political storms created by its more controversial decisions.

Lazarus, Edward. *Closed Chamber.* New York: Times Books, 1998. An eyewitness account of how the Supreme Court operates. Written by a former law clerk, it is filled with both interesting facts and personal opinions.

McCloskey, Robert G. *The American Supreme Court.* 4th ed. Edited by Sanford Levinson. Chicago: University of Chicago Press, 2005. Superb brief history of the Supreme Court, updated by one of McCloskey's former students who now teaches law at the University of Texas.

Rabkin, Jeremy. *Judicial Compulsions.* New York: Basic Books, 1989. Explains (and argues against) the extensive Court intervention in the work of administrative agencies.

Wolfe, Christopher. *The Rise of Modern Judicial Review.* New York: Basic Books, 1986. An excellent history of judicial review from 1787 to the present.

PART IV

The Politics of Public Policy

In the extended republic of the United States, and among the great variety of interests, parties, and sects which it embraces, a coalition of a majority of the whole society could seldom take place on any other principles than those of justice and the general good.

FEDERALIST No. 51

CHAPTER 17

Politics and Public Policy

How the American System Affects Policy-Making

How the American System Has Changed

Restraints on Growth

Relaxing the Restraints
  The Old System ● The New System ●
  Polarized Politics

Should the System Be Changed?
  Reducing the Barriers to Action ●
  Increasing the Barriers to Action ●
  Term Limits ● Who Is Right?

WHO GOVERNS?

1. What changes have occurred in who has power in the federal government?
2. Should the Constitution be modified to make it either harder or easier to govern?

TO WHAT ENDS?

1. What does the federal government do today that it did not do in the past?

*T*alk to almost any citizen about American government and you will get a long list of complaints that generally fall into two groups. The first are gripes about politics: "Politicians are self-serving captives of special-interest groups, interested only in their own reelection. Judges are too liberal (or too conservative). The media are too interested in trivial scandals (or not interested enough in important scandals). The president and Congress are in gridlock, unable or unwilling to take decisive action." The second group are grievances about policies: "It's outrageous that we have this budget deficit; why can't we manage to live within our means? Why can't the government do something about (take your pick) crime, drug abuse, racism, poor schools, air pollution, or Japanese competition?"

A lot of people think that there is a connection between our political problems and our policy failures. In their opinion we don't solve the problems of the deficit, crime, or racism *because* our politicians are self-serving, the press doesn't do its job right, the courts are filled with wrong-headed judges, and special-interest groups are too powerful. Many people who think that way decided to support Ross Perot when the Texas businessman announced that he would run for president as an independent in 1992 and 1996. They apparently were saying that we could solve our problems if only we had strong, dedicated leaders.

This view of how to fix the system, or of whether the system even needs fixing at all, has some truth to it, but for the most part it is too simple. Having read this book so far, you should understand that the way our system works is not mainly the result of the people in charge of it, but mainly (though not entirely) the result of the constitution that shapes it. The Constitution was written not to make governing easy but to make it hard, not to facilitate choices but to impede them, not to empower leaders but to frustrate them. The written and unwritten constitutions of European democracies are very different: they were designed to allow the government to govern, subject only to the periodic checks of a popular election. Here popular participation is encouraged; there it is discouraged. Here the courts can overturn presidential and congressional actions; there they usually cannot. Here many officials have the power to say no, and none has the power to say yes and make it stick; there a prime minister can say yes and make it stick.

☆ How the American System Affects Policy-Making

This system for making policy creates quite predictable results, and among them are the very aspects of politics that so many Americans find distasteful. Consider the effects of four constitutional provisions on how we make policy:

1. *The separation of powers:* This has at least two important results. First, the president and Congress will be rivals, even when they are from the same political party. The White House and Congress will compete for power over the policies and personnel of the government. Stalemates will be the rule, not the exception, and they will only be overcome by a national crisis, a powerful tide of public opinion, or tough political bargaining. For example, if the president wants to cut the deficit by reducing spending and Congress wants to cut it by increasing taxes, a political standoff will occur, as happened during much of the Reagan and Bush administrations and during Clinton's first term. Second, members of Congress will first and foremost represent their districts and states. Virtually no bill will become a law unless it is first adjusted to reflect the differing demands of local constituencies. A president may complain that members of Congress work to get "unnecessary" benefits—roads, bridges, parks, and airports—for their districts, but he forgets that this is exactly what the voters want from their members. Calling it "pork-barrel politics" doesn't change that fundamental political reality.

2. *Federalism:* The states have an independent political position. As a result it is very hard to have a truly "national" policy on anything. And even when we do have a national policy, the states play a big role in implementing it. For example, the states have major responsibility for enforcing pollution control programs and building major highways, even though most of the money comes from Washington. And they play the dominant role in schooling, law enforcement, and land-use controls and pay most of those bills.

3. *Judicial review:* The federal courts can declare an act of the president or Congress unconstitutional and can decide suits brought by people arguing either that a federal agency has exceeded its legal authority or that it has not done all that the law

requires. The courts have obviously played a decisive role in racial integration and civil liberties cases, but they also play an important, though less visible, role in implementing laws affecting the environment, occupational safety and health, and highway construction.

4. *Freedom of speech and assembly:* The First Amendment guarantees the right of individuals to speak their minds and lobby their senators and representatives. This right cannot be preserved for individuals and denied to groups; after all, groups are just collections of like-minded individuals. As a result placing any meaningful restrictions on the activities of lobbyists is next to impossible (except, of course, to ensure that they do not engage in corruption, such as bribery).

When you add together the effects of these four features of our Constitution, you get a uniquely American system of policy-making. Though it has many distinctive features, the best word to describe our system of government is *adversarial*—that is, a system that encourages participation by people who have an incentive to fight rather than cooperate. Freedom of speech protects each person's right to participate; the separation of powers and federalism means that any participant can usually find a political ally; the decentralized structure of Congress (which is one effect of federalism and the separation of powers) gives each member an incentive to call attention to himself or herself by making speeches, taking positions, and (above all) attacking adversaries; and the courts provide a convenient (though expensive) arena in which to wage endless struggles.

One can see our adversarial system at work in many policy arenas. Business and government fight over what environmental protection rules to enforce. (You may be surprised to learn that in much of Europe, they cooperate rather than fight in deciding these rules.) Pro-environment groups attack business, portraying it in the worst possible light; antiabortion groups attack pro-choice groups (and vice versa). Anyone offering a plan to reduce the deficit quickly discovers that every interest that might be adversely affected (either by paying higher taxes or receiving smaller benefits) is highly organized and ready to do battle. When a government agency issues an unpopular order, we don't usually respond by obeying but by claiming that our rights have been violated and threatening to sue or hold a protest march.

Not all of these situations occur as the inevitable result of the Constitution, and historical forces have intensified these problems in recent decades. But however much events have aggravated these tendencies, the tendencies themselves arise directly from the kind of government that we have chosen.

Adversarial politics puts a premium on the ability to dramatize issues, gain publicity, mount demonstrations, and attack opponents. It downplays the ability to conduct quiet negotiations, make commitments, and accept personal responsibility.

In a participatory, adversarial system, politicians have no incentive to say that the government shouldn't tackle a problem or doesn't know how to solve it, and they have every incentive to claim that government must "do something" and that they know just what to do. The more such things are done, the more interest groups will have an incentive to organize lobbying efforts and open offices in Washington. The more such offices are opened, the greater the pressure to draft more bills and the smaller the chances that any given bill will make much sense.

Adversarial politics also colors our judgement as to the actual level of corruption and misconduct in our government. The checks and balances of our constitutional system and the individualistic style of political campaigning in our country give everybody an incentive to dig up dirt and blow the whistle on a rival. By contrast, in parliamentary regimes such as those in Europe, these checks and balances and individualistic rivalries are much less common, and therefore the incentive to expose a rival also diminishes. As a result lying and corruption seem more prevalent here than abroad, when in fact we may have less; it is just that here more gets exposed—or invented.

Given these features of our system, what is surprising is that anything gets done at all. But it does. Preoccupied as we are with all the government's failings, we sometimes forget its accomplishments. Since the end of World War II our government has built an interstate highway system, passed a set of civil rights laws, created the Medicare program for the elderly, adopted a series of increasingly tough environmental laws, explored outer space, deregulated the airlines, waged and won a forty-five-year cold war against the former Soviet Union, and sustained a level of economic growth and freedom sufficient to make millions of people from all parts of the world want to immigrate to this country. It paid a price, of course, for all of this: higher taxes, more regulations, and new groups to assimilate.

The "Rules" of Politics

Some "Rules" of Politics

Here are some generalizations about American politics, distilled from what has been said in this book, offered in nervous awareness that our political system has a way of proving everybody wrong. (Before the 1960s it was a "rule" of politics that no Catholic could be elected president. John F. Kennedy took care of that.)

- Policies once adopted tend to persist, whatever their value. (It is easier to start new programs than to end old ones.)

- Almost all electoral politics is local politics. (Members of Congress who forget "home base" tend not to remain in Congress for long.)

- Whatever the size of their staff and budget, Congress and the White House will always be overworked. (More resources produce more work, which produces more resources.)

- Each branch of government tends to emulate the others. (Congress will become more bureaucratized to cope with an executive branch that is becoming more bureaucratized; judges will become more activist as Congress becomes more activist.)

- Proposals that seem to confer widespread and immediate benefits will be enacted, whatever their long-term costs.

- Proposals that seem to confer delayed benefits will be enacted only if their costs are unknown, concealed, or deferred.

- Nobody—businesspeople, bureaucrats, members of Congress, judges, professors—likes competition, and everybody will do whatever he or she can to reduce or eliminate it.

- "Planning" in government takes place after a crisis takes place.

- The mass media never cover a story about things that are going well. Thus the number of "problems" in society is a function of the number of reporters.

- If you want something, you are claiming a right; if your opponent wants something, he or she is protecting a vested interest.

Despite the growth of the federal government, state and local governments retain more power in the United States than in almost any other nation. This is the Texas legislature.

Since our complex political system makes it easy for all kinds of people and groups to wield at least some power, we should not expect policies to get made in only one way. If we had a less participatory, less adversarial system, it would be much easier to explain policy-making. In Japan, for example, appointed officials—bureaucrats—have much more power than their American counterparts, and much Japanese policy is the result of government agency proposals that are only modestly changed, if changed at all, by the legislature. In Great Britain the prime minister enjoys a great deal of power for as long as his or her party has a majority in the House of Commons, and so discussing British policy-making involves explaining why the prime minister favors one policy over another.

In the United States everybody gets into the act. Some policies are proposed by the president and enacted (after many changes) by Congress; others are proposed by members of Congress and enacted despite presidential objections. (Congress may override the president's veto or sufficiently modify the proposal to get him to withhold his veto.) When a congressional majority forms around a proposal, it is not always the result of one party (say, the Democrats) outvoting the other (the Republicans); rather, the majority often consists of a coalition of Democrats and Republicans winning out over a smaller coalition of other Democrats and Republicans.

☆ How the American System Has Changed

Our political system has always been adversarial and participatory to some degree, but in recent decades it has become much more so. One of the main reasons for this change is that the federal government now does more things affecting more people than ever before. In 1950 Washington played little or no role in health care, civil rights, worker safety, environmental protection, or the control of crime and drug abuse. Today it plays an important role in all these matters. Since Washington touches the lives of more people than once was the case, more people try to influence Washington. And when they do, they find that everybody else has also gotten into the act. The result is an unprecedented amount of pushing and shouting. Some people find all this exciting; some are completely turned off by it.

But the Constitution was written so as to make this huge growth in government activity difficult if not impossible. For any new policy to take effect, the House and the Senate have to agree on a bill, the president has to sign it, and the courts have to accept it as constitutional. Since the president and the members of Congress are elected separately, neither branch of government can readily use a political party to control the other branch, and so no party system can (except under unusual circumstances) centralize by informal means what the Constitution has decentralized by formal ones.

Moreover, the states enjoy special constitutional protection (for a while the state legislatures even chose U.S. senators); this means that the sphere in which the federal government can act—assuming it decides to take any action at all—is quite limited. To obtain a new policy its proponents have to navigate a difficult obstacle course, persuading hundreds of independent legislators that the new policy is in their interests, does not violate states' rights, and will serve the common good. To defeat a new policy its opponents need only persuade the majority of one key committee.

If the American political system is biased against action, then how has it become so large, powerful, and expensive? If it is so hard for Congress and the president to agree, then how is it that the federal government now spends a sum one-fifth the size of the gross national product, has piled up a federal debt of around six trillion dollars, and employs more than three million civilians and over one million military personnel? If the federal government is so hedged in with constitutional restrictions, then what enables that government to manage a vast retirement system, set rules determining how factories and businesses shall operate, strike down laws banning abortions, require that private colleges allow women to participate in intercollegiate sports, search our luggage before we board an airplane, compel all eighteen-year-old males to register for the draft, and (until recently) insist that the states impose a fifty-five-mile-per-hour speed limit on all their highways?

The most striking change in the American government since its founding has been the vast increase in the scope of its activities and the reach of its powers. For the first century and a half, the government in Washington behaved pretty much as the

Framers had anticipated. It regulated foreign commerce, distributed the mail, and occasionally went to war. It carried on passionate debates about slavery and the right of women to vote, but it dealt with the former only when an irrepressible conflict broke out and with the latter only after decades of agitation. Generally it spent no more money than it took in from taxes, and these taxes were mostly on imported goods, not on personal incomes. During wartime the government would get larger and run up a debt, but after the war it would shrink in size and return to pay-as-you-go financing. The standing army was minuscule. During an economic recession a major argument would arise over whether something other than gold should be the basis for American currency (if dollar bills could be redeemed for silver, for example, more dollar bills could be printed, and so money would be easier to get), but for the most part the advocates of maintaining a hard, gold-backed currency prevailed. A few efforts were made to regulate large corporations, especially the railroads, but in general government regulation of business was left to the states. And sometimes the Supreme Court prevented even the states from regulating businesses.

Until the mid–twentieth century, who ruled in Washington—and to what ends—made little difference in the lives of most citizens, except in time of war or economic crisis. Governors and mayors were more in the public eye than presidents or members of Congress. Most senators and representatives served only one or two terms in office; there didn't seem to be much point in becoming a career legislator since Congress didn't do much, didn't pay much, and wasn't in session very often. If the Republicans were in power, the government tended to seek high tariffs; if the Democrats were in power, it sought lower tariffs. Today who rules and to what ends affects almost every aspect of our lives. Members of the House serve, on average, at least three terms in office. What can explain the growth of the federal government?

In a sense the question ought to be turned around. In a government whose leaders are chosen by a competitive struggle for the people's votes, candidates for office have a strong incentive to offer new programs to voters in order to win their support. It is hard to excite people by promising to do less for them; it is only natural, therefore, that politicians usually promise to do more. In acting this way politicians are not behaving badly; they are behaving democratically. If politicians foster new programs, the interesting questions become these: What kept the federal government from growing rapidly in size from its very first years of existence? Why did it not become large and powerful until nearly the middle of the twentieth century?

☆ Restraints on Growth

There were three restraints on the growth of the U.S. government in the nineteenth and early twentieth centuries. First, the Constitution was interpreted in a way that sharply limited what policies the federal government could adopt. For a century or more the Supreme Court held that the federal government had only very limited powers to regulate business and commerce and that Congress could not delegate such powers as it had to administrative agencies. Similarly, the Supreme Court for a long time maintained that the Bill of Rights limited only what the federal government could do, and so there was little or no basis for challenging in federal court what state governments were doing. For example, not until 1963 was there a federal constitutional right to have a lawyer appointed to represent a poor person in a state criminal trial. The ratification of the Fourteenth Amendment in 1868 in theory brought more state action under federal court scrutiny (it held that no state could "deprive any person of life, liberty, or property without due process of law"), but the Court interpreted this provision narrowly, so that, for example, the amendment provided no basis for attacking school segregation as unconstitutional. The Court even held that a federal income tax was unconstitutional.

The Supreme Court could not have maintained its interpretation for as long as it did if that position had not been pretty much in accord with public opinion. This opinion was the second restraint on the growth of the federal government. There was little or no popular demand for a federal welfare or retirement system, federal aid to local public education, a federal program to deal with crime, or federal action against segregation. Not even organized labor demanded a major federal role in industrial affairs. The American Federation of Labor, led by Samuel Gompers, resisted federal involvement in labor-management disputes and was not especially outspoken in calling for a national social security program. Even as late as the 1930s, during the depths of the Great Depression, public opinion polls suggested that as many as half the voters were opposed to a federal unemployment

compensation program. There were frequent popular demands by farmers for federal control over the railroads and by progressives for reforming the federal civil service, but these were matters well within the accepted limits of federal constitutional authority.

Even if people had wanted the federal government to do more, many of them lacked the political resources to back up their demands. This is the third reason that Washington had so small an agenda for so long. Although labor unions existed in the nineteenth century, it was not until after their right to organize was guaranteed in 1935 that they grew rapidly in numbers and influence. Whatever policies women might have wanted to see adopted did not stand much chance until women had won the vote, and that did not occur until 1920. Those elites who wanted to organize people concerned about the environment, consumer safety, and public health did not have the computerized mailing lists, foundation grants, and sympathetic journalists necessary to convert a cause into a campaign. Public-interest law firms, willing and able to pursue policy goals through the courts, scarcely existed.

☆ Relaxing the Restraints

In recent decades each of these constraints on federal action has weakened or disappeared altogether. First, the courts have altered their interpretation of the Constitution in ways that have not only permitted but sometimes even required government action. The Bill of Rights has been extended so that almost all of its important provisions are now regarded as applying to the states (by having been incorporated into the due-process clause of the Fourteenth Amendment). This means that a citizen can use the federal courts to alter state policy to a greater degree than ever before. (Overturning state laws that ban abortions or require racially separate schools are two important examples of this change.) The special protection that the courts once granted property rights has been substantially reduced so that business can be regulated to a greater degree than previously. The Court has permitted Congress to give broad discretionary powers to administrative agencies, allowing bureaucrats to make decisions that once only Congress could make.

Second, public opinion has changed in ways that support an expanded role for the federal government.

The public demanded action to deal with the Great Depression (the programs that resulted, such as Social Security, survived in part because the Supreme Court changed its mind about the permissible scope of federal action). Political elites changed their minds faster than the average citizen. Well-educated, politically active people began demanding federal policies regarding civil rights, public welfare, environmental protection, consumer safety, and foreign aid well before the average citizen became concerned with such things.

Once in place most of these programs proved popular, and so their continuance was supported by mass as well as elite opinion. The cumulative effect of this process was to blur, if not erase altogether, the line that once defined what the government had the authority to do. At one time a new proposal was debated in terms of whether it was legitimate for the federal government to do it at all. Federal aid to education, for example, was usually opposed because many people feared it would lead to federal control of local schools. But after so many programs (including federal aid to education) had been passed, people stopped arguing about whether a certain policy was *legitimate* and argued instead about whether it was *effective*.

Third, political resources have become more widely distributed. The number and variety of interest groups have increased enormously. The funds available from foundations for organizations pursuing specific causes have grown. It is now easier to get access to the federal courts than formerly was the case, and once in the courts, plaintiffs are more likely to encounter judges who believe that the law and the Constitution should be interpreted broadly to permit particular goals (for example, prison reform) to be attained by legal rather than legislative means. Hundreds of magazines and newsletters have arisen to provide policy information to specialized segments of the public. The techniques of mass protest, combined with the desire of television to show pictorially interesting accounts of social conflict, have been perfected in ways that convey the beliefs of a few into the living rooms of millions.

Campaign finance laws and court rulings have given legal status and constitutional protection to thousands of political action committees (PACs) that raise and spend tens of millions of dollars from millions of small contributors. A college education, once the privilege of a tiny minority, has become the common experience of millions of people, so that the effects of college—in encouraging political participation and in shaping political beliefs—are now widespread. The ability of candidates to win nomination for office no longer depends on their ability to curry favor with a few powerful bosses; it now reflects their skill at raising money, mobilizing friends and activists, cultivating a media image, and winning a primary election.

So great have been the changes in the politics of policy-making in this country starting in the 1930s that we can refer, with only slight exaggeration, to one policy-making system having been replaced by another (see the box on page 476).

The Old System

The Old System had a small agenda. Though people voted at a high rate and often took part in torchlight parades and other mass political events, political leadership was professionalized, in the sense that the leadership circle was small, access to it was difficult, and the activists in social movements were generally kept out. Only a few major issues were under discussion at any time. A member of Congress had a small staff (if any at all), dealt with his or her colleagues on a personal basis, deferred to the prestige of House and Senate leaders, and tended to become part of some stable coalition (the farm bloc, the labor bloc, the southern bloc) that persisted across many issues.

When someone proposed adding a new issue to the public agenda, a major debate often arose over whether it was legitimate for the federal government to take action at all on the matter. A dominant theme in this debate was the importance of "states' rights." Except in wartime, or during a very brief period when the nation expressed an interest in acquiring colonies, the focus of policy debate was on domestic affairs. Members of Congress saw these domestic issues largely in terms of their effect on local constituencies. During this time the presidency was small and somewhat personal; there was only a rudimentary White House staff. The president would cultivate the press, but there was a clear understanding that what he said in a press conference was never to be quoted directly.

For the government to take bold action under this system, the nation usually had to be facing a crisis. War presented such a crisis, and so the federal government during the Civil War and World Wars I and II acquired extraordinary powers to conscript soldiers, control industrial production, regulate the

⋆ HOW THINGS WORK ⋆

How American Politics and Government Have Changed

Old System	New System
Congress	
Chairmen relatively strong	Chairmen relatively weak
Small staffs	Large staffs
Few subcommittees	Many subcommittees
Interest Groups	
A few large blocs (farmers, business, labor)	Many diverse interests that form ad hoc coalitions
Rely on "insider" lobbying	Mobilize grassroots
Presidency	
Small staff	Large staff
Reaches public via press conferences	Reaches public via radio and television
Courts	
Allow government to exercise few economic powers	Allow government to exercise broad economic powers
Take narrow view of individual freedoms	Take broad view of individual freedoms
Political Parties	
Dominated by state and local party leaders meeting in conventions	Dominated by activists chosen in primaries and caucuses
Policy Agenda	
Brief agenda	Long agenda
Key Questions	
Should the federal government enter a new policy area?	How can we fix or pay for an existing policy?
Key Issue	
Would a new federal program abridge states' rights?	Would a new federal program prove popular?

flow of information to citizens, and restrict the scope of personal liberty. Each succeeding crisis left the government bureaucracy somewhat larger than it had been before, but when the crisis ended, the exercise of extraordinary powers ended. Once again the agenda of political issues became small, and legislators argued about whether it was legitimate for the government to enter some new policy area, such as civil rights or industrial regulation.

The New System

The New System began in the 1930s but did not take its present form until the 1970s. It is characterized by a large policy agenda, the end of the debate over the legitimacy of government action (except in the area of First Amendment freedoms), the diffusion and decentralization of power in Congress, and the multiplication of interest groups. The government has grown so large that it has a policy on almost every conceivable subject, and so the debate in Washington is less often about whether it is right and prudent to take some bold new step and more often about how the government can best cope with the strains and problems that arise from implementing existing policies. As someone once said, the federal government is now more concerned with managing than with ruling.

Senior citizens rallying to get prescription drugs included in Medicare.

For example: In 1935 Congress debated whether the nation should have a Social Security retirement system at all; in the 1980s and 1990s it debated whether the system could best be kept solvent by raising taxes or by cutting benefits. In the 1960s Congress argued over whether there should be any federal civil rights laws at all; by the 1980s it was arguing over whether those laws should be administered in a way that simply eliminated legal barriers to equal opportunity for racial minorities or in a way that through affirmative action would make up for the disadvantages that had burdened such minorities in the past. As late as the 1950s the president and Congress argued over whether it was right to adopt a new program if it meant that the government had to borrow money to pay for it. During the 1970s and 1980s the existence of a huge federal deficit was taken for granted, and the debate in Washington focused on the best way to slow its rate of growth or cut it back slightly. As late as the 1960s many members of Congress believed that the federal government had no business paying for the health care of its citizens; today hardly anyone argues against having Medicare, but many worry about how best to control its rising cost.

The differences between the Old and New Systems should not be exaggerated. The Constitution still makes it easier for Congress to block the proposals of the president, or for some committee of Congress to defeat the preferences of the majority of Congress, than is true in almost any other democratic government. The system of checks and balances operates as before. The essential differences between the Old and the New Systems are these:

1. Under the Old System the checks and balances made it difficult for the federal government to *start* a new program, and so the government remained relatively small. Under the New System these checks and balances make it hard to *change* what the government is already doing, and so the government remains large.

2. Under the Old System power was *somewhat centralized* in the hands of party and congressional leaders. There was still plenty of conflict, but the number of people who had to agree before something could be done was not large. Under the New System power is much more *decentralized*, and so it is harder to resolve conflict, because so many more people—party activists, interest group leaders, individual members of Congress, heads of government agencies—must agree.

The transition from the Old to the New System occurred chiefly during two periods in American politics. The first was in the early 1930s, when a catastrophic depression led the government to explore new ways of helping the needy, regulating business, and preventing a recurrence of the disaster. Franklin Roosevelt's New Deal was the result. The huge majorities enjoyed by the Democrats in Congress, coupled with popular demands to solve the problem, led to a vast outpouring of new legislation and the creation of dozens of new government agencies. Though initially the Supreme Court struck down some of these measures as unconstitutional, a key member of the Court changed his mind, and others retired from the bench; by the late 1930s the Court had virtually ceased opposing any economic legislation.

The second period was in the mid-1960s, a time of prosperity. There was no crisis akin to the Great Depression or World War II, but two events helped change the face of American politics. One was an intellectual and popular ferment that we now refer to as the spirit of "the sixties"—a militant civil rights movement, student activism aimed at resisting the Vietnam War, growing concern about threats to the environment, the popular appeal of Ralph Nader and his consumer protection movement, and an optimism among many political and intellectual leaders that the government could solve whatever problems it was willing to address. The other was the 1964 election that returned Lyndon Johnson to the presidency with a larger share of the popular vote than any other president in modern times. Johnson swept into office with huge Democratic majorities in both the House and Senate.

The combination of organized demands for new policies, elite optimism about the likely success of those policies, and extraordinary majorities in Congress meant that President Johnson was able, for a few years, to get almost any program he wanted enacted into law. So large were his majorities in Congress that the conservative coalition of Republicans and southern Democrats was no longer large enough to block action; northern Democratic liberals were sufficiently numerous in the House and Senate to take control of both bodies. Thus much of Johnson's "Great Society" legislation became law. This included (1) the passage of Medicare (to help pay the medical bills of retired people) and Medicaid (to help pay the medical bills of people on welfare); (2) greatly expanded federal aid to the states to assist them in fighting crime, rebuilding slums, and running transit systems; (3) the enactment of major civil rights laws and of a program to provide

President Roosevelt meets with members of the Civilian Conservation Corps, which put unemployed young men to work; he feared that Long might challenge him in the 1936 election.

federal aid to local schools; (4) the creation of a "War on Poverty" that included various job-training and community-action agencies; and (5) the enactment of a variety of laws regulating business for the purpose of reducing auto fatalities, improving the safety and health of industrial workers, cutting back on pollutants entering the atmosphere, and safeguarding consumers from harmful products.

These two periods—the early 1930s and the mid-1960s—changed the political landscape in America. Of the two the latter was perhaps the more important, for not only did it witness the passage of so much unprecedented legislation, but it also saw major changes in the pattern of political leadership. It was during this time that the great majority of the members of the House of Representatives came to enjoy relatively secure seats, primary elections came to supplant party conventions as the decisive means of selecting presidential candidates, interest groups increased greatly in number, and television began to play an important role in shaping the political agenda and perhaps influencing the kinds of candidates that are nominated. (At least one major change in the political process occurred after the 1960s—the passage of the campaign finance laws.)

Some people believed that the election of Ronald Reagan in 1980 meant that we had begun a new era of bold changes. No doubt the Reagan administration was more conservative than any other in a half a century; no doubt it made a major effort to alter how certain laws (such as in the area of civil rights) are administered. But rather little in the way of a legislative breakthrough occurred compared to the breakthroughs of Franklin Roosevelt and Lyndon Johnson. Domestic spending was cut in certain areas, and though the effect of a few of these cuts has been keen, there was no reduction in total outlays. (Federal spending, domestic as well as military, *increased* during the Reagan years.) There was a significant personal income tax cut in 1981, but it was partially offset by increases in Social Security and business taxes in subsequent years. There was a buildup in our military, but even before Reagan left office, the buildup had ended.

The politics of the deficit illustrate the features of the New System. The huge gap between what the government took in from taxes and what it spent on programs in the 1980s and early 1990s would not exist in a government that had not acquired a large policy agenda—an expensive medical care program, high levels of peacetime military spending, and many subsidies to various domestic interest groups. But the great difficulty the government experienced in trying to cut the deficit revealed, among other things, the effects of decentralized and fragmented political power: no group of officials could impose its preferences on the others.

Polarized Politics

Since the 1990s our New System of national government has become intensely polarized. By *polarized* we mean that the opposition between Democrats and Republicans in Congress and in our political parties has become more intense. Compared with the politics in the 1960s, there is less bipartisan negotiation, fewer bipartisan bills, and more angry talk between the two parties.

In 1993 the budget proposed by President Clinton passed a Democratic-controlled Congress without a single Republican in either the House or the Senate voting for it. In 1995 a disagreement about federal spending between Clinton and a Republican-controlled Congress led to many parts of the federal government being shut down. In 1998 when an effort

The "Rules" of Politics

Three Simple Rules for Improving Government

1. **No law is valid unless the members of Congress voting for it have read it.** The Ninety-seventh Congress considered over ten thousand bills and enacted over five hundred. The tax bill alone ran to several hundred pages. What is your guess as to the number of these bills that the average member of Congress read?

2. **No law or regulation is valid if it is incomprehensible to the average citizen.** Section 509(a) of the Internal Revenue Code reads as follows: "For purposes of paragraph (3), an organization described in paragraph (2) shall be deemed to include an organization described in section 501 (c) (4), (5), or (6) which would be an organization described in paragraph (2) if it were an organization described in section 501 (c) (3)." Any questions?

3. **No law is valid if it does not clearly state its goals and the means to attain them.** The law creating the Federal Communications Commission instructs it to award radio and television licenses on the following principle: to serve "the public interest, convenience, or necessity." Now you know.

Source: Reprinted with permission of the author, Irving Younger. Excerpt from a speech titled, "The Trial of Socrates, the Congress of the United States and US." Available from The Professional Education Group, Inc. <www.proedgroup.com>. 800.229.2531.

was made to impeach Clinton, all but four Republican members of the House voted to impeach him and all but five Democrats voted against it. In the Senate where the Clinton impeachment was put on trial, every Democrat voted for acquittal and 91 percent of the Republicans voted for conviction.

Party-line votes have become more common in Congress, and the verbal hostility between Democrats and Republicans has intensified. On at least one occasion, many House members had a private meeting to see if they could persuade themselves to be more polite. Not much came of the meeting.

One reason for this polarization has been a realignment in American politics. Once the Democratic party was composed of liberal northerners and conservative southerners. Today the South elects almost no conservative Democrats; their places have been taken by southern Republicans. Once the Republican party was composed of liberal easterners and conservative midwesterners. Today there are far fewer liberal Republicans and many more conservative ones. As a result of these changes, Congress is now composed of two parties whose members are either almost all liberal (the Democrats) or almost all conservative (the Republicans).

This polarization may even affect how voters feel. In the 2004 presidential election, the great majority of Democrats detested George W. Bush and the great majority of Republicans detested John F. Kerry. It was common for Bush to be described as a fool and for Kerry to be called a war criminal. Turnout in the election was higher than it has been since 1968, and hardly any voters made up their minds at the last moment.

For now, the New System of politics is an intensely polarized one, at least in Congress. This does not mean our two parties operate as they would in a parliamentary system, but it does mean that members of Congress no longer spend much time getting along with one another in relaxed, private meetings.

☆ Should the System Be Changed?

Almost from the day it was ratified, the Constitution has been the object of debate over ways in which it might be improved. These debates have rarely involved the average citizen, who tends to revere the document even if he or she cannot recall all of its details. Because of this deep and broad popular support, scholars and politicians have been wary of attacking it or suggesting many wholesale changes. But such attacks have occurred, and during 1987, when we celebrated the bicentennial of its adoption, we heard a variety of suggestions for improving the Constitution, ranging from particular amendments to wholesale revisions. In general there are today, as in the eighteenth century, two kinds of critics—those who think the federal government is too weak and those who think it is too strong.

Reducing the Barriers to Action

To the first kind of critic, the chief difficulty with the Constitution is the separation of powers. By making every decision the uncertain outcome of the pulling and hauling between the president and Congress, the Constitution precludes the emergence, except perhaps in times of crisis, of the kind of effective national leadership the country needs. In this view our nation today faces a number of challenges that require prompt, decisive, and comprehensive action. Our position of international leadership and the need to find ways of stimulating economic growth (while reducing our dependence on foreign oil and conserving our environment) all require that the president be able to formulate and carry out policies free of numerous pressures and delays from interest groups and local-minded members of Congress.

Such an increase in presidential authority would not only make for better policies, these critics argue, but also would help the voters hold the president and his party accountable for their actions. As matters now stand, nobody in government can be held responsible for policies: everybody takes the credit for successes, and nobody takes the blame for failures. This is because the president, who tends to be the major source of new programs, cannot get his policies adopted by Congress without long delays and much bargaining, the result of which may be some watered-down compromise that neither the president nor Congress really likes but which each must settle for if anything is to be done at all.

Finally, critics of the separation of powers complain that the government agencies responsible for implementing a program are exposed to undue interference from members of Congress and the special interests that can capture a member's ear. In this view the president is supposed to be in charge of the bureaucracy, but in fact he has to share that authority with countless legislators and legislative committees.

Not all critics of the separation of powers agree with all these points, nor do they all agree on what should be done about the problems. But they all have in common a fear that the separation of powers makes the president too weak and insufficiently accountable.

Their proposals for reducing the separation of powers include the following:

• Allow the president to appoint members of Congress to serve in the cabinet (the Constitution forbids members from holding any federal appointive office while in Congress).

- Allow the president to dissolve Congress and call for a special election (elections now can be held only on the schedule determined by the calendar).
- Allow Congress to require a president who has lost its confidence to face the country in a special election before his term would normally end.
- Require the presidential and congressional candidates to run as a team in each congressional district so that each voter would have to vote for the team as a whole. Thus a presidential candidate who carries a given district could be sure that the congressional candidate of his party would also win in the district.
- Have the president serve a single six-year term instead of being eligible for up to two four-year terms; this would presumably free him to lead without having to worry about reelection.
- Lengthen the terms of members of the House of Representatives from two to four years so that the entire House would stand for reelection at the same time as the president.

Some of these proposals are offered out of a desire to make the American system of government work a bit more like the British parliamentary system, in which the prime minister is the undisputed leader of the majority in the British Parliament. The parliamentary system is the major democratic alternative to the American separation-of-powers system in the world today. Another way of describing the aims of these reforms is that they would combine the somewhat greater centralization of power characteristic of the Old System of making policy with the larger agenda and bigger government characteristic of the New System.

Both the diagnosis and the remedies proposed by these critics of the separation of powers have been challenged. Many defenders of the Constitution believe that other nations with a more unified political system, such as Great Britain, have done no better than the United States in dealing with the problems of economic growth, national security, and environmental protection. Moreover, they argue, close congressional scrutiny of presidential proposals has improved those policies more often than it has weakened them. Finally, congressional "interference" in the work of government agencies is a good way of ensuring that the average citizen can fight back against the bureaucracy. Without that so-called interference citizens and interest groups might be helpless before big, powerful agencies.

Each of the specific proposals, defenders of the present system argue, would either make matters worse or have at best uncertain effects. Adding a few members of Congress to the president's cabinet would not help him much in getting his programs through Congress: of the 535 senators and representatives, only about half a dozen would probably be in the cabinet. Giving either the president or Congress the power to call a special election between the regular elections (every two or four years) would cause needless confusion and great expense; the country would live under the threat of being in a perpetual political campaign, with even weaker political parties. Linking the fate of the president and representatives by having them run as a team in each district would reduce the stabilizing and moderating effect of having them separately elected: if a Republican presidential candidate won, he would have a Republican majority in the House; if a Democratic candidate won, he would have a Democratic majority. With a linked ticket we might expect dramatic changes in policy as the political pendulum swung back and forth. Giving the president a single six-year term would indeed free him from the need to worry about reelection, but it is precisely that worry that keeps the president reasonably concerned about what the American people want.

Finally, defenders of the present system simply do not agree that the separation of powers makes government inert. They marvel at the sweeping domestic- and foreign-policy initiatives taken during this century. How, they ask, can a government system capable of launching a New Deal, a Great Society, and a rocket to the moon; of mobilizing for World War I, World War II, Vietnam, and Iraq; and of readying to impeach a president for violating his oath of office be characterized as antiquated or prone to inaction?

Defenders believe that problems in the system may result less from the separation of powers and more from the inability (or unwillingness) of key political leaders to work within it. They point, for example, to the early years of the Carter and Clinton administrations. These presidents found it hard to persuade Congress to support their domestic initiatives. Their party had a majority in both houses of

Congress, but that did not seem to matter. If the separation of powers, and not a lack of political skills, explains the policy stalemate suffered by Carter and Clinton, then how, defenders ask, did Ronald Reagan succeed in getting Congress to act quickly on his major domestic proposals?

Increasing the Barriers to Action

The second kind of critic of the Constitution thinks the government does too much, not too little. Though the separation of powers at one time may have slowed the growth of government and moderated the policies it adopted, in the last few decades government has grown helter-skelter. The problem, these critics argue, is not that democracy is a bad idea but that democracy can produce bad, or at least unintended, results if the government caters to the special-interest claims of the citizens rather than to their long-term values.

To see how these unintended results might occur, imagine a situation in which every citizen thinks the government is too big, taxes too heavily, and spends too much. Each citizen wants the government made smaller by reducing the benefits other people get—but not by reducing the benefits he or she gets. In fact the citizen may even be willing to see his or her own benefits cut, provided everybody else's are cut as well, and by a like amount.

But the political system attends to individual wants, which may or may not be in the public interest. It gives aid to farmers, contracts to industry, grants to professors, pensions to the elderly, and loans to students. As someone once said, the government is like an adding machine: during elections candidates campaign by promising to do more for whatever group is dissatisfied with what the present officeholders are doing for it. As a result most elections bring to office men and women who are committed to doing more for somebody. The grand total of all these additions is more for everybody. No politician has an incentive to do less for anybody.

Moreover, a big government is hard to manage. When the government tries to do too much, it does nothing well. To the critics our government is big without being strong, fat but not effective.

To remedy this state of affairs these critics suggest various mechanisms, but principally a constitutional amendment that would either set a limit on the amount of money the government could collect in taxes each year or require that each year the government have a balanced budget (that is, not spend more than it collects in taxes), or both. In some versions of these plans an extraordinary majority (say, 60 percent) of Congress could override these limits, and the limits would not apply in wartime.

The effect of such amendments, the proponents claim, would be to force Congress and the president to look at the big picture—the grand total of what they are spending—rather than just to operate the adding machine by repeatedly pushing the "add" button. If they could spend only so much during a given year, they would have to allocate what they spend among all the rival claimants, comparing the worth of each claimant to that of every other one. For example, if more money were spent on the poor, less would be spent on the military, and vice versa. In this way we could no longer add to the national debt by continuing to run up big deficits.

Some critics of an overly powerful federal government think these amendments will not be passed or may prove unworkable. Instead they favor enhancing the president's power to block spending through the line-item veto. The theory is that this power will better equip the president to stop unwarranted spending without vetoing the other provisions of a bill that he approves of.

Finally, some of these critics of a powerful government feel that the real problem arises not only from an excess of "adding machine" democracy but also from the growth in the power of the federal courts. These critics would like to devise a set of laws or constitutional amendments that would narrow the authority of federal courts.

Congress and Clinton agreed on a law that would give the President a kind of line-item veto, but the Supreme Court has declared the law to be unconstitutional. Others argue that to restrict the level of taxes and to require a balanced budget are unworkable suggestions, even assuming—which these opponents do not—that a smaller government is desirable. There is no precise, agreed-upon way to measure how much the government spends or to predict in advance how much it will receive in taxes during the year; thus defining and enforcing a "balanced budget" is no easy matter. The government has shown great ingenuity in spending money in ways that never appear as part of the regular budget (for example, Social Security).

The line-item veto may or may not be a good idea, these people argue. We may discover that the president will use it not to spend less but to spend more—by threatening to veto something of a modest cost that Congress wants in order to get Congress to vote for something expensive that the president wants.

Finally, some argue that proposals to curtail judicial power are thinly veiled attacks on the ability of the courts to protect essential citizen rights. If Congress and the people do not like the way the Supreme Court has interpreted the Constitution in a particular case, they can always amend the Constitution to change the specific ruling. There is no need to adopt some general, across-the-board limitation on court powers.

Term Limits

A change that might make our system either more or less democratic is to limit the number of terms that people can serve in Congress. Already the president is limited to two terms. The most common proposal is to limit members of the House to six terms (a total of twelve years) and members of the Senate to two (also a total of twelve years).

Between 1992 and 1994 the people in twenty-two states adopted proposals that would have imposed term limits on their delegations to Congress. But federal courts have held these limits to be unconstitutional. The Constitution makes Congress the sole judge of the qualifications of its members and limits the states to determining the time, place, and manner of holding congressional elections.

It is also not clear what effect such limits might have, even if they were constitutional. Proponents argue that they would once again make members of Congress "citizen legislators," not career politicians. Knowing that they could serve for only twelve years, they would be free, at least during their last term in office, to do what is right rather than what is demanded by interest groups or required by their own desire for reelection.

But opponents argue that short-term legislators will never master the intricacies of federal politics and policies, and so they will become dependent on unelected staff members and Washington lobbyists. And they point to the many long-term legislators who are widely admired. Finally, they argue that the voters are the best judges of who should stay in office and so should have the right to keep reelecting their own representatives and senators if they wish.

There is no way to settle this issue by arguments or theories. We will learn what difference term limits make only if we try them. But there is a risk: if we try them and don't like them, it will be very hard to get rid of them. In any event term limits may be hard to try, because Congress doesn't like them and Congress must approve a constitutional amendment to impose them (unless, of course, two-thirds of the state legislatures demand the calling of a constitutional convention to consider them). We can, of course, learn something about term limits in the states that impose them on state officials.

Who Is Right?

Some of the arguments of these various critics of the Constitution may strike you as plausible or even entirely convincing. But one should not make or remake a Constitution based entirely on abstract reasoning or unproven factual arguments. Even when the Constitution was first written in 1787, it was not an exercise in abstract philosophy but rather an effort by the Framers to solve pressing, practical problems in the light of a theory of human nature, the lessons of past experience, and a close consideration of how governments in other countries had worked.

Just because the Constitution is now over two hundred years old does not mean that it is out-of-date. The crucial questions are these: How well has it worked over the long sweep of American history? And how well has it worked compared to the constitutions of other democratic nations?

The only way to answer these questions is to study American government closely, with special attention to its historical evolution, the way it makes particular policies, and the practices of other nations. This book has provided only the briefest introduction to the workings of American government and has said very little about how it works in comparison to other governments or how it handles particular policy issues. Therefore you should not try to make up your mind about what, if anything, needs to change in our Constitution from what you have learned here. Learn more.

Nonetheless, by reviewing these competing proposals for revising the Constitution, you will at least be able to understand the central features of our system of government and the controversies that system has engendered, as well as how that system has changed over the past half century.

RECONSIDERING WHO GOVERNS?

1. What changes have occurred in who has power in the federal government?

Under the New System, the president has gained more power owing to the increased importance of foreign and military affairs. The courts have become more important because there are many more new laws to be interpreted. Congress has become more polarized because the parties are now either almost entirely liberal (the Democrats) or entirely conservative (the Republicans). There has been a large growth in the federal bureaucracy and the size of congressional staffs.

2. Should the Constitution be modified to make it either harder or easier to govern?

During the 1970s and 1980s there was a lot of talk about changing the Constitution to make it either easier or harder to govern. Those who wanted to make it easier argue that we should increase the authority of the president. Those who wanted to make it harder argue that we should have a balanced budget amendment, give the president a line-item veto, or impose term limits on members of Congress. None of these ideas has gotten anywhere, and it is not obvious that the arguments are persuasive.

RECONSIDERING TO WHAT ENDS?

1. What does the federal government do today that it did not do in the past?

Almost everything. Before the mid-1960s, there was scarcely any federal action regarding crime, education, civil rights, health care, or the environment. Many members of Congress thought that these matters did not belong on the federal agenda and that

any federal action on these issues would violate states' rights. Today hardly anyone argues that the federal government lacks the authority to act or that it can afford to ignore public demands for federal policies about these and almost any other matter one can imagine.

WORLD WIDE WEB RESOURCES

Nonpartisan reviews of public policy issues:
www.publicagenda.org

For partisan discussion of issues, use the World Wide Web addresses of the Washington, D.C., think tanks listed in Chapter 14.

☆ THE DECLARATION OF INDEPENDENCE

In Congress, July 4, 1776

The Unanimous Declaration of the Thirteen United States of America

When, in the course of human events, it becomes necessary for one people to dissolve the political bands which have connected them with another, and to assume, among the powers of the earth, the separate and equal station to which the laws of nature and of nature's God entitle them, a decent respect to the opinions of mankind requires that they should declare the causes which impel them to the separation.

We hold these truths to be self-evident: That all men are created equal; that they are endowed by their Creator with certain unalienable rights; that among these are life, liberty, and the pursuit of happiness; that, to secure these rights, governments are instituted among men, deriving their just powers from the consent of the governed; that whenever any form of government becomes destructive of these ends, it is the right of the people to alter or to abolish it, and to institute new government, laying its foundation on such principles, and organizing its power in such form, as to them shall seem most likely to effect their safety and happiness. Prudence, indeed, will dictate that governments long established should not be changed for light and transient causes; and accordingly all experience hath shown that mankind are more disposed to suffer, while evils are sufferable, than to right themselves by abolishing the forms to which they are accustomed. But when a long train of abuses and usurpations, pursuing invariably the same object, evinces a design to reduce them under absolute despotism, it is their right, it is their duty, to throw off such government, and to provide new guards for their future security. Such has been the patient sufferance of these colonies; and such is now the necessity which constrains them to alter their former systems of government. The history of the present King of Great Britain is a history of repeated injuries and usurpations, all having in direct object the establishment of an absolute tyranny over these states. To prove this, let facts be submitted to a candid world.

He has refused to assent to laws, the most wholesome and necessary for the public good.

He has forbidden his governors to pass laws of immediate and pressing importance, unless suspended in their operation till his assent should be obtained; and, when so suspended, he has utterly neglected to attend to them.

He has refused to pass other laws for the accommodation of large districts of people, unless those people would relinquish the right of representation in the legislature, a right inestimable to them, and formidable to tyrants only.

He has called together legislative bodies at places unusual, uncomfortable, and distant from the depository of their public records, for the sole purpose of fatiguing them into compliance with his measures.

He has dissolved representative houses repeatedly, for opposing, with manly firmness, his invasions on the rights of the people.

He has refused for a long time, after such dissolutions, to cause others to be elected; whereby the legislative powers, incapable of annihilation, have returned to the people at large for their exercise; the state remaining, in the mean time, exposed to all dangers of invasions from without and convulsions within.

He has endeavored to prevent the population of these states; for that purpose obstructing the laws for naturalization of foreigners; refusing to pass others to encourage their migration hither, and raising the conditions of new appropriations of lands.

He has obstructed the administration of justice, by refusing his assent to laws for establishing judiciary powers.

He has made judges dependent on his will alone, for the tenure of their offices, and the amount and payment of their salaries.

He has erected a multitude of new offices, and sent hither swarms of officers to harass our people, and eat out their substance.

He has kept among us, in times of peace, standing armies, without the consent of our legislatures.

He has affected to render the military independent of, and superior to, the civil power.

He has combined with others to subject us to a jurisdiction foreign to our constitution, and unacknowledged by our laws, giving his assent to their acts of pretended legislation:

For quartering large bodies of armed troops among us:

For protecting them, by a mock trial, from punishment for any murders which they should commit on the inhabitants of these states;

For cutting off our trade with all parts of the world;

For imposing taxes on us without our consent;

For depriving us, in many cases, of the benefits of trial by jury;

For transporting us beyond seas, to be tried for pretended offenses;

For abolishing the free system of English laws in a neighboring province, establishing therein an arbitrary government, and enlarging its boundaries, so as to render it at once an example and fit instrument for introducing the same absolute rule into these colonies;

For taking away our charters, abolishing our most valuable laws, and altering fundamentally the forms of our governments;

For suspending our own legislatures, and declaring themselves invested with power to legislate for us in all cases whatsoever.

He has abdicated government here, by declaring us out of his protection and waging war against us.

He has plundered our seas, ravaged our coasts, burned our towns, and destroyed the lives of our people.

He is at this time transporting large armies of foreign mercenaries to complete the works of death, desolation, and tyranny already begun with circumstances of cruelty and perfidy scarcely paralleled in the most barbarous ages, and totally unworthy the head of a civilized nation.

He has constrained our fellow-citizens, taken captive on the high seas, to bear arms against their country, to become the executioners of their friends and brethren, or to fall themselves by their hands.

He has excited domestic insurrection among us, and has endeavored to bring on the inhabitants of our frontiers the merciless Indian savages, whose known rule of warfare is an undistinguished destruction of all ages, sexes, and conditions.

In every stage of these oppressions we have petitioned for redress in the most humble terms; our repeated petitions have been answered only by repeated injury. A prince, whose character is thus marked by every act which may define a tyrant, is unfit to be the ruler of a free people.

Nor have we been wanting in our attentions to our British brethren. We have warned them, from time to time, of attempts by their Legislature to extend an unwarrantable jurisdiction over us. We have reminded them of the circumstances of our emigration and settlement here. We have appealed to their native justice and magnanimity; and we have conjured them, by the ties of our common kindred, to disavow these usurpations, which would inevitably interrupt our connections and correspondence. They, too, have been deaf to the voice of justice and of consanguinity. We must, therefore, acquiesce in the necessity which denounces our separation, and hold them, as we hold the rest of mankind, enemies in war, in peace friends.

We, therefore, the representatives of the United States of America, in General Congress assembled, appealing to the Supreme Judge of the world for the rectitude of our intentions, do, in the name and by the authority of the good people of these colonies, solemnly publish and declare, that these United Colonies are, and of right ought to be, FREE AND INDEPENDENT STATES; that they are absolved from all allegiance to the British crown, and that all political connection between them and the state of Great Britain is, and ought to be, totally dissolved; and that, as free and independent states, they have full power to levy war, conclude peace, contract alliances, establish commerce, and do all other acts and things which independent states may of right do. And for the support of this declaration, with a firm reliance on the protection of Divine Providence, we mutually pledge to each other our lives, our fortunes, and our sacred honor.

JOHN HANCOCK [*President*]
[*and fifty-five others*]

☆ THE CONSTITUTION OF THE UNITED STATES

Preamble

We the People of the United States, in Order to form a more perfect Union, establish Justice, insure domestic Tranquility, provide for the common defence, promote the general Welfare, and secure the Blessings of Liberty to ourselves and our Posterity, do ordain and establish this Constitution for the United States of America.

ARTICLE I.

Bicameral Congress

Section 1.   All legislative Powers herein granted shall be vested in a Congress of the United States, which shall consist of a Senate and House of Representatives.

Membership of the House

Section 2.   The House of Representatives shall be composed of Members chosen every second Year by the People of the several States, and the Electors in each State shall have the Qualifications requisite for Electors of the most numerous Branch of the State Legislature.

No person shall be a Representative who shall not have attained to the age of twenty five Years, and been seven Years a Citizen of the United States, and who shall not, when elected, be an Inhabitant of that State in which he shall be chosen.

Representatives and direct Taxes shall be apportioned among the several States which may be included within this Union, according to their respective Numbers, which shall be determined by adding to the whole Number of free Persons, including those bound to Service for a Term of Years, and excluding Indians not taxed, three fifths of all other Persons.[1] The actual Enumeration shall be made within three Years after the first Meeting of the Congress of the United States, and within every subsequent Term of ten Years, in such Manner as they shall by Law direct. The Number of Representatives shall not exceed one for every thirty Thousand, but each State shall have at Least one Representative; and until such enumeration shall be made, the State of New Hampshire shall be entitled to chuse three, Massachusetts eight, Rhode-Island and Providence Plantations one, Connecticut five, New-York six, New Jersey four, Pennsylvania eight, Delaware one, Maryland six, Virginia ten, North Carolina five, South Carolina five, and Georgia three.

When vacancies happen in the Representation from any State, the Executive Authority thereof shall issue Writs of Election to fill such Vacancies.

Power to impeach

The House of Representatives shall chuse their Speaker and other Officers; and shall have the sole Power of Impeachment.

Membership of the Senate

Section 3.   The Senate of the United States shall be composed of two Senators from each State, *chosen by the Legislature thereof,*[2] for six Years; and each Senator shall have one Vote.

NOTE: The topical headings are not part of the original Constitution. Excluding the Preamble and Closing, those portions set in italic type have been superseded or changed by later amendments.
1. Changed by the Fourteenth Amendment, section 2.
2. Changed by the Seventeenth Amendment.

Immediately after they shall be assembled in Consequence of the first Election, they shall be divided as equally as may be into three Classes. The Seats of the Senators of the first class shall be vacated at the Expiration of the second Year, of the second Class at the Expiration of the fourth Year, and of the third Class at the Expiration of the sixth Year, so that one third may be chosen every second Year; *and if Vacancies happen by Resignation, or otherwise, during the Recess of the Legislature of any State, the Executive thereof may make temporary Appointments until the next Meeting of the Legislature, which shall then fill such Vacancies.*[3]

No Person shall be a Senator who shall not have attained to the Age of thirty Years, and been nine Years a Citizen of the United States, and who shall not, when elected, be an Inhabitant of that State for which he shall be chosen.

The Vice President of the United States shall be President of the Senate, but shall have no Vote, unless they be equally divided.

The Senate shall chuse their other Officers, and also a President pro tempore, in the Absence of the Vice President, or when he shall exercise the Office of President of the United States.

Power to try impeachments

The Senate shall have the sole Power to try all Impeachments. When sitting for that Purpose, they shall be on Oath or Affirmation. When the President of the United States is tried the Chief Justice shall preside: And no Person shall be convicted without the Concurrence of two thirds of the Members present.

Judgment in Cases of Impeachment shall not extend further than to removal from Office, and disqualification to hold and enjoy any Office of honor, Trust or Profit under the United States: but the Party convicted shall nevertheless be liable and subject to Indictment, Trial, Judgment and Punishment, according to Law.

Laws governing elections

Section 4. The Times, Places and Manner of holding Elections for Senators and Representatives, shall be prescribed in each State by the Legislature thereof; but the Congress may at any time by Law make or alter such Regulations, except as to the Places of chusing Senators.

The Congress shall assemble at least once in every Year, and such Meeting shall be on the *first Monday in December, unless they shall by Law appoint a different Day.*[4]

Rules of Congress

Section 5. Each House shall be the Judge of the Elections, Returns and Qualifications of its own Members, and a Majority of each shall constitute a Quorum to do Business; but a smaller number may adjourn from day to day, and may be authorized to compel the Attendance of absent Members, in such Manner, and under such Penalties as each House may provide.

Each House may determine the Rules of its Proceedings, punish its Members for disorderly Behaviour, and, with the Concurrence of two thirds, expel a Member.

Each House shall keep a Journal of its Proceedings, and from time to time publish the same, excepting such Parts as may in their Judgment require Secrecy; and the Yeas and Nays of the Members of either House on any question shall, at the Desire of one fifth of those Present, be entered on the Journal.

---

3. Changed by the Seventeenth Amendment.
4. Changed by the Twentieth Amendment, section 2.

Neither House, during the Session of Congress, shall, without the Consent of the other, adjourn for more than three days, nor to any other Place than that in which the two Houses shall be sitting.

Salaries and
immunities of members

Section 6.   The Senators and Representatives shall receive a Compensation for their Services, to be ascertained by Law, and paid out of the Treasury of the United States. They shall in all Cases, except Treason, Felony and Breach of the Peace, be privileged from Arrest during their Attendance at the Session of their respective Houses, and in going to and returning from the same; and for any Speech or Debate in either House, they shall not be questioned in any other Place.

Bar on members of Congress
holding federal appointive
office

No Senator or Representative shall, during the Time for which he was elected, be appointed to any civil Office under the Authority of the United States, which shall have been created, or the Emoluments whereof shall have been encreased during such time; and no Person holding any Office under the United States, shall be a Member of either House during his Continuance in Office.

Money bills originate in
House

Section 7.   All Bills for raising Revenue shall originate in the House of Representatives; but the Senate may propose or concur with Amendments as on other Bills.

Procedure for enacting
laws; veto power

Every Bill which shall have passed the House of Representatives and the Senate, shall, before it become a Law, be presented to the President of the United States; If he approve he shall sign it, but if not he shall return it, with Objections to that House in which it shall have originated, who shall enter the Objections at large on their Journal, and proceed to reconsider it. If after such Reconsideration two thirds of that House shall agree to pass the Bill, it shall be sent, together with the Objections, to the other House, by which it shall likewise be reconsidered, and if approved by two thirds of that House, it shall become a Law. But in all such Cases the Votes of both Houses shall be determined by yeas and Nays, and the Names of the Persons voting for and against the Bill shall be entered on the Journal of each House respectively. If any Bill shall not be returned by the President within ten Days (Sundays excepted) after it shall have been presented to him, the Same shall be a Law, in like Manner, as if he had signed it, unless the Congress by their Adjournment prevent its Return, in which Case it shall not be a Law.

Every Order, Resolution, or Vote to which the Concurrence of the Senate and House of Representatives may be necessary (except on a question of Adjournment) shall be presented to the President of the United States; and before the Same shall take Effect, shall be approved by him, or being disapproved by him, shall be repassed by two thirds of the Senate and House of Representatives, according to the Rules and Limitations prescribed in the Case of a Bill.

Powers of Congress
—*taxes*

Section 8.   The Congress shall have Power To lay and Collect Taxes, Duties, Imposts and Excises, to pay the Debts and provide for the common Defence and general Welfare of the United States; but all Duties, Imposts and Excises shall be uniform throughout the United States.

—*borrowing*

To borrow Money on the credit of the United States;

—*regulation of commerce*

To regulate Commerce with foreign Nations, and among the several States, and with the Indian Tribes;

—*naturalization and bankruptcy*

To establish an uniform Rule of Naturalization, and uniform Laws on the subject of Bankruptcies throughout the United States;

—money

To coin Money, regulate the Value thereof, and of foreign Coin, and fix the Standard of Weights and Measures;

—counterfeiting

To provide for the Punishment of counterfeiting the Securities and current Coin of the United States;

—post office

To establish Post Offices and post Roads;

—patents and copyrights

To promote the Progress of Science and useful Arts, by securing for limited Times to Authors and Inventors the exclusive Right to their respective Writings and Discoveries;

—create courts

To constitute Tribunals inferior to the Supreme Court;

—punish piracies

To define and punish Piracies and Felonies committed on the high Seas, and Offences against the Law of Nations;

—declare war

To declare War, grant Letters of Marque and Reprisal, and make Rules concerning Captures on Land and Water;

—create army and navy

To raise and support Armies, but no Appropriation of Money to that Use shall be for a longer Term than two Years;

To provide and maintain a Navy;

To make Rules for the Government and Regulation of the land and naval Forces;

—call the militia

To provide for calling forth the Militia to execute the Laws of the Union, suppress Insurrections and repel Invasions;

To provide for organizing, arming, and disciplining, the Militia, and for governing such Part of them as may be employed in the Service of the United States, reserving to the States respectively, the Appointment of the Officers, and the Authority of training the Militia according to the discipline prescribed by Congress;

—govern District of Columbia

To exercise exclusive Legislation in all Cases whatsoever, over such District (not exceeding ten Miles square) as may, by Cession of Particular States, and the Acceptance of Congress, become the Seat of the Government of the United States, and to exercise like Authority over all Places purchased by the Consent of the Legislature of the State in which the Same shall be, for the Erection of Forts, Magazines, Arsenals, dock-Yards and other needful Buildings;—And

—"necessary-and-proper" clause

To make all Laws which shall be necessary and proper for carrying into Execution the foregoing Powers, and all other Powers vested by this Constitution in the Government of the United States, or in any Department or Officer thereof.

Restrictions on powers of Congress

—slave trade

Section 9.   The Migration or Importation of such Persons as any of the States now existing shall think proper to admit, shall not be prohibited by the Congress prior to the Year one thousand eight hundred and eight, but a Tax or duty may be imposed on such Importation, not exceeding ten dollars for each Person.

—habeas corpus

The Privilege of the Writ of Habeas Corpus shall not be suspended, unless when in Cases of Rebellion or Invasion the public Safety may require it.

—no bill of attainder or ex post facto law

No bill of Attainder or ex post facto Law shall be passed.

No Capitation, or other direct, Tax shall be laid, *unless in Proportion to the Census or Enumeration herein before directed to be taken.*[5]

—no interstate tariffs

No Tax or Duty shall be laid on Articles exported from any State.

—no preferential treatment for some states

No Preference shall be given by any Regulation of Commerce or Revenue to the Ports of one State over those of another; nor shall Vessels bound to, or from, one State, be obliged to enter, clear or pay Duties in another.

---

5. Changed by the Sixteenth Amendment.

—appropriations

No Money shall be drawn from the Treasury, but in Consequence of Appropriations made by Law; and a regular Statement and Account of the Receipts and Expenditures of all public Money shall be published from time to time.

—no titles of nobility

No Title of Nobility shall be granted by the United States: And no Person holding any Office of Profit or Trust under them, shall, without the Consent of the Congress, accept of any present, Emolument, Office, or Title, of any kind whatever, from any King, Prince, or foreign State.

Restrictions on powers of states

Section 10.   No State shall enter into any Treaty, Alliance, or Confederation; grant Letters of Marque and Reprisal; coin Money; emit Bills of Credit; make any Thing but gold and silver Coin a Tender in Payment of Debts; pass any Bill of Attainder, ex post facto Law, or Law impairing the Obligation of Contracts, or grant any Title of Nobility.

No State shall, without the Consent of Congress, lay any Imposts or Duties on Imports or Exports, except what may be absolutely necessary for executing its inspection Laws; and the net Produce of all Duties and Imposts, laid by any State on Imports or Exports, shall be for the Use of the Treasury of the United States; and all such Laws shall be subject to the Revision and Controul of the Congress.

No State shall, without the Consent of Congress, lay any Duty of Tonnage, keep Troops, or Ships of War in time of Peace, enter into any Agreement or Compact with another State, or with a foreign Power, or engage in War, unless actually invaded, or in such imminent Danger as will not admit of delay.

ARTICLE II.

Office of president

Section 1.   The executive Power shall be vested in a President of the United States of America. He shall hold his Office during the Term of four Years, and, together with the Vice President, chosen for the same Term, be elected, as follows:

Election of president

Each State shall appoint, in such Manner as the Legislature thereof may direct, a Number of Electors, equal to the whole Number of Senators and Representatives to which the State may be entitled in the Congress: but no Senator or Representative, or Person holding an Office of Trust or Profit under the United States, shall be appointed an Elector.

The Electors shall meet in their respective States, and vote by Ballot for two Persons, of whom one at least shall not be an Inhabitant of the same State with themselves. And they shall make a List of all the Persons voted for, and of the Number of Votes for each; which List they shall sign and certify, and transmit sealed to the Seat of the Government of the United States, directed to the President of the Senate. The President of the Senate shall, in the Presence of the Senate and House of Representatives, open all the Certificates, and the Votes shall then be counted. The Person having the greatest Number of Votes shall be the President, if such Number be a Majority of the whole Number of Electors appointed; and if there be more than one who have such Majority, and have an equal Number of Votes, then the House of Representatives shall immediately chuse by Ballot one of them for President; and if no Person have a Majority, then from the five highest on the List said House shall in like Manner chuse the President. But in chusing the President, the Votes shall be taken by States, the Representation from each State having one Vote; a quorum for this Purpose shall consist of a Member or Members from two thirds of the States, and a Majority of all the States shall be necessary to a Choice. In every Case, after the Choice of the President, the Person having the greatest Number of Votes of the Electors shall be the Vice President. But if there should remain two or more who have equal Votes, the Senate shall chuse from them by Ballot the Vice President.[6]

The Congress may determine the Time of chusing the Electors, and the Day on which they shall give their Votes, which Day shall be the same throughout the United States.

Requirements to be president

No Person except a natural born Citizen, or a Citizen of the United States, at the time of the Adoption of this Constitution, shall be eligible to the Office of President; neither shall any person be eligible to that Office who shall not have attained to the Age of thirty five Years, and been fourteen Years a Resident within the United States.

In Case of the Removal of the President from Office, or of his Death, Resignation, or Inability to discharge the Powers and Duties of the said Office, the Same shall devolve on the Vice President, and the Congress may by Law provide for the Case of Removal, Death, Resignation or Inability, both of the President and Vice President, declaring what Officer shall then act as President, and such Officer shall act accordingly, until the Disability be removed, or a President shall be elected.[7]

Pay of president

The President shall, at stated Times, receive for his Services, a Compensation, which shall neither be increased nor diminished during the Period for which he shall have been elected, and he shall not receive within that Period any other Emolument from the United States, or any of them.

Before he enter on the Execution of his Office, he shall take the following Oath or Affirmation:—"I do solemnly swear (or affirm) that I will faithfully execute the Office of President of the United States, and will to the best of my Ability preserve, protect and defend the Constitution of the United States."

**Powers of president
—*commander in chief***

Section 2.   The President shall be Commander in Chief of the Army and Navy of the United States, and of the Militia of the several States, when called into the actual Service of the United States; he may require the Opinion, in writing, of the principal Officer in each of the executive Departments, upon any Subject relating to the Duties of their respective Offices, and he shall have Power to grant Reprieves and Pardons for Offences against the United States, except in Cases of Impeachment.

—*pardons*

—*treaties and appointments*

He shall have Power, by and with the Advice and Consent of the Senate, to make Treaties, provided two thirds of the Senators present concur; and he shall nominate, and by and with the Advice and Consent of the Senate, shall appoint Ambassadors, other public Ministers and Consuls, Judges of the supreme Court, and all other Officers of the United States, whose Appointments are not herein otherwise provided for, and which shall be established by Law: but the Congress may by Law vest the Appointment of such inferior Officers, as they think proper, in the President alone, in the Courts of Law, or in the Heads of Departments.

The President shall have Power to fill up all Vacancies that may happen during the Recess of the Senate, by granting Commissions which shall expire at the End of their next Session.

Relations of president with Congress

Section 3.   He shall from time to time give to the Congress Information of the State of the Union, and recommend to their Consideration such Measures as he

---

6. Superseded by the Twelfth Amendment.
7. Modified by the Twenty-fifth Amendment.

shall judge necessary and expedient; he may, on extraordinary Occasions, convene both Houses, or either of them, and in Case of Disagreement between them, with Respect to the Time of Adjournment, he may adjourn them to such Time as he shall think proper; he shall receive Ambassadors and other public Ministers; he shall take Care that the Laws be faithfully executed, and shall Commission all the Officers of the United States.

Impeachment

Section 4. The President, Vice President and all civil Officers of the United States, shall be removed from Office on Impeachment for, and Conviction of, Treason, Bribery, or other high Crimes and Misdemeanors.

ARTICLE III.

Federal courts

Section 1. The judicial Power of the United States, shall be vested in one supreme Court, and in such inferior Courts as the Congress may from time to time ordain and establish. The Judges, both of the supreme and inferior Courts, shall hold their Offices during good Behaviour, and shall, at stated Times, receive for their Services, a Compensation, which shall not be diminished during their Continuance in Office.

Jurisdiction of courts

Section 2. The judicial Power shall extend to all Cases, in Law and Equity, arising under this Constitution, the Laws of the United States, and Treaties made, or which shall be made, under their Authority;—to all Cases affecting Ambassadors, other public Ministers and Consuls;—to all Cases of admiralty and maritime Jurisdiction;—to Controversies to which the United States shall be a Party;—to Controversies between two or more States;—*between a State and Citizens of another State;*[8]—between Citizens of different States;—between Citizens of the same State claiming Lands under Grants of different States, and between a State, or the Citizens thereof, and foreign States, Citizens or Subjects.

—original

—appellate

In all Cases affecting Ambassadors, other public Ministers and Consuls, and those in which a State shall be Party, the supreme Court shall have original Jurisdiction. In all the other Cases before mentioned, the supreme Court shall have appellate Jurisdiction, both as to Law and Fact, with such Exceptions, and under such Regulations as the Congress shall make.

The Trial of all Crimes, except in Cases of Impeachment, shall be by Jury; and such Trial shall be held in the State where the said Crimes shall have been committed; but when not committed within any State, the Trial shall be at such Place or Places as the Congress may by Law have directed.

Treason

Section 3. Treason against the United States, shall consist only in levying War against them, or in adhering to their Enemies, giving them Aid and Comfort. No Person shall be convicted of Treason unless on the Testimony of two Witnesses to the same overt Act, or on Confession in open Court.

The Congress shall have Power to declare the Punishment of Treason, but no Attainder of Treason shall work Corruption of Blood, or Forfeiture except during the Life of the Person attainted.

---

8. Modified by the Eleventh Amendment.

ARTICLE IV.

Full faith and credit

Section 1. Full Faith and Credit shall be given in each State to the public Acts, Records, and judicial Proceedings of every other State. And the Congress may by general Laws prescribe the Manner in which such Acts, Records and Proceedings shall be proved, and the Effect thereof.

Privileges and immunities

Section 2. The Citizens of each State shall be entitled to all Privileges and Immunities of Citizens in the several States.

Extradition

A person charged in any State with Treason, Felony, or other Crime, who shall flee from Justice, and be found in another State, shall on Demand of the executive Authority of the State from which he fled, be delivered up, to be removed to the State having Jurisdiction of the Crime.

No Person held to Service or Labour in one State, under the Laws thereof, escaping into another, shall, in Consequence of any Law or Regulation therein, be discharged from such Service or Labour, but shall be delivered up on Claim of the Party to whom such Service or Labour may be due.[9]

Creation of new states

Section 3. New States may be admitted by the Congress into this Union; but no new State shall be formed or erected within the Jurisdiction of any other State; nor any State be formed by the Junction of two or more States, or Parts of States, without the Consent of the Legislatures of the States concerned as well as of the Congress.

Governing territories

The Congress shall have Power to dispose of and make all needful Rules and Regulations respecting the Territory or other Property belonging to the United States; and nothing in this Constitution shall be so construed as to Prejudice any Claims of the United States, or of any particular State.

Protection of states

Section 4. The United States shall guarantee to every State in this Union a Republican Form of Government, and shall protect each of them against Invasion; and on Application of the Legislature, or of the Executive (when the Legislature cannot be convened) against domestic Violence.

ARTICLE V.

Amending the Constitution

The Congress, whenever two thirds of both Houses shall deem it necessary, shall propose Amendments to this Constitution, or, on the Application of the Legislatures of two thirds of the several States, shall call a Convention for proposing Amendments, which, in either Case, shall be valid to all Intents and Purposes, as Part of this Constitution, when ratified by the Legislatures of three fourths of the several States, or by Conventions in three fourths thereof, as the one or the other Mode of Ratification may be proposed by the Congress; Provided that no Amendment which may be made prior to the Year One thousand eight hundred and eight shall in any Manner alter the first and fourth Clauses in the Ninth Section of the first Article; and that no State, without its Consent, shall be deprived of its equal Suffrage in the Senate.

---

9. Changed by the Thirteenth Amendment.

ARTICLE VI.

Assumption of debts of
Confederation

All Debts contracted and Engagements entered into, before the Adoption of this Constitution, shall be as valid against the United States under this Constitution, as under the Confederation.

Supremacy of federal laws and
treaties

This Constitution, and the Laws of the United States which shall be made in Pursuance thereof; and all Treaties made, or which shall be made, under the Authority of the United States, shall be the Supreme Law of the Land; and the Judges in every State shall be bound thereby, any Thing in the Constitution or Laws of any State to the Contrary notwithstanding.

No religious test

The Senators and Representatives before mentioned, and the Members of the several State Legislatures, and all executive and judicial Officers, both of the United States and of the several States, shall be bound by Oath or Affirmation, to support this Constitution; but no religious Test shall ever be required as a Qualification to any Office or public Trust under the United States.

ARTICLE VII.

Ratification procedure

The Ratification of the Conventions of nine States, shall be sufficient for the Establishment of this Constitution between the States so ratifying the Same.

Done in Convention by the Unanimous Consent of the States present the Seventeenth Day of September in the Year of our Lord one thousand seven hundred and Eighty seven and of the Independence of the United States of America the Twelfth In witness whereof We have hereunto subscribed our Names,

G⁰. WASHINGTON—*Presidᵗ.*
and deputy from Virginia

New Hampshire	{ John Langdon Nicholas Gilman	*Connecticut*	{ Wᴹ. Samˡ. Johnson Roger Sherman
Massachusetts	{ Nathaniel Gorham Rufus King	*New York*	Alexander Hamilton
New Jersey	{ Wil: Livingston David Brearley Wᴹ. Paterson Jona: Dayton	*Maryland*	{ James McHenry Dan of Sᵗ Thoˢ Jenifer Danˡ Carroll
		Virginia	{ John Blair— James Madison Jr.
Pennsylvania	{ B Franklin Thomas Mifflin Robᵗ. Morris Geo. Clymer Thoˢ FitzSimons Jared Ingersoll James Wilson Gouv Morris	*North Carolina*	{ Wᴹ. Blount Richᴰ. Dobbs Spaight Hu Williamson
		South Carolina	{ J. Rutledge Charles Cotesworth Pinckney Charles Pinckney Pierce Butler

Delaware { GEO: READ
GUNNING BEDFORD jun
JOHN DICKINSON
RICHARD BASSETT
JACO: BROOM

Georgia { WILLIAM FEW
ABR BALDWIN

[The first ten amendments, known as the "Bill of Rights," were ratified in 1791.]

AMENDMENT I.

Freedom of religion, speech, press, assembly

Congress shall make no law respecting an establishment of religion, or prohibiting the free exercise thereof, or abridging the freedom of speech, or of the press; or the right of the people peaceably to assemble, and to petition the Government for a redress of grievances.

AMENDMENT II.

Right to bear arms

A well regulated Militia, being necessary to the security of a free State, the right of the people to keep and bear Arms, shall not be infringed.

AMENDMENT III.

Quartering troops in private homes

No Soldier shall, in time of peace be quartered in any house without the consent of the Owner, nor in time of war, but in a manner to be prescribed by law.

AMENDMENT IV.

Prohibition against unreasonable searches and seizures

The right of the people to be secure in their persons, houses, papers, and effects, against unreasonable searches and seizures, shall not be violated, and no Warrants shall issue, but upon probable cause, supported by Oath or affirmation, and particularly describing the place to be searched, and the persons or things to be seized.

AMENDMENT V.

Right when accused; "due-process" clause

No person shall be held to answer for a capital, or otherwise infamous crime, unless on a presentment or indictment of a Grand Jury, except in cases arising in the land or naval forces, or in the Militia, when in actual service in time of War or public danger; nor shall any person be subject for the same offence to be twice put in jeopardy of life or limb; nor shall be compelled in any criminal case to be a witness against himself, nor be deprived of life, liberty, or property, without due process of law, nor shall private property be taken for public use, without just compensation.

AMENDMENT VI.

Rights when on trial

In all criminal prosecutions, the accused shall enjoy the right to a speedy and public trial, by an impartial jury of the State and district wherein the crime shall have been committed, which district shall have been previously ascertained by law, and to be informed of the nature and cause of the accusation; to be confronted with the witnesses against him; to have compulsory process for obtaining witnesses in his favor, and to have the Assistance of Counsel for his defence.

AMENDMENT VII.

Common-law suits

In Suits at common law, where the value in controversy shall exceed twenty dollars, the right of trial by jury shall be preserved, and no fact tried by a jury, shall be otherwise reexamined in any Court of the United States, than according to the rules of the common law.

AMENDMENT VIII.

Bail; no "cruel and unusual" punishments

Excessive bail shall not be required, nor excessive fines imposed, nor cruel and unusual punishments inflicted.

AMENDMENT IX.

Unenumerated rights protected

The enumeration in the Constitution, of certain rights, shall not be construed to deny or disparage others retained by the people.

AMENDMENT X.

Powers reserved for states

The powers not delegated to the United States by the Constitution, nor prohibited by it to the States, are reserved to the States respectively, or to the people.

AMENDMENT XI.
[*Ratified in 1795.*]

Limits on suits against states

The Judicial power of the United States shall not be construed to extend to any suit in law or equity, commenced or prosecuted against one of the United States by Citizens of another state, or by Citizens or Subjects of any Foreign State.

AMENDMENT XII.
[*Ratified in 1804.*]

Revision of electoral-college procedure

The Electors shall meet in their respective states and vote by ballot for President and Vice President, one of whom, at least, shall not be an inhabitant of the same state with themselves; they shall name in their ballots the person voted for as President, and in distinct ballots the person voted for as Vice President, and they shall make distinct lists of all persons voted for as President, and of all persons voted for as Vice President, and of the number of votes for each, which lists they shall sign and certify, and transmit sealed to the seat of government of the United States, directed to the President of the Senate;—The President of the Senate shall, in the presence of the Senate and House of Representatives, open all the certificates and the votes shall then be counted;—The person having the greatest number of votes for President, shall be the President, if such number be a majority of the whole number of Electors appointed; and if no person have such majority, then from the persons having the highest numbers not exceeding three on the list of those voted for as President, the House of Representatives shall choose immediately, by ballot, the President. But in choosing the President, the votes shall be taken by states, the representation from each state having one vote; a quorum for this purpose shall consist of a member or members from two-thirds of the states, and a majority of all the states shall be necessary to a choice. *And if the House of Representatives shall not choose a President whenever the right of choice shall devolve upon them, before the fourth day of March next following, then the Vice President shall act as President, as in the case of the death or other constitutional disability of the President.*—[10] The person having the greatest number of votes as Vice President, shall be the Vice President, if such number be a majority of the whole number of Electors appointed, and if no person have a majority, then from the two highest numbers on the list, the Senate shall choose the Vice President; a quorum for the purpose shall consist of two-thirds of the whole number of Senators, and a majority of the whole number shall be necessary to a choice. But no person constitutionally ineligible to the office of President shall be eligible to that of Vice President of the United States.

AMENDMENT XIII.
[*Ratified in 1865.*]

Slavery prohibited

Section 1.   Neither slavery nor involuntary servitude, except as a punishment for crime whereof the party shall have been duly convicted, shall exist within the United States, or any place subject to their jurisdiction.

Section 2.   Congress shall have power to enforce this article by appropriate legislation.

AMENDMENT XIV.
[*Ratified in 1868.*]

Ex-slaves made citizens

"Due-process" clause applied to states

"Equal-protection" clause

Section 1.   All persons born or naturalized in the United States and subject to the jurisdiction thereof, are citizens of the United States and of the State wherein they reside. No State shall make or enforce any law which shall abridge the privileges or immunities of citizens of the United States; nor shall any State deprive any person of life, liberty, or property, without due process of law; nor deny to any person within its jurisdiction the equal protection of the laws.

Reduction in congressional representation for states denying adult males the right to vote

Section 2.   Representatives shall be apportioned among the several States according to their respective numbers, counting the whole number of persons in each State, excluding Indians not taxed. But when the right to vote at any election for the choice of electors for President and Vice President of the United States, Representatives in Congress, the Executive and Judicial officers of a State, or the members of the Legislature thereof, is denied to any of the male inhabitants of such State, being *twenty-one*[11] years of age and citizens of the United States, or in any way abridged, except for participation in rebellion, or other crime, the basis of representation therein shall be reduced in the proportion which the number of such male citizens shall bear to the whole number of male citizens twenty-one years of age in such State.

Southern rebels denied federal office

Section 3.   No person shall be a Senator or Representative in Congress, or elector of President and Vice President, or hold any office, civil or military, under the

---

10. Changed by the Twentieth Amendment, section 3.
11. Changed by the Twenty-sixth Amendment.

United States, or under any State, who, having previously taken an oath, as a member of Congress, or as an officer of the United States, or as a member of any State legislature, or as an executive or judicial officer of any State, to support the Constitution of the United States, shall have engaged in insurrection or rebellion against the same, or given aid or comfort to the enemies thereof. But Congress may by a vote of two-thirds of each House, remove such disability.

Rebel debts repudiated

Section 4.   The validity of the public debt of the United States, authorized by law, including debts incurred for payment of pensions and bounties for services in suppressing insurrection or rebellion, shall not be questioned. But neither the United States nor any State shall assume or pay any debt or obligation incurred in aid of insurrection or rebellion against the United States, or any claim for the loss or emancipation of any slave; but all such debts, obligations and claims shall be held illegal and void.

Section 5.   The Congress shall have power to enforce, by appropriate legislation, the provisions of this article.

AMENDMENT XV.
[*Ratified in 1870.*]

Blacks given right to vote

Section 1.   The right of citizens of the United States to vote shall not be denied or abridged by the United States or by any State on account of race, color, or previous condition of servitude.

Section 2.   The Congress shall have power to enforce this article by appropriate legislation.

AMENDMENT XVI.
[*Ratified in 1913.*]

Authorizes federal income tax

The Congress shall have power to lay and collect taxes on incomes, from whatever source derived, without apportionment among the several States, and without regard to any census or enumeration.

AMENDMENT XVII.
[*Ratified in 1913.*]

Requires popular election of senators

The Senate of the United States shall be composed of two Senators from each State, elected by the people thereof, for six years; and each Senator shall have one vote. The electors in each State shall have the qualifications requisite for electors of the most numerous branch of the State legislatures.

When vacancies happen in the representation of any State in the Senate, the executive authority of such State shall issue writs of election to fill such vacancies: Provided, That the legislature of any State may empower the executive thereof to make temporary appointments until the people fill the vacancies by election as the legislature may direct.

This amendment shall not be so construed as to affect the election or term of any Senator chosen before it becomes valid as part of the Constitution.

AMENDMENT XVIII.
[*Ratified in 1919.*]

Prohibits manufacture and sale of liquor

Section 1.   *After one year from the ratification of this article the manufacture, sale, or transportation of intoxicating liquors within, the importation thereof into, or the exportation thereof from the United States and all territory subject to the jurisdiction thereof for beverage purposes is hereby prohibited.*

Section 2.   *The Congress and the several States shall have concurrent power to enforce this article by appropriate legislation.*

Section 3.   *This article shall be inoperative unless it shall have been ratified as an amendment to the Constitution by the legislatures of the several States, as provided in the Constitution, within seven years from the date of the submission hereof to the States by the Congress.*[12]

AMENDMENT XIX.
[*Ratified in 1920.*]

Right to vote for women

The right of citizens of the United States to vote shall not be denied or abridged by the United States or by any State on account of sex.

Congress shall have power to enforce this article by appropriate legislation.

AMENDMENT XX.
[*Ratified in 1933.*]

Federal terms of office to begin in January

Section 1.   The terms of the President and Vice President shall end at noon on the 20th day of January, and the terms of Senators and Representatives at noon on the 3d day of January, of the years in which such terms would have ended if this article had not been ratified; and the terms of their successors shall then begin.

Section 2.   The Congress shall assemble at least once in every year, and such meeting shall begin at noon on the 3d day of January, unless they shall by law appoint a different day.

Emergency presidential succession

Section 3.   If, at the time fixed for the beginning of the term of the President, the President elect shall have died, the Vice President elect shall become President. If a President shall not have been chosen before the time fixed for the beginning of his term, or if the President elect shall have failed to qualify, then the Vice President elect shall act as President until a President shall have qualified; and the Congress may by law provide for the case wherein neither a President elect nor a Vice President elect shall have qualified, declaring who shall then act as President, or the manner in which one who is to act shall be selected, and such person shall act accordingly until a President or Vice President shall have qualified.

---

12. Repealed by the Twenty-first Amendment.

Section 4.   The Congress may by law provide for the case of the death of any of the persons from whom the House of Representatives may choose a President whenever the right of choice shall have devolved upon them, and for the case of the death of any of the persons from whom the Senate may choose a Vice President whenever the right of choice shall have devolved upon them.

Section 5.   Sections 1 and 2 shall take effect on the 15th day of October following the ratification of this article.

Section 6.   This article shall be inoperative unless it shall have been ratified as an amendment to the Constitution by the legislatures of three-fourths of the several States within seven years from the date of its submission.

AMENDMENT XXI.
[*Ratified in 1933.*]

Repeals Prohibition

Section 1.   The eighteenth article of amendment to the Constitution of the United States is hereby repealed.

Section 2.   The transportation or importation into any State, Territory, or possession of the United States for delivery or use therein of intoxicating liquors, in violation of the laws thereof, is hereby prohibited.

Section 3.   This article shall be inoperative unless it shall have been ratified as an amendment to the Constitution by conventions in the several States, as provided in the Constitution, within seven years from the date of submission hereof to the States by the Congress.

AMENDMENT XXII.
[*Ratified in 1951.*]

Two-term limit for president

Section 1.   No person shall be elected to the office of the President more than twice, and no person who has held the office of President, or acted as President, for more than two years of a term to which some other person was elected President shall be elected to the office of President more than once. But this Article shall not apply to any person holding the office of President when this Article was proposed by the Congress, and shall not prevent any person who may be holding the office of President, or acting as President, during the term within which this Article becomes operative from holding the office of President or acting as President during the remainder of such term.

Section 2.   This Article shall be inoperative unless it shall have been ratified as an amendment to the Constitution by the legislatures of three-fourths of the several States within seven years from the date of its submission to the States by the Congress.

AMENDMENT XXIII.
[*Ratified in 1961.*]

Right to vote for president in District of Columbia

Section 1.   The District constituting the seat of Government of the United States shall appoint in such manner as the Congress may direct:

A number of electors of President and Vice President equal to the whole number of Senators and Representatives in Congress to which the District would be entitled if it were a State, but in no event more than the least populous State; they shall be in addition to those appointed by the States, but they shall be considered, for the purposes of the election of President and Vice President, to be electors appointed by a State; and they shall meet in the District and perform such duties as provided by the twelfth article of amendment.

Section 2. The Congress shall have power to enforce this article by appropriate legislation.

AMENDMENT XXIV.
[*Ratified in 1964.*]

Prohibits poll taxes in federal elections

Section 1. The right of citizens of the United States to vote in any primary or other election for President or Vice President, for electors for President or Vice President, or for Senator or Representative in Congress, shall not be denied or abridged by the United States or any State by reason of failure to pay any poll tax or other tax.

Section 2. The Congress shall have the power to enforce this article by appropriate legislation.

AMENDMENT XXV.
[*Ratified in 1967.*]

Presidential disability and succession

Section 1. In case of the removal of the President from office or of his death or resignation, the Vice President shall become President.

Section 2. Whenever there is a vacancy in the office of the Vice President, the President shall nominate a Vice President who shall take office upon confirmation by a majority vote of both Houses of Congress.

Section 3. Whenever the President transmits to the President pro tempore of the Senate and the Speaker of the House of Representatives his written declaration that he is unable to discharge the powers and duties of his office, and until he transmits to them a written declaration to the contrary, such powers and duties shall be discharged by the Vice President as Acting President.

Section 4. Whenever the Vice President and a majority of either the principal officers of the executive departments or of such other body as Congress may by law provide, transmit to the President pro tempore of the Senate and the Speaker of the House of Representatives their written declaration that the President is unable to discharge the powers and duties of his office, the Vice President shall immediately assume the powers and duties of the office as Acting President.

Thereafter, when the President transmits to the President pro tempore of the Senate and the Speaker of the House of Representatives his written declaration that no inability exists, he shall resume the powers and duties of his office unless the Vice President and a majority of either the principal officers of the executive department[s] or of such other body as Congress may by law provide, transmit within four days to the President pro tempore of the Senate and the Speaker of the House of Representatives their written declaration that the President is unable to discharge the powers and duties of his office. Thereupon Congress shall decide the issue, assembling within forty-eight hours for that purpose if not in session. If the Congress, within twenty-one days after receipt of the latter written declaration, or, if Congress is not in session, within twenty-one days after Congress is required to assemble, determines by two-thirds vote of both Houses that the President is unable to discharge the powers and duties of his office, the Vice President shall continue to discharge the same as Acting President; otherwise, the President shall resume the powers and duties of his office.

AMENDMENT XXVI.
[Ratified in 1971.]

Voting age lowered to eighteen

Section 1.   The right of citizens of the United States, who are eighteen years of age or older, to vote shall not be denied or abridged by the United States or by any State on account of age.

Section 2.   The Congress shall have power to enforce this article by appropriate legislation.

AMENDMENT XXVII.
[Ratified in 1992.]

Congressional pay raises

No law varying the compensation for the services of the Senators and Representatives shall take effect, until an election of Representatives shall have intervened.

★ THE FEDERALIST NO. 10

November 22, 1787

James Madison

TO THE PEOPLE OF THE STATE OF NEW YORK.

Among the numerous advantages promised by a well constructed Union, none deserves to be more accurately developed than its tendency to break and control the violence of faction. The friend of popular governments, never finds himself so much alarmed for their character and fate, as when he contemplates their propensity to this dangerous vice. He will not fail therefore to set a due value on any plan which, without violating the principles to which he is attached, provides a proper cure for it. The instability, injustice and confusion introduced into the public councils, have in truth been the mortal diseases under which popular governments have every where perished; as they continue to be the favorite and fruitful topics from which the adversaries to liberty derive their most specious declamations. The valuable improvements made by the American Constitutions on the popular models, both ancient and modern, cannot certainly be too much admired; but it would be an unwarrantable partiality, to contend that they have as effectually obviated the danger on this side as was wished and expected. Complaints are every where heard from our most considerate and virtuous citizens, equally the friends of public and private faith, and of public and personal liberty; that our governments are too unstable; that the public good is disregarded in the conflicts of rival parties; and that measures are too often decided, not according to the rules of justice, and the rights of the minor party; but by the superior force of an interested and over-bearing majority. However anxiously we may wish that these complaints had no foundation, the evidence of known facts will not permit us to deny that they are in some degree true. It will be found indeed, on a candid review of our situation, that some of the distresses under which we labor, have been erroneously charged on the operation of our governments; but it will be found, at the same time, that other causes will not alone account for many of our heaviest misfortunes; and particularly, for that prevailing and increasing distrust of public engagements, and alarm for private rights, which are echoed from one end of the continent to the other. These must be chiefly, if not wholly, effects of the unsteadiness and injustice, with which a factious spirit has tainted our public administrations.

By a faction I understand a number of citizens, whether amounting to a majority or minority of the whole, who are united and actuated by some common impulse of passion, or of interest, adverse to the rights of other citizens, or to the permanent and aggregate interests of the community.

There are two methods of curing the mischiefs of faction: the one, by removing its causes; the other, by controlling its effects.

There are again two methods of removing the causes of faction: the one by destroying the liberty which is essential to its existence; the other, by giving to every citizen the same opinions, the same passions, and the same interests.

It could never be more truly said than of the first remedy, that it is worse than the disease. Liberty is to faction, what air is to fire, an aliment without which it instantly expires. But it could not be a less folly to abolish liberty, which is essential to political life, because it nourishes faction, than it would be to wish the annihilation of air, which is essential to animal life, because it imparts to fire its destructive agency.

The second expedient is as impracticable, as the first would be unwise. As long as the reason of man continues fallible, and he is at liberty to exercise it, different opinions will be formed. As long as the connection subsists between his reason and his self-love, his opinions and his passions will have a reciprocal influence on each other; and the former will be objects to which the latter will attach themselves. The diversity in the faculties of men from which the rights of property originate, is not less an insuperable obstacle to a uniformity of interests. The protection of these faculties is the first object of Government. From the protection of different and unequal faculties of acquiring property, the possession of different degrees and kinds of property immediately results: and from the influence of these on the sentiments and views of the respective proprietors, ensues a division of the society into different interests and parties.

The latent causes of faction are thus sown in the nature of man; and we see them every where brought into different degrees of activity, according to the different circumstances of civil society. A zeal for different opinions concerning religion, concerning Government and many other points, as well of speculation as of practice; an attachment to different leaders ambitiously contending for pre-eminence and power; or to persons of other descriptions whose fortunes have been interesting to the human passions, have in turn divided mankind into parties, inflamed them with mutual animosity, and rendered them much more disposed to vex and oppress each other, than to cooperate for their common good. So strong is this propensity of mankind to fall into mutual animosities, that where no substantial occasion presents itself, the most frivolous and fanciful distinctions have been sufficient to kindle their unfriendly passions, and excite their most violent conflicts. But the most common and durable source of factions, has been the various and unequal distribution of property. Those who hold, and those who are without property, have ever formed distinct interests in society. Those who are creditors, and those who are debtors, fall under a like discrimination. A landed interest, a manufacturing interest, a mercantile interest, a monied interest, with many lesser interests, grow up of necessity in civilized nations, and divide them into different classes, actuated by different sentiments and views. The regulation of these various and interfering interests forms the principal task of modern Legislation, and involves the spirit of party and faction in the necessary and ordinary operations of Government.

No man is allowed to be judge in his own cause; because his interest would certainly bias his judgment, and, not improbably, corrupt his integrity. With equal, nay with greater reason, a body of men, are unfit to be judges and parties, at the same time; yet, what are many of the most important acts of legislation, but so many judicial determinations, not indeed concerning the rights of single persons, but concerning the rights of large bodies of citizens, and what are the different classes of legislators, but advocates and parties to the causes which they determine? Is a law proposed concerning private debts? It is a question to which the creditors are parties on one side, and the debtors on the other. Justice ought to hold the balance between them. Yet the parties are and must be themselves the judges; and the most numerous party, or, in other words, the most powerful faction must be expected to prevail. Shall domestic manufactures be encouraged, and in what degree, by restrictions on foreign manufactures? are questions which would be differently decided by the landed and the manufacturing classes; and probably by neither, with a sole regard to justice and the public good. The apportionment of taxes on the various descriptions of property, is an act which seems to require the most exact impartiality; yet, there is perhaps no legislative act in which greater opportunity and temptation are given to a predominant party, to trample on the rules of justice. Every shilling with which they over-burden the inferior number, is a shilling saved to their own pockets.

It is in vain to say, that enlightened statesmen will be able to adjust these clashing interests, and render them all subservient to the public good. Enlightened statesmen will not always be at the helm: Nor, in many cases, can such an adjustment be made at all, without taking into view indirect and remote considerations, which will rarely prevail over the immediate interest which one party may find in disregarding the rights of another, or the good of the whole.

The inference to which we are brought, is, that the *causes* of faction cannot be removed; and that relief is only to be sought in the means of controlling its *effects*.

If a faction consists of less than a majority, relief is supplied by the republican principle, which enables the majority to defeat its sinister views by regular vote: It may clog the administration, it may convulse the society; but it will be unable to execute and mask its violence under the forms of the Constitution. When a majority is included in a faction, the form of popular government on the other hand enables it to sacrifice to its ruling passion or interest, both the public good and the rights of other citizens. To secure the public good, and private rights, against the danger of such a faction, and at the same time to preserve the spirit and the form of popular government, is then the great object to which our inquiries are directed: Let me add that it is the great desideratum, by which alone this form of government can be rescued from the opprobrium under which it has so long labored, and be recommended to the esteem and adoption of mankind.

By what means is this object attainable? Evidently by one of two only. Either the existence of the same passion or interest in a majority at the same time, must be prevented; or the majority, having such co-existent passion or interest, must be rendered, by their number and local situation, unable to concert and carry into effect schemes of oppression. If the impulse and the opportunity be suffered to coincide, we well know that neither moral nor religious motives can be relied on as an adequate control. They are not found to be such on the injustice and violence of individuals, and lose their efficacy in proportion to the number combined together; that is, in proportion as their efficacy becomes needful.

From this view of the subject, it may be concluded, that a pure Democracy, by which I mean, a Society, consisting of a small number of citizens, who assemble and administer the Government in person, can admit of no cure for the mischiefs of faction. A common passion or interest will, in almost every case, be felt by a majority of the whole; a communication and concert results from the form of Government itself; and there is nothing to check the inducements to sacrifice the weaker party, or an obnoxious individual. Hence it is, that such Democracies have ever been spectacles of turbulence and contention; have ever been found incompatible with personal security, or the rights of property; and have in general been as short in their lives, as they have been violent in their deaths. Theoretic politicians, who have patronized this species of Government, have erroneously supposed, that by reducing mankind to a perfect equality in their political rights, they would, at the same time, be perfectly equalized and assimilated in their possessions, their opinions, and their passions.

A republic, by which I mean a government in which the scheme of representation takes place, opens a different prospect, and promises the cure for which we are seeking. Let us examine the points in which it varies from pure democracy, and we shall comprehend both the nature of the cure and the efficacy which it must derive from the union.

The two great points of difference, between a democracy and a republic, are, first, the delegation of the government, in the latter, to a small number of citizens, elected by the rest; secondly, the greater number of citizens, and greater sphere of country, over which the latter may be extended.

The effect of the first difference is, on the one hand, to refine and enlarge the public views, by passing them through the medium of a chosen body of citizens, whose wisdom may best discern the true interest of their country, and whose patriotism and love of justice, will be least likely to sacrifice it to temporary or partial considerations. Under such a regulation, it may well happen, that the public voice, pronounced by the representatives of the people, will be more consonant to the public good, than if pronounced by the people themselves, convened for the purpose. On the other hand the effect may be inverted. Men of factious tempers, of local prejudices, or of sinister designs, may by intrigue, by corruption, or by other means, first obtain the suffrages, and then betray the interest of the people. The question resulting is, whether small or extensive republics are most favorable to the election of proper guardians of the public weal, and it is clearly decided in favor of the latter by two obvious considerations.

In the first place, it is to be remarked that, however small the republic may be, the representatives must be raised to a certain number, in order to guard against the cabals of a few; and that however large it may be, they must be limited to a certain number, in order to guard against the confusion of a multitude. Hence, the number of representatives in the two cases not being in proportion to that of the constituents, and being proportionally greatest in the small republic, it follows, that if the proportion of fit characters be not less in the large than in the small republic, the former will present a greater option, and consequently a greater probability of a fit choice.

In the next place, as each Representative will be chosen by a greater number of citizens in the large than in the small Republic, it will be more difficult for unworthy candidates to practise with success the vicious arts, by which elections are too often carried; and the suffrages of the people being more free, will be more likely to center on men who possess the most attractive merit, and the most diffusive and established characters.

It must be confessed, that in this, as in most other cases, there is a mean, on both sides of which inconveniences will be found to lie. By enlarging too much the number of electors, you render the representatives too little acquainted with all their local circumstances and lesser interests; as by reducing it too much, you render him unduly attached to these, and too little fit to comprehend and pursue great and national objects. The Federal Constitution forms a happy combination in this respect; the great and aggregate interests being referred to the national, the local and particular, to the state legislatures.

The other point of difference is, the greater number of citizens and extent of territory which may be brought within the compass of Republican, than of Democratic Government; and it is this circumstance principally which renders factious combinations less to be dreaded in the former, than in the latter. The smaller the society, the fewer probably will be the distinct parties and interests composing it; the fewer the distinct parties and interests, the more frequently will a majority be found of the same party; and the smaller the number of individuals composing a majority, and the smaller the compass within which they are placed, the more easily they will concert and execute their plans of oppression. Extend the sphere, and you take in a greater variety of parties and interests; you make it less probable that a majority of the whole will have a common motive to invade the rights of other citizens; or if such a common motive exists, it will be more difficult for all who feel it to discover their own strength, and to act in unison with each other. Besides other impediments, it may be remarked, that where there is a consciousness of unjust or dishonorable purposes, communication is always checked by distrust, in proportion to the number whose concurrence is necessary.

Hence it clearly appears, that the same advantage, which a Republic has over a Democracy, in controlling the effects of factions, is enjoyed by a large over a small Republic—is enjoyed by the Union over the States composing it. Does this advantage consist in the substitution of Representatives, whose enlightened views and virtuous sentiments render them superior to local prejudices, and to schemes of injustice? It will not be denied, that the Representation of the Union will be most likely to possess these requisite endowments. Does it consist in the greater security afforded by a greater variety of parties, against the event of any one party being able to outnumber and oppress the rest? In an equal degree does the increase variety of parties, comprised within the Union, increase this security? Does it, in fine, consist in the greater obstacles opposed to the concert and accomplishment of the secret wishes of an unjust and interested majority? Here, again, the extent of the Union gives it the most palpable advantage.

The influence of factious leaders may kindle a flame within their particular States, but will be unable to spread a general conflagration through the other States: a religious sect, may degenerate into a political faction in a part of the Confederacy but the variety of sects dispersed over the entire face of it, must secure the national Councils against any danger from that source: a rage for paper money, for an abolition of debts, for an equal division of property, or for any other improper or wicked project, will be less apt to pervade the whole body of the Union, than a particular member of it; in the same proportion as such a malady is more likely to taint a particular county or district, than an entire State.

In the extent and proper structure of the Union, therefore, we behold a Republican remedy for the diseases most incident to Republican Government. And according to the degree of pleasure and pride, we feel in being Republicans, ought to be our zeal in cherishing the spirit, and supporting the character of Federalists.

PUBLIUS

☆ THE FEDERALIST NO. 51

February 6, 1788

James Madison

TO THE PEOPLE OF THE STATE OF NEW YORK.

To what expedient then shall we finally resort for maintaining in practice the necessary partition of power among the several departments, as laid down in the constitution? The only answer that can be given is, that as all these exterior provisions are found to be inadequate, the defect must be supplied, by so contriving the interior structure of the government, as that its several constituent parts may, by their mutual relations, be the means of keeping each other in their proper places. Without presuming to undertake a full development of this important idea, I will hazard a few general observations, which may perhaps place it in a clearer light, and enable us to form a more correct judgment of the principles and structure of the government planned by the convention.

In order to lay a due foundation for that separate and distinct exercise of the different powers of government, which to a certain extent, is admitted on all hands to be essential to the preservation of liberty, it is evident that each department should have a will of its own; and consequently should be so constituted, that the members of each should have as little agency as possible in the appointment of the members of the others. Were this principle rigorously adhered to, it would require that all the appointments for the supreme executive, legislative, and judiciary magistracies, should be drawn from the same fountain of authority, the people, through channels, having no communication whatever with one another. Perhaps such a plan of constructing the several departments would be less difficult in practice than in it may in contemplation appear. Some difficulties however, and some additional expense, would attend the execution of it. Some deviations therefore from the principle must be admitted. In the constitution of the judiciary department in particular, it might be inexpedient to insist rigorously on the principle; first, because peculiar qualifications being essential in the members, the primary consideration ought to be to select that mode of choice, which best secures these qualifications; secondly, because the permanent tenure by which the appointments are held in that department, must soon destroy all sense of dependence on the authority conferring them.

It is equally evident that the members of each department should be as little dependent as possible on those of the others, for the emoluments annexed to their offices. Were the executive magistrate, or the judges, not independent of the legislature in this particular, their independence in every other would be merely nominal.

But the great security against a gradual concentration of the several powers in the same department, consists in giving to those who administer each department, the necessary constitutional means, and personal motives, to resist encroachments of the others. The provision for defense must in this, as in all other cases, be made commensurate to the danger of attack. Ambition must be made to counteract ambition. The interest of the man must be connected with the constitutional right of the place. It may be a reflection on human nature, that such devices should be necessary to control the abuses of government. But what is government itself but the greatest of all reflections on human nature? If men were angels, no government would be necessary. If angels were to govern men, neither external nor internal controls on government would be necessary. In framing a government which is to be administered by men over men, the great difficulty lies in this: You must first enable the government to control the governed; and in the next place, oblige it to control itself. A dependence on the people is no doubt the primary control on the government; but experience has taught mankind the necessity of auxiliary precautions.

This policy of supplying by opposite and rival interests, the defect of better motives, might be traced through the whole system of human affairs, private as well as public. We see it particularly displayed in all the subordinate distributions of power; where the constant aim is to divide and arrange the several offices in such a manner as that each may be a check on the other; that the private interest of every individual, may be a sentinel over the public rights. These inventions of prudence cannot be less requisite in the distribution of the supreme powers of the state.

But it is not possible to give each department an equal power of self defense. In republican government the legislative authority, necessarily, predominates. The remedy for this inconvenience is, to divide the legislative into different branches; and to render them by different modes of election, and different principles of action, as little connected with each other, as the nature of their common functions, and their common dependence on the society, will admit. It may even be necessary to guard against dangerous encroachments by still further precautions. As the weight of the legislative authority requires that it should be thus divided, the weakness of the executive may require, on the other hand, that it should be fortified. An absolute negative, on the legislature, appears at first view to be the natural defense with which the executive magistrate should be armed. But perhaps it would be neither altogether safe, nor alone sufficient. On ordinary occasions, it might not be exerted with the requisite firmness, and on extraordinary occasions, it might be prefidiously abused. May not this defect of an absolute negative be supplied, by some qualified connection between this weaker department, and the weaker branch of the stronger department, by which the latter may be led to support the constitutional rights of the former, without being too much detached from the rights of its own department?

If the principles on which these observations are founded be just, as I persuade myself they are, and they be applied as a criterion, to the several state constitutions, and to the federal constitution, it will be found, that if the latter does not perfectly correspond with them, the former are infinitely less able to bear such a test.

There are moreover two considerations particularly applicable to the federal system of America, which place the system in a very interesting point of view.

First. In a single republic, all the power surrendered by the people, is submitted to the administration of a single government; and usurpations are guarded against by a division of the government into distinct and separate departments. In the compound republic of America, the power surrendered by the people, is first divided between two distinct governments, and then the portion allotted to each, subdivided among distinct and separate departments. Hence a double security arises to the rights of the people. The different governments will control each other; at the same time that each will be controlled by itself.

Second. It is of great importance in a republic, not only to guard the society against the oppression of its rulers; but to guard one part of the society against the injustice of the other part. Different interests necessarily exist in different classes of citizens. If a majority be united by a common interest, the rights of the minority will be insecure. There are but two methods of providing against this evil: The one by creating a will in the community independent of the majority, that is, of the society itself, the other by comprehending in the society so many separate descriptions of citizens, as will render an unjust combination of a majority of the whole, very improbable, if not impracticable. The first method prevails in all governments possessing an hereditary or self appointed authority. This at best is but a precarious security; because a power independent of the society may as well espouse the unjust views of the major, as the rightful interests, of the minor party, and may possibly be turned against both parties. The second method will be exemplified in the federal republic of the United States. While all authority in it will be derived from and dependent on the society, the society itself will be broken into so many parts, interests and classes of citizens, that the rights of individuals or of the minority, will be in little danger from interested combinations of the majority. In a free government, the security for civil rights must be the same as for religious rights. It consists in the one case in the multiplicity of interests, and in the other, in the multiplicity of sects. The degree of security in both cases will depend on the number of interests and sects; and this may be presumed to depend on the extent of country and number of people comprehended under the same government. This view of the subject must particularly recommend a proper federal system to all the sincere and considerate friends of republican government: Since it shows that in exact proportion as the territory of the union may be formed into more circumscribed confederacies or states, oppressive combinations of a majority will be facilitated, the best security under the republican form, for the rights of every class of citizens, will be diminished; and consequently, the stability and independence of some member of the government, the only other security, must be proportionally increased. Justice is the end of government. It is the end of civil society. It ever has been, and ever will be pursued, until it be obtained, or until liberty be lost in the pursuit. In a society under the forms of which the stronger faction can readily unite and oppress the weaker, anarchy may as truly be said to reign, as in a state of nature where the weaker individual is not secured against the violence of the stronger: And as in the latter state even the stronger individuals are prompted by the uncertainty of their condition, to submit to a government which may protect the weak as well as themselves: So in the former state, will the more powerful factions or parties be gradually induced by a like motive, to wish for a government which will protect all parties, the weaker as well as the more powerful. It can be little doubted, that if the state of Rhode Island was separated from the confederacy, and left to itself, the insecurity of rights under the popular form of government within such narrow limits, would be displayed by such reiterated oppressions of factious majorities, that some power altogether independent of the people would soon be called for by the voice of the very factions whose misrule had proved the necessity of it. In the extended republic of the United States, and among the great variety of interests, parties and sects which it embraces, a coalition of a majority of the whole society could seldom take place on any other principles than those of justice and the general good; and there being thus less danger to a minor from the will of the major party, there must be less pretext also, to provide for the security of the former, by introducing into the government a will not dependent on the latter; or in other words, a will independent of the society itself. It is no less certain than it is important, notwithstanding the contrary opinions which have been entertained, that the larger the society, provided it lie within a practicable sphere, the more duly capable it will be of self government. And happily for the *republican cause,* the practicable sphere may be carried to a very great extent, by a judicious modification and mixture of the *federal principle.*

PUBLIUS

☆ PRESIDENTS AND CONGRESSES, 1789–2006

Year	President and vice president	Party of president	Congress	House Majority party	House Minority party	Senate Majority party	Senate Minority party
1789–1797	**George Washington** John Adams	None	1st 2d 3d 4th	38 Admin 37 Fed 57 Dem-Rep 54 Fed	26 Opp 33 Dem-Rep 48 Fed 52 Dem-Rep	17 Admin 16 Fed 17 Fed 19 Fed	9 Opp 13 Dem-Rep 13 Dem-Rep 13 Dem-Rep
1797–1801	**John Adams** Thomas Jefferson	Federalist	5th 6th	58 Fed 64 Fed	48 Dem-Rep 42 Dem-Rep	20 Fed 19 Fed	12 Dem-Rep 13 Dem-Rep
1801–1809	**Thomas Jefferson** Aaron Burr (to 1805) George Clinton (to 1809)	Dem-Rep	7th 8th 9th 10th	69 Dem-Rep 102 Dem-Rep 116 Dem-Rep 118 Dem-Rep	36 Fed 39 Fed 25 Fed 24 Fed	18 Dem-Rep 25 Dem-Rep 27 Dem-Rep 28 Dem-Rep	13 Fed 9 Fed 7 Fed 6 Fed
1809–1817	**James Madison** George Clinton (to 1813) Elbridge Gerry (to 1817)	Dem-Rep	11th 12th 13th 14th	94 Dem-Rep 108 Dem-Rep 112 Dem-Rep 117 Dem-Rep	48 Fed 36 Fed 68 Fed 65 Fed	28 Dem-Rep 30 Dem-Rep 27 Dem-Rep 25 Dem-Rep	6 Fed 6 Fed 9 Fed 11 Fed
1817–1825	**James Monroe** Daniel D. Tompkins	Dem-Rep	15th 16th 17th 18th	141 Dem-Rep 156 Dem-Rep 158 Dem-Rep 187 Dem-Rep	42 Fed 27 Fed 25 Fed 26 Fed	34 Dem-Rep 35 Dem-Rep 44 Dem-Rep 44 Dem-Rep	10 Fed 7 Fed 4 Fed 4 Fed
1825–1829	**John Quincy Adams** John C. Calhoun	Nat-Rep	19th 20th	105 Admin 119 Jack	97 Jack 94 Admin	26 Admin 28 Jack	20 Jack 20 Admin
1829–1837	**Andrew Jackson** John C. Calhoun (to 1833) Martin Van Buren (to 1837)	Democrat	21st 22d 23d 24th	139 Dem 141 Dem 147 Dem 145 Dem	74 Nat Rep 58 Nat Rep 53 AntiMas 98 Whig	26 Dem 25 Dem 20 Dem 27 Dem	22 Nat Rep 21 Nat Rep 20 Nat Rep 25 Whig
1837–1841	**Martin Van Buren** Richard M. Johnson	Democrat	25th 26th	108 Dem 124 Dem	107 Whig 118 Whig	30 Dem 28 Dem	18 Whig 22 Whig
1841	**William H. Harrison*** John Tyler	Whig					
1841–1845	**John Tyler** (VP vacant)	Whig	27th 28th	133 Whig 142 Dem	102 Dem 79 Whig	28 Whig 28 Whig	22 Dem 25 Dem
1845–1849	**James K. Polk** George M. Dallas	Democrat	29th 30th	143 Dem 115 Whig	77 Whig 108 Dem	31 Dem 36 Dem	25 Whig 21 Whig
1849–1850	**Zachary Taylor*** Millard Fillmore	Whig	31st	112 Dem	109 Whig	35 Dem	25 Whig
1850–1853	**Millard Fillmore** (VP vacant)	Whig	32d	140 Dem	88 Whig	35 Dem	24 Whig
1853–1857	**Franklin Pierce** William R. King	Democrat	33d 34th	159 Dem 108 Rep	71 Whig 83 Dem	38 Dem 40 Dem	22 Whig 15 Rep

NOTES: Only members of two major parties in Congress are shown; omitted are independents, members of minor parties, and vacancies.

Party balance as of beginning of Congress.

Congresses in which one or both houses are controlled by party other than that of the president are shown in color.

During administration of George Washington and (in part) John Quincy Adams, Congress was not organized by formal parties; the split shown is between supporters and opponents of the administration.

ABBREVIATIONS: **Admin** = Administration supporters; **AntiMas** = Anti-Masonic; **Dem** = Democratic; **Dem-Rep** = Democratic-Republican; **Fed** = Federalist; **Jack** = Jacksonian Democrats; **Nat Rep** = National Republican; **Opp** = Opponents of administration; **Rep** = Republican; **Union** = Unionist; **Whig** = Whig.

* Died in office.

Year	President and vice president	Party of president	Congress	House Majority party	House Minority party	Senate Majority party	Senate Minority party
1857–1861	**James Buchanan** John C. Breckinridge	Democrat	35th 36th	118 Dem 114 Rep	92 Rep 92 Dem	36 Dem 36 Dem	20 Rep 26 Rep
1861–1865	**Abraham Lincoln*** Hannibal Hamlin (to 1865) Andrew Johnson (1865)	Republican	37th 38th	105 Rep 102 Rep	43 Dem 75 Dem	31 Rep 36 Rep	10 Dem 9 Dem
1865–1869	**Andrew Johnson** (VP vacant)	Republican	39th 40th	149 Union 143 Rep	42 Dem 49 Dem	42 Union 42 Rep	10 Dem 11 Dem
1869–1877	**Ulysses S. Grant** Schuyler Colfax (to 1873) Henry Wilson (to 1877)	Republican	41st 42d 43d 44th	149 Rep 134 Rep 194 Rep 169 Dem	63 Dem 104 Dem 92 Dem 109 Rep	56 Rep 52 Rep 49 Rep 45 Rep	11 Dem 17 Dem 19 Dem 29 Dem
1877–1881	**Rutherford B. Hayes** William A. Wheeler	Republican	45th 46th	153 Dem 149 Dem	140 Rep 130 Rep	39 Rep 42 Dem	36 Dem 33 Rep
1881	**James A. Garfield*** Chester A. Arthur	Republican	47th	147 Rep	135 Dem	37 Rep	37 Dem
1881–1885	**Chester A. Arthur** (VP vacant)	Republican	48th	197 Dem	118 Rep	38 Rep	36 Dem
1885–1889	**Grover Cleveland** Thomas A. Hendricks	Democrat	49th 50th	183 Dem 169 Dem	140 Rep 152 Rep	43 Rep 39 Rep	34 Dem 37 Dem
1889–1893	**Benjamin Harrison** Levi P. Morton	Republican	51st 52d	166 Rep 235 Dem	159 Dem 88 Rep	39 Rep 47 Rep	37 Dem 39 Dem
1893–1897	**Grover Cleveland** Adlai E. Stevenson	Democrat	53d 54th	218 Dem 244 Rep	127 Rep 105 Dem	44 Dem 43 Rep	38 Rep 39 Dem
1897–1901	**William McKinley*** Garret A. Hobart (to 1901) Theodore Roosevelt (1901)	Republican	55th 56th	204 Rep 185 Rep	113 Dem 163 Dem	47 Rep 53 Rep	34 Dem 26 Dem
1901–1909	**Theodore Roosevelt** (VP vacant, 1901–1905) Charles W. Fairbanks (1905–1909)	Republican	57th 58th 59th 60th	197 Rep 208 Rep 250 Rep 222 Rep	151 Dem 178 Dem 136 Dem 164 Dem	55 Rep 57 Rep 57 Rep 61 Rep	31 Dem 33 Dem 33 Dem 31 Dem
1909–1913	**William Howard Taft** James S. Sherman	Republican	61st 62d	219 Rep 228 Dem	172 Dem 161 Rep	61 Rep 51 Rep	32 Dem 41 Dem
1913–1921	**Woodrow Wilson** Thomas R. Marshall	Democrat	63d 64th 65th 66th	291 Dem 230 Dem 216 Dem 240 Rep	127 Rep 196 Rep 210 Rep 190 Dem	51 Dem 56 Dem 53 Dem 49 Rep	44 Rep 40 Rep 42 Rep 47 Dem
1921–1923	**Warren G. Harding*** Calvin Coolidge	Republican	67th	301 Rep	131 Dem	59 Rep	37 Dem
1923–1929	**Calvin Coolidge** (VP vacant, 1923–1925) Charles G. Dawes (1925–1929)	Republican	68th 69th 70th	225 Rep 247 Rep 237 Rep	205 Dem 183 Dem 195 Dem	51 Rep 56 Rep 49 Rep	43 Dem 39 Dem 46 Dem
1929–1933	**Herbert Hoover** Charles Curtis	Republican	71st 72d	267 Rep 220 Dem	167 Dem 214 Rep	56 Rep 48 Rep	39 Dem 47 Dem
1933–1945	**Franklin D. Roosevelt*** John N. Garner (1933–1941) Henry A. Wallace (1941–1945) Harry S Truman (1945)	Democrat	73d 74th 75th 76th 77th 78th	310 Dem 319 Dem 331 Dem 261 Dem 268 Dem 218 Dem	117 Rep 103 Rep 89 Rep 164 Rep 162 Rep 208 Rep	60 Dem 69 Dem 76 Dem 69 Dem 66 Dem 58 Dem	35 Rep 25 Rep 16 Rep 23 Rep 28 Rep 37 Rep
1945–1953	**Harry S Truman** (VP vacant, 1945–1949) Alben W. Barkley (1949–1953)	Democrat	79th 80th 81st 82d	242 Dem 245 Rep 263 Dem 234 Dem	190 Rep 188 Dem 171 Rep 199 Rep	56 Dem 51 Rep 54 Dem 49 Dem	38 Rep 45 Dem 42 Rep 47 Rep

* Died in office.

Year	President and vice president	Party of president	Congress	House Majority party	House Minority party	Senate Majority party	Senate Minority party
1953–1961	**Dwight D. Eisenhower** Richard M. Nixon	Republican	83d 84th 85th 86th	221 Rep 232 Dem 233 Dem 283 Dem	211 Dem 203 Rep 200 Rep 153 Rep	48 Rep 48 Dem 49 Dem 64 Dem	47 Dem 47 Rep 47 Rep 34 Rep
1961–1963	**John F. Kennedy*** Lyndon B. Johnson	Democrat	87th	263 Dem	174 Rep	65 Dem	35 Rep
1963–1969	**Lyndon B. Johnson** (VP vacant, 1963–1965) Hubert H. Humphrey (1965–1969)	Democrat	88th 89th 90th	258 Dem 295 Dem 247 Dem	177 Rep 140 Rep 187 Rep	67 Dem 68 Dem 64 Dem	33 Rep 32 Rep 36 Rep
1969–1974	**Richard M. Nixon†** Spiro T. Agnew†† Gerald R. Ford§	Republican	91st 92d	243 Dem 254 Dem	192 Rep 180 Rep	57 Dem 54 Dem	43 Rep 44 Rep
1974–1977	**Gerald R. Ford** Nelson A. Rockefeller§	Republican	93d 94th	239 Dem 291 Dem	192 Rep 144 Rep	56 Dem 60 Dem	42 Rep 37 Rep
1977–1981	**Jimmy Carter** Walter Mondale	Democrat	95th 96th	292 Dem 276 Dem	143 Rep 157 Rep	61 Dem 58 Dem	38 Rep 41 Rep
1981–1989	**Ronald Reagan** George Bush	Republican	97th 98th 99th 100th	243 Dem 269 Dem 253 Dem 257 Dem	192 Rep 165 Rep 182 Rep 178 Rep	53 Rep 54 Rep 53 Rep 54 Dem	46 Dem 46 Dem 47 Dem 46 Rep
1989–1993	**George Bush** Dan Quayle	Republican	101st 102d	262 Dem 267 Dem	173 Rep 167 Rep	55 Dem 56 Dem	45 Rep 44 Rep
1993–2000	**Bill Clinton** Albert Gore, Jr.	Democrat	103d 104th 105th 106th	258 Dem 230 Rep 228 Rep 223 Rep	176 Rep 204 Dem 206 Dem 211 Dem	57 Dem 53 Rep 55 Rep 54 Rep	43 Rep 47 Dem 45 Dem 46 Dem
2000–2009	**George W. Bush** Dick Cheney	Republican	107th 108th 109th	220 Rep 229 Rep 233 Rep	215 Dem 204 Dem 206 Dem	50 Rep 51 Rep 55 Rep	50 Dem 48 Dem 44 Dem

*Died in office.   †Resigned from the presidency.   ††Resigned from the vice presidency.   §Appointed vice president.

☆ GLOSSARY

activist approach The view that judges should discern the general principles underlying laws or the Constitution and apply them to modern circumstances. (16)

activists People who tend to participate in all forms of politics. (8)

ad hoc structure Several subordinates, cabinet officers, and committees report directly to the president on different matters. (14)

adversarial press The tendency of the national media to be suspicious of officials and eager to reveal unflattering stories about them. (12)

affirmative action Programs designed to increase minority participation in some institution (businesses, schools, labor unions, or government agencies) by taking positive steps to appoint more minority-group members. (6)

amendment A new provision in the Constitution that has been ratified by the states. (2)

amicus curiae A brief submitted by a "friend of the court." (16)

Antifederalists Those who favor a weaker national government. (2)

appropriation A legislative grant of money to finance a government program or agency. (15)

Articles of Confederation A weak constitution that governed America during the Revolutionary War. (2)

Australian ballot A government-printed ballot of uniform dimensions to be cast in secret that many states adopted around 1890 to reduce voting fraud associated with party-printed ballots cast in public. (8)

authority The right to use power. (1)

authorization legislation Legislative permission to begin or continue a government program or agency. (15)

background A public official's statement to a reporter that is given on condition that the official not be named. (12)

bicameral legislature A lawmaking body made up of two chambers or parts. (13)

bill of attainder A law that declares a person, without a trial, to be guilty of a crime. (2)

Bill of Rights First ten amendments to the Constitution. (2)

blanket primary A primary election in which each voter may vote for candidates from both parties. (10)

block grants Money from the national government that states can spend within broad guidelines determined by Washington. (3)

blog A series, or log, of discussion items on a page of the World Wide Web. (12)

brief A written statement by an attorney that summarizes a case and the laws and rulings that support it. (16)

bully pulpit The president's use of his prestige and visibility to guide or enthuse the American public. (14)

bureaucracy A large, complex organization composed of appointed officials. (15)

bureaucratic view View that the government is dominated by appointed officials. (1)

cabinet The heads of the fifteen executive branch departments of the federal government. (14)

categorical grants Federal grants for specific purposes, such as building an airport. (3)

caucus A meeting of party members to select delegates backing one or another primary candidates. (9, 10, 13)

checks and balances Authority shared by three branches of government. (2)

circular structure Several of the president's assistants report directly to him. (14)

civic competence A belief that one can affect government policies. (4)

civic duty A belief that one has an obligation to participate in civic and political affairs. (4)

civil disobedience Opposing a law one considers unjust by peacefully disobeying it and accepting the resultant punishment. (6)

civil rights The rights of people to be treated without unreasonable or unconstitutional differences. (6)

class consciousness A belief that you are a member of an economic group whose interests are opposed to people in other such groups. (4)

class-action suit A case brought by someone to help him or her and all others who are similarly situated. (16)

clear-and-present-danger test Law should not punish speech unless there was a clear and present danger of producing harmful actions. (5)

closed primary A primary election in which voting is limited to already registered party members. (10)

closed rule An order from the House Rules Committee that sets a time limit on debate; forbids a bill from being amended on the floor. (13)

cloture rule A rule used by the Senate to end or limit debate. (13)

coalition An alliance of factions. (2)

coattails The alleged tendency of candidates to win more votes in an election because of the presence at the top of the ticket of a better-known candidate, such as the president. (10)

committee clearance The ability of a congressional committee to review and approve certain agency decisions in advance and without passing a law. (15)

competitive service The government offices to which people are appointed on the basis of merit, as ascertained by a written exam or by applying certain selection criteria. (15)

concurrent powers Powers shared by the national and state governments. (2)

concurrent resolution An expression of opinion without the force of law that requires the approval of both the House and the Senate, but not the president. (13)

concurring opinion A signed opinion in which one or more members agree with the majority view but for different reasons. (16)

conditions of aid Terms set by the national government that states must meet if they are to receive certain federal funds. (3)

conference committees A joint committee appointed to resolve differences in the Senate and House versions of the same bill. (13)

congressional campaign committee   A party committee in Congress that provides funds to members and would-be members. (9)

conservative coalition   An alliance between Republican and conservative Democrats. (13)

Constitutional Convention   Meeting in Philadelphia in 1787 that produced a new constitution. (2)

constitutional court   A federal court authorized by Article III of the Constitution that keeps judges in office during good behavior and prevents their salaries from being reduced. They are the Supreme Court (created by the Constitution) and appellate and district courts created by Congress. (16)

courts of appeals   Federal courts that hear appeals from district courts; no trials. (16)

critical or realignment period   Periods when a major, lasting shift occurs in the popular coalition supporting one or both parties. (9)

de facto segregation   Racial segregation that occurs in schools, not as a result of the law, but as a result of patterns of residential settlement. (6)

de jure segregation   Racial segregation that is required by law. (6)

democracy   The rule of the many. (1)

devolution   The effort to transfer responsibility for many public programs and services from the federal government to the states. (3)

direct or participatory democracy   A government in which all or most citizens participate directly. (1)

discharge petition   A device by which any member of the House, after a committee has had the bill for thirty days, may petition to have it brought to the floor. (13)

discretionary authority   The extent to which appointed bureaucrats can choose courses of action and make policies that are not spelled out in advance by laws. (15)

dissenting opinion   A signed opinion in which one or more justices disagree with the majority view. (16)

district courts   The lowest federal courts; federal trials can be held only here. (16)

diversity cases   Cases involving citizens of different states who can bring suit in federal courts. (16)

divided government   One party controls the White House and another party controls one or both houses of Congress. (14)

division vote   A congressional voting procedure in which members stand and are counted. (13)

double-tracking   A procedure to keep the Senate going during a filibuster in which the disputed bill is shelved temporarily so that the Senate can get on with other business. (13)

dual federalism   Doctrine holding that the national government is supreme in its sphere, the states are supreme in theirs, and the two spheres should be kept separate. (3)

due process of law   Denies the government the right, without due process, to deprive people of life, liberty, and property. (5)

electoral college   The people chosen to cast each state's votes in a presidential election. Each state can cast one electoral vote for each senator and representative it has. The District of Columbia has three electoral votes, even though it cannot elect a representative or senator. (14)

elite   Persons who possess a disproportionate share of some valued resource, like money or power. (1, 7)

enumerated powers   Powers given to the national government alone. (2)

equal protection of the law   A standard of equal treatment that must be observed by the government. (5)

equal time rule   An FCC rule that if a broadcaster sells time to one candidate, it must sell equal time to other candidates. (12)

equality of opportunity   Giving people an equal chance to succeed. (6)

equality of result   Making certain that people achieve the same result. (6)

establishment clause   First Amendment ban on laws "respecting an establishment of religion." (5)

ex post facto law   A law that makes an act criminal although the act was legal when it was committed. (2)

exclusionary rule   Improperly gathered evidence may not be introduced in a criminal trial. (5)

exit polls   Polls based on interviews conducted on Election Day with randomly selected voters. (7)

external efficacy   The willingness of the state to respond to the citizenry. (4)

faction   A group with a distinct political interest. (2)

feature stories   Media stories about events that, though public, are not regularly covered by reporters. (12)

federalism   Government authority shared by national and state governments. (2)

Federalists   Those who favor a stronger national government. (2)

federal-question cases   Cases concerning the Constitution, federal laws, or treaties. (16)

fee shifting   A rule that allows a plaintiff to recover costs from the defendant if the plaintiff wins. (16)

filibuster   An attempt to defeat a bill in the Senate by talking indefinitely, thus preventing the Senate from taking action to the bill. (13)

527 organizations   Organizations that, under section 527 of the Internal Revenue Code, raise and spend money to advance political causes. (10)

franking privilege   The ability of members to mail letters to their constituents free of charge by substituting their facsimile signature for postage. (13)

freedom of expression   Right of people to speak, publish, and assemble. (5)

freedom of religion   People shall be free to exercise their religion, and government may not establish a religion. (5)

free-exercise clause   First Amendment requirement that law cannot prevent free exercise of religion. (5)

gender gap   Difference in political views between men and women. (7)

general election   An election held to choose which candidate will hold office. (10)

gerrymandering   Drawing the boundaries of legislative districts in bizarre or unusual shapes to favor one party. (10)

good-faith exception   An error in gathering evidence sufficiently minor that it may be used in a trial. (5)

grandfather clause   A clause in registration laws allowing people who do not meet registration requirements to vote if they or their ancestors had voted before 1867. (8)

grants-in-aid   Money given by the national government to the states. (3)

Great Compromise   Plan to have a popularly elected House based on state population and a state-selected Senate, with two members for each state. (2)

gridlock   The inability of the government to act because rival parties control different parts of the government. (14)

habeas corpus   An order to produce an arrested person before a judge. (2)

ideological interest groups   Political organizations that attract members by appealing to their political convictions or principles. (11)

ideological party   A party that values principled stands on issues above all else. (9)

impeachment   Charges against a president approved by a majority of the House of Representatives. (14)

in forma pauperis   A method whereby a poor person can have his or her case heard in federal court without charge. (16)

incentive   Something of value one cannot get without joining an organization. (11)

incumbent   The person already holding an elective office. (10)

independent expenditures   Spending by political action committees, corporations, or labor unions that is done to help a party or candidate but is done independently of them. (10)

initiative   Process that permits voters to put legislative measures directly on the ballot. (3)

insider stories   Media stories about events that are not usually made public. (12)

internal efficacy   The ability to understand and take part in politics. (4)

iron triangle   A close relationship between an agency, a congressional committee, and an interest group. (15)

issue network   A network of people in Washington, D.C.–based interest groups, on congressional staffs, in universities and think tanks, and in the mass media, who regularly discuss and advocate public policies. (15)

joint committees   Committees on which both senators and representatives serve. (13)

joint resolution   A formal expression of congressional opinion that must be approved by both houses of Congress and by the president; constitutional amendments need not be signed by the president. (13)

judicial review   The power of the courts to declare laws unconstitutional. (2, 16)

laissez-faire   An economic theory that government should not regulate or interfere with commerce. (15)

lame duck   A person still in office after he or she has lost a bid for reelection. (14)

legislative courts   Courts created by Congress for specialized purposes whose judges do not enjoy the protections of Article III of the Constitution. (16)

legislative veto   The authority of Congress to block a presidential action after it has taken place. The Supreme Court has held that Congress does not have this power. (14, 15)

legitimacy   Political authority conferred by law or by a state or national constitution. (1)

libel   Writing that falsely injures another person. (5)

line-item veto   An executive's ability to block a particular provision in a bill passed by the legislature. (2, 14)

literacy test   A requirement that citizens pass a literacy test in order to register to vote. (8)

litmus test   An examination of the political ideology of a nominated judge. (16)

loaded language   Words that imply a value judgment, used to persuade a reader without having made a serious argument. (12)

majority leader   The legislative leader elected by party members holding the majority of seats in the House or the Senate. (13)

malapportionment   Drawing the boundaries of legislative districts so that they are unequal in population. (10)

mandates   Terms set by the national government that states must meet whether or not they accept federal grants. (3)

marginal districts   Political districts in which candidates elected to the House of Representatives win in close elections, typically by less than 55 percent of the vote. (13)

Marxist view   View that the government is dominated by capitalists. (1)

material incentives   Money or things valued in monetary terms. (11)

minority leader   The legislative leader elected by party members holding a minority of seats in the House or the Senate. (13)

mugwumps or progressives   Republican party faction of the 1890s to the 1910s composed of reformers who opposed patronage. (9)

multiple referral   A congressional process whereby a bill may be referred to several committees. (13)

name-request job   A job that is filled by a person whom an agency has already identified. (15)

national chairman   Day-to-day party manager elected by the national committee. (9)

national committee   Delegates who run party affairs between national conventions. (9)

national convention   A meeting of party delegates held every four years. (9)

"necessary and proper" clause   Section of the Constitution allowing Congress to pass all laws "necessary and proper" to its duties, and which has permitted Congress to exercise powers not specifically given to it (enumerated) by the Constitution. (3)

New Jersey Plan   Proposal to create a weak national government. (2)

norm   A standard of right or proper conduct. (7)

nullification   The doctrine that a state can declare null and void a federal law that, in the state's opinion, violates the Constitution. (3)

office-bloc ballot   A ballot listing all candidates for a given office under the name of that office; also called a "Massachusetts" ballot. (9)

open primary   A primary election in which voters may choose in which party to vote as they enter the polling place. (10)

open rule   An order from the House Rules Committee that permits a bill to be amended on the floor. (13)

opinion of the court   A signed opinion of a majority of the Supreme Court. (16)

orthodox   A belief that morality and religion ought to be of decisive importance. (4)

party polarization A vote in which a majority of Democratic legislators oppose a majority of Republican legislators. (13)

party-column ballot A ballot listing all candidates of a given party together under the name of that party; also called an "Indiana" ballot. (9)

per curiam opinion A brief, unsigned court opinion. (16)

personal following The political support provided to a candidate on the basis of personal popularity and networks. (9)

plaintiff The party that initiates a lawsuit. (16)

pluralist view The belief that competition among all affected interests shapes public policy. (1)

plurality system An electoral system in which the winner is the person who gets the most votes, even if he or she does not receive a majority; used in almost all American elections. (9)

pocket veto A bill fails to become law because the president did not sign it within ten days before Congress adjourns. (14)

police power State power to enact laws promoting health, safety, and morals. (3, 6)

political action committee (PAC) A committee set up by a corporation, labor union, or interest group that raises and spends campaign money from voluntary donations. (10)

political cue A signal telling a legislator what values are at stake in a vote, and how that issue fits into his or her own political views on party agenda. (11)

political culture A coherent way of thinking about how politics and government ought to be carried out. (4)

political efficacy A belief that you can take part in politics (internal efficacy) or that the government will respond to the citizenry (external efficacy). (4)

political elites Persons with a disproportionate share of political power. (7)

political ideology A more or less consistent set of beliefs about what policies government ought to pursue. (7)

political machine A party organization that recruits members by dispensing patronage. (9)

political party A group that seeks to elect candidates to public office. (9)

political question An issue the Supreme Court will allow the executive and legislative branches decide. (16)

political socialization Process by which background traits influence one's political views. (7)

poll A survey of public opinion. (7)

poll tax A requirement that citizens pay a tax in order to register to vote. (8)

pork-barrel legislation Legislation that gives tangible benefits to constituents in several districts or states in the hope of winning their votes in return. (13)

position issues An issue about which the public is divided and rival candidates or political parties adopt different policy positions. (10)

power The ability of one person to get another person to act in accordance with the first person's intentions. (1)

power elite view View that the government is dominated by a few top leaders, most of whom are outside of government. (1)

primary election An election held to choose candidates for office. (10)

prior restraint Censorship of a publication. (5)

private bill A legislative bill that deals only with specific, private, personal, or local matters. (13)

probable cause Reasonable cause for issuing a search warrant or making an arrest; more than mere suspicion. (5)

progressive A belief that personal freedom and solving social problems are more important than religion. (4)

prospective voting Voting for a candidate because you favor his or her ideas for handling issues. (10)

public bill A legislative bill that deals with matters of general concern. (13)

public opinion How people think or feel about particular things. (7)

public-interest lobby A political organization whose goals will principally benefit nonmembers. (11)

purposive incentive A benefit that comes from serving a cause or principle. (11)

pyramid structure A president's subordinates report to him through a clear chain of command headed by a chief of staff. (14)

quorum The minimum number of members who must be present for business to be conducted in Congress. (13)

quorum call A roll call in either house of Congress to see whether the minimum number of representatives required to conduct business is present. (13)

random sample Method of selecting from a population in which each person has an equal probability of being selected. (7)

ratings Assessments of a representative's voting record on issues important to an interest group. (11)

recall Procedure whereby voters can remove an elected official from office. (3)

red tape Complex bureaucratic rules and procedures that must be followed to get something done. (15)

referendum Procedure enabling voters to reject a measure passed by the legislature. (3)

registered voters People who are registered to vote. (8)

remedy A judicial order enforcing a right or redressing a wrong. (16)

representative democracy A government in which leaders make decisions by winning a competitive struggle for the popular vote. (1)

republic A government in which elected representatives make the decisions. (2)

reserved powers Powers given to the state government alone. (2)

restrictive rule An order from the House Rules Committee that permits certain kinds of amendments but not others to be made into a bill on the floor. (13)

retrospective voting Voting for a candidate because you like his or her past actions in office. (10)

reverse discrimination Using race or sex to give preferential treatment to some people. (6)

revenue sharing Federal sharing of a fixed percentage of its revenues with the states. (3)

roll-call vote A congressional voting procedure that consists of members answering "yea" or "nay" to their names. (13)

routine stories Media stories about events that are regularly covered by reporters. (12)

runoff primary A second primary election held when no candidate wins a majority of the votes in the first primary. (10)

safe districts Districts in which incumbents win by margins of 55 percent or more. (13)

sampling error   The difference between the results of random samples taken at the same time. (7)

search warrant   A judge's order authorizing a search. (5)

select committees   Congressional committees appointed for a limited time and purpose. (13)

selective attention   Paying attention only to those news stories with which one already agrees. (12)

selective incorporation   Court cases that apply Bill of Rights to states. (5)

separate-but-equal doctrine   The doctrine established in *Plessy v. Ferguson* (1896) that African Americans could constitutionally be kept in separate but equal facilities. (6)

separation of powers   Constitutional authority is shared by three different branches of government. (2)

sequential referral   A congressional process by which a Speaker may send a bill to a second committee after the first is finished acting. (13)

Shays's Rebellion   A 1787 rebellion in which ex-Revolutionary War soldiers attempted to prevent foreclosures of farms as a result of high interest rates and taxes. (2)

simple resolution   An expression of opinion either in the House or Senate to settle procedural matters in either body. (13)

social movement   A widely shared demand for change in some aspect of the social or political order. (11)

soft money   Funds obtained by political parties that are spent on party activities, such as get-out-the-vote drives, but not on behalf of a specific candidate. (10)

solidary incentives   The social rewards (sense of pleasure, status, or companionship) that lead people to join political organizations. (9, 11)

sophomore surge   An increase in the votes congressional candidates usually get when they first run for reelection. (10)

sound bite   A radio or video clip of someone speaking. (12)

sovereign immunity   The rule that a citizen cannot sue the government without the government's consent. (16)

split ticket   Voting for candidates of different parties for various offices in the same election. (9)

sponsored party   A local or state political party that is largely supported by another organization in the community. (9)

standing   A legal rule stating who is authorized to start a lawsuit. (16)

standing committees   Permanently established legislative committees that consider and are responsible for legislation within a certain subject area. (13)

stare decisis   "Let the decision stand," or allowing prior rulings to control the current case. (16)

straight ticket   Voting for candidates who are all of the same party. (9)

strict scrutiny   A Supreme Court test to see if a law denies equal protection because it does not serve a compelling state interest and is not narrowly tailored to achieve that goal. (6)

strict-constructionist approach   The view that judges should decide cases strictly on the basis of the language of the laws and the Constitution. (16)

superdelegates   Party leaders and elected officials who become delegates to the national convention without having to run in primaries or caucuses. (9)

suspect classifications   Classifications of people on the basis of their race or ethnicity. (6)

symbolic speech   An act that conveys a political message. (5)

teller vote   A congressional voting procedure in which members pass between two tellers, the "yeas" first and the "nays" second. (13)

trial balloon   Information leaked to the media to test public reaction to a possible policy. (12)

trust funds   Funds for government programs that are collected and spent outside the regular government budget. (15)

two-party system   An electoral system with two dominant parties that compete in national elections. (9)

unalienable   A human right based on nature or God. (2)

unified government   The same party controls the White House and both houses of Congress. (14)

valence issue   An issue about which the public is united and rival candidates or political parties adopt similar positions in hopes that each will be thought to best represent those widely shared beliefs. (10)

veto message   A message from the president to Congress stating that he will not sign a bill it has passed. Must be produced within ten days of the bill's passage. (14)

Virginia Plan   Proposal to create a strong national government. (2)

voice vote   A congressional voting procedure in which members shout "yea" in approval or "nay" in disapproval, permitting members to vote quickly or anonymously on bills. (13)

voting-age population   Citizens who are eligible to vote after reaching the minimum age requirement. (8)

wall of separation   Court ruling that government cannot be involved with religion. (5)

whip   A senator or representative who helps the party leader stay informed about what party members are thinking. (13)

white primary   The practice of keeping blacks from voting in the southern states' primaries through arbitrary use of registration requirements and intimidation. (8)

writ of certiorari   An order by a higher court directing a lower court to send up a case for review. (16)

☆ NOTES

Chapter 1 *The Study of American Government*

1. National Commission on Terrorist Attacks Upon the United States, *The 9/11 Commission Report: Final Report of the National Commission on Terrorist Attacks Upon the United States* (New York and London: W.W. Norton, 2004), 399.
2. Ibid., 419.
3. Aristotle, *Politics*, iv, 4, 1290[b]. More precisely, Aristotle's definition was this: Democracy is a "constitution in which the free-born and poor control the government—being at the same time a majority." He distinguished this from an oligarchy, "in which the rich and well-born control the government—being at the same time a minority." Aristotle listed several varieties of democracy, depending on whether, for example, there was a property qualification for citizenship.
4. Joseph A. Schumpeter, *Capitalism, Socialism, and Democracy*, 3d ed. (New York: Harper Torchbooks, 1950), 269. (First published in 1942.)
5. Karl Marx and Friedrich Engels, "The Manifesto of the Communist Party," in *The Marx-Engels Reader*, 2d ed., ed. Robert C. Tucker (New York: Norton, 1978), 469–500.
6. C. Wright Mills, *The Power Elite* (New York: Oxford University Press, 1956).
7. H. H. Gerth and C. Wright Mills, eds., *From Max Weber: Essays in Sociology* (London: Routledge and Kegan Paul, 1948), 232–235.
8. Among the authors whose interpretations of American politics are essentially pluralist is David B. Truman, *The Governmental Process*, 2d ed. (New York: Knopf, 1971).
9. Kay L. Schlozman et al., "Inequalities of Political Voice: A Background Memo to the American Political Science Association Task Force on Inequality and American Democracy," Washington, D.C.: American Political Science Association, January 2004, p. 1. Also see Larry M. Bartels et al., "Inequality in American Governance: A Background Memo to the American Political Science Association Task Force on Inequality and American Democracy," Washington, D.C.: American Political Science Association, January 2004; and Jacob Hacker et al., "How Policies Affect Equality—Stratification, Citizenship, and American Public Policy: A Background Memo to the American Political Science Association Task Force on Inequality and American Democracy," Washington, D.C.: American Political Science Association, January 2003.
10. Schlozman, 21.
11. Alexis de Tocqueville, *Democracy in America*, vol. 2, ed. Phillips Bradley (New York: Knopf, 1951), book 2, ch. 8, 122.
12. Derek C. Bok and John T. Dunlop, *Labor and the American Community* (New York: Simon and Schuster, 1970), 134.

Chapter 2 *The Constitution*

1. Quoted in Bernard Bailyn, *The Ideological Origins of the American Revolution* (Cambridge: Harvard University Press, 1967), 61, n. 6.
2. Quoted in Bailyn, ibid., 135–137.
3. Quoted in Bailyn, ibid., 77.
4. Quoted in Bailyn, ibid., 160.
5. *Federalist* No. 37.
6. Gordon S. Wood, *The Creation of the American Republic* (Chapel Hill: University of North Carolina Press, 1969). See also *Federalist* No. 49.
7. Letter of George Washington to Henry Lee (October 31, 1787), in *Writings of George Washington*, vol. 29, ed. John C. Fitzpatrick (Washington, D.C.: Government Printing Office, 1939), 34.
8. Letters of Thomas Jefferson to James Madison (January 30, 1787) and to Colonel William S. Smith (November 13, 1787), in *Jefferson Himself*, ed. Bernard Mayo (Boston: Houghton Mifflin, 1942), 145.
9. *Federalist* No. 51.
10. *Federalist* No. 48.
11. *Federalist* No. 51.
12. Ibid.
13. Ibid.
14. "The Address and Reasons of Dissent of the Minority of the State of Pennsylvania to Their Constituents," in *The Anti-Federalist*, ed. Cecelia Kenyon (Indianapolis: Bobbs-Merrill, 1966), 39.
15. Max Farrand, *The Framing of the Constitution of the United States* (New Haven, Conn.: Yale University Press, 1913), 185.
16. See, for example, John Hope Franklin, *Racial Equality in America* (Chicago: University of Chicago Press, 1976), ch. 1, esp. 12–20.
17. Max Farrand, *The Records of the Federal Convention of 1787*, 4 vols. (New Haven, Conn.: Yale University Press, 1911–1937).
18. Theodore J. Lowi, *American Government: Incomplete Conquest* (Hinsdale, Ill.: Dryden Press, 1976), 97.
19. Article I, section 2, para. 3.
20. Article I, section 9, para. 1.
21. Article IV, section 2, para. 3
22. Charles A. Beard, *An Economic Interpretation of the Constitution* (New York: Macmillan, 1913), esp. 26–51, 149–151, 324–325.
23. Forrest McDonald, *We the People* (Chicago: University of Chicago Press, 1958); Robert E. Brown, *Charles Beard and the Constitution* (Princeton: Princeton University Press, 1956).
24. Robert A. McGuire, "Constitution Making: A Rational Choice Model of the Federal Convention of 1787," *American Journal of Political Science* 32 (May 1988): 483–522. See also Forrest McDonald, *Novus Ordo Seclorum* (Lawrence: University of Kansas Press, 1985), 221.
25. McDonald, *Novus Ordo Seclorum*, 202–221.
26. Robert A. McGuire and Robert L. Ohsfeldt, "Economic Interests and the American Constitution: A Quantitative Rehabilitation of Charles A. Beard," *Journal of Economic History* 44 (June 1984): 509–519.
27. Lloyd N. Cutler, "To Form a Government," *Foreign Affairs* (Fall 1980): 126–143.

Chapter 3 *Federalism*

1. Woodrow Wilson, *Constitutional Government in the United States* (New York: Columbia University Press, 1961), 173. (First published in 1908.)
2. David B. Truman, "Federalism and the Party System," in *Federalism: Mature and Emergent*, ed. Arthur MacMahon (Garden City, N.Y.: Doubleday, 1955), 123.
3. Ibid.
4. Harold J. Laski, "The Obsolescence of Federalism," *New Republic* (May 3, 1939): 367–369.
5. William A. Riker, *Federalism: Origin, Operation, Significance* (Boston: Little, Brown, 1964), 154.
6. Daniel J. Elazar, *American Federalism: A View from the States* (New York: Crowell, 1966), 216.
7. Martin Diamond, "The Federalists' View of Federalism," in *Essays in Federalism*, ed. George C. S. Benson (Claremont, Calif.: Institute for Studies in Federalism, 1961), 21–64; and Samuel H. Beer, "Federalism, Nationalism, and Democracy in America," *American Political Science Review* 72 (March 1978): 9–21.
8. *United States v. Sprague*, 282 U.S. 716 (1931).
9. *Garcia v. San Antonio Metropolitan Transit Authority*, 105 S. Ct. 1005 (1985), overruling *National League of Cities v. Usery*, 426 U.S. 833 (1976).
10. *McCulloch v. Maryland*, 4 Wheat. 316 (1819).
11. *Pollock v. Farmers' Loan & Trust Co.*, 157 U.S. 429 (1895); *South Carolina v. Baker*, No. 94 (1988).
12. *Texas v. White*, 7 Wall. 700 (1869).
13. *Champion v. Ames*, 188 U.S. 321 (1903).
14. *Hoke v. United States*, 227 U.S. 308 (1913).
15. *Clark Distilling Co. v. W. Md. Ry.*, 242 U.S. 311 (1917).
16. *Hipolite Egg Co. v. United States*, 220 U.S. 45 (1911).

17. *United States v. E. C. Knight Co.*, 156 U.S. 1 (1895).
18. *Paul v. Virginia*, 8 Wall. 168 (1869).
19. *Veazie Bank v. Fenno*, 8 Wall. 533 (1869).
20. *Brown v. Maryland*, 12 Wheat. 419 (1827).
21. *Wickard v. Filburn*, 317 U.S. 111 (1942); *NLRB v. Jones & Laughlin Steel Corp.*, 301 U.S. 58 (1937).
22. *Kirschbaum Co. v. Walling*, 316 U.S. 517 (1942).
23. *Goldfarb v. Virginia State Bar*, 421 U.S. 773 (1975); *Flood v. Kuhn*, 407 U.S. 258 (1972); *Gonzales v. Raich* (03-1454), 2005.
24. *United States v. California*, 332 U.S. 19 (1947).
25. Morton Grodzins, *The American System* (Chicago: Rand McNally, 1966), 49–50.
26. Max Sawicky, Economic Policy Institute Brief #176, Washington, D.C., February 14, 2002; U.S. Office of Management and Budget, *Summary Composition of Total Outlays for Grants to State and Local Governments, 1940–2001* (Washington, D.C.: Government Printing Office, 2002).
27. Martha Derthick, *Keeping the Compound Republic: Essays on American Federalism* (Washington, D.C.: Brookings Institution, 2001), 140.
28. Donald F. Kettl, ed., *The Department of Homeland Security's First Year: A Report Card* (New York: Century Foundation Report, 2004), 18, 102.
29. Samuel H. Beer, "The Modernization of American Federalism," *Publius* 3 (Fall 1973): esp. 74–79; and Beer, "Federalism," 18–19.
30. R. Douglas Arnold, "The Local Roots of Domestic Policy," in *The New Congress*, ed. Thomas E. Mann and Norman J. Ornstein (Washington, D.C.: American Enterprise Institute, 1981), 268.
31. Congressional Budget Office, *Federal Constraints on State and Local Government Actions* (Washington, D.C.: Government Printing Office, 1979).
32. *Federally Induced Costs Affecting State and Local Governments* (U.S. Advisory Commission on Intergovernmental Relations, September 1994).
33. Stephen V. Monsma, *Putting Faith in Partnerships: Welfare-to-Work in Four Cities* (Ann Arbor: University of Michigan Press, 2004). Also see Richard P. Nathan, *The "Nonprofitization" Movement as a Form of Devolution* (New York: The Nelson A. Rockefeller Institute of Government, October 1996).
34. Will Marshall, "After Dependence," *Blueprint* (January/February 2002): 18.
35. R. Kent Weaver, "Deficits and Devolution in the 104th Congress," unpublished draft paper, Washington, D.C., Brookings Institution, April 1996.
36. *The Public Perspective* (April/May 1995): 5.

Chapter 4   *American Political Culture*

1. Alexis de Tocqueville, *Democracy in America*, ed. Phillips Bradley (New York: Knopf, 1951), vol. 1, 288. (First published in 1835.)
2. Ibid., vol. 1, 319–320.
3. Ibid., 319.
4. Donald J. Devine, *The Political Culture of the United States* (Boston: Little, Brown, 1972), 185; Herbert McClosky and John Zaller, *The American Ethos: Public Attitudes Toward Capitalism and Democracy* (Cambridge: Harvard University Press, 1984), ch. 3, esp. 74–75.
5. McClosky and Zaller, *The American Ethos*, 74–77.
6. Ibid., 66.
7. Gunnar Myrdal, *An American Dilemma: The Negro Problem in Modern Democracy* (New York: Harper, 1944), intro. and ch. 1.
8. Frank R. Westie, "The American Dilemma: An Empirical Test," *American Sociological Review* 30 (August 1965): 536–537.
9. Eric L. McKitrick, "Party Politics and the Union and Confederate War Efforts," in *The American Party Systems*, ed. William Nisbet Chambers and Walter Dean Burnham, 2d ed. (New York: Oxford University Press, 1975), 117–121.
10. McClosky and Zaller, *The American Ethos*, 174.
11. Sidney Verba and Gary R. Orren, *Equality in America: The View from the Top* (Cambridge: Harvard University Press, 1985), 146–147.
12. McClosky and Zaller, *The American Ethos*, 82–84.
13. Ibid., 93, 95.
14. Verba and Orren, *Equality in America*, 74; McClosky and Zaller, *The American Ethos*, 126.
15. Verba and Orren, *Equality in America*, 72, 254.
16. Donald Kinder and David Sears, "Symbolic Racism Versus Racial Threats to the Good Life," *Journal of Personality and Social Psychology* 40 (1981): 414–431.
17. Paul M. Sniderman and Michael Gray Hagen, *Race and Inequality: A Study in American Values* (Chatham, N.J.: Chatham House, 1985), 111.
18. Ibid., 37–38.
19. Theodore Caplow and Howard M. Bahr, "Half a Century of Change in Adolescent Attitudes: A Replication of a Middletown Survey by the Lynds," *Public Opinion Quarterly* 43 (1979): 1–17, table 1.
20. Thomas J. Anton, "Policy-Making and Political Culture in Sweden," *Scandinavian Political Studies* 4 (1969): 88–100; M. Donald Hancock, *Sweden: The Politics of Post-Industrial Change* (Hinsdale, Ill.: Dryden Press, 1972); Sten Johansson, "Liberal-Democratic Theory and Political Processes," in *Readings in the Swedish Class Structure*, ed. Richard Scarse (New York: Pergamon Press, 1976); Steven J. Kelman, *Regulating America, Regulating Sweden: A Comparative Study of Occupational Safety and Health Policy* (Cambridge, Mass.: MIT Press, 1981), 118–123.
21. Lewis Austin, *Saints and Samurai: The Political Culture of American and Japanese Elites* (New Haven, Conn.: Yale University Press, 1975).
22. Gabriel Almond and Sidney Verba, *The Civic Culture* (Princeton, N.J.: Princeton University Press, 1963), 169, 185. See also Gabriel Almond and Sidney Verba, eds., *The Civic Culture Revisited* (Boston: Little, Brown, 1980).
23. Sidney Verba et al., *Voice and Equality: Civic Voluntarism in American Politics* (Cambridge: Harvard University Press, 1995), 69, 70.
24. Kenneth Newton and Pipa Norris, "Confidence in Public Institutions: Faith, Culture or Performance?," paper presented at the Annual Meeting of the American Political Science Association, Atlanta, Ga., September 1999, tables 8.1 and 8.3.
25. Paul M. Sniderman, *A Question of Loyalty* (Berkeley: University of California Press, 1981).
26. Verba and Orren, *Equality in America*, 255.
27. George Gallup, Jr., and Thomas Jones, *The Next American Spirituality: Finding God in the Twenty-First Century* (Colorado Springs, Colo.: Cook, 2000); Kenneth D. Wald, *Religion and Politics in the United States*, 3d ed. (Washington, D.C.: Congressional Quarterly Press, 1997); Samuel P. Huntington, *American Politics: The Promise of Disharmony* (Cambridge: Harvard University Press, 1981), 154–166; Seymour Martin Lipset, *The First New Nation* (New York: Doubleday Anchor Books, 1967), 170, 171.
28. Gallup and Jones, *The Next American Spirituality*, 25.
29. Ibid., 94.
30. Ram A. Cnaan et al., *The Newer Deal: Religion and Social Work in Partnership* (New York: Columbia University Press, 1999).
31. Pew Center for the People and the Press, *Religion and Politics: The Ambivalent Majority* (Washington, D.C.: Author, 2000).
32. Pew Forum on Religion and Public Life, *Lift Every Voice: A Report on Religion in American Public Life 2002* (Washington, D.C.: Author, 2001).
33. Max Weber, *The Protestant Ethic and the Spirit of Capitalism*, trans. Talcott Parsons (New York: Scribner's, 1930). (First published in 1904.)
34. Erik H. Erikson, *Childhood and Society* (New York: Norton, 1950), ch. 8.
35. The phrase "culture war" is from James Davison Hunter, *Culture Wars: The Struggle to Define America* (New York: Basic Books, 1991). This discussion draws heavily on Professor Hunter's analysis.
36. Ibid., 96–97, 116–117. See also Robert Lerner, Stanley Rotham, and S. Robert Lichter, "Christian Religious Elites," *Public Opinion* 11 (March/April 1989): 54–58.
37. Gary Orren, "Fall From Grace: The Public's Loss of Faith in Government," in Joseph Nye, Jr., Philip D. Zelikow, and David C. King, eds., *Why People Don't Trust Government* (Cambridge, MA: Harvard University Press, 1997), 77–107, and Robert J. Blendon, et al., "Changing Attitudes in America," in ibid., 205–216.
38. Ibid.
39. The Gallup Organization, *Poll Releases* (June 19, 1997), 3–6.

40. Samuel H. Barnes and Max Kaase, eds., *Political Action: Mass Participation in Five Democracies* (Beverly Hills, Calif.: Sage, 1979), 541–542, 574.

41. Marc J. Hetherington, "The Effect of Political Trust on the Presidential Vote, 1968–96," *American Political Science Review*, 93 (June 1999): 311–327.

42. James W. Prothro and Charles M. Grigg, "Fundamental Principles of Democracy: Bases of Agreement and Disagreement," *Journal of Politics* 22 (Spring 1960): 275–294.

43. James A. Davis, "Communism, Cohorts, and Categories: American Tolerance in 1954 and 1972–1973," *American Journal of Sociology* 81 (1975): 491–513; and Clyde A. Nunn, Harry J. Crockett, Jr., and J. Allen Williams, Jr., *Tolerance for Nonconformity: A National Survey of Changing Commitment to Civil Liberties* (San Francisco: Jossey-Bass, 1978). But compare the different conclusion in John L. Sullivan, James Piereson, and George E. Marcus, *Political Tolerance and American Democracy* (Chicago: University of Chicago Press, 1982).

44. See, for example, John L. Sullivan, James Piereson, and George F. Marcus, *Political Tolerance and American Democracy* (Chicago: University of Chicago Press, 1982), 194–202.

Chapter 5 *Civil Liberties*

1. *Zamora v. Pomeroy*, 639 F.2d 662 (1981); *Goss v. Lopez*, 419 U.S. 565 (1975); *Tinker v. Des Moines Community School District*, 393 U.S. 503 (1969); *Smith v. Goguen*, 415 U.S. 566 (1974); *New Jersey v. T.L.O.*, 469 U.S. 325 (1985).

2. *Sheppard v. Maxwell*, 384 U.S. 333 (1966); *New York Times Co. v. United States*, 403 U.S. 713 (1971); *Kunz v. New York*, 340 U.S. 290 (1951).

3. *Barron v. Baltimore*, 7 Pet. 243 (1833).

4. *Chicago, Burlington, and Quincy Railroad Co. v. Chicago*, 166 U.S. 226 (1987); *Gitlow v. New York*, 268 U.S. 652 (1925).

5. *Palko v. Connecticut*, 302 U.S. 319 (1937).

6. William Blackstone, *Commentaries*, vol. 4 (1765), 151–152.

7. Jefferson's remarks are from a letter to Abigail Adams (quoted in Walter Berns, *The First Amendment and the Future of American Democracy* [New York: Basic Books, 1976], 82 and from a letter to Thomas McKean, governor of Pennsylvania, February 19, 1803 (Paul L. Ford, ed., *The Writings of Thomas Jefferson: 1801–1806*, vol. 8 [New York: Putnam, 1897], 218.

8. *Schenck v. United States*, 249 U.S. 47 (1919), 52.

9. *Gitlow v. New York*, 268 U.S. 652 (1925), 666.

10. *Fiske v. Kansas*, 274 U.S. 380 (1927); *Stromberg v. California*, 283 U.S. 359 (1931); *Near v. Minnesota*, 283 U.S. 697 (1931); *De Jonge v. Oregon*, 299 U.S. 353 (1937).

11. *Dennis v. United States*, 341 U.S. 494 (1951), 510ff. The test was first formulated by Judge Learned Hand of the court of appeals: see *Dennis v. United States*, 183 F.2d 201 (1950), 212.

12. *Yates v. United States*, 354 U.S. 298 (1957).

13. *Brandenburg v. Ohio*, 395 U.S. 444 (1969).

14. *Village of Skokie v. National Socialist Party*, 432 U.S. 43 (1977); 366 N.E.2d 349 (1977); and 373 N.E.2d 21 (1978).

15. *R.A.V. v. City of St. Paul*, 112 S. Ct. 2538 (1992).

16. *Wisconsin v. Mitchell*, No. 92–515 (1993).

17. C. Herman Pritchett, *Constitutional Civil Liberties* (Englewood Cliffs, N.J.: Prentice-Hall, 1984), 100.

18. *New York Times v. Sullivan*, 376 U.S. 254 (1964); but compare *Time, Inc. v. Firestone*, 424 U.S. 448 (1976).

19. Henry J. Abraham, *Freedom and the Court*, 4th ed. (New York: Oxford University Press, 1982), 193, fn 189.

20. Justice Stewart's famous remark was made in his concurring opinion in *Jacobellis v. Ohio*, 378 U.S. 184 (1964), 197.

21. *Miller v. California*, 413 U.S. 15 (1973).

22. *Jenkins v. Georgia*, 418 U.S. 153 (1974).

23. *Schad v. Borough of Mt. Ephraim*, 452 U.S. 61 (1981).

24. *Barnes v. Glen Theatre*, 111 S. Ct. 2456 (1991).

25. *American Booksellers Association v. Hudnut*, 771 F.2d 323 (1985), affirmed at 475 U.S. 1001 (1986).

26. *Renton v. Playtime Theatres*, 475 U.S. 41 (1986). See also *Young v. American Mini-Theatres, Inc.*, 427 U.S. 50 (1976).

27. *Reno v. American Civil Liberties Union*, 521 U.S. 844 (1997); *Ashcroft v. Free Speech Coalition*, 122 S. Ct. 1389 (2002).

28. *United States v. O'Brien*, 391 U.S. 367 (1968).

29. *Texas v. Johnson*, 109 S. Ct. 2533 (1989).

30. *U.S. v. Eichman*, 496 U.S. 310 (1990).

31. *First National Bank of Boston v. Bellotti*, 435 U.S. 765 (1978); *Federal Election Commission v. Massachusetts Citizens for Life, Inc.*, 479 U.S. 238 (1986).

32. *44 Liquormart v. Rhode Island*, 517 U.S. 484 (1996); *Greater New Orleans Broadcasting Association v. United States*, 527 U.S. 173 (1999).

33. *Pacific Gas and Electric Co. v. Public Utilities Commission*, 475 U.S. 1 (1986). Some limitations on corporate speech have been upheld, including a state law prohibiting a firm from spending money on candidates for elective office. *Austin v. Michigan Chamber of Commerce*, 100 S. Ct. 1391 (1990).

34. *Board of Trustees of the State University of New York v. Fox*, 492 U.S. 469 (1989).

35. *Bates v. State Bar of Arizona*, 433 U.S. 350 (1977); *Edenfield v. Bane*, 113 S. Ct. 1792 (1993).

36. *McConnell v. Federal Election Commission*, 124 S. Ct. 619 (2003).

37. *Hazelwood School District v. Kuhlmeier, et al.*, 484 U.S. 260 (1988).

38. *Murdock v. Pennsylvania*, 319 U.S. 105 (1943).

39. *Church of the Lukumi Babalu Aye v. City of Hialeah*, No. 91–948 (1993).

40. *Reynolds v. United States*, 98 U.S. 145 (1878).

41. *Jacobson v. Massachusetts*, 197 U.S. 11 (1905).

42. *Employment Division, Department of Human Resources of Oregon v. Smith*, 110 S. Ct. 1595 (1990).

43. *Society for Krishna Consciousness v. Lee*, 112 S. Ct. 2701 (1992).

44. *Welsh v. United States*, 398 U.S. 333 (1970); Pritchett, *Constitutional Civil Liberties*, 140–141.

45. *Sherbert v. Verner*, 374 U.S. 398 (1963); *Wisconsin v. Yoder*, 406 U.S. 205 (1972); *Hobbie v. Unemployment Appeals Commission of Florida*, 480 U.S. 136 (1987); *Estate of Thornton v. Caldor, Inc.*, 472 U.S. 703 (1985).

46. Berns, *The First Amendment*.

47. Pritchett, *Constitutional Civil Liberties*, 145–147.

48. *Everson v. Board of Education*, 330 U.S. 1 (1947).

49. *Engel v. Vitale*, 370 U.S. 421 (1962).

50. *Lubbock Independent School District v. Lubbock Civil Liberties Union*, 669 F.2d 1038.

51. *School District of Abington Township v. Schempp*, 374 U.S. 203 (1963).

52. *Lee v. Weisman*, 112 S. Ct. 2649 (1992); *Santa Fe Independent School District v. Jane Doe*, 530 U.S. 290 (2000).

53. *Epperson v. Arkansas*, 393 U.S. 97 (1968); *McLean v. Arkansas Board of Education*, 529 F. Supp. 1255 (1982).

54. *McCollum v. Board of Education*, 333 U.S. 203 (1948); *Zorach v. Clauson*, 343 U.S. 306 (1952).

55. *Tilton v. Richardson*, 403 U.S. 672 (1971).

56. *Board of Education v. Allen*, 392 U.S. 236 (1968).

57. *Walz v. Tax Commission*, 397 U.S. 664 (1970).

58. *Mueller v. Allen*, 463 U.S. 388 (1983).

59. *Zobrest v. Catalina Foothills School District*, 509 U.S. 1 (1993); *Mitchell v. Helms*, 2000 Lexis 4485.

60. *Lemon v. Kurtzman*, 403 U.S. 602 (1971).

61. *Committee for Public Education v. Nyquist*, 413 U.S. 756 (1973).

62. *Meek v. Pittenger*, 421 U.S. 349 (1975); *Wolman v. Walter*, 433 U.S. 229 (1977).

63. *Edwards v. Aguillard*, 482 U.S. 578 (1987); *Board of Education of Kiryas Joel Village School v. Louis Grumet*, 114 S. Ct. 2481 (1994).

64. *Agostini v. Felton*, 521 U.S. 203 (1997) overruled *Aguilar v. Felton*, 473 U.S. 402 (1985).

65. *Zelman v. Simmons-Harris*, 536 U.S. 639 (2002).

66. *Lemon v. Kurtzman*, 403 U.S. 602 (1971).

67. *Lynch v. Donelly*, 465 U.S. 668 (1984); *Allegheny v. ACLU*, 109 S. Ct. 3086 (1989).

68. *Marsh v. Chambers*, 492 U.S. 573 (1983).

69. Yale Kamisar, "Does (Did) (Should) the Exclusionary Rule Rest on a 'Principled Basis' Rather Than an 'Empirical Proposition'?" *Creighton Law Review* 16 (1982–1983): 565–667.

70. *Wolf v. Colorado*, 338 U.S. 25 (1949).

71. *Mapp v. Ohio*, 367 U.S. 643 (1961).

72. *Chimel v. California*, 395 U.S. 752 (1969).

73. *Washington v. Chrisman*, 455 U.S. 1 (1982).

74. *Oliver v. United States*, 466 U.S. 170 (1984).

75. *Arkansas v. Sanders*, 442 U.S. 753 (1979); *Robbins v. California*, 453 U.S. 420 (1981).

76. *United States v. Ross*, 456 U.S. 798 (1982); *Maryland v. Dyson*, 199 S. Ct. 2013 (1999); *Wyoming v. Houghton*, 119 S. Ct. 1297 (1999); *Whren v. United States*, 517 U.S. 806 (1996).

77. *Winston v. Lee*, 470 U.S. 753 (1985).

78. *South Dakota v. Neville*, 459 U.S. 553 (1983); *Schmerber v. California*, 384 U.S. 757 (1966).

79. *United States v. Dunn*, 480 U.S. 294 (1987); *California v. Ciraolo*, 476 U.S. 207 (1986); *California v. Carney*, 471 U.S. 386 (1985).

80. *O'Connor v. Ortega*, 480 U.S. 709 (1987).

81. *Escobedo v. Illinois*, 378 U.S. 478 (1964); *Miranda v. Arizona*, 384 U.S. 436 (1966).

82. *Malloy v. Hogan*, 378 U.S. 1 (1964).

83. *Miranda v. Arizona*, 384 U.S. 436 (1966).

84. *Gilbert v. California*, 388 U.S. 263 (1967); *Kirby v. Illinois*, 406 U.S. 682 (1972).

85. *Estelle v. Smith*, 451 U.S. 454 (1981).

86. *Brewer v. Williams*, 430 U.S. 387 (1977).

87. *Illinois v. Perkins*, 496 U.S. 292 (1990).

88. *Missouri v. Seibert*, 02-1317 (2004).

89. *Dickerson v. U.S.*, 120 S. Ct. 2826 (2000).

90. *Fare v. Michael C.*, 442 U.S. 707 (1979).

91. *United States v. Leon*, 468 U.S. 897 (1984); *Massachusetts v. Sheppard*, 468 U.S. 981 (1984).

92. *New York v. Quarles*, 467 U.S. 649 (1984); *Arizona v. Fulminante*, 111 S. Ct. 1246 (1991).

93. *Nix v. Williams*, 467 U.S. 431 (1984).

94. Ex parte *Quirin*, 317 U.S. 1 (1942).

95. *Rasul v. Bush*, 03-334 (2004).

96. *Hamdi v. Rumsfeld*, 03-6696 (2004).

Chapter 6   *Civil Rights*

1. *United States v. Carolene Products Co.*, 304 U.S. 144 (1938); *San Antonio Independent School District v. Rodriguez*, 411 U.S. 1 (1973).

2. Gunnar Myrdal, *An American Dilemma* (New York: Harper, 1944), ch. 27.

3. Richard Kluger, *Simple Justice* (New York: Random House/Vintage Books, 1977), 89–90.

4. Paul B. Sheatsley, "White Attitudes Toward the Negro," in *The Negro American*, ed. Talcott Parsons and Kenneth B. Clark (Boston: Houghton Mifflin, 1966), 305, 308, 317.

5. *Strauder v. West Virginia*, 100 U.S. 303 (1880).

6. *Civil Rights Cases*, 109 U.S. 3 (1883).

7. *Plessy v. Ferguson*, 163 U.S. 537 (1896).

8. *Cumming v. Richmond County Board of Education*, 175 U.S. 528 (1899).

9. *Missouri ex rel. Gaines v. Canada*, 305 U.S. 337 (1938).

10. *Sipuel v. Board of Regents of the University of Oklahoma*, 332 U.S. 631 (1948).

11. *Sweatt v. Painter*, 339 U.S. 629 (1950); *McLaurin v. Oklahoma State Regents for Higher Education*, 339 U.S. 637 (1950).

12. *Brown v. Board of Education of Topeka*, 347 U.S. 483 (1954).

13. *Brown v. Board of Education of Topeka*, 349 U.S. 294 (1955). This case is often referred to as "Brown II."

14. Frederick S. Mosteller and Daniel P. Moynihan, eds., *On Equality of Educational Opportunity* (New York: Random House, 1972), 60–62.

15. *Brown v. Board of Education of Topeka*, 347 U.S. 483 (1954).

16. C. Herman Pritchett, *Constitutional Civil Liberties* (Englewood Cliffs, N.J.: Prentice-Hall, 1984), 250–251, 261.

17. *Green et al. v. County School Board of New Kent County*, 391 U.S. 430 (1968).

18. *Swann v. Charlotte-Mecklenburg Board of Education*, 402 U.S. 1 (1971).

19. Busing *within* the central city was upheld in *Armour v. Nix*, 446 U.S. 930 (1980); *Keyes v. School District No. 1*, Denver, 413 U.S. 189 (1973); *Milliken v. Bradley*, 418 U.S. 717 (1974); *Board of School Commissioners of Indianapolis v. Buckley*, 429 U.S. 1068 (1977); and *School Board of Richmond v. State Board of Education*, 412 U.S. 92 (1972). Busing *across* city lines was upheld in *Evans v. Buchanan*, 423 U.S. 963 (1975), and *Board of Education v. Newburg Area Council*, 421 U.S. 931 (1975).

20. *Pasadena City Board of Education v. Spangler*, 427 U.S. 424 (1976).

21. See, for example, Herbert McClosky and John Zaller, *The American Ethos* (Cambridge: Harvard University Press, 1984), 92, 100; and data reported in Chapter 5 of this text.

22. NES, *1952–1990 Cumulative Data File, 1992 NES Pre/Post Election Study* (1992).

23. *Freeman v. Pitts*, 112 S. Ct. 1430 (1992).

24. Robert S. Erikson and Norman R. Luttbeg, *American Public Opinion* (New York: Wiley, 1973), 49; Hazel Erskine, "The Polls: Demonstrations and Race Riots," *Public Opinion Quarterly* 31 (Winter 1967–1968): 654–677.

25. Howard Schuman, Charlotte Steeh, and Lawrence Bobo, *Racial Attitudes in America* (Cambridge: Harvard University Press, 1985), 69, 78–79.

26. Ibid., 102, 110, 127–135.

27. *Grove City College v. Bell*, 465 U.S. 555 (1984).

28. *United States v. Armstrong*, 116 S. Ct. 1480 (1996).

29. *Promoting Cooperative Strategies to Reduce Racial Profiling: A Technical Guide*, chap. 9 (Santa Monica, CA: RAND, April 2004).

30. *Mueller v. Oregon*, 208 U.S. 412 (1908).

31. Equal Pay Act of 1963; Civil Rights Act of 1964, Title VII, and 1978 amendments thereto; Education Amendments of 1972, Title IX.

32. *Reed v. Reed*, 404 U.S. 71 (1971).

33. *Frontiero v. Richardson*, 411 U.S. 677 (1973).

34. *Stanton v. Stanton*, 421 U.S. 7 (1975).

35. *Craig v. Boren*, 429 U.S. 190 (1976).

36. *Dothard v. Rawlinson*, 433 U.S. 321 (1977).

37. *Cleveland Board of Education v. LaFleur*, 414 U.S. 632 (1974).

38. *Fortin v. Darlington Little League*, 514 F.2d 344 (1975).

39. *Roberts v. United States Jaycees*, 468 U.S. 609 (1984); *Board of Directors Rotary International v. Rotary Club of Duarte*, 481 U.S. 537 (1987).

40. *Arizona Governing Committee for Tax Deferred Annuity and Deferred Compensation Plans v. Norris*, 463 U.S. 1073 (1983).

41. *E.E.O.C. v. Madison Community Unit School District No. 12*, 818 F.2d 577 (1987).

42. *Michael M. v. Superior Court*, 450 U.S. 464 (1981).

43. *Vorchheimer v. School District of Philadelphia*, 430 U.S. 703 (1977).

44. *Kahn v. Shevin*, 416 U.S. 351 (1974).

45. *Schlesinger v. Ballard*, 419 U.S. 498 (1975).

46. *Bennett v. Dyer's Chop House*, 350 F. Supp. 153 (1972); *Morris v. Michigan State Board of Education*, 472 F.2d 1207 (1973); *Fitzgerald v. Porter Memorial Hospital*, 523 F.2d 716 (1975); *Kruzel v. Podell*, 226 N.W.2d 458 (1975).

47. *United States v. Virginia*, 116 S. Ct. 2264 (1996).

48. *Rostker v. Goldberg*, 453 U.S. 57 (1981).

49. *Gebser v. Lago Vista School District*, 118 S. Ct. 1989 (1998); *Faragher v. Boca Raton*, 118 S. Ct. 2275 (1998); *Burlington Industries v. Ellerth*, 118 S. Ct. 2257 (1998).

50. *Griswold v. Connecticut*, 381 U.S. 479 (1965).

51. *Roe v. Wade*, 410 U.S. 113 (1973).

52. Though the constitutionality of the Hyde Amendment was upheld in *Harris v. McRae*, 448 U.S. 297 (1980), other limitations on access to abortions were struck down in *Planned Parenthood Federation of Central Missouri v. Danforth*, 428 U.S. 52 (1976); *Akron v. Akron Center for Reproductive Health*, 462 U.S. 416 (1983); and *Thornburgh v. American College of Obstetricians and Gynecologists*, 476 U.S. 747 (1986).

53. *Planned Parenthood v. Casey*, 112 S. Ct. 2791 (1992).

54. *Schenck v. Pro-Choice Network of Western New York*, 519 U.S. 357 (1997).

55. For an argument in support of a color-blind Constitution, see Andrew Kull, *The Color-Blind Constitution* (Cambridge: Harvard University Press, 1992).

56. *Regents of the University of California v. Bakke*, 438 U.S. 265 (1978).

57. *Fullilove v. Klutznick*, 448 U.S. 448 (1980).

58. *City of Richmond v. J.A. Croson Co.*, 488 U.S. 469 (1989).

59. *Metro Broadcasting v. FCC*, 497 U.S. 547 (1990).

60. *Northeastern Florida Contractors v. Jacksonville*, No. 91–1721 (1993).

61. *Firefighters Local Union No. 1784 v. Stotts*, 467 U.S. 561 (1984); *Wygant v. Jackson Board of Education*, 476 U.S. 267 (1986); *City of Richmond v. J.A. Croson Co.*, 488 U.S. 469 (1989).

62. *Local No. 28 of the Sheet Metal Workers' International Association v. Equal Employment Opportunity Commission*, 478 U.S. 421 (1986); *Wards Cove Packing Co. v. Atonio*, 490 U.S. 642 (1989); *Price Waterhouse v. Hopkins*, 490 U.S. 228 (1989). (Note: *Wards Cove* and *Price* were both superseded in part by the Civil Rights Act of 1991.)

63. *Fullilove v. Klutznick*, 448 U.S. 448 (1980); *Metro Broadcasting v. FCC*, 497 U.S. 547 (1990).

64. *United Steelworkers of America v. Weber*, 443 U.S. 193 (1979); *Johnson v. Santa Clara County Transportation Agency*, 480 U.S. 616 (1987).

65. *Wygant v. Jackson Board of Education*, 476 U.S. 267 (1986); *U.S. v. Paradise*, 480 U.S. 149 (1987).

66. Seymour Martin Lipset and William Schneider, "An Emerging National Consensus," *The New Republic* (October 15, 1977): 8–9.

67. John R. Bunzel. "Affirmative Re-Actions," *Public Opinion* (February/March 1986): 45–49; *New York Times* (December 14, 1997).

68. *Adarand Constructors v. Pena*, 515 U.S. 200 (1995).

69. *Hopwood v. Texas*, 78 F. 3d 932 (1996).

70. *Gratz v. Bollinger*, 539 U.S. 244 (2003).

71. *Grutter v. Bollinger*, 539 U.S. 306 (2003).

72. *Bowers v. Hardwick*, 478 U.S. 186 (1986).

73. *Romer v. Evans*, 517 U.S. 620 (1996).

74. *Lawrence v. Texas*, 539 U.S. 558 (2003).

75. *Goodridge v. Department of Public Health*, 440 Mass. 309 (2003) and 440 Mass. 1201 (2004).

76. *Boy Scouts of America v. Dale*, 530 U.S. 640 (2000).

Chapter 7 *Public Opinion*

1. George W. Bishop, Alfred J. Tuchfarber, and Robert W. Oldendick, "1984: How Much Can We Manipulate and Control People's Answers to Public Opinion Surveys?" paper delivered at the 1984 annual meeting of the American Political Science Association; Howard Schuman and S. Presser, *Questions and Answers in Attitude Surveys* (New York: Academic Press, 1981), ch. 5.

2. For example, see Bernard Berelson et al., *Voting: A Study of Opinion Formation in a Presidential Campaign* (Chicago: University of Chicago Press, 1954), and Phillip E. Converse, "The Nature of Belief Systems in Mass Publics," in *Ideology and Discontent*, ed. David E. Apter (New York: Free Press, 1964).

3. For example, see V. O. Key, *The Responsible Electorate* (Cambridge: Harvard University Press, 1966); Samuel Popkin, *The Reasoning Voter: Communication and Persuasion in Presidential Campaigns* (Chicago: University of Chicago Press, 1991); Benjamin I. Page and Robert Y. Shapiro, *The Rational Public: Fifty Years of Trends in Americans' Policy Preferences* (Chicago: University of Chicago Press, 1991).

4. Terry M. Moe, *Schools, Vouchers, and the American Public* (Washington, D.C.: Brookings Institution, 2001), 253.

5. Ibid.

6. Michael W. Traugott, "Can We Trust the Polls?" *The Brookings Review* (Summer 2003): 9.

7. M. Kent Jennings and Richard G. Niemi, "The Transmission of Political Values from Parent to Child," *American Political Science Review* 62 (March 1968): 173; Robert D. Hess and Judith V. Tomey, *The Development of Political Attitudes in Children* (Chicago: Aldine, 1967), 90.

8. Several studies of child-parent agreement on party preference are summarized in David O. Sears, "Political Behavior," in *The Handbook of Social Psychology*, ed. Gardner Lindzey and Elliot Aronson, 2d ed. (Reading, Mass.: Addison-Wesley, 1969), vol. 5, 376.

9. Norman H. Nie, Sidney Verba, and John R. Petrocik, *The Changing American Voter* (Cambridge: Harvard University Press, 1976), ch. 4.

10. Karen M. Kaufman and John R. Petrocik, "The Changing Politics of American Men: Understanding the Sources of the Gender Gap," *American Journal of Political Science* 43 (1999): 864–887.

11. National Election Studies, University of Michigan. Updated by Marc Siegal, 2005.

12. Steve Saler, "Analysis: The Voting Gender Gap Narrows," United Press International (www.upi.com), November 20, 2003, based on election night surveys of 17,872 voters.

13. Alexander M. Astin, *Four Critical Years: Effects of College on Beliefs, Attitudes, and Knowledge* (San Francisco: Josey-Bass, 1978), 36–38.

14. Terry S. Weiner and Bruce K. Eckland, "Education and Political Party: The Effects of College or Social Class?" *American Journal of Sociology* 84 (1979): 911–928.

15. Kenneth Heineman, *Put Your Bodies Upon the Wheels: Student Revolt in the 1960s* (Chicago: Ivan R. Dee, 2001), 62.

16. Elizabeth Hamel et al., "Younger Voters: Age and the American Electorate," *Public Perspective* (May/June 1993): 13.

17. Russell Jacoby, *Dogmatic Wisdom: How the Culture Wars Divert Education and Distract America* (New York: Doubleday, 1994), 3; and William Korn, *The American Freshman: Twenty Year Trends, 1966–1985* (Los Angeles: Higher Education Institute, 1987), as cited in Kevin Matson, *Engaging Youth: Combating the Apathy of Young Americans Toward Politics* (New York: The Century Foundation Press, 2003), 18, 57.

18. Robert Putnam et al., *Better Together: Final Report of the Saguaro Seminar* (Cambridge: John F. Kennedy School of Government, 2001), 77–78; and Sidney Verba et al., *Voice and Equality: Civic Voluntarism in American Politics* (Cambridge: Harvard University Press, 1995), 420.

19. Jane Eisner, *Taking Back the Vote: Getting American Youth Involved in Our Democracy* (Boston: Beacon Press, 2004), chs. 5 and 6.

20. John Zaller, "Information, Values, and Opinion," *American Political Science Review* 85 (1991): 1215–1238.

21. Stephen Earl Bennett, "Young Americans' Indifference to Media Coverage of Public Affairs," *PS: Political Science* (Summer 1998): 535–541.

22. Kay Lehman Schlozman and Sidney Verba, *Insult to Injury: Unemployment, Class, and Political Response* (Cambridge: Harvard University Press, 1979), 115–118; and David Butler and Donald E. Stokes, *Political Change in Great Britain* (New York: St. Martin's Press, 1969), 70, 77.

23. V. O. Key, Jr., *Public Opinion and American Democracy* (New York: Knopf, 1961), 122–138.

24. Richard E. Dawson, *Public Opinion and Contemporary Disarray* (New York: Harper & Row, 1973), ch. 4.

25. David A. Bositis, *Public Opinion 1998: Political Attitudes* (Washington, D.C.: Joint Center for Political and Economic Studies (October 1998), table 18A.

26. *The American Enterprise* (November/December 1998): 91, reporting data from a *Time/CNN* survey, August 1997.

27. David A. Bositis, foreword by Eddie N. Williams, *Dividing Generations: The Transformation of African American Policy Views* (Washington, D.C.: Joint Center for Political and Economic Studies, 2001).

28. Bruce Cain and Roderick Kiewiet, "California's Coming Minority Majority" *Public Opinion* (February/March 1986): 50–52.

29. Lisa J. Montoya et al., "Latina Politics: Gender, Participation, and Leadership," *PS: Political Science and Politics* 33 (September 2000): 557.

30. Cain and Kiewiet, "California's Coming Minority Majority," 50–52.

31. F. Chris Garcia et al., "The Effects of Ethnic Partisanship on Electoral Behavior: An Analysis and Comparison of Latino and Anglo Voting in the 1988 United States Presidential Election," paper delivered at the Annual Meeting of the American Political Science Association, September 3–6, 1992.

32. Michael Barone, "We've Been Here Before: Ethnicity and America, 1900 and 2000," Bradley Lecture, American Enterprise Institute, October 4, 1999, 21, 22.

33. Nie, Verba, and Petrocik, *The Changing American Voter*, 247–250.

34. ICPSR National Election Studies, Cumulative Data File, 1952–1996.

35. *The American Enterprise* (January/February 1999): 51, citing surveys by CBS/*New York Times*.

36. Philip E. Converse, "The Nature of Belief Systems in Mass Publics," in *Ideology and Discontent*, ed. David Apter (Glencoe, Ill.: Free Press, 1964), 206–261.

37. Christopher H. Achen, "Mass Political Attitudes and the Survey Response," *American Political Science Review* 69 (December 1975): 1218–1231.

38. Seymour Martin Lipset and Earl Raab, *The Politics of Unreason* (New York: Harper & Row, 1970), ch. 11; James A. Stimson, "Belief Systems: Constraint, Complexity, and the 1972 Election," *American Journal of Political Science* 19 (1975): 393–417; and Herbert McClosky and John Zaller, *The American Ethos* (Cambridge: Harvard University Press, 1984), ch. 8.

39. William S. Maddox and Stuart A. Lilie, *Beyond Liberal and Conservative* (Washington, D.C.: Cato Institute, 1984), 5, 68, 96, 104.

40. Zaller, "Information," and Stimson, "Belief Systems." See also Allen H. Barton and R. Wayne Parsons, "Measuring Belief System Structures," *Public Opinion Quarterly* 41 (1977): 159–180.

41. Gary C. Jacobson, "The Electoral Basis of Partisan Polarization in Congress," paper delivered at the annual meeting of the American Political Science Association, August 31–September 3, 2000.

42. Larry M. Bartels, "Partisanship and Voting Behavior, 1952–1996," *American Journal of Political Science* 44 (2000): 35–50.

43. Melissa P. Collie and John Lyman Mason, "The Electoral Connection Between Party and Constituency Reconsidered: Evidence from the U.S. House of Representatives, 1972–1994," in *Continuity and Change in House Elections*, ed. David W. Brady et al. (Stanford, Calif.: Hoover Institution, 2000).

44. John Zaller, *The Nature and Origins of Mass Opinion* (Cambridge: Cambridge University Press, 1992).

45. Lawrence R. Jacobs and Robert Y. Shapiro, "Debunking the Myth of the Pandering Politician," *The Public Perspective* (April/May 1997): 3–5.

Chapter 8   *Political Participation*

1. David Glass, Peverill Squire, and Raymond Wolfinger, "Voter Turnout: An International Comparison," *Public Opinion* (December/January 1984): 49–55. See also G. Bingham Powell, Jr., "Voting Turnout in Thirty Democracies: Partisan, Legal, and Socio-Economic Influences," in *Electoral Participation: A Comparative Analysis*, ed. Richard Rose (Beverly Hills, Calif.: Sage Publications, 1980).

2. Donald P. Green and Alan S. Gerber, *Get Out the Vote!: How to Increase Voter Turnout* (Washington, D.C.: Brookings Institution, 2004).

3. Ibid., 92.

4. Raymond E. Wolfinger and Jonathan Hoffman, "Registering and Voting with Motor Voter," *PS: Political Science and Politics*, 34 (March 2001): 90.

5. Morton Keller, *Affairs of State* (Cambridge: Harvard University Press, 1977), 523.

6. *United States v. Reese*, 92 U.S. 214 (1876); *United States v. Cruikshank*, 92 U.S. 556 (1876); and *Ex parte Yarbrough*, 110 U.S. 651 (1884).

7. *Guinn and Beall v. United States*, 238 U.S. 347 (1915).

8. *Smith v. Allwright*, 321 U.S. 649 (1944).

9. *Schnell v. Davis*, 336 U.S. 933 (1949).

10. Jane Eisner, *Taking Back the Vote: Getting American Youth Involved in Our Democracy* (Boston: Beacon, 2004), 49.

11. Kevin Matson, *Engaging Youth: Combatting the Apathy of Young Americans Toward Politics* (New York: Century Foundation Press, 2003), 2, 4; and 2002 figures from U.S. Bureau of Census data compiled by Marc Siegal.

12. Robert Putnam et al., *Better Together: Final Support of the Saguaro Seminar* (Cambridge, Mass.: John F. Kennedy School of Government, Harvard University, 2001), 77; Eisner, *Taking Back the Vote*, ch. 5.

13. Paul Wellstone, quoted in Elizabeth Crowley, "More Young People Turn Away from Politics," *Wall Street Journal* (June 16, 1999).

14. Putnam et al., *Better Together*; Eisner, *Taking Back the Vote*; and Matson, *Engaging Youth*.

15. *Historical Statistics of the United States: Colonial Times to 1970*, part 2, 1071–1072.

16. Walter Dean Burnham, "The Changing Shape of the American Political Universe," *American Political Science Review* 59 (March 1965): 11; and William H. Flanigan and Nancy H. Zingale, *Political Behavior of the American Electorate*, 3d ed. (Boston: Allyn and Bacon, 1975), 15.

17. Burnham, "Changing Shape;" E. E. Schattschneider, *The Semisovereign People* (New York: Holt, Rinehart and Winston, 1960), chs. 5, 6.

18. Philip E. Converse, "Change in the American Electorate," in *The Human Meaning of Social Change*, ed. Angus Campbell and Philip E. Converse (New York: Russell Sage Foundation, 1972), 263–338.

19. Michael P. McDonald and Samuel L. Popkin, "The Myth of the Vanishing Voter," *American Political Science Review* 95 (December 2001): table 1, 966.

20. Ibid.

21. Raymond Wolfinger and Benjamen Highton, "What If They Gave an Election and Everyone Came?" Public Affairs Report, Institute of Governmental Studies, University of California at Berkeley, June 1999, 11–13.

22. Ibid., 13.

23. Ibid.

24. Sidney Verba and Norman H. Nie, *Participation in America* (New York: Harper & Row, 1972), 30. See also Aage R. Clausen, "Response Validity: Vote Report," *Public Opinion Quarterly*, 32 (1968–1969): 588–606.

25. Michael W. Traugott and John P. Katosh, "Response Validity in Surveys of Voting Behavior," *Public Opinion Quarterly* 43 (1979): 359–377; Aage R. Clausen, "Response Validity: Vote Report," *Public Opinion Quarterly* 32 (1969): 588–606.

26. Sidney Verba et al., *Voice and Equality: Civic Voluntarism in American Politics* (Cambridge: Harvard University Press, 1995), 79.

27. Ibid., 77.

28. Verba and Nie, *Participation in America*, ch. 6.

29. Lester W. Milbrath and M. I. Goel, *Political Participation*, 2d ed. (Chicago: Rand McNally, 1977); Raymond E. Wolfinger and Steven J. Rosenstone, *Who Votes?* (New Haven, Conn.: Yale University Press, 1980); W. Russell Neuman, *The Paradox of Mass Voting* (Cambridge: Harvard University Press, 1986), ch. 4.

30. Wolfinger and Rosenstone, *Who Votes?*, esp. 102, and John P. Katosh and Michael W. Traugott, "Costs and Values in the Calculus of Voting," *American Journal of Political Science* 26 (1982): 361–376.

31. David C. Leege and Lyman A Kellstedt, *Rediscovering the Religious Factor in American Politics* (Armonk, N.Y.: M. E. Sharpe, 1993), 129–131.

32. Verba and Nie, *Participation in America* 151–157; Milbrath and Goel, *Political Participation*, 120.

33. Jack Citrin, "The Alienated Voter," *Taxing and Spending* (October 1978), 1–7; Austin Ranney, "Nonvoting Is Not a Social Disease," *Public Opinion* (October/November 1983): 16–19; Glass, Squire, and Wolfinger, "Voter Turnout."

34. *Dunn v. Blumstein*, 405 U.S. 330 (1972).

35. Wolfinger and Rosenstone, *Who Votes?*

36. Richard G. Smolka, *Election Day Registration: The Minnesota and Wisconsin Experience* (Washington, D.C.: American Enterprise Institute, 1977), 5.

37. Gary R. Orren, "The Linkage of Policy to Participation," in *Presidential Selection*, ed. Alexander Heard and Michael Nelson (Durham, N.C.: Duke University Press, 1987).

38. Glass, Squire, and Wolfinger, "Voter Turnout," 52.

39. Powell, "Voting Turnout"; Robert W. Jackman, "Political Institutions and Voter Turnout in Industrial Democracies," *American Political Science Review* 81 (1987): 405–423.

40. Roy Texeira, "Will the Real Nonvoter Please Stand Up?" *Public Opinion* (July/August 1988): 43; Texeira, "Registration and Turnout," *Public Opinion* (January/February 1989): 12.

41. Richard A. Brody, "The Puzzle of Political Participation in America," in *The New American Political System*, ed. Anthony King (Washington, D.C.: American Enterprise Institute, 1978): 315–323.

42. Richard Smolka, quoted in William J. Crotty, *Political Reform and the American Experiment* (New York: Crowell, 1977), 86–87.

43. For Japan: The Society for Promotion of Clear Elections, *Survey of 34th General Election, 1976*. See Gary Orren, "Political Participation and Public Policy: The Case for Institutional Reform," Cambridge, Mass., November 1985, 16A. For U.S. and Sweden: Samuel P. Huntington and Joan M. Nelson, *No Easy Choice* (Cambridge: Harvard University Press, 1976), 88.

44. Sidney Verba et al., "Race, Ethnicity, and the Resources for Participation: The Role of Religion," paper delivered at the 1992 annual meeting of the American Political Science Association, September 3–6, 1992.

Chapter 9   *Political Parties*

1. Leon D. Epstein, "Political Parties," in *Handbook of Political Science*, ed. Fred I. Greenstein and Nelson W. Polsby (Reading, Mass.: Addison-Wesley, 1975), vol. 4, 230.

2. Quoted in Henry Adams, *History of the United States of America During the Administrations of Jefferson and Madison*, ed. Ernest Samuels, abridged edition (Chicago: University of Chicago Press, 1967), 147.

3. Walter Dean Burnham, *Critical Elections and the Mainsprings of American Politics* (New York: Norton, 1970), 10.

4. James L. Sundquist, *Dynamics of the Party System* (Washington, D.C.: Brookings Institution, 1973), ch. 7.

5. Edward G. Carmines and James A. Stimson, "Issue Evolution, Population Replacement,

and Normal Partisan Change," *American Political Science Review* 75 (March 1981): 107–118; and Gregory Markus, "Political Attitudes in an Election Year," *American Political Science Review* 76 (September 1982): 538–560.

6. Ray Wolfinger and Michael G. Hagen, "Republican Prospects: Southern Comfort," *Public Opinion* (October/November 1985): 8–13. But compare Richard Scammon and James A. Barnes, "Republican Prospects: Southern Discomfort," *Public Opinion* (October/November 1985): 14–17.

7. Jerold G. Rusk, "The Effect of the Australian Ballot Reform on Split-Ticket Voting: 1876–1908," *American Political Science Review* 64 (December 1970): 1220–1238.

8. Morton Keller, *Affairs of State* (Cambridge: Harvard University Press, 1977), 239.

9. Quoted in Keller, ibid., 256.

10. Martin Shefter, "Parties, Bureaucracy, and Political Change in the United States," in *The Development of Political Parties*, Sage Electoral Studies Yearbook, vol. 4, ed. Louis Maisel and Joseph Cooper (Beverly Hills, Calif.: Sage, 1978).

11. James Q. Wilson, *The Amateur Democrat: Club Politics in Three Cities* (Chicago: University of Chicago Press, 1962).

12. Samuel J. Eldersveld, *Political Parties: A Behavioral Analysis* (Chicago: Rand McNally, 1964), 278, 287.

13. Robert H. Salisbury, "The Urban Party Organization Member," *Public Opinion Quarterly* 29 (Winter 1965–1966): 550–564.

14. Ibid., 557, 559.

15. Eldersveld, *Political Parties;* and J. David Greenstone, *Labor in American Politics* (New York: Knopf, 1969), 187.

16. David R. Mayhew, *Placing Parties in American Politics* (Princeton, N.J.: Princeton University Press, 1986), chs. 2, 3.

17. *Boston Globe* (July 9, 1984): 1.

18. William Nisbet Chambers and Walter Dean Burnham, eds., *The American Party Systems: Stages of Political Development*, 2d ed. (New York: Oxford University Press, 1975), 6.

19. *Williams v. Rhodes*, 393 U.S. 23 (1968).

20. James Q. Wilson, *Political Organizations* (New York: Basic Books, 1973), ch. 12; and Samuel Stouffer, *Communism, Conformity, and Civil Liberties* (Garden City, N.Y.: Doubleday, 1955).

21. Updated from Jeane Kirkpatrick, *The New Presidential Elite* (New York: Russell Sage Foundation and Twentieth Century Fund, 1976), 297–315.

22. Nelson W. Polsby, *Consequences of Party Reform* (New York: Oxford University Press, 1983), 9–11, 64.

23. Ibid., 158. But compare John G. Geer, "Voting in Presidential Primaries," paper delivered to the 1984 annual meeting of the American Political Science Association.

24. Center for the Study of the American Electorate, April 2000.

25. Michael J. Malbin, "Democratic Party Rules Are Made to Be Broken," *National Journal* (August 23, 1980): 1388.

Chapter 10 *Elections and Campaigns*

1. *Wesberry v. Sanders*, 376 U.S. 1 (1964).

2. Richard F. Fenno, Jr. "U.S. House Members and Their Constituencies: An Exploration," *American Political Science Review* 71 (September 1977): 883–917, esp. 914.

3. John A. Ferejohn, *Pork Barrel Politics* (Stanford, Calif.: Stanford University Press, 1974).

4. Douglas Arnold, *Congress and the Bureaucracy* (New Haven, Conn.: Yale University Press, 1979).

5. Fred Barnes, "Charade on Main Street," *The New Republic* (June 15, 1987): 15–17. See also Hugh Winebrenner, *The Iowa Precinct Caucuses: The Making of a Media Event* (Ames: Iowa State University Press, 1987).

6. Arthur H. Miller et al., "A Majority Party in Disarray: Policy Polarization in the 1972 Election," *American Political Science Review* 70 (1976): 757.

7. Donald E. Stokes and John J. DiIulio, Jr., "Valence Politics in Modern Elections," in *The 1992 Elections*, ed. Michael J. Nelson (Washington, D.C.: Congressional Quarterly Press, 1993), ch. 1.

8. Michael Kelley, "The Making of a First Family: A Blueprint," *New York Times* (November 14, 1992): 1, 9.

9. Ibid.

10. Thomas E. Patterson and Robert D. McClure, *The Unseeing Eye: The Myth of Television Power in National Politics* (New York: Putnam, 1976); and Xandra Kayden, *Campaign Organization* (Lexington, Mass.: D. C. Heath, 1978), ch. 6.

11. Gerald M. Pomper et al., *The Election of 1980* (Chatham, N.J.: Chatham House, 1981), 75, 105–107.

12. *Public Opinion Strategies: American Monitor* (November 2004).

13. Gary C. Jacobson, *The Politics of Congressional Elections*, 2d ed. (Boston: Little, Brown, 1987), 49.

14. Donald Philip Green and Jonathan S. Krasno, "Salvation for the Spendthrift Incumbent: Reestimating the Effects of Campaign Spending in House Elections," *American Journal of Political Science* 32 (1988): 884–960; Stephen Ansolabehre, "Winning Is Easy but It Sure Ain't Cheap," Working Paper 90–1, Center for American Politics and Public Policy, UCLA, 1990; Robert S. Erickson and Thomas R. Palfrey, "The Puzzle of Incumbent Spending in Congressional Elections," Social Science Working Paper 806, California Institute of Technology, August 1992.

15. Angus Campbell, Philip E. Converse, Warren E. Miller, and Donald E. Stokes, *The American Voter* (New York: Wiley, 1960), ch. 8.

16. V. O. Key, Jr., *The Responsible Electorate* (Cambridge: Harvard University Press, 1966).

17. Morris P. Fiorina, *Retrospective Voting in American National Elections* (New Haven, Conn.: Yale University Press, 1981).

18. Jay P. Greene, "Forewarned Before Forecast: Presidential Election Forecasting Models and the 1992 Election," *P.S.: Political Science and Politics* (March 1993): 20.

19. Paul Freedman and Ken Goldstein, "Measuring Media Exposure and the Effects of Negative Campaign Ads," *American Journal of Political Science* 43 (October 1999): 1189–1208.

20. Robert Axelrod, "Where the Votes Come From: An Analysis of Electoral Coalitions, 1952–1968," *American Political Science Review* 66 (1972): 11–20; and Axelrod, "Communication," *American Political Science Review* 68 (1974): 718–719.

21. Gerald M. Pomper, *Elections in America* (New York: Dodd, Mead, 1971), 178.

22. Benjamin Ginsberg, "Elections and Public Policy," *American Political Science Review* 70 (March 1976): 41–49.

Chapter 11 *Interest Groups*

1. L. Harmon Zeigler and Hendrik van Dalen, "Interest Groups in the States," in *Politics in the American States*, ed. Herbert Jacob and Kenneth N. Vines, 2d ed. (Boston: Little, Brown, 1974), 122–160; Edward C. Banfield and James Q. Wilson, *City Politics* (Cambridge: Harvard University Press, 1963), chs. 18, 19.

2. Joseph LaPalombara, *Interest Groups in Italian Politics* (Princeton, N.J.: Princeton University Press, 1964).

3. Kay Lehman Schlozman and John T. Tierney, "More of the Same: Washington Pressure Group Activity in a Decade of Change," *Journal of Politics* 45 (1983): 356.

4. The use of injunctions in labor disputes was restricted by the Norris-LaGuardia Act of 1932; the rights to collective bargaining and to the union shop were guaranteed by the Wagner Act of 1935.

5. *Historical Statistics of the United States, Colonial Times to 1970*, vol. 1, 386.

6. The distinction is drawn from Kay Lehman Schlozman and John T. Tierney, *Organized Interests and American Democracy* (New York: Harper and Row, 1985).

7. Jeffrey M. Berry, *The Interest Group Society* (Boston: Little, Brown, 1984), 20–21.

8. Ibid., 24, 130.

9. Gabriel A. Almond and Sidney Verba, *The Civic Culture* (Princeton, N.J.: Princeton University Press, 1963), 302; Derek C. Bok and John T. Dunlop, *Labor and the American Community* (New York: Simon and Schuster, 1970), 49; *Statistical Abstract of the United States, 1975*, 373.

10. Almond and Verba, *The Civic Culture*, 194.

11. Ibid., 207.

12. Mancur Olson, Jr., *The Logic of Collective Action* (Cambridge: Harvard University Press, 1965), 153–157.

13. Ellen Nakashima, "Study: Contracts Given to Repeat Violators," *Washington Post* (May 7, 2002): A19.
14. Bok and Dunlop, *Labor,* 134.
15. Jane J. Mansbridge, *Why We Lost the ERA* (Chicago: University of Chicago Press, 1986), ch. 10.
16. Joyce Gelb and Marian Lief Palley, *Women and Public Choices* (Princeton, N.J.: Princeton University Press, 1982), ch. 3; Jo Freeman, *The Politics of Women's Liberation* (New York: McKay, 1975), ch. 3; Maren Lockwood Carden, "The Proliferation of a Social Movement: Ideology and Individual Incentives in the Contemporary Feminist Movement," *Research in Social Movements* 1 (1978): 179–196; and Dom Bonafede, "Still a Long Way to Go," *National Journal* (September 13, 1986): 2175–2179.
17. *Statistical Abstract of the United States, 2000,* 445; Mansbridge, *Why We Lost, 130–131.*
18. Jeffrey M. Berry, *Lobbying for the People* (Princeton, N.J.: Princeton University Press, 1977), 71–76.
19. Berry, *Interest Group Society,* 88.
20. General Accounting Office (GAO), *Managing for Results* (Washington, D.C.: GAO-01-592, 2001), 10; *Unlevel Playing Field: Barriers to Participation by Faith-Based and Community Organizations in Federal Social Service Delivery Programs* (Washington, D.C.: White House Office of Faith-Based and Community Initiatives, August 2001).
21. *Unlevel Playing Field,* op. cit.
22. Ibid., and John J. DiIulio, Jr., "Government-By-Proxy: A Faithful Overview," *Harvard Law Review* 116, no. 5 (March 2003): 1274.
23. Schlozman and Tierney, *Organized Interests and American Democracy,* table 5-4.
24. *New York Times* (December 8, 1983): 1.
25. Raymond A. Bauer, Ithiel de Sola Pool, and Lewis Anthony Dexter, *American Business and Public Policy* (New York: Atherton, 1963), ch. 30.
26. Berry, *Lobbying for the People,* 136–140.
27. Margaret Ann Latus, "Assessing Ideological PACs: From Outrage to Understanding," in *Money and Politics in the United States,* ed. Michael J. Malbin (Chatham, N.J.: Chatham House, 1984), 143; data supplied by the Federal Election Commission, March 1992.
28. Latus, *Assessing,* 144.
29. Malbin, *Money and Politics,* table A.8, 290–291.
30. Michael J. Malbin, "Looking Back at the Future of Campaign Finance Reform: Interest Groups and American Elections," in Malbin, *Money and Politics,* 248; James B. Kau and Paul H. Rubin, *Congressmen, Constituents and Contributors* (Boston: Martinus Nijhoff, 1982); Henry W. Chappell, Jr., "Campaign Contributions and Voting on the Cargo Preference Bill: A Comparison of Simultaneous Models," *Public Choice* 36 (1981): 301–312; W. P. Welch, "Campaign Contributions and Voting: Milk Money and Dairy Price Supports," *Western Political Quarterly* 35 (1982): 478–495; John R. Wright, "PACs, Contributions, and Roll Calls: An Organizational Perspective," *Ameri-*

can Political Science Review 79 (1985): 400–414. But compare Benjamin Ginsberg and John C. Green, "The Best Congress Money Can Buy," in *Do Elections Matter?,* ed. Benjamin Ginsberg and Alan Stone (Armonk, N.Y.: M. E. Sharpe, 1986), 75–89.
31. William T. Gormley, "A Test of the Revolving Door Hypothesis at the FCC," *American Journal of Political Science* 23 (1979): 665–683; Paul J. Quirk, *Industry Influence in Federal Regulatory Agencies* (Princeton, N.J.: Princeton University Press, 1981); Jeffrey E. Cohen, "The Dynamics of the 'Revolving Door' on the FCC," *American Journal of Political Science* 30 (1986): 689–708.
32. Suzanne Weaver, *Decision to Prosecute* (Cambridge, Mass.: MIT Press, 1977), 154–163.
33. *United States v. Harriss,* 347 U.S. 612 (1954).
34. *United States Code,* Title 26, section 501(c)(3).

Chapter 12 *The Media*

1. Karin Deutsch Karleka, ed. *Freedom of the Press 2004* (New York: Freedom House, 2004).
2. David E. Butler, "Why American Political Reporting Is Better Than England's," *Harper's* (May 1963): 15–25.
3. *New York Times* (January 28, 1974).
4. Douglass Cater, *The Fourth Branch of Government* (Boston: Houghton Mifflin, 1959), 76; and William L. Rivers, "The Press as a Communication System," in *Handbook of Communication,* ed. Ithiel de Sola Pool et al. (Chicago: Rand McNally, 1973), 522–526.
5. Quoted in F. L. Mort, *American Journalism, 1690–1960,* 3d ed. (New York: Macmillan, 1962), 529.
6. Center for Media and Public Affairs, "The Incredible Shrinking Sound Bite," Press Release, Washington, D.C., September 28, 2000.
7. U.S. Census Bureau, *Home Computers and Internet Use in the United States: August 2000* (Washington, D.C.: Census Bureau, 2001).
8. Edward Jay Epstein, *News from Nowhere: Television and the News* (New York: Random House, 1973), 37.
9. *Near v. Minnesota,* 283 U.S. 697 (1931).
10. *New York Times v. United States,* 403 U.S. 713 (1971).
11. *New York Times v. Sullivan,* 376 U.S. 254 (1964).
12. *Miami Herald Publishing Co. v. Tornillo,* 418 U.S. 241 (1974).
13. *Yates v. United States,* 354 U.S. 298 (1957).
14. *Branzburg v. Hayes,* 408 U.S. 665 (1972).
15. *Zurcher v. Stanford Daily,* 436 U.S. 547 (1978), overturned by the Privacy Protection Act of 1980 (P.L. 96–440).
16. S. Robert Lichter, Stanley Rothman, and Linda S. Lichter, *The Media Elite* (Bethesda, Md.: Adler and Adler, 1986); Stanley Rothman and Amy Black, "Elites Revisited: American Social and Political Leadership in the 1990s," *International Journal of Public Opinion Research* 11 (1999): 169–195; William Schneider and I. A. Lewis, "Views on the News," *Public Opinion* (August/September 1985): 7.
17. Rothman and Black, "Elites Revisited," 182.

18. Ibid., 177.
19. Gallup Poll, February 2003; Pew Research Center for the People and the Press poll, July 2003.
20. William G. Mayer, "Why Talk Radio Is Conservative," *The Public Interest* (Summer 2004): 86–103.
21. David W. Brady and Jonathan Ma, "Spot the Difference," *Wall Street Journal* (November 12, 2003).
22. Lichter, Rothman, and Lichter, *Media Elite.*
23. John R. Lott, Jr., and Kevin A. Hassett, "Is Newspaper Coverage of Economic Events Politically Biased?" unpublished paper, American Enterprise Institute (September 1, 2004). See also Tim Groseclose and Jeff Milyo, "A Measure of Media Bias," unpublished paper, Department of Political Science, UCLA (September 2003).
24. David Okrent, "Is the New York Times a Liberal Newspaper?" *New York Times* (July 25, 2004).
25. David O. Sears and Richard E. Whitney, "Political Persuasion," in Pool, *Handbook of Communication,* 253–289.
26. Robert S. Erickson, "The Influence of Newspaper Endorsements in Presidential Elections: The Case of 1964," *American Journal of Political Science* 20 (May 1976): 207–233.
27. Kim Fridkin Kahn and Patrick J. Kenney, "The Slant of the News: How Editorial Endorsements Influence Campaign Coverage and Citizens' Views of Candidates," *American Political Science Review* 96 (2002): 381–394.
28. Maxwell E. McCombs and Donald R. Shaw, "The Agenda Setting Function of the Mass Media," *Public Opinion Quarterly* 36 (Summer 1972): 176–187; Shanto Iynegar and Donald R. Kinder, *News That Matters* (Chicago: University of Chicago Press, 1987).
29. G. Ray Funkhouser, "The Issues of the Sixties," *Public Opinion Quarterly* 37 (Spring 1973): 62–75.
30. Benjamin I. Page, Robert Y. Shapiro, and Glenn R. Dempsey, "What Moves Public Opinion?" *American Political Science Review* 81 (March 1987): 23–43; Benjamin I. Page, "The Media as Political Actors," *PS: Political Science and Politics* (March 1996): 21.
31. George Jergens, "Theodore Roosevelt and the Press," *Daedalus* (Fall 1982): 113–133; Henry Fairlie, "The Rise of the Press Secretary," *The New Republic* (March 18, 1978): 20–23.
32. Michael J. Robinson, "A Twentieth Century Medium in a Nineteenth Century Legislature: The Effects of Television on the American Congress," in *Congress in Change,* ed. Norman J. Ornstein (New York: Praeger, 1975): 240–261.
33. Pew Research Center for the People and the Press, "Media Seen as Fair, But Tilting to Gore," Press Release, Washington, D.C., October 15, 2000.
34. Center for Media and Public Affairs, "Public to Press: Keep in Touch!," Press Release, Washington, D.C., 1996.
35. Pew Center for the People and the Press, "Terror Coverage Boost News Media's Images," Press Release, November 28, 2001.

36. Will Lester, "Poll: Interest in News Stabilizes," *The Macon Telegraph* (June 9, 2002).

Chapter 13 *Congress*

1. Continuity of Government Commission, *Preserving Our Institutions: The Continuity of Congress* (Washington, D.C.: American Enterprise Institute and Brookings Institution, May 2003).
2. H. Douglas Price, "Careers and Committees in the American Congress," in *The History of Parliamentary Behavior*, ed. William O. Aydelotte (Princeton, N.J.: Princeton University Press, 1977), 28–62; John F. Bibby, Thomas E. Mann, and Norman J. Ornstein, *Vital Statistics on Congress, 1980* (Washington, D.C.: American Enterprise Institute, 1980), 53–54; Thomas E. Cavanaugh, "The Dispersion of Authority in the House of Representatives," *Political Science Quarterly* 97 (1982–1983): 625–626; *Congressional Quarterly Weekly Reports*.
3. David R. Mayhew, *Congress: The Electoral Connection* (New Haven, Conn.: Yale University Press, 1974); Bibby, Mann, and Ornstein, *Vital Statistics*, 14–15.
4. Mayhew, *Congress*; Morris P. Fiorina, *Congress: Keystone of the Washington Establishment* (New Haven, Conn.: Yale University Press, 1977).
5. Rhodes Cook, "House Republicans Scored a Quiet Victory in '92," *Congressional Quarterly* (April 17, 1993): 966.
6. Bruce E. Cain and David Butler, "Redrawing District Lines: What's Going On and What's at Stake," *The American Enterprise* (July/August 1991): 37.
7. Walter Dean Burnham, as quoted in Fred Barnes, "Realignment, Now More Than Ever," *The Weekly Standard* (November 22, 2004): 11.
8. Warren E. Miller and Donald E. Stokes, "Constituency Influence in Congress," in *Elections and the Political Order*, ed. Angus Campbell et al. (New York: Wiley, 1966), 359.
9. John E. Jackson, *Constituencies and Leaders in Congress* (Cambridge: Harvard University Press, 1974).
10. Jerrold E. Schneider, *Ideological Coalitions in Congress* (Westport, Conn.: Greenwood Press, 1979), 134, 195.
11. Michael Foley, *The New Senate: Liberal Influence on a Conservative Institution, 1959–1972* (New Haven, Conn.: Yale University Press, 1980), 242.
12. Tim Groseclose, Steven D. Levitt, and James M. Snyder, Jr., "Comparing Interest Group Scores Across Time and Chambers," *American Political Science Review* 93 (1999): 33–50.
13. *Congressional Quarterly Weekly Report* (December 3, 1994): 3430–3435.
14. In 1993 the 103d Congress also contained a lot of newly elected Democratic members eager to change House rules. They voted for the old rules and procedures, however, because that is what their party leaders wanted.
15. Barbara Sinclair, *The Transformation of the United States Senate* (Baltimore: Johns Hopkins University Press, 1989).

16. Norman J. Ornstein, Thomas E. Mann, and Michael J. Malbin, *Vital Statistics on Congress, 1995–1996* (Washington, D.C.: Congressional Quarterly Press, 1996), 199–200.
17. Gary C. Jacobson, "The Electoral Basis of Partisan Polarization in Congress," paper delivered at the annual meeting of the American Political Science Association, August 31–September 3, 2002; Larry M. Bartels, "Partisanship and Voting Behavior, 1952–1996," *American Journal of Political Science* 44 (2000): 35–50.
18. Marc J. Hetherington, "Resurgent Mass Partisanship: The Role of Elite Polarization," *American Political Science Review* 95 (2001): 619–631.
19. Keith T. Poole and Howard Rosenthal, *Congress: A Political Economic History of Roll Call Voting* (New York: Oxford University Press, 1997), 8.
20. Nolan McCarty, Keith T. Poole, and Howard Rosenthal, "The Hunt for Party Discipline in Congress," *American Political Science Review* 95, no. 3 (September 2001): 686.
21. Susan Webb Hammond, "Congressional Caucuses in the 104th Congress," in *Congress Reconsidered*, ed. Lawrence C. Dodd and Bruce I. Oppenheimer, 6th ed. (Washington, D.C.: Congressional Quarterly Press, 1997), 6.
22. Ibid., 34.
23. Steven S. Smith, "Revolution in the House: Why Don't We Do It on the Floor?" discussion paper no. 5, Brookings Institution, Washington, D.C., September 1986.
24. Richard F. Fenno, Jr., *Congressmen in Committees* (Boston: Little, Brown, 1973).
25. Michael J. Malbin, "Delegation, Deliberation, and the New Role of Congressional Staff," in *The New Congress*, ed. Thomas E. Mann and Norman J. Ornstein (Washington, D.C.: American Enterprise Institute, 1981), 134–177, esp. 170–171.
26. Lawrence H. Chamberlain, "The President, Congress, and Legislation," in *The Presidency*, ed. Aaron Wildavsky (Boston: Little, Brown, 1969), 444–445; Ronald C. Moe and Steven C. Teel, "Congress as a Policy-Maker: A Necessary Reappraisal," *Political Science Quarterly* 85 (September 1970): 443–470.
27. Richard E. Cohen, "Challenging the House's Traffic Cop," *National Journal* (April 4, 1993): 1002.
28. Thomas E. Mann and Norman J. Ornstein, *Renewing Congress: A Second Report* (Washington, D.C.: American Enterprise Institute, 1993), 49.
29. Malcolm E. Jewell and Samuel C. Patterson, *The Legislative Process in the United States*, 3d ed. (New York: Random House, 1977), 439.
30. National Commission on Terrorist Attacks Upon the United States, *The 9/11 Commission Report: Final Report of the National Commission on Terrorist Attacks Upon the United States* (New York and London: W.W. Norton & Company, 2004), 420.
31. Ibid.
32. Ibid., 419.
33. Continuity of Government Commission, 2.
34. Ibid., 3, 4.

Chapter 14 *The Presidency*

1. Jean Blondel, *An Introduction to Comparative Government* (New York: Praeger, 1969), as cited in Nelson W. Polsby, "Legislatures," in *Handbook of Political Science*, ed. Fred I. Greenstein and Nelson W. Polsby (Reading, Mass.: Addison-Wesley, 1975), vol. 5, 275.
2. Donald F. Kettl, *Deficit Politics: Public Budgeting in Its Institutional and Historical Context* (New York: Macmillan, 1992), 13.
3. Morris P. Fiorina, *Divided Government* (New York: Macmillan, 1992), 86–111.
4. David Mayhew, *Divided We Govern: Party Control, Lawmaking, and Investigations, 1946–1990* (New Haven, Conn.: Yale University Press, 1991), 76.
5. Mark A. Peterson, *Legislating Together: The White House and Congress from Eisenhower to Reagan* (Cambridge: Harvard University Press, 1990).
6. Richard E. Cohen, *Washington at Work: Back Rooms and Clean Air* (New York: Macmillan, 1992), 154–155.
7. Ibid., 169.
8. Kettl, *Deficit Politics*, 138.
9. Woodrow Wilson, *Congressional Government* (New York: Meridian Books, 1956), 167–168, 170. (First published in 1885.)
10. Stephen Hess, *Organizing the Presidency* (Washington, D.C.: Brookings Institution, 1976), 3; R. W. Apple, "Clinton's Refocusing," *New York Times* (May 6, 1993): A22; Michael K. Frisby, "Power Switch," *Wall Street Journal* (March 26, 1993): A1, A7.
11. David T. Stanley et al., *Men Who Govern* (Washington, D.C.: Brookings Institution, 1967), 41–42, 50.
12. Daniel J. Elazar, "Which Road to the Presidency?" in *The Presidency*, ed. Aaron Wildavsky (Boston: Little, Brown, 1969), 340.
13. Richard E. Neustadt, *Presidential Power*, rev. ed. (New York: Wiley, 1976), ch. 4.
14. Walter D. Burnham, "Insulation and Responsiveness in Congressional Elections," *Political Science Quarterly* 90 (Fall 1975): 412–413; George C. Edwards III, *Presidential Influence in Congress* (San Francisco: Freeman, 1980), 70–78; Warren E. Miller, "Presidential Coattails: A Study in Political Myth and Methodology," *Public Opinion Quarterly* 19 (Winter 1955–1956): 368; and Miller, "The Motivational Basis for Straight and Split Ticket Voting," *American Political Science Review* 51 (June 1957): 293–312.
15. *Clinton v. City of New York*, 118 S.Ct. 2091 (1998).
16. *Marbury v. Madison*, 1 Cranch 137 (1803).
17. *United States v. Nixon*, 418 U.S. 683 (1974).
18. *Clinton v. Jones*, 520 U.S. 681 (1997); *In Re Grand Jury Subpoena Duces Tecum*, 112 F.3d 910 (1997); *In Re Sealed Case*, 121 F.3d 729 (1997).
19. Marcus Cunliffe, *American Presidents and the Presidency* (New York: American Heritage Press/McGraw-Hill, 1972), 63, 65.

20. Ibid., 214.
21. Adapted from Paul C. Light, *The President's Agenda* (Baltimore, Md.: Johns Hopkins University Press, 1982), 217–225.

Chapter 15   *The Bureaucracy*

1. Charles E. Lindblom, *Politics and Markets* (New York: Basic Books, 1977), 114.
2. Article II, section 2, para. 2.
3. Article II, section 3.
4. Calculated from data in *Historical Statistics of the United States: Colonial Times to 1970* (Washington, D.C.: Government Printing Office, 1975), vol. 2, 1102–1103.
5. *Panama Refining Co. v. Ryan*, 293 U.S. 388 (1935).
6. *Hampton Jr. & Co. v. United States*, 276 U.S. 394 (1928).
7. Edward S. Corwin, *The Constitution and What It Means Today*, 13th ed. (Princeton, N.J.: Princeton University Press, 1973), 151.
8. Bruce D. Porter, "Parkinson's Law Revisited: War and the Growth of American Government," *Public Interest* (Summer 1980): 50–68.
9. See the cases cited in Corwin, *The Constitution*, 8.
10. *U.S. Statutes*, vol. 84, sec. 799 (1970).
11. *Historical Statistics of the United States*, vol. 2, 1107.
12. Donald F. Kettl et al., *Civil Service Reform: Building a Government That Works* (Washington, D.C.: Brookings Institution, 1996), 18.
13. Ibid., 15.
14. Hugh Heclo, "Issue Networks and the Executive Establishment," in *The New American Political System*, ed. Anthony King (Washington, D.C.: American Enterprise Institute, 1978), 87–124.
15. Quoted in Hugh Heclo, *A Government of Strangers* (Washington, D.C.: Brookings Institution, 1977), 225.
16. Alexis Simendinger, "Of the People, for the People," *National Journal* (April 18, 1998): 852–855. Data from the Pew Charitable Trusts Research Center for the People and the Press.
17. Stanley Rothman and S. Robert Lichter, "How Liberal Are Bureaucrats?" *Regulation* (November/December, 1983): 17–18.
18. Kenneth Meier and Lloyd Nigro, "Representative Bureaucracy and Policy References: A Study of the Attitudes of Federal Executives," *Public Administration Review* 36 (July/August 1976): 458–467; Bernard Mennis, *American Foreign Policy Officials* (Columbus: Ohio State University Press, 1971).
19. Joel D. Aberbach and Bert A. Rockman, "Clashing Beliefs Within the Executive Branch: The Nixon Administration Bureaucracy," *American Political Science Review* 70 (June 1976): 456–468.
20. David Stockman, *The Triumph of Politics* (New York: Harper and Row, 1986).
21. James Q. Wilson, *Bureaucracy* (New York: Basic Books, 1989), ch. 6.
22. Heclo, "Issue Networks and the Executive Establishment," 87–124.

23. Richard F. Fenno, Jr., *The Power of the Purse* (Boston: Little, Brown, 1966), 450, 597.
24. John E. Schwartz and L. Earl Shaw, *The United States Congress in Comparative Perspective* (Hinsdale, Ill.: Dryden Press, 1976), 262–263; *National Journal* (July 4, 1981): 1211–1214.
25. *Immigration and Naturalization Service v. Chadha*, 462 U.S. 919 (1983); *Maine v. Thiboutot*, 448 U.S. 1 (1980).
26. See cases cited in Corwin, *The Constitution*, 22.
27. Steven Kelman, "The Grace Commission: How Much Waste in Government?" *Public Interest* (Winter 1985): 62–87.
28. Daniel Katz et al., *Bureaucratic Encounters* (Ann Arbor: Survey Research Center, University of Michigan, 1975), 63–69, 118–120, 184–188.
29. *From Red Tape to Results: Creating a Government That Works Better and Costs Less*, report of the National Performance Review, Vice President Al Gore, September 7, 1993.

Chapter 16   *The Judiciary*

1. Henry J. Abraham, *The Judicial Process*, 3d ed. (New York: Oxford University Press, 1975), 279–280.
2. Robert G. McCloskey, *The American Supreme Court* (Chicago: University of Chicago Press, 1960), 27.
3. *Marbury v. Madison*, 5 U.S. 137 (1803); and *McCulloch v. Maryland*, 17 U.S. 316 (1819).
4. *Martin v. Hunter's Lessee*, 14 U.S. 304 (1816); and *Cohens v. Virginia*, 19 U.S. (1821).
5. *Gibbons v. Ogden*, 22 U.S. (1824).
6. Quoted in Albert J. Beveridge, *The Life of John Marshall* (Boston: Houghton Mifflin, 1919), vol. 4, 551.
7. *Dred Scott v. Sandford*, 60 U.S. 393 (1857).
8. Abraham, *The Judicial Process*, 286.
9. *In re Debs*, 158 U.S. 564 (1895).
10. *Pollock v. Farmers' Loan & Trust Co.*, 157 U.S. 429 (1895).
11. *United States v. Knight*, 156 U.S. 1 (1895).
12. *Cincinnati, N.O. & T.P. Railway Co. v. Interstate Commerce Commission*, 162 U.S. 184 (1896).
13. *Hammer v. Dagenhart*, 247 U.S. 251 (1918).
14. *Lochner v. New York*, 198 U.S. 45 (1905).
15. McCloskey, *The American Supreme Court*, 151.
16. *Munn v. Illinois*, 94 U.S. 113 (1877).
17. *Dayton-Goose Creek Railway Co. v. United States*, 263 U.S. 456 (1924).
18. *Atchison, Topeka, and Santa Fe Railroad Co. v. Matthews*, 174 U.S. 96 (1899).
19. *Mugler v. Kansas*, 123 U.S. 623 (1887).
20. *St. Louis Consolidated Coal Co. v. Illinois*, 185 U.S. 203 (1902).
21. *New York Central Railroad Co. v. White*, 243 U.S. 188 (1917).
22. *German Alliance Insurance Co. v. Lewis*, 233 U.S. 389 (1914).
23. Morton Keller, *Affairs of State* (Cambridge: Harvard University Press, 1977), 369. See also Mary Cornelia Porter, "That Commerce Shall Be Free: A New Look at the Old Laissez-Faire Court," in *The Supreme Court Review*, ed.

Philip B. Kurland (Chicago: University of Chicago Press, 1976), 135–159.
24. *Chief of Capitol Police v. Jeannette Rankin Brigade*, 409 U.S. 972 (1972).
25. *Aptheker v. Secretary of State*, 378 U.S. 500 (1964).
26. *Trop v. Dulles*, 356 U.S. 86 (1958); *Afroyim v. Rusk*, 387 U.S. 253 (1967); and *Schneider v. Rusk*, 377 U.S. 163 (1964).
27. *Lamont v. Postmaster General*, 381 U.S. 301 (1965); and *Blount v. Rizzi*, 400 U.S. 410 (1971).
28. *Richardson v. Davis*, 409 U.S. 1069 (1972); *U.S. Department of Agriculture v. Murry*, 413 U.S. 508 (1973); *Jimenez v. Weinberger*, 417 U.S. 628 (1974); and *Washington v. Legrant*, 394 U.S. 618 (1969).
29. *United States v. Lopez*, 514 U.S. 549 (1995).
30. *Seminole Tribe of Florida v. Florida*, 517 U.S. 44 (1996); *Alden v. Maine*, 527 U.S. 706 (1999); *Florida v. College Savings Bank*, 527 U.S. 627 (1999).
31. Daniel R. Pinello, "Linking Party to Judicial Ideology in American Courts: A Meta-analysis," *Justice System Journal* 20 (1999): 219–254.
32. An opinion survey of federal judges shows how party affects ideology: see Althea K. Nagai, Stanley Rothman, and S. Robert Lichter, "The Verdict of Federal Judges," *Public Opinion* (November/December 1987): 52–56.
33. *United States v. Lanza*, 260 U.S. 377 (1922). Cf. *Abbate v. United States*, 359 U.S. 187 (1959), and *Bartkus v. Illinois*, 359 U.S. 121 (1989).
34. *Gideon v. Wainwright*, 372 U.S. 335 (1963). The story is told in Anthony Lewis, *Gideon's Trumpet* (New York: Random House, 1964).
35. Erwin Griswold, "Rationing Justice: The Supreme Court's Case Load and What the Court Does Not Do," *Cornell Law Review* 60 (1975): 335–354.
36. Joseph Weis, Jr., "Disconnecting the Overloaded Circuits—A Plan for a Unified Court of Appeals," *St. Louis University Law Journal* 39 (1995): 455.
37. *Alyeska Pipeline Service Co. v. Wilderness Society*, 421 U.S. 240 (1975).
38. *Flast v. Cohen*, 392 U.S. 83 (1968), which modified the earlier *Frothingham v. Mellon*, 262 U.S. 447 (1923); *United States v. Richardson*, 418 U.S. 166 (1947).
39. *Brown v. Board of Education of Topeka*, 347 U.S. 483 (1954).
40. *Baker v. Carr*, 369 U.S. 186 (1962).
41. See Louise Weinberg, "A New Judicial Federalism?" *Daedalus* (Winter 1978): 129–141.
42. Quoted in Abraham, *The Judicial Process*, 330.
43. Carolyn D. Richmond, "The Rehnquist Court: What Is in Store for Constitutional Precedent?" *New York Law Review* 39 (1994): 511.
44. *Colegrove v. Green*, 328 U.S. 549 (1946).
45. The Court abandoned the "political question" doctrine in *Baker v. Carr*, 369 U.S. 186 (1962), and began to change congressional-district apportionment in *Wesberry v. Sanders*, 376 U.S. 1 (1964).

46. Donald L. Horowitz, *The Courts and Social Policy* (Washington, D.C.: Brookings Institution, 1977), 6.

47. *Gates v. Collier*, 349 F. Supp. 881 (1972).

48. *Lau v. Nichols*, 414 U.S. 563 (1974).

49. Jane Burnbaum, "Guilty! Too Many Lawyers and Too Much Litigation," *Business Week* (April 13, 1992), 60–61.

50. Joel B. Grossman and Austin Sarat, "Litigation in the Federal Courts: A Comparative Perspective," *Law and Society Review* 9 (Winter 1975): 321–346.

51. Administrative Office of the U.S. Courts, *Annual Report, 1988,* 109.

52. Jack W. Peltason, *Fifty-eight Lonely Men: Southern Federal Judges and School Desegregation* (New York: Harcourt Brace, 1961).

53. Anthony Patridge and William B. Eldridge, *The Second Circuit Sentencing Study* (Washington, D.C.: Federal Judicial Center, 1974).

54. *Abington School District v. Schempp*, 374 U.S. 203 (1963).

55. Robert H. Birkby, "The Supreme Court and the Bible Belt," *Midwest Journal of Political Science* 10 (1966): 3.

56. Cass R. Sunstein, "Impeaching the President," *University of Pennsylvania Law Review* 147 (1998): 279.

57. *United States v. Butler*, 297 U.S. 1 (1936).

58. *Ex parte McCardle*, 74 U.S. 506 (1869).

59. Walter F. Murphy, *Congress and the Court* (Chicago: University of Chicago Press, 1962); and C. Herman Pritchett, *Congress Versus the Supreme Court* (Minneapolis: University of Minnesota Press, 1961).

60. Gregory A. Caldeira, "Neither the Purse nor the Sword: Dynamics of Public Confidence in the U.S. Supreme Court," *American Political Science Review* 80 (1986): 1209–1226. See also Joseph T. Tannenhaus and Walter F. Murphy, "Patterns of Public Support for the Supreme Court: A Panel Study," *Journal of Politics* 43 (1981): 24–39.

☆ INDEX

AARP (American Association of Retired Persons), 270–271, 287
ABC network, 296, 299, 310
Abortion, 28(fn.),172, 227, 253
  as interest group issue, 281
  "culture war" and, 86
  judiciary on, 59, 143–144, 448, 464
  landmark cases, 143
  NARAL, 274, 275
  public funding of, 71
  views of Congress on, 331, 338–339
Acheson's Rule, 426
ACLU. *See* American Civil Liberties Union
Activism, 81, 238
  barriers to, in government, 479–482
  consumer, 427
  federal government, 61–62
  interest groups and, 269, 280
  judicial, 439, 444, 459–460, 463, 464
  partisan, 225, 390
  political, 162, 171, 188, 215–216, 255
  student activism, 135, 159, 161–162, 272, 285
  union, 216
ADA (Americans with Disabilities Act) of 1990, 66–67, 147
Adams, John, 5, 18, 20, 201
  Congress and, 322
  Constitution and, 24, 85
  Marbury v. Madison and, 440, 441
  presidency of, 374, 384, 388
  vice presidency of, 401, 412
Adams, John Quincy, 240, 388
Adams, Samuel, 24, 30
Adarand case, 148, 149
"Adding-machine" democracy, 481
Ad hoc staff structure, 381, 382
Administration Committee (House), 345
Administrative Procedure Act (1946), 424
Adversarial press, 292, 309, 310, 311
Adversary culture, 411, 459, 470
Advertising
  campaign, 234, 240, 242, 244, 257
  freedom of expression in, 109
  negative campaign ads, 234, 257, 261, 310
  television, 302–303
Advocacy organizations, 304
AFBF (American Farm Bureau Federation), 266, 267
AFDC (Aid to Families with Dependent Children), 68, 69
Affirmative action, 144–149, 169, 399, 448, 476
  equality of opportunity, 145–149
  Supreme Court on, 146–147, 148, 149
Afghanistan, U.S. invasion of, 88, 120, 399
AFL-CIO, 11, 109, 217, 266, 276, 280, 455
African Americans. *See also* Race; Slavery
  in bureaucracy, 421
  civil rights of, 125, 126–127, 138, 331
  in Congress, 325–326, 325(tab.), 340–341
  Democratic party and, 222, 258, 259
  discrimination against, 3–4, 95(fig.)
  as elected officials, 140(fig.)
  in judiciary, 447(fig.)

NAACP and, 269
  opinions of, 164–165, 164(tab.), 224
  political alliances of, 221
  political participation of, 188, 191, 193(fig.)
  in president's cabinet, 387
  racial equality and, 78
  on Supreme Court, 442, 443, 461
  trust in institutions by, 88–89
  voting rights of, 138, 180–181, 182
Age. *See also* Youth
  generation gaps on issues, 159(fig.)
  political participation and, 183, 188, 189(fig.)
Age Discrimination Act, 358
Agency for International Development, 424
Agnew, Spiro, 402–403
Agriculture, Nutrition, and Forestry Committee (Senate), 344
Agriculture Committee (House), 345
Agriculture Department, 413, 426, 427
AIDS, discussion of, 174
Aid to Families with Dependent Children (AFDC), 68, 69
Airline industry, 280
Alabama, 135, 137, 183(tab.), 217, 457
Albany, Georgia, 106
Albany, New York, 214
Alden v. Maine (1999), 58
Alger, Horatio, 86
Aliens, civil rights of, 146, 181
Almond, Gabriel, 80, 269
Al Qaeda, 120
Amblach v. Norwich (1979), 146
Amendments to bills, 352, 354, 356
Amendments to Constitution. *See* Constitutional Amendments
America Coming Together, 252
America for Job Security, 252
American Association of Retired Persons (AARP), 270–271, 287
American Civil Liberties Union (ACLU), 99, 109, 251, 272, 451
American Cotton Manufacturers Institute, 268–269
American Council on Education, 269, 276
American Enterprise Institute, 273
American Farm Bureau Federation (AFBF), 266, 267
American Federation of Labor, 473. *See also* AFL-CIO
American Independent party, 220–221
American Indian Movement, 285
Americanism, 78–79
American Jewish Committee, 267
American Legion, 270, 426
American Medical Association, 267, 280
American Nazi party, 105
American Political Science Association, 10
American Public Transit Association, 269
American Revolution, 17, 18, 20–21, 38, 84
Americans for Constitutional Action, 280
Americans for Democratic Action, 280
Americans with Disabilities Act (ADA) of 1990, 66–67, 147
American system, 469

American way of life, 78
America Votes, 252
Amicus curiae, 455
Amish sect, 111
Anderson, John, 242
Andrus, Cecil D., 272
Annapolis, Maryland, 22
Anti-Defamation League, 267
Antifederalists, 31, 34, 35, 39, 201
Anti-Jackson Republicans, 203
Anti-Masonic party, 203, 212
Anti-Saloon League, 223
Antislavery organizations, 267
Antitrust legislation, 58
Antiwar movement, 161, 221–222, 286
AP (Associated Press), 295, 299, 305, 306
Appellate courts. *See* Courts of appeals
Appropriations bills, 351, 428
Appropriations Committee (House), 342, 345, 428–429
Appropriations Committee (Senate), 344
Approval ratings, 392–393(fig.)
Aristocracy, 25
Aristotle, 6, 30
Arkansas, 183(tab.)
Armed Services Committee (House), 345
Armed Services Committee (Senate), 344
Arthur, Chester, 378
Articles of Confederation, 17, 21–22, 37, 52
  Constitution and, 24, 25, 26, 31, 34
Ash Council (1969-1971), 432
Asian American Legal Defense Fund, 272
Asian Americans, 165
Assistant minority leader (Senate), 336
Associated Press (AP), 295, 299, 305, 306
Atlantic Legal Foundation, 272
Atlantic Monthly (magazine), 295
Attack journalism, 309
Attitudinal voting, 331, 332–333
Australia, 190, 438
Australian ballot, 185
Austria, 81, 90, 266
Authority, 5, 200. *See also* Presidential power (authority)
  centralized, 52, 200
  delegation of, to bureaucracy, 415
  discretionary, 415
  enhanced rescission authority, 45, 395
  formal, political power and, 5
  political authority, 20, 46, 200, 265
Authorization legislation, 428

Babbitt, Bruce, 572
Background story, 313
Baker, Howard, 233, 382
Bakke, Allan, 149, 455
Balanced budget amendment, 28(fn.), 43, 45, 481
Ballots, 149, 185, 198, 207, 236
Banking, Housing and Urban Affairs Committee (Senate), 344
Bargaining
  in Congress, 356
  over conditions of aid, 68
Bayh, Birch, 217

Beard, Charles, 38
Beliefs, 11, 77, 91, 92(fig.), 159, 160
Berman, Howard L., 215
Bernstein, Carl, 300
Bias, 278–279
    in media, 293, 303–307
Bicameral legislature, 25, 321
Bilingual education, 101
Bill of attainder, 35
Bill of Rights (1791), 34–36, 98–99, 111,
    450
    See also Constitution of U.S.; *specific*
        amendments
    applied to states, 35, 102, 104, 473
    text of, A13–A14
Bills, 347–356
    amendments to, 352, 354, 356
    congressional calendar, 352
    floor debate of, 353–355
    introduction of, 348, 350
    riders to, 354
    steps in legislative process, 348–349
    study by committees, 348, 350–353
    voting methods, 355–356
Bimodal distribution of votes, 338
Binding presidential preference primary, 241
Bin Laden, Osama, 88, 120
Bipartisan Campaign Finance Reform Act
    (2002), 250, 251–252
Black, Hugo, 106, 439
Blackmun, Harry, 447, 464
Blacks. *See* African Americans; Race; Slavery
Blackstone, William, 102–103
Blair, Tony, 370
Blanket primary, 241
Block grants, 63–64, 65
    devolution and, 49, 50, 68–69
Blogs (web logs), 292, 293, 297
Blount, William, 38
Blue-collar workers, 163
"Blue Dog Democrats" (The Coalition), 341
"Blue slip," 447
Border Patrol, 424
Boren's Laws, 426
Bork, Robert, 438
Boston, Massachusetts, 133, 266, 298
Boston Tea Party, 25, 30
Bowers v. Hardwick (1986), 150
Boy Scouts of America, 101, 268
Boy Scouts of America v. Dale (2000), 150, 151
Bradley, Bill, 225, 233
Brady, Jim, 282
Brady bill (1993), 282, 445
Brandeis, Louis, 446, 461
Brandenburg, Clarence, 104
Braun, Carol Moseley, 325–326
Breckinridge, John C., 205–206
Brennan, William, 132
Breyer, Stephen, 454(tab.), 456
Bribery, 285, 359. *See also* Corruption
Briefs, 455
Broad-based aid, 63–64
Broadcast media. *See* Media
Broder, David, 233
Brown, Corrine, 341
Brown, Linda, 129, 131, 132, 453
Brown, Pat, 217
Brown, Ronald H., 212
Brownlow Commission (1936–1937), 432
Brown v. Board of Education (1954), 129, 131,
    134, 453, 462

Bryan, William Jennings, 203, 206
Buchanan, James, 388
Buchanan, Pat, 250
Buddy system, in bureaucracy, 418–419
Budget and Accounting Act (1921), 380
Budget Committee (House), 345
Budget Committee (Senate), 344
Budget deficits, 70, 70(fig.), 359, 428–429,
    476, 478, 481
    See also Federal budget
Budget Reform Act (1974), 397
"Bull Moose" (Progressive) party, 221, 222,
    223
Bully pulpit, 390
Bureaucracy, 40, 213, 409–436, 480
    agency allies, 426–427
    appointment of officials in, 417–418, 434
    buddy system, 418–419
    bureaucratized parties, 208–209
    change of role of, 423
    congressional, 345
    congressional oversight of, 420–421, 423,
        424, 427–430, 433
    constraints on, 424–426
    culture of, 423
    distinctiveness of, 410–411
    divided government and, 433
    economic policy and, 423
    growth of, 411–414, 475
    in Japan, 471
    language of, 425
    "laws" of, 426
    modern, 414–427
    under parliamentary systems, 410
    "pathologies," 430–432
    policy-making and, 422
    power of, 415, 473
    presidency and, 397, 398, 433
    red tape and, 425–426, 430, 431, 432–433
    reform movements, 412, 417–418, 432–433
    service role of, 412–414
    spoils system (patronage), 412, 417, 418
    White House, 381, 382
Bureaucrats
    agency culture and, 423
    agency point of view and, 420–421
    behavior of, 423
    daily duties, 418
    firings, 419–420
    personal attributes of, 421–422
    power of, 9, 423
    recruitment and retention, 415–419
    sabotage of superiors, 420, 422–423
Bureau of Competition, 423
Bureau of Economics, 423
Burger, Warren, 133, 447, 464
Burnett, Carol, 105
Burnham, Walter Dean, 329
Burr, Aaron, 376
Bus boycott, 135
Bush, George H. W. (elder), 144, 216–217, 313
    appointments by, 427
    battles with Congress, 370–371, 469
    character of, 389
    election of 1988 and, 234, 237, 239, 256
    election of 1992 and, 187, 243
    judicial appointments by, 438, 448
    opposition to mandates, 66, 67
    presidency of, 369, 378, 392, 393(fig.),
        398, 400
    vice presidency of, 233, 401

Bush, George W. (younger), 11, 61, 64, 233
    on affirmative action, 148
    appointments by, 417
    cabinet of, 369, 386, 387
    character of, 389
    community-serving organizations and, 62
    Court nominations of, 438
    election of 2000 and, 84, 225, 234, 248,
        251, 309, 376
    election of 2004 and, 186, 211, 219, 239,
        240, 242, 248–249, 250, 479
    first inauguration of, 374
    funding for faith-based organizations, 277
    interest groups and, 272
    judicial appointments by, 448
    Latinos and, 166, 303
    white male support for, 160
    NAACP and, 165
    national crises under, 398
    personal following of, 216, 217
    popularity of, 393(fig.)
    on racial profiling, 139
    unified government and, 370
    veto power and, 396
    war on terrorism and, 120, 360, 368, 389,
        399, 400
Bush, Jeb, 216, 217
Bush v. Gore (2000), 251
Business
    institutional interests, 267, 278
    power elite in, 9
    public confidence in, 309
    red tape in, 430
    regulation of, 443, 472, 473
Business-oriented interest groups, 267, 278
Busing, 133–134, 463
    federal mandates for, 67
Byrd, Harry, Jr., 218
Byrd family, 217

CAB (Civil Aeronautics Board), 280
Cabell v. Chavez-Salido (1982), 146
Cabinet
    African Americans in, 387
    choosing members of, 369
    conflict with presidential staff, 387–388
    member of Congress in, 479–480
    president and, 369, 384–385, 384(tab.),
        385(tab.), 411–412
Cable News Network (CNN), 243, 297, 299,
    311
Cable television, 297, 298, 308, 311
Calendar of business (Senate), 352
"Calendar Wednesday procedure," 353
Calhoun, John C., 56, 376
California, 52, 149, 165, 215, 235
    no-fault auto insurance in, 272
    redistricting in, 329
    same-sex marriage in, 151
    state constitution of, 59
California Public Utility Commission, 108
Calorie Control Council, 282
Cambridge, Massachusetts, 219
Cameron, Simon, 386
Campaign debate, 242, 244, 302
Campaigners, 188
Campaign financing, 8, 233, 244–247,
    250–253
    federal grants, 244–245, 246–247
    new sources of, 251–252
    PACs and, 245, 282–283, 284, 474

reform of, 282
rules of, 109, 246–247, 250–251, 287
soft money, 209, 247, 250
sources of, 244–246
winning and, 252–253
Campaigns, 230–262, 256–257. *See also*
Congressional campaigns; Presidential
campaigns
debates, 242, 244, 302
direct-mail, 209, 215, 243–244, 247, 257
franked mail and, 253
Internet and, 209, 243, 297, 303
kinds of issues in, 239–240
negative ads, 234, 257, 261, 310
partisan loyalty and, 256–257
primary *vs.* general, 237–244
strategy and themes, 234, 257
television and, 240, 242, 243, 244, 257
Campaign speeches, 242–243
Campaign staff, 233–234
Campbell, Ben Nighthorse, 326
Canada, 21, 80, 84(tab.), 189–190, 438
judicial review in, 462
Candidates, 474
character of, 252, 257
congressional, 318, 480
financing for, 233, 250–253, 282, 283
"mention" and, 233, 300
presidential, 231, 297, 300, 302, 480
and Spanish-speaking voters, 303
Cannon, Joseph G., 321, 323, 342
Capital grants, 69
Capitalists, 9, 79
Capital punishment, 458
Capitol building, map of, 337
Carlyle, Thomas, 432
Carnal Knowledge (film), 106
Carter, Jimmy, 167, 206, 233
character of, 389
Congress and, 480–481
election of 1976 and, 234, 239, 240
election of 1980 and, 242, 255
energy bill of, 351, 356
judgeships and, 461
media and, 313
"mentioned," 300
national crises under, 398
policies of, 397
presidency of, 272, 369, 370, 382, 388,
391, 392, 393(fig.), 394, 427, 447
Senate and, 368, 371
Categorical grants, 63–65, 66, 68
Catholic Charities, 277
Catholics, 85, 87, 95(fig.), 100, 159, 160(tab.),
206, 212
Kennedy and, 253, 258, 469
parochial schools, 99, 111–112
Cato Institute, 273
Caucuses, 202, 225, 231, 237
congressional, 340–341, 341(tab.), 343
Democratic, 342
Iowa caucus, 237–238, 300
women's issues and, 275
CBC (Congressional Black Caucus), 340–341
CBO (Congressional Budget Office), 70, 347
CBS network, 292, 296, 299, 307, 310, 452
CEA (Council of Economic Advisors), 383
Censorship, 99, 103, 107, 300
Census, U.S.
distributional formulas and, 65, 248
redistricting and, 327, 329, 330

Center for Defense Information, 273
Center for Individual Rights, 272, 451
Center for Strategic and International Studies,
273
Center on Budget and Policy Priorities, 273
Central Intelligence Agency (CIA), 383, 417,
424, 453
Centralized power (authority), 52, 200
Certiorari, writ of, 450–451, 455
Chadha case (1983), 429
Chairman of the Caucus (House), 336
Chairman of the Conference (House), 336
Chairman of the Conference (Senate), 336
Chamber of Commerce, U.S., 109, 267, 269,
280
Chaplinsky v. New Hampshire (1942), 109
Chapman's Rules of Committees, 426
Character
of candidates, 252, 257
of presidents, 388–389
Charter of Rights (Canada), 462
Chase, Samuel P., 386, 461
Checks and balances, 29, 30, 470, 476
Cheney, Dick, 299, 335, 402
Chew v. Colding (1953), 146
Chicago, Illinois, 67, 214, 266, 298
Chief justice, Supreme Court, 349(tab.), 455
Child pornography, 107
Children's Defense Fund, 273
Chinese Americans, 181
Chinese Revolution, 17
Christian Coalition, 83, 269, 280
Christmas tree bill, 354
CIA (Central Intelligence Agency), 383, 417,
424, 453
Cincinnati, Ohio, 298
Circular staff structure, 381, 382
Cities
existence of, 59
federal agencies and, 411
interest groups in, 266
intergovernmental lobbies, 62
municipal bonds, 56
municipal elections, 219
Citizenship, 35, 67, 145
City government, 57, 63
Civic competence, 80
Civic duty, 77, 80, 82–83
Civic participation, 8, 82, 162
Civic problems, values and, 91
Civil Aeronautics Board (CAB), 280
Civil disobedience, 135
Civilian Conservation Corps, 477
Civility in Congress, decline of, 333–334
Civil liberties, 97–123. *See also* First
Amendment
civil rights and, 99
crime and due process, 113–121
cultural conflicts and, 100–102
politics, culture and, 99–100
Supreme Court and, 462
terrorism and, 119–121
Civil rights, 124–152, 416
affirmative action, 144–149, 169, 399, 448
black predicament and, 125, 126–127
Brown v. Board of Education (1954), 129,
131, 134, 453, 462
campaign in Congress, 134–139
campaign in federal courts, 127–134, 462
citizenship and, 145
civil liberties and, 99

of disabled persons, 66–67, 147
of homosexuals. *See* Homosexual (gay)
rights
of illegal aliens, 146, 181
opinion on, 169
racial profiling and, 139
separate-but-equal doctrine and, 128–129
of women. *See* Women's rights
Civil Rights Act of 1957, 137
Civil Rights Act of 1964, 137, 141, 182, 457,
459
Civil Rights Act of 1965, 137
Civil Rights Act of 1968, 137
Civil Rights Act of 1972, 141
Civil Rights Act of 1988, 137, 141
Civil Rights Act of 1991, 141
Civil rights cases, 451–452, 460. *See also specific case*
Civil rights legislation, 51, 141, 476, 477
Congress and, 137–138, 350–351
key provisions of, 138
labor unions and, 11, 273
mandates, 66, 67
representational voting on, 331
Southern Democrat support for, 139(fig.)
vague language in, 459
Civil rights movement, 127, 135, 286
See also National Association for the
Advancement of Colored People
disruptive tactics of, 135, 136, 273
in federal courts, 127–134
religion and, 83
white opposition to, 136–137
Civil service, 214. *See also* Bureaucracy
reform of, 213–214, 417–418, 419
Civil Service Reform Act (1978), 419
Civil War, 5, 78, 378
bureaucratic growth in, 412
national supremacy and, 54, 442
party realignment and, 205–206
sectionalism in, 203–204
slavery and, 37, 56, 205–206
veterans' pensions, 267, 413
Clarity standard, 107
Class-action suits, 453–454
Class consciousness, 86. *See also* Social class;
specific class
Clay, Henry, 376
Clean Air Acts (1970, 1990), 378
Clear-and-present-danger test, 103–104
Cleveland, Grover, 204, 240, 377, 378,
380
patronage jobs and, 417
veto power and, 395
Client politics, 280, 284, 426
Clinton, Bill, 69, 167, 234, 242
affirmative action and, 399
appointments by, 385, 421–422, 427, 447,
448
budget proposal of, 478
cabinet of, 387
character of, 389
Congress and, 371, 469, 480–481
election of 1992 and, 167, 187, 219,
239–240, 243, 256, 309, 371
as governor, 233, 369
health care plan of, 280, 368, 381
impeachment of, 87, 331, 333, 338, 368,
403, 478
line-item veto and, 43, 481
national crises under, 398

policies of, 397
popularity of, 392, 393(fig.)
presidency of, 151, 272, 368, 374, 387, 400
on racial profiling, 139
reelection of, in 1996, 262
sexual conduct of, 142, 310, 311, 396
staff organization of, 383
welfare reform and, 68, 378–379
Clinton, George, 23
Clinton, Hillary Rodham, 240, 309, 381
Clinton et al. v. New York et al. (1998), 45
Closed primary, 241
Closed rule, 352
Clothespin vote, 239
Cloture, 354, 355
CNN (Cable News Network), 243, 297, 299, 311
Coalition, The ("Blue Dog Democrats"), 341
Coalitions, 34, 341
  Christian Coalition, 83, 269, 280
  in Congress, 471, 474
  conservative coalition, 330, 333, 477
  divided government and, 372
  in Europe, 219–220
  "New Deal" coalition, 206, 259
  parliamentary, 369
  party organization and, 200, 202, 206, 219
  winning, in elections, 257–259
Coattails, 232, 391
Coca-Cola Company, 282
Colleges and universities
  See also under Student; *specific institutions*
  admissions policies of, 147, 149, 448
  freedom of speech in, 93
  integration of, 129, 130, 132
  land-grant colleges, 60
  liberalizing effect of, 136, 161, 267
  political correctness on, 162
  sex discrimination and, 141
  voting and, 188, 191
Collin v. Smith (1978), 109
Colonists, views of liberty, 84
Colorado, 148, 149, 150, 377
Columbus Dispatch (newspaper), 300
Commander in chief, 378, 379–380, 440
  See also Presidential power (authority)
Commentaries (Blackstone), 103
Commerce, regulation of, 53–54, 412, 413, 442, 445
Commerce, Science and Transportation Committee (Senate), 344
Commerce Department, 413
Committee clearance, 429
Committee of Detail, 27
Committee on Aging (Senate), 344
Committee on Committees (Senate), 335, 336, 337
Committees (Congress). *See also* Congressional committees; *specific committee*
  conference committees, 356
  legislative, 428
  select committees, 342
  seniority and chairmanship in, 323, 338, 339–340, 342, 363
  standing committees, 342, 344, 345
  subcommittees, 341, 342, 343, 346
Common Cause, 277
Communalists, 188
Communist Control Act (1954), 100
Communist party, 100, 104, 221

Communists, 92, 92(fig.)
Community-based organizations, 69
Community Development Block Grants, 64
"Community-needs" broadcasting, 301
Community service, 80, 162, 183, 188
  relgious-based, 82, 84, 94
Competition, 469
  for federal jobs, 416
  in media, 298–299, 310–311
Competitive Enterprise Institute, 273
Competitive service, 416
Computerized mailings, 208. *See also*
  Direct-mail solicitation
Computers, 413. *See also* Internet
Concurrent powers, 29
Concurrent resolution, 350
Concurring opinion, 455
Condit, Gary, 311
Confederal system, 51, 53(fig.)
Confederation, 51, 53(fig.)
Conference committees, 342
Confessions, involuntary, 117–118
Confidentiality, presidential, 396
Confidentiality of sources, media and, 301
Conflict
  in bureaucracies, 430, 431
  between cabinet and staff, 387–388
  cultural, 86–87, 100–101
  in federal-state relations, 49
  in interest group politics, 281
  over slavery, 49, 205–206. *See also* Civil War
  in politics, 281, 476
  within upper-middle class, 278
Conflict of interest, 285
Congress
  appointment of officials and, 412, 419–420
  attitudinal voting in, 331, 332–333
  Bill of Rights and, 35
  budget and, 379, 397, 428–429
  bureaucracy of, 411
  bureaucratic oversight by, 420–421, 423, 424, 427–430, 433
  bureaucratic power and, 415
  campaign finance reform and, 250
  caucuses. *See* Caucuses
  changes in, 475
  checks and balances and, 29
  church and state and, 111
  civil rights legislation and, 137–138
  civil service reform and, 419
  commerce and, 413
  committees of. *See* Congressional committees; *specific committees*
  congressional calendar, 352
  constituencies and, 320, 330–334, 469
  Constitutional amendments and, 28, 42
  Constitutional powers of, 26, 27, 55–56
  courts and, 446, 460, 461–463
  decentralization trend in, 320, 322, 342–343, 470, 476
  Democratic majority in, 260, 370, 371, 477
  desegregation and, 131, 134–139
  devolution and, 68–69
  districts of. *See* Congressional districts; Redistricting
  divided government and, 370–372
  ethics rules, 360
  evolution of, 321–325
  exclusionary rule and, 118–119
  exempt from laws, 358
  federal aid and, 61, 64–66

  federalism and, 53, 66–67, 70, 72
  flag-burning law and, 108
  floor debate in, 353–355
  House-Senate differences, 323, 356
  ideology and civility in, 333–334
  impoundment of funds and, 396–397
  incumbency and. *See* Incumbency
  independent counsel and, 404
  interest groups and, 281, 320, 332, 344, 351
  labor disputes and, 267
  legislative process in, 347–356, 358
  legislative veto and, 400, 429
  lobbying and, 287
  map of Capitol building, 337
  104th Congress, 49, 69, 340, 342, 358
  organizational voting in, 331, 332
  organization of, 345–347
  PACs and, 282–283, 284(tab.)
  parliament compared, 318–321, 359, 371
  party unity in, 338–340
  pay raise for, 362
  polarization in, 478–479
  policy preferences in, 171
  political elites in, 171
  political parties and, 200, 319, 328–330, 334–337
  pork-barrel legislation, 358, 359, 477
  power of, 317, 320, 321, 364–365, 472
  powers and perks, reducing, 358–359
  prayer in, 113
  presidency and, 373, 375–379, 380, 390–391, 391(tab.), 393(fig.)
  presidential veto and, 43–45, 348, 358, 395, 396, 471
  qualifications and privileges of, 238
  regulation of commerce by, 53–54, 57, 413
  representational voting in, 331–332
  scandals in, 330, 333
  sedition law and, 100, 103
  seniority system in. *See* Seniority
  separation of powers and, 40, 42–43, 479–481
  size of, 357
  slavery and, 19, 36, 37
  standing and, 452, 453
  state militias and, 60
  state sovereignty and, 58
  Supreme Court and, 438, 459
  television coverage of, 307, 308
  term limits in, 327, 342, 345, 358, 482
  terrorist legislation and, 120, 121, 359–362
  treaty with Britain (1783), 21
  voting in, 236–237, 331–333, 338, 344, 355–356
  women and minorities in, 325–326, 325(tab.)
  women's rights and, 140
  workload of, 478
Congressional Accountability Act (1995), 358
Congressional Black Caucus (CBC), 340–341
Congressional Budget Office (CBO), 70, 347
Congressional calendar, 352
Congressional campaign committee, 208
Congressional campaigns, 232–237, 331
  funding for, 244–245, 245(fig.), 246
  presidential campaigns and, 232–234
  TV ads in, 302–303
Congressional Committee (Democratic), 209
Congressional committees, 319, 336, 341–345
  See also specific committee

conference committee, 356
growth in, 346(fig.)
hearings, 308, 351
House, 342, 343, 345
legislative process and, 350–353
reform of, 342
Senate, 342, 343, 344
seniority in, 323, 338, 339–340
subcommittees, 341, 342, 343, 346
Congressional districts, 327
1990 census and, 327, 329, 330
courts and, 457
marginal *vs.* safe, 327
pork-barrel legislation and, 359
redistricting, 235–236, 339
Congressional elections, 181, 225, 482
of 1938, 390
of 1974, 333
of 1982, 260
of 1986, 183
of 1994, 333
of 2002, 183
gender gap in, 160–161
incumbency advantage in, 253(tab.), 282, 327–328
PAC financing, 283
partisan gains in, 394(tab.)
presidential popularity and, 391
Republican success in, 328–329, 329(tab.)
ticket-splitting in, 207
turnout in, 187
Congressional ethics, rules of, 360
Congressional Government (Wilson), 379
Congressional investigations, 307, 308, 431–432
Congressional oversight, 420–421, 423, 424, 427–430, 433
Congressional Record, 238
Congressional reforms, 317
Congressional Research Service, 347
Congressional staffs, 345–347, 346(fig.)
Connecticut, 20, 27(fn.), 37, 306
Connecticut Compromise, 26–27
Connor, Eugene ("Bull"), 136
Consent calendar (House), 352
Conservatism, 170(tab.), 215
in bureaucracy, 422
congressional Republicans, 171, 339
interest groups, 451, 452
judges, 446
judicial review and, 439
meaning of term, 168–169
public-interest law firms, 272
in Senate, 332, 333
talk shows, 303, 304–305
think tanks, 273
Conservative coalition, 330, 333, 477
Conservative party (Great Britain), 260
Considine, Bob, 99
Constituencies, 320, 330–334, 469
attitudinal voting and, 332–333
organizational voting and, 331, 332
representational voting and, 331–332
Constituency-based caucuses, 340, 341(tab.)
Constitution, English, 18
Constitutional Amendments, 5
First Amendment. *See* First Amendment (1791), A13
Second Amendment (1791), 36, 102, A13
Third Amendment (1791), 102, A13
Fourth Amendment (1791), 36, 41, 114, A13

Fifth Amendment (1791), 36, 41, 102, 114, A13
Sixth Amendment (1791), 36, 41, A13
Seventh Amendment (1791), 36, 102, A14
Eighth Amendment (1791), 36, 102, 457, A14
Ninth Amendment (1791), 36, A14
Tenth Amendment (1791), 36, 53, 58, 66, 67, 142, A14
Eleventh Amendment (1795), 58, 445, 461, A14
Twelfth Amendment (1804), 376, A14
Thirteenth Amendment (1795), 461, A15
Fourteenth Amendment. *See* Fourteenth Amendment (1868), A15
Fifteenth Amendment (1870), 181, 443, 461, A16
Sixteenth Amendment (1913), 414, A16
Seventeenth Amendment (1913), 324, 361, A16
Eighteenth Amendment (1919), A17
Nineteenth Amendment (1920), 41, 140, 182, A17
Twentieth Amendment (1933), A17
Twenty-first amendment (1933), 28, 41, A18
Twenty-second Amendment (1951), 373, 401, A18
Twenty-third Amendment (1961), 183, A18
Twenty-forth Amendment (1964), A19
Twenty-fifth Amendment (1967), 384, 402, A19
Twenty-sixth Amendment (1971), 183, 461, A20
text of, A13–A20
Constitutional amendments, proposed
balanced budget amendment, 28(fn.), 43, 45, 481
Equal Rights Amendment, 274, 275
flag-burning, 108
Constitutional Convention (1787), 5, 22–27
See also Framers of Constitution
economic interests, 37–38
plan for federalism, 52–53
political history and, 22–23
Shays's Rebellion and, 23–24, 25
state constitutions and, 22–23
Constitutional Council (France), 438, 462
Constitutional courts, 446
Constitutional Union party, 205
Constitution of U.S., 7, 16–47, 60, 200. *See also* Constitutional Convention; Framers of Constitution
Amendments to. *See* Constitutional Amendments
authority of, 5
Bill of Rights. *See* Bill of Rights
checks and balances in, 29
criticism of, 40, 42–45, 85
democracy and, 25, 27–30
elections in, 181
equal protection of law, 127–128
Great Compromise, 26–27
guarantee of individual liberty in, 24–25
homosexual rights and, 149–151
on House of Representatives, 235
improvements on, 479, 482
judicial review and, 45, 439, 440, 441
language of, 41
liberty and, 17–19, 30–31, 34–35, 84

need for bill of rights, 34–36
New Jersey Plan for, 25–26
policy-making and, 469–470
power-sharing and, 309, 379
on powers of Congress, 26, 27, 55–56, 320
preamble to, 155
presidency and, 397
ratification of, 31, 38–39
separation of powers. *See* Separation of powers
signing of, 21
silence on slavery, 36–37, 38
on state-federal relations, 53, 55, 594
states and, 50
text of, A4–A20
Virginia Plan for, 25, 26
ways of amending, 28, 28(fn.), 42
women and, 41
Consumer activists, 419, 427
See also Nader, Ralph
Consumer Federation of America, 280
Consumer protection laws, 12
Continental Congress, 37
Continuity of Government Commission, 317, 360–361, 362
Contracts, 35
Cook County, Illinois, 214
Coolidge, Calvin, 378, 401
Cornell University Medical School, 125
Corporate funding, 250
PACs and, 282, 283
Corporations, 443, 472
free-speech rights of, 103, 108–109
Corruption
bribery, 285, 359
in Defense Department, 284
reform era and, 204
regulation of lobbying, 287
Cosmopolitan (magazine), 295
Cost of Living Council, 414
Council of Economic Advisors (CEA), 383
Council of State Governments, 62
Counties, 57, 59, 62, 69
Court of Military Appeals, 446, 449(fig.)
Courts. *See also* Federal courts; Supreme Court
changes in, 475
checks and balances and, 29
mandates and, 67
power of, 438
state, 59, 448, 449, 449(fig.), 450, 454
Courts of appeals, 84, 445, 446, 448
jurisdiction of, 449(fig.), 450–451
Cox Broadcasting Corp. v. Cohn (1975), 113, 117
Crack cocaine, 138–139
Craig v. Boren (1976), 142
Crime
civil rights and, 138–139, 169
due process and, 113–121
media and, 299, 301
Criminal Justice Legal Foundation, 272
Crisis, The (magazine), 128, 129, 269
Cronkite, Walter, 307
CRS (Congressional Research Service), 347
C-SPAN TV network, 308
Cuba, 120, 295
Cuban Americans, 165, 258
Cultural conflict, immigration and, 100–101
"Culture war," 86–87
Cummings, Elijah, 341
Cumming v. Richmond County Board of Education (1899), 128

Cuomo, Mario, 233
Currency, 56, 61, 472
Customs Service, 399, 424

Daily Mirror (newspaper), 298
Daily Telegraph (newspaper), 298
Damage suits, 452–453
Darwinism, 268
Daschle, Tom, 248
Davis, Gray, 165
Davis, John W., 212
Dean, Howard, 239, 250, 307
    Internet campaign of, 209, 243, 297
Death penalty, 458
Deaver, Michael K., 284
Debate, by presidential candidates, 242, 244, 302
Debs, Eugene V., 220, 221, 222
Decentralization, in Congress, 320, 322,
    342–343, 470, 476
Declaration of Independence (1776), 17, 18,
    35–36, 83
    on slavery, 19
    text of, A1–A3
De facto segregation, 132
Defense Department, 422, 424, 428. *See also*
    Military
    corruption in, 284
    employees in, 421(fig.)
Defense of Marriage Act (1996), 151
Deficit. *See* Budget deficit
De jure segregation, 132
DeKalb County, Georgia, 134
Delaware, 35, 37, 237(fn.)
Delegate model, 399
Delegate selection, 225, 241
    delegate allocation formulas, 209–210
    superdelegates, 211
    winner-reward systems, 212
Democracy, 6–10, 76
    "adding-machine," 481
    Constitution and, 25
    direct, 6–8, 59
    distribution of power in, 8–10
    human nature and, 29–30
    intraparty, 210
    political culture and, 77
    representative, 6–8, 27–28
    self-interest and, 10
    terrorism and, 7
Democracy in America (Tocqueville), 77
Democratic caucus, 342, 343
Democratic Congressional Campaign Commit-
    tee, 336
Democratic National Committee (DNC), 209,
    211–212, 246
Democratic party. *See also* Political parties;
    Republican party
    African Americans and, 222, 258, 259
    antiwar movement and, 221–222
    conservative coalition in, 333
    control of Congress, 260, 370, 371, 477
    control of House, 328, 330
    factionalization of, 208
    gridlock and, 371
    identification with, 199, 199(fig.)
    Iowa caucus and, 237, 238
    Jacksonian, 202–203, 204, 375
    nominating conventions of, 203, 209–212,
        217, 222, 224
    527 organizations and, 252
    polarization of Congress and, 478–479

presidency and, 225–226, 254–255,
    258(tab.), 259
redistricting and, 329
reform groups in, 215
South and, 167, 203, 204
split in (1860), 205–206
two-party system and, 217–220
unions and, 216, 222, 258
voter turnout and, 190
women and, 160
Democratic-Republicans. *See* Jeffersonian
    Republicans
Democratic Study Group, 332, 340
Demonstrations, 88, 192, 476
    civil rights movement, 135, 136, 137, 273
    interest groups and, 274, 285–286
    public policy and, 190
Denver, Colorado, 298
Departments. *See specific departments*
Deregulation, 280, 301–302
Desegregation. *See also Brown v. Board of
    Education*
    busing and, 67, 133–134, 463
    compliance with Civil Rights Act of 1964,
        137, 460
    federal mandates, 66, 67
    "freedom of choice" plan, 132, 134
    integration contrasted, 132–134
    racial quotas in, 169, 451
    of schools, 129, 131, 380, 459
    social science as rationale for, 131–132
    Supreme Court rulings, 129, 131–134
Detroit, Michigan, 215–216, 298
Devolution, 49, 50, 68–70
Dickerson v. United States (2000), 121
Dickinson, John, 18
Dillon's rule, 57
Direct democracy, 6–8, 59
Direct-mail solicitations
    campaigning, 243–244, 247, 257
    fund-raising, 209, 215, 283
    by interest groups, 277–278, 282
Direct primary elections, 204, 222
Dirksen, Everett, 137
Disabled (handicapped) persons, 431
    rights of, 66–67, 147
Discharge calendar (House), 352
Discharge petition, 352, 353
Discretionary authority, 415
Discrimination, 457
    in employment, 138, 145, 148
    on gender bias, 138, 141
    intent to discriminate, 133
    racial, 3–4, 95(fig.), 148, 149
    reverse discrimination, 145, 148, 455
    strict scrutiny of, 125
Disruptive tactics, 285–286. *See also* Protests
Dissenting opinion, 456
Distributional formulas, 65
District courts, 445, 446, 448
    jurisdiction of, 449(fig.), 450
District of Columbia, 7, 183, 278, 298
Diversity
    affirmative action and, 144
    federalism and, 70, 72
    religious, 85
Diversity cases, 448
Divided government, 370–372, 433
Division (standing) vote, 355
"Dixiecrat" (States' Rights) party, 220, 221,
    223

DNC (Democratic National Committee), 209,
    211–212, 246
Doctrines
    of dual sovereignty, 450
    of nullification, 56
    of "privileged speech," 238
    of sovereign immunity, 452
    of state sovereignty, 21, 58–60, 455
Dole, Bob, 187, 233, 237
Domestic policy. *See* Policy
Double tracking, 355
Douglas, Stephen A., 205
Douglas, William O., 461
Douglass, Frederick, 212
Draft, military
    protests, 108, 110
    women excluded from, 140, 141–142
Dred Scott case, 442, 461, 463
"Driving while black," 139
Drug Enforcement Administration, 424
Dual federalism, 57
Dual sovereignty doctrine, 450
Du Bois, W. E. B., 129, 269
Due process, 113–121, 473
    confessions and self-incrimination, 117–118
    exclusionary rule, 114–116, 118–119
    good-faith exception, 119
    landmark cases, 121
    search and seizure, 113–114, 116–117
    terrorism and civil liberties, 119–121
Due process clause, 102, 104, 110
Dukakis, Michael, 225, 233, 234, 256, 309
Dunlop, John, 387
Duplication, bureaucratic, 430, 431

Economic interests, 37–39
Economic Interpretation of the Constitution, An
    (Beard), 38
Economic policy, 169
Economic Policy Institute, 273
Economic protest parties, 220, 221
Economic system (economy)
    government role in, 413, 442–443
    other nations compared, 81–82
    party realignment and, 206
    political culture and, 77, 79–80
    voting and, 252, 255–256
Economists, bureaucracy and, 423
Education. *See also* Schools
    bilingual, 101
    desegregation of. *See Brown v. Board of Edu-
        cation;* Desegregation
    federal grants for, 60, 62, 65–66
    liberalizing effect of, 136, 161, 162, 267
    public opinion and, 161–162
    sex discrimination in, 138
    voting and, 188, 189(fig.), 191
Education and the Workforce Committee
    (House), 345
Education Department, 385, 411
Eighteen-year-olds, voting by, 183, 461
Eighth Amendment (1791), 36, 102, 457
Eisenhower, Dwight, 233, 259
    cabinet of, 384
    character of, 388
    popularity of, 392(fig.)
    presidency of, 369, 375, 380, 391, 400
    veto power and, 395
Elazar, Daniel J., 51
Elections, 43, 181, 192, 230–262
    campaigns and. *See* Campaigns

congressional. *See* Congressional elections
deciding factors in, 253–259
effects on policy, 259–260, 262
forecasting outcomes of, 256
issues and, 255–256
kinds of, 241
municipal, 219
party affiliation and, 252, 254
plurality system, 217–218
presidential. *See* Presidential elections
primary. *See* Primary elections
prospective voting, 255
reelection of incumbents, 232
retrospective voting, 255–256
role of parties in, 254–255
state and municipal, 213, 214
winner-take-all, 211, 217, 218–219, 220, 376
winning coalitions, 257–259
Electoral college, 27, 372, 373, 376–377
winner-take-all principle in, 218–219, 376
Electorate, 180–187
federal control of, 181–183
party identification, 199
voter turnout. *See* Voter turnout
Electronic media, 296–297. *See also* Internet; Radio; Television
Electronic roll-call voting, 356
Eleventh Amendment (1795), 58, 445, 461
Elites
interest group bias and, 278
pluralist view of, 9–10
political. *See* Political elites
power elite in business, 9
Employment
during and after government service, 284–285
conditions of aid and, 67
disabled and, 147
discrimination in, 59, 138, 145, 148
federal employees, 416(fig.)
hiring quotas and, 79
of illegal aliens, 146
sexual harassment and, 142
unemployment, 69
Employment and Training Administration, 411
Energy and Commerce Committee (House), 345
Energy and Natural Resources Committee (Senate), 344
Energy Department, 428
Engel v. Vitale (1962), 114
England. *See* Great Britain
Enhanced rescission authority, 45, 395
Entitlement grants, 69–70
Entitlement programs, 359
Entrepreneurial function of staffs, 346
Enumerated powers, 29
Environmental Action, 274, 282
Environmental Defense Fund, 274, 276
Environmental protection
mandates, 66, 67
movement for, 273, 274
Environmental Protection Agency (EPA), 271, 411, 422, 427, 452
Environment and Public Works Committee (Senate), 344
EPA. *See* Environmental Protection Agency
Episcopal church, 87
Equal Employment Opportunities Commission, 142

Equality, 10
Constitution and, 39–40
income, 81–82, 82(tab.)
political culture and, 77
race relations and, 78
Equality of opportunity, 79, 145–149, 476
Equality of results, 79, 144, 145
Equal justice principle, 457
Equal Pay Act, 358
Equal protection of law, 102, 127–128, 131, 140, 146, 150
Equal Rights Amendment (ERA), 142, 274, 275
Equal time rule, 302
ERA. *See* Equal Rights Amendment (ERA)
Erikson, Erik, 85–86
Erznoznik v. Jacksonville (1975), 113, 117
Escobedo case, 118
Espionage Act (1917), 100, 103
Establishment clause, 101, 110, 111–113
Ethic of self-reliance, 79
Ethics and Public Policy Center, 273
Ethics Committee (Senate), 344
Ethics in Government Act (1978), 284, 285
Ethics rules in Congress, 360
Ethnic minorities, 164–167. *See also* Minorities; Race
Europe, 231, 368, 561(fn.). *See also specific country*
bureaucracy in, 411
class cleavage in, 163
coalition parties in, 219–220
judicial review in, 462
parliamentary systems in, 231, 368, 470
political participation in, 192, 192(tab.)
political parties in, 199–200
political association in, 269
sense of efficacy in, 90
voter turnout in, 178
European Court of Human Rights, 462
Evangelical Christians, 86, 159, 160(tab.)
Everson v. Board of Education (1947), 114
Exclusionary rule, 114–116, 118–119
Exclusive committees (House), 345
Executive agencies, 386
Executive branch, 20. *See also* Presidency
conflicts of interest and, 285
reorganization of, 399–400
veto power of, 25
Executive Calendar (Senate), 352
Executive Office of the President, 383–384
Executive privilege, 396
Exit polls, 157
Ex post facto laws, 35, 102
External efficacy, 90

Factional parties, 203–204, 220–221, 223
Factions, 30, 32–33, 85
Madison on, 32, 51, 265
within political parties, 201–202, 215
Fairness Doctrine, 302
Fair-share formulas, 61
Faith-based programs, 94
Family, political socialization and, 85–86, 158–159
Family and Medical Care Leave Act, 358
Family Assistance Plan of 1969, 167
Farber, Myron, 301
Farmers, 258–259, 427. *See also under* Agriculture
interest groups and, 266, 267, 270, 278
protests by, 279

Farmers' Union, 266, 267, 280
FBI (Federal Bureau of Investigation), 136, 411, 417, 424, 428
FCC. *See* Federal Communications Commission
FDA (Food and Drug Administration), 282, 284, 422
FEA (Federal Energy Administration), 280
Feature news stories, 305
Federal agencies. *See also specific agency*
"activist" agencies, 422
culture of, 423–424
growth of, 413, 477
heads of, subordinates and, 422–423
political ideologies of, 422
president and, 386, 399, 417
recruitment and retention, 415–419
regulatory agencies, 284, 415
states and, 415
Federal aid. *See* Federal grants; Grants-in-aid
Federal budget, 380, 383–384, 398
balancing of, 262, 338
budget deficits, 70, 70(fig.), 359, 428–429, 476, 478
Clinton and, 371
Congress and, 379, 397, 428–429
proposed balance budget amendment, 28(fn.), 43, 45, 481
surplus, 61
Federal bureaucracy. *See* Bureaucracy
Federal Bureau of Investigation (FBI), 136, 411, 417, 424, 428
Federal Communications Commission (FCC), 243, 280, 299, 301, 427, 450
licensing by, 293, 478
Federal Constitutional Court (Germany), 462
Federal courts. *See also* Supreme Court
activism of. *See* Judicial activism
campaign finance suit in, 251
civil rights movement in, 127–134
class-action suits in, 453–454
on confidentiality of sources, 301
Congress and, 460, 461–463
development of, 439–445
fee shifting, 452, 454
getting to, 451–454
judicial review, 28, 438–439, 469–470
jurisdiction of, 448–451, 449(fig.)
lawsuits in, 451–454
legislation and, 460
mandates by, 67
map of, 445
Marbury v. Madison and, 440–441
nation-state relationship and, 441–442, 473
policy-making of, 439
power of, 456–457, 459, 481, 482
public interest lobbies and, 443
public opinion and, 444, 463–464
selecting judges for, 446–448, 447(tab.)
standing and, 452–453, 454
structure of, 446–448
Federal Deposit Insurance Corporation, 424
Federal Emergency Management Agency, 399
Federal Energy Administration (FEA), 280
Federal government. *See also* Congress; Government; House of Representatives; Judiciary; Presidency; President; Senate; Supreme Court
activism of, 61–62
Bush's reorganization of, 399
constraints on, 406
employment by, 416(fig.)

power to regulate commerce, 442, 443
social welfare programs. *See* Welfare
supremacy of, 441–442
wartime powers of, 474–475
Federal grants, 271. *See also* Grants-in-aid
for campaigns, 233, 244–246, 250, 288
discrimination and, 138
for interest groups, 276–277
Federal highway program, 63
Federal Housing Finance Board, 424
Federal income tax, 3, 460
cuts in, 478
exemption from, 287
grants-in-aid and, 61
Sixteenth Amendment and, 414, 461
wartime taxes, 414
Federalism, 30, 39, 48–73, 469
Congress and, 53, 66–67, 70, 72
controversy surrounding, 50–52
devolution and, 49, 50, 68–70
dual federalism, 57–58
federal-state relations, 60–68
goals of Founders and, 51, 52–54, 85
governmental structure under, 50–52
as innovation, 52–53
mandates and, 67–68
meaning of, 54–60
nullification and, 56
political activity under, 52, 61–62
political party organization and, 200
representative democracy and, 28–29
state sovereignty and, 58–60
Supreme Court on, 54–56, 58
terminology of, 51
Federalist papers, 22, 25, 32–33
No. 10, 32, 33, 34, 51, 153, 265
No. 28, 53
No. 39, 51
No. 45, 54
No. 46, 53
No. 51, 1, 32, 33, 34, 315, A26–A29
No. 78, 440
Federalist party, 201–202, 294, 440, 463
*Federal Maritime Commission v. South Carolina
Ports Authority* (2002), 58
Federal-question cases, 448
Federal regime, 51
Federal Regulation of Lobbying Act (1946),
286–287
Federal Reserve Board, 424
Federal spending, 398, 416(fig.). *See also* Bud-
get deficits; Federal budget
grants. *See* Grants-in-aid
presidential attempts to limit, 394,
396–397, 398, 478
red tape and, 431
Federal-state relations, 60–68. *See also*
Grants-in-aid
Federal system, 51
Federal Trade Commission (FTC), 284, 422, 423
Federation of Business and Professional
Women, 274
Fee shifting, 452, 454
Feingold, Russell, 109, 252
Feminine Mystique, The (Friedan), 140
Feminist movement, 106, 274–275
Ferraro, Geraldine, 240
Fifteenth Amendment (1870), 181, 443, 461
Fifth Amendment (1791), 36, 41, 102, 114
Filibuster, 235, 324, 354–355, 438
Finance Committee (Senate), 344, 345

Financial disclosure, 285
Financial Services Committee (House), 345
Firings "rules," 419, 420
First Amendment (1791), 36, 102–113, 146,
286
    See also Freedom of expression
    freedom of religion, 101, 102, 110–113, 453
    inclusive definition of "person," 108–110
    interpreting and applying, 102–105
    media and, 300, 313. *See also* Free press
First Great Awakening, 83
First Hoover Commission (1947–1949), 432
"Fitness" for office, 375
527 organizations, 252
Flag-burning, 108
"Floaters" (repeat voters), 185
Floor debate (House), 353–354
Floor debate (Senate), 354–355
Florida, 183(tab.), 186, 248, 251, 376, 464
Flowers, Gennifer, 310, 311
Foley, Tom, 337
Foley v. Connelie (1978), 146
Food and Drug Administration (FDA), 282,
284, 422
Ford, Gerald, 134, 240, 309
    character of, 388–389
    election of 1976 and, 224, 242
    pardon of Nixon by, 404
    popularity of, 392, 393(fig.)
    presidency of, 386, 387, 394
    as vice president, 233, 403
Ford Foundation, 276
Foreign affairs, history of, 11–12
Foreign policy, 6, 331
Foreign Relations Committee (Senate), 344
Foreign service jobs, 422
Forest Service, 428
Formal authority, power and, 5
Foundation grants, 276
Founders. *See* Framers of Constitution
Fourteenth Amendment (1868), 148, 461
    Bill of Rights extended to states, 35, 102,
    111, 473
    citizenship and, 145
    desegregation and, 127–128, 131, 132
    due process clause of, 104, 110, 473
    equal protection of law, 102, 127–128,
    131, 140, 146, 150
    illegal aliens and, 146
    state law and, 439, 443
    women's rights and, 140
Fourth Amendment (1791), 36, 41, 114
Fox News television, 299, 303
Framers of Constitution (Founders), 24–25, 155
    Bill of Rights and, 84, 98
    compromise with slavery, 36–37
    concerns about presidency, 372–373
    Congress and, 321
    goals of, federalism and, 30, 51, 52–54
    judiciary and, 438–439
    motives of, 29–30, 37–40
    political parties and, 201–202
    ratification and, 31
    on representative democracy, 8, 27–28
France, 23, 82(tab.), 198
    bureaucracy in, 411
    Constitutional Council, 438, 462
    interest groups in, 266
    media in, 293
    multiparty system of, 377
    patriotism in, 81, 81(tab.)

plurality system in, 217–218
religion in, 83(tab.), 84(tab.)
Revolution in (1789), 17, 100, 169, 374
unitary government of, 50, 51
working class in, 163
Frankfurter, Felix, 457
Franking privilege, 253, 319, 358
Franklin, Benjamin, 24, 26
Fraternal Order of the Police, 99
Free Congress Foundation, 273
"Freedom-of-choice" desegregation plan, 132,
134
"Freedom of contract," 439
Freedom of expression, 99
    free press and, 105, 109, 113, 117, 292–293
    inclusive definition of "person," 108–110
    libel and, 105, 293
    national security and, 102–105
    obscenity and, 105–107
    symbolic speech, 108
    testing restrictions on, 107
Freedom of Information Act (1966), 293, 424
Freedom of religion, 102, 110–113, 114
Freedom rides, 135
Free-exercise clause, 110–111
"Free love" primary, 241
Free press, 105, 113, 117, 292–293
    landmark cases on, 109
Free-Soil party, 221
Free speech, 109, 251, 470. *See also* Freedom of
expression
French Revolution (1789), 17, 100, 169, 374
Freneau, Philip, 294
Freshmen members of Congress, 326–327,
326(fig.)
Friedan, Betty, 140
Frist, Bill, 318
FTC (Federal Trade Commission), 284, 422, 423
Fulton, Robert, 442
Fundamentalist religious groups, 206, 268
Funding. *See also* Campaign financing
    abortion-funding policies, 71
    growth of PACs and, 282–284, 283(tab.)
    for interest groups, 276–278
Funding formulas, 61

Gaines, Lloyd, 129
Gallup poll, 303, 391, 392–393(fig.)
GAO (General Accounting Office), 347
Gardner, John, 277
Garfield, James A., 401, 402, 417
Garner, John Nance, 401
Garrity, W. Arthur, 133
Gatekeeper function of media, 299
Gay (same-sex) marriage, 5, 150–151, 159(fig.),
161, 286. *See also* Homosexual rights
Gazette of the United States, 294
Gender discrimination, 142. *See also* Women's
rights
Gender gap, in political attitudes, 160–161,
161(tab.)
General Accounting Office (GAO), 347
General-act charter, 57
General elections, 241
General Motors, 268, 271
General revenue sharing (GRS), 63–64
General Services Administration, 432
Geographical region, 167
George III, King of England, 19
Georgia, 27(fn.), 35, 113, 134, 149, 183(tab.),
203, 217, 442

Gephardt, Richard, 233
Gerber, Alan S., 178
Germany, 82(tab.), 83(tab.), 84(tab.), 90, 269, 438
    judicial review in, 462
    patriotism in, 81, 81(tab.)
Gerry, Elbridge, 28, 35, 38, 39, 234
Gerrymandering, 234, 235, 236
Gettysburg Address (Lincoln), 155
Gideon, Clarence Earl, 450, 451
Gideon v. Wainwright (1964), 121
Gingrich, Newt, 323, 333, 337–338, 342
Ginsburg, Ruth Bader, 454(tab.), 456
Gitlow, Benjamin, 104
Gitlow v. New York (1925), 102, 103, 104
Giuliani, Rudy, 11
Glenn, John, 233
Goldwater, Barry, 169, 224, 225, 226, 242
Gompers, Samuel, 473
"Good behavior," 403, 403(fn.), 446
Goode, Virgil H., Jr., 218
Good-faith exception, 119
Gore, Al, 84, 225, 240, 309
    Florida vote-count controversy and, 248, 251, 376
    as vice president, 233, 401
Government, 3–15. *See also* Federal government
    achievements of, 4
    barriers to action in, 479–482
    change in vision of, 20–21
    changes in, 471–473
    constraints on journalists, 311, 313
    creation of interest groups and, 267
    democratic. *See* Democracy
    divided government, 370–372, 433
    goals of, 3–4
    growth of, 11, 472
    human nature and, 29–30
    importance of, 4
    media and, 292, 309
    mistrust of. *See* Mistrust of government
    New system, 475–478
    Old system, 474–475, 476
    polarized politics and, 478–479
    political change and, 11–12
    political participation and, 179–180
    political power and, 4–6
    regulation by. *See* Government regulation
    relaxing restraints on growth of, 473–479
    restraints on growth of, 473
    restraints on journalists by, 311, 313
    rules for improving, 478
    unified government, 370
Governmental Affairs Committee (Senate), 344
Government employee unions, 275, 276(tab.)
Government Performance and Results Act (1993), 432
Government Printing Office, 295
Government programs, disabled and, 147
Government Reform Committee (House), 345
Government regulation, 416(fig.)
    of commerce, 53–54, 442, 443
    deregulation of broadcast media, 301–302
    of economy, 413
    of interest groups, 286–287
    regulatory agencies, 284, 460
Government workers, unionization of, 275, 276, 276(tab.)
Governors, 43, 63
    federalism and, 61, 62
    presidency and, 372

GPRA Government Performance and Results Act (1993), 432
Grace, J. Peter, 431
Grace Commission, 431
Graham v. Richardson (1971), 146
Grand Army of the Republic, 267
Grandfather clause, 181
Grand jury information, 120
Grand Rapids, Michigan, 66
Grange, 266, 267
Grant, Ulysses S., 378
Grants-in-aid, 60–66, 415. *See also* Federal grants
    block grants, 49, 50, 63–64, 65, 69
    categorical grants, 63–65, 66, 68
    conditions of aid and, 66, 67–68
    distributional formulas, 65
    entitlements and, 69–70
    federal-state relations and, 60–62
    intergovernmental lobby and, 62
    interstate rivalry, 65–66
    mandates, 66–67
Grassroots, partisan, 390
Grassroots lobbying, 281–282, 287
Gratz v. Bollinger (2003), 149
Gravel, Mike, 238
Great Britain (England), 49, 82(tab.), 90, 374
    civic duty in, 80
    colonial views of, 17–18, 24
    legal tradition of, 103, 114
    libel law in, 105, 293
    national newspapers in, 298
    Official Secrets Act, 293, 309
    parliamentary system of, 28, 42, 231, 259–260, 319, 369, 371, 410, 438, 480
    political authority in, 265
    political organizations in, 269
    prime minister in, 308, 309, 368–370, 471, 480
    religion in, 83(tab.), 84(tab.)
    slavery and, 36
    U.S. treaty with (1783), 21
    working class in, 163
Great Compromise, 26–27
Great Depression, 394, 473
    election of 1932 and, 206
    government programs of, 474. *See also* New Deal
    union movement and, 275
"Great Mentioner, The," 233
"Great Society" legislation, 477
Greek *polis*, 6
Green, Donald P., 178
Greenback party, 206, 221
Green party, 221, 271
Green v. County School Board of New Kent County (1968), 132, 134
Greer v. Spock (1976), 113, 117
Gridlock, 40, 371–372
Griswold v. Connecticut (1965), 143
GRS (General revenue sharing), 63–64
Grutter v. Bollinger (2003), 149
Guantanamo prison, 120
Guardian (newspaper), 298
Gun control, 274, 282, 331, 445

Habeas corpus, writ of, 35, 102, 462
Haddon, William, Jr., 281
Hagen, Michael Gray, 79
Haig, Alexander, 385–386

Haldeman, H. R., 382
Hamilton, Alexander, 6, 18, 26, 372, 384
    on federalism, 54, 85
    Federalist papers, 32, 53, 440
    Gazette of the United States, 294
    Jefferson and, 201
    ratification of Constitution and, 35
    as secretary of Treasury, 369, 374, 375, 386
    views on government, 22
Hammond, Susan Webb, 340, 341
Hampton v. Mow Sun Wong (1976), 146
Hancock, John, 21, 22
Handgun Control, Inc., 282
Handicapped Children's Protection Act (1986), 66
Handicapped (disabled) persons, 431
    rights of, 66–67, 147
Hannity, Sean, 303
Harding, Warren G., 104, 214, 243
Hare Krishnas, 110
Harkin, Tom, 233
Harlan, John (elder), 461
Harlan, John (younger), 461
Harper's (magazine), 295
Harrison, Benjamin, 243
Harrison, William Henry, 378, 388, 401
Hart, Gary, 300, 310
Harvard Law Review, 455
Hastert, Dennis, 323, 331
Hastings, Alice, 461
Hatch Act (1939), 214
Hate crimes, 105
Hawaii, 272
Hayes, Rutherford B., 212, 378
Health, Education, Labor and Pensions Committee (Senate), 344
Health and Human Services (HHS) Department, 384, 411
Health care, federal grants for, 62
Health Care Financing Administration, 411
Hearst, William Randolph, 295
Heclo, Hugh, 427
Heinz, John, III, 297
Henry, Patrick, 18, 24, 35
Heritage Foundation, 273
HHS (Health and Human Services) Department, 384, 411
Hialeah, Florida, 110
Hill, Anita, 448
Hispanics (Latinos), 161, 459
    in Congress, 325, 325(tab.), 326
    cultural conflicts and, 100, 101
    in judiciary, 447(fig.)
    political participation of, 192, 193, 193(fig.)
    public opinion and, 165–167, 166(fig.)
    voting of, 191, 258
Hollerith, Herman, 413
Holmes, Oliver Wendell, 103, 104, 447
Homeland security, 70, 399
Homeland Security, Department of (DHS), 49, 61, 359–360, 399, 414
Home-rule charter, 57
Homosexual (gay) rights, 86, 95(fig.), 101, 149–151
    AIDS and, 174
    gay marriage, 5, 150–151, 159(fig.), 161, 286
    landmark cases, 150
"Honeymoon" of president, 394
Honoraria, ban on, 360, 362
Hoover, Herbert, 307, 390, 399, 432

House calendars, 352
House of Representatives, 34, 37. *See also* Congress; Senate; Speaker of the House
  campaign costs for, 244–246, 245(fig.)
  campaign for, 234–235
  changing organization of, 322–323, 343
  committees of. *See specific committees*
  Constitution and, 27, 28
  Democratic control of, 207, 260
  devolution and, 69, 70
  "Dirty Dozen" in, 282
  election to. *See* Congressional elections
  floor debate of bills in, 353
  impeachment and, 87, 403
  legislative process and, 352
  media coverage of, 308
  party structure in, 335–337
  polarization in, 333
  presidential elections and, 220, 372, 373, 376, 377
  qualifications and privileges of, 238, 319
  Republican control of, 232, 328–330, 338, 342, 344
  revenue bills and, 351
  standing committees of, 345
  terms of, 42
  voting for, 181
Housing, discrimination in, 138
Housing and Urban Development (HUD), 64, 384–385, 411, 427
Hughes, Charles Evans, 461
Human nature, democracy and, 29–30, 84
Humphrey, Hubert, 217, 221, 224, 242, 401
Hunt, James B., 210
Hunt Commission, 210
Hussein, Saddam, 172, 248
Hyde, Henry, 143, 342, 403
Hyde Amendment (1976), 143

ICC (Interstate Commerce Commission), 413, 443
Idaho, 141
Ideological interest groups, 271, 283
Ideological parties, 215, 220, 221
Ideological purity, 447–448
Ideological self-identification surveys, 168(fig.)
Ideology. *See* Political ideology(ies)
"I Have a Dream" speech (King), 136
Illegal aliens, rights of, 146
Illinois, 219
Illinois Farm Bureau, 270
Immigration, 78
  1840–1996, 101(fig.)
  cultural conflict and, 100–101
  curbs on legal, 173
  illegal aliens, 146
  political machine and, 213
  terrorist law and, 120, 121
Immigration and Naturalization Service (INS), 146, 399
Immigration Reform and Control Act (1986), 146
Imminent danger, 107
Impeachment, 403–404, 461
  of Clinton, 87, 331, 333, 338, 368, 403, 478
Imperialism, bureaucratic, 430, 431
"Imperial presidency," 368
Implied powers, 378
Impoundment of funds, 396–397

Incentives to join organizations, 270–272
Income
  election results and, 256
  equity in, 81–82, 82(tab.)
  security, federal grants for, 62
Income tax. *See* Federal income tax
Incorporation, 102, 103. *See also* Corporations
Incumbency, 282
  campaign funds for, 246
  growth of, 326–328, 326(tab.), 327(tab.), 329
  newspaper endorsment of, 306
  PAC funding and, 283
  reelection of, 232, 234–235, 236, 256, 262, 328(tab.)
  retrospective voting and, 255–256
  spending by, 253, 253(tab.)
Independence Hall (Philadelphia), 26
Independent agencies, 386
Independent counsel, 404
Independent expenditures, 250
Independents, 158–159, 207
Independent voters, 254–255
India, 438
Indiana, 106, 213, 217
"Indiana" ballot, 207
Indian Affairs Committee (Senate), 344
Individual contributions, 250
Individual effort, 231
Individual responsibility, 77, 79
  member of Congress and, 232
Industry. *See also* Business; *specific industry*
  Defense Department and, 284
  interest groups and, 267, 278, 280
  state law and, 443
Inequality, views of, 39. *See also* Equality
In forma pauperis, 451
Information. *See* Political information
Initiative, legislation by, 13, 59, 149, 204
  See also Referendum
Insider news stories, 305
Insider strategy, 280–281
INS (Immigration and Naturalization Service), 146, 399
Institute for Policy Studies, 273
Institutional interests, 268–269
Institutions, trust in, 12, 88–89, 89(fig.)
INS v. Delgado (1984), 146
INS v. Lopez-Mendoza (1984), 146
Intelligence Committee (Senate), 344
Intent to discriminate, 133
Interest groups, 255, 264–290. *See also* Political action committees (PACs)
  activities of, 279–286
  bias in, 278–279
  bureaucracy and, 427
  campaign finance and, 234, 282
  conflict of interest and, 285
  Congress and, 281, 320, 332, 344, 351
  courts and, 451–452, 454, 455
  environmental movement, 273, 274
  feminist movement, 274–275
  formation of PACs, 282–284
  funding of, 276–278
  incentives to join, 270–272
  influence of staff on, 272–273
  as information suppliers, 279–280
  institutional interests, 268–269
  kinds of organizations, 268–273
  lobbying by, 271, 280–282, 470. *See also* Lobbying

  membership organizations, 269–270
  origins of, 266–268
  president and, 397
  proliferation of, 265–266, 474, 475
  public-interest law firms, 272
  public support of, 280–282
  "revolving door" and, 284–285
  social movements and, 267, 273–276
  think tanks, 273
  union movement, 266, 267, 273, 275–276
Intergovernmental lobby, 62
Interior Department, 414, 427
Internal efficacy, 90, 90(fig.)
Internal Revenue Service, 287, 411
Internal Revenue Code, 478
Internal Security Act (1940), 100
International City/Council Management Association, 62
International Relations Committee (House), 345
Internet, 120, 297–298
  campaigning and, 209, 243, 297, 303
  pornography on, 107
  "Rock the Vote" website, 185
  web logs (blogs), 292, 293, 297
Internet taps, 120
Interstate commerce, 57–58, 412, 413, 442, 445
Interstate Commerce Commission (ICC), 413, 443
Intraparty caucuses, 340–341, 341(tab.)
Intrastate commerce, 57–58
"Investigative reporting," 295, 305
Involuntary confessions, 117–118
Iowa caucus, 237–238, 300
Iran, arms sales to, 311
Iraq, U.S. war in, 88, 157, 248
Iron triangle, 426–427
Irving, Washington, 432
Israel, 231, 368
Issue network, 427
Issue public, 281
Italy, 82(tab.), 83(tab.), 190, 198, 411
  interest groups in, 266
  media monopoly in, 293
  multiparty system of, 377

Jackson, Andrew, 180
  election of 1824 and, 202, 376
  presidency of, 202–203, 322, 375–377
  states' rights and, 442
  Washington Globe and, 294
Jackson, Jesse, 191, 211, 222, 225
Jacksonian Democrats, 202–203, 204, 375
Jacobson, Gary C., 253
Japan, 80, 192, 368
  bureaucracy in, 471
Japanese Americans, 125, 165
Jay, John, 32
Jefferson, Thomas, 5, 56, 100, 103
  Congress and, 322
  Constitution and, 22, 23, 39, 85
  Declaration of Independence, 18, 19, 35–36
  election of 1800 and, 240, 376
  on established religion, 111
  National Gazette and, 294
  presidency of, 201–202, 378, 384, 388, 396, 440
  as Secretary of State, 369, 374, 386, 411
  states' rights and, 54
  as vice president, 401

Jeffersonian Republicans, 442, 463
  conflict with Federalists, 85
  founding of, 201–202, 201(fn.), 203
  Marbury v. Madison (1803), 440, 441
  newspapers controlled by, 294
Jeffords, James, 335, 370
Jehovah Witnesses, 110
Jewish Federations, 277
Jews, 87, 95(fig.), 99, 159, 160(fig.), 206
  anti-Semitism and, 105, 125
  cultural conflict and, 100, 101
  party loyalty of, 258, 259
  on Supreme Court, 446, 461
Johnson, Andrew, 240, 388, 403
Johnson, Hiram, 204, 222
Johnson, Lyndon B., 222, 233, 369
  character of, 388
  civil rights and, 137, 139
  Congress and, 370, 371, 394
  election of 1964 and, 167, 240, 242, 258, 306, 477
  election of 1968 and, 250
  media and, 313
  presidency of, 390, 392, 392(fig.), 398, 400
  as Senate majority leader, 334–335
  vice presidency of, 374, 401
  Vietnam war and, 307, 368, 371, 392
Joint Center for Political and Economic Studies, 273
Joint Committees, 342
Joint operating agreement, 298
Joint resolution, 350
Jones, Paula Corbin, 142, 310, 311, 396
Jordan, Hamilton, 382
Journalism
  "attack journalism," 309
  confidentiality of sources, 301
  electronic, 296–298. *See also* Internet
  government restraints on, 311, 313
  opinion magazines, 295–296
  party press, 294–295
  political history of, 283–298
  popular press, 295
  "yellow journalism," 295
Judges. *See also specific judges*
  appointment of. *See* Judicial appointments
  behavior of, 460
  court-ordered remedies and, 457
  impeachment of, 403
  mandates from, 67
  political ideology of, 446, 448
  selection of, 446–448, 447(tab.)
Judicial activism, 439, 440, 443, 444, 459–460, 463, 464
Judicial appointments, 385, 444, 461. *See also under specific presidents*
  litmus test, 447–448
  selection of, 446–448, 447(tab.)
  Senate approval of, 438, 447, 448
Judicial power, 45, 446
Judicial review, 28, 438–439, 469–470
Judiciary, 437–465. *See also* Courts; *specific cases*
  checks on power of, 460–464
  federal courts. *See* Federal courts
  independence of, 438
  Supreme Court. *See* Supreme Court
  under Virginia Plan, 25
Judiciary Act of 1789, 441
Judiciary Committee (House), 308, 345, 403
Judiciary Committee (Senate), 136, 137, 344, 448

Juries, racially segregated, 128
Jurisdiction
  of federal courts, 448–451, 449(fig.)
  of Supreme Court, 441, 449(fig.), 450, 451, 462–463
Jury trial, 35
Justice Department, 121, 287, 424, 428, 447

Kamarck, Elaine, 381
Kansas, 129
Katzenbach, Nicholas, 132
Kefauver, Estes, 307, 308
Kemp, Jack, 233
Kennedy, Anthony M., 58, 144, 147, 454(tab.), 456, 463
Kennedy, Edward M. ("Ted"), 278, 282
  on pocket veto, 395
Kennedy, John F., 136, 167, 216, 233
  assassination of, 137, 374, 401
  campaign debates, 242, 244
  character of, 388
  Congress and, 370
  Democratic machine and, 214
  election of 1960 and, 391
  media and, 310, 313
  national crises under, 398
  presidency of, 369, 384, 392(fig.), 394, 396, 400
  religion of, 253, 258, 469
  Vietnam war and, 368
Kennedy, Joseph P. II, 216
Kennedy, Robert F., 216, 222
Kentucky Resolution, 56
Kerrey, Bob, 233
Kerry, John F., 233, 250, 297
  election of 2004 and, 160, 186, 219, 219(tab.), 239, 240, 242, 248–249, 254(tab.), 479
Key, V. O., Jr., 163, 255
Kinder, Donald, 79
King, Martin Luther, Jr., 83, 135, 136, 139, 310
King, Rodney, 449–450
Kirk, Paul, 211
Kissinger, Henry, 382, 383, 387
"Know-Nothing" (American) party, 221
Knox, Henry, 369
Korean Americans, 165
Korean War, 100, 104
Kristol, William, 280
Ku Klux Klan, 104, 105, 285
Kunz, Carl Jacob, 99

Labor Department, 387, 413
Labor unions, 109, 163, 473. *See also specific unions*
  civil rights legislation and, 11, 273
  decline in membership, 275(fig.)
  Democratic party and, 216, 222, 254, 258
  government employee, 275, 276, 276(tab.)
  political funding by, 282, 283
  union movement, 266, 267, 273, 275–276
Labour party (G. Britain), 163
La Follette, Robert, 204, 217, 223
La Follette Progressive party, 221, 223
Laissez-faire economy, 413
Lame duck, 404
Land-grant colleges, 60
Land grants, 60
Landmark Legal Foundation, 272

Language
  bureaucratese, 425
  in newspapers, 304, 305
  political participation and, 193, 303
  in schools, 459
  of U.S. Constitution, 41
"Larry King Live" (TV program), 297
Laski, Harold, 51
Latinos. *See* Hispanics (Latinos)
Law clerks, influence of, 451
Law Enforcement Assistance Act, 64
Lawrence v. Texas (2003), 150, 151
Lawsuits. *See also* Supreme Court
  civil rights cases, 451–452, 453
  class-action suits, 453–454
  in federal court, 451–454
  fee shifting and, 452, 454
  by interest groups, 272
  private, state immunity from, 58
  standing and, 452–453, 454
Lawyers, 449
  activist courts and, 459
  bureaucracy and, 423
  class-action suits and, 453–454
  interest groups and, 268
  before Supreme Court, 455, 462
Lawyers' Committee for Civil Rights, 272
Leadership, 199, 267, 474, 479
  changing patterns of, 477
  party, 319
Leadership Forum, The, 252
League of Conservation Voters, 280
League of Women Voters, 268, 270, 274, 302
"Leaks," 308–310
Least-restrictive means, 107
Lee v. Weisman (1971), 114
Legal Defense and Education Fund (NAACP), 272, 287
Legal periodicals, 455
Legislation. *See also* Civil Rights legislation; *specific laws*
  authorization, 428
  campaign finance laws, 245, 246–247, 250
  courts and, 460
  pork-barrel legislation, 358, 359, 469
  president's program, 397–400
  revenue legislation, origin of, 351
Legislation by initiative, 13, 59, 149, 204
Legislative branch, 20
Legislative committees, 428
Legislative court, 446
Legislative function of staffs, 346
Legislative process, 347–356, 358
  floor debate, 348, 353–355
  introduction of bills, 348, 350
  riders to bills, 354
  study by committees, 348, 350–353
  synopsis of steps in, 348–349
Legislative veto, 400, 429
Legislature. *See also* Congress; House of Representatives; Senate; State legislature
  bicameral, 25, 321
  Great Compromise and, 27
Legitimacy
  of political parties, 201
  political power and, 5, 20
  of president, 375
Lemon v. Kurtzman (1971), 114
"Letterhead" organizations, 268
Lewinsky, Monica, 310, 311, 392, 403, 404
Libel, 105, 238, 293, 300–301

Liberalism
  defined, 168–169
  education and, 136, 161, 162, 267
  in media, 303, 305, 306
Liberals, 170(tab.), 215, 224(tab.)
  in bureaucracy, 422
  caucus participation of, 237
  college students as, 161, 162
  congressional Democrats, 171, 333, 339
  judicial review and, 439, 446
  public-interest law firms, 272
  in Senate, 332–333
  think tanks, 273
Libertarian party, 170, 215, 221
Liberty, 17–19, 34. *See also* Civil liberties
  Constitution and, 24–25, 39, 40
  equality and, 39
  factions and, 32
  as natural right, 18–19, 24
  political authority and, 20
  political culture and, 77, 84
  Supreme Court on, 443–445
  tolerance and, 91, 92
Library of Congress, 347
Limbaugh, Rush, 302, 303
Lincoln, Abraham, 205, 206
  assassination of, 401
  cabinet of, 384, 386
  Civil War and, 374, 378
  Gettysburg Address, 155
  presidency of, 377, 379, 380
  Republican machine and, 214
Line-item veto, 43–45, 395, 481–482
Line Item Veto Act (1996), 43–45
Linmark Associates, Inc. v. Willingboro (1977), 113, 117
Lipset, Seymour Martin, 169
Literacy tests, for voting, 138, 181
Litmus test, 447–448
Little Rock, Arkansas, 131, 380
Liuzzo, Viola, 137
Livermore, Kentucky, 126
Loaded language, 304, 305
Lobbying groups (lobbyists), 277, 344, 346, 470
  See also Interest groups
  grassroots lobbying, 281–282, 287
  as information suppliers, 279–280
  insider *vs.* outsider strategy of, 280–281
  intergovernmental, 62
  public interest, 268, 271
  regulation of, 286–287
Local government, 57, 59, 411, 452, 471
  bureaucracy and, 378
  federal grants to, 62(fig.), 63–64, 67–68
  local organizations and, 270
  political party organization and, 213–217
Localism, 237
Local media, 298–299, 313
Locke, John, 24
London *Times*, 298
Long, Huey, 223, 477
Long family, 217
Los Angeles, California, 215, 266, 298, 449
Louisiana, 128, 183(tab.), 217
Lowi, Theodore, 37
Lutheran Social Services, 277
Lynching, 126–127, 135
McCain, John, 109, 225, 250, 252

McCain-Feingold campaign finance reform law (2002), 109, 252
McCardle case, 462
McCarthy, Eugene, 221–222, 250
McCarthy, Joseph R., 79, 100
McCarthyism, 79
McClosky, Herbert, 169
McClure's (magazine), 295
McConnell v. Federal Election Commission (2003), 109
McCorvey, Norma, 144
McCulloch, James, 55–56
McCulloch v. Maryland (1819), 55–56, 441
McDonald, Michael P., 186
McGovern, George, 210, 222, 239, 242
  campaign financing, 247, 250
McKinley, William, 206, 295, 401
McLaurin, George, 129
McNamara, Robert S., 396
Madison, James, 85, 201, 202
  background of, 38
  on factions, 32, 51, 265
  Federalist papers, 32–33, 34, 51, 53
  on land grants, 60
  Marbury v. Madison and, 440–441
  on nullification, 56
  ratification of Constitution and, 35
  Senate and, 27
  State Department and, 411–412
  states' rights and, 54
  U.S. Constitution and, 22, 23, 24, 30, 35, 39
Magazines of opinion, 295–296
Maine, 189, 376
Majoritarian politics, 9
Majority leaders (Congress), 334–335, 336, 337, 353
Majority rule, 25
Majority whips (Congress), 336
Malapportionment, 235, 236
Mandates, 66–67
Mansbridge, Jane, 274
Mansfield, Mike, 335
Mapp, Dollree, 116
Mapp v. Ohio (1961), 116, 121
Marbury, William, 440
Marbury v. Madison (1803), 440–441
March on Washington (1963), 136
Marginal districts, 327, 328, 331–332
Market, media and, 302, 310
Marriage
  Polygamous (Mormons), 110
  same-sex, 5, 150–151, 159(fig.), 161, 286
Marshall, John, 55–56, 440, 441, 442, 463
Marshall, Thurgood, 461, 462, 463
Marshall Plan (1946), 371
Marx, Karl, 9
Marxists, 220, 222. *See also* Socialist party
Marxist view, 9, 86
Maryland, 27(fn.), 55–56
Mason, George, 6, 28, 37, 38
Massachusetts, 35, 37, 67, 203, 322
  constitution of, 23
  executive power in, 372
  gay marriage in, 150–151, 286
  Shays's rebellion in, 23–24, 25
"Massachusetts" ballot, 207
Massachusetts Citizens for Life, 108
Massachusetts Spy (newspaper), 18
Mass transit, 66, 269
Matching funds, 250

Material incentives, 270
Mayer, William G., 305
Mayhew, David, 217, 371
Mayors, 63
Mecklenburg County, North Carolina, 133
Media, 251, 291–314, 469
  bias in, 293, 303–307
  civil rights protests and, 136
  competition in, 298–299
  confidentiality of sources, 301
  congressional coverage, 307, 308
  "culture war" and, 87
  effects on politics, 293–298
  elites and, 171, 299
  FCC and, 293, 299, 301
  foreign, 293, 298
  free press, 105, 109, 113, 117, 292–293
  government regulation of, 293, 298
  how to read newspapers, 304
  Internet. *See* Internet
  interpreting news. *See* News
  journalism. *See* Journalism; Newspapers
  liberalism in, 303–305
  local, 298–299, 313
  market and, 302, 310
  mistrust of, 306
  national, 299–300
  objectivity in, 305
  president and, 307–308, 390
  press secretaries and, 307–308
  public perception of, 306, 307(fig.)
  radio. *See* Radio
  relationship with government, 292
  "rules" for, 308
  rules governing, 300–303
  scandal and, 333
  sensationalism in, 295, 310–311
  structure of, 298–303
  television. *See* Television
  voters and, 346
Media elites, 171, 299
Media Fund, 252
Medicaid, 143, 260, 477
  grants-in-aid and, 60, 69, 70
Medicare, 260, 318, 476, 477
Meet the Press (TV program), 299
Membership interests, 269–270
Mental tune-out, 306
"Mention," as candidate, 233, 300
Merit system, 417–418, 430
Meskimen's Law, 426
Mexican American Legal Defense Fund, 272
Mexican Americans, 165–166, 258, 272
Mexico, 84(tab.), 341
Miami Herald (newspaper), 300
Miami Herald Publishing Co. v. Tornillo (1974), 113, 117, 302
Michigan, 7
Middle class, 86, 87, 211, 267, 274
Mikulski, Barbara, 210
Military. *See also* Defense Department
  civilian access to, 113, 117
  Court of Military Appeals, 446, 449(fig.)
  National Guard, 68, 131
  presidential power and, 379–380
  women in, 140, 141–142
Military draft
  protests, 108, 110
  women excluded from, 140, 141–142
Military tribunals, 120, 121
Miller v. California (1973), 109

"Millionaire's Club," Senate as, 324
Million Moms March (2004), 274
Mills, C. Wright, 9
Minnesota, 189, 215, 217
Minorities. *See also specific minorities*
  affirmative action and, 146, 147, 148, 149, 476
  in bureaucracy, 421, 421(fig.), 422(tab.)
  in Congress, 325(tab.)
  in judiciary, 447(fig.)
  political participation and, 193, 193(fig.)
  preferential hiring of, 79
Minority leader, 334, 335, 336, 337, 353
Minority Whip, 336
Minor parties, 219, 220–223, 250
  economic protest, 220, 221
  factional parties, 203–204, 220–221, 223
  ideological parties, 215, 220, 221
  one-issue, 221
  presidential elections and, 220
  third parties, 7, 215, 219, 220, 223, 377
  winner-take-all system and, 221
Miranda, Ernesto A., 118, 119
Miranda rules, 118–119
Miranda v. Arizona (1966), 118, 121
Mississippi, 182, 183(tab.), 203
Missouri Compromise, 442
Mistrust of government, 426
  attack journalism and, 309
  mistrust of bureaucracy and, 430, 432
  mistrust of Congress, 317, 320
  political culture and, 84–85, 87–89, 89(fig.), 91
  political participation and, 189
Mistrust of media, 306, 307(fig.)
Mob rule, 25
Moe, Terry M., 156–157
Mondale, Walter, 210–211, 233, 242, 401
Money laundering, 120
Monroe, James, 202, 374, 388
Montesquieu, Baron de, 34
Montgomery, Alabama, 135
Morality
  orthodox *vs.* progressive, 86–87
  views of, 93(fig.)
Moral Majority, 83
Mormons, polygamy and, 110
Morris, Gouverneur, 27, 373
Morris, Robert, 38
Motor-voter law (1993), 179, 180(fig.)
Mountain States Legal Foundation, 272
Mount Vernon, 22
Moynihan, Daniel Patrick, 317, 387
MSNBC (TV network), 299
Muckrakers, 295
Mugwumps, 203–204, 223
Multiple referrals, 351
Muncie, Indiana, 80
Municipal bonds, taxation of, 56
Municipal elections, 219
Municipal government, 57, 63. *See also* Cities
Murphy's Law, 426
Muskie, Edmund, 281
Myrdal, Gunnar, 78

NAACP. *See* National Association for the Advancement of Colored People
Nader, Ralph, 267, 281, 427, 477
  organizations of, 271–272, 419
  as presidential candidate, 250, 271
Name recognition, 253

Name-request job, 418
NARAL (National Abortion Rights Action League), 274, 275
Narrowcasting, 297
NASA (National Aeronautics and Space Administration), 428
Nassau County, New York, 214
National Abortion Rights Action League (NARAL), 274, 275
National Aeronautics and Space Administration (NASA), 428
National Association for the Advancement of Colored People (NAACP), 128–129, 165, 267, 269–270, 280, 455
  Brown v. Board of Education and, 129, 453, 462
  civil rights cases and, 451–452
  Legal Defense and Education Fund, 272, 287
National Association of Counties, 62, 268, 269
National Association of Manufacturers, 267
National Bureau of Standards, 413
National Catholic Welfare Conference, 267
National chairman, 208
National Commission on Terrorist Attacks, 3, 359
National committee, 208
National Conference of State Legislatures, 62
National crises, presidency and, 378, 394, 398, 399, 413
National debt, 472, 481
National Education Association, 217
National Endowment for the Arts, 86
National Environmental Policy Act (NEPA, 1969), 424
National Farmers' Union, 266
National Federation of Republican Women, 275
National Gazette (newspaper), 294
National Governors Association, 62
National Guard, 68, 131
National Independent Retail Jewelers, 268
National intelligence director, 414
National Intelligencer (newspaper), 294
National League of Cities, 62
National Legal Center for the Public Interest, 276
National nominating conventions, 209–213, 241
  caucus system replaced with, 203
  characteristics of delegates, 212(tab.)
  costs of, 245
  delegate allocation formulas, 209–210
  Democratic, 203, 209–212, 217, 222, 224
  Republican, 209–210, 211, 225
National Opinion Research Center (NORC), 251
National Organization for Women (NOW), 217, 274, 275
National Performance Review (NPR), 432, 433
National Republican Congressional Committee (House), 336
National Rifle Association (NRA), 109, 282
National Right to Life Committee, 251
National security, 248. *See also* Homeland security
  free speech and, 102–105
National supremacy, 54, 55–56, 441–442
National Urban League, 165
National Wildlife Foundation, 274
National Women's Political Caucus, 275
Nation (magazine), 295

Native Americans, 429
  in Congress, 326
  religious beliefs of, 110
  removal of, 125
Natural right, liberty as, 18–19, 24
Nazis, 120
  freedom of speech and, 105
NBC network, 296, 299, 310
Near v. Minnesota (1931), 302
NEAs (Noncareer executive assignments), 417
Nebraska, 376
"Necessary and proper" clause, 56
Negative campaign ads, 234, 257, 261, 310
NEPA (National Environmental Policy Act, 1969), 424
Neshoba County, Mississippi, 126, 136
Netherlands, 81, 90, 231
Neustadt, Richard, 386, 390
Neutrality, 107
New Deal, 5, 169, 222, 260, 262, 414
  Supreme Court and, 444, 477
"New Deal coalition," 206, 259
New England town meeting, 6, 27
New Hampshire, 27(fn.), 35
New Hampshire primary, 300
New Haven, Connecticut, 306
New Jersey, 27(fn.), 35, 41, 139, 180
New Jersey Plan, 25–26, 29, 31(fn.)
New Kent County, Virginia, 132
New politics, 280–282
News. *See also* Journalism; Media; Newspapers
  beliefs of media and, 305
  bias in, 293, 303–307
  government and, 307–313
  influence on public, 306
  Internet as source of, 297
  leaks, 308–310
  sensationalism in, 295, 310–311
Newsom, Gavin, 151
Newspapers, 293. *See also* Journalism; *specific newspapers*
  competition among, 295, 298–299
  decline of, 298
  freedom of press and, 99, 109, 113, 117
  how to read, 304
  incumbent endorsement and, 306
  libel and, 105
  party press, 294–295
  popular press, 295
  sensationalism and, 295
  watchdog role of, 300
Newsweek (magazine), 306
New system, 475–478
New York City, 35, 233, 298
  after Revolutionary War, 21
  proportional representation in, 219
  Tammany machine in, 213, 215
  transit subsidy, 66
  World Trade Center attack (9/11), 7, 10, 88
New York state, 27(fn.), 56, 203, 322, 442
New York Times, 299, 301, 305, 306
  Pentagon Papers and, 99, 300
New York Times v. Sullivan (1964), 109, 302
Nie, Norman, 187
Nineteenth Amendment (1920), 41, 140, 182
Ninth Amendment (1791), 36
Nixon, Richard, 134
  attacks on press by, 313
  cabinet of, 387
  character of, 388
  court appointments by, 447, 463, 464

debate with Kennedy, 242, 244
election of 1968 and, 221, 239
election of 1972 and, 239, 247, 254, 391
Ford's pardon of, 404
impeachment of, 308
impoundment of funds by, 396–397
national crises under, 398
popularity of, 392, 392(fig.)
presidency of, 369, 383, 394, 400
resignation of, 403
as vice president, 233, 401
wage and price controls of, 368, 414
Watergate scandal, 87, 246, 396
Nixon, Walter, 461
NLRB (National Labor Relations Board), 481–482
Nofziger, Lyn, 284
Nomenklatura (Soviet elite), 171
Noncareer executive assignments (NEAs), 417
Nonprofit organizations, 69, 84, 250, 277, 287
Nonvoting, 178–180
demographics of, 187
fines for, 190, 194
poverty and, 188, 191, 193
NORC (National Opinion Research Center), 251
Norms, 174
North, Oliver, 382
North Carolina, 27(fn.), 31, 133, 180, 183(tab.), 306
NOW (National Organization for Women), 217, 274, 275
NPR (National Performance Review), 432, 433
NRA (National Rifle Association), 109, 282
Nude dancing, 106
Nullification doctrine, 56

Obama, Barack, 319
Obscenity, 105–107
Occupational Safety and Health Administration (OSHA), 411, 427
Ocean Dumping Ban Act (1988), 66
O'Connor, Sandra Day, 144, 147, 454(tab.), 456, 461, 463, 464
Office-block ballot, 207
Office of Compliance, 358
Office of Homeland Security, 399
Office of Management and Budget (OMB), 380, 383, 422
Office of Personnel Management (OPM), 383, 416, 417, 418
Office of Special Counsel, 423
Office of Technology Assessment (OTA), 347
Office of the U.S. Trade Representative, 383
Office of Thrift Supervision, 424
Official Secrets Act (Great Britain), 293, 309
"Off the record," 313
Oil industry, 278, 280
Oil rights, state-federal relations and, 60
"Old boys' network," 419
Old system, 474–475, 476
OMB (Office of Management and Budget), 380, 383, 422
O'Neill, Thomas P. "Tip," 237, 337
One-issue parties, 221
"On the record," 313
Open Meeting Law (1976), 424
Open primary, 241
Open rule, 353
Operational grants, 69

Opinion magazines, 295–296
Opinion of the Court, 455–456
Opinion-policy congruence, 157
Opinion polls, 157, 303, 391, 392–393(fig.)
See also Public opinion
OPM (Office of Personnel Management), 383, 416, 417, 418
Oral arguments, 455
"Ordering the bill," 348
Oregon, 189
Organization, campaign, 233–234
Organizational decision, 231
Organizational entrepreneurs, 267
Organizational voting, 331, 332
Orren, Gary, 81
Orthodox belief, 86–87
OSHA (Occupational Safety and Health Administration), 411, 427
OTA (Office of Technology Assessment), 347
Otis, James, 37
O'Toole's Corollary to Murphy's Law, 426
Outsider strategies, 280–281

Pacific Gas and Electric Company, 108
Pacific Legal Foundation, 272
PACs. See Political action committees
Paine, Thomas, 23
Palko v. Connecticut (1937), 102, 103
Palmer, A. Mitchell, 100
Panama Canal treaty, 281
Panetta, Leon E., 381
Parent Teacher Association (PTA), 270
Parkinson's Laws, 426
Parks, Rosa, 135
Parliamentary systems, 200, 470
bureaucracy in, 410
Congress compared, 318–321, 359, 371
elections in, 217–218
in Great Britain, 28, 42, 231, 259–260, 319, 369, 371, 410, 438, 480
popular consent and, 28
prime minister in, 308, 309, 368–370, 471, 480
public policy in, 259–260
Parochial participants, 188
Parochial schools, aid to, 99, 111–112, 453
Participatory democracy, 6–8, 59
Partisanship. See Party identification
Party activists, 225, 390
Party-column ballot, 207
Party delegates, 212, 212(tab.)
Party identification, 158–159, 198, 252
Congress and, 339, 340
decline in, 189, 198, 199(fig.)
elections and, 206
judges and, 446
of labor unions, 216, 222, 254, 258
race and, 222, 258, 259
Party loyalty, 200, 206, 255–256, 258, 259
See also Party identification
gender and, 160
Party platforms, 262
Party polarization, 338–339, 339(tab.)
Party press, 294–295
Paterson, William, 25
Patriotism, 81(tab.), 88
Patronage, 203, 213, 214, 336
bureaucracy and, 412, 417, 418
Pawtucket, Rhode Island, 112
Pay raises, Congressional, 362
Peckham, Rufus, 439

Peers, 171
Pelosi, Nancy, 335
Pembroke, second earl of, 438
Pendleton Act (1883), 417
Pennsylvania, 21, 22–23, 24, 27(fn.), 35, 37, 203, 361
Pension. See also Social Security
for president, 375
Pension Office, 412–413
Pentagon, 7
Pentagon Papers, 99, 238, 300
Penthouse (magazine), 105
Per curiam opinion, 455
Perkins, Frances, 387
Perot, Ross, 223, 243, 256, 297, 371, 468
Personal attitudes of bureaucrats, 423
Personal attributes of bureaucrats, 421–422
Personal campaigns, 236
Personal following, 216–217, 236
Personal-interest caucuses, 340, 341(tab.)
Personal liberties. See Civil liberties
Personal responsibility, 77, 79
Persuasion of president, 390–394
Peter Principle, 426
Philadelphia, Pennsylvania, 17, 67, 214, 298
Constitutional Convention in, 22, 23, 26, 53–54
Philosophy, influence of, 24
"Photo op," 308
Pittsburgh, Pennsylvania, 112–113
Plaintiff, 452
Planned Parenthood v. Casey (1992), 143, 144
Playboy (magazine), 242
Pledge of Allegiance, 84
Plessy, Adolph, 128
Plessy v. Ferguson (1896), 128, 129, 134
Pluralist view, 9–10
Plurality system, 217–218
Plural national executive, 372
Plyler v. Doe (1982), 146
Pocketbook vote, 252
Pocket veto, 348, 394–395, 395(tab.), 397
Poindexter, John, 382
Poland, 374
Polarized politics, 478–479
Police
civil rights violence and, 136–137
due process rights and, 114, 117–119
power of, 59, 99, 142
Policy, 9, 156
bureaucrats and, 422
client politics and, 284
Congress and, 378
demonstrations and, 190
elections and, 259–260, 262
elites and, 171–172, 174, 474
gridlock and, 371, 372
interest groups and, 267, 268, 281
judiciary and, 439, 456–457, 459
media influence and, 306
Old system and, 474–475
preferences. See Policy preferences
president and, 397, 417
public opinion and, 79, 156, 157, 281
Policy agenda, 475
Policy Committee (House), 336, 337
Policy Committee (Senate), 335, 336
Policy-making, 468–471
Constitutional effects on, 469–470
failures in, 468

Policy preferences, 12, 14, 171–172, 171(tab.)
   of convention delegates, 223–224, 225
   party, 259–260, 262
Polis (city-state), 6
Political action committees (PACs), 233,
      284(tab.), 287
   campaign finance and, 245, 282–283, 284,
      474
   growth of, 246(fig.)
Political associations, 266. *See also* Interest
      groups
Political attitudes
   family and, 158–159
   gender and, 160–161, 161(tab.)
   of media elite, 299
   religion and, 159–160, 161(tab.)
   role of education in, 161, 162
Political authority, 20, 46, 200, 265
Political change, history of, 11–12
Political conduct, 169
Political consultants, 208
Political cues, 280
Political culture, 75–96, 148
   civic role of religion in, 82, 83(tab.), 86–87,
      92(fig.)
   compared with other nations, 80–84
   "culture war" and, 86–87
   defined, 77
   economic system and, 77, 79–80
   mistrust of government and, 84–85, 87–89,
      89(fig.), 91
   parties and, 200–201
   political efficacy and, 89–91, 90(fig.)
   political system and, 77–79
   political tolerance and, 91–95
   role of religion in, 83–84, 84(tab.), 85
   sources of, 84–87
Political efficacy, 89–91, 90(fig.)
Political elites
   attitudinal voting and, 332
   courts and, 446, 463
   ideology and, 171–172, 174, 332, 446
   influence of, 8–10
   media elites, 299, 307
   norms stated by, 174
   public opinion and, 158, 162, 474
   self-interest of, 10–11
   on Vietnam war, 299
Political ideology(ies), 167–172, 225, 371
   analyzing consistency in, 169–171
   of bureaucrats, 422
   categories of opinion, 169
   Congress divided by, 332, 335, 339, 340
   consistency of attitudes, 168
   ideological parties, 215, 221
   interest groups, 271, 283
   of judges, 446, 448
   political elites and, 171–172, 174, 332, 446
   political parties and, 215, 221
   public opinion and, 167–172
   role of family in, 159
   self-identification surveys, 168(fig.),
      170(tab.)
   terminology of, 168–169, 170(tab.)
Political inactives, 188. *See also* Nonvoting
Political information
   on Internet, 297–298
   liberalism and, 162, 171, 188
   sources of, 304
   supplied by interest groups, 279–280
   voting patterns and, 188, 254

Political institutions, trust in, 81
Political machines, 185, 213–215
Political name, 216–217
Political participation, 177–195, 216. *See also*
      Voting
   alternate activities, 191(fig.)
   American electorate, 180–187
   causes of, 188–191
   education and, 162, 188, 191
   effects on government, 179–180
   under federalism, 52
   forms of, 187–188
   Jacksonian era, 180–181
   nonvoting. *See* Nonvoting
   other than voting, 187, 191(tab.), 192(tab.),
      193(tab.)
   political machines and, 214
   rates of, meaning of, 191–193, 193(fig.)
Political parties, 197–229. *See also specific
      parties*
   activism, 225, 390
   campaign funding and, 250
   caucuses and, 202
   changes in, 475
   Civil War and, 203–204
   Congress and, 318, 328–330, 332, 334–340
   decline of, 200, 207, 266
   delegates, to national conventions, 217,
      224, 226
   economic protest parties, 221
   factional parties, 203–204, 221
   founding of, 201–202
   global comparison of, 198–201
   ideological parties, 215, 220, 221
   Jacksonian era, 202–203
   leadership of, 319
   lump-sum grants to, 245
   machine politics, 213–215
   minor. *See* Minor parties
   modern structure, 207–209
   newspapers controlled by, 294–295
   nominating conventions. *See* National nomi-
      nating conventions
   nominating role of, 231
   one-issue parties, 221
   party platforms, 262
   personal following and, 216–217
   policy preferences, 259–260, 262
   presidential nomination and, 223–225
   primary voting and, 211, 224–225
   realignments, 205–207, 239, 463
   in reform era, 204–205
   rise and decline of, 201–207
   sectionalism and, 203–204
   solidary groups, 215–216
   sponsored parties, 216
   state and local, 213–217
   stigma attached to, 374–375
   third parties. *See* Minor parties
   trivia, 212
   two-party system, 208, 209(fig.), 217–220
   unity in, 338–340
   voting and, 185, 189, 225–226
Political power, 14, 18
   bureaucratic, 415, 425, 473
   competition for, 309
   of Congress, 317, 320, 321, 364–365, 472
   distribution of, 8–10, 12, 39
   of federal courts, 456–457, 459, 481, 482
   federalism and, 51, 59
   Hispanic, 258

   of incumbency, 328
   legitimacy and, 5, 20
   nature of, 4–6
   of president. *See* Presidential power
   separation of. *See* Separation of powers
   state parties and, 213
Political pressure, 281
Political privilege, 39
Political question, 457
Political reform, 295. *See also under* Reform
Political resources, distribution of, 10
Political socialization, 158–159
Political system
   other nations compared, 80–84
   political culture and, 77–79
   two-party system, 208, 209(fig.), 217–220
Political tolerance, 91–93, 92(fig.), 93(fig.),
      94(fig.)
Politicians, media and, 292, 309
Politics
   civil liberties and, 99–100
   client politics, 280, 284, 426
   conflict in. *See* Conflict
   crisis politics, 398, 399
   media effects on, 293–298
   nature of, 12
   "new politics," 280–282
   polarized, 478–479
   religion and, 85, 86–87
   "rules" of, 469
   women's activism and, 275
Polk, James, 377
Polls. *See* Opinion polls
Poll tax, 181
Polygamy, Mormons and, 110
Poole, Keith T., 340
Poor people. *See* Poverty (poor people)
Popkin, Samuel L., 186
Popular consent, 25, 46
Popularity of president, 390–392,
      392–393(fig.), 394
Popular opnion. *See* Public opinion
Popular press, 295
Populist party, 170, 206, 220, 221
Pork-barrel legislation, 358, 359, 469
Pornography, 102, 106, 107
   See also Obscenity
Position issues, 239, 240
Position papers, 234
Postal Service, 411, 412, 417, 421(fig.), 433
Poverty (poor people), 259
   courts and, 451
   nonvoters and, 188, 191, 193
   "War on Poverty" programs and, 477
Powell, Colin, 387
Power. *See* Political power
Power elite theory, 9
Prayer
   in Congress, 113
   in schools, 86, 111, 112, 160(fig.), 460
Precedent principle, 457
Preference systems, 148
Preferred position, 107
Prescription drugs, Medicare and, 476
Presidency, 367–406
   administrative powers of, 373, 379
   changes in, 475
   concerns of Founders and, 372–373
   under Confederation, 21, 22
   Congress and, 200, 373, 375–379,
      390–391, 391(tab.), 393(fig.)

contrasting views of, 368
divided government and, 370–372
early presidents, 374–375
electoral college and, 372, 373
evolution of, 372–379
Executive Office, 380–385
federal agencies and, 386, 399, 417
"imperial presidency," 368
Jacksonians, 375–377
legitimacy of, 375
national crises and, 378, 394, 398, 399, 413
orderly transition in, 401–406
plural, 372
presidential character, 388–389
presidential program, 378, 397–400
presidential staffs, 380–385, 387–388
press coverage, 310, 474
prime ministers compared, 368–370
qualifications and benefits, 380
succession of vice-president, 401–402
term of office, 27, 42, 373–374, 405, 480
trivia, 388
White House Office, 381–383
President
    appointments by. *See* Presidential appointments
    authority of. *See* Presidential power
    cabinet and, 369, 384–385, 384(tab.), 385(tab.), 411–412
    character of, 388
    checks and balances and, 29
    chronology of presidents, A30–A32
    confidentiality, 396
    constraints on program planning, 398–399
    executive privilege and, 396
    impeachment of, 403–404
    impoundment of funds by, 396–397
    legislative program of, 378, 397–400
    media and, 307–308
    as outsider, 369
    popularity. *See* Popularity of president
    presidential persuasion, 390–394
    reorganization of executive branch, 399–400
    separation of powers and, 40, 42, 479–481
    sexual affairs of, 310
    veto by. *See* Veto powers
Presidential appointments, 381, 385–387
    agencies and commissions, 385
    bureaucracy and, 411–412, 417, 420, 427, 436
    cabinet appointments, 369, 384–387
    fitness rule and, 375
    judges, 385, 438, 444, 447, 448, 461
    patronage and, 417, 418
    Senate approval of, 411, 412, 438, 447, 448
Presidential campaigns. *See also* Campaigns; Congressional campaigns
    of 1992, 371
    congressional campaigns and, 232–234
    factors in, 233–234
    funding for, 244–245, 247, 252
    position issues in, 239, 240
    television and, 296–297, 302
    valence issues in, 239–240
Presidential candidates, 231, 297, 300, 302, 480
    See also specific candidates
Presidential character, 388–389

Presidential elections, 238, 254–256, 254(tab.)
    See also Campaigns; Electoral college
    of 1796, 201
    of 1800, 85, 201, 205, 376
    of 1804, 202
    of 1816, 202
    of 1820, 202
    of 1824, 202, 376
    of 1828, 202, 204, 205
    of 1832, 202, 203
    of 1840, 202
    of 1860, 204, 205–206, 219, 260
    of 1892, 220
    of 1896, 205, 206, 259, 260
    of 1912, 220, 221, 259
    of 1916, 259
    of 1924, 223
    of 1932, 205, 206, 259, 260
    of 1936, 444
    of 1948, 220, 221
    of 1952, 259
    of 1960, 254(tab.), 391
    of 1964, 137, 226, 254(tab.), 260, 306
    of 1968, 220, 221, 254(tab.)
    of 1972, 183, 254(tab.), 391
    of 1976, 189, 254(tab.)
    of 1980, 206, 220, 254(tab.), 260
    of 1984, 191, 206, 254(tab.), 262
    of 1988, 191, 207, 219(tab.), 254(tab.)
    of 1992, 187, 219, 219(tab.), 220, 226, 254(tab.), 309
    of 1996, 183, 186, 187, 219(tab.), 254(tab.), 262
    of 2000, 83–84, 183, 186, 219(tab.), 254(tab.), 309, 376, 464
    of 2004, 5, 160, 185, 186, 219(tab.), 248–249, 254(tab.)
    divided government and, 371–372
    economy and, 256(fig.)
    Electoral college. *See* Electoral college
    exit polls at, 157
    gender gap in, 160
    House of Representatives and, 220, 372, 373, 376, 377
    parties *vs.* voters in, 225
    partisan gains in, 391(tab.)
    primaries. *See* Presidential primary
    trivia, 240
    voter turnout in, 184(fig.), 186–187, 186(tab.), 189(fig.)
    winning coalitions in, 257–259
Presidential electors, 181
Presidential nomination, 202–203, 208, 223–225, 231
Presidential power (authority)
    accountability and, 479
    analysis of, 373, 406
    military powers, 378, 379–380, 400
    national crisis and, 378, 398, 399, 413
    power to persuade, 390–394
    power to say no, 394–397
    separation of powers and, 40, 42–43
Presidential Power (Neustadt), 390
Presidential powers (administrative), 373
    sole and shared powers, 379
    veto powers. *See* Veto powers
Presidential primary, 211, 224–225, 239, 241, 307. *See also* Primary elections
    funding for, 246, 247, 250
    New Hampshire primary, 300

Presidential program, formulating, 378, 397–400
Presidential transition, 401–406
    impeachment and, 403–404
    lame duck presidents, 404
    problems of succession, 374, 402–403
    vice president's role, 401–402
President pro tempore (Senate), 336, 402
Press. *See* Journalism; Newspapers
    adversarial, 29, 309, 310, 311
Press, freedom of. *See* Free press
Press conferences, 310, 474
Press secretaries, 307–308
Price and wage controls, 368, 414
Primary elections, 200, 222, 477. *See also* Presidential primary
    congressional candidates and, 318
    voting in, 224–225, 236
    white primary, 181
    winning, 236, 257
Prime ministers, 308, 309, 368–370, 471, 480
Printz v. United States (1997), 58
Prior restraint, 103, 107, 300. *See also* Censorship
Prisoners' rights, 120–121, 457, 459, 460
Prison systems, 67
Privacy Act (1974), 424
Privacy rights, 113, 117
    landmark cases, 143
    and sex, 142–144, 150
Private bills, 350
Private calendar (House), 352
Private organizations, 81
Private property, 443. *See also* Property rights
"Private Sector Survey on Cost Control," 431
"Privileged speech" doctrine, 238
Probable cause, 116
"Professional" politicians, 327, 330
Professional societies, 267
Profit motive, 310
Progress for America, 252
Progressive belief, 86–87
Progressive ("Bull Moose") party, 221, 222, 223
Progressive Policy Institute, 273
Progressives, 203–205, 295
Prohibition, 42, 223
Prohibition party, 221, 223
"Pro-life" groups, 227
Property rights, 18, 23, 33, 443, 473
Propinquity, rule of, 381
Proportional representation, 27, 219
Prospective voting, 255
Protective paternalism, 140
Protestant ethic, 85
Protestantism, 85, 86–87, 206. *See also specific sect*
Protest marches, 136, 190
Protest parties, 221
Protests, 135, 161, 192, 474. *See also* Demonstrations; Student activism
Proxmire, William, 238
Proxy voting, 344
PTA (Parent Teacher Association), 270
Public, government insulated from, 34
Public accommodations, 128, 138, 147
Public bills, 350. *See also* Bills
Public Citizen, 272
Public confidence
    in business, 309
    in institutions, 88–89, 89(fig.)
    in Supreme Court, 444, 463, 464(fig.)

Public debt, 38. *See also* National debt
Public interest, 109
    courts and, 443, 460
    media and, 301
Public-interest law firms, 272
Public-interest lobbies, 268
Public Interest Research Groups (PIRGs), 272
Publicly-owned enterprises, 411
Public opinion, 154–174, 378
    accuracy in media, 307(fig.)
    on big business, 309
    on bureaucracy, 432
    on busing for racial integration, 134
    cleavages in, 162–167
    on Congress, 330
    constituency, 331, 332
    defined, 156–157
    elites, public policy and, 171–172, 174,
        474
    family and, 158–159
    generation gaps in, 159(fig.)
    geographic region and, 167
    grassroots lobbying and, 281–282
    on growth of government, 473–474
    journalist opinion compared, 303(tab.)
    mistrust of government and, 87–89
    origins of political attitudes, 157–162
    policy and, 79, 156, 157, 281
    political ideology and, 159, 167–172
    political tolerance and, 91
    president and, 380, 390, 399
    public policy and, 79
    race and ethnicity, 164–167
    religion and, 159–160, 161(tab.)
    schooling and information, 161–162
    school integration and, 136
    social class and, 163–164
    of toleration and morality, 91–93, 92(fig.),
        93(fig.), 94(fig.)
    two-party system and, 219, 220(tab.)
Public policy. *See* Policy
Public schools. *See* Schools
"Publius," 32
Puck (magazine), 324
Puerto Ricans, 165, 258
Pulitzer, Joseph, 295
Pure conservatives, 170
Pure liberals, 170
Puritan tradition, 85
Purposive incentive, 271, 274
Pyramid staff structure, 381–382, 383

Quakers, 23
Quayle, Dan, 309
Quorum, 353
Quorum call, 353
Quotas, 79, 146–148, 149

Raab, Earl, 169
Race
    cleavages in public opinion, 164–167
    party identification and, 164, 222, 258,
        259
    political participation and, 188, 189(fig.)
    in public accommodations, 126, 138, 147
Race relations, 78
Racial discrimination, 148, 149
Racial profiling, 139
Racial quotas, 169, 451
Racism, 79, 174
Radical Republicans, 322

Radio, 293, 296, 297, 298
    regulation of, 299, 301–302
    talk shows, 302, 303–304, 313
Randolph, Edmund, 25, 27, 369, 372
Random sample, 157
Rangel, Charles, 283
Rasul v. Bush (2004), 121
Ratification of Constitution, 31, 38–39
Ratings of legislators, 280
Rayburn, Sam, 321, 336–337
Reagan, Ronald, 11, 224, 262, 272
    appointments by, 422, 427
    assassination attempt on, 282, 401, 402
    budget and, 371
    busing and, 134
    campaigning by, 233, 234, 391
    character of, 389
    election of 1980 and, 242, 255, 257, 391
    ethics violations in administration of, 284
    federal aid and, 66, 68
    governing style of, 397–398
    judges appointed by, 144, 147, 438, 447,
        448, 461, 463, 464
    liberal lobbies and, 277
    national crises under, 398
    popularity of, 393(fig.)
    presidency of, 368, 369, 385, 388, 394,
        400, 469
    reelection of, in 1984, 206–207, 239, 240,
        254, 255–256
    spending cuts by, 478
    staff organization of, 383
    veto of, 137
Realigning periods, 205–207, 239, 463
Reapportionment, 235–236
"Reasonable expectation of privacy," 117
Reasonableness standard, 140
Recall procedure, 59
Recession (1981–1982), 256
Reconstruction, 378, 462
Recruitment and retention, 415–419
"Red-diaper babies," 159
Redistricting, 235–236, 339
    1990 census and, 327, 329, 330
Red Scare, 99, 104. *See also* McCarthy, Joseph
Red tape, 425–426, 430, 431, 432–433
Reed, Thomas B., 321, 322–323, 342
Reed v. Reed (1971), 142
Referendum, 7, 8, 59, 204. *See also* Initiative,
    legislation by
Reform era, 204–205
Reform factions, 203–204, 215
Reform party, 221, 223
Reforms
    campaign finance, 250
    of civil service, 412, 417–418, 432–433
    of Congress, 317
Regan, Donald, 382
Regents of the University of California v. Bakke
    (1978), 147, 149
Regulatory agencies, 284, 460. *See also* Gov-
    ernment regulation; *specific agency*
Rehabilitation Act (1973), 431
Rehnquist, William, 58, 448, 454(tab.), 456,
    463
Reindeer Service, 414
Religion. *See also specific religion*
    civic role of, 82, 83(tab.) 92(fig.)
    First Amendment and, 101, 102, 110–113,
        453
    freedom of, 102, 110–113, 114

fundamentalist groups, 206, 268
    landmark cases, 114
    political belief and, 85, 86–87
    political participation and, 188, 193
    role in political attitudes, 159–160,
        161(tab.), 219
    separation of church and state, 110,
        111–113, 453
Religious nonprofit organizations, 277
"Religious Right," 86–87
Remedy, judicial, 131, 457
Remington, Frederic, 295
Reno v. ACLU (1997), 109
Reorganization Act (1939), 400
Representational voting, 331–332
Representative democracy, 6–8, 27–28
Representatives, 477. *See also* Congress; House
    of Representatives
    constituency opinion and, 331–332
    direct election of, 28, 181
    interest groups and, 282
    personal PACs of, 282–283
    power of, 323
    qualifications and privileges, 238, 319–320
    term of office for, 480
Republican caucus, 237–238
Republican Committee on Committees (Senate),
    335, 336, 337
Republican National Committee (RNC), 163,
    208–209, 211, 224
Republican party. *See also* Democratic party; Jef-
    fersonian Republicans; Political parties
    action against caucuses, 340
    bureaucratization of, 208–209
    Civil War and, 203, 205, 206
    coalitions in, 258–259
    control of House by, 232, 328–330, 338,
        342, 344
    delegate allocation formulas, 209–210
    devolution and, 68, 69, 70
    election of 1860 and, 205–206, 219
    election of 2004 and, 248
    gender and, 160
    identification with, 199, 199(fig.)
    independent voters and, 254–255
    527 organizations and, 252
    origins of, 205–206
    polarization of Congress and, 478–479
    political elites of, 171
    presidency and, 259
    reform factions in, 203–204, 215
    Senate and, 248, 345
    South and, 218(tab.), 248, 327, 330, 333,
        479
    split-offs from, 221, 222, 322
    two-party system and, 217–220
    voter turnout and, 190
    vote-seat gap, 328–329, 329(tab.)
Republican Senatorial Committee, 336
Republican Study Group, 332
Republics, 27, 34
Research Committee (House), 336
Reserved powers, 29
Resolution Funding Corporation, 424
Resolution Trust Corporation, 424
Resources Committee (House), 345
Responsibility, denial of, 232, 479
Restrictive rule, 353
Retrospective voting, 255–256
Revenue legislation, origin of, 351
Revenue sharing, 63–64, 66

Reverse discrimination, 145, 148, 455
Revolutionary War. *See* American Revolution
"Revolving door," 284–285
Rhode Island, 21, 24, 27(fn.), 31, 37, 112
Rice, Condoleezza, 387
Rice, Donna, 300
Richmond v. Croson (1989), 149
Rider, legislative, 354
Ridge, Tom, 399
Rights, unalienable, 19
Right-to-life movement, 215, 275
Riker, William H., 51
RNC (Republican National Committee), 163,
    208–209, 211, 224
Roberts, Owen J., 444
Robertson, Pat, 225, 237
Robertson's Rule, 426
Rockefeller, Nelson, 242, 403
Rockefeller Family Fund, 276
Roe v. Wade (1973), 143–144
Roll-call votes, 331, 355, 356
Roman Catholic Church. *See* Catholics
Roosevelt, Franklin D., 125, 167, 212, 214,
    233
    attempt to assassinate, 401
    bureaucracy and, 400
    cabinet of, 384, 387
    Congress and, 370, 371, 394
    national crises under, 398
    New Deal of, 5, 169, 206, 222, 259, 414,
        444, 477
    polls and, 399
    presidency of, 369, 373, 381, 388, 390
    press and, 307, 310
    Socialist proposals and, 222–223
    Supreme Court and, 444, 461, 462, 477
    veto power and, 395
Roosevelt, Theodore, 105, 221, 222, 447
    presidency of, 378, 388
    press and, 307, 309
    as vice president, 401
Rosenthal, Howard, 340
Rostker v. Goldberg (1981), 141–142
Rotary Club, 270
Routine news stories, 305
Rules
    bureaucratic, 433. *See also* Red tape
    campaign finance rules, 109, 246–247,
        250–251
    congressional ethics rules, 360
    for court standings, 452–453
    governing media, 300–303
    House rules, changes in, 343–344,
        352–353
    for improving government, 478
    of politics, 469
Rules and Administration Committee (Senate),
    344
Rules Committee (House), 136, 137, 321, 336,
    345, 352–353
    Speaker of the House and, 322, 323, 353,
        364
Rule 22 (Senate), 324, 325. *See also* Filibuster
Rumsfeld, Donald, 386
Runoff primary, 218, 241
Russian Revolution (1917), 17. *See also* Soviet
    Union (former)

Sabotage, bureaucratic, 420, 422–423
Safe districts, 327–328
St. Louis County, Missouri, 216

Salary, of representatives, 319
Salvation Army, 277
Same-sex (gay) marriage, 5, 150–151,
    159(fig.), 161, 286
Sampling error, 157
Sanchez, Loretta, 156
San Francisco school system, 459
Santa Fe Independent School District v. Doe
    (2000), 114
Santeria religion, 110
SBA (Small Business Administration), 427
Scaife Foundation, 276
Scalia, Antonin, 58, 147, 454(tab.), 456, 463
Scandals
    Clinton administration, 142, 310, 311, 396
    in Congress, 330, 333
    media coverage of, 300
    Watergate, 87, 246, 311, 392, 396, 463
"Schedule C" appointments, 417
Schenck, Charles T., 103, 104
Schenck v. United States (1919), 103, 104, 109
Schneider v. New Jersey (1939), 146
School districts, 57
Schools, 78, 100. *See also* Education
    bilingual education in, 101, 459
    desegregation of. *See* Desegregation
    free-speech rights in, 109–110
    parochial, public aid to, 99, 111–112, 453
    prayer in, 86, 111, 112, 160(fig.), 460
    school vouchers, 112, 159(fig.), 161
Schumer, Charles, 11
Schumpeter, Joseph, 6, 7
Schwarzenegger, Arnold, 297
Science Committee (House), 345
Scorekeeper function of media, 299–300
Scott, Dred, 442
Scribner's (magazine), 295
Search and seizure, 113–114, 116–117, 119
Search warrant, 116, 301
Sears, David, 79
Seattle, Washington, 88, 298
Secretary of State, 402
    Jefferson as, 369, 374, 386, 411
Secret ballot, 185
Sectionalism, 203–204
"Section 1983" suits, 452
Secular humanism, 87
Sedition Act (1798), 100, 103
Sedition Act (1918), 100, 103
Sedition laws, 100, 103–104
Segregation. *See also Brown v. Board of
    Education*
    de facto and *de jure*, 132
    in public accommodations, 128, 138, 147
    racially segregated juries, 128
Select committees, 342
Selective attention, 306
Self-incrimination, 117
Self-interest, 10–11, 30
Self-reliance, ethic of, 79
Senate
    approval of judges by, 438, 447, 448
    approval of officials by, 411, 412
    calendars, 352
    changing ideology in, 332–333
    changing organization of, 343
    Constitution and, 27, 28
    domination of, 373
    election to. *See* Congressional elections
    evolution of, 323–325
    filibuster (Rule 22) in, 235, 324, 354–355

    floor debate in, 354–355
    impeachment and, 403
    legislative process in, 352, 353
    party organization of, 334–335
    party voting in, 338
    presidential appointments and, 385
    Republican control of, 248, 329, 345
    standing committees of, 344
    television coverage of, 308
    treaty ratification by, 368, 371, 372, 373,
        375
    vice president and, 401–402
    voting in, 356
Senatorial Committee (Democrats), 209
Senators
    direct election of, 324, 361
    power of, and benefits to, 319–320
    public opinion and, 332
    qualifications and privileges, 238
    state legislature selection of, 28, 321,
        323–324
Seneca Falls Convention (1848), 140
Senior citizens, 271. *See also* Social Security
Senior Executive Service (SES), 420
Seniority
    in House committees, 323, 338, 339–340,
        342, 363
    in Supreme Court, 454(tab.), 455
Sensationalism, 295, 310–311
Sensenbrenner, James, 342
Separate-but-equal doctrine, 128–129
Separation of church and state, 110, 111–113,
    453
Separation of powers, 23, 28, 30, 40, 358, 469
    as barrier to action, 479–481
    modifications to, 42–43
September 11 terrorist attacks, 7, 10, 88, 90,
    119, 139, 311, 389. *See also* Terrorism
    9/11 Commission, 3, 359–360, 361
    homeland security and, 61, 359–360, 399,
        414
Sequential referral, 352
Service role of bureaucracy, 412–414
SES (Senior Executive Service), 420
Set aside laws, 147
Seventeenth Amendment (1913), 324, 361
Seventh Amendment (1791), 36, 102
Seventh Day Adventists, 111
Sex. *See also* Pornography
    politics and, 310
    privacy and, 142–144, 150
Sex discrimination. *See also* Homosexual (gay)
    rights; 138, 141
Sexism, 174
Sexual harassment, 142, 448
Shalala, Donna E., 381
Sharon, Ariel, 105, 301
Shays, Daniel, 23
Shays's Rebellion, 23–24, 25
Sheppard, Samuel H., 99
Sherman, Roger, 28, 35
Sierra Club, 269, 270, 274, 287
Simon, Paul, 233
Simple resolution, 350
Simpson, O. J., 164
Sinclair, Barbara, 338
Single-issue groups, 257
Sipuel, Ida Lois, 129
Sit-in demonstrations, 135, 190, 273, 285
Sixteenth Amendment (1913), 414, 461
    See also Federal income tax

Sixth Amendment (1791), 36, 41
"Sixties, the" (1960s), 267, 477
    social movements in, 268, 286
    student radicals in, 159, 161
60 Minutes (TV program), 292
Slander, 105. *See also* Libel
Slavery, 102, 260
    conflict over, 49, 205–206
    Constitution of U.S. silent on, 36–37, 38
    Declaration of Independence and, 19
    Dred Scott decision, 442, 461
    national supremacy and, 441–442
    nullification doctrine and, 56
    Senate and, 323
Small Business Administration (SBA), 427
Small Business Committee (House), 345
Small Business Committee (Senate), 344
Smith, Al, 212
Smith, Howard, 136
Smith, Samuel Harrison, 294
Smith Act (1940), 100, 104
Smith's Principle, 426
Sniderman, Paul M., 79
Snowbelt states, 65
Social class
    class consciousness, 86
    in Marxism, 9
    middle class, 86, 87, 211, 267, 274
    political participation and, 188, 192
    public opinion and, 163–164
    upper-middle class, 163, 193, 278
    workers, 9, 163, 267
Social diversity, federalism and, 72
Socialist Labor party, 221
Socialist party, 222–223
Socialists, 92, 220, 221
Socialist Workers party, 215, 221
Social movements, 215. *See also specific*
        movements
    interest groups and, 267, 273–276
    1960s, 268, 286
Social policy, 79–80
Social Security, 159(fig.), 428, 476, 478
Social services, 84, 422
Social welfare. *See* Welfare programs
Soft money, 209, 247, 250, 252, 288
Soil Conservation Service, 424, 428
Solicitor general of U.S., 455
Solidary incentives, 215–216, 270
Sophomore surge, 236
Soros, George, 252
Sound bites, 296
Sources of information, 301, 304
Souter, David, 144, 448, 454(tab.), 456
South, the, 65, 167
    black vote in, 126, 138, 180–181, 182
    Democratic party in, 167, 203, 204
    desegregation and, 131
    politicians with personal followings in, 217
    presidential elections in, 206, 207
    Republican party in, 218(tab.), 248, 327,
        330, 333, 479
    slavery and, 37
    voting registration in, 183(tab.)
South America, 76
South Carolina, 27(fn.), 183(tab.), 203
"Southern Manifesto" (1956), 131
Sovereign immunity, 452
Sovereignty
    federalism and, 51
    state, 21, 58–60, 445

Soviet Union (former), 50, 171
Spain, 21, 84(tab.), 295
Speaker of the House, 335–337, 344, 402
    Gingrich as, 323, 333, 337–338, 342
    power of, 321, 322–323, 336
    referral of bills by, 352, 353
    Rules Committee and, 322, 323, 353, 364
Special-act charter, 57
Special-district governments, 57
Special election, 43, 480
Special interests, 320. *See also* Interest groups
Special revenue sharing, 63
Speech, freedom of, 286, 470. *See also* Freedom
        of expression
Speechmaking, 242–243, 296, 390
"Spinning" news, 311
Split-ticket voting, 207, 208(fig.), 372, 480
Spock, Benjamin, 113, 117
Spoils system (patronage), 203, 213, 336, 412,
        417, 418
Sponsored parties, 216
Spots (TV ads), 240
Staff
    campaign, 233–234
    congressional, 345–347, 346(fig.)
    White House staff, 307, 381–383, 387–388
Standards of Official Conduct Committee
        (House), 345
Standing, courts and, 452–453, 454
Standing committees, 342, 344, 345
Standing (division) vote, 355
Stare decisis, 457
Starr, Kenneth, 311, 403
State and Local Fiscal Assistance Act (1972),
        64
State and local political parties
    distribution of power in, 213–214
    ideological parties, 215
    machine politics, 213–215
    one-party states, 217
    organization and, 200, 213–217
    party bosses, 213
    personal followings, 216–217
    solidary groups, 215–216
    sponsored parties, 216
    two-party system, 217
State constitutions, 20–21, 59
    Constitution of U.S. and, 22–23, 27
    state bills of rights, 34
State courts, 59, 448
    class action suits in, 454
    jurisdiction of, 449, 449(fig.), 450
State Department, 411–412, 422, 424, 428
State Farm Insurance, 454
State legislatures, 100, 471
    election to, 219
    governmental structure and, 50, 51–52
    leadership in, 322
    reapportionment of, 28(fn.)
    U.S. Senator selection by, 28, 321, 323–324
State of the Union Address, 308, 378
States, 55, 452, 469
    abortion rights and, 143
    Bill of Rights applied to, 35, 102, 104, 473
    changing representation in House, 236(tab.)
    conditions of federal aid to, 66, 67–68
    elections and, 181, 219, 482
    electoral college and, 373
    federal grants to, 62(fig.), 63, 64, 477
    Great Compromise and, 27
    intergovernmental lobbies, 62

    interstate commerce and, 53–54, 442, 443,
        445
    interstate rivalry for federal money, 65–66
    leadership in, 72
    mandates and, 66–67
    media regulation and, 301
    tobacco-settlement payments to, 70
State sovereignty, 21, 58–60, 455
States' rights, 31, 54, 442, 474. *See also*
        Antifederalists
States' Rights ("Dixiecrat") party, 220, 221,
        223
Steering and Policy Committee (House), 336,
        337, 364
Steering Committee (Senate), 335
Steffens, Lincoln, 295
Stenberg v. Carhart (2000), 143
Stephanopoulos, George, 382
Stevens, John Paul, 454(tab.), 456
Stevens, Thaddeus, 322
Stevenson, Adlai, 224, 307
Stewart, Potter, 106
Stockman, David, 383–384, 422
STOP ERA, 275
Straight-ticket voting, 207
Strict-constructionist approach, 439
Strict scrutiny standard, 125, 140–141, 148,
        149
Student activism, 159, 272, 285
    politics and, 161–162
    protests by, 135, 161
Student rights, 109–110
    See also Colleges and universities
Students for a Democratic Society, 285
Subcommittees (Congress), 341, 342, 343,
        346
Subsidies, 415
Succession Act (1886), 402
Sunbelt states, 65
Superdelegates, 211
Supreme Court, 27, 31
    See also Federal courts; Judiciary; *specific*
        cases
    on abortion and privacy, 143–144
    in action, 454–456
    activism of, 440, 443, 444, 463, 464
    administrative agencies and, 414
    on affirmative action, 146–147, 148, 149
    on African American voting rights, 181
    attempts to regulate commerce, 57–58
    Bill of Rights applied to states by, 35, 102,
        104, 473
    on bureaucratic power, 415
    on campaign finance reform, 251, 288
    chief justices, 349(tab.), 455
    on church-state separation, 110, 111–113,
        453
    class action suits and, 453, 454
    on confidentiality of sources, 301
    Congress and, 321
    on corporate rights, 108
    desegregation and, 128–134, 137
    development of, 439–445
    election of 2000 and, 251, 464
    on Eleventh Amendment, 58
    on exclusionary rule, 114–116
    on executive privilege, 396
    on Fourteenth Amendment, 35, 104,
        128–129
    government and economy, 442–443
    government and political liberty, 443–445

on hate crime, 105
on homosexual rights, 101, 149–150, 151
on individual rights, 67
on involuntary confessions, 117–118
judicial review and, 28, 438, 439, 441
jurisdiction of, 441, 449(fig.), 450, 451, 462–463
on legislative veto, 400, 429
on line-item veto, 44, 45, 395, 481
on lobbying restriction, 287
on national conventions, 241
on national supremacy, 54–56, 441–442
on obscenity, 105–107
on oil rights, 60
power of, 457, 459, 460–464
public opinion of, 463, 464(fig.)
redistricting and, 236
on regulatory agencies, 413
revival of state sovereignty and, 445
Roosevelt and, 444, 461, 462, 477
on school prayer, 86
sedition law and, 100, 103, 104
Senate approval of nominees to, 438
seniority in, 454(tab.), 455
on symbolic speech, 108
on taxation, 55–56
on Tenth Amendment, 53, 67
on term limits, 327
trivia, 461
on voting age, 183
women's rights and, 139–142
workload of, 450, 451, 454
writs of *certiorari* and, 450–451, 455
Sure-Tan v. National Labor Relations Board (1984), 146
Suspect classifications, 125
Swann v. Charlotte-Mecklenburg Board of Education (1971), 133, 134
Sweatt, Heman, 129
Sweden, 81–82, 82(tab.), 84(tab.), 192, 198, 411
Symbolic racism, 79
Symbolic speech, 108

Taft, William Howard, 221, 267, 374, 388, 461
Taliban regime (Afghanistan), 88, 120, 399
Talk shows, 296, 297, 302, 303–304, 313
Talmadge family, 217
Tammany Hall, 213, 215
Taney, Roger B., 442, 444, 461, 463
Tariffs, 56, 61, 239, 472
Task Force on Inequality and American Democracy, 10
Taxation, 18, 125, 472
  federal-state relations and, 55–56, 61, 68
  House of Representatives and, 351
  on imports. *See* Tariffs
  federal income tax, 3, 61, 287, 414, 460, 461, 478
  nonprofit exemption, 287
  poll tax, 181
  reform of, 262, 371, 481
  Shays's Rebellion and, 23
Tax-exempt organizations, 287
  See also Nonprofit organizations
Taxpayer status, lawsuits and, 452, 453
Tax Reform Act (1986), 371
Taylor, Zachary, 378, 401
Telecommunications Act (1996), 301
Telegraph, invention of, 295

Telephone services, 147, 281
Telephone taps, 120
Television, 298, 474
  "big three" networks, 296, 297(tab.), 310
  cable, 297, 298, 311
  campaigns, 240, 242, 243, 244, 257, 302–303
  candidate coverage by, 307
  competitiveness in, 310–311
  coverage of Congress on, 307, 308
  FCC and, 293, 299
  news programs, 292
  political agenda and, 477
  presidential campaigns and, 296–297, 302
  right to privacy and, 113, 117
  on segregationist violence, 136
  watchdog role of, 300
Teller votes, 355, 356
Tenth Amendment (1791), 36, 53, 58, 66, 67, 142
Term limits, 327, 342, 345, 358, 480, 482
Term of office, presidency, 27, 42, 373–374, 405, 480
Terrorism, 3, 88, 90, 139, 248
  See also September 11 terrorist attacks
  civil liberties and, 119–121
  Congress and, 359–362
  democracy and, 7
  Department of Homeland Security, 49, 61, 70, 359–360, 399, 414
  war on, 120, 360, 368, 389, 399, 400
Texas, 150, 165, 183(tab.), 329, 471
Texas v. Johnson (1989), 109
Thematic campaigning, 234
Think tanks, 273
Third parties, 215, 219, 220, 223, 377
  See also Minor parties
Thirteenth Amendment (1795), 461
Thomas, Clarence, 58, 438, 439, 448, 454(tab.), 456
Thune, John, 248
Thurmond, J. Strom, 221
Tilden, Samuel J., 212
Time (magazine), 105, 301, 306
Tinsdale, Elkanah, 234
Tobacco settlements, 70
Tocqueville, Alexis de, 10, 76, 77, 82
"Tonight Show with Jay Leno" (TV program), 297
Topeka, Kansas, 129, 453. *See also Brown v. Board of Education*
Trade. *See* Commerce, regulation of
Transportation, 62, 147
Transportation and Infrastructure Committee (House), 345
Transportation Department, 431
Treasury Department, 375, 412, 414, 424
Treaties, Senate approval of, 368, 371, 372, 373, 375
Treaty of Versailles, 325
Trial balloon, 304, 305
Trial by jury, 35
Truman, David B., 50
Truman, Harry S, 224, 394, 400
  election of 1948 and, 221
  popularity of, 392, 392(fig.)
  steel mill seizure and, 460–461
  veto power and, 395
  as vice president, 233, 401
Trustee approach, 399
Trustee *vs.* delegate debate, 237

Trust funds, 428
Twenty-first Amendment (1931), 42
Twenty-second Amendment (1951), 373, 401
Twenty-third Amendment (1961), 183
Twenty-fifth Amendment (1967), 384, 402
Twenty-sixth Amendment (1971), 183, 461
Two-party system, 208, 209(fig.), 217–220
Tyler, John, 401
Tyner, James N., 213

UAW (United Auto Workers), 216
Unalienable rights, 19
Un-American Activities Committee (House), 78–79
Unemployment, 69. *See also* Employment
Unified government, 370
Unimodal distribution of votes, 338
Union calendar (House), 352
Union movement, 266, 267, 273, 275–276
  See also Labor unions; *specific unions*
Unitarian Church, 87
Unitary system, 50, 51, 52
United Airlines flight 93, 361
United Auto Workers (UAW), 216
United Kingdom, 81. *See also* Great Britain
United Press International (UPI), 299
U.S. Council of Mayors, 62
U.S. Maine (battleship), 295
U.S. News & World Report, 299
U.S. v. Brignoni-Price (1975), 146
USA Patriot Act (2001), 120, 121
USA Today (newspaper), 299
United States Code, Section 1983, 452
United States v. Leon (1984), 121
United States v. Lopez (1995), 58
United States v. Morrison (2000), 58
United States v. Nixon (1973), 396
United States v. Virginia (1996), 142
United Steel Workers v. Weber (1979), 149
United We Stand America, 223
Universities. *See* Colleges and Universities
University of Alabama, 132
University of California, 455
University of California at Davis, 147, 149
University of California at Los Angeles, 60
University of Chicago, 251
University of Michigan, 149
University of Oklahoma, 129
University of Texas Law School, 129, 149
Unpopular ideas, tolerance of, 92(fig.)
UPI (United Press International), 299
Upper-middle class, 163, 193, 278. *See also* Elites
Urban League, 267

Vacancies Act (1868), 385
Valence issues, 239–240
Values, 77–78, 80, 85, 91
  See also Morality
Van Buren, Martin, 203, 401
Van Essen, Thomas, 11
VAP. *See* Voting-age population (VAP)
VEP (voting-eligible population), 186–187, 186(tab.), 329
Verba, Sidney, 80–81, 187, 269
Vermont, 22, 151
Versailles, Treaty of, 325
Veterans' Affairs Committee (House), 345, 426
Veterans' Affairs Committee (Senate), 344, 426
Veterans' Affairs Department, 426
Veterans' groups, 267, 413, 426

Veto message, 394
Veto powers, 25, 137, 378, 394–396
    Andrew Jackson and, 322, 375
    Congress and, 43–45, 348, 358, 395, 396, 471
    legislative, 400, 429
    line-item, 43–45, 395, 481–482
    pocket veto, 348, 394–395(tab.), 395, 397
    Senate and judicial nominees, 447
Vice president, 401–402
Vietnam war, 299, 307, 368, 371, 392
    elite opinion and, 299
    press coverage of, 299, 307
Violence
    police and, 136–137
    race riots, 135
Violence Against Women Act (1994), 58
Virginia, 21, 27(fn.), 132, 183(tab.), 217, 441
Virginia Military Institute, 141
Virginia Plan, 25, 26, 29
Virginia Resolution, 56
Virtue, cultivation of, 30
Visuals (TV), 240, 242
Voice votes, 355
Volunteering, 162, 183, 187(fig.)
    in campaigns, 234
Voter registration, 178–179
    blacks and, 138
    Motor-voter law, 179, 180(fig.)
    political machine and, 213
    regulations, 185–186, 189, 204, 213
    in South, 183(tab.)
Voters
    African American, 126, 138, 180–181, 188
    apathy of, 178. *See also* Nonvoting
    character and, 252
    congressional elections and, 318
    delegate opinion and, 224, 226(tab.)
    direct democracy and, 59
    Hispanic, 191, 258
    incumbency and, 330
    independent, 254–255
    media and, 346
    partisanship of, 172, 252, 260(fig.), 306, 339
    policy preferences of, 171(tab.)
    political parties and, 185, 189, 225–226
    presidential election and, 373
    recruiting, critical elections and, 206
    Spanish-speaking, 303
    split-ticket voting by, 372
    targeting, in presidential campaigns, 234
Voter turnout, 178–179, 192
    calculating, 179(tab.), 186–187, 186(tab.)
    in congressional elections, 183, 329
    decline in, 188–191
    election of 2004, 248, 479
    globally, 179(tab.), 192
    Hispanic, 258
    machine politics and, 213
    negative ads and, 257, 310
    political party and, 190–191
    in presidential elections, 183, 184(fig.), 186(tab.), 225
Voting. *See also* Nonvoting
    age and, 183, 188, 189(fig.), 461
    attitudinal, 332–333
    civil rights and. *See* Voting rights
    compulsory, 190
    in Congress, 236–237, 331–333, 338, 344, 355–356

economic interests and, 252, 255–256
    by eighteen-year-olds, 183, 461
    global comparison of, 163, 198
    loyalty in. *See* Voters, partisanship of
    multi-lingual instructions for, 190
    political information and, 188
    political parties and, 185, 189
    primary voting, 224–225, 236
    property requirements for, 180
    prospective voting, 255
    retrospective voting, 255–256
    schooling and, 188, 189(fig.), 191, 474
    self-reports of, 187
    social class and, 163
    split-ticket voting, 207, 208(fig.), 372
    straight-ticket voting, 207
    women, 41, 52, 181, 286
Voting-age population (VAP), 178, 179, 183(tab.), 184, 186–187, 186(tab.), 248
Voting-eligible population (VEP), 186–187, 186(tab.), 329
Voting fraud, 185, 204, 213, 214
Voting rights
    of African Americans, 138, 180–181, 182
    of women, 52, 181, 182, 184, 274, 286, 473
Voting Rights Act (1965), 182, 260
Voting Rights Act (1970), 183
Voting Rights Act Amendments (1982), 66
Voting specialists, 188

Wage and price controls, 368, 414
"Walk-in schools," 133
Wallace, George, 132, 167, 182, 217, 223
    election of 1968 and, 218, 220, 221
Wallace, Henry, 221
Wall-of-separation principle, 111–113
Wall Street Journal, 299
Walsh, Lawrence, 311
War. *See also* Military; *specific war*
    bureaucratic power in, 413–434
    civil liberties restricted in, 100
    federal power in, 474–475
    presidency and, 400
War Department, 412. *See also* Defense Department
"War on Poverty," 477
War on terrorism, 120, 360, 368, 389, 399, 400
Warren, Earl, 129, 444, 464
Washington, D.C., 7, 183, 278, 298
Washington, George, 5, 21, 22, 38, 201
    cabinet of, 369, 384, 386
    Congress and, 322
    Constitution and, 23, 25
    presidency of, 35, 369, 373, 374, 375
    presidential succession and, 404
    self-restraint of, 372
Washington Globe (newspaper), 294
Washington Legal Foundation, 272
Washington Post, 299, 300, 305, 311
Waste, bureaucratic, 430, 431
Watchdog function of media, 300
Watergate scandal, 87, 396, 463
    press coverage of, 246, 311, 392
Watt, James, 272
Watt, Melvin, 341
Watts, J. C., 340
Waxman, Henry A., 215

"Waxman-Berman organization," 215
Ways and Means Committee (House), 342, 345, 351
WEAL (Women's Equity Action League), 275
Weather Underground, 285
Weaver, R. Kent, 70
Weaver, Robert, 387
Weber, Max, 9, 79
Web logs (blogs), 292, 293, 297
Webster, Daniel, 376, 401
Webster v. Reproductive Health Services (1989), 143, 144
Wednesday Club, 332
Welfare programs, 94
    Clinton's reform of, 68, 378–379
    court-ordered, 457
    devolution reform, 68, 69, 70
    political machine and, 214
    states sovereignty and, 58–59
Welfare Reform Act (1996), 378–379
Welfare-to-work programs, 69
Wellstone, Paul, 183
Westmoreland, William, 452
Whig party, 203, 205, 219, 378
Whip, 334, 335, 336, 337
Whistle Blower Protection Act (1989), 423
White-collar workers, 416–417
"White flight", 113, 117, 134
White House, 375, 381
White House Office, 381–383
White House Office of Faith-Based and Community Initiatives, 62
White House press conferences, 310
White House press corps, 308, 310
White House staff, 307, 381–383, 387–388
White primary, 181
Whites, 164–165, 164(tab.), 165(tab.), 182, 258, 331
    "white flight", 113, 117, 134
Whitewater scandal, 309
Wilderness Society, 274
Wilson, James, 27, 28, 38, 39, 372
Wilson, Woodrow, 49–50, 221, 259, 374, 402
    as author, 379
    presidency of, 378, 379
    Senate filibuster and, 325
    wartime powers of, 413
Winchell, Walter, 99
Winner-reward systems, 212
Winner-take-all elections, 211, 217, 218–219, 220, 376
Winograd, Morley, 210
Wisconsin, 189, 203, 204, 215, 217, 241
Woman's party, 221
Women, 95(fig.)
    in civil service, 421(fig.)
    in Congress, 325–326, 325(tab.), 335
    Constitution and, 41
    demonstrations by, 274
    feminist movement, 106, 274–275
    in government jobs, 419
    in judiciary, 447(fig.), 456, 461
    in military, 140, 141–142
    at national party conventions, 212
    pornography and, 106
    preferential hiring of, 79
    in president's cabinet, 387
    rights of. *See* Women's rights
    welfare reform and, 68
Women's Equity Action League (WEAL), 275

Women's Legal Defense Fund, 272
Women's rights, 139–144, 159(fig.). *See also*
    Abortion
    affirmative action and, 146
    landmark cases, 142
    voting rights, 52, 181, 182, 184, 274, 286,
        473
Woodward, Bob, 300
Workers (working class), 9, 163
    unions and, 267
Work ethic, 79, 85. *See also* Employment
World Trade Center attack, 7, 88. *See also*
    September 11 terrorist attacks
World Trade Organization, protest of, 88
World War I
    Espionage and Sedition Acts (1917–1918),
        100, 103
World War II, 414
    Smith Act of 1940 and, 100, 104
    work of women in, 140

World Wide Web. *See* Internet
Wright, Jim, 333, 337
Writ of *certiorari*, 450–451, 455
Writ of *habeas corpus*, 35, 102, 462
Wyoming Territory, 41, 52

Yale Law Journal, 455
Yellow journalism, 295
Youth. *See also under* Student
    community service and, 183
    eighteen-year-old vote, 183, 461
    interest in political news, 298, 298(fig.)
    1960s social movements and, 268, 286

Zacchini, 113, 117
Zacchini v. Scripps-Howard Broadcasting Co.
    (1977), 113, 117
Zaller, John, 162, 169, 174
Zelman v. Simmons-Harris (2000), 114
Zorauch v. Clauson (1952), 114